Traumatic Brain Injury

Methods for Clinical and Forensic Neuropsychiatric Assessment

Second Edition

Traumatic Brain Injury

Methods for Clinical and Forensic Neuropsychiatric Assessment

Second Edition

Robert P. Granacher, Jr.

CRC Press
Taylor & Francis Group
Boca Raton   London   New York

CRC Press is an imprint of the
Taylor & Francis Group, an **informa** business

The book cover depicts a magnetic resonance spectroscopy probe of right frontal encephalomalacia seen within the window over the right frontal pole. (See Figure 5.13 for definitions of specific chemicals.)

CRC Press
Taylor & Francis Group
6000 Broken Sound Parkway NW, Suite 300
Boca Raton, FL 33487-2742

© 2008 by Taylor & Francis Group, LLC
CRC Press is an imprint of Taylor & Francis Group, an Informa business

No claim to original U.S. Government works
Printed in the United States of America on acid-free paper
10 9 8 7 6 5 4 3 2 1

International Standard Book Number-13: 978-0-8493-8138-6 (Hardcover)

Visit the Taylor & Francis Web site at
http://www.taylorandfrancis.com

and the CRC Press Web site at
http://www.crcpress.com

Contents

xvi

Preface to the Second Edition

Since the first edition of this text, the number of traumatic head injuries that occur in the United States on a yearly basis has risen to almost 3 million. These, in turn, produce considerable morbidity and death. This text has two purposes. The first purpose is to provide a physician or a psychologist with a neuropsychiatric schema for the evaluation of a patient who has sustained a traumatic brain injury (TBI), and for whom the clinician wishes to develop a treatment plan. The second purpose is for forensic neuropsychiatric evaluations. As an added benefit, the methods in this book can be used to evaluate and treat any neuropsychiatric disorder, with the addition of appropriate laboratory studies and treatments specific to the pathology. The first eight chapters of this text focus upon evaluations for treatment. Chapters 9 through 11 provide a focus for physicians performing forensic TBI examinations. As the medical examination format is no different when examining a patient for treatment than it is when examining a patient for forensic purposes, the first eight chapters can be read by the treatment clinicians, and if they have no interest in forensic issues, Chapters 9 through 11 can be avoided. On the other hand, the physician wishing to perform a competent forensic neuropsychiatric examination will find it necessary to utilize all 11 chapters.

The logic of clinical TBI examination formulated in the first edition remains in the second edition. That is, the examination techniques follow standard medical concepts but with a significant neuropsychiatric focus. In other words, the evaluation techniques are not psychologically based; they are brain based. Moreover, there are exciting new clinical findings regarding TBI since the first edition was written. These have been added to improve the quality of the text and enhance the learning experience for the reader. These include the recent reports of blast overpressure brain injury as seen in combat veterans and civilians injured in conflicts in Kosovo, Lebanon, Iraq, Afghanistan, and other world areas. An enlarged review of sports injuries in children, high school students, and college and professional athletes has been added. Inflicted brain injury in children receives more attention. A larger emphasis has been placed on mild traumatic brain injury (MTBI), particularly from a forensic standpoint, owing to the contribution of litigation to increased symptom expression. Neuroimaging techniques have been considerably expanded so that the neuropsychiatric examiner can provide a better clinical correlation between imaging and the findings from direct medical examination. The literature on outcomes in adults and children following TBI has been expanded to make it of more use for the forensic examiner.

This text is not a comprehensive review of all knowledge of TBI. Moreover, it is not to be used as an encyclopedia. Its purpose is to provide a physician or a psychologist with a practical method for an effective evaluation of TBI using state-of-the-art techniques. The techniques described in this text come from known standards within the world medical and psychological literature as well as from the author's large database of TBI examinations. The procedures and recommendations in this book come from almost 4000 cases wherein the author has personally examined persons with TBI, or those claiming to have a TBI.

Preface to the First Edition

Approximately 2 million traumatic head injuries occur in the U.S. yearly. These in turn produce more than 50,000 deaths annually. There is a biphasic distribution of brain injury, with the highest incidence found among young people 15 to 24 years of age and a second group of citizens greater than 75 years of age. Almost 25% of head injuries require hospitalization, and nearly 100,000 persons yearly are left with some level of chronic brain impairment.

This text has a specific focus. It provides not only methods for clinical examination but also the forensic evaluation of traumatically brain-injured persons. The reader can be selective in using this book. If he or she is interested only in clinical assessment, treatment planning, and neuropsychiatric treatment, the first eight chapters of the book will suffice. On the other hand, for the physician performing a forensic neuropsychiatric examination, the entire book should be useful. If the clinician is already highly skilled in the clinical evaluation of traumatic brain injury but wishes to learn further forensic issues, he or she may focus only on the last four chapters of this text.

There is a simple logic to the book. It follows traditional medical evaluation concepts with a neuropsychiatric focus. It demarcates differences in the adult evaluation vs. the child evaluation. Chapter 8 integrates the clinical section of this text, whereas Chapter 11 integrates the forensic section of the text. The seven preceding chapters in the clinical section of the book proceed logically to a culmination of data analysis and case studies in Chapter 8. The same format applies to the forensic section, Chapter 9 to 12. Chapters 9 to 11 provide the forensic analysis database, and Chapter 12 offers the forensic expert guidance for the writing of neuropsychiatric traumatic brain injury reports and the providing of neuropsychiatric testimony.

This text is not intended to provide complete information regarding the multiple advances within the entire field of traumatic brain injury. For instance, it provides only a limited focus on management of acute traumatic brain injury. This is better left to neurosurgeons and trauma physicians. Its primary intent is to provide the physician, at some time well after the brain injury, with a clinically tested schema for either evaluating and treating a patient or examining a plaintiff or defendant. The genesis for this text comes from the author's database of almost 3000 traumatically brain-injured persons, or those alleging a traumatic brain injury, examined by extensive historical, physical, imaging, neuropsychological, and laboratory procedures. It is hoped that the reader will find this to be a practical text providing pragmatic information either for evaluation and treatment of one's patient or for providing a state-of-the-art forensic examination of an alleged traumatic brain injury.

Acknowledgments

Robert P. Granacher, Jr., congratulates the superb and energetic work of Barbara Norwitz and her colleagues at Taylor & Francis CRC Press for their untiring support and dedication to the production of this text. He also thanks Jasmine Adkins, who devoted hundreds of hours to the transcription of this work and did so with precision and skill. Lastly, he thanks and celebrates the lights of his life—his wife Linda and his son Phillip.

Author

Robert P. Granacher, Jr., M.D., M.B.A., is president and executive director of the Lexington Forensic Institute in Lexington, Kentucky. He is a clinical professor of psychiatry in the Department of Psychiatry of the University of Kentucky College of Medicine. He has a full-time office practice as a treating neuropsychiatrist and as a forensic psychiatrist, and he provides neuropsychiatric consultation on complex cases to a large tertiary care hospital.

Dr. Granacher received his B.S. in chemistry from the University of Louisville, and his M.D. from the University of Kentucky, Lexington, and he served as resident and chief resident in psychiatric medicine at the University of Kentucky Hospital. He later served as resident and fellow at the Harvard Medical School and the Massachusetts General Hospital and other Harvard University teaching hospitals in Boston. Since the first edition of this book, he has received his M.B.A. from the University of Tennessee in Knoxville. He has specialized in the neuropsychiatric treatment and evaluation of traumatic brain injury, perinatal birth injury, toxic brain injury, and other complex neurobehavioral disorders for almost 30 years. His forensic neuropsychiatry practice is national in scope.

Dr. Granacher is board certified by the American Board of Psychiatry and Neurology in general psychiatry, with added qualifications in geriatric psychiatry and forensic psychiatry. He is also board certified in forensic psychiatry by the American Board of Forensic Psychiatry, Inc. He is a diplomate of and is board certified in sleep medicine by the American Board of Sleep Medicine. He has been certified in psychopharmacology by the American Society of Clinical Psychopharmacology. He is a distinguished life fellow of the American Psychiatric Association and a member of the American Neuropsychiatric Association. Dr. Granacher is a member of the deans' council at the University of Kentucky College of Medicine.

Dr. Granacher is a director of the Kentucky Psychiatric Medical Association. He serves on the board of directors of Saint Joseph Healthcare, Lexington, Kentucky, a corporation managing a number of hospitals and other healthcare facilities in the central Kentucky area. He formerly served as chair of the board of directors of the same corporation. He also is a director and shareholder of C.B.A. Pharma, an oncology research pharmaceutical company based in Lexington. He serves at the pleasure of the governor on the board of the Kentucky Traumatic Brain Injury Trust Fund.

1 The Epidemiology and Pathophysiology of Traumatic Brain Injury

INTRODUCTION

Traumatic brain injury has been recognized as an affliction of humankind since the Stone Age. Anthropological evidence from mass graves of ancient battle fields has demonstrated trephination holes across fracture lines of skulls.[1] It is postulated that these drill holes were perhaps for release of pressure from hematoma following head injury. In the eighteenth century, Pott, LeBran, and Heister related altered mental status and severity of head injury to pressure on the brain rather than damage to the skull itself.[2] By the turn of the twentieth century, neurosurgery had progressed to the point that it was conclusively known that intracranial pressure increased in head injury, and Jaboulay in France emphasized the need for opening the skull to release intracranial pressure.[3] Jefferson introduced us to uncal herniation as a consequence of sustained intracranial hypertension.[4] Continuous intracerebral pressure monitoring was introduced in the late 1950s and early 1960s.[5] In the three decades from the 1970s to the 1990s, studies revealed that there were two major components to traumatic brain injury (TBI): primary injury and secondary injury.[6–9] From the early 1990s onward, the neurosurgical profession has made significant strides in improving survivability following TBI.

It is the issue of survivability that heralds the heavy toll of neuropsychiatric psychopathology that remains following brain trauma. Improved survival rates following brain trauma have led to a dramatic increase in the number of cognitively and behaviorally impaired persons who then develop long-term neuropsychiatric disorders as a consequence of traumatic injury. Presently, three million cases per year of brain injury from mild to severe occur in the United States. Characterizing the epidemiology of brain trauma in the United States is very difficult. Brain injury definitions, criteria for diagnoses, and sources of data vary from study to study throughout North America. There is no universal systematic data collection available to enable precision in the determination of brain injury rates. The Centers for Disease Control and Prevention maintain data on injury and adverse effects, but their data inputs come from extremely variable sources. At the present time in the United States, it is not possible to precisely state the incidence of TBI nor the prevalence of brain-injured persons in the population. In 1996, prevalence of traumatic brain injury was estimated to be between 2.5 and 6.5 million persons.[10] The variance is so large that it currently lacks usefulness to predict needed services.

There are other significant confounding factors affecting attempts to provide incidence and prevalence rates for TBI. The data for cases with injuries admitted to hospital, and later discharged, are fairly well documented. However, the vast majority of mild traumatic brain injury (MTBI) is seen in an emergency department, treated, and released. These data are sketchy, maldistributed, and poorly reported. There is a very poor database for expressing MTBI flowing through emergency departments in the United States. The rate of persons discharged with a brain injury from a short-stay hospitalization during 1998 was approximately 87 per 100,000 population. The Popovic and Kozak study[11] indicates that the brain injury rate for males was twice as high as that for females and that most persons discharged from a hospital with brain injury received a diagnosis of hemorrhage, contusion, or scalp laceration without fracture of the skull.

The neuropathology of brain trauma has gone through rapid scientific advancements in recent years. The primary traumatic effects following head trauma involve receptor dysfunction, free-radical effects, calcium damage, cell dysfunction, and cell death.[12] The cellular and molecular consequences of TBI are becoming better understood, and neuropathological damage can be complicated by secondary injuries occurring after head trauma. These include intracranial hyper-tension, vascular failure, ischemia, endogenous brain defenses, axonal injury, and neuronal injury.[13]

Head injury classification is varied among neurosurgeons and neuropathologists. The types of head and brain injury are anatomically straightforward and include scalp injury, skull fracture, epidural hemorrhage, subdural hemorrhage, subarachnoid hemorrhage, cerebral contusion, diffuse TBI, penetrating head injury, and child abuse.[14] More recently, the connection between apolipo-protein E genotypes on chromosome 19 and neurodegeneration from TBI have become much more elucidated through research.[12] Moreover, the identification of neuron-specific enolase and the S-100 protein offers new promise in the biochemical detection of TBI in the emergency department because of their specificity.[15]

This chapter reviews the epidemiology of brain injury and the biomechanics, neuropathology, and pathophysiology of TBI. Various classification systems for categorizing the severity of head and brain injury are reviewed. When compared to the first edition of this book, enlargements on new data regarding blast and explosion overpressure injuries, sports injuries, and inflicted child brain injury are reviewed. Biochemical and genetic markers of acute trauma and predictors of later neurodegeneration are explained. A recent review of neurosurgical advancements in the neuro-trauma unit is explained.

EPIDEMIOLOGY OF TRAUMATIC BRAIN INJURY

There is an inherent difficulty in attempting to gather incidence and prevalence figures using standard epidemiological techniques. Epidemiological research studies of patients with brain injur-ies are few in number and rarely undertaken. Since the mid-1990s there has been a shift in data-gathering techniques to those using administrative data sets to extrapolate the incidence and features of individuals with TBI. Much of the current U.S. data comes from hospital sources, such as the United States National Hospital Discharge Survey (NHDS), the United States National Hospital Ambulatory Medical Care Survey (NHAMCS), and the U.S. National Health Interview Survey (NHIS). Other data sets are reported from individual states. These data have reasonable reliability in those cases of moderate to severe brain injury requiring hospitalization and subsequent discharge. However, the data on MTBI are probably quite unreliable, as there is no uniform reporting system for emergency department visits, physician office visits, diagnoses, and discharges.

The occurrence of recent brain injury reports ranges from a low of 92 per 100,000 population in a seven-state study[16] to a high of 618 per 100,000 population in a U.S. national survey.[17] Obviously, this is a huge variance and is of little use in community treatment planning. With regard to deaths from brain injury, the data is equally variable. Sosin et al. reported that an average of approximately 28% of all injury deaths involve significant brain trauma.[18] On the other hand, Sosin et al. reported an estimate of the actual proportion of fatal brain injury varying from 23% to 44% of all head injuries.[19] The National Health Interview Survey for 1985–1997 was extrapolated to the 1990 United States Census population of about 249 million residents at that time. This survey reported that about 1,975,000 head injuries occur per year in the United States.[20] Fifteen years later, it is reported that more than three million people a year in the United States sustain a TBI.[21]

There are a number of demographic variables that determine the risk of TBI. These include age, gender, ethnicity, substance use, recurrent TBI, and socioeconomic level. Persons between the ages of 15 and 24 years are at the highest risk to sustain a brain injury in the United States.[22] With regard to gender, males outnumber females by a ratio of approximately 2:1.[17,23] With regard to race,

TABLE 1.1

Epidemiology of Traumatic Brain Injury (TBI)

- 3,000,000 per year in the United States
- 175–200 per 100,000 population
- 50–50,000 deaths per year
- Rates are comparable in industrialized countries
- Each subsequent TBI exponentially increases future risks

a review of the U.S. literature indicates extremely large variances recording ethnicity or race in medical records with regard to TBI. These data are probably not usable to extrapolate race or ethnicity numbers for the United States. Obviously in countries consisting of other races, it would be unreliable to report these figures against the U.S. figures. Correlation of substance abuse with TBI is fraught with error as a result of huge variances among emergency departments obtaining blood–alcohol and drug-of-abuse urine determinations in traumatized persons. There is a general consensus that positive blood–alcohol concentration increases risk of injury for all external causes. Kraus et al. found that 56% of adults with a brain injury diagnosis had a positive blood–alcohol concentration.[24]

The Mayo Clinic study was the first to measure an initial recurrent TBI as a risk for a second TBI. It determined that an earlier TBI increased the risk of a second injury 2.8–3.0 times that of the general noninjured population. Moreover, the relative risk of a third TBI, given a second brain injury, was between 7.8 and 9.3 times that of initial head injury in the population.[25] Thus, each subsequent brain injury exponentially increases the risk of a second or third brain injury. Recurrent head trauma risk has been particularly emphasized recently in sports injuries, as we shall see below. Jordan and Zimmerman have admonished the need of parents and coaches to monitor carefully the head-concussed athlete before permitting a return to contact sports.[26] For socioeconomic status, the consensus among studies is that the rate of brain injury per 100 people per year is highest in families at the lowest income levels.[27–29] Table 1.1 summarizes TBI in industrialized nations.

When one examines rates of brain injury in most developed nations outside the United States, the brain injury rates are comparable. For instance, in a university hospital in Norway during 1993, the annual incidence of hospital-referred head injury was 229 per 100,000 population with a male preponderance of 1.7:1.0.[30] In south Australia, a higher than expected incidence of TBI was discovered. The rate of 322 brain injuries per 100,000 population annually exceeded the average rates reported for the United States and the European Union. The elevated rates were seen mostly in young males living in rural areas working in manual trades.[31] Estimated incidence rates in France have been reported recently to be between 150–300 per 100,000 inhabitants. The annual incidence of severe head injury was estimated to be approximately 25 per 100,000 inhabitants for cerebral trauma with intracranial injuries and around 9 per 100,000 for the most severe level of head injury with coma.[32]

CLASSIFICATION OF HEAD INJURY

GENERAL CLASSIFICATION OF HEAD INJURY

Multiple classifications of head injury are available to the reader and range from classification by level of severity, level of consciousness, mental status following head injury, and location of body injury.[33] The Abbreviated Injury Scale is primarily an anatomical system but it also scores for severity, and it is based on the relative seriousness of the lesion and its effect upon mental state.[34] A seven-digit code number is assigned that reflects the location of the lesion and its size and severity. The final digit of this code is related to severity and is scored on a scale of 1–6. The Glasgow Coma Scale (GCS) was introduced to modern medicine by Teasdale and Jennett.[35]

TABLE 1.2
Glasgow Coma Scale (GCS)

Eye-opening (E)	
Spontaneous	4
To voice	3[a]
To pain	2
No response	1
Verbal response (V)	
Oriented conversation	5
Confused, disoriented	4
Inappropriate words	3[a]
Incomprehensive sounds	2
No response	1
Best motor response (M)	
Obeys commands	6
Localizes	5
Withdraws (flexion)	4[a]
Abnormal flexion (posturing)	3
Extension (posturing)	2
No response	1

[a] GCS = 10: E = 3, V = 3, M = 4.

Source: From Teasdale, G. and Jennett, B., *Lancet*, 1, 81, 1974. With permission.

This system is the most widely used scoring procedure for mental and neurological status following head injury in the United States and in most developed countries. Its score is based on the sum of three components: eye-opening, verbal response, and best motor response. For instance, if an individual at the accident scene opened eyes to voice, used inappropriate words, and demonstrated a flexion response to motor stimulation, the scoring would be E + V + M = 3 + 3 + 4 = 10 (please see Table 1.2). This in turn produces a graded score in the moderate severity range. The GCS can be further subdivided into mild injury (GCS = 13–15), moderate injury (GCS = 9–12), and severe injury (GCS = 3–8). The clinical features of mild injury are loss of consciousness ≤20 min, no focal neurological signs, no intracranial mass lesion, and no requirement for intracranial surgery. Regardless of mental state, a focal CT lesion places the patient into the moderate category. Coma duration ≥6 h places the patient into the severe category regardless of subsequent mental state. However, these classes of severity are poor statistical predictors of outcome (see Chapter 9).

In terms of outcome, the most commonly used current scales are the Glasgow Outcome Scale[36] (Table 1.3) and the Rancho Los Amigos Level of Cognitive Functioning[37,38] (Table 1.4). The Rancho Scale is widely used by rehabilitation facilities after the patient leaves the neurosurgical intensive care unit or neurosurgical floor for post-acute care. Generally, a final grading using the Rancho Scale is made before the patient's discharge from a brain injury rehabilitation unit if such is required.[38]

BLUNT HEAD TRAUMA

The best example of blunt head trauma is the classic closed head injury, wherein brain injury results from impact to the head causing deformation of the brain that results in characteristic pathological changes discussed more fully below. Broadly speaking, these are due to intentional injuries as a result of assault and battery or suicides, and unintentional injuries due to motor vehicle accidents,

TABLE 1.3
Glasgow Outcome Scale (GOS)

Categories	Clinical Features
Death	
Vegetative state	Absence of cognitive function with total abolition of communication
Severe disability	Conscious but dependent patient
Moderate disability	Independent but disabled
Good recovery	Independent patient who may return to work or premorbid activity Mild cognitive or neurological deficits may persist

Reprinted from Elsevier Science, Jennett, B. and Bond, M. *The Lancet*, 1, 480, 1975. With permission.

falling objects, or falls. Blunt head trauma is the leading cause of death under the age of 45 years in industrialized nations, and among those, closed head injury accounts for 25%–33% of all deaths from trauma. Kraus and McArthur report a prevalence of disabled brain injury survivors in the United States of 24 per 100,000 population per year.[39] Those with major persisting impairment are about 64,600 individuals. As the reader will note, this estimation is much less than earlier studies reported in the United States because of a 25% decline in hospital admission rates seen in recent years. It is hoped that at least part of this decrease is due to a reduction in the incidence of head trauma. There is recent evidence that head injuries due to road traffic accidents are being mitigated by modern protective devices such as seat belts, airbags, and stability control units added to automobiles since the 1970s. The evidence is consistent with a reduction in the number of severe brain injuries due to these modern devices.[40]

The mechanical loading to the head necessary to produce a closed head injury occurs by static loading and various types of dynamic loading.[41] Static loading occurs when forces are applied to the head gradually, and it is usually a slow process. Examples are a squeezing injury due to compression by a large object, or a head injury sustained in an earthquake or landslide. Another example is a head injury sustained by a person at work under an automobile that settles from the jack, crushing the head. The time sequence usually requires more than 200 ms for a brain injury to develop. If force is sufficient, the skull will sustain multiple, comminuted fractures of an eggshell type at the vault or base of the skull. Coma and severe neurological signs are generally not prominent unless cranial

TABLE 1.4
Rancho Los Amigos Level of Cognitive Functioning

Levels	Clinical Signs
I. **No response**	Unresponsive to any stimulus
II. **Generalized response**	Nonpurposeful responses, usually to pain only
III. **Localized responses**	Purposeful; may follow simple commands
IV. **Confused, agitated**	Confused, disoriented, aggressive; unable to perform self-care
V. **Confused, inappropriate**	Nonagitated; appears alert; responds to commands; verbally inappropriate; does not learn
VI. **Confused, appropriate**	Can relearn old skills; serious memory defects; some awareness of self and others
VII. **Automatic, appropriate**	Oriented; robot-like in daily activities; minimal confusion; lacks insight or planning ability
VIII. **Purposeful, appropriate**	Alert and oriented; independent in living skills; capable of driving; defects may remain in judgment; stress tolerance and abstract reasoning may not be at pre-injury cognitive ability

Source: Rancho Los Amigos National Rehabilitation Center, Downey, California.

nerves are damaged. If deformation of the skull is severe, the brain becomes compressed and distorted during fatal laceration.

Dynamic loading is subdivided into categories of impulsive or impact. The forces act in less than 200 ms; in most cases, the forces act in less than 20 ms. Impulsive loading is uncommon and occurs when the head is set in motion, and then the moving head is stopped abruptly without it being either directly struck or impacted. This could occur, for instance, in a person violently struck in the thorax or the face, setting the head violently in motion.[12,37] The resulting head injuries are solely due to the inertia produced by the manner in which the head has been moved by a force to the body elsewhere. It has been questioned whether real-world accidents produce sufficiently high levels of inertial forces to produce serious internal injuries of the brain if impact to the head or face does not occur.[42] Impact loading occurs when a blunt object strikes the head. In the United States, this is most commonly caused by motor vehicle accidents, as it is in most industrialized countries. It results from a combination of contacts and inertia following the sudden deceleration of the head when the cranial vault strikes an object (such as the head of a passenger inside a motor vehicle or the head of a worker falling from a scaffold to the sidewalk). The response of the head to impact varies with the type of blunt object that strikes the head. Inertia is reduced during certain impact conditions, such that the head is prevented from moving when it is struck. As a result, most of the impact energy is delivered to the head at contact, and this produces contact phenomena. The magnitude and importance of this event varies with the size of the impacting object and with the magnitude of the force delivered to the contact point. The latter is determined by the mass, surface area, velocity, and hardness of the impacting objects. These factors determine the manner in which energy is transferred to the head. For objects larger than 5.0 cm^2, localized skull deformation occurs, as the skull bends inward immediately below the point of impact, an outbending of the skull occurs peripheral to the impact site. If skull deformation in the area of impact exceeds the tolerance of the skull, a fracture will result. In those instances where the offending object has a surface area less than 5.0 cm^2, penetration, perforation, or localized depressed fracture of the skull is more likely. After impact, shock waves traveling at the speed of sound propagate throughout the skull from the point of impact, as well as directly through the brain. These shock waves cause local changes in tissue pressure. If these changes cause sufficient brain distortion, then small localized interparenchymal petechial hemorrhages will result.[12] If the skull strikes a hard surface, like a steel plate, it takes approximately 33.3–75 ft-lb of energy to produce a linear fracture. The energy is absorbed in approximately 0.0012 s. The first 0.0006 s deforms and compresses the scalp tissue while the residual 0.0006 s deforms the bone. Only a slight increase in energy is required to produce a stellate fracture or multiple linear fractures. A free fall backward from 6 ft for a head weighing 10 lb, gives 60 ft-lb of available energy. The velocity of the head is approximately 20 ft/s or 13.5 mph at impact to the occipital skull[43] (see Table 1.5).

Brain deformation caused by strain is the proximate cause of tissue injury, whether induced by inertia or by contact. Strain is of three forms: compression, tension, and shear. Strain is the amount of deformation that a tissue undergoes as a result of a mechanical force being applied. Tensile strain is the amount of elongation that occurs when a material is stretched. Characteristically, brain tissue withstands strain better if it is deformed slowly rather than quickly. As the rate of strain increases, brain tissue exponentially becomes more brittle, and it will tear at lower strain levels under rapidly applied loads. Within the skull, there are three principal tissues affected in a blunt head trauma: bone, blood vessels, and brain parenchyma. These vary widely in density and tolerance to deformation. Obviously, the skull bone is considerably stronger than blood vessels or brain tissue, and more force is required to induce damaging strain. However, the strain that bone can tolerate is less than that needed to injure the brain. Bone will break at a strain of 1%–2%, whereas brain and vascular tissue may not tear until a 10%–20% strain is applied. On the other hand, it takes considerably more force to cause a 1%–2% strain in bone than it does to produce a 10%–20% strain in brain tissue. Since the brain is virtually incompressible in the living state, and since it has a very low tolerance to tensile and shear strain, it is these two types of strains that are the usual causes

TABLE 1.5

Biomechanical Mechanisms of Traumatic Brain Injury

Mechanism	Features
Static loading	≥200 ms to develop[12,41]
Skull bending	
Skull volume change	
Dynamic loading	≤20 ms to develop impulsive or impact[12,37,41]
Impact	
Impulsive	
Acceleration	
Translational	All particles move simultaneously in same direction, linear[12,41,46]
Rotational-angular	Particles move angular to others, shear forces common, causes diffuse axonal injury[12,41,42,46]
Coup lesions	Predominate if head is accelerated[12]
Contrecoup lesions	Predominate if head is decelerated[12]
Strain	Compression, tension or shear[12,41]
Skull fracture	Requires 33.3–75 ft-lb of energy. A 6 ft person with a 10 lb head falling backward will produce available energy of 60 ft-lb causing the head to strike at 13.5 mph[43]

of physical brain damage. The same holds true for vascular tissue. Vascular tissue tends to fail under more rapidly applied loads than does the brain. There are some conditions that can cause relatively pure injury to the vascular tissue or tissues of the brain within the skull without a fracture to the skull.[12] The mechanical events that contribute to brain injury are presented in Figure 1.1.

Coup injuries (under the blow) are more common when the head is accelerated. This causes contusions beneath the site of impact. Contrecoup injuries (across from the blow) do not require a direct impact. Movement of the brain toward the site of impact (coup) will cause tensile strains within brain tissue in the area opposite that to the site of impact. If the tensile strains that result are greater than the vascular tolerance, a contusion will result.[44,45] The frequently occurring contusions to the frontal and temporal poles are almost always contrecoup, regardless of head impact site. It is

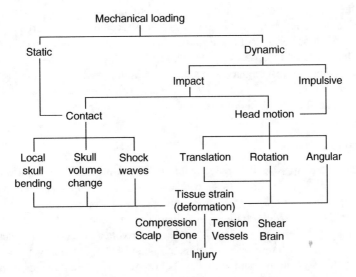

FIGURE 1.1 Mechanical events that contribute to traumatic brain injury (TBI). (From Graham, D.I., Gennarelli, T.A., and McIntosh, T.K., Trauma, in *Greenfield's Neuropathology,* 7th edition, Graham, D.I. and Lantos, P.L., Eds., Arnold, London, 2002. With permission.)

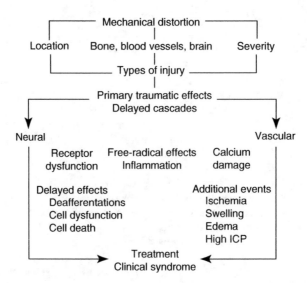

FIGURE 1.2 Mechanisms of brain injury. (From Graham, D.I., Gennarelli, T.A., and McIntosh, T.K., Trauma, in *Greenfield's Neuropathology*, 7th edition, Graham, D.I. and Lantos, P.L., Eds., Arnold, London, 2002. With permission.)

extremely common when an individual falls backward on ice, striking the occiput to the pavement, to develop bifrontal contusions as a result of impact, with little or no contusions under the site of the occipital skull's impact with the sidewalk.

The internal structure of the skull dictates the most probable location of traumatic injuries of the brain in most cases of closed head injury. The skull surfaces above the eyes are quite rough, and the most anterior frontal vault of the skull is limited in size. As the brain accelerates forward or rotates into the frontal areas of the skull, the infraorbital frontal lobes are often contused or impacted by the rough prominences above the orbits. At the same time, the sphenoid ridges of the skull provide a significant structural impediment to the temporal poles which in turn produces an accordion-like compression of the temporal tips. The temporal lobes contain numerous structures such as the amygdalae, hippocampi, and limbic structures which may account for disturbances of memory, mood, or complex emotions because of the temporal lobe deformation while frontal lobe injury may result in specific frontal lobe syndromes[46] (see Chapter 2). Recent study has led to mathematical models that enable biomechanical engineers to study head injury mechanisms and the forces at play within the skull during trauma.[47–53] Figure 1.2 delineates further biomechanical mechanisms as a cause of cascading microstructural, cellular, chemical, and genetic effects.

PENETRATING HEAD TRAUMA

Penetrating head trauma by missiles is less frequent than blunt force trauma to the head. However, in certain cities in the world, missile injury to the head exceeds motor vehicle accident blunt trauma as a cause for TBI. Obviously, in military situations, missile injury to the head is more common than blunt trauma. Missiles are usually bullets, but they also include knives, crossbow bolts, and shrapnel. As we shall see, even dog teeth, nails, and screwdrivers can become missiles. In Phoenix, Arizona, 10% of all admissions to a level 1 trauma clinic are from gunshot wounds. These have a mortality of 60%.[54] In 1988, in the United States, 33,000 gunshot wound deaths occurred.[55]

The differences between missile head injury in civilian life and military practice are usually quite distinct. Military shoulder- or vehicle-fired weapons are of high velocity, which generally cause deep penetration of the skull and a severe forward-concussive wave through the brain.

The muzzle velocities generally range from 731 to 975 m/s, and in most direct calvarial injuries, death is instantaneous.[12] Most civilian gunshot wounds to the head occur by handguns, and these have a relatively lower muzzle velocity, usually less than 305 m/s. Many of these individuals reach a hospital for treatment and survive. However, the muzzle velocity of handguns and ammunition has changed considerably in the last 10 years. Higher velocity handguns are now available to civilians, which has blurred the distinction between military and civilian injuries.[56]

The availability of CT scanners for use in military medicine has dramatically improved the survivability of soldiers injured in the field by gunshot wound to the head, as bony and metallic fragments and the relation of hematomas to the missile tract can be detected easily. Follow-up examination for brain abscess is also easier to complete with military mobile CT scanners.[57] Soldiers who do survive a penetrating head injury due to a missile usually have higher rates of complications. This finding has been seen particularly in recent regional wars. During the Croatian homeland war, the complications of penetrating head injuries consisted of postoperative hematomas, infections, seizures, and cerebrospinal fluid fistulas. Intracranial migration of foreign bodies and posttraumatic hydrocephalus were seen. The complication rate of 176 soldiers with well-defined head injuries from missiles was 35%. Cerebrospinal fluid fistulas occurred at a rate of 12%. Of those with fistulas, almost 50% developed intracranial infections.[58] Thus, the person providing a neuropsychiatric evaluation to a soldier who sustained penetrating missile brain trauma should be prepared for ultra-complex and widely diffuse or penetrating cerebral injuries. During Operation Desert Storm, the VII Corps was studied with regard to brain wounds and field neurosurgical support for these troops. Only 1 of 22 soldiers who sustained a head wound died. As a result of this study, the Kevlar helmet design appeared to be successful in reducing the rate of TBI and death. Those wounds that did occur were basilar in location, and the rate of brain wounds for American soldiers was less than expected. The Iraqis, on the other hand, had wounds that were randomly distributed about the head.[59] They did not have access to the Kevlar helmet.

Pathologists classify missile head injury as depressed, penetrating, or perforating.[60] In the depressed injury, the missile does not enter the cranial vault but causes a depressed fracture of the skull and contusions adjacent to the fracture. Brain damage is focal if it occurs, and if consciousness is lost, it frequently is only brief or not at all. In a penetrating injury, the missile enters the cranial cavity but does not pass through it. If the object is small, such as a nail, there may be very little direct injury to the skull or the brain. Nail injuries to the skull and brain may escape clinical detection. Brain damage is again focal, and loss of consciousness is unusual. Frequently, patients injured by penetrating missiles such as a screwdriver or a nail are admitted to a neurosurgical unit with the missile still in position and the patient fully conscious.[61,62] Emergency room physicians are cautioned that small missiles can cause unsuspecting penetration into the brain, which may not be apparent immediately or upon close inspection. This has occurred from dog bites to infant heads.[63]

The amount of brain damage depends on many factors such as the mass, shape, and velocity of the missile, and the damage is proportional to the amount of energy released by the missile during its passage through the head. Greater brain damage is associated with a missile that yaws as it moves rather than tumbles—one that is a hollow-point bullet rather than one that does not shatter—and injury due to a shotgun blast.[12] If the missile deforms on impact, brain injury is usually greater. In a perforating injury, the missile or bullet traverses the cranial cavity and leaves through an exit wound. Brain damage is often severe, but in unusual occasions, a high-velocity bullet may pass through the head without knocking the victim down or causing impairment of consciousness.[64] Owing to the advancing shockwave as the bullet enters the brain, the exit wound in the skull is characteristically larger than the entry wound. Bullets of low-velocity, such as 0.22-caliber rifle bullets or handgun bullets, cause more damage at the site of entry and rarely pass completely through the skull. The bullet may ricochet inside the skull and traverse the brain in various directions.[65] Low-velocity bullet injuries tend to produce complicated injuries. Often, fragments of bone, scalp, hair, or clothing are driven into the intracranial cavity.[66] With penetrating injuries, particularly those contaminated with foreign bodies, there is an 11% risk of intracranial infection. Of these infections, 67% develop within six weeks after the injury.[67]

In nonsurvivors, the wound canals have been evaluated at autopsy. Three fairly distinct zones are described by neuropathologists after a missile enters the brain.[12] The cross section of the missile tract is slightly larger than the diameter of the missile in most instances and will be filled with blood. Enveloping the central cavity of the missile tract is an intermediate band of hemorrhagic tissue necrosis. This, in turn, is surrounded by a marginal layer of pinkish-gray discolored tissue. Both of these findings follow the creation of a temporary cavity, which is blasted forward by the shockwave and collapses rapidly after formation around the permanent missile tract. This temporary cavity, which occurs at the time of impact, may be up to 30 times the diameter of the missile and is largely dependent on the mass and velocity of the missile. The temporary cavity is smaller in low-velocity than in high-velocity missile injuries. The shock waves radiating out from the temporary cavity frequently produce remote contusions affecting the frontal and temporal poles and the undersurface of the cerebellum. Associated findings include bleeding into the basal ganglia, hypothalamus, and upper brainstem. Large subdural hematomas may develop as a consequence of the concussive force. Contrecoup fractures may also occur in the orbital plates.[68,69] Table 1.6 summarizes penetrating head trauma.

Koszyca et al. studied 14 patients who survived between 1.5 and 86 h after head shots. Studies for beta-amyloid precursor protein (β-APP) revealed widely distributed axonal damage diffuse through the cerebral hemispheres and also in the brainstem.[70] Oehmichen et al. reported on 20 cases with survival of less than 1.5 h. The histopathological changes identified along the missile tract extended about 18 mm radially from the center of the wound and tapered gradually along the tract of the wound from entry point to the exit point.[71] Gunshot wounds damage blood vessels and produce traumatic false aneurysms,[72] and there is also a high frequency of epilepsy (32%–51%) following gunshot wounds to the brain.[73] Obviously, if an individual survives with an extensive missile tract representing substantial advancing shockwave trauma to the brain, the neuropsychiatrist can expect significant neuropsychological dysfunction. The physician providing an examination after a gunshot wound to the head obviously will be examining a survivor. Generally, survivors have higher GCS scores when received in the emergency department than those who die from the gunshot wound after emergency treatment.[74,75]

A number of individuals survive self-inflicted gunshot wounds to the head during suicide attempts. Survival is more likely if the individual shoots himself with a submental or transoral gunshot using a low-velocity handgun. These individuals usually shoot themselves in a suicide attempt with .22-caliber, .25-caliber, or .32-caliber weapons and suffer predominately unilateral frontal brain injuries. The resulting neuropsychiatric syndromes generally will present with executive dysfunction and frontal lobe syndromes specific to the site that is damaged.[76] Moreover, physicians examining persons following gunshot wounds to the head are more likely to see a person who has undergone an anteroposterior gunshot wound rather than a lateral penetrating gunshot wound. The mortality rate is 25% for anteroposterior wounds versus 83% for the lateral injury group.[77]

TABLE 1.6
Penetrating Head Trauma

- Survivors sustain low-velocity injuries.
- Intracranial infection rate is high.
- Damage is proportional to missile size and energy release.
- Seizures, blood vessel damage, and false aneurysms are frequent.

BLAST OR EXPLOSION OVERPRESSURE TRAUMA

At the time of the writing of this chapter, the United States was involved in warfare in Iraq and Afghanistan. Numerous U.S. soldiers were returning to the United States with brain injuries not formerly seen at any level in American civilian life. There has been a significant lack of study, because closed brain injuries due to blast have been uncommon in civilians. Dr. Deborah Warden, Director of the Defense and Veteran's Brain Injury Center at Walter Reed Army Medical Center in Washington DC, has focused the attention of the neuroscience community toward blast-induced brain injury.[78] The highest ranking U.S. Army officer to be wounded, General Patt Maney, sustained a blast overpressure brain injury in Afghanistan.[259]

The injuries of blast overpressure are often associated with high-powered explosives that can cause occult injuries to multiple internal organs, even in the absence of observable signs of injury. U.S. troops generally use Kevlar helmets in combat along with other body armor. These uses have significantly reduced the frequency of penetrating injuries to the head and to vital organs within the torso. However, these protective devices offer limited protection against nonpenetrating injuries from blasts and high-impact falls.[79] The U.S. military has coined the term "polytrauma" to describe this increasing population of patients.[80] The brain itself is particularly vulnerable to high-impact injuries because of the delicate compositions of the cerebral cortex and axonal fibers, as well as potential contusion and shearing by bony protuberances in the skull base. Ordinary TBI is usually readily detected by CT imaging in the field. Closed brain injuries from blast overpressure are often missed, particularly in the presence of externally evident injuries such as burns, fractures, and hemorrhages. The U.S. Veterans Administration and the Department of Defense have worked as a team to establish the Seamless Transition Office, which functions as the liaison between military treatment facilities and the Veterans Administration Polytrauma Rehabilitation Centers. Four Veterans Administration medical centers are designated in this category currently: Minneapolis, Palo Alto, Richmond, and Tampa.[81]

Table 1.7 lists the classes, types of injuries, and explosive causes neuropsychiatric physicians and physiatrists can expect to result therefrom. As expressed in Table 1.7, the four basic mechanisms of blast injury are termed as primary, secondary, tertiary, and quaternary. Primary injuries occur due to the intense over-pressurization impulse created by a detonated high explosive. The advancing blast wave travels at the speed of sound and at a pressure much higher than atmospheric pressure. Blast injuries are characterized by anatomical and physiological changes from the direct or reflective over-pressurization force impacting the body's surface.[81] Explosives are categorized as high-order explosives (HEs) or low-order explosives (LEs). HEs produce a defining supersonic over-pressurization shockwave. Examples of HEs include TNT, C-4, Semtex, nitroglycerin, dynamite, and ammonium nitrate/fuel oil (such as used in the Oklahoma City bombing in the United States). LEs tend to cause shrapnel-type injuries to humans, as they lack the over-pressurization wave of HEs. Terrorists use whatever is available, and the term of art as a result of the overthrow of Saddam Hussein is "IEDs": improvised explosive devices. These may be composed of HEs, LEs, or both.[81]

While this section focuses upon blast injuries to the brain, the individual who suffers a blast over-pressurization wave also has other organs commonly injured, as noted in Table 1.7. Blast lung is a direct consequence of HE over-pressurization waves. It is the most common fatal primary blast injury

TABLE 1.7
Blast or Explosion Overpressure Trauma

- Intense overpressurization impulse causes primary, secondary, tertiary, and quaternary injuries.
- High-order explosives: TNT, C-4, Semtex, nitroglycerin, dynamite, and ammonium nitrate/fuel oil.
- Injuries to lung, brain, auditory system, bowel, and testicles.
- Cognitive and emotional changes common.

among initial survivors and is more common than blast brain injury. (This apparently led to the death of Abu Musab al-Zarqawi when two 500-lb bombs were dropped on his safe house in Iraq.[126]) Signs of blast lung are usually present at the time of initial evaluation, but they have been reported as late as 48-h after explosion. Blast lung is characterized by the clinical triad of apnea, bradycardia, and hypotension. Pulmonary injuries vary from scattered petechiae to confluent hemorrhages. Blast lung should be suspected for anyone with dyspnea, cough, hemoptysis, or chest pain following blast exposure.[82] Other commonly injured organ systems include the ears and the abdomen. Primary blast injuries of the auditory system cause significant morbidity and are easily overlooked. Primary blast injury of the auditory complex includes hearing loss, tinnitus, otalgia, vertigo, and bleeding from the external auditory canal. Abdominal injuries are common because gas-containing sections from the gastrointestinal system are the most vulnerable to primary blast effect. The blast can lead to immediate bowel perforation, hemorrhage, mesenteric shear injuries, solid organ lacerations, and testicular rupture. Blast abdominal injuries should be suspected in anyone exposed to an explosion with abdominal pain, nausea, vomiting, hematemesis, rectal pain, tenesmus, testicular pain, unexplained hypovolemia, or any finding suggestive of an acute abdomen.[83]

For the physician performing neuropsychiatric evaluation of potential brain injury in a person who has suffered blast over-pressure injury, it is not necessary to understand the surgical and internal medical consequences of blast injury in their entirety. However, the importance of this information is that brain injury may be overlooked, particularly if it is mild, at the time of the blast over-pressurization injury to other organs. Thus, well after the person who suffered blast injury has rehabilitated, the person may present with headache, fatigue, poor concentration, lethargy, depression, anxiety, insomnia, or posttraumatic stress disorder. The physician must be vigilant to the consideration of TBI as a result of blast over-pressurization in these persons. Individuals working in healthcare facilities in any country that receives combat veterans who have sustained injury from IEDs or HEs should consider TBI. Over 50% of injuries sustained in combat are now the result of explosive munitions, including bombs, grenades, land mines, missiles, mortar and artillery shells, and IEDs, unlike prior armed conflicts.[84] The statistics on the rate of blast injuries and the resulting percent of brain injuries is marginal. When the U.S. Marine barracks was bombed in Saudi Arabia, October 23, 1983, the blast was equivalent to approximately 12 tons of TNT. This resulted in 234 immediate deaths and at least 122 injured survivors. Of the immediate deaths, 167 demonstrated evidence of head injury. Of the 356 victims, there was 59% rate of head injury. The fatality rate from head injury was 70%. Between July and November 2003, the Walter Reed Army Medical Center in Washington DC screened 155 patients from another war theatre who had returned from Iraq and were deemed as being at risk for brain injury. Of the 155 patients screened, 96 were identified as having sustained a brain injury. Of the 155 screened, 88 were blast cases, and 61% of the blast cases had sustained a brain injury.[85] The Defense and Veterans Brain Injury Center noted that soldiers with TBI as a result of blast injury have symptoms and findings affecting several areas of brain function. Sleep disturbances, headaches, and sensitivity to light and noise are common initial symptoms. Cognitive changes occur and are detectable through neuropsychological testing; they may include disturbances in attention, memory, or language, as well as delayed reaction time during problem solving. The most troubling symptoms often are behavioral: mood changes, depression, anxiety, impulsiveness, emotional outbursts, or inappropriate laughter. Many symptoms of TBI in these veterans include those of posttraumatic stress disorder (PTSD) superimposed on TBI. Thus, the physician examining veterans returning from conflict who have sustained blast injuries should always be suspicious of the comorbid presence of PTSD and TBI.[86]

SPORTS INJURIES

Sports-related concussions result in 300,000 brain injuries per year in the United States.[87] Between 1945 and 1999 in the United States, there have been 712 fatalities from high school and college football.[88] Approximately 70% of these deaths were from brain injury, and subdural hematomas contributed to 75% of the fatalities. Powell and Barber-Foss produced one of the best recent studies of varsity athletic sports. They reviewed 1219 mild traumatic brain injuries at 235 high schools. This was 5.5% of the total injuries that occurred to students at these institutions. Football accounted for 63% of concussions, wrestling 11%, female soccer 6%, male soccer 6%, and female basketball 5%. In soccer, the majority of the brain injuries occurred during heading. These authors extrapolated their data to predict 62,816 MTBI cases across 10 popular high school sports with the majority occurring in football.[89]

Football Injuries

It has been known for some time that serious injuries occur while playing football. It is only relatively recently that football has been studied scientifically with regard to TBI. A recent study at Virginia Tech University used a helmet system with spring-mounted accelerometers and an antenna that transmitted data via radio frequency to a sideline receiver and laptop computer system. Recordings were made throughout the 2003–2004 football season during 22 games and 60 practices, comprising 52 players. A total of 11,604 head impacts were recorded by this method. For the 52 players, this was an average of 224 head impacts each throughout the football season.[87] Concussion and brain responses in the National Football League of the United States have only been recently examined. Viano et al.[90] simulated brain responses from concussive impacts by finite element analysis using a detailed anatomic model of the brain and head accelerations from laboratory reconstructions of game impacts. This brain response model was based upon a paradigm developed at Wayne State University in Detroit, and it has fine anatomic detail of the cranium and brain with more than 300,000 elements. This model has 15 different material properties for brain and surrounding tissues. The model includes viscoelastic gray and white matter, membranes, ventricles, cranium and facial bones, soft tissues, and slip interface conditions between the brain and dura. Strain responses were compared with signs and symptoms of concussion. For instance, early after impact, the strain is located in the temporal lobe adjacent to the impact site and then migrates to the far temporal lobe after head acceleration. In all cases, the largest strains occur later in the fornix, midbrain, and corpus callosum. They significantly correlated with removal from play, cognitive and memory problems, and loss of consciousness. Dizziness correlated with early strain in the orbital-frontal cortex and temporal lobe. Concussion injuries happen during the rapid displacement and rotation of the cranium, after peak head acceleration and momentum transfer in helmet impacts.[90]

The National Football League, through its Mild Traumatic Brain Injury Committee, undertook a study to test helmets for impact performance. For players in the National Football League, concussions occur with an impact velocity of 9.3 ± 1.9 m/s (20.8 ± 4.2 mph) oblique on the face mask, side, and back of the helmet. Pendulum impacts were used on helmets to simulate 7.4 and 9.3 m/s impacts causing concussion in NFL players. A second study was undertaken to evaluate helmets at 9.3 m/s and during elite impact condition at 11.2 m/s. The pendulum test closely simulated the conditions causing concussion in NFL players. These studies determined that risk of concussion was reduced in the 7.4 and 9.3 m/s impacts oblique on the face mask and lateral on the helmet shell, but no helmet designs currently used in the NFL address the elite impact condition at 11.2 m/s, as the padding bottomed out, and head responses within the helmet dramatically increased.[91] Pellman's group[92] conducted another study to determine rates of recovery in NFL and high school football players. They assessed and evaluated a sample of NFL and high school athletes within days of a concussion. A computer-based neuropsychological test was used with a symptom inventory protocol. Test performance was compared to a pre-injury baseline level of a similar, but not identical, group of athletes who had undergone preseason testing. A multivariate analysis of variance demonstrated that high school players demonstrated more prolonged neuropsychological effects of concussion but NFL players did not demonstrate decrements in neuropsychological performance beyond one week of injury.

The most sophisticated MTBI study done to date on college athletes was completed at the University of Virginia as part of the Sports Laboratory Assessment Model (SLAM).[93] This study examined 2300 football players at 10 universities and used preseason testing and postseason testing by neuropsychological assessment. A matched control group was also in place, and it used individuals as their own controls as well. Baseline pre-injury data were collected during the football preseason and then compared to postseason data. To evaluate severity of concussion and make eventual return-to-play decisions, the methodology used by SLAM is now the gold standard for sports-related head impact analysis. A variety of assessment methods may be used including traditional paper and pencil neuropsychological tests, computerized assessment methods, or the newer internet-based evaluation procedures. Neuropsychological screening of athletes usually takes 20–30 min and should include measures of cognition known to be sensitive to the sequelae of concussion. These include measures of mental processing speed, attention and concentration, and memory.[94] It is essential to have preseason screening to determine the individual athlete's baseline level of cognitive functioning. Otherwise, premorbid cognitive dysfunction such as learning disabilities, attention-deficit/hyperactivity disorder, a history of concussion, depression, or anxiety may confound the test results after a suspected concussion. Learning disability and a history of more than two concussions confound testing in some investigations.[95] Studies by Barth et al.[93] have determined the recovery curve for MTBI in young, healthy, well-motivated athletes. Athletes who demonstrated mild neurocognitive deficits after concussion demonstrated a 5–10 day natural recovery curve.

The question any physician working in the brain injury arena may be asked is, "When can my athlete return to play after a concussion?" Table 1.8 provides guidelines for returning athletes to play after concussion. The athlete must be asymptomatic following the guidelines of Table 1.8. Asymptomatic is defined as having no evidence of headache, dizziness, impaired orientation, poor concentration, or memory dysfunction during rest or exertion.[96] For further information regarding the postconcussion syndrome, the reader is referred to Chapter 2. Grading of concussion is also described in Chapter 2. Computerized tests will probably see increased use for the screening of large numbers of athletes at the high school and collegiate levels. These neuropsychological procedures have many advantages over paper and pencil tests. They do not require a neuropsychologist to be face to face with the athlete, and there is ease and speed of statistical comparisons. Databases can be maintained so that individual students are compared instantly to their own baseline or compared to group baselines. Individually purchased software for tests such as the Automated Neuropsychological Assessment Metric (ANAM)[97] have been developed recently and utilized. The Concussion Resolution Index is a set of neurocognitive tests that measure attention, reaction time, memory, and problem solving.[98] Trainers are taught to be supervisors, and athletes may log into the system at any time to take a standard 20–30 min neurocognitive battery. The test results are then instantly compared with previous test results to determine any decline or improvement. The results can be

TABLE 1.8
Return-To-Play Guidelines for Young Athletes

	Mild Grade 1	Moderate Grade 2	Severe Grade 3
First concussion	Asymptomatic for one week	Asymptomatic for one week	No play for one month or until asymptomatic for one week
Second concussion	Return in two weeks if asymptomatic for one week	No play for one month; consider sitting out the season	Terminate the season; consider next season
Third concussion	Terminate season; consider next season	Terminate season; consider next season	Do not return to play

accessed by physicians or athletic personnel who will make return-to-play decisions. Testing allows progress to be charted, and testing can be performed on a daily basis.

Soccer Injuries

Whereas football in the United States is the major impact sport, for most of the rest of the world it is soccer. In fact, in many countries outside the United States, "football" is the common term for soccer. While there is less physical contact between players of soccer than players of American football, aggressive play and an unprotected head increase the likelihood of brain injury. It has been a controversial question whether heading the ball causes brain injury or increases the risk of brain injury in soccer players. A Swedish study[99] recently reviewed serum concentrations of the bio-chemical markers of brain damage, S-100B and neuron-specific enolase (see "Acute Biochemical Markers"). Blood samples were taken in players before and after a competitive game, and the number of headers and trauma events during soccer play were assessed. Playing competitive elite soccer was found to cause an increase in serum concentrations of S-100B. This biological marker significantly correlated to the number of headers. These subtle changes of biochemical markers may not translate to neuropsychological changes as recently suggested in Norway. Players in the Norwegian Professional Football League (Tippeligaen) performed two consecutive baseline neuro-psychological tests (CogSport) before the 2004 season. A questionnaire was completed by 271 athletes that assessed previous concussions, match heading exposure (self-reported number of heading actions per match), player career duration, and other factors. The number of previous concussions was positively associated with lifetime heading exposure, but there was no relation between previous concussions and neuropsychological test performance. Computerized neuro-psychological testing revealed no evidence of neuropsychological impairment due to heading exposure or previous concussions.[100] In Canada, the biomechanics of head impacts in soccer was investigated.[101] Game video footage of 62 cases of head impact caused by the upper extremity or by the head of the opposing player was reviewed. By reviewing video, a laboratory enactment by five volunteer football players striking a pedestrian model manikin was developed. Instruments were placed into the manikin, and elbow-to-head impacts measured 1.7–4.6 m/s, and lateral hand strikes measured 5.2–9.3 m/s. These resulted in a low risk of concussion or severe neck injury. Head-to-head impacts at 1.5–3.0 m/s resulted in high concussion risk (up to 67%) but a low risk of severe neck injury.

There appears to be less risk of head injury in soccer today than during previous years. It is suggested that a heavier ball, with potentially more damaging mass, was used previously. Also, younger players now benefit from technologically improved equipment. Previously, the presence of learning disorders was rarely accounted for in early research and created the potential for skewed results because of preexisting factors. Also, earlier research often failed to accurately measure the history of concussion and brain injury outside of soccer play in athletes. Research during the mid-1980s did not always fully appreciate the contribution of multiple concussions.[102]

Boxing and Other Sports Injuries

Boxing has traditionally been known to produce TBI and is the only international sport that sanctions repeated blows to the head (kickboxing and other forms of full-body boxing and contact are included). Inducing loss of consciousness in one's adversary is an acceptable goal. Martland in 1928 introduced the term "punch-drunk."[103] The neurological changes observed by those who followed the brilliant boxing career of Muhammad Ali cannot be ignored. It has been estimated that between 10% and 25% of professional boxers ultimately develop a postboxing neurological syndrome.[104] The neuropathology of boxing injury has been described with cerebral atrophy, cellular loss in the cerebellum, and increased cortical and subcortical neurofibrillary tangles.[105] Those boxers developing the neurobehavioral picture of memory loss and Parkinson-like symptoms develop diffuse amyloid-β deposits and neurofibrillary tangles.[106] A recent Swedish review concluded that the more head punches a boxer takes during his career, the greater the risk of chronic brain damage.[107]

Brain injury has been reported in many other sports, too numerous to mention here. Neuropsychological dysfunction has been reported in jockeys who fall from horses,[108] rugby players,[109] field hockey athletes,[110] and in children associated with or on golf courses.[111] It is the author's experience that most athletes who are examined for a potential sports-related brain injury have not had neuroimaging or biochemical marker assay (see "Acute Biochemical Markers") at the time of the alleged injury. When an athlete gives a history of repeated concussions, it is probably wise to obtain magnetic resonance imaging at a minimum and to provide a complete neuropsychological assessment. The technique for examination is the same as that applied to a person who has sustained an injury in a motor vehicle accident or a fall. If the physician or psychologist is providing consultation to a school, it will be wise to review the return-to-play recommendations of Table 1.8.

HEAD INJURY IN INFANCY AND CHILDHOOD

Kraus has projected the average incidence rate of all levels of brain injury severity in children younger than 15 years to be approximately 180 per 100,000 children each year.[112] Males predominate over females with regard to childhood injuries. For the first 5 years of life, the incidence rates for brain injury are about the same for males and females. However, as children increase in age, the male rate begins to surpass that of females to the point that it exceeds 2:1 by late childhood and adolescence.[113]

Head injury is the single most common cause of death and new disability in childhood, and it is the third leading cause of death in children less than age 12 months.[114,115] Fracture of the skull occurs in roughly 20%–40% of child head injury cases, and a surgical lesion is found in about 9% of children admitted to a hospital after a TBI. The overall mortality in cases with a GCS score of less than 8 varies in numerous studies from 9% to 52%.[115] Child abuse accounts for almost 25% of all children admitted to the hospital under the age of two and is second only to car accidents as the cause of death.[116] Between the ages of 2 years and 4 years, falls are the most common cause of TBI. In older children, bicycling, falling, and automobile accidents are the most common causes of injury.

Skull fracture in infancy is not uncommon during the first year of life. The skull is thin and breaks easily after impact. Most skull fractures in infants are linear and are usually not associated with underlying focal brain damage. Intracranial bleeding is common, however. Neurosurgeons generally manage simple depressed skull fractures without operation. If the skull is significantly deformed, surgery may be undertaken primarily for cosmetic reasons. There are two major complications associated with fracture of the skull in infancy. The first is the development of a subepicranial hygroma when the dura is torn and allows cerebrospinal fluid to dissect between the periosteum and skull bone.[117] These bony membrane disturbances are called pseudomeningoceles, and they generally resolve spontaneously without the need for surgery. The second complication unique to infants following a skull fracture is a growth of the skull fracture, which results from the herniation of contused and swollen brain outward through the torn dura mater. This separates the bones along the line of the fracture, and then the fracture tends to enlarge during the period of rapid growth of the underlying brain. The opposed fracture lines cannot fuse, and dense scarring at the junction between the brain and dura mater prevents secondary closure of the dura. This perpetuates the growing fracture, and neurosurgical repair is required.[118]

Child abuse is a special cause of head injury in infants. Incidence figures are not reliable at this time. Terms of art for head injury child abuse syndromes include "battered child" and "the shaken baby syndrome." However, recent research calls into question whether to-and-fro shaking of a child's body producing whiplash motion is sufficient to cause brain injury. Many experts believe that impact of the head in conjunction with shaking is required. Attempts to model the injury mechanism for shaken baby syndrome is difficult, and researchers are now focusing on injury mechanisms involved in low-energy cyclic loading.[119] Another confounding factor is that cervical spine injury is almost nonexistent in children who are supposedly injured by violent upper body shaking. Biomechanical studies in the laboratory indicate that forces to the infant neck would far exceed the limits for structural failure of the cervical spine during the head velocity and acceleration reported to exist in shaken baby syndrome. These findings call into question whether the syndrome can exist without also the concurrence of head impact.[120]

Leestma, at the Department of Pathology at Children's Memorial Hospital in Chicago, Illinois, reviewed the English language medical case literature for apparent or alleged child abuse between the years 1969 and 2001. Individual case information was available for 324 cases; these were analyzed, yielding 54 cases in which a person was recorded as having admitted, in some fashion, to shaking the injured baby. Only 11 cases of admittedly shaken babies showed no sign of cranial impact (thus apparently free-shaken). Leestma concluded that this small number of cases does not prevent valid statistical analysis or support for many of the commonly stated aspects of the so-called shaken baby syndrome.[121] Leestma's analysis indicates that shaking alone is apparently sufficient in a minority of cases to produce brain injury. This has been confirmed by an analysis from Australia. A retrospective study of infant abusive head trauma was undertaken in cases investigated by the State Crime Operations Command, Queensland Police Service, Brisbane, Australia.[122] Over a 10-year period, cases of head trauma involving subdural or subarachnoid hematoma and retinal hemorrhages, in the absence of any evidence of impact, were defined as shaking-induced. Retrospective examination of perpetrator statements was made for further evidence to support the shaking hypothesis, and for descriptions of the victim's immediate neurological response to a shaking event. From a total of 52 serious infant abusive head trauma cases, 25% was found to have no medical or observer evidence of impact. In 5 of those 13 cases, there was a statement by the perpetrator to the effect that the victim was subjected to a shaking event. In several cases, both with and without evidence of associated impact, perpetrator accounts described an immediate neurological response on the part of the victim. The authors of the study opined that serious neurological impairment can be induced by shaking alone.

The term "battered child" was the first widely recognized syndrome of child abuse. Caffey (1974) introduced the term "shaken baby syndrome."[123] He described abused infants as presenting with acute subdural hematoma and subarachnoid hemorrhage, retinal hemorrhages, and periosteal new bone formations at epiphyseal regions of long bones; he attributed this to the to-and-fro shaking of a child's body, producing whiplash motion of a child's head upon the neck. Graham et al. have described an autopsy series of 87 children.[124] They contrasted their data with CT imaging from 262 children studied after acute head injury.[125] Zimmerman et al.[125] had argued earlier that only 16% of CT studies of abused children produced evidence of brain contusions. At autopsy, the Graham et al. study found 90% evidence of contusions in their series of 87 children. Thus, the later autopsy study suggests that CT imaging may not detect many of the traumatic contusions probably present within the brains of children who have sustained inflicted head abuse. The study by Graham et al. further documented that 61 of the 87 children showed postmortem evidence of swelling of the brain, and in 45 of these children the swelling was bilateral. In 27 of the 45 cases, the swelling was attributable to ischemic damage, contusions, intracranial hematomas, or to a combination of these factors. In the remaining 18 children, an underlying cause could not be found. Children with hematological disorders, especially those with hemophilia, are at particular risk for developing intracranial hemorrhage after a trivial head injury. Another special at-risk group of children are those who have been shunted for hydrocephalus.[12]

There is a confounding issue that neuropsychiatric examiners should consider with abused or head injured children. It is important to rule out whether or not the child sustained any form of birth trauma at the time the examination is undertaken, to determine whether there has been a superimposed brain injury caused by blunt head trauma later in childhood. Birth trauma refers to injury of the central nervous system or peripheral nervous system in the premature or full-term infant caused by mechanical factors during labor or delivery.[127] Caput succedaneum is a common lesion consisting of localized hemorrhagic edema of the subcutaneous tissues in the presenting part of the head at birth. It almost always resolves without medical problems. Cephalohematoma is a collection of blood between the periosteum and the outer surface of the skull, limited by suture lines. It is associated with skull fracture in 25% of cases.[128] Its incidence increases proportionally with use of forceps, and it also usually resolves without problems.[129] Epidural hematomas rarely occur; this is blood between the skull and the periosteum on its inner aspect, and it is usually related to birth trauma. They may require surgical removal.[130] Subdural hematoma, blood between the dura and the leptomeninges, typically occurs in the full-term infant. Volpe states that subdural hemorrhage is more likely to occur when the infant is relatively large and the birth canal is relatively small. It is complicated if the skull is unusually compliant, as in premature infants, or if the pelvic structures are unusually rigid, as in primigravidas or older multiparous mothers. If the duration of labor is unusually brief, not allowing enough time for dilatation of the pelvic structures, or if the labor is unusually long, subjecting the head to prolonged compression and molding, while there is breech or footling presentation, or face or brow presentation, necessitating difficult forceps extraction, vacuum extraction or rotational maneuvers, can lead to hemorrhage.[131] The examiner should remember that prenatal or intrauterine subdural hematomas also occur secondary to maternal abuse, severe factor V deficiency, high-dose aspirin in the mother, medulloblastoma with hemorrhage, and neonatal vitamin K deficiency.

NEUROPATHOLOGY OF TRAUMATIC BRAIN INJURY

The initial event of brain trauma is mechanical distortion of brain tissue. Instantaneous cell death is relatively uncommon in TBI.[12] In the last 20 years, most animal studies of TBI have been carried out primarily in rodents. Recently, neurosurgeons are arguing that the pig is a better model with which to study human TBI. A swine model results in a defined and reproducible injury with pathological features similar to human TBI. Physiological parameters of pigs after injury are readily monitored in settings that mimic the conditions of a human intensive care unit. This in turn establishes a more clinically relevant experimental model for future investigations.[132] It is postulated that the initial abnormality in TBI occurs through mechanoporation. Mechanoporation is the creation of a traumatic defect in the cell membrane that occurs within the lipid bilayer of the cell. It is transiently separated from the more stiff protein inclusions in the cell wall such as receptors and channels.[133] As a result of the rent in the lipid bilayer, various ions can move rapidly into or out of the cell following their pre-injury concentration gradients. Initially, this would provide for potassium to move to the outside, and sodium, chloride, and calcium to move to the inside of the cell. The rent in the lipid bilayer is thought to be present for only a brief period. Within minutes, or at most a few hours, the defect closes by flow of the lipid bilayer, or by an active process due to calcium-activated phospholipase A_2, which generates lysolecithin that produces a patch or fusion of the membrane.[134] There is evidence that measurement of transient rises in intracellular calcium covary in direct proportion to the amount of injury delivered to the central nervous system.[135]

After the initial mechanical events of TBI, delayed cellular dysfunction occurs by four principal mechanisms. These include inflammation, receptor-mediated dysfunction, free-radical and oxidative damage, and calcium or other ion-mediated damage.[12] These processes in turn modulate gene expression or protein regulation, and they ultimately lead either to cell death or to putative repair mechanisms. At this time, these central nervous system repair mechanisms are poorly understood. The remainder of this neuropathology section will concern itself with the molecular, genetic, and cellular consequences of TBI. Figure 1.3 displays the interaction of the four principal mechanisms of cellular injury following TBI.

POTENTIAL NEURODEGENERATION

Head injury has been convincingly implicated as a risk factor for Alzheimer's disease in several epidemiological studies.[12] As noted above, boxing often leads to permanent brain injury. The punch-drunk syndrome presents with memory loss and Parkinson-like symptoms; the syndrome

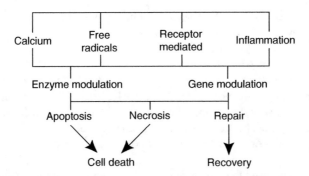

FIGURE 1.3 The four pillars of cellular damage following traumatic brain injury (TBI). (From Graham, D.I., Gennarelli, T.A., and McIntosh, T.K., Trauma, in *Greenfield's Neuropathology*, 7th edition, Graham, D.I. and Lantos, P.L., Eds., Arnold, London, 2002. With permission.)

also demonstrates β-amyloid deposits and neurofibrillary tangles, both of which have been identified pathologically and associated with brain trauma.[106]

It is recognized that the ε4 allele of the apolipoprotein E gene is a major genetic risk factor for the development of Alzheimer's disease. Patients demonstrating the apolipoprotein E ε4 allele who died from head injury have been shown to be more than four times as likely to have β-amyloid deposits than patients who lack the ε4 allele. Several studies in the last 10 years have demonstrated that patients with apolipoprotein E ε4 have a worse outcome after TBI than those who do not have the ε4 allele. Teasdale's group in Scotland studied a prospectively recruited series of patients. Fifty-seven percent of patients with ε4 alleles had an unfavorable outcome (died, continued in a vegetative state, or had severe disability) six months after their injury, compared with 27% of patients who did not possess the ε4 allele.[136] This study demonstrated significant negative outcome findings for persons possessing ε4 alleles when controls were put in place for age, severity of the initial injury, and the initial CT scan findings. A study of 30 professional boxers (ages 23–76 years) demonstrated that those athletes with more than 12 professional bouts who had the ε4 allele had significantly greater scores on a clinical scale of chronic TBI.[137]

Mouse studies have determined that presence of the ε4 allele results in dramatic blood–brain barrier defects following brain trauma.[138] Other mouse data support the hypothesis that Apo ε4 influences the neurodegenerative cascade after TBI by affecting β-amyloid.[139] In humans, the presence of ε4 alleles of apolipoprotein E is associated with impairment of memory. In a Johns Hopkins School of Public Health study, 87 adult patients presenting with mild or moderate TBI to a shock trauma center were enrolled prospectively. A battery of 13 neuropsychological tests was administered twice at approximately three and six weeks after injury. All patients were genotyped for apolipoprotein E using a buccal swab technique. Of the patients studied, 90% had mild brain injury (GCS score of 13–15), and the remainder were in the moderate range (GCS score of 9–12). Of these patients 23% had one allele of ε4 and none had two ε4 alleles. Patients positive for the ε4 allele had lower mean scores on 12 of the 13 neuropsychological outcomes measured in this study.[140] A University of South Florida study examined 110 veterans enrolled in the Defense and Veterans Head Injury Center (DVHIC) program. This study demonstrated that memory performance was worse in those veterans who had at least one ε4 allele when compared to those who had no ε4 alleles. In this study 30 of 110 veterans were positive for at least one allele of ε4. There were no differences between the groups on demographics or injury variables, and there were no differences on measures of executive function. The authors concluded that these data support a specific role for the apolipoprotein E protein in memory outcome following TBI.[141]

Teasdale's Glasgow group has demonstrated recently that late decline may occur following head injury. However, they were unable to find a clear relationship between this decline and the Apo E genotype. They studied a cohort of 396 subjects who had an initial assessment at the time of their brain injury between 1968 and 1985. Outcome data six months following injury was available, and the ages ranged between 2 and 70 years. The 396 subjects were reassessed an average of 18 years following their original injury. They had the Apo E genotype determined and a detailed neuro-psychological testing. Twice as many patients had deteriorated as had improved between six months after injury and the assessment 18 years later. Of the ε4 carriers 22% had a good late outcome, whereas 31% of the noncarriers had a good late outcome. This was statistically significant. This study was unable to differentiate between ε4 carriers and noncarriers in terms of neuropsychological assessment, but the authors conceded that the duration of the study may be too short to detect changes.[142]

Recent studies have reviewed the influence of apolipoprotein E polymorphism and outcome for various clinical groups. For instance, ethnicity and regional differences have been studied in South Africa. A cohort of black African patients from a Zulu-speaking region who presented with traumatic cerebral contusions was studied. Of these persons 24% with a ε4 allele experienced poor outcome compared with 15% of persons without this allele. This study revealed no significant relationship between the ε4 allele and factors of age, GCS score, contusion volume, and type of neurosurgical management. The risk of poor outcome was greater in patients who possessed the ε4 allele (relative risk = 1.59).[143]

In a study of elderly patients in Finland who sustained TBI by falling, TBI predicted earlier onset of dementia in a study of 325 patients. Those patients who possessed the ε4 phenotype of apolipoprotein E had a much higher likelihood of developing dementia than those that did not. These patients were followed up to 9 years.[144] The University of Glasgow TBI group found a relationship between possession of the ε4 allele and an increased likelihood of severe ischemic brain damage following TBI. This group examined 239 fatal cases of TBI between 1987 and 1999 for which Apo E genotypes were determined from archival tissue. Of these cases 35% were ε4 carriers, and 65% were noncarriers. Possession of the ε4 allele was associated with a greater incidence of moderate or severe contusions versus the non-ε4 carriers. There was a trend toward a greater incidence of severe ischemic brain damage in the ε4 group.[145] The overall scientific evidence at this time is that there is a synergistic interaction between brain injury and possession of the apolipo-protein E ε4 allele as a risk factor for Alzheimer's-like neurodegeneration following brain trauma.[146]

DAMAGE TO THE NEUROFILAMENTOUS CYTOSKELETON

We have learned from Alzheimer's disease research that neurofibrillary tangles are a feature of this illness and consist of abnormally phosphorylated tau protein.[147] We have seen above the relation-ship of apolipoprotein E ε4 carriers to brain trauma. Neurofibrillary tangles have been found within the brains of ex-boxers and have tested positive for the tau protein suggesting that tau pathology may be a feature of the dementia syndrome associated with this sport.[106] When the cerebrospinal fluid of brain-injured humans is tested, cleaved forms of tau proteins are found to be markedly elevated.[148]

In axonal swellings following TBI, immunochemical reactions indicate that neurofilamentous protein accumulates as a consequence of traumatic axonal injury.[149] This traumatic disruption of the neurofilamentous cytoskeleton and loss of neurofilamentous proteins such as tau occurs in regions of both gray and white matter following TBI.[12] Unfortunately, it is not well understood presently how disturbances in the neurofilament cytoskeleton contribute to the clinical aftereffects of TBI.

Other markers of neuron structure have been identified that are associated with degeneration following TBI. These include tau, ubiquitin, α-, β-, and γ-synuclein. The University of Pittsburgh Department of Neurology has reviewed the histopathology of temporal cortex following resection from individuals treated surgically for severe TBI. Tau-positive neurofibrillary tangles were detected in only 2 of 18 subjects. Both of these individuals were of more advanced age. However, other neurode-generative changes of the cytoskeleton, evidenced by ubiquitin and synuclein-immunoreactive neurons, were abundant in the majority of cases.[150] The University of Cincinnati Department of Psychiatry evaluated use of tau protein as a biomarker of neuronal damage after TBI. This study was conducted in rats rather than in humans. However, their results suggest that C-tau is a reliable, quantitative biomarker for evaluating TBI-induced neuronal injury and a potential biomarker to test the neuroprotectant efficacy of therapeutic drugs.[151] A recent autopsy of a retired National Football League professional football player was undertaken. Following brain resection, this patient demonstrated sparse neurofibrillary tangles and tau-positive neuritic threads in neocortical areas. The apolipoprotein E genotype was ε3/ε3. There was mild neuronal dropout in the frontal, parietal, and temporal neocortex. This autopsy was performed approximately 12 years following his retirement from football after he died as a result of a coronary artery event. The University of Pittsburgh Department of Pathology suggested that this case highlighted potential long-term neurodegenerative outcomes in retired professional National Football League players subjected to repeated MTBI. They recommended comprehensive clinical and forensic approaches to understand and further elucidate this emergent professional sport hazard.[152]

Povlishock's group at the Medical College of Virginia has recently summarized the cytoskeleton dynamics following TBI and the resulting local axonal failure and disconnection. His group points out that classic theories had suggested that traumatically injured axons were mechanically torn at the moment of injury. Studies in the last two decades have not supported this premise in the majority of injured axons that have been histopathologically studied. Current thought considers traumatic axonal injury to be a progressive process which is evoked by the tensile forces of injury, which then gradually evolves from focal axonal alteration to ultimate disconnection (see Ref. 133). Recent observations have demonstrated that traumatically induced focal axolemmal permeability leads to the local influx of calcium ions. This produces a subsequent activation of the cysteine proteases, calpain, and caspase. These then play a pivotal role in the pathogenesis of axonal injury by way of proteolytic digestion of brain spectrin, a major constituent of the cytoskeletal network, the "membrane skeleton." Local calcium ion overloading, with the activation of calpains, initiates mitochondrial injury resulting in the release of cytochrome *c*, with the activation of caspase. Both activated calpain and caspases then participate in the degradation of the axonal cytoskeleton causing local axonal failure and ultimately the disconnection of the axon from the cell body.[153]

ALTERATIONS OF CALCIUM HOMEOSTASIS

Regional cerebral edema, vasospasm, and delayed cell death (apoptosis) are common outcomes of TBI. These outcomes have been linked to alterations in brain calcium homeostasis and certain receptor/channels associated with calcium entry. These are voltage-sensitive channels or ion-sensitive channels, such as glutamate receptors mediated by *N*-methyl-D-aspartate (NMDA). Direct brain trauma, brain ischemia, or anoxic injury to neurons is associated with widespread neuronal depolarization. This in turn releases excitatory amino acid neurotransmitters such as glutamate, which cause opening of NMDA receptor-associated ion channels and the immediate influx of calcium.[12] These posttraumatic increases in intracellular calcium may precipitate an attack against the cellular membrane by way of activating calcium-dependent phospholipases. Logically, one might conclude that calcium channel blockers, along with competitive and noncompetitive NMDA receptor antagonists, might assist in the treatment of TBI. To date, human studies using these substances have been disappointing.[154]

Calcium mediates in other ways to produce direct neuronal injury. Increased intracellular calcium may stimulate the release of reactive oxygen species (ROS) for mitochondria, or this can be generated by the cytoplasm. These are highly reactive molecules, and they may cause peroxidative destruction of the cell membrane, oxidized cellular protein and nucleic acids, or attack the cerebral blood vessels. Macrophages and neutrophils may excrete excitatory amino acid neurotransmitters or nitric acid synthase, which also can produce ROS.[155] The immediate-early genes *c-fos* and *c-jun* are induced by ROS.[156]

Calcium may also irreversibly activate the nonlysosomal cysteine protease calpain, which can proteolyse a wide range of cytoskeletal proteins. Calpain can also be involved in the degradation of other enzymes (kinases, phosphatases) and membrane-associated proteins, including ion channels and transporters, glutamate receptors, neurotrophin receptors, and adhesion molecules.[157] It is this activation of calpain, when it is prolonged and unregulated, that produces irreversible structural and functional alterations to the cytoskeleton that have been implicated in neuronal toxicity.[158]

Excitotoxic damage through alterations of the NMDA receptor, alterations in calcium homeostasis, and free-radical-induced damage are thought to be key pathways in the pathophysiology of brain tissue degradation following trauma. It is believed that the final target of all these pathways is the mitochondria, through the alteration of the mitochondrial permeability transition pore. Moreover, the inflammatory response that occurs after trauma may be important in the exacerbation of secondary damage as well.[159] Mitochondria serve as the powerhouse of the cell by maintaining ratios of ATP/ADP (adenosine triphosphate and -diphosphate) that thermodynamically favor the hydrolysis of ATP/ADP. A byproduct of this process is the generation of ROS. Protein pumping by components of the electron transport system generates a membrane potential that can then be used to phosphorylate ADP or sequester calcium ions out of the cytosol into the mitochondrial matrix. This allows mitochondria to act as cellular calcium ion sinks and to be in phase with changes in cytosolic calcium ion levels. Under extreme loads of calcium ion influx however, opening of the mitochondrial permeability transition pore results in the extrusion of mitochondrial calcium ions and other high and low-molecular weight components. This catastrophic event discharges the membrane potential and uncouples the electron transport system from ATP production. These recent findings at the Spinal Cord and Brain Injury Research Center at the University of Kentucky in Lexington have found that by adding cyclosporin A, a potent immunosuppressive drug, mitochondrial permeability is inhibited and attenuates mitochondrial dysfunction and neuronal damage in rat models. This study potentially opens the way for therapeutically targeting the mitochondrial permeability transition pore to reduce the aftereffects of brain trauma.[160]

The effects of alterations of calcium homeostasis following TBI, cell death, and dysfunction following TBI consists of a primary phase, which causes immediate consequences to cells by direct mechanical destruction of the brain. A secondary phase ensues, which consists of delayed events initiated at the time of insult (see Figure 1.4). One of the major culprits that contribute to delayed

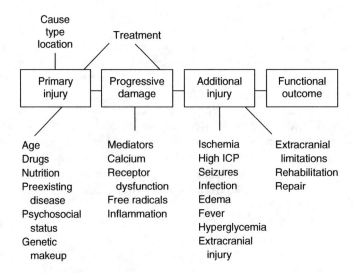

FIGURE 1.4 The process of traumatic brain injury (TBI). (From Graham, D.I., Gennarelli, T.A., and McIntosh, T.K., Trauma, in *Greenfield's Neuropathology*, 7th edition, Graham, D.I. and Lantos, P.L., Eds., Arnold, London, 2002. With permission.)

neuronal damage and death after traumatic insult is the calcium ion. The original calcium hypothesis suggested that a large, sustained influx of calcium into neurons initiates cell death by signaling cellular toxic cascades. Much of this original hypothesis remains true, but recent findings suggest that the role of calcium in traumatic neuronal injury is much more complex. For example, it has been found that a sustained level of intracellular free calcium is not necessarily lethal, but the specific route of calcium entry may couple calcium directly to cell death pathways. Other sources of calcium such as that within the cell itself can also cause cell damage. In addition, calcium-mediated signal transduction pathways have been found to be altered following brain injury. These alterations are sustained for several hours after the injury and may contribute to dysfunction in neurons that did not necessarily die after a traumatic episode.[161] Figure 1.4 dramatically demonstrates that TBI is a process, not an instantaneous event.

APOPTOSIS AND CELLULAR DEATH

Apoptosis, or programmed cell death, is a physiological form of cellular death that is important for normal embryologic development and cell turnover in adult organisms. Central nervous system research suggests that apoptosis can also be triggered in tissues without a high rate of cell turnover, such as brain tissue. Apoptosis is emerging as a cause for delayed neuronal loss after both acute and chronic brain injury.[162] In the immature brain, this can be even more dramatic than in the adult brain. Head trauma is the leading cause of death and disability in the pediatric population. Biochemical studies indicate that both the extrinsic and the intrinsic apoptotic pathways are involved in the pathogenesis of apoptotic cell death following trauma in the developing brain, and that caspase inhibition ameliorates apoptotic neurodegeneration in an infant head trauma model.[163]

While it is beyond the scope of this chapter, TUNEL (terminal deoxynucleotidyl transferase-mediated dUTP nick-end labeling) immunohistochemistry has been used since the early 1990s to establish that neural cell apoptosis is a component of the pathology of neurodegenerative diseases such as Alzheimer's, Parkinson's, and Huntington's.[12] Rink et al.[164] were the first to report that between 12 h and 3 days after a lateral fluid percussion brain injury in the rat, a small but significant number of injured neurons in the cortex and hippocampus exhibited TUNEL reactivity. Conti et al.[165] extended these initial observations by demonstrating that there was a biphasic increase at 24 h and 1 week post-injury in the number of apoptotic cells in the cortex. The presence of apoptotic cell death has been suggested by the presence of TUNEL-positive neurons and oligodendrocytes in human head-injured tissue. Graham et al.[12] argue that although TUNEL methodology has been widely used to visualize apoptotic cells and tissue sections, these results must be cautiously interpreted in humans, as DNA degradation leading to the formation of hydroxyl groups can occur in the late phases of necrosis. It has been argued further that a continuum between apoptosis and necrosis exists (see Figure 1.3). The presence of a continuum suggests that intracellular pathways leading to apoptosis and necrosis may not be mutually exclusive. Even though it has been proposed that calcium-activated neutral proteases (calpains) may mediate necrosis and that caspase-3 is only activated in apoptotic cells, calpain activation may also lead to apoptosis.[12] Despite three decades of preclinical research, the pathological mechanisms underlying cell death and behavioral dysfunction after TBI are not fully understood. The current literature suggests that a complex mechanism involving altered anti- and pro-cell death signaling pathways is likely to play a major role in mediating posttraumatic apoptotic cell death.[12]

ACUTE BIOCHEMICAL MARKERS

There is emerging scientific evidence that biochemical markers may enable the diagnosis of TBI to be made more confidently in the acute setting when clinical or pathological evidence of brain injury is not obvious or is equivocal. The two most common markers developed recently for the detection of brain injury following acute trauma are the S-100 protein and neuron-specific enolase. These two substances are quite specific. S-100 protein is produced by Schwann cells or oligodendroglia. Their presence in the cerebrospinal fluid or serum is indicative of neuronal or glial damage from trauma.[12] These findings are highly significant for the clinician, as both S-100 and enolase can be detected in serum, and a lumbar puncture is not necessarily required. Moreover, the release of these neurobiochemical markers of brain damage has been directly associated with intracranial pathology detected by computerized tomography.[166] It has been known for 10 years that neuropsychological function following minor head injury is positively correlated with increased serum levels of protein S-100,[167] and it has been known for more than 10 years that alteration of neuron-specific enolase and myelin basic protein elevation are diagnostic for cellular injury following acute head injury.[168]

S-100 protein is an acidic calcium-binding protein. It is much more abundant in the brain than in other tissues of the body. It exists as a mixture of S-100a and S-100b. This has been termed S-100β. These two isoforms are predominately synthesized and secreted by glial cells. Structural damage of these cells causes leakage of the S-100β protein into the extracellular compartment and into cerebrospinal fluid, further entering the bloodstream.[169] Potentially, after minor head trauma, detection of S-100β could prove difficult. A United Kingdom study[170] has recently noted the rapid clearance of S-100β from the serum. A study at the Hull Royal Infirmary found the mean half-life following mild head injury to be 97 min (95% confidence interval of 75–136 min). These authors cautioned that variation in the time elapsed between injury and sampling is likely to influence the accuracy of head injury outcome prediction based on S-100β concentrations in serum, and this should be considered when designing future studies. Notwithstanding the warnings of Townend et al.,[170] the rate of clearance may be related to the volume of injury. Herrmann's group in Magdeburg, Germany,[166] examined 66 patients following TBI. Their serum was analyzed 1–3 days after injury by immunoluminometric assay. Volumetric evaluation of CT scans were performed on all patients. All serum concentrations of S-100β were significantly correlated with the volume of contusion. Protein S-100β levels in serum also correlated directly with ultimate brain death. A Greek study followed 47 patients to a maximum of six consecutive days and compared S-100β serum levels between those who survived and those who did not. An odds ratio of 2.09 indicated more than twice the probability of deteriorating to brain death. This statistical prediction between those who survived and those who did not was quite high ($p < .0001$).[171]

Recent studies have attempted to predict posttraumatic symptomatic complaints and return to work following mild head injury using biochemical markers as a predictor. A study from the Netherlands[172] found that the presence of headache, dizziness, or nausea in the emergency department after MTBI was strongly associated with the elevation of neuron-specific enolase and S-100β in serum. This series of 79 patients demonstrated that all 10 patients presenting to the emergency department without symptoms and normal biochemical markers recovered fully versus the twofold increased severity of cognitive and psychiatric complaints in those with increased concentrations of the biochemical markers at the time of injury.[172] Another Greek study[173] followed 100 patients after a mild head injury. All subjects had a GCS score of 15, either with or without loss of consciousness. Serum S-100β was collected within 3 h of the injury. An independent observer measured the return-to-work rate within one week of injury. The failure to return to work or to normal daily activities was significantly correlated with elevated S-100β ($p < .0001$). This study's authors suggested that the S-100β assay might be useful in selecting patients who need closer observation after minor head injury. Further use of S-100β has helped distinguish primary brain damage in intoxicated patients where assessment is often difficult.[174] To further enlarge the discussion about soccer players, a Swedish study has found that both S-100β and neuron-specific enolase were increased in elite female soccer players. These markers were significantly related to the number of headers and other trauma events that these women sustained during the game.[175]

With regard to biochemical markers in children, serum neuron-specific enolase and S-100β are elevated both in children who sustain noninflicted brain trauma and inflicted brain trauma.[176] Berger's group at the Child Advocacy Center in Pittsburgh, Pennsylvania argues that identification of inflicted TBI in well-appearing infants may be augmented by using biochemical markers as a possible screening tool.[177] Her group prospectively followed 98 well-appearing infants who presented with nonspecific symptoms and no history of trauma. Serum or cerebrospinal fluid was collected. Neuron-specific enolase and S-100β were assayed. Fourteen patients received a clinical diagnosis of inflicted TBI using established cutoffs. Neuron-specific enolase was 77% sensitive and 66% specific. Myelin basic protein was also assayed. It had a lower sensitivity of 36% but was 100% specific for inflicted TBI. It was concluded that S-100β was neither sensitive nor specific for inflicted brain trauma. Emory University[178] has attempted to use neuron-specific enolase as a predictor of short-term outcome in children who sustain closed TBI. The study group consisted of 90 children in whom neuron-specific enolase levels had been determined. Seven subjects had poor outcome based on the GCS. There was a significant difference in neuron-specific enolase levels between the poor and good outcome groups. A serum neuron-specific enolase level of 21.2 ng/dl was 86% sensitive and 74% specific in predicting poor outcome.

THE PATHOLOGY OF HEAD INJURY

SKULL FRACTURE

The presence of skull fracture indicates that impact to the head has occurred with force.[179] Interestingly, some patients with a skull fracture may have no evidence of brain damage and make an uneventful recovery. It is hypothesized that the energy producing the fracture is dissipated by the fracture itself, which in turn displaces the focus of energy into the skull bones rather than into the brain parenchyma. However, patients suffering a skull fracture because of head trauma have a much higher incidence of intracranial hematoma than those who do not sustain a fracture.[180,181] The type of fracture found following trauma is dictated in part by the shape of the object that makes contact with the head. Flat-shaped objects tend to produce fissure fractures, which can extend into the base of the skull, while angled or pointed objects produce a localized or stellate fracture.[182] Fractures at the base of the skull may give rise to infection. These fractures often pass through the petrous bone or the anterior cranial fossa (cribriform plate) and cause leakage of cerebrospinal fluid through the nose, mouth, or ear. Up to 30% of patients who have skull fractures producing leakages of cerebrospinal fluid develop tumor-like complications when the resulting cavity distends as a result of trapped air (aerocoele).

Contrecoup fractures (fractures located at a distance from the point of injury that are not direct extensions of a fracture originating at the point of injury) occur principally in the roofs of the orbits and the ethmoid plates after falls that cause trauma to the back of the skull[12] (the classic "slip and fall"). Linear fractures are a direct consequence of contact effects to the skull because of impact. Head motion, acceleration, and inertia do not play a role as they do in contrecoup fractures. Linear fractures are interesting in that most of the impact energy is not utilized to set the head in motion, and the available energy deforms the skull producing the fracture. The object striking the skull generally has a surface area larger than 5 cm². An acceleration injury could occur if substantial head motion follows after impact.[12] Depressed fractures are similar physically to linear fractures except that there are more contact forces, usually because the impact surface is smaller than 5 cm². Since the contact phenomena are much more focused and more intense, they exceed the elasticity of the skull causing a perforation inward of the bone.[12] Basal fractures are due either to direct impact to the skull base (osteoid, mastoid) or due to the energy transmitted to the skull base downward from the face. In the latter case, stress waves propagate from the point of impact with sufficient force to cause a fracture. Common mechanisms for skull-based fractures are impact to the chin (this usually results in mandibular fracture), a force transmitted up the temporomandibular joints, or a head whip. Head whipping occurs usually in frontal car crashes when the torso is well restrained by a shoulder restraint, and the head is free to move violently forward. A special case of skull base fracture is the so-called ring fracture. This occurs because of abrupt hyperextension of the head and because of the tenacious attachment of the neck muscles to the base of the skull producing a ring avulsion fracture. This may result in a pontomedullar vascular stretch or rent.[183]

Obviously, fracture can occur from a penetrating head injury as well. The most common penetrating head injuries are gunshot wounds. In these cases, management of the fracture is secondary to the management of the bullet path, if the person survives the initial impact of the bullet. Craniotomy is required for most of these individuals. The physician providing a late examination to a surviving person should review the records carefully for postgunshot complications such as infection, intracranial hemorrhage, cerebrospinal fluid leak, and epileptic seizures.[184] These complications may augment neuropsychiatric deficits. Commonly, the cribriform plate is fractured in closed head injury. However, comminuted fractures of the anteriocranial base often result from gunshot injuries producing significant CSF rhinorrhea. Cerebrospinal fluid fistulas commonly occur following these injuries, and currently these may be treated by an endonasal endoscopic approach.[185]

Skull fractures in children present certain challenges. Skull fracture during infancy can result in enduring impairment of specific cognitive skills related to the processing of complex nonverbal stimuli.[186] However, routine skull fracture in children following closed head injury, even in uncomplicated cases, can result in meningitis.[187] The physician or psychologist examining children who sustained basilar skull fracture should review carefully to determine whether the child has a complicating secondary brain injury from meningitis.

FOCAL HEAD INJURY

Contusions and Lacerations

A contusion is a bruise that occurs focally in the brain and is caused mainly by contact between the surface of the brain and a bony protuberance within the skull or by rapid acceleration–deceleration.[12] By definition, the membranes of the pia–arachnoid remain intact over surface contusions, but following lacerations they are torn. The biomechanics of closed head injury are such that contusions generally distribute over the frontal poles, the orbital gyri, the cortex above and below the Sylvian fissures, the tips of the temporal poles, and lateral and inferior aspects of the temporal lobes. Less frequently, the inferior surfaces of the cerebellar hemispheres may be affected as well.[46] Contusions can occur but are rarely found over the parietal and occipital lobes unless there is a skull fracture in these areas.[182] Table 1.9 reveals the characteristic distribution of brain traumatic contusions following head injury without depressed skull fracture. DiMaio and DiMaio[43] have reported that the initial appearance of a brain contusion evolves over time. Shortly following the injury, the contusion will be visible as microscopic regions of perivascular hemorrhage that follow tracts along the small vessels within the cortex. These usually run perpendicular to the cortical surface, and they may occur almost instantaneously following injury. As time progresses, blood products seep into the adjacent cortex, and neuronal structures in the immediate vicinity begin to degenerate. The cascade of events described in "Neuropathology of Traumatic Brain Injury" begin to take place.

TABLE 1.9

Characteristic Distribution of Brain Traumatic Contusions

- Frontal poles
- Orbital surfaces of the frontal lobes
- Temporal poles
- Lateral and inferior surfaces of the temporal poles
- Cortex adjacent to the sylvian fissures

Morphologically, as neurons degenerate, a glial scar is subsequently produced. Potentially, the hemorrhage will extend into the white matter, causing demyelination of axons and eventual loss of neuronal tracts. As necrotic tissue is produced, it is eventually removed by macrophages, and the contusion develops into a shrunken scar. At autopsy, this is apparent to the naked eye. Residual hemosiderin fills the macrophages, and in many instances the scar will have a brown appearance. Magnetic resonance imaging may detect hemosiderin deposits (gradient echo sequences) resulting from contusions at a time distant from the original injury (see Chapter 5). After the contusion ages, it may develop a pyramidal shape, with the apex of the pyramid deep into the cortex and the base of the pyramid at the crest of the gyrus.[182] Coup contusions occur beneath the site of impact and are due to local tissue strains arising from local bending of the skull as it exceeds the tolerances of the local pial, vascular, and cortical brain tissue. As seen above, the impact of the object must be relatively small and hard, and the area of the skull that is struck must remain elastic. Rupture of pial vessels usually occurs because of high tensile strains, such as suction, that are produced when the focally depressed elastic skull rapidly accelerates back to its normal configuration and away from the traumatized brain. If skull elasticity is exceeded by the force of the blow, a direct compressive injury will occur to the cortical surface.[12] On the other hand, contrecoup contusions are focal areas of vascular disruption and cortical damage that are remote from the site of impact. These occur principally because of head motion (acceleration) and can result from translational (linear) or angular (following a curve) movements of the head. Movement of the brain toward the site of impact causes tensile strains to occur in the area opposite to that of the impact. When tensile strains are greater than the vascular tolerance, a contusion results at a site distant from the point of impact. However, it is most important to understand, particularly for forensic purposes, that impact over the site of the bruise is not necessary for contrecoup contusions to occur. Pathologists point out that the term "coup" is therefore a misnomer, since the critical mechanism is most often acceleration rather than the impact producing the lesion. For instance, in those situations where the head undergoes impulsive loading, contrecoup contusions occur solely because of the effects of acceleration. Also, if an impact causes considerable global deformation to the skull, tensile strains can occur at sites distant from impact and produce contusional damage. However, the predominant mechanism for contrecoup contusions is rapid acceleration of the head.[12]

Cerebral contusions have a 51% incidence of evolution in the first hours after injury. Evolution is associated with clinical deterioration, and this is why neurosurgeons place intracerebral pressure monitors or proceed to surgical intervention. If a CT scan is obtained, the absence of pericontusional edema may be a useful marker to predict that the contusion will not evolve.[188] Many contusions are not detected by CT at the time of injury, and arguments are made by radiologists that early phase MRI is essential to the detection of brain injury, at least using conventional imaging techniques.[189] The contusions that develop following trauma apparently develop ischemia. The ischemia follows a centrifugal gradient with the highest levels of ischemia central in the lesion, and lower levels present more peripherally at greater distances from the center of the lesion. This has been confirmed by cerebral blood flow measures utilizing xenon-enhanced computerized tomography (XeCT).[190] If regional cerebral blood flow is measured, most ischemia is in the hemorrhagic core; the perihematoma edematous area surrounding the core has a higher level of blood flow than the center, the highest flow being within a 1 cm rim of perihematoma, and otherwise normal appearing brain tissue surrounding the edematous area.

Pure lacerations are not very common, but when they do occur, they present significant clinical findings. Of patients with cerebral lacerations 20% will present with a lucid interval and no significant mental status changes. However, as the laceration evolves through hemorrhage, the mental state will deteriorate, and the GCS score will reduce. Lacerations will often progress to coma together with ventricular shift, and they are frequently found in the presence of bilateral skull fractures.[191] When a brain laceration occurs, the presence of considerable blood on CT suggests an unfavorable prognosis. The site of the laceration and the mass effect from the laceration do not seem to influence the course or progression of the complications.[192]

Extradural (Epidural) Hematoma

The classic case of the epidural hematoma is the patient who is in a motor vehicle accident, lucid at the scene with a GCS score of 15, who then rapidly progresses to coma during transit to the emergency department. Fracture of the skull is present in the great majority of these patients, but it can occur in the absence of fracture, especially in children. This type of hemorrhage usually takes place from disruption of meningeal blood vessels. As the hematoma enlarges, it strips the dura from the skull to form a circumscribed ovoid mass that progressively indents and flattens the subjacent brain.[12] Epidural hematoma occurs in approximately 2% of brain injuries according to Lindenberg.[193] In the Glasgow database, epidural hematomas are present in about 8% of the cases.[194] Classically, this hematoma results from tearing of the middle meningeal artery (about 50% of the cases) in the region of the squamous part of the temporal bone where the bone is thin and easily fractured. However, 20%–30% of epidural hematomas occur at other anatomical sites within the skull, such as the frontal regions, parietal regions, or posterior fossa.[195]

Since the temporal bone is more flexible than other parts of the skull, it will often deform inward following a direct impact, develop a fracture line, and transect or rupture a meningeal artery or an occasional vein. These vessels lie on the inner table of the skull, and in cases where an artery is ruptured, the arterial pressure quickly forces blood into the potential space between the skull and the dura. This produces an enlarging space-occupying mass. It is this potential for the rapid enlargement of the mass that may produce a life threatening situation to the patient because of pressure transfer throughout the brain. Epidural hematomas can enlarge to the point of causing downward herniation of the inferior brain producing uncal herniation at the foramen magnum.

Surgical evacuation is not always required, particularly for small masses. Where the mass continues to enlarge or the size of the mass is producing midline shift or downward herniation, neurosurgical intervention will be required. In those hematomas that are not evacuated, they will eventually undergo partial organization, and their centers may remain cystic and filled with dark viscous fluid.[196] After the clot liquefies, the hematoma gradually shrinks, and in the majority of patients, it may be completely resolved by the fourth to the sixth week post-injury.

When epidural hematoma occurs, it is frequently associated with diffuse axonal injury.[197] Interestingly, the use of motorcycle helmets to prevent head injuries has been very controversial in the United States. Many states refuse to mandate helmet use for motorcycle riders, even in those states where use of seat belt restraints is mandatory for drivers of automobiles. Italy put in place a motorcycle helmet law and recently reviewed its data from 1999 to 2001. Following implementation of the law, the Romagna region increased helmet use from less than 20% to over 96%. The TBI incidence in the Romagna region was compared before and after helmet law implementation. The rate of TBI admissions to neurosurgical departments in this region decreased by over 31%, and epidural hematomas almost completely disappeared in crash-injured motorcycle or moped riders.[198]

There are some significant clinical differences in epidural hematomas found in children versus adults. Epidural hematoma in newborn infants is rare, but it is always a posttraumatic lesion, and it is only possible if the insult has produced a cleavage of the dura mater from the bone. Epidural hematoma results from the mechanical forces exerted on the fetal head during birth, with or without instrument interference. It is still unclear whether this injury is directly caused by forceps, when used, or is already inflicted by natural forces of uterine compression and birth canal pressure. While epidural hematoma is rare, it remains an ever-present cause of morbidity in the neonatal population.[199] Many times surgical decompression is not required in a neonate. However, if the child tolerates the mass poorly, surgery will be required, and it is usually successful.[200]

Intradural (Subdural) Hematoma

Subdural hematomas are usually caused by rupture of the bridging veins, and there may be little other evidence of intracranial injury. Subdural hematoma usually takes three forms. Pure subdural hematoma is caused by rupture of the bridging veins, which allows blood to pool in the subdural space between the dura and the meningeal tissues. The other two forms are contusions on the surface of the brain with localized bleeding and adjacent intracerebral hematoma. This has been referred to by neuropathologists and neurosurgeons as a "burst" lobe.[12] Rarely, subdural hematomas are arterial in origin, and the hemorrhage arises from a cortical artery.[195] The principal causes of subdural hematoma are falls, motor vehicle accidents, and physical assault. They also have been reported to occur by whiplash injury only with no injury to the head.[201] Unlike the epidural hematoma, which produces a lenticular or ovoid appearance on imaging, subdural blood can spread freely throughout the subdural space and follows the gyral pattern of the brain surface. They are usually larger and more extensive than extradural hematomas. Many cases of subdural hematoma are associated with considerable tissue brain damage, and the mortality and morbidity is greater in subdural hematomas than it is in extradural hematomas. In infants, subdural hematomas are the most common type of intracranial injury following child abuse.[202] Table 1.10 lists the location of hemorrhages that occur following head injury.

Graham[194] has described well the clinical evolution of the subdural hematoma clot. If the hematoma does not require surgical evacuation, the blood will remain clotted for about 48 h. The blood may remain clotted for several days, but subsequently, a mixture of blood clot and fluidized blood occurs. In most cases, the clot will be absorbed in about three weeks. After the clot is absorbed, the gyral and sulcal patterns under the hematoma will remain preserved. While the convolutions over the surface of the brain do not flatten under the hematoma, there is often marked flattening of the convolutions over the opposite hemisphere. This is because the subdural blood is in direct contact with both the gyri and sulci and exerts a uniform compression on the underlying brain tissue, which prevents flattening of the contiguous surface.[194] Blood is quite frequently noxious to brain tissue, and in about 25% of patients who require a neurosurgical evaluation of the clot, acute brain swelling occurs within the hemisphere directly beneath the clot. This often results in a poor prognosis.[203]

The chronic subdural hematoma is a special case when compared to the acute clot. Classically, these are seen in patients who present to an emergency department with neurological changes weeks or months following an acute injury. However, a history of head injury is absent in about 25%–50% of cases.[204] The individual may deteriorate neurologically because the hematoma becomes encapsulated within the membrane and then slowly increases in size, possibly as a result of repeated small hemorrhages into its substance rather than as an osmotic effect.[205] Chronic subdural hematoma is commonly found in older patients, and 75% of these individuals are over 50 years of age. This is thought to occur because cerebral atrophy may be associated with aging; since the hematoma expands slowly, the period of spatial compensation may be so long that the cerebral hemispheres may become severely distorted before there is any significant increase in intracranial pressure. Chronic subdural hematoma is not infrequently bilateral, and most large series report a mortality rate of about 10%.[206] One of the more frequent problems in the elderly, relative to subdural hematoma, are those persons whose hematomas are anticoagulated. Most of the chronic subdural hematomas found in this population are due to falls. Following a fall, the initial CT scan may be negative, but then may reveal a delayed acute subdural hematoma within a matter of days.[207] In children, CT

TABLE 1.10

Hemorrhages Occurring after Head Injury

- Within the extradural, subdural, or subarachnoid spaces
- Intraparenchymal
- Into the ventricles
- Within the brainstem

---

scans are more likely to miss small subdural bleeding. In children who are suspected to have had inflicted head damage, CT may require supplementation with MRI.[208]

Subdural Hygroma

A subdural hygroma is a collection of clear, xanthochromic, or blood-stained fluid within the subdural space.[12] Unlike the subdural hematoma, which contains blood, the hygroma is thought to develop as the result of a valve-like tear in the arachnoid membrane, which allows central cerebrospinal fluid to escape into the subdural space. It is an epiphenomenon of head injury. It is easily detected on CT, and this is the preferred diagnostic imaging modality if it is suspected.[209] However, MRI can clearly differentiate this as well. The differential diagnosis of subdural hygroma has to be made with that of chronic subdural hematoma and atrophy with enlargement of the subarachnoid space. Over time, the subdural hygroma either resolves, or it becomes a chronic subdural hematoma through evolution. Neurosurgical evacuation is required only when a mass effect creates central nervous system compromise. Membrane formation surrounding the hygroma is unusual. Hygromas have been reported in between 7% and 12% of all intracranial mass lesions.[210]

Traumatic subdural hygroma is frequently bilateral and locates at the top of the head in a supine position. This suggests that gravity in cranial posture acts in a certain role. A Korean study[211] attempted to test the effects of gravity. These authors found that traumatic subdural hygroma was more commonly bilateral in patients with a symmetrical cranium than in those with an asymmetrical cranium. They concluded that gravity and cranial posture, particularly in the ICU, can predict the location of traumatic subdural hygroma. When subdural hygromas are acute following trauma, they can mimic acute subdural hematoma and may require surgical evacuation. They provide a mass effect to the brain similar to that of a subdural hematoma.[212]

Subarachnoid Hemorrhage

A subarachnoid hemorrhage is blood located between the meninges and the surface of the brain.[14] Subarachnoid hemorrhage often accompanies other brain injuries such as contusions or intraventricular hemorrhage. It is a frequent occurrence in patients who sustain diffuse axonal injury. Standard T1- or T2-weighted images on MRI display subarachnoid hemorrhage poorly, but it can usually be confirmed with fluid-attenuated inversion recovery imaging (FLAIR) on MRI. CT imaging in the acute setting is the preferred method for demonstrating subarachnoid hemorrhage.[213] There is often a close correlation between the main site of the subarachnoid blood and the location of focal severe vasospasm in the same anatomic area.[214]

Traumatic subarachnoid hemorrhage can be associated with adverse outcome. It is still unclear whether the relationship between traumatic subarachnoid hemorrhage and poor outcome in TBI is merely an epiphenomenon or a direct cause and effect. Vasospasm and ischemia are at the heart of the issue in this disagreement. Some argue that traumatic subarachnoid hemorrhage is merely a marker of severe TBI, while others argue it directly causes vasospasm and ischemia. Serial head CT is required in neurotrauma units once subarachnoid hemorrhage has been detected.[215]

More recently, direct brain tissue oxygen monitoring will soon become routine in patients with detected subarachnoid hemorrhage.[216]

One common complication of subarachnoid hemorrhage is hypopituitarism. Physicians and psychologists examining persons following TBI well after the fact are advised to consider whether endocrine failure has occurred. It is not unusual to see the person a year or more after injury for a neuropsychiatric or neuropsychological evaluation. Hypothyroidism or failure of the adrenal glands can independently exacerbate or cause neuropsychiatric presentations. It is recommended that brain-injured patients undergo neuroendocrine follow-up over time in order to monitor pituitary function.[217] Recent clinical investigations have suggested that hypopituitarism is frequent after subarachnoid hemorrhage but often undetected.[218] Physicians working in rehabilitation units should consider this as a cause of impaired recovery or continued long-term morbidity in individuals with a prior history of significant subarachnoid hemorrhage.

Intraparenchymal (Intracerebral) Hemorrhage

All the hemorrhages discussed in this chapter heretofore are above the surface of the brain. A pure intracerebral hemorrhage (hematoma) is one that is not in contact with the surface of the brain.[12] In the Glasgow database, pure intracerebral hematomas are present in 15% of the cases. In closed head trauma particularly, they are usually found in the frontal and temporal regions, though they may also occur deep within the hemispheres and are often found in the cerebellum. The etiology is thought to be a direct rupture of intrinsic cerebral blood vessels instantaneous with the time of injury. Sequential CT scans have shown that these hemorrhages are often multiple, and their appearance on CT scan is often delayed; they may become apparent only within several hours following trauma, or they may not be detected until the day following admission.[219] The current definition of a delayed hematoma is "a lesion of increased attenuation (verified by CT scan) developing after admission to hospital, in a part of the brain which the admission CT scan had suggested was normal."[220] If a solitary hematoma is found deep within the brain of a patient following head injury, the differential diagnosis includes either a hypertensive bleed or the rupture of a saccular aneurysm because of the head injury.[221] If the bleeding is deep into the brain such as in the basal ganglia, the patient is likely to have sustained diffuse brain damage at the time of the injury in association with the focal bleeding.[222,124]

Intraventricular Hemorrhage

Intraventricular hemorrhage is an uncommon feature of TBI but often associated with severe morbidity or lethality. The Emergency Medicine Center at the David Geffen School of Medicine at UCLA in Los Angeles, California, recently conducted a large trauma review of the prevalence and prognosis of traumatic intraventricular hemorrhage.[223] Eighteen centers in North America were enrolled in the National Emergency X-Radiography Utilization Study (NEXUS) II. Patients were prospectively enrolled if they received a CT scan of the head. Clinical data were collected at the time of enrollment, and CT reports were compiled at least one month later. The prevalence was calculated and demographics were collected from the 18 centers. Outcome data were gathered from the medical records of patients with traumatic intraventricular hemorrhage who were seen at any of six centers that participated in the follow-up portion of the study. The prevalence of traumatic intraventricular hemorrhage among all trauma patients who received head CT was 118 per 8374 patients. This was 1.14% of all trauma patients who received a head CT scan. Among the traumatic intraventricular hemorrhage patients, 70% had a poor outcome. A poor outcome appeared to be associated with an abnormal presenting GCS score and involvement of the third or fourth ventricle. Age appeared to be unrelated. Overall conclusions from the study indicated that traumatic intraventricular hemorrhage is rare and associated with poor outcomes that seem to be the consequence of other associated bodily injuries. The study did not identify any case of isolated traumatic intraventricular hemorrhage combined with a normal neurological examination, resulting in a poor outcome. For penetrating ventricular injuries, particularly by gunshot, intraventricular hemorrhage is a poor prognostic indicator. Ventricular injury and cranial gunshot wounds are complex and severe types of trauma that require extreme and often radical intervention.[224]

DIFFUSE (MULTIFOCAL) BRAIN DAMAGE

With regard to blunt trauma, immediate prolonged unconsciousness unaccompanied by an intracranial mass lesion occurs in almost half of severely head-injured patients and is associated with 35% of all head injury deaths.[12] In those patients who have sustained a minor head injury, there may be persisting mild diffuse damage in the brain for approximately 100 days after the trauma.

TABLE 1.11

Causes of Diffuse Brain Injury

- Diffuse axonal injury
- Ischemic injury
- Brain swelling
- Vascular injury

The focal brain damage reviewed above is in most cases obvious by detection with imaging studies. Diffuse brain damage is both more difficult to define and also more difficult to delineate than these obvious focal types of damage, as macroscopic abnormalities may be minimal or even trivial; much of it can only be recognized microscopically at autopsy when the brain has been properly fixed before dissection. There are four principal types of diffuse brain damage. Three of these are seen frequently in patients who survive their injuries long enough to be admitted to a hospital: diffuse axonal injury, ischemic brain injury, and brain edema. The fourth principal type is diffuse vascular injury, but the mortality rate is much higher in these individuals than the former three categories.[225] Table 1.11 lists common causes of diffuse TBI.

Diffuse Axonal Injury

Today's concept of diffuse axonal injury (DAI) was first defined by Strich[226] when he described the occurrence of diffuse degeneration of the cerebral white matter in a series of patients presenting with severe posttraumatic dementia. The particular neuropathological changes that occur in the axon following the cascade of events after brain trauma has been noted above. Strich's original descriptors have come to be known as DAI, a term first introduced in the early 1980s.[227] More recent studies by the University of Glasgow group have concluded that neuropathologically the principal structural basis of both the severely disabled person and the vegetative person is traumatic diffuse axonal injury (DAI) with widespread damage to white matter and pathological changes in the thalami.[228] For the less severely injured, isolated DAI detected by MRI is associated with persistent cognitive impairment in most persons.[229]

Diffuse axonal injury is extremely difficult to detect noninvasively and is poorly defined as a clinical syndrome.[230] Magnetic resonance diffusion tensor imaging is improving the ability to detect DAI (see Chapter 5). Recently, it has been determined that diffusion-weighted imaging is as useful as FLAIR imaging in detecting DAI lesions.[231] However, for hemorrhagic DAI in the acute care setting, gradient-echo MR imaging is superior to both (see Chapter 5).

There are three distinctive features of the neuropathology of DAI in the more severe forms: (1) diffuse damage to axons, (2) a focal lesion in the corpus callosum, and (3) focal lesions in the dorsal lateral sector of the rostral brainstem adjacent to the superior cerebellar peduncles. The appearances of individual lesions depend on the length of survival after injury. In the early stages after injury (hours to days), focal lesions in the corpus callosum are typically hemorrhagic. These lesions generally occur in the inferior part of the corpus callosum and on one side of the midline. In some cases, they extend to the midline and involve the interventricular septum (which is often ruptured and may be a cause of associated intraventricular hemorrhage) and the fornix. Hemorrhagic lesions may be restricted to the splenium of the corpus callosum where they are frequently bilateral, particularly along the lateral margins.[12] Diffuse axonal injury should be suspected strongly if there are focal lesions in the corpus callosum and appropriate areas of the brainstem noted either by CT scan or MRI.

The direction in which the head moves plays an important role in the amount and distribution of axonal damage. The brain is most vulnerable if it is moved laterally rather than front-to-back, as the brain tolerates sagittal movement best.[12] Although some degree of axonal damage can occur in any direction of head movement, widely scattered DAI in the cerebral hemispheres and brainstem along with tissue tear hemorrhages occur most probably because of geometrical changes in the strain pattern induced by the falx and tentorium during lateral motions.[12] These neuropathological findings suggest that side impact in a motor vehicle accident is more deleterious to the brain than forward impact. That of course assumes that the patient's head remains with eyes forward at the time of impact.

Ischemic Brain Injury

Cerebral ischemia is implicated in poor outcome after brain injury, and it is a very common postmortem finding. Moreover, it is one of the leading contributors to the secondary causes of injury after head trauma, as noted below. The inability of the brain to store metabolic substrates in the face of high oxygen and glucose requirements after injury makes it very susceptible to ischemic damage.[232] Ischemic brain damage occurs soon after injury, but the pathogenesis of ischemic brain damage is not fully understood at this time. Recent research has attempted to quantify ischemic events after TBI in humans by using a simple scoring system. The Medical College of Virginia has devised a simple five-item scoring system taking into account the occurrence of specific potentially brain-damaging events of hypoxemia, hypotension, low cerebral blood flow, herniation, and low cerebral perfusion pressure.[233] This scoring system was tested in a large population of severe TBI patients. In a population of 172 patients, a significant correlation was found between the ischemic score from the five-item system and neurologic outcome at three months and at six months. The correlation at both time points was statistically significant. Much new information regarding cerebral ischemia is being obtained by using O_2 positron emission tomography. Positron emission tomography using isotopes of oxygen can image cerebral blood flow, cerebral blood volume, cerebral metabolic rate for oxygen, and oxygen extraction fraction. This allows a robust and specific delineation of true ischemia. Neurotrauma critical care units are now bringing online this technology in an effort to provide clinical guidance for the management of ischemia in the neurotrauma unit.[234]

Brain Swelling and Edema

Brain swelling frequently occurs following traumatic head injury and may be a major factor contributing to increased intracerebral pressure. Its pathogenesis has been a question for decades. Recent neurosurgical studies have used diffusion-weighted imaging methods to determine whether the edema is primarily cellular or vasogenic. The Medical College of Virginia studied 45 severely injured patients with a GCS score of 8 or less. Of these 32 patients had diffuse injury, 13 had focal injury, and 8 were normal volunteers. Apparent diffusion coefficients were calculated, and brain water and cerebral blood flow were also measured using magnetic resonance and xenon CT techniques. Cerebral blood flow was well above ischemic thresholds within the course of this study. The authors concluded that the predominant form of edema responsible for brain swelling and increased intracranial pressure is cellular in nature rather than vasogenic.[235]

Swelling commonly occurs in the white matter adjacent to contusions. When the brain is physically disrupted and necrotic tissue develops, there is a zone of damaged blood vessels wherein there is increased permeability at the capillary level and loss of normal physiological regulation at the arteriolar level. The water content of the brain tissue around cerebral contusions is increased. A similar consequence of events may occur around an intracerebral hematoma.[12] CT studies have recently been used to predict the evolution of a contusion after closed head injury. Gennarelli's group[236] studied this issue and found that a higher proportion of patients without contusion evolution had perilesional edema present on the first CT scan after trauma. They concluded that the absence of pericontusional edema on early CT scans may be a useful marker to predict a lower likelihood of contusion evolution.

Diffuse swelling in one cerebral hemisphere is most often seen in association with ipsilateral acute subdural hematoma. When the hematoma is evacuated, the brain simply expands to fill the space that was created. This type of brain swelling can occur very soon after the occurrence of subdural hematoma. If a craniectomy is undertaken to evacuate the hematoma with the aim of reducing intracerebral pressure, the brain tissue simply herniates through the craniectomy. Pathologists have concluded that it is likely that this type of swelling is due to vasodilatation with or without significant preexisting ischemia. In fact, with patients in whom a subdural hematoma does not become clinically manifest until two to three days after the injury, progressive development of brain swelling is more likely to be the cause of clinical deterioration with a resulting increase in intracranial pressure than is enlargement of the hematoma itself.[237]

Where the patient continues to deteriorate and develops medically uncontrollable intracerebral pressure or brain herniation, decompressive craniectomy is required. The University of Maryland studied 967 consecutive patients with closed TBI who experienced diffuse brain swelling. Of these 50 patients underwent decompressive craniectomy without removal of clots or contusion to control intracranial pressure or reverse dangerous brain shifts. Diffuse injury was demonstrated in 44 of these patients. In 10 patients, the surgery was performed urgently before intracerebral pressure monitoring, while in 40 patients the procedure was performed after intracranial pressure had become unresponsive to conventional medical management. Fourteen of 50 patients died, 7 patients remained in a vegetative state, and 9 were severely disabled. Twenty patients had a good outcome with a GCS of 4–5. The authors concluded that decompressive craniectomy was associated with a better than expected functional outcome in patients with medically uncontrollable intracerebral pressure or brain herniation compared with outcomes in other control cohorts reported in the medical literature.[238]

Whereas focal swelling is common in adults, diffuse swelling of the entire brain occurs mainly in children and adolescents.[124] In the living child, its presence is indicated by the demonstration of small symmetrical ventricles and occlusion of the basal cisterns on CT. Neuropathologists and neurosurgeons believe that the available evidence suggests that the diffuse swelling is brought about by an increase in cerebral blood volume. If this hyperemia persists, it is likely that true cerebral edema will subsequently occur.

Diffuse Vascular Injury

This is the fourth type of injury seen in diffuse brain damage. Unfortunately, patients who sustain this generally do not survive and they die very soon after their head injuries.[225] Recently, researchers in Tokyo[239] have noted that the degree of cerebral endothelial injury depends on the type of head injury; the measurements of two substances, thrombomodulin and von Willebrand factor, are useful for predicting delayed traumatic intracerebral hematoma. This study demonstrated that the degree of endothelial activation in focal brain injury was significantly higher than that seen in diffuse brain injury. This suggests that focal brain injury is more likely to harm the vascular system than diffuse injury. A Brazilian study[240] has found evidence that diffuse vascular injury and severe diffuse axonal injury depend on the same biomechanical mechanism. The degree of axonal and vascular damage is determined by the intensity of head acceleration. A common secondary cerebral insult following TBI is intravascular coagulation. This occurs fairly frequently in humans, and it has been proved by comparing tissue sampled from surgical specimens of human cerebral contusions with samples from rats that had sustained lateral fluid-percussion injuries, and from pigs with head rotational acceleration injuries. Intravascular coagulation was found in all specimens, and microthrombi had formed in arterioles and venules of all sizes. This phenomenon is more pronounced in focal lesions of more severe injuries, but considerable intravascular coagulation was also observed in mild and diffuse brain injuries.[241]

SECONDARY INJURY AFTER HEAD TRAUMA

The most obvious cause of brain injury is acute physical insult or primary injury to the brain parenchyma itself. This occurs following translation of the kinetic energy of blunt trauma into tissue damage, and thus primary injury is produced. Neurosurgeons and neuropathologists struggle with

---

TABLE 1.12

Potential Causes of Reduced Cerebral Perfusion Pressure

- Arterial hypotension
  Hypovolemia
  Cardiodepressant drugs
  Sepsis
- Intracranial hypertension
  Mass lesions such as hematoma
  Vascular engorgement
  Cerebral edema
  Acute hydrocephalus
  Brain shift and herniation

---

determining how much of the clinical picture of a patient with TBI is related to the primary injury and how much is due to the secondary injury. Secondary injury occurs when mechanical loading of the brain produces primary injury, but it in turn ignites a set of biochemical reactions and cascades that may take several hours to days to manifest, as described in "Neuropathology of Traumatic Brain Injury." Neuropathologically, secondary injury is most often associated with three intracerebral issues: vascular failure, intracranial hypertension, and brain shifting. Brain swelling, as noted above, is a focal phenomenon in most adults. It has also been noted that swelling occurs adjacent to contusions and may be in one hemisphere or bilateral. However, cerebral hypoperfusion caused by ischemia, intravascular clotting, and elevated intracranial pressure is associated with an alteration in the autoregulation of cerebral blood flow.[242] Cerebral perfusion pressure is the difference between the mean arterial pressure and intracranial pressure. It can be reduced following head injury simply by an increase in the intracranial pressure or a decrease in the arterial pressure, bringing blood to the brain.[243] Table 1.12 reviews the major causes of reduced cerebral perfusion pressure.

Vascular Failure

Cerebral ischemia is at the core of secondary injuries to the brain following trauma.[244] Ischemia in the brain is not always a local phenomenon. Brain traumatized patients often are traumatized diffusely in other parts. Central brain ischemia can also be caused by anemia, shock due to blood loss, or low saturated oxygen levels. Central pathogenic mechanisms may occur as well, such as low microcirculatory flow, high intracerebral pressure, diffusion impairment, or deficiencies of electron transfer at the mitochondrial level.[245] More than 90% of patients who die from head trauma have evidence of hypoxic brain damage at autopsy, and up to 36% of patients in the neurointensive care unit (NICU) will have, at one point during their hospitalization, global desaturation of jugular venous oxygen detected during brain tissue oxygen monitoring.[246] The prevention of ischemic episodes due to secondary injury has been markedly improved in the last decade by the application of advanced trauma life support before hospitalization and special trauma care algorithms in emergency departments. Neurosurgeons refrain from excessive dehydration and hyperventilation of patients with TBI. These neurointensive care improvements have contributed to the prevention of ischemic episodes. Prevention of vascular failure is critical during the first 24 h after TBI, as cerebral blood flow is decreased at this time. It is especially critically impaired in the first 6 h, and this may contribute to poor outcomes. After the first 24 h, and the next three to five days thereafter, cerebral blood flow will increase and then drop within the following two weeks.[247]

While it has been thought that TBI causes cerebral vascular dysfunction as a result of endothelial and smooth muscle alteration, recent research suggests that neurogenic damage occurs following TBI and may be a contributor to some of the associated vascular abnormalities. Significant injury to perivascular nerves appears to occur.[248] Vascular autoregulation failure following brain trauma has been assessed by perfusion CT at the University of California, San Francisco.[249] The investigators were able to use perfusion CT in severe head trauma patients and provide direct and quantitative assessment of cerebral vascular autoregulation using a single measurement. The authors argue that this may be used henceforth as a guide for brain edema therapy, and also to monitor efficacy of treatment following severe brain injury.

Another cause of cerebral ischemia following TBI is posttraumatic vasospasm. In a study of 299 patients, hemodynamically significant vasospasm was found in the anterior circulation in 45% of the patients.[250] The most common day of onset for vasospasm was post-injury day two. The highest risk of developing hemodynamically significant vasospasm in the anterior and frontal lobe circulation was found on post-injury day three. The daily prevalence of vasospasm in patients in the intensive care unit was 30% between post-injury day 2 to post-injury day 13. In 50% of the patients, vasospasm resolved after five days. The authors concluded that the incidence of vasospasm after TBI is similar to that following a subarachnoid hemorrhage due to a ruptured intracranial aneurysm.

INTRACRANIAL HYPERTENSION

Intracranial hypertension comes about after injury. It is a secondary consequence of injury and not part of the primary parthophysiology of cellular damage, as discussed above. In the neurointensive care unit, generally intracerebral pressure monitoring (ICP) is appropriate in patients with severe head injury demonstrating an abnormal admission CT scan. Severe head injury is defined as a GCS score of 3 through 8,[246] and an abnormal CT scan of the head (see Chapter 5). If the CT scan is normal with a low GCS score, ICP monitoring is appropriate.[251] Neurosurgical intervention may be required at a threshold of ICP at 20–25 mmHg. Mortality and morbidity increases dramatically thereafter as intracranial pressure exceeds 20 mmHg.[246]

Should ICP increase, intervention is required.[252] In the Glasgow database, there is evidence that ICP had been high in 75% of monitored patients.[222] In those cases where ICP was high, there was a high incidence of secondary hemorrhage or infarction in the brainstem (68%) with a contralateral peduncular lesion in the midbrain (17%), and of infarction in the territories supplied by the posterior cerebral arteries (36%), the anterior cerebral arteries (12%), and the superior cerebellar arteries (6%).[12]

The dominating cause of death in patients with severe brain trauma is an intractable increase in intracranial pressure, leading to a progressive decrease in cerebral perfusion pressure and thereby loss of cerebral blood flow. Once carotid cerebral perfusion pressure is exceeded by ICP, ischemia is manifest. An increase in cerebral perfusion pressure will cause a net transport of water across the blood–brain barrier along with a further elevation in intracerebral pressure.[253] When ICP does not respond to neurointensive care medical management, neurosurgeons often undertake a decompressive craniectomy. However, there is a substantial lack of class I evidence relevant to this topic. There are a very small number of well-designed prospective randomized control trials to determine the efficacy of decompressive craniectomy.[254] In the absence of surgery, hyperosmolar agents are widely used in neurosurgical practice. Mannitol has been a mainstay for decades, but currently hypertonic saline is emerging as an alternative to mannitol in some cases.[255]

BRAIN SHIFT AND HERNIATION

If a hematoma continues to enlarge, or focal swelling of adjacent brain tissue increases, the brain is shifted away from the growing mass, and structures that normally lie in the midline may be displaced. The falx is a very tough and adherent tissue and tends to remain in the midline. As a result, the cingulate gyrus may be herniated under the free edge of the falx and cause compression or distortion of the pericallosal arteries.[256] Because the foramen of Monro becomes occluded in this process of midline shift, the contralateral cerebral ventricle may become dilated while the ventricle on the side of the mass becomes compressed. This sign on CT scan is a reliable indication that intracranial pressure is increased.[257]

There are three major types of brain swelling encountered in patients who have sustained a TBI: swelling adjacent to contusions and intraparenchymal hemorrhages, diffuse swelling of one cerebral hemisphere, and diffuse swelling of both cerebral hemispheres.[12] Swelling of white matter adjacent to contusions is common. The water content of brain tissue around cerebral contusions is increased, and this form of edema has been generally referred to as vasogenic (see edema controversy above). A similar sequence of events may occur around an intraparenchymal hematoma. Local hypoxia increases the regional breakdown of the blood–brain barrier to circulating protein.

Diffuse swelling of one cerebral hemisphere is most often seen in association with an ipsilateral acute subdural hematoma. If the hematoma is surgically evacuated, the brain simply expands to fill the space thus created, a situation similar to that which has been created in experimental studies. Diffuse brain swelling is more difficult to account for. Diffuse swelling of the entire brain is more likely to occur in children and adolescents than it is in adults. The CT scan will demonstrate small symmetrical ventricles with a slit-like appearance and occlusion of the basal cisterns.[257]

Some brain swelling occurs in almost every patient with severe TBI, and in 5%–10% of patients with moderate TBI.[258] There has been significant controversy as to whether the increase in brain volume after TBI is due to vasogenic edema as noted above. It is felt to be more likely at this time in medical science that there is a net shift of small ions together with obligated water from the intravascular to the extracellular compartment: within about 60 min of the injury the extracellular volume decreases as water and ions become intracellular. At the most severe end of the spectrum, the injured brain is unable to restore ionic homeostasis, intracerebral pressure rises, cerebral perfusion pressure is compromised, and death may ensue if neurosurgical treatment is not successful. The CT scan appearances are those of "loss of gray-white definition" or the "ground glass appearance" (see Chapter 5), but such changes do not occur in all patients with diffuse injuries. Vasogenic edema probably becomes important around focal contusions on the second through the tenth to the fifteenth day post-injury.[12]

REFERENCES

1. Thorell, W. and Aarabi, B., History of neurosurgical techniques of head injury. *Neurosurg. Clin. North Am.*, 12, 311, 2001.
2. Forcht, T., The management of head trauma, in *A History of Neurosurgery*, Greenblatt, S.H., Dagi, T.F., and Epstin, M.H., Eds., The American Association of Neurological Surgeons, Park Ridge, IL, 1997, p. 289.
3. Jaboulay, M., La trepanation decompressive. *Lyon Med.*, 83, 73, 1896.
4. Jefferson, G., The tentorial pressure cone. *Arch. Neurol. Psychiatry*, 40, 857, 1938.
5. Lundberg, N., Continuous recording and control of ventricular fluid pressure in neurosurgical practice. *Acta Psychol. Neurol. Scand.*, 36 (149), 1, 1960.
6. Becker, D.P., Miller, J.D., Ward, J.D., et al., The outcome from severe head injury with early diagnosis and intensive management. *J. Neurosurg.*, 47, 491, 1977.
7. Chesnut, R.N., The management of severe traumatic brain injury. *Emerg. Med. Clin. North Am.*, 15, 581, 1997.
8. Andrews, B.J., Levy, M.L., and Pitts, L.H., Implications of systemic hypotension for the neurological examination in patients with severe head injury. *Surg. Neurol.*, 28, 419, 1987.
9. Miller, J.D. and Becker, D.P., Secondary insults to the injured brain. *J. R. Coll. Surg. Edinb.*, 27, 292, 1982.
10. Kraus, J.F. and McArthur, D.L., Epidemiologic aspects of brain injury. *Neurol. Clin.*, 14, 435, 1996.
11. Popovic, J.R. and Kozak, L.J., National hospital discharge survey: Annual summary, 1998. *Vit. Health Stat.*, 13, 1, 2000.
12. Graham, D.I., Gennarelli, T.A., and McIntosh, T.K., Trauma, in *Greenfield's Neuropathology*, 7th edition, Graham, D.I. and Lantos, P.L., Eds., Arnold, London, 2002, p. 823.
13. DeKosky, S.T., Kochanek, P.M., Clark, R.S.B., et al., Secondary injury after head trauma: Subacute and long-term mechanisms. *Sem. Clin. Neuropsychiatr.*, 3, 176, 1998.

14. Dolinak, D., Trauma, in *Neuropathology*, Preyson, R.A. and Goldblum, J.R., Eds., Elsevier Churchill Livingstone, Philadelphia, PA, 2005, p. 73.
15. McKeating, E.G., Andrews, P.J., and Mascia, L., Relationship of neuron-specific enolase and protein S-100 concentrations in systemic and jugular venous serum to injury severity and outcome after traumatic brain injury. *Acta Neuro. Chir. Suppl. (Wien)*, 71, 117, 1998.
16. Thurman, D.J. and Guerrero, J., Trends and hospitalization associated with traumatic brain injury. *JAMA*, 282, 954, 1999.
17. Sosin, D.M., Sniezek, J.E., and Thurman, D.J., Incidence of mild and moderate brain injury in the United States, 1991. *Brain Inj.*, 10, 47, 1996.
18. Sosin, D.M., Sniezek, J.E., and Waxweiler, R.J., Trends in death associated with traumatic brain injury, 1979–1992. *JAMA*, 273, 1778, 1995.
19. Sosin, D., Sacks, J., and Smith, S., Head injury-associated deaths in the United States from 1979 to 1986. *JAMA*, 262, 2251, 1989.
20. Collins, J.G., Types of injuries by selected characteristics, United States, 1985–1987. *Vital Health Stat.*, 10, 175, 1990.
21. Silver, J.N., McAllister, T.W., and Yudofsky, S.C., Eds., *Textbook of Traumatic Brain Injury*, American Psychiatric Press, Washington, D.C., 2005, p. xix.
22. Thurman, D.J., Alverson, C., Brown, D., et al., *Traumatic Brain Injury in the United States: A Report to Congress.* Centers for Disease Control and Prevention, Atlanta, GA, 1999.
23. Thurman, D.J., Jeppson, L., Burnett, C.L., et al., Surveillance of traumatic brain injuries in Utah. *West. J. Med.*, 165, 192, 1996.
24. Kraus, J.F., Morgenstern, H., Fife, D., et al., Blood alcohol test, prevalence of involvement and outcomes following brain injury. *Am. J. Public Health*, 79, 294, 1989.
25. Annegers, J.F., Grabow, J.D., Kurland, L.T., et al., The incidence, causes, and secular trends in head injury in Olmsted County, MN, 1965–1974. *Neurology*, 30, 912, 1980.
26. Jordan, B.D. and Zimmerman, R.D., Computed tomography and magnetic resonance imaging comparisons in boxers. *JAMA*, 263, 1670, 1990.
27. Collins, J.G., *Types of Injuries by Selected Characteristics: United States, 1985–1987 (Vital and Health Statistics, Series 10: Data from the National Health Survey, #175) (DHHS Publication No. DHS-91-1503)*, U.S. Department of Health and Human Services, Hyattsville, MD, 1990.
28. Kraus, J.F., Fife, D., Ramstein, K., et al., The relationship of family income to the incidence, external causes, and outcome of serious brain injury, San Diego County, CA. *Am. J. Public Health*, 76, 1345, 1986.
29. Whitman, S., Coonley-Hoganson, R., and Desai, B.T., Comparative head trauma experiences in two socioeconomically different Chicago-area communities: A population study. *Am. J. Epidemiol.*, 119, 570, 1984.
30. Mortensen, K., Romner, B., and Ingebrigtsen, T., Epidemiology of head injuries in Troms. *Tidsskr. Nor. Laegeforen*, 119, 1870, 1999.
31. Hillier, S.L., Hiller, J.E., and Metzer, J., Epidemiology of traumatic brain injury in south Australia. *Brain Inj.*, 11, 649, 1997.
32. Masson, F., Epidemiology of severe cranial injuries. *Ann. Fr. Anesth. Reanim.*, 19, 261, 2000.
33. Stein, S.C., Classification of head injury, in *Neurotrauma*, Narayn, R.K., Wilberger, J.E., and Povlishock, J.T., Eds., W.B. Saunders, Philadelphia, PA, 1996, p. 31.
34. *Association for the Advancement of Automotive Medicine: The Abbreviated Injury Scale, 1990 revision*, Association for the Advancement of Automotive Medicine, Des Plaines, IL, 1990, p. 15.
35. Teasdale, G. and Jennett, B., Assessment of coma and impaired consciousness. *Lancet*, 1, 81, 1974.
36. Jennett, B., Snoek, J., Bond, M.R., et al., Disability after severe head injury: Observation on the use of the Glasgow Outcome Scale. *J. Neurol. Neurosurg. Psychiatry*, 44, 285, 1981.
37. Gouvier, W.D., Blanton, P.D., Laporte, K.K., et al., Reliability and validity of the Disability Rating Scale and the levels of the Cognitive Functioning Scale in monitoring recovery from severe head injury. *Arch. Phys. Med. Rehab.*, 68, 94, 1987.
38. Taylor, C.A. and Price, T.R.P., Neuropsychiatric assessment in, *Neuropsychiatry of Traumatic Brain Injury*, Silver, J.M., Yudofsky, S.C., and Hales, R.E., Eds., American Psychiatric Press, Washington, D.C., 1994, p. 89.
39. Kraus, J.F. and McArthur, D.L., Epidemiology of head injury, in *Head Injury*, 4th edition, Cooper, P.R. and Golfinos, J.F., Eds., McGraw-Hill, New York, 2000, p. 1.

40. Pintar, F.A., Yoganadan, N., and Gennarelli, T.A., Airbag effectiveness on brain trauma in frontal crashes. *Annu. Proc. Assoc. Adv. Automot. Med.*, 44, 149, 2000.
41. Gennarelli, T.A. and Meaney, D.F., Mechanisms of primary head injury, in *Neurosurgery,* 2nd edition, Wilkins, R.H. and Rengachary, S.S., Eds., McGraw-Hill, New York, 1996, p. 2611.
42. Meaney, D.F., Thibault, L.E., and Gennarelli, T.A., Rotational brain injury tolerance criteria as a function of vehicle crash parameters, in *Proceedings of International Research Council on the Biokinetics of Impact (IRCOBI)*, Bron, France, 1994, p. 234.
43. DiMaio, V.J. and DiMaio, D., *Forensic Pathology,* 2nd edition, CRC Press, Boca Raton, FL, 2001, p. 147.
44. Ommaya, A.K. and Gennarelli, T., Cerebral concussion and traumatic unconsciousness. *Brain*, 97, 633, 1974.
45. Ommaya, A.K., Grubb, R.L., and Naumann, R.A., Coup and contrecoup injury: Observations on the mechanics of visible brain injuries in the Rhesus monkey. *J. Neurosurg.*, 35, 503, 1971.
46. Graham, D.I. and Gennarelli, T.A., Trauma, in *Greenfield's Neuropathology*, 6th edition, Arnold, London, 1997, p. 197.
47. Bandak, F.A., On the mechanics of impact neurotrauma: A review and critical synthesis. *J. Neurotrauma*, 12, 635, 1995.
48. Ommaya, A.K., Head injury mechanisms in the concept of preventive management: A review and critical synthesis. *J. Neurotrauma*, 12, 527, 1995.
49. King, A.I., Ruan, J.S., Zhou, C., et al., Recent advances in biomechanics of brain injury research: A review. *J. Neurotrauma*, 12, 651, 1995.
50. Vossoughi, J. and Bandak, F.A., Mechanical characteristics of vascular tissue and their role in brain injury modeling: A review. *J. Neurotrauma*, 12, 755, 1995.
51. Pintar, F.A., Kumaresan, S., Yoganandan, N., et al., Biomechanical modeling of penetrating traumatic head injuries: A finite element approach. *Biomed. Sci. Instrum.*, 37, 429, 2001.
52. McIntosh, T.K., Smith, D.H., Meaney, D.F., et al., Neuropathological sequelae of traumatic brain injury: Relationship to neurochemical and biomechanical mechanisms. *Lab. Invest.*, 74, 315, 1996.
53. Hwang, H.M., Lee, M.C., Lee, S.Y., et al., Finite element analysis of brain contusion: An indirect impact study. *Med. Biol. Eng. Comput.*, 38, 253, 2000.
54. Petersen, S. and Bowlby, K.J., *Trauma Report*, St. Joseph's Hospital and Medical Center, Phoenix, AZ, 1997.
55. Carey, M.E., Sarna, G.S., Farrell, J.B., et al., Experimental missile wound to the brain. *J. Neurosurg.*, 71 (5 Pt. 1), 754, 1989.
56. Harrington, T. and Apostolides, P., Penetrating brain injury, in *Head Injury,* 4th edition, Cooper, P.R. and Golfinos, J.G., Eds., McGraw-Hill, New York, 2000, p. 349.
57. Rappaport, Z.H., Sahar, A., Shaked, I., et al., Computerized tomography in combat-related craniocerebral penetrating missile injuries. *Isr. J. Med. Sci.*, 20, 668, 1984.
58. Tudor, M., Tudor, L., and Tudor, K.I., Complications of missile craniocerebral injuries during the Croatian Homeland War. *Mil. Med.*, 170, 422, 2005.
59. Carey, M.E., Joseph, A.S., Morris, W.J., et al., Brain wounds and their treatment in VII Corps during Operation Desert Storm, February 20 to April 15, 1991. *Mil. Med.*, 163, 581, 1998.
60. Lindenberg, R., Trauma of meninges and brain, in *Pathology of the Nervous System, Volume II*, Minckler, J., Ed., McGraw-Hill, New York, 1971, p. 1705.
61. Litvack, Z.N., Hunt, M.A., Winstein, J.S., et al., Self-inflicted nail-gun injury with twelve cranial penetrations and associated cerebral trauma. Case report and review of the literature. *J. Neurosurg.*, 104, 828, 2006.
62. deAndrade, A.F., deAlmeida, A.N., Muoio, V.M., et al., Penetrating screwdriver injury to the brainstem. Case illustration. *J. Neurosurg.*, 104, 853, 2006.
63. Iannelli, A. and Lupi, G., Penetrating brain injuries from a dog bite in an infant. *Pediatr. Neurosurg.*, 41, 41, 2005.
64. Strich, S.J., Cerebral trauma, in *Greenfield's Neuropathology*, 3rd edition, Blackwood, W. and Corsellis, J.A.N., Eds., Arnold, London, 1976, p. 327.
65. Freytag, E., Autopsy findings in head injuries from firearms. *Arch. Pathol.*, 76, 215, 1963.
66. Sights, W.P., Ballistic analysis of shotgun injuries to the central nervous system. *J. Neurosurg.*, 31, 25, 1969.

67. Taha, J.N., and Haddad, F.S., Central nervous system infections after cranial cerebral missile wounds, in *Missile Wounds of the Head and Neck, Volume II*, Aarabi, B. and Kaufman, H.H., Eds., AANS Publications Committee, Park Ridge, IL, 1999, p. 271.

68. Campbell, G.A., The pathology of penetrating wounds of the brain and its enclosures, in *Missile Wounds of the Head and Neck, Volume I*, Aarabi, B. and Kaufman, H.H., Eds., AANS Publications Committee, Park Ridge, IL, 1999, p. 73.

69. Karger, B., Puskas, Z., Rewald, B., et al., Morphological findings in the brain after experimental gunshots using radiology, pathology, and histology. *Int. J. Legal Med.*, 111, 314, 1998.

70. Koszyca, V., Blumberg, P.C., Manavis, J., et al., Widespread axonal injury in gunshot wounds to the head using amyloid precursor protein as a marker. *J. Neurotrauma*, 15, 674, 1998.

71. Oehmichen, M., Meissner, C., and Konig, H.G., Brain injury after gunshot wounding: Morphometric analysis of cell destruction caused by temporary cavitation. *J. Neurotrauma*, 17, 155, 2000.

72. Haddad, F.S., Haddad, G.F., and Taha, J., Traumatic aneurysms caused by missiles: Their presentation and management. *Neurosurgery*, 28, 1, 1991.

73. Salazar, A.N., Aarabi, B., Levi, L., et al., Posttraumatic epilepsy following craniocerebral missile wounds in recent armed conflicts, in *Missile Wounds of Head and Neck, Volume II*, Aarabi, B. and Kaufman, H.H., Eds., AANS Publications Committee, 1999, p. 281.

74. Murano, T., Mohr, A.M., Lavery, R.F., et al., Civilian craniocerebral gunshot wounds: An update in predicting outcomes. *Am. Surg.*, 71, 1009, 2005.

75. Martins, R.S., Siqueira, M.G., Santos, M.T., et al., Prognostic factors in treatment of penetrating gunshot wounds to the head. *Surg. Neurol.*, 60, 98, 2003.

76. Kriet, J.D., Stanley, R.B., and Grady, M.S., Self-inflicted submental and transoral gunshot wounds that produce nonfatal brain injuries: Management and prognosis. *J. Neurosurg.*, 102, 1029, 2005.

77. Izci, Y., Kayali, H., Daneyemez, M., et al., Comparison of clinical outcomes between anteroposterior and lateral penetrating craniocerebral gunshot wounds. *Emerg. Med. J.*, 22, 409, 2005.

78. Sullivan, M.G., Returning soldiers may have blast injury to brain: Possibly undiagnosed (clinical rounds). *Fam. Prac. News*, 34, 24, 2004.

79. Lew, H.L., Poole, J.H., Alvarez, S., et al., Soldiers with occult traumatic brain injury. *Am. J. Phys. Med. Rehabil.*, 84, 393, 2005.

80. Guest Editorial, Rehabilitation needs of an increasing population of patients: Traumatic brain injury, polytrauma, and blast-related injuries. *J. Rehabil. Res. Dev.*, 42, xiii, 2005.

81. Explosions and blast injuries: A primer for clinicians, Centers for Disease Control, Injury Prevention. http://www.bt.cdc.gov/masstrauma/pdf/explosions-blast-injuries.pdf, site visited June 24, 2006.

82. Whightman, J.M. and Gladish, S.L., Explosions and blast injuries. *Ann. Emerg. Med.*, 37, 664, 2001.

83. Stein, M. and Hirshberg, A., Trauma care in the new millennium: Medical consequences of terrorism, the conventional weapon threat. *Surg. Clin. North Am.*, 1999, Vol. 79.

84. Coupland, C.R.M. and Meddings, D.R., Mortality associated with use of weapons in armed conflicts, wartime atrocities, and civilian mass shootings, literature review. *Br. Med. J.*, 319, 410, 1999.

85. Defense and Veterans Brain Injury Center, Blast Injury. http://dvbic.org, site visited April 23, 2006.

86. Okie, S., Traumatic brain injury in the war zone. *N. Eng. J. Med.*, 352, 2043, 2005.

87. Brolinson, P.G., Manoogian, S., McNeely, D., et al., Analysis of linear head accelerations from collegiate football impacts. *Curr. Sports Med. Rep.*, 5, 23, 2006.

88. Mueller, F.O., Catastrophic head injuries in high school and collegiate sports. *J. Athl. Train.*, 36, 312, 2001.

89. Powell, J.W. and Barber-Foss, K.D., Traumatic brain injury in high school athletes. *JAMA*, 282, 958, 1999.

90. Viano, D.C., Casson, I.R., Pellman, E.J., et al., Concussion in professional football: Brain responses by finite element analysis: Part 9. *Neurosurgery*, 57, 891, 2005.

91. Pellman, E.J., Viano, D.C., Withnall, C., et al., Concussion in professional football: Helmet testing to assessed impact performance: Part 11. *Neurosurgery*, 58, 78, 2006.

92. Pellman, E.J., Lovell, M.R., Viano, D.C., et al., Concussion in professional football: Recovery of NFL and high school athletes assessed by computerized neuropsychological testing: Part 12. *Neurosurgery*, 58, 263, 2006.

93. Barth, J.T., Alves, W.M., Ryan, T., et al., Mild head injury in sports: Neuropsychological sequelae and recovery of function, in *Mild Head Injury*, Levin, H.S., Eisenberg, H.M., and Benton, A.L., Eds., Oxford University Press, New York, 1989, p. 257.

94. Lovell, M.R. and Collins, M.W., Neuropsychological assessment of the college football player. *J. Head Trauma Rehabil.*, 13, 9, 1998.
95. Collins, M.W., Grindel, S.H., Lovell, M.R., et al., Relationships between concussions and neuropsychological performance in college football players. *JAMA*, 282, 964, 1999.
96. Cantu, R.C., Return-to-play guidelines after head injury. *Clin. Sports Med.*, 17, 56, 1998.
97. Bleiberg, J., Kane, R.L., Reeves, D.L., et al., Factor analysis of computerized and traditional tests used in mild brain injury research. *Clin. Neuropsychol.*, 14, 287, 2000.
98. Erlanger, D.M., Feldman, D., Kutner, K., et al., Development and validation of a Web-based neuropsychological test protocol for sports-related return-to-play decision making. *Arch. Neuropsychol.*, 18, 293, 2003.
99. Stalnacke, B.M., Tegner, Y., and Sojka, P., Playing soccer increases serum concentrations of the biochemical markers of brain damage S-100B and neuron-specific enolase in elite players: A pilot study. *Brain Inj.*, 18, 899, 2004.
100. Straume-Naesheim, T.M., Andersen, T.E., Dvorak, J., et al., Effects of heading exposure in previous concussions on neuropsychological performance among Norwegian elite footballers. *Br. J. Sports Med.*, 39 (suppl. 1:i), 70, 2005.
101. Withnall, C., Shewchenko, N., Gittens, R., et al., Biomechanical investigation of head impacts in football. *Br. J. Sports Med.*, 39 (suppl. 1:i), 49, 2005.
102. Freeman, J.R., Barth, J.T., Broshek, D.K., et al., Sports injuries, in *Textbook of Traumatic Brain Injury*, Silver, J.M., McAllister, T.W., and Yudofsky, S.C., Eds., American Psychiatric Press, Washington, D.C., 2005, p. 453.
103. Martland, H.S., Punch-drunk. *JAMA*, 19, 1103, 1928.
104. Ryan, A.J., Intracranial injuries resulting from boxing: A review (1918–1985). *Clin. Sports Med.*, 6, 31, 1987.
105. Corsellis, J.A., Bruton, C.J., and Freeman-Brone, D., The aftermath of boxing. *JAMA*, 3, 270, 1973.
106. Tokuda, T., Ikeda, S., Yanagisawa, N., et al., Reexamination of ex-boxers' brains using immunohistochemistry with antibodies to amyloid-β protein and tau protein. *Acta Neuropathol.*, 82, 281, 1991.
107. Blennow, K., Popa, C., Rasulzada, A., et al., There is strong evidence that professional boxing results in chronic brain damage. The more head punches during a boxer's career, the bigger is the risk. *Lakartidningen*, 102, 2468, 2005.
108. Wall, S.E., Williams, W.H., Cartwright-Hatton, S., et al., Neuropsychological dysfunction following repeat concussions in jockeys. *J. Neurol. Neurosurg. Psychiatry*, 77, 518, 2006.
109. McIntosh, A.S., Rugby injuries. *Med. Sport Sci.*, 49, 120, 2005.
110. McManus, A., Management of brain injury in non-elite field hockey and Australian football—a qualitative study. *Health Promot. J. Aust.*, 17, 67, 2006.
111. Rahimi, S.Y., Singh, H., Yeh, D.J., et al., Golf-associated head injury in the pediatric population: A common sports injury. *J. Neurosurg.*, 102, 163, 2005.
112. Kraus, J.F., Epidemiological features of brain injury in children: Occurrence, children at risk, causes and manner of injury, severity, and outcomes, in *Traumatic Head Injury in Children*, Broman, S.H. and Michel, N.E., Eds., Oxford University Press, New York, 1995, p. 22.
113. Max, J.E., Children and adolescents, in *Textbook of Traumatic Brain Injury*, Silver, J.M., McAlister, T.W., and Yudofsky, S.C., Eds., American Psychiatric Press, Washington, D.C., 2005, p. 477.
114. Luerssen, T., Head injuries in children. *Neurosurg. Clin. North Am.*, 2, 399, 1991.
115. Weiner, H.L. and Weinberg, J.S., Head injury in the pediatric age group, in *Head Injury*, 4th edition, Cooper, P.R. and Golfinos, J.G., Eds., McGraw-Hill, New York, 2000, p. 419.
116. Billmire, M.E. and Myers, P.A., Serious head injury in infants: Accident or abuse? *Pediatrics*, 75, 340, 1985.
117. Epstein, J.A., Epstein, B.S., and Small, M., Subepicranial hygroma. A complication of head injuries in infants and children. *J. Pediatr.*, 59, 562, 1961.
118. Scarfo, G.B., Mariottini, A., Tamaccini, D., et al., Growing skull fractures: Progressive evolution of brain damage and effectiveness of surgical treatment. *Childs Nerv. Syst.*, 173, 653, 1989.
119. Wolfson, D.R., McNally, D.S., Clifford, M.J., et al., Rigid-body modelling of shaken baby syndrome. *Proc. Inst. Mech. Eng.*, 209, 63, 2005.
120. Bandak, F.A., Shaken baby syndrome: A biomechanics analysis of injury mechanisms. *Forensic Sci. Int.*, 151, 71, 2005.

121. Leestma, J.E., Case analysis of brain-injured admittedly shaken infants: 54 cases, 1969–2001. *Am. J. Forensic Med. Pathol.*, 26, 199, 2005.

122. Biron, D. and Shelton, D., Perpetrator accounts in infant abusive head trauma brought about by a shaking event. *Child Abuse Negl.*, 29, 1347, 2005.

123. Caffey, J., The whiplash shaken infant syndrome—manual shaking by the extremities with whiplash-induced intracranial and intraocular bleedings, linked with residual permanent brain damage and mental retardation. *Pediatrics*, 54, 396, 1974.

124. Graham, D.I., Ford, I., Adams, J.H., et al., Fatal head injury in children. *J. Clin. Pathol.*, 42, 18, 1989.

125. Zimmerman, R.A., Bilaniuk, L.T., Bruce, D.A., et al., Computed tomography of craniocerebral injury in the abused child. *Radiology*, 130, 687, 1979.

126. Gamel, K., al-Zarqawi lived for 52 minutes after strike. Associated Press, 6/12/06.

127. Kinney, H.C. and Armstrong, D.D., Perinatal neuropathology, in *Greenfield's Neuropathology,* 7th edition, Graham, D.I. and Lantos, P.L., Eds., Arnold, London, 2002, p. 519.

128. Kendall, N. and Wolochin, H., Cephalhematoma associated with fracture of the skull. *J. Pediatr.*, 41, 125, 1952.

129. Churchill, J.A., Stevenson, L., and Habhab, G., Cephalhematoma in natal brain injury. *Obstet. Gynecol.*, 27, 580, 1966.

130. Hendrick, A.B., Harwood-Hash, D.C., and Hudson, A.R., Head injuries in children: A survey of 4465 consecutive cases at the Hospital for Sick Children, Toronto, Canada. *Clin. Neurosurg.*, 11, 46, 1964.

131. Volpe, J.J., *Neurology of the newborn,* 3rd edition, W.B. Saunders, Philadelphia, PA, 1995.

132. Manley, G.T., Rosenthal, G., Lam, M., et al., Controlled cortical impact in swine: Pathophysiology of biomechanics. *J. Neurotrauma*, 23, 128, 2006.

133. Gennarelli, T.A., Thibault, L.E., and Graham, D.I., Diffuse axonal injury: An important form of traumatic brain injury. *Neuroscientist*, 4, 2002, 1998.

134. Yawo, H. and Kuno, M., How a nerve fiber repairs its cut end: Involvement of phospholipase A_2. *Science*, 222, 1351, 1983.

135. Galbraith, J.A., Thibault, L.E., and Matteson, R.A., Mechanical and electrical responses of the squid giant axon to simple elongation. *J. Biomech. Eng.*, 115, 13, 1993.

136. Teasdale, G.M., Nicoll, J.A., Murray, G., et al., Association of apolipoprotein E polymorphism with outcome after head injury. *Lancet*, 350, 1069, 1997.

137. Jordan, B.D., Relkin, N.R., Ravdin, L.D., et al., Apolipoprotein E epsilon 4 associated with chronic traumatic brain injury in boxing. *JAMA*, 278, 136, 1997.

138. Methia, N., Andre, P., Hafezi-Moghadam, A., et al., Apo E deficiency compromises the blood–brain barrier especially after injury. *Mol. Med.*, 7, 810, 2001.

139. Hartman, R.E., Laurer, H., Longhi, L., et al., Apolipoprotein E4 influences amyloid deposition but not cell loss after traumatic brain injury in a mouse model of Alzheimer's disease. *J. Neurosci.*, 22, 10083, 2002.

140. Liberman, J.N., Stewart, W.F., Wesnes, K., et al., Apolipoprotein E epsilon 4 and short-term recovery from predominately mild brain injury. *Neurology*, 58, 1038, 2002.

141. Crawford, F.C., Vanderploeg, R.D., Freeman, M.J., et al., APO E genotype influences acquisition and recall following traumatic brain injury. *Neurology*, 58, 1115, 2002.

142. Millar, K., Nicoll, J.A., Thornhill, S., et al., Long term neuropsychological outcome after head injury: Relation to Apo E genotype. *J. Neurol. Neurosurg. Psychiatry*, 74, 1047, 2003.

143. Nathoo, N., Chetry, R., vanDellen, J.R., et al., Apolipoprotein E polymorphism and outcome after closed traumatic brain injury: Influence of ethnic and regional differences. *J. Neurosurg.*, 98, 302, 2003.

144. Luukinen, H., Viramo, P., Herala, M., et al., Fall-related brain injuries and the risk of dementia in elderly people: A population-based study. *Eur. J. Neurol.*, 12, 86, 2005.

145. Smith, C., Graham, D.I., Murray, L.S., et al., Association of Apo e4 and cerebrovascular pathology in traumatic brain injury. *J. Neurol. Neurosurg. Psychiatry*, 77, 363, 2006.

146. Mayeux, R., Ottman, R., Maestre, G., et al., Synergistic effects of traumatic head injury in apolipoprotein ε4 in patients with Alzheimer's disease. *Neurology*, 45, 555, 1995.

147. Grundke-Iqbal, I., Iqbal, K., Tung, Y.C., et al., Abnormal phosphorylation of the microtubule-associated protein tau in Alzheimer cytoskeletal pathology. *Proc. Natl. Acad. Sci. U.S.A.*, 83, 4913, 1986.

148. Zemlan, F.P., Rosenderg, W.S., Luebbe, P.A., et al., Quantification of axonal damage in traumatic brain injury: Affinitive purification and characterization of cerebrospinal fluid tau proteins. *J. Neurochem.*, 72, 741, 1999.

149. Maxwell, W.L., Povlishock, J.T., and Graham, D.I., A mechanistic analysis of nondisruptive axonal injury: A review. *J. Neurotrauma*, 14, 419, 1997.

150. Ikonomovic, M.D., Uryu, K., Abrahamson, A.E., et al., Alzheimer's pathology in human temporal cortex surgically excised after severe brain injury. *Exp. Neurol.*, 190, 192, 2004.

151. Gabbita, S.P., Scheff, S.W., Menard, R.N., et al., Cleaved-tau: A biomarker of neuronal damage after traumatic brain injury. *J. Neurotrauma*, 22, 83, 2005.

152. Omalu, B.I., DeKosky, S.T., Minster, R.L., et al., Chronic traumatic encephalopathy in a National Football League player. *Neurosurgery*, 57, 128, 2005.

153. Buki, A. and Povlishock, J.T., All roads lead to disconnection?—Traumatic axonal injury revisited. *Acta Neurochir. (Wein)*, 148, 181, 2006.

154. Doppenberg, E.M.R. and Bullock, R., Clinical neuro-protection trials in severe traumatic brain injury: Lessons from previous studies. *J. Neurotrauma*, 14, 71, 1997.

155. Dugan, L.L. and Choi, D.W., Excitotoxicity, free radicals and cell membrane changes. *Ann. Neurol.*, 35, S17, 1994.

156. Amstad, P.A., Krupitza, G., and Cerutti, P.A., Mechanism of c-fos induction by active oxygen. *Cancer Res.*, 52, 3952, 1992.

157. Takahashi, K., *Calpain Substrate Specificity in Intracellular Calcium-Dependent Proteolysis*. Mellgrin, R.L. and Murachi, T., Eds., CRC Press, Boca Raton, FL, 1990, p. 55.

158. Bartus, R.T. The calpain hypothesis of neurodegeneration: Evidence for common cytotoxic pathway. *Neuroscientist*, 3, 314, 1997.

159. Enriquez, P. and Bullock, R., Molecular and cellular mechanisms in the pathophysiology of severe head injury. *Curr. Pharm. Des.*, 10, 2131, 2004.

160. Sullivan, P.G., Ravchevsky, A.G., Waldmeier, P.C., et al., Mitochondrial permeability transition in CNS trauma: Cause or effect of neuronal cell death? *J. Neurosci. Res.*, 79, 231, 2005.

161. Weber, J.T., Calcium homeostasis following traumatic neuronal injury. *Curr. Neurovasc. Res.*, 1, 151, 2004.

162. Zhang, X., Chen, Y., Jenkins, L.W., et al., Bench-to-bedside review: Apoptosis/programmed cell death triggered by traumatic brain injury. *Crit. Care*, 9, 66, 2005.

163. Bittigau, P., Sifringer, M., Felderhoff-Meuser, U., et al., Apoptotic neurodegeneration in the context of traumatic injury to the developing brain. *Exp. Toxicol. Pathol.*, 56, 83, 2004.

164. Rink, A., Fung, K.-M., Trojanowski, J.Q., et al., Evidence of apoptotic cell death after experimental traumatic brain injury in the rat. *Am. J. Pathol.*, 147, 1575, 1995.

165. Conti, A.C., Raghupathi, R., Trojanowski, J.Q., et al., Experimental brain injury induces regionally distinct apoptosis during the acute and delayed post-traumatic period. *J. Neurosci.*, 18, 5663, 1998.

166. Herrmann, M., Jost, S., Kutz, S., et al., Temporal profile of release of neurobiochemical markers of brain damage after traumatic brain injury is associated with intracranial pathology as demonstrated in cranial computerized tomography. *J. Neurotrauma*, 17, 113, 2000.

167. Waterloo-K., Ingebrigtesten, T., and Romner, V., Neuropsychological functions in patients with increased serum levels of protein S-100 after minor head injury. *Acta Neurochir. (Wein)*, 139, 26, 1997.

168. Yamazaki, Y., Yada, K., Morii, S., et al., Diagnostic significance of serum neuron-specific enolase and myelin basic protein assay in patients with acute head injury. *Surg. Neurol.*, 43, 267, 1995.

169. Beaudeux, J., Dequen, L., and Foglietti, M., Pathophysiologic aspects of S-100 beta protein: A new biological marker of brain pathology. *Ann. Biol. Clin.(Paris)*, 57, 261, 1999.

170. Townend, W., Dibble, C., Abid, K., et al., Rapid elimination of protein S-100B from serum after minor head trauma. *J. Neurotrauma*, 23, 149, 2006.

171. Dimopoulou, I., Korfias, S., Dafni, U., et al., Protein S-100β serum levels in trauma-induced brain death. *Neurology*, 60, 947, 2003.

172. DeKruijk, J.R., Leffers, P., Menheere, P.P., et al., Prediction of posttraumatic complaints after mild traumatic brain injury: Early symptoms and biochemical markers. *J. Neurol. Neurosurg. Psychiatry*, 73, 737, 2002.

173. Stranjalis, G., Korfias, S., Papapetrou, C., et al., Elevated serum S-100β protein as predictor of failure to short-term return to work or activities after mild head injury. *J. Neurotrauma*, 21, 1070, 2005.

174. Mussack, T. and Ladurner, R., Role of S-100β for evaluation of traumatic brain injury in patients with alcohol intoxication. *Recenti. Prog. Med.*, 96, 77, 2005.

175. Stalnacke, B.M., Ohlsson, A., Tegner, Y., et al., Serum concentrations of two biochemical markers of brain tissue damage S-100β and neuron-specific enolase are increased in elite female soccer players after a competitive game. *Br. J. Sports Med.*, 40, 313, 2006.

176. Berger, R.P., Adelson, P.D., Pierce, N.C., et al., Serum neuron-specific enolase, S-100β and myelin basic protein concentrations after inflicted and noninflicted traumatic brain injury in children. *J. Neurosurg.*, 103 (Suppl. 1) 61, 2005.

177. Berger, R.P., Dulani, T., Adelson, P.D., et al., Identification of inflicted traumatic brain injury in well-appearing infants using serum and cerebrospinal markers: A possible screening tool. *Pediatrics*, 117, 325, 2006.

178. Bandyopadhyay, S., Hennes, H., Gorelick, M.H., et al., Serum neuron-specific enolase as a predictor of short-term outcome in children with closed traumatic brain injury. *Acad. Emerg. Med.*, 12, 732, 2005.

179. DiMaio, V.J. and DiMaio, D., *Forensic Pathology*, 2nd edition, CRC Press, Boca Raton, FL, 2001, p. 147.

180. Cooper, P.R., Skull fracture and traumatic cerebral spinal fluid fistulas, in *Head Injury*, Cooper, P.R., Ed., Williams & Wilkins, Baltimore, 1993, p. 115.

181. Mendelow, A.D., Teasdale, G., Jennett, B., et al., Risks of intracranial hematoma in head injury adults, *BMJ*, 287, 1173, 1983.

182. Roberts, G.W., Leigh, P.N., and Weinberger, D.R., *Neuropsychiatric Disorders*, Wolfe, London, 1993, p. 5.1.

183. Kondo, T., Saito, K., Nishigami, J., et al., Fatal injuries of the brain stem and/or upper cervical spinal cord in traffic accidents: Nine autopsy cases. *Sci. Justice*, 35, 197, 1995.

184. Gonul, E., Erdogan, E., Taser, N., et al., Penetrating orbital cranial gunshot injuries. *Surg. Neurol.*, 63, 24, 2005.

185. Tosun, F., Gonul, E., Yetiser, S., et al., Analysis of different surgical approaches for the treatment of cerebrospinal fluid rhinorrhea. *Minim. Invasive Neurosurg.*, 48, 355, 2005.

186. Marsh, N.V. and Whitehead, G., Skull fracture during infancy: A five year follow-up. *J. Clin. Exp. Neuropsychol.*, 27, 352, 2005.

187. Servais, L., Fonteyne, C., Christophe, C., et al., Meningitis following basilar skull fracture in two in-line skaters. *Childs Nerv. Syst.*, 21, 339, 2005.

188. Beaumont, A. and Gennarelli, T., CT prediction of contusion evolution of closed head injury: The role of pericontusional edema. *Acta Neurochir. Suppl.*, 96, 30, 2006.

189. Brandstack, N., Kurki, T., Tenovuo, O., et al., MR imaging of head trauma: Visibility of contusions and other intraparenchymal injuries in early and late stage. *Brain Inj.*, 20, 409, 2006.

190. Chieragto, A., Fainardi, E., Servadei, F., et al., Centrifugal distribution of regional cerebral blood flow and its time course in traumatic intracerebral hematomas. *J. Neurotrauma*, 21, 655, 2004.

191. Servadei, F., Piazza, G.C., Padovani, R., et al., "Pure" traumatic cerebral lacerations. A review of 129 cases with long-term follow-up. *Neurochirurgia (Stuttg.)*, 28, 170, 1985.

192. Manfredini, M. and Marliana, A.F., CT and plain X-ray examination of the skull in pure traumatic laceration of the brain. *Neuroradiology*, 24, 249, 1983.

193. Lindenberg, R., Trauma of meninges and brain, in *Pathology of the Nervous System, Vol. 2*, Minckler, J., Ed., McGraw-Hill, New York, 1971, p. 1705.

194. Graham, D.I., Neuropathology of head injury, in *Neurotrauma*, Narayn, R.K., Wilberger, J.E., and Povlishock, J.T., Eds., W.B. Saunders, Philadelphia, PA, 1996, p. 43.

195. Cooper, P.R., Posttraumatic intracranial mass lesions, in *Head Injury,* 4th edition, Cooper, P.R. and Golfinos, J.G., Eds., McGraw-Hill, New York, 2000. p. 293.

196. Bullock, R., and Teasdale, G., Surgical management of traumatic intracranial hematomas, in *Handbook of Clinical Neurology, Vol. 15, Head Injury*, Braackman, R., Ed., Elsevier, Amsterdam, 1990, p. 249.

197. Gusmao, S.N. and Pittella, J.E., Extradural haematoma and diffuse axonal injury in victims of fatal road traffic accidents. *Br. J. Neurosurg.*, 12, 123, 1998.

198. Servadei, F., Begliomini, C., Gardini, E., et al., Extradural hematoma and diffuse axonal injury in victims of fatal road traffic accidents. *Inj. Prev.*, 9, 257, 2003.

199. Hamlat, A., Heckly, A., Adn, M., et al., Pathophysiology of intracranial epidural hematoma following birth. *Med. Hypotheses*, 66, 371, 2006.

200. Vinchon, M., Pierrat, V., Tchofo, P.J., et al., Traumatic intracranial hemorrhage in newborns. *Childs Nerv. Syst.*, 21, 1042, 2005.

201. Ommaya, A.K. and Yarnell, P., Subdural hematoma after whiplash injury. *Lancet*, 2, 237, 1969.

202. Leestma, J.E., Neuropathology of child abuse, in *Forensic Neuropathology*, Leestma, J.E. and Kirpatrick, J.B., Eds., Raven Press, New York, 1988, p. 333.

203. Lobato, R.D., Sarabia, R., Cordobes, F., et al., Posttraumatic cerebral hemispheric swelling: Analysis of 55 cases studied with computerized tomography. *J. Neurosurg.*, 68, 417, 1988.
204. Fogelholm, R. and Waltimo, O., Epidemiology of chronic subdural hematoma. *Acta Neurochir.*, 32, 247, 1975.
205. Markwalder, T.-M., Chronic subdural hematomas: A review. *J. Neurosurg.*, 54, 637, 1981.
206. Mellergard, P. and Wisten, O., Operations and reoperations for chronic subdural hematomas during a 25 year period in a well defined population. *Acta Neurochir. (Wein)*, 138, 708, 1996.
207. Itshayek, E., Rosenthal., G., Fraifeld, S., et al., Delayed posttraumatic acute subdural hematoma in elderly patients on anticoagulation. *Neurosurgery*, 58, E851, 2006.
208. Datta, S., Stoodley, N., Jayawant, S., et al., Neuroradiological aspects of subdural hemorrhages. *Arch. Dis. Child.*, 90, 947, 2005.
209. Deltour, P., Lemmerling, M., Bauters, W., et al., Posttraumatic subdural hygroma: CT findings and differential diagnosis. *JBR-BTR*, 82, 155, 1999.
210. Stone, J.L., Lang, R.G.R., Sugar, O., et al., Traumatic subdural hygroma. *Neurosurgery*, 8, 542, 1981.
211. Lee, K.S., Bae, W.K., Yoon, S.M., et al., Location of the traumatic subdural hygroma: Role of gravity and cranial morphology. *Brain Inj.*, 14, 355, 2000.
212. Kamezaki, T., Yanaka, K., Fujita, K., et al., Traumatic acute subdural hygroma mimicking acute subdural hematoma. *J. Clin. Neurosci.*, 11, 311, 2004.
213. Tsurushima, H., Meguro, K., Wada, M., et al., FLAIR images of patients with head injuries. *No Shinkei Geka*, 24, 891, 1996.
214. Taneda, M., Kataoka, K., Akai, F., et al., Traumatic subarachnoid hemorrhage as a predictable indicator of delayed ischemic symptoms. *J. Neurosurg.*, 84, 762, 1996.
215. Armin, S.S., Colohan, A.R., and Zhang, J.H., Traumatic subarachnoid hemorrhage: Our current understanding and its evolution over the past half century. *Neurol. Res.*, 28, 445, 2006.
216. Hemphill, J.C., Morabito, D., Farrant, M., et al., Brain tissue oxygen monitoring and intracerebral hemorrhage. *Neurocrit. Care*, 3, 260, 2005.
217. Giordano, G., Aimaretti, G., and Zhigo, E., Variations of pituitary function over time after brain injuries: The lesson from a prospective study. *Pituitary*, 8, 227, 2005.
218. Kreitschmann-Andermahr, I., Subarachnoid hemorrhage as a cause of hypopituitarism. *Pituitary*, 8, 219, 2005.
219. Roberts, G.W., Leigh, P.N., and Weinberger, D.R., *Neuropsychiatric Disorders*, Wolfe, London, 1993, p. 5.8.
220. Gentleman, D., North, F., and MacPherson, P., Diagnosis and management of delayed traumatic haematomas. *Br. J. Neurosurg.*, 3, 367, 1989.
221. Graham, D.I., Neuropathology of head injury, in *Neurotrauma*, Narayn, R.K., Wilberger, J.E., and Povlishock, J.T., Eds., W.B. Saunders, Philadelphia, PA, 1996, p. 31.
222. Graham, D.I., Lawrence, A.E., Adams, J.E. et al., Brain damage in non-missile head injuries secondary to a high ICP. *Neouropathol. Appl. Neurobiol.*, 13, 209, 1987.
223. Atzema, C., Mower, W.R., Hoffman, J.R., et al., Prevalence and prognosis of traumatic intraventricular hemorrhage in patients with blunt head trauma. *J. Trauma*, 60, 1010, 2006.
224. Erdogan, E., Izci, Y., Gonul, E., et al., Ventricular injury following cranial gunshot wounds: Clinical study. *Mil. Med.*, 169, 691, 2004.
225. Gennarelli, T.A. and Graham, D.I., Neuropathology of the head injuries, *Semin. Clin. Neuropsychiatr.*, 3, 160, 1998.
226. Strich, S.J., Diffuse degeneration of the cerebral white matter in severe dementia following head injury. *J. Neurol. Neurosurg. Psychiatry*, 19, 163, 1956.
227. Gennarelli, T.A., Thibault, L.E., Adams, J.H., et al., Diffuse axonal injury and traumatic coma in the primate. *Ann. Neurol.*, 12, 564, 1982.
228. Graham, D.I., Adams, J.H., Murray, L.S., et al., Neuropathology of the vegetative state after head injury. *Neuorpsychol. Rehabil.*, 15, 198, 2005.
229. Scheid, R., Walter, K., Guthke, T., et al., Cognitive sequelae of diffuse axonal injury. *Arch. Neurol.*, 63, 418, 2006.
230. Smith, D.H., Meaney, D.F., and Shull, W.H., Diffuse axonal injury in head trauma. *J. Head Trauma Rehabil.*, 18, 307, 2003.
231. Kinoshita, T., Moritani, T., Hiwatashi, A., et al., Conspicuity of diffuse axonal injury lesions on diffusion-weighted MR imaging. *Eur. J. Radiol.*, 56, 5, 2005.

232. Nortje, J. and Gupta, A.K., The role of tissue oxygen monitoring in patients with acute brain injury. *Br. J. Anaesth.*, 97, 95, 2006.

233. Mazzeo, A.T., Kunene, N.K., Choi, S., et al., Quantitation of ischemic events after severe traumatic brain injury in humans: A simple scoring system. *J. Neurosurg. Anesthesiol.*, 18, 170, 2006.

234. Menon, D.K., Brain ischaemia after traumatic brain injury: Lessons from 15 O_2 postitron emission tomography. *Curr. Opin. Crit. Care*, 12, 85, 2006.

235. Marmarou, A., Signoretti, S., Aygok, G., et al., Traumatic brain edema in diffuse and focal injury: Cellular or vasogenic? *Acta Neurochir. Suppl.*, 96, 24, 2006.

236. Beaumont, A. and Gennarelli, T., CT prediction of contusion evolution after closed head injury: The role of pericontusional edema. *Acta Neurochir. Suppl.*, 96, 30, 2006.

237. Miller, J.D. and Corales, R.L., Brain edema as a result of head injury: Fact or fallacy, in *Brain Edema*, Vieger, M., Lange, S.A., and Becks, J.W.S., Eds., John Wiley & Sons, New York, 1981, p. 99.

238. Aarabi, B., Hesdorffer, D.C., Ahn, E.S., et al., Outcome following decompressive craniectomy from malignant swelling due to severe head injury. *J. Neurosurg.*, 104, 469, 2006.

239. Yakota, H., Naoe, Y., Nakabayashi, M., et al., Cerebral endothelial injury in severe head injury: The significance of measurements of serum thrombomodulin and the von Willebrand factor. *J. Neurotrauma*, 19, 1007, 2002.

240. Pittella, J.E. and Gusmao, S.N., Diffuse vascular injury in fatal road traffic accidents: Its relationship to diffuse axonal injury. *J. Forensic Sci.*, 48, 626, 2003.

241. Stein, S.C., Chen, X.H., Sinson, G.P., et al., Intravascular coagulation: A major secondary insult in nonfatal traumatic brain injury. *J. Neurosurg.*, 97, 1373, 2002.

242. Miller, J.D., Piper, I.R., and Jones, P.A., Pathophysiology of head injury, in *Neurotrauma*, Narayn, R.K., Wilberger, J.E., and Povlishock, J.T., Eds., W.B. Saunders, Philadelphia, PA, 1996, p. 61.

243. Miller, J.D., Stanek, A.E., and Langfitt, T.W., Concepts of cerebral perfusion pressure and vascular compression during intracranial hypertension, in *Progress in Brain Research, Vol. 35, Cerebral Blood Flow*, Meyer, J.S. and Schade, J., Eds., Elsevier, Amsterdam, 1972, p. 411.

244. Manley, G., Nudson, M.M., Morabito, D., et al., Hypotension, hypoxia, and head injury: Frequency, duration, and consequences. *Arch. Surg.*, 136, 1118, 2001.

245. Chesnut, R.N., Marshall, S.B., Pick, J., et al., Early and late systemic hypotension as a frequent and fundamental source of cerebral ischemia following severe brain injury in the Traumatic Coma Databank. *Acta Neurochir. (Wein)*, 59, 121, 1993.

246. Aarabi, B., Eisenberg, H.M., Murphy, K., et al., Traumatic brain injury: Management and complications, in *Textbook of Neurointensive Care*, Layon, A.J., Gabrielli, A., and Friedman, W.A., Eds., W.B. Saunders, Philadelphia, PA, 2004, p. 771.

247. Marion, D.W., Darby, J., and Yonas, H., Acute regional cerebral blood flow changes caused by severe head injuries. *J. Neurosurg.*, 74, 407, 1991.

248. Ueda, Y., Walker, S.A., and Povlishock, J.T., Perivascular nerve damage in the cerebral circulation following traumatic brain injury. *Acta Neuropathol. (Berl.)*, 112, 85, 2006.

249. Wintermark, M., Chiolero, R., VanMelle, G., et al., Cerebral vascular autoregulation assessed by perfusion-CT in severe head trauma patients. *J. Neuroradiol.*, 33, 27, 2006.

250. Oertel, M., Boscardin, W.J., Obrist, W.D., et al., Posttraumatic vasospasm: The epidemiology, severity, and time course of an underestimated phenomenon: A prospective study performed in 299 patients. *J. Neurosurg.*, 103, 812, 2005.

251. Marshall, L.F., Marshall, S.B., Klauber, M.R., et al., A new classification of head injury based on computerized tomography. *J. Neurosurg.*, 75, S-14, 1991.

252. Adams, J.H., Graham, D.I., and Gennarelli, T.A., Contemporary neuropathological considerations regarding brain damage and head injury, in *Central Nervous System Trauma Status Report*, Becker, D.P. and Povlishock, J.T., Eds., National Institute of Neurological Communicative Disorders and Stroke, Washington, D.C., 1985, p. 65.

253. Nordstrom, C.H., Assessment of critical thresholds for cerebral perfusion pressure by performing bedside monitoring of cerebral energy metabolism. *Neurosurg. Focus*, 15, E5, 2003.

254. Winter, C.D., Adamides, A., and Rosenfeld, J.V., The role of decompressive craniectomy in the management of traumatic brain injury: A critical review. *J. Clin. Neurosci.*, 12, 619, 2005.

255. Ogden, A.T., Mayer, S.A., and Connolly, E.S., Hyperosmolar agents in neurosurgical practice: The evolving role of hypertonic saline. *Neurosurgery*, 57, 207, 2005.

256. Miller, J.D. and Adams, J.H., The pathophysiology of raised intracranial pressure, in *Greenfield's Neuropathology,* 5th edition, Adams, J.H. and Duchen, E., Eds., Arnold, London, 1992, p. 69.
257. Teasdale, E., Cardoso, E., Galbraith, S.E., et al., CT scan in diffuse head injury: Physiological and clinical correlation. *J. Neurol. Neurosurg. Psychiatry,* 47, 600, 1984.
258. Marmarou, A., Traumatic brain edema: An overview. *Acta Neurochir.,* 60 (Suppl.), 421, 1994.
259. Warren, J., A hero finally heads home. *Lexington Herald Leader,* December 23, 2006.
260. Jennett, B. and Bond, M., Assessment of outcome after severe brain damage. *Lancet,* 1, 480, 1975.

2 Neuropsychiatric and Psychiatric Syndromes following Traumatic Brain Injury

NEUROPSYCHIATRIC SYNDROMES

INTRODUCTION

Human behavior may be conceptualized in terms of three basic functional systems: (1) cognition, which is the information processing aspects of behavior (analogous to a computer); (2) emotionality, which concerns feelings and motivation; and (3) executive functions, which governs how behavior is expressed and managed (the chief executive officer of our brain). Lezak et al.[48] provide the basic definitions for these three functional systems. The four major classes of cognitive function borrow from the language of computer operations. These classes include input, storage, processing, and output. Brain receptors and sensory systems select, acquire, classify, and integrate input information; informational storage and retrieval are the memory and learning portions of human mental function. Thinking occurs during the mental organization and reorganization of input information and storage of information. The expressive portions of cognition are the means through which information is communicated or acted upon.[48] Human executive functions consist of those capacities that enable a person to engage successfully in independent, purposive, self-serving behavior. They differ significantly from cognitive functions in a number of ways. Executive function begs the question as to how or whether a person goes about doing an act or task. On the other hand, questions about cognitive function are generally phrased in terms of what or how much. This further begs questions of how much a person knows or what that person can do. So long as the executive functions are reasonably intact, a person can sustain considerable cognitive loss and still continue to be independent, constructively self-serving, and productive.

The neuropsychiatric, neurobehavioral, and psychiatric disorders seen by physicians following traumatic brain injury (TBI) are very poorly delineated. Psychiatric nosology handles these disorders too simply and has only a rudimentary diagnostic system. One of the great strengths of the *Diagnostic and Statistical Manual of Mental Disorders*, however, is the systematic descriptive terminology and descriptive diagnostic labels for most of the major psychiatric conditions. On the other hand, this diagnostic classification system has yet to offer medical practice an effective model for diagnosing the many behavioral syndromes seen following trauma to or disease of the central nervous system. Table 2.1 lists the current *DSM-IV-TR* diagnoses appropriate for an individual who has sustained TBI.[1] With regard to cognitive disorders, about the best that can be obtained for a diagnosis is cognitive disorder, not otherwise specified (294.9). The extremely common postconcussional disorder is addressed in Appendix B of the *DSM-IV-TR* and is a new category which requires further study. This follows three decades of scientific research into the psychiatric, neurological, and neurosurgical literature concerning postconcussional syndromes. Another common disorder, particularly with mild traumatic brain injury (MTBI) or postconcussion

TABLE 2.1
***DSM-IV-TR* Diagnoses Appropriate for TBI**

• Amnestic disorder due to head trauma	(294.0)
• Anxiety disorder due to head trauma	(293.89)
• Cognitive disorder not otherwise specified	(294.9)
• Dementia due to head trauma	(294.1)
• Mood disorder due to head trauma	(293.83)
• Personality change due to head trauma	(310.1)
• Psychotic disorder due to head trauma	(293.xx)
• Sleep disorder due to head trauma	(780.xx)

syndrome, is mild neurocognitive disorder. This also is addressed in Appendix B of the *DSM-IV-TR* as a category for further study. The reader can ascertain the picture. Psychiatric nosology has not kept pace with the emerging body of evidence in neuropsychiatry, neurology, and neuropsychology regarding the multiple cognitive and behavioral syndromes seen following brain trauma. It is hoped that our colleagues developing the *DSM-V* will accept these criticisms as constructive and encourage neuropsychiatrists to assist the task force of the *DSM-V* with a more appropriate neuropsychiatric nosology for mental disorders often seen as outcomes following TBI.

ADULT COGNITIVE DISORDERS

Disorders of Attention

Attention is the sine qua non of sensory input to the brain. Each sensory modality has an attentional system. In other words, there is visual attention, auditory attention, tactile attention, olfactory attention, and gustatory attention. From a practical standpoint, only visual function, auditory function, and tactile function are assessed in most neuropsychiatric or neuropsychological examinations. There is no practical or clinically useful measuring system for detecting alterations of attention within taste and smell modalities. Moreover, when assessing clinically the traumatized patient, it is important to determine first the individual's level of attention and vigilance. If attention cannot be maintained, it is almost impossible to get an accurate assessment of neurocognitive status. Therefore, attention is the first cognitive domain to be addressed within a neurocognitive examination. About 9% of consecutively referred patients suffering severe head trauma have impairments in vigilance (the maintenance of attention longitudinally over time), whereas 77% of remaining patients will show increased distractibility within the context of normal vigilance.[2,3]

One portion of attention particularly sensitive to injury in TBI is the operation of control processes that are "slow" and "effortful."[4] Control processes are much more vulnerable to TBI than other forms of attention, and they include sustained, divided, and selective attention. Sustained attention is often termed "vigilance," and refers to the ability to maintain concentration on a task over a continuous period. On the other hand, divided attention refers to the ability to attend to two or more tasks simultaneously (multitask). Selective attention is the ability to focus on a specific target or task while being distracted. Impairments of attention in TBI are more marked within those cognitive tasks that require processing of multiple stimuli or tasks. Subtle defects in attention may occur even in MTBI, probably because divided attention requires a greater degree of central processing.[5] Parasuraman et al. have reported that in MTBI, attentional performance on visual vigilance testing is normal but worsened when stimuli are degraded and made more difficult to detect.[6]

Specific tests to measure attention are discussed in greater detail in Chapter 6 when the neurocognitive examination is considered. However, information processing in TBI patients has been assessed extensively by a common test, the Paced Auditory Serial Addition Test

(PASAT).[7] When Gronwall first reported these data, subjects were presented auditorily with a series of single digits at different speeds, and they were asked to add the first digit to the second digit, the second digit to the third digit, and so forth. This test can discriminate between mildly brain-injured subjects and normal controls, and it has been used as a gauge of recovery in MTBI. Other tests such as the Symbol Digit Modality Test and the Stroop Color-Word Test will demonstrate similar findings. They will also detect that TBI affects speed of processing more than it affects focused attention or sustained attention.[8] There are a variety of additional tests that might be useful for assessing attention in patients with TBI. These include the WAIS-III subtests such as Digit Span and Letter-Number Sequencing, the WMS-III mental control subtests, and the Brief Test of Attention[9] (see Chapter 6).

Following MTBI, performance on simple measures of attentional capacity, such as the Digit Span subtest of the Wechsler Intellectual Scales, may recover to relatively normal levels. Alterations in attention may not be uncovered unless more sophisticated neuropsychological measures are used, and then prominent deficits may be noted in these same patients. In addition, slowed information processing speed is a sensitive and well-documented cognitive sequela of head trauma. During face-to-face mental status examination, little may be noted by the clinician other than a perception that the patient is not thinking very quickly. When more sophisticated neuropsychological measures are applied, deficits in the application of divided attention under progressively increasing rates of information processing speed may be noted. In those patients with mild head injury only, reduction in mental processing speed tends to be restricted to the first 1–3 months after recovery. Thereafter in most patients, mental processing speed returns to near baseline levels.[13]

The appearance of attentional deficits may be dependent upon the cognitive load placed on the injured person. In other words, these deficits may not appear until sufficient cognitive loading is placed as a demand on the individual's brain. The more effort required for the person to pay attention, the more likely the attentional deficit will be detected. Moreover, patients may also demonstrate difficulty refocusing their attention after a period of delay from stimuli. If the task is short, such as that commonly performed in a face-to-face mental status examination, the attentional deficit may not be detected. More sophisticated attentional tasks, such as presented by neuropsychological evaluation, will generally reveal these deficits. One form of cognitive load testing is to provide the individual with a distracting stimulus while he attempts to focus attention on a target or other stimulus. Responses may be omitted within this type of assessment. On the other hand, patients may have difficulty inhibiting responses when asked to do so. Sensitive executive tests such as the Wisconsin Card Sorting Test or the Category Test may detect these impairments that will otherwise not be revealed by ordinary mental status examination (see Chapter 6). Table 2.2 reviews common attentional issues following TBI.

When attention is impaired following TBI, it is often mild, and it is less likely to become chronically impaired than memory or executive function.[10] With regard to visual attention, even patients with apparent mild outcomes may show deficits in predictive smooth pursuit eye movements (SPEM) associated with impairment of other cognitive functions. These processes are dependent on common white matter connections between multiple cerebral and cerebellar

---

TABLE 2.2

Attentional Disorders

- Attention is the *sine qua non* of sensory input to the brain.
- Attention should be measured before attempting to measure other neuropsychological domains.
- Attentional deficits may not appear without cognitive loading.
- Digit span subtest may recover to normal while other attentional deficits remain.

regions.[11] The University of Oregon, Department of Human Physiology, recently noted that temporal constraints of attention are subtly but systematically affected by MTBI. They presented a task with a stream of rapidly presented letters displayed with target and probe letters, separated by varying durations. The study subjects were required to identify the target letter and determine whether the probe letter was present or not. Those patients with MTBI had difficulty with attentional competition and made more errors in identifying the target letter when compared with controls.[12] The more sophisticated aspects of attentional testing following TBI are presented in Chapter 6.

Disorders of Memory

Memory disorders following TBI are confusing and perplexing. Memory is discussed in greater detail in Chapter 6, but for purposes of the memory disorders seen clinically following brain injury, an understanding of a model of memory organization is useful. Figure 2.1 displays a useful schema for understanding memory based upon the work of Squire.[14] For purposes of this chapter, the two major forms of memory are "declarative" and "procedural." Declarative memory is often called factual memory. Simply put, it is the memory system that enables one to consciously know that something is learned (such as algebra or literature), whereas procedural memory is the ability to perform a learned skill in the absence of conscious awareness of the learning experience (such as shooting a basketball or riding a bicycle). Some authors and memory experts use synonymous terms for declarative and procedural memories. Declarative memory is often termed "explicit," whereas procedural memory is termed "implicit." As noted in Figure 2.1, declarative memory is subdivided into episodic and semantic memories. Episodic memory is termed by some as autobiographical memory. Episodic memory can be stored long term. While performing a mental status examination, psychiatrists often test the limits of episodic memory at the bedside when asking a person to describe their morning, what they had for breakfast, and what their doctor told them during consultation. Episodic memory is highly autobiographical. It is critical to humans, as it enables social functioning, maintenance of relationships, judgment, goal-directed behavior, and the continuous sense of self across time.[15]

Semantic memory contrasts strongly with episodic memory. In semantic memory, general knowledge, recognition and meaning of words, objects, and actions are utilized. Facts are remembered that are not necessarily tied to a specific time or place of learning. One can have a TBI leading to amnesia. Yet the individual can retain intellectual, linguistic, perceptual, and semantic knowledge and skills while showing profound deficits in the ability to recall specific details and episodes of newly learned information.[16]

When reviewing procedural memory, sensory and motor skills are self-evident and make up a large component of this domain. It is thought that the basal ganglia are very much involved in this type of skill learning. This correlates clinically with specific neuropsychiatric diseases such as Huntington's disease and Parkinson's disease, where a patient will demonstrate specific deficits in

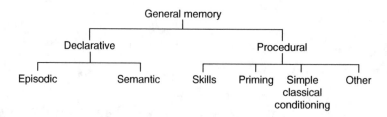

FIGURE 2.1 A schema of memory. (From Squire, L.R., *Memory and Brain*, Oxford University Press, New York, 1987, p. 170. With permission.)

motor skill learning but not necessarily in declarative memory. On the other hand, priming refers to enhanced processing of memory information because of preceding exposure to a specific stimulus or cue. There may not be conscious awareness of this. One example of priming used for learning is when students and scholars scan the elements of a book chapter to get the general layout of the book before they undertake reading and learning that particular chapter. Another form of procedural learning includes simple classical conditioning that all college students learn about in Psychology 101. Other more complex issues regarding memory are deferred to Chapter 6.

Declarative memory disorders are frequent after TBI, whereas procedural memory disorders rarely, if ever, occur to any significant degree. Retrograde amnesia occurs at the moment of impact or shortly thereafter and refers to the inability to remember events before the trauma. It typically demonstrates a temporal gradient, i.e., events nearer to the time of the impact are more likely to be forgotten, whereas remote events such as one's childhood or marriage would rarely be expected to show loss. Retrograde amnesia tends to shrink over time as the patient heals. On the other hand, anterograde amnesia (posttraumatic amnesia) usually covers a greater time span than retrograde amnesia. Episodic memory in particular seems impaired after impact, and patients who demonstrate posttraumatic amnesia do not maintain a coherent permanent record of ongoing environmental and autobiographical events. A summary of current scientific evidence regarding memory disorders following TBI indicates the following: (1) the greater the likelihood of memory impairment, the more severe the TBI; (2) most patients with MTBI, who show no other risk factors for memory impairment and no intercurrent complications, will recover to normal or near-normal levels of memory functioning; and (3) retrograde amnesia after TBI usually shrinks over time and is usually brief relative to posttraumatic anterograde amnesia.

Ribot's law is worth understanding, as it classically relates to memory disorders following brain trauma.[17] According to Ribot's law, there is a gradient of memory loss wherein the loss of recent memory is greater than the loss of remote memory. Many authors assert that if the traumatic brain-injured person recovers from posttraumatic amnesia, the person has regained a grossly normal level of orientation and awareness of ongoing events. However, this does not imply that the patient's memory has returned to normal. Levin has found that, among patients who recovered normal intellectual functioning (full-scale IQ greater than or equal to 85), disproportionately severe memory deficit was found in 16% of those recovered from moderate head trauma and 25% of those recovered from severe head trauma. Patients tend to report a lower rate of memory complaints than relatives' reports, and this probably reflects their lack of insight or the presence of organic denial (agnosia) affecting self-monitoring following head trauma.[18]

The cause of memory disorders following TBI is likely secondary to the relatively predictable pattern of diffuse and focal neuropathology sustained by persons with head trauma. This in turn results in high concentrations of parenchymal and extraparenchymal lesions in the frontal and anterior temporal lobes, the anatomical areas most likely to subserve memory.[19] These areas contain the hippocampus and other neuronal structures that are purported to be anatomical areas involved in the storage and retrieval of newly formed memories.[20,21] The orbitofrontal lobes, as previously noted, are particularly sensitive to injury during closed-head trauma. Moreover, the lateral areas of the temporal poles are also very susceptible to contusions or bruises. Hippocampal damage may result from release of excitotoxic amino acids after the injury.[22–24]

When evaluating traumatic brain-injured patients, it is often useful to ask the last event remembered before the traumatic impact, whether they remember the impact itself, and the first thing they remember following impact. These are crude historical markers for retrograde and anterograde posttraumatic memory deficits. Retrograde amnesia extends backward in time from the moment of trauma, whereas anterograde amnesia extends forward in time from the moment of that trauma.[25,26] The classical studies by Russell and Nathan[26] found that in patients who recovered from TBI the duration of their retrograde amnesia is almost always much shorter than the duration of the anterograde amnesia. Thus, the majority of patients who sustain a TBI will report a residual retrograde amnesia of only seconds or minutes in duration, whereas the anterograde amnesia will

TABLE 2.3

Elements of Memory Disorders in the Traumatically Brain-Injured Patient

- Memory is usually the most affected cognitive function.
- Ribot's Law: There is a gradient of memory loss: recent > remote.
- Explicit memory affected > implicit memory (factual > procedural).
- Patients report greater memory loss than their relatives.
- The duration of anterograde amnesia is almost always longer than the duration of retrograde amnesia.

almost always be much longer than this by their reports. It was Ribot[17] who first wrote of a large survey of patients reporting memory disorders following trauma. His work proposed a temporal gradient of retrograde memory loss for head trauma patients, which was subsequently confirmed by Levin et al.[27] Table 2.3 lists the salient features of memory disorders seen in the traumatically brain-injured patient.

Language Disorders

The patient examined after a TBI likely will complain of difficulty with language. However, a true aphasia is extremely rare following TBI. This may be because following TBI the neural pathways for language are seldom injured selectively. About 2% of patients admitted to a neurosurgery head trauma service are aphasic and have left perisylvian contusions. Approximately one-third of these patients manifest one of the classic aphasic disorders. When examined for language, 51% will demonstrate a fluent aphasia, 35% will demonstrate a nonfluent aphasia, and 14% will demonstrate a global aphasia. Approximately another third of patients are nonaphasic but demonstrate dysarthria. Most language disorders following TBI are subclinical. That is to say, the examiner will have to perform sophisticated language testing such as described in Chapter 6 to detect language differences that are not apparent during conversation.[28] The most prevalent language disorders that can be detected by a face-to-face examination are word-finding impairment or anomia. The Boston Naming Test described in Chapter 6 will assist the examiner in detecting anomia. Word-finding or retrieval problems may require more complicated language batteries. As noted in the forensic section of this text (see Chapter 10), language can be a prominent impairment where there is a question of competency or understanding of the information relevant to informed consent, decision making, and planning. In those cases, it is recommended that the examiner provide formal neuropsychological testing of language comprehension with a standardized test such as the Boston Diagnostic Aphasia Battery (see Chapter 6).

Anomia, the inability to name common objects, is the most common language disturbance seen following head trauma. It spares fluency, and the ability to repeat and comprehend, both of which are impaired in the more classic language disorders.[29,30] The paraphasias may be more difficult to detect for the uninitiated examiner. However, the examiner may notice that the patient speaks by circumlocution and may demonstrate semantic paraphasias. Semantic paraphasia may present by switching one word term for another. During neuropsychological testing of patients who have aphasia-related head injury, the highest rate of defective performance will be seen in confrontational naming. Deficits in comprehension, writing praxis, and verbal associative fluency will be seen at lower rates of occurrence. The ability to repeat words remains relatively preserved on neuropsychological testing.[29]

In patients who sustain aphasia after TBI, fluent aphasias are more common than nonfluent aphasias, as noted above. Global aphasia is rare and is usually a transient condition; it is associated with severe generalized cognitive defects and is more likely to occur in an older person. Following TBI, patients may have significant impairment in discourse and use of pragmatic and practical language, such as understanding indirect requests, hints, or jokes. Recovery of language ability tends to be strong following TBI and often exceeds recovery of other cognitive impairments, such as attention, executive function, and memory. Some experts think this reflects the fact that language is a highly practiced skill mediated by structures that generally are not in the line of injury at the time of head trauma.[31] A very recent rehabilitation outcome study in patients with aphasic and nonaphasic TBI demonstrated that there were no significant differences in functional and cognitive gains between those patients who were aphasic following TBI versus those who were not aphasic.[32]

The symbolic aspects of language tend to transfer across hemispheres through the corpus callosum independent of whether it is phonetic language or semantic language. For instance, a recent Japanese study demonstrated language disturbance in a man who sustained a traumatic callosal hemorrhage following brain injury; the entire corpus callosum was severed with exception of the lower part of the genu and the lower part of the splenium.[33] This patient wrote with jargon when he used the right hand but not so when he used the left. He also demonstrated right unilateral tactile anomia and right tactile alexia with right ear extinction on a dichotic listening test for verbal stimuli. Since this patient learned to write with his right hand, kinesthetic images of Japanese language characters were thought to be formed and stored dominantly in the left hemisphere. Since his right hand could not connect to the left hemisphere following his lesion, he wrote jargon.

Some patients may show a foreign accent syndrome following TBI.[34] This is a very rare disorder caused by lesions within the dominant hemisphere. Foreign accent syndrome is defined as a loss of normal phonetic contrast while using the mother language. When native speakers listen to the injured person, the pronunciation is perceived to be a foreign accent. Further close listening and analysis of language following TBI may detect that the person's language has become semantically less complex. One way to detect this is by listening to propositions. The mean number of propositions within a sentence will drop off in some brain-injured persons following their injury.[35] Adolescents may demonstrate problems coping in high school, as TBI is noted to affect their ability to comprehend language inferences when the storage demands become high, such as during formal education by learning literature, history, etc.[36]

If aphasic TBI patients recover their basic language abilities, the conversational discourse of these patients is often characterized by deficits that are not easily related to standard language parameters of fluency, repetition, comprehension, and naming. For instance, it has been demonstrated that, in patients who have preferentially left prefrontal traumatic lesions, communication is characterized by disorganized and impoverished narratives. In contrast to this, the communication of patients who have suffered right prefrontal injuries tends to be tangential and socially inappropriate.[37,38]

Visual-Perceptual Disorders

Most individuals who suffer a closed TBI display normal visual-perceptual abilities.[39] However, in patients who sustain brain contusions or hematomas, those who have right hemisphere bruising or bleeding are more likely to show a deficit of visual perception. Visual-spatial function remains relatively preserved in patients even following severe head trauma.[40] Constructional ability or drawing praxis is also generally preserved in these individuals.[41]

A complicating factor in disorders of visual perception can be lesions which may or may not be confined entirely to the right hemisphere. Many persons following TBI complain of impaired vision. There can be direct injury to the visual pathways. Trauma to the occiput or contrecoup injury to the occiput and posterior temporal areas affects the primary and secondary visual association cortex. A variety of visual field defects can occur, as well as the neuropsychiatric syndromes of alexia, visual agnosia, prosopagnosia, and achromatopsia.[31] In Chapter 6 there will be exploration of the rare Bálint syndrome that occurs with occipital–parietal lesions.

If the lesions are confined to the left parietal area following TBI, patients will tend to show confusion, simplification, and concrete handling of visual designs. During neuropsychological assessment, they are likely to work from left than right as they approach a visual task. On the other hand, patients whose brain lesions are mostly right-sided may begin at the right of the page and work to the left. Their drawings may demonstrate distortions of the entire design or misperceptions of the design as they attempt to reproduce a drawing such as the Rey-Osterrieth Figure (see Chapter 6). Patients with the right-sided lesions are much more likely to demonstrate a visual-perceptual deficit with distortions of the design or misperceptions of the design. If the visual-perceptual deficit is quite prominent, they may not square a corner, or they may not appreciate the format of the design. Lezak has noted that the Block Design subtest from the Wechsler Intelligence Scales is an excellent measure of visual-spatial ability.[42] The Block Design subtest is not specific to right hemisphere injury, and it may be impaired in the presence of any kind of brain injury. However, it has been demonstrated to be the most impaired when the traumatic lesion involves the posterior right brain.[43] Lezak quotes Edith Kaplan in calling our attention to the performance of brain-injured patients that have right parietal lobe components to their injury. These individuals will cluster their errors at the bottom of the visual field, whereas patients with lesions in the temporal lobe are more likely to cluster errors in the upper visual fields. This may give some indication of the anatomical site of the lesion.[42]

There is a biomechanical basis that explains the lack of visual-perceptual deficits in most traumatic brain injuries. As discussed previously, there is an anterior posterior gradient to tissue destruction in most closed-head trauma. That is to say the frontal parts of the brain are more likely to be injured than the posterior parts. Most of the components of visual-perceptual processing systems are located in the posterior portions of the brain, and thus visual perception is preferentially spared.[44] The reader is referred to Table 2.4 for a listing of common visual-perceptual disorders that occur following TBI.

Prosopagnosia may occur following TBI. This is discussed more fully in Chapter 6. However, early after brain trauma, it is not unusual for injured persons to be unable to recognize previously known family members or friends. In fact, there may be focal prosopagnosia present, wherein the individual can detect the lower half of the face of a loved one but not the upper half.[45] The Glasgow group has recently provided information that indicates individuals with prosopagnosia are unable to use the visually detected information around the person's eyes to identify a familiar face. They are more likely to focus on the lower part of the face, including the mouth and the external contours. The brain-injured person processes faces by focusing on the suboptimal information points of the face rather then the more optimal periorbital areas.[46] Moreover, patients with recently acquired TBI are impaired in their ability to perceive emotions in faces.[47] This may explain some of the personality changes noted by loved ones and other observers in patients following TBI.

Intellectual Disorders

Piaget has said that intellect is what we use when we do not know what to do.[49] However, with TBI, the untoward effects on intellectual functioning are often indirect rather than direct. In fact,

---

TABLE 2.4

Visual-Perceptual Disorders following Traumatic Brain Injury (TBI)

- Visual-perceptual disorders are usually absent following TBI.
- Hematomas or contusions may predispose to visual-perceptual impairment.
- Left parietal lesions can cause confusion, simplification, and concrete handling of designs.
- Right parietal lesions may cause distortions or misperceptions of the design.
- Usually the anterior–posterior gradient of head trauma spares the more posterior visual-perceptual cortex.

intelligence testing using instruments such as the Wechsler Adult Intelligence Scale-III is poor at detecting brain injury, and full-scale intellectual changes measured by similar test instruments after head injury may not be significantly different from those of normal age-matched controls. On the other hand, certain subtest scores measured by the Wechsler Memory Scale-III are very likely to show diminishment following TBI when compared with those of controls.[50] In fact, use of deviation IQ scores alone is not an appropriate yardstick when determining cognitive changes following TBI. The predominant reason that IQ testing alone is a poor choice for injury assessment is that intelligence testing does not tap into many of the critical areas of a person's cognitive functioning, such as personality regulation, short-term memory, attentional capacity, and executive function.[51]

Cattelani et al. have shown in adults who were head-injured as children that changes in intellectual functioning are less important years after a TBI than the prevailing problems of social maladjustment and poor quality of life, which seem related to behavioral and psychosocial disorders.[52]

As we shall see in Chapter 6, assessment of intellect following brain injury has no meaning unless an estimation of pre-injury IQ can be made. Within the last one to two decades, multiple test instruments have come to the forefront to enable neuropsychologists and psychologists to provide a reasonably accurate estimate of pre-injury intellectual ability before the fact of a TBI. Whereas estimation of premorbid intellectual ability has become commonplace in the English-speaking world, it is more recently coming to less developed nations. China has recently published information using the Chinese Revised Version of the Wechsler Adult Intelligence Scale. In those cases where pre-injury and post-injury IQ scores were available, they are adopting premorbid ability assessment in their forensic institutions for consideration of post-injury assessments following TBI.[53] While there may be a significant dose–response relationship between TBI severity and IQ scores and index scores, use of the summary test scores alone is not recommended.[54] However, there is some recent Japanese evidence that verbal intelligence quotients (VIQs) following TBI are preferentially lower than performance intelligence quotients (PIQs) following injury.[55] It is recommended that the subtest scores on a complete intellectual assessment such as the Wechsler Adult Intelligence Scales be used to supplement information where a significant discrepancy between PIQ and VIQ is noted following TBI.

In general, intellectual functions improve over time after a TBI, from the acute stages following trauma to the chronic period wherein the neuropsychiatric or neuropsychological examination is most likely to be undertaken. More than 30 years ago, Mandleberg and Brooks[56] studied 40 men with TBI of varying severity, defined by the duration of posttraumatic amnesia. Initial scores on most subscale tests of the Wechsler Adult Intelligence Scales were below those of a control group. However, there was no significant difference in VIQ between the two groups 10 months after injury. Performance subscale scores of the TBI group showed slower improvement and did not approach that of the control group until 3 years post-injury. In this study, and in many other studies of IQ after TBI, the verbal subtest scores were not as low as the performance subtest scores, in contrast to the Japanese study above. Also, the verbal scores improved to premorbid levels more quickly. This pattern probably reflects the relative novelty of performance subscale tasks, which are generally more sensitive to brain dysfunction than verbal subscale tasks.[42] Usually, patients with TBI will show intellectual deficits that generally correlate with the severity of the trauma. While IQ tests are useful in the assessment of cognitive changes following brain trauma, in order to understand specific cognitive abilities, the examiner must use specific subscales such as those within the Wechsler Adult Intelligence Scales.

ADULT EXECUTIVE DISORDERS

Deficits in executive function will be a critical determinant of functional outcome following TBI in the adult. Anatomically, executive function is considered the domain of the prefrontal and

TABLE 2.5

Executive Dysfunction due to Traumatic Brain Injury

- Human executive function = volitional behavior, planning for the future, purposeful action, and regulating one's behavior.
- Impairment of executive function leads to disorders of emotional intelligence.
- The standard psychiatric mental status examination may be inadequate to uncover executive disorders; a precise history is generally more revealing.

---

frontal lobes and their projections.[57] Table 2.5 lists the common components of executive functions that may be impaired following TBI. While there is significant variation among the disciplines of behavioral neurology, neuropsychiatry, and neuropsychology as to the exact domain of executive function, for purposes of this text, executive function refers to higher-level abilities such as judgment, decision making, social conduct, organizational skills, and planning. Decision-making impairments may reflect failure to respond to changing contingencies, inhibit inappropriate responses, and appreciate future consequences of actions.[58] As noted in Chapter 1, damage to the orbital surfaces of the frontal lobes is common, and injury to the frontal and temporal lobes is extremely common during TBI. Executive dysfunction is difficult to detect even by the best psychiatric or neurological examination. Collateral interviews may be much more diagnostic. Obviously, the patient should be interviewed directly for symptoms of executive impairment (see Chapter 3). However, collateral informants such as a spouse, family members, friends, or employers can provide important ancillary information regarding the patient's social behavior, judgment, and decision making.

Adult patients with executive dysfunction disorders following TBI may demonstrate deficient self-awareness of impairment (anosognosia). Patients are unaware of their deficits and are unable to self-monitor. They are less likely to take compensatory steps to mitigate their difficulties. The physician may receive complaints from the physical therapist, occupational therapist, or speech pathologist that the patient is unwilling to participate in rehabilitation or other interventions. Family members may exclaim that the patient will not follow directions for medication or may engage in unsafe behaviors. Anosognosia often has an associated disorder, anosodiaphoria. This is the lack of mood-appropriate emotional reactions to the acquired deficits. The patient may appear indifferent to these deficits and deny all medical impairments, orthopedic as well as cognitive. Anosognosia generally demonstrates a recovery curve similar to other cognitive functions. Most patients will eventually recover some awareness of their medical condition and cognitive impairments although there is usually a dose–response relationship to the level of severity of the TBI.[31]

A frequent marker of reduced executive function is a reduction in verbal fluency. This often covaries with the expressed executive dysfunction.[59] The standard psychiatric clinical interview or basic psychological evaluation often fails to detect the presence of significant executive deficits. However, head trauma patients with executive dysfunction may lack the initiative to manage their lives once they leave the professional's office. The adaptive functioning of these patients is often impaired because they lack the necessary flexibility of reasoning and problem-solving to respond to a complex environment.

In the standard clinical examination, the psychiatrist usually asks leading questions and actively guides the interview while the patient passively provides what may well be habitual answers based on pre-injury knowledge. Moreover, most psychological evaluations follow standard psychometric procedures, and the person is examined using highly structured tasks with explicit instructions. Often, situations are not open-ended enough to detect the executive dysfunction present following TBI, as these do not adequately measure performance that requires self-initiation and active self-monitoring of performance. The adaptive functions necessary to lead satisfactory lives are often termed emotional intelligence. It is probably more important to human efficiency and success than is test IQ. The brain-injured individual may lack the necessary flexibility of reasoning and problem-solving to respond to the environment as it challenges the individual with novel or complex situations.[60]

One of the more common features that the neuropsychiatric examination will detect when interviewing collateral sources is that patients with executive dysfunction often develop associated personality changes (see "Personality Changes following Traumatic Brain Injury"). The family, and occasionally the patient, may report adverse changes in the patient's judgment, organizational ability, initiation, and regulation of behavior. Coworkers or family members may report the presence of apathy, depression, and irritability. It is thought that these neurobehavioral changes are direct outcomes of damage to limbic and frontal lobe systems in the anterior brain that are associated with mood and emotional regulation, or they reflect language dysprosody (see Chapter 6). These changes can be overlooked, or they can be misconstrued as due to external stressors thought to be a result of the patient's reaction to the injury. Thus, when examining for behavioral outcomes following TBI, the impact of potential dysexecutive syndromes must be taken into account or interpretive errors may occur when ascertaining causes of behavioral change. Persons with frontal lobe damage and dysexecutive syndromes will generally elevate certain scales on the MMPI-2, particularly scales 1 and 3 associated with somatization tendencies, and scale 8, associated with apathy (see Chapter 7). Of particular importance in the assessment of executive function is the question of *ecological validity*. This is a term of art that has come about recently questioning the usefulness and validity of neuropsychological assessments and how well they predict day-to-day and real world function. For example, the widely used executive function tests, the Wisconsin Card Sorting Test, the Trailmaking Tests, and the Category Test may produce results failing to validate the expected relation between frontal lobe injury and day-to-day executive function. These tests clearly have value in a neuropsychological battery and may aid decisions relevant to management and rehabilitation. However, the examiner should consider newer tests that have been developed that may be more sensitive to specific aspects of executive function.[48,61]

CHILD COGNITIVE DISORDERS

Persons uninitiated to the consequences of pediatric TBI often implicitly assume that the young brain, due to its plasticity during development, will recover function, leaving the growing child time for cerebral growth to overcome the TBI. There is a caveat: the effects of diffuse insult produced by TBI in young children may ultimately result in greater cognitive impairment in a developing brain than in a mature brain. There is an inverse age-related gradient in young children who sustain TBI. Children below 10 years of age are more at risk for significant cognitive impairment following brain injury than are adolescents. Infants and toddlers are at the greatest risk for brain damage following trauma to the head than are children of preschool or kindergarten age[62,63] (see Table 2.6). Moreover, there is a known pattern that children who become brain

---

TABLE 2.6

Unique Characteristics of Pediatric Traumatic Brain Injury (TBI)

- TBI affects a developing brain more so than a mature brain.
- Children below age five are much more affected by TBI than older children.
- Brain plasticity does not benefit the very young child after traumatic injury.
- Three-fourths of preschool brain-injured youngsters may not work as adults.

---

injured are overrepresented with pre-injury learning disability and academic dysfunction from developmental disorders.[64]

However, all is not doom even in children who sustain moderate to severe brain injury. A recent Finnish study[65] followed a cohort of 22 traumatic brain-injured patients for four decades in relation to eventual vocational outcome. These patients had suffered moderate to severe TBI in traffic accidents as preschoolers. The cognitive performance of full-time working patients was compared with those who were not working. As expected, the patients working full time had significantly better intellectual performance than those patients who were not at work. Memory performance was substandard in both groups, but neither group had subjective memory complaints at examination. All patients working full time lived in a marital relationship and had less obvious neurobehavioral problems than the patients not at work. The authors concluded that good intellectual capacity, verbal memory, and marital status were connected with a positive outcome following childhood TBI. It was concluded that it is still possible for a subgroup of patients to live a normal and productive life even though they sustained moderate to severe brain injury in young childhood. On the other hand, some children do retain lack of functional capacity into adulthood following brain injury. For instance, quantitative measurement of the corpus callosum on MRI reflects neuropsychological outcome better than ventricular dilation in pediatric patients.[66] Corpus callosum atrophy on MRI is the best predictor of long-term outcome in pediatric patients with cognitive disorders following TBI when compared with other affected anatomical structures.[67] Other questions have been raised about the quality of life in children following TBI. Johns Hopkins University School of Medicine recently published a study of 330 youngsters with TBI. The children were followed over time, and the primary caregiver was interviewed by telephone at baseline following brain injury, at 3 months, and at 12 months post-injury, to measure the child's health-related quality of life. At 3 months post-injury, 42% of children continued to have a negative impact on quality of life. At 12 months, 40% of children were negatively affected after injury. The authors concluded that moderate or severe TBI in children resulted in measurable declines of health-related quality of life in the first year after injury.[68]

In summary, children who suffer TBI frequently make a good physical recovery and appear outwardly normal. This raises expectation above their abilities, because there is a bias by their relatively healthy presentation, despite ongoing significant cognitive and behavioral difficulties. Children who sustain mild TBI may perform adequately on neuropsychological testing but continue to experience problems when faced with the complexities of everyday life, in particular learning, new skill acquisition, and psychological functioning with peers.[69]

Attentional Disorders

In children who develop attentional deficits following TBI, the attentional symptomatology in the first 2 years after injury in both children and adolescents is significantly related to the severity of injury. Moreover, the overall symptomatology in a 2-year period is also significantly related to the level of family dysfunction.[70] Since the frontal lobes are often impacted, similar to that seen in adult patients, attentional control has a high likelihood of being affected adversely.[71] Attentional deficits are prominent in children who sustained inflicted TBI.[72] Whether inflicted or noninflicted, there is a detrimental impact of external interference on attentional performance in children. Also, adults and children appear to show differential difficulties.[73]

Attentional deficits in a young child probably have much more affect upon outcome during maturation than in the mature adult. Deficits in attention will impede input of information for learning and accumulation of new knowledge. This can possibly result in global cognitive dysfunction, as has been reported in the long-term follow-up with childhood TBI.[74] There is a specific contrast in children versus adults. Adults show psychomotor slowing after moderate to severe TBI, whereas children are more likely to present with global attentional deficits. Many of these problems persist beyond the acute recovery stage, whereas they are more likely to improve in the adult.

As noted, there is an inverse gradient for injury in children. The younger the child at injury, the more likely a poor outcome, and this is true for attentional deficits as well. When specific attentional components are localized and measured in children, the results consistently show relatively intact sustained attention capacity (vigilance), but difficulty with rate of motor execution and with response selection. Children are also more likely to fluctuate in attention, which may be difficult to detect on the more traditional measures of attention.[69] This is probably because the attentional development is at a relatively immature stage at the time of brain injury. Also, the normal components of attention emerge in the developing child later in life and fail to develop due to interruptions with the substrates within frontal attentional systems. Thus, children differ distinctly from adults in that they may have a two-fold strike against them. In addition to the cognitive impairment associated with initial injury, there may be a later ongoing impact on cerebral development as well as an inability to acquire new skills. This may lead to increasing lags in knowledge and skills relative to their peers, and a failure to differentiate further cognitive and attentional abilities.[69] Studies of attentional deficits in brain-injured preschool children between the ages of 3 and 8 years indicate that youngsters recover many of the deficits of arousal and motivation over time, whereas focused attention, impulsivity, and hyperactivity often remain as prominent chronic features.[75,76]

Memory Disorders

For almost three decades, it has been known that the most likely cognitive domain to show impairment after childhood TBI is memory. Those children with the greatest impairment tend to have the poorest recovery.[77,78] The number of memory studies in children following TBI compared with that in adults is relatively low. Most studies have measured verbal memory impairment, and a few studies have examined nonverbal memory disorders. Verbal memory impairment has been documented for recognition memory for words, word-list learning, paired-associates learning, and story recall.[79–82] Nonverbal studies have reported impairments in the recall of shapes from the Tactual Performance Test and impairment in the reproduction of simple and complex geometric shapes.[83,84]

The impact of memory impairment on the development of the child is substantial. The day-to-day tasks of childhood require acquiring knowledge and learning along with perfecting new skills. Memory impairment will interfere with this process and can result in failure to develop at an age-appropriate rate. Kinsella and colleagues have demonstrated the strong impact of impaired learning capacity in that verbal learning skills after TBI are predictive of educational progress at 2 years post-injury. Children with learning deficits following TBI are more likely to be in a special school environment or in need of individual remedial intervention.[85]

Generally, if children have memory measures applied during the acute phase of TBI recovery, no reliable dose–response relationship between injury severity and memory function can be found. If children are measured 1 year or more following brain injury, the dose–response relationship can be shown to develop over time. The more severe the injury, the greater the memory deficit measured at 12 months or more post-injury.[86] When memory is measured implicitly and explicitly, children show more impairment of explicit memory than they do of implicit memory[87,88] (i.e., more impairment of factual memory exists than that of procedural memory). Since the cognitive demands for adolescents are different than young children, adolescents are more sensitive to the attentional demands of working memory. This generalizes into the language area as well and produces difficulty for those comprehension tasks with high working memory demands.[89]

Language Disorders

As was noted above, the classic aphasic disorders are rare in adult head injuries. The same can be said for childhood TBI. On the other hand, children are more likely than adults to have language difficulties following TBI. These disorders differ from classic aphasic syndromes and are more likely to present as communication deficits, slowed speech, dysfluency, poor logical sequencing of ideas, and word-finding difficulties. Substantial articulatory dysfunction may be present.[90] Children following TBI may display pronounced difficulties with the pragmatic, everyday aspects of language. In those children demonstrating impairment in expressive language skills, writing abilities are often impaired as well.[91] Children display distinct and different language disorders than adults do following TBI. The child may demonstrate difficulty interpreting ambiguous sentences, making inferences, formulating sentences from individual words, and explaining figurative expressions. Studies of narrative discourse in children as they tell a story indicate that children who sustain TBI use fewer words in sentences within their stories than control subject children.[78] The most consistent finding of language disorders in children following TBI is that those youngsters injured at an early age consistently predict poor performance on language tasks versus older children or adolescents with a similar injury. The child injured very young loses the ability to acquire communicative skills. In fact, the severity of the brain injury in a child does not predict language performance as strongly as being injured before age five.[92]

In children who sustain inflicted head injury at a young age, speech and language difficulties in a Canadian study were present in 64% of children. These youngsters had other neurological evidence of injury such as cranial nerve abnormalities (20%) or visual defects and epilepsy (25%).[93] In the adolescent attempting high school and injured before age 10, a New Zealand study demonstrates that language comprehension tasks with high working memory demands pose the most difficulty.[89]

Not only do brain-injured children often show impairment of articulatory speed and linguistic processing but they may show a reduction in the speaking rate. These impairments are demonstrated by a reduction in speed of forming words and an increased time between the expression of these words. The addition of reduced articulatory speed and reduced linguistic processing contributes independently to slowed speaking rates in youngsters. This can be manifest in the slowed expression of a story or narration, and it is significant enough that peers are burdened by listening.[94,95]

Since children are learning to communicate, much of the recent TBI research in children is focused on the examination of functional language skills that are important for day-to-day communication. These studies have shown that when performances on standardized language tests are intact, children with a history of TBI demonstrate functional difficulties. These children produce less information content and poor organizational structure during conversation. As the child develops, the negative impact on language development is such that it may cause increased difficulty over time. By high school age, the quality of conversation and syntax in the teenager may be so simple and reduced in complexity that it is well below that of peers.[69] To date, the medical literature demonstrates no relationship between reduced discourse ability and the locus of the brain injury lesion in injured children younger than 5 years. For children older than 5 years at the time of TBI, the size and laterality of the lesion tend to produce language disorders similar to those seen in adolescents and adults.[96] With regard to nonverbal aspects of communication, children may understand emotional communication and the spontaneous externalization of emotion, but they do not express well affective signals to influence others (expressive dysprosody).[97] Table 2.7 describes common language disorders seen following pediatric TBI.

Intellectual Disorders

To be purposely redundant, IQ scores are insufficient to fully demonstrate the range of impairments or changes following TBI in children, as they are in adults. However, brain-injured children who recover from head trauma generally reveal post-injury deficits in intelligence as measured by the Wechsler Intelligence Scales for Children, regardless of the edition administered. During recovery, serial IQ testing will show progressive increments in IQ improvement.[19] Chadwick et al.[98] demonstrated that children who suffer moderate to severe head trauma had mean verbal intelligence

TABLE 2.7

Language Disorders following Pediatric Traumatic Brain Injury (TBI)

- Children are more likely than adults to develop disorders of language following TBI.
- Pragmatic aspects of ordinary daily language often are affected.
- Problems are commonly seen with interpreting ambiguous sentences, making inferences, or explaining figurative expressions (abstract language).
- Speaking rate, articulatory speed, and linguistic processing often are reduced.
- Injury below age five often reduces ability for discourse.

quotient (VIQ) deficits of 10 points, and mean performance intelligence quotient (PIQ) deficits of 30 points when compared to matched controls. In these children, at 1 year follow-up, the mean VIQ had recovered to within two points of the controls. However, the mean PIQ remained at 11 points below controls. As with adults, the subscale scores are far more meaningful neuropsychologically when determining the impact of TBI upon child intelligence tests. Unlike adults, the IQ scores of children may drop over time, as children fail to develop appropriately, and social learning is deficient.[99] Since there are many neuropsychological domains IQ tests do not tap, the effect of deficiencies in attention, speed of processing, memory, and learning may not be apparent on IQ testing in a child until some time after the injury.

Another factor to consider is the altered behavior of youngsters who sustain TBI. This may have a substantially negative impact upon test performance and could lead to a reduction in IQ scores. A recent study in the United Kingdom noted that teachers of more structured subjects such as mathematics and science perceive the brain-injured child as excitable but performing at average or above-average levels. On the other hand, teachers of less structured subjects such as art, drama, and music perceive the pupil to be attention seeking and disruptive in class.[100] This same author studied 67 school-age children with TBI and assessed them using the Vineland Adaptive Behavior Scales and the Wechsler Intelligence Scales for Children-III. Two-thirds of the children with TBI exhibited significant behavioral problems, statistically more than controls. Those children with behavioral problems had a mean IQ of approximately 15 points lower than those without behavioral problems. At school, 76% of the children with behavioral problems also had difficulties with schoolwork.[101]

A child who has been brain injured sustains a greater negative impact upon mathematics performance in school than upon reading and spelling performance. This is probably because mathematic skill requires more attentional input than verbal skills.[80] The child who has sustained a TBI requires a comprehensive, multidisciplinary evaluation during the rehabilitation phase to facilitate a smooth transition to home and school. Optimizing the child's reentry into the academic setting requires significant communication and close coordination among rehabilitation specialists, family members, and educators.[102] Many youngsters injured traumatically have a learning disability before their brain injury. A moderate to severe TBI will cause a significant additional cognitive impairment in those youngsters having a pre-injury learning disorder. Thus, even greater modification and adjustment of the academic curriculum may be required in these children after brain injury.[103] Table 2.8 summarizes intellectual outcomes in traumatically brain-injured children.

CHILD EXECUTIVE DISORDERS

Since the first edition of this book, there has been growing recognition that executive function, the superordinate managerial capacity for directing more modular abilities, is frequently impaired by TBI in children and mediates the neurobehavioral sequelae exhibited by these youngsters.[104] As noted in Chapter 1, the mechanisms involved in TBI often result in frontal lobe injury. The

TABLE 2.8

Intellectual Outcomes in Traumatically Brain-Injured Children

- Performance IQ may be permanently reduced relative to verbal IQ owing to task novelty demands and reduced mental and motor processing speed.
- The younger the child at the time of injury, the less IQ recovery will be.
- Traditional achievement tests may be insensitive to IQ-driven academic deficits.
- Mathematics performance sustains a greater negative impact than reading or spelling skills, probably because of increased attentional demands of calculation.
- A child learning-disabled before brain injury will sustain an additional cognitive decrement.

frontal brain regions are believed to subsume much of executive function. As in adults, executive functioning in the child broadly refers to a set of interrelated skills necessary to maintain an appropriate problem-solving set for the attainment of a future goal and may include cognitive functions such as attentional control, planning, problem-solving, cognitive flexibility, abstraction, and information processing.[71] A recent study by Ewing-Cobbs' group[105] at the University of Texas Health Science Center at Houston enlarged the study of executive function to children who had sustained inflicted TBI. They examined social and cognitive competence in 25 infants, ages 3–23 months who had sustained moderate to severe inflicted TBI. They were compared to 22 healthy community-comparison children. The evaluations occurred on average 1.6 months after injury. Inflicted TBI was associated with reduction in (1) initiation of social interactions, (2) responsiveness to interactions initiated by the examiner, (3) a positive affect, and (4) compliance. They concluded that early inflicted brain injury causes significant disruption in behaviors regulating initiation and responsiveness in social contexts. It seems obvious that this will reduce the effectiveness of the children as they attempt social interaction in older childhood and adulthood.

One great weakness in the TBI literature of children is the lack of studies determining the rate and extent of recovery of executive skills following pediatric TBI. Catroppa's group[106] in Australia employed a prospective, longitudinal design with participants recruited at the time of injury and followed over a 2-year period. They studied 69 children who had sustained a mild, moderate, or severe TBI. Four components of executive function were assessed: (1) attentional control; (2) planning, goal setting, and problem-solving; (3) cognitive flexibility; and (4) abstract reasoning. The results of this study demonstrated that while children with severe TBI performed most poorly during the acute post-injury stage, they exhibited greatest recovery of executive function over a 24-month period. Regardless, functional deficits of executive function remained for this group 2 years after injury. Pre-injury abilities and age at injury were identified as significant predictors of executive function and functional skills. The authors concluded that children sustaining severe TBI at a young age are particularly vulnerable to impairments in executive function. While these difficulties show some recovery with time after injury, long-term deficits remain and may have a negative impact on ongoing development. As these children progress through school, many of the deficits caused by executive dysfunction within academic settings are related to emotional or social intelligence.[107]

Postconcussion Syndrome

Postconcussion syndrome is probably the most controversial neuropsychiatric disorder thought to occur following head injury. Moreover, three terms are in current use within the TBI literature causing further confusion: (1) concussion, (2) postconcussion syndrome, and (3) mild traumatic brain injury. Using the Glasgow Coma Scale system, scores of 13 or greater are usually considered to be consistent with mild brain injury. However, it is not clear in the Glasgow Coma Scale system if a GCS score of 13–15 is consistent with concussion. The American Congress of Rehabilitation Medicine defines mild traumatic brain injury (MTBI) as a traumatically induced disruption of brain function that results in a loss of consciousness of less than 30 min duration or in an alteration of consciousness manifested by incomplete memory of the event and being dazed and confused. The period of posttraumatic amnesia should not last longer than 24 h, and the individual may or may not have focal neurological deficits.[230] The International Classification of Diseases, 9th Revision, includes a diagnostic category of concussion defined as "transient impairment of function as a result of a blow to the brain."[231] To complicate our journey further, the Centers for Disease Control and Prevention define TBI as "an occurrence of injury to the head that is documented in a medical record, with one or more of the following conditions attributed to head injury: (1) observed or self-report of decreased level of consciousness, (2) amnesia, (3) skull fracture, (4) objective neurological or neuropsychological abnormality, or (5) diagnosed intracranial lesion.[232] Obviously, these are of no help whatsoever with regard to truly classifying brain injury by level of severity, level of consciousness, or in terms of a postconcussion syndrome.

Cantu[233] has published an excellent guide for grading the severity of concussion. His work comes from the area of clinical sports injuries. Concussion is graded numerically as, 1 (mild), 2 (moderate), and 3 (severe). Table 2.9 demonstrates this classification system. Mild concussion can have a duration of posttraumatic amnesia up to 30 min, whereas the duration of posttraumatic amnesia varies from 30 min to less than 24 h in grade 2 concussion. Grade 3 concussion is defined by duration of posttraumatic amnesia greater than 24 h. The loss of consciousness allowed is none for grade 1, less than 5 min for grade 2, and greater than or equal to 5 min for grade 3. The American Academy of Neurology published a grading system for concussion in 1997.[234] A grade 1 (mild) concussion consisted of transient confusion and symptoms of mental status abnormality which resolved in less than 15 min with no loss of consciousness. Grade 2 (moderate) concussions demonstrated transient confusion with symptoms of mental status abnormalities on examination that lasted greater than 15 min with no loss of consciousness. Grade 3 (severe) concussions included any loss of consciousness classified as either brief (seconds) or prolonged (minutes). This definition differs somewhat from that of Cantu in that a moderate concussion allows no loss of consciousness under the American Academy of Neurology guidelines, whereas with Cantu, the loss of consciousness may last less than 5 min.

Recent information about concussion indicates that approximately 10% of individuals will develop persistent signs and symptoms of postconcussion syndrome (PCS). There are no scientific established treatments for concussion or PCS. The recent review by Willer and Leddy[235] concluded that there was limited evidence-based pharmacological treatment of acute concussion symptoms or PCS symptoms. However, their article presented a clinical model to suggest that concussion can evolve to become MTBI after PCS developed. This represents a more severe form of brain injury than ordinary concussion.

As discussed previously, the *DSM-IV* leaves a lot to be desired in terms of diagnostic criteria following TBI. Levin's group at the Baylor College of Medicine has recently reviewed diagnostic criteria for both the *DSM-IV* and the *ICD-10*. They applied diagnostic criteria for

TABLE 2.9
The Grading of Concussion

	Grade	Loss of Consciousness	Length of Posttraumatic Amnesia
Mild	1	None	<30 min
Moderate	2	<5 min	>30 min <24 h
Severe	3	>5 min	>24 h

postconcussional syndrome in 178 adults with mild to moderate TBI and 104 adults with extra-cranial trauma. The results showed that prevalence of postconcussion syndrome was higher using the *ICD-10* criteria (64%) than *DSM-IV* criteria (11%). Specificity to TBI was limited, as PCS criteria were often fulfilled by patients with extracranial trauma. The authors concluded that further refinement of the *DSM-IV* and *ICD-10* criteria for PCS is needed before these criteria are reasonably employed.[236,237]

The natural history of concussion is poorly explained in many studies. McHugh et al. followed-up 26 MTBI patients[238] who received comprehensive neuropsychological assessment at three intervals: one week, four months, and seven months postconcussion. *DSM-IV* criteria were used. Asymptomatic MTBI participants improved in overall level of functioning from four to seven months but remained significantly different from normal control participants in their reduced verbal fluency and working memory function. To further confuse the picture regarding concussion, a University of Melbourne study reviewed the association between self-reported history of concussion and current neurocognitive status. This particular study found no relation between the number of previous self-reported episodes of concussion and current cognitive state, directly contradicting the findings of previous research.[239] This study is reported for purposes of balance, but it may be an outlier. A University of Utah study looked at litigation issues and MTBI. Sixty-seven adults with disappointing recoveries after MTBI were evaluated. The majority of these participants were involved in a compensation or litigation context. The authors concluded that in cases of poor recovery after mild TBI where compensation or litigation may be a factor, most of the variants in recovery seem to be explained by depression, pain, and symptom invalidity rather than the injury variables themselves.[240] Lastly, a large study in Lithuania reviewed findings in over 600 children.[241] Of these 301 children aged 4–15 years who had sustained an isolated brain concussion were compared against a group of 301 matched children who sustained any other mild body injury excluding the head. The severity of complaints was rated on the Visual Analogue Scale. After final exclusions, 102 pairs strictly matched by sex, age, and the date of trauma were analyzed. Neuropsychological testing was not performed in this study, and this is a great weakness, unfortunately. However, parental complaints were reviewed, and the differences of parental concern regarding the health condition of their children between the head injury cases and control groups were statistically insignificant for all symptoms, except parental concerns about their child having brain damage, which were significantly higher in the case group. The likelihood of parental concerns about the possibility of their child having brain damage was 2.7 times higher than that of the case group. Headache, learning difficulties, and sleep disorders were significant variables predicting parental concerns. The results of this study caused the authors to question the validity of the postconcussion syndrome in children. Thus, at the time of the writing of this text, the validity of significant postconcussion syndrome persisting beyond a number of months remains in question, particularly if litigation is a factor. See Table 2.9 to review the grading of concussion.

FRONTAL LOBE SYNDROMES

The first edition of this book focused upon frontal lobe syndromes as if they were discrete disorders. As executive function research has evolved, particularly in the past 10 years, the designation of particular syndromes following TBI specific to the frontal lobes has lost its appeal. Adult executive disorders and child executive disorders have been discussed above. This section takes a critical look at a more complex schema of frontal lobe dysfunction in terms of a central executive system impairment or dysexecutive syndrome. The central executive system is a term of art within cognitive neuroscience, whereas a dysexecutive syndrome has cache in the discipline of behavioral neurology. Neuropsychiatry tends to speak still of "frontal lobe syndromes." However, there is no *DSM-IV-TR* diagnosis specific to frontal lobe disorders. Table 2.10 describes the historical descriptors of frontal lobe disorders and is provided as a

---

TABLE 2.10

Frontal Lobe Disorders following Traumatic Brain Injury

Disinhibited (orbitofrontal) syndromes
- Behavioral disinhibition
- Acquired sociopathy
- Impulsive, socially inappropriate behaviors
- Lack of affective modulation

Disorganized (dorsolateral) syndromes
- Inability to integrate sensation into a whole
- Inability to switch sets with alternating paradigms
- Inflexible, perseverative responses
- Poor self-monitoring ability

Apathetic (mediofrontal) syndromes
- Can cause akinetic mutism
- Amotivational syndrome
- Lack of intentional behavior
- May cause severe environmental inattention

---

baseline from which to move to a more sophisticated understanding of central executive system impairment or dysexecutive syndrome. The famous case of Phineas Gage described by Harlow[108] is explored further as a model during the discussion of personality changes following brain injury.

From a gross anatomical standpoint, each frontal lobe is divided into primary motor, premotor, and prefrontal regions. These cortical areas are anatomically and functionally distinct. The prefrontal cortex is one of the most important cortical regions involved in cognition, behavior, and emotion. Neuroscientists have not been able to place the diverse aspects of behavior from this anatomical area within a single construct or process. However, recent research has pointed to three functional areas of behavioral mediation: (1) long-term knowledge storage, (2) learning and short-term representational knowledge, and (3) executive functions and self-regulation.[109]

With regard to long-term knowledge storage, the prefrontal cortex stores substantial amounts of acquired knowledge that is important for decision making and adaptation. An enigma for neuropsychologists and cognitive neuroscientists alike is that patients with prefrontal cortex damage often do not demonstrate deficits in measured intelligence on standardized instruments such as the Wechsler Adult Intelligence Scales. Except in cases of massive frontal damage or specific penetrating frontal damage, most persons perform within the pre-injury range on standard tests of intelligence following prefrontal cortex injury. A patient with a prefrontal cortex lesion following TBI can be a significant enigma for the uninitiated examiner. The standard mental status examination performed by psychiatrists or neurologists is insufficient to assess this area of cortical functioning (see Chapter 6). With regard to learning and short-term representational knowledge, the prefrontal cortex influences learning through its role in attention, analytical processing, and working memory (the attentional component of memory). These processes are necessary for the acquisition of new information, and they separate active from passive learning. The prefrontal cortex has some specific and focal areas of function. For instance, Tulving et al.[110] have demonstrated by functional imaging studies that normal individuals selectively activate the left prefrontal cortex during verbal learning (or encoding) but activate the right prefrontal cortex when engaging in verbal retrieval processes. For executive functions and self-regulation, Eslinger[111] has described executive functions as processes that

- Control the activation and inhibition of response sequences that are guided by internal neural representations (e.g., verbal rules, biologic needs, somatic states, emotions, goals, and mental models)
- Act for the purpose of meeting a balance of immediate situational, short-term, and long-term goals and demands
- Span physical–environmental, cognitive, behavioral, emotional, and social domains of functioning

The clinical presentations are varied following frontal lobe injury. For instance, damage to the primary motor and premotor areas of the frontal lobes causes contralateral limb and facial weakness. This varies from a mild hemiparesis to complete hemiplegia. The loss of motor function is expressed according to the homuncular representation of the body. Dysarthria may occur due to lesions in this area, and limb and buccofacial forms of apraxia may be evident (see Chapter 4). Damage to the left anterior inferior premotor region causes Broca's aphasia in the left hemisphere and expressive dysprosody in the right hemisphere. Superior medial lesions are located in the interhemispheric fissure of the frontal lobes. This area contains a supplementary motor area (SMA) but also has some of the anterior cingulate gyrus within it. Patients can exhibit behaviors noted in the apathetic or mediofrontal syndrome described previously (Table 2.10). Loss of behavior initiation and spontaneity affecting speech and goal-directed behaviors may occur. The most dramatic presentation occurs from a bilateral lesion in this anatomical area, which produces akinesia and mutism, in which patients fail to respond to their environment, including other persons they know, despite being fully awake, alert, and capable of movement and speech (Table 2.10).

If the inferior medial frontal lobes are affected (Brodmann's areas 10, 12; parts of areas 14, 24, 25, and 32), significant impairments in emotional processing may occur. These can affect motivation, memory, and emotional self-regulation, including displays of depression and bipolar-like disorders.[112] (See Chapter 6 for Brodmann's cortical localizations.) The basal forebrain encompasses a small anatomical area clustered along the inferior medial aspects of the posterior frontal lobe. It includes the septum, nucleus basalis of Meynert, the precommissural fornix, nucleus accumbens, and nucleus of the diagonal band of Broca.[109] This area is rarely injured in brain trauma except by missile penetration. It is usually damaged by an anterior communicating artery aneurysm rupture rather than by TBI. Injuries in this particular area produce clinical amnesia with prominent confabulations. Basal forebrain amnesia is characterized by temporal and spatial context confusion that not only limits the accuracy of memories but also may cause the person to utter spontaneous confabulations.[113] When damage is to the orbitofrontal region, prominent personality changes usually occur. The individual is often disinhibited, impaired in social judgment and emotion-based learning, and lacking in self-awareness[114] (Table 2.10). Alterations in the orbitofrontal regions have been linked to increased risk-taking behavior and reduction in judgment that depends upon learning from contingency-based outcomes. Damasio and colleagues have proposed that this defect includes loss of somatic markers of experience that impairs a person's anticipation of future consequences.[115] Patients with orbitofrontal damage are impaired in emotion-based learning, and they cannot guide their responses based on these social contingencies. Medial orbitofrontal damage can cause impulsive actions and poor social judgment despite evidence of any significant change in intellect, memory, attention, perception, or language. Strikingly, some persons after orbitofrontal damage have reduced or absent empathy. The acquired sociopathy syndrome is discussed later in this chapter in "Personality Changes following Traumatic Brain Injury."

There are large areas of deep white matter within the frontal lobes. These pathways link frontal regions with other regions of the cortex, the basal ganglia and thalamus, and limbic and brainstem structures. These frontal–cortical and frontal–subcortical circuits are critical for behavioral adaptation across motor, cognitive, and emotional domains.[116] Traumatic brain injury may disconnect these important pathways producing changes in emotions, personality, cognition, and interpersonal processes. Prominent irritability with reduced empathy, motivation, and self-awareness may be present. The dorsolateral aspects of the frontal lobes contain multimodal convergence areas. These important frontal brain areas integrate with higher cognitive processes of attentional control, planning, organization, working memory, and decision making. It is thought that this dorsolateral frontal area is the one most likely to be affected and produce alterations on the Wisconsin Card Sorting Test. Functional brain imaging studies (see Chapter 6) note that the dorsolateral prefrontal cortex is activated during paradigms that require making a decision, analyzing the interrelationship of task elements, and keeping information temporarily in mind (working memory) until used in a response pattern. Lastly, the frontal poles remain poorly understood. Hebb[117] first called our attention to these anatomical areas. More recently, Moll et al. reported that the frontal poles are activated in healthy persons during a cognitive task of social–moral judgment.[118]

Moving from specific anatomical areas to the frontal lobes in general, a recent study in Italy investigated whether cognitive impairment after TBI is a consequence of a speed processing defect or an impairment of the central executive system of working memory.[119] This study determined, by multiple regression analyses of neuropsychological test data on 37 TBI patients, that cognitive impairment following TBI is primarily caused by an impairment of the central executive system rather than a defect of mental speed processing. Robinson's group at the University of Iowa has further delineated differences in patients with lateral or medial frontal brain damage. Lateral prefrontal damage disrupts mood regulation and drives while leaving intact the ability to experience negative emotions. Medial frontal injury inhibits the experience of mood changes, anxiety, or apathy.[120] A recent CT scan study revealed that impaired self-awareness after TBI is significantly associated with the number of lesions, but not with the location and volume of focal lesions, early after TBI.[121] The Stuss group in Boston determined a differential response for impaired concentration following frontal lobe damage from two distinct lesion sites. Left lateral lesions caused defective setting of specific stimulus–response contingencies. On the other hand, right superomedial lesions caused an insufficient energizing of attention to respond.[122]

Owing to the delayed maturation of the frontal lobes in human beings, which often does not occur until approximately age 25, children with prefrontal executive function syndromes differ substantially in clinical presentation to those of adults. However, children will show impaired regulation of cognition, attention, behavior, arousal, and emotion. These have serious and pervasive consequences for later child development.[123] Personality change from frontal lobe TBI is common in children. Max et al.[124] have looked at the phenomenology and predictive factors of personality change due to TBI 6–24 months after injury in children ages 5–14 years. These findings were interesting in that 13% of children showed personality changes between 6 and 12 months after injury, whereas another 12% did not demonstrate these changes until the second year after injury. The severity of the injury covaried in a linear fashion with personality change. The pre-injury adaptive function of the child predicted personality change only in the second year after injury. In the first year after injury, lesions of the superofrontal gyrus were associated with personality change, whereas in the second year, only lesions in the frontal lobe white matter were significantly related to personality change. This probably explained the differences between the early personality changes and the late personality changes.

POSTTRAUMATIC SEIZURE DISORDERS

Posttraumatic seizures following TBI are divided into two groups. The first group consists of early seizures generally seen in a neurointensive care unit. The second group consists of late-onset seizures that usually occur as a focal seizure with or without secondary generalization or generalized tonic–clonic seizure.[125] Many seizures occur subclinically, and recent continuous EEG monitoring in neurointensive care unit (NICU) patients with TBI reveals a higher incidence of epileptiform activity than previously considered. Seventy TBI patients requiring NICU were followed with digital EEG recordings continuously in Uppsala, Sweden.[126] The recordings were analyzed 5 min every hour off-line. Of these patients, 33% developed seizures, 74 ± 47 h after trauma. The seizures were brief and responded to phenytoin, or they were persistent and required the use of propofol or barbiturate sedation. In eight patients who had persistent seizures, six of these had intracerebral contusions. Eighteen patients displayed focal high-frequency activity that proceeded later to seizures in eight cases. Twelve patients developed recurrent paroxysmal delta activity on EEG. The patients in the seizure group were significantly older (62 years $\pm$ 12 years) versus the nonseizure group (28 years $\pm$ 17 years); they were more often exposed to low-energy trauma (87% versus 22%).

As the neuropsychiatric examiner reviews medical records following brain trauma, the NICU records may reveal that phenytoin, carbamazepine, phenobarbital, or valproate were used to control early posttraumatic seizures. On the other hand, these seizure medications are not useful to prevent late posttraumatic seizures after release from the NICU.[127] The risk factors in the NICU for development of seizures have been studied at the University of Washington in Seattle. Temkin reported 783 cases at high risk of developing seizures, who were followed for 2 years as part of a seizure prophylaxis study.[128] Subgroups of patients with significantly elevated risk for seizures included those with the following: evacuation of a subdural hematoma, surgery for an intracerebral hematoma, Glasgow Coma Scale score in the range of 3–8 at admission, delayed early seizures, skull fracture that was not surgically elevated, penetration of the dura by injury, at least one nonreactive pupil, a parietal lesion on CT scan, and a delay to following commands of a week or more. After the patient leaves the NICU, the ability to control seizures thereafter is poor. The neuropsychiatric examiner may see an individual 1 or 2 years after injury who is sustaining posttraumatic seizures refractory to complete control. This may worsen neurocognitive function as time progresses. Antiepileptic drug prophylaxis is effective in protecting against acute seizures occurring within seven days after injury. However, no antiepileptic drug treatment has been found to protect against the development of posttraumatic epilepsy. Therefore, long-term anticonvulsant prophylaxis is presently not recommended by neurologists.[129] Table 2.11 describes the common qualities of posttraumatic seizure disorders following TBI. With regard to children, those with a normal neurological examination and normal cranial CT scan seen in the emergency department or hospital after immediate posttraumatic seizures are at low risk for further short-term complications that require immediate hospitalization. These children may be considered for discharge to home from the emergency department. Children with blunt head trauma and a positive finding on CT scan, who then develop a seizure, will usually require hospitalization and further evaluation.[130] Children often have untoward reactions to posttraumatic seizures that differ considerably from those of adults. Seizures can be a serious

---

TABLE 2.11

Posttraumatic Seizure Disorders following Traumatic Brain Injury

- Seizure incidence is higher in children than adults.
- Depressed skull fracture or hemorrhagic contusions predispose to seizures.
- Early seizures (first seven days post-injury) tend to be focal with or without secondary generalization.
- Late seizures are more likely to occur in adults or following penetrating missile injury.
- Many early seizures are nonconvulsive and thus not detected.
- No antiepilepsy drugs protect against posttraumatic epilepsy.

complication to head injury in children, because their incidence is higher than adults, and they can worsen secondary brain damage.[131]

Early seizures are more likely to be focal with or without secondary generalization and are seen in about 75% of people with early posttraumatic seizures. The remaining seizures consist of generalized tonic–clonic seizures. Focal seizures are more likely to be seen in children or adults who have missile wounds to the head. Late closed-head injury seizures (more than seven days post-injury) decrease in frequency as time increases following the injury. A Vietnam Head Injury Study revealed that 18% of late-onset penetrating injury seizures develop within the first month, and 57% began within the first year. Brain volume loss positively correlates with increasing risk of late seizures. The main risk factors for seizures in a civilian population are intracranial hematomas, depressed skull fractures, early seizures, and focal neurological signs.[125,132,133]

POSTTRAUMATIC HEADACHES

Headache is the most common neurologic symptom following minor closed-head injury. The onset of head pain often leads to other psychiatric disorders such as depression or anxiety. Moreover, chronic head pain can induce minor neuropsychological abnormalities such as impaired attention and vigilance. Just as the exact pathophysiology is unknown for migraine headaches, the exact pathophysiology of posttraumatic headache is still unknown in many cases.[134] The term posttraumatic headache is often used as a term of art rather than a specific diagnosis. Differentiation of trauma as a cause from other myriad etiologies for headache is difficult.[135]

Chronic posttraumatic headache is often part of the so-called postconcussion or posttraumatic syndrome (see above). The pathophysiology of posttraumatic headaches includes biological, psychological, and social factors. The most common manifestation is the tension-type headache, but exacerbations of classic migraine-like headaches often occur following TBI as well. After the physician has ruled out a structural lesion as cause for the headache, the treatment of posttraumatic headache syndrome is similar to that of other primary headaches.[136] By definition, headache that develops within one week after head trauma (or within one week after regaining consciousness) is referred to as posttraumatic headache. These usually resolve within 6–12 months after injury, but 18%–33% of posttraumatic headaches persist beyond 1 year. A recent systematic literature review[137] found that 37% of all posttraumatic headaches were tension type and 29% were migraine type. The authors noted that well-controlled studies in this field are a paucity, and double-blind, placebo-controlled treatment trials and other evidence-based studies are lacking.

Whereas headache is the most common symptom following concussion and other minor closed-head injuries, headache syndromes following TBI do not correlate with injury severity. The Veterans Affairs Medical Center in Richmond, Virginia[138] conducted a recent study of 109 military or veteran beneficiaries with moderate or severe brain injury. While in acute rehabilitation, these veterans consented to data collection, and they completed 6- and 12-month follow-up evaluations. Approximately 38% of the patients had acute posttraumatic headache symptoms, most often in a frontal location, and most often of daily frequency. These headache syndromes showed no relation to injury severity, emotional variables, or demographic variables. When subjects complained of posttraumatic headache symptoms at the 6-month follow-up, more than 90% reported symptoms again at the 12-month follow-up period.

A recent study of high school athletes demonstrated that persistence of headache seven days after injury correlated with significantly worse performance on reaction time and memory neurocognitive scores than those athletes not reporting headaches seven days after a sports-related concussion.[139] The authors suggested that any degree of postconcussion headache in high school athletes seven days after injury is likely associated with an incomplete recovery after concussion. Overall, the data from multiple TBI headache studies suggest that the risk of developing posttraumatic chronic daily headache is greater for the less severe head-injured person than for those who sustain a moderate to severe TBI. The possible reasons for this relationship are unclear.[140]

Normal-Pressure Hydrocephalus

In the neurological and neurosurgical literature, normal-pressure hydrocephalus (NPH) is a term commonly used for a syndrome seen mostly in elderly individuals. It is classically characterized by disturbance of gait with a widening of the stride, progressive dementia associated with slowing of cognitive processes, and urinary incontinence.[141] Although the lateral ventricles are widely enlarged on neuroimaging, the mean cerebrospinal fluid pressure at lumbar puncture is not elevated. With regard to TBI, in some patients there is a known antecedent cause such as head injury associated with subarachnoid hemorrhage or brain infection following a penetrating head injury. Posttraumatic ventriculomegaly determined by CT or MRI may be misleading to the clinician, and particularly misleading to the neuropsychiatric examiner. When the patient is examined well after the time of the TBI, it is difficult for the clinician to know whether he or she is dealing with increased ventricular pressure or *ex vacuo* changes. *Ex vacuo* changes in the ventricular size are due to brain atrophy following trauma. Since the neuropsychiatric examination usually takes place well after the TBI, normal-pressure hydrocephalus (NPH) could present to the neuropsychiatric examiner as a new disorder, which may not have been present weeks or months following the original injury. Cerebrospinal fluid dynamic testing may be useful to distinguish between atrophy and hydrocephalus as two possible causes for the ventriculomegaly.[142] If this disorder is detected before the neuropsychiatric examination, a ventriculoperitoneal shunt may be in place. Currently, most shunts are programmable. Therefore, if the neuropsychiatric examiner intends to perform an MRI, it must be remembered that the shunt will have to be reprogrammed, and the person will need to be sent straight away to the neurosurgeon after the MRI for reprogramming of the shunt electronics.[143] The absence of deep white matter lesions on MRI is a good prognostic sign. If NPH is first detected at the neuropsychiatric examination, the examiner will have to reschedule a second examination after a shunt is placed in order to determine the adverse contribution to cognition from direct tissue injury during trauma versus that caused by temporarily increased cerebrospinal fluid pressure.

Posttraumatic Fatigue and Excessive Daytime Somnolence

Fatigue is a frequent and disabling symptom in patients with TBI. Its exact incidence and prevalence are unknown. It is one of the commonest symptoms included in the postconcussion syndrome. A recent review of fatigue and TBI indicated that this symptom is present in 43%–73% of patients with TBI. It does not seem to be significantly related to injury severity or time since injury.[144] A recent Dutch study looked at fatigue and MTBI versus a control group. The base rate for severe fatigue in the control group was 12%, while report of severe fatigue in the MTBI group was 32%.[145] These authors concluded that one-third of a large sample of MTBI patients experienced severe fatigue six months after injury, and their experience is associated with limitations in daily functioning. This study further concludes that the mechanism of injury is more important than injury severity to causation of fatigue. Those injuries that produced nausea and headache at the time of presentation to the emergency department were significantly related to higher levels of fatigue at six months.

There is an association between fatigue and reduced vigilance, and also between fatigue and selective attention deficits. An Australian study[146] found that TBI patients performed at a lower level on vigilance tasks compared to controls. The same Australian group noted that the subjective complaint of fatigue correlated positively with impairment on tasks requiring higher order attentional processes.[147] Interestingly, this Australian group found evidence on an earlier study that fatigue was positively correlated with TBI in those patients with higher educational levels and a greater elapsed time since injury. Administration of the Visual Analogue Scale-Fatigue (VAS-F) found fatigue to vary independent of the effects of mood. Moreover, injury severity and age were not found to be significant predictors of subjective fatigue severity in TBI participants.[148]

While fatigue is related in many instances to excessive daytime somnolence and insomnia, in other cases it is not. In fact, idiopathic hypersomnia is a disorder independent of both fatigue and insomnia and must be differentiated from several disorders of excessive daytime sleepiness such as narcolepsy, obstructive sleep apnea syndromes, periodic limb movement disorders, depression, and posttraumatic hypersomnia.[149] Some patients with posttraumatic hypersomnolence may develop progressive increasing hypersomnia in the months after injury. This is in contrast to the usual frequent complaint of excessive daytime somnolence and hypersomnia immediately after head injury, which progressively declines post-injury.[150] Multiple sleep latency testing in an accredited sleep laboratory may produce positive findings of excessive daytime somnolence as a sequela of severe head trauma.[151] A University of Texas at Houston study using nocturnal polysomnography followed by a multiple sleep latency test found evidence of sleep disordered breathing, narcolepsy, and posttraumatic hypersomnia in patients following TBI. The authors concluded that treatable sleep disorders are common in the sleepy TBI population but are largely undiagnosed and untreated.[152] There is recent evidence from Australia that TBI affects the chronobiology of sleep and produces a circadian rhythm disorder, most commonly delayed sleep phase syndrome.[153] This study revealed that the TBI and control groups reported similar habitual sleep times as reflected on the Morning-Eveningness Questionnaire. However, there was significant variability in the TBI groups' change from the pre-injury score to the post-injury score. Saliva melatonin samples were collected half hourly according to a standard protocol. There was no statistical difference between the timing of melatonin onset between the two groups. This study suggests evidence of a shift in circadian timing of sleep following TBI, but further studies are required to confirm this claim. Overall, a recent Canadian review of TBI sleep studies indicates the prevalence to be about 30%–70% of patients.[154] These authors point out that very little scientific attention has been given to sleep disorders following TBI.

BALANCE DISORDERS

The pathophysiology of TBI suggests that balance disorders in TBI populations may be associated with multisystem dysfunction.[155] Twenty-seven patients were recruited who had a mean GCS score of 9.6 after injury. Deficits were observed across a wide range of domains at both individual and group levels. The overall level of balance dysfunction was high. A Finnish study examined motor performance in physically well-recovered men over time. In this study, 34 TBI patients were compared against 36 healthy controls.[156] Men with TBI had impaired balance and agility compared with healthy men. In a rhythm coordination test, they had difficulties in starting and sustaining simultaneous rhythmical movements of hands and feet. The most sensitive clinical test for detecting these disorders in TBI patients included asking them to run a figure of 8 test of agility, tandem walk forward, and complete a rhythm coordination test with fast tempo. All three of these tests were highly sensitive and specific for distinguishing between men with TBI and a healthy population. A recent Pennsylvania State University study found physiological correlates for alterations of posture. Athletes were studied at 3, 10, and 30 days after MTBI. Movement-related cortical potentials were evaluated (MRCP). The frontal lobe MRCP effects were larger than that of posterior areas. There was a persistent reduction of MRCP amplitude before initiation of postural movement up to 30 days after injury, although abnormal postural responses clinically recovered within 10 days post-injury. The authors suggested that these findings may indicate residual disturbance of neuronal networks involved in execution preparation of postural movements following TBI.[157]

SEXUAL DISORDERS

In general, sexual disorders following TBI present in two broad categories: behavioral and physical/physiological. Patients with frontal lobe pathology, both men and women, may demonstrate sexual impulsiveness and inappropriateness. Since attentional systems are required to produce an orgasm, alteration of frontal attentional pathways may impair or impede sexual orgasm, whereas other frontal lobe pathology may produce sexual disinhibition. The Department of Rehabilitation Medicine at Mount Sinai School of Medicine in New York City examined 322 individuals with TBI (193 men and 129 women), and contrasted their reports of sexual dysfunction to 264 persons without disability (152 men and 112 women). After extensive statistical analysis, individuals with TBI reported higher rates of (1) physiological difficulties influencing their energy for sex, sex drive, ability to initiate sexual activities, and achieve orgasm; (2) physical difficulties influencing body positioning, body movement, and sensation; and (3) body image difficulties influencing feelings of attractiveness and with comfort of having a partner view one's body during sexual activity.[158] In comparison to gender-matched groups without disability, males with TBI reported less frequent involvement in sexual activity in relationships and more frequent difficulties sustaining an erection; women with TBI reported more frequent difficulties in sexual arousal, pain with sex, difficulties with masturbation, and vaginal lubrication. Age was the only demographic variable that was related to reports of sexual difficulties in individuals with TBI when compared to men without disability. In males, the most sensitive predictor of sexual dysfunction was the level of depression. For women without disability, an endocrine disorder was the most sensitive predictor of sexual dysfunction. For women with TBI, an endocrine disorder and the level of depression combined were the most sensitive predictors of sexual difficulties. In general, the number of research articles regarding human sexuality following TBI is extremely sparse. This area of medicine has received scant attention until the last 10 years, and few large, controlled, systematic studies exist.

PSYCHIATRIC SYNDROMES

As noted in Chapter 1, the primary anatomical areas affected by TBI are frontal brain systems including the prefrontal cortex, the frontal lobes, anterior lobe structures, anterior temporal lobes, and the anterior cingulate. These areas contain numerous mood-regulating systems. Thus, the regulation of affect and mood can be adversely affected by TBI. Many of the classic psychiatric syndromes are seen following brain injury.[159] Mood disorders, psychotic disorders, and anxiety disorders occur with significantly increased frequency in those who sustain TBI.[160] O'Donnell et al. in Australia recently concluded that even with conservative methodology, about one-fifth of persons with TBI meet criteria for one or more psychiatric diagnoses 1 year after injury.[161] Another Australian study evaluated 7485 participants. This was a community-based sample that determined whether self-purported TBI, occurring up to 60 years previously, is associated with current psychiatric symptoms, suicidality, or psychologic morbidity. The participants were administered scales measuring anxiety, depression, suicidality, positive and negative affect, personality traits, and physical health status. Of this sample, 5.7% reported a prior history of TBI involving loss of consciousness for at least 15 min. The brain injury occurred on average 22 years previous to the time of the study. A history of TBI was statistically associated with increased symptoms of depression, anxiety, negative affect, and suicidal ideation. The effect was greatest for those persons injured as young adults.[162] The Mount Sinai School of Medicine conducted a study of 188 persons who had sustained TBI within 4 years of enrollment into the research.[163] The study occupied 6 years, and each assessment was approximately 1 year apart. Several Axis I psychiatric diagnoses were analyzed to detect cross-sectional differences and average individual changes over the multiple assessment time points. The odds ratios changed longitudinally within each subject, indicating a decreased probability of having an Axis I diagnosis over time. Age at the time of injury in this study had little impact on resulting Axis I diagnoses. After controlling for cross-sectional effects, the frequencies of Axis I disorders increased in depression, anxiety, and posttraumatic stress disorders (PTSD) in the first assessment post-injury and declined in all subsequent assessments.

DEPRESSION

In the early 1990s, Federoff et al. and Jorge et al. reported a rate of depression of approximately 25% in patients following TBI.[164,165]

A recent study in the geriatric population noted that major depression in the first few months after a TBI had persisting adverse effects on outcome. In this study, the rate of major depression was about 16%, which is lower than that of most studies.[166] Another segment of this study noted that depressed persons performed significantly more poorly on various measures of memory, attention, and executive functioning. In mild to moderate TBI, these study subjects demonstrated deficits that were linked in large measure to comorbid major depression.[167] Psychosocial disabilities are more strongly associated with development of a mood disorder than to the presence of physical disabilities.[168] Comorbidity is high, and in one study, 44% of individuals presented with two or more Axis I diagnoses following TBI.[169] Most studies show little relationship between the level of severity of brain injury and the development of depression. Holsinger et al. stand out in this regard. Their long-term findings indicate a correlation between severity and onset of depression.[170]

Jorge and Robinson's group recently followed 91 patients with TBI. They evaluated these individuals at 3, 6, and 12 months following the traumatic episode. Psychiatric diagnosis was made utilizing the Structured Clinical Interview using *DSM-IV* criteria. Neuropsychological testing and quantitative magnetic resonance imaging were performed at the 3-month follow-up visit. Major depressive disorder was observed in one-third of the 91 patients during the first year after sustaining a TBI. This diagnosis was significantly more frequent among patients with TBI than among the study controls. However, patients who developed depression were more likely to have a pre-injury history of mood and anxiety disorders than patients who did not exhibit major depression. The level of comorbid anxiety was 77% in those with major depression, and aggressive behavior was comorbid in 57%. Those patients displaying major depression had significantly greater impairment in executive functions than their nondepressed counterparts. At the 6- and 12-month follow-up examinations, those with major depression demonstrated poorer social functioning than controls as well as significantly reduced left prefrontal gray matter volumes, particularly in the ventrolateral and dorsolateral regions, as detected by MRI.[171]

Prediction of those who might develop depression following TBI has proved elusive. Levin's group at the Baylor College of Medicine recently produced a study after following prospectively a cohort of 129 adults with MTBI. The Structured Clinical Interview for the *DSM-IV* and CT scans of intracranial lesions yielded 93% sensitivity and 62% specificity for identifying patients at high risk for depression. The predictors for depression at three months after TBI included elevated depression scores, older age, and positive CT scan lesion.[172] A second study attempting to predict behavior following TBI originated from the New York State Psychiatric Institute. The study hypothesis was that MTBI would be associated with suicidal behavior at least partly because of shared risk factors contributing to the diathesis for suicidal acts. A backward stepwise logistic regression model on 255 patients examined the relationship between suicide attempter status and variables that differed in the TBI and non-TBI patients. Of these subjects 44% reported MTBI. Subjects with TBI were more likely to be male, have a history of substance abuse, have Cluster B personality disorder as noted in the *DSM-IV*, and be more aggressive and hostile compared with subjects without TBI. They were also more likely to have made a suicide attempt. Interestingly, the prediction of whether one will attempt suicide, within this study model, is predicted mostly by the presence of aggressive and hostile features before TBI, and not merely the presence of TBI.[173] Table 2.12 describes common features of depression following TBI.

Recent studies have assisted in the delineation of the pathophysiologic aspects of major depression following TBI and relationships to MRI findings. In Finland 58 patients were studied at Tirku University Hospital recently. The association between psychiatric disorder and the presence

TABLE 2.12

Depression following Brain Injury

- Level of severity poorly predicts depression; pre-injury depression common.
- Anxiety highly comorbid with depression.
- Reduced left prefrontal gray matter volume correlates with depression.
- Pre-injury aggressive and hostile features may predict suicidal behavior.

and location of traumatic lesions on MRI was assessed on all 58 patients, on average 30 years after a TBI. A 1.5 Tesla MRI scanner was used. One-third of the subjects had traumatic lesions visible on MRI. In subjects with evidence of contusion, three psychiatric disorders were significantly more common: delusional disorder, dementia, and disinhibited organic personality syndrome. The personality syndrome with its disinhibited subtype was associated with frontal lesions; major depression was inversely associated with temporal lesions. This particular study did not find a convincing correlation between location or presence of contusion and type of psychiatric disorder.[174]

Hippocampal volume has been reported in association with major depression, as well as other cognitive and memory disorders, following TBI. In all, 423 studies were reviewed by Dutch authors recently.[175] A strong relationship was seen between loss of hippocampal volume in major depression, PTSD, and many other neuropsychiatric conditions. While this study does show a relationship, the number of studies included was so large that there is no specificity to the findings with regard to major depression. Much remains to be done to delineate more fully the relationship of major depression to TBI. Suffice it to say that there is a strong relationship, but Jorge and Starkstein have called for an integration of major depression following TBI into a comprehensive pathophysiologic model.[176]

MANIA

Mania is not common following TBI. The earliest classic article on this subject was by Krauthammer and Klerman.[177] They defined secondary mania as a psychotic disorder because of a medical, pharmacologic, or other organic dysfunction. Their classic article did not mention head injury or TBI as one of the potential causes. However, the term "secondary mania" has crept into the literature since that time. Klerman et al. redefined the manic syndrome following head injury as secondary mania in 1987.[178] Jorge was the first to publish incidence figures for mania following TBI. He and Robinson found a rate of about 9% for secondary mania following TBI.[179] Since the lifetime prevalence of bipolar I disorder in the general population is roughly 0.4%–1.6%,[180] the incidence of secondary mania following TBI seems to be raised above the baseline. Since these earlier studies, rapid-cycling bipolar disorder has been described following TBI,[181] and recurrent mania has also been described following repeated TBI.[182]

When Jorge et al.[179] first described clinical aspects of secondary mania following TBI, they noted an association with the presence of basopolar temporal lesions. The manic episodes lasted approximately 2 months, and the elevated or expansive mood had a mean duration of 5.7 months. Poor cognition was associated with the presence of those individuals developing mania. However, there is insufficient specificity to predict mania based on the site of a focal lesion on neuroimaging. The general features of mania following TBI resemble those of classic mania. Table 2.13 summarizes the general aspects of secondary mania following TBI.

TABLE 2.13
Mania following Brain Injury

- Mania not as common as depression.
- Mania of brain injury termed secondary mania.
- Mania usually associated with poor cognition.
- Lesion location not predictive of developing mania.
- Manic features resemble those of classical mania.
- Rapid-cycling disorder may occur after repeated TBI.

ANXIETY DISORDERS

Anxiety disorders other than posttraumatic stress disorders are discussed in this section. Posttraumatic stress disorder is uniquely connected in some respects to TBI and is discussed separately below. Anxiety disorders have been described following TBI with a range and frequency from 11% to 70% in older studies of adults and children.[183,184] Acute stress disorder has been described in 14% of patients following TBI.[185] Eighty percent of persons who met the criteria for acute stress disorder following TBI were diagnosed with posttraumatic stress disorder (PTSD) 2 years later.[186]

The non-PTSD anxiety syndromes have been studied and reported less frequently in the literature. Fann et al. studied 50 consecutive patients referred to a university brain rehabilitation clinic.[187] They found evidence of generalized anxiety disorder in 24% of the patients. However, the study is somewhat contaminated, as some of these patients also had concurrent major depression. Moreover, the authors noted a pre-injury history of generalized anxiety disorder in 34% of the patients. A very recent review of the psychiatric literature underscores the difficulties in making an association between discrete anxiety disorders and TBI.[188] The research data of mild TBI is rife with inconsistencies concerning prevalence rates, the magnitude and implications of anxiety, and whether anxiety disorders can exist at all in the face of TBI. Panic disorder and obsessive-compulsive disorder have been reported following TBI. Again, though, the exact relationship of these disorders to TBI is poorly detailed.[189,190] Particularly with anxiety disorders, and their relationship to TBI, the current literature calls loudly for randomized, double-blind, placebo-controlled trials to establish the most effective treatments for psychiatric conditions related to TBI.[191]

POSTTRAUMATIC STRESS DISORDER

Unlike the non-PTSD anxiety disorders, PTSD has been better studied and is better delineated in terms of its relationship to TBI. However, it is also probably the most controversial psychiatric disorder that can be diagnosed following TBI. In particular, it begs the question, How does a person with amnesia for the events following TBI develop PTSD? The famous Coconut Grove disaster in a Boston nightclub was the first major study of memory and trauma. Adler presented his findings in 1943 in the *Journal of the American Medical Association*[192] and noted that survivors who sustained a loss of consciousness longer than 1 h were less likely to develop psychiatric complications following their injuries. Moreover, there is evidence that psychiatrists frequently misdiagnose PTSD after brain trauma.[193] Sumpter and McMillan reported 34 persons in a community treatment center for acquired brain injury in Glasgow, Scotland. Screening measures and self-report questionnaires were administered followed by a structured interview. Of these persons 59% fulfilled criteria for PTSD on the Posttraumatic Diagnostic Scale, and 44% met criteria on the Impact of Events Scale. The structured interview (Clinician-Administered PTSD Scale) revealed that only 3% met criteria. These authors recommend that after TBI, PTSD diagnosis by self-report might be used as a screening tool, but not for diagnostic purposes. In a further review of data, Sumpter and McMillan reported a second study[194] pointing out that the diagnosis of PTSD by questionnaire can lead to erroneous conclusions, and other factors related to brain injury must be carefully considered when investigating PTSD. These factors will have considerable importance when the forensic aspects of TBI assessment are discussed later in the book. Further criticism of the diagnosis of PTSD in persons who sustain memory impairment and loss of consciousness following TBI has been raised from Israel.[195]

On the other hand, there is a substantial body of literature suggesting that persons with amnesia following TBI can sustain PTSD. McMillan reported 10 persons out of 312 evaluated who met criteria for PTSD. However, they had no vivid reexperiencing.[196] Most of the studies reporting PTSD in patients who experience amnesia following TBI, are short case studies, presented with limited data, and are based upon self-report questionnaires administered well after the event.[197] Finally, another more recent study by Glaesser et al.[198] reports a prospective study of admissions to a rehabilitation unit and notes that PTSD is much less likely to develop in TBI patients with more prolonged loss of consciousness. Thus, within the last decade, the wealth of studies suggests that the longer the loss of consciousness or posttraumatic amnesia is present, the less likely one is to develop PTSD as a consequence of TBI. This is consistent with the Coconut Grove report in 1943.

There is evidence that trauma modulates the amygdala and medial prefrontal areas as a response to consciously attended fear. A study from New South Wales, Australia, used functional MRI to elucidate the effect of trauma reactions on amygdala function during an overt fear of perception task. However, this form of study has not been replicated in TBI patients.[199] In line with the controversial discussion noted above, Gil et al.[200] recently reported further on their experience with PTSD in TBI patients. They studied 120 subjects with MTBI who were hospitalized for observation. They were followed by investigation at one week, three months, and six months later. All participants underwent psychiatric evaluation and self-assessment of their memory regarding the traumatic events. This study indicated that memory of a traumatic event is a strong predictor and a potential risk factor for subsequent development of PTSD. This adds further credence to the argument that amnesia for the event lessens or obviates the risk of PTSD following traumatic brain injury. On the other hand, Creamer et al.[201] evaluated 307 consecutive admissions to a level 1 trauma center. Amnesia did not always occur concurrently with MTBI, and 18% of those with mild injury had full recall; over half had partial recall of the event. Just over 10% of these participants developed PTSD by 12 months post-injury. The authors concluded that PTSD may develop following head trauma despite amnesia for the event. It is noteworthy that none of these patients had moderate or severe brain trauma. Table 2.14 summarizes the relationship of PTSD to brain trauma based on current medical literature.

TABLE 2.14
Anxiety and Posttraumatic Stress Disorder (PTSD)

- Non-PTSD anxiety is poorly studied following TBI.
- Inability to remember the trauma may ameliorate PTSD.
- Diagnosis of PTSD by self-report is criticized.
- Diagnosis of PTSD by questionnaire is criticized.
- Some persons with amnesia may also experience PTSD symptoms.
- The greater the LOC, the less the risk of PTSD.

PSYCHOSIS

As with most traumatic brain injury disorders, there is no *DSM-IV-TR* diagnostic rubric for TBI-induced psychosis. The closest one can come to a diagnosis to fit psychosis in TBI is psychotic disorder due to a general medical condition.[1] Davison and Bagley reported a series of psychotic patients following traumatic brain injury from eight long-term follow-up studies published between 1917 and 1964. They described the psychosis as a schizophrenia-like disorder, and most of these patients did not have a family history of schizophrenia. They reported an incidence of 0.7%–9.8% of psychosis following brain injury.[202] Lishman gave an early account of 670 soldiers with penetrating head injuries and followed them for 4 years subsequent to their trauma. He found the incidence of psychotic syndromes to be about 0.7%.[203] Hillbom studied 415 Finnish war veterans with head injuries. He found an 8% incidence of psychosis in these men. Only one of the veterans had a psychosis similar to that seen in schizophrenia. Temporal lobe lesions occurred in 40% of this veteran group.[204] In the more modern era, the rate of psychosis following TBI is similar to that reported earlier. Achte et al.[205] found posttraumatic delusional states in 3.4% of 530 patients reviewed within a neurosurgical unit at a Belgian hospital. One-third of these patients had a chronic course similar to schizophrenia. However, the data appear not to follow traditional *DSM-IV-TR* criteria. Some studies have been published utilizing the Minnesota Multiphasic Personality Inventory (MMPI) to determine evidence of psychosis. These studies demonstrate elevations on Scale 8, which can elevate with psychosis.[206–208]

There is no classic form of psychosis seen following traumatic brain injury. Psychosis is generally defined as a mental disorder presenting with delusions or hallucinations in which the patient has no insight that either the delusions or the hallucinations are abnormal. The general aspects of positive and negative affect associated with schizophrenia are usually not found within most descriptions of psychosis following traumatic brain injury. McAllister's group at Dartmouth notes that the onset of symptoms can be early or late, and psychosis can occur during the period of posttraumatic amnesia and in association with posttraumatic epilepsy. It is also seen in TBI-related mood disorders. It is thought that TBI can interact with genetic vulnerability to increase the risk of developing illnesses such as schizophrenia at a later time. Atypical antipsychotic drugs have recently become first-line treatment for psychotic disorders associated with traumatic brain injury. The addition of anticonvulsants or antidepressants may also be needed.[209] Other recent reviews of the topic of psychosis following TBI come from Australia and the United States.[210–212] The clinical presentation has considerable overlap with primary schizophrenic disorder, and it generally displays a prominence of persecutory and other delusions, auditory hallucinations, and a lack of negative symptoms. The mean onset is described as 4–5 years after TBI with the majority of cases occurring within 2 years. Most reviews suggest that psychosis is linked with damage to frontal and temporal lobe systems with probable alteration of dopaminergic pathways. Table 2.15 summarizes elements of psychosis following brain injury.

TABLE 2.15
Psychosis following Brain Injury

- Psychosis is usually persecutory with delusions and auditory hallucinations.
- There is no pathognomonic form of psychosis after TBI.
- Psychotic syndromes can appear early or late.
- MMPI profiles often show elevations on Scale 8.
- Negative symptoms are not seen.

Personality Changes

Personality change is the disorder most likely to be described by family members after a loved one has sustained a traumatic brain injury. This report holds true whether they are asked at 1, 5, or 15 years post-injury.[213] Rarely is a new personality put in place as a result of traumatic brain injury, and in most instances, the injury exaggerates pre-injury personality traits. To date, attempts to measure personality change following traumatic brain injury have not been very successful. Rather than a personality change, what is often present is disinhibition of aggressive and other unpleasant personality traits that were present in the individual before the brain injury. However, the clearest historical example of personality change is that of Phineas Gage. Dr. Harlow reported on his patient in two separate publications.[108,214] Harlow described Gage as a responsible, socially well-adjusted, and popular person with coworkers and supervisors until an iron tamping rod was blown by dynamite under his left zygomatic arch, subsequently protruding through the anterior medial skull. Afterwards, Harlow described Phineas Gage as "fitful, irreverent, indulging at times in the grossest profanity (which was not previously his custom), manifesting but little deference for his fellows, impatient of restraint or advice when it conflicts with his desires, at times pertinaciously obstinate, yet capricious and vacillating, devising many plans of future operation, which are no sooner arranged than they are abandoned and turned for others appearing more feasible." Tranel's group at the University of Iowa[215] has focused upon prefrontal brain injury, particularly in the area of the ventromedial prefrontal cortex. These individuals display a number of characteristic features: inability to organize future activity and hold gainful employment, diminished capacity to respond to punishment; a tendency to present an unrealistic, favorable view of themselves; and a tendency to display inappropriate, emotional reactions. These characteristics have been called "acquired sociopathy," and the antisocial personality characteristics bear striking similarities to those described by Cleckley[216] and Hare.[217] The full features of acquired sociopathy and psychopathy following ventromedial prefrontal brain injury are described at length by Granacher and Fozdar.[218] Hannah Damascio has reconstructed virtual images of Gage's injury by the tamping rod (Figure 2.2).[242]

Children often show substantial personality change after traumatic brain injury. Max et al.[219] have studied personality changes in children extensively following traumatic brain injury. He reported a sample of 37 severe traumatically brain-injured children. The labile subtype of personality change was most common in this group, seen in almost half of the children. It was followed in frequency by an aggressive and disinhibited subtype of personality change in another 38% of the children. The remaining subjects of the study were either apathetic or paranoid at a 14% and 5% rate, respectively. Perseveration in the classic style was seen in one-third of the children. Max and his group have carried their work further. They recently reported a study of 177 children, ages 5–14 years, with traumatic brain injury.[220] These children had consecutive admissions to five trauma centers and were followed prospectively at baseline and 6 months later with semistructured psychiatric interviews. Personality change occurred in 22% of the youngsters in the first 6 months after injury. The severity of the injury predicted the personality change, whereas none of the psychosocial variables predicted a personality change. Lesions of the dorsal prefrontal cortex, specifically the superior frontal gyrus, were associated with personality changes after controlling for severity of injury or the presence of other lesions. Max et al. extended this study to 24 months post-injury. Personality change occurred in 13% of participants between 6 and 12 months after injury, and in 12% at the end of the second year after injury. Whereas the dorsal prefrontal cortex had been involved in early personality change, in those youngsters who showed personality change into the second year, only lesions in the frontal lobe white matter were significantly related to these changes.[124] Table 2.16 describes common personality changes after traumatic brain injury.

Aggression

Following traumatic brain injury, families, caregivers, and medical nursing personnel report that the major stress they experience following TBI is aggressiveness on the part of the patient.[221] Initially

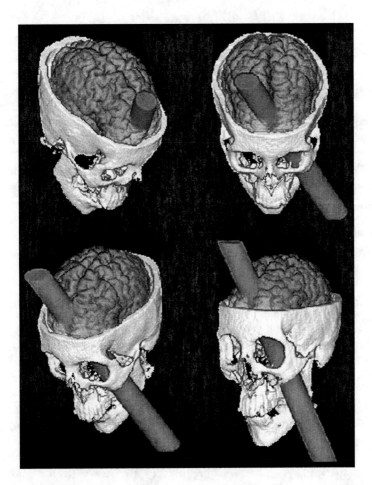

FIGURE 2.2 The ventromedial lesion of Phineas Gage. (From Damasio, H., Gravowski, T., Frank, R., Galaburda, A.M., Damasio, A.R., *Science*, 1102, 264, 1994. With permission. Courtesy of Dr. Hanna Damasio, The Dana and David Domsife Cognitive Neuroscience Imaging Center and Brain Creativity Institute, University of Southern California.)

following brain injury in the neurosurgical intensive care unit or rehabilitation facility, agitation is the most frequent accelerated behavior following TBI. Agitation is most frequent in the first two weeks of hospitalization following brain injury and generally resolves slowly over time. In the subacute phase of recovery, restlessness is common, and it may appear within two months, persisting as long as 4–6 weeks. Within the acute recovery period, agitated behaviors are reported in one-third to two-thirds of patients.[222] The prevalence figures for aggression show such variance

---

TABLE 2.16
Personality Changes after Brain Injury

- Cited by families as the most significant changes.
- Measurement of personality changes difficult at best.
- Development of sociopathic or borderline traits may occur.
- Children more likely to show labile subtype of personality change.
- Persistent change in children related to frontal white matter injury.

---

that they have little use in prediction. It must be assumed that many individuals following TBI will in fact become aggressive.

Since frontal systems are frequently injured as a result of traumatic brain injury, it is not unexpected that disinhibited and aggressive syndromes will occur. As noted above, the orbitofrontal syndrome may be associated with impulsivity, disinhibition, hyperactivity, and lability of mood. Damage to the inferior orbital surfaces of the frontal lobes and the anterior temporal lobes is often associated with rage and misdirected violence. If the *DSM-IV* classification system is used, patients with aggressive behavior would be noted under the "Personality Change Due to a General Medical Condition" rubric, and they would be subtyped as "Aggressive Type." Those patients with predominance of mood lability rather than aggression would be specified under the personality change rubric as "Labile Type." Neuroanatomical substrates of aggression following TBI are thought to lie in the hypothalamus, limbic system, amygdala, temporal cortex, and frontal neocortex. The hypothalamus may be involved in sympathetic arousal and inability to monitor appropriately one's internal state. The amygdala provides activation or suppression of the hypothalamus. The temporal cortex, sometimes in a subclinical seizure manner, may be associated with aggression. The frontal neocortex provides the braking system for behavior and modulates limbic and hypothalamic activity associated with social and judgmental aspects of aggression.[221] The Vietnam Head Injury Study made a comparison between 279 veterans with penetrating brain injury and 85 age-matched control veterans who spent equivalent time in Vietnam. The controls did not sustain a head injury during combat. Those veterans with ventromedial frontal lobe injuries (e.g., Phineas Gage) had the highest ratings for violence as reported by relatives and friends. Veterans with orbitofrontal lesions, while reported to be aggressive, had the least amount of insight into their aggression. No relationship was demonstrated between the size of the brain injury lesion, the presence of seizures, and aggression.[223]

Alcohol consumption at high rates both before and after the TBI is correlated highly with aggressive behavior following the traumatic brain injury. Kreutzer et al.[224] studied 327 patients whose brain injury varied in severity. This study reviewed alcohol use patterns, arrest histories, behavioral characteristics, and psychiatric treatment histories. They were compared to an uninjured control group. The study analysis revealed a high incidence of heavy alcohol consumption both before and after injury, particularly among those patients who had a history of arrest. Those persons who had been arrested before brain injury were associated with a greater likelihood of having been psychiatrically treated before their TBI. Aggressive behaviors were very high in this group of patients. Table 2.17 summarizes aggression due to TBI.

A recent Australian study attempted again to assess the prevalence and predictors of aggressive behavior among persons with traumatic brain injury. This study followed 228 patients with moderate to severe TBI and reviewed their behavior at 6, 24, and 60 months postdischarge. The outcome measures were the Overt Aggression Scale and the Glasgow Coma and Outcome Scales. At any given follow-up period, 25% of the participants in this study were classified as aggressive. In those persons who were aggressive, they had a consistent association with complaints of depression. Most of the aggressive persons were of younger age at injury. Post-injury depression was the single

---

TABLE 2.17

Brain-Injury-Induced Aggression

- Aggression is more likely with frontal cortex injuries.
- Sexual offenders are over-represented.
- Aggressive behaviors are high in those with pre-injury alcohol abuse.
- Brain injury is a risk factor for being murdered.
- Post-injury depression and aggression covary.
- Aggression does not positively correlate with lesion size or posttraumatic seizures.

most important factor significantly associated with aggressive behavior, followed by younger age at the time of injury.[225]

Sexual offenses seem overly represented in the brain-injured population as well. Langevin[226] studied 476 male sexual offenders, seen at a university psychiatric hospital for forensic assessment. Of these men 49% had sustained head injuries that led to unconsciousness. Of those who were unconscious, 23% sustained a significant neurological insult. Motor vehicle accident was the most common cause of brain injury and was associated highly with alcohol abuse, drug abuse, and a prior history of violence. The brain-injury group had been convicted for a wide range of sexual offenses and was comparable to the non-brain-injured group in that respect. However, they tended more often to offend against adults rather than against children, and they were more exhibitionistic and polymorphous in their sexual behavior. With regard to younger patients, an Italian study recently reviewed 96 posttraumatic patients ranging from 0 to 18 years of age. They were divided into three different age groups (0–6 years; 7–13 years; and 14–18 years). The subjects received a protocol made of age-appropriate scales. Aggression was more common in the older youngsters and less common in the children. The younger children were more internalizing and withdrawn.[227]

Overall, aggressive and violent behaviors are wide ranging, and they are often the largest barrier to reintegration into the community for patients with TBI. Aggressive behaviors interfere with social integration and personal and family function. Brain-injured males are more likely to batter their partners.[228] These persons often exhibit substantial neuropsychological impairment when appropriate testing is undertaken. Lastly and remarkably, brain injury is a risk factor for being murdered. A Swedish study of 1739 homicides between 1978 and 1994 revealed that traumatic brain injury, in both men and women, increased the risk of one being murdered.[229]

REFERENCES

1. American Psychiatric Association, *Diagnostic and Statistical Manual of Mental Disorders,* 4th edition, *Text Revision*, American Psychiatric Association, Washington, D.C., 2000.
2. Levin, H.S., Sustained attention and information processing speed in chronic survivors of severe closed head injury. *Scand. J. Rehabil. Med.*, 17, 33, 1988.
3. Risser, A.H., Vigilance and distractibility on a continuous performance task by severely head-injured adults. *J. Clin. Exp. Neuropsychol.*, 12, 35, 1990.
4. Parasuraman, R. and Davies, D.R., *Varieties of Attention*, Academic Press, Orlando, FL, 1984.
5. Stuss, D.T., Stetham, L.L., Hugenholtz, H., et al., Reaction time after head injury: Fatigue, divided and focused attention, and consistency of performance. *J. Neurol. Neurosurg. Psychiatry*, 52, 742, 1989.
6. Parasuraman, R., Mutter, S.A., and Molloy, R., Sustained attention following mild closed-head injury. *J. Clin. Exp. Neuropsychol.*, 13, 789, 1991.
7. Gronwall, D., Paced auditory serial addition task: A measure of recovery from concussion. *Percept. Motor Skills*, 44, 367, 1977.
8. Ponsford, J. and Kinsella, G., Attentional deficits following closed head injury. *J. Clin. Exp. Neuropsychol.*, 14, 822, 1992.
9. Spreen, O. and Strauss, E., *A Compendium of Neuropsychological Tests: Administration, Norms, and Commentary, Ed.*, 2. Oxford University Press, New York, 1998.
10. Scheid, R., Walter, K., Guthke, T., et al., Cognitive sequelae of diffuse axonal injury. *Arch. Neurol.*, 63, 418, 2006.
11. Suh, M., Kolster, R., Sarkar, R., et al., Deficits in predictive smooth pursuit after mild traumatic brain injury. *Neurosci. Lett.*, 401(1 & 2), 108, 2006.
12. McIntire, A., Langan, J., Halterman, C., et al., The influence of mild traumatic brain injury on the temporal distribution of attention. *Exp. Brain Res.*, 174, 361, 2006.
13. Gronwall, D., Memory and information processing capacity after closed heads injury. *J. Neurol. Neurosurg. Psychiatry*, 44, 889, 1981.
14. Squire, L.R., *Memory and Brain*. Oxford University Press, New York, 1987.
15. Levine, B., Black, S.E., Cabesa, R., et al., Episodic memory and the self in a case of isolated retrograde amnesia. *Brain*, 121, 1951, 1998.

16. Deluca, J., Lengenfelder, J., and Eslinger, P.J., Memory and learning, in *Principles and Practice of Behavioral Neurology and Neuropsychology*, Rizzo, M. and Eslinger, P.J., Eds., W.B. Saunders, Philadelphia, PA, 2004, p. 247.

17. Ribot, T., *Diseases of Memory: An Essay on the Positive Psychology*, Appleton, New York, 1882.

18. Levin, H., Long-term neuropsychological outcome of closed head injury. *J. Neurosurg.*, 50, 412, 1979.

19. Capruso, D.X. and Levin, H.S., Neurobehavioral outcome of head trauma, in *Neurology and Trauma*, Evans, R.W., Ed., W.B. Saunders, Philadelphia, PA, 1996, p. 201.

20. Milner, B., Hemisphere specialization: Scope and limits, in *The Neurosciences, Third Study Program*, Schmitt, F.O. and Warden, F.G., Eds., Massachusetts Institute of Technology Press, Cambridge, MA, 1974.

21. Newcombe, F., *Missile Wounds of the Brain: A Study of Psychological Deficits*, Oxford University Press, New York, 1969.

22. Gentry, L.R., Godersky, J.C., and Thompson, B., MR imaging of head trauma, review of the distribution and radiopathologic features of traumatic lesions. *Am. J. Forentgenol.*, 150, 663, 1988.

23. Gurdjian, E.S., Cerebral contusions: Reevaluation and the mechanism of their development. *J. Trauma*, 15, 35, 1976.

24. Kotapka, M.J., Graham, D.I., Adams, J.H., et al., Hippocampal pathology in fatal non-missile head injury. *Acta Neuropathol.*, 83, 530, 1992.

25. Russell, W.R., *The Traumatic Amnesias*, Oxford University Press, New York, 1971.

26. Russell, W.R. and Nathan, P.W., Traumatic amnesia. *Brain*, 69, 183, 1946.

27. Levin, H.S., High, W.M., Meyers, C.A., et al., Impairment of remote memory after closed head injury. *J. Neurol. Neurosurg. Psychiatry*, 48, 556, 1985.

28. Sarno, M.T., Buonaguro, A., and Levita, E., Characteristics of verbal impairment in closed head patients. *Arch. Phys. Med. Rehabil.*, 67, 400, 1986.

29. Levin, H.S., Aphasia after head injury, in *Acquired Aphasia,* 2nd edition, Sarno, M.T., Ed., Academic Press, New York, 1991.

30. Levin, H.S., Grossman, R.G., and Kelly, P.J., Aphasic disorder in patients with closed head injury. *J. Neurol. Neurosurg. Psychiatry*, 39, 1062, 1976.

31. Jones, R.D. and Rizzo, M., Head trauma and traumatic brain injury, in *Principles and Practice of Behavioral Neurology and Neuropsychology*, Rizzo, M. and Eslinger, P.J., Eds., W.B. Saunders, Philadelphia, PA, 2004, p. 615.

32. Ozbudak, D.S., Gorgulu, G., and Koseogelu, F., Comparison of rehabilitiation outcome in patients with aphasic and non-aphasic traumatic brain injury. *J. Rehabil. Med.*, 38, 68, 2006.

33. Ihori, N., Murayama, J., Mimura, M., et al., Right unilateral jargon agraphia as a symptom of callosal disconnection. *Cortex*, 42, 28, 2006.

34. Lippert-Gruener, M., Weinert, U., Greisbach, T., et al., Foreign accent syndrome following traumatic brain injury. *Brain Inj.*, 19, 955, 2005.

35. Coelho, C.A., Grela, B., Corso, M., et al., Microlinguistic deficits in the narrative discourse of adults with traumatic brain injury. *Brain Inj.*, 19, 1139, 2005.

36. Morien, C. and Gillon, G., Inference comprehension of adolescents with traumatic brain injury: A working memory hypothesis. *Brain Inj.*, 19, 743, 2005.

37. Alexander, M.P., Benson, D.F., and Suss, D.T., Frontal lobes and language. *Brain Lang.*, 37, 656, 1989.

38. Novoa, O.P. and Ardila, A., Linguistic abilities in patients with prefrontal damage. *Brain Lang.*, 30, 206, 1987.

39. Levin, H.S., Grossman, R.G., and Kelly, P.J., Impairment of facial recognition after closed head injuries of varying severity. *Cortex*, 13, 119, 1977.

40. Levin, H.S., Goldstein, F.C., Williams, D.H., et al., The contribution of frontal lobe lesions to the neurobehavioral outcome of closed head injury, in *Frontal Lobe Function and Dysfunction*, Levin, H.D., Eisenberg, H.M., and Benton, A.L., Eds., Oxford University Press, New York, 1991, p. 318.

41. Levin, H.S., Gary, H.E., Eisenberg, H.M., et al., Neurobehavioral outcome one year after injury: Experience of the Traumatic Coma Data Bank. *J. Neurosurg.*, 73, 699, 1990.

42. Lezak, M.D., *Neuropsychological Assessment,* 3rd edition, Oxford University Press, New York, 1995.

43. Warrington, E.K., James, M., and Maciejewski, C., The WAIS as a lateralizing and localizing diagnostic instruement. *Neuropsychologia*, 24, 223, 1986.

44. Adams, J.H., Graham, D., Scott, G., et al., Brain damage in fatal nonmissile head injury. *J. Clin. Pathol.*, 33, 1132, 1980.
45. Bukach, C.M., Bub, D.N., Gauthier, I., et al., Perceptual expertise effects are not all or none: Spatially limited perceptual expertise for faces in a case of prosopagnosia. *J. Cogn. Neurosci.*, 18, 48, 2006.
46. Caldara, R., Schyns, P., Mayer, E., et al., Does prosopagnosia take the eyes out of face representations? Evidence for a defect in representing diagnostic facial information following brain damage. *J. Cogn. Neurosci.*, 17, 1652, 2005.
47. Green, R.E., Turner, G.R., and Thompson, W.F., Deficits in facial emotion perception in adults with recent traumatic brain injury. *Neuropsychologia*, 42, 133, 2004.
48. Lezak, M.D., Howieson, D.B., and Loring, D.W., *Neuropsychological Assessment*, 4th edition, Oxford University Press, New York, 2004.
49. Piaget, J., *The Origins of Intelligence in Children*, International Universities Press, New York, 1952.
50. Fisher, D.C., Ledbetter, M.F., Cohen, N.J., et al., WAIS-III and WMS-III profiles of mildly to severely brain-injured patients. *Appl. Neuropsychol.*, 7, 126, 2000.
51. Cahn, G. and Gould, R.E., Understanding head injury and intellectual recovery from brain damage: Is IQ an adequate measure? *Bull. Am. Acad. Psychiatry Law*, 24, 135, 1996.
52. Cattelani, R., Lombardi, F., Brianti, R., et al., Traumatic brain injury in childhood: Intellectual, behavioral, and social outcome into adulthood. *Brain Inj.*, 12, 283, 1998.
53. Gao, B., Jiang, S., Wang, X., et al., The role of pre-injury IQ in the determination of intellectual impairment from traumatic brain injury. *J. Neuropsychiatr. Clin. Neurosci.*, 12, 385, 2000.
54. Langeluddecke, P.N. and Lucas, S.K., Wechsler Adult Intelligence Scale-Third Edition, findings and relation to severity of brain injury in litigants. *Clin. Neuropsychol.*, 17, 273, 2003.
55. Kamikubo, T., Ohashi, M., Hashimoto, K., et al., Lowered VIQ level following traumatic brain injury. *No To Shinkei*, 56, 952, 2004.
56. Mandleberg, I.A. and Brooks, D.N., Cognitive recovery after severe head injury, 1. Serial testing on the Wechsler Adult Intelligence Scale. *J. Neurol. Neurosurg. Psychiatry*, 38, 1121, 1975.
57. Stuss, D.T. and Levine, B., Adult clinical neuropsychology: Lessons from studies of the frontal lobes. *Annu. Rev. Psychol.*, 53, 401, 2002.
58. Best, M., Williams, J.M., and Coccaro, A.F., Evidence for a dysfunctional prefrontal circuit in patients with an impulsive aggressive disorder. *Proc. Nat. Acad. Sci. U.S.A.*, 99, 8448, 2002.
59. Mathias, J.L. and Coats, J.L., Emotional and cognitive sequelae to mild traumatic brain injury. *J. Clin. Exp. Neuropsychol.*, 21, 200, 1999.
60. Lezak, M.D. Assessment of psychological dysfunctions resulting from head trauma, in *Assessment of the Behavioral Consequences of Head Trauma*, Lezak, M.D., Ed., Allan R. Liss, New York, 1989, pp. 113–189.
61. Bechara, A., Tranel, D., Damasio, H., et al., Failure to respond anatomically to anticipated future outcomes following damage to prefrontal cortex. *Cereb. Cortex*, 6, 215, 1996.
62. Brink, J.D., Garrett, A.L., Hale, W.R., et al., Recovery of motor and intellectual function in children sustaining severe head injuries. *Dev. Med. Child Neurol.*, 12, 565, 1970.
63. Lange-Cosack, H., Wider, B., Schlesner, H.J., et al., Prognosis of brain injuries in young children (1 until 5 years of age). *Neuropaediatrics*, 10, 105, 1979.
64. Capruso, D.X. and Levin, H.S., Neurobehavioral outcome of head trauma, in *Neurology and Trauma*, Evans, R.W., Ed., W.B. Saunders, Philadelphia, PA, 1996, p. 201.
65. Nybo, T., Sainio, M., and Muller, K., Middle age cognition and vocational outcome of childhood brain injury. *Acta Neurol. Scand.*, 112, 338, 2005.
66. Verger, K., Junque, C., Levin, H.S., et al., Correlation of atrophy measures on MRI with neuropsychological sequelae in children and adolescents with traumatic brain injury. *Brain Inj.*, 15, 211, 2001.
67. Narberhaus, A., Segarra-Castells, M.D., Verger-Maestre, K., et al., Evaluation of diffuse cerebral atrophy in patients with a history of traumatic brain injury and its relation to cognitive deterioration. *Rev. Neurol.*, 36, 925, 2003.
68. McCarthy, M.L., MacKenzie, E.J., Durbin, D.R., et al., Health-related quality of life during the first year after traumatic brain injury. *Arch. Pediatr. Adolesc. Med.*, 160, 252, 2006.
69. Anderson, V.A., Pediatric head injury, in *Principles and Practice of Behavioral Neurology and Neuropsychology*, Rizzo, M. and Eslinger, P.J., Eds., W.B. Saunders, Philadelphia, PA, 2004, p. 863.

70. Max, J.E., Arndt, S., Castillo, C.S., et al., Attention-deficit hyperactivity symptomatology after traumatic brain injury: A prospective study. *J. Am. Acad. Child Adoles. Psychiatry*, 37, 841, 1998.

71. Catroppa, C. and Anderson, V., Planning, problem-solving and organizational abilities in children following traumatic brain injury: Intervention techniques. *Pediatr. Rehabil.*, 9, 89, 2006.

72. Barlow, K.M., Thomson, E., Johnson, D., et al., Late neurologic and cognitive sequelae of inflicted traumatic brain injury in infancy. *Pediatrics*, 116, e174, 2005.

73. Salmond, C.H. and Sahakian, B.J., Cognitive outcome in traumatic brain injury survivors. *Curr. Opin. Crit. Care*, 11, 111, 2005.

74. Dennis, N., Wilkinson, M., Koski, L., et al., Attention deficits in the long-term after childhood head injury, in *Traumatic Head Injury in Children*, Broman, S. and Michel, M.E., Eds., Oxford University Press, New York, 1995, p. 165.

75. Bakkr, K. and Anderson, V., Assessment of attention following preschool traumatic brain injury: A behavioral attention measure. *Pediatri. Rehabil.*, 3, 149, 1999.

76. Anderson, V., Fenwick, T., Manly, T., et al., Attentional skills following traumatic brain injury in childhood: A componential analysis. *Brain Inj.*, 12, 937, 1998.

77. Levin, H. and Eisenberg, H., Neuropsychological impairment after closed head injury in children and adolescents. *J. Pediatr. Psychol.*, 4, 389, 1979.

78. Catroppa, C. and Anderson, V., Attentional skills in the acute phase following pediatric traumatic brain injury. *Neuropsychol. Dev. Cognit. Sect. C Child Neuropsychol.*, 5, 251, 1999.

79. Levin, H.S., Eisenberg, H.M., Wigg, N.R., et al., Memory and intellectual ability after head injury in children and adolescents. *Neurosurgery*, 11, 668, 1982.

80. Yeates, K.O., Blumenstein, E., Patterson, C.M., et al., Verbal learning and memory following pediatric closed-head injury. *J. Int. Neuropsychol. Soc.*, 1, 78, 1995.

81. Chadwick, O., Rutter, M., Brown, G., et al., A prospective study of children with head injuries: II. Cognitive sequelae. *Psychol. Med.*, 11, 49, 1981.

82. Bassett, S.S. and Slater, E.J., Neuropsychological function in adolescents sustaining mild closed-head injury. *J. Ped. Psychol.*, 15, 225, 1990.

83. Klonoff, H., Low, M.D., and Clark, C., Head injuries in children: A prospective 5-year follow-up. *J. Neurol. Neurosurg. Psychiatry*, 40, 1211, 1977.

84. Yeates, K.O., Patterson, C.M., Waber, D.M., et al., Constructional and figural memory skills following pediatric closed-head injury. *J. Clin. Exp. Neuropsychol.*, 15, 58, 1993.

85. Kinsella, G., Prior, M., Sawyer, M., et al., Predictors and indicators of academic outcome in children two years following traumatic head injury. *J. Int. Neuropsychol. Soc.*, 3, 608, 1997.

86. Anderson, V.A., Catroppa, C., Morse, S.A., et al., Functional memory skills following traumatic brain injury in young children. *Pediatr. Rehabil.*, 3, 159, 1999.

87. Shum, D., Jamieson, E., Bahr, M., et al., Implicit and explicit memory in children with traumatic brain injury. *J. Clin. Exp. Neuropsychol.*, 22, 149, 1999.

88. Ward, H., Shum, D., Dick, B., et al., Interview study of the effects of paediatric traumatic brain injury on memory. *Brain Inj.*, 18, 471, 2004.

89. Moran, C. and Gillon, G., Language and memory profiles of adolescents with traumatic brain injury. *Brain Inj.*, 18, 273, 2004.

90. Kahill, L.M., Murdoch, B.E., and Theodoros, D.G., Articulatory function following traumatic brain injury in childhood: A perceptual and instrumental analysis. *Brain Inj.*, 19, 41, 2005.

91. Ewing-Cobbs, L., Fletcher, J., Levin, H., et al., Longitudinal neuropsychological outcome in infants and preschoolers with traumatic brain injury. *J. Int. Neuropsychol. Soc.*, 3, 581, 1997.

92. Didus, E., Anderson, V.A., and Catroppa, C., The development of pragmatic communication skills in head-injured children. *Pediatr. Rehabil.*, 3, 177, 1999.

93. Barlow, K., Thompson, E., Johnson, D., et al., The neurological outcome of non-accidental head injury. *Pediatr. Rehabil.*, 7, 195, 2004.

94. Campbell, T.F. and Dollaghan, C.A., Speaking rate, articulatory speed and linguistic processing in children and adolescents with severe traumatic brain injury. *J. Speech Hear. Res.*, 38, 864, 1995.

95. Biddle, K.R., McCabe, A., and Bliss, L.S., Narrative skills following traumatic brain injury in children and adults. *J. Commun. Disord.*, 29, 447, 1996.

96. Chapman, S.B., Levin, H.S., Wanek, A., et al., Discourse after closed-head injury in young children. *Brain Lang.*, 61, 420, 1998.

97. Dennis, M., Barnes, M.A., Wilkinson, M., et al., How children with head injury represent real and deceptive emotion in short narratives. *Brain Lang.*, 61, 450, 1998.

98. Chadwick, O., Rutter, M., Shaffer, D., et al., A prospective study of children with head injuries: IV. Specific cognitive deficits. *J. Clin. Neuropsychol.*, 3, 101, 1981.

99. Levine, S.C., Kraus, R., Alexander, E., et al., IQ decline following early unilateral brain injury: A longitudinal study. *Brain Cogn.*, 59, 114, 2005.

100. Hawley, C.A., Saint or sinner? Teacher perceptions of a child with traumatic brain injury. *Pediatr. Rehabil.*, 8, 117, 2005.

101. Hawley, C.A., Behaviour and school performance after brain injury. *Brain Inj.*, 18, 645, 2004.

102. Farmer, J.E., Clippard, D.S., Luehr-Weimann, Y., et al., Assessing children with traumatic brain injury during rehabilitation: Promoting school and community reentry. *J. Learn. Disabil.*, 29, 532, 1996.

103. Donders, J. and Strom, D., The effect of traumatic brain injury on children with learning disability. *Pediatr. Rehabil.*, 1, 179, 1997.

104. Levin, H.S. and Hanten, G., Executive functions after traumatic brain injury in children. *Pediatr. Neurol.*, 33, 79, 2005.

105. Landry, S.H., Swank, P., Stuebing, K., et al., Social competence in young children with inflicted traumatic brain injury. *Dev. Neuropsychol.*, 26, 707, 2004.

106. Anderson, V. and Catroppa, C., Recovery of executive skills following paediatric brain injury (TBI): A 2 year follow-up. *Brain Inj.*, 19, 459, 2005.

107. Sattler, J.M., *Assessment of Children: Cognitive Applications*, 4th edition, Jerome Sattler, San Diego, CA, 2001.

108. Harlow, J., Passage of an iron rod through the head. *Boston Med. Surg. J.*, 39, 389, 1848.

109. Eslinger, P.J. and Chakara, F., Frontal lobe and executive functions, in *Principles and Practice of Behavioral Neurology and Neuropsychology*, Rizzo, M. and Eslinger, P.J., Eds., W.B. Saunders, Philadelphia, PA, 2004, p. 435.

110. Tulving, E., Kapur, S., Kraik, F.I.M., et al., Hemisphere encoding/retrieval symmetry in episodic memory: Positron emission tomography findings. *Proc. Natl. Acad. Sci. U.S.A.*, 91, 2016, 1994.

111. Eslinger, P.J., Conceptualizing, describing and measuring components of executive functions, in *Attention, Memory, and Executive Function*. Lyon, G.R. and Krasenger, D.A., Eds., Paul H. Brookes, Baltimore, 1996, p. 367.

112. Eslinger, P.J. and Geder, L., Behavioral and emotional changes after focal frontal lobe damage, in *Focal Brain Lesions and Emotions*, Bogousslavsky, J. and Cummings, J.L., Eds., Cambridge University Press, Cambridge, 2000, p. 217.

113. Ptak, R. and Schnider, A., Spontaneous confabulations after orbital frontal damage: The role of temporal context confusion and self-monitoring. *Neurocase*, 5, 243, 1999.

114. Eslinger, P.J. and Damasio, A.R., Severe disturbance of higher cognition after bilateral frontal lobe ablation: Patient EVR. *Neurology*, 49, 764, 1985.

115. Damasio, A.R., Tranel, D., and Damasio, H.C., Somatic markers in the guidance of behavior: Theory and preliminary testing, in *Frontal Lobe Function and Dysfunction*, Levin, H.S., Eisenberg, H.M., and Benton, A.L., Eds., Oxford University Press, New York, 1991, p. 217.

116. Mega, M.S. and Cummings, J.L., Frontal–subcortical circuits and neuropsychiatric disorders. *Neuropsychiatr. Clin. Neurosci.*, 6, 358, 1994.

117. Hebb, D.O., Man's frontal lobes: A critical review. *Arch. Neurol. Psychiatry*, 54, 10, 1945.

118. Moll, J., Oliveira-Souza, R., and Eslinger, P.J., Morals in the human brain: A working model. *NeuroReport*, 14, 299, 2003.

119. Serino, A., Ciaramelli, E., Di Santantonio, A., et al., Central executive system impairment in traumatic brain injury. *Brain Inj.*, 20, 23, 2006.

120. Paradiso, S., Chemerinski, E., Yazici, K.M., et al., Frontal lobe syndrome reassessed: Comparison of patients with lateral or medial frontal damage. *J. Neurol. Neurosurg. Psychiatry*, 67, 664, 1999.

121. Sherer, M., Hart, T., Whyte, J., et al., Neuroanatomical basis of impaired self-awareness after traumatic brain injury: Findings from early computed tomography. *J. Head Trauma Rehabil.*, 20, 287, 2005.

122. Alexander, M.P., Stuss, D.T., Shallice, T., et al., Impaired concentration due to frontal lobe damage from two distinct lesion sites. *Neurology*, 65, 572, 2005.

123. Powell, K.B. and Voeller, K.K., Prefrontal executive function syndromes in children. *J. Child Neurol.*, 19, 785, 2004.

124. Max, J.E., Levin, H.S., Schachar, R.J., et al., Predictors of personality change due to traumatic brain injury in children and adolescents 6 to 24 months after injury. *J. Neuropsychiatr. Clin. Neurosci.*, 18, 21, 2006.

125. Temkin, N.R., Haglund, M., and Winn, H.R., Posttraumatic seizures, in *Neurotrauma*, Narayn, R.K, Wilberger, J.E., and Povlishock, J.T., Eds., W.B. Saunders, Philadelphia, PA, 1996, p. 611.

126. Ronne-Engstrom, E. and Winkler, T., Continuous EEG monitoring in patients with traumatic brain injury reveals a high incidence of epileptiform activity. *Acta Neurol. Scand.*, 114, 47, 2006.

127. Aarabi, B., Eisenberg, H.M., Murphy, K., et al., Traumatic brain injury: Management and complications, in *Textbook of Neurointensive Care*, Layon, A.J., Gabrielli, A., and Friedman, W.A., Eds., W.B. Saunders, Philadelphia, PA, 2004, p. 771.

128. Temkin, N.R., Risk factors for posttraumatic seizures in adults. *Epilepsia*, 44, Suppl. 10, 18, 2003.

129. D'Ambrosio, R. and Perucca, E., Epilepsy after head injury. *Curr. Opin. Neurol.*, 17, 731, 2004.

130. Holmes, J.F., Palchak, M.J., Conklin, M.J., et al., Do children require hospitalization after immediate posttraumatic seizures? *Ann. Emerg. Med.*, 43, 706, 2004.

131. Chiaretti, A., DeBenedictis, R., Polidori, G., et al., Early posttraumatic seizures in children with head injury. *Childs Nerv. Syst.*, 16, 862, 2000.

132. Pagni, C.A., Posttraumatic epilepsy: Incidence and prophylaxis. *Acta Neurochir. Suppl*, 50, 38, 1990.

133. Salazar, A.M., Jabbari, B., Vance, S.C., et al., Epilepsy after penetrating head injury: I. Clinical correlates: A report of the Vietnam Head Injury Study. *Neurology*, 33, 1406, 1985.

134. Packard, R.C., Epidemiology and pathogenesis of posttraumatic headache. *J. Head Trauma Rehabil.*, 14, 9, 1999.

135. Solomon, S., Posttraumatic migraine. *Headache*, 38, 772, 1998.

136. Solomon, S., Posttraumatic headache. *Med. Clin. North Am.*, 85, 987, 2001.

137. Lew, H.L., Lin, P.H., Fuh, J.L., et al., Characteristics and treatment of headaches after traumatic brain injury: A focused review. *Am. J. Phys. Med. Rehabil.*, 85, 619, 2006.

138. Walker, W.C., Seel, R.T., Curtiss, G., et al., Headache after moderate and severe traumatic brain injury: A longitudinal analysis. *Arch. Phys. Med. Rehabil.*, 86, 1793, 2005.

139. Collins, M.W., Field, M., Lovell, M.R., et al., Relationship between postconcussion headache and neuropsychological test performance in high school athletes. *Am. J. Sports Med.*, 31, 168, 2003.

140. Couch, J.R. and Bearss, C., Chronic daily headache in the posttrauma syndrome: Relation to extent of head injury. *Headache*, 41, 559, 2001.

141. Ironside, J.W. and Pickard, J.D., Raised intracranial pressure, oedema, and hydrocephalus, in *Greenfield's Neuropathology,* 7th edition, Graham, D.I. and Lantos, P.L., Eds., Arnold, London, 2002, p. 222.

142. Marmarou, A., Foda, M.A., Bandoh, K., et al., Posttraumatic ventriculomegaly: Hydrocephalus or atrophy? A new approach for diagnosis using CSF dynamics. *J. Neurosurg.*, 86, 1026, 1996.

143. Bergsneider, M., Management of hydrocephalus with programmable valves after traumatic brain injury and subarachnoid hemorrhage. *Curr. Opin. Neurol.*, 13, 661, 2000.

144. Belmont, A., Agar, N., Hugeron, C., et al., Fatigue and traumatic brain injury. *Ann. Readapt. Med. Phys.*, 49, 370, 2006.

145. Stulemeijer, M., van der Werf, S., Bleijenberg, G., et al., Recovery from mild traumatic brain injury: A focus on fatigue. *J. Neurol.*, May 17 (epub ahead of print), 2006.

146. Ziino, C. and Ponsford, J., Vigilance and fatigue following traumatic brain injury. *J. Int. Neuropsychol. Soc.*, 12, 100, 2006.

147. Ziino, C. and Ponsford, J., Selective attention deficits and subjective fatigue following traumatic brain injury. *Neuropsychology*, 20, 383, 2006.

148. Ziino, C. and Ponsford, J., Measurement and prediction of subjective fatigue following traumatic brain injury. *J. Int. Neuropsychol. Soc.*, 11, 416, 2005.

149. American Sleep Disorders Association, *The International Classification of Sleep Disorders: Diagnostic and Coding Manual*, American Sleep Disorders Association, Rochester, NY, 1990, p. 48.

150. Guillenminault, C., van den Hoed, J., and Miles, L., Posttraumatic excessive daytime sleepiness. *Neurology*, 33, 1584, 1983.

151. Kryger, M.H., Roth, T., and Dement, W.C., *Principles and Practice of Sleep Medicine,* 3rd edition, W.B. Saunders, Philadelphia, PA, 2000, p. 689.

152. Castriotta, R.J. and Lai, J.M., Sleep disorders associated with traumatic brain injury. *Arch. Phys. Med. Rehabil.*, 82, 1403, 2001.

153. Steele, D.L., Ragaratnam, S.N., Redman, J.R., et al., The effect of traumatic brain injury on the timing of sleep. *Chronobiol. Int.*, 22, 89, 2005.
154. Ouellet, M.C., Savard, J., and Morin, C.N., Insomnia following traumatic brain injury: A review. *Neurorehabil. Neural Repair*, 18, 187, 2004.
155. Campbell, M. and Parry, A., Balance disorder in traumatic brain injury: preliminary findings of a multifactorial observational study. *Brain Inj.*, 19, 1095, 2005.
156. Rinne, M.B., Pasanen, M.E., Vartiainen, N.V., et al., Motor performance in physically well-recovered men with traumatic brain injury. *J. Rehabil. Med.*, 38, 224, 2006.
157. Slobounov, S., Sebastianelli, W., and Moss, R., Alteration of posture-related cortical potentials in mild traumatic brain injury. *Neurosci. Lett.*, 383, 251, 2005.
158. Hibbard, M.R., Gordon, W.A., Flanagan, S., et al., Sexual dysfunction after traumatic brain injury. *NeuroRehabilitation*, 15, 107, 2000.
159. *The Frontal Lobes and Neuropsychiatric Illness*. Salloway, S.P., Malloy, P.F., and Duffy, J.D., Eds., American Psychiatric Press, Washington, D.C., 2001.
160. McAllister, T.W. and Green, R.L., Traumatic brain injury: A model of acquired psychiatric illness? *Semin. Clin. Neuropsychiatr.*, 3, 158, 1998.
161. O'Donnell, M.L., Creamer, M., Pattison, P., et al., Psychiatric morbidity following injury. *Am. J. Psychiatry*, 162, 629, 2005.
162. Anstey, K.J., Butterworth, P., Jorn, A.F., et al., A population survey found an association between self-reports of traumatic brain injury and increased psychiatric symptoms. *J. Clin. Epidemiol.*, 57, 1202, 2004.
163. Ashman, T.A., Spielman, L.A., and Hibbard, M.R., et al., Psychiatric challenges in the first six years after traumatic brain injury: Cross-sequential analyses of Axis I disorders. *Arch. Phys. Med. Rehabil.*, 85 (4 suppl. 2), S36, 2004.
164. Federoff, J.P., Starkstein, S.E., Forrester, A.W., et al., Depression in patients with traumatic brain injury. *Am. J. Psychiatry*, 149, 918, 1992.
165. Jorge, R.E., Robinson, R.G., Arndt, S.V., et al., Comparison between acute and delayed-onset depression following traumatic brain injury. *J. Neuropsychiatr.*, 5, 43, 1993.
166. Rapoport, M.J., Kiss, A., and Feinstein, A., The impact of major depression on outcome following mild-to-moderate traumatic brain injury in older adults. *J. Affect. Disord.*, 92, 273, 2006.
167. Chamelian, L. and Feinstein, A., The effect of major depression on subjective and objective cognitive deficits in mild-to-moderate traumatic brain injury. *J. Neuropsychiatr. Clin. Neurosci.*, 18, 33, 2006.
168. Bowen, A., Neumann, V., Conner, M., et al., Mood disorders following traumatic brain injury: Identifying the extent of the problem and the people at risk. *Brain Inj.*, 12, 177, 1998.
169. Hibbard, M.R., Uysal, S., Kepler, K., et. al., Axis I psychopathology in individuals with traumatic brain injury. *J. Head Trauma Rehabil.*, 13, 24, 1998.
170. Holsinger, T., Steffens, D.C., Phillips, C., et al., Head injury in early adulthood and the lifetime risk of depression. *Arch. Gen. Psychiatry*, 59, 17, 2002.
171. Jorge, R.E., Robinson, R.G., Moser, D., et al., Major depression following traumatic brain injury. *Arch. Gen. Psychiatry*, 61, 42, 2004.
172. Levin, H.S., McCauley, S.R., Josic, C.P., et al., Predicting depression following mild traumatic brain injury. *Arch. Gen. Psychiatry*, 62, 523, 2005.
173. Oquendo, M.A., Friedman, J.H., Grunebaum, M.F., et al., Suicidal behavior in mild traumatic brain injury and major depression. *J. Nerv. Ment. Dis.*, 192, 430, 2004.
174. Koponen, S., Taiminen, T., Kurki, T., et al., MRI findings in Axis I and II psychiatric disorders after traumatic brain injury: A 30-year retrospective follow-up study. *Psychiatry Res.*, 146, 263, 2006.
175. Geuze, E., Vermetten, E., and Bremner, J.D., MR-based *in vivo* hippocampal volumetrics: II. Findings in neuropsychiatric disorders. *Mol. Psychiatry*, 10, 160, 2005.
176. Jorge, R.E. and Starkstein, S.E., Pathophysiologic aspects of major depression following traumatic brain injury. *J. Head Trauma Rehabil.*, 20, 475, 2005.
177. Krauthammer, C. and Klerman, G.L., Secondary mania. *Arch. Gen. Psychiatry*, 35, 1333, 1978.
178. Riess, H., Schwartz, C.W., and Klerman, G.L., Manic syndrome following head injury: Another form of secondary mania. *J. Clin. Psychiatry*, 48, 29, 1987.
179. Jorge, R.E., Robinson, R.G., Starkstein, S.E., et al., Secondary mania following traumatic brain injury. *Am. J. Psychiatry*, 150, 916, 1993.

180. American Psychiatric Association. *Diagnostic and Statistical Manual of Mental Disorders*, 4th edition, American Psychiatric Association, Washington, D.C., 1994, p. 353.

181. Monji, A., Yoshida, I., Koga, H., et al., Brain injury-induced rapid-cycling affective disorder successfully treated with Valproate. *Psychosomatics*, 40, 448, 1999.

182. Heinrich, T.W. and Junig, J.T., Recurrent mania associated with repeated brain injury. *Gen. Hosp. Psychiatry*, 26, 490, 2004.

183. Klonoff, H., Head injuries in children: Predisposing factors, accident conditions, accident proneness, and sequelae. *Am. J. Public Health*, 61, 2405, 1971.

184. Lewis, A., Discussion on differential diagnosis and treatment of post-concussional states. *Proc. R. Soc. Med.*, 35, 607, 1942.

185. Harvey, A.G. and Bryant, R.A., Acute stress disorder after mild traumatic brain injury. *J. Nerv. Ment. Dis.*, 186, 333, 1998.

186. Harvey, A.G. and Bryant, R.A., Two-year prospective evaluation of the relationship between acute stress disorder and posttraumatic stress disorder following mild traumatic brain injury. *Am. J. Psychiatry*, 157, 626, 2000.

187. Fann, J., Uomoto, J.M., and Katun, W.J., Sertreline in the treatment of major depression following mild traumatic brain injury. *Brain Inj.*, 12, 226, 2000.

188. Moore, E.L., Terryberry-Spohr, L., and Hope, D.A., Mild traumatic brain injury and anxiety sequelae: A review of the literature. *Brain Inj.*, 20, 117, 2006.

189. Bryant, R.A. and Panasetis, P., The role of panic and acute dissociative reactions following trauma. *Br. J. Clin. Psychol.*, 44 (Pt 4), 489, 2005.

190. Coetzer, B.R., Obsessive-compulsive disorder following brain injury: A review. *Int. J. Psychiatry Med.*, 34, 363, 2004.

191. Jorge, R.E., Neuropsychiatric consequences of traumatic brain injury: A review of recent findings. *Curr. Opin. Psychiatry*, 18, 289, 2005.

192. Adler, A., Neuropsychiatric complications in victims of Boston's Coconut Grove disaster. *JAMA*, 123, 1098, 1943.

193. Sumpter, R.E. and McMillan, T.M., Misdiagnosis of posttraumatic stress disorder following severe traumatic brain injury. *Br. J. Psychiatry*, 186, 423, 2005.

194. Sumpter, R.E. and McMillan, T.M., Errors in self-reports of posttraumatic stress disorder after severe traumatic brain injury. *Brain Inj.*, 20, 93, 2006.

195. Gil, S., Caspi, I.Y., and Klein, E., Memory of the traumatic event as a risk factor for the development of PTSD: lessons from the study of traumatic brain injury. *CNS Spectr.*, 11, 603, 2006.

196. McMillan, T., Posttraumatic stress disorder following minor and severe closed head injury: Ten single cases. *Brain Inj.*, 10, 749, 1996.

197. Warden, D.L. and Labvate, L.A., Posttraumatic stress disorder and other anxiety disorders, in *Textbook of Traumatic Brain Injury*, Silver, J.M., McAllister, T.W., and Yudofsky, S.C., Eds., American Psychiatric Press, Washington, D.C., 2005, p. 231.

198. Glaesser, J., Neuner, F., Lutgehetmann, R., et al., Posttraumatic stress disorder in patients with traumatic brain injury. *BMC Psychiatry*, 4, 5, 2004.

199. Williams, L.M., Kemp, A.H., Felmingham, K., et al., Trauma modulates amygdala and medial prefrontal responses to consciously attended fear. *Neuroimage*, 29, 347, 2006.

200. Gil, S., Caspi, Y., Ben-Ari, I.Z., et al., Does memory of a traumatic event increase the risk for posttraumatic stress disorder in patients with traumatic brain injury? A prospective study. *Am. J. Psychiatry*, 162, 963, 2005.

201. Creamer, M., O'Donnell, M.L., and Pattison, P., Amnesia, traumatic brain injury, and posttraumatic stress disorder: a methodological inquiry. *Behav. Res. Ther.*, 43, 1383, 2005.

202. Davison, K. and Bagley, C.K., Schizophrenia-like psychosis associated with organic disorder of the CNS. *Br. J. Psychiatry*, 4 (Suppl. 4), 113, 1969.

203. Lishman, W.A., Brain damage in relation to psychiatric disability after head injury. *Br. J. Psychiatry*, 114, 373, 1968.

204. Hillbom, E., After-effects of brain injuries. *Acta Psychiatr. Neurol. Scand. Suppl.*, 142, 1, 1960.

205. Achte, K., Jarho, L., Kyykka, T., et al., Paranoid disorders following war brain damage: preliminary report. *Psychopathology*, 24, 309, 1991.

206. Burke, J.M., Imhoff, C.L., and Kerrigan, J.M., MMPI correlates among post-acute TBI patients. *Brain Inj.*, 4, 223, 1990.
207. Burke, J.M., Smith, S.A., and Imhoff, C.L., The response styles of post-acute traumatic brain injured patients on the MMPI. *Brain Inj.*, 3, 35, 1989.
208. Dikmen, S. and Reitan, R.M., MMPI correlates of adaptive ability deficits in patients with brain lesions. *J. Nerv. Ment. Dis.*, 165, 247, 1977.
209. McAllister, T.W. and Ferrell, R.B., Evaluation and treatment of psychosis after traumatic brain injury. *NeuroRehabilitation*, 17, 357, 2002.
210. Zhang, Q. and Sachdev, P.S., Psychotic disorder in traumatic brain injury. *Curr. Psychiatry Rep.*, 5, 197, 2003.
211. Arciniegas, D.B., Harris, S.N., and Brousseau, K.M., Psychosis following traumatic brain injury. *Int. Rev. Psychiatry*, 15, 328, 2003.
212. Fujii, D. and Ahmed, I., Psychotic disorder following traumatic brain injury: a conceptual framework. *Cognit. Neuropsychiatr.*, 7, 41, 2002.
213. O'Shanick, G.J. and O'Shanick, A.M., Personality and intellectual changes, in *Neuropsychiatry of Traumatic Brain Injury*, Silver, J.M., Yudofsky, S.C., and Hales, R.E., Eds., American Psychiatric Press, Washington, D.C., 1994, p. 163.
214. Harlow, J.M., Recovery from the passage of an iron bar through the head. *Pub. Mass. Med. Soc.*, 2, 327, 1868.
215. Tranel, D., Emotion, decision-making, and the ventromedial prefrontal cortex, in *Principles of Frontal Lobe Function*, Stuss, D. and Knight, R., Eds., Oxford University Press, New York, 2002, p. 338.
216. Cleckley, H., *The Mask of Sanity,* 5th edition, C.V. Mosby, St. Louis, 1976.
217. Hare, R., *The Hare Psychopathy Checklist, Revised.* Multi-health Systems, Toronto, 1991.
218. Granacher, R.P. and Fozdar, M.A., Acquired psychopathy and the assessment of traumatic brain injury, *The International Handbook of Psychopathic Disorders and the Law*, Felthous, A. and Sass, H., Eds., John Wiley & Sons, New York, 2007.
219. Max, J.E., Robertson, B.A., and Lansing, A.E. The phenomenology of personality change due to traumatic brain injury in children and adolescents. *J. Neuropsychiatr. Clin. Neurosci.*, 13, 161, 2001.
220. Max, J.E., Levin, H.S., Landis, J., et al., Predictors of personality change due to traumatic brain injury in children and adolescents in the first six months after injury. *J. Am. Acad. Child Adolesc. Psychiatry,* 44, 434, 2005.
221. Silver, J.M. and Yudofsky, S.C., Aggressive disorders, in *Neuropsychiatry of Traumatic Brain Injury*, Silver, J.M., Yudofsky, S.C., and Hales, R.E., Eds., American Psychiatric Press, Washington, D.C., 1994, p. 313.
222. Rao, N., Jellinek, H.M., and Woolston, D.C., Agitation in closed head injury: Haloperidol effects on rehabilitation outcome. *Arch. Phys. Med. Rehabil.*, 66, 30, 1985.
223. Grafman, J., Schwab, K., Warden, D., et al., Frontal lobe injuries, violence and aggression: a report of the Vietnam Head Injury Study. *Neurology*, 46, 1231, 1996.
224. Kreutzer, J.S., Marwitz, J.H., and Witol, A.D., Interrelationships between crime, substance abuse, and aggressive behaviors among persons with traumatic brain injury. *Brain Inj.*, 9, 757, 1995.
225. Baguley, I.J., Cooper, J., and Felmingham, K., Aggressive behavior following traumatic brain injury: How common is common? *J. Head Trauma Rehabil.*, 21, 45, 2006.
226. Langevin, R., Sexual offenses in traumatic brain injury. *Brain Cogn.*, 60, 206, 2006.
227. Geraldina, P., Mariarosaria, L., Annarita, A., et al., Neuropsychiatric sequelae in TBI: a comparison across different age groups. *Brain Inj.*, 17, 835, 2003.
228. Cohen, R.A., Rosenbaum, A., Kane, R.L., et al., Neuropsychological correlates of domestic violence. *Violence Vict.*, 14, 397, 1999.
229. Allgulander, C. and Nilsson, B., Victims of criminal homicide in Sweden: A matched case-control study of health and social risk factors among all 1,739 cases during 1978–1994. *Am. J. Psychiatry*, 157, 244, 2000.
230. Kay, T., Harrington, D.E., Adams, R., et al., Definition of mild traumatic brain injury. *J. Head Trauma Rehabil.*, 8, 86, 1993.
231. *World Health Organization: International Classifications of Diseases, 9th Revision*, Clinical Modifications, 3rd edition. U.S. Department of Health and Human Services, Washington, D.C., 1989.

232. Thurman, D.J., Sniezek, J.E., Johnson, D., et al., *Guidelines for Surveillance of Central Nervous System Injury*, Centers for Disease Control and Prevention, Atlanta, GA, 1995.
233. Cantu, R.C., Return-to-play guidelines after a head injury. *Clin. Sports Med.*, 17, 52, 1998.
234. Kelly, J.P. and Rosenburg, J.H., The diagnosis and management of concussion in sports. *Neurology*, 48, 575, 1997.
235. Willer, B. and Leddy, J.J., Management of concussion and postconcussion syndrome. *Curr. Treat. Options Neurol.*, 8, 415, 2006.
236. McCauley, S.R., Boake, C., Pedroza, C., et al., Postconcussional disorder: Are the DSM-IV criteria an improvement over the ICD-10? *J. Nerv. Ment. Dis.*, 193, 540, 2005.
237. Boake, C., McCauley, S.R., Levin, H.S., et al., Diagnostic criteria for postconcussional syndrome after mild to moderate traumatic brain injury. *J. Neuropsychiatr. Clin. Neurosci.*, 17, 350, 2005.
238. McHugh, T., Laforce, R., Gallagher, P., et al., Natural history of the long-term cognitive, affective, and physical sequelae of mild traumatic brain injury. *Brain Cogn.*, 60, 209, 2006.
239. Collie, A., McCrory, P., and Makdissi, N., Does history of concussion affect current cognitive status? *Br. J. Sports Med.*, 40, 550, 2006.
240. Mooney, G., Speed, J., and Sheppard, S., Factors related to recovery after mild traumatic brain injury. *Brain Inj.*, 19, 975, 2005.
241. Nacajuskaite, O., Endziniene, M., Jureniene, K., et al., The validity of postconcussion syndrome in children: A controlled historical cohort study. *Brain Dev.*, 28, 507, 2006.
242. Damasio, H., Gravowski, T., Frank, R., et al., The return of Phineas Cage: Clues about the brain from the skull of a famous patient. *Science*, 1102, 264, 1994.

3 Gathering the Neuropsychiatric History following Brain Trauma

INTRODUCTION

Traditionally, psychiatry has termed the gathering of oral history from a patient in the psychiatric interview. In neuropsychiatry, the psychiatric interview takes a different path from traditional psychiatric examination. The strengths of the traditional psychiatric interview approach remain, but the examiner should focus more on cerebral dysfunction than on psychological abnormality while collecting neuropsychiatric data. While it is not precise, localization as a paradigm for a neuropsychiatric examination is more systematized scientifically than the general and traditional psychiatric symptoms.[1,2]

Within psychiatric medicine, the gathering of history has been the *sine qua non* of the practice of medicine since the time of Hippocrates.[3] Within the United States, one of the signers of the Declaration of Independence, Benjamin Rush, first provided American medical practice with the schema for taking a psychiatric history while making medical inquiry of the mind.[4] Gowers developed a manual for use while exploring diseases of the nervous system, which was published in the late 1880s.[5] More recently, Ovsiew has provided an excellent overview of bedside neuropsychiatry, and his chapter provides a broad review of methods used for gathering neuropsychiatric data at the bedside.[6] In this chapter, gathering history is separated from the mental status examination. This is unlike the traditional psychiatric interview technique, which combines the interview, history, and mental status examination.[7] With regard to children, the reader is referred to Larsen.[8] With particular reference to traumatic brain injury (TBI) in children, the reader is referred to Arffa.[9] This exploration of gathering neuropsychiatric history following brain trauma will separate taking the adult history from the child history. The taking of history will be augmented by exploring the use of collateral historians such as parents, spouses, and caregivers. Special emphasis will be given to collecting data from the available medical records. This provides background information for the treating psychiatrist. For the forensic psychiatrist, however, reviewing records is critical in determining causation and the presence of prior cerebral disorders or brain trauma that may have a bearing on apportionment within a civil tort action. Also, in neuropsychiatry, while attention is focused on cerebral symptomatology, one must not neglect psychosocial variables, as these may have substantial impact on symptom expression, level of impairment, and disability.[6] Moreover, it is important for the neuropsychiatric practitioner to remember there is no substitute for the taking of an adequate history. One should not fall prey to the use of rapidly advancing neuroimaging techniques and cognitive neuropsychology as substitutes for a complete neuropsychiatric history.

Taking a history following brain trauma is no different from taking a history following any kind of accident or taking a history for any suspected psychiatric condition. The following is a suggested medical history questionnaire. It is quite long, but it provides to the neuropsychiatric examiner a general comprehensive medical history format. When the information has been placed on this questionnaire, before the face-to-face examination by the physician, it then forms a useful guide to ask specific neuropsychiatric questions relevant to TBI. These will be outlined below within the content of this chapter. It is recommended that the physician write onto the document produced by the patient. This enables the physician to add contemporaneous notes to the document that are specific to the medical history following TBI. Thus, when the physician writes a report following the examination, a comprehensive and complete medical history will have been obtained, and it will be augmented by questioning specific to TBI outlined within the remainder of this chapter.

PATIENT QUESTIONNAIRE (FOR TREATMENT)

ALL QUESTIONS MUST BE ANSWERED!

WARNING: Because of managed care insurance practices, and possible intrusion of your medical insurer or disability carrier into your privacy, please be aware that if you sign authorization to release your medical records to your insurer, or for disability or legal reasons, others may see this information.

PLEASE BE ADVISED: If you are in a lawsuit, workers' compensation claim, social security claim or criminal charge, Dr. Pleasant will testify only as your treating doctor, not as an expert witness.

GENERAL INFORMATION

Name:_____ Today's Date:_____

Address:_____ City:_____State:_____

Zip code:_____ Date of birth:_____ Age:_____

Phone number:_____ Social Security number:_____

Which is your dominant hand? (right, left, both):_____ Your present weight _____

Can you read a newspaper? Yes _____ No _____ Education (highest grade completed):_____

Employment (current):_____

Address:_____ Phone:_____

Did you drive yourself here today? Yes_____ No_____. If no, who brought you? _____

What is their relation to you (friend, relative, hired by your lawyer, etc.)?_____

Who do you live with at this time?_____

HISTORY OF PRESENTING PROBLEM

Have you been experiencing any mental or nervous problems in the last month? Yes ___No_____
If yes, describe:_____

Which year did your mental problems first begin? _____

Have you been experiencing any physical problems in the last month? Yes _____ No _____ If yes,
describe:_____

_____

Which year did your physical problems first begin? _____

ACTIVITIES OF DAILY LIVING

Are you currently working? _____ How many hours per week? _____

Does your town contain more than 2500 people? Yes _____ No _____

What time do you get up in the morning? _____ What time do you go to bed at night? _____ Who fixes your breakfast?_____ Do you drive your car or truck? _____Do you use a checkbook? _____ Who pays your bills? _____Who cleans your home?_____

Who fixes your meals? _____Do you attend church?_____How often?_____

What hobbies do you now have?_____

What video games do you play?_____
What do you read? _____ Can you write?_____

Do you watch TV?_____ How many hours per day?_____
What do you do with your children? _____

What was your last overnight trip? _____

Who mows your yard? _____

What work do you do around your home or farm? _____

How many movies do you rent per month?_____ How many times do you go to the movie theater a year?_____ How many times do you sleep away from home in a year? _____ How many ball games do you attend in a year? _____ How many times do you hunt in a year? _____ How many times do you fish per year? _____

How many times do you eat out in a month? _____ How many times a month do friends or family visit you in your home? _____ How many times a week do you call someone on your phone? _____ What plants do you grow? _____ Can you dress yourself? _____ Can you bathe yourself or shower yourself? _____ Can you have sex? _____

Do you have any problems using the bathroom? _____

PAST MEDICAL HISTORY

List any serious childhood illnesses you had:_____

Were you born prematurely? Yes _____ No _____ What did you weigh at birth? _____

Did you have growth problems? Yes _____No _____ Did you have a birth injury? _____,

As a baby: How old were you when you could sit alone? _____, crawl? _____,

Pull yourself up? _____ Stand alone? _____ Walk alone? _____

Were you potty trained? _____

Were you sad or depressed or happy as a child? Sad _____ Happy _____

List any permanent physical or mental problems from childhood: _____

As a child, did you have trouble sitting still in school? Yes _____ No _____ Did you have trouble learning in school? Yes _____ No _____ Did you have trouble keeping your mind on tasks as a child? Yes _____ No _____ Did you have trouble learning to read? Yes _____ No _____

Did teachers complain you were too active? Yes _____ No _____

Check any serious illnesses you have now or have been treated for in the past.

_____ Seizures (Epilepsy)	_____ Attention deficit disorder
_____ Cancer	_____ Stomach or bowel disease
_____ Diabetes	_____ Female problems
_____ Thyroid disease	_____ Pregnancy problems
_____ Anemia (low blood)	_____ Bladder problems
_____ High blood pressure	_____ Sexual problems
_____ Heart disease	_____ Prostate problems
_____ Lung or breathing problems	_____ Sleep problems
_____ Kidney disease	_____ HIV or AIDS
_____ Joint or back disease	_____ Learning disorder
_____ Depression	_____ Manic–depressive illness (bipolar)
_____ Panic disorder	_____ Schizophrenia
_____ Alcoholism	_____ Eating disorders (e.g., anorexia)
_____ Drug abuse	_____ Neurological disease
_____ Overdoses of medication	_____ Spouse abuse
_____ Suicide attempts	_____ Child abuse or neglect
_____ Violence toward others	_____ Pain disorder

If you were hospitalized for any of these illnesses, list the hospital(s):_____

_____

Have you been injured in any motor vehicle accidents? Yes _____ No _____ If yes, list below:

Year	Your Age at the Time	Type of Injury	Treatment/by Whom

Have you ever been knocked unconscious, or had a brain injury? Yes _____ No _____

If yes, describe what happened: _____

Have you ever been in a coma? Yes _____ No _____

Have you ever broken any bones? Yes _____ No _____

If yes, describe which bones were broken, right or left side: _____

Have you had any surgeries or operations? Yes _____ No _____ If yes, list below:

Year	Your Age at the Time	Hospital Where Performed	Type of Surgery

Are you now taking any medications? Yes _____ No _____

If yes, please list the milligrams and how often you take your medicine.

Medications	Milligrams	Times per Day

Are you taking any over-the-counter medicines (you do not need a prescription)? Yes_____ No_____ If yes, list them: _____

Are you taking any herbs or natural products? Yes _____ No _____

If yes, list them: _____

Who keeps track of your medications? You _____ Your spouse _____ Someone else _____

Do you have any drug allergies or reactions? Yes _____ No _____ If yes, list below:

Drugs	Allergic Reaction
	Rash, nausea, hives, trouble breathing, etc.

Do you use tobacco now? Yes _____ No _____ Not now but previously _____ If answered yes or have used tobacco in the past, please describe how much and when you started and when you stopped:_____

Do you use alcohol now? Yes _____ No _____ Not now but in the past _____ If yes to any use of alcohol, then describe:_____

Type of alcohol you currently use (whiskey, beer, wine, etc.): _____

Number of alcohol drinks you have per day: _____

When did you first start using alcohol? When did you stop? _____

Describe any past alcohol problems in your life (DUIs, AIs, alcoholism, etc.): _____
_____

Describe any medical treatment for alcohol problems: _____
_____

Have you ever taken a medication or drug that you bought off the street? Yes _____ No _____

If yes, describe: _____

Have you ever used illegal drugs, (i.e., marijuana, heroin, cocaine, uppers, downers, crack, etc.)? Yes _____ No _____

Have you ever sniffed paint, glue, or gasoline to get high? Yes _____ No _____ If yes, what did you sniff and how long? _____

Have you ever used LSD, peyote, mescaline, PCP, mushrooms? Yes _____ No _____

If yes, what and when? _____

Have you ever used Ecstasy or meth? Yes _____ No _____

Have you ever injected illegal drugs (IV drugs)? Yes _____ No _____

Have you ever received treatment for drug/substance abuse? Yes _____ No _____ If yes, what hospital? Which year? _____

_____

Do you drink coffee or tea? Yes _____ No _____ How many cups per day?_____

Do you drink caffeinated soft drinks? Yes _____ No _____ What soft drinks? _____

_____ How many per day? _____

Next Five Questions for Women:

1. How many pregnancies have you had? _____ How many living children have you had? _____ How many miscarriages have you had? _____
2. Were you depressed after having a baby or miscarriage? Yes _____ No _____ If yes, when? _____Were you medically treated? Yes _____No _____
3. Have you had any babies by caesarean section? Yes _____ No _____
4. Could you be pregnant? Yes _____ No _____
5. When was your last menstrual period?_____

PAST PSYCHIATRIC HISTORY

Have you ever been hospitalized for psychiatric, drug abuse, alcohol, or mental problems?

Yes _____ No _____ If yes, please explain below:

Psychiatric Hospital Admissions	Year Hospitalized	Hospital Name	Treating Physician or Psychiatrist	Diagnosis or Reason for Admission	Type of Treatment Received
First admission					
Second admission					
Third admission					
Fourth admission					

Have you ever been discharged from any hospital against medical advice (AMA)?

Yes_____ No_____ If yes, describe: _____

Have you ever been prescribed any form of nerve medicines, antidepressants, tranquilizers, or other psychiatric medications? Yes _____ No _____ If yes, describe: _____

_____

When is the first time in your life you ever took nerve medicines, tranquilizers, or antidepressants?

_____

Have you ever stopped prescribed nerve pills without asking the doctor? Yes _____ No _____

Have you ever had shock treatments (ECT or vagus nerve stimulator insertion)? Yes _____
No _____ If yes, describe when and where:_____

Have you ever been advised by any doctor or health practitioner to get mental or psychological
treatment? Yes _____ No _____ If yes, describe: _____

Have you ever been legally committed or admitted involuntarily to a mental hospital or psychiatric
unit? Yes _____ No _____ If yes, describe: _____
_____

Have you ever refused mental treatment when recommended by a doctor? Yes _____
No _____ If yes, describe:_____

Have you ever received any type of office treatment by your family doctor, psychiatrist, internist,
psychologist, or therapist (medication, counseling, therapy) for any nervous condition, psychological, psychiatric, family, or marital problem? Yes _____ No _____ If yes, describe:

Year of Treatment	Treating Therapist/Physician	Diagnosis or Problem	Type of Treatment (e.g., Drugs, Therapy)

Have you ever intentionally overdosed yourself on drugs or medicines? Yes _____ No _____
If yes, describe: _____

Have you ever attempted to take your life? Yes _____ No _____ If yes, describe:
_____

Have you ever intentionally cut, burned, or disfigured yourself? Yes _____ No _____ If yes,
describe: _____

Did you set fires as a child? Yes _____ No _____

Did you harm or kill animals as a child? Yes _____ No _____

FAMILY HISTORY

Please check if any of these illnesses or acts have occurred in any of your parents, brother/sisters,
or children (do not list grandparents, aunts/uncles, or cousins).

_____High blood pressure		_____Nervous breakdown	
_____Thyroid illness		_____Mental illness/nerve problem	
_____Diabetes		_____Depression	
_____Cancer		_____Alcohol/drug problems	
_____Heart disease		_____Eating disorder (anorexia nervosa, bulimia)	
_____Lung disease		_____Attention deficit disorder	
_____Kidney disease		_____Learning disorder	

_____Liver or gastrointestinal disease   _____Killing another person

_____Seizures (epilepsy)   _____Child abuse

_____Neurological disease   _____Suicide

_____Alzheimer's disease   _____Violence toward others

_____Strokes   _____Spouse abuse

_____HIV or AIDS

If you checked any of the above, please explain which relatives had the illness or performed the violent act: _____

_____

If father is now alive, his age? _____ If mother is now alive, her age? _____

If a relative is dead, list what your father, mother, brothers/sisters, or child died of and their ages at death: _____

_____

SOCIAL HISTORY

Where were you born? _____

Date of birth: _____

Of your siblings, how many sisters? _____ brothers? _____ Where do you come in the family? (First child, last child, etc.) _____

What did your father do for a living? _____

What did your mother do for a living? _____

Did your family have enough money? _____Not enough money? _____Live in poverty? _____

Is your father living? _____ Year he died? _____ Your mother? _____Year she died? _____

Are (were) your parents divorced?_____ If yes, when? _____ How old were you at the time?

_____

Who raised you? _____ Did your parent(s) own your home? Yes _____ No _____

Was you home life happy? Yes _____ No _____ Abusive? Yes _____ No _____ Threatening? Yes _____ No _____. Hard on you? Yes _____ No _____ Make you depressed? Yes ___ No _____

Did your father abuse your mother? Yes _____ No _____ If yes, explain: _____

Have you ever been sexually abused? Yes _____ No _____ If yes, explain: _____

Have you ever been raped? Yes _____ No _____ If yes, explain: _____

Have you ever been physically abused? Yes _____ No _____ If yes, explain: _____

_____

Are you presently being sexually or physically abused by anyone? Yes _____ No _____ If yes, who? _____

Have you ever been violent to or harmed a person? Yes _____ No _____

Have you ever shot, stabbed, or beaten another person? Yes _____ No _____

Have you ever threatened to kill another person? Yes _____ No _____

Have you ever torn up property? Yes _____ No _____

Have you ever killed another person, even if by accident? Yes _____ No _____

Are there guns in your home? Yes _____ No _____ If yes, what type or caliber (e.g., .357 handgun, 12 gauge shotgun) _____

Have you ever been in legal trouble for your sexual behavior? Yes _____ No _____

Have you ever sexually abused or harassed a child or adult? Yes _____ No _____

Highest grade you completed in school? _____

If you did not finish high school, what was the reason you quit? _____

_____

_____

What were your grades in high school? _____ Did you require special education classes? Yes _____ No _____ In grade school or high school, did the teachers think you were hard to control or was it hard to get your attention? Yes _____No _____

If yes, explain: _____

_____

If you attended any college or trade school, list degree, diploma, date of graduation, and college/university, or trade school you attended:

Degree/Diploma/Major	Dates of Graduation	College/University/Trade School

How many times have you been married? _____

How many times have you been divorced? _____

Are you now: Divorced? _____ Married? _____

How long have you been divorced or married? _____

Please complete:

Marriage	Year Married	Year Divorced	Spouse's Name	Any Natural Children and Their Ages	Reason for Divorce
First marriage					
Second marriage					
Third marriage					
Fourth marriage					

How many natural children do you have? _____

How many stepchildren do you have? _____

How would you describe your marriage if you are presently married?_____

Good relationship _____ Bad relationship _____

Fair relationship _____ Terrible or abusive relationship _____

If you are not married but have a lover, describe your relationship:

Good _____ Fair _____ Bad _____ Terrible or abusive _____.

Describe your relationship with your children:

Close _____ Could be better _____ Distant _____ Poor _____.

If you do not have a relationship at this time, how do you feel about this?

Satisfied _____   Not satisfied and want a relationship _____

Lonely but OK _____   Very sad or lonely _____

LEGAL HISTORY

Have you ever been in prison or jail? Yes _____ No _____ If yes, where and when?

_____

_____

_____

Have you had any criminal felony or misdemeanor convictions, drug arrests, DUIs, or public intoxication arrests? Yes _____ No _____ If yes, fill in below:

Arrest Date	Charge(s)	Where (City or State)	Were You Convicted	Length of Time in Prison/Jail

Have you been involved in any lawsuits as either the plaintiff or defendant?

Yes _____ No_____ If yes, describe: _____

Has your spouse or anyone else, ever gotten a restraining order or emergency protective order against you? Yes _____ No _____ If yes, describe: _____

_____

Have you ever gotten a restraining order or emergency protective order against your spouse, or anyone else? Yes _____ No _____ If yes, describe: _____

_____

Have you ever been charged with spouse abuse, child abuse or neglect, or terroristic threatening? Yes _____ No _____ If yes, describe: _____

Have you ever filed a workers' compensation claim? Yes _____ No _____ If yes, what was (were) the work injury(ies)? _____

Have you ever been declared bankrupt? Yes _____ No _____

EMPLOYMENT/VOCATIONAL HISTORY

Employment status: (check one)

Full time _____ Part time _____ Not employed _____ Student _____ Retired _____

If not employed, reason you are not presently employed? _____

_____

If presently employed, who is your employer? _____

Employer address: _____

Describe your job duties: _____

Length of time on this employment: _____

If you are presently disabled, year of and reason for your disability: _____

_____

What are your present sources of all monthly income? _____

_____

Were you ever fired or asked to resign from employment? Yes _____ No _____

If yes, reason: _____

Have you ever threatened an employer or a coworker? Yes _____ No _____

Where is your spouse or housemate or partner presently employed? _____

_____

If you are not working, do you plan to return to work at anytime in the future?

Yes _____ No _____

List past employment (beginning with your most recent job):

Employer	Job Title	Start Date	Finish Date	Reason for Leaving	Other

MILITARY HISTORY

Have you ever tried to enter military service or a service academy (e.g., Naval Academy, West Point)? Yes _____ No _____

Were you ever turned down for military service? Yes _____ No _____

If you have had any military service, list below:

Branch of Service	Years Served	Rank at Time of Discharge	Type of Discharge	Job Duties

Were there any disciplinary actions against you? Yes _____ No _____

If yes, describe: _____

Were you ever in the brig or stockade? Yes _____ No _____

Where was your basic training? _____

Where was your advanced training? _____

If you ever served in a combat zone, list year and area: _____

_____

If wounded in military service, describe: _____

_____

Describe any military pension or disability you may receive: _____

REVIEW OF SYSTEMS

(CIRCLE THOSE SYMPTOMS PRESENT)

GENERAL: Fever, shaking, chills, change in appetite, loss in weight, gain in weight, fatigue, change in sleeping patterns, soaking night sweats
Explain any circled items. If you have lost or gained weight, how many pounds in the last three months?

_____
_____
_____

HEAD   Headache, changes in vision, double vision, blurred vision, eye pain,
EYES   excessive tearing, discharge from the eyes, changes in hearing, ringing in
EARS   ears, ear pain, discharge from ears, nosebleeds, odd odors, hoarseness,
NOSE   dental pain, sore tongue, sore throat, mouth sores, trouble swallowing
THROAT: Explain any circled items: _____

_____
_____
_____

CHEST: Cough, sputum production, shortness of breath, wheezing, blood in sputum, abnormal chest x-ray, positive TB test, lump(s) in breast, nipple discharge, nipple bleeding, breast pain
Explain any circled items: _____

_____
_____
_____

HEART: Chest pain with exercise, shortness of breath while walking, shortness of breath upon lying down, heart murmur, rheumatic fever, shortness of breath that wakes you up at night, swelling in legs, fainting

Explain any circled items:_____
_____
_____
_____
_____

STOMACH: Change in appetite, nausea, vomiting, blood in vomit, dark brown vomit

BOWEL: Diarrhea, constipation, change in stool size, blood in stool, dark black tarry colored stool, food intolerance, trouble swallowing, heartburn, indigestion, laxative use, excessive gas, abdomen pain, weight loss, weight gain

Explain any circled items: _____
_____
_____
_____

URINARY,   Trouble starting urination, excessive urination, dribbling of urine, pain upon
GENITAL: urination, blood in urine, excessive urination after going to bed, unable to hold urine, bedwetting, sores on genitals

Explain any circled items: _____
_____
_____
_____

FEMALE: Menstrual irregularity, premenstrual distress, menopause symptoms, excessive female bleeding

Explain any circled items: _____
_____
_____
_____

MENTAL: Do you have a present plan to kill yourself? Yes _____ No _____

Do you have a plan to kill someone else? Yes _____ No _____

Depression, sadness, nervousness, panic, thoughts of suicide, poor concentration, loss of memory, too happy, word-finding difficulty, confusion, inability to know month/year, hearing voices, seeing things, paranoid thoughts, irritability, excessive anger, arguing, crying for no reason, trouble thinking, flashbacks, thoughts of killing another person, counting things, checking things, afraid of germs, afraid to touch doorknobs, wash hands more than 10 times daily, take more than two baths or showers daily

Explain any circled items: _____
_____
_____

NEUROLOGIC: Blackouts, seizures, double vision, partial blindness, headaches, numbness, tingling, weakness, poor balance, shaking or tremors, abnormal movements of face or body, poor coordination, paralysis, loss of reflexes, pain

Explain any circled items: _____

_____

_____

_____

MUSCLES   Muscle spasms, joint pain, bone disorders, difficulty walking, difficulty sitting,
SKELETAL: difficulty using hands, difficulty bending, difficulty lifting

Explain any circled items: _____

_____

_____

_____

SLEEP: How many hours do you sleep at night? _____.

How many days weekly do you nap? _____.

Cannot fall asleep, cannot stay asleep, wake up too early, fall asleep anytime, night terrors, nightmares, sleep walking, restless legs before sleep, cannot stay awake during or while sitting, severe snoring that bothers others, choking during sleep, cannot stay awake to drive, others have observed you to stop breathing during sleep, fall or stagger if angry or laugh, hear things when falling asleep or waking up, paralyzed for short time after waking up

Explain any circled items: _____

_____

_____

_____

SEXUAL: Men: Cannot get erection, cannot ejaculate, ejaculate too soon, no sexual desire, partner does not meet my needs

Women: Cannot lubricate, cannot have orgasm, no sexual desire, partner does not meet my needs

How many times per month do you engage in sexual activity with another person or a spouse?

_____

Explain any circled items: _____

_____

_____

_____

HIV: Have you been tested for HIV? Yes _____ No _____

Results if tested: Positive _____ Negative _____

AUTHORIZATION INFORMATION

I authorize Dr. Pleasant, MD, to examine, test and treat me. (If you are under 18 years of age, your parent or guardian must sign this form.)

_____

Signature

_____

Date

I authorize Dr. Pleasant, MD, to send a copy of this evaluation to the person or agency who requested me to be examined or to those parties involved in my treatment.

_____
Signature

_____
Date

I authorize the licensed or certified psychologists consulting my doctor to test me psychologically.

_____
Signature

_____
Date

By my signature, I certify all statements I answered on this questionnaire are true and accurate.

_____
Signature

_____
Date

If this form was filled out by someone other than you, please give name:

_____

Relationship to you (spouse, friend, parent, guardian, etc.) _____

TAKING THE ADULT BRAIN INJURY HISTORY

POSTTRAUMA SYMPTOMS AND TREATMENT

The reader will note that this book follows a classical schema of reviewing domains of neuropsychological function. Table 3.1 reviews those domains, and each one should be individually assessed to determine if there are important symptoms to report from each neuropsychological domain. For instance, in Table 3.1 the reader can see that attention is the first neuropsychological domain to query. In an effort to determine other areas of cerebral disorder, the examiner should question the patient regarding speech and language, memory and orientation, visuospatial or constructional ability, executive function, and the more classical psychiatric disorders, respectively. A review of treatment following injury should be undertaken. This will generally include various

---

TABLE 3.1

The Adult Neuropsychiatric Symptom History following Brain Trauma

- Chief complaint
- Are there problems with
  Attention
  Speech and language
  Memory or orientation
  Visuospatial or constructional ability
  Executive function
  Affect and mood
  Thought processing or perception
  Risk to self or others

---

psychotropic medications and various efforts at cognitive rehabilitation. It is important to remember other aspects of injury that may have occurred concomitant with TBI. The patient who has sustained severe trauma may also have numerous orthopedic injuries, abdominal injuries, cardiac contusion, or other substantial organ injuries that may have a bearing on the person's ability to rehabilitate following TBI.

Taking a neuropsychiatric history directly from a person who has sustained significant brain trauma can be a challenge. Obviously, amnesia may play a role by impeding inquiry. If individuals have a substantial posttraumatic amnesia, they probably will be unable to tell the examiner salient features of their hospital stay and rehabilitation. Therefore, this is another reason for critical review of medical records, as this may be the only way the neuropsychiatric examiner can obtain and verify treatment information.

Attention

Recall from Chapter 2 that sensory information cannot be processed by a person if the individual cannot attend to stimuli. If attention is severely impaired, it will impact the entire neuropsychiatric examination. Recall that in most neuropsychiatric examinations, only auditory, visual, and occasionally tactile attention are measured. There is no practical reason to measure the level of attention to odors or tastes, but smell detection is part of the neurological examination (Chapter 4). The individual should be asked about fluctuating awareness or difficulty paying attention to what is heard or what is seen. Traumatic brain injury may affect differentially auditory versus visual attention. The individual may have more difficulty paying attention to what is heard than what is seen, or the opposite may be true. Probing the details of attentional deficits depends on the lifestyle and background of the individual being examined. Attentional deficits for a Wall Street executive require a different inquiry than the attentional deficits of a farmer or lobster fisherman. Therefore, the examiner should use creativity in inquiring about deficits of attention, and the exploration should follow the kinds of stimuli that the individual is likely to experience on a daily basis within his occupation or lifestyle. From Chapter 2, fatigue and hypersomnolence were explored. These have to be considered in the differential aspects of attentional deficits. If the individual is extraordinarily fatigued or hypersomnolent as a result of TBI, these factors alone may account for fluctuating awareness and attention rather than discreet injury to the attentional apparatus.

Once the lifestyle and occupational background of the individual has been determined briefly, the examiner then should focus specific questions to elicit information about the person's attentional operation when performing tasks. For instance, for the executive, specific questions about ability to pay attention auditorily in a meeting when a number of persons are speaking simultaneously could be important. Can the executive visually focus on a laptop computer, PDA, Blackberry, or written material? Can a college student auditorily attend to an instructor in a classroom? Can that student maintain attention at a college sporting event during the cacophony of noises and speech? Can the college student pay attention while typing assignments on a laptop computer? For the farmer or skilled tradesman, the examination should probably focus more on visual attention than auditory attention. Can the electrician pay attention to schematic diagrams? Can the cattle farmer read and follow a herd report? Can a lobster fisherman pay attention to the radar or sonar? The reader can see the logic behind this, and it is not possible to describe every possible lifestyle or occupation in this book. The creativity and life experience of the examiner will determine the quality of the history taken from an individual person.

While forming questions regarding history, it is important to remember the differential aspects of attention. For instance, focused attention to a specific auditory or visual stimulus is quite different than the longitudinal attention (vigilance) required for observing the chalkboard, LCD screen, or listening to a 50 min lecture regarding differential calculus. Simply put, attention can be instantaneous or it can require concentration (vigilance). With vision, tracking is another element of attention that is more important to visual input than to auditory input in most instances. Visual tracking is an important component of reading, and the tracking must occur over time. Auditory attention also has a point source or a longitudinal quality. Immediate attention to a fire truck siren is one thing, while maintaining auditory vigilance to a lecture is another. Finer questioning is required to pinpoint specifically the precise disturbance in the attentional matrix. For instance, the brain-injured adult may experience a slowing of information processing as a component of attentional deficit. On the other hand, attentional deficits may present as impersistence, perseveration, distractibility, or an inability to inhibit immediate but inappropriate responses (lack of executive attention).[10] These fine points of inquiry into attentional deficits may be beyond the scope of what a severely brain-injured person can self-detect and report. Therefore, it may be necessary to take collateral information. Also, particularly in those injured in the right brain, neglect to a particular auditory or visual stimulus may occur. The individual may not be aware of the neglect, which is the usual presentation to the examiner, or the individual may have a component of anosognosia complicating his ability to provide historical information. Many brain-injured persons with a working memory (attentional component of memory) deficit may be unaware that they perseverate and repeat themselves to family members or to others. If the attentional deficits are extreme, the inability to self-monitor causes the person to be unable to report to the examiner specific attentional deficits. It is important to ask the person if it takes longer to react or if one's performance has slipped while performing tasks that require speed.[11,12]

Table 3.2 lists simple screening questions that may be used to detect attentional deficits by way of history. These are useful if the examiner remembers the caveat noted above. That is, questions regarding attention must be specific to the lifestyle of the individual or important historical information will be missed. However, a simple question such as, "Are you thinking slower than you used to?" may be important. Individuals with attentional deficits often feel as if the environment or others are moving faster than they are, and this is a common presentation with a reduction in attention and a reduction in mental processing speed. These two separate domains can be parsed out more accurately by techniques noted in Chapter 6. Tromp and Mulder have noted that memory activation is a critical problem for many brain-injured patients, and the lack of activation of memory may cause the individual to feel as if he is performing more slowly than before his injury.[12] This differentiation also will require some of the techniques noted in Chapter 6 to detect.

Speech and Language

Speech is the motor manifestation of language, and it is produced by the articulating muscles of the face and oropharynx in concert with airflow produced through the vocal cords and lips during exhalation. On the other hand, language is the symbolic representation of syntax and grammatical elements of oral and written expression. Language drives speech. As noted in Chapter 4, difficulty articulating may be associated with specific brainstem or cranial nerve injuries as well as certain portions of cerebral function. The examiner should ask the brain-injured person whether difficulty is noted in articulating or pronouncing words. While this is a subject for the mental status examination, obviously much of the mental status examination will be performed while taking a history.

TABLE 3.2

Screening Questions for Attentional Deficits

- Can you pay attention while others are speaking?
- Can you concentrate when reading a magazine or book?
- Can you repeatedly point and click when using the computer?
- Are others speaking too fast for you?
- Do others say you repeat yourself?
- Can you follow the story line in a television program or movie?

Therefore, articulation is best determined by listening to the person's speech and determining whether the language is fluent (flows well). The examiner should focus upon listening for discreet problems of either articulation or language during a portion of the historical examination. Since self-monitoring may be impaired, skillful questions may be necessary to cue individuals that their articulation is impaired. The examiner can ask if the person notices difficulty repeating prayers in his place of worship or if impairment while reading aloud is noted. Often, the best information regarding lack of articulatory ability or language impairment comes from collateral sources of others who live with the individual or hear the individual's speech patterns on a daily basis.

When presented with a potential language disorder following TBI, other causes of abnormal communication must be excluded. First, it is necessary to exclude a developmental or congenital language disorder, which can occur as an isolated language dysfunction or as part of a more general condition associated with mental retardation syndromes. This can be detected during the collection of information regarding developmental history. Second, one must exclude motor speech disorders. These disturb only spoken language output, and comprehension of spoken and written language remains intact. Third, disorders of language content secondary to psychiatric disorders must be excluded. This could prove particularly difficult in the psychotic patient who sustains a superimposed TBI. In psychosis, the mechanics of speech and language are normal, but the underlying thought process or manipulation of language concepts is abnormal. The psychotic patient may articulate well-constructed sentences and display normal word choice and grammar, but the content of the language is bizarre or illogical.[13] By taking a careful history of the antecedent uses of language by the patient and the developmental history, it should be easy to separate in most instances language disorders following TBI from those associated with developmental issues or more classic psychiatric disorders.

Simple screening questions for language disorder following TBI can be constructed by focusing upon the simple elements of language function. Asking the patient to name, repeat, read, and write will screen for most potential language dysfunctions. The two commonest language disorders following TBI are difficulty with naming or word-finding difficulty. Several questions can be asked regarding word finding. How difficult is it for the person to find words when he wishes to speak with someone? Does the person use the wrong word or misplace an initial sound in a word? Is there confusion with meaning of words? Does the individual find himself speaking slower or with more effort than before the injury? As noted in Chapter 4, the examiner will be on notice as to fluency merely by speaking with the individual. Speech is "fluent" if the phrase length and melody are appropriate and "nonfluent" if phrase length is less than four words and the speech is halting, effortful, or dysarthric. Anterior brain lesions in the dominant hemisphere are more likely to result in nonfluent language, whereas posterior lesions tend to result in fluent but paraphasic speech (phonemic misstatements or misuse of word meaning).

Detection of language errors in locations other than the dominant cerebral hemisphere by history alone may be difficult. For instance, injury in the medial portions of the frontal lobes can affect the initiation and maintenance of speech. These also play a significant role in attentional and emotional influences upon speech. Damage in these areas will not cause a pure language disorder but rather varying degrees of difficulty in the initiation of speech, or it may even produce mutism.[14] Since the drive to communicate is no longer present, the individual may not be able to tell the examiner of the reduction in speech rate or of the difficulty in producing speech. Table 3.3 outlines language-deficit screening questions.

It is important to discuss with patients whether they have had a change in the ability to communicate with others, particularly in the ability to obtain meaning from the communication with others. As the reader will see in Chapters 4 and 6, the dominant hemisphere controls the expression and reception of symbolic language, but the emotional coloring (affective prosody) is supplied by the nondominant hemisphere. In most individuals, the nondominant side is within the right hemisphere, and the prosody of language and the kinesics (motor gestures) of language constitute the paralinguistic portions of language reception and expression. It may be useful to

---

TABLE 3.3
Screening Questions for Language Deficits

- Can you find words while speaking?
- Can you name common objects?
- Has your ability to communicate changed?
- Have others said you speak differently?
- Can you repeat prayers or songs?

---

ask the patient if anyone has noticed a change in the pitch, intonation, tempo, stresses, cadence, and loudness of the individual's language since brain injury (how it sounds to others).[15] Kinesics refers to the limb, truncal, and facial movements that accompany language output. The gesturing and facial expression associated with language modulates the verbal message being communicated.[16] Since impaired communication is one of the major variables that will determine whether a brain-injured patient can return to functional life or to the workplace, the examiner should ask whether or not the patient has noted difficulties expressing ideas and whether it has been brought to their attention that there has been a change in facial expression. Oftentimes, the "flatness" described in brain-injured patients is actually an element of aprosodia or dysprosody (an impairment of the production, comprehension, and repetition of affective melody without disrupting the propositional elements of language).[17] The detection of aprosodia or dysprosody requires a significant amount of skill; more discussion about this matter is presented in Chapters 4 and 6.

Memory and Orientation

The examiner will have determined orientation during the mental status examination and during formal questioning of the individual. It is usually not practical to ask significant questions about orientation, as a truly disoriented person often is not aware that he or she is disoriented. It is probably simpler to ask, "Do you often find that you cannot remember the month, the year, or your location in the city where you live?" This will provide sufficient information to determine whether a more detailed examination of orientation is required. Thus, disorientation is not a common complaint after TBI, but memory difficulty is probably the commonest complaint following head trauma.[18] The reader may wish to refer back to Figure 2.1 in Chapter 2 to refresh information as to Squire's schema of memory. Questions regarding memory function should focus primarily on issues of declarative memory rather than procedural memory. In most instances, as seen in Chapter 2, procedural memory is changed little, if at all, following TBI, whereas episodic memory (autobiographical) and semantic (factual) memory are much more likely to be impaired following TBI. Further inquiry can be made whether individuals can listen to what they are told and retain the information, or if they have to write a list. The writing of lists takes the place of converting episodic memory to short-term storage or long-term storage; the list replaces these storage portions of memory and becomes a memory device external to the brain. Individuals with episodic memory impairment cannot retain the information long enough to convert it to storage. Many patients with episodic memory impairment following TBI lose confidence in themselves to remember and become almost slaves to diaries or notebooks. In fact, many TBI patients are instructed in rehabilitation units to acquire and use such notebooks to assist them both with rehabilitation and to compensate for chronic memory dysfunction.

Questions regarding impairment of long-term memory are basically used to determine whether or not the patient is able to learn information. Long-term memory refers to information that has been encoded and further consolidated to a degree that is sufficient to permit that information to be held in the brain. As has been previously noted, it is often useful to ask the patient about anterograde and retrograde amnesia. In taking the neuropsychiatric history following TBI, the most important elements to be determined are whether or not the person has impairment of anterograde memory (however, retrograde amnesia may have forensic importance). Anterograde memory refers to learning and memory that occurs after damage to the brain. As noted in Chapter 2, Ribot proposed that a temporal gradient in retrograde memory can be observed, and patients have better recall the farther back in time events were acquired before TBI. It is possible, although extremely rare, that the examiner may confront a case of focal retrograde amnesia with normal or near-normal antero-grade memory.[19] However, the major reference regarding focal retrograde amnesia is Kapur,[19] and these cases primarily represent various forms of brain disease, not TBI. To the author's knowledge, there are no credible references in the medical literature demonstrating that TBI will produce a focal retrograde amnesia in the absence of anterograde amnesia (an important point to remember during forensic examinations).

Declarative memory is primarily limbic based, and therefore subject to substantial disruption owing to the frontal physical injury bias that occurs to the brain during trauma. Questioning a patient regarding episodic memory can be focused if the examiner remembers that episodic memory is primarily autobiographical and unconsciously catalogs what the individual experiences while moving through life. Thus, after TBI, questions should be framed regarding personal events that the examiner is aware the individual may have experienced since TBI. A general discussion about what the patient remembers regarding a recent birthday, death, or the trip to the examiner's office may provide insight into the functioning of episodic memory. It is useful to remember that episodic information is actively remembered, while semantic information is only known.[20] If the neuropsychiatric examiner has a family member present, by speaking briefly with the family member, enough biographical information since the TBI can be gleaned to frame further questions to assist in the possible discovery of episodic memory impairment. Specific measures of memory are included in most memory batteries and are a component of the Wechsler Memory Scale-III and the WAIS-III IQ batteries (see Chapter 6).

When the examiner focuses on semantic memory, the ordinary and simple memory questions posed during the mental status examination will provide a general screening of the intactness of this component of declarative memory (see Chapter 4). The general questions learned during psychiatric residency will suffice: "Who is the president of the United States?" "What is the capital of this state?" "Who is the mayor of your town?" "Who attacked the World Trade Center?" Another simple statement regarding declarative memory is that semantic memory is used to know the present, while episodic memory is used for remembering the past.[21] The examiner will have to be somewhat skillful in constructing memory screening questions during the neuropsychiatric history. Obviously, the questions have to be relevant to the person's life, where the person is in life according to age, and consistent with the person's life experience and level of education. For a 19 year old college student, questioning can focus upon the ability to remember classroom assignments and social functions in college. For an individual who is not a student or has limited education, questions can focus upon what the individual reads or what is presently available on television relative to the person's social experience. Current events are frequently useful as fodder for developing questions. However, there will be overlap in using this material between episodic memory and semantic memory. Since family members and others often comment to an individual following TBI that their memory seems poor, it is wise to ask the patient if others have commented that their memory is weak.

For specific occupations, some screening questions regarding procedural memory may be necessary. For the individual who drives a city bus, flies an airplane, operates heavy machinery, or is engaged in other motor-skilled labors, procedural memory questioning may be required. Generally, the individual will not report defects in these areas unless the brain injury has been quite severe or there was a penetrating brain injury. Almost 100 years ago, Schneider[22] noted that an amnesic person could learn to solve a jigsaw puzzle even if the person could not remember new episodes of the puzzle. Probably the most famous memory case in medical history, H.M., was able

---

TABLE 3.4

Screening Questions for Memory Deficits

- Can you keep track of dates and important events?
- Do you need to keep lists or a journal?
- Can you remember what you read or see on television?
- How did you get here today?
- Tell me how you will return to your home.
- Have you lost memory for any skills (e.g., recipes, computer tasks)?

---

to learn new motor skills without noticeable difficulty, such as those involved in a rotor pursuit task.[23] Most individuals who will demonstrate procedural memory deficits have sustained injury to the upper brainstem or basal ganglia rather than limbic systems. Persons who sustain lesions within the basal ganglia generally will show motor signs associated with procedural memory loss.[24] Suggested simple memory screening questions are displayed in Table 3.4.

Visuospatial and Constructional Ability

Dysfunction in the areas of visuospatial perception and constructional ability are associated with complex visual processing. The neuropsychiatric examiner should be aware that if defects in these areas are present, examination beyond the neuropsychiatric may be required including neuropsychological, neuroimaging, or neuroophthalmological. Patients who have alteration of visual ability because of lesions in the occipital striate cortex or optic radiations may have remnants of visual function even though they claim blindness. Detection of these difficulties is probably beyond the scope of most neuropsychiatric examiners and usually requires consultation from a neuroophthalmologist. Other visual analysis errors can occur, which also may require consultation. These include disorders of color perception, the presence of visual agnosia, disorders of face perception (prosopagnosia), disorders of motion perception (akinetopsia), disorders of spatial perception (Bálint's syndrome), and topographagnosia (getting lost in familiar surroundings). Disorders of color are described as cerebral dyschromatopsia. These individuals see the world in shades of gray. If color perception is present, it will be faded or reduced in its range of hues. Patients with visual agnosia cannot recognize or remember what they have seen before, and they cannot name a previously familiar but unrecognized object; they show no knowledge of its use, context, or history. Patients with prosopagnosia cannot recognize the faces of familiar people or learn new faces. A patient with akinetopsia is very difficult to detect. Patients with motion perception deficits from unilateral lesions are either asymptomatic or have more subtle complaints such as "feeling disturbed by visually cluttered moving scenes" and trouble judging the speed and direction of cars.[25] Bálint's syndrome consists of a loosely associated triad of simultanagnosia, optic ataxia, and ocular motor apraxia. Patients with this disorder have deficits in distributing spatial attention, and they cannot pay attention to more than a few objects at a time. They cannot tolerate attentionally demanding visual search tasks. They often can perceive individual elements of a complex scene but cannot integrate the scene (simultanagnosia). Optic ataxia is the inability to judge the spatial position and distance of objects. Ocular motor apraxia is the inability to direct gaze voluntarily. The diagnosis of Bálint's syndrome is probably best left to neuroophthalmologists. Topographagnosia describes patients who get lost within their own hometown. The defect causing this disorder is usually within the ventral or dorsal visual association cortices. Ventral lesions usually have associated prosopagnosia and achromatopsia. Further review of these visual defects can be found in Barton.[26]

The purpose in presenting this complex material regarding visual defects is not to confuse the neuropsychiatrist or neuropsychologist. It is helpful to know of these disorders so that one can ask intelligent questions regarding visuospatial function.

Topographic orientation is easy to query. This defect generally reflects impairment in visuospatial memory, and simple questions as to the person's ability to locate their surroundings in a city, find a room at home, or use a map will usually delineate the presence or absence of the problem. Geographic disorientation is not infrequent following moderate to severe head injury, and it occurs in patients with both bilateral and unilateral posterior cerebral lesions.[27,28] With regard to visual agnosia, questions can be framed for the patient or family as to whether or not the individual can recognize objects seen before. Questions to elicit the presence of prosopagnosia are more complicated. Many times persons with prosopagnosia are not aware of the defect. In its purest form, a husband may not be able to recognize the face of his wife and may become delusional, thinking she has been replaced by a usurper. Lesions are almost always bilateral when prosopagnosia extends beyond the acute phase of TBI.[29] With regard to color vision, while taking the history, the patient should be asked if he has noted differences in the ability to perceive colors, name colors, or associate colors with specific items, such as the color of blood or the color of a banana. Disorders of motion perception are simple to detect in a person who hunts. The eye–hand coordination necessary to hit a moving target with a gun quickly displays itself if akinetopsia is present. For nonhunters, questions as to the patient's ability to pursue movements by eye should be simple and straightforward.

Constructional ability can be assessed by asking if the patient has difficulty keeping handwriting on the line or if the patient can write well without using lined paper. The Clock Writing Test is a simple bedside screening tool to detect lack of constructional ability. The Judgment of Line Orientation Test (see Chapter 6) is useful for detection of visuospatial dysfunction.[30] If the patient cannot complete this task well, this usually clinically correlates with lesions in the right posterior brain.[31] Chapter 4 will delineate bedside screening tests to detect constructional difficulties. Table 3.5 contains suggested screening questions for visuospatial/constructional deficits.

Executive Function

The prefrontal and frontal cortex of the human separates us from other mammals on this planet. The multimodal convergence in cortical association areas within these structures points to three areas of behavioral mediation: long-term knowledge storage, learning and short-term representational knowledge, and executive functions and self-regulation.[32] The prefrontal cortex has neurons that appear to be associated with long-term motor-related knowledge underlying skilled movements, by manual coordination and speech. Moreover, the prefrontal cortex is believed to be a storehouse for acquired knowledge used during decision making and adaptation. Grafman suggests that the prefrontal cortex is specialized for acquisition and storage of more complex types of knowledge and operations than the more general and routine knowledge associated with the temporal, parietal, and occipital cortices.[33] With regard to learning and short-term representational knowledge, the prefrontal cortex influences learning, as it is related to attention, analytical processing, and working memory. For instance, Tulving et al.[34] have demonstrated by functional imaging studies that normal individuals

---

TABLE 3.5

Screening Questions for Visuospatial/Constructional Deficits

- Can you find your way alone to an office within a building?
- Can you name the color of a banana, blood, or a crow?
- Can you keep your handwriting on a line?
- Can you draw objects?
- Can you describe the routes you will take to return home?

selectively activate the left prefrontal cortex during verbal learning or encoding verbal material, but the right prefrontal cortex is activated in verbal retrieval processes. These functions are thought to be compliments of the hippocampus and mediotemporal lobes during memory consolidation processes. It is observed that patients with frontal lobe damage generally do not demonstrate clinical amnesias such as seen following mediotemporal lobe damage, but they develop inefficiencies and disorganization as they learn and retrieve memory processes. The term of art for this is "forgetting to remember." Physicians have seen this in persons who keep lists after TBI but then forget to look at the list in order to remember.

The other important contribution of the frontal lobes to memory concerns working memory. As noted previously, working memory is an attentional component of memory, and it is active during the temporary and changing representations of knowledge that permit us to keep new information active or in mind. We then use these representations for comprehension, problem solving, sequencing, and multitasking. Working memory dysfunction is often detected during executive function examinations as noted in Chapter 6. Functional imaging studies have demonstrated consistent evidence that the prefrontal cortex, in combination with the posterior sensory association areas, becomes active during working memory tasks.[35]

Behavioral neurologists and neuropsychiatrists correlate the prefrontal cortex and other frontal lobe components with the long-term and short-term storage and representational use of knowledge. These disciplines also recognize executive functions and self-regulation as a portion of frontal lobe capacity. Neuropsychologists are mostly in agreement with the positions of neuropsychiatry and behavioral neurology, but they tend to describe executive functions in a more dynamic descriptive sense. For instance, Lezak describes executive functions by four main components: (1) volition, (2) planning, (3) purposive action, and (4) affective performance.[36] Stuss and Benson have taken a more neurological approach and describe the behavioral characteristics of executive function as anticipation, goal selection, preplanning, monitoring, and use of feedback.[37] More recently, Eslinger and Chakara[32] describe executive functions as diverse psychological processes that

- Control the activation and inhibition of response sequences that are guided by internal neural representations (e.g., biologic needs, somatic states, emotions, goals, mental models)
- Meet a balance of immediate situational, short-term, and long-term goals and demands
- Span physical–environmental, cognitive, behavioral, emotional, and social domains of functioning

Clearly, these more recent descriptors are far more complex and expansive as behavioral models than those purported earlier. Regardless of which orientation one follows in terms of the exact constituents of executive function, it is simple to ask questions about these particular domains of patients. Keep in mind that persons being examined may be unaware of their deficits, or they may be unable to sufficiently self-monitor or provide accurate history, and collateral sources may be required. However, one can explore volition or drive by asking the patient about any changes in motivation or ability to stay interested. Planning may be assessed by inquiry into the person's post-injury ability, such as the ability to plan a dinner, to plan a school event for his child, to plan a course of a study if a student, or to plan something as simple as a game or birthday party. These areas of life function would come under "effective performance" as defined by Lezak,[36] or "self-monitoring and use of feedback" as defined by Stuss and Benson.[37] Further areas of inquiry regarding self-monitoring and self-regulation include asking about impulsiveness, aggressiveness, and the ability to change direction if a plan is not going forward as intended. This is important as many persons with TBI and executive dysfunction are unable to make moment-to-moment adjustments or course changes as required by the vagaries of life. Screening questions for executive deficits are outlined in Table 3.6. Also, the reader can refer to Chapter 2 to review again the three broad types of frontal lobe syndrome and formulate historical questions to inquire about the

---

TABLE 3.6
Screening Questions for Executive Deficits

- Could you plan a party if you wished?
- Has your motivation or interest changed?
- Can you control aggressive or angry impulses?
- Are you as creative as you used to be?
- Are you less able to control your emotions?
- Do you have difficulty controlling your sexual impulses?

---

potential of these behaviors. If significant executive dysfunction appears to be present in the person following TBI, collateral information can be most important in assisting the examiner to delineate the extent of potential executive dysfunction.

Obtaining the History of Affective and Mood Changes

Risk factors for the development of psychiatric illness after TBI include the premorbid personality predisposition of the person, the presence of a history of psychiatric illness before injury, the concomitant presence of cognitive impairment following TBI, and premorbid low levels of formal education and social functioning.[38] Interestingly, there is some evidence that focal lesions of left brain versus right brain may modify in some fashion how affective and mood changes are expressed by a patient after TBI. These so-called focal differences of affective expression have been controversial. However, in reviewing all the data available, there is a suggestion that right hemisphere injury is dominant in causing persons to be emotionally indifferent following TBI. Moreover, the research data to present indicates that it is too simple to consider this lack of emotional expression to be simply a consequence of a defect of emotional communication. Research has shown that right brain-damaged patients are consistently impaired in recognizing emotions expressed through tone of voice, in the identification of facial emotional expressions, and in the ability to express emotions through facial movements or with the prosodic (melody) contours of speech.[39] The best evidence for a relationship between cerebral hemisphere localization and affect has been provided by the studies of poststroke depression with lesions of the left frontal cortex. However, these studies probably are not representative of TBI patients with primarily left hemisphere lesions. Most of the stroke work has been done by Robinson et al.,[40] but to the best of the author's knowledge, there is no consistent evidence in the TBI literature that lesions following TBI preferential to the left hemisphere are more important for emotional regulation than those more focal to the right hemisphere.

It is not unusual for patients following TBI to become extremely labile in emotions. They may demonstrate fluctuating mood, extreme tearfulness, and significant lability of emotional expression while with the examiner. It is thought that some of these difficulties may result from trauma to the amygdala, as this anatomical structure plays a crucial role in modulating the neural impact of sensory stimuli. The amygdala places an emotional valence upon a sensory stimulus, and the valence determines the strength of the input to the individual. Direct damage to the amygdala can produce states of hypoemotionality in humans.[41] While reviewing mood with the patient, recall that mood is the subjective experience of emotions by the patient, whereas affect is the external manifestation of mood that can be observed by the examiner. This distinction should help the examiner in forming questions. For instance, it is worthwhile to ask patients if they have noticed difficulties controlling their emotions, or if they have felt depressed, sad, or irritable. It is appropriate to follow *DSM-IV-TR* formats for the questioning associated with mood changes following TBI. As noted in Chapter 2, classical major depressive disorders or bipolar syndromes can occur following TBI. Thus, inquiries can be made as to whether the normal diurnal variation of mood is present, as this is commonly seen with major depression. Following TBI, the diurnal variation of depression commonly seen with classical major depression may not be present. Moreover, a report of depression following TBI may be associated with lethargy, as discussed in Chapter 2. This can be confusing to the examiner, as lethargy is often a component of depression associated with bipolar illness, but following TBI, lethargy is a common physical manifestation of brain injury and may covary with the depressive syndromes seen following TBI. If the neuropsychiatric examiner is seeing the individual years after the TBI, recall that recent longitudinal studies of brain injury in military veterans indicate that chronic mood changes following TBI may persist for decades.[42] This is pointed out because some clinicians may not see a mood disorder until years after a TBI, and they may miss its relation to the original brain injury.

As is standard while taking any good psychiatric history, it is best after listening to open-ended discourse from the patient to then ask some direct screening questions regarding mood. One simple formula is to ask persons if they have noticed any change in their mood or how they feel. Asking them if they have been uncomfortable, tense, overly vigilant, or sad is appropriate. It is particularly important to look for dysphoric mood, and patients should be asked if they have noticed unpleasant or negative mood states or a sense of feeling low or blue. On the other hand, since mood can be discordant between observed affects, it is also important to ask patients if they have noted elevations in mood, increased intensity of feelings, or feelings of aggression, anger, irritability, or anxiety. Table 3.7 lists common inquiries of affective and mood changes.

The issues of affect and mood are discussed in more detail in Chapter 4. In neuropsychiatrically intact individuals, affect remains congruent with the mood state. Neuropsychiatric disorders following brain injury can disconnect affect from mood and disrupt a person's ability to effectively and accurately communicate their prevailing mood. Some persons with mood changes following TBI develop alexithymia. This term describes a person who cannot assign descriptors for emotions and cannot use the vocabulary necessary to describe emotions.

Affective dysregulation can occur following TBI and produce pathological crying or laughing. This has been termed emotional incontinence or pseudobulbar affect. Affective dysregulation of the pseudobulbar type is relatively infrequent following TBI, but it has been reported to occur in approximately 5% of cases.[43] Patients who describe this unusual form of affective incontinence experience episodes of involuntary crying or laughing that may occur many times during the day and can be provoked by trivial stimuli which are not sentimental. The response is stereotyped, uncontrollable, and is not associated with a persistent change in prevailing mood, such as noted in more classic forms of major depression. This disorder must be distinguished from affective lability. This differs from the affective dysregulation of pseudobulbar affect in that both affective expression and experience are episodically dysregulated. The precipitating stimulus is much more likely to be sentimental. The patient will describe to the examiner that it is easier for them to control affective lability. Patients with pathological crying or laughing generally cannot control the behavior. Jorge and Robinson have noticed a 1 year prevalence of affective lability of 12% following TBI.[44]

Alterations of mood can be the only neuropsychiatric finding in a person following TBI. On the other hand, TBI can present with substantial cognitive disorders, which can be complicated further

---

TABLE 3.7

Screening Questions for Affective and Mood Changes

- Has your mood changed since your injury?
- Do you ever feel sad or possibly too happy?
- Have you been nervous, easily startled, or tense?
- Do you relive the injury in your mind?
- Do you have nightmares about the injury?
- Do certain events cause you to relive the injury?

by the contribution of abnormal mood to cognitive dysfunction. Depression very likely coexists with memory disturbance in a person who has sustained a TBI. Therefore, while the examiner is questioning about mood, it is important to listen for complaints of symptoms of cognitive importance.

The History of Thought Processing

Early in the history of psychiatry, thought disorders were divided into a functional versus organic dichotomy. This is no longer considered appropriate, and many psychiatric experts now divide thought disorders into primary (e.g., manic episode due to bipolar I disorder) and secondary (e.g., substance-induced mania due to steroids). Secondary thought disorders are common during psychiatric consultation in a general hospital and frequently are associated with delirium, dementia, and substance-induced mental disorders. Primary thought disorders are generally confined to the classic psychiatric syndromes of schizophrenia, mania, and major depression with psychosis. The thought disorder of TBI would be in the secondary category. Patients with primary thought disorders usually are younger and have no related medical illness, no clouding of consciousness, and no disorientation. They generally have a positive psychiatric history for a major psychiatric illness. For the TBI patient, there is generally no evidence of primary psychiatric illness producing a disorder of thought, and the problems of thinking are a direct outcome of disordered brain function as a result of TBI.[45]

While evaluating thought processing, it is important to look at other components associated with thought disorders. These include disorders of perception such as illusions, hallucinations, delusions, and ideas of reference. An attempt to explore issues of judgment and insight may be necessary as well during this component of history taking. However, to question a person about how he thinks is a difficult matter. It can be a particularly difficult matter in the post-TBI person who has sufficient impairment to interfere with thinking or self-monitoring skills. This person may not be able to perceive alterations of thinking or alterations of self-monitoring, particularly if the person has any elements of neglect or anosognosia. To explore thinking following TBI, it may be useful to ask patients if they have been addled or have found it difficult to think. Further inquiry can be made to determine if their ideas are not connected or they cannot find thoughts while scanning for them in their minds. Since the thought disorders that occur following TBI most likely arise from structurally or functionally based neurologic dysfunction,[46] multiple neural systems may be involved within the underlying pathology of the thought disorder. Table 3.8 outlines general questions that may be used while exploring thought processing following TBI. If a thought disorder is present, it is probably important to interview family members or caregivers who may observe disorders of thinking not detected during the neuropsychiatric examination. Observations by others often are more objective, particularly when the thinking disturbance may include paranoia, delusions, or hallucinations.

Risk to Self or Others

As a general statement, it is not possible for a psychiatrist to foresee an act of suicide beyond a very short interval of time. In fact, most experts believe a psychiatrist's ability to predict a suicidal act is

---

TABLE 3.8

Screening Questions for Changes in Thinking

- Do you ever hear voices or see things others cannot see?
- Do you ever feel you would be better off dead?
- Have you made plans to take your life?
- Has your ability to think changed in any way?
- Can you connect ideas in your head?

TABLE 3.9

Questions for Exploring Active Thinking of or Planning of Suicide

- Has your status in life changed so much that you wish you were dead?
- Are you unable to get pleasure from life since your injury?
- Do you feel like your life is no longer worth living?
- Do you ever wish that you would die or that you would not wake up in the morning?
- Have you ever made a plan as to how you would take your life?

---

no better than that of a layman. On the other hand, psychiatrists are expected to be skilled at determining suicide risk. Therefore, a risk analysis of the potential for suicide should be part of any new patient evaluation following TBI. Suicide attempts are almost unheard of in an acutely brain-injured patient. There is no significant medical evidence that suicide risk is increased immediately following acute TBI. Risk of suicide in the chronically brain-injured patient is another matter. Particularly at risk is the TBI patient with a pre-injury history of bipolar affective illness, recurrent major depression, or recurrent major depression with psychosis. Of even greater probable risk is the schizophrenic person who has sustained a TBI. However, it has been observed that suicide risk increases in the chronic phase of TBI even in the absence of premorbid psychiatric illness.[47,48]

When taking the history, the examiner should diplomatically but explicitly inquire as to suicidal ideation or plans. Direct questioning is required, as some patients passively think of suicide ("I wish I would not wake up in the morning.") or have active thoughts of suicide ("I will keep my gun by my bedside in case I feel the need to shoot myself."). Most patients who contemplate suicide have active thoughts about killing themselves but no specific plan to do so. The examiner must carefully distinguish between active and passive thoughts of suicide, as active thoughts carry a greater risk than passive thoughts. Moreover, if a specific plan has been made, this further increases risk. Risk analysis of suicidal thoughts in depressed persons is expertly delineated by Simon and Hales.[49] Table 3.9 provides explicit questions for exploring active thinking or planning of suicide. One will not increase suicide risk by politely inquiring with these questions. Also, the examiner must consider other premorbid aspects of personality that may increase suicidal risk following TBI. These include the borderline personality disordered patient or the antisocial patient with impulsivity who sustains a TBI, acquires personality changes, and becomes even more impulsive as a result of frontal lobe disinhibition. With the borderline patient, inquiries should be made as to whether she has increased thoughts of cutting herself, harming others, burning herself, or causing self-mutilation.

Behavioral Treatment History following Traumatic Brain Injury

The point where the post-TBI patient is within the rehabilitation process will dictate how the history of behavioral treatment is taken at this point in the examination. A neuropsychiatric examiner evaluating a person 4 years after TBI will obviously develop a different database than the neuropsychiatric examiner seeing a patient 2 months after leaving a rehabilitation unit. However, in both instances, it is important to develop a history of psychopharmacologic treatment. Since the first edition of this book, there have been advances in the use of neurological and psychiatric medications following TBI. While unfortunately the level of psychopharmacology research directed at TBI remains sparse, it is improving. Table 3.10 lists the common classes of psychotropic agents now used to assist TBI patients. Almost all of these uses will be off label. However, it is important to inquire about these medications during the history taking, as they assist the examiner in understanding what symptoms other physicians have attempted to treat. At the current examination, the neuropsychiatric examiner must establish whether or not certain psychotropic medications are assisting or working adversely to the TBI patient's benefit. Careful inquiry should be made as to any possible medication side effects that may contribute to cognitive dysfunction during the

TABLE 3.10

Classes of Psychotropic Agents Used to Assist TBI Patients

- Antidepressants
- Antiepileptic drugs
- Lithium salts
- Neuroleptic drugs
- Anxiolytics
- Cholinergics
- Psychostimulants
- Dopamine agonists
- NMDA receptor antagonists (e.g., memantine)
- Hypothalamic stimulants

neuropsychiatric examination. This is particularly important for the forensic examiner, as an attorney may raise the issue that the person's cognitive impairments are due to the medications they are receiving rather than a putative TBI. For instance, during rehabilitation, the patient may have developed substantial difficulties from medications that have since been discontinued.[50,51] Certain antiepileptic drugs used as mood stabilizers have been known to produce cognitive slowing and adversely affect vigilance.[52] Many patients are now taking cholinesterase inhibitors following TBI, and these are commonly prescribed during acute rehabilitation.[53] The commonest psychotropic medication used following TBI is an antidepressant.[54,55] As seen in Chapter 2, it may be necessary to treat psychosis, mood disorders, anger, and aggression.[56–58] More careful delineation of psychotropic drugs and their current uses following TBI are discussed in Chapter 8.

ACTIVITIES OF DAILY LIVING

A question for the neuropsychiatric examiner following TBI is what is the patient's current functioning? A review of activities of daily living provides a wealth of information. For the treating psychiatrist or clinician, the activities of daily living are helpful in determining the strengths and weaknesses of patients as they cope with real-world situations in their daily lives. For the clinician examining a person for forensic purposes, the activities of daily living survey is critical. It is here that the physician will in part determine functionality as it applies to the damages portion of a personal injury litigation, or to answer questions of functionality in a workers' compensation or Social Security Administration examination. The reader is referred to the medical questionnaire introduced early in this chapter.

For those clinicians treating patients following a TBI, daily activities are often one of the most useful portions of the history-gathering process. Obviously, the brain-injured patient who has been rendered quadriplegic will report a severely reduced level of activity, whereas the person who sustained a mild TBI with little cognitive impairment may report few, if any, alterations of daily activities. In general, it is useful to begin with where the patient is currently living. Many times, living situations have changed following a brain injury. Moreover, if the patient's injuries have been a sufficient stress upon the family, divorce or separation may have occurred. Owing to the physical changes that may occur in association with a TBI, it is useful to inquire about biological markers of vegetative function. Ask patients what time they retire at night and what time they arise. An inquiry should be made whether there has been a change in bathroom functions or sexual functions.

Questions about activities that most normal people engage in are the most informative. For instance, do patients have hobbies they pursue, and if they no longer pursue hobbies, why not? Can the person watch television, and if so, how much? Has there been any alteration in the person's ability to read or write? What literature does the individual read, and has there been any alteration in the complexity of literature that the person can understand? How many hours of television does the person watch daily, and has there been an increase or decrease in the level of viewing? Does the person fix his own breakfast? Can he drive an automobile or other vehicle, and if not, has there been a change in his ability to do so? Can the person prepare meals, wash dishes, clean his home, and see to ordinary household and daily activities? If the person is ambulatory, can he leave his home to purchase groceries and other household items? Is he able to organize his day and activities sufficiently to leave home and see to his daily needs?

One of the major purposes in taking a history of activities of daily living is to determine two fundamental issues about the patient's life: (1) Has there been a change in the individual's ability to care for herself? (2) If there has been a change, how significant has it been? For instance, can the individual now maintain a checkbook? Is she able to pay her own bills? Can she compose a simple letter? Does she use the telephone, and if so, how many times weekly? Is she able to eat outside her home socially, and if so, how many times monthly? Does she have friends or visitors into her home, and if so, how often monthly? Can the patient garden, tend to houseplants, or care for pets? Other questions regarding activities of daily living are specific to the individual's lifestyle. It is one thing to ask questions of a 61 year old widowed woman who was living alone at the time of her TBI, and another to ask questions of a 47 year old accountant who was operating his own firm. Thus, the creativity of the examiner will be called into play to determine lifestyle-specific changes in activities of daily living. The accumulation of this data, especially information about one's work product, will be covered in greater detail where it is relative to forensic applications.

Past Medical History

With a brain-injured adult, it is important to take a good childhood history of basic development to determine if there are any preexisting brain or mental difficulties that may interact with the brain injury or exacerbate cognitive symptoms of brain injury. Most people know their birth weights, and that should be asked. Persons born prematurely, or those persons who spent a considerable portion of their early lives in neonatal units may have some preexisting neurobehavioral difficulties before TBI. Problems of development are also important to note. These may be markers of childhood developmental delays that have persisted into adulthood. Were there any childhood illnesses that impact upon injury? For instance, is there a history of learning disability, attention deficit disorder (ADD), Tourette's syndrome, or other common childhood neuropsychiatric conditions that may have persisted into adulthood?

As the history becomes more focused upon adult health problems, it is important to determine whether there is a prior history of trauma. In other words, the brain injury being evaluated at the present time may not be the index brain injury (see Chapter 2). It is particularly important to inquire about prior motor vehicle accidents and their association with loss of consciousness, skull fractures, or head trauma. Has the person been in a motor vehicle accident sufficient to break bones and require a stay in a hospital? The patient should always be asked about a prior history of bone fractures. Many times, these are associated with slips and falls, significant work-related trauma, physical abuse, or other aspects of trauma wherein the person may have incidentally also sustained a blow to the head.

In discussing pre-injury medical problems with the patient, of course, all medical problems have some importance. However, the focus will clearly be upon those medical problems that may have a direct bearing on how the person's brain injury affects the person or has a direct bearing upon diseases that may have an adverse impact upon function following a brain injury. The neuropsychiatric history of pre-injury medical problems should be fairly extensive, but certainly not at the level of an internal medicine physician. In fact, it is important to focus upon diseases of the nervous system, as they are the most likely pre-injury medical problems to impact directly upon functioning following brain injury. One should inquire whether the patient has had any adult forms of meningitis, encephalitis, or other infections of the central nervous system. Moreover, did the individual have childhood or adult epilepsy of some form? Has there been a pre-injury stroke? It is not unusual to find a middle-age person who has had a stroke and subsequently sustains a TBI in a motor vehicle accident. In most instances, the pre-injury stroke would play some role in the post-injury symptomatology of the patient. Clearly, the examiner wants to know if there is any past history of intracranial hematomas, arteriovenous malformations, or multiple sclerosis. Diabetes is particularly problematic for a person who sustains a TBI if the diabetes has been in place sufficiently long to cause angiopathy of the brain. Endocrinopathies are likewise important factors to consider in the medical history of a brain-injured patient, particularly hypothyroidism (see subarachnoid hemorrhage), which can impact adversely upon cognition. Heart disease is often a marker for possible cerebrovascular disease. The menopausal woman who needs, but yet is not receiving, estrogen replacement should be noted, particularly those women who sustain posttrauma depression and who may be estrogen deficient. Recent evidence suggests that these women do poorly on antidepressants unless they also receive estrogen supplementation.[59]

A pre-injury surgical history should be taken and recorded. It is especially important to focus upon intracranial surgery that may have occurred before brain injury. Cardiovascular surgery also plays an important role. There is significant evidence available that many coronary artery bypass surgeries result in substantial cognitive dysfunction following surgery.[60] Thus, a person may have had heart disease and subsequent surgery 2 years before brain injury. Cognitive disturbance could be present following the heart surgery, which is then exacerbated by a closed-head injury. Other surgeries may be important markers for potential diseases that could have an impact upon posttrauma brain function. In particular, peripheral vascular surgery or carotid endarterectomy should be noted. The need for carotid endarterectomy is often associated with cognitive disturbance from cerebrovascular disease, and complications from carotid endarterectomy can lead to cognitive dysfunctions.[61]

Careful history of pre-injury medication usage should be obtained if possible. What medications the patient has used before brain trauma may be a marker for diseases that were present before brain trauma that currently affect the outcome of the injury. For instance, a long history of hypertension and the need for multiple antihypertensives to control the hypertension could be revealing regarding potential hypertensive brain changes. Diabetic medications and their length of usage are important subjects to note. Endocrine disorders, particularly thyroid function, may provide the examiner with insight regarding possible hypothyroidism. A prior history of cancer and use of chemotherapeutic agents is important. There is substantial evidence that chemotherapy may cause lasting cognitive disturbance after its use.[62] Clearly, if the patient has been prescribed cognitive enhancers, such as cholinesterase inhibitors, the patient probably had a cognitive disorder before brain injury.[63]

PAST NEUROPSYCHIATRIC HISTORY

The reason for taking neuropsychiatric history is self-evident. With the adult, it is important to determine if there were psychiatric syndromes that developed in childhood, even if they did not require treatment. As noted previously, a history of attention deficit hyperactivity disorder or Tourette's syndrome may play a role in adult behavior and adversely affect symptomatology following TBI. Other disorders, such as autism spectrum disorder, may never have been diagnosed.[64] The taking of the psychiatric history in an adult is fairly standard and has been well covered in many modern textbooks of psychiatry.[65,66] Common sense dictates that TBI will rarely improve most existing psychiatric disorders. In a person who had a pre-injury psychiatric syndrome or illness, the TBI may produce a comorbid or dual-diagnosis situation. A person with bipolar I disorder with a rapid cycling variant, who then develops an orbitofrontal syndrome following a TBI, may become an extremely difficult patient to manage. Those physicians treating the homeless or impoverished should recall that many homeless schizophrenic persons sustain TBIs because of assaults.[67]

A careful inquiry of psychiatric treatment is important. Has the patient been treated on a chronic basis for a psychiatric disorder? What medications did the patient take before brain injury? How old were the patients at the time of their first manifestation of psychiatric illness? The examiner should carefully inquire regarding pre-injury mood disorders, anxiety disorders, obsessional syndromes, psychotic conditions, and personality disorders, as all of these may be exacerbated or complicated by a TBI. It is important to determine if there have been any psychiatric hospitalizations, as these are important markers for serious mental disorder.

With regard to pre-injury neuropsychiatric conditions, it is important to inquire as to the pre-injury presence of epilepsy and related syndromes, when they occurred, and how they were treated. Pre-injury strokes have been mentioned previously. Pre-injury dementias are a common complicating factor in TBI, particularly in slips and falls among the elderly. In addition, it is important to inquire as to pre-injury aggressive syndromes, antisocial personality, borderline personality disorders, and other syndromes that may have a brain-behavior basis.

FAMILY HISTORY

The purpose of the family history is to differentiate preexisting brain injury factors that may play a role in the patient's biological and psychological response to the brain injury. Taking a family history is essentially taking a history of genetic patterns of disease within the patient's family and attempting to identify disease patterns that may have a familial basis. For instance, in neuropsychiatry, it is incontrovertible that alcoholism is familial and apparently can be specifically transmitted from parent to child whether or not the child is exposed to the alcoholic parent.[68] Antisocial personality is probably overrepresented with a genetic tendency in families. Antisocial personality disorder is clearly more common among the first-degree biological relatives of those with the disorder than among the general population.[69]

In taking the family history, it is important to focus upon illnesses in first-degree relatives. The neuropsychiatric examiner should not only screen for basic neurological and psychiatric conditions but also give attention to hypertension, thyroid illnesses, diabetes, cancer, heart disease, lung disease, kidney disease, and liver or gastrointestinal disease. Specific inquiries should be made regarding the frequency in the patient's first-degree relatives of epilepsy, neurological disease, Alzheimer's disease, and stroke. In the psychiatric portion of the family history, the language should be appropriate to the person being examined. The examiner might initially ask if anyone in the family has had a nervous breakdown. If the answer is affirmative, then more specific questions can be directed to determine if the disorder was a bipolar affective illness, major depression, schizophrenia, or any other more specific psychiatric condition. One should also ask the patient about a family history of markers that may represent psychiatric illness in families. This would include asking about the presence of suicides, homicides, violence toward others, child abuse, and spouse abuse within the family.

SOCIAL HISTORY

Recording the patient's social history, within the context of a TBI examination, is quite helpful in terms of treatment planning for the patient. The social context of a traumatized individual is always important, and it may be predictive of how the patient will fare in rehabilitation. The history should first put the brain-injured individual into social context. This is best determined by developing a profile of the patient's home of origin. It is important to ask where the patient was born, how many siblings the patient had, and if employed, what occupations the patient's parents pursued. One should ask if the parents are currently living, how they are doing, and whether the injured patient was involved in caregiving of the parents, particularly if the parents are elderly.

A simple question to ask is, "Who raised you?" We often assume as physicians that people are raised by their parents. However, by age 18, approximately 20% of youngsters have lost one of their parents through death or divorce. Moreover, it is surprising how many youngsters are raised by grandparents, aunts, or other care providers, rather than the biological parents. Simple inquiry can be made as to whether the person's home life was happy. Was there abuse in the home, or was it a threatening place in which to live? Was the home of origin abusive, and did it cause the patient to feel depressed when young? It is now customary to ask men and women if they have ever been sexually or physically abused. This includes asking men and women whether they have ever been raped. It is amazing what answers are returned from this inquiry. Persons struggling with issues of abuse who then become brain damaged may have an extraordinarily difficult time with recovery because of unresolved issues of past abuse.

As noted in Chapter 2, aggression may be an outcome of brain injury. Thus, it is important to ask in the social history if the patient has a pre-injury history of violence to others. It is important to determine if the patient has ever harmed another person or shot, stabbed, or beaten another person. It is useful to ask if the person has ever killed another person, even by accident. Specific inquiries should be made as to whether guns are in the home. Have the individuals ever been in legal or personal difficulty because of their sexual behavior?

The educational history is an important marker for the patient's pre-injury academic attainment. More specific inquiry into educational history will be noted in the forensic section, where level of education has importance in determining causation. However, in the clinical brain-injured patient, treatment planning may change direction, depending upon the level of pre-injury education. If the patient did not finish high school, it is important to determine the reason behind the person's lack of education. Also, it is important to ask if the individual required special education classes, or while in grade school or high school, did the teachers think the person was difficult to control or was it difficult to obtain the person's attention? Further inquiry should be made as to post-high-school education, whether or not the person attended vocational school, and if the person is a high school dropout, did the person attain a GED?

The person's marital status should be asked or if divorced how many times? If more than one marriage is involved, it is worthwhile to learn why the person divorced and which party asked for the divorce. Direct questions should be asked generally regarding the quality of the present marriage, if the patient is in a stable marital situation. It is important to distinguish whether the quality of the marriage has been impacted by the brain injury in the spouse. Moreover, it is important to determine if the brain injury has had an impact upon the present relationship with regard to aggression, sexual dysfunction, and intimacy. As discussed in Chapter 4, alterations of prosody may impact the maintenance of romantic relationships.

Within the context of social history, the examiner should inquire as to any legal history. Specific questions as to whether the individual has ever been convicted of a felony or misdemeanor are important. Many brain injuries occur within the context of assaults or other criminal activities. Moreover, those persons with a predisposition to criminal activity are more likely to suffer a brain injury. A useful question is whether anyone has ever received a restraining order or emergency protective order against self, and likewise, has the person in turn ever obtained a restraining order or emergency protective order against another person? A useful follow-up question is to determine if the patient has ever been charged with spouse abuse, child abuse, child neglect, or terroristic threatening.

The employment-vocational history is important in the brain-injured individual. The examinee may be involved in consultation with vocational rehabilitation specialists, or the person may need assistance with obtaining disability benefits. A simple chronology of pre-injury employments should be obtained, and a rough job description of the patient's most recent employment may be a useful addition. Ask about military history in all patients who have been brain injured. Historically, the majority of those who served in the military were males. That, of course, is no longer true. Important social information is gleaned regarding military history. Not only should persons be asked if they have ever been involved in military service, but it is also useful to know if persons have ever attempted to enlist into military service or a service academy and been denied induction. If the individual has served in the military, it is important to determine the branch of service, years served, and rank at the time of discharge. Specifically, the individual should be asked if there has been an honorable discharge. Those persons who were found unfit for military duty because of psychiatric disorder or inability to adjust to military life will have a military discharge other than an honorable one. While it may not be a dishonorable discharge, it may be given under medical conditions, or it could be a general discharge under honorable conditions. Further inquiry should be made if there were any disciplinary actions taken against the individual while in the military service and, of course, if in the military service, whether the person served in a combat zone and whether the person was wounded. Pre-injury issues of posttraumatic stress disorder (PTSD) or undetected blast overpressure brain injury from military action are obvious possibilities.

REVIEW OF SYSTEMS

The general review should focus upon vegetative signs and general health. Has the person had a change in weight, either up or down, or a change in sleeping pattern since the trauma? Has the person noticed fatigue or a change in appetite? In taking the head, eye, ear, nose, and throat history, careful attention should be paid to this area in the review of systems. Maxillofacial and scalp injuries are a frequent comorbid condition in TBI for obvious reasons.[70] Mandibular fractures may result in TMJ syndromes, and fractures into the maxillary and frontal sinuses may result in significant nasal airflow dysfunction and even increase the likelihood of obstructive sleep apnea. Orbital fractures can result in diplopia. Surgical techniques have advanced greatly the management of these fractures, but multiple residual symptoms may persist.[71,72]

In the system review of the chest, it is important to determine if posttraumatic complications persist that may have an effect upon the person's psychological or cognitive state. It is important to remember that severe trauma sufficient to injure the brain oftentimes produces thoracic vascular or lung injury in patients.[73] The patient may have sustained bleeding, embolization, or thrombosis of blood vessels that supply neurological structures. A careful review of the medical records, as noted in "Review of Medical Records," will determine whether the patient sustained an aortic arch injury, injury to the descending thoracic aorta, or had embolization due to foreign bodies or air. The neuropsychiatric examiner is more likely to encounter complaints of causalgia because of thoracic outlet vascular injury as a result of trauma to the chest. Even more frequently encountered, though, are seat belt injures to the carotid artieries.[74,75]

In the cardiovascular review, it must be remembered that myocardial injury may occur in up to 50% of head-injured patients, even in the absence of coronary artery disease. Some myocardial damage is due to direct blunt-force trauma to the anterior chest wall, resulting in myocardial contusion. However, even more difficult to understand is the apparent distant cerebral effect upon the myocardium itself.[76] Penetrating wounds of the chest are common in trauma sufficient to produce brain injury as well, particularly in urban centers. These may result in direct damage to the myocardium or to the great vessels surrounding the heart.[77] Thus, it is important to ask the usual cardiac questions. Has the patient experienced chest pain with exercise, shortness of breath on walking, collection of fluid in the lungs associated with swelling in the legs, or shortness of breath that awakens the patient at night?

The combination of abdominal and head injuries has been found to be particularly lethal.[78] Particularly in motor vehicle accidents, blunt abdominal trauma associated with a TBI is very common. The patient may also have sustained a diaphragmatic rupture or a duodenal or colonic injury. Gastric injury is fairly rare from blunt trauma, with a 5%–15% incidence.[79] Owing to bowel injury, the patient may have a malabsorption syndrome, chronic diarrhea, chronic constipation, nausea, or other abdominal symptomatology. Moreover, not infrequently following injuries of this type, the patient will complain of excessive gas or abdominal pain. With constipation, of course, inquiry should be made about laxative use.

In the genitourinary system review, the examiner should recall that injury to the urinary system or the genitals themselves occurs not infrequently in association with TBI.[80] Contusions of the kidney are not uncommon at all, nor are contusions of the bladder or outright urinary bladder rupture. In the male, penetrating penile or testicular injury may have occurred. Chronic urinary tract difficulty may persist following brain injury. If the patient has been rendered paraplegic or quadriplegic, chronic need for catheterization may result in frequent urinary tract infections and their attendant morbidity.

Orthopedic injuries are extremely common in persons who have sustained TBI. Obviously, many of the traumas to the body are as severe as the trauma to the head. However, there is an interesting aspect to this issue that some physicians do not consider. There is some evidence that suggests that the rate of fracture healing is accelerated in patients with a severe head injury, although the mechanism for this is not well elucidated by research or clinical experience.[81] The issue of enhanced bone healing in patients with fractures associated with neurological impairment was first reported by Riedel in 1883.[82] Rapid callus formation occurring in fractures associated with significant neurological insult or closed-head injury was reported by Benassy et al. in 1963.[83] Even more unusual, heterotopic bone formation may occur in soft tissues outside the skeleton in association with head injury.[84] However, not all orthopedic surgeons agree that excess callus formation or heterotopic ossification occurs. In fact, there is a present controversy in the orthopedic profession as to whether this is the case.[85] Be that as it may, orthopedists seem to be unified in their opinion that closed-head injury patients who have concomitant orthopedic injuries require meticulous care to maintain alignment during fixation of fractures.[86] Thus, it is important to take a careful history regarding orthopedic complications following TBI. Brain-injured patients may be sufficiently impaired that they cannot see to their physical rehabilitation. Moreover, significant pain and dysfunction may result from alterations of ossification during bone healing following TBI.

TAKING THE CHILD BRAIN INJURY HISTORY

The approach to the child is of course different than the approach to the adult with regard to taking a history. Traditionally, focus with the child is upon the family, the parents, and the neurodevelopmental history of the child. Thus, one of the immediate and obvious differences between the examination of the adult and the child is that the child is a work-in-progress and the adult is essentially a finished work. Moreover, it is essential to tailor the neuropsychiatric examination of the child to the age and developmental level of that particular child. In addition, it is necessary and essential to interpret the clinical findings within the context of the developmental expectations for the child's age. Clearly, the examination of a 3-year-old child is much different than the examination of a 10-year-old child, which is again different from the examination of a 17-year-old child. A suggested general history format for the child or adolescent is noted below. It will be augmented by specific neuropsychiatric questions within the history that should be used to buttress the overall examination and history taking from the child and the parent. Obviously, the parent cannot be left out of this process. Children are minors (legally), and while a direct examination of the child must be undertaken, for younger children, the majority of the history will come from the parent.

PATIENT QUESTIONNAIRE (FOR TREATMENT)

ALL QUESTIONS MUST BE ANSWERED!

> WARNING: Because of managed care insurance practices, and possible intrusion of your child's medical insurer or disability carrier into your privacy, please be aware that if you sign authorization to release your child's medical records to your insurer, or for disability or legal reasons, others may see this information.

> PLEASE BE ADVISED: If your child is in a lawsuit, workers' compensation claim, social security claim, or criminal charges, Dr. Pleasant will testify only as your child's treating doctor, not as an expert witness.

GENERAL INFORMATION

Name:_____ Today's date:_____

Address:_____ City:_____

Zip code:_____ Date of birth: _____ Age:_____

Phone number:_____ Social security number:_____

Which is the child's dominant hand? (right, left, both): _____ Child's present weight_____

Can the child read a newspaper? Yes_____ No_____ Education (highest grade completed)_____

Physician or person who referred the child to this office: _____

If the child is involved in other actions for disability, social security, a lawsuit, or criminal charges, who is the child's lawyer?_____

Who drove the child here today?_____ What is his/her relation to the child (parent, friend, relative, hired by the child's lawyer, etc.)?_____

Who does the child live with at this time?_____

HISTORY OF PRESENTING PROBLEM

Has the child been experiencing any mental or nervous problem is the last month? Yes_____ No_____ If yes, describe: _____

When did the mental problems first begin?_____

Has the child been experiencing any physical problems in the last month? Yes_____ No_____If yes, describe: _____

When did the physical problems first begin? _____

ACTIVITIES OF DAILY LIVING

What time does the child get up in the morning? _____ What time does the child go to bed at night? _____ Who fixes breakfast? _____ Does the child drive a car or truck? _____ Does the child attend church? _____ How often?_____ Where is the child between 3:00 and 6:00 p.m. on school days?
_____

Who cares for the child during this time?_____

What hobbies does the child have?_____

What does the child read?_____

What TV shows are presently the child's favorite?_____

What video games or computer games does the child play?_____

What was the child's last overnight trip?_____

How many movies does the child rent per month?_____
How many times does the child go to the movie theater a year?_____ How many times does the child sleep away from home in a year?_____ How many sports does the child play in a year?_____ How many times does the child hunt in a year?_____

How many times does the child fish per year?_____ How many times does the child eat out in a month?_____ How many times a month do friends or family visit the child at home? _____ How many times a week does the child call someone on the phone?_____

Can the child dress him/herself? _____ Can the child bathe him/herself?_____

PAST MEDICAL HISTORY

List any serious childhood illnesses: _____

Was the child born prematurely? Yes_____ No_____ What was the weight at birth? _____

Does the child have growth problems? Yes_____ No_____

As a baby: How old was the child when it could sit alone? _____ Crawl? _____
Pull itself up? _____ Stand alone? _____ Walk alone? _____ Potty trained?
_____

Is the child sad, depressed, or happy? Sad_____ Happy _____

List any permanent physical or mental problems from childhood or birth: _____
_____

Does the child have trouble sitting still in school? Yes_____ No_____

Does the child have trouble learning in school? Yes_____ No_____

Does the child have trouble keeping its mind on tasks? Yes_____ No_____

Does the child have trouble learning to read? Yes_____ No_____

Do teachers complain the child is too active? Yes_____ No_____

Check any serious illnesses the child has now or has been treated for in the past:

_____Seizures	_____Depression
_____Cancer	_____Panic disorder
_____Diabetes	_____Alcoholism
_____Thyroid disease	_____Drug abuse
_____Anemia (low blood)	_____Overdoses of medication
_____High blood pressure	_____Suicide attempts
_____Heart disease	_____Violence toward others
_____Lung or breathing problems	_____Attention deficit disorder
_____Kidney disease	_____Learning disorder
_____Joint or back disease	_____Manic–depressive illness
_____Stomach or bowel disease	_____Schizophrenia
_____Female problems	_____Eating disorders (e.g., anorexia)
_____Pregnancy problems	_____Neurological disease
_____Urinary tract problems	_____Child abuse or neglect
_____Sleep problems	_____HIV or AIDS

If the child was hospitalized for these illnesses, list the hospitals:_____

Has the child been injured in any motor vehicle accidents? Yes_____ No_____ If yes, list them:

Date	Age at the Time	Type of Injury	Treatment/By Whom

Has the child ever been knocked unconscious, or had a brain injury? Yes_____ No_____

If yes, describe what happened: _____

Has the child ever been in a coma? Yes_____ No_____

Has the child ever broken any bones? Yes_____ No_____

If yes, describe which bones were broken, right or left side: _____

_____

Has the child had any surgeries or operations? Yes_____ No_____ If yes, list below:

Date	Age at the Time	Hospital Where Performed	Type of Surgery

Is the child now taking any medications? Yes_____ No_____ If yes, please list milligrams and how often the medicine is taken:

Medications	Milligrams	Times per Day

Is the child taking any over-the-counter medicines (do not need a prescription)? Yes_____

No_____ If yes, list them: _____

Who keeps track of the child's medications? Child_____ Parent_____ Someone else_____

Does the child have any drug allergies or reactions? Yes_____ No_____ If yes, list below:

Drugs	Allergic Reaction
	Rash, nausea, hives, etc.

Does the child use tobacco now? Yes_____ No_____ Not now but previously _____

If yes or has used tobacco in the past, please describe how much and when the child started and when the child stopped: _____

_____

Does the child use alcohol now? Yes _____ No_____ Not now but in the past _____

If yes to any use of alcohol then describe: _____

Type of alcohol (whiskey, beer, wine, etc.)_____

Number of alcohol drinks the child has or had per day:

_____

When did the child start using alcohol? When did the child stop? _____

Describe any past alcohol problem in the child's life (DUIs, AIs, alcoholism, etc.):

_____

_____

Describe any medical treatment for alcohol problems: _____

_____

Has the child ever taken a medication or drug received from friends or family or bought off the street? Yes_____ No_____

If yes describe: _____

Has the child ever used illegal drugs (i.e., marijuana, heroin, cocaine, uppers, downers, crack, etc.)? Yes_____ No_____

Has the child ever sniffed paint, glue, or gasoline to get high? Yes_____ No_____ If yes, what did the child sniff and how long? _____

Has the child ever used LSD, peyote, mescaline, PCP, mushrooms? Yes_____ No_____

If yes, what and when? _____

Has the child ever injected illegal drugs (IV drugs)? Yes_____ No_____

Has the child ever received treatment for drug/substance abuse? Yes_____ No_____ If yes, which hospital; which year? _____

Drug/Substance	Age at Use	How Long Used	Last Date Used

Does the child drink coffee or tea? Yes _____ No_____ How many cups per day? _____

Does the child drink caffeinated soft drinks? Yes_____ No_____ What soft drinks? _____

_____ How many per day?_____

Next Five Questions for Girls/Teenagers:

1. How many pregnancies has the child had? _____ How many living children has the child had?_____ How many miscarriages has the child had?_____
2. Was the child depressed after having a baby or miscarriage? Yes_____ No_____
   If yes, when?_____ Was the child medically treated? Yes_____ No_____
3. Has the child had any babies by caesarean section? Yes_____ No_____
4. Could the child be pregnant at this time? Yes_____ No_____
5. When was the child's last menstrual cycle? _____

PAST PSYCHIATRIC HISTORY

Has the child ever been hospitalized for psychiatric, drug abuse, alcohol, or mental problems? Yes_____ No_____ If yes, please explain below:

Psychiatric Hospital Admissions	Year Hospitalized	Hospital Name	Treating Physician or Psychiatrist	Diagnosis or Reason for Admission	Type of Treatment Received
First admission					
Second admission					
Third admission					
Fourth admission					

Has the child ever been discharged from any hospital against medical advice (AMA)? Yes_____ No_____ If yes, describe: _____

Has the child ever been prescribed any form of nerve medicines, antidepressants, tranquilizers, or other psychiatric medications? Yes _____ No _____ If yes, describe:_____
_____

When is the first time in the child's life it ever took nerve medicines, tranquilizers, or antidepressants? _____

Has the child ever stopped prescribed nerve pills without asking the doctor?
Yes_____ No_____

Has the child ever had shock treatments (ECT)? Yes_____ No_____ If yes, describe when and where:_____

Has the child ever been advised by any doctor, health practitioner, or school counselor/teacher to receive mental or psychological treatment? Yes_____ No_____ If yes, describe: _____
_____

Has the child ever been legally committed or admitted involuntarily to a mental hospital or psychiatric unit? Yes_____ No_____ If yes, describe: _____
_____

Has the child, parent, or guardian ever refused mental treatment when recommended by a doctor? Yes_____ No_____ If yes, describe:_____

Has the child ever received any type of office treatment by a family doctor, psychiatrist, pediatrician, psychologist, or therapist (medication, counseling, therapy) for any nervous condition, psychological, psychiatric, or family problems? Yes_____ No_____ If yes, describe: _____
_____

Year of Treatment	Treating Therapist/Physician	Diagnosis or Problem	Type of Treatment (e.g., Drugs, Therapy)

Has the child ever intentionally overdosed on drugs or medicines? Yes_____ No_____

If yes, describe: _____

Has the child ever attempted to take its life? Yes _____ No_____ If yes, describe:_____

_____

Has the child ever intentionally cut, burned, or disfigured himself/herself? Yes_____ No_____ If yes, describe: _____

Has the child ever hurt, abused, or killed animals? Yes_____ No_____ If yes, describe:

_____

FAMILY HISTORY

Please check if any of these illnesses or acts have occurred in any of the child's parents, brother/sisters, or children: (do not list grandparents, aunts/uncles or cousins.)

_____High blood pressure   _____Nervous breakdown

_____Thyroid illnesses   _____Mental illness/nerve problems

_____Diabetes   _____Insanity, lost their mind

_____Cancer   _____Alcohol/drug problems

_____Heart disease   _____Eating disorder (anorexia, bulimia)

_____Lung disease   _____Attention deficit disorder

_____Kidney disease   _____Learning disorder

_____Liver or gastrointestinal disease   _____Suicide

_____Seizures (epilepsy)   _____Killing another person

_____Neurological disease   _____Violence toward others

_____Alzheimer's disease   _____Child abuse

                                                    _____Spouse abuse

If any of the above were checked, please explain which relative had the illness or did the violent act:

_____

Father's age if living: _____ Mother's age if living: _____

If a relative is dead, list what the child's father, mother, brothers/sisters, or child died of and their ages at death: _____

_____

SOCIAL HISTORY

Where was the child born? _____

Date of birth: _____ How many children are in the child's family of origin? _____

Of the child's siblings, how many are sisters? _____ Brothers? _____ Where does the child come in the family? (first child, last child, etc.)_____

What does the child's father do for a living? _____

What does the child's mother do for a living? _____

Does the family have enough money?_____ Not enough money?_____ Live in poverty?_____

Is the father living? _____ Year he died? _____ The mother?_____ Year she died?_____

Are the child's parents divorced? _____ If yes, when? _____

How old was the child at the time?_____

Who raises the child?_____ Do the parent(s) own their own home? Yes_____ No_____

Is the home life happy? Yes_____ No_____ Abusive? Yes_____ No_____ Threatening? Yes_____ No_____ Hard on the child? Yes_____ No_____ Make the child depressed? Yes_____ No_____

Does the father abuse the child's mother? Yes_____ No_____ If yes, explain:_____

Has the child ever been sexually abused? Yes_____ No_____ If yes, explain: _____

Has the child ever been raped? Yes_____ No_____ If yes, explain: _____

Has the child ever been physically abused: Yes_____ No_____ If yes, explain: _____

_____

Is the child presently being sexually or physically abused by anyone? Yes_____ No_____

If yes, who?_____

Has the child been bullied at school? Yes_____ No_____

Has the child been a firesetter? Yes _____ No_____

Has the child ever been violent to or harmed a person, or torn up property? Yes_____ No_____

Has the child ever shot, stabbed, or beaten another person? Yes_____ No_____

Has the child ever threatened to kill another person or classmate? Yes_____ No_____

Has the child ever killed another person, even by accident? Yes_____ No_____

Are there guns in the child's house? Yes_____ No_____ Does the child have access to them? Yes_____ No_____

Has the child ever been in legal trouble for his or her sexual behavior? Yes_____ No_____

_____

Has the child ever sexually abused or harassed another child? Yes_____ No_____

_____

Highest grade completed in school? _____

If the child did not finish high school, what was the reason for quitting?

_____

What were the child's grades in school? _____ Did the child require special education classes? Yes_____ No_____ In grade school or high school, did the teachers think the child was hard to control or was it hard to get the child's attention? Yes _____ No_____ If yes, explain:

_____

LEGAL HISTORY

Has the child ever been in a juvenile corrections facility? Yes_____ No_____ If yes, where and when? _____

_____

Has the child had any juvenile arrests? Yes_____ No_____ If yes, fill in below:

Arrest Date	Charge(s)	Where (City or State)	What Did the Juvenile Judge Do?	Length of Time in Juvenile Facility

Has the child been involved in any lawsuits as either the plaintiff or defendant? Yes_____
No _____If yes, describe:_____

EMPLOYMENT/VOCATIONAL HISTORY

Employment status (check one): Full time_____ Part time_____
Not employed_____ Student _____
If presently employed, who is the child's employer?_____
Employer address:_____
Describe job duties: _____
Length of time on last permanent job: _____
Job duties/position of that job: _____
List past employment (beginning with the child's most recent job):

Employer	Job Title	Start Date	Finish Date	Reason for Leaving	Other

REVIEW OF SYSTEMS
(CIRCLE THOSE SYMPTOMS PRESENT)

GENERAL: Fever, shaking, chills, change in appetite, loss in weight, change in weight, fatigue, change in sleeping patterns, soaking night sweats

Explain any of the circled items, if the child has lost or gained weight, how many pounds in the last 3 months?

_____

HEAD, EYES, EARS, NOSE, THROAT:	Headache, changes in vision, double vision, blurred vision, eye pain, excessive tearing, discharge from the ears, changes in hearing, ringing in ears, discharge from ears, nosebleeds, odd odors, hoarseness, dental pain, sore tongue, sore throat, mouth sores, trouble swallowing

Explain any circled items:_____

_____

_____

CHEST:	Cough, sputum production, shortness of breath, wheezing, blood in sputum, abnormal chest x-ray, positive TB test, lump(s) in breast, nipple discharge, nipple bleeding, breast pain

Explain any circled items: _____

_____

_____

HEART:	Chest pain with exercise, shortness of breath while walking, shortness of breath upon lying down, heart murmur, rheumatic fever, shortness of breath that wakes the child at night, swelling in legs, fainting

_____

_____

STOMACH:	Change in appetite, nausea, vomiting, blood in vomit, dark brown vomit
BOWEL:	Diarrhea, constipation, change in stool size, blood in stool, dark black tarry colored stool, food intolerance, trouble swallowing, heartburn, indigestion, laxative use, excessive gas, abdomen pain, weight loss, weight gain

Explain any circled items: _____

_____

_____

URINARY: GENITAL:	Trouble starting urination, excessive urination, dribbling of urine, pain upon urination, blood in urine, excessive urination after going to bed, unable to hold urine, bedwetting, sores on genitals

Explain any circled items: _____

_____

_____

FEMALE:	Menstrual irregularity, premenstrual distress, excessive female bleeding

Explain any circled items: _____

_____

_____

_____

MENTAL: Depression, sadness, nervousness, panic, thoughts of suicide, poor concentration, loss of memory, too happy, word-finding difficulty, confusion, inability to know month/year, hearing voices, seeing things, paranoid thoughts, irritability, excessive anger, aggressive behavior, arguing, crying for no reason, trouble thinking, flashbacks, thoughts of killing another person, counting things, checking things, afraid of germs, afraid to touch doorknobs, wash hands more than 10 times daily, take more than two baths or showers daily. Does the child have a present plan to kill himself? Yes_____ No_____ Does the child have a plan to kill someone else? Yes_____ No_____Explain any circled items:_____

_____

_____

_____

NEUROLOGIC: Blackouts, seizures, double vision, partial blindness, headaches, numbness, tingling, weakness, poor balance, shaking or tremors, abnormal movements of face or body, poor coordination, paralysis, loss of reflexes, pain

Explain any circled items:_____

_____

_____

_____

MUSCLES: SKELETAL: Muscle spasms, joint pain, bone disorders, difficulty walking, difficulty, sitting, difficulty using hands, difficulty bending, difficulty lifting

Explain any circled items:_____

_____

_____

_____

SLEEP: Cannot fall asleep, cannot stay asleep, wake up too early, fall asleep anytime, night terrors, nightmares, sleep walking, restless legs before sleep, cannot stay awake during or while sitting, severe snoring that bothers others, choking during sleep, cannot stay awake to drive, others have observed the child to stop breathing during sleep, fall or stagger if angry or laugh, hear things when falling asleep or waking up, paralyzed for short time after waking up

Explain any circled items: _____

_____

_____

HIV: Has the child been tested for HIV? Yes _____ No _____

Results if tested: Positive: _____ Negative: _____

AUTHORIZATION INFORMATION

I authorize Dr. Pleasant to examine and test the child. (The parent or guardian must sign this form.)

_____

Signature

_____

Date

I authorize Dr. Pleasant to send a copy of this evaluation to the referring doctor or agency who requested the child to be examined.

_____

Signature

_____

Date

I authorize the psychological associates or examiners of Dr. Pleasant to perform whatever psychological testing Dr. Pleasant thinks is necessary to evaluate the child.

_____

Signature

_____

Date

By my signature, I certify all statements I answered on this questionnaire are true and accurate.

_____

Signature

_____

Date

If this form was filled out by someone other than the child, please give name:

_____

Relationship to child (friend, parent, guardian, etc.)_____

POSTTRAUMA SYMPTOMS AND TREATMENT

To lay the groundwork for differences that may occur in a child following trauma versus those of the adult, it is important to focus upon issues of relevance to the developing child. Posttraumatic seizures may be a complication more likely in children than among adults. In young children, seizure incidence is higher than among older children, and higher yet than among adults. Seizure incidence in young children is about 10%.[87] However, these are early seizures rather than late seizures. Seizures beyond the first week following TBI occur in about 4%–7% of adults but are even less frequent in children. Academic functioning is another issue for the child, and it is important to take a pre-injury social history of academic function with particular inquiry as to skill deficits that may have been present or whether special education was required. The younger a child at the point of injury, the more vulnerable the child may be to persistent deficits in academic skills.[88] Word recognition scores may be relatively spared, whereas arithmetic scores and reading comprehension scores seem more vulnerable to TBI in the child.[89] Even if scores on standardized academic tests recover to the average range, classroom performance and academic achievement may not. This suggests that standardized tests used for academic achievement are relatively insensitive to detecting the aftereffects of TBI in the child.

As discussed in Chapter 2, there are some distinct neuropsychiatric differences in brain trauma outcomes seen in children versus those in adults. However, extensive research indicates that brain injury in children can produce deficits similar to those in adults in various domains. Thus, the history of neurobehavioral consequences can be taken from the child in a manner very similar to that from the adult. With the very young child or the middle school-age child, clearly many of the questions will have to be posed to the parents or custodian of the child. Many prominent research centers have published studies outlining the neurobehavioral consequences of TBI in children, and it is suggested that if required, these sources be consulted.[90–94]

Attention

A secondary attentional disorder may arise following TBI in the child. The term "secondary" is used for symptoms of ADD that develop after TBI to distinguish those symptoms from the more classical idiopathic or genetic-onset ADD seen in children. Interestingly, those children that develop attentional deficits within the ADD spectrum following TBI are associated with a much lower level of functioning within the family before injury.[95] Use of a continuous performance test in the acute period after child TBI predicts later development of secondary ADD symptomatology in those children that have a significant number of omission errors.[96] In a child with attentional deficits following TBI who presents with oppositional defiant disorder (ODD) behavior, increased severity of TBI predicts ODD symptomatology 2 years after injury. However, one study has shown that ODD symptomatology in the first year after a TBI is related to pre-injury family dysfunction, lower social class, and pre-injury ODD symptomatology in the child before injury.[97]

While parents and children alike complain of attentional problems following traumatic head injury, the research studies supporting an objective measure of attentional deficits in children following head injury are rare. One way to get at potential attentional deficits in children is to ask whether the child is easily distracted. It is also useful to ask if the child is slower in reaction time than before the injury. As noted in Chapter 2, expect that the deficits will be greater in children injured quite early in life versus their older counterparts.[98] Most of the research on children with attentional deficits following head injury has focused upon continuous-performance tasks. This appears to result from the continuing low development of psychological tests in young children that measure the entire panoply of attention deficits.

Attention may be found to be particularly impaired in children following closed-head injures who are examined in the early post-injury period. These children may develop disorientation and confusion. Thus, if the evaluator is seeing the child within the first 3 months following a TBI, specific questions regarding orientation and confusion are appropriate, if the child is old enough to be oriented. A number of standardized methods have been developed for measuring posttraumatic amnesia and orientation in children following head injury. These include the Children's Orientation and Amnesia Test.[99] Table 3.11 describes approaches to exploring attention and language deficits in younger children.

Speech and Language

As we have been reminded elsewhere in this text, children with closed-head injuries may display more pronounced difficulties with the pragmatic aspects of language than their adult counterparts.[100] While taking the history of speech and language changes in children, it is best to ask if notice has

---

TABLE 3.11

Taking the Child's History of Attention/Language

- Is the child easily distracted or poor at tasks?
- Has the child's ability to converse or use language changed?
- Does the teacher report a deterioration of verbal skills in speaking, reading, or writing?
- Does the child read less at home or display disinterest in television?
- Can the child tell a story or a joke?
- Can the child focus upon video games?

---

been made of difficulty formulating sentences from individual words. Has there been any change in the child's ability to carry on discourse? Of course, one has to take into account the age of the child when asking these questions. However, Chapter 4 points out that most children after age 7 can use six- or seven-word sentences and recite their numbers into the 30s. If the child had a severe closed-head injury, the child may use fewer words in sentences when narrating stories. The stories may contain less information and may not be as well organized. In the child from kindergarten age upward, this type of information can be obtained more easily from teachers possibly than parents, unless the more observant parent is intimately involved in assisting the child with homework. Deficits in discourse can cause substantial academic difficulties in children with closed-head injuries. Thus, the parents should be asked if teachers have written notes to the home regarding changes in the child's language skills following injury. Children, like adults, rarely develop a full aphasia or substantial dysphasia following closed-head injury, so these are generally not likely to be seen except in a very small percentage of children.

Memory and Orientation

Memory is a global rather than specific concept for most adults. Therefore, when discussing memory deficits in children with the parent, it is important to bring some focus to the history taking. Parents generally do not describe their children in terms of having verbal memories versus visual memories, and this differentiation should be made clear for parents. In taking the history, it will be beyond most parents to differentiate more specific verbal memory disorders in their child. It is known that memory deficits occur in a variety of amnestic components, including problems of storage, retention, and retrieval.[101] Yet, it is not likely that a parent will be able to differentiate this for the examiner, and if this differentiation is required, it is best secured from teachers or from neuropsychological data as described in Chapter 6.

Since explicit memory involves the recollection of past events or facts, and implicit memory involves performance in the absence of conscious recollection, it is important to distinguish with the parent whether the child's memory deficit is for facts and events or for skills. Memory for skills generally remains intact in children following brain trauma. The child may well have motor impairment from a TBI that interferes with the child's ability to perform skills, but the child should remember how to use a computer or ride a bicycle, even after brain injury. On the other hand, factual memory in the child may show glaring deficits following brain injury.[102]

Visuospatial and Constructional History

Generally, children who have been brain-injured demonstrate a decline in performance IQ relative to verbal IQ as measured by standard intellectual assessment batteries (e.g., Wechsler Intelligence Scales for Children-IV). Many nonverbal skills, including both visuospatial and constructional abilities, may be impaired following brain trauma, thus driving down the performance IQ. This is

---

TABLE 3.12

Uncovering Memory or Visuospatial Deficits in Children

- Has the child displayed memory deficits for facts?
- Has the child deteriorated in skills?
- Can the child write on a line (if old enough to do so)?
- Has the child's drawing skill deteriorated?
- Can the child name common objects in the child's room?
- Have the child's cutting skills deteriorated?

---

covered in more detail in Chapter 6, but constructional dysfunction has been reported using a three-dimensional block task.[103] Thus, it is useful to ask the parent if the youngster has demonstrated impairment in playing checkers, drawing two-dimensional objects, or handwriting. Most of the studies in children have included measures of visual–perceptual or visual–spatial skills requiring motor ability. Two studies noted that some children with closed-head injuries show deficits on tasks involving facial discrimination[103] and picture matching.[104] It might be useful to ask the parent if the child demonstrated any inability to recognize known relatives or friends following the brain injury. Further information can be obtained from school teachers of young children. It may be useful to inquire whether there has been deterioration in the child's constructional ability in cutting paper if the child is a preschooler, or in drawing and artistic skills if the child is kindergarten or early school age. Table 3.12 provides guidance for taking a history of child memory or visuospatial dysfunction.

Executive Function History

Current research evidence indicates that maturation of the frontal lobes extends in the human at least into adolescence, if not into young adulthood.[105,106] The child with executive dysfunction may not be able to filter out interfering or competing stimuli. The Stroop Test discussed in Chapter 6 may prove abnormal in children with this tendency. Children have poor judgment to begin with, but generally childhood judgment deteriorates following frontal lobe injury. The child may become irritable, assaultive, or even sexually disinhibited. Verbal fluency may be impaired, and the child may also perseverate on drawing tasks or writing numbers. Thus, it is useful to ask the parent about these possible dysfunctions in a child who has sustained frontal lobe injury. Again, inquiry of school authorities or school psychologists may be useful as well.

Baddeley and Wilson have characterized a childhood dysexecutive syndrome associated with "metamemory."[107] This is characterized by poor attentional control, diminished speed of information processing, and a breakdown of boundaries between different memory domains for various categories of information. This results in confabulation, intrusions, faulty retrieval, or memory deficits for semantic information. The patient is unable to set goals and carry them out, and the child may demonstrate poor organization and poor planning skills.

Obtaining the History of Affective and Mood Changes

It is well recognized that it is difficult to diagnose a mood disorder in a prepubertal child, particularly if the child is below 7 years of age. Verbal communication is paramount in diagnosing a mood disorder in either adults or children, and most children under age 7 lack sufficient communication skills to describe their moods adequately. However, preschoolers with depression may look sad and have reduced verbal communication following brain injury. The parent or guardian should be asked about this in detail. Moreover, the child may move or talk more slowly. The normal communication of happiness through facial expression may alter following a brain injury. Common symptoms of depression in preschoolers also include loss of weight, a left shift on the growth curve, increased irritability and tearfulness, and somatic symptoms, particularly gastro-intestinal discomfort.[108] With the older child, the examiner may be able to take the history directly from the youngster. The parents or school authorities may be able to tell the examiner about alterations in concentration, suicidal ideation, or if the child is expressing a desire not to live. Somatic symptoms are very common in this age group, and the most common symptoms following a brain injury are headaches and abdominal pain. The parents should be asked if the number of pediatrician visits has increased owing to nonspecific complaints for which no sound medical basis can be found. These increased doctor visits may signal depression or anxiety. The diagnosis of a depression or anxiety disorder following brain injury in children will follow the *DSM-IV* (*Diagnostic and Statistical Manual of Mental Disorders, 4th edition*) guidelines for a mood disorder because of a general medical condition.

A high proportion of children who develop depressive disorders following TBI have pre-injury depressive disorders or first-degree relatives with major depression.[109] Max and his group have collected data which substantiates that most children who manifest depressed mood after TBI have a pre-injury personal history of depressive disorders, and that most of the remaining children have identifiable risk factors for a new-onset depressive disorder.[109] It has also been noted that suicide attempts in adults who develop major depression and give a remote history of prior TBI often have a history of pre-injury aggression in childhood.[110] As it was noted during the discussion on secondary mania following TBI in Chapter 2, there are a few reports of apparent secondary mania in children following TBI.[109] Max, in a 1977 study, found 8% of 50 children in a prospective study developed mania or hypomania.[111] Psychosis seems even more rare than mania following TBI in children. A number of studies were combined to report that 224 children were consecutively admitted to hospital following TBI. Standardized psychiatric interviews were used in these studies, and only two cases of new-onset nonaffective psychosis were reported in these children. The studies of psychosis available in children following TBI are almost nonexistent.[109] Posttraumatic stress disorder does occur in children following TBI. Posttraumatic stress disorder symptoms at 1 year post-injury were predicted by pre-injury psychosocial adversity, pre-injury anxiety symptoms, and injury severity, as well as early post-injury depression symptoms and nonanxiety psychiatric diagnoses. The children in this study who met the criteria for PTSD had significantly fewer lesions in the limbic system structures in the right cerebrum than subjects who did not meet criteria. Similarly, the presence of left temporal lesions and the absence of left orbitofrontal lesions were significantly related to PTSD symptoms and hyperarousal symptoms.[112,113]

When discussing mood or affective changes with the parent of the brain-injured child, the examiner should recall that behavioral functioning following childhood closed-head injury does not closely correlate with cognitive outcomes. The cognitive and behavioral outcomes in children may be somewhat independent and not concordant following a closed-head injury. Thus, the examiner should not make any assumptions about mood changes in children and attempt to relate them to severity of brain injury. Careful inquiry regarding affective changes in children must be made on a case-by-case basis. Table 3.13 provides suggested questions regarding executive changes and affective or mood changes in the child.

There are no good studies on suicidal behavior following TBI in children to guide us. However, since the late 1970s, the CDC in Atlanta has been focusing upon suicidal behavior as a national mental health problem of youth. As part of the affective history, it is important to inquire of parents, caregivers, and the child itself whether or not suicidal ideas have increased since the TBI. Also, it is necessary to pay particular attention to the child with depressive affect following TBI who is treated with SSRI antidepressants.[114,115] Since suicidal behavior is not a psychiatric diagnosis but is considered a psychiatric symptom, clinicians must be very careful when assessing for the presence of this type of behavior in children. Suicidal ideation or acts may occur in the preschool period, the preadolescent period, or in adolescence. Although intent to cause self-injury or to die is an essential element of the definition of suicide, it is not necessary that a child has a mature concept of the finality of death.[116]

TABLE 3.13

Asking about Childhood Executive Dysfunction or Affective/Mood Changes

- Is the child more irritable, assaultive, or sexually disinhibited?
- Does the child now fight with peers?
- Can the child resist focusing on extraneous stimuli?
- Is the child sad, or does the child speak of death?
- Are gastrointestinal complaints more frequent?
- Have general pediatric visits increased?

ACTIVITIES OF DAILY LIVING

The reader should refer to the pediatric history form noted above. Much of the information in the remaining sections within "Taking the Child Brain Injury History" can be gleaned from that document. It is basically a review of a psychiatric pediatric history, and the remaining portions of this particular section of pediatric brain injury require the addition of neuropsychiatric history as relevant to TBI. The purpose of reviewing activities of daily living is to determine if observable behavior of ordinary daily activities has been affected by TBI.

NEUROPSYCHIATRIC DEVELOPMENTAL HISTORY

Much of the information in the pediatric history form noted above is similar to what all physicians learn during their pediatric rotation in medical school. However, it is more important to focus on developmental milestones while taking a child TBI history. It is significant to determine whether before TBI the child experienced learning disorder, growth delay, perinatal birth injury, or other neuropsychiatric disorders that can complicate the outcome from TBI.

Moreover, it is important to get some determination of the pre-injury childhood temperament. The mother in particular should be interviewed if possible concerning social interaction problems, eccentric and odd personality styles, learning disorders, dyslexia, or need for special education. The mother should be asked if the child demonstrated pre-injury hyperactivity, motor clumsiness, tics, epilepsy, eating disorders, or aberrations of thinking before the injury. It is important to ask the mother regarding her prenatal history and whether she had complications during the prenatal period or during labor and delivery. The mother should be diplomatically asked regarding her use of alcohol or drugs during pregnancy or whether she had an eating disorder.

It is mandatory to make an inquiry regarding the child's academic progress before the brain injury. This helps establish a baseline of pre-injury cognitive ability and also provides a benchmark for determining any posttraumatic changes in academic performance. It is important to determine if the child had difficulty sitting still in school. Were there any noteworthy learning difficulties in school? Was the child able to keep its mind on tasks in the classroom, and did teachers bring any neurobehavioral issues to the parents' attention? If the child is of appropriate age, did the child have difficulty learning to read? Did teachers complain that the child was too active in the classroom? Was there any evidence that the child had a behavioral problem before the brain injury? Have there been legal issues with juvenile authorities?

PAST PEDIATRIC HISTORY

Continuation of a review of the mother's pregnancy, labor, and delivery is important here. Complications of the pregnancy and information about fetal movement and results of fetal ultrasound or other pregnancy diagnostic tests should be noted. The mother should be questioned about the labor, delivery, and nursery course of her baby. Questions regarding the pediatrician's comments about developmental milestones and whether or not the child met these appropriately should be undertaken.

The past pediatric history should include hospitalizations, surgeries, significant illnesses, prior trauma, medications used, and allergies. A careful review of the child's medication history in the year before the TBI is important. The examiner should not forget to inquire regarding the use of over-the-counter medications, herbs, or natural products, as parents often do not recognize these as drugs. Does the child have any history of drug allergies or drug reactions? This would include contrast dyes or other imaging substances. In today's cultural climate, careful inquiry should be made regarding the child's use of tobacco products, alcohol-containing substances, or illicit substances. Is there any prior history of glue sniffing, gasoline sniffing, paint huffing, or other organic solvents? Has the child ever received treatment for drug, alcohol, or substance abuse? Does the child consume caffeinated beverages of any kind, and if so, how many per day? For postpubertal girls, inquiry should be made as to any possible pregnancies, menstrual irregularity, or other gynecological issues.

PAST PEDIATRIC NEUROPSYCHIATRIC HISTORY

In general, if a child has a pre-injury neuropsychiatric disorder, TBI worsens or exacerbates the condition in most instances. Thus, it is important to carefully inquire about pre-injury neuropsychiatric conditions that may subsequently result in comorbid neurobehavioral pathology. Other authors have reviewed these issues extensively and in more detail than will be covered in this text.[117,118] Indirect inquiry may determine whether there was an undiagnosed neuropsychiatric condition present before the brain trauma. For instance, the parents should be asked if the child has ever been hospitalized for psychiatric, drug abuse, alcohol, or mental problems. Has the child ever been discharged from a hospital against medical advice? This is often a revealing question, as the parent may have been advised to admit the child and refused to do so. Has the child ever been prescribed any form of nerve medicines, antidepressants, tranquilizers, or other psychiatric medicines? Has the parent ever been advised by any doctor, health practitioner, or school counselor to get mental or psychological treatment for the child? Has the parent or guardian ever refused mental treatment when recommended by a doctor? Has the child ever received any type of office treatment by a family doctor, psychologist, nonmedical therapist, or psychiatrist for any nervous condition, psychological, psychiatric, or family problem?

More specific inquiry for markers of childhood mental disorders should be undertaken. For instance, has the child ever intentionally overdosed on drugs or medicines? Has the child ever attempted to take its life? Has the child ever intentionally cut, burned, or disfigured itself? Has the child ever hurt, abused, or killed animals? Specific inquiry regarding preexisting brain trauma syndromes should be made. As noted previously, it is important to inquire as to whether learning disabilities were present before the trauma. Is there any pre-injury history of epilepsy or seizures? Is there a pre-injury history of ADD, Tourette's syndrome, or motor tics? In today's infectious disease climate, it is important to determine if there are any neurobehavioral manifestations related to pediatric AIDS or HIV infection. Inquiry as to odd behaviors or lack of social reciprocity that may be associated with autism spectrum disorders should be made.

FAMILY HISTORY

Genetic diseases in the family may play a role in neurodevelopmental difficulties, and this history should be explored in detail. For the adopted child, this, of course, may be impossible. However, the limitations resulting from adoption should be noticed in the neuropsychiatric history. In a neuro-psychiatric examination, the family history focuses upon neurobehavioral disorders rather than general pediatric conditions. It is important to inquire of the parent whether first-degree relatives (parents and siblings) have evidenced conduct problems, violence toward others, suicides, ADDs, mood disorders, anxiety disorders, psychotic illnesses, or substance abuse and alcoholism.[119] More specific neurobehavioral inquiry should be made as well, and this would include a review of familial mental retardation syndromes, learning disabilities, dementias, movement disorders, early-onset strokes, migraine headaches, or specific genetic illnesses such as Huntington's disease. The purpose of the neuropsychiatric family history is to determine if possible genetic predispositions to disease exist, which may play a role in the genesis of illness in the child.

SOCIAL HISTORY

Recent studies have demonstrated that the role of environmental influences as predictors of outcome following childhood TBI is quite important. Environmental influences are a significant predictor of both cognitive and behavioral outcome following TBIs in children as well as adults. Socioeconomic status, family demographics, family status, and social environment are specific and consistent predictors of neurobehavioral outcome following TBI in children.[120] The pediatric history form noted above contains most of the important general pediatric information that one should attempt to glean when examining a child following TBI.

REVIEW OF SYSTEMS

The review of systems follows the same format as noted earlier for the adult historical inquiry. Obviously, specific factors regarding pediatric issues must be taken into account. However, the comorbid injuries to other body parts associated with TBI are essentially the same in the child as they are in the adult. The examiner may be guided in taking the review of systems by information gleaned from review of the medical records. A review of systems format is noted above within the pediatric medical history questionnaire.

REVIEW OF THE MEDICAL RECORDS

EMERGENCY ROOM RECORDS

Probably the most important record to review following TBI is the emergency room record. This is the initial contact of the TBI patient with the healthcare system. It is at this point that medical assessment of mental and physical functions first occurs. Since the first edition of this book, substantial changes have been made, and protocols have been put in place within emergency room departments treating the brain-injured patient. Within the United States, multilevel trauma centers have been established in almost all geographic areas. Therefore, the initial emergency department record may reflect triage and movement of the patient to a more specialized treatment center. Thus, it may be necessary to obtain more than one emergency department record following TBI. In the United States, the first use of the *Glasgow Coma Scale* (GCS) is generally at the accident scene by emergency medical services (EMS), and the second point of application of this instrument is usually in the emergency department. As discussed in Chapter 1, the fully oriented and functional patient will score 15 points on the GCS, whereas the patient in full coma will score 3 points. Most single scores within the range of 3–15 on this instrument form a basis for the diagnosis of coma. However, there is general agreement among neurosurgeons that 90% of all patients with a GCS score of 8 or less, and none of those with a score of 9 or more, are found to be in coma as defined as the inability to obey commands, utter words, and open the eyes.[121] Therefore, a GCS score of 8 or less has become the generally accepted emergency department definition of coma.

Limited studies are available to determine what percentages of patients following head injury are admitted to hospital from the emergency department. The Centers for Disease Control and Prevention (CDC) recently published figures on 12 states from the year 2002. An estimated 74,517 persons (79 per 100,000 population) were hospitalized with TBI-related diagnoses in the 12 reporting states. Unintentional falls, motor vehicle traffic accidents, and assaults were the leading contributors to these hospitalizations.[122] As the neuropsychiatric examiner reviews the emergency department records, if the patient has had a severe injury, it will be noteworthy to determine the approach to the comatose patient. Most emergency departments today recognize this, and management of impaired consciousness includes prompt stabilization of vital physiologic functions to prevent secondary neurologic injury (see Chapter 1), etiological diagnoses, and institution of brain-directed therapeutic or preventative measures.[123] Recent epidemiologic studies have identified certain risk factors for TBI in the United States. Interestingly, some states in the United States have passed laws wherein a motorcycle rider does not have to wear a helmet, but most states require drivers of automobiles and their passengers to be belted. A recent West Virginia University study[124] reviewed cross-sectional analyses of hospital discharge data from 33 states participating in the Healthcare Cost and Utilization project in 2001. Results revealed that motorcyclists hospitalized from states without universal helmet laws are more likely to die during the hospitalization following TBI, be discharged to long-term care facilities, and lack private health insurance. This study demonstrated the substantial increased burden of hospitalization and long-term care seen in states that lack universal motorcycle helmet use laws.

The examiner may have to track records to various locations (this will be particularly important if a forensic evaluation is performed). As noted above, trauma centers within states either receive patients who have been triaged or receive them directly by air or ambulance transport. Some trauma centers cover wide geographic areas and have instituted protocols for prehospital management of TBI. Cornell University published a recent study[125] reporting on 1449 patients with severe TBI (GCS < 9) treated at 22 trauma centers enrolled in a New York state quality improvement program between the years 2000 and 2004. The prehospital data collected on these patients included time of injury, time of arrival to the trauma center, mode of transport, type of EMS provider, direct or indirect transport, blood pressure and pulse oximetry values, GCS score, pupillary assessment, and airway management procedures. Direct transport to a trauma center was found to result in significantly lower mortality than indirect transport to a triage center, and later to a level-1 trauma center. Transport mode, time to admission, and prehospital intubation were found not to be related to 2 week mortality. The authors concluded that a 50% increase in mortality was associated with indirect transfer of TBI patients. They concluded further that patients with severe TBI should be transported directly to a level-1 or level-2 trauma center with capabilities delineated in the *Guidelines for the Prehospital Management of Traumatic Brain Injury*, even if the trauma center may not be the closest hospital. The examiner may note that some emergency departments, trauma centers, and EMS squads use the Trauma Score and Injury Severity Score (TRISS) as well as the GCS. TRISS scores are being used epidemiologically and at a research level throughout the United States to provide follow-up data and predictions of outcome in brain-injured persons.[126]

Thus, the evaluating physician or neuropsychologist should review carefully the emergency room record to see if commonly associated factors have occurred with the brain injury. A careful review of what physicians did in the emergency department should be undertaken. Important information can be gleaned from the modern trauma reporting sheets now being used. Further determination should be undertaken to detect if the patient was intoxicated at the time of injury, if the patient had nontraumatic coma (e.g., diabetic coma), if there was an associated spinal cord injury or other orthopedic injuries, if transfusions were required, and if there was evidence of secondary factors contributing to the injury.

THE HOSPITAL RECORD

Neurosurgical management of brain trauma has been revolutionized in the last 10 years. If the patient is removed from the emergency department and placed into the hospital, the course of care varies; in most modern hospitals, the patient will be sent to a neurosurgical intensive care unit (NICU). Some hospitals supporting level-1 trauma centers now use neurointensivists to manage TBI patients. The hospital record in those instances will contain information often not found in general hospital records without neurointensive care units. Patient outcomes have been dramatically improved in those centers that have neurointensivists, and the Medical College of Wisconsin has recently presented data demonstrating this.[127] This study was headed by world renowned neuropathologist Thomas Gennarelli. The mortality rate, length of stay, and discharge disposition of all patients with head trauma who had been admitted to a 10 bed tertiary care university hospital NICU were compared between two 19 month periods before and after the appointment of a neurointensivist. The authors analyzed data pertaining to 328 patients before the addition of the neurointensivist, and in 264 patients admitted after this person's appointment. There was a 50% reduction in the NICU-associated mortality rate, a 12% shorter hospital stay, and 50% greater odds of being discharged to home or to rehabilitation using multivariate models after controlling for baseline differences between the two periods. The authors concluded that institution of a neurointensivist-led team model had an independent and positive impact on patient outcomes. Examiners of TBI patients can expect these models to be spread throughout large tertiary care hospital systems with attendant improvements in mortality rates. However, as noted elsewhere in this book, the resulting neuropsychiatric pathology will increase because of persons who would not have otherwise survived.

When reviewing a hospital record, it is important that the examiner reviews data beyond that of the mental state. It is important to know if other complications have arisen. For instance, direct injury to the myocardium may occur in up to 50% of head-injured patients who sustain significant motor vehicle trauma, even in the absence of coronary artery disease.[128] Myocardial dysfunction following brain trauma has been well described in adults, but it is also seen in children.[129] These lesions have a characteristic feature and are similar to those seen following an acute myocardial infarction. They may occur independent of chest trauma, resembling myocardial lesions seen following pheochromocytoma or catecholamine infusion. At autopsy, subendocardial hemorrhages are commonly found in TBI-injured persons. It has been speculated that there may be an association between hypothalamic injury and myocardial damage.[130] Further review of the hospital record may detect respiratory dysfunction following TBI, and this is not an unusual complication of TBI. Neurogenic pulmonary edema can occur, and this is a variant of the adult respiratory distress syndrome (ARDS) seen with general body trauma and other diseases. A common cause of death in patients who have sustained an intracranial hemorrhage or severe head injury is neurogenic pulmonary edema.[131] Earlier studies of patients following TBI found a high association of pneumonia in the brain-injured patient. Recent changes in ICU management have reduced this. Many of these pneumonias were related to neutralization of gastric pH by antacids and were associated with gastroesophageal reflux. Raising the head of the bed 25°–30° in most ICUs has markedly diminished this, and sucralfate became more commonly used rather than H_2 blockers. Proton pump inhibitors are now more commonly used as well.[132]

Head-injured patients, like most trauma patients, are at increased risk for deep vein thrombosis and secondary pulmonary embolus. The placement of a Greenfield filter in the vena cava may be required to prevent clots from moving to the lungs.[133] On the other hand, the anticoagulated patient who sustains a TBI is at risk for bleeding complications. These findings are more likely in elderly patients who are anticoagulated and fall, sustaining a subdural or epidural bleed. All trauma patients on warfarin should have an INR performed in the emergency department, and a CT scan should be done in most of these patients, as the mortality is quite high if head injury is not detected early.[134] In contrast to bleeding, coagulopathy is another common adverse outcome following TBI, and the examiner may find evidence of this in the hospital record. Brain tissue itself is a potent stimulator of disseminated intravascular coagulopathy (DIC). Brain tissue injury additive with injury to endothelial cells of local vessels can initiate DIC. This can be exacerbated by the accompanying catecholamine release that occurs during severe injury.[135] Some patients require ventriculostomy or placement of ventricular monitoring systems. These individuals may develop a hematoma along the path of the catheter.[136]

It is important for the examiner to determine if neuroendocrine changes have occurred following TBI. Not only does severe physiological stress elevate adrenocorticotropic hormone (ACTH), injury to the frontal brain parts may damage the hypothalamus and pituitary. The patient may develop a syndrome of inappropriate antidiuretic hormone secretion (SIADH) or panhypopituitarism. Loss of thermoregulation can occur because of hypothalamic damage. These are low likelihood events and occur in less than 1% of brain-injured persons, but the possibility for these should be reviewed by the examiner while observing the hospital record. When they do occur, they can cause significant morbidity to the patient.[130] Gastrointestinal complications are frequent following TBI. Enteral feeding is often required in TBI patients. Some of those individuals may develop multiple-organ failure syndromes if they do not receive early institution of feedings.[137] Stress gastritis is common, and proton pump inhibitors are frequently used to combat this.[138]

COGNITIVE REHABILITATION RECORDS

Following acute hospitalization for TBI, many patients are then referred to a rehabilitation center specializing in brain trauma for further assistance. A recent Baylor College of Medicine study[139] compared postacute rehabilitation early after injury with persons receiving postacute rehabilitation 12 or more months post-injury. Both groups displayed effectiveness of postacute rehabilitation and improved in functional outcome. This study was conducted in a not-for-profit outpatient community reentry program affiliated with an inpatient rehabilitation hospital. The outcome measures were undertaken using the Disability Rating Scale, the Supervision Rating Scale, and the Community Integration Questionnaire. For the group beginning postacute rehabilitation at the earliest point, independence continued to improve after discharge. As the examiner goes through rehabilitation records, the examiner may note use of the Barthel Index. The Barthel Index has the capacity to detect serial changes in functional independence during rehabilitation.[140]

There are many models of cognitive rehabilitation following TBI, and this book will not discriminate among those models, as it is beyond the scope of this text. Moreover, the models vary from country to country and world region. As the examiner reviews cognitive rehabilitation, it may be worthwhile to detect what models were used. However, these have no significant neuropsychiatric importance to the examiner, and the obvious and most important variable is outcome. Our European colleagues often use the European Brain Injury Questionnaire and determine needs of TBI patients and their outcomes by having relatives and caregivers complete this instrument.[141] Most cognitive rehabilitation centers, regardless of country of origin, will assist TBI patients with memory deficits. In general, these therapeutic procedures will consist of establishing self-awareness of memory deficits in the patient, introducing a customized compensatory tool, teaching the patient a cueing system, and teaching organizational strategies.[142] With regard to the overall rehabilitation of TBI patients, three major foci of rehabilitation are undertaken: (1) attentional rehabilitation, (2) feature identification rehabilitation, and (3) categorization rehabilitation.

Many brain-injured persons perseverate. Perseveration is thought by many to be an inability to shift a focus of attention, and therefore the person continually repeats the behavior or task. The perseveration behavior may coexist with inability to maintain vigilance. Vigilance often refers to an individual's ability to maintain a focus of attention and self-monitor incoming stimuli to screen for a specific set of features. Vigilance is one of the most complicated attentional skills, and therapy may concentrate on maintaining a focus of attention in a stimulus-rich environment where multiple distracters are present. Another attentional deficit often seen and treated during cognitive rehabilitation is the inability to cognitively shift. It is more complicated than either vigilance or suppression of perseveration. Cognitive shifting requires the person to mentally shift between activities with the least amount of disruption to the information being received and stored. Generally, a therapist will have the patient begin with shifting physical tasks from one task to another, then progress to shifting from a physical task to a mental task, and then lastly focus upon shifting strictly from one mental task to another.

Feature identification is done automatically by all of us. However, brain-injured persons have specific difficulties performing this skill. From the time of early infant development, all individuals must learn to attend to and identify the iconic features of objects. This includes such features as color, shape, texture, weight, etc. Individuals with language disorders may become unable to describe or name an object and instead will mention its function. For instance, instead of naming a cup, the individual may describe its use as a drinking utensil. The remediation of deficits of feature identification generally requires the individual to focus on a checklist of seven or eight iconic features such as color, shape, etc. Then persons progress through steps in the hierarchy to gradually increase their skills at feature identification.

After a person relearns to identify features of objects, the rehabilitation then helps the individual learn to categorize. Categorization is learned very much like feature identification in that the person is guided to separate the color from the form of an object. For instance, an apple, fire truck, and cardinal all share the same red color. The individual is gradually challenged in an increasingly difficult hierarchy to define symbolic or functional categories and separate these from features such as color that place separate categories into the same group.

OCCUPATIONAL AND PHYSICAL THERAPY RECORDS

Occupational therapy and physical therapy are usually both major components of postacute TBI rehabilitation. Important neuropsychiatric information can be obtained by reviewing the rehabilitation records for these two components. The motor manifestations of TBI are often profound. Spasticity is often an outcome of TBI as a result of damage to cortical or subcortical motor centers. Spasticity is often very difficult to manage, but the examiner may note within rehabilitation records the use of botulinum toxin to reduce spasticity, improve function, and reduce pain. Botulinum toxin is usually administered with physical therapy while the patient is in rehabilitation.[143] If required, baclofen therapy is also used and may be injected intrathecally.[144]

With regard to classical physical therapy, the examiner may note various rating scales within the rehabilitation records. These are used to keep track of ambulation training after TBI. Some of these scales include the Functional Ambulation Category, Standing Balance Scale, Rivermeade Mobility Index, and the High-Level Mobility Assessment Tool.[145,146] The rehabilitation records should contain considerable information regarding the person's ability to manipulate objects. Moreover, documentation of balance is usually available. However depending on the level of skill of the examiner in the rehabilitation facility, it may not provide the neuropsychiatric examiner with adequate information. This, of course, can be obtained during psychiatric observation or neurological testing. The record should be examined for complaints of headache, blurred vision, or nausea, particularly after physical activity or a change in the attitude of the head in space. This may indicate vestibular dysfunction.[147]

Generally, information will be contained in these records regarding the range of motion of extremities and trunk. Also, statements about the neurologic status and whether hemiparesis is present can be found generally. Physical therapy records will be most important in determining the strength in extremities and overall physical endurance of the person. If the person is hemiparetic, or has quadriparesis, the physical and occupational therapy records will yield information generally regarding the quality of movement. Information explaining how the injured person transfers from wheelchair to car, from car to wheelchair, from bed to wheelchair, from bed to commode, and other important motor information can be determined. This information is very useful to the neuropsychiatric examiner, as the examination may take place a significant time following discharge from rehabilitation. Thus, a comparison of continued progress can be made qualitatively.

SPEECH AND LANGUAGE PATHOLOGY RECORDS

These records are most important, and if a patient is sent to rehabilitation following acute treatment for TBI, most centers use speech and language pathologists as part of the overall treatment plan. The examiner should review these records to determine if the patient was successfully able to complete the goals of speech and language therapy. For instance, some individuals will require orientation training before they can engage in speech–language therapy.[148] Since dysarthria is a common sequel of TBI, impairment-based therapy and a wide variety of compensatory management strategies are often undertaken by speech and language therapists in this patient population. A recent Cochrane database review found no trials for dysarthria that met their criteria.[149] However, it is generally accepted that brain systems respond to practice, and most TBI treatment centers are of the opinion that speech and language therapy play prominent roles in assisting rehabilitation in those patients demonstrating dysarthria. The reader should consult Chapter 4 to understand better language disorders and their relationship to TBI. This will assist in the examination of speech and language pathology records. Also, some rehabilitation centers apply treatment goals to aprosodia and dysprosodic disorders (see Chapters 4 and 6). Aprosodia is the inability to either produce or comprehend the affective components of speech or gesture. This is a common occurrence after brain injury, particularly with damage preferentially to the right cerebral hemisphere. The prosodic components of speech assist a person to infer the attitude and emotion of the speaker, which is vital to all of us in everyday communication. It is generally accepted that the left cerebral hemisphere is responsible for modulating the linguistic components of prosody (e.g., timing), whereas the right hemisphere is predominately responsible for modulating the affective components of prosody (e.g., spectral information or pitch).[150]

Other important information that may be learned from the speech record during rehabilitation is the swallowing integrity of the patient. If the patient has a brainstem injury (see Chapter 4), speech and language therapists often assist radiologists in performing cineographic swallowing studies. These are important to complete in a patient who may be at risk for aspiration. They also enable the speech pathologist to determine the integrity of the velopharyngeal complex and whether this leads to communication impairment in the patient.

TAKING THE COLLATERAL HISTORY

Taking collateral history is rudimentary within psychiatric medicine. For the neuropsychiatric examiner evaluating a patient following TBI, it may be critical. Obviously, the more severely the patients are injured, the less likely patients are competent to give their own history. Collateral history is generally obtained from the patient's family, guardian, or other interested caregiver. If the patient is being examined well after the TBI occurred, the examiner will want to focus on two major issues while taking collateral history: (1) information regarding the injured person's physical and mental deficits as seen by others and (2) whether or not caregiver stress exists within the living structure of the patient. Review the adult and child histories above and note the activities of daily living. The information regarding these can be enhanced by asking observers in the patient's environment if the patient is capable of completing daily living tasks. In particular, questions should be asked to determine patient function in the areas of hygiene, toileting, dressing, grooming, feeding, meal planning, meal preparation, shopping, laundry, medication taking, telephone usage, computer usage, motor vehicle operation, hobbies, time management, and the ability to attend to health and safety issues. Those patients with significant executive dysfunction may neither be able to meet these needs, nor may they be able to set goals, plan, have foresight to the future, and maintain persistence and initiation to complete tasks.[151] Since elements of anosognosia may be present in patients, the collateral history may be more accurate in the determination of the impact of residual frontal lobe impairment than is information received from patients who may not be aware of their deficits. Also, regarding issues of aggression, the patient may be reluctant to admit these, and the collateral historian will probably be more accurate in providing this information to the examiner. Further information is needed to determine how well the patient is integrating into the community. Can the patient drive a vehicle or use community transportation? Is the patient capable of communicating effectively and socializing with others? Does the patient have special needs that should be addressed for transportation, ambulation, toileting, feeding, and other aspects of daily function?

REFERENCES

1. Damasio, H. and Damasio, A.R., *Lesion Analysis in Neuropsychology*. Oxford University Press, New York, 1989.
2. Kertez, A., Ed., *Localization in Neuroimaging and Neuropsychology*. Academic Press, San Diego, CA, 1994.
3. Adams, F., *The Genuine Works of Hippocrates: Translated from the Greek with a Preliminary Discourse and Annotations, Vol. 1*. Sydenham Society, London, 1849.
4. Rush, B., *Medical Inquiries and Observations upon the Diseases of the Mind*. Kimber and Richardson, Philadelphia, PA, 1812.
5. Gowers, W.R., *A Manual of Diseases of the Nervous System*. American edition. P. Blakiston, Philadelphia, PA, 1888.
6. Ovsiew, F., Bedside neuropsychiatry: Eliciting the clinical phenomena of neuropsychiatric illness, in *The American Psychiatric Publishing Textbook of Neuropsychiatry and Clinical Neurosciences*, 4th edition, Yudofsky, S.C. and Hales, R.E., Eds., American Psychiatric Press, Washington, D.C., 2002, p. 153.
7. Cheiber, S.C., The psychiatric interview, psychiatric history, and mental status examination, in *The American Psychiatric Publishing Textbook of Clinical Psychiatry*, 4th edition, Hales, R.E. and Yudofsky, S.C., Eds., American Psychiatric Press, Washington, D.C., 2003, p. 155.
8. Larsen, P.D., Clinical neuropsychiatric assessment of children and adolescents, in *Pediatric Neuropsychiatry*. Coffey, C.E. and Brumback, R.A., Eds., Lippincott, Williams & Wilkins, Philadelphia, PA, 2006, p. 49.
9. Arffa, S., Traumatic brain injury, in *Pediatric Neuropsychiatry*, Coffey, C.E. and Brumback, R.A., Eds., Lippincott, Williams & Wilkins, Philadelphia, PA, 2006, p. 507.
10. Mesulam, M.M., *Principles of Behavioral and Cognitive Neurology*, 2nd edition, Oxford University Press, New York, 2000, p. 121.
11. Brouwer, W.H. and VanWolffelar, P.C., Sustained attention and sustained efforts after closed head injury: Detection and $0.10H_2$ heart rate variability in low event rate vigilance task. *Cortex*, 21, 111, 1985.
12. Tromp, E. and Mulder, T., Slowness of information processing after traumatic head injury. *J. Clin. Exp. Neuropsychol.*, 13, 821, 1991.
13. Docherty, N.M., DeRosa, M., and Andreaseu, N.C., Communication disturbances in schizophrenia and mania. *Arch. Gen. Psychiatry*, 53, 358, 1996.
14. Damasio, A.R. and Damasio, H., Aphasia and the neural basis of language, in *Principles of Behavioral and Cognitive Neurology*, 2nd edition, Mesulam, M.M., Ed., Oxford University Press, New York, 2000, p. 294.
15. Emmorey, K., The neurologic substrates for the prosodic aspects of speech. *Brain Lang.*, 30, 305, 1987.
16. Critchley, M., *The Language of Gesture*, Edward Arnold, London, 1939.
17. Bowers, D., Bauer, R.M., and Heilman, K.M., The nonverbal affect lexicon: Theoretical perspectives from neuropsychological studies of affect perception. *Neuropsychology*, 7, 433, 1993.
18. Ruff, R.M., Levin, H.S., Mattis, S., et al., Recovery of memory after a mild head injury: A three-center study, in *Mild Head Injury*, Levin, H.D., Eisenberg, H.M., and Benton, A.L., Eds., Oxford University Press, New York, 1989, p. 176.
19. Kapur, N., Focal retrograde amnesia in neurological disease: A critical review. *Cortex*, 29, 217, 1993.
20. Squire, L.R. and Zola, S.M., Structure and function of declarative and nondeclarative memory systems. *Proc. Natl. Acad. Sci. U.S.A.*, 93, 13515, 1996.
21. Markowitch, H.J., Memory and amnesia, in *Principles of Cognitive and Behavioral Neurology*, 2nd edition, Mesulam, M.M., Ed., Oxford University Press, New York, 2000, p. 257.
22. Schneider, K., Uber Einige Klinisch-Psychologische Untersuchungsmethoden und Ihre Ergebnisse, Zugleich ein Beitrag zur Psychopathologie der Korsakowschen Psychose. *Z. Neurol. Psychiatr.*, 8, 553, 1912.
23. Milner, B., Memory in the medial temporal regions of the brain, in *Biology of Memory*, Primbram, K.H. and Broadbent, D.E., Eds., Academic Press, New York, 1970, p. 29.
24. Wise, S.P., The role of the basal ganglia in procedural memory. *Semin. Neurosci.*, 8, 39, 1996.

25. Vaina, L. and Cowey, A., Impairment of the perception of second order motion but not first order motion in a patient with unilateral local brain damage. *Proc. R. Soc. Lond. B Biol. Sci.*, 263, 1225, 1996.

26. Barton, J.J.S., Visual dysfunction, in *Principles and Practice of Behavioral Neurology and Neuropsychology*, Rizzo, M. and Eslinger, P., Eds., W.B. Saunders, Philadelphia, PA, 2004, p. 267.

27. Benton, A.L., Levin, H.S., and VanAllen, M.W., Geographic orientation in patients with unilateral cerebral disease. *Neuropsychologia*, 12, 183, 1974.

28. Hecaen, H. and Angelergues, R., Agnosia for faces (prosopagnosia). *Arch. Neurol.*, 7, 92, 1962.

29. Damasio, A.R., Tranel, D., and Rizzo, M., Disorders of complex visual processing, in *Principles of Behavioral and Cognitive Neurology,* 2nd edition, Mesulam, M.M., Ed., Oxford University Press, New York, 2000, p. 332.

30. Benton, A.L., Varney, N.R., and Hamsher, K., Visuospatial judgment: A clinical test. *Arch. Neurol.*, 35, 364, 1978.

31. Benton, A.L., Hamsher, K., Varney, N.R., et al., *Contributions to Neuropsychological Assessment*, Oxford University Press, New York, 1983.

32. Eslinger, P.L. and Chakara, F., Frontal lobe and executive functions, in *Principles and Practice of Behavioral Neurology and Neuropsychology*, Rizzo, M. and Eslinger, P., Eds., W.B. Saunders, Philadelphia, PA, 2004, p. 435.

33. Grafman, J., Similarities and distinctions among current models of prefrontal cortical functions. *Ann. N.Y. Acad. Sci.*, 769, 337, 1995.

34. Tulving, E., Kapur, S., Craik, F.I.N., et al., Hemisphere encoding/retrieval symmetry in episodic memory: Positron emission tomography findings. *Proc. Natl. Acad. Sci. U.S.A.*, 91, 2016, 1994.

35. Ungerlider, L.G., Courtneyi, S.M., and Haxbry, J.V., A neural system for human visual working memory. *Proc. Natl. Acad. Sci. U.S.A.*, 95, 883, 1998.

36. Lezak, M.D., *Neuropsychological Assessment,* 3rd edition, Oxford University Press, New York, 1995, p. 650.

37. Stuss, D.T. and Benson, D.F., *The Frontal Lobes*, Raven Press, New York, 1986, p. 244.

38. Erhan, H.N. and Feinberg, T.E., Emotional disorders in relation to nonfocal brain dysfunction, in *Behavioral Neurology and Neuropsychology,* 2nd edition, Feinberg, T.E. and Farah, M.J., Eds., McGraw-Hill, New York, 2003, p. 735.

39. Gainotti, G., Emotional disorders in relation to unilateral brain damage, in *Behavioral Neurology and Neuropsychology,* 2nd edition, Feinberg, T.E. and Farah, M.J., Eds., McGraw-Hill, New York, 2003, p. 725.

40. Robinson, R.G., Kubos, K.L., Starr, L.B., et al., Mood disorders in stroke patients: Importance of location of lesion. *Brain*, 107, 81, 1984.

41. Aggleton, J.P., The contribution of the amygdala to normal and abnormal emotional states. *Trends Neurosci.*, 16, 328, 1993.

42. Holsinger, T., Steffins, D.C., Phillips, C., et al., Head injury in early adulthood and the lifetime risk of depression. *Arch. Gen. Psychiatry*, 59, 17, 2002.

43. Zeilig, G., Drubach, D.A., Katz-Zeilig, M., et al., Pathological laughter and crying patients with closed traumatic brain injury. *Brain Inj.*, 10, 591, 1996.

44. Jorge, R. and Robinson, R.G., Mood disorders following traumatic brain injury. *Int. Rev. Psychiatry*, 15, 317, 2003.

45. Weise, M.G. and Servis, M.E., Mental status examination and diagnosis, in *The American Psychiatric Publishing Textbook of Consultation-Liaison Psychiatry: Psychiatry in the Medically Ill,* 2nd edition, Weise, M.G. and Rundell, J.R., Eds., American Psychiatric Press, Washington, D.C., 2002, p. 61.

46. Benson, D.F., *The Neurology of Thinking*, Oxford University Press, New York, 1994.

47. Kishi, Y., Robinson, R.G., and Kosier, J.T., Suicidal ideation among patients with acute life-threatening physical illness: Patients with stroke, traumatic brain injury, myocardial infarction, and spinal cord injury. *Psychosomatics*, 42, 382, 2001.

48. Leon-Carrion, J., DeSerdio-Arias, M.L., Cabezas, F.M., et al., Neurobehavioral and cognitive profile of traumatic brain injury patients at risk for depression and suicide. *Brain Inj.*, 15, 175, 2001.

49. Simon, R.I. and Hales, R.E., *The American Psychiatric Publishing Textbook of Suicide Assessment and Management*, American Psychiatric Press, Washington, D.C., 2006.

50. Wilkinson, R., Meythaler, J.M., and Guin-Renfroe, S., Neuroleptic malignant syndrome induced by haloperidol following traumatic brain injury. *Brain Inj.*, 13, 1025, 1999.
51. Hensley, P.L. and Reeve, A., A case of antidepressant-induced akathisia in a patient with traumatic brain injury. *J. Head Trauma Rehabil.*, 16, 302, 2001.
52. Kennedy, R., Burnett, D.M., and Greenwald, B.D., Use of antiepileptics in traumatic brain injury: A review for psychiatrists. *Ann. Clin. Psychiatry*, 13, 163, 2001.
53. Whelan, F.J., Walker, M.S., and Schultz, S.K., Donepezil in the treatment of cognitive dysfunction associated with traumatic brain injury. *Ann. Clin. Psychiatry*, 12, 131, 2000.
54. Fann, J.R., Uomoto, J.M., and Katon, W.J., Sertraline in the treatment of major depression following traumatic brain injury. *J. Neuropsychiatr. Clin. Neurosci.*, 12, 226, 2000.
55. Fann, J.R., Uomoto, J.M., and Katon, W.J., Cognitive improvement with treatment of depression following mild traumatic brain injury. *Psychosomatics*, 42, 48, 2001.
56. McAllister, T.W., Traumatic brain injury and psychosis: What is the connection? *Semin. Clin. Neuropsychiatr.*, 3, 211, 1998.
57. Taylor, C.A. and Jung, H.Y., Disorders of mood after traumatic brain injury. *Semin. Clin. Neuropsychiatr.*, 3, 224, 1998.
58. Anderson, K. and Silver, J.M., Modulation of anger and aggression. *Semin. Clin. Neuropsychiatr.*, 3, 232, 1998.
59. Schneider, L.S., Small, G.W., and Clary, C.M., Estrogen replacement therapy and antidepressant response to sertraline in older depressed women. *Am. J. Geriatr. Psychiatry*, 9, 393, 2001.
60. Grocott, H.P., Mackensen, G.B., Grigore, A.M., et al., Postoperative hyperthermia is associated with cognitive dysfunction after coronary artery bypass graft surgery. *Stroke*, 33, 537, 2002.
61. Heyer, E.J., Sharma, R., Rampersad, A., et al., A controlled prospective study of neuropsychological dysfunction following carotid endarterectomy. *Arch. Neurol.*, 59, 217, 2002.
62. Olin, J.J., Cognitive function after systematic therapy for breast cancer. *Oncology*, 15, 613, 2001.
63. Greig, N.H., Vtsuki, T., Yu, Q., et al., A new therapeutic target in Alzheimer's disease treatment: Attention to butylcholinesterase. *Curr. Med. Res. Opin.*, 17, 159, 2001.
64. Ratey, J.J. and Johnson, C., *Shadow Syndromes*, Pantheon Books, New York, 1997, p. 214.
65. Manley, M.R.S., Psychiatric interview history and mental status examination, in *Comprehensive Textbook of Psychiatry*, 7th edition, Saddock, B.J. and Saddock, V.A., Eds., Lippincott, Williams & Wilkins, Philadelphia, PA, 2000, p. 652.
66. Mohl, P.C. and McLaughlin, G.D.W., Listening to the patient, in *Psychiatry*, Tasman, A., Kay, J., and Lieberman, J.A., Eds., W.B. Saunders, Philadelphia, PA, 1997, p. 3.
67. Vincett, J.D., Brain injury: A society within a society. *A.A.B.N. News Lett.*, 51, 19, 1995.
68. Taylor, M.A., *The Fundamentals of Clinical Neuropsychiatry*, Oxford University Press, New York, 1999, p. 398.
69. *Diagnostic and Statistical Manual of Mental Disorders*, 4th edition, American Psychiatric Association, Washington, D.C., 1994, p. 648.
70. Shenaq, S.M. and Dinh, T., Maxillofacial and scalp injury in neurotrauma, in *Neurotrauma*, Narayan, R.K., Wilberger, J.E., and Povlishock, J.T., Eds., McGraw-Hill, New York, 1996, p. 225.
71. Manson, P.N., Management of facial fractures. *Perspect. Plast. Surg.*, 2, 1, 1988.
72. Rohrich, R.J. and Hollier, L.H., Management of frontal sinus fractures: Changing concepts. *Clin. Plast. Surg.*, 19, 219, 1992.
73. Mattox, K.L. and Wall, M.J., Thoracic vascular injury in patients with neurological injury, in *Neurotrauma*, Narayan, R.K., Wilberger, J.E., and Povlishock, J.T., Eds., McGraw-Hill, New York, 1996, p. 285.
74. Baik, S., Uku, J.M., and Joo, K.G., Seatbelt injuries to the left common carotid artery and left internal carotid artery. *Am. J. Forensic Med. Pathol.*, 9, 38, 1988.
75. Chedid, M.K., Deeb, Z.L., Rothfus, W.E., et al., Major cerebral vessels injury caused by a seatbelt shoulder strap: Case report. *J. Trauma*, 29, 1601, 1989.
76. Colice, G.L., Neurogenic pulmonary edema. *Clin. Chest Med.*, 6, 472, 1985.
77. Mattox, K.L., Feliciano, D.V., Beall, A.C., et al., Five thousand seven hundred and sixty cardiovascular injuries in 4459 patients: Epidemiologic evolution 1958–1988. *Ann. Surg.*, 209, 698, 1989.
78. Boone, D.C. and Peitzman, A.B., Abdominal injuries, in *Neurotrauma*, Narayan, R.K., Wilberger, J.E., and Povlishock, J.T., Eds., McGraw-Hill, New York, 1996, p. 295.

79. Flint, L.M., Small and large bowel injuries, in *Current Surgery Therapy,* 4th edition, Cameron, J.L., Ed., Mosby Yearbook, St. Louis, 1992, p. 853.
80. Coburn, M., Genitourinary injuries, in *Neurotrauma*, Narayan, R.K., Wilberger, J.E., and Povlishock, J.T., Eds., McGraw-Hill, New York, 1996, p. 303.
81. Lindsey, R.W. and Cash, C., Orthopedic injuries, in *Neurotrauma*, Narayan, R.K., Wilberger, J.E., and Povlishock, J.T., Eds., McGraw-Hill, New York, 1996, p. 269.
82. Riedel, B., Demonstration eines durchachtagiges Umhergehen total destruirten Kniegelenkes von einem Patienten mit Stichverletzung des Ruckens. *Verh. Dtsch. Ges. Chir.*, 12, 93, 1883.
83. Benassy, J., Mazabraud, A., and Diverres, J., L'osteogenese neurogene. *Rev. Chir. Orthoped.*, 49, 117, 1963.
84. Cope, R., Heterotopic ossification. *South. Med. J.*, 83, 1058, 1990.
85. Garland, D.E., Clinical observations on fractures and heterotopic ossification in spinal cord and traumatic brain injured population. *Clin. Orthopaed.*, 233, 86, 1988.
86. Wood, D. and Hoffer, M.M., Tibial fracture in head-injured children. *J. Trauma*, 27, 65, 1987.
87. Yablon, S.A., Posttraumatic seizures. *Arch. Phys. Med. Rehabil.*, 74, 983, 1993.
88. Ewing-Cobbs, L., Barnes, N., Fletcher, J.M., et al., Modeling of longitudinal achievement scores after pediatric traumatic brain injury. *Dev. Neuropsychol.*, 25, 107, 2004.
89. Ewing-Cobbs, L., Fletcher, J.N., Levin, H.S., et al., Academic achievement and academic placement following traumatic brain injury in children and adolescents: A two-year longitudinal study. *J. Clin. Exp. Neuropsychol.*, 20, 769, 1998.
90. Levin, H.S. and Eisenberg, H.M., Neuropsychological impairment after closed head injury in children and adolescents. *J. Pediatr. Psychol.*, 4, 389, 1979.
91. Klonoff, H., Low, M.D., and Clark, C., Head injuries in children: A prospective five-year follow-up. *J. Neurol. Neurosurg. Psychiatry*, 40, 1211, 1977.
92. Chugani, H. and Phelps, M., Imaging human brain development with positron emission tomography. *J. Nucl. Med.*, 32, 23, 1991.
93. Passler, M., Isaac, W., and Hynd, G., Neuropsychological development of behavior attributed to frontal lobe functioning in children. *Dev. Neuropsychol.*, 1, 349, 1985.
94. Baddeley, A. and Wilson, B., Frontal amnesia and the dysexecutive syndrome. *Brain Cognit.*, 7, 212, 1988.
95. Max, J.E., Arndt, S., Castillo, C.S., et al., Attention-deficit hyperactivity symptomatology after traumatic brain injury: A prospective study. *J. Am. Acad. Child Adolesc. Psychiatry*, 37, 841, 1998.
96. Wassenberg, R., Max, J.E., Lindgren, S.D., et al., Sustained attention in children and adolescents after traumatic brain injury: Relation to severity of injury, adaptive functioning, ADHD, and social background, *Brain Inj.*, 18, 751, 2004.
97. Max, J.E., Castillo, C.S., Bokura, H., et al., Oppositional defiant disorder symptomatology after traumatic brain injury: A prospective study. *J. Nerv. Ment. Dis.*, 186, 235, 1998.
98. Dennis, M., Wilkinson, M., Koski, L., et al., Attention deficits in the long term after childhood lead injury, in *Traumatic Head Injury in Children*, Broman, S.H. and Michel, M.E., Eds., Oxford University Press, New York, 1995, p. 165.
99. Ewing-Cobbs, L., Levin, H.S., Fletcher, J.M., et al., The Children's Orientation and Amnesia Test: Relationship to severity of acute head injury and to recovery of memory. *Neurosurgery*, 27, 683, 1990.
100. Chapman, S.B., Discourse as an outcome measure in pediatric head-injured populations, in *Traumatic Head Injury in Children*, Broman, S.H. and Michel., M.E., Eds., Oxford University Press, New York, 1995, p. 95.
101. Roman, M.J., Delis, D.C., Willerman, L., et al., Impact of pediatric traumatic brain injury on components of verbal memory. *J. Clin. Exp. Neuropsychol.*, 20, 245, 1998.
102. Vakil, E., Jaffe, R., Eluze, S., et al., Word recall versus reading speed: Evidence of preserved priming in head-injured patients. *Brain Cognit.*, 31, 75, 1996.
103. Levin, H.S. and Eisenberg, H.M., Neuropsychological impairment after closed head injury in children and adolescents. *J. Pediatr. Psychol.*, 4, 389, 1979.
104. Klonoff, H., Low, M.D., and Clark, C., Head injuries in children: A prospective five-year follow-up. *J. Neurol. Neurosurg. Psychiatry*, 40, 1211, 1977.
105. Chugani, H. and Phelps, M., Imaging human brain development with positron emission tomography. *J. Nucl. Med.*, 32, 23, 1991.

106. Passler, M., Isaac, W., and Hynd, G., Neuropsychological development of behavior attributed to frontal lobe functioning in children. *Dev. Neuropsychol.*, 1, 349, 1985.

107. Baddeley, A. and Wilson, B., Frontal amnesia and the dysexecutive syndrome. *Brain Cognit.*, 7, 212, 1988.

108. Weller, E.B. and Weller, R.A., Mood disorders in prepubertal children, in *Textbook of Child and Adolescent Psychiatry*, 2nd edition, Wiener, J.M., Ed., American Psychiatric Press, Washington, D.C., 1997, p. 333.

109. Max, J.E., Children and adolescents, in *Textbook of Traumatic Brain Injury*, Silver, J.N., McAllister, T.W., and Yudofsky, S.C., Eds., American Psychiatric Press, Washington, D.C., 2005, p. 477.

110. Oquendo, M.A., Friedman, J.H., Grunebaum, M.F., et al., Mild traumatic brain injury in suicidal behavior and major depression. *J. Nerv. Ment. Dis.*, 192, 430, 2004.

111. Max, J.E., Smith, W.L., Sato, Y., et al., Mania and hypomania following traumatic brain injury in children and adolescents. *Neurocase*, 3, 119, 1997.

112. Herskovits, E.H., Gerring, J.P., Davatzikos, C., et al., Is a spatial distribution of brain lesions associated with closed head injury in children predictive of subsequent development of posttraumatic stress disorder? *Radiology*, 224, 345, 2002.

113. Vasa, R.A., Grados, M., Slomine, B., et al., Neuroimaging correlates of anxiety after pediatric traumatic brain injury. *Biol. Psychiatry*, 55, 208, 2004.

114. Food and Drug Administration. FDA statement on recommendations of the psychopharmacologic drugs and pediatric advisory committees. *www.FDA.gov/bds/topics/news/2004/new01116.html*. Accessed September 23, 2006.

115. Food and Drug Administration. Suicidality in Children and Adolescents Being Treated with Antidepressant Medications. *www.FDA.gov/cder/drug/antidepressants/SSRIPHA200410.html*. Accessed September 23, 2006.

116. Pfeffer, C.R., Suicide and suicidality, in *The American Psychiatric Publishing Textbook of Child and Adolescent Psychiatry*, 3rd edition, Wiener, J.N. and Dulcan, M.K., Eds., American Psychiatric Press, Washington, D.C., 2004, p. 891.

117. Nass, R. and Stiles, J., Neurobehavioral consequences of congenital focal lesions, in *Pediatric Behavioral Neurology*, Frank, Y., Ed., CRC Press, Boca Raton, FL, 1996, p. 149.

118. Arffa, S., Traumatic brain injury, in *Textbook of Pediatric Neuropsychiatry*, Coffey, C.E. and Brumback, R.A., Eds., American Psychiatric Press, Washington, D.C., 1998, p. 1093.

119. Neeper, R., Huntzinger, R., and Gascon, G.G., Examination1: Special techniques for the infant and young child, in *Textbook of Pediatric Neuropsychiatry*, Coffey, C.E. and Brumback, R.A., Eds., American Psychiatric Press, Washington, D.C., 1998, p. 153.

120. Taylor, H.G., Yeates, K.O., Wade, S.L., et al., Influences in first-year recovery from traumatic brain injury in children. *Neuropsychology*, 13, 76, 1999.

121. Vladka, A.B. and Narayan, R.K., Emergency room management of the head-injured patient, in *Neurotrauma*, Narayan, R.K., Wilberger, J.E., and Povlishock, J.T., Eds., McGraw-Hill, New York, 1996, p. 119.

122. Centers for Disease Control and Prevention (CDC). *Morb. Mortal. Wkly. Rep.*, 55, 201, 2006.

123. Stevens, R.D. and Bhardwaj, A., Approach to the comatose patient. *Crit. Care Med.*, 34, 31, 2006.

124. Coben, J.H., Steiner, C.A., and Miller, T.R., Characteristics of motorcycle-related hospitalizations: Comparing states with different helmet laws. *Accid. Anal. Prev.*, 39, 190, 2006.

125. Hartl, R., Gerber, L.M., Iacono, L., et al., Direct transport within an organized state trauma system reduces mortality in patients with severe traumatic brain injury. *J. Trauma*, 60, 1250, 2006.

126. Davis, D.P., Serrano, J.A., Vilke, G.M., et al., The predictive value of field versus arrival Glasgow Coma Scale score and TRISS calculations in moderate-to-severe traumatic brain injury. *J. Trauma*, 60, 985, 2006.

127. Varelas, P.N., Eastwood, D., Yun, H.J., et al., Impact of a neurointensivist on outcomes in patients with head trauma treated in a neurosciences intensive care unit. *J. Neurosurg.*, 104, 713, 2006.

128. Colice, G.L., Neurogenic pulmonary edema. *Clin. Chest Med.*, 6, 472, 1985.

129. Perkin, R.M., Anas, N., and Lubinisky, P., Myocardial ischemia and disparate ventricular function after pediatric head injury. *Crit. Care Med.*, 19, 587, 1991.

130. Kaufman, H.H., Timberlake, G.A., and Voelker, J., Medical complications of head injury, in *Neurology and Trauma*, Evans, R.W., Ed., W.B. Saunders, Philadelphia, PA, 1996, p. 186.

131. Simmons, R.L., Martin, A.M., Heisterkamp, C.A., et al., Respiratory insufficiency in combat casualties: II. Pulmonary edema following head injury. *Ann. Surg.*, 170, 39, 1969.

132. Tryba, M., Risk of acute stress bleeding in nosocomial pneumonia in ventilated intensive care patients: Sucralfate versus antacids. *Am. J. Med.*, 83 (Suppl. 3B), 117, 1987.

133. Rogers, F.B., Shackford, S.R., Wilson, J., et al., Prophylactic vena cava filter insertions in severely injured trauma patients: Indications and preliminary results. *J. Trauma*, 35, 637, 1993.

134. Cohen, D.B., Rinker, C., and Wilberger, J.E., Traumatic brain injury in anticoagulated patients. *J. Trauma*, 60, 553, 2006.

135. Kearney, T.J., Bentt, L., Grode, M., et al., Coagulopathy and catecholamines in severe head injury. *J. Trauma*, 32, 608, 1992.

136. Kaufman, H.H., Delayed posttraumatic intracerebral hematoma, in *Intracerebral Hematomas: Etiology, Pathophysiology, Clinical Presentation and Treatment*. Kaufman, H.H., Ed., Raven Press, New York, 1992, p. 173.

137. Young, B. and Ott, L., Nutritional and metabolic management of the head-injured patient, in *Neurotrauma*. Narayan, R.K., Wilberger, J.E., and Povlishock, J.T., Eds., McGraw-Hill, New York, 1996, p. 345.

138. Kamada, T., Fusamoto, H., Kawano, S., et al., Gastrointestinal bleeding following head injury: A clinical study of 433 cases. *J. Trauma*. 17, 44, 1997.

139. High, W.M., Roebuck-Spencer, T., Sander, A.M., et al., Early versus later admission to postacute rehabilitation: Impact on functional outcome after traumatic brain injury. *Arch. Phys. Med. Rehabil.*, 87, 334, 2006.

140. Houlden, H., Edwards, N., McNeil, J., et al., Use of the Barthel Index and the Functional Independence Measure during early inpatient rehabilitation after single incident brain injury. *Clin. Rehabil.*, 20, 153, 2006.

141. Schonberger, M., Humle, F., Zeeman, P., et al., Patient compliance in brain injury rehabilitation in relation to awareness and cognitive and physical improvement. *Neuropsychol. Rehabil.*, 16, 561, 2006.

142. Fleming, J.M., Shum, D., Strong, J., et al., Prospective memory rehabilitation for adults with traumatic brain injury: A compensatory training programme. *Brain Inj.*, 19, 1, 2005.

143. Bergfeldt, U., Borg, K., Kullander, K., et al., Focal spasticity therapy with botulinum toxin: Effects on function, activities of daily living and pain in 100 adult patients. *J. Rehabil. Med.*, 38, 166, 2006.

144. Francisco, G.E., Hu, M.M., Boake, C., et al., Efficacy of early use of intrathecal baclofen therapy for treating spastic hypertonia due to acquired brain injury. *Brain Inj.*, 19, 359, 2005.

145. Wilson, D.J., Powell, N., Gorham, J.L., et al., Ambulation training with and without partial weight bearing after traumatic brain injury: Results of a randomized controlled trial. *Am. J. Phys. Med. Rehabil.*, 85, 68, 2006.

146. Williams, G.P., Greenwood, K.N., Robertson, V.J., et al., High-Level Mobility Assessment Tool (HiMAT): Interrater reliability, retest reliability, and internal consistency. *Phys. Ther.*, 86, 395, 2006.

147. Pender, D.J., *Practical Otology*, J.B. Lippincott Company, Philadelphia, PA, 1992.

148. Gentry, B., Smith, A., and Dancer, J., Relation of orientation, verbal aggression, and physical aggression to compliance in speech–language therapy for adults with traumatic brain injury. *Percept. Mot. Skills*, 96 (3 Pt. 2), 1311, 2003.

149. Sellars, C., Hughes, T., and Langhorne, P., Speech and language therapy for dysarthria due to nonprogressive brain damage. *Cochrane Database Syst. Rev.*, 20, CD002088, 2005.

150. Wymer, J.H., Lindman, L.S., and Booksh, R.L., A neuropsychological perspective of aprosody: Features, function, assessment, and treatment. *Appl. Neuropsychol.*, 9, 37, 2002.

151. Levin, H.S., Grafman, J., and Eisenberg, H., *Neurobehavioral Recovery from Head Injury*, Oxford University Press, New York, 1987.

4 The Neuropsychiatric Mental Status and Neurological Examinations following Traumatic Brain Injury

INTRODUCTION

Once the neuropsychiatric interview and history taking are complete, the examiner moves to the core components of a neuropsychiatric assessment of any kind, including traumatic brain injury (TBI). The two principal sources of information on which a neuropsychiatric and neurobehavioral diagnosis is based are the neuropsychiatric history and the neuropsychiatric mental status and neurological examinations. This chapter describes first the detailed mental and neurological examinations of the adult patient and then follows that with a similar detailed explanation of these examinations in the child. The neuropsychiatric mental examination expands upon the classic mental status examination taught within a psychiatric residency and during medical school training. This examination was initially based upon mental examination techniques Adolf Meyer first proposed almost 100 years ago at Johns Hopkins University. However, moving from the more classic examination of mental status to a neuropsychiatric mental status examination requires the examiner to focus upon a brain-based examination rather than the more traditional emotional and mind-based examination. Those wishing to follow the more classical and updated mental status examination of modern psychiatry can consult Trzepacz and Baker.[1] If the examiner wishes a more neurological approach to the mental status examination, the text by Strub and Black is recommended.[2] For those examiners practicing neuropsychology, the techniques of Lezak[3] are recommended. To make the mental examination even more cerebral based, the recent text by Cummings and Mega is highly recommended.[4]

The neuropsychiatric mental status examination of the TBI patient will focus upon specific neuropsychiatric disorders commonly encountered. These are outlined in Table 4.1. The reader should consult Chapter 2 for delineation of some of these syndromes. The neurologic examination of the adult and child following TBI has a specific physical focus rather than the mental focus of the neuropsychiatric mental status examination. The examiner may have to modify the clinical focus of each examination to comport to the age and developmental stage of the patient (e.g., child, adolescent, adult, geriatric). With regard to the forensic aspects of these examinations, most neuropsychiatric examiners will be evaluating the TBI person late after injury. The neuropsychiatric mental status and neurological examinations at this point in the recovery process will focus upon residual impairment and damages as they comport to the litigation. For the treating examiner, the examinations should focus upon deficits that may need further remediation through psychotherapy, cognitive therapy, pharmacologic therapy, or physical therapy.

TABLE 4.1

Specific Neuropsychiatric Disorders

- Frontal lobe disorders: apathetic, disinhibited, and dysexecutive syndromes
- Temporal lobe disorders: amnestic disorders, personality dysfunction, and temporal lobe based seizure syndromes
- Basal ganglia or brainstem dysfunctions: movement disorders, arousal disorders, and subcortical cognitive dysfunction
- Language and prosody disorders
- Visual processing disorders
- Disorders of motor or sensory behaviors
- Denial and neglect syndromes

THE ADULT MENTAL EXAMINATION

APPEARANCE AND LEVEL OF CONSCIOUSNESS

This section stresses the measurement of mental function as it applies to TBI. However, the examiner must also be an acute and astute observer of appearance and behavior of the patient. Table 4.2 lists common features that the examiner should detect rather quickly following initial establishment of rapport with the adult person. The general behavior should be described in terms of whether the patient is normal in activity, hyperactive, agitated, quiet, immobile, or poorly ambulatory. The question of whether the person is dressed neatly or slovenly often coincides with elements of neglect, anosognosia, and self-monitoring. Do persons dress and behave in accordance with their age, that of their peers, their gender, and their social background? Does the individual make appropriate eye contact? This is important in terms of initially determining visual neglect, homonymous hemianopia, or paranoia. In terms of verbal output, does the patient converse with the examiner in a normal fashion? What is the rate of speech? Particularly in patients with frontal lobe injuries, is the phrase length reduced and is the absolute word content within a sentence reduced? Does the motoric behavior represent hemiparesis, reduction of motor speed, a movement disorder, or other indicia of motor syndromes? While observing the patient and making initial verbal contact, it is important to determine the speed of mental and motor function. Often times this is reduced following TBI. The best way to determine alterations of thought or perception is by quiet listening rather than direct inquiry. Can the individual go from point A to point B when answering questions? Is the language output reflective of tangential thinking, loosening of associations, or circumstantiality?

With regard to consciousness, not everyone can describe it well, including most physicians. William James, the philosopher, reminds us that "everyone knows what *consciousness* is, until he tries to define it."[5] However, most central nervous system clinicians distinguish five levels of

TABLE 4.2

Common Mental Examination Elements of Appearance/Level of Consciousness

- Apparent age versus chronological age
- General behavior
- Level of consciousness
- Dress and grooming
- Eye contact
- Verbal output and comprehension
- Physical abnormalities
- Motoric behavior
- Speed of mental/motor function

consciousness: (1) alertness, (2) lethargy, (3) obtundation, (4) stupor, and (5) coma.[6] It is not possible to perform a comprehensive psychiatric examination while a person is in stupor or coma, and therefore, the neuropsychiatric examiner will generally be examining people who are either alert, lethargic, or mildly obtunded. The alert patient is fully awake and responds appropriately to external and internal stimuli. However, the person may be cognitively impaired or even disoriented and still be described as alert. The reader will probably acknowledge that many times emergency room patients who have an altered state of consciousness are still described as alert by the emergency department personnel. On the other hand, the lethargic patient is not fully alert and may drift in awareness or consciousness while not actively stimulated. Lethargic patients usually have a reduction in mental speed. Recall from Chapter 2 that lethargy is often a permanent feature in the postacute TBI patient. The lethargic patient may attend poorly to the examination because of lethargy rather than as a specific defect of attention. The obtunded patient generally presents with a level of consciousness between that of lethargy and stupor. This individual may be difficult to arouse and may appear overtly confused. A complete neuropsychiatric examination may be impossible in the obtunded patient, and it may be necessary to apply less stringent examination techniques. A test battery for determining the level of severe impairments is discussed in Chapter 6. The obtunded patient will be marginal in ability to cooperate and pay attention.

Attention

Traumatic brain injury often affects attentional components of mental function, particularly since anterior brain injury is so common.[7,8] It has been repeated elsewhere in this book that one cannot perform a detailed neuropsychiatric examination in a person without first determining the level of attention. If the examinee or patient cannot pay attention during questioning or when asked to perform tasks, the examination will probably be suboptimal. Thus, attention and concentration must be assessed in all patients, as any disturbance of these domains will result in failures throughout the mental status examination. Many of the tests discussed in Chapter 6 have timed components, and the inattentive or lethargic patient will have difficulty in performing memory tests, calculations, tests of language comprehension, and other explicit functions. Cummings and Mega[4] point out three major types of attentional disturbances that may be identified during the face-to-face examination. These include (1) drowsiness or deficits of alertness, (2) deficits in concentration, demonstrated as distractibility and fluctuating attention, and (3) unilateral neglect or hemispatial inattention. Drowsiness may reflect alterations of the reticular-activating system, and posttraumatic hypersomnia has been discussed previously in this text. Distractibility is a common feature of frontal lobe injury. Sensory unilateral neglect may point to injury within the thalamus or parietal lobe, and motor neglect may result from injury in the caudate nucleus or frontal lobe.

Attention is the patient's ability to bring focus to a specific external stimulus while at the same time filtering out distractions from extraneous internal or environmental stimuli.[9] Vigilance is a term of art for attention maintained longitudinally over time. Other neuropsychological or neurological terms for vigilance are "sustained attention" or "concentration." Attention is more focused and requires a specific orienting response, whereas vigilance is nonspecific and refers to the more basic tonic arousal process of the reticular-activating system during which an awake patient can respond to any stimulus appearing in his environment.[2] Attention is directed to any of the five senses. There is a specific attentional capacity for each sense. As mentioned previously in this text, most neuropsychiatric and neuropsychological assessments will measure auditory and visual attention and possibly tactile attention, but rarely is olfactory or gustatory attention measured. Olfactory sensation (cranial nerve I) is generally examined during the neurological examination (see below), but the attentional aspects of olfaction are almost never determined except in experimental paradigms.

While attention can be measured electrophysiologically and by using neuropsychological means, the examiner should remember that a clinician's own experience and training are as qualitatively valid at detecting inattention as quantitative measurements. In the inattentive patient, the examiner will notice distractibility or difficulty in attending to the examiner's questions. At a very basic level, one can screen auditory attention with the classical digit span testing. Single digits are recited to the patient in a series of increasing length. After each series is repeated to the patient, the patient is then asked to repeat it back to the examiner aloud. Writing should not be permitted, as this introduces a language and motor component, or a proprioceptive component, to a simple test of auditory attention. The examiner can initiate the examination by saying, for example, "I want you to repeat the following numbers after I say them: 3-1-9-2." If the patient has attended, the patient should reply back exactly, "3-1-9-2." The examiner should take care to repeat the digits in a monotonous voice, except for the last digit, which should be said at a slightly lowered pitch so the patient can understand that this is the final digit of the series. (The dysprosodic patient with a comprehension deficit may not detect this subtle change in tone.) The monotonous speech pattern is used by the examiner so as not to provide a cue to the patient and inadvertently improve the patient's ability to repeat digits. Most experts believe that about a one second interval should exist between each digit as it is recited to the patient. Normal digit span length is 6 ± 1 digit. The ability to recite back at least six digits should remain stable well into old age. Most normal and healthy adults can perform seven digits forward and five digits backward. However, the examiner must recall that reciting digits backward is not a pure measure of auditory attention, as it also introduces a parallel-processed working memory task. Patients must divide their attention by first remembering the forward order of the digits, and then mentally reversing them before repeating them back to the examiner. In the TBI patient, reciting digits backward can be quite challenging to those with frontal lobe injury (impaired set switching). This challenge arises because of the recitation of a digit span backward, while requiring divided attention, and it also measures concentration and vigilance. The Folstein Mini-Mental State Exam[10] requires spelling the word "world" backward. This is used as an alternative to the digit span repetition or the serial 7s test. This apparently simple test of the Mini-Mental State Exam measures divided attention and concentration as well as pure auditory attention. If a language disorder is present, it should be recalled that most aphasic patients cannot produce valid results on digit repetition or a visual letter cancellation task. Table 4.3 lists common facts about the measurement of auditory and visual attention.

Another popular test used during the bedside evaluation of vigilance is the serial 7 subtraction. Neurologists and psychiatrists have used this technique for almost a century. It is a measurement of vigilance, dual tracking, and concentration rather than focused attention. The patient is asked to start at 100 and subtract 7 from this number, and then to keep subtracting 7 from each subsequent answer. The expected response in the patient is "100, 93, 86, 79, 72, 65 . . . ." If the patient can complete at least seven subtractions, this is considered to be within normal limits.[1] The greater the number of errors produced, the more impaired the concentrating ability of the patient. Some neuropsychologists screen language using the Wepman tasks from the Halstead–Reitan Battery.[11] However, this technique is not recommended.[3]

TABLE 4.3
The Face-to-Face Assessment of Attention

- Each sensory modality has an orienting or attentional component.
- The neuropsychiatric mental status examination generally evaluates only auditory attention, sometimes visual attention, and sometimes tactile attention.
- Auditory attention can be tested by digit repetition.
- Visual attention can be tested by a letter cancellation or similar task.
- In aphasic persons, digit repetition or letter cancellation cannot be tested validly.
- See Chapter 6 for measures of tactile attention.

Speech and Language

Speech generally refers to the motor-driven articulatory component of language. Language, on the other hand, is the symbolic representation within the brain used for communication by speaking, reading, computation, and writing. Like all brain disorders affecting language, language skills are more likely to be impaired following TBI to the dominant cerebral hemisphere. In Chapter 2 we learned that language disorders occur on a permanent basis in about only 2% of persons following TBI. We also learned in Chapter 2 of distinct differences between language disorders in children following TBI when compared with adults. The approach to language should be systematic, and Table 4.4 lists the principal language functions that should be assessed during a neuropsychiatric examination. During spontaneous speech, the examiner should listen carefully to determine fluency. Nonfluent speech is characterized by a decrease in verbal output, effort during production of speech, dysarthria, decreased phrase length, dysprosody (loss of speech rhythm and music), and agrammatism (omission of the small relational words). Nonfluent speech has a normal verbal output, or at times is increased. Articulation is usually normal, and phrase length is normal. The prosody is preserved. However, the speech is often empty and circumstantial or paraphasic.[12,13] If the examiner hears nonfluent speech, in nearly all right-handed persons and a majority of left-handed persons, nonfluent aphasia reflects structural changes in the left frontal lobe. On the other hand, if the aphasia is fluent, this is usually indicative of damage to the left posterior temporal, inferior parietal, or temporoparietal–occipital junction.[13] If the examiner detects a lack of prosody, this is usually a right cerebral disorder. Expressive dysprosody is usually associated with a frontal lobe lesion, but it also may involve subcortical dysfunction in the basal ganglia.[14,15]

The examiner must be careful not to confuse dysarthria with dysprosody. Dysarthria is an impairment of articulation. It is common after TBI and is generally caused by incoordination of pharyngeal muscles. It occurs particularly in those individuals who sustained brainstem or complex facial injuries. Injury to cranial nerve XII may cause unilateral tongue weakness and difficulty in articulating lingual consonants (T, D, L, R, N). Patients with substantial nerve VII weakness may have difficulty with labial and dentilabial consonants (P, B, M, W, F, V). Bilateral involvement of corticobulbar pathways in the brainstem results in pseudobulbar speech, which is characterized by a slow laborious speech production with a strained quality to the speech as the patient attempts to produce sounds. Cerebellar damage may cause dysrhythmic speech associated with irregularities in pitch and loudness. Basal ganglia injuries may result in jerky, dysrhythmic speech and are often associated with movement disorders such as choreoathetosis or loss of prosody and may contain Parkinsonian features.[16] Table 4.5 outlines particular impairments of speech articulation.

Language comprehension is difficult to assess in the best of circumstances, and it may require use of the Boston Diagnostic Aphasia Examination if it is necessary to precisely establish the level of comprehension (such as in a competency evaluation for forensic purposes). A classic question to

---

TABLE 4.4

Principal Language Functions to Be Tested or Observed during the Mental Status Examination

- Spontaneous speech
- Comprehension
- Repetition
- Naming
- Reading (aloud and for comprehension)
- Writing
- Word-list generation
- Prosody of speech

TABLE 4.5
Impairment of Speech Articulation

- Dysarthria is distortion or slurring of speech sounds.
- Nerve XII impairment affects lingual consonants T, D, L, R, N.
- Facial nerve (VII) weakness affects labial consonants P, B, M, W, F, V.
- Cerebellar lesions cause irregularities of pitch and loudness.
- Basal ganglia injury may result in dysrhythmic speech sounds with choreoathetotic movements.

test comprehension may be used: "Is my wife's brother a man or a woman?"[17] Nonfluent speech is often difficult to detect, whereas fluent aphasic speech is easily recognizable as a language. The sounds flow easily and seem normal. The striking finding of fluent speech is the lack of nouns and verbs. The content of the speech output consists mostly of small words such as articles, conjunctions, interjections, or even curse words. If nouns and verbs are used, they are often paraphasic. Paraphasias exist in two forms, and the examiner must listen carefully to detect these. In the first form, the meaning may be substituted (semantic paraphasia) for the correct word (e.g., "I wore my car"). The other form is a phonemic paraphasia, and a syllable may be substituted (e.g., "I wore my pat"). If the person substitutes nonsense words, this is called a neologistic paraphasia (e.g., "I wore my pash"). The most common language disorder the examiner will hear following TBI is a naming impairment. The patient will have difficulty in producing the names of common items in the environment during the face-to-face mental examination. On a more formal examination, such as the Boston Naming Test, the patient will usually demonstrate impairment that correlates with what the examiner can hear.

Most examiners who are experienced with detecting language disorders can determine the overall fluency by listening to the patient's spontaneous speech. More subtle difficulties with fluency may require specific testing such as outlined in Chapter 6. These could include the Animal Naming Test[18] and the FAS test.[19] Strub and Black[2] enjoy using the Animal Naming Test during their examinations. They find it particularly useful in patients with severe injury who demonstrate significant deterioration of cognitive function. The test is simple, and the patient is instructed to recall and name as many animals as possible within 60 s. The score is the number of correct responses as well as any paraphasic productions that occur. A normal individual should produce 18–22 animal names in 1 min, with the expected variation being plus or minus 5–7 names.[18] However, this test is age sensitive, and normal individuals above age 70 produce approximately 17 names ± 2.8 names in the eighth decade, and 15.5 names ± 4.8 names in the ninth decade. A score below 13 in an otherwise normal person is consistent with impaired verbal fluency.

Repetition is normal in aphasias only if they are transcortical. In ordinary fluent or nonfluent aphasias, the patient usually lacks the ability to repeat. In the classic mental status examination, most psychiatrists have learned phrases such as, "The quick brown fox jumped over the lazy dog," and complex and linguistically irregular phrases such as, "No ifs, ands, or buts."[17] The examiner must be aware that deficits of attention or concentration will interfere with all but the most simple tests of repetition. Anatomically, failure of repetition occurs in those aphasias with lesions situated adjacent to the Sylvian fissure in the dominant hemisphere. Aphasias with preserved repetition have intact perisylvian structures.[13] Table 4.6 lists the distinction between perisylvian and nonperisylvian syndromes detected by repetition ability. Another quick way to assess language is to remember "the four Ds" of speech. The examiner can ask the question: "Does the patient have dysphonia, dyarthria, dysprosody, or dysphasia?" Table 4.7 lists the four items that the neuropsychiatric examiner should listen for while reviewing language function during the neuropsychiatric mental status examination.

Naming disturbances are the most common language disorders seen following TBI, but they lack specificity for the type of language impairment. Anomia is common following TBI, but the

TABLE 4.6

Repetition Syndromes

Impaired Repetition	Intact Repetition
Perisylvian Syndromes	**Nonperisylvian Syndromes**
Broca's aphasia	Anomic aphasias
Wernicke's aphasia	Transcortical aphasias
Conduction aphasia	Subcortical aphasias
Global aphasia	

examiner should remember that it also is occasionally evident in toxic-confusional states and also with evidence of increased intracranial pressure or other nonfocal disturbances.[20] The ability to name objects is acquired very early in our development and is one of the most basic of language functions. This ability stays remarkably stable over decades, and normal 80-year-olds generally perform as well as normal 25-year-old persons.[21] Naming is invariably disturbed in all types of aphasia. Naming may be impaired in some traumatically brain-injured persons who otherwise do not demonstrate classic aphasia. Word-finding difficulty is closely related to anomia, and this is the reduced ability to retrieve the nouns and verbs used in spontaneous speech. It is also frequently abnormal in persons who have suffered TBI. Patients with word-finding difficulty may show impairment on the picture completion test of the Wechsler Adult Intelligence Scale-III. Anomia can be objectively tested face-to-face by asking the patient to name objects or pictures that the examiner points to in the room.

The detection of disturbances of reading, writing, and spelling is easily done. As the reader is probably aware, we are not born into the world knowing how to read. Virtually everyone who is born learns to speak one's language, assuming one has sufficient hearing and central nervous function to do so. However, reading is a complex neurological function that must be learned, and it is subject to cultural and educational influences. The examiner can consider difficulties of reading only by applying those to the person's level of educational achievement. The ability to read aloud and also to read with comprehension must be tested separately. Some lesions of the brain will disrupt oral reading but leave reading comprehension intact, whereas other disorders may impair reading comprehension but spare the ability to read aloud. Rarely, the examiner may detect hemialexia, which is the occurrence of ignoring one-half of the word.[12] Writing is also an acquired task and must be learned. An acquired disturbance of writing is called agraphia, and it may occur due to aphasia secondary to an interruption of linguistic function. It also may occur from a non-aphasic cause produced by impairment of the motor system and the mechanical aspects of writing.[4] A very important function of language disturbance must be remembered by the examiner. All aphasics will make errors in their written as well as their oral production, and the characteristics of the written language closely resemble those of the spoken output.[22] If repetition is impaired,

TABLE 4.7

The Four Ds of Speech Evaluation

- Dysphonia: Difficulty in producing voice sounds (phonating)
- Dysarthria: Difficulty in articulating the individual sounds or the sound units of speech (phonemes, the Fs, Rs, Gs, vowels, consonants, labials (cranial nerve VII), gutturals (cranial nerve X), and linguals (cranial nerve XII)
- Dysprosody: Difficulty with the melody and rhythm of speech, the accent of syllables, the inflections, intonations, and pitch of the voice, the affective components of speech
- Dysphasia: Difficulty in expressing or understanding words as the symbols of communication

the anatomical localization is in the perisylvian area of the dominant cerebral hemisphere (see Table 4.6). Anterior aphasias will have the characteristics of a Broca's language disturbance, whereas posterior aphasias will have the characteristics of a Wernicke's disorder. Persons with conduction and global aphasias also demonstrate impaired repetition. On the other hand, if the patient can repeat the short phrases required, the aphasia is anatomically outside the perisylvian area and is usually an anomic, transcortical, or subcortical disorder. Subcortical aphasias can infrequently be an element of TBI syndromes, particularly with brainstem involvement. Transcortical aphasias are rarely, if ever, seen in traumatic brain injuries but are more likely to be found in hypoxic or toxic brain syndromes affecting the vascular watershed areas of the cerebral hemispheres.

Prosody refers to the melodic, rhythmic, affective, and inflectional elements of speech associated with gestural aspects of speech. At the face-to-face examination, it is sufficient to evaluate the presence of spontaneous prosody and prosodic comprehension. Spontaneous prosody is judged by watching the patient and listening to the patient so as to determine the prosodic quality of verbal utterances during the course of conversation. To test for prosodic comprehension, the examiner can have the patient, with eyes closed, listen to a neutral sentence executed by the examiner in four prosodic styles: surprise, happy, angry, and sad.[4] The examiner should then ask the patient to identify the emotional state of the speaker based on the way the sentence was inflected. Impaired spontaneous prosody is an anterior disturbance produced by right frontal lesions and extrapyramidal disorders, whereas prosodic comprehension is more likely to occur following right temporoparietal injuries.[14]

Memory and Orientation

Mild TBI generally does not lead to severe compromise of memory functions. On the other hand, moderate to severe brain injury can lead to chronic memory disorder, confusion, and disorientation. Questions of orientation are always asked during a formal mental status examination. In the TBI patient, if the individual remains disoriented following injury, it is most often a consequence of diffuse cerebral injury, particularly affecting anterior areas of limbic structures. During examination of memory functions, the examiner must account for other potential confounding factors affecting memory such as psychotropic medications, metabolic disorders, endocrine dysfunction, and impairment of the hypothalamic-pituitary axis as a result of TBI.

The basic rule of testing orientation is to inquire as to the person's ability to temporally localize by person, place, and time. Orientation to person can be assessed simply by asking the person's name. Place can be determined by asking for the current physical or geographic location. Time is easily determined by asking the patient the day of the week, the month, and the current year. If the patient exhibits lack of orientation to these questions, the examiner should determine if the patient knows the season of the year. Location can be examined by asking the location of the examiner's officer, the city that the office occupies, the building where the office is located, and, if necessary, the state the office occupies. The ability to temporally sequence and maintain orientation can be determined by asking the patient's birth date and age; however, this also tests certain aspects of past memory and these questions are not directed purely toward orientation.

Recall in Chapter 3 that it was recommended to ask the TBI patient the last thing the patient remembered before impact, whether or not the patient remembers the impact, and other aspects of being removed from the accident scene, and lastly what is the first thing the patient remembers when memory awareness returns. This tests episodic memory. Memory, like the attentional system noted above, has a specific memory for each sensory modality. The location of memory storage is thought to be in heteromodal centers associated with the focal representation of the sensory modality in each cerebral hemisphere. The reader may wish to review Figure 2.1, which represents Squire's formulation of memory. From a practical standpoint, memory is often divided into three functions: (1) immediate, (2) recent, and (3) remote. Immediate memory is also called working memory, and it is the attentional aspects of memory tested by digit span repetition. Immediate memory is best considered an attentional capacity, whereas recent memory refers to the ability to learn and recall new information. Orientation in time and space must be learned on a daily basis and is part of the autobiographical aspects of living associated with episodic memory. There are two types of recent memory disturbances: amnesias and retrieval deficit syndromes. In amnestic disorders, there is a failure to store information, whereas in the retrieval deficit syndrome, there is an impairment of timely recall of stored data.[4] The examiner should expect a significantly brain-injured person to be amnestic for the impact and information immediately following the impact. This information can never be recalled, as it is never stored. The person with a true amnesia cannot spontaneously recall this information, and even by giving the patient cues or clues, the individual will not be able to report information, as there is nothing stored to remember. On the other hand, a patient with retrieval deficit syndrome will benefit from cues, and this individual is able to distinguish between targets and foils on tests of recognition memory.[23] The truly amnestic patient generally has brain dysfunction that has affected temporarily or permanently the hippocampus in the mediotemporal regions, the fornix, mammary bodies, mammillothalamic tract, or the medial thalamus nuclei. On the other hand, retrieval deficit syndrome is often associated with disturbances affecting the dorsolateral prefrontal cortex or caudate nucleus. This individual might also display abnormalities on the Wisconsin Card Sorting Test if the dorsolateral prefrontal cortex is involved.

When information is first registered within the brain, it does not require focused attention by the primary sensory cortex to which the information is being sent (e.g., primary auditory cortex if information is conveyed by voice). If the brain does not attend to this input within a few seconds, the information is not remembered nor stored. Part of initial registration requires the immediate organization of memory data into patterns by a secondary sensory cortex which lies anatomically near the primary sensory cortex. Attention is paid cognitively to the input at this stage in memory. For instance, in the input of auditory information, individuals self-monitor their language as they speak to another person. They can immediately relate their conversation to others and by self-monitoring they maintain their place in the flow and sequence of their oral communication. In brain-injured patients, this pattern is often disrupted; the patient cannot self-monitor, and the speech output is fragmented or rambling. This rambling speech often presents as circumstantial thinking.

Working memory is not a true memory but is an attentional process that holds information for 20 or 30 s until it is processed further. This stage of memory function is tested by measurement of digit span or by the immediate recall of words (verbal) or diagrams (visual). Memory can be consolidated if an effort is made to remember the information by rehearsing it. This is a form of new learning and it requires from seconds to extended minutes to be completed. Any sensory modality can "remember" in this fashion but in the mental status examination, generally, only verbal and visual components are tested. As shall be seen in later chapters, tactile learning can also be tested by procedures such as fingertip writing and finger naming while the person is blindfolded. During the mental status examination, verbal new learning ability can be tested easily by asking the person to learn a series of eight or nine words by repeating the list until it is memorized. Recall then can be tested 20 or 30 min later to confirm the level of learning that has taken place. The words chosen for the person to remember should not be easy to link phonetically or semantically as this will provide memory cues and falsely increase the efficiency of the learning process.[2] Another good test of verbal learning is to read a short paragraph to the person being tested, and after 20 min, ask for a recall of the story. The specific number of memory elements in the story must be known by the examiner beforehand. This technique is used in the Wechsler Memory Scale-III. Most persons without a brain dysfunction can recall 15–17 items of a 25-item story, and after 20 min, they should be able to remember two-thirds of their original score.[24] Standardized methods for assessing verbal memory are explained further in Chapter 6. Strub and Black[2] recommend hiding five objects in front of the person to test visual memory, and then after a period, asking the person to find the objects.

To test long-term memory, examiners have to know either something specific about the individual's life, or they should ask the patient about commonly known historical facts. Adequacy of long-term memory is influenced by educational level and intellect, but most neurologically intact

TABLE 4.8

A Functional Schema for Memory Functions

- Data are registered without requiring focused attention by the primary sensory cortex. If attention to the stimulus does not occur, data are lost in 1–2 s.
- Data are organized by the secondary sensory cortex and attention is brought to bear.
- If effort is made, seven to nine items can be held. This is working memory or short-term memory and data are held for approximately 15–20 s if no effort is made to remember it.
- With rehearsal or memory work, memory becomes consolidated in 30 s to 30 min.
- Long-term memory is stored in secondary and tertiary (heteromodal) areas. Affect paired with a memory increases the strength of long-term storage (e.g., death of a loved one). Long-term memory is of two types: procedural/implicit (e.g., driving a vehicle, a skill) and declarative/explicit (semantic/factual).
- Declarative memory (explicit) is composed of semantic memory (general information or facts) and episodic memory (autobiographical experiences).

persons should be able to name the current president of the United States or the governor of their state. Moreover, they should be aware of major historical events or persons that have had historical impact (e.g., the World Trade Center bombing or Who was Hitler?).

There is no singular or universally accepted theory of memory. In fact, the diversity of approaches to memory research is the rule rather than the exception. Multiple reviews of memory studies have been written and all current theories divide memory into different psychological or neurophysiological processes.[24–28] Five such processes have been described by Signoret.[29] He suggests that a holding process occurs in which information is retained momentarily until other memory processing can take place. This has been referred to in Table 4.8 as working memory. An acquiring process then follows that encodes data selected for placement into general memory. The acquiring process can be subdivided into "chunking," which is the efficient gathering of information and subsequent "linking" (the correlation of discrete elements of information). The storing process is often called consolidation. During this function, information is placed into a permanent or semipermanent storage system that includes new memory traces, rehearsal, and maintenance of the memory information. The recall of memory is a retrieval process wherein previously learned information is recaptured and made useable. Furthermore, a scanning process occurs that allows items relevant to the person's current environmental situation to be selected from a vast array of stored memory traces.

Visuospatial and Constructional Ability

Assessment of visuoconstructive ability is performed by using simple screening methods. The examiner may use the intersecting pentagons from Folstein's Mini-Mental State Examination.[10] Asking the patient to draw a three-dimensional cube is a sensitive detector of visuoconstructive impairment. Obviously, the patient must have relatively normal motor skills in the writing hand or these screening tests will have no validity. Most idiopathic psychiatric disorders spare constructional ability, but lesions of the frontal or parietal occipital regions of either hemisphere may disrupt visuoconstructive ability.[30] Neglect of one side of the figure is consistent usually with a posterior hemispheric lesion contralateral to the neglected hemispace. Right cerebral dysfunction seems more likely to produce left neglect than left cerebral dysfunction causing right neglect.[31]

Visuoconstructive ability is also called visuospatial ability in some texts. Visuospatial ability can be entirely a cognitive ability. When constructional ability is added to the screening for visuospatial skills, it must be remembered that the prerequisites for constructional ability are not only intact vision, but intact motor coordination, strength, praxis, and tactile sensation. Patients who fail constructional tasks may require testing for other disorders that could interfere with their ability to complete the task. For instance, in addition to visual deficits, the patient also could have writing dyspraxia or visual agnosia.

The impaired patient, when drawing two- or three-dimensional figures, often omits major elements of the figure being copied. Angles often are rounded; the form of the figure may be lost, or the patient is unable to copy alternating designs. The clock test is a useful screening device for visuospatial neglect.[57] If the patient has, for instance, a right hemisphere lesion, the individual may neglect the left hemispace and place all the clock numbers to the right side of the clock. Drawing tasks may also demonstrate perseverative responses in the patient. The patient may continue to draw repeating lines without closing in a figure or, for instance, when drawing numbers on a clock, may repetitively draw 1 and forget the numerical sequence 1, 2, 3 . . . .

Constructional ability and visuospatial function are absolutely essential to performing many everyday activities. In fact, neuropsychiatric and neuropsychological testing has been discussed in the medical and psychological literature under the topic of ecological validity. Does this mean that there is a relation between test performance and real-world abilities? Constructional ability and visuospatial functions are necessary to drive vehicles, function in a kitchen, use a vacuum cleaner, read maps, drive around a city, use a computer, operate Excel spread sheets, and generally function within the environment and remain topographically and geographically oriented. Impairment of constructional ability and visuospatial ability is seen generally in individuals sustaining TBI sufficient to produce tissue-based brain injury. Often this level of injury is demonstrable on structural or functional brain imaging. Table 4.9 outlines important elements of visuospatial and constructional ability.

Some traumatically injured persons who sustain a brain injury may also have an inability to use their upper extremities. In examining visuospatial ability in these individuals, one cannot rely on motor activity for the assessment. An alternative approach is to ask the patient to identify particular geometric figures among a series of figures oriented in different planes. These are presented to the patient visually, and the person can then respond verbally to the examiner's questions about figure orientation. These tasks require cognitive manipulation of figures without the need for motor output.

Executive Function

Executive functions for neurologists are higher-ordered cognitive abilities thought to be mediated primarily by the dorsolateral prefrontal cortex and various subcortical structures linked to this region. Psychiatrists may call functions from this area frontal lobe abilities.[24] Clinical psychiatrists have also used terms previously such as abstraction ability, conceptualization, insight, and judgment.[1] The term executive function probably comes from neuropsychologists. Lezak has conceptualized executive functions as having four components: (1) volition, (2) planning, (3) purposive action, and (4) affected performance.[3] Stuss and Benson have proposed four higher control

---

TABLE 4.9

Assessment of Visuospatial/Constructional Ability

- These skills usually are assessed by paper-and-pencil copying of two- or three-dimensional figures.
- Skills can be disrupted by visual field cuts from retinal, optic nerve, chiasmal, optic tract, lateral geniculate body, optic radiation, or primary visual cortex damage.
- For those patients who cannot use their hands, cognitive identification of geometric shapes in different planar orientations can be attempted.
- Focal injuries to the parietal right hemisphere are more likely to impair visuospatial function than analogous left hemisphere injuries.
- The person will demonstrate impairment while using Excel for computation or spreadsheets, if previously skilled, due to Excel's inherent spatial characteristics.

functions attributed to the prefrontal cortex. They include (1) sequencing, (2) drive, (3) executive control, and (4) future memory.[32]

When the examiner tests attention and concentration, a portion of this examination is subsumed under executive function. Many patients with executive dysfunction will have alterations of attention. Use of a word-list generator (see Chapter 6) also relies upon frontal circuits, and this can be tested with the use of the FAS test described above or the Controlled Oral Word Association Test. Retrieval of stored information from memory is mediated by frontal–subcortical circuits, and the retrieval deficit syndrome has been discussed above. These syndromes are often seen in patients who have sustained frontal injury and who present with executive deficits. Perseveration, as may be detected on the Clock Drawing Test,[57] would be another manifestation of being stimulus bound. This is often a feature of patients who have sustained frontal lobe injury. Motor programming skills depend on intact frontal–subcortical circuits. The reader can consult Strub and Black's text[2] for information regarding alternating written sequences used to detect executive dysfunction. These tests reveal the patient's ability to program motor responses in a specific repeating or alternating sequence. Using the Strub and Black technique, the patient is asked to copy an alternating sequence or a looped figure provided by the examiner; the patient is then asked to continue the same repeating pattern across the page. Another simple bedside technique is to ask the patient to tap once each time the examiner taps twice and tap twice whenever the examiner taps once. The examiner should alternate the sequences on a random basis and then observe whether the patient can respond in a reciprocal fashion.

The screening of executive function by face-to-face examination has been systematized recently by a number of authors. Power and colleagues have developed a screening test for detecting dementia in patients with AIDS. This instrument includes measures of attention (repeating four words), measures of memory, free and semantically cued recall of words, measures of psychomotor speed (writing the alphabet), visuospatial function (copying a cube), and response inhibition (antisaccadic eye movements).[33] The Executive Interview (EXIT)[34] has been tested and proves to be a better predictor of independent functioning in several geriatric test samples than the Mini-Mental State Examination of Folstein.[10] The Behavioral Dyscontrol Scale[35] is designed specifically to predict everyday functional capacity. This test instrument uses go/no-go motor sequencing and alphanumeric sequencing tasks to analyze the ability to organize goal-directed behavior. The alphanumeric sequencing portion provides a brief measure of psychomotor speed and working memory. For those patients with motor or movement disorders, the Frontal Assessment Battery[36] may be useful. This instrument requires 5 min to perform and surveys motor sequencing, spontaneous word-list generation, and response inhibition on a go/no-go task. Table 4.10 describes common signs and symptoms of executive dysfunction.

TABLE 4.10

Signs and Symptoms of Executive Dysfunction

- Outrageous, disinhibited behavior
- Impulsiveness or perseveration of oral or written information
- Reduced ability to express words
- Poor visual or auditory attention
- Reduction in motivation or drive
- Inability to switch sets or inhibit responses
- Inability to plan for the future
- Inability to organize

Affect and Mood

Traumatic brain injuries are frequently accompanied by psychiatric disturbances, which can vary from striking to relatively minor alterations in personality, behavior, and emotional regulation.[37] Mood disorders, anxiety disorders, and substance abuse disorders are the more prevalent classical psychiatric diagnoses seen among TBI patients.[38] Specifically, major depression is noted to be a large contributor to mood disturbances seen following TBI. In fact, in mild to moderate TBI, subjective cognitive deficits are linked in large measure to comorbid major depression. However, other mechanisms may also account for these deficits.[39] When examining for mood changes following TBI, the neuropsychiatric examiner may experience substantial difficulty in contrast to the relative ease of detecting these disorders in classic psychiatric patients. A New South Wales study reports that the majority of participants in a research protocol with TBI reported some change in the post-injury experience of everyday emotion, although the pattern of changes differed greatly among individuals. Reduced subjective experience, especially of sadness and fear, was associated with poor emotion matching but not emotion labeling.[40] The findings of this group suggest elements of dysprosody as a cause for the difficulty with emotion matching of facial expressions. Moreover, some of the examples described by these authors suggest components of alexithymia. The alexithymia concept consists of difficulty in identifying emotions, difficulty in describing emotions, and a tendency to externally oriented thinking.[41]

In classical psychiatry affect refers to the outward display of emotions. These are emotions that the examiner can visually or auditorily perceive and detect. On the other hand, mood is the term for the unobserved internal, perceived, or felt aspects of emotions (see the somatic marker hypothesis in Chapter 2). The display of affect and the content of thinking generally are congruous and well correlated. If the examiner detects a significant lack of correlation between the outward display of emotion (affect) and the content of thought as expressed by the patient (mood), the differential considerations include a classical psychiatric disorder, an anatomical functional disconnection of limbic or subcortical areas associated with emotional regulation, or a metabolic–toxic derangement of emotional control.[42] Where the neuropsychiatrist is likely to have the most difficulty in detecting mood changes following TBI will be in the patient who demonstrates neglect syndromes, anosognosia, or disturbances of higher-order cognitive processing. The more classically oriented psychiatrist often describes mood as a consistent sustained-feeling state, whereas affect is experienced as the moment-to-moment expression of the feelings related to the mood or distinct from the mood.[1] Mood disturbances following TBI are probably the most common psychiatric manifestations, and as Holsinger et al. have noted, these may persist for decades following TBI.[43]

In the neuropsychiatric examination, the physician or psychologist will note that mood and affect permeate the entire interview process and are assessed in an ongoing manner throughout the examination. Since there may be a disparity between observed mood and perceived mood, it is important to verify one's observation of the affect by asking specifically what mood the patient is experiencing. If patients cannot describe their emotional state in their own words (alexithymia), open-ended questions should be asked such as, "How have you been feeling in the last few days?" or "How have you been feeling lately?" or "How do you feel right now?" Follow-up questions are required to determine whether the mood described at the time of the neuropsychiatric examination has changed in any way from prior mood states the patient may have experienced since injury. The term "depression" does not have the same meaning to everyone. Patients will rarely use the term depression, and they are more likely to describe mood changes with terms such as "sadness" or "nervousness." Once the level of affect and mood has been determined by the examiner, it will be important to confirm the examiner's observation. This can be done with standardized test instruments such as the Minnesota Multiphasic Personality Inventory-2 or the Personality Assessment Inventory. These are discussed further in Chapter 6. Also, it is important that the examiner recalls that what appears to be expressed affect may not be. For instance, recall from Chapter 2 that following TBI, apathy, somnolence, fatigue, and other alterations of behavior and consciousness

TABLE 4.11
Descriptors of Affect/Mood

Dysphoric	Sad, hopeless, grieving, despondent, distraught
Euthymic	Well feeling, comfortable, happy, friendly, pleasant
Euphoric	Elated, ecstatic, hyperthymic, giddy
Apathetic	Flat, bland, dull, lifeless, nonspontaneous
Angry	Irritable, argumentative, irate, belligerent, confrontational
Apprehensive	Angry, fearful, scared, worried, nervous, frightened

may accompany brain injury and be mistaken for changes in affect. A medial frontal syndrome (Chapter 2) may produce a profound picture of apathy that can be misconstrued for depression. However, persons with frontal lesions in the medial brain generally will not affirm sadness or depression and are much more likely to provide information consistent with anosognosia. Further confounding factors may occur in the patient with significant right cerebral hemisphere injury who displays prominent aspects of expressive dysprosody. In the patient who appears too happy, the examiner must distinguish between secondary mania versus orbitofrontal pseudoeuphoria or other aspects of disinhibition. Table 4.11 reviews clusters of descriptors for affect (observable) and mood (internal and subjective) in TBI patients.

When assessing mood and affect, it is important to remember that the examiner's own non-dominant hemisphere detector systems are useful in distinguishing affective states. The examiner's right brain posterior language decoding systems may use mirror neurons to assist the examiner to feel sad himself while examining a depressed patient. When we as humans use the expression, "I feel your pain," we may not realize how literally it could be true.[44] Our subtle detector systems are part of us all, and the examiner should pay careful attention to these during a neuropsychiatric observation. Many messages from those who are examined are expressed emotionally and with kinesics rather than verbally. The examiner's own emotional detector systems may be acutely sensitive to expressed affect of another person. When the examiner reports on affect, it is usually done within five basic parameters: (1) appropriateness, (2) intensity, (3) mobility, (4) range, and (5) reactivity.[1] Appropriateness enables the examiner to determine whether the affect is congruent or incongruent with the mood. The intensity level of affect enables the examiner to determine whether the person is apathetic or disinhibited. The mobility level of affect is often described as labile or constrictive. The range of affect may be reduced in patients with alterations of motivation and drive, whereas reactivity of affect can vary from hyperreactive to nonreactive or even nonresponsive.

Thought Processing, Content, and Perception

Two of the greatest books written in the English language regarding thought processing with regard to organic mental conditions are the British texts by Lishman[45] and Fish.[46] Table 4.12 lists common thought-processing defects. Psychiatrists tend to think that thought processing and content disorders

TABLE 4.12
Thought-Processing Defects

Perseveration	Neologisms
Circumstantiality	Echolalia
Loose associations	Clang associations
Tangentiality	Thought blocking
Flight of ideas	Witzelsucht (moria)

as primarily associated with the classic psychiatric illnesses that can produce psychosis. Neuropsychiatrically, many of the thought-processing defects of Table 4.12 can also be seen following TBI. When the examiner listens for a thought disorder, this must be inferred from abnormalities within what the patient says. When conceptualizing thought disorders, it is often useful to think of them in terms of a disorder of the form of thought versus a disorder of the content of thinking. Disturbed thought form refers to abnormal relationships between ideas within the flow of conversation. These can represent themselves as a loosening of associations, a flight of ideas, perseverative thinking, or abnormally slow or fast thinking. Loosening of associations describes a loss of the link between logical associations within a sentence structure, and these are classical findings in schizophrenia-like thought disorders. Tangential thinking refers to digression in the stream of thought without returning to the point of departure. This is to be contrasted with circumstantiality, which is digression from the topic with an eventual return to the intended point. Another way of conceptualizing circumstantiality is as the person goes from point A to point B, they take all of the back roads in the country rather than use the more direct high-speed highway. They will eventually get to point B but will travel more miles than necessary to get there. Circumstantiality is a frequent finding in persons with organic brain disease of many kinds including TBI. Flight of ideas is a formal thought disorder characteristic of mania and hypomanic disorders demonstrated by a rapid flow of ideas. This may be associated with rhyming, punning, or clanging. Witzelsucht or moria is an uncontrollable tendency to pun or tell irrelevant jokes. It is common with lesions of the orbitofrontal cortex. Perseveration is also common in persons with organic mental conditions of many etiologies. This can present itself as perseverating on a theme, a word, or even a written number. The patient repeats the word, phoneme, or number multiple times.

The classic finding of a disorder of thought content is the delusion. Delusions are false ideas for which no consensual validation can be obtained from others. Generally speaking, religious ideas are excluded from delusional thinking unless they are so outlandish they cannot be validated by a believing consensus. Disorders of thought content can take many forms including ideas of reference, mind reading, thought broadcasting, grandiose beliefs, persecutory beliefs, and theme-specific delusions. These can occur in the form of misidentification syndromes that are seen within the context of an organic mental disorder. Delusions are usually described either as persecutory or grandiose in nature. Confabulation is a disorder of thought content seen in persons with disorders of memory who fabricate responses in order to make the stream of thinking believable.

As discussed in Chapter 2, psychosis following brain injury does occur. It is relatively rare, and it is thought to represent abnormalities within the temporal and frontal brain areas. The general presentation of post-TBI psychosis includes persecutory delusions and auditory hallucinations with an absence of the negative symptoms classically seen in schizophrenia. The mean onset is 4–5 years after TBI, with the majority of cases occurring within 2 years post-injury.[47] The most prominent risk factor for psychosis following TBI is injury to the temporal and frontal lobes. Genetic loading from family origins of schizophrenia and other psychotic illnesses may also be a contributor to post-TBI psychosis.[48] Within the context of thought disorders, paranoid disorders are reported following brain injury. A study in 3000 war veterans from Finland demonstrated that psychotic disorders were found in approximately 750 cases of war veterans with moderate or severe brain injury. This study noted that paranoid schizophrenia and paranoid schizophreniform psychosis developed earlier (in 23% of cases within 1 year) than delusional psychosis, which tends to occur much later, and in 40% of the cases appeared more than 5 years after injury. Jealousy or fear of being sexually betrayed constituted the most prominent individual content of the delusions.[49]

The content of thought is particularly important for the examiner to determine when assessing mood or anxiety in posttraumatic brain disorders. Traumatized patients may have recurring intrusive preoccupations with sounds, images, and other stimuli that remind them of the accident. As noted in Chapter 2, many brain-injured patients may develop a posttraumatic stress disorder. As Harry Stack Sullivan said many years ago, one must "listen with a third ear" when assessing patients. This important admonition remains valid today. The examiner should pay special attention to the opening minute of the examination and to any unstructured moments throughout the interview.[1] The unstructured portion of the interview allows one to gauge the processes of thinking and also to assess the themes that are important to the patient. For instance, the patient's thought may be replete with themes of anger, guilt, diminished self-esteem, fear of intimacy, and desire for closeness. Brain-injured patients often see themselves as different from others and not capable of being loved. Moreover, patients with an organic neglect or denial syndrome generally will demonstrate a large discrepancy between the content of their thinking and the problems within their observed behavior. Open-ended questions without structure are more fruitful in gaining the content of thinking. For instance, the examiner might ask, "What kinds of problems have you been having lately?" or "Tell me something about yourself." If the patient is too disorganized in thinking or too language impaired to provide useful information, then the examiner will have to move on to a more structured form of interview. If the examiner learns of specific problem areas in the thinking, these will require interview follow-up. It is particularly important for the clinician to explore delusional content, homicidal ideas, paranoid themes, phobic statements, preoccupation with traumas or healing, ruminations, and suicidal ideas. If any of these themes are discovered, then it is paramount for the examiner to explore the level of distress these themes may cause the patient. In a person who has suspended reality, abnormal ideas may cause little distress, whereas some brain-injured persons may be so worried and focused upon the aversive content of their thinking that they cannot maintain a goal direction for rehabilitation. As we shall see later in this text, the level of disorganization and the level of communication difficulty are inversely proportional to how the brain-injured person will function postrecovery.

Hallucinations can occur in any sensory modality. They are not very common following head injury unless there has been some substantial injury to the limbic or deep subcortical brain systems. Hallucinations can be auditory, visual, tactile, olfactory, or gustatory (taste). These are perceptual experiences in the mind or consciousness of the patient without a sensory input. On the other hand, illusions are sensory misinterpretations of real stimuli. For instance, a visual image is misinterpreted to be an object that it is not. Autoscopy is the hallucinatory experience of seeing oneself. Its best common description is that often reported when patients describe "near death experiences." Déjà vu is the perception of having previously seen or lived in the current setting. It is a sense that one has "been here before." On the other hand, jamais vu is just the opposite. That is to say, the present familiar environment seems strange and alien and as if one has not been there previously.

Visual hallucinations are more common following TBI than auditory hallucinations unless the traumatically brain-injured person has a prior history of schizophrenia or other psychosis. Visual hallucinations, of course, are much more likely to occur if there is damage to the visual system, particularly the heteromodal processing centers in the vicinity of the calcarine fissure. Patients with cortical blindness due to bilateral occipital lesions may confabulate the description of what they cannot see (Anton's syndrome). This is in actuality a type of visual neglect syndrome.[2] Olfactory hallucinations are relatively rare but can occur with the frontal injuries commonly associated with TBI as the anterior brain structures are more likely to be injured than more posterior structures. Olfactory and gustatory hallucinations are most frequently encountered following temporal lobe injury which in turn may lead to seizures in the uncal or entorhinal areas. Somatic (tactile or haptic) hallucinations are rarely, if ever, seen following TBI. Déjà vu and jamais vu not only occur following parietal lobe injury but also are frequently encountered in temporal lobe injuries, leading to posttraumatic seizure disorders. Derealization and depersonalization are most likely to be seen in traumatically brain-injured patients in the acute care setting, and these may accompany delirium or encephalopathy following trauma. If present in the acute care setting, these generally do not persist into the rehabilitation period or chronic phase of the brain injury disorder. It should be fairly obvious that within the context of a brain injury mental examination, these perceptual disturbances must be explored through the interview process as there is no standardized means to measure perceptual distortions within a face-to-face examination. Table 4.13 lists common perceptual distortions and their definitions.

TABLE 4.13
Perceptual Distortions

Form	Distortion
Hallucination	Perceptual experience in the mind without a sensory stimulus
Illusion	Sensory misinterpretation of external stimuli
Derealization	The external environment is unreal
Depersonalization	One's self is unfamiliar
Autoscopy	A hallucination of seeing oneself
Déjà vu	Having previously lived the present setting
Jamais vu	The current previously known setting is not familiar

Risk to Self or Others

There is no evidence in the world literature that an acute TBI is associated with an increased risk of suicide. As we have seen in previous chapters however, chronic depression occurring after TBI can certainly be associated with an increased suicidal risk. Since forensic and treatment examiners will be evaluating TBI persons after they have had an injury, it is necessary to determine what risk, if any, exists with regard to suicidal thoughts and suicidal actions. The reader is referred to the current text by Simon and Hales[50] for guidance in this area. This is probably the preeminent text at the present regarding suicide assessment and management. As has been stated previously, no psychiatrist is expected to foresee suicide in a person. However, not assessing suicide risk in a person who is potentially or actively suicidal is medically negligent. In the chronic phase of TBI, suicide risk increases and covaries with the level of depression.[51,52] Table 4.14 notes the common assessment factors that should be taken into consideration in determining the risk of suicide in any person, including one who may have sustained a TBI and who is now depressed.

In determining the elements within Table 4.14, the individual factors to be considered include a distinctive clinical syndrome or prodrome, whether or not the person has reasons to continue living, and whether religious beliefs play a role in suicidal intent or lack of intent. Under the clinical factors, the examiner should consider the lethality of the planned suicidal attempt if possible, whether or not there is rapport or a relationship with a treatment person, whether suicidal ideation is present, and particularly whether command hallucinations are present. If there is a plan, how well formed is it? Does the individual have any sense of hopelessness? Has the individual made prior attempts, and how potentially lethal were those attempts? Is suicidal ideation associated with panic attacks, psychic anxiety, or other anxiety disorders? How significant is the relationship with alcohol or substance abuse? Is global insomnia present? What is the current psychiatric diagnosis, severity of symptoms, and comorbidity of other disorders? Has the individual recently been discharged from a psychiatric hospital? How impulsive is the individual, and is agitation or physical illness present?

TABLE 4.14
Systematic Suicide Risk Assessment

Assessment Factors
- Individual
- Clinical
- Interpersonal relations
- Situational
- Demographic
- Overall risk rating

TABLE 4.15

Suicide Screening Questions and Guidelines for Assessment of Suicide Risk

- Have you had symptoms or feelings of depression/sadness that have led you to think you might be better off dead?
- During the past week, have you had any thoughts that your life is not worth living or that you would be better off dead?
- Have you had any thoughts about hurting or even killing yourself? If yes, what thoughts of self-harm have you had? Have you actually done anything to hurt yourself? Have you made a plan to take your life?

Risk	Thoughts	Action Plan
Low risk	No current thoughts present; no major risk factors present	Continue regular follow-up visits and monitoring of the patient.
Intermediate risk	Patient has current thoughts of suicide but no specific plans even though risk factors may be present	Question patient carefully at each visit for suicide risk. Ask patient to call you if suicide thoughts become more prominent. Consult with an expert (psychiatrist) if the examiner is not a psychiatrist.
High risk	Active current thoughts with a plan	Defer emergency management to a qualified expert (psychiatrist).

Is there a family history of mental illness, childhood sexual or physical abuse, and is the individual mentally competent? With regard to interpersonal relations, these should be determined within the context of employment, family, spouse or partner, and one's children, if present. Situational factors include the living circumstances, employment or academic status, financial status, and the availability of guns or other lethal means. One demographic factor to consider is age. Suicide is more common in males in their twenties or elderly males. Another demographic factor includes gender, as males are more likely to use lethal means to attempt suicide than females. Marital status is important. Single males are at the highest risk as a demographic group. Race is important, as Caucasians are more likely to attempt suicide than persons of color. The overall risk rating is based upon a judgment as to low, moderate, high, or a range of risks. For example, a homeless schizophrenic 27-year-old male with a prior history of suicide attempts who sustained a TBI 9 months before the current neuropsychiatric examination would warrant significant consideration as a potential risk of suicide. The above factors can be used as one part of the clinical assessment in an attempt to determine risk.

Once risk has been determined, it should be explicitly stated within the record. A note should be included in the assessment stating what suicide risk factors have been identified and how they have been weighted; what protective factors have been identified to reduce the risk of suicide; the overall assessment as to risk of suicide; what treatment and management interventions have been put in place to reduce the risk of suicide; if the patient is being seen on a continuous basis; and a statement about effectiveness of prior intervention or lack of effectiveness should be included in the note.[53] Table 4.15 lists suicide questions and guidelines for assessment of suicide risk.

Overall Mental Screening Examination

Table 4.16 enables the neuropsychiatric examiner to provide a comprehensive screening of attention, memory, language, visuospatial ability, executive function, and animal naming at the bedside or in the office. Following this screening, more sophisticated measurements can be undertaken if required. If a forensic examination is undertaken, it is necessary to quantify for a trier of fact measurements of cognitive function, and these techniques are discussed in great detail in Chapters 6 and 9.

One of the simplest tests of concentration is to ask the patient to count backward from 20 to 1. However, any sequence can be used since this is such a simple test of concentration that even those of limited intelligence and education should be able to pass if concentration is intact. Trzepacz and

TABLE 4.16

Face-to-Face Neuropsychiatric Screening Methods for Trauma-Induced Brain Injury in Adults

Mental Domain	Task	Poor Performance Significance
Attention	"Count from 20 to 1 backwards." (See Trzepacz and Baker.)[1]	Concentration impairment
	Serial 7s: "subtract 7 from 100, then 7 from that answer and continue." (See Trzepacz and Baker.)[1]	Impairment of working memory
Memory	Short-term verbal memory: "Remember brown, tulip, eyedropper, honesty."[2]	Less than 3 words after 10 min: Impaired frontosubcortical function of verbal memory[2]
	Short-term visual memory: "Copy these three shapes and remember them: square, triangle, circle" (see Folstein et al.)[10]	Two or less drawn after 3 min is impaired.
	Evaluate orientation to person, place or time. Past memory: "Who is the President?" "Which country bombed Pearl Harbor?"[55] "In which city is the World Trade Center?"	Normal is perfect responses or off by one day on date. Sensitive to low educational level.[54]
Language	Ask for names of common objects in visual space.[2]	Left perisylvian damage if attention is normal.[2]
	Repeat: "Methodist-Episcopal; triangle, Massachusetts"	If intact, language dysfunction outside perisylvian area. If impaired, Broca's, Wernicke's, or conduction aphasia.[2,27]
Visuospatial	Copy square, cross, triangle. Copy two intersecting pentagons.	If impaired, right hemisphere damage.[35]
	"Draw a clock and put the numbers in place. Set the time for 3 o'clock."[57]	If numbers skewed to right or left, check for visual neglect. Distortion of numbers may represent right hemisphere damage.[57]
Executive	Response inhibition: "Place your left hand to your right ear"; "Place your left hand to your left elbow."	If impaired, orbitofrontal damage.[56]
Animal naming (Strub and Black)	Frontal lobe word generator: "Say as many animal names as you can in one minute."	If impaired, dorsolateral frontal lobe or semantic memory system.[56,18] (Normal = 18–22 names, ±5–7.)

Baker[1] point out that this test is simple for the elderly. Some elderly patients find serial 7s too difficult, even those who are demonstrating cognitive impairment because of the normal effects of aging. The serial 7s test in patients younger than 60–65 years of age is very sensitive for detecting impairment of working memory and vigilance. The individual must parallel track and maintain two operations in the mind at once. After the person subtracts 7 from 100, the number 93 is held in mind. Then the person must keep that number in mind while the person subtracts 7 to produce 86. This double tracking method is a sensitive test of working memory.[56] The four particular words chosen for measurement of short-term verbal memory include brown, tulip, eyedropper, and honesty. These words are chosen for their semantic and phonemic diversity. This avoids memory cues, and they are recommended by Strub and Black.[2] The short-term visual memory test comes from Folstein et al.[10] The square, triangle, and circle are placed in the memory, and after 3 min the patient is asked to draw these again. Only the most significantly impaired person or seriously mentally retarded person will fail this test. However, since it is so easy to pass, it is not a sophisticated measure of visual memory, and if necessary, the examiner may need to apply the Wechsler Memory Scale-III (see Chapter 6).

By copying a square, cross, and triangle, sufficient angles are required, particularly in the drawing of the cross to pick up most constructional disorders. By drawing a clock, the examiner will screen for any spatial neglect, perseveration while writing, and comprehension. The simple test of executive function will detect comprehension as well as response inhibition when the person is asked to "place your left hand to your left elbow." The frontal lobe generator can be quickly screened by asking the person to say all the words beginning with the letter S that can be thought of within 1 min. This is a subsection of the Controlled Oral Word Association test or FAS test (see Chapter 6).

THE ADULT NEUROLOGICAL EXAMINATION

Clinical psychiatry focuses little on the neurological examination. However, a comprehensive neuropsychiatric examination begs the neurological examination to be performed. If the psychiatric examiner is ill equipped to perform this, it can be deferred to a neurologist or internist if the neuropsychiatric examiner wishes. Moreover, if the person has had a substantial TBI, it is likely that multiple neurological examinations have been performed by neurosurgeons, neurologists, or physiatrists, and the neuropsychiatric examiner can use these. The author recommends performing the neurological examination at the time of the neuropsychiatric examination, as it maintains the skill of the neuropsychiatric physician and also adds significant contemporary information to the database at the time of the neuropsychiatric examination. For instance, if a person had a TBI 9 months before the neuropsychiatric examination and in the postacute phase demonstrated a mild left hemiparesis, the physical representation of the hemiparesis may no longer be obvious while the patient is walking or manipulating objects. This detection may rely entirely on alteration of reflexes or subtle changes in muscular tone or strength that would be missed if the neurological examination is not performed contemporaneously with the neuropsychiatric examination. In those cases where the neuropsychiatric examination is performed for forensic purposes, if even the slightest hint of prior focal neurological findings is present in the trauma records, it is incumbent upon the neuropsychiatric examiner to perform a neurological examination, or see that another competent physician does so at the request of the neuropsychiatric examiner. For those psychiatrists and neuropsychiatrists who perceive their neurological examination skills to be weak, recall procedural learning discussed previously in this text. That learning is still present in the neuropsychiatric physician's brain and can be quickly ramped up to effectiveness by practice. It is also recommended to consult DeMyer.[58] Dr. DeMyer's teaching in the *Technique of the Neurologic Examination* is now in its fifth edition and is considered by many to be the greatest programmed text available for learning proper neurological examination techniques. Most neurologists conduct a simple mental status screening test at the time of their comprehensive neurologic examination. That will not be covered in this section, as this text focuses upon a much more detailed mental neuropsychiatric examination than generally practiced by neurologists.

CRANIAL NERVE EXAMINATION

Cranial Nerve I

Following TBI, all cranial nerves (except IX to XII) are at significant risk. The olfactory nerve and the facial nerve are the first and second most likely to sustain injuries.[59] Hematoma of the olfactory bulbs occurs following cranioencephalic trauma.[60] In those TBI patients who suffered a loss of consciousness, olfactory dysfunction may present in as high as 20% of the injured population.[61] The incidence of olfactory dysfunction is approximately 7% of all patients sustaining TBI.[16] The presentation of cranial nerve I dysfunction is usually partial anosmia. The frontal brain parts may be contused or slide forward within the anterior cranial vault. The olfactory epithelium to the entorhinal cortex may be affected.[62] Some patients report they can smell, but they may also report a distortion of the normal sense of smell (parosmia). In those instances, the injury is to the orbitofrontal and temporal lobes in most cases.[63] As a consequence, taste ability is generally affected as well. Much of our taste function as humans arises from food vapors traveling into the nasopharynx and being detected by the olfactory nervous system. Food substances in the mouth send aromatic molecules upward through the nasal passages to the olfactory apparatus, which contributes to the appreciation of taste. For the forensic psychiatrist, loss of the ability to smell may be a significant contribution to legal damages, as the inability to smell smoke, gas, or other noxious substances may place the affected individual at risk of harm.[64]

To test smell, the examination can vary from simple to complex. For those physicians requiring a complex examination, the University of Pennsylvania Smell Identification Test is available.[65] The use of a three-item screening measure as a gross indicator is about 80% effective in detecting anosmia. However, 20% of patients who perform perfectly on a three-item screening test will score in the anosmic range on the full University of Pennsylvania Smell Identification Test. Using a three-item screening test, the author chooses essential oils that can be purchased online from pharmaceutical supply companies. These essential oils are often used in making candy. The oils used should be common food and flavoring odors that most reasonable people will find familiar. This can include essential oils such as lemon, peppermint, spearmint, or anise. Depending on the patient's country of origin and culture, other essential oils consistent with foods in the particular culture of the patient may be chosen. The examiner says to the patient, "Close your eyes. Sniff and try to identify this odor." Compress one of the patient's nostrils, and hold the vial in front of the open nostril while asking the patient to sniff. Wait a moment and then ask the patient to identify the odor. For the second trial, compress the opposite nostril and do not present a stimulus. This will test the suggestibility and attentiveness of the patient. Thereafter, two other essential oils can be presented. Do not test smell ability with strong noxious chemicals, as the examiner will get a false-positive result. Strong chemicals and alcohol will stimulate the trigeminal nerve within the mucous membranes of the nose rather than the olfactory nerve. From a neuroimaging standpoint, a recent study was able to identify an altered perfusion pattern by SPECT scan in patients with impaired smell ability who had otherwise normal anatomic structures noted on MRI.[66] If a patient has a lesion to the mediotemporal lobe it is possible to develop olfactory hallucinations. These are more common in tumors and epilepsies but have been reported following TBI. They may present as olfactory déjà vu, in which the patient senses a familiar odor without a stimulus. The stimulus of olfaction becomes paired with a peculiar feeling of familiarity. If not previously ordered, an MRI should be obtained.

Cranial Nerve II

The optic nerve receives information from the retina, relays it through the nerve posterior to the eye, and crosses to the opposite side at the optic chiasm. The optic tract then travels from the chiasm to the lateral geniculate body and from there through the geniculocalcarine tract to the calcarine fissure of the occipital lobe and Brodmann area 17. This calcarine area is the primary visual cortex. Information from Brodmann area 17 then radiates to areas 18 and 19 in the adjacent visual association cortex. Further visual analysis may take place in the posterior temporal cortex. Approximately 3% of patients who sustain a TBI will demonstrate a persistent visual field defect, impaired visual acuity, or blindness.[67] The optic nerve alone is affected in approximately 5% of persons who sustain a TBI.[68] Direct trauma may cause injury to the optic nerve, but since most traumatic brain injuries are associated with frontal injuries to cerebral structures, the optic nerve and its pathways may also be injured by bone fracture, shearing forces, stretching, contusion, or loss of blood supply to the optic structures.[69] Table 4.17 lists the lesion location and the resulting visual impairment. The reader can consult a neuroanatomical text or ophthalmology text for further elucidation in this area. A neuropsychiatric examiner is not expected to be expert in optic lesion analysis nor ophthalmology, and Table 4.17 will provide assistance in determining the type of blindness. Analysis thereafter will

TABLE 4.17

Lesion Location in the Optic Tract: Type of Blindness

Lesion Location	Type of Blindness
Optic nerve (left)	Complete blindness, left eye
Optic chiasm	Complete bitemporal hemianopia
Optic tract (left)	Complete nasal hemianopia, left eye
Lateral geniculate body (left)	Complete right homonymous hemianopia
Inferior geniculocalcarine tract (left)	Complete right superior homonymous quadrantanopia
Superior geniculocalcarine tract (left)	Complete right inferior homonymous quadrantanopia
Calcarine fissure of occipital lobe (left)	Complete right homonymous hemianopia
	Right-sided lesions will produce blindness to the left side

require ophthalmologic consultation. Occipital lesions affecting the calcarine fissure are rare. When they occur, they are more likely to be seen following head injury in children than adults, and they are usually transient.[70]

Examination of vision is performed by confrontational testing while standing directly in front of the patient. If there is a unilateral optic nerve injury, neither the ipsilateral nor the contralateral pupil will be constricted when light is directed into the injured eye. On the other hand, both pupils will constrict when light is directed into the unaffected eye. The swinging flashlight test can be used to measure pupillary light response if the lesion is prechiasmatic. By shining a light in one eye and swinging it back and forth to the other eye, the pupil on the injured side will dilate as the light is swung to that eye (Marcus–Gunn phenomenon). If the optic nerve is atrophied, during funduscopic examination the clinician will note that the optic disc is pale. If there is no optic nerve or prechiasmatic injury, visual acuity can be tested using the hand-held Snellen acuity chart or a near-vision reading card. If these are not available, the person can be asked to read simple materials such as a newspaper.[69]

Visual fields are also assessed by confrontational testing. The neurological terms used for visual field descriptors are confusing and the reader will find some texts describing visual field-cuts as hemianopsia, while other texts will call it hemianopia. These terms are equivalent. When testing visual acuity, the patient should wear prescription glasses if the patient has them. This is because poor visual acuity caused by retinal or optic pathway dysfunction cannot be corrected by eyeglasses. If visual acuity is corrected by eyeglasses, the abnormality is generally in the ocular lens or other parts of the refraction system and not in the visual pathway.

Trauma to the optic chiasm has been reported but its incidence is low. However, previous research may be underreported. A study from Switzerland reviewed 91 patients with a diagnosis of traumatic optic neuropathy. Of these, 10 patients showed evidence of optic chiasm involvement. In some cases, the visual defect was obvious, but in others it was more subtle. Visual prognosis for these persons was generally poor.[71] The lesion analysis described above may not be as clear-cut as neuroanatomy texts would lead us to believe. Emory University School of Medicine examined 904 patients between 1989 and 2004 with homonymous hemianopia. Of these patients, 37% were complete and 62.4% were incomplete. Homonymous quadrantanopia (29%) was the most common type of incomplete homonymous hemianopia followed by homonymous scotomatous defects (13.5%). Of the 904 cases, 13% was due to brain trauma. The authors concluded that although the characteristics of the visual field defects can be helpful in lesion location, specific visual field defects do not always indicate specific brain locations. This underscores the need for expert consultation in those patients seen neuropsychiatrically and present with homonymous hemianopia.[72] In trauma-induced homonymous hemianopia, most cases are from motor vehicle accidents, and the patients are usually younger, more often male and have had multiple brain lesions. A median delay of 5 months has been observed before documentation of the homonymous hemianopia.[73] Therefore, the neuropsychiatric examiner conceivably could be the first physician to detect the defect.

Cranial Nerves III, IV, and VI

Cranial nerves III, IV, and VI are responsible for the peripheral optomotor system. The optomotor system foveates. This means that the optomotor system finds, fixates, focuses/aligns on, and follows visual targets. To foveate means to align each eye so as to cause the central light ray to fall on the fovea and the entire retinal image to fall on corresponding retinal points of both eyes.[58] Traumatic head injury leads to injury of the oculomotor, trochlear, or abducens nerve in 2%–8% of TBI patients. The most common causes of injury to these nerves come from orbital wall fractures or fracture into the cavernous sinus due to a basilar skull fracture.[74,75] Also, brainstem injury may occur during TBI, and this may in turn directly injure cranial nerve nuclei or their intranuclear pathways.[76]

Conjugate horizontal gaze requires coordination in contractions between one lateral rectus muscle (nerve VI) and the medial rectus muscle of the contralateral or opposite eye (nerve III). The frontal gaze center within the frontal lobe initiates voluntary horizontal conjugate gaze and projects nervous impulses to the contralateral (opposite) pons. When one examines the patient for horizontal conjugate gaze to command, such as when examining for horizontal nystagmus, this function is a response to vestibular input and is under cerebellar control, and thus is an alternative neuroanatomical pathway for conjugate horizontal gaze and differs from that which is initiated voluntarily. However, both voluntary and involuntary horizontal gazes use the pontine visual center for lateral gaze. This center in the pons has several names associated with it, including the paramedian pontine reticular formation (PPRF) and the para-abducens nucleus. Discharges from the horizontal gaze center in the pons permit simultaneous stimulation of the ipsilateral sixth nerve and contralateral third nerve. As a result, conjugate horizontal gaze moves the eyes toward the side of the discharging gaze center. Thus, horizontal gaze to the patient's right is using the discharging gaze center of the right pons. Dysconjugate gaze, as a result of injury to gaze structures, may cause the patient to complain of double vision or diplopia.

Vertical gaze depends upon coordinated contractions of eye muscles innervated by nerves III and IV. These nuclei are innervated by an anatomically different control locus as the vertical gaze center lies in the roof of the midbrain (the tectum) and not the pons. Paresis of ocular movement may cause functional impairment by interfering with visuomotor tasks. The inability to move the eye upward, inward, or downward, with preserved lateral movement, suggests injury to nerve III. This often is accompanied by an enlarged pupil and a droopy eyelid on the side of the injury. Injury to nerve IV may manifest as the inability to turn the eye inward or move it downward and is often accompanied by head tilt.[77] The inability to move the eye laterally, with other ocular movements preserved, is consistent with an injury to nerve VI.[78]

Recent causes of oculomotor palsy following head trauma include posttraumatic pneumocephalus,[79] and minor head trauma has been noted to produce isolated oculomotor palsy without affecting the trochlear and abducens nerves.[80] Trochlear nerve palsies have been reported. A recent Swiss study demonstrated 39 cases of isolated trochlear nerve palsy following TBI. Of these 46% occurred in patients with cerebral contusions, 39% occurred within the context of cerebral concussion, and 15% had a minor head trauma. The authors emphasized a hitherto underestimated fact in the literature—that even a relatively mild head trauma can cause isolated trochlear nerve palsies.[81] Superior oblique muscle palsy is the most frequent cause of acquired vertical strabismus, which produces anomalous head posturing and torsional diplopia.[82] Bilateral fourth-nerve palsy has been reported following shaken baby syndrome.[83] With regard to isolated traumatic sixth-nerve palsy (abducens) the Mayo clinic undertook a 24-year retrospective chart review. Patients who were first seen more than 6 weeks after injury were excluded to reduce bias toward nonrecovery.[84] Spontaneous recovery at 6 months was 27% in those with unilateral traumatic sixth-nerve palsy and 12% in bilateral traumatic sixth-nerve palsy. This study indicates that spontaneous recovery from isolated traumatic sixth-nerve palsy may be lower than previously reported.

Cranial Nerve V

Cranial nerve V lesions occur in about 3.6% of head-injured patients.[85] Isolated paratrigeminal motor neuropathy has been reported following brain trauma.[86] It has also been reported following epidural hematoma over the clivus occurring as a result of an automobile accident in a patient presenting with a Glasgow Coma Scale (GCS) score of 13. This woman also had bilateral sixth-nerve palsy, bilateral numbness within the mandibular territory of the trigeminal nerve, and a left hypoglossal palsy (cranial nerve XII).[87] Other causes of trigeminal nerve injury during TBI are basilar skull fracture into the petrous bone or brainstem trauma.[88]

In examining cranial nerve V, the motor component of nerve V only innervates the muscles used for chewing. The motor axons innervating the chewing muscles include the masseter, temporal, and lateral and medial pterygoids. The sensory component of the trigeminal nerve has three branches: ophthalmic, maxillary, and mandibular. These sensory branches convey touch and other sensations bilaterally from the face within these three divisions. There are some sensory-mediated reflexes within the trigeminal nerve distribution. These include the corneal reflex, the corneal mandibular reflex, and the glabellar blink reflex. Assessment of cranial nerve V is simple. Determining the presence of the corneal reflex will test the sensory ophthalmic branch of the trigeminal nerve, and facial sensation over the lateral maxillary and mandibular areas can be tested as well with a cotton swab. Motor function can be tested by asking the patient to vigorously clench the jaw, and the examiner can palpate the masseter and temporalis muscles as they contract. Pterygoid muscle strength can be assessed by asking the patient to move the jaw laterally. With a unilateral trigeminal nerve injury, the jaw will deviate toward the paralyzed side. Separation of the medial from the lateral pterygoid muscle function is difficult.

Cranial Nerve VII

Approximately 3% of head trauma patients will sustain a facial nerve injury. This usually results from a fracture of the temporal bone.[16] The facial nerve injury results in weakness or palsy of the muscles of the upper and lower face on the side of the injury. Bilateral facial paralysis can occur due to basilar skull fracture.[89] Since there is no facial asymmetry, this can be difficult to recognize, as both sides of the face will be paralyzed. This usually requires basilar skull fracture with bilateral temporal bone fractures. If the corticobulbar pathway is affected as a result of injury to the frontal lobe, injury to the internal capsule, or injury to the upper brainstem, a facial weakness will be present on the same side of the lesion, but the upper facial muscles of expression will be spared. The person will be able to raise the muscles of the forehead even though the lower facial muscles may be paralyzed. Facial nerve function is assessed by asking the patient to grin, purse the lips, raise the eyebrows or forehead, and tightly close the eyes. Except for the mandible movement and eyelid elevation, cranial nerve VII innervates every other movement that the face can make. DeMyer[58] teaches with an interesting mnemonic for the student to remember the important functions of cranial nerve VII: It tears, snots, tastes, salivates, moves the face, and dampens sounds.

The sensory portion of nerve VII carries taste sensation on the anterior two-thirds of the tongue. It is difficult to differentiate between nerves VII and IX if one attempts to measure taste. If measurement of the taste sensation in nerve VII is necessary, the patient can be instructed to leave the tongue extended while a dilute salt or sugar solution is placed to the anterior portion of each side of the tongue. The mouth should be rinsed with water between applications of this solution. If the sensory portion of nerve VII is intact, the patient will be able to identify these fundamental tastes. Aromatic substances should not be used, as nerve I will receive the aromas and confound the testing. Unilateral facial nerve damage causing paresis of the upper and lower facial muscles may not be accompanied by loss of taste sensation.

Cranial Nerve VIII

Traumatic brain injury is frequently accompanied by hearing loss, tinnitus, or vertigo. The incidence of hearing changes following TBI ranges from 18% to 56%.[90,91] The etiology of injury to nerve VIII is usually concussion or petrous bone fractures. The most common injury follows a longitudinal fracture of the temporal bone following a lateral blow to the head, which produces a conductive hearing loss due to dislocation and disruption of the ossicles. Cranial nerve VIII consists of two divisions: cochlear (auditory) and vestibular (labyrinthine). The cochlear and vestibular divisions of nerve VIII travel through the internal auditory canal accompanied by nerve VII. The cochlear nerve transmits auditory impulses from the middle and inner ear mechanisms to the superior temporal gyri of both cerebral hemispheres (Brodmann areas 41 and 42). Hearing is represented bilaterally on the cortex. Therefore, a unilateral lesion of nerve VIII will not cause hearing impairment. However, temporal bone fractures can result in sensorineural hearing loss, vertigo, and disequilibrium as a result of direct injury to either the acoustic branch of nerve VIII or the cochlea or labyrinth structures in the inner ear.[16] Those patients who sustain a brainstem contusion may present with impairment of the auditory and vestibular nuclei. The examiner will probably not be able to detect functional impairment since the deficit is usually unilateral, and the bilateral representation of hearing results in compensation. The more common outcome of head injury is tinnitus or other impairment of vestibular function leading to dizziness and impairments of balance and coordination. Loss of hearing as an outcome of TBI is rare, whereas tinnitus, hyperacusis, difficulty listening, and background noise are common symptoms reported by patients following TBI.[92]

With regard to vestibular function, benign paroxysmal positional vertigo is frequently a cause of dizziness after TBI.[93] About half of patients with severe TBI will complain later about positional vertigo. Dynamic visual acuity testing (DVAT) and the Dizziness Handicap Index can be used as reliable outcome measures of patients after head injury who are demonstrating balance disorders.[94] During examination of nerve VIII, hearing is tested initially by whispering into each of the patient's ears while covering the other or rubbing one's index finger and thumb together while covering the nontested ear. Air conduction versus bone conduction is assessed by the Rinné and Weber tests. In the Rinné test, the vibrating tuning fork is held first against the mastoid process. When the sound is no longer heard by bone conduction, air conduction is tested by holding the tines outside the auditory canal. In sensorineural hearing loss, air conduction usually outlasts bone conduction. In conductive deafness, bone conduction is superior. A vibrating tuning fork is placed at the center of the forehead during the Weber test and the patient reports whether the sound appears to originate from the right, the left, or the center of the head. If the sound lateralizes to either side during the Weber test, this is abnormal and indicates that bone conduction is transmitting the sound rather than air conduction. Sound lateralizes away from the side of sensorineural hearing loss because the acoustic nerve cannot detect the impulses and the sound lateralizes to the good ear. If the patient has conductive hearing loss, the auditory apparatus responds to bone conduction with less competition from external sound and the patient will report hearing the sound better toward the side of the conductive hearing loss.

The presence of direction-fixed horizontal nystagmus usually suggests a unilateral injury to the vestibular apparatus. As noted above, vertical nystagmus usually results from brainstem injury. However, nystagmus may also occur as a consequence of sedative–hypnotic medications, anticonvulsant medications, alcohol, and other specific medications. If vestibular injury is suspected, it is best to seek consultation from an otolaryngologist or otoneurologist.

Cranial Nerves IX and X

These cranial nerves generally are tested together, as clinical separation in an ordinary neurological examination is difficult at best. They also are generally injured together. Collet–Sicard syndrome may be seen even after minor head trauma. This is a palsy of cranial nerves IX through XII because of a fracture of the occipital condyle,[95] but they can also be injured as a result of a basilar skull fracture that extends into the foramen magnum.[96] The skeletal muscles supplied by cranial nerves IX and X originally came from branchial arches. Cranial nerve IX supplies only one muscle exclusively (stylopharyngeus). Because this muscle aids in swallowing, its isolated functioning cannot be tested clinically. The remaining branchial efferent fibers of cranial nerves IX and X supply the pharyngeal constrictors. Because they act as a unit in swallowing, one cannot isolate the function of the individual constrictors at the bedside. Cranial nerve X innervates the palatal muscles and is aided by cranial nerve V in this function, which supplies the pharyngeal constrictors. Cranial nerve IX aids as well. Complete interruption of cranial nerve V has little clinical effect on palatal function, and therefore the motor functions of the palate, pharynx, and larynx are functionally completely innervated by cranial nerves IX and X. However, cranial nerves IX and X also mediate sensation from the palate and pharynx and cranial nerve X alone from the pharynx. Therefore, cranial nerves IX and X function as the motor and sensory sentinels of the palatal orifice and the pharynx. Cranial nerve X alone is a sensory motor nerve of the larynx. Cranial nerve IX also carries afferents from the carotid sinus that mediate baroceptive and chemoceptive reflexes.[58] Thus, the gag reflex is composed of a reflex arc between cranial nerves IX and X.

To assess function of these two nerves, the examiner should listen to spontaneous speech during casual conversation. The patient may be asked to repeat syllables that require lingual (la), labial (pa), and guttural (ga) speech control. If a patient has cerebellar dysfunction instead of injury to nerves IX and X, the patient generally will demonstrate irregularities in the rhythm of speech similar to dystaxia, but the ability to form syllables should be mostly intact. Moreover, injury to nerves IX and X should not be confused with dysphasic patients as the patient with brainstem injury to these cranial nerves will be able to provide full meaning when speaking, and verbal comprehension will be normal. Moreover, a patient with injury to cranial nerves IX and X can write without language errors. For instance, the aphasic patient when directed, "Please, raise your right hand and touch your right ear," would be unable either to comprehend or be unable to comply with the request. A patient with injury to nerves IX and X would completely understand the command and be able to execute it.

In testing the gag reflex, with injury to nerves IX and X, the reflex is diminished or absent on the side of the nerve injury. Moreover, the palate and uvula may be deviated to the opposite side. If there is an upper motor neuron (UMN) lesion above the brainstem nuclei of cranial nerves IX and X, the gag reflex may be pathologically brisk and the patient may retch or even vomit. This is sometimes seen as a consequence of extensive injury to the frontal lobes or deep white matter structures. In this case, usually there is an associated pseudobulbar palsy consisting of dysarthria, dysphasia, and emotional lability. Head trauma has been shown to produce injury to the vagus nerve (cranial nerve X) and has been described in trauma patients with delayed gastric emptying. It is noted that the heart rate response to deep oropharyngeal suctioning may lead to the diagnosis of this vagus dysfunction syndrome.[97] In children, vagus nerve dysfunction following brain trauma has been associated with reduced lower esophageal sphincter pressure.[98]

Cranial Nerve XI

Cranial nerve XI, the spinal accessory nerve, has two parts, spinal and accessory. The spinal part supplies the sternocleidomastoid muscle and the rostral portions of the trapezius muscles. The accessory portion functions as an accessory agent to the vagus nerve. The accessory fibers arise in the nucleus ambiguus of the medulla and hitchhike along the proximal part of cranial nerve XI before joining cranial nerve X for distribution to the pharynx and larynx. The action of the sternocleidomastoid muscle thrusts the head forward and turns it to the opposite side while tilting the head to the same side as the muscle. Rarely is nerve XI isolated in injury, and it often accompanies injury to cranial nerve XII following fracture of the occipital condyle.[99] One must remember the rule of opposites when examining the SCM. For instance, when the right SCM is activated, the head turns to the left, and the opposite holds for activating the left SCM. By asking the patient to rotate the head to the right and push upon the examiner's fist, the examiner is testing the left sternocleidomastoid muscle. Weakness in the trapezius muscle will be demonstrated if the patient has difficulty in shrugging the shoulder on the same side of the lesion.

Cranial Nerve XII

The hypoglossal nerve (cranial nerve XII) travels under the tongue and thus its name, hypoglossal. It innervates the genioglossus muscle. Like examination of the sternocleidomastoid muscle, when only the right genioglossus muscle contracts, it pulls the right-sided base of the tongue forward and thereby protrudes and deviates the tip of the tongue to the left (side opposite). This function of the genioglossus mirrors what we learned about the function of the lateral pterygoid muscle above. For instance, the muscle that turns the tongue to the right is the left genioglossus, and the muscle that turns the mandible to the right is the left lateral pterygoid innervated by cranial nerve V. There have been rare reports of bilateral paralysis of the hypoglossal nerve.[100] Isolated unilateral hypoglossal nerve palsy has also been reported following fracture to the occipital condyle, but it is rare.[101]

The tongue is tested first by inspection to observe for atrophy. At times it may be necessary to palpate the tongue with a gloved hand to detect questionable hemiatrophy. Asking the patient to stick out the tongue will enable the examiner to check for alignment. Testing of muscular strength is fairly easy. Have the patient leave the tongue inside the mouth while the examiner places a finger against the cheek. The patient is then asked to press against your finger with his tongue. As noted above, if the hypoglossal nerve has been injured, the tongue will deviate to the same side as the lesion. Using our example above, if the left genioglossus is injured, the power of the right genioglossus will deviate the tongue toward the dysfunctional left genioglossus since the right muscle is unopposed. Also, recall above that the hypoglossus nerve may be injured as part of Collet–Sicard syndrome. Table 4.18 lists a simple checklist for examination of cranial nerve function.

MOTOR EXAMINATION

The motor examination begins the instant the examiner meets the patient. The examiner's eye should follow how the patient sits, stands, walks, and gestures; the postures; and the general activity level of the patient. This is easier to accomplish if the examiner meets the patient in the waiting area and walks with the patient to the examination room. Particularly in brain-injured patients, muscular atrophy usually occurs as a result of an immobilization syndrome following prolonged coma or inability to move. Focal muscle atrophy is invariably associated with a lower motor neuron (LMN) injury and should alert the examiner to possible peripheral nerve injury or radiculopathy (nerve root injury). It is not expected that the neuropsychiatric neurological examination will be as thorough as that provided by a neurologist. However, general observation and palpation will reveal the muscle bulk of the patient. Focal atrophy can be discerned by comparing the circumference of the limb in question, and measurements around the biceps, forearm, quadriceps, or gastrocnemius may be useful for side-to-side comparison. For the hemiparetic patient, spasticity is usually present. This is due to a UMN lesion.

Muscle Tone

Muscle tone is the muscular resistance that the examiner feels while manipulating a patient's resting joint. The tone of the muscle is dependent on the number and rate of motor unit discharges. The two common alterations of muscle tone are hypertonia (too much tone) and hypotonia (too little tone). The two most common hypertonic states are spasticity and rigidity. A less common hypertonic state is paratonia (Gegenhalten). Spasticity is an initial catch or resistance and then a yielding when the examiner briskly manipulates the patient's resting extremity. Rigidity is an increased muscular resistance felt throughout the entire range of movement as the examiner slowly manipulates a resting joint. It has been termed lead-pipe rigidity. The presence of lead-pipe rigidity indicates an

TABLE 4.18

Traumatic Cranial Nerve Injuries

Nerves	Usual Cause of Trauma	Clinical Testing
I	Frontal blows, fracture of the cribriform plate, contusion of the entorhinal cortex	Nonirritating stimuli such as anise or peppermint oils
II	Fractures of orbital bones, shearing forces, mechanical stretching, contusions, or vascular injury	Pupillary light response, funduscopic examination, visual field testing, and measurement of visual acuity
III, IV, and VI	Fractures of the orbital walls, basilar skull fracture extending into cavernous sinus	Eye tracking right, left (nerve VI); up, down (nerve III); in and down (nerve IV); in and up (nerve III); raise eyelid, pupillary light response (nerve III)
V	Facial fractures; rarely brainstem injury or petrous bone fracture	Corneal reflex; sensation of lateral face, gums, inner cheek (sensory limb); masseter, pterygoids, temporalis strength testing (motor limb)
VII	Temporal bone fractures, brainstem trauma to nerve nucleus (lower motor neuron); injury to frontal lobe or internal capsule (upper motor neuron)	Squeeze eyes closed, raise eyebrows, purse lips, grin (UMN lesion spares forehead raising); sensory arm tested with sweet or salt solution to anterior tongue
VIII	Longitudinal fracture of temporal bone, transverse fracture of temporal bone, petrous bone concussion or fracture	Hearing check, Weber and Rinné tests, check for horizontal nystagmus, ice-water caloric test
IX and X	Basilar skull fracture extending into foramen magnum, Collet–Sicard syndrome	Test gag reflex; repeat "la," "pa," and "ga"; examine uvular and palatal movement
XI	Basilar skull fracture, Collet–Sicard syndrome, or occipital condyle fracture	Turn head to right (L. SCM) and left (R. SCM) against force, raise shoulder toward ears (trapezius)
XII	Basilar skull fracture or atlanto-occipital injury, occipital condyle fracture, or Collet–Sicard syndrome	Protrude tongue; deviation is to the side of the injury; atrophy to side of injury

extrapyramidal dysfunction in the basal motor circuitry, more specifically in the dopaminergic projections from the substantia nigra to the striatum.[58] Cogwheel phenomena often occur while the examiner passively manipulates a joint, and it will feel like a series of ratchet-like catches. Paratonia is the resistance, equal in degree and range, that the patient presents to each attempt of the examiner to move a part of a limb in any direction. Paratonia is a frequent occurrence in dementia. Spasticity is the commonest outcome of TBI and can be so severe as to immobilize the patient. Recent use of botulinum toxin offers some relief to many TBI patients.[102] Spasticity can be so severe as to cause contractures of a joint. Ankle contractures often occur after moderate to severe TBI, and they may deform the ankle.[103]

Spasticity has significant negative implications for the rehabilitation of traumatically brain-injured patients. Spasticity in the affected limb may impede mobility and transferability. Upper extremity spasticity may affect the patient's ability to perform daily care activities. Spasticity of the neck or head can lead to difficulties with feeding, and spasticity of the pharyngeal and laryngeal muscles may interfere with oral communication, swallowing, and even breathing. If tone is increased in the trunk muscles, patients may experience problems positioning themselves in bed, a wheelchair, or during standing and attempts at ambulation. Spasticity associated with paresis may result in joint contractures of the affected extremity. These are most likely to be seen in the wrist, elbow, knee, or ankle. The examination of muscle tone occurs with the patient fully relaxed. Passive movements of the upper and lower extremities are elicited. Flexing and extending the wrist, elbow, shoulder, knee, or hip may elicit abnormalities of tone. If range of motion is limited, the examiner

TABLE 4.19

Signs of UMN versus LMN Lesions

UMN	LMN
1. Hyperreflexia	1. Hyporeflexia
2. Spasticity	2. Flaccidity
3. Babinski sign	3. Atrophy
4. Clonus	4. Fasciculations
5. Weakness	5. Weakness

should consider contracture or a heterotopic overgrowth of bone in the affected joint region leading to ossification.[104] Table 4.19 differentiates the physical signs of UMN versus LMN lesions.

Muscle Strength

When the examiner tests muscular strength, it should be remembered that the muscles are strongest when acting from their shortest position, and they have little or no strength when acting from their longest position. Thus, to test the strength of the biceps muscle, if the patient has flexed that muscle with the hand against the head of the biceps, the biceps muscle will have its greatest strength. The examiner should test a few simple powerful muscles. The neuropsychiatric examiner is not expected to isolate individual muscles in the manner of a neurologist or physiatrist. Start from the top and work downward. The SCM muscle has been tested, as noted above, and so has the trapezius muscle. For testing shoulder girdle strength, have the patient hold the arms straight out to the sides and then press down on both arms where you expect your strength to approximate that of the patient. Perform a similar maneuver with the arms extended to the sides to test downward adduction. To test the pectoralis muscles, have the patient extend the arms straight in front while crossed at the wrists, and then try to pull them apart. For scapular adduction, have the patient stand with the hands on the hips. The examiner should be behind the patient and then ask the patient to force the elbows backward as hard as possible while the examiner tries to push them forward at the elbow. Scapular winging can be detected by having the patient lean forward against a wall supporting the body with outstretched arms. Similar maneuvers at the elbow can isolate the biceps and triceps muscles, and at the wrist, the wrist extensors and flexors.

Testing for weakness of the hip girdle is accomplished with the patient sitting at first. Ask the patient to lift a knee off the table surface, and with the butt of your palm try to push the knee back down. To measure thigh abduction and adduction, have the patient hold the legs apart while you try to press them together with your hands and the lateral sides of the knees. Then have the patient hold the knees together as you place your hands on the medial sides of the knees and try to pull the legs apart. Hip extension is measured with the patient in the prone position. Have the patient lift the knee from the table surface and hold it up. Place your hand on the popliteal space and try to press the knee back down.[58] Ankle flexion and extension can be tested while pushing the toes toward the head against the patient's resistance for extension power and pulling the toes toward the plantar surface to measure flexion power. Obviously, a patient with hemiparesis will be weaker on the side that is hemiparetic. Refer to Table 4.19 and note that weakness is the only notable sign seen in both UMN and LMN lesions. Moreover, UMN lesions will present with hyperreflexia, whereas LMN lesions will present with hyporeflexia.

ABNORMAL INVOLUNTARY MOVEMENTS

As defined by neurologists, involuntary movements mean those patterns of muscle contractions (tremors and other movement sequences) caused by identifiable structural or biochemical lesions in the circuitry of the basomotor nuclei, reticular formation, and cerebellum. Broadly construed, the concept of involuntary movements can also include the gamut of muscle fiber contractions of peripheral and central origins, extending from fibrillations of muscles to epileptic seizures.[58] Traumatic brain injury, particularly injury to the basal ganglia, can produce dystonia, dyskinesia, choreoathetosis, ballismus, myoclonus, asterixis, or parkinsonism.[105–108] Some patients can present with paroxysmal autonomic instability and dystonia after brain injury. This presents with intermittent agitation, diaphoresis, hyperthermia, hypertension, tachycardia, tachypnea, and extensor posturing.[109]

Dystonia is an involuntary sustained contraction of both agonist and antagonist muscles. It may cause repetitive, twisting movements or abnormal postures.[110,111] The psychiatrist or neurologist will be familiar with this disorder as it frequently is caused by high-potency neuroleptic medicines such as haloperidol or fluphenazine. Dystonia generally has two causes following brain trauma: injury to the basal ganglia or as a side effect of neuroleptic medications. Dyskinesias are stereotyped, automatic movements of the limbs or oral–facial muscles and may also result from injury to the basal ganglia or from neuroleptic medication side effects. Choreoathetosis (choreo = dance, athetosis = wormy or writhing) is a slow spasmodic involuntary writhing or dancing movement of the limbs or face muscles. It is commonly seen as a side effect of neuroleptic medications, adrenergic medications, or anticonvulsants. It also is reported as an outcome from traumatic injury to the basal ganglia.[112] Ballismus is a violent flinging of the upper extremity, usually at the proximal shoulder, and generally is an outcome of injury to the subthalamic nucleus.[16] Tremor is a frequent outcome as a medication side effect, but it has also been reported as a consequence of head injury. In the traumatically brain-injured patient, it is most frequently seen as a postural tremor and it may involve the head, upper extremities, or legs.[113]

Myoclonus is a shock-like or brief contraction of voluntary muscles. It can occur throughout the whole body but it is found generally in a group of muscles. It is sometimes induced by an auditory stimulus, such as a loud noise or clap of the hands. It has been reported as an outcome of TBI and it is usually associated with cerebellar, basal ganglia, or pyramidal signs.[114] It is a common side effect from dopaminergic medications used in the treatment of parkinsonism, and it often is an outcome of hypoxic brain injury. Asterixis is an involuntary lapse of posture or a flapping of the hands. It is most likely to be detected as a wrist flap, and physicians are aware of this as an outcome of hepatic failure. However, it also has been reported as an outcome of thalamic, internal capsule, midbrain, or parietal cortex injury.[115] Posttraumatic parkinsonism has been described as a result of TBI[116] and most readers will be familiar with the posttraumatic parkinsonism present in a former world-famous heavyweight boxer.

Examination of the patient to detect abnormal involuntary movements is primarily visual. However, choreoathetotic movements of the hands and face often can be detected by activating movements. Having the patient walk down the hall may activate choreoathetotic movements in the fingers and wrists. With the patient sitting in front of the examiner, the patient can be asked to tap the hand rapidly on the thigh and while the examiner observes the mouth parts or the contralateral hand, dyskinetic movements may become manifest.

SENSORY EXAMINATION

In orienting oneself for this portion of the neurological examination, it should be remembered that the sensory dermatomes are mapped over the human body. Table 4.20 lists eight upper body dermatomes and six lower body dermatomes. Remember that the C1 dermatome does not exist, and the first clinical dermatome is C2 found at the occiput. The T4 dermatome marks the nipple line and the T10 dermatome marks the umbilicus. Sensory perception is often dysfunctional in patients following TBI. The sensory deficits may be of little consequence to the patient and are generally masked or outweighed by impairment in motor and cognitive systems. Two-point discrimination perception is often impaired following TBI. The loss of two-point discrimination is not affected by the GCS at the time of injury or the duration of posttraumatic amnesia.[117]

TABLE 4.20
Sensory Dermatomal Patterns

Upper Body			Lower Body
C1	Does not exist	L1	Groin
C2	Occipital area	L2	Lateral thigh
C4	Above collarbone	L3	Medial thigh
C6	Thumb	L4	Medial leg
C7	Middle fingers	L5	Lateral leg, large toe
C8	Little finger	S1	Little toe, sole of foot
T4	Nipple line		
T10	Umbilicus		

An injury to one of the thalami causes an impairment of all sensory modalities on the opposite side of the face and body, whereas, in parietal lobe injuries, sensory loss affects localization of the site of sensory stimulation. However, pain and temperature sensation are preserved following parietal lobe injuries. In addition to inability to localize the sensory input following parietal lobe injuries, the examiner will also find an impairment of stereognosis (the ability to manipulate shapes with the hand and identify them by tactile sensations, e.g., a coin). Joint-position sense is also impaired by parietal lobe injuries as is graphesthesia (the ability to recognize figures written on the skin while blindfolded or with eyes closed). In nondominant or right hemisphere injuries, sensory neglect is often apparent in the left hemispace.

Assessment of the primary sensory modalities is easily accomplished by face-to-face neurological examination. Examination should include determination of sensation to pain, light touch, vibration, and joint-position sense. Once it has been established that the primary sensory modalities are intact, one can then check higher cortical sensory functions subserved by the parietal lobe. These include graphesthesia, stereognosis, and locating a sensory stimulus. Patients who have a neglect syndrome will be easily identified at this point in the examination as they will be able to detect a stimulus such as a pin prick on either limb when the limb is tested individually, but they will neglect the affected side when the limbs are touched simultaneously. The examiner should ask that the patient's eyes be closed during this portion of the examination to disallow visual cues.

REFLEXES

As has been noted in Table 4.19, examination of the reflexes is very important to determine whether there is an UMN or LMN lesion and to find lateralizing signs. Hyperreflexia is a consequence of injury to the UMNs, whereas injury to the LMNs causes hyporeflexia. Spasticity covaries with the hyperreflexia, whereas flaccidity generally accompanies hyporeflexia. The tendon stretch reflex tests the sensory–motor arc at the spinal cord level of the specific reflex. For instance, the biceps reflex tests the integrity of the C5–C6 spinal cord level. A hyperreflexic biceps tendon, in association with spasticity, would point to an UMN lesion in the contralateral brain or brainstem. The UMN pathway crosses the midline primarily in the pyramidal decussation of the lower medulla which is immediately above the foramen magnum in a normal person. The first synapse in the direct corticospinal pathway from brain to spinal cord is in the anterior horn of the spinal cord. Table 4.21 delineates the muscles associated with spinal nerve roots and the reflex that will test a particular nerve root. During examination, the reflex is elicited with a brisk tap from a reflex hammer over the tendon. Neurologists generally grade the level of the reflex, but for purposes of neuropsychiatric screening, this probably is not necessary and the important analysis is whether the reflexes are symmetrical from right side to left side and whether there is evidence of hyperreflexia or hyporeflexia.

TABLE 4.21
Muscle Stretch Reflexes

Roots	Muscles	Actions	Reflexes
Nerve V	Masseter	Clench jaw	Jaw reflex
C5	Deltoid	Abduct shoulder	—
C5–C6	Biceps	Flex elbow	Biceps reflex
C5–C6	Brachioradialis	Flex elbow	Brachioradialis reflex
C7	Triceps	Extend elbow	Triceps reflex
C8	Intrinsic hand	Abduct/adduct fingers	—
L3–L4	Quadriceps	Extend lower leg	Patellar reflex
L4–L5	Anterior tibial	Dorsiflex foot and large toe	—
S1	Gastrocnemius	Plantarflex foot	Achilles reflex

The reflexes clearly help localize the site of a TBI. A hyperactive reflex is consistent with an injury to the corticospinal tract and one should find associated muscle weakness (Table 4.19) and possibly an upgoing large toe upon stroking the sole of the foot (Babinski sign). Hypoactive reflexes are seen often with injury of the LMN. Focal hyporeflexia in one nerve root system should alert the examiner to injury in a spinal root, plexus, or peripheral nerve. Diffuse hyporeflexia is seen following cerebellar injury, but it is also common in the peripheral neuropathy often associated with hypothyroidism, diabetes mellitus, alcoholism, or renal disease. As noted previously, a hyperactive jaw jerk suggests bilateral corticospinal tract injury above the level of the middle pons.

COORDINATION AND GAIT

Coordination is controlled by various brain and peripheral nervous system structures. These include the corticospinal tracts, the basal ganglia, the cerebellum, and the sensory pathways. The most important area of the brain that contributes to coordination is the cerebellum. Before one can attribute incoordination to cerebellar dysfunction, it must be determined that the other four systems contributing to coordination are intact. Therefore, vision must be intact to coordinate movement; the motor system must be intact enough to provide strength sufficient to perform a task; proprioceptive sensation must be intact for the person to detect the attitude of his limbs in space; and the vestibular system must be intact so that the patient can integrate rotational movement and position in space.[118]

There is a relationship between strength, balance, and swallowing deficits following TBI. Assessments of these abilities in addition to assessment of the dynamic balance during rehabilitation are helpful as screening tests in predicting the need for assistance by another person when the patient is discharged from rehabilitation. This association remains strong at 1 year after TBI.[119] Physiatrists use a number of measures to determine quality of gait and balance after TBI. These can include the Dizziness Handicap Inventory, caloric irrigation of the ear canals, optokinetic testing, the Dix-Hallpike Test, posturography, and center-of-mass movement.[120] The University of Oregon measures dynamic instability by having TBI patients walk over obstacles. This is a real-world test to determine whether TBI patients are at risk before discharge. Patients are instructed to perform unobstructed level walking and to step over obstacles that correspond to 2.5%, 5%, 10%, and 15% of their height.[121] This provides an objective measurement that reflects the complaints of instability that may not be observable in a clinical examination. The neuropsychiatric examiner should be aware that despite the apparent good recovery of locomotor functioning following TBI, this may be valid only at normal walking speeds. Patients with moderate or severe TBI generally will demonstrate residual deficits in relation to greater difficulties in dealing with environments that challenge their locomotor and attentional abilities. They may demonstrate significant dynamic instability while making turns in hallways, going up and down stairs, conducting a simultaneous visual task during locomotion, and other ordinary activities of daily living that exceed walking on a level surface.[122]

Examination of upper extremity coordination is fairly simple. The examiner should ask the patient alternately to touch the nose and then the examiner's finger, which is placed at an arm's length from the patient. Intention tremor can be detected as a fine rhythmic, regular movement of the outstretched finger that intensifies as the patient attempts to touch the examiner's finger or hand. This is different than dysmetria which is "past-pointing," a jerky irregular movement and over-shooting of the patient's arm or finger when the patient tries to touch the examiner's hand or finger target. Should dysmetria or intention tremor be present, the patient can be asked to produce hand-writing. Intention tremor will affect the smoothness and accuracy of the handwriting movements, whereas dysmetria may result in the patient being unable to maintain handwriting upon a straight line. To test for dysdiadochokinesia, the patient should be sitting comfortably in front of the examiner. The examiner should then ask the patient to place the right hand on the knee. Alterna-tively, the patient can place the palm of the hand on a table. The examiner should then demonstrate how to rapidly turn his palm up and then palm down and ask the patient to repeat the maneuver, first with the right hand and then with the left hand. Another simple measure of dysdiadochokinesia is to ask the patient to alternately touch fingers two through five with the thumb in rapid succession. The speed of movement, the rhythm of movement, and the smoothness of the movement should be assessed as well as the accuracy of point-to-point contact.

Lower extremity coordination may be assessed with the patient sitting on the examination table in front of the clinician or sitting in a chair facing the examiner. The patient is asked to touch the heel to the knee and then slide the heel up and down the lower leg. Smoothness and accuracy are again assessed. If this is not practical for the patient, for instance, owing to hip dysfunction, the patient can be asked to draw a figure 8 or circle in the air with the large toe. Dysdiadochokinesia of the foot can be assessed by asking the patient rapidly to tap the foot on the floor. Dystaxia is best tested by observing the patient while walking. One can ask the patient to perform "the drunk test" by placing the feet heel-to-toe. However, the examiner should exercise caution in asking signifi-cantly weak patients or elderly patients to perform this maneuver, as they may fall.

Persons who have a true sensory loss in both feet because of neuropathy or other cause will be unable to maintain their posture during the Romberg maneuver. Also, this will be found in patients who have injury to the posterior columns of their spinal cord from trauma, multiple sclerosis, syphilis, or vitamin B_{12} deficiency. The Romberg sign is easily elicited by having the patient stand in front of the examiner, stretch the patient's arms at 90° forward from the body, close the eyes, and then the clinician asks the person to maintain balance. Be prepared to catch the patient if necessary. When the patient closes the eyes, the ability to visually compensate for body position in space is lost and if the posterior columns cannot transmit sensory information from the feet or if the patient cannot feel the floor with the feet, the patient may fall. Table 4.22 describes the simple maneuvers for evaluating coordination.

TABLE 4.22
Examination of Coordination

Defect	Maneuver
Dysmetria	Finger-to-nose test, toe-to-finger test
Intention tremor	Same as above, handwriting analysis
Dyssynergia	Thumb-to-fingers in rapid succession
Dysdiadochokinesia	Rapid supination–pronation of hand, rapid tapping of toe upon floor
Dystaxia	Heel-to-toe walking, observe gait and turns
Romberg sign	Stand with heels together, arms stretched forward, close eyes, maintain posture

Patients should be observed as they stand or sit. This will give an index of hip strength and static balance. By asking the patient to stand with the feet together and arms outstretched, static balance can be assessed further. While walking, the gait should be assessed to determine if the patient's head and trunk are in the proper position and whether arm swing is normal and symmetrical. The heels should fall on the midline while walking. Assessment of posture and gait should be coupled with the examination of coordination.

MOTOR VEHICLE DRIVING AFTER TRAUMATIC BRAIN INJURY

There is evidence that following severe brain injury and coma lasting for at least 48 h, an individual has a statistically significant higher risk of being involved in a road traffic accident.[123] The data for accidents in persons who have sustained mild or moderate TBI is lacking. It is generally accepted among physicians that drivers with neurobehavioral disorders are at risk for a crash resulting from cognitive impairment.[124] However, evidence-based data for this statement is also lacking. The neurocognitive algorithm for driving includes three major elements: (1) perceive and attend to a stimulus and interpret the situation on the road, (2) formulate a plan based on the particular driving situation and relevant previous experience or memory, and (3) execute an action by use of various motor vehicle controls. Errors at any point at any stage can result in unsafe or harmful driving. From a neuropsychiatric point of view, driving skill may be altered substantially following TBI as a result of impairment in various cognitive and behavioral systems. Perception is highly involved in driving ability, and motor vehicle driving is a highly visual task.[125] Any cerebral lesion which produces alterations of visual perception can negatively impact driving. Current cognitive driving tests often measure the Useful Field of View (UFOV). This is the visual area from which information can be acquired without moving either the eyes or the head. While this test has found usefulness in persons with moderate to severe TBI, its usefulness has recently been questioned in persons who have mild TBI. It is recommended that its use be limited to more severely impaired persons.[126] Executive function is also an important factor in driving skill, as decision making during driving requires the evaluation of immediate and long-term consequences of planned actions. Moreover, driving behavior can be influenced by poor impulse control, insight, and judgment or planning in those individuals with executive function disorders. Memory and language ability also plays a role in driving. Aphasics may experience difficulties in interpreting information from glimpses of maps or roadway signs. Drivers may fail to recognize important landmarks and may misinterpret previously familiar road signs or symbols.[127] Brainstem and reticular-activating functions are important variables during driving. Alterations of consciousness or alertness may negatively impact the ability to drive. This can come directly from brain trauma or indirectly from brain trauma-induced sleep dysfunction. These factors have been measured during deteriorating driving simulator performance in healthy, sleep-deprived persons.[128] Emotional factors can contribute to poor driving performance. Dysregulation of emotions or induction of aggressiveness by TBI patients may negatively impact driving skill. These factors have been measured using the Dula Dangerous Driver Index.[129] Lastly, one would have to consider the effect of medications prescribed to persons following TBI and assess their impact upon alertness, cognition, and the potential for inducing drowsiness.

The assessment of driving performance is often performed by occupational therapists working in brain injury rehabilitation units or hospitals. If the neuropsychiatric examiner feels the need to determine, by standardized assessment, driving performance, it is best to consult with occupational therapists skilled in driving assessment. The assessment of driving performance can be conducted by the following: (1) road test, (2) use of a dual instrumented vehicle, (3) a driving simulator, and (4) cognitive and computer-based tests designed to assess driving using a laboratory model. Three cognitive tests have been found to correlate highly with the ability to predict impaired driving performance. These include the Controlled Oral Word Association test, the Rey-Osterrieth Complex Figure Test, and Trail-Making Test Part B.[124] The question for the neuropsychiatric examiner is whether cognitively based laboratory tests can provide ecologically valid measures that will predict

driving performance on the road? Cognitive laboratory assessment should probably be supple-
mented either with a direct driving examination or a simulated test. Simulator-based assessments of
patients with brain injuries have recently been found to be ecologically valid as measures. In fact,
they may be more sensitive than a traditional road test as predictors of long-term driving performance in a community.[130] While direct measurements are important in determining driver performance following TBI, particularly if the information is to be used in a forensic setting, premorbid
factors are also quite useful in predicting safe return to driving after TBI. In particular, the examiner
should probe for prior motor vehicle accidents, prior driving violations, prior driving under-the-
influence convictions, and evidence of risky personality traits or impulsive behavior. An Italian
study found these factors to have high validity in predicting future risky driving behavior.[131]
A recent survey of occupational therapists in Canada or the United States noted that approximately
75% used the following off-road assessments during the examination of persons for driving ability
following TBI: (1) Brake Reaction Timer, (2) Trailmaking Tests, Parts A and B, and (3) Motor
Free Visual Perception Test. It is recommended that a comprehensive evaluation following TBI
for ability to drive include either a road test or a simulator test combined with appropriate
cognitive measures. These testings are particularly important for individuals possessing a commercial driver's license or those persons operating heavy motorized equipment. It goes without saying
that any individual driving a school bus who has sustained a TBI should be assessed face-to-face for
driving skill.

THE CHILD MENTAL EXAMINATION

The mental status examination may be conducted at the beginning or end of the pediatric neuropsychiatric examination. Oftentimes, the child's neurological examination provides helpful data
on the mental status. For example, can the child pay attention to the examiner; does the child follow
the examiner's simple directions; is the child impulsive; does the examiner have to repeat questions;
how does the child respond socially?[132] Obviously, in assessing the child, if the child is a competent
historian, the chief informant is the child. In examination of the minor child, while the child's
information is very important, the parent or guardian generally represents the child. The child's
psychiatric interview is thus more complex than that of the adult. The examiner must take into
account the child's age, level of cognitive development, and willingness to discuss problems.[133]
While some experts may examine children younger than 3 years to determine cognitive capacity,
cognitive examinations of children younger than 3 years are difficult if not impossible to complete
with objective data. Since standardized neuropsychological test instruments exist for the 3 year old
child and older, it is probably best to wait until the brain-injured child is age 3 to assess cognitive
deficits objectively.

A child aged 3–6 years can usually provide the examiner correct information if the questions are
framed in a manner consistent with his level of development.[132] However, as we will see later in this
text, the examiner must use care and not make assumptions about the validity of the child's report
in situations where child abuse issues or litigation may be involved. Younger children are suggestible and they may repeat information given to them by a hostile or litigious parent.[134,135] The
neuropsychiatric mental examination of a very young child is essentially a neurodevelopmental
examination. The Folstein et al. Mini-Mental State Examination has been adapted for use with
children by Ouvier et al.[136] and Weinberg et al.[137] have developed the Symbol Language Battery for
use in the physician's office to screen child cognition.

ATTENTION

The most difficult quandary for the neuropsychiatric examiner will be to distinguish attention deficit
disorder as a diagnosis from attentional deficits due to TBI. Some experts are now calling attention
deficits following TBI secondary ADHD. Max and his group at the University of California,

San Diego, have recently reviewed predictors of ADHD within 6 months and within 6–24 months in children following TBI. These researchers evaluated children ages 5–14 years and excluded those with pre-injury ADHD. They took patients from five trauma centers and observed them prospectively for 6 months. They evaluated the children with semistructured psychiatric interviews. Secondary ADHD was detected in the first 6 months after injury in 18 of 115 children (16%). All subtypes of ADHD were detected. Lesions of the orbitofrontal gyrus were connected to ADHD at a statistically significant level.[138] This same research group continued their study, prolonging it to 24 months. In the second year after injury, another 21% of these youngsters demonstrated secondary ADHD. They also discovered that pre-injury adaptive function was a consistent predictor of secondary ADHD. Children raised in psychosocial adversity acted as an independent predictor of secondary ADHD in the second year after injury.[139] The Kennedy Krieger Institute in Baltimore, Maryland, recently published data comparing children with ADHD before TBI versus those children who developed secondary ADHD after TBI. They studied 82 children with severe TBI, and these children underwent neuropsychological testing 1 year after injury. There were greater deficits in memory skills in the secondary ADHD group when compared with the pre-injury ADHD group. However, this preliminary study was unable to clearly differentiate the two groups of children based on neuropsychological data alone.[140]

Attention can be evaluated in the young child by observing the youngster's ability to attend to the examiner or to listen to the topic of discussion. The degree to which the child jumps from one activity to another or needs restructuring is an important marker of poor attention. If the child is easily distractible to noises outside the examination area or quickly drawn to objects in the room and is unable to resist grabbing the objects, then it is fairly obvious the child's attention is impaired. For a child greater than age 8 years, attention can be assessed by having the youngster count from 1 to 20. If vigilance is assessed, generally children over age 9 can perform serial 7s or spell "WORLD" backwards. The reader should consult Chapter 6 for more specific child-oriented tests of attentional ability.

SPEECH AND LANGUAGE

When children sustain TBI of significant proportions, they may show persisting deficits in higher level discourse abilities throughout life. When these children are compared to typically developing youngsters, the children injured earliest in life are the most likely to demonstrate written and oral difficulties with discourse.[141] A recent Canadian study has determined that the American Speech-Language-Hearing Association National Outcome Measures System (Birth to Kindergarten NOMS/School-Aged Healthcare) is sufficient to detect changes in language ability within children and adolescents who have sustained a TBI.[142] Language disorders may be particularly prevalent in children injured at a very tender age by inflicted harm. In one study, speech and language difficulties were present in 64% including autistic spectrum disorder. The range and degree of severity of neurological abnormalities, including speech and language disorders in survivors of inflicted head injury, is extremely variable, with the majority of these children being moderately or severely abnormal.[143]

The evaluation of speech and language, of course, depends upon the age of the child and the development of language appropriate to the child's age. As noted above with the adult mental examination, the examination of child language is no different. The examiner must listen to the articulation, inflection, and the rhythm and fluency of the child's speech. Analysis of language is based on whether the child speaks with idiosyncratic aspects and if the vocabulary and syntax are correct. With a young child, it is important to note whether there is misuse of pronouns and gender. A judgment can be made about the overall intelligence of the child based on how the language is produced and whether or not it is appropriate to the child's age. Can the child tell a small story or a joke (narrative discourse)? The nonverbal aspects of language are evaluated in the child the same as the adult. Does the child have appropriate facial expression, speech melody, and intonation and

TABLE 4.23

Important Childhood Speech and Language Milestones

Receptive Language	Age	Expressive Language
Turns to sound of bell	6 months	Cries, laughs, babbles
Waves "bye-bye"	9 months	Imitates sounds and makes dental sounds during play (e.g., "da-da")
Knows meaning of "no" and "don't touch"	12 months	Uses one to two words (e.g., "da-da," "mama," "bye")
Responds to "come here"	15 months	Uses jargon (speech-like babbling during play)
Points to nose, eyes, hair	18 months	Uses 8–10 words (one-third are nouns)
		Puts two words together (e.g., "more cookie")
		Repeats requests
Points to a few named objects	24 months	Asks one- to two-word questions (e.g., "Where kitty?")
Obeys simple commands		
Repeats two numbers	30 months	Uses "I," "you," "me"
Can identify by name "What barks?" and "What blows?"		Names objects
		Uses three word simple sentences
Responds to prepositions "on" and "under"	3 years	Masters consonants b, p, m
Responds to prepositions "in," "out," "behind," "in front of"	4 years	Speaks in three- to four-word sentences
		Uses future and past tenses
		Masters consonants d, t, g, k
Can repeat a seven-word sentence	6.5 years	Masters th sound
		Uses six- to seven-word sentences
		Says numbers up to 30s

Source: Reprinted from Olson, W.H., Brumback, R.A., Gascon, G.G., et al., in *Handbook of Symptom-Oriented Neurology*, 2nd edition, Mosby, St. Louis, 1994, p. 347. With permission.

make eye contact with the examiner? If the child appears to have a formal language disorder, it may be necessary to consult with a speech and language pathologist for more definitive evaluation. The important speech and language milestones of the child below 7 years are noted in Table 4.23.

MEMORY AND ORIENTATION

The reader is referred to Chapter 6 for specific memory tests useful in children. For the face-to-face examination or bedside examination of a child, techniques are fairly straightforward and simple. However, in the special case where a child is being examined within a forensic context, performance of tests of memory must be checked for malingering. Children are not likely to malinger, but they may unconsciously malinger by proxy if they feel particular pressure from the parent or guardian. Recently, children were evaluated to determine if the Test of Memory Malingering (TOMM) was appropriate for use in a child sample. One hundred consecutively referred 6- to 16-year-old children with a wide range of clinical diagnoses were tested using the TOMM. Two children were correctly identified as providing suboptimal effort, and only one case was a possible false positive. Performance did not vary with gender, ethnicity, parental occupation, performance on an independent memory test, or length of coma. Younger children tended to be somewhat less efficient on the TOMM than older children, but more than 90% of the children in the 6- to 8-year range met criteria originally developed for adults for sufficient effort on the TOMM. The author concluded that the TOMM is a potentially useful measure of effort in the clinical neuropsychological evaluation of school-age children.[144] With regard to lesion location and its effects upon memory, the California

Verbal Learning Test—Children's Version was used to determine the relationship of memory impairment in children to lesion location. These children were measured and were compared by MRI brain scans using volumetric analysis. The GCS score at the time of injury was not predictive of performance on the memory test when a factor analysis was applied. Unexpectedly in this study, the lesion volume outside the frontotemporal areas was predictive of the outcome 1 year after injury. It is suggested that this finding may relate to widespread diffuse axonal injury lying outside frontal–temporal circuits.[145]

Children ages 3–7 years are able to answer general orientation questions.[146] For instance, children of this age are able to give their first and last name and tell how old they are. Children generally know the month and day of their birthday and what city they live in. The child is able to relate his father's name and his mother's name. If in school, he can generally name his school and what grade he is in. Most children of this age will be able to tell the examiner where they are at present, for instance, in a hospital or doctor's office. Children within this age range are able to state whether it is daytime or nighttime.[132,133]

A child aged between 8 and 15 years is oriented more specifically in time. Children in this age group will be able to tell the examiner the current time and day of the week. They know the day of the month and the name of the month. They are also able to give the year, generally unlike most children in the 3–7 year age group.[132,133] A child younger than 8 years can usually learn and repeat three simple objects if the child is given sufficient rehearsals to learn all three. For instance, the child can be asked to remember ball, cup, and doll. Most normal children will remember two or three of these objects. Visual memory can be tested by hiding three objects as the child watches. The child can be asked to retrieve the objects 5 min later and even the younger child should be able to do so unless visual memory is impaired. Remote memory can be evaluated by asking even a young child to relate the favorite television show or if in preschool or school, the teacher's name.

VISUOSPATIAL AND CONSTRUCTIONAL ABILITY

Pencil and paper tests can be used to assess visuospatial abilities in young children. A 3-year-old child should be able to copy a circle drawn by the examiner in front of the child. A 4-year-old should be able to copy an X and a +. A 5-year-old can copy a triangle and a 6-year-old can copy a square. Children older than age 7 generally can copy intersecting diamonds.[132] Most children ages 9 or older should be able to draw a clock and place the numbers in the appropriate locations and draw hands to four o'clock.

EXECUTIVE FUNCTION

In children who sustain moderate to severe TBI before age 6, the executive function is difficult to measure. Youngsters in this age group can be tested for working memory, and the ability to control inhibitions but more complex measures of executive function such as discussed in Chapter 6 are difficult to determine.[147] Some measure of executive function can be obtained using NEPSY. This test can be used to measure executive function in children as young as 3 years.[148] On the other hand, there is growing recognition that executive function, the superordinate managerial capacity for directing more modular abilities, is frequently impaired by TBI in children and mediates the neurobehavioral sequelae exhibited by these patients. Executive dysfunction in the child may present as an impairment of motivation, self-regulation, and social cognition as well as the more specific functions discussed in previous chapters of this book. Domains of executive function in the young child are more difficult to describe or measure and include the basic processes of working memory and inhibition as well as more complex processes such as decision-making.[149] Moreover, while executive function disorders in children show some recovery after injury, long-term deficits often remain and may impact adversely the continuing development of the child.[150] Tests with more specific application to executive function in the brain-injured child will be discussed more fully in

Chapter 6. These tests include the Tower of London, which measures planning skills; the Controlled Oral Word Association test, which measures verbal fluency; and the Wisconsin Card Sorting Test, which measures concept formation and mental flexibility.[151]

AFFECT AND MOOD

Mood disorders are extremely common in the brain-injured child. Depressive disorders are very common. Mood disorders with internalization are more likely to resolve in youngsters injured at a tender age in contrast to those who have more externalizing features. There seems to be a direct relationship between the level of stress experienced by the child after injury and also the severity of the brain injury to the prediction of a new-onset mood disorder following pediatric brain trauma.[152] The examiner must also recognize and be aware that posttraumatic stress disorder symptomatology is a common consequence of traffic accidents in children. Also, no significant group differences are noted between children who sustain a TBI and develop PTSD versus children who do not sustain a TBI but also develop PTSD.[153]

Stability of moods normally is evident in children by ages 2 to 3 years. Usually at this point, there is a diminishment of crying and separation anxiety. Most children by preschool age have learned not to show anger or not to be abusive to others. The child can be asked very simple questions as outlined by Weinberg et al.[154] Simple questions include: "Can I ask you some very personal important questions? Are you having mostly good, mixed, or bad days in your feelings? Is it so bad you sneak off to your room and cry? Are you able to have fun or not when you feel badly? Have you been thinking about dying or wish that you were dead? Would you like to leave and go to heaven?" Also, as noted, the child may be irritable or assaultive. The child may have been noted to speak of death. In young children, in particular, depression and sadness may manifest as gastrointestinal complaints.

THOUGHT PROCESSING, CONTENT, AND PERCEPTION

Determining thought content in the child is difficult at best. The problem of assessing thought disorder in children has been addressed by others.[155,156] Children can develop delusions and even hallucinations. Detecting this in very young children is difficult but Caplan et al.[157] have developed an instrument that reliably and validly measures illogical thinking and loose associations in children. The development cut-off age is 7 years in nonschizophrenic children. The Kiddie Formal Thought Disorder Rating Scale (K-FTDS) is useful to assist the neuropsychiatric examiner if consideration is given that children between 3 and 7 years are demonstrating formal thought disorders. Table 4.24 outlines face-to-face neuropsychiatric screening methods for the child who has sustained brain trauma.

CHILD NEUROLOGICAL EXAMINATION

When examining the child who may have been traumatized and spent many days in a hospital, it is useful to keep a few simple pediatric pearls in mind. In younger children, the neurological examination will be a catch-as-catch-can procedure. A considerable amount of information can be obtained merely by observing the youngster play or interact with her parents. The dominant handedness of the child or the presence of cerebellar deficits, hemiparesis, or even visual field defects may become apparent with this approach. It is best not to wear a white coat as children equate this with injections or immunizations. For the 3- to 7-year old child, a few small items are useful for the examination such as: a tennis ball, small toys, a small car or truck that can be used to assess fine motor coordination, a bell, and a bright or shiny object that will attract the child's attention.

When examining a 3- or 4-year-old child, it is best to have the child seated in his mother's or father's lap and talk to the child while facing him. Defer touching the child until some degree of rapport has been established both with the parent and the child. For a 3- or 4-year-old child, handing

TABLE 4.24

Face-to-Face Neuropsychiatric Screening Methods for the Brain Traumatized Child 8–15 Years

Domain	Task
Orientation	"What is the year, the season, the date, the day, and the month?"
Attention	"Count from 20 to 1 backward."
Vigilance	"Subtract 7 from 100; now subtract 7 from that answer; keep subtracting 7 from each answer."
Memory	"Repeat after me: ball, cup, doll. Repeat them again. Now I want you to remember these. I will ask you to repeat them later."
	"I'm going to hide these objects here in the room (3 common items). Watch me and then I will see if you can find them."
Language	Point to a pen; your watch; your nose. Ask the child to name each one.
	"Repeat: no ifs, ands, or buts."
	"Take this paper, fold it in half, carry it across the room and place it on the desk."
	Show a paper or card with large print: "CLOSE YOUR EYES."
Visuospatial	Have the child copy two intersecting diamonds. Ask the child to draw a clock, place numbers on the clock, and place hands at four o'clock.

him a toy or a bright object may improve the development of rapport. Patience is required as once frightened, most young children are difficult to reassure and the examination may not proceed well.

Appearance

The general appearance of the child is carefully noted, in particular her facial configuration and the presence of any dysmorphic features or structural alterations of the face. Cutaneous lesions are clues to the presence of phakomatoses. These include lesions such as *café au lait*, angiomas, facial pigmentations, etc. Some pediatric neurologists take particular note of the location of the hair whorl as abnormalities of whorl patterns may indicate the presence of a cerebral malformation.[158] The neuropsychiatric examiner is clearly not expected to be an expert pediatrician nor pediatric neurologist. If unusual facial features are found, a consultation may be required as clearly what may appear to be cognitive changes from a traumatic head injury may in fact have a contributing factor or causation from a congenital or genetic disorder.

The general appearance of the skull can suggest the presence of macrocephaly, microcephaly, or craniosynostosis. Prominence of the venous pattern over the scalp might accompany increased intracranial pressure. Biparietal enlargement suggests the presence of subdural hematomas and, in certain situations, should raise the suspicion of child abuse. Palpation of the skull can disclose ridging of the sutures as occurs in craniosynostosis. The head circumference of the child should be measured and compared to a standard international and interracial head circumference graph.[159] One may review most standard textbooks of pediatrics for this information.

Cranial Nerves

As with the adult, a child may lose olfactory nerve function due to infraorbital or temporal lobe brain trauma or a fracture through the cribriform plate. Olfactory sensation is not functional in a newborn but is present by at least 5–7 months of age. By the time an accurate brain injury examination of a child can be made at age 3, full olfactory function should be present. However, a newborn will respond to inhalation of irritants such as ammonia or vinegar as this is transmitted by nerve V. Even a child born without an olfactory apparatus will respond to irritation of nerve V.[160]

The optic nerve in the child can be injured in the same manner as injury occurring to the adult optic nerve. The macular light reflex is absent until approximately 4 months of age, but clearly by age 3, the child will have a physiological reflex. Visual acuity can be tested in the older child by standard means. In the 3- or 4-year-old, approximation of visual acuity can be obtained by observing him or her at play and by offering toys of various sizes into the visual field. In a very small child or a child who is severely injured, the blink reflex, closure of the eyelids when an object is suddenly moved toward the eyes, may be used to determine the presence of functional vision. This reflex is absent in the newborn and does not appear until approximately 3–4 months of age. It is present in about half of normal 5-month-olds, but certainly by age 1, all normal children should have a physiological blink reflex.[161]

Nerves III, IV, and VI are evaluated after first noting the position of the child's eyes at rest. Observation of the points of reflection of light from the illuminating instrument will assist the examiner in detecting nonparallel alignment of the eyes. Paralysis of nerve III results in a lateral and slightly downward deviation of the affected eye. If the sixth nerve is paralyzed, a medial deviation of the affected eye will be noted. Paralysis of the fourth nerve produces little eye position change at rest. Eye movements are examined by having the very young child visually follow a shiny object. Mother should hold the child's head to prevent rotation. If the young child will permit the examiner to do so, each eye should be examined separately while the other one is kept covered. Sometimes, the child is able to assist with this and at other times, the parent may be asked to assist. There should be no difficulty in detecting abnormalities in a young child as eye excursion is completely developed in all directions by about 4 months of age. Eye movements directed toward a sound appear at about 5 months of age and depth perception is present at 2–4 months of age.[162] In a palsy of nerve VI, failure of the affected eye to move laterally should be readily demonstrable. For a pure third-nerve palsy, the defective eye will appear outwardly and downwardly displaced. Lateral movement will be defective. If the fourth nerve is palsied, the eye fails to move down and in. This defect is often accompanied by head tilt.

A simple test for the motor component of nerve V is performed by asking the child to demonstrate how to chew gum. If the child seems to fully comprehend this instruction, the examiner can chew appropriately in front of the child so the child can attempt to mimic the examiner's movements. In a unilateral lesion of the trigeminal nerve, the jaw will deviate to the paralyzed side and there should be atrophy of the temporalis muscle present some months after the injury. A UMN lesion above the level of the pons will result in an exaggerated jaw jerk. The sensory branch of the trigeminal nerve is tested by the corneal reflex and lateral facial sensation.

Injury to nerve VII should result in facial asymmetry. As noted above, if the facial nucleus and branches distal to this site are injured, LMN weakness in which both upper and lower parts of the face are paralyzed will be present. Normal wrinkling of the forehead cannot be performed; the eyebrows cannot be elevated, and the affected eye cannot be closed. Weakness of the face will be obvious on observation and the asymmetry should be accentuated when the child laughs or cries. Recall that facial weakness due to a UMN lesion above the facial nucleus or in the cerebral structures will spare the upper face musculature. The upper facial motor neurons receive little direct cortical input, whereas, the lower facial neurons apparently do.[163] The sensory arm of the facial nerve can be tested with a weak salt or sweet solution as described above with adult testing.

Hearing can be tested in the younger child[159] using a tuning fork or a bell. By age 3, all normal children will have the ability to turn the eyes to the direction of the sound, as this becomes evident by 7 to 8 weeks of age, and turning the eyes and head to stimuli appears at about 3–4 months of age. If there is a question of hearing loss in the child, audiometric evaluation may be required. Vestibular function can be assessed by observing for nystagmus. It is not recommended during a neuropsychiatric examination that caloric testing of a young child be performed and should this be required, consultation with an otolaryngologist is recommended.

Examination of nerves IX and X can be performed during the oral examination. The resting uvula and palate should function during phonation and a failure to elevate indicates impaired nerve X function. The gag reflex tests both arms of the vagus-glossopharyngeal nerve arc. Measuring taste carried by nerve IX over the posterior part of the tongue is extremely difficult and is not recommended in children. Testing of nerve XI can be accomplished by having the child rotate her head against resistance from the examiner's fist or hand. Most children age 3 and older can mimic shoulder shrugging of the examiner. During examination of the mouth, the resting tongue can be observed for vesiculations. Nerve XII is easy to test in children as they enjoy sticking their tongue out to mimic the examiner and a paretic tongue will deviate toward the side of the lesion.

Motor

The child's station can be observed at a distance. It is worthwhile to watch the child stand and then ask the youngster to run down the hallway. This enables assessment of running gait. Throwing a tennis ball down the hallway and asking the youngster to retrieve it is an excellent way to observe bilateral motor function, as most children enjoy performing for the examiner. This will provide sufficient information in the younger child to determine muscle strength and other examinations of strength are merely confirmatory. In the child older than age 5, evaluation of the motor system can be done in a more formal manner. Muscle tone is examined by manipulating the major joints. It is necessary to rule out alterations of tone, particularly in children who may have had a perinatal birth injury and later sustained a TBI.

A sensitive test for hypotonia of the upper extremities is to ask the child to raise his hands over his head. The pronator sign will appear in the hand on the hypotonic side as it hyperpronates to palm outward as the arms are raised. The elbow may flex as well. In the lower extremities, weakness of the flexors of the knee can be tested readily by having the child lie on her tummy and asking her to maintain her legs in flexion at right angles to the knee. The weak flexors will not allow her to maintain the leg at a 90° angle.

Sensory

Sensory examination is almost impossible to assess in a toddler. However, since adequate neuro-psychiatric examination of a brain-injured child is difficult to perform before age 3, the examinations of children in this circumstance will focus on age 3 and above. Sensory modalities can be tested in a 3- or 4-year-old if the child is comforted on the parent's lap. Using a tracing wheel is the preferred modality. Pins appear too much like injection needles to a youngster. Likewise, most children can cooperate for vibratory testing if the child is told that it will tickle. Object discrimination can be determined in children older than age 5 by the use of paperclips, coins, or rubber bands.

Coordination

The younger child enjoys performing the finger–nose test if the child's attention span will permit it. Coordination can be tested by having the youngster reach for toys and manipulate the toys. The older child can perform not only finger–nose testing, but also heel–shin testing. The ability to perform rapidly alternating movements (diadochokinesia) can be tested by having the child repeatedly tap the clinician's hand or by having him perform rapid pronation and supination of the hand on the knee. Rapid tapping of the foot on the floor will evaluate diadochokinesia of the foot. The heel-to-shin test is more difficult for children to comprehend than the finger-to-nose test. Children 9 years of age and older generally can perform the heel-to-shin maneuver, but children ages 7 and below may have difficulty with this performance. Observation of the child is best to determine abnormal involuntary movements and the procedures used for the adult can be applied here. Athetoid and choreiform movements may activate during walking or by rapidly slapping one's thigh. Dystonic posturing is detected best by observation.

Reflexes

The younger the child, the less information is obtained from deep tendon reflexes. With a child, reflex inequalities are common and less reliable than inequalities of muscle tone in terms of determining the presence of a UMN lesion.[95] The major deep tendon reflexes are noted in Table 4.21. The Babinski sign is a significant indicator of impaired pyramidal tract function. Some young children cannot tolerate having the sole of their foot stroked, but stimulation of the outer side of the foot is less problematic for these youngsters. Babinski response in the child is identical to the response in the adult and an extensor plantar response can be distinguished from voluntary withdrawal. Withdrawal is seen after a moment's delay, whereas the extension of the great toe and the fanning of the toes are immediate following stimulation. A Babinski sign is seen normally in the majority of 1-year-old children and in many children up to 2½ years of age. However, by age 3, almost all children will no longer demonstrate a Babinski sign.[164] Clonus is a regular repetitive movement of a joint caused by sudden stretching of the muscle. It is easiest to demonstrate by dorsiflexion of the foot. The examiner can press on the anterior sole of the foot and flex the ankle. Several beats of clonus can be demonstrated in very young children but a sustained ankle clonus in a child older than age 3 is abnormal and suggests a lesion of the pyramidal tract. It is due to increased reflex excitability.[159] Young children often can perform tandem walking. This will be difficult for a 3- or 4-year-old child, but forward tandem gait is performed successfully in 90% of children 5 years of age or older. Hopping in place on one leg generally is difficult for a 3- or 4-year-old. However, by age 7, 90% of children will be able to hop in place on one leg.[165]

REFERENCES

1. Trzepacz, P.T. and Baker, R.W., *The Psychiatric Mental Status Examination*, Oxford University Press, New York, 1993.
2. Strub, R.L. and Black, F.W., *The Mental Status Examination in Neurology*, 4th edition, F.A. Davis Company, Philadelphia, PA, 2000.
3. Lezak, M.D., *Neuropsychological Assessment*, 4th edition, Oxford University Press, New York, 2004.
4. Cummings, J.L. and Mega, M.S., *Neuropsychiatry and Behavioral Neuroscience*, Oxford University Press, New York, 2003.
5. James, W., *The Principles of Psychology*, Holt, New York, 1890.
6. Plum, F. and Posner, J.B., *The Diagnosis of Stupor and Coma*, 3rd edition, F.A. Davis Company, Philadelphia, PA, 1980.
7. McAllister, T.W., Neuropsychiatric sequelae of head injuries. *Psychiatr. Clin. North Am.*, 15, 395, 1992.
8. Brooks, N., Behavioral abnormalities in head injured patients. *Scand. J. Rehabil. Med. Suppl.*, 17, 41, 1988.
9. Umilta, C., Orienting of attention, in *Handbook of Neuropathology*, Vol. 1, Boller, F. and Grafman, J., Eds., Elsevier Science Publishers, Amsterdam, 1988, p. 115.
10. Folstein, M.F., Folstein, F.E., and McHugh, J.R., A practical method for grading the cognitive state of patients for the clinician. *J. Psychiatr. Res.*, 12, 189, 1975.
11. Reitan, R.M. and Wolfson, D., *The Halstead–Reitan Neuropsychological Test Battery. Theory and Clinical Interpretation*, 2nd edition, Neuropsychology Press, Tucson, AZ, 1993.
12. Benson, D.F., *Aphasia, Alexia, and Agraphia*, Churchill Livingstone, New York, 1979.
13. Damasio, A.R., Aphasia. *New Engl. J. Med.*, 326, 531, 1992.
14. Ross, E.D. and Mesulim, M.M., Dominant language functions of the right hemisphere? Prosody and emotional gesturing. *Arch. Neurol.*, 36, 144, 1979.
15. Cancelliere, A.E.B. and Kertesz, A., Lesion localization and acquired deficits of emotional expression and comprehension. *Brain Cogn.*, 13, 133, 1990.
16. Gelber, D.A., The neurologic examination of the traumatically brain-injured patient, in *Traumatic Brain Injury Rehabilitation*, Ashley, M.J. and Krych, D.K., Eds., CRC Press, Boca Raton, FL, 1995, p. 23.
17. Goodglass, H. and Kaplan, E., *The Assessment of Aphasia and Related Disorders*, 2nd edition, Lea and Febiger, Philadelphia, PA, 1983.
18. Goodglass, H. *Understanding Aphasia*, Academic Press, San Diego, CA, 1993.
19. Borkowski, J.G., Benton, A.L., and Spreen, O., Word fluency in brain damage. *Neuropsychologia*, 5, 135, 1967.

20. Benson, D.F., Neurological correlates of anomia, in *Studies in Neurolinguistics*, Whittaker, H. and Whittaker, H.A., Eds., Academic Press, New York, 1979, p. 293.
21. Tombaugh, T.N. and Hubley, A.M., The 60-item Boston Naming Test: Norms for cognitively intact adults aged 25 to 80 years, *J. Clin. Exp. Neuropsychol.*, 19, 922, 1997.
22. Benson, D.F. and Cummings, J.L., Agraphia, in *Clinical Neuropsychology, Volume 45. Handbook of Clinical Neurology*, Frederick, J.A.N., Ed., Elsevier, New York, 1985, p. 457.
23. Cummings, J.L., Amnesia and memory disturbances in neurologic disorders, in *Review of Psychiatry*, Oldham, J.M., Riba, M.B., and Tasman, A., Eds., American Psychiatric Press, Washington, D.C., 1993, p. 725.
24. Taylor, M.A., *The Fundamentals of Clinical Neuropsychiatry*, Oxford University Press, New York, 1999.
25. Squire, L.R., *Memory and Brain*, Oxford University Press, New York, 1987.
26. Mesulam, M.M., *Principles of Behavioral Neurology*, F.A. Davis, Philadelphia, PA, 1985.
27. Benson, D.F. and McDaniel, K.D., Memory disorders, in *Neurology and Clinical Practice*, Vol. II, Bradley, W.G., Daroff, R.B., Fenichel, G.M., et al., Eds., Butterworth-Heinemann, Boston, 1991.
28. Benson, D.F., *The Neurology of Thinking*, Oxford University Press, 1994.
29. Signoret, J.L., Memory and amnesias, in *Principles of Behavioral Neurology*, Mesulam, M.M., Ed., F.A. Davis, Philadelphia, PA, 1985, p. 169.
30. Holland, A.L., Fromm, D., and Greenhouse, J.B., Characteristics of recovery of drawing ability in left and right brain-damaged patients. *Brain Cogn.*, 7, 16, 1988.
31. Carlesimo, G.A., Fadda, I., and Caltagirone, C., Basic mechanisms of constructional apraxia in unilateral brain-damaged patients: Role of visuoperceptual and executive disorders. *J. Clin. Exp. Neuropsychol.*, 15, 342, 1993.
32. Stuss, D.T. and Benson, D.F., *The Frontal Lobes*, Raven Press, New York, 1986.
33. Power, C., Selnes, O.A., Grim, J.A., et al., HIV Dementia Scale: A rapid screening test. *J. Acquir. Immune Defic. Syndr.*, 8, 273, 1995.
34. Royall, D.R., Mahurin, R.K., and Gray, K.F., Bedside assessment of executive cognitive impairment: The Executive Interview. *J. Am. Geriatr. Soc.*, 40, 1221, 1992.
35. Grigsby, J. and Kaye, K., *Behavioral Dyscontrol Scale*, Manual, 2nd edition, Denver, CO, 1996.
36. Dubois, B., Slachevsky, A., Litvan, I., et al., The FAB: A frontal assessment battery at the bedside. *Neurology*, 55, 1621, 2000.
37. Warriner, E.M. and Velikonja, D., Psychiatric disturbances after traumatic brain injury. Neurobehavior and personality changes. *Curr. Psychiatry Rep.*, 8, 73, 2006.
38. Jorge, R.E., Neuropsychiatric consequences of traumatic brain injury: A review of recent findings. *Curr. Opin. Psychiatry*, 18, 289, 2005.
39. Chamelian, L. and Feinstein, A., The effect of major depression on subjective and objective cognitive deficits in mild to moderate traumatic brain injury. *J. Neuropsychiatr. Clin. Neurosci.*, 18, 33, 2006.
40. Croker, V. and McDonald, S., Recognition of emotion from facial expression following traumatic brain injury. *Brain Inj.*, 19, 787, 2005.
41. Henry, J.D., Phillips, L.H., Crawford, J.R., et al., Cognitive and psychosocial correlates of alexithymia following traumatic brain injury. *Neuropsychologia*, 44, 62, 2006.
42. Mueller, J. and Fogel, B.S., Neuropsychiatric examination, in *Neuropsychiatry*, Fogel, B.S., Schiffer, R.B., and Rao, S.M., Eds., Williams & Wilkins, Baltimore, 1996, p. 11.
43. Holsinger, T., Steffens, D.C., Phillips, C., et al., Head injury in early adulthood and the lifetime risk of depression. *Arch. Gen. Psychiatry*, 59, 17, 2002.
44. Rizzolatti, G., Fogassi, L., and Gallese, V., Mirrors in the mind. *Sci. Am.*, 295, 54, 2006.
45. Lishman, W.A., *Organic Psychiatry: The Psychological Consequences of Cerebral Disorder*, 2nd edition, Blackwell Scientific Publications, Oxford, 1987.
46. Fish, F., *Fish's Clinical Psychopathology: Signs and Symptoms in Psychiatry*, Hamilton, M., Ed., John Wright & Sons, Bristol, 1974.
47. Fujii, D. and Ahmed, I., Psychotic disorder following traumatic brain injury: A conceptual framework. *Cognit. Neuropsychiatry*, 7, 41, 2002.
48. Zhang, Q. and Sachdev, P.S., Psychotic disorder in traumatic brain injury. *Curr. Psychiatry Rep.*, 5, 197, 2003.

49. Achte, K., Jarho, L., Kyykka, T., et al., Paranoid disorders following war brain damage. Preliminary report. *Psychopathology*, 24, 309, 1991.

50. Simon, R.I. and Hales, R.E., Eds., *The American Psychiatric Publishing Textbook of Suicide Assessment and Management*, American Psychiatric Press, Washington, D.C., 2006.

51. Kishi, Y., Robinson, R.G., and Kosier, J.T., Suicidal ideation among patients with acute life-threatening physical illness: Patients with stroke, traumatic brain injury, myocardial infarction, and spinal cord injury. *Psychosomatics*, 42, 382, 2001.

52. Leon-Carrion, J., DeSerdio-Arias, M.L., Carbezas, F.M., et al., Neurobehavioral and cognitive profile of traumatic brain injury patients at risk for depression and suicide. *Brain Inj.*, 15, 175, 2001.

53. Simon, R.I., Discharging sicker, potentially violent psychiatric inpatients in the managed care era: Standard of care and risk management. *Psychiatr. Ann.*, 27, 726, 1997.

54. Adams, J.H., Graham, D., Scott, G., et al., Brain damage in fatal non-missile head injury. *J. Clin. Pathol.*, 33, 1132, 1980.

55. Lezak, M.D., *Neuropsychological Assessment*, 3rd edition, Oxford University Press, New York, 1995.

56. Ovsiew, F. and Bylsma, F.W., The three cognitive examinations. *Sem. Clin. Neuropsychiatr.*, 7, 54, 2002.

57. Freedman, M., Leach, L., Kaplan, E., et al., *Clock Drawing: A Neuropsychological Analysis*, Oxford University Press, New York, 1994.

58. DeMyer, W.E., *Technique of the Neurologic Examination*, 5th edition, McGraw-Hill, New York, 2004.

59. Kruse, J.J. and Awasthi, D., Skull-based trauma: Neurosurgical prospective. *J. Craniomaxillofac. Trauma*, 4, 8, 1998.

60. Toledano, A., Gonzalez, E., Ferrando, J., et al., Hematoma of the olfactory bulbs following cranioence-phalic trauma. *Acta Otorrinolaringol. Esp.*, 56, 280, 2005.

61. Sumner, D., Disturbances of the senses of smell and taste after head injuries, in *Handbook of Clinical Neurology*, Vol. 24, Vinken, P.J. and Bruyn, C.W., Eds., North-Holland Publishing, Amsterdam, 1976, p. 1.

62. Hendricks, A.P.J., Olfactory dysfunction. *Rhinology*, 26, 229, 1988.

63. Levin, H.S., High, W.M., and Eisenberg, H.M., Impairment of olfactory recognition after closed head injury. *Brain*, 108, 579, 1985.

64. Jennett, B. and Teasdale, G., *Management of Head Injuries*, F.A. Davis Company, Philadelphia, PA, 1981.

65. Callahan, C.D. and Hinkebein, J.H., Assessment of anosmia after traumatic brain injury: Performance characteristics of the University of Pennsylvania Smell Identification Test. *J. Head Trauma Rehabil.*, 17, 251, 2002.

66. Mann, N.M. and Vento, J.A., The study comparing SPECT and MRI in patients with anosmia after traumatic brain injury. *Clin. Nucl. Med.*, 31, 458, 2006.

67. Roberts, A.H., *Severe Accidental Head Injury: An Assessment of Long-Term Prognosis*, The Macmillan Press, Ltd., London, 1979.

68. Gjerris, F., Traumatic lesions of the visual pathways, in *Handbook of Clinical Neurology*, Vol. 24, Vinken, P.J. and Bruyn, C.W., Eds., North-Holland Publishing, Amsterdam, 1976, p. 27.

69. Kline, L.B., Morawetz, R.B., and Swaid, S.N., Indirect injury to the optic nerve. *Neurosurgery*, 14, 756, 1984.

70. Chadwick, O., Rutter, M., Brown, G., et al., A prospective study of children with head injuries. II: Cognitive sequelae. *Psychol. Med.*, 11, 49, 1981.

71. Atipo-Tsiba, P.W. and Borruat, F.X., Traumatic dysfunction of the optic chiasm. *Klin. Monatsbl. Augenheilkd.*, 220, 138, 2003.

72. Zhang, X., Kedar, S., Lynn, M.J., et al., Homonymous hemianopias: Clinical-anatomic correlations in 904 cases. *Neurology*, 66, 906, 2006.

73. Bruce, B.B., Zhang, X., Kedar, S., et al., Traumatic homonymous hemianopia. *J. Neurol. Neurosurg. Psychiatry*, 77, 986, 2006.

74. Baker, R.S. and Epstein, A.D., Ocular motor abnormalities from head trauma. *Surv. Opthalmol.*, 35, 245, 1991.

75. Shokunbi, T. and Agbeja, A., Ocular complications of head injury in children. *Child's Nerv. Syst.*, 7, 147, 1991.

76. Hardman, J.M., The pathology of traumatic brain injury, in *Advances in Neurology: Complications of Central Nervous System Trauma*, Vol. 22, Thompson, R.A. and Green, J.B., Eds., Raven Press, New York, 1979, p. 15.

77. Kushner, B.J., Ocular causes of abnormal head postures. *Ophthalmology*, 86, 2115, 1979.

78. Sydnor, C.F., Seaber, J.H., and Buckley, E.G., Traumatic superior oblique palsies. *Ophthalmology*, 89, 134, 1982.

79. Aygun, D., Doganay, Z., Baydin, A., et al., Posttraumatic pneumoencephalus-induced bilateral oculo-motor nerve palsy. *Clin. Neurol. Neurosurg.*, 108, 84, 2005.

80. Levy, R.L., Geist, C.E., and Miller, N.R., Isolated oculomotor palsy following minor head trauma. *Neurology*, 65, 269, 2005.

81. Muri, R., Meienberg, O., and Wieser, D., Isolated trochlear nerve paralysis following head trauma. *Schweiz. Med. Wochenschr.*, 120, 1223, 1990.

82. Bixenman, W.W., Diagnosis of superior oblique palsy. *J. Clin. Neuroophthalmol.*, 1, 199, 1981.

83. Cackett, P., Fleck, B., and Mulhivill, A., Bilateral fourth-nerve palsy occurring after shaking injury in infancy. *J. AAPOS.*, 8, 280, 2004.

84. Mutyala, S., Holmes, J.M., Hodge, D.O., et al., Spontaneous recovery rate in traumatic sixth-nerve palsy. *Am. J. Ophthalmol.*, 122, 898, 1996.

85. Yadav, Y.R. and Khosla, V.K., Isolated fifth to tenth cranial nerve palsy in closed head trauma. *Clin. Neurol. Neurosurg.*, 93, 61, 1991.

86. Ko, K.F. and Chan, K.L., A case of isolated paratrigeminal motor neuropathy. *Clin. Neurol. Neurosurg.*, 97, 199, 1995.

87. Ratilal, B., Castanho, P., VaraLuiz, C., et al., Traumatic clivus epidural hematoma: Case report and review of the literature. *Surg. Neurol.*, 66, 2000, 2006.

88. Schecter, A.D. and Anziska, B., Isolated complete posttraumatic trigeminal neuropathy. *Neurology*, 40, 1634, 1990.

89. Li, J., Goldberg, G., Munin, M.C., et al., Post-traumatic bilateral facial palsy: A case report and literature review. *Brain Inj.*, 18, 315, 2004.

90. Sakai, C.C. and Mateer, C.A., Otological and audiological sequelae of closed head trauma. *Semin. Hear.*, 5, 157, 1984.

91. Kochhar, L.K., Deka, R.C., Kacker, S.K., et al., Hearing loss after head injury. *Ear Nose Throat J.*, 69, 537, 1990.

92. Attias, J., Zwcker-Lazar, I., Nageris, V., et al., Dysfunction of the auditory efferent system in patients with traumatic brain injuries with tinnitus and hyperacusis. *J. Basic Clin. Physiol. Pharmacol.*, 16, 117, 2005.

93. Motin, M., Keren, O., Groswasser, Z., et al., Benign paroxysmal positional vertigo as the cause of dizziness in patients after severe traumatic brain injury: Diagnosis and treatment. *Brain Inj.*, 19, 693, 2005.

94. Gottshall, K., Drake, A., Gray, N., et al., Objective vestibular tests as outcome measures in head injury patients. *Laryngoscope*, 113, 1746, 2003.

95. Hashimoto, T., Watanabe, O., Takase, M., et al., Collet–Sicard syndrome after minor head trauma. *Neurosurgery*, 23, 367, 1988.

96. Yadav, Y.R. and Khosla, V.K., Isolated fifth to tenth cranial nerve palsy in closed head trauma. *Clin. Neurol. Neurosurg.*, 93, 61, 1991.

97. Haig, A.J., Ho, K.C., and Ludwig, G., Clinical, physiologic and pathologic evidence for vagus dysfunction, a case of traumatic brain injury. *J. Trauma*, 40, 441, 1996.

98. Vane, D.W., Shiffler, M., Grosfeld, J.L., et al., Reduced lower esophageal sphincter (LES) pressure after acute and chronic brain injury. *J. Pediatr. Surg.*, 17, 960, 1982.

99. Schliack, H. and Schafer, P., Hypoglossal and accessory nerve paralysis and a fracture of the occipital condyle. *Nervenartz*, 36, 362, 1965.

100. Engelhardt, P., Traumatic bilateral paralysis of hypoglossal nerve. *Nervenartz*, 48, 109, 1977.

101. Kaushik, V., Kelly, G., Richards, S.D., et al., Isolated unilateral hypoglossal nerve palsy after minor head trauma. *Clin. Neurol. Neurosurg.*, 105, 42, 2002.

102. Bergfeldt, U., Borg, K., Kullander, K., et al., Focal spasticity therapy with botulinum toxin: Effects on function, activities of daily living and pain in 100 adult patients. *J. Rehabil. Med.*, 38, 166, 2006.

103. Singer, B.J., Jegasothy, G.N., Singer, K.P., et al., Incidence of ankle contracture after moderate to severe acquired brain injury. *Arch. Phys. Med. Rehabil.*, 85, 1465, 2004.

104. Garland, D.E. and Rhoades, M.E., Orthopedic management of brain-injured adults: Part II. *Clin. Orthopaed. Relat. Res.*, 131, 111, 1978.

105. Sandyk, R., Hemichorea–A late sequel of an extradural hematoma. *Postgrad. Med. J.*, 59, 462, 1983.

106. Drake, M.E., Jackson, R.D., and Miller, C.A., Paroxysmal choreoathetosis after head injury. *J. Neurol. Neurosurg. Psychiatry*, 49, 837, 1986.
107. Frei, K.P., Pathak, M., Jenkins, S., et al., Natural history of posttraumatic cervical dystonia. *Mov. Disord.*, 19, 1492, 2004.
108. Francisco, G.E., Successful treatment of posttraumatic hemiballismus with intrathecal baclofen therapy. *Am. J. Phys. Med. Rehabil.*, 85, 779, 2006.
109. Blackman, J.A., Patrick, P.D., Buck, M.L., et al., Paroxysmal autonomic instability with dystonia after brain injury. *Arch. Neurol.*, 61, 321, 2004.
110. Marsden, C.D., Obeso, J.A., Zarranz, J.J., et al., The anatomical basis of symptomatic hemidystonia. *Brain*, 108, 463, 1985.
111. Pettigrew, L.C. and Jankovic, J., Hemidystonia: A report of 22 patients and a review of the literature. *J. Neurol. Neurosurg. Psychiatry*, 48, 650, 1985.
112. Robin, J.J., Paroxysmal choreoathetosis following head injury. *Ann. Neurol.*, 2, 447, 1977.
113. Biary, N., Cleeves, L., Findley, L., et al., Posttraumatic tremor. *Neurology*, 39, 103, 1989.
114. Fahn, S., Marsden, C.D., and VanWoert, M.H., Definition and classification of myoclonus, in *Advances in Neurology: Myoclonus*, Vol. 43, Fahn, S., Marsden, C.D., and VanWoert, M.H., Eds., Raven Press, New York, 1986, p. 1.
115. Lance, J.W., Action myoclonus, Ramsay Hunt syndrome, and other cerebellar myoclonic syndromes, in *Advances in Neurology: Myoclonus*, Vol. 43, Fahn, S., Marsden, C.D., and VanWoert, M.H., Eds., Raven Press, New York, 1986, p. 33.
116. Nayernouri, T., Posttraumatic Parkinsonism. *Surg. Neurol.*, 24, 263, 1985.
117. Heriseanu, R., Baguley, I.J., and Slewa-Younan, S., Two-point discrimination following traumatic brain injury. *J. Clin. Neurosci.*, 12, 156, 2005.
118. Haerer, A.F., *DeJong's The Neurologic Examination*, 5th edition, J.B. Lippincott Company, Philadelphia, PA, 1992.
119. Duong, T.T., Englander, J., Wright, J., et al., Relationship between strength, balance and swallowing deficits in outcome after traumatic brain injury: A multicenter analysis. *Arch. Phys. Med. Rehabil.*, 85, 1291, 2004.
120. Basford, J.R., Chou, L.S., Kaufman, K.R., et al., An assessment of gait and balance deficits after traumatic brain injury. *Arch. Phys. Med. Rehabil.*, 84, 343, 2003.
121. Chou, L.S., Kaufman, K.R., Walker-Rabatin, A.E., et al., Dynamic instability during obstacle crossing following traumatic brain injury. *Gait Posture*, 20, 245, 2004.
122. Vallee, M., McFadyen, B.J., Swaine, B., et al., Effects of environmental demands on locomotion after traumatic brain injury. *Arch. Phys. Med. Rehabil.*, 87, 806, 2006.
123. Formisano, R., Bivona, U., Brunelli, S., et al., A preliminary investigation of road traffic accident rate after severe brain injury. *Brain Inj.*, 19, 159, 2005.
124. Rizzo, M., Safe and unsafe driving, in *Principles and Practice of Behavioral Neurology and Neuropsychology*, Rizzo, M. and Eslinger, P.L., Eds., W.B. Saunders, Philadelphia, PA, 2004, p. 197.
125. Hills, V.L., Vision, visibility and driving. *Perception*, 9, 183, 1980.
126. Schneider, J.J. and Gouvier, W.T., Utility of the UFOV test with mild traumatic brain injury. *Appl. Neuropsychol.*, 12, 138, 2005.
127. Uc, E.Y., Smothers, J.L., Shi, Q., et al., Driver navigation and safety errors in Alzheimer's disease and stroke. (abstract). *Second International Driving Symposium on Human Factors in Driver Assessment, Training, and Vehicle Design*, Park City, UT, July 21–24, 2003.
128. Reyner, L.A. and Horne, J.A. Falling asleep while driving: Are drivers aware of prior sleepiness? *Int. J. Legal Med.*, 111, 120, 1998.
129. Dula, C.S. and Ballard, N.E., Development and evaluation of a measure of dangerous, aggressive, negative emotional and risky driving. *J. Appl. Soc. Psychol.*, 33, 263, 2003.
130. Lew, H.L., Poole, J.H., Lee, E.H., et al., Predictive validity of driving-simulator assessments following traumatic brain injury: A preliminary study. *Brain Inj.*, 19, 177, 2005.
131. Pietrapiana, P., Tanietto, M., Torrini, G., et al., Role of premorbid factors in predicting safe return to driving after severe TBI. *Brain Inj.*, 19, 197, 2005.
132. Neeper, R., Huntzinger, R., and Gascon, G.G., Examination I: Special techniques for the infant and young child, in *Textbook of Pediatric Neuropsychiatry*, Coffey, C.E. and Brumback, R.A., Eds., American Psychiatric Press, Washington, D.C., 1998, p. 153.

133. Kestenbaum, C.J., The clinical interview of the child, in *Textbook of Child and Adolescent Psychiatry*, 2nd edition, Wiener, J.M., Ed., American Psychiatric Press, Washington, D.C., 1997, p. 79.

134. Ornstein, P.A., Larus, D.M., and Clubb, P.A., Understanding children's testimony: Implications of research in the development of memory. *Ann. Child Dev.*, 8, 145, 1991.

135. Ceci, S.S., Ross, D.F., and Tuglia, M.P., Suggestibility of children's memory: Psychological implications. *J. Exp. Psychol. Gen.*, 116, 338, 1987.

136. Ouvier, R.A., Goldsmith, R.F., Ouvier, S., et al., The value of the Mini-Mental State Examination in childhood: A preliminary study. *J. Child Neurol.*, 8, 145, 1993.

137. Weinberg, W.A., Harper, C.R., and Brumback, R.A., Use of the Symbol Language Battery in the physician's office for assessment of higher brain function. *J. Child Neurol.*, 10 (Suppl. 1), 23, 1994.

138. Max, J.E., Schachar, R.J., Levin, H.S., et al., Predictors of attention-deficit/hyperactivity disorder within 6 months after pediatric traumatic brain injury. *J. Am. Acad. Child Adolesc. Psychiatry*, 44, 1032, 2005.

139. Max, J.E., Schachar, R.J., Levin, H.S, et al., Predictors of secondary attention-deficit/hyperactivity disorder in children and adolescents 6 to 24 months after traumatic brain injury. *J. Am. Acad. Child Adolesc. Psychiatry*, 44, 1041, 2005.

140. Slomine, B.S., Salorio, C.F., Grados, M.A., et al., Differences in attention, executive function and memory in children with and without ADHD after severe traumatic brain injury. *J. Int. Neuropsychol. Soc.*, 11, 645, 2005.

141. Chapman, S.B., Sparks, G., Levin, H.S., et al., Discourse macrolevel processing after severe pediatric traumatic brain injury. *Dev. Neuropsychol.*, 25, 37, 2004.

142. Thomas-Stonell, N., Johnson, P., Rumney, P., et al., An evaluation of the responsiveness of a comprehensive set of outcome measures for children and adolescents with traumatic brain injuries. *Pediatr. Rehabil*, 9, 14, 2006.

143. Barlow, K., Thompson, E., Johnson, D., et al., The neurological outcome of non-accidental head injury. *Pediatr. Rehabil.*, 7, 195, 2004.

144. Donders, J., Performance on the test of memory malingering in a mixed pediatric sample. *Child Neuropsychol*, 11, 221, 2005.

145. Salorio, C.F., Slomine, B.S., Grados, N.A., et al., Neuroanatomic correlates of CVLT-C performance following pediatric traumatic brain injury. *J. Int. Neuropsychol. Soc.*, 11, 686, 2005.

146. Ewing-Cobbs, L., Levin, H.S., Fletcher, J.M., et al., The Children's Orientation and Amnesia Test: Relationship to severity of acute head injury and to recovery of memory. *Neurosurgery*, 27, 683, 1990.

147. Ewing-Cobbs, L., Prasad, M., Landry, S.H., et al., Executive functions following traumatic brain injury in young children: A preliminary analysis. *Dev. Neuropsychol.*, 26, 487, 2004.

148. Corkman, M., Kirk, U., and Kemp, S., *NEPSY: A Developmental Neuropsychological Assessment*, Manual. The Psychological Corporation, San Antonio, TX, 1998.

149. Levin, H.S. and Hanten, G., Executive functions after traumatic brain injury in children. *Pediatr. Neurol.*, 33, 79, 2005.

150. Anderson, V. and Katroppa, C., Recovery of executive skills following paediatric traumatic brain injury (TBI): A two year follow-up. *Brain Inj.*, 19, 459, 2005.

151. Yeates, K.O., Closed head injury, in *Pediatric Neuropsychology: Research, Theory and Practice*, The Guilford Press, New York, 2000, p. 92.

152. Luis, C.A. and Mittenberg, W., Mood and anxiety disorders following pediatric traumatic brain injury: A prospective study. *J. Clin. Exp. Neuropsychol.*, 24, 270, 2002.

153. Mather, F.J., Tate, R.L., and Hannan, T.J., Posttraumatic stress disorder in children following road traffic accidents: A comparison of those with and without mild traumatic brain injury. *Brain Inj.*, 17, 1077, 2003.

154. Weinberg, W.A., Harper, C.R., and Brumback, R.A., Examination II: Clinical evaluation of cognitive/behavioral function, in *Textbook of Pediatric Neuropsychiatry*, Coffey, C.E. and Brumback, R.A., Eds., American Psychiatric Press, Washington, D.C., 1998, p. 171.

155. Arboleda, C. and Holzman, P.S., Thought disorder in children at risk for psychosis. *Arch. Gen. Psychiatry*, 42, 1004, 1985.

156. Caplan, R., Thought disorder in childhood. *J. Am. Acad. Child Adolesc. Psychiatry*, 33, 605, 1994.

157. Caplan, R., Guthrie, D., Fish, V., et al., The Kiddie-Formal Thought Disorder Rating Scale: Clinical assessment, reliability and validity. *J. Am. Acad. Child Adolesc. Psychiatry*, 28, 408, 1989.

158. Tirosh, E., Jaffe, N., and Dar, H., The clinical significance of multiple hair whorls and their association with unusual dermatoglyphics and dysmorphic features in mentally retarded Israeli children. *Eur. J. Pediatr.*, 146, 568, 1987.

159. Menkes, J.H., *Textbook of Child Neurology*, 5th edition, Williams & Wilkins, Baltimore, 1995, p. 1.

160. Peiper, A., *Cerebral Function in Infancy and Childhood*, Consultants Bureau, New York, 1963, p. 49.

161. Kasahara, M. and Inamatsu, S., Der Blinzelreflex im Säuglingsalter. *Arch. Kinderhk.*, 92, 302, 1931.

162. Jampel, R.S. and Quaglio, N.D., Eye movements in Tay-Sachs disease. *Neurology*, 14, 1013, 1964.

163. Jenny, A.B. and Saper, C.B., Organization of the facial nucleus and corticofacial projection in the monkey: A reconsideration of the upper motor neuron facial palsy. *Neurology*, 37, 930, 1987.

164. Paine, R.S. and Oppe, T.E., *Neurological Examination of Children. Clinics in Developmental Medicine*, Vol. 20–21, William Heinemann, London, 1966.

165. Denckla, N.B., Development of motor coordination in normal children. *Dev. Med. Child Neurol.*, 16, 729, 1974.

5 The Use of Structural and Functional Imaging in the Neuropsychiatric Assessment of Traumatic Brain Injury

INTRODUCTION

It is not possible to provide a comprehensive neuropsychiatric assessment of a person following traumatic brain injury (TBI) without also including at a minimum structural brain imaging. Functional brain imaging may be useful in particular and special circumstances as noted further in this chapter. The use of electroencephalographic evaluation also plays an important role in certain situations following TBI. Table 5.1 is a listing of the common structural and functional procedures available to the neuropsychiatric examiner. Physicians performing a neuropsychiatric examination are not expected to understand neuroimaging at the level of a radiologist or neuroradiologist, nuclear medicine physician or neurologist-electroencephalographer. However, physicians functioning in the neuropsychiatric realm are expected to understand and use neuroimaging where appropriate, particularly in the postacute evaluation of cognitive status following TBI. It is important that the neuropsychiatric examiner develops a professional relationship with radiologists or neuroradiologists, nuclear medicine physicians and neurologists performing electroencephalograms. Neuroimaging to the neuropsychiatric examiner is no different than any other laboratory examination. The images are obtained using standardized protocols and are interpreted in standardized manners based on the particular standards for the profession involved in the interpretation of the images. The neuropsychiatric examiner then obtains these images and overreads them. Thus, stems the necessity for a good relationship with imaging physicians. It is recommended that the neuropsychiatric examiners, early in their career, overread each image with the imaging physician when it is obtained during a neuropsychiatric TBI examination. Over time, the neuropsychiatric examiner will develop skill in the understanding and detection of TBI lesions identified by functional and structural imaging. This will enhance the skill set of the neuropsychiatric examiner to provide a comprehensive and quality examination of the post-TBI patient. It goes without saying that in a forensic situation, structural and functional imaging is a must for providing the trier of fact with images to establish the integrity of the brain following TBI. This chapter introduces to the examiner performing neuropsychiatric brain injury assessment issues that are primarily related to imaging of acute brain trauma. However, most of the imaging performed in a neuropsychiatric evaluation will be well after the fact of the brain injury and will be used to determine outcomes, damages, and as an adjunct to treatment planning in therapy. It is necessary for the examiner to be aware of imaging obtained either in the emergency department or the acute care setting following TBI. Otherwise, when the examiner reviews medical records, the clinical correlation between the original acute injury and the current findings on neuropsychiatric examination will be poorly understood by the physician. This chapter presents structural and functional imaging figures that correspond to the real life chronic lesions that

---

TABLE 5.1

Structural and Functional Neuroimaging of the Brain in Traumatic Brain Injury

Structural imaging
- Computed tomography (CT)
- Magnetic resonance imaging (MRI)

Functional imaging
- Single-photon emission computed tomography (SPECT)
- Positron emission tomography (PET)
- Functional magnetic resonance imaging (fMRI)
- Magnetic resonance spectroscopy (MRS)
- Electroencephalography (EEG)

---

may be detected during neuropsychiatric examination. Imaging from acute care settings after TBI will be described and some are figuratively displayed. The reader is referred to expert sources for acute imaging exemplars.[1,16,25,27,44,75,78,89,110,121,127]

STRUCTURAL IMAGING OF BRAIN TRAUMA

COMPUTED TOMOGRAPHY

Use in the Acute Care Setting

Computed tomography (CT) is the most common means used for intracranial evaluation following trauma.[1] The principles of CT are similar to those of standard planar radiography, except that the former uses stationary detectors rather than radiographic film to capture images. Planar x-ray functions like an ordinary photographic camera, except instead of light striking film, an x-ray beam is attenuated as it passes through tissues before striking the detector. CT also uses an x-ray beam and is counterbalanced with an x-ray detector bank situated within the outer ring of the scan gantry. The degree to which the x-ray beam is absorbed or scattered (attenuated) determines the radiographic density of the structure being scanned. When an x-ray beam enters two separate but contiguous structures, the structure that is composed of the densest material will absorb more of the beam than its neighbor allowing fewer x-ray photons to reach the detectors. A diminished detector signal is translated into a lighter shade of gray on the image gray scale than that of its less dense neighbor. This allows the radiologist to differentiate tissues based on contrast resolution. CT can also be performed with a variety of postacquisition electronic filters. These filters selectively add or remove various frequencies from the raw data and change the limits of the gray scale producing either a smoothing or an accentuation of the edges. Filters are applied to the raw digital data during postacquisition manipulation. If needed, ionic and nonionic forms of contrast media are available for CT. Ionic contrast agents are much less costly than the nonionic forms. However, the nonionic contrast agents have substantially fewer side effects. Contrast is rarely used to detect CT lesions of TBI in the chronic phase. They may be used if there is a question of acute ischemic stroke as a result of mass effects from intracranial traumatic lesions.[1]

CT is the imaging modality of choice in the evaluation of acute head trauma, because of its widespread availability and speed and compatibility with life support and monitoring devices. Motion artifact as a result of uncooperative patients has become less important with the increasing availability of fast multidetector scanners and with the emergence of the new 64-slice scanning systems. For instance, if images are degraded by motion artifact, those particular slices can be selectively rescanned without repeating the entire scan. CT scanners have "windows" wherein the electronic scanning parameters are changed depending on the tissue being scanned. For instance, a brain window format evaluates for parenchymal lesions. The subdural window is used for extra-axial assessment. Bone windows are used to detect skull and facial fractures. Subdural windows are particularly useful in detecting superficial hemorrhage, shallow contusions, and small extra-axial collections of blood, where the high attenuation of blood may blend into the adjacent high attenuation of bone. Limitations of using CT include beam-hardening effects, which may partially obscure blood in the posterior fossa. This also may obscure blood in the subtemporal and subfrontal regions. In those instances where the CT scan produces equivocal findings, small lesions such as small subdural hematomas will be more readily apparent using magnetic resonance imaging.[2] Recent Japanese studies also conclude that while MRI is more sensitive and accurate in diagnosing cerebral pathology, CT is considered the most critical imaging technique for the management of closed head-injured patients in the acute stage.[3]

The epidemiology of emergency department patients with blunt head injury undergoing cranial CT scanning has recently been evaluated in a very large study. Holmes et al.[4] at the University of California Davis School of Medicine enrolled 13,728 patients in a prospective, multicenter, observational study of emergency department patients undergoing cranial CT after blunt head injury. Of this group, 65% were men and 1193 (8.7%) had a significant acute TBI. Among these patients selected for cranial CT scanning, increased risk of TBI was noted for patients younger than 10 years and those older than 65 years (relative risk = 1.44 and 1.59, respectively). The early days of CT use following blunt head trauma had limited clinical guidelines. Marshall et al. at the University of California Medical Center, San Diego, described a classification scheme to be used both as a research and clinical tool in association with other predictors of neurologic status.[5] However, more recent researchers have found the Marshall criteria to be incomplete as CT predictors. Neurosurgeons at the Erasmus Medical Center in Rotterdam, the Netherlands, tested the Marshall classification system in 2269 patients. This system was investigated during the tirilazad trials (trials to test a cerebral rescue drug after TBI). The researchers concluded that it is preferable to use combinations of individual CT predictors rather than the Marshall CT classification alone for prognostic purposes in TBI. They recommend that such models include at least the following CT parameters: status of the basal cisterns; presence of shift; presence of traumatic subarachnoid or intraventricular hemorrhage; and presence of different types of mass lesions.[6] This study is noteworthy, as Marshall participated in the data analysis.

Decision rules for whether or not CT is required when a potential TBI patient presents to an emergency department have recently been tested. The same group in the Netherlands completing the test of the Marshall classification system recently reviewed and evaluated the Canadian CT Head Rule and the New Orleans Criteria for CT scanning. This study followed 3181 consecutive adult patients with minor head injury who presented with Glasgow Coma Scale (GCS) scores of 13–14 or with a GCS score of 15 and at least one risk factor. The data were collected between February 2002 and August 2004. For patients with mild head injury and a GCS score of 13–15, the Canadian CT Head Rule has a lower sensitivity than the New Orleans Criteria for neurocranial traumatic or clinically important CT findings, but it identifies all cases requiring neurosurgical intervention and has greater potential for reducing the use of CT scans in the emergency department.[7]

One question commonly asked is, "When is it appropriate to avoid CT scanning following head injury?" This is a polarizing question, and neurosurgeons have a clear admonition for this issue. Surgeons at the University of Pennsylvania School of Medicine concluded that although the incidence of intracranial lesions, especially those that require surgery, is low in mild TBI, the consequences of delayed diagnosis are forbidding. Adverse outcome of an intracranial hematoma is so costly that it more than balances the expense of CT scans.[8] Another question often posed is, Should the initial CT scan of minor head injury be repeated? A Massachusetts General Hospital study reviewed the records of 692 consecutive trauma patients with GCS scores of 13 to 15 and a head CT scan (cases between October 2004 and October 2005). Patients with a worse and unchanged routine repeat head CT scan (RRHCT) were compared, and independent predictors of a worse RRHCT were identified by stepwise logistic regression. Twenty-one percent of patients showed signs of injury evolution on RRHCT, and 4% required neurosurgical intervention. However, the 4% group had observable clinical deterioration preceding RRHCT. In no patient without clinical deterioration did RRHCT cause a change in management. The authors concluded that RRHCT is unnecessary in patients with mild head injury. Thus, after the first CT scan, if there is no clinical change in the patient, it is not necessary to repeat the CT scan. Clinical examination will identify accurately the few patients who will show significant evolution and require intervention.[9] These issues in neurosurgical management are discussed to provide the neuropsychiatric examiners with an overview while they are reviewing the acute care records of a person being examined well after the original injury.

The indications for CT of the head after trauma are debated in the medical literature. However, a summary of the published findings suggest clinical indications for CT of the head in patients who sustained head trauma. These include[10,11] (1) a GCS score of less than 15, (2) clinical signs of basilar skull fracture or depressed skull fracture, (3) all penetrating head injuries, (4) anisocoria or fixed and dilated pupils, (5) neurologic deficit including focal motor paralysis, (6) cranial nerve deficit, (7) abnormal Babinski reflex, (8) known bleeding disorder or patient on anticoagulation medication, (9) loss of consciousness for more than 5 min, and (10) anterograde amnesia.

Skull Fracture

The incidence of skull fracture increases in relation to the severity of brain injury. However, a skull fracture provides evidence of bone injury from trauma, but it does not necessarily mean that the brain or spinal cord has been injured. MRI does not usually reveal fractures, because the protons of cortical bone are nonmobile during image acquisition. Thus, cortical bone appears as a linear hypointensity or blackness that cannot be discerned from air or cerebral spinal fluid. CT with bone window settings is now the method of choice for determining the presence of skull fracture, rather than standard planar cranial x-rays. However, when the neuropsychiatric examiner reviews medical records and observes prior evidence of a skull fracture shortly after the time of trauma, it must be remembered that bony injury is significant, not only as a sign of potential brain injury, but also often as a pathway for the spread of infection. Moreover, skull fracture often has associated cranial nerve palsy. (Please see Chapter 4.) If the records indicate that blood is present behind the tympanic membranes without direct ear trauma, or there is evidence of otorrhea or rhinorrhea or presence of a subcutaneous hematoma around the mastoid process (Battle sign), or when bruising around the orbits without direct orbital trauma (raccoon sign) is present, evidence of a basilar skull fracture should be sought. Skull x-rays have generally been suboptimal in demonstrating these fractures, but now high-resolution cranial CT with thin sections is the best modality for demonstrating such fractures.[12]

Linear fractures or separation of sutures with no underlying brain injury are generally not clinically significant. A "growing fracture" is very rare and is usually seen in children. It may produce a leptomeningeal cyst as the meninges are trapped by the opposing edges of the fracture. Fractures through the base of the skull or paranasal sinuses may produce pneumocephalus, cerebrospinal fluid (CSF) leaks and may lead to meningitis. Fractures through the temporal bone may give origin to gas in the temperomandibular joint and venous sinus. In a depressed skull fracture by definition, fragments are displaced by more than 0.5 cm (12–13 mm). Most depressed skull fractures have underlying brain contusions, and contrecoup injures are present in 30% of patients. Most depressed skull fractures are considered to be open by neurosurgeons and require surgical debridement. However, most skull fractures have no underlying brain injury, and most severe brain injuries have no skull fractures. Skull radiographs may be ordered to document fractures which could be missed by CT scan if they are oriented parallel to the CT slice.[13] Table 5.2 outlines the classification of patterns displayed by skull fractures.

TABLE 5.2
Classification of Skull Fractures

Classification	Features
Linear fractures	A straight crack or break in the calvarium or skull bony structures and is produced by a blow to the skull. These are common in children.
Depressed fractures	Commonly result from low velocity impacts to a limited area of the calvarium. Such fractures commonly form in the frontal and parietal regions.
Bursting fractures	Fractures which bend outward distal to the impact site.
Diastatic fractures	Demonstrate separation of the cranial sutures. Diastatic fractures usually form between the petrous portion of the temporal bone, the greater wing of the sphenoid bone, and the petrosquamosal fissures.
Hinge fractures	Result when the head is run over and crushed by a heavy object such as a truck wheel. These fractures commonly cross the dorsum sellae to allow the base of the skull to move like a hinge.
Ring fractures	Circumscribe the foramen magnum like a ring and may result from impacts to the base of the spine, such as a fall impacting on the buttocks.
Remote fractures	Occur at a distance from the point of cranial impact. These are commonly found in the orbital roofs of the ethmoid plates following crushing injuries, falls, and gunshot wounds. "Raccoon eyes" herald the presence of these fractures.
Compound basal fractures	May produce cerebrospinal fluid fistulae when the fractures traverse the paranasal sinuses. Fractures of the petrous portion of the temporal bones may cause otorrhea. CNS infection can occur with these fractures.
Growing fractures	Result with an enlarging traumatically induced leptomeningeal cyst. These fractures nearly always occur in children less than 3 years old and are generally not associated with any significant injury to the brain. Erosion of the bone may occur because of pulsation of the brain.

Missile and Penetrating Injury

Missile and penetrating injuries are usually caused by gunshot, particularly in the United States. However, improvised explosive devices (IEDs) have increased in worldwide use with sectarian violence, and these are an emerging cause of penetrating injury to the brain. Depending on where the neuropsychiatric examiner lives and practices, the missile involved in head penetration may vary. From a neuropsychiatric standpoint, most people do not survive a substantial gunshot wound to the head, particularly if it is a military missile or a missile fired by a heavy high-velocity handgun such as a .44 magnum, a .357 magnum, or a .40 caliber. Four types of cranial gunshot injuries are classically described, based on the degree of penetration of the cranial vault.[14] Superficial injuries are defined as bullets trapped within the scalp or skull at impact without penetrating the cranial vault. Tangential injuries are produced by bullets that graze the head, again without penetration of the cranial vault. Even though the missile does not penetrate the calvarium, both superficial and tangential gunshot wounds can result in significant intracranial lesions, either through direct energy transfer (see Chapter 1) or through the production of secondary penetrating missiles, such as bone fragments. Penetrating injuries result from bullets that enter into and lodge within the cranial vault. Perforating injuries describe through-and-through lesions having both an entrance and an exit wound to the cranial vault.[15] With the evolution of modern neurosurgical care, some of these patients may survive and come to the attention of a neuropsychiatric examiner for clinical and forensic assessment.

The findings at CT imaging are extremely variable and depend on the size, shape, and number of projectiles. The projectile velocity is a significant variable in the size and shape of the intraparenchymal wound if the missile penetrates the calvarium (see Chapter 1). CT findings will delineate the entry and exit site, the presence of skull fractures, and whether the bullet remains embedded and

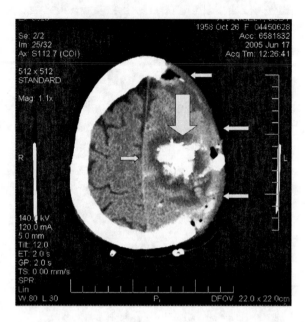

FIGURE 5.1 Small caliber gunshot wound to left vertex (southward-facing arrow). Observe effacement and loss of gyral pattern. Note rightward bowing of falx (eastward-facing arrow). The left calvarium has been surgically removed.

has impaled bone fragments into the parenchyma. Pneumocephalus will be apparent if present. Secondary epidural, subdural, and subarachnoid hemorrhage may be apparent on CT scan. Missile penetration can also produce intracerebral and intraventricular hemorrhage. If vascular structures are harmed, ischemia and infarction may result.[16] Figures 5.1 and 5.2 reveal a gunshot wound to the vertex and its downward path into the left midbrain.

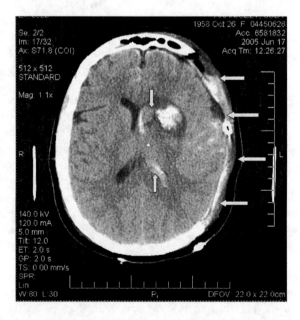

FIGURE 5.2 Compression of left ventricles due to mass effect from edema (ventricle arrows). The left calvarium is surgically absent (westward-facing arrows).

Contusions

The brain contusion is an injury to a brain surface involving superficial gray matter. It is usually a contact injury that results from the cerebral gyrus striking the inner surface of the skull. Pathologically, it appears to the eye as a bruise to a surface of the brain.[17] If a contusion is not initially hemorrhagic, it then tends to develop a hemorrhage during the first 72 h after the trauma. A CT scan obtained 24–48 h after injury usually shows contusions to be larger and more numerous than immediately following the injury. Of all traumatic brain injuries, contusions represent approximately 44% of injuries. The anatomical location of a contusion usually is in the tips of the frontal and temporal lobes, the undersurfaces of the frontal lobes, and the dorsolateral midbrain. In 30% of patients, multiple contusions will be found. In patients with severe head trauma, the incidence of contusions is 5%–10%. Intraventricular hemorrhage coexists with contusions in 1%–5% of patients and is due to tearing of the subependymal veins and the choroid plexus.[13]

The characteristic CT findings are poorly defined hypodensity and swelling early, and in fact the CT scan may be normal early even if a contusion has occurred. The appearance of the contusion is a patchy, ill-defined, low-density lesion with small hyperdense foci of petechial hemorrhage. Generally after 24 to 48 h evolution, multiple new hypodense lesions may appear. These lesions often contain edema and will increase in size and produce a mass effect with bowing of the falx or tentorium. Petechial hemorrhages may evolve to hematomas. Over time, the lesion becomes isodense. If encephalomalacia occurs, there will be parenchymal volume loss.[16] Figure 5.3 demonstrates a characteristic CT appearance of encephalomalacia from TBI (this is the case of E.L. in Chapter 11).

Contusions can be missed because of volume averaging by the computer during image acquisition. When a thin stripe of high-density cortical blood lies next to high-density bone, an artifact may obscure the blood in the hemorrhage. Blood on the surface of the brain adjacent to bone may produce a beam-hardening artifact. Contusions of the parietal vertex and inferior temporal lobe may be partially volumed with contiguous bone on the axial CT slice resulting in an overall bone density that obscures the presence of the contusion. Usually, coronal images are not obtained during CT studies in the emergency department. As a result, such contusions are frequently missed.[18,19]

As discussed in Chapter 1, with frontal impact trauma, the brain moves over the roughened edges of the inner table of the skull. This occurs particularly on the floor of the anterior cranial fossa. During impact, the brain slams forward into the sphenoid wings and the petrous ridges. This explains why contusions occur most commonly on the inferior frontal, anterior temporal, and lateral temporal regions. Paramedian bony irregularities may cause superficial frontal and parasagittal contusions.[2] Table 5.3 lists a classification of intra- and extra-axial TBI lesions.

FIGURE 5.3 Demonstration of residual encephalomalacia from case 11.1.

TABLE 5.3

Neuroimaging Classification of Traumatic Brain Lesions

Intra-axial lesions
- Contusion
- Intraparenchymal hematoma
- Diffuse axonal injury (DAI)
- Brainstem injury

Extra-axial lesions
- Subdural hematoma (SDH)
- Epidural hematoma (EDH)
- Subarachnoid hemorrhage (SAH)
- Intraventricular hemorrhage (IVH)

Brainstem Injury

Traumatic injury to the thalamus, basal ganglia, and brainstem is relatively uncommon. CT imaging is a very poor modality for detecting this type of injury, as only 10% of brainstem injuries are clearly delineated on CT scan. When they are detected, they are usually associated with diffuse axonal injury.[13,17] Severe shearing forces associated with diffuse axonal injury may disrupt small perforating vessels into the brainstem. A CT image may be normal or it may demonstrate multiple hemorrhagic foci near the lentiform nucleus and external capsule. After brainstem injury, it may be suspected as the basal cisterns are often obliterated due to diffuse cerebral edema. Magnetic resonance imaging is a better evaluation technique for suspected brainstem contusion and hemorrhage since it is more sensitive for nonhemorrhagic lesions and less susceptible to artifacts caused by the bone of the posterior fossa. Frequently, subarachnoid hemorrhage coexists with brainstem contusions. If a brainstem contusion occurs, poor prognosis is reliably predicted by age greater than 60 years, a low GCS score, abnormal pupil response, abnormal occulocephalic response, and abnormal motor response to painful stimuli.[2,20] Figure 5.4 reveals a midbrain hemorrhage detected by CT.

Extradural (Epidural) Hematoma

Only 1%–4% of patients with head trauma have epidural hematomas. Since the overall mortality in these patients is 5% or less, the neuropsychiatric examiner will encounter many survivors of epidural hematoma. More than 90% of epidural hematomas in adults are associated with skull fractures.[21] The epidural space is a potential space between the cranial periosteum and the inner table of the skull. The dura and periosteum are anatomically inseparable. This potential epidural space is tightly bound at the sutural margin. Blood supply to the dura lies on the inner table of the skull between the skull and the dura. Therefore, if a fracture of the inner table occurs, it often lacerates a meningeal artery. However, not all epidural hematomas are arterial in origin. An epidural hematoma of nonarterial origin should be suspected if the CT image shows a hematoma overlying a dural venous sinus or if it is in the posterior fossa and convexity. The sinus origin group has a high frequency of fractures that cross the sinuses.[22] In children, epidural hematomas can occur without fracture because of the increased plasticity of the skull.

The CT appearance of an epidural hematoma is quite characteristic. The periosteal dura has its strongest attachment at the suture lines. Therefore, in contrast to subdural hematomas, epidural hematomas do not cross sutures, and they have a characteristic convex lens-like shape. While they do not cross sutures, they may cross the falx. Unilateral epidural hematomas classically occur in the temporoparietal region. Of all epidural hematomas 95% are supratentorial. Epidural hematomas

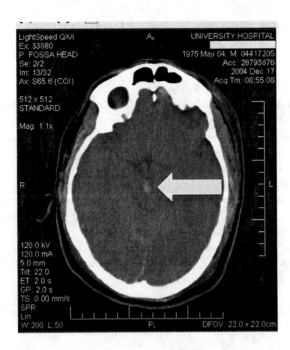

FIGURE 5.4 Midbrain hemorrhage is often difficult to detect on CT. The westward-facing arrow depicts a midbrain hemorrhage from TBI.

in the posterior fossa are much rarer than those in the anterior brain and have a higher morbidity and mortality.[2]

A "lucid interval" is seen in one-half of patients who develop an epidural hematoma, and it precedes clinical deterioration. It is not unusual for a person to be quite lucid at the emergency scene and then deteriorate markedly during transport by ambulance or helicopter. A hematoma at the vertex is always epidural, crosses a superior sagittal sinus, and displaces it inferiorly.[13] An acute epidural hematoma on CT imaging is hyperdense in appearance in two-thirds of cases; in one-third of cases, it is mixed with hyperdense and hypodense features. If the hematoma is actively bleeding at the time of the CT scan, a "swirl sign" may be seen. If air is detected within an epidural hematoma (which occurs in 20% of cases), this suggests that a sinus or mastoid air cell has been fractured.[16,21]

Subdural Hematoma

An acute subdural hematoma (SDH) with a thickness greater than 10 mm or a midline shift greater than 5 mm on CT scan should be surgically evacuated regardless of the patient's GCS score. All patients with acute SDH in coma (GCS score less than 9) should undergo intracranial pressure (ICP) monitoring.[23] Thus, the neuropsychiatric examiner will likely see a number of patients who have had brain surgery as a result of an acute subdural hematoma. Subdural hematomas are found in 10%–20% of severe head trauma victims. These carry a high mortality rate of 60%–90%. About 95% of subdural hematomas occur in the frontoparietal regions because of tearing of bridging veins. Approximately 10%–15% of subdural hematomas are bilateral. An interhemispheric location present in children suggests inflicted trauma and blunt trauma to the head. The CT finding in the acute phase of subdural hematoma (less than 3 days) includes hyperdense lesions. In the subacute phase (3–21 days duration) the blood is isodense, and in the chronic phase (greater than 3 weeks of age) the blood products are hypodense. Thus, a CT scan can be used to stage the approximate age of the hematoma. If CT contrast is used, both the isodense and hypodense subdural hematomas may reveal inner membrane enhancement. Very small subdural hematomas require the use of intermediate CT window settings. These may not be detected easily, and MRI may be required for detection. There is a coexistence of contusions in patients with subdural hematomas, and about 50% of patients with subdural hematoma will demonstrate a coincidental contusion. Subdural hygromas may also occur, and these are CT lesions of cerebrospinal fluid in the subdural space caused by a tear in the arachnoid membrane allowing leakage of CSF. Most of these will be found in older persons who sustain head trauma.[13] Figure 5.5 is a hygroma that appears after a right temporal tip injury.

The characteristic finding of subdural hematomas, unlike the lens-shaped feature of the epidural hematoma, is a crescent-shaped lesion on CT scan. The collection of blood spreads diffusely over the gyri of the affected hemisphere. This generally produces a mass effect, which displaces the gray–white matter junction. Thus, the sulcal pattern remains, but it will show itself to be some distance from the inner table of the calvarium.[16] With subdural hematomas of considerable size, there is often a midline shift of the falx.[17] Moreover, a subdural hematoma does not cross the midline (unlike the epidural hematoma) because it is fixed by the sites of dural attachment at the falx and the tentorium.[24] A word of caution: an acute subdural hematoma can appear isodense against gray matter if the patient has bled significantly and the hemoglobin concentration is below 10–11 g/dl. Subdural hematomas are often bilateral, and if they are isodense, this may cause diagnostic difficulty. They can usually be detected if the examiner pays attention to identifying the displacement of gray matter, and usually the ventricles are compressed and may present themselves as a

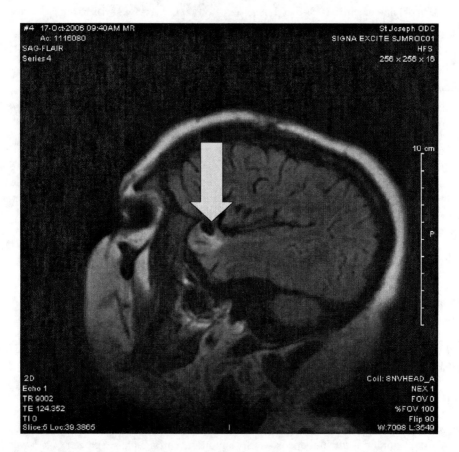

FIGURE 5.5 Hygromas are CSF lesions in the subdural space. This one is at the polar area of the right temporal lobe as seen on a sagittal FLAIR MRI.

slit-like appearance. Sometimes contrast enhancement is necessary to assist with the diagnosis of suspected bilateral isodense subdural hematomas.[25]

Subarachnoid Hemorrhage

Subarachnoid hemorrhage (SAH) occurs in approximately 11% of traumatic brain injuries.[26] This type of hemorrhage usually occurs as a result of injury to small bridging cortical vessels lying on or within the pia or arachnoid meningeal structures crossing the subarachnoid space. There is a biphasic appearance to these bleeds, and they occur in the very young and the very old at a higher frequency than others. They may also occur as a result of blood from an intracerebral hematoma decompressing directly into the subarachnoid space or dissecting into the ventricular system. Not uncommonly, subarachnoid hemorrhage is focal and found next to a contusion. Figure 5.6 shows SAH along the falx with a right frontal intraparenchymal hemorrhage, right lenticular hemorrhage and IVH in both occipital horns. A pressure catheter tip is present in the right anterior horn.

On CT imaging, the subarachnoid blood will appear as a high density in the subarachnoid spaces or cisterns. This may be the only manifestation of subtle subarachnoid hemorrhage. It is more likely to be found in the sulci of convexities than in the basal cisterns.[16] It occurs most frequently in moderate and severe head injuries, and it is less likely in a mild head injury. Also, there is usually less blood in SAH due to head injury than that caused by rupture of an aneurysm. The blood from SAH almost never induces vasospasm, but it may produce posttraumatic communicating hydrocephalus at a later time and a picture consistent with normal pressure hydrocephalus (see Chapter 1). Other CT findings include a "pseudodelta" sign, as hyperdense blood is found layering along the posterior superior sagittal sinus. Blood in the interpeduncular cistern needs to be differentiated from brainstem hematoma or basilar artery apex aneurysm. The sensitivity of CT imaging to detection of SAH is more than 90% in the first 20 h. However, this degrades to less than 50% by the third day post-injury.[13] Thus, CT is a procedure of choice for identifying radiographic findings of early subarachnoid hemorrhage. When the patient is examined long after the initial trauma, blood in the

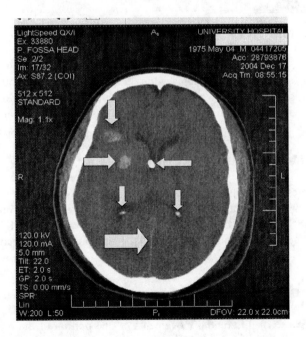

FIGURE 5.6 CT revealing (1) a right frontal contusion, (2) a right lenticular contusion, (3) dependent IVH in both ventricular posterior horns, and (4) SAH layering over the posterior falx. Note the catheter tip in the right anterior ventricular horn.

subarachnoid space may have decreased in density and now appears as an isodense finding so that the subarachnoid spaces appear obliterated. Subarachnoid hemorrhage is difficult to appreciate when the CT study is done more than several days after trauma, and MRI will be more sensitive for detecting free blood in the subarachnoid spaces at that time, as noted below.

Intraparenchymal Hemorrhage

Since intraparenchymal hematomas are rarely found unrelated to contusions, when they occur, they are usually the result of penetrating trauma such as gunshot or stab wounds into the brain. If missile trauma leaves metallic objects behind (such as bullet fragments), this may preclude accurate MRI as a diagnostic modality. Noncontrast CT will demonstrate a homogenous high attenuation consolidation with well-defined margins. Surrounding edema increases and peaks at one week post-injury.[2]

Subacute interparenchymal hematomas between 3 and 7 days age may give the appearance on CT of layering fluid-blood levels within the blood clot or clot retraction. Interparenchymal hematomas between 7 and 14 days age will decrease in attenuation from the periphery inward, of approximately 1 to 2 Hounsfield units each day. These units are the standard attenuation units of CT imaging named for the developer of CT, Godfrey Hounsfield, who later received the Nobel prize.[27] Intercerebral hematomas more than two weeks in age are composed primarily of intracellular ferritin and lysosomal hemosiderin. On CT imaging, the hematoma will continue to decrease in attenuation over time. Within 3–10 weeks, chronic intercerebral hematomas will become isodense contrasted with normal brain parenchyma, and they will be very difficult to detect at this time. Continued proteolysis, phagocytosis, and adjacent cellular atrophy will eventually replace the hematoma with an area of encephalomalacia.[2] This area can be detected on late CT many weeks after injury, and this is the most likely finding during neuropsychiatric examination in a patient who has sustained a traumatic intraparenchymal hematoma. Figure 5.6 demonstrates a right frontal intraparenchymal hemorrhage and a right lenticular hemorrhage.

Intraventricular Hemorrhage

Intraventricular hemorrhage occurs in approximately 3% of all persons who sustain blunt head trauma in the United States.[28] The incidence of intraventricular hemorrhage increases dramatically in those patients whose GCS score is in the severe range (score of less than 8).[29] In LeRoux's paper[28] intracranial pressure monitors were placed in 39 patients with intraventricular hemorrhage. Intracranial pressure rose in 46% of these patients, and acute hydrocephalus developed in 7% of those. Ventricular drainage was required in 10% of the patients. Mortality in patients with intraventricular hemorrhage has been reported to range from 21% to 77%. However, experts believe the outcome is more likely related to the severity of the brain injury than directly to the intraventricular hemorrhage.[2] Figure 5.6 reveals bilateral occipital horn IVH.

On CT, it is not unusual to see layering of hemorrhage within the ventricular system owing to the antithrombotic properties of fibrinolytic activators within the CSF. Noncontrast CT will demonstrate a fluid–fluid layer with high attenuation blood lying below lower attenuation blood within the ventricle. The lowest density CSF will be on top. There is evidence that FLAIR sequences on MR reveal acute intraventricular hemorrhage during the first 48 h more precisely than noncontrast CT.[30]

Diffuse Axonal Injury

Diffuse axonal injury (DAI) was discussed in Chapter 1. Recall that the mechanism is thought to be a shear–strain injury. Shear–strain deformation develops upon exposure of axons to rotational acceleration forces because of differential movements of one portion of the brain with respect to another. These portions vary in density.[31] The commonest locations for lesions of DAI are in the frontotemporal cerebral hemispheres at the gray–white matter junctions. Fifty percent of DAI will be seen in these areas. DAI is also commonly found in the basal ganglia, at the splenium of the

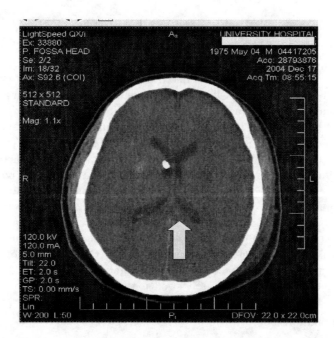

FIGURE 5.7 A separate cut from Figure 5.6 showing evidence of left shear injury near the splenium of the corpus callosum.

corpus callosum, and in the dorsal midbrain. In patients sustaining DAI, overall mortality can be as high as 50%. The initial CT scan of a person sustaining DAI may be normal in 50%–85% of patients. Lesions generally become more prominent during the first 24 h and may be detected on subsequent CT scans. DAI is the most common cause of posttraumatic vegetative states.[13] See Figure 5.7 for shear hemorrhage near the left splenium of the corpus callosum.

Thirty percent of patients with DAI will have positive findings on MRI. On the CT, the lesions appear as small hypodense foci corresponding to edema at the site of shearing injury. They may correlate with foci of petechial hemorrhages in 20%–50% of cases. Approximately 10%–20% of DAI lesions will evolve to a focal mass lesion, which can be seen as an admixture of hemorrhage and edema on CT. Delayed CT scans taken in the neurointensive care unit often reveal "new" lesions when CT scans are compared serially.[16] The presence of a small amount of intraventricular blood in the occipital horn of one or both ventricles (see IVH in occipital horns bilaterally on Figure 5.6) should arouse suspicion that there has been a tear of the corpus callosum with transependymal extension of the bleeding.[29] After edema resolves and the hemorrhage is physiologically removed, the CT scan may appear normal even though the patient has significant cognitive and behavioral abnormalities. In other cases, the follow-up CT scan may show only generalized cerebral atrophy.[32] On CT, the foci of DAI are typically less than 1 cm in size and spare the adjacent cortical surface of the brain. The lesions may be located entirely within the white matter rather than the gray matter.[33]

If the neuropsychiatric examiner reviews carefully the original trauma records, prognostic statements can be made based on acute findings as a result of DAI. The outcome of patients with DAI is directly proportional to severity variables, the most sensitive being the duration of posttraumatic amnesia (PTA). Patients with PTA of less than 12 weeks had a much more favorable recovery after rehabilitation than patients with PTA lasting for more than 12 weeks. Age has a complex effect on recovery. Age does not contribute to the duration of coma but rather to the duration of PTA. The age effect is apparent in patients older than 40 years and very significant in patients older than 60 years.[34] On the other hand, CT has proven of low prognostic value in patients with DAI when used in the absence of severity variables.[33]

Cerebral Edema

Recall from Chapter 1 that cerebral edema is a type of secondary brain injury. As a result of edema, severe vascular compromise can result in ischemic brain injury. The CT findings of traumatic cerebral edema are compressed ventricles and effaced sulci. The lateral ventricles may assume a slit-like appearance on cranial CT. As a result of alterations of blood flow, the brain parenchyma may present as a low attenuation pattern, and white matter will show less attenuation than gray matter. This is because cortical white matter is less resistant to fluid accumulation than gray matter. Also, on CT images, the normal gray matter or white matter interface may be obliterated. A vasogenic edema pattern will be more prominent in the white matter, whereas a cytotoxic pattern will be more prominent in the gray matter. Cerebral edema is thought to be a dynamic process involving glutamate-mediated excitotoxicity resulting in cellular damage. In addition to the compressed ventricles on CT scan, sulci are effaced as they press against the calvarium because of focal or diffuse increase in brain water. Figure 5.2 reveals closure of the left ventricles and extrusion of the left cerebrum due to edema from a GSW. Obviously, substantial edema can result in herniation of the brain, and vascular compression can lead to infarction.[16] On CT using soft tissue window settings, the cerebellum, the cerebral vasculature, and the dural surfaces (falx and tentorium) appear hyperdense against the background of diffusely swollen edematous hypodense brain tissue.[17]

Brain Shift and Herniation

Herniation of the brain is defined as a movement of brain tissue from one compartment (normally separated by calvarial and dural boundaries) to another compartment.[16] Four main types of brain displacements can occur following trauma: (1) subfalcine, (2) descending and ascending transtentorial, (3) descending and ascending transalar, and (4) cerebellar tonsillar herniation.[11] Subfalcine herniation occurs when the cingulate gyrus is pushed laterally under the falx. This is usually secondary to a unilateral frontal lobe mass effect and can be seen with a large frontal lobe intracerebral hematoma. Transtentorial herniation can be unilateral or bilateral. In unilateral herniation, a medial temporal lobe is pushed inferiorly through the incisura. The uncus and para-hippocampal gyrus will be displaced medially. The brainstem can become compressed and displaced by the herniating temporal lobe pressing against it. It will shove the brainstem against the opposite tentorial margin (the Kernohan notch). Cranial nerve III will become compressed and affect pupillary size ipsilaterally. With bilateral or central herniation, the diencephalon and midbrain are displaced inferiorly. Both temporal lobes herniate into the tentorial hiatus, and on CT scan, the quadrigeminal cistern will be deformed. With tonsillar herniation, the cerebellar tonsil herniates into the spinal canal. This may obstruct the fourth ventricle and produce obstructive hydrocephalus. With transalar herniation, brain contents herniate across the sphenoid wing. This is very uncommon.

A midline shift of 5 mm or more is considered significant from a surgical standpoint. A shift of this magnitude is associated with a 50% mortality rate,[35] and thus the neuropsychiatric examiner will likely never see these persons. Either CT or MRI is effective at establishing the diagnosis of cerebral herniation, which guides the neurosurgeon or emergency department physician regarding therapeutic options and prognosis.[36] Survivors of herniation may have substantial cognitive and behavioral deficits, which will require neuropsychiatric evaluation. Figure 5.2 demonstrates massive edema from a left hemisphere GSW. Note that the left cranium is removed for decompression. Also note that the left ventricles are compressed due to swelling.

Posttraumatic Neurodegeneration

The neuropsychiatric examiner will be involved in the detection of late posttraumatic neurodegeneration. These findings occur after the patient has left the acute care setting and a brain injury rehabilitation unit. Thus, it is incumbent upon the neuropsychiatric examiner to detect potential neurodegenerative changes, as these will account for measured neuropsychological and psychological deficits at the time of examination. Certain neuropathological changes take place following a traumatic hemorrhagic contusion. The evolution of these changes can be correlated with imaging studies.[37] Four distinct phases occur: (1) acute damage, (2) liquefaction of the contusion with the development of edema, (3) repair during which macrophages remove blood elements and damaged tissue causing proliferation of blood vessels, and (4) sloughing of necrotic tissue and formation of cystic cavities.[27] During the liquefaction phase, the softening and swelling that result from edema formation occur between the third and seventh days after injury. At this time, the components of hemorrhage are converted from deoxyhemoglobin to methemoglobin. Subsequently, the CT scan will reveal a volume averaging that may appear as an area of decreased density at the site of contusion.[37] This CT finding is dependent upon the relative proportions of globin and water within the brain tissue. This is a critical time during the acute care of the brain-injured patient, as swelling and edema may increase the mass effect and produce cerebral herniation.

During the third phase, new blood vessels proliferate around the area of healing. However, a blood–brain barrier disturbance is present. At this point with CT imaging, if a contrast agent is given, enhancement analogous to that seen with a cerebral infarction occurs at the margin of the contusion.[37] During the fourth stage, evolution occurs slowly over a 6–12 month period. Contused brain tissue may be sloughed into the cerebrospinal fluid pathways such that an irregular surface of the contused portions of the hemisphere results. CT scan at this time will show an area of decreased density within the brain parenchyma, often with enlargement of the overlying cerebrospinal fluid spaces. The size of the cortical gyri may diminish, and the adjacent underlying ventricle may increase in size.[37] Figure 5.3 reveals multiple areas of posttraumatic encephalomalacia. Table 5.4 summarizes CT findings in TBI.

MAGNETIC RESONANCE IMAGING

Use in the Acute Care Setting

Magnetic resonance imaging (MRI), at the time of the writing of this book, remains an alternative initial modality for evaluating TBI in the acute care setting. It has a greater sensitivity for detecting abnormalities in predicting prognosis than does CT.[38] However, MRI is inferior to CT in evaluation of injuries to the skull vault or for detecting bone fractures. Contraindications to MRI include cardiac pacemakers, noncompatible vascular clips, metallic implants, and ocular ferromagnetic foreign bodies.[2]

Magnetic resonance imaging compares the relative intensity differences between anatomic subunits of tissue that are exposed to both a constant magnetic field and intermittently exposed to a changing set of secondary gradients (to give spatial resolution) and also to an external radio frequency (RF) pulse to energize the nuclear spin of ions[39] (see Table 5.5). Signal intensity is a measure of how all protons within any small block of tissue (voxel) respond to the RF signal. This signal is then digitally compared to its neighbors and represented on film or computer imaging as a shade on a gray scale. If tissue within a voxel behaves discordantly, then the overall signal of that voxel is diminished or lost and will be described as a "susceptibility artifact." These artifacts can be used for clinical detection; for instance, hemosiderin is detected in this manner. The process of deriving signal from the magnetic response of most stationary brain tissue during MR is referred to as "relaxivity." The measurable response time is called the "relaxation rate." Types of tissues can be detected by their relative relaxation rates. Some have faster rates while others have slower rates. These differences are portrayed on MR images as differences in shades-of-gray. Before the signal is read-out (detected), it is refocused either by using a second RF pulse (i.e., the spin-echo) or by using magnet gradients (i.e., gradient-echo or GRE). The spin-echo technique has better contrast resolution, whereas the gradient-echo technique is substantially faster. Numerous MRI sequences are used to change the detection ability of the instrument.[1] These are described in Table 5.5. If the reader needs specific magnetic resonance protocols, such as those for tumor, trauma or stroke, it is best to consult a technical manual such as Castillo.[13]

TABLE 5.4

Computed Tomography (CT) and Traumatic Brain Injury (TBI)

Lesion	Image Findings[2,12,13,16,27]
Skull fracture	Calvarial disruption on bone window setting.
Contusions	Usually found adjacent to anterior and middle cranial fossae, sphenoid wings and petrous ridges—most frequent in frontal and temporal poles and undersurfaces of frontal lobes. Hemorrhagic lesions are high density; nonhemorrhagic lesions are low density.
Epidural hematoma	Usually presents as a high-density biconvex lens. Does not cross suture margins. Focal iso- or hypodensity consistent with active bleeding or coagulopathy.
Subdural hematoma	Acute: Isodense against gray matter if hemoglobin <10–11 gm/dl. If not isodense, presents as a crescent-shaped hyperdense collection which conforms to the gyral–sulcal pattern. Does not cross the falx.
	Chronic: Fluid usually appears hypodense due to blood product breakdown but density is higher than CSF due to protein content. Upon complete breakdown of blood products, fluid may be isodense to brain.
Subarachnoid hemorrhage	Linear hyperdense fluid collections are within sulci and fluid cisterns.
Intraparenchymal hemorrhage	Mostly found in frontal and temporal brain areas. Usually is hyperdense in appearance. Serum from a clot may cause a rim of hypodensity. Edema may produce a mass effect. In older lesions, new vessel formation may enhance as a rim with contrast agents. Clot resorption may leave a cavity.
Intraventricular hemorrhage	Focal and diffuse hyperdensity is within the ventricles. Blood tends to settle in the occipital horns. Correlates with diffuse axonal injury (DAI).
Diffuse axonal injury	Most injuries are in lobar white matter at the corticomedullary junction of frontal and temporal lobes. Also appears in the corpus callosum and dorsolateral brainstem. Usually appears as small hyperdense bleeds in these areas.
Brain swelling	Obliteration of cerebral sulci and basal cisterns occurs. Effacement of gray–white matter interface is present. Edematous brain is usually hypodense.
Chronic neurodegeneration	Irregular brain surface presents with hypodensity within parenchyma. Overlying cerebrospinal fluid spaces may enlarge. Cortical gyri size may diminish with compensatory increased ventricular size (*ex vacuo* dilatation).

Routine clinical brain MRI sequences are being used much more frequently in the acute care setting following TBI since the first edition of this book. Particularly in those centers having 3 T magnets, the speed of image acquisition has increased to the point where safety is less a consideration. Recent Johns Hopkins University studies have noted that when parameters are adjusted for changes in relaxation rates, routine clinical scans at 3 T can provide similar image appearances as 1.5 T (the standard for most MRIs today), but with superior image quality and increased speed.[40]

Gentry[41] believes that all moderate to severe head injury patients should be evaluated with MRI at some point during the first two weeks after injury. The extent of TBI will not be determined fully if only CT is used to evaluate this group of patients. MRI is clearly more valuable than CT for assessing the magnitude of injury. It also provides more accurate information regarding the expected degree of final neurologic recovery.[41]

Skull Fracture

MRI is not useful for detecting skull fractures. In general, CT is superior even to planar skull x-ray for assessing depressed skull fractures. High-resolution CT with thin slices will easily evaluate facial fractures, orbital fractures, and basilar skull fractures.

TABLE 5.5
Magnetic Resonance Imaging Sequences

Sequence	Basis[2,13,16,121,127,128]
T1-weighted (T1)	T1 and T2 are time constants that provide the basis for MRI tissue contrast. These are differing tissue relaxation rates during radio frequency (RF) delivery. (The signal intensity increases over time.) T1-weighting is best for imaging normal anatomy.
T2-weighted (T2)	Similar in basis to T1. The signal intensity decreases over time. The greater the fluid content of tissue, the greater the intensity of T2 images. T2-weighting is useful for detecting CSF, widening of sulci, and fluid-filled spaces.
Proton density (PD)	The density of protons has a direct effect upon signal intensity. Only protons in hydrogen nuclei contribute to MR signals. PD is falling out of favor due to the addition of GRE and FLAIR sequencing.
Fluid-attenuated inversion recovery (FLAIR)	This is a computer-aided reconstruction of T2-weighted sequences. High signals from ventricles and sulci are suppressed. This aids detection of increased signal from abnormal fluid in parenchyma. Lesions next to CSF can now be discriminated. FLAIR is especially good for detecting edema and demyelination.
Diffusion-weighted imaging (DWI)	This modality detects small changes in diffusion of differing groups of H_2O molecules. It is superior to all MRI sequences for detecting acute ischemia and transient ischemic attacks (TIAs). It can detect abnormalities even if focal neurologic signs have normalized.
Gradient-echo (GRE)	MRI is weak at detecting acute hemorrhage or bleeding less than 48 h old. GRE displays acute and chronic hemorrhage as very low signal which appears black. GRE can detect SDH, EDH, SAH, and intraparenchymal hemorrhage. It easily detects punctuate hemorrhages of TBI.
Diffusion tensor imaging (DTI)	DTI images the direction of water diffusion. Diffusion vectors become the diffusion tensor. In white matter, H_2O diffusion is usually parallel to the axon. DTI is experimental at this time. It is superior to all MRI sequences for evaluating white matter tracts.
MR contrast	Contrast is paramagnetic and is usually based on gadolinium. It is useful for detecting breaches in the blood–brain barrier.

Note: Proton density and the variance of T1 and T2 relaxation effects are properties of brain tissue. Their measurements are the bases for differential contrast of tissue imaging with MRI.

Missile and Penetrating Injury

The use of MRI for cranial gunshot injuries has been relatively rare; probably because cranial gunshot wounds render the patient severely injured and in need of instrumentation, CT has been almost entirely the imaging modality of choice for GSW patients. Also, bullet fragments produce susceptibility artifact and interfere with accurate detection of tissue integrity. However, most bullets contain nonferromagnetic material and generate only minor image-degrading artifacts. MRI shows good spatial resolution for bullet localization and proximity to vital structures, often better than CT scan, which may be limited by streak artifacts.[15] The recent use of fluid-attenuated inversion-recovery (FLAIR) techniques allows MRI detection of acute extra-axial hemorrhage, including subarachnoid hemorrhage with a greater degree of sensitivity than CT.[42] Diffusion-weighted imaging (DWI) has facilitated earlier imaging diagnosis of early acute infarction; however, the primary limitations of MRI in the acute setting of trauma continue to be logistical and related to scan acquisition times, scanner availability, and difficulty in monitoring critically ill patients. With gunshot injuries, the consistent additional risk of potentially hazardous ferromagnetic metal bullet fragments in skull fractures, which MRI plays little role in assessing, leads to the obvious choice of CT as the primary imaging modality of cranial gunshot injuries in the acute setting where the added information provided by MRI is very unlikely to affect surgical management.[15] Thus, the neuropsychiatric examiner will likely obtain early CT films if the person survives a gunshot wound and comes to neuropsychiatric assessment (see Figures 5.1 and 5.2). However, it is recommended that the late evaluation of survivors of gunshot wounds includes MRI. It is useful at this later point in the evaluation in order to detect encephalomalacia and blast overpressure injury distant from the missile tract (see Chapter 1).

Contusions

Recall that contusions are found primarily in superficial gray matter. Contusions, when present, tend to be multiple and bilateral.[43] Temporal lobe lesions are most likely to occur just above the petrous bone or slightly behind the greater sphenoid wing. Frontal lobe contusions tend to lie just above the cribriform plate, the orbits, the planum sphenoidale, or the lesser sphenoid wing. The parietal and occipital lobes are the least likely anatomical areas to sustain cortical contusions. However, approximately 10% of frontal brain contusions may also show lesions in the cerebellum. These are typically found in the superior vermis, tonsils, and inferior hemispheres.[44] Gentry's series of trauma patients revealed that cortical contusions are much less likely to be associated with severe initial impairment of consciousness than diffuse axonal injury. If a severe impairment of consciousness is present with a contusion, typically there will be found very large multiple, bilateral lesions or the contusions are associated with diffuse axonal injury.[45]

The MR finding of contusion in the acute phase is an admixture of edema and hemorrhage on T1-weighted images. At the time of neuropsychiatric examination in the chronic phase, the T1-weighted images may demonstrate focal or diffuse atrophy. On FLAIR images, the acute phase demonstrates hyperintense cortical edema, which is easily detected by FLAIR, and it may also show hyperintense subarachnoid hemorrhage associated with the contusion. In the chronic phase, FLAIR may demonstrate hemosiderin or ferritin deposits in the parenchyma with hyperintense Wallerian-type axonal degeneration. Cystic encephalomalacia may be present. The neuropsychiatric examiner may notice on late gradient-echo (GRE) sequences that ferritin and hemosiderin deposits "bloom" within the scarred residual parenchyma. Clot resorbtion within the contusion begins from the periphery inward, and depending on the size of the hematoma, may vary from one to six weeks in duration. It is during neuropsychiatric examination that the physician may detect necrotic tissue on MRI that has been sloughed, and cystic cavities are formed over the next 6–12 months. Focal atrophy may be present and is characterized by a decrease in the size of the cortical gyri, with compensatory enlargement of cerebrospinal fluid spaces and dilatation of the adjacent ventricle. Figure 5.8 reveals encephalomalacia in the right temporal tip with atrophy of the right hippocampus on an axial FLAIR image. Cystic cavities will demonstrate increased signal because of gliosis and hemosiderin scarring.[2]

Brainstem Injury

MRI provides better evaluation for brainstem contusion and hemorrhage than CT, since it is more sensitive for nonhemorrhagic lesions and less susceptible to the artifact from the bony posterior fossa. Also, brainstem hemorrhage frequently coincides with subarachnoid hemorrhage.[2] FLAIR sequences may demonstrate traumatic brainstem injury impossible to detect by CT imaging.[46] The most common area of injury is within the dorsolateral aspect of the upper midbrain and usually occurs because the brainstem strikes the edge of the tentorium (Kernohan's notch). Secondary brainstem injury can occur due to prolonged hypoxia or ischemic injury and may be associated with Duret's hemorrhages. These hemorrhages are caused by prolonged transtentorial herniation and are usually located in the midline within the midbrain and the pontine tegmentum.[17] The hypothalamus and pituitary may be coincidentally injured at the time of brainstem injury.[47] Pituitary injuries have been discussed previously in this text. Injury to this structure often leads to the syndrome of inappropriate antidiuretic hormone causing a diabetes insipidus disorder. It may not be revealed on MRI.

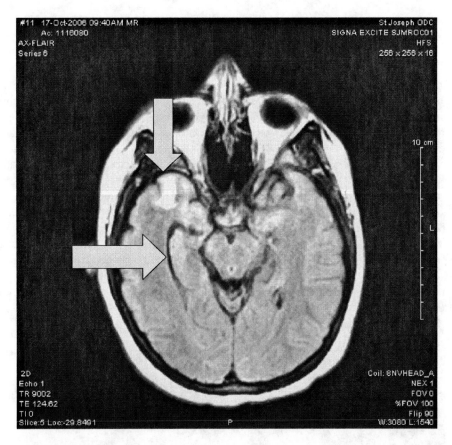

FIGURE 5.8 Axial FLAIR MRI revealing encephalomalacia at the right temporal tip and right hippocampal atrophy.

Extradural (Epidural) Hematoma

This biconvex extra-axial mass is seen on MRI, and the anatomical appearance is similar to that seen on CT. On T1-weighted imaging, the acute EDH is isointense, and as it becomes subacute or early in the chronic phase, it may appear hyperintense. On T2-weighted imaging, the acute phase is variable from hyper- to hypointensity.[16] In the subacute phase, it becomes hypointense, and in the chronic phase, it becomes hyperintense. Thus, a chronic epidural hematoma detected at neuropsychiatric examination will exhibit signal intensity similar to CSF on both T1- and T2-weighted images. The CSF in the ventricular spaces will appear about the same density as the epidural hematoma.[2] If the MRI is of particularly good quality, the dura often can be seen to be displaced away from the inner table of the skull by the enlarging mass of blood. It may be visualized as a thin line of low-signal intensity between the brain and the biconvex-shaped hematoma. If the dura can be visualized on MRI, this unequivocally proves the diagnosis of epidural hematoma. As discussed previously, venous bleeding can produce an epidural hematoma, even though most causes are arterial. If differentiation is required, magnetic resonance venography may be of assistance.[16]

Subdural Hematoma

The outcome from subdural hematoma induced by TBI is poor as noted above. This is primarily because of secondary forms of injury and the associated brain injury lying under the hematoma.[41] Diffusion-weighted imaging (DWI) is very helpful in evaluating SDH. It is capable of demonstrating areas of secondary ischemic injury and vascular compromise secondary to the hematoma. The signal of SDH is quite variable on MRI, and it generally evolves in a pattern similar to the changes found in interparenchymal hemorrhage.[16] The acute subdural hematoma will be of little interest to the neuropsychiatric examiner, and that is best left to neurosurgeons and trauma physicians to evaluate. However, chronic subdural hematomas can remain and may be detected by the neuropsychiatric examiner. MRI has revolutionized the ability to identify chronic subdural hematomas, because with coronal imaging, the relationship between the brain and the inner table of the skull can be exquisitely demonstrated.[27] On T1-weighted images, the hematoma is isointense to CSF if it is stable or chronic. On T2-weighted imaging, the signal is usually hypointense in the majority of chronic SDH. FLAIR sequencing is the most sensitive sequence for detection of SDH. GRE sequencing reveals a hypointense signal from subacute-chronic blood products within the hematoma. DWI produces a variable signal.[16] Gadolinium contrast can be used to bring out subdural membranes in an area of increased contrast enhancement on T1-weighted images. This helps differentiate subdural hygromas, which do not demonstrate membrane formation with contrast, and they will not enhance with gadolinium. They behave in the manner of a cerebrospinal fluid-filled subdural space on T1-weighted images, proton density-weighted images, and T2-weighted images.[27] Figure 5.9 demonstrates a concave pressure defect of the right hemi-cerebrum following extraction of an SDH. Note the shunt catheter into the right posterior ventricle. Also observe multiple areas of posttraumatic encephalomalacia.

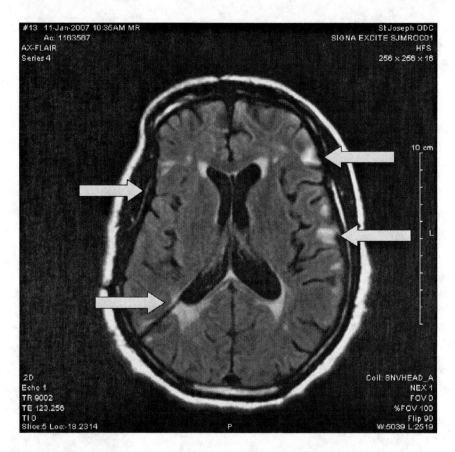

FIGURE 5.9 Axial FLAIR MRI revealing postsurgical evacuation of SDH with residual pressure deformation of right frontotemporal lobes (superior eastward-facing arrow), right hemisphere catheter tract (inferior eastward-facing arrow), and left frontal and left temporal encephalomalacia (westward-facing arrows).

Subarachnoid Hemorrhage

The low hematocrit within acute subarachnoid blood, and the low content of deoxyhemoglobin, gives a signal similar to brain parenchyma on T1- and T2-weighted spin-echo images.[48] Therefore, MRI may underestimate or fail to detect the subarachnoid hemorrhage. As a result, FLAIR may detect small areas of acute or subacute subarachnoid hemorrhage that are not detected by conventional MRI. These images can be seen as hyperintense signals within the Sylvian fissures or cerebral sulci.[49]

The reader should recall that hydrocephalus is the most common complication after subarachnoid hemorrhage. Obstruction may occur within the first week because of ependymitis or intraventricular blood obstructing the aqueduct of Sylvius or outlet of the fourth ventricle.[2] Thus, the neuropsychiatric examiner may detect a pattern of normal pressure hydrocephalus with enlarged lateral ventricles and no gyral effacement when MRI is obtained at the time of the neuropsychiatric examination.

Intraparenchymal Hemorrhage

After the clot is no longer visible on CT, it may remain highly visible on MRI. Intraparenchymal hemorrhage may be visible indefinitely on MRI owing to persistent hemosiderin deposits within machrophages around the lesion. If there is a reason to suspect prior hemorrhage, gradient-echo (GRE) sequences should be used. The neuropsychiatric examiner should ask the radiologist to use GRE sequences if the records indicate a prior intraparenchymal hemorrhage at some time distant from the current neuropsychiatric examination. About 90% of intraparenchymal hemorrhage will leave hemosiderin deposits well after the time of the original injury.[50]

One of the powerful uses of MRI is to detect the evolution of blood and blood products inside the brain following trauma. Blood goes through a sequence of changes during detection by MRI if imaging is performed on a serial basis. Blood in arteries or veins is in the oxyhemoglobin state. When it becomes a clot, it is changed to deoxyhemoglobin and later to methemoglobin.[51] On MRI, the deoxyhemoglobin is hypointense to isointense on T1-weighted images. On T2-weighted images, it is markedly hypointense (a susceptibility effect). Susceptibility refers to the inherent magnetic fields within the different tissues that constitute the brain. Intact red blood cells containing deoxyhemo-globin have a susceptibility different from that of the surrounding extracellular fluid. If a proton is exposed to the varying local magnetic fields, one due to intracellular deoxyhemoglobin and one due to surrounding extracellular fluid, it will have its spin thrown out of phase so that it does not give back a signal. This appears as an area of blackness on MRI. About three days after the formation of the hematoma, deoxyhemoglobin is oxidized to methemoglobin. It now will appear as high-signal intensity on T1-weighed images. This occurs first at the periphery of the hematoma. On T2-weighted images, the hematoma appears black. As red blood cells die and rupture, a solution of methemoglobin is formed which is then bright on both T1- and T2-weighted images.[52]

Intracellular methemoglobin is found first around three days after the formation of the hema-toma. The formation of intracellular methemoglobin progresses from the periphery of the hematoma toward the center.[54] Extracellular methemoglobin is found about the end of the first week post-injury. Deoxyhemoglobin within the center of the hematoma may persist for weeks. Macrophages are mobilized and move in to digest the hematoma. As a result of the ingestion of blood products, hemosiderin is found within the lysosomes of the macrophage.[53] Again, this creates a susceptibility effect that makes the area of hemosiderin black on T2-weighted images. It then is found within the brain tissue at sites of traumatic bleeding, perhaps for the rest of the patient's life. Methemoglobin has been found for months to years following a brain injury, but it is eventually resorbed. However, the neuropsychiatric examiner should specifically ask the radiologist to look for hemosiderin when evaluating patients by MRI some length of time following their brain injury. FLAIR and GRE sequences are classically used for estimating the age of hematomas. However, a Swedish study recently questioned whether the relationship to the age of the hematoma can be accurately graded with spin-echo FLAIR and GRE sequencing.[55] Figure 5.10 is a GRE sequence demonstrating black hemosiderin deposits in the right cerebellum and right posterior temporal lobe.

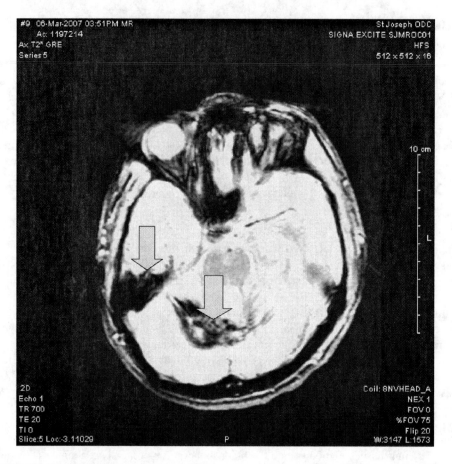

FIGURE 5.10 Axial T2 gradient-echo MRI demonstrating right posterior temporal hemosiderin and right cerebellar hemosiderin (black areas under arrows).

Intraventricular Hemorrhage

The MRI appearance of intraventricular hemorrhage is variable. The blood is almost always hyperintense relative to cerebrospinal fluid on T1-weighted images. It is especially hyperintensive on FLAIR scans, and usually this allows easy detection.[39] On T2-weighted MRI, the layering of acute blood will appear isointense to hypointense inferiorly and equivalent to CSF intensity superiorly. This is due to the layering effect. Acute blood will appear hyperintense on FLAIR sequences sensitive to T2 prolongation while nulling the normal cerebrospinal fluid background. There is evidence that FLAIR and fast spin-echo FLAIR sequences more conspicuously show acute intraventricular hemorrhage during the first 48 h than will a noncontrast CT.[30] T1- and T2-weighted images will show acute intraventricular hemorrhage isointense or hypointense. Cerebrospinal fluid pulsation artifacts within the ventricles, particularly within the posterior fossa, may be confused for intraventricular hemorrhage.[2] These findings will be of little consequence to the neuropsychiatric examiner at the time of examination except to signal that careful neuropsychiatric assessment must be done. Recall that the sign of intraventricular hemorrhage is often associated to injuries of the corpus callosum or brainstem and commonly associated with diffuse axonal injury. The deleterious effects of acute axonal injury will probably be detected during the neuropsychiatric examination. That is because intraventricular hemorrhage in most cases is due to rotation of the brain tearing subependymal veins on the ventral surface of the corpus callosum and along the fornix and septum pellucidum. During the torsional and stretching forces that cause diffuse axonal injury, these veins are often disrupted by that same force. Gentry et al.[56] found that intraventricular hemorrhage occurred in 60% of patients with diffuse axonal injury of the corpus callosum. However, about 12% of patients had diffuse axonal injury without evidence of callosal injury. In those cases, the hemorrhage was invariably due to dissection of a large intracerebral hematoma into the ventricular system.

Diffuse Axonal Injury

As seen elsewhere in this text, diffuse axonal injury is thought to be shear–strain injury. Deceleration of the head in a linear or rotational manner is associated with motor vehicle accidents and other violent head traumas. Holbourn[57] reported as early as 1945 that as the skull rotates, the brain has to "depend on its rigidity to avoid being left behind." However, during rapid deceleration, some brain structures are left behind to a considerable degree, and anatomic distortion occurs. Because of the relative fixation of certain parts of the brain to the rigid skull, the deep and superficial portions of the brain may not move at the same rate and can move in different directions during rotational acceleration or deceleration. This will result in shear–strain that manifests across the axons and results in axonal injury and rupture (see Chapter 1). Since different brain parts have differing consistencies and masses, depending on cell morphology and cell concentration, strains usually result at their junctions.[33]

The MRI findings in DAI are often unremarkable on T1-weighted images. This can cause the overlooking of DAI and may have importance in forensic cases. On the other hand, there is limited evidence in the medical literature that a mild TBI produces significant levels of DAI. However, if DAI is present on T2-weighted images, multifocal hyperintense foci are seen at characteristic locations as described elsewhere in this text. If this is a hemorrhagic lesion, the MRI may demonstrate hemoglobin products, but the signal is dependent on the age of the hemoglobin, as discussed above. Multifocal hypointense residuals may remain for years. On FLAIR imaging, multiple high signal foci are seen at characteristic anatomical locations as well. With gradient-echo imaging, multifocal hypointense foci on T2 GRE sequences are secondary to susceptibility from blood products. These lesions will be seen on the MRI at characteristic anatomical locations. Using DWI, hyperintense foci of restricted diffusion are seen. In more recent research studies, diffusion tensor imaging may show the severity of white matter injury.[16] MR spectroscopy (MRS) offers a noninvasive, nonradioactive method of assessing microscopic injury and predicting outcome. This is discussed in more detail below.

Diffuse axonal injury may be seen rarely without evidence of direct head trauma and with a delayed onset of coma.[58] This can occur in high-velocity accidents without immediate evidence of head injury. Other studies have confirmed findings of diffuse axonal injury on MRI following minor brain injury (GCS score = 15).[59] However, diffuse axonal injury in the aforementioned cases cannot be assumed without visual evidence on MRI. Recent studies have confirmed again the usefulness of detecting diffuse axonal injury lesions on diffusion-weighted MRI.[60,61] While diffusion tensor imaging (DTI) remains somewhat experimental at the time this book is published, numerous studies are beginning to point out that diffusion tensor imaging changes can be detected at both early and late time points following injury. They may represent an early indicator and a prognostic measure of subsequent brain damage.[62]

Posttraumatic Neurodegeneration

Posttraumatic changes over the long term are where the neuropsychiatric examiners will bring most of their professional value to the examination. It is the complex behavioral and cognitive changes occurring following TBI that will be of most interest from a neuropsychiatric perspective. Studies have demonstrated changes over the long term that can be detected by MRI. A recent Italian study[63] evaluated 19 closed-head TBI patients and compared them against 19 control subjects. MRIs were processed in a fully automatic system using voxel-by-voxel methods. The corpus callosum, fornix, anterior limb of the internal capsule, superior frontal gyrus, para-hippocampal gyrus, optic radiation, and the chiasma showed significant white matter density reduction when compared to control subjects. However, these findings did not correlate between days of coma and memory performance scores on neuropsychological testing with the exception of a significant negative correlation between white matter density in the mid-body of the corpus callosum and short-story delayed recall. The neuropsychiatric examiner should pay careful attention to hippocampal cross section volume and whether or not there have been changes with enlargement of the hippocampal cisterns. TBI causes hippocampal damage, and the hippocampus can be macroscopically divided into the head, body, and tail, which differ in terms of their sensitivity to trauma induced excitotoxic agents and also in terms of their cortical connections.[64] Memory is worse on neuropsychological testing in those patients demonstrating bilateral hippocampal atrophy, mainly involving the hippocampal head. A recent United Kingdom study[65] demonstrated that in children suffering severe TBI with resulting loss of hippocampal volume, despite adequate growth and stature, the effects of TBI on brain growth and hippocampal volume extend into adulthood. In those patients who sustained severe TBI (GCS score of less than 9), some may show no significant evidence of neuroradiological lesions. Tomaiuolo's group in Rome[66] used high spatial resolution T1-weighted MRI scans of the brain and compared these to neuropsychological evaluations at least three months after trauma. In their 19 patients, they found a clear reduction in hippocampal, fornix, and callosal volume. The length of coma did predict the callosal volume reduction. This was considered to be a marker of the severity of axonal loss. However, since memory scores did not correlate well with callosal loss, the authors concluded that the relationship with memory performance and anatomical volume loss may reflect the diffuse nature of the damage, indicating that neural circuits have been disrupted at multiple levels. Figure 5.11 displays posterior temporal and cerebellar encephalomalacia in the right cerebrum on a T1-weighted image and it corresponds to the GRE-weighted sequence in Figure 5.10.

Atrophy of the cerebrum may occur focally or diffusely in patients following TBI. MRI will show widening of the cortical sulci with concordant ventriculomegaly in the affected areas. Cerebellar atrophy is demonstrated by prominence of subarachnoid and cisternal spaces in the posterior fossa. Time-dependent atrophic changes occurring after TBI can be quantified using MR volumetric studies. In the chronic stage of TBI, MR volumetric studies may predict eventual cognitive outcome.[67] Focal atrophy may present on MRI as areas of encephalomalacia or may even contain cystic structures because of necrosis of tissue. On MRI, a porencephalic cyst can be easily differentiated from a posttraumatic cyst on the FLAIR sequences; a porencephalic cyst will show low-signal intensity on the FLAIR sequence, whereas encephalomalacia demonstrates high-signal intensity.[68] Figure 8.6 demonstrates atrophy and enlargement of the hippocampal cisterns.

Where the radiologists report back to the neuropsychiatric examiner that there is atrophy of the corpus callosum (best seen on sagittal views), the degree of corpus callosal atrophy correlates significantly with the chronicity of the injury. This also correlates with the severity of diffuse axonal injury.[69] If the radiologist reports back to the neuropsychiatric examiner evidence of significant callosal atrophy, the neuropsychological portion of the examination should focus closely on this issue in an attempt to correlate clinically elements of posttraumatic hemispheric disconnection.[70] Table 5.6 summarizes MRI findings of lesions often detected during TBI evaluation.

High-Field Magnetic Resonance Imaging

High-field magnetic resonance imaging (HFMRI) was originally developed to assist with spectroscopy and functional MRI. However, at the time of the preparation of this text, it is now moving into clinical practice for static imaging, and many centers across the United States and large urban centers in other parts of the world are adding 3 Tesla-dedicated MRI installations. High magnetic fields during MRI afford a better signal/noise ratio, and consequently the spatial resolution is improved and acquisition time is shortened. When 3 T MRI is compared to 1.5 T MRI, the main advantage of the HFMRI is that the stronger magnetic field is associated with a proportional increase

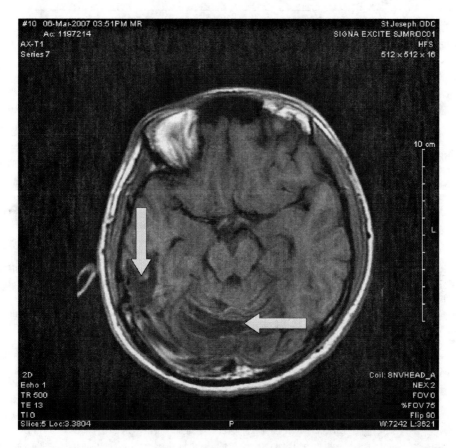

FIGURE 5.11 Axial T1 MRI at same level as 5.10 demonstrating structural brain tissue loss at sites of hemosiderin.

in the percentage of hydrogen protons oriented parallel to the static magnetic field. This results in increased macroscopic longitudinal magnetization and a better signal/noise ratio. The resulting greater spatial resolution makes 3 T imaging more accurate when fine morphological detail is required such as in volumetric studies of the hippocampus and in improving the early detection of structural changes associated with Alzheimer's disease.[71]

HFMRI in patients following TBI is advantageous when compared to 1.5 T MRI. Theoretically, performance of a 3 T MR imager should double that of a 1.5 T machine. However, artifacts and technical limitations do not allow a doubling to be achieved, although a close approximation is generally obtained.[72] HFMRI shows an advantage when compared to 1.5 T MRI for detecting diffuse axonal injury, hemoglobin within brain tissue, and study of intracranial vessels.[73] Within the near future, it is anticipated that most large tertiary care medical centers will replace current MRI equipment with 3 T MRI instruments.

FUNCTIONAL IMAGING OF BRAIN TRAUMA

Single-Photon Emission Computed Tomography

Single-photon emission computed tomography (SPECT) is based upon an indirect determination of blood flow using the distribution of a radiopharmaceutical agent in the brain to approximate almost on a 1:1 basis regional cerebral blood flow. A radiotracer is injected into the person for imaging by SPECT. After appropriate distribution the tracer decays, emitting a photon, which is detected and

TABLE 5.6

Magnetic Resonance Imaging (MRI) and Traumatic Brain Injury (TBI)

Lesion	Image Findings[13,16,29,121,127,128]
Contusions	Both T1- and T2-weighted spin-echo sequences will demonstrate hemorrhagic contusions. T2-weighted spin-echo sequences are superior for demonstrating nonhemorrhagic contusions. Hemosiderin blooms on GRE of chronic injury. FLAIR can detect axonal degeneration.
Brainstem injury	Detected by sagittal or coronal T2-weighted or FLAIR axial sequences.
Epidural hematoma	High-signal intensity extruded serum seen as a biconvex form. T1- and T2-weighted sequences will detect acute lesions while subacute stages may be seen by T1-weighted sequences. Displaced dura may be seen on T2-weighted sequences.
Subdural hematoma	Subacute cresentic lesion detected by T1- and T2-weighted sequences. Isodense subdural on CT detected by T1- and T2-weighted sequences. FLAIR sequences may detect subtle coincidental subarachnoid hemorrhage. Chronic subdural hematoma is seen as high-signal-intensity methemoglobin, low-signal-intensity protein fluid on T1-weights. FLAIR is the most sensitive sequence for SDH.
Subararachnoid hemorrhage	T2-weighted FLAIR sequences are quite sensitive. Sulci and cisterns are hyperintense. GRE is useful.
Intraparenchymal hemorrhage	Deoxyhemoglobin signal is hypointense to isointense on T1-weighted sequences. It is markedly hypointense on T2-weighted images. Methemoglobin is high-signal intensity on T1-weights. On T2-weighted sequences it is black. Hemosiderin is black on T2-weighted sequences. GRE is probably the superior sequence for detection of blood or blood products.
Intraventricular hemorrhage	Hyperintense relative to CSF on T1-weighted sequences. Especially intense on T2-weighted FLAIR images. GRE sequences are also sensitive for detection.
Diffuse axonal injury	Small punctate areas of hyperintense signal on T2-weighted sequences early after injury. Hypointense T2-weighted signal is seen as the lesion ages due to hemosiderin deposits. GRE sequences are superior for detecting old DAI hemorrhages. T1 may be unremarkable.
Chronic neurodegeneration	Encephalomalacia is detected as a hypointense signal on T1-weighted sequences and FLAIR sequences with high-signal intensity on T2-weighted sequences. Ventricular dilatation and cortical atrophy are common and can be detected by FLAIR sequences.

recorded by a gamma camera. The data are then reconstructed by computer and tomographic sectioning is undertaken. The functional slices produced by SPECT are displayed in a manner similar to CT or MRI. SPECT is usually displayed with coronal, sagittal, and axial views. Three-dimensional reconstruction is also available, and computer programs can rotate the three-dimensional figure for visual analysis. Various analytical programs are available as well. Recently, voxel-based statistical analysis using technetium-99 labeled tracer has been analyzed using SPECT in patients with TBI and then comparing group and individual differences.[74] The most common tracer used in the United States is technetium-99m-hexamethylpropyleneamine oxime (Tc-99m-HMPAO). Another tracer is often used in countries outside the United States, technetium-99m-ethylcysteinate dimer (Tc-99m-ECD). Tc-99m-ECD has less extracerebral uptake, which produces dramatically different patterns when compared with Tc-99m-HMPAO. Concentrations of either HMPAO or ECD SPECT are highest in brain lesions receiving the most plentiful blood flow shortly after injection and remain so up to 24 h. One advantage to using SPECT is that the individual can be injected and the scan can be made an hour or so later at the convenience of the scanning department without alteration of the data. This is because the radioisotopes themselves are absorbed in the glial cells that are proximal to the active neurons, but these isotopes are not immediately excreted. The absorbed radioisotopes remain in greater concentration in the more active blood flow areas of the brain.

SPECT has some advantages when compared with positron emission tomography (PET) or functional magnetic resonance imaging (fMRI). For instance, the radioisotopes that are typically used for SPECT imaging can be ordered and delivered in advance of the patient, thus not requiring an on-site cyclotron and nuclear chemist as is usually required for PET. SPECT can be used to image change in resting blood flow from one well-defined event to another (e.g., from pre-ictal to the ictal state), but it is not appropriate to use this for mapping blood flow changes that occur rapidly over time (such as those encountered in most states of cognitive activity) or for making direct inferences about brain metabolism owing to the time required for radioactive decay of the isotopes.[75] The use of SPECT generally produces spectacular color imaging. Images are visually striking, but these can be quite misleading to the evaluator. It is recommended that to ensure reliable and valid interpretations, quantitative pixel counts be used.[76] However, quantitative assessment using pixel counts is generally not available in most SPECT centers. Images are usually interpreted qualitatively, and interpretations may vary from clinician to clinician to a significant degree.[77]

SPECT has several sources of potential measurement error. Unlike PET, SPECT imaging requires that regional radiation counts be normalized to a brain area that is theoretically free from injury. This sets a standard of Relative Flow values in SPECT. Nuclear medicine physicians often base these relative values upon a region such as the thalamus or cerebellum, which is assumed to be uninjured. These assumptions may be valid for some populations with focal lesions such as in a stroke, but they may not be valid for populations wherein the neuropathology is much more diffuse, such as occurs in TBI. Particularly when using SPECT in TBI, an initial SPECT scan done acutely may be predictive of a good clinical outcome. However, use of an abnormal scan for prognosis is less clear at this time.[78] Other issues of error include depressed mood. This can affect adversely SPECT results, as can certain brain active medications and substance abuse. The studies on SPECT at this time are sparse and inadequate, and they have not been shown to clearly correlate with behavioral changes or neuropsychological deficits. Discrimination of neural or anatomical detail is not possible, even when paired or fused with CT or MRI. SPECT and CT/MRI fusion improve anatomical localization, but the disparity between the poor resolution of the SPECT and the higher resolution of CT or MRI cannot be overcome at this time. The American College of Radiology rates SPECT 1/9 for mild or minor acute closed-head injury (GCS $\geq$ 13), without risk factors or neurologic deficit (where 1 = least appropriate and 9 = most appropriate).[105]

SPECT and Traumatic Brain Injury

In India, Tc-99m-ECD SPECT was used as a complementary technique to CT in the initial evaluation of patients with mild TBI. This study was done in patients receiving evaluation within 12 h of injury.[79] However, there are no follow-up studies presently available to determine whether the acute findings hold up during the chronic phase. The critical factor for using brain SPECT in TBI and having it be clinically relevant is a carefully designed clinical protocol.[80] However, these protocols do not exist in most hospitals. Most studies on SPECT and TBI are done at a time quite distant from the original injury. Moreover, SPECT scans are usually interpreted separately, and they are not coregistered with a structural image such as CT or MRI. Most of the studies that purport SPECT to be useful in TBI are more than 10 years old, and they have not been replicated in large-scale studies.[81–87] Table 5.7 outlines SPECT usage for evaluating TBI.

The neuropsychiatric examiner using SPECT for treatment evaluation is probably on reasonably safe ground if the SPECT scan is made close in time to the original injury. However, for most forensic cases, particularly if the SPECT scan is made years after the original injury, if it does not correlate well with a concurrent structural scan such as CT or MRI, it may not meet a *Daubert* standard.[88] Presently, there are few consistent data regarding validity and reliability of SPECT techniques in clinical cases of TBI. Almost all that have been applied are single case studies or small group studies. The examiner should be very careful applying SPECT studies as a sole measure in a legal case. There is no particular SPECT profile that is solely pathognomonic for any level of TBI,[89,90] and false positives are high.[91] Thus, the promise of SPECT imaging and application to TBI remains lacking until large-scale prospective studies can be completed. It is useful in selected cases particularly where it can be correlated with structural scanning. The American College of

TABLE 5.7

Single-Photon Emission Computed Tomography (SPECT) and Traumatic Brain Injury (TBI)

- SPECT studies months or years after moderate or severe TBI have demonstrated decreased cerebral blood flow. The presence of decreased blood flow is not, by itself, evidence of nonfunctional brain tissue.[75]
- There is no SPECT profile that is pathognomonic for any level of TBI.[89,90]
- SPECT is routinely positive in a variety of medical and neurological disorders,[91] thus false positives are high.
- The American College of Radiology has rated SPECT as inappropriate (a rating of 2 on a scale of 1–9, with 1 = least appropriate and 9 = most appropriate) for clinically evaluating postconcussion syndrome.[75] It rates SPECT 1/9 for acute head injury (minor or mild) and 4/9 for chronic head injury (with cognitive or neurological deficits).[105]
- At present, SPECT should be used in the evaluation of chronic head injury only when imaging findings correlate with structural imaging or MRS.

Radiology rates the appropriateness of SPECT in chronic head injury, with cognitive or neurologic deficits, at 4/9.[105]

POSITRON EMISSION TOMOGRAPHY

A decade ago, positron emission tomography (PET) seemed likely to emerge as a reliable way to assess cognitive changes following TBI.[92] A present review of one of the world's standard textbooks on positron emission tomography,[93] published in 2003, demonstrates not a single chapter on PET use in brain trauma, and the index of this book contains no entries for trauma-related uses of PET imaging of the brain. Like SPECT, positron emission tomography is a radioisotope-based imaging technology. Typically, current PET studies utilize intravenous tracers such as 18F-flurodeoxyglucose (FDG) for the quantification of regional brain metabolism. For the measurement of blood flow or dynamic changes associated with motor or cognitive activity, a tracer of radioactive oxygen is usually used such as oxygen-15.[99] Current research of cognition and behavior is undertaken with radio-labeled ligands that bind selectively with dopaminergic, serotonergic, and other known neurotransmitter receptor systems.[98] Recently, the ability to evaluate the dopamine transport system has become available.[75]

With regard to using PET for the evaluation of chronic symptoms thought to be related to TBI, this seems at first to be an intuitive choice. However, when one reviews the world literature of PET use in TBI, particularly since it has been used for TBI evaluation since 1970, few studies can be found that directly relate functional imaging findings with PET and cognition after TBI. Most of the studies from neuropsychological and other psychological assessments have been obtained at points in time that were quite disparate from the time at which the imaging occurred.[94] In contrast to the poorly designed study just described,[94] more carefully designed studies do find localized abnormal cerebral metabolic rates in the frontal and temporal regions that correlate with subjective complaints and neuropsychological test results obtained during the chronic phase of recovery.[95] Other PET studies have demonstrated frontal hypometabolism with related decreased performance on neuropsychological tests that are thought to be mediated by frontal lobe functioning.[96] PET has been noted to correlate with post-TBI anosmia and hypometabolism of orbitofrontal brain tissue.[97] However, even with these findings that correlate somewhat with symptomatic TBI patients, there are no systematic, long-term, large-scale studies of PET imaging in TBI patients that allow examiners to have standards for the interpretation of PET when used for examination of TBI symptoms. Moreover, there are no pathognomonic features on PET imaging that are specific for TBI. There are no published radiological or nuclear medicine standards for PET use in TBI. The same difficulty with interpretation of SPECT applies to PET imaging. That is to say, multiple neurological, psychiatric, metabolic, and medical causes are known for altered brain metabolism detectable by PET imaging. For instance, use of PET to evaluate post-TBI cognitive changes 3 years

TABLE 5.8

Positron Emission Tomography (PET) and Traumatic Brain Injury (TBI)

- PET using 18-FDG is used to detect hypometabolism. PET using O-15 labeled water is used to measure blood flow associated with cognitive tasks.[98,99]
- The use of PET in TBI has been minimally investigated.[75]
- PET can demonstrate that functional injury is beyond the boundaries of demonstrated CT or MRI structural injury. These occur less acutely in gray matter than in white matter.[100,101]
- Most PET studies are quite distant in time from the acute injury.
- There are no pathognomonic signs of PET imaging for any level of TBI. There are no published criteria or classification for PET interpretation in TBI.[75] PET is inappropriate for use in acute minor head injury and below average in appropriateness for chronic head injury with cognitive or neurologic deficits.[105]
- At present PET should probably not be used for the evaluation of late TBI without CT or MRI correlation.

after the head trauma poses difficult problems of interpretation. This is particularly true if the data are to be used for forensic purposes. The reader is referred to Chapter 10 for further discussion of the medical–legal issues associated with presentation of TBI data to a trier of fact. Table 5.8 lists guidelines for PET use to evaluate TBI. Unlike CT and MRI, to date no atlas of SPECT or PET imaging has been published that demonstrates pathognomonic or functional lesions following TBI, which can be correlated with behavioral and cognitive deficits. The American College of Radiology rates PET use as inappropriate (1/9) for minor acute head trauma and 4/9 on a nine-point scale for use to evaluate chronic head trauma with cognitive or neurologic deficits.[105] Thus, it is recommended that PET be used as an adjunct imaging modality where differentiation of Alzheimer's disease from post-TBI symptoms is necessary, or in those cases where CT or MRI has demonstrated previous lesions secondary to TBI that now may be explained functionally by the use of PET. It is recommended that PET analysis of TBI neuropsychiatric examinations be paired with a concomitant structural image for clinical correlation. Figure 5.12 is a PET scan of case E.L. in Chapter 11. This scan was made at the time of the CT portrayed in Figure 5.3.

FUNCTIONAL MAGNETIC RESONANCE IMAGING

In ordinary static MRI, when the nuclei of hydrogen atoms in water encounter a strong magnetic field, they align parallel to the field's direction. Radio frequency (RF) pulses are presented at an angle that is 90° relative to this magnetic field. This causes approximately 1% of the hydrogen nuclei to realign and begin spinning in a different direction (excitation). When the RF pulse is discontinued, the nuclei return to their original alignment and spin dynamics. During the process of returning to the previous resting status, an electrical signal is emitted from the nuclei that is detectable by the scanner and allows reconstruction of static anatomic images. Functional MRI (fMRI) is a variant of structural MRI. The primary difference between the two is that the dependent variable of interest in fMRI is the change in intensity of electrical signal emissions related to increases in blood flow (that are presumably caused by changes in neural activity). The focus of fMRI is on regional changes in brain activity rather than anatomic structure alone. During fMRI, specific stimuli can be presented in the same manner that occurs during O-15 PET. When neural activity increases in a brain region, there is a corresponding increase in blood flow to that region. This blood flow may increase by over 50% beyond the metabolic needs of a tissue. This excess of flow to the region results in a localized surplus of oxyhemoglobin relative to deoxyhemoglobin in the cerebral venous and capillary beds. Oxyhemoglobin is naturally diamagnetic while deoxyhemoglobin is paramagnetic (becomes readily magnetized within a magnetic field). There is a net decrease in the paramagnetic material resulting in an increased signal intensity that can be detected

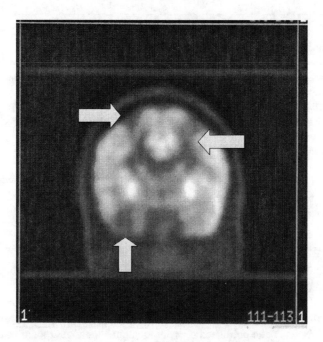

FIGURE 5.12 PET scan of E.L., case 11.1. This coronal view corresponds to Figure 5.3 (CT encephaloma-lacia). Note bilateral frontal hypometabolism and right inferior temporal lobe hypometabolism.

externally. Most contemporary MRI scanners can be adapted to perform fMRI. However, this technique is still investigational in most clinical populations including brain injury.[102–104]

At the time this book is written, few fMRI studies of individuals with TBI exist. Moreover, no studies of fMRI in large-scale populations of persons with TBI have ever been completed. Many research medical centers have ongoing protocols that are currently addressing the lack of evidence-based literature using fMRI in working memory following injury, and these show an increased recruitment of cerebral resources following severe diffuse TBI, particularly during response inhibition or when task difficulty is increased.[106,107] Very recent fMRI studies by McAllister's group at Dartmouth University have found evidence for the role of catecholaminergic dysregulation in the etiology of working memory complaints after mild and moderate TBI.[109] This need for a greater expenditure of cerebral effort to achieve overtly normal behavior has been demonstrated in a finger tapping paradigm several years after injury.[108] However, although fMRI represents a very advanced approach to brain imaging, the advanced approach has not met the criteria of real-world data usage to evaluate TBI. Even when compared to SPECT or PET, it has not reached an efficient threshold of scientific evidence for routine use at any level of injury severity after head trauma. This procedure is classified as investigational by the American College of Radiology (see Table 5.9).[75,105]

TABLE 5.9

Functional Magnetic Resonance Imaging (fMRI) and Traumatic Brain Injury (TBI)

- fMRI can correlate blood flow with working memory, response inhibition, psychomotor execution, and improved cognitive status.[106–109]
- fMRI does not automatically generate brain maps, and there are no normative values for fMRI scans.[75]
- This technique is rated as investigational for use in head trauma by the American College of Radiology.[105]

MAGNETIC RESONANCE SPECTROSCOPY

Magnetic resonance spectroscopy (MRS) is a noninvasive modality that provides information about the neurochemical status of the brain. Some imaging centers are now suggesting a multifunctional approach to cerebral injuries by obtaining MRI using diffusion-weighted imaging, proton-weighted imaging, and magnetic resonance spectroscopy. When used together, they increase the specificity and diagnostic capabilities of static MRI.[110] Protein MRS can identify markers of neuronal viability (N-acetyl-aspartate, NAA), metabolism of cellular membranes (choline) and cellular energy metabolism (creatine or lactate). MRS allows the physician to measure the quantity of these compounds. Changes in the quantities of these chemicals (or changes in the ratio between them) correlate with the extent of cellular damage after neural insult.[111] Studies are demonstrating that people with TBI differ from controls in the variance of the above compounds in that the relative concentrations correlate with concurrent neuropsychological performance or GCS categories.[112,113] Other studies have demonstrated that certain chemical ratios (decreased NAA/CR, decreased NAA/CHO, and increased CHO/CR) correlate with the GCS and posttraumatic amnesia.[114]

In the acute phase, MRS can depict injury in the brain that appears normal on static imaging.[115] Moreover, MRS has been approved by the United States Food and Drug Administration as a noninvasive method providing metabolic information about the brain.[110] MRS is relatively easy to perform and can be completed on any high quality static MRI system that has the appropriate software. It relies on the same physical principles to collect signal as static MRI but then differs in the way the data are processed, displayed, and interpreted. Instead of structural images of brain anatomy, a plot with peak amplitudes of the chemicals being studied is obtained[110] (see Figure 5.13).

In diffuse axonal injury, the main abnormalities found following TBI are a reduction of NAA levels and a reduction in the NAA/creatine ratio. If the injury is mild, there may be no significant reduction in these substances. DAI is also associated with an increase in choline levels and an increase in the choline/creatine ratio. Choline is associated with myelin and membrane breakdown,

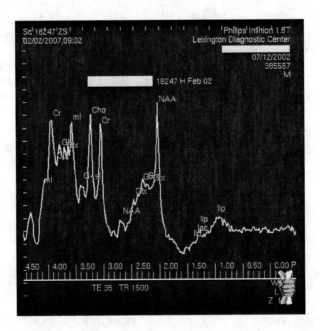

FIGURE 5.13 Magnetic resonance spectroscopy (MRS) of case 8.4, D.H. NAA, N-acetyl aspartate; Cr, creatine; Cho, choline; Ml, myo-inositol; lac, lactate; and glx, glutamate.

TABLE 5.10

Magnetic Resonance Spectroscopy (MRS) and Traumatic Brain Injury (TBI)

- MRS provides chemical data that correlate more strongly with neuronal dysfunction than the structural information provided by conventional MRI.[111]
- MRS can detect a reduction in the NAA/creatine ratio in the parietal white matter and splenium of the corpus callosum up to 3 years after TBI.[116]
- MRS is FDA approved for brain study.[110]
- MRS detects NAA, creatine, and choline in TBI.[110]

and therefore it is believed to be consistent with DAI. In the acute phase of DAI, where spectroscopy is used in the neurointensive care unit, creatine is typically normal and enables differentiation of brain trauma from a hyperosmolar state. Hyperosmolar states affect white matter and are characterized by an increase in creatine and especially in choline and myoinositol.[110]

Neuronal damage is usually characterized by reduction in the NAA/creatine ratio in parietal white matter near the corpus callosum. It can be seen by MRS from the second day after injury up to 3 years posttrauma.[116] It is hoped that continued research using MRS will enable neurosurgeons and physiatrists to predict outcomes more accurately during the acute phase of brain trauma. On the other hand, the ability to detect the presence of brain injury when not imaged well by static imaging such as CT and MRI may be accomplished currently using appropriate MRS techniques.[111] Figure 5.13 is an MRS of the right hippocampus made at the time of the neuropsychiatric examination of case D.H. in Chapter 8.

ELECTROENCEPHALOGRAPHY

There are four basic frequencies detected by electroencephalography (EEG) of the human brain. Beta rhythm oscillates at a frequency of greater than 12.5 Hz. Alpha rhythm, the predominant rhythm of the brain and most frequently found in the posterior head, oscillates at a frequency of 8.0–12.5 Hz. Theta rhythms are found at a frequency of 3.5–8.0 Hz, and delta rhythms are at a frequency less than 3.5 Hz. Recently, gamma frequencies (20–60 Hz) are receiving attention as probable neuropsychiatric markers of tonic consciousness.[139] EEG rhythm is produced by a thalamic pacemaker and corticocortical and thalamocortical networks. The oscillating frequency of the thalamic pacemaker is modulated by the nucleus reticularis, one of the predominant nuclei of the thalamus.[129] Each of the four basic EEG frequencies has a principal neural generator. Beta activity is generated by corticocortical and thalamocortical networks involving information processing, and it is found maximally over the frontal and central regions. It is increased and made more prominent by many psychiatric and brain active medications. Alpha rhythms are generated by thalamic pacemaker neurons, and as noted, these frequencies are most prominent over the occipital head region. Theta rhythms also come from the thalamic pacemaker neurons, but they are under significant inhibitory influence from the reticular nucleus of the thalamus. Limited amounts of theta are present in the waking state, and as individuals become drowsy or proceed into sleep, theta rhythms become more prominent. Delta rhythms are "bad" in the awake state and "good" in the sleeping state. They are not typically seen in the awake EEG of healthy adults. These rhythms come from oscillatory neurons lying deep in the gray matter cortical layers, and they are also found within the thalamus. During the waking state, they are prominently detected in neurodegenerative states and focal brain lesions.[130]

Williams and Denny-Brown[131] were the first to experimentally demonstrate EEG abnormalities after TBI, including attenuation of the amplitude and slowing of the frequency followed by resolutions of these abnormalities over time. Following mild TBI, the EEG is typically normal immediately after the injury or only mildly abnormal. The EEG may demonstrate slowing of the background rhythm into the theta range, and alpha activity may become attenuated with an increase in the presence of delta activity. If TBI is more severe, delta activity may become even more prominent and much more diffuse with a dropout of alpha frequencies and even theta frequencies.[132] If injuries following TBI are focal in the brain, then the EEG changes may include focal or asymmetrical slowing into the delta range. Following acute head injury, EEG abnormalities may be present for a short period of time (a few days) even in the absence of CT or MRI abnormalities. This is particularly true in children.[133]

As the neuropsychiatric examiner reviews medical records following TBI, it is not uncommon to find evidence of EEG monitoring in the neurointensive care unit. This is becoming more frequent in neurosurgical and neurointensive care units.[134] The EEG output is usually not monitored by the intensivist but rather by a neurophysiologist, neurologist, or anesthesiologist. Nurses are trained to detect burst suppression or generalized seizures.[135] EEG can be used as a monitor of regional cerebral blood flow. Gray matter receives approximately 80% of the cerebral blood flow, and cortical and electrical activity requires roughly 50% of the total oxygen consumed by the brain. The EEG begins to become abnormal when cortical blood flow decreases below 20 ml/100 g of brain tissue per minute. A margin of safety is present between the time at which the EEG becomes abnormal and that at which cellular damage begins to occur, as cellular survival is not threatened until cortical blood flow falls below 12 ml/100 g per minute.[136] Seizures are a common problem in the neurointensive care unit and are sometimes difficult to detect clinically. If an EEG processor is being used in an ICU, it is important to maintain the raw EEG tracing. The processor may miss sharp waves, spikes or spike and dome complexes, which are best appreciated by an electrophysiologically trained neurologist visually reviewing the raw EEG tracing.[137] Obviously, the EEG is helpful in the neurointensive care unit in determining the presence of coma or brain death.[134] EEG analyses may provide some prognostic information for patients who have sustained severe TBI, but there are significant detection issues with their application to mild TBI. In many mild TBI patients, no EEG abnormalities can be detected. Even in some patients with structural lesions detected by MRI, no focal change in EEG frequency or rhythms is noted. EEG analysis is not highly regarded for diagnostic or prognostic purposes in evaluating persons with mild TBI.[138] Table 5.11 reviews critical issues using EEG following TBI.

SPECIAL PROBLEMS IN PEDIATRICS

GENERAL PEDIATRIC PERSPECTIVES

Of all children who sustain traumatic brain injuries, 95% will survive. With regard to the specific issue of severe TBI, only 65% survive.[117] The highest mortality is seen in children who are less than 2 years of age. The mortality rates gradually decline through age 12, and then a second peak in mortality is seen at age 15.[118] For very young children, recent data from the Centers for Disease Control and Prevention in Atlanta, Georgia, describe 2536 nonfatal TBI-related hospitalizations in 15 states for children younger than 2 years of age.[119] These data found that the overall rate

---

TABLE 5.11

Electroencephalography (EEG) and Traumatic Brain Injury (TBI)

- EEG rhythms are generated primarily by the thalamus.[129]
- Beta rhythm (>12.5 Hz) is maximal over frontal and central head regions.[130]
- Alpha rhythm (8.0–12.5 Hz) is the predominant waking rhythm and is maximal over the occipital region.[130]
- Theta rhythm (3.5–8.0 Hz) becomes more obvious with sleep and drowsiness. It can increase with injury.[130]
- Delta rhythm (<3.5 Hz) is bad when awake and good when asleep. It may occur focally over injured brain regions and during encephalopathic states.[130]

of nonfatal TBI-related hospitalization peaked at 1 month of age (178 cases per 100,000 person-years) and was followed by a secondary peak at 8 months of age (128 cases per 100,000 person-years). Rates for unintentional fall and inflicted head injury were significantly higher for infants ages 0–11 months of age than for children 12–23 months of age. Recent German data demonstrate that falls from less than 1.5 m height lead only in a very few cases to severe brain injury.[120]

The sequelae of head trauma in children include infarction from severe brain edema and vascular injury, infections, leptomeningeal cysts, and hydrocephalus.[121] As medical knowledge about pediatric head injury is developed, it is now probably incontrovertible that TBI in children, particularly those under age 5, demonstrates unique biochemical, molecular, cellular, and physiological facets when compared to adults.[122]

NONACCIDENTAL TRAUMA (CHILD ABUSE)

As noted earlier in this book, the scientific evidence of child-inflicted trauma is changing rapidly. "Shaken baby syndrome" is no longer *en vogue*, and the previous term "inflicted trauma" is now termed "nonaccidental trauma." Nonaccidental trauma is a euphemism for child abuse. The reader may wish to review Chapter 1 regarding head injury in infancy and childhood. Nonaccidental trauma of children is an increasing problem, and 3 million cases of suspected child abuse were reported from the United States in the year 2000. Of these, nearly half resulted in disfigurement, permanent neurological or psychological deficit or death. In the year 2002, approximately 896,000 children in the United States were determined to be victims of child abuse or neglect, and 1400 children died from inflicted trauma or neglect. Head trauma is the leading cause of morbidity and mortality in the abused child, especially in patients under the age of 2 years.[121] The so-called shaken baby syndrome is currently characterized by the following clinical indicators: retinal hemorrhage, subdural or subarachnoid hemorrhage, cerebral contusion, and diffuse cerebral edema with minimal evidence of external trauma. The direct injuries can result in skull fractures, subdural hematomas, and cerebral contusions of the contrecoup-type. Axonal injuries were classically thought to be due to tissue shearing in these children, but they are now considered to be the result of probable diffuse hypoxia and edema.[121]

The imaging findings in nonaccidental child trauma most commonly reveal subdural hematoma, subarachnoid hemorrhage, or cerebral contusion when CT scans are used. CT is the imaging modality of choice in the acutely injured child. However, the neuropsychiatric examiner working on a potential criminal case, for instance, must remember that hemorrhage becomes more difficult to detect by CT after approximately one week, as the blood becomes isodense with brain; at this point MRI is more sensitive than CT in diagnosing subacute hematomas, whether they are subdural or intraparenchymal. While child abuse is by far the most common cause of subdural hematoma in infants, it is important to consider metabolic diseases that can also cause bilateral subdural hematoma. These include Menkes' kinky hair disease, glutaricaciduria type I, and Hermansky–Pudlak syndrome. These can cause both subdural hematomas and retinal hemorrhages.[123] Table 5.12 summarizes important findings in child abuse.

TABLE 5.12

Features of Nonaccidental Child Head Trauma (Child Abuse)

- The classic presentation of an abused child is with retinal hemorrhages, subdural or subarachnoid hemorrhage, cerebral contusion, and diffuse cerebral edema with minimal evidence of external trauma.[121]
- Falls from less than 1.5 m (4.9 ft) lead to severe TBI only in very rare cases.[120]
- The young child brain has unique biochemical, molecular, cellular, and physiological facets of TBI when compared with the adult brain.[122]

In the acute phase, edema and parenchymal injury of the cortex and white matter are commonly present and are easier to detect using MRI than CT. Diffusion-weighted imaging (DWI) makes the lesions more conspicuous.[124] Concomitant injury to the spine and spinal cord is far more common in nonaccidental child abuse than it is in the child who falls or who is traumatized in an automobile. The cervical spine is particularly affected by severe shaking injury or swinging by the legs and striking the child's head into a hard object. The neuropsychiatric examiner should review medical records carefully to determine if cervical injuries in particular have occurred in the infant or child concomitant with brain injury. In a child, it has been rather unequivocally stated by radiologists, that the presence of subdural hemorrhage of any age is strongly suggestive of nonaccidental trauma.[121] In one series of 93 children ages 3 years or less, with extraparenchymal hematomas, 47% of those children with subdural hematomas were ultimately diagnosed as having been abused.[125] Particularly with children who may have been abused, fast spin-echo and FLAIR sequences, which are relatively insensitive to paramagnetic substances, should not be used as primary sequences in trauma cases of children, as the presence of old and new hemorrhages is of critical importance.[121] Many children have been head abused more than once by the time they come to medical attention. Recently, it has been suggested that proton MRS obtained in the subacute phase may be useful to assess prognosis in children who have suffered inflicted trauma. In particular, the presence of elevated lactate or the reduction of NAA on MRS studies obtained 5–7 days after the injury indicates significant damage. Preliminary studies suggest that these patients will have a poor prognosis and require intensive intervention.[126]

REFERENCES

1. Quisling, R.G. and Sohn-Williams, L., Neuroradiologic imaging, in *Textbook of Neurointensive Care*, Layon, A.J., Gabrielli, A., and Friedman, W.A., Eds., W.B. Saunders, Philadelphia, PA, 2004, p. 47.
2. Young, R.J. and Destian, S., Imaging of traumatic intracranial hemorrhage. *Neuroimaging Clin. N. Am.*, 12, 189, 2002.
3. Toyama, Y., Kobayashi, T., Nishiyama, Y., et al., CT for acute stage of closed head injury. *Radiat. Med.*, 23, 309, 2005.
4. Holmes, J.F., Hendey, G.W., Oman, J.A., et al., Epidemiology of blunt head injury victims undergoing ED cranial computed tomographic scanning. *Am. J. Emerg. Med.*, 24, 167, 2006.
5. Marshall, L.F., Marshall, S.B., Klauber, M.R., et al., The diagnosis of head injury requires a classification based on computed axial tomography. *J. Neurotrauma*, 9 (Suppl. 1), S287, 1992.
6. Maas, A.I., Hukkelhoven, C.W., Marshall, L.F., et al., Prediction of outcome in traumatic brain injury with computed tomographic characteristics: A comparison between the computed tomographic classification and combinations of computed tomographic predictors. *Neurosurgery*, 57, 1173, 2005.
7. Smits, M., Dippel, D.W., de Haan, G.G., et al., External validation of the Canadian CT Head Rule and the New Orleans Criteria for CT scanning in patients with minor head injury. *JAMA*, 294, 1519, 2005.
8. Stein, S.C., Burnett, M.G., and Glick, H.A., Indications for CT scanning in mild traumatic brain injury: A cost-effectiveness study. *J. Trauma*, 61, 558, 2006.
9. Velmahos, G.C., Gervasini, A., Petrovick, L., et al., Routine repeat head CT for minimal head injury is unnecessary. *J. Trauma*, 60, 494, 2006.
10. Cihangiroglu, M., Ramsey, R.G., and Dohrmann, G.J., Brain injury: Analysis of imaging modalities. *Neurol. Res.*, 24, 7, 2002.
11. Zee, C.S. and Go, J., CT of head trauma. *Neuroimaging Clin. North Am.*, 8, 525, 1998.
12. Zimmerman, R.A., *Evaluation of Head Injury: Supratentorial*, in Taveras, J. and Ferrucci, E., Eds., Lippincott, Philadelphia, PA, 1986.
13. Castillo, M.A., *Neuroradiology Companion: Methods, Guidelines, and Imaging Fundamentals*, 3rd edition, Lippincott, Williams & Wilkins, Philadelphia, PA, 2006.
14. Hardman, J.N. and Manoukian, M.D., Pathology of head trauma. *Neuroimaging Clin. N. Am.*, 12, 175, 2002.

15. Kim, P.E., Go, J.L., and Zee, C.S., Radiographic assessment of cranial gunshot wounds. *Neuroimaging Clin. N. Am.*, 12, 229, 2002.
16. Osborn, A.G., Blaser, S.I., and Salzman, K.L., et al., *Diagnostic Imaging: Brain*, Amirys, Inc., Salt Lake City, 2005.
17. Diaz-Marchan, P.J., Hayman, L.A., Carrier, D.A., et al., Computed tomography of closed head injury, in *Neurotrauma*, Narayan, R.K., Wilberger, J.E., and Povlishock, J.T., Eds., McGraw-Hill, New York, 1996, p. 137.
18. Schunk, J.E., Rodgerson, J.D., and Woodward, G.A., The utility of head computed tomographic scanning in pediatric patients with normal neurologic examination in the emergency department. *Pediatr. Emerg. Care*, 12, 160, 1996.
19. Zimmerman, R.A., Bilaniuk, L.T., Gennarelli, T., et al., Cranial computed tomography in diagnosis and management of acute head trauma. *Am. J. Radiol.*, 131, 27, 1978.
20. Lee, J.P. and Wang, A.D., Posttraumatic basal ganglia hemorrhage: Analysis of 52 patients with emphasis on the final outcome. *J. Trauma*, 31, 376, 1991.
21. Zimmerman, R.A. and Bilaniuk, L.T., Computed tomographic staging of traumatic epidural bleeding. *Radiology*, 144, 809, 1982.
22. Yilmazlar, S., Kocaeli, H., Dogan, S., et al., Traumatic epidural haematomas of non-arterial origin: Analysis of 30 consecutive cases. *Acta Neurochir. (Wein)*, 147, 1241, 2005.
23. Bullock, M.R., Chesnut, R., Ghajar, J., et al., Surgical management of acute subdural hematomas. *Neurosurgery*, 58 (3 Suppl.), S16, 2006.
24. Reed, D., Robertson, W.D., Graeb, D.A., et al., Acute subdural hematomas: Atypical CT findings. *Am. J. Neuroradiol.*, 7, 417, 1986.
25. Osborn, A.G., *Diagnostic Neuroradiology*, Mosby, St. Louis, 1994.
26. Greene, K.A., Marciano, F.F., Johnson, B.A., et al., Impact of traumatic subarachnoid hemorrhage on outcome in nonpenetrating head injury. Part I: A proposed computerized tomography grading scale. *J. Neurosurg.*, 83, 445, 1995.
27. Zimmerman, R.A., Craniocerebral trauma, in *Cranial MRI and CT*, 4th edition, Lee, S.H., Rao, K.C.V.G., and Zimmerman, R.A., Eds., McGraw-Hill, New York, 1999, p. 413.
28. LeRoux, P.D., Haglund, M.M., Newell, D.W., et al., Intraventricular hemorrhage in blunt head trauma: An analysis of 43 cases. *Neurosurgery*, 31, 678, 1992.
29. Abraszko, R.A., Zurynski, Y.A., and Dorsch, N.W., The significance of traumatic intraventricular hemorrhage in severe head injury. *Br. J. Neurosurg.*, 9, 769, 1995.
30. Bakshi, R., Kamran, S., Kinkel, P.R., et al., Fluid-attenuated inversion-recovery MR imaging in acute and subacute cerebral intraventricular hemorrhage. *Am. J. Neuroradiol.*, 20, 629, 1999.
31. Gentry, L.R., Head trauma, in *Magnetic Resonance Imaging of the Brain and Spine*, 3rd edition, Atlas, S.W., Ed., Lippincott, Williams & Wilkins, Philadelphia, PA, 2001, p. 1069.
32. Groswasser, Z., Reider-Groswasser, I., Soroker, N., et al., Magnetic resonance imaging in head injured patients with normal late computed tomography scans. *Surg. Neurol.*, 27, 331, 1987.
33. Hammoud, D.A. and Wasserman, B.A., Diffuse axonal injuries: Pathophysiology and imaging. *Neuroimaging Clin. N. Am.*, 12, 205, 2002.
34. Katz, D.I. and Alexander, M.P., Traumatic brain injury: Predicting course of recovery in outcome for patients admitted to rehabilitation. *Arch. Neurol.*, 51, 661, 1994.
35. Marshall, L.F., Marshall, S.B., Klauber, M.R., et al., A new classification of head injury based on computerized tomography. *J. Neurosurg.*, 75, S14, 1991.
36. Johnson, P.L., Eckerd, D.A., Chason, D.P., et al., Imaging of acquired cerebral herniations. *Neuroimaging Clin. N. Am.*, 12, 217, 2002.
37. Koo, A.H. and LaRoque, R.I., Evaluation of head trauma by computed tomography. *Radiology*, 123, 345, 1977.
38. Paterakis, K., Karantanas, A.H., Konnos, A., et al., Outcome of patients with diffuse axonal injury: The significance and prognostic value of MRI in the acute phase. *J. Trauma*, 49, 1071, 2000.
39. Atlas, S.W., *Magnetic Resonance Imaging of the Brain and Spine*, Raven Press, New York, 1991.
40. Lu, H., Nagae-Poetscher, L.M., Golay, X., et al., Routine clinical brain MRI sequences for use at 3.0 Tesla. *J. Magn. Reson. Imaging*, 22, 13, 2005.
41. Gentry, L.R., Head trauma, in *Magnetic Resonance Imaging of the Brain and Spine*, 3rd edition, Atlas, S.W., Ed., Lippincott, Williams & Wilkins, Philadelphia, PA, 2002, p. 1059.

42. Noguchi, K., Seto, H., Kamisaki, Y., et al., Comparison of fluid-attenuated inversion-recovery MRI imaging with CT of a simulated model of acute subarachnoid hemorrhage. *A.J.N.R. Am. J. Neuroradiol.*, 21, 923, 2000.

43. Adams, J.H., Head injury, in *Greenfield's Neuropathology*, 4th edition, Adams, J.H., Corsellis, J.A.N., and Duchen, L.W., Eds., John Wiley & Sons, New York, 1984, p. 85.

44. Hankins, L., Taber, K.H., Yeakley, J., et al., Magnetic resonance imaging in head injury, in *Neurotrauma*, Narayan, R.K., Wilberger, J.E., and Povlishock, J.T., Eds., McGraw-Hill, New York, 1996, p. 151.

45. Gentry, L.R., Thompson, B., and Godersky, J.C., Trauma to the corpus callosum: MR features. *Am. J. Neuroradiol.*, 9, 1129, 1988.

46. Aguas, J., Begue, R., and Dies, J., Brainstem injury diagnosed by MRI. An epidemiologic and prognostic reappraisal. *Neurocirugia (Astur)*, 16, 14, 2005.

47. Chung, S.M., Fenton, G.A., Schmidt, J.G., et al., Trauma to the cranial nerves and brainstem, in *Neurotrauma*, Narayan, R.K., Wilberger, J.E., and Povlishock, J.T., Eds., McGraw-Hill, New York, 1996, p. 621.

48. Barkovich, A.J. and Atlas, S.W., Magnetic resonance imaging of intracranial hemorrhage. *Radiol. Clin. N. Am.*, 26, 801, 1988.

49. Singer, M.B., Atlas, S.W., and Drayer, B.P., Subarachnoid space disease: Diagnosis with fluid-attenuated inversion-recovery MR imaging and comparison with gadolinium-enhanced spin-echo MR imaging— blinded reader study. *Radiology*, 208, 417, 1998.

50. Wardlaw, J.M. and Statham, P.F., How often is haemosiderin not visible on routine MRI following traumatic intracerebral hemorrhage? *Neuroradiology*, 42, 81, 2000.

51. Gomori, J.M. and Grossman, R.I., Mechanisms responsible for the MR appearance and evolution of intracranial hemorrhage. *Radiology*, 161, 364, 1986.

52. Zimmerman, R.A., Bilaniuk, L.T., Hackney, D.B., et al., Head injury: Early results of comparing CT and high-field MR. *Am. J. Neuroradiol.*, 7, 757, 1986.

53. Gomori, J.M., Grossman, R.I., Bilaniuk, L.T., et al., High-field MR imaging of superficial siderosis of the central nervous system. *J. Comput. Assist. Tomgr.*, 9, 972, 1985.

54. Zimmerman, R.A., Bilaniuk, L.T., Grossman, R.I., et al., Resistive NMR of intracranial hematomas. *Neuroradiology*, 27, 16, 1985.

55. Alemany Ripoll, M., Stenborg, A., Sonninen, P., et al., Detection and appearance of interparenchymal hematomas of the brain at 1.5 T with spin-echo, FLAIR and GE sequences. Poor relationship to the age of the hematoma. *Neuroradiology*, 46, 435, 2004.

56. Gentry, L.R., Thompson, B., and Godersky, J.C., Trauma to the corpus callosum: MR features. *Am. J. Neuroradiol.*, 9, 1129, 1988.

57. Holbourn, A.H.S., The mechanics of brain injuries. *Br. Med. Bull.*, 3, 147, 1945.

58. Gieron, M.A., Korthals, J.K., and Riggs, C.D., Diffuse axonal injury without direct head trauma and with delayed onset of coma. *Pediatr. Neurol.*, 19, 382, 1998.

59. Voller, B., Benke, T., Benedetto, K., et al., Neuropsychological, MRI and EEG findings after very mild traumatic brain injury. *Brain Inj.*, 13, 821, 1999.

60. Ezaki, Y., Tsutsumi, K., Morikawa, M., et al., Role of diffusion-weighted magnetic resonance imaging in diffuse axonal injury. *Acta Radiol.*, 47, 773, 2006.

61. Kinoshita, T., Moritani, T., Hiwatashi, A., et al., Conspicuity of diffuse axonal injury lesions on diffusion-weighted MR imaging. *Eur. J. Radiol.*, 56, 5, 2005.

62. Inglese, M., Makani, S., Johnson, G., et al., Diffuse axonal injury in mild traumatic brain injury: A diffusion tensor imaging study. *J. Neurosurg.*, 103, 298, 2005.

63. Tomaiuolo, F., Worsley, K.J., Lerch, J., et al., Changes in white matter in long-term survivors of severe non-missile traumatic brain injury: A computational analysis of magnetic resonance images. *J. Neurotrauma*, 22, 76, 2005.

64. Ariza, M., Serra-Grabulosa, J.M., Junque, C., et al., Hippocampal head atrophy after traumatic brain injury. *Neuropsychologia*, 44, 1956, 2006.

65. Tasker, R.C., Salmond, C.H., Westland, A.G., et al., Head circumference and brain and hippocampal volume after severe traumatic brain injury in childhood. *Pediatr. Res.*, 58, 302, 2005.

66. Tomaiuolo, F., Carlesimo, G.A., DiPaola, M., et al., Gross morphology and morphometric sequelae in the hippocampus, fornix and corpus callosum of patients with severe non-missile traumatic brain injury

without macroscopically detectible lesions. A T1-weighted MRI study. *J. Neurol. Neurosurg. Psychiatry*, 75, 1314, 2004.

67. Blatter, D.D., Bigler, E.D., Gale, S.D., et al., MR-based brain and cerebrospinal fluid measurement after traumatic brain injury: Correlation with neuropsychological outcome. *Am. J. Neuroradiol.*, 18, 1, 1997.

68. Zee, C.S., Hovanessian, A., Go, J.L., et al., Imaging of sequelae of head trauma. *Neuroimaging Clin. N. Am.*, 12, 325, 2002.

69. Levin, H.S., Grossman, R.G., Rose, J.E., et al., Long-term neuropsychological outcome of closed head injury. *J. Neurosurg.*, 50, 412, 1979.

70. Benavidez, D.A., Fletcher, J.M., Hannay, H.J., et al., Corpus callosum damage and interhemispheric transfer of information following closed head injury in children. *Cortex*, 35, 315, 1999.

71. Scarabino, T., Giannatempo, G.M., Popolizio, T., et al., 3.0T MRI diagnostic featuers: Comparison with lower magnetic fields, in *High Field Brain MRI: Use in Clinical Practice*, Salvolini, U. and Scarabino, T., Eds., Springer, Berlin, 2006, p. 10.

72. Giugni, E., Luccichenti, G., Hagberg, G.E., et al., High-field neuroimaging in traumatic brain injury, in *High Field Brain MRI: Use in Clinical Practice*, Salvolini, U. and Scarabino, T., Eds., Springer, Berlin, 2006, p. 169.

73. Bernestein, M.A., Houston, J., Lin, C., et al., High-resolution intracranial and cervical MRA at 3.0T: Technical considerations and initial experience. *Magn. Reson. Med.*, 46, 955, 2001.

74. Shin, Y.B., Kim, S.J., Kim, I.J., et al., Voxel-based statistical analysis of cerebral blood flow using Tc-99m ECD brain SPECT in patients with traumatic brain injury: Group and individual analyses. *Brain Inj.*, 20, 661, 2006.

75. Ricker, J.H. and Arenth, P.N., Functional neuroimaging of TBI, in *Brain Injury Medicine: Principles and Practice*, Zasler, N.D., Katz, D.I., and Zafonte, R.D., Eds., Demos, New York, 2007, p. 149.

76. Audenaert, K., Jensen, H.M.L., Otte, A., et al., Imaging of mild traumatic brain injury using 57 CO and 99m Tc HMPAO SPECT as compared to other diagnostic procedures. *Med. Sci. Monit.*, 9, 112, 2003.

77. van Laere, K.J., Warwick, J., Versijpt, J., et al., Analysis of clinical brain SPECT data based on anatomic standardization and reference to normal data: An ROC-based comparison of visual, semiquantitative, and voxel-based methods. *J. Nucl. Med.*, 43, 458, 2002.

78. Anderson, K.E., Taber, K.H., and Hurley, R.A., Functional imaging, in *Textbook of Traumatic Brain Injury*, Silver, J.N., McAllister, T.W., and Yudofsky, S.C., Eds., American Psychiatric Press, Washington, D.C., 2005, p. 107.

79. Gowda, N.K., Agrawal, D., Bal, C., et al., Technetium Tc-99m ethyl cysteinate dimer brain single-photon emission CT in mild traumatic brain injury: A prospective study. *A.J.N.R. Am. J. Neuroradiol.*, 27, 447, 2006.

80. Pavel, D., Jobe, T., Devore-Best, S., et al., Viewing the functional consequences of traumatic brain injury by using SPECT. *Brain Cogn.*, 60, 211, 2006.

81. Masdeu, J.C., VanHeertum, R.L., Kleinman, A., et al., Early single photon emission computed tomography in mild head trauma: A controlled study. *J. Neuroimaging*, 4, 177, 1994.

82. Alexander, M.P., In the pursuit of proof of brain damage after whiplash injury (editorial). *Neurology*, 51, 336, 1998.

83. Choksey, M.S., Costa, D.C., Iannotti, F., et al., 99mTc HMPAO SPECT studies in traumatic intracerebral hematoma. *J. Neurol. Neurosurg. Psychiatry*, 54, 6, 1991.

84. Abdel-Dayem, H.M., Sadek, S.A., Kouris, K., et al., Changes in cerebral perfusion after acute head injury: Comparison of CT with Tc-99m HMPAO SPECT. *Radiology*, 165, 221, 1987.

85. Roper, S.N., Mena, I., King, W.A., et al., An analysis of cerebral blood flow in acute closed head injury using technetium-99m-HMPAO-SPECT and computed tomography. *J. Nucl. Med.*, 32, 1684, 1991.

86. Nedd, K., Sfakiankis, G., Ganz, W., et al., 99mTc-HMPAO SPECT of the brain in mild to moderate traumatic brain injury patients: Compared with CT—a prospective study. *Brain Inj.*, 7, 469, 1993.

87. Oder, W., Goldenberg, G., Podreka, I., et al., HMPAO-SPECT in persistent vegetative state after head injury: Prognostic indicator of the likelihood of recovery? *Intensive Care Med.*, 17, 149, 1991.

88. *Daubert v. Merrell Dow*, 509, 579 (U.S. 1993).

89. Ricker, J.H., Functional neuroimaging in medical rehabilitation populations, in *Rehabilitation Medicine*, 4th edition, Delisa, J. and Gans, B., Eds., Lippincott, Williams & Wilkins, Baltimore, 2004, p. 229.

90. Herscovitch, P., Functional brain imaging: Basic principles and application to head trauma, in *Head Injury and the Postconcussive Syndrome*, Rizzo, M. and Tranel, D., Eds., Churchill Livingstone, New York, 1996, p. 89.

91. Dougherty, D.D., Rauch, S.L., and Rosenbaum, J.F., *Essentials of Neuroimaging for Clinical Practice*, American Psychiatric Press, Washington, D.C., 2004.

92. Granacher, R.P., Functional imaging techniques, in *Head Trauma Cases: Law and Medicine*, 2nd edition, Vol. 1, Roberts, A.C., Ed., John Wiley & Sons, New York, 1996, pp. 10–11.

93. *Positron Emission Tomography: Basic Science and Clinical Practice*, Valk, P.E., Bailey, D.L., Townsend, D.W., and Maisey, M.N., Eds., Springer, Berlin, 2003.

94. Ruff, R., Crouch, J.A., Troester, A.I., et al., Selected cases of poor outcome following a minor brain trauma: Comparing neuropsychological and PET assessment. *Brain Inj.*, 8, 297, 1994.

95. Gross, H., Kling, A., Henry, G., et al., Local cerebral glucose metabolism in patients with long-term behavioral and cognitive deficits following mild head injury. *J. Neuropsychiatr. Clin. Neurosci.*, 8, 324, 1996.

96. Fontaine, A., Azouvi, P., Reymy, P., et al., Functional anatomy of neuropsychological deficits after severe traumatic brain injury. *Neurology*, 53, 1963, 1999.

97. Varney, N.R., Pinksont, J.B., and Wu, J.C., Quantitative PET findings in patients with posttraumatic anosmia. *J. Head Trauma Rehabil.*, 16, 253, 2001.

98. Buckner, R.I. and Logan, J.M., Functional neuroimaging methods: PET and fMRI, in *Handbook of Functional Neuroimaging of Cognition*, Cabeza, R. and Kingstone, A., Eds., MIT Press, Cambridge, MA, 2001.

99. Coles, J.P., Fyer, D.T., Smielewski, P., et al., Defining ischemic burden after traumatic brain injury using 15-O PET imaging of cerebral physiology. *J. Cereb. Blood Flow Metabol.*, 24, 191, 2004.

100. Langfitt, T.W., Obrist, W.D., Alavia, A., et al., Computerized tomography, magnetic resonance imaging and positron emission tomography in the study of brain trauma. *J. Neurosurg.*, 64, 760, 1986.

101. Wu, H.M., Huan, S.C., Hattori, M., et al., Selective metabolic reduction in gray matter acutely following human traumatic brain injury. *J. Neurotrauma*, 21, 149, 2004.

102. Springer, C.S., Patlak, C.S., Playka, I., et al., Principles of susceptibility contrast-based functional MRI: The sign of the functional response, in *Functional MRI*, Moonen, C.T. and Bandettini, P.A., Eds., Springer-Verlag, Berlin, 2000, p. 91.

103. Chen, W. and Ogawa, S., Principles of BOLD functional MRI, in *Functional MRI*, Moonen, C.T. and Bandettini, P.A., Eds., Springer-Verlag, Berlin, 2000, p. 103.

104. Weisskoff, R.M., Basic theoretical models of BOLD signal change, in *Functional MRI*, Moonen, C.T. and Bandettini, P.A., Eds., Springer-Verlag, Berlin, 2000, p. 115.

105. Davis, P.C., Seidenwurm, D.J., Brunberg, J.A., et al., American College of Radiology appropriateness criteria: Head trauma. www.guideline.gov, site visited 12/01/06.

106. Perlstein, W.M., Cole, N.A., Demery, J.A., et al., Parametric manipulation of working memory load in traumatic brain injury: Behavioral and neural correlates. *J. Int. Neuropsychol. Soc.*, 10, 724, 2004.

107. Scheibel, R.S., Pearson, D.A., Faria, L.P., et al., An fMRI study of executive functioning after severe diffuse TBI. *Brain Inj.*, 17, 919, 2003.

108. Prigatano, G.P., Johnson, S.C., and Gale, S.D., Neuroimaging correlates of the Halstead Finger Tapping Test several years after posttraumatic brain injury. *Brain Inj.*, 18, 661, 2004.

109. McAllister, T.W., Flashman, L.A., McDonald, B.C., et al., Mechanisms of working memory dysfunction after mild and moderate TBI: Evidence from functional MRI and neurogenetics. *J. Neurotrauma*, 23, 1450, 2006.

110. Brandão, L.A. and Domingues, R.C., *MR Spectroscopy of the Brain*, Lippincott, Williams & Wilkins, Philadelphia, PA, 2004.

111. Kothari, S., Prognosis after severe TBI: A practical, evidence-based approach, in *Brain Injury Medicine: Principles and Practice*, Zasler, N., Katz, D.I., and Zafonte, R.D., Eds., Demos, New York, 2007, p. 169.

112. Friedman, S., Brooks, W., Jung, R., et al., Proton MR spectroscopic findings correspond to neuropsychological function in traumatic brain injury. *Am. J. Neuroradiol.*, 19, 1879, 1998.

113. Choe, B., Suh, T., Choi, K., et al., Neuronal dysfunction in patients with closed head injury evaluated by *in vivo* 1H magnetic resonance spectroscopy. *Invest. Radiol.*, 30, 502, 1995.

114. Garnett, M., Blemire, A., Rajagopalan, R., et al., Evidence for cellular damage in normal appearing white matter correlates with injury severity in patients following traumatic brain injury. *Res. Spectroscop. Study Brain*, 123, 1403, 2000.

115. Holshouser, V.A., Tong, K.A., and Ashwal, S., Proton MR spectroscopic imaging depicts diffuse axonal injury in children with traumatic brain injury. *A.J.N.R. Am. J. Neuroradiol.*, 26, 1276, 2005.

116. Sinson, G., Bagley, L.J., Cecil, K.M., et al., Magnetization transfer imaging in proton MR spectroscopy in the evaluation of axonal injury: Correlation with clinical outcome after traumatic brain injury. *A.J.N.R. Am. J. Neuroradiol.*, 22, 143, 2001.

117. Sumich, A.I., Nelson, M.R., and McDeavitt, J.T., TBI: A pediatric perspective, in *Brain Injury Medicine: Principles and Practice*, Zasler, N., Katz, D.I., and Zafonte, R.D., Eds., Demos, New York, 2007, p. 305.

118. Luerssen, T.G., Claubert, M.R., and Marshall, L.F., Outcome from head injury related to patient's age: A longitudinal prospective study of adult and pediatric head injury. *J. Neurosurg.*, 68, 409, 1988.

119. Eisele, J.A., Kegler, S.R., Trent, R.B., et al., Nonfatal traumatic brain injury-related hospitalizations of very young children—15 states, 1999. *J. Head Trauma Rehabil.*, 21, 537, 2006.

120. Oehmichen, M., Meissner, C., and Saternus, K.S., Fall or shaken: Traumatic brain injury in children caused by falls or abusive home—a review on biomechanics and diagnosis. *Neuropediatrics*, 36, 240, 2005.

121. Barkovich, A.J., *Pediatric Neuroimaging*, 4th edition, Lippincott, Williams & Wilkins, Philadelphia, PA, 2005, p. 190.

122. Kochanek, P.M., Pediatric traumatic brain injury: Quo vadis? *Dev. Neurosci.*, 28, 244, 2006.

123. Menkes, J.H., Commentary: Subdural hematoma, nonaccidental head injury or . . . ? *Eur. J. Paediatr. Neurol.*, 5, 175, 2001.

124. Parizel, P.N., Ceulemans, B., Laridon, A., et al., Cortical hypoxic-ischemic brain damage in shaken-baby (shaken impact) syndrome: Value of diffusion-weighted MRI. *Pediatr. Radiol.*, 33, 868, 2003.

125. Shugerman, R.P., Paez, A., Grossman, D.C., et al., Epidural hemorrhage: Is it abuse? *Pediatrics*, 97, 664, 1996.

126. Hasler, L.J., Phil, M., Arcinue, E., et al., Evidence from proton magnetic resonance spectroscopy for a metabolic cascade of neuronal damage in shaken baby syndrome. *Pediatrics*, 99, 4, 1997.

127. Atlas, S.W., Ed., *Magnetic Resonance Imaging of the Brain and Spine*, 3rd edition, Lippincott, Williams & Wilkins, Philadelphia, PA, 2002.

128. Goldstein, M.A. and Price, B.H., Magnetic resonance imaging, in *Essentials of Neuroimaging for Clinical Practice*, Doughtery, D.D., Rauch, S.L., and Rosenbaum, J.F., Eds., American Psychiatric Press, Washington, D.C., 2004, p. 21.

129. Mesulam, M.-M., *Principles of Behavioral and Cognitive Neurology*, 2nd edition, F.A. Davis, Philadelphia, PA, 2000.

130. Hughes, J.R., EEG in *Clinical Practice*, Butterworth Publishers, New York, 1982.

131. Williams, S.D. and Denny-Brown, D., Cerebral electrical changes in experimental concussion. *Brain*, 64, 223, 1941.

132. Theilen, H.J., Ragller, N., Tscho, U., et al., Electroencephalogram silence ratio for early outcome prognosis in severe head trauma. *Crit. Care Med.*, 28, 3522, 2000.

133. Liguori, G., Foggia, L., Buonaguro, A., et al., EEG findings in minor head trauma as a clue for indication to CT scan. *Child's Nerv. Syst.*, 5, 160, 1989.

134. Seubert, C.N. and Mahla, M.E., Neurologic monitoring in the neurointensive care unit, in *Textbook of Neurointensive Care*, Layon, A.J., Gabrielli, A., and Friedman, W.A., Eds., W.B. Saunders, Philadelphia, PA, 2004, p. 619.

135. Jordan, K.G., Continuous EEG and evoked potential monitoring in the neuroscience intensive care unit. *J. Clin. Neurophysiol.*, 10, 445, 1993.

136. Guerit, J.N., The usefulness of EEG, exogenous evoked potentials and cognitive evoked potentials in the acute stage of post-anoxic and posttraumatic coma. *Acta Neurol. Belg.*, 100, 229, 2000.

137. Gotman, J., Automatic detection of seizures and spikes. *J. Clin. Neurophysiol.*, 16, 130, 1999.

138. Lew, H.L., Lee, E.H., Pan, S.S., et al., Electrophysiological assessment techniques: Evoked potentials and electroencephalography, in *Brain Injury Medicine: Principles and Practice*, Zasler, N.D., Katz, D.I., and Zafonte, R.D., Eds., Demos, New York, 2007, p. 157.

139. McCarley, R.W., Human electrophysiology and basic sleep mechanisms, in The American Psychiatric Publishing Textbook of Neuropsychiatry and Clinical Neurosciences, Yudofsky, S.C. and Hales, R.E., Eds., American Psychiatric Press, Washington, D.C., 2002, p. 43.

6 Standardized Neurocognitive Assessment of Traumatic Brain Injury

INTRODUCTION

Owing to the complexities of potential cognitive injury following traumatic brain injury (TBI), it is important to quantify the measurement of cognitive status following TBI. This is necessary in order to document the deficits of the patient and necessary in order to develop a comprehensive treatment plan for the patient. For instance, without baseline memory testing, how does one document memory change after prescription of cognitive enhancers? This chapter focuses on the strengths and weaknesses of neuropsychological assessment. Our neuropsychology colleagues have contributed greatly to the understanding of cognitive measurement. Adolf Meyer[1] also contributed to the consistency of the examination of human mental status. When the formal mental status examination was introduced by Meyer at Johns Hopkins University Medical School in 1918, the procedure became the *sine qua non* for the training of American psychiatrists to this day. However, its inherent weakness is its lack of standardization, and it contains no significant reproducible metrics. On the other hand, its qualitative power is immense, and it has been incorporated into the mental examinations of persons with psychiatric diseases in every country in the world where psychiatrists practice. To say that it is not standardized means that it was not empirically tested and it contains neither precise rules for administration nor precise rules for scoring. It is an extensive narrative description of patient behavior based on face-to-face observation by the physician and the application of a few bedside oral tests. It retains significant subjectivity. This examination, while an important part of clinical psychiatry, is not sufficiently quantified to detect the often subtle changes that may occur in the mental status of persons afflicted with TBI. Lord Kelvin has reminded us of the importance of measurement,[2] and his admonition applies to cognitive examination as well:

> When you can measure what you are speaking about, and express it in numbers, you know something about it; but when you cannot measure it, when you cannot express it in numbers, your knowledge is of a meager and unsatisfactory kind: it may be the beginning of knowledge, but you have scarcely in your thoughts, advanced to the stage of science.[2]

Psychiatrists have applied recently many qualitative questionnaires and standardized forms for recording various aspects of mental status including depression, anxiety, psychosis, and others.[3] These are widely useful when applied to the longitudinal assessment of patients receiving treatment with antidepressants, antipsychotics, and in various research paradigms where the study of new psychiatric medicines is undertaken during phase II and phase III clinical studies before marketing. Table 6.1 outlines the strengths and weaknesses of these examinations. The reader requiring further information or the direct use of forms such as the Beck,[3] Hamilton,[3] and others should consult with reference 3.

TABLE 6.1

Strengths and Weaknesses of Brief, Structured Mental Status Examinations

Strengths
- Brief and nondemanding for the patients.
- Reveal little practice effect.
- Require little formal training for their use.
- Physicians find them familiar as they derive from traditional exams.
- Uniformity is present in administration and scoring.
- Quantified results show comparisons over time.

Weaknesses
- Questions are easy to answer and thus producing high false-negative rates.
- Low intelligence, race, and old age lead to high false-positive rates.
- Differentiate organic from functional disturbances poorly.
- Differentiate acute from chronic organicity poorly.

It is recommended that the physician undertaking neuropsychiatric examination of patients following TBI utilizes the services of a psychologist or neuropsychologist expert and skilled in the application and interpretation of standardized neuropsychological test instruments. Recently, psychological testing has been exhaustively reviewed by respected research and clinical psychologists.[4] These authors reviewed data from more than 125 meta-analyses covering test validity. Of these 800 samplings examined multimethod assessment and the authors came to four general conclusions regarding psychological testing within psychological assessment: (1) psychological test validity is strong and compelling, (2) psychological test validity is comparable to medical test validity, (3) distinct assessment methods provide unique sources of information, and (4) clinicians who rely exclusively on interviews are prone to incomplete understandings. On the other hand, certain caveats are required with the use of neuropsychological testing. Unlike the breadth of clinical medicine techniques, neuropsychologists are hung on their own laboratory assessment petard. Their entire profession rests on the use of neuropsychological testing alone to confirm their conclusions about a person's neuropsychological mental state. It must be remembered by the physician that neuropsychological tests are human effort dependent and no different in purpose than a medical laboratory test. A physician using the services of a neuropsychologist in a TBI assessment should not accept neuropsychological test data unless the person being examined has been subjected to two tests of cognitive distortion at a minimum, and three tests of cognitive distortion are recommended to verify that optimum effort was exercised by the patient during examination. The neuropsychologist is at a distinct disadvantage in clinical assessment compared to the neuropsychiatric physician. We have at our disposal a comprehensive history including past medical history, social history, and the genetic history found within families. The physical and neurological examinations afford us an opportunity to collect data in a very personal nonlaboratory fashion. Structural neuroimaging cannot be controlled in any way by the patient with the exception of artifact due to bodily movement. Functional imaging is subject to some control by the patient in terms of what drugs they may have taken, what mental stimuli they perform during scanning, or whether or not they have a concurrent psychiatric illness. Electrophysiological data collected during the neuropsychiatric examination also has a low likelihood of influence by the patient being examined.

BASIC STATISTICS OF PSYCHOLOGICAL TESTING

Many physicians have a poor understanding of the fundamental mathematical principles involved in the analysis and numerical representation of psychological measurements. A simple review of these principles will remove much of the aura of psychological testing and help the examiner understand

TABLE 6.2

Glossary of Psychological Testing Terms

Term	Meaning
Deviation IQs	Standard IQ scores have a mean of 100 and a standard deviation of 15 (e.g., WAIS-III IQ scores).
Ecological validity	Predictive relationship between neuropsychologist test performance and real-world function (e.g., does an IQ test predict driving ability?)
Median	The exact midpoint of a group of numerical data or scores.
Percentile	The point on a distribution at or below which there is a given percentage of individuals.
Practice effect	Increases in test performance resulting from having practiced on preceding tests (e.g., if a woman takes the WAIS-III in March, will her verbal IQ increase slightly if she retakes the test the following May?).
Reliability	A special type of correlation that measures consistency of observations or scores (e.g., will a person produce the same verbal IQ on the WAIS-III if it is administered again 9 months apart?)
SAT scores	Standard scores having a mean of 500 and a standard deviation of 100.
Sensitivity	This refers to the probability of correctly detecting abnormal function in an impaired individual (e.g., abnormal memory function in an injured person with abnormal memory).
Specificity	This refers to the probability of correctly identifying a normal person with normal function in the domain being tested (e.g., normal memory ability in a normal person).
Standard deviation	A measure of the extent to which scores cluster around the mean.
Standardization	Uniformity of procedure in administering and scoring the test.
Standard scores	Scores expressed in standard deviation units.
Stanine scores	Divides the normal curve into nine equal units, each interval represents 1/2 standard deviation; each interval is numbered 1–9 (e.g., a verbal IQ of 100 would lie within a stanine score of 5).
T-scores	Standard scores having a mean of 50 and a standard deviation of 10 (e.g., MMPI-2 scores).
Validity	The extent to which measurements are useful in making decisions relevant for a given purpose (e.g., does the WAIS-III validity measure verbal IQ?).
Z-score	The number of standard deviation units that a particular score is above or below the mean of the distribution.

the simple logic behind psychological measurement as it has been developed by our psychological colleagues. Table 6.2 outlines common definitions used within the language of psychological testing. Upon review of Figure 6.1, it can be seen that certain probabilities exist within the normal distribution. For instance, approximately 68% (68.26%) of a normally distributed population lies between ± 1 standard deviation (SD) of the mean of that distribution. If one were reviewing Wechsler IQ scores, it can be seen that 68% of the normally distributed population would have an IQ that lies between the standard scores of 85 and 115 (± 1 SD; SD = 15). Also by reviewing Figure 6.1, it can be noticed that a deviation IQ of 130 on the Wechsler-III corresponds to a T-score of 70 or a percentile of approximately 97. The reader is cautioned that data points in Figure 6.1 cannot be used to equate scores on one test to scores on another. For instance, a T-score of 70 on scale 2 of the Minnesota Multiphasic Personality Inventory (MMPI) means one thing, whereas a deviation full-scale IQ of 130 on the Wechsler Adult Intelligence Scale-III (WAIS-III) means another. Both scores on these testes are 2 SDs above their respective group means, but they do not represent "equal" standings because the scores were obtained from different samples within the individual normative data for the tests.[5] However, the examiner clearly can use the data in Figure 6.1 to compare the same test to itself. For instance, if within the context of a brain injury evaluation a man produces a verbal IQ of 117 on the WAIS-III for his rehabilitation psychologist in August but a verbal IQ of 94 when he is examined by a neuropsychologist the following November; clearly an explanation for this difference must be sought. One would not expect this variance by chance alone. In fact, if the reader refers below, it can be seen that a practice effect would be expected, and one would expect the neuropsychologist to have found a slightly higher verbal IQ in most instances, unless there has been brain function deterioration from

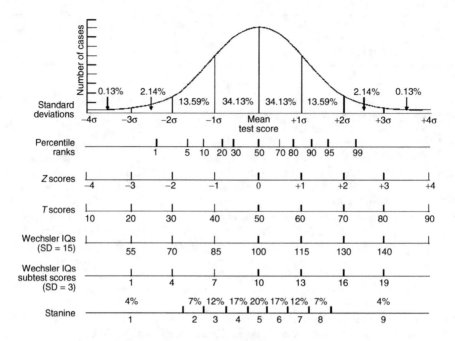

FIGURE 6.1 Relationship of the normal curve to various types of standard scores.

disease, intercurrent psychiatric illness, use of medications, poor performance, faking, or other factors. The same can be said for an individual producing a T-score of 62 on the depression scale of the MMPI-2 (scale 2) and later producing a T-score of 115 on the same MMPI-2 scale when examined by a psychiatrist 6 weeks later. Clearly, this difference must be explained, and obviously it is not expected unless there has been an interval change in the person's mood between the two testings, or as we shall see in Chapters 7 and 9, the person may be symptom magnifying or faking at the second examination. The use of standardized test data is a powerful tool for making intertest comparisons over a time interval. For a more precise analysis of the statistics of psychological testing, refer to comprehensive texts.[5–10]

ADULT NEUROCOGNITIVE ASSESSMENT

As described earlier, neuropsychologists have formed almost the entirety of their profession around the use of neuropsychological tests. There is a majority component of laboratory assessment to their profession. Thus, another word of caution is needed when using neuropsychological tests in neuro-psychiatric assessment. This chapter will delineate many of the emerging neuroanatomical and neuroimaging bases for various cognitive domains such as attention, memory, language, etc. Almost all neuropsychological test instruments in current use throughout the world were developed before the developing marriage of cognitive neuroscience and functional brain imaging. Therefore, there is limited empirical or historical data to enable neuropsychologists to delineate a functional neuroanat-omy based upon neuropsychological testing alone. In fact, almost all neuropsychological tests have no well-defined or empirically tested functional neuroanatomical basis. Therefore, it is probably best to think of neuropsychological tests as measuring a particular psychological function. To attempt to clinically correlate a particular neuropsychological test result with a known functional neuroanatom-ical area lends credibility to neuropsychological assessment where it may not be justified. As stated above, neuropsychological testing forms a core component of the neuropsychiatric assessment of TBI. However, the examiner must be well versed in the limitations of neuropsychological test data when data are applied neuropsychiatrically (see Table 6.3).

TABLE 6.3

Various Methods Used for Neuropsychological Assessment

- Batteries for general use (e.g., Halstead–Reitan Test Battery, Luria–Nebraska Neuropsychological Battery, and NEPSY)[11–13]
- Analytical approach (a flexible San Diego Neuropsychological Test Battery[14] and eclectic use of tests of intelligence, visual perception, semantics, literacy, language, event memory, reasoning, and behavior)[14,15]
- The Boston process approach[15]
- The Iowa–Benton School of Neuropsychological Assessment[16]
- The Lezak approach[8]

MEASURING COGNITIVE DISTORTION

This section will devote itself to examining cognitive distortion[17] during TBI examination; the reader should be aware that there are three ways that any person can distort the results of a medical examination. These include (1) distortion of or falsifying psychological symptoms and signs, (2) distortion of or falsifying cognitive symptoms and signs, and (3) distortion of or falsifying physical symptoms and signs.[19] Cognitive distortion can be performed by slowing performance speed during the timed portions of neuropsychological testing. Many neuropsychological tests are extremely sensitive to the timed portions, and by deliberate slowing, the person will appear far more impaired than he/she actually is. It is also possible to provide false responses, such as during memory tests, other factually based tests, or during the administration of intellectual assessments. Since one can never perform better than one's theoretical maximal ability, an individual's test performance depends on cooperation and motivation to produce optimal effort and optimal test answers. On the other hand, any person can reduce effort and motivation to function below his theoretical upper limit. Therefore, the neuropsychiatric examiner should ensure that the psychologist or neuropsychologist providing testing services examines the individual carefully for cognitive effort at the time the person is tested.[18] It is also important that tests used to measure cognitive effort be based on binomial probability theory or forced-choice recognition techniques. Tests not based on binomial probability or forced-choice recognition are less sensitive to questionable effort than tests that are based on these paradigms.[20] Table 6.4 lists suggested tests that may be used to test cognitive effort at the time of neuropsychological assessment. This table is not all inclusive, however.

The fundamental property present in all tests purported to measure cognitive malingering or cognitive effort is that these tests must be easy for even a brain-injured person to pass. If this were not so, the examiner could not distinguish whether persons with mild Alzheimer's disease, TBI, or mild mental retardation were providing adequate effort at the time they were neuropsychologically

TABLE 6.4

Tests Useful for Measuring Neuropsychological Effort

Tests Based on Binomial Probability
- Portland Digit Recognition Test (PDRT)
- Test of Memory Malingering (TOMM)
- Validity Indicator Profile (VIP)
- Victoria Symptom Validity Test (VSVT)
- Word Memory Test (WMT)

Tests Not Based on Binomial Probability
- Dot Counting: Ungrouped Dots
- Dot Counting: Grouped and Ungrouped Dots
- Rey 15-Item Test

tested. The power of tests based on binomial probability is that they push an individual into one of two statistically measured groups. These tests are based on a simple proposition: if the examiner asks a person to make choices between two alternatives, and if a large number of choices are offered, the responses will statistically sort into equally represented populations. For instance, most of us learned during high school algebra that if one flips a two-sided coin into the air 100 times and allows it to land randomly on the floor, approximately 50 heads and 50 tails will appear. This is a two-alternative probability task, and it represents the purest form of the binomial distribution. During cognitive effort testing, the individual is forced to choose between two alternatives, the correct one and the incorrect one. If she properly chooses the correct one most times, her responses will exceed chance (50% probability) by a considerable degree. On the other hand, if she deliberately chooses wrong answers, her responses will dramatically fall below chance levels. If a person is truly confused or brain injured and cannot make a choice between "correct" and "wrong," she will produce a random response by guessing. This will produce approximately 50% correct answers and 50% wrong answers.

Tests not based on the binomial probability theory have a long history of use in neuropsychology. The dot-counting tests were first proposed in 1941, and the Rey 15-Item Test was later proposed in 1964.[21,22] Of these, the most widely used today by psychologists is the Rey 15-Item Test. This is performed with a card that contains 15 visual items. However, there are really only nine items, as the card consists of A, B, C and a, b, c; 1, 2, 3 and I, II, III. The last three items are a square, triangle, and circle. Thus, in reality, the person looks at the card and has to remember only nine items, as two sets are repeated. There is some argument as to the specific cutoff score for an abnormal response. Some define cutoff scores as low as 7, while others define them as 9. Several investigators have reported that this test lacks sensitivity in identifying malingerers or those providing poor effort. Its efficacy to detect feigned memory impairment appears to be limited.[23] No assessment of effort or malingering should be based solely on this test.[24] The dot-counting measures have been found to have a 40% false-negative rate, and thus their use is no longer recommended.[25]

Portland Digit Recognition Test

The Portland Digit Recognition Test (PDRT) is a forced-choice test that is an outgrowth of the earlier Hiscock and Hiscock procedures that required subjects to identify, after a brief delay, which of two five-digit numbers shown on a card was the same as a number seen on a prior card.[26] The PDRT consists of a total of 72 items of digit recognition using an auditory stimulus presentation. Five-digit numbers are orally presented at the rate of one digit per second by the examiner. Following presentation, the subject counts backward aloud until interrupted visually with a 3-by-5 index card containing one distracter number (the false number) and the correct five-digit number. The brilliance of this test is its simplicity. The distracter number is off by only one digit in either the first or last digit. Thus, the person being examined can quickly scan the cards and determine the correct from the noncorrect response. The first 18 trials include 5s of counting backward from 20 before the second card is shown. The second block of 18 trials involves counting backward from 50 for 15s, and the third and fourth blocks of 18 trials both involve counting backward from 100 for 30s. Although 72 trials are conducted, there are only 18 correct target items, and thus 18 items are administered four times. The target items are no different for counting backward from 100 for 30s than the targets for counting backward from 20. Patients are more likely to fake bad when the activity interval increases.[27] For obvious reasons, statistically accurate cutoff scores on tests measuring malingering or effort will not be put into the public domain in this text.

Test of Memory Malingering

The Test of Memory Malingering (TOMM) is used for discriminating between memory-impaired persons and those who are either malingering or providing poor effort for other reasons. The TOMM is a 50-item recognition test that includes two learning trials and a retention trial. During the two learning trials, the patient is shown 50 line drawings (target pictures) of common objects for 3s each, given at 1s intervals. The patient is then shown 50 panels to recognize, one at a time. Each panel contains one of the previously presented target pictures and a new picture (a distracter). The patient is required to select the correct picture (i.e., the picture shown during the learning trial). The same procedure is used on the optional retention trial, except target pictures are not readministered.

To assess effort or malingering, the learning trials alone are usually sufficient. Use of the retention trial (which is optional) adds only a few minutes to the test time and helps corroborate the results. It takes about 15 min to administer the two learning trials. The power of this test lies in the impression to the patient that it is much more difficult than it really is. By administering a large number of visual stimuli, the test leads malingerers to believe that it will be difficult for people with genuine memory impairments, and thus, they intentionally perform poorly. The other major power of the TOMM is that, while it is sensitive to malingering, it is insensitive to a person with true neurological impairment. Almost all individuals with neurological impairment have a remarkably high capacity for storing and retrieving simple pictures of common everyday objects. The validation data of the TOMM include head-injured subjects.[28]

Validity Indicator Profile

The Validity Indicator Profile (VIP) contains 100 nonverbal abstraction items and 78 word definition problems, both of which are presented in a two-choice recognition format. The nonverbal stimuli are presented as an incomplete design matrix very similar to those in Raven's Matrices (see below). These nonverbal items are modifications from the Test of Nonverbal Intelligence (TONI).[29] The test items purposefully vary in difficulty to create the impression to the examinee that this is an ability test. Test response patterns are classified into four groups to reflect the inner actions of effort (high versus low) and motivation (to excel versus to fail). If valid performance results from high effort to excel, it is termed "compliant." If the test scores are in the malingering range, this is reflective of a high effort to perform poorly. There are two intermediate categories that are termed "careless" due to poor effort to respond correctly and "irrelevant" indicating effort to respond incorrectly. Unfortunately, since this test has verbal and nonverbal sections as independent measures, when both are used, it is possible to have a valid response in one measure and an invalid response on the other. There are significant scoring complexities for this test, and it is recommended by the author of this test that a scoring service be used,[30] which can entail some extra cost and probably decreases the routine use of this instrument. This test has been found to have 51% sensitivity for the verbal subtest and 60% sensitivity for the nonverbal subtest.[8]

Victoria Symptom Validity Test

The Victoria Symptom Validity Test (VSVT) includes a total of 48 items, presented in 3 blocks of 16 items each. During each block of 16 items, there is a study trial and a recognition trial. This test is administered visually by computer. During the study trial, a single five-digit number is presented on the screen for 5s. Following the presentation of this number, there is a retention time interval during which the patient views a blank computer screen. This interval is then followed by the recognition trial in which the correct study number is shown and a five-digit distracter number is displayed as well. The patient is asked to choose the number he saw in the study trial. In the second block of 16 items, the retention interval is increased to 10s, and in the third block, the retention interval is increased to 15s.

Much of the power of this test to detect poor effort or malingering lies in the standard instructions. Patients are told that they are "taking a test of memory that requires concentration," and that "people with memory problems often find this test to be difficult." Instructions indicating that the patient may find the items becoming more difficult are given to minimize deception. Research has found that a majority of patients with real memory problems did not make significantly more errors when the retention interval was increased.[31]

Within each trial or block, items are given that appear to be either easy or difficult. For easy items, the study numbers and the distracters share no common digits (unlike the PDRT). Thus, the recognition of any one of the digits in the five digits will allow the patient to make the correct choice. For the difficult items, the distracter is identical to the study number with the exception that the second and third, or third and fourth digits have been transposed. To choose the correct answer on the difficult items, the patient must recall the order of the middle digits. Recognition of the first or last digit will not aid in choosing the right answer. All three blocks contain an equal number of easy and difficult items. Like the PDRT and the TOMM, a person providing poor effort will perform significantly below chance levels, whereas a person providing good effort will perform significantly above chance levels.

Word Memory Test

Philosophically, this test assesses response bias in the context of memory assessment similar to that of the TOMM. Instead of visual symbols of the TOMM, a list of 20 word pairs with strong semantic associations is used and presented orally twice. This is a forced-choice recognition format, and each of the 40 words comprises 20 word pairs with strong semantic similarity such as dog–cat. On the first recognition trial, each target word is paired with another word having a much lower association (e.g., dog–rat) and the subject is not told whether his responses are correct. A second recognition trial is administered, and targets are paired with new foils following a 30 min delay to determine response consistency. After the delayed two-choice recognition, a multiple choice trial is presented with target words within a list of eight words. Paired associate recall is tested next during which the examiner recites the first word (e.g., dog) for the subject to recall its pair (i.e., cat). This is followed by a test of free recall, and after 20 min elapse, a second free recall test is administered.

When Green et al.[32] developed this test, it was devised so that it could be administered individually or by a computer. When it is given in its entirety, the Word Memory Test (WMT) contains separate validity and ability measures, and it produces a gradient of difficulty across these measures. Thus, internally, the performance decrement across tasks provides an additional way for the examiner to determine performance validity.[8] When Green and others tested patients who had sustained clearly documented brain injuries, these injured persons performed better than patients with less severe injuries who were engaged in litigation.[33]

ESTABLISHING A PRE-INJURY COGNITIVE BASELINE

It is very rare for the neuropsychiatric examiner to have pre-injury or premorbid measurements of cognitive capacity in order to draw a comparison between a person's pre-injury cognitive status and her cognitive status following apparent brain injury. Thus, comparison standards must be determined in order to accomplish this task. Comparison standards can be derived directly from population norms, premorbid test data of the individual being examined, historical or demographic information, or indirectly extrapolated from current test findings and observation.[8] While normative standards are available on a population basis for the United States and most other developed countries, the difficulty is knowing where the person being examined fits on the normal curve before injury (see Figure 6.1). It is one thing to know that the mean standard score on an IQ test in the United States is 100 and knowing where the person being examined fits in relation to that cognitive ability indicator premorbidly. Most cognitive abilities distribute normally in the population at large. If one determines that a deficit exists in a specific ability following TBI, that deficit can be assessed directly if there is a normative comparison standard for the ability or by indirect measurement when the examiner compares the present performance of the individual on a neuropsychological test with an estimate of the person's original ability level (this is how it is usually measured in most examinations). Table 6.5 lists various ways and methods for estimating pre-injury mental abilities in order to establish a comparison standard or pre-injury cognitive baseline.

TABLE 6.5

Methods for Estimating Pre-injury Mental Abilities

Demographic tests (after injury)	• Barona Index
	• The Oklahoma Estimate
	• Wilson's Formula
Reading-based tests (after injury)	• National Adult Reading Test
	• North American Adult Reading Test
	• Wechsler Test of Adult Reading
	• Wide Range Achievement Test
Academic or institutional sources (pre-injury data)	• Academic grades
	• ACT scores
	• Armed Services Vocational Aptitude Battery (ASVAB)
	• SAT scores
	• School-based IQ scores

Wilson et al. devised a formula using the demographic variables of age, sex, race, education, and occupation.[34] However, this formula has been found weak and will predict only two-thirds of premorbid Wechsler IQ scores within a 10-point error range. Barona et al. elaborated on the work of Wilson et al. and included variables of geographic region, urban–rural residence, and the handedness of the person into the estimation formula first proposed by Barona et al.[35] They devised three formulae for predicting each of the Wechsler IQ scores directly from these data. They caution that where the premorbid full-scale IQ was above 120 or below 69, serious under- or overestimation errors may occur. Some studies have claimed that at best, the Wilson and Barona estimates misclassify more than half of patients, which of course is no better than a chance level prediction or by guessing. Krull et al. used demographic variables similar to those of Wilson and Barona, but they combined these with either the vocabulary or picture completion test scores from the Wechsler IQ scales to estimate premorbid IQ.[36]

From Table 6.5 it can be seen that there may be data available from pre-injury sources to enable the examiner to make a direct comparison between post-injury neuropsychological test data and pre-injury test data. For instance, academic grades may be available. However, grades are highly motivation-dependent and extremely variable from school system to school system and from state to state. Thus, they are a marginal estimate of a person's cognitive capacity. More accurate information can be drawn from population-based standardized tests such as ACT scores and SAT scores. Some individuals who sustain a TBI have served in the U.S. military. In those cases, the Armed Services Vocational Aptitude Battery (ASVAB) is a useful source for determining pre-injury cognitive capacity. A section of this battery directly measures cognitive capacity in a fashion similar to standardized intelligence tests. Also, for individuals who have learning disabilities or other impairments, a referral may have been made to school authorities, and an individualized educational plan (IEP) may have been developed. In those instances, cognitive measurements may have been made, and the school-based IQ scores may be available within the academic records. If they can be found for individuals with pre-injury impairments, this would be the most accurate normative data available from which to draw comparisons between after injury and before injury abilities.

After injury, a number of tests estimating pre-injury cognitive ability have been developed. In general, these tests rely on measurement of post-injury reading ability. Reading ability is considered to be a highly crystallized cognitive function that changes little even in the face of TBI, unless the injury has occurred as a result of a depressed skull fracture or a penetrating wound directly into anatomical areas subserving reading. Vocabulary and related verbal skill scores may provide the best estimates of the general premorbid cognitive ability level if pre-injury measures are not available. However, the vocabulary subscale on the Wechsler IQ test requires the patient to produce

TABLE 6.6
Classification of Ability Levels

Classification	Z-Score	Percent Under Normal Curve	Lower Limit of Percentile
Very superior	+2.0 and >	2.2	98
Superior	+1.3 to 2.0	6.7	91
High average	+0.6 to 1.3	16.1	75
Average	±0.6	50.0	25
Low average	−0.6 to −1.3	16.1	9
Borderline	−1.3 to −2.0	6.7	2
Retarded	−2.0 and <	2.2	—

oral definitions. Therefore, this test is more vulnerable to brain damage than verbal tests that can be answered in a word or two, or those that call on practical experience or recognition, such as in the reading tests noted below. Moreover, if the patient's brain injury is focally to the dominant cerebral hemisphere, vocabulary ability may be impaired as well. In an attempt to improve upon vocabulary-based methods, the use of reading scores derived by the Wide Range Achievement Test (WRAT), National Adult Reading Test (NART), and Wechsler Test of Adult Reading (WTAR) have been used. The original NART was first standardized on British subjects, but there is now a North American version available (NAART). The very recent Wechsler Test of Adult Reading is probably superior to both the WRAT and the NART because, similar to the Oklahoma estimate, the WTAR is based upon reading measures and demographics, and also has been standardized on TBI patients. The classification of both pre-injury and post-injury ability levels can be done in many fashions. Lezak[5,8] argues that the classification of ability levels should be based on Z-scores or percentiles as one way to avoid the many difficulties inherent in test score reporting. Table 6.6 lists classification of ability levels based upon Z-scores and percentile ranges (see Figure 6.1 for further analysis).

National Adult Reading Test

The National Adult Reading Test (NART)[37] has been restandardized against the Wechsler Adult Intelligence Scale-Revised (WAIS-R).[39] This restandardization allows the reading score taken from the NART to be used to predict the WAIS-R full-scale, verbal, and performance IQs, which are predicted from the number of errors made on the NART. This allows the estimation of a predicted full-scale IQ within the interval of 69 to 131. If a person has a language disturbance following a brain injury, the NART may underestimate premorbid ability. Therefore, patients who are aphasic, dyslexic, or who have articulatory or visual acuity defects probably should not be screened using this instrument.[38] Moreover, the standardization sample did not include subjects of more than 70 years of age. Be aware that the WAIS-R is outdated and supplanted by the WAIS-III (see below).

Reading Subtest of the Wide Range Achievement Test-4

The WRAT-III has been standardized on thousands of persons across the United States in nearly half of the 48 continental states and Alaska. The data were compiled using a stratified sampling of nearly 5000 individuals. This test can be used to measure reading recognition levels in persons aged 5–75 years.[39] The first Wide Range Achievement Test was developed as an unpublished assessment instrument 70 years ago when the original author, Joseph F. Jastak, a psychologist, created three tests to augment the pioneering work that was being done by David Wechsler on the Wechsler-Bellvue Scales. The Wide Range Achievement Test, 4th edition (WRAT-4) supplants the WRAT-III. Several new features have been added to the WRAT-4. These include updated norms and an entirely new measure of reading achievement, Sentence Comprehension, has been added.

This enhances the scope of the content measured and meets a need often expressed by users of previous editions. The WRAT-4 includes the following four subtests: (1) Word Reading to measure letter and word decoding through letter identification and word recognition; (2) Sentence Comprehension to measure an individual's ability to gain meaning from words and to comprehend ideas and information contained in sentences; (3) Spelling to measure an individual's ability to encode sounds into written form through the use of a dictated spelling format containing both letters and words; and (4) Math Computation to measure an individual's ability to perform basic mathematical computations through counting, identifying numbers, solving simple oral problems, and calculating written mathematics problems.[91] For purposes of developing a pre-injury cognitive baseline, only word reading is used. The other three subtests are used with word reading when the examiner wishes to understand the level of academic development of the person being tested.

Wechsler Test of Adult Reading

The Wechsler Test of Adult Reading (WTAR) was developed specifically to provide clinicians with an assessment tool for estimating premorbid intellectual functioning of adults ages 16–89. It has been developed and conormed with the WAIS-III and the Wechsler Memory Scale-III (WMS-III). This codevelopment of the WTAR with the WAIS-III and the WMS-III provided data for direct comparison between predicted and actual intelligence and memory function of a large sample of functionally normal adults.[40] With regard to TBI, this test has been specifically evaluated in persons who have sustained TBI, both adults and adolescents. It was found that WTAR performance by the brain-injured group did not differ significantly from that of the control group. Thus, the WTAR appears capable of predicting premorbid intellectual test scores and memory scores following TBI based on the Wechsler IQ and memory scales.

The WTAR is probably the most powerful test available at this time for estimation of premorbid intellectual and memory abilities in traumatically brain-injured persons. It has increased power in this ability because the predictions are based not only upon reading scores, but the WTAR also specifically includes a combination of WTAR reading scores and a demographics prediction of WAIS-III and WMS-III scores. Thus, the WTAR builds upon the goal of the Oklahoma premorbid test and has expanded that format.

For those examiners performing neuropsychiatric evaluations within the context of litigation, particular care must be used for establishing a pre-injury cognitive baseline. Examination must be made to ensure that cognitive effort is adequate at the time of neuropsychological testing. Unfortunately, many neuropsychologists in the United States do not provide adequate screening of cognitive effort at the time of their examination.[41] Mittenburg's group[42] reviewed 33,531 annual neuropsychological cases in personal injury ($n = 6,371$), disability claims ($n = 3,688$), criminal ($n = 1,341$), or medical examinations ($n = 22,131$). Base rates of malingering did not differ among geographic regions or practice settings but were related to the proportion of plaintiff versus defense referrals. Reported rates would be 2%–4% higher if variance due to referral sources were controlled. Twenty-nine percent of personal injury, 30% of disability, 19% of criminal, and 8% of medical cases involved probable malingering and symptom exaggeration. Thirty-nine percent of mild head injury, 35% of fibromyalgia/chronic fatigue, 31% of chronic pain, 27% of neurotoxic, and 22% of electrical injury claims resulted in diagnostic impressions of probable malingering. Diagnosis was supported by multiple sources of evidence including severity (65% of cases) or pattern (64% of cases) of cognitive impairment that was inconsistent with the condition and did not clinically correlate. Other data supporting the diagnosis of malingering were scores below empirical cutoffs on forced-choice tests (57% of cases), discrepancies among records, self-report, and observed behavior (56%), implausible self-reported symptoms in interview (46%), implausible changes in test scores across repeated examinations (45%), and abnormal validity scale scores on objective personality tests (38% of cases). This is probably the largest number of neuropsychological cases reported to date where malingering base rates were established. Thus, the evaluation of response bias and malingering in cases of mild head injury in particular should not rely on a single test to detect cognitive effort. Initial injury severity, typical neuropsychological test or performance patterns, preexisting emotional stress or chronic social difficulties, history of previous neurological or psychiatric disorders, other system injuries sustained in the accident, pre-injury alcohol abuse and a propensity to attribute benign cognitive and somatic symptoms to a brain injury must be considered during the examination, along with performances on specific measures of response bias (tests to detect cognitive distortion).[43]

Practice Effects from Cognitive Retesting

Repeated examinations by psychological and neuropsychological testing can produce a learning effect, which is termed "practice effect." McCaffrey et al. have made the greatest contribution to date in the evaluation of this bias in testing. Their recent texts contain norms that can be used by psychological examiners to determine the potential for practice effects biasing the test data.[44,45] Psychological tests that have a large speed component requiring an unfamiliar or infrequently practiced mode of response or having a single solution, particularly if it can be easily conceptualized once it is attained, are more likely to show significant practice effects.[8] The Wechsler Intelligence Scale tests demonstrate that the more unfamiliar tasks on the Performance Scale tests show greater practice effects than do those tasks on the Verbal Scale tests.[44,46] Practice effects are particularly important in memory testing, as the examinee can, in some cases, learn the material. This occurs in all but seriously memory-impaired patients.[8] Possible biasing effects during testing have particular importance in forensic evaluations. However, Lezak points out that except for single-solution tests and others with a significant learning component, large changes between the first test and the retest are not common.[8] On retesting, the Wechsler Intelligence Scale test scores have proven to be quite stable.

The Grooved Pegboard test contains unfamiliar motor responses and tends to show large practice effects upon retesting.[47] On the other hand, the Block Design subtest of the WAIS-III is difficult to conceptualize, and patients are unlikely to improve with practice alone. In tests similar to the Block Design subtest, improvements in test scores attributable to practice tend to be minimal. This has been found to vary with the location of the brain injury and the age of the patient.[48] Practice effects are difficult to attribute solely to retaking the same test. There is psychological data in the literature that demonstrates by taking a psychological test of any kind, one can substantially improve subsequent performance on unrelated tests. This phenomenon has been referred to as test sophistication.[6] Current psychological literature offers limited guidance to the neuropsychiatric examiner about practice effects within brain injury assessment. Even a large academic text such as Lezak et al.[8] offers no specific guidance. Particularly in forensic situations, the lawyer for either side may claim that test–retest intervals have inflated the scores. The clinical folklore of neuropsychological testing has suggested that six months is an adequate length of time to diminish or remove practice effects. To verify this argument, it is probably wise to consult the guidance of McCaffrey et al.[44,45]

Neuropsychological approaches across the United States and much of the world have significant variance when compared against the medical art forms of physical and mental examination. A mental status examination in Moscow contains the same basic elements as a mental status examination performed in California. Moreover, a neurological examination of a patient following TBI is performed the same in Buenos Aries as it is in New York City. A brain MRI will be interpreted by the same technique in Dallas as one in London or Zurich. On the other hand, a Halstead–Reitan examination in Los Angeles will be an entirely different test paradigm when compared to the Lezak neuropsychological approach in Portland, Oregon. That is not to say that neuropsychological examinations are poor because of their variance, but caveat emptor to the neuropsychiatric examiner. As a result, it is incumbent upon the medical examiner of a brain-injured person who uses neuropsychological test data to be highly aware of the training, background, and skills of the psychologists and neuropsychologists upon whom the physician intends to rely. This is the nature of the beast and is not meant to be a criticism. On the other hand, a confident full neuropsychiatric examination of a person following TBI is not complete without neuropsychological examination. The reader is referred to multiple sources describing the various neuropsychological approaches to examination.[8-18] The tests reviewed for the physician in this chapter are not meant to be comprehensive of all available neuropsychological test instruments. Moreover, the reader is advised not to place particular importance on any test referenced in this book; likewise the absence of a particular test or neuropsychological instrument in this chapter represents no value judgment due to its omission. The tests selected for review in this book are representations of all possible neuropsychological measurement techniques.

MEASURING ATTENTION

The Neuroanatomical and Neuroimaging Bases of Attention

An attentional domain exists for each of the five senses. However, during a neuropsychiatric examination, generally only three senses (auditory, visual, and tactile) are measured for an attentional component or a tracking component. Rarely if ever in an ordinary neurocognitive examination are olfaction and gustation metrically examined. The modulation of attentional tone exists for all five senses and occurs in a bottom-up fashion from the brainstem. The bottom-to-top arousal mechanisms are transmitted through the ascending reticular activating system (ARAS).[49] The ARAS influences the cerebral cortex by direct stimulation and also by relays of information through the thalamus. The projections from the brainstem to the thalamus are mediated mostly by cholinergic neurons. These neurons originate in the pons and nuclei of the brainstem reticular formation.[50]

   In normal vernacular, we use the term "paying attention" to a stimulus or a person. However, attention as a practical matter is difficult to define, and the neuropsychiatric examiner must be explicit in its definition due to the numerous variations and intepretations among differing languages and cultures. From a process orientation, several factors determine when attention is necessary to restrict processing of some items versus others in our extrapersonal space:[51]

(1) Attention may be required when a person's cognitive resources are insufficient to process stimuli. This is termed resource-allocation, and attention restricts the processing of stimuli to allow limited cognitive resources to be allocated to the item of attention. If the stimuli are so great that they exceed the capacity of the individual's working memory, attention may exclude some items from the working memory system.[51]

(2) Focus of attention may reduce the person's uncertainty in making judgments about a stimulus. This decision-noise account will demonstrate a reduction in optimum performance as the number of stimuli increases since each stimulus contains some uncertainty (noise). Attention may be used to enhance the signal-to-noise ratio of items in the attentional field.[51]

(3) Attention may be needed to bind together the features of an object under consideration. For instance, if the individual is viewing a red circle, how does she avoid the error of binding "red" to a "square"? One solution is to intensely focus attention on a single stimulus, which glues or binds the features together.[51] Table 6.7 lists the major forms of attention.

   Spatial attention has been studied usually with visual search paradigms and cueing. Posner's study is a classic in this regard.[52] Peripheral and central cues control attention differently. Observers cannot ignore peripheral cues, which appear to attract attention to the cued location almost automatically. However, they can ignore these central cues if instructed to do so. It takes at least 200 ms to program and execute a saccadic eye movement to a cued location.[51] A peripheral cue is a target well off to the right or left hemispace, whereas a central cue is a symbol presented to the front of the person. Peripheral cues are executed faster than central cues. This problem operates in daily

TABLE 6.7

Major Forms of Human Attention

Form	Function
Spatial attention	This is closely associated with early processing before stimulus identity is determined. Attention is directed to a location in personal space before the stimulus item is physically identified.
Object-based attention	Object of attention (visual) can occur independent of where the object exists in space. This is consistent with separate functional processes for object-based and spatial attention.
Working memory	This is a nonpersistent selection process. It enables the ability to briefly hold sensory stimuli for potential higher order processing.
Executive attention	This functions to select and put into a queue sensory stimuli for higher-order processing. One task may be selected at the expense of another. It enables the ability to voluntarily switch to the task the person is prepared to perform (switch the task set).

life. We may slam into the back of a vehicle sitting on the road in front of us while driving, but we are less likely to hit a vehicle entering the roadway from the periphery.

Object attention may rely on mechanisms separate from spatial attention, but some forms of object selection may involve a modified form of spatial attention. If more than one object is present, humans group the features according to principles such as similarity, color, form, and other such identifying items. This principle is used to screen stimuli in the Wisconsin Card Sorting Test as discussed below. However, object-based attention appears to be distinct and separate from spatial attention, and persons can select objects irrespective of their positions in space.

Working memory is used as a storage mechanism to hold objects, sounds, tactile perceptions, tastes, or odors for higher order processing. The master wine taster can hold a number of tastes and odors of a fine Bordeaux in working memory to process out distinct flavors and aromas such as cassis, blackberry, black cherry, or cedar. Attentional processing helps information to enter into working memory, and it acts as a protective gate (probably in the reticular nucleus of the thalamus) that prevents working memory from being overloaded with more information than can be used or processed.

Executive attention is used to select one task from among many possible tasks that can be performed. As noted below, executive function is much more complex than executive attention. Executive attention is one component of executive function. A general finding of numerous studies of humans is that performance is impaired dramatically when multiple tasks are performed concurrently or alternated among or between in succession. These attentional costs occur even when the individual tasks are highly practiced.[51] The Stroop Test, as noted below, is often used to measure this portion of executive function. However, it may involve more than task-based attention, particularly on the third portion of the Stroop task where color of words is added to the paradigm of a printed word (e.g., "blue" is printed in red ink; "yellow" is printed in blue ink).

Spatial attention can become quite disordered following TBI and other lesions of brain origin. The posterior parietal lobes have been studied most extensively with regard to spatial attention, particularly in the clinical domains of neglect and extinction syndromes.[53] Neglect and extinction are far more likely to occur following right parietal damage than left parietal damage. Clinical symptoms are most evident within the left side of extrapersonal space. In addition to attentional deficits associated with neglect and extinction, patients can also demonstrate motor neglect. The person might not move a limb to the side opposite the brain lesion even though strength is normal.[53] If motor neglect appears present, it must be distinguished from general hemiparesis. Neglect and extinction in the visual system can often be determined at the bedside using the Clock Drawing Test, or a psychologist may use the Rey Complex Figure Test. The disorder of attention in parietal lobe damaged patients appears to involve the bottom-up control discussed above. General perceptual processing is largely intact in patients who demonstrate neglect, but attention is not effectively captured by stimuli on the side opposite the lesion. Although the stimuli have intact perceptual representations with regard to the retina or to the auditory and tactile process, the perceptual representations are not fully captured and do not drive the damaged attentional processes.[51]

With regard to spatial attention, there are three major anatomical areas controlling this domain. These include (1) the parietal lobes, (2) the frontal lobes, and (3) the superior colliculus and pulvinar. Unilateral damage to the human parietal lobe can result in a profound syndrome of neglect or hemineglect.[54] Patients can present either with attentional neglect or motor and sensory neglect. The neglect features are contralateral to the affected parietal lobe. This is not a sensory-level impairment. There is evidence that the sensory amplifiers of the heteromodal parietal lobe centers, when damaged, result in neglect.[55] Spatial attention deficits due to parietal lobe damage have been studied more than other anatomical areas causing spatial attention defects. However, there is evidence that frontal lobe damage also negatively affects spatial attention, particularly the ability to produce eye movements necessary for directing visual attention to a hemispace. Lesions of the superior frontal lobe areas that include the frontal eye fields disrupt some types of eye movements. When lesions occur in the frontal eye field regions, eye movements are disrupted to peripheral targets. However, not all eye movements are disrupted equally. Voluntary over-orienting to a visual stimulus is impaired in persons sustaining damage to the frontal eye fields. These patients are only slowed in directing eye movements to the contralesional field, and damage to the frontal eye field does not abolish visual orienting entirely.[51] Obviously, the parietal lobe control of spatial attention and the frontal lobe control of spatial attention is executed through cortical influence. The superior colliculus is probably involved with the visual movement required for spatial attention. The reader is reminded that patients with progressive supranuclear palsy have a marked impairment of voluntary gaze control, particularly due to degeneration of dorsal midbrain structures including the superior colliculus.[56] Lesions in the midbrain are involved in inhibition of return. This is the decreased tendency to reorient attention to a previously attended location. In addition to the superior colliculus, the pulvinar nucleus of the thalamus appears involved in the subcortical control of spatial attention as well. Pulvinar lesions can also cause neglect, and after neglect is recovered, these patients exhibit attentional impairments.[57]

Object-based attention is the visual process that selects one shape from several others.[58] Most studies of object-based attention investigate either the time to switch attention within an object or between objects, or the effect of focusing attention on one object after dividing attention across objects.[51] In patients with parietal lobe lesions, object-based selection is often impaired. Patients with right parietal lesions demonstrate a fairly normal object effect; they are faster to detect invalid targets that appear in the cued object than those that appear in the uncued object, regardless of the target field. However, patients with left parietal lesions show a larger object effect in their contralesional field than in the ipsilesional field, suggesting that it is difficult for them to switch attention between the objects appearing in the contralesional field. It has been argued by Egly et al.,[59] that object-based attention may involve left parietal lobe processes to a greater degree while spatial attention may involve right parietal lobe processes to a greater degree. Another feature of object-based attention is the "attentional blink" associated with visual working memory. The attentional blink can increase pathologically after cerebral lesions. Visual neglect appears to be a disorder that affects a patient's ability to direct attention in time as well as space. Husain et al.[60] studied eight patients with visual neglect defined clinically by a shaped cancellation task, and they could not identify the second target in a dual-target task until 1440 ms had elapsed after they had identified the first target. These subjects had right hemisphere lesions in the superior parietal lobe, temporal lobe, medial frontal lobe, or subcortical regions. The study authors concluded that visual neglect is a disorder that affects the patient's ability to direct attention in time as well as space and suggested the need to reformulate prevailing spatial accounts of visual neglect. Attentional impairments following damage to the frontal lobes are heterogeneous including those deficits of object-based attention. Patients with frontal lobe damage can exhibit a constellation of impairments that includes distractibility, working memory impairments, difficulties learning new tasks, and inhibiting well-learned responses. The one paradigm perhaps most closely associated with frontal lobe impairments is the Wisconsin Card Sorting Test (see below). Another widely studied cognitive paradigm that manipulates the consistency of information is the Stroop task (see below). Patients with damage to the right frontal lobe but not the left, show more errors on the Stroop task than noninjured patient groups.

Using neuroimaging data to map functional neuroanatomical systems, irrespective of stimulus modality, there seems to exist a mostly right hemispheric frontal, parietal, thalamic, and brainstem network, which is coactivated by alerting and orienting attentional demands. Both PET and fMRI data have delineated the cortical and subcortical networks subserving alertness and sustained attention. These studies demonstrate that intrinsic and phasic alertness are the most basic aspects of attention intensity and probably constitute the basis for the more complex and capacity-demanding aspects of attentional selectivity.[61] Studies at the University of Wisconsin have demonstrated through functional MRI that successful inhibition can be demonstrated by fMRI recorded activation occurring predominately in the right prefrontal and parietal regions.[62] The National Institute of Mental Health, using PET experiments, has demonstrated that the Digits Forward task and Digits Backward task use overlapping functional neural systems associated with working memory. These systems, as detected by PET imaging, are most notably in the right dorsolateral prefrontal cortex, bilateral inferior parietal lobule, and the anterior cingulate.[63] Muller and Knight[64] in Germany remind us of the continuing importance of lesion studies even in the face of functional neuroimaging. They have provided an excellent review of the functional neuroanatomy of working memory. Their lesion studies suggest a functional subdivision of the visuospatial sketch pad of working memory with a ventral stream reaching from the occipital to the temporal cortex for support of object recognition. A dorsal stream connects the occipital lobe with the parietal cortex and enables spatial operations. The phonological loop of working memory can be divided into a short-term store lying in the inferior parietal cortex and an articulatory subvocal rehearsal process in Broca's area. The supplemental motor association cortex and possibly the cerebellum also may play a role in the phonological loop. The data of these researches argue against the modulatory view of the prefrontal cortex in working memory and suggests that working memory processes are distributed along the ventral and dorsolateral prefrontal cortex.

What do the various studies above tell us, in a summary fashion, about the frontoparietal control network? Giesbercht et al.[65] have found the key areas of attentional orienting to lie within the neuroanatomical areas of the inferior parietal sulcus and the precentral gyrus and frontal eye fields of the frontal lobe. Results from their laboratories provide the first direct evidence that both spatial and nonspatial attention draw on similar control systems using these networks. They ask within their studies whether the functional components of the frontal parietal control network could be specified more completely? The anatomical areas are so large that this begs the question whether there is more specificity within the network. Woldorff et al.[66] have reported that portions of the medial frontal and medial parietal cortex are involved in orienting to spatial locations. However, at this time, more significant specificity within the general attentional control networks of the frontal and parietal lobes are not well delineated. The reader is referred to Table 6.8, which outlines in a summary fashion the neuroanatomy of attention. Figure 6.2 enables the reader to find Brodmann's numbers of cortical localization as they are discussed further in this chapter.

The Neuropsychological Measurement of Attention

Lezak[8] parses the measurement of the complex area of attention into subdivisions of orientation, attention, and perception. Some experts have argued that attention cannot be tested. vanZomeren and Brouwer[67] have stated that attention cannot be tested and that when an assessment of attention is undertaken, only a certain aspect of human behavior with special interest for its attentional component can be measured. Lezak argues that while attention, concentration, and mental tracking

TABLE 6.8
The Neuroanatomy of Attention

Function	Purported Location
Bottom-to-top arousal (stimulus driven)	Projections of ARAS from the brainstem reticular formation and pons to the thalamus[51,52]
Top-down modulation of arousal by on-line maintenance of information (goal driven)	Prefrontal cortex (frontal eye fields) posterior cingulated gyrus and parietal cortex[51,79]
Executive aspects of working memory	Dorsolateral prefrontal cortex[80]
Mood and motivational modulation of attention	Top-down projections from limbic system[81]
Modulation of responses to facial expressions	Amygdala[81]
Improvement of performance within vigilance and spatial attention	Anterior cingulated gyri[82]
Attentional valance upon sensory events	Limbic, posterior parietal, and prefrontal cortex[83]
Sustained attention and divided attention	Preferentially right prefrontal and posterior cortex[84,85]
Exploratory attention (reaching, grasping, searching with hands)	Posterior and medial parietal cortex[86]
Visual stimulation during scanning for a target	Brodmann's area 7 and Brodmann's area 6.[87]
Selective spatial orienting of attention	Right intraparietal sulcus[88]
Selective temporal orienting of attention	Left intraparietal sulcus[88]

can be theoretically differentiated in practice, these are very difficult to separate.[5] Attentional defects may appear as distractibility or impaired ability for focused behavior. Intact attention is a necessary precondition both for concentration and for mental tacking activities. Problems of concentration may be an outcome of simple attentional disturbance or, on the other hand, the inability to maintain an attentional focus. Moreover, slowed processing speed often underlies attentional deficits, and simple reaction time is often slowed following TBI. The slowing increases disproportionately as the complexity of the task increases. It has been pointed out that TBI patients may be distinguished from normal controls due to their relatively huge variability during testing and their inconsistencies in performance.[68] As has been previously stated in this text, attentional measures following brain injury are usually only performed within the visual, auditory, and tactile domains, but almost never in the olfactory or gustatory domains.

Table 6.9 lists the multiple ways that orientation, attention, and perception can be subdivided. There are numerous neuropsychological test instruments used for measuring each of these three subdivisions of attention. The reader is referred to Lezak[8] for a more complete understanding of the various instruments available. The reader can see obviously in Table 6.9 that when an examiner states that attention was measured, clarity is necessary to report exactly what was measured. Twenty-eight separate subdivisions of orientation, attention, and perception are noted in Table 6.9 emphasizing the complexity of attention and the difficulties with its measurement. To further complicate the assessment of attention, many recent studies suggest that tasks thought to occupy the attentional domain in fact overlap into executive areas or executive control. For instance, the Connor's Continuous Performance Test (CPT) is often administered as a measure of attention and is widely used for the clinical assessment of attention deficit disorder in children and adults. However, recent studies suggest that it may measure executive control rather than sustained attention and, therefore, may represent functions of more than one brain system. The executive control issue has been further enlarged by consideration that TBI patients have working memory impairment in most instances, and this appears to be due to dysfunction of the central executive system as measured by standard neuropsychological testing.[69,70]

With regard to whether attentional deficits improve following TBI, arousal and motivation seem to improve over time, whereas focused attention, impulsivity, and hyperactivity, if present

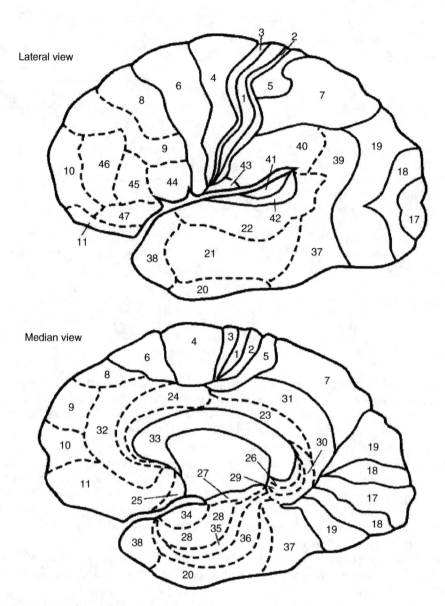

FIGURE 6.2 Brodmann's cortical localization.

following brain injury, may remain stable. As far as motivation is concerned, it has been noted that, while self-motivation may be impaired with regard to attention following TBI, external motivators may improve the attentional performance of brain-injured persons.[71,72] Assessment of attention following mild TBI may be the most demanding aspect of detecting change within the neuropsychiatric examination. Paricularly in forensic issues, as noted in previous chapters, this can present a particular challenge to the examiner. Therefore, it is extremely important that significant measures of cognitive effort are performed concurrent with the attempt to measure attentional deficits following purported mild TBI. Failure to maintain attention is easy to fake. If a person has truly sustained a mild TBI, her brain must be put under significant cognitive load before attentional systems fail. Cicerone, for one, has found that patients with mild TBI exhibit relatively subtle cognitive deficits that are apparent only under conditions that require effort for controlled cognitive processing exceeding the patient's cognitive resources.[89] Table 6.10 lists common tests of attention.

TABLE 6.9

Subdivisions of Orientation, Attention, and Perception[8]

Orientation	• Time
	• Place
	• Body orientation
	• Finger agnosia
	• Right–left orientation
	• Space
Attention	• Reaction time
	• Short-term storage capacity
	• Working memory
	• Complex attention tasks
Perception	• Visual inattention
	• Visual scanning
	• Color perception
	• Visual recognition
	• Visual organization
	• Visual interference
	• Auditory acuity
	• Auditory discrimination
	• Aphasia
	• Auditory inattention
	• Auditory-verbal perception
	• Auditory comprehension
	• Nonverbal auditory reception
	• Tactile sensation
	• Tactile inattention
	• Tactile recognition
	• Olfaction
	• Gustation

TABLE 6.10

Neuropsychological Tests of Attention

Test	Measurement
Brief Test of Attention	Auditory divided attention
Color Trails Test	Visual tracking attention (excellent where English skills are lacking)
Continuous Performance Test-II	Visual target vigilance
Digit Span Test (of WAIS-IV)	Auditory working memory
Paced Auditory Serial Addition Test	Divided auditory attention (sensitive to subtle alterations of sustained and divided auditory attention)
Ruff 2 & 7 Selective Attention Test	Visual selective attention (can be administered at the bedside)
Stroop Color and Word Test-Revised	Visual attention and concentration (sensitive to poor patient effort)
Symbol Digit Modalities Test	Complex visual scanning and tracking
Trailmaking Test	Visual conceptual and visuomotor tracking

Brief Test of Attention

The Brief Test of Attention (BTA) is a relatively simple and easily administered test of auditory divided attention. It is designed to be sensitive to subtle auditory attentional impairments and to reduce confounding task demands such as psychomotor speed and conceptual reasoning.[73] The BTA consists of two parallel forms: Form N (numbers) and Form L (letters), which are presented by an audiocassette. Each form requires about 10 min to administer. The normative sample was a reference group of 740 persons, which included 667 adults between ages 17 and 82 years, and 74 children between ages 6 and 14 years.

The BTA has been used to assess patients who have sustained TBIs and has been found to be sensitive to the auditory attentional problems of these patients for assessments even as long as 8 years after injury. It appears to possess some ecological validity in that it may predict the driving outcome of elderly patients.[74] Its chief limitation is that it may not be appropriate for individuals from different cultural backgrounds or those whose primary language is not English. Also, obviously this test instrument would not be appropriate for a patient with significant hearing impairment or aphasia.

Conners Continuous Performance Test-II

Conners has updated his original test, and the second edition has a larger normative sample, including data both from adults with brain disorders as well as persons who suffer attention deficit disorders.[90] It takes approximately 15 min to administer this test, and as a result of this fact, it also measures the person's ability to sustain attention over a relatively long period of time with a monotonous task. This test instrument is used for persons who have sustained TBI as well as adults and children who may have attention deficit disorder or attention deficit disorder with hyperactivity. Adults with attention deficit disorder have a higher rate of commission errors than control subjects. This suggests that they have impaired ability to inhibit their responses. They also make omission errors and have high reaction time variability. The same findings can be seen in TBI patients with frontal lobe impairment. A computer version of this test is available, and most brain-injured persons are able to master easily the test requirements to complete it by computer.

Digit Span Subtest

This is a subtest of the WAIS-III. It consists of an oral presentation of random number sequences at a rate of approximately one per second. The patient must repeat the digits in the exact sequence in which they are presented. After each correct performance, the examiner adds a digit until the patient fails. Most patients are able to recall six digits forward and four digits backward. A difference of three or more digits between the patient's forward and backward scores is observed more commonly in brain-damaged patients than in intact individuals.[75]

Poor performance on this test can be due to many factors besides TBI, such as anxiety, depression, being preoccupied, and poor effort. The Digit Span Subtest seems more sensitive to left hemisphere brain damage than to right-sided brain damage. It is fairly resistant to the aging process. It is primarily a test of auditory working memory. Moreover, it does not correlate highly with the other 10 subtests on the Wechsler Adult Intelligence Scales. It appears to measure a very specific skill or ability. The digits-backward score appears to be more sensitive to brain damage and the effects of aging than is the forward score.[18]

Ruff 2 & 7 Selective Attention Test

The Ruff 2 & 7 Selective Attention Test (2 & 7 Test) was developed to measure two overlapping aspects of visual attention: sustained attention and selective attention. Within this testing format, sustained attention is defined as the ability to maintain a consistent level of performance over an extended period, while selective attention refers to the ability to select relevant stimuli (targets) while ignoring salient but irrelevant stimuli (distracters).[76]

The normative group consisted of 360 normal volunteers. These persons were stratified by age, gender, and education. Of these, 100 subjects were later retested to establish test reliability.[77] Ruff reported that this test can be administered easily and is sensitive to patients with brain damage involving the frontal lobes as well as temporal, parietal, and occipital lobes. This is thought to be one of the key predictors whether patients who have sustained TBIs are capable of returning to work or to school. The majority of patients with major depression are not impaired on this test, particularly if they do not exhibit clinical evidence of psychomotor retardation.[78]

The major strength of this test is its easy administration and the fact that it can be given at the patient's bedside. Not only is it sensitive for patients who have sustained TBI, but also it has been shown to be sensitive to early attentional changes in those afflicted with cerebral AIDS. It may not be appropriate for individuals who demonstrate poor vision or those who are severely anxious at the time of testing. Patients with significant motor impairment or psychomotor retardation may perform poorly on this test.[18]

Stroop Color and Word Test: Revised

Since the last edition of this book, a revised version of the Stroop Color and Word Test (Stroop) has been published. The present version attempts to update both the scoring and interpretive strategies used with the Stroop, as well as to improve clinical awareness of the meaning of Stroop's scores. A modified scoring system is introduced for adults, and it provides a better and more extensive age and education correction. The Stroop was developed from the observations by early experimental psychologists that the naming of color hues is always slower than the reading of color names in literate adults. Neuropsychological studies have suggested that Stroop interference occurs not at the response stage or due to the confusion of the subject, but as a result of interference of verbal processing. The uniqueness of the Stroop lies in the fact that the colored word invokes an automatic verbal response that requires many of the same neuropsychological functions as the requested color naming response. Overall, analysis suggests that the Stroop Interference Color-Word page basically tests the ability of the individual to separate the word and color naming stimuli. If this can be done, the individual can suppress the reading response and proceed with color naming. Thus, in the adult with normal reading skills, the Stroop stimuli involve at a basic level the ability of an individual to sort information from his or her environment and to selectively react to this information. The first page (Word page) contains color names printed in black ink. The second page (Color page) contains groupings of four Xs printed in colors. The third page (Word-Color page) contains words from the first page printed in colors from the second page (the interference task).[92]

The main strength of this test is its ease of administration to patients. It usually takes only 5–10 min to administer the test. It appears to be sensitive to subtle attentional and cognitive difficulties in patients who have sustained TBIs. However, it is also sensitive to dementia. Its weakness lies in possible false positives due to anxiety, depression, or poor motivation on the part of the patient. Individuals who deliberately fake on this test may be inaccurately diagnosed as brain impaired. When using the Stroop Test, it is recommended that effort testing be included in the overall assessment process.[18]

Trailmaking Test

The Trailmaking Test is an integral part of the Halstead–Reitan Battery. This is a timed paper and pencil test that consists of parts A and B. On each part, the patient is given a sample page that is used for practice to aid in understanding instructions. The examiner then gives the patient part A, which is a white sheet of paper with 24 numbered circles distributed in a random pattern, and the patient is required to connect the circles with lines in numerical order as quickly as possible. Part B consists of 25 circles. Some are numbered from 1 to 13, and the remainder are lettered from A to L. The patient is required to connect the circles beginning with number 1, then going to A, and then from A to 2, 2 to B, B to 3, and so on, in an alternating sequence.[93]

This test is widely used as a measure of attention, visual scanning and visuomotor tracking. Thus, it is not a pure test of attention. Part B is more difficult than part A, as it requires the patient to shift sets (switch from a number to a letter and vice versa), rather than connecting only numbers.

One of the chief strengths of this test is that it is widely used since it is a component of the Halstead–Reitan Battery. It appears to be sensitive to various forms of brain damage. Moreover, a skilled examiner can observe the patient's behavior while he takes the test and easily detect qualitative errors. It is backed by a solid body of research data and normative data. The weakness of the test lies in negative effects from patients with low educational backgrounds or low intellectual functioning. Thus, it may misclassify normal adults as brain damaged if these persons have low levels of education or intelligence. Moreover, the test may not be appropriate for persons whose native language is not English. Since it is a timed test, it may provide false positives in persons who are anxious or depressed. It is not useful as a stand-alone test to differentiate brain-injured patients from psychiatric patients, and it discriminates poorly between these populations.[18]

MEASURING MEMORY

The Neuroanatomical and Neuroimaging Bases of Memory

The reader is referred to Figure 2.1 in order to review again the organizational hierarchy of general memory. General memory is subdivided into two major divisions: declarative (explicit) and procedural (implicit) memories. For further discussions of memory in this book, working memory is considered to be a component of executive function and attentional networks within executive function rather than a component of general memory. Declarative memory is sometimes called factual memory, and this enables the individual to consciously know that something is learned. On the other hand, procedural memory is the ability to perform a learned skill in the absence of conscious awareness of the learning experience. Declarative memory is further divided into episodic (autobiographical) and semantic (factual) memories.

The neuroanatomy of human memory is a work in progress, and much remains to be elucidated. However, quite a bit is known of the functional neuroanatomy of human memory systems based on recent functional neuroimaging. Ramón y Cajal first described dendritic spines.[94] These have been historically assumed to underlie the physical substrate of long-term memory in the brain. Recent time-lapse imaging of dendritic spines in live tissue, using confocal microscopy, have revealed these to be amazingly plastic in their structure. Segal's studies in Israel[94] demonstrated that dendritic spines can be formed, can change their shape, and can disappear in response to afferent (input) stimulation. These changes occur in a dynamic fashion and are consistent with spine morphology as an important vehicle for structuring synaptic interactions useful for long-term memory.[94] Recent PET studies[95] have demonstrated that dopamine D_2 receptors in the hippocampus affect local hippocampus function during memory storage, but these also exert functions outside the hippocampus such as in the prefrontal cortex. In older persons with TBI, the differentiation of post-TBI memory impairment from possible concurrent Alzheimer's disease has recently been conducted by Small's group at UCLA.[96] PET scanning uses FDDNP 2-(1-{6-[2-[^{18}F] fluoroethyl)(methyl)amino]-2-naphthyl} ethylidene)malononitrile, a molecule that binds to plaques and tangles *in vitro*. FDDNP-PET scanning is able to differentiate persons with mild cognitive impairment from those with Alzheimer's disease and those with no cognitive impairment. This technique is showing potential usefulness as a noninvasive method to determine regional cerebral patterns of amyloid plaques and tau neurofibrillary tangles.

Larry Squire[97] has spent his career studying the medial temporal lobe. He has demonstrated that the medial temporal lobe includes a system of anatomically related structures that are essential for declarative memory. This system consists of the hippocampus region (CA fields, dentate gyrus, and subicular complex) and the adjacent perirhinal, entorhinal, and parahippocampal cortices. His group recently reviewed findings from humans, monkeys, and rodents to show that this system (1) principally is concerned with memory, (2) operates with the neocortex to establish and maintain long-term memory, and (3) ultimately, through a process of consolidation, becomes independent of long-term memory. Their work indicates further that the functions of the hippocampus and the adjacent medial temporal cortex, such as associative versus nonassociative memory, episodic versus semantic memory and recollection versus familiarity, are not simple dichotomies and are more complex than previously suspected. Gold and Squire[98] have recently added three autopsy cases to the literature of anterograde and retrograde amnesia. Only eight such cases have been reported previously for a total now of 11 cases. All three patients reported in this most recent study exhibited a similar phenotype of amnesia with markedly impaired declarative memory (anterograde and retrograde amnesia), but exhibited normal performance on neuropsychological tests of nondeclarative memory (e.g., priming and adaptational-level effects) as well as on tests of other cognitive functions. One patient revealed damage to the hippocampus in the dentate gyrus and the CA1 and CA3 fields and in layer 3 of the entorhinal cortex, but with relative sparing of the CA2 field and the subiculum. The second patient revealed damage to the internal medullary lamina and medial dorsal thalamic nuclei, while the third patient had damage to the mammillary nuclei, mammillothalamic tracts, and the anterior thalamic nuclei. These findings illuminated the relationship between the diencephalic regions and the medial temporal lobe regions in declarative memory amnesia.

Studies from Germany have recently separated out the encoding processes related to priming versus explicit (declarative) memory.[99] Priming is a facilitation of cognitive processing with stimulus repetition that can occur without explicit memory. More simply put, priming refers to enhanced processing of memory information because of preceding exposure to specific stimuli or cues. There is usually no conscious awareness of these cues. Event-related functional magnetic resonance imaging demonstrated that activations in the medial temporal lobe were specific for explicit memory, whereas priming occurred in the bilateral extrastriate occipital lobe cortex, left fusiform gyrus, and the bilateral inferior prefrontal cortex. These areas were linked with stimulus identification. It is well recognized that memory of any event can be enhanced by the power of the emotions occurring at the time of the event. The key brain areas involved in emotional memory are the amygdala and hippocampus. A recent aversive event study, using fMRI, demonstrated that the bilateral dorsal amygdalae and the anterior hippocampi were highly activated, and this enhanced immediate recognition memory.[100] This study confirmed previous reported sex differences of emotional memory associations with the left amygdala for women and the right amygdala for men. Recognizing that emotion contributes to the strength of the memory trace and its subsequent storage, neuroimaging studies of the human cortical and subcortical physical pain response have identified a neural network consistently referred to as the "pain matrix." A study in the United Kingdom at the University of Liverpool used fMRI to investigate whether the pain matrix could be activated through the retrieval of memories relating to previous painful events, in the absence of any direct peripheral noxious input. Memories in pain-free participants were primed by explicitly instructing the subjects to recall autobiographical memories of painful episodes in response to pain-related words and nonpainful episodes in response to equally salient but nonpain words. Memories triggered by pain-related words produced significantly greater activation of the left caudal anterior cingulate cortex (Brodmann's area 32) and left inferior frontal gyrus (BA 44 extending to BA 47–45). The activations were much greater than memories triggered by equally salient but nonpain words.[101]

Let us leave these general discussions of the functional neuroanatomy of memory and focus further on three specific properties of general memory: episodic memory, semantic memory, and skill learning. Dobbins and Davachi[102] ask the question, "How do episodic memories form?" They point out that the mere perception and global attention given to a stimulus or event does not guarantee long-term autobiographical memory formation for that particular stimulus. Obviously, we remember only a small percentage of what we perceive or experience in our daily lives. It has been shown that we do not necessarily encode these events, or we may be blind to the seemingly relevant aspects of the event, such as the identity of a person with whom we are conversing.[103] Further mechanisms are needed to ensure the longevity of the autobiographical stimulus. These mechanisms are encoding or processing that leads to the formation of an enduring memory. Following brain trauma, some patients have a dense amnesia of the events surrounding their injury, hospitalization, and rehabilitation. They do not form new episodic memories after the traumatic onset of their amnesia. Recently, PET scanning is falling out of favor for studies of episodic memory, and fMRI using event-related designs is now *en vogue*. The power of fMRI is that it allows estimation of brain activation to be related to a single trial or a single event unlike the more diffuse capture of putative stimuli using PET. Encoding-related activation can be either processed- or content-specific. During episodic or autobiographical stimulation, if the stimuli are verbally semantic or phonological, the anterior and posterior portions of the left inferior frontal gyrus are preferentially engaged,[104] while pictorial and unnamable stimuli preferentially engage the right prefrontal cortex.[105] Almost every study within the last 10 years has found that activation within the medial temporal lobe correlates with episodic memory formation during fMRI studies.[102] However, the precise division of labor among the various subregions within the medial temporal lobe remains to be fully elucidated. How the various elements making up the autobiographical memory trace are linked or constructed into a coherent unit is not fully understood at this time. Purely semantic information appears to be associated with activation in the anterior inferior frontal gyrus, whereas phonological episodic memory activates the left prefrontal and parietal cortex. Thus, the episodic memory formation of autobiographical data is augmented by increased activation in brain regions selective to the task being performed. If the stimulus differs by class (e.g., words, pictures, etc.) this causes a differentiation of cortical processing (e.g., left versus right hemisphere), or a differentiation among brain structures associated with episodic memory.[102] Once the autobiographical information is encoded, how is it then retrieved? The overall picture is one of a highly flexible set of retrieval operations that are specific to different types of episodic memory demands.[102] However, most studies indicate that the prefrontal cortex is involved during retrieval. Lepage et al.[106] examined data across four different PET studies and isolated specific prefrontal cortex regions that appear to be systematically recruited during episodic (autobiographical) recognition regardless of whether the recognitions were predominantly new or old. These regions included Brodmann's areas 45–47, 10, 8–9, and 32. Apparently, these regions are activated while one mentally holds in the background of focal attention the segment of one's personal past and then consciously becomes aware of these products as a remembered event.[107] Further work by Dobbins et al.[108] has led to a working hypothesis that left frontal polar and dorsal regions are involved in the online monitoring of autobiographical recollections, whereas the left anterior ventrolateral region is involved in the semantic or conceptual elaboration of the data that is retrieved. The left prefrontal cortex appears to be engaged whenever retrieval is aimed at recovering evidence about one's prior systematic processing of autobiographical information.[109]

Now moving to the other major arm under declarative memory (Figure 2.1), semantics is used to refer to the meaning of a word or a phrase. However, Tulving borrowed the word "semantic" to refer to a memory system for "words and other verbal symbols, their meaning and referents, about relations among them, and about rules, formulas, and algorithms" for manipulating them.[110] Word knowledge has been expanded by Thompson-Schill et al.[111] to refer to world knowledge. Tulving has argued for a specific functional differentiation of episodic memory from semantic memory within the overall declarative memory concept.[110] He has argued vehemently for two functionally distinct memory systems based on multiple sources of evidence.[112] More modern studies using functional neuroimaging have compared episodic and semantic memory. A summarization to date of these findings indicates that semantic memory and episodic memory systems rely in part on common neural circuitry. However, semantic memory retrieval has a distinct neural signature, which includes regions of temporal and frontal cortex that differentiates it on a neuroimaging basis from episodic memory function. To further complicate the reader's understanding, semantic memory can be categorized into various category-specific domains. These include (1) visual attribute domains, (2) nonvisual attribute domains, and (3) abstract semantic representations.[111] Taking visual attribute domains separately, neuroimaging studies have found activation within the visual cortex while a person is employing only mental imagery. The visual attribute domains can be parsed further into color, motion, size, and form. Nonvisual attribute domains can be split into action or other sensory domains, whereas abstract representations are a single attribute. Knowledge of color and its relation to its perception of color is the most widely studied neuroimaging attribute of all forms of semantic memory.[111] Activation of the color attributes of memory are typically observed on neuroimaging in the left or bilateral ventral temporal cortex. The ventral temporal cortex may be active specifically during color retrieval in contrast to retrieval of object size knowledge.[113] The retrieval of action knowledge activates the left middle temporal gyrus, which is anterior to a region associated with motion perception. In addition to object motion, the lateral temporal lobe has also been implicated in the memory of biological motion. Specifically, the superior temporal sulcus, which is slightly anterior and dorsal to the medial temporal area has shown to be involved when persons observe face and leg motion, mouth movements, eye movements, and body movements.[115] The parietal cortex seems activated during retrieval of size knowledge. It remains equivocal whether the lateral or the medial parietal lobe is involved during this retrieval. Kellenbach et al.[114] argue for the medial parietal cortex activation, whereas a recent study suggests that it occurs in the lateral, not the medial parietal lobe.[116] Activation of memories for form have been reported in the ventral occipitotemporal cortex during mental imagery of object shape or during semantic decisions based on object form. Even in blind subjects, retrieval of shape knowledge activates the occipitotemporal cortex to the same extent as sighted subjects.[117]

With regard to nonvisual attribute domains, the term "functional knowledge" typically was used to contrast this domain with visual knowledge when discussing various forms of semantic memory. This term of art is now rarely used. Many neuroimaging studies have investigated the neural bases of action knowledge retrieval.[111]

The anatomical areas consistently identified as playing a role for these memory representations are distributed in the left ventral prefrontal, posterior temporal, and parietal areas. Particularly, an area of left ventral lateral premotor cortex is activated by imagined grasping and other hand movements with the right hand. It has been argued that knowledge of tool use is stored in this region.[118] While action knowledge seems stored in the described anatomical areas, information about the function of the object depends on more abstract representations and is probably stored at sites beyond these.[119]

Other sensory domains excluding the visual domain have been investigated only slightly. Retrieval of auditory knowledge has been found to have selective activity in the superior aspect of the temporal lobe and the temporoparietal cortex near the auditory association areas, as well as the superotemporal gyrus.[111,114] Recent research has found that in large part, the regions associated with olfactory perception, including the orbitofrontal, pyriform, and insular cortex, are involved in the identification of odors.[120] Lastly, what are the neuroanatomical underpinnings of abstract semantic representations? This is particularly a conundrum presently, and to date no well circumscribed anatomical area has been found to be activated during memory representations of abstract concepts. Many cognitive models of semantic memory have described hierarchical networks that reflect abstract regions between concepts (e.g., a tree is a plant, and a plant is a living thing). Recent studies have articulated formal models of semantic memory that include units integrating information across all of the attribute domains (including verbal descriptions and object names). As a consequence, abstract memory probably occurs by cross-modal mappings of many interconnected sites with different perceptual-motor areas.[111,121]

Lastly, using again the pictorial representation of general memory in Figure 2.1, we explore the neuroanatomy of skill learning. This is under the general memory dichotomy and falls into the procedural memory domain. The classic clinical case of amnesia represented by the patient, H.M., noted that he was able to acquire motor skills in a normal manner even though he suffered from dense amnesia for episodic information.[122] Subsequent studies have demonstrated that amnesic patients are also able to normally acquire a range of perceptual skills even though they have impairment of declarative memory.[123] The neuroimaging of skill learning involves a number of difficult conceptual and methodological issues that are not encountered in imaging of static performance on cognitive tasks. Skill learning is almost invariably associated with changes in task performance (e.g., faster, more accurate responses).[123] As the learning curve improves, the individual's skill ability improves as well. Because functional imaging signals are not linear to the amount of time spent on a task, it becomes difficult to determine whether changes in activation on neuroimaging reflect the neural changes that result in skill learning or the neural effects that come from changes in performance. Moreover, some skills do not require learning sequences of motor acts, but rather require learning new relationships between perceptual stimuli and motor behaviors. Most studies of sequence learning report the premotor cortex (lateral Brodmann's area 6; posterior parietal Brodmann's areas 7 and 40; and prefrontal cortices, Brodmann's areas 45 and 46) is activated early in the training; as one obtains skill, due to practice effects, the supplemental motor area is activated later in training.[123] With advanced training, such as the skill level of an Olympic diver, the striatal activation in the basal ganglia becomes much more prominent. Furthermore, there is some reason to believe that the striatum may be involved very generally in the acquisition of perceptual skills as well.[123] The basal ganglia seem to play a central role in many forms of skill learning, and according to Squire is consistent with a number of earlier proposals based on neuropsychological data.[124] This finding is not surprising, particularly for motor skills, given the importance of the basal ganglia for motor control. However, later studies have demonstrated that the basal ganglia play significant roles in perceptual and cognitive skill learning. The basal ganglia do not perform their functions in isolation, but are part of large-scale "loops" from the cortex to the striatum and back to the cortex by way of the pallidum and the thalamus.[125] There is recent evidence that habit learning, such as simple classical conditioning, occurs within the tail of the caudate nucleus. Brain imaging studies have shown caudate activation associated with learning arbitrary visuomotor associations. The tail of the caudate nucleus is strongly connected to higher-order visual cortices in primates, suggesting that it may serve to connect visual representations with particular motor actions.[126] Table 6.11 lists the putative neuroanatomy of memory functions.

The Neuropsychological Measurement of Memory

It should be clear from the preceding discussion that memory occupies many different regions of brain function, and complex neuroanatomy is the substrate. Therefore, in the evaluation of TBI, where memory dysfunction is a primary complaint, it is not possible to define all of the potential memory disorders that may exist following TBI. Moreover, a comprehensive neuropsychological testing of memory function alone could occupy more than 20 different neuropsychological test instruments to measure the multiple areas of episodic, semantic, skill learning, and further subdivide these into a learning concept for each sense. Since there are five senses, there are five memories, one

---

TABLE 6.11

The Neuroanatomy of Memory

Function	Purported Location
Procedural (implicit or skill) memory	Cerebellum, basal ganglia, and probably dorsolateral prefrontal cortex[129,130]
Visual priming of memory	Peristriate, temporal, and parietal cortices[131]
Retrieval of memory	Preferentially right prefrontal cortex[132]
Encoding of stored information	Preferentially left prefrontal cortex[132]
Retrieving autobiographical memories (episodic)	Right hemisphere more critical[133]
Retrieving factual memories (semantic)	Left hemisphere more critical[133]
Naming objects and reading words	Bilateral fusiform gyri, left activation greater during reading[134–136]
Identifying and naming animals	Lateral fusiform gyrus, medial occipital cortex, and superior temporal sulcus[135]
Visual processing pictures of tools	Medial fusiform gyrus, left middle temporal gyrus, and left premotor cortex[135]

for each of the five senses. As noted previously in this text, rarely are taste and olfaction measured. With regard to memory, almost all memory testing at a neuropsychological level is performed on auditory or visual information only, and occasionally on tactile information (Halstead–Reitan test battery). The reader should be aware again that if someone performs poorly on simple attentional tasks, such as span of immediate verbal retention (e.g., Digit Span Forward) or simple mental tracking (e.g., counting backwards by 7s), it may not be possible to get a valid measure of retention.[8] Lezak proposes that a comprehensive neuropsychological memory evaluation should include the following: (1) orientation to time and place; (2) prose recall to examine learning and retention of meaningful information which resembles what one hears in conversation (such as Wechsler's Logical Memory stories); other stories can be used as well to develop tests of verbal recall; (3) rote learning ability that gives a learning curve and is tested with both free and recognition trials, such as the Auditory-Verbal Learning Test or the California Verbal Learning Test; (4) visuospatial memory such as the Complex Figure task, followed by a recognition trial when available; (5) remote memory, such as fund of information; and (6) personal memory (autobiographical).[8] Obviously, some of these measures are quantifiable and will use published test instruments, whereas others will come from a mental status examination, such as orientation to time and place, fund of information, and autobiographical memory. Table 6.12 lists various neuropsychological tests often used for measurement of memory. The reader can select from these tests for particular needs during examination.

Auditory-Verbal Learning Test

The Auditory-Verbal Learning Test (AVLT) began with the work of Claparède and was later used by Rey to form the AVLT.[127] The power of this test is that it enables the examiner to develop a learning curve. It is easily administered and provides an analysis of learning and retention while using a five-trial presentation of a 15-word list (list A), a single presentation of an interference list (list B), two postinterference recall trials, one immediate and one delayed, and a recognition of the target words presented with distracters.[8] There are language versions other than English, which include Flemish, Hebrew, and Spanish.

Most young adults (ages 20–39) will recall 6 or 7 words on trial 1 and achieve 12 or 13 words by the fifth trial. The change in the number of words recalled from trials 1 to 5 shows the rate of learning (the learning curve) or will reflect little or no learning if the number of words recalled on later trials is not much different than that given initially on trial 1. In general, the patient will lose approximately 1.5 words while going from trial 5 to trial 6 (following the interference trial, List B). However, after age 64, the spread between trials 5 and 6 gradually increases to about 2.0 words.

TABLE 6.12

Neuropsychological Tests of Memory

Test	Measurement
Auditory-Verbal Learning Test	Immediate memory span (provides a learning curve)
Benton Visual Retention Test	Visual recall
Brief Visuospatial Memory Test-Revised	Visual learning, delayed recall, and recognition
Buschke Selective Reminding Test	Short-term verbal retention
California Verbal Learning Test	Verbal short-term retention, storage, and retrieval
Complex Figure Test	Verbal memory and verbal learning strategies
Recognition Memory Test	Immediate and delayed visual recall
Rivermead Behavioral Memory Test	Recall of words and faces
Brown–Peterson Technique	Tests everyday verbal and visual memory
Ruff-Light Trail Learning Test	Visuospatial learning
Wechsler Memory Scale-III	Complex battery for testing verbal and visual memories, working memory

Little if any loss occurs between trials 6 and 7 (the delayed recall trials). Interestingly, even most patients with brain disorders, such as TBI, will show a learning curve over the five trials. They may not be able to learn as much information as they could before brain injury, but most brain injuries do not abolish their ability to demonstrate a learning curve.[8] The appearance of a curve, even at a low level, (e.g., from 3 or 4 words on trial 1 to 8 or 9 on trial 5), demonstrates some ability to learn if some of the gain is maintained on the delayed recall, trial 7. These patients may be capable of benefiting from cognitive retraining and other forms of speech pathology or occupational rehabilitation training. Some TBI patients will have a reduced recall for each measure but will demonstrate a learning curve with some loss on delayed recall with a near normal performance on the recognition trial. This indicates a significant verbal retrieval problem. These patients tend to make a few intrusion errors. The AVLT has been effective in predicting psychosocial outcome after TBI.[128]

Complex Figure Test
Please see the section "Neuropsychological Measurement of Visuospatial and Perceptual Ability."

Ruff-Light Trail Learning Test
The Ruff-Light Trail Learning Test assesses visuospatial learning and memory in adults. The test was specifically developed to avoid requiring the patient to possess drawing skills, keen eyesight, good motor control, and refined visuospatial integration. Thus, it is very useful in traumatically brain-injured persons with comorbid orthopedic injuries.[137] This test makes a direct measure of immediate visual memory as well as visuospatial learning. It also has a delayed recall section, and it allows for the development of learning curves over the course of the testing. It has been standardized for use with individuals aged 16–70 years, and normative data are available for two age groups: 16–54 and 55–70 years. It is not validated for individuals under the age of 16.

Wechsler Memory Scale-III
Wechsler Memory Scale-III (WMS-III) is a revision of the Wechsler Memory Scale-Revised (WMS-R). The basic structure of the WMS-III is the same as that of the WMS-R, and it retains the tradition of assessing memory and attentional functioning within both auditory and visual stimuli.[138] Changes in the WMS-III relative to the WMS-R include the addition of new subtests, a revision of memory stimuli, an expansion of scoring options, an addition of subtest scaled scores, and an expansion of indices in both content and number.

The scores from WMS-III are organized into summary index scores. The primary index scores are as follows:

1. Auditory immediate: The ability to remember information immediately after it is orally presented
2. Visual immediate: The ability to remember information immediately after it is visually presented
3. Immediate memory: The ability to remember both visual and auditory information immediately after it is presented
4. Auditory delayed: The ability to recall orally presented information after a delay of approximately 30 min
5. Visual delayed: The ability to recall visually presented information after a delay of approximately 30 min
6. Auditory recognition delayed: The ability to recognize auditory information after a delay of approximately 30 min
7. General memory: The delayed memory capacity based upon scores from Logical Memory II, Verbal Paired Associates II, Faces II, and Family Pictures II
8. Working memory: The capacity to remember and manipulate visually and orally presented information in short-term memory storage using performance data from the Spatial Span and Letter–Number Sequencing subtests

The WMS-III is one of the most widely used scales to assess memory. It is correlated with the WTAR for pre-injury memory skill prediction. It now supplants the very widely used WMS-R. The tests are relatively easy for an experienced psychologist to administer and score. Normative data are available for persons ranging from 16 to 89 years. However, WMS-III takes much longer to administer than the older edition, WMS-R, especially if it is administered to brain-injured patients. Many neuropsychologists avoid administering the full WMS-III battery due to that limitation, and it may not be appropriate for a severely brain-injured person who is extremely impaired cognitively or physically. However, prorated scores are not recommended in forensic cases. Currently, no normative data are available on the test instrument for persons for whom English is the second language.

Unlike the WMS-R, the WMS-III contains four supplementary auditory composites:

1. Single-trial learning: The capacity to immediately recall auditory data after a single exposure to material
2. Learning slope: The ability to acquire new auditory information after repeated exposures
3. Retention: The delayed recall capacity as a function of immediate recall performance after a delay of approximately 35 min
4. Retrieval: The retrieval for recall versus recognition memory

MEASURING LANGUAGE

The Neuroanatomical and Neuroimaging Bases of Language

As the reader will recall, language disorders are not common following TBI. Aphasias occur in approximately 2% of persons, on a persistent basis, following a TBI. Language disorders are seen not only in audio-based languages such as English, French, or German but also ideogrammatic languages. Persons who must use American Sign Language for communication can demonstrate aphasia while using only visuomotor signs. Moreover, languages such as Chinese or Japanese will also demonstrate a classic aphasia if this occurs. The Damasios have described three major domains of language processing dysfunction: (1) syntax, the grammatical structures of sentences and paragraphs; (2) lexicon, the words available within the person's brain in the particular language being used to denote meanings; and (3) the morphology and phonology of words, how individual speech sounds are combined from phonemes.[139] The current classification of language disorders is extremely complex. To assist the reader, Table 6.13 outlines the aphasias, alexias, agraphias, and acalculia. This table follows the work of Kirshner,[140] and the descriptions of language disorders also correlate closely with Geschwind, Ross, Mesulam et al.[139,141–144] It is important to remember that the descriptions of language disorders in Table 6.13 are based on the classic descriptions of language disorders within the medical literature of the last 100 years. These are based almost entirely on the interruption of vasculature in the brain causing strokes in language centers. Therefore, these descriptors do not translate directly to all language syndromes seen following TBI. Traumatic brain injury language syndromes tend to present themselves with aspects of stroke-language disorders, but they do not mimic them precisely.

Much of what we know about language disorders comes from the nineteenth century. Broca described patients with acquired language disorders and studied their brains anatomically after death. He created the original clinical correlations of structure with function that have formed the model for the behavioral neurological study of language ever sinice.[140] These findings were further refined in the twentieth century primarily by Geschwind[141] and Damasio and Damasio.[139] A bedside diagnostic schema for the detection of aphasic disorders following TBI is presented in Table 6.13. In diagnosing a patient with language difficulty following TBI, the examiner must take a comprehensive history and first exclude confounding conditions. These include three other frequent causes of abnormal communication in humans. First one must exclude the developmental or congenital language disorders, which can occur either as isolated "dysphasia" or as part of a

TABLE 6.13
Language Disorder Syndromes

A. Bedside Language Examination
- Is spontaneous speech fluent or nonfluent?
- Can the patient name objects, parts of objects, colors, body parts, and actions?
- Can the patient repeat (no = perisylvian injury; yes = extraperisylvian injury)?
- Does the patient comprehend the examiner's questions?
- Can the patient read aloud for meaning?
- Can the patient copy, write to dictation, and write spontaneously?

B. Aphasia Syndromes
- Broca's aphasia: Nonfluent, hesitant, impaired naming; impaired repetition; poor reading aloud; difficulty writing with either hand; usually a right hemiparesis present and patient appears depressed and frustrated.
- Aphemia: Nonfluent speech with normal comprehension and writing.
- Wernicke's aphasia: Fluent with phonemic and verbal paraphasic errors; impaired naming; impaired auditory comprehension; impaired repetition; usually impaired reading; writing well formed but paragraphic; possible right hemianopia with sparing of motor and sensory function and behavior may be happy, angry or paranoid.
- Pure word deafness: Selective deafness for auditory language; impaired repetition and comprehension is severely impaired but speech, writing, naming, and reading are normal.
- Global aphasia: Nonfluent or mute with impairment in all language areas; most have right hemipareses and depressed affect.
- Conduction aphasia: Relatively uncommon with literal paraphasic errors and fluent speech; repetition is poor; naming, reading, and writing are variable; right hemiparesis present with right visual field defect and nothing typical is seen with behavior.
- Anomia aphasia: Naming is the primary abnormality and speech is fluent; comprehension, repetition, reading, and writing are intact; word-finding difficulty may be present.
- Transcortical aphasias: Motor resembles Broca's aphasia but repetition is preserved and sensory resembles Wernicke's with sparing of repetition.
- Subcortical aphasia: Thalamic aphasia may be fluent with paraphasic errors but better comprehension and repetition than Wernicke's aphasia; anterior subcortical aphasia is usually nonfluent with dysarthria and hemiparesis but the language errors are mild.

C. Alexias
- Pure alexia with agraphia: Speech is fluent, often paraphasic and anomic with spared comprehension and repetition; reading and writing are impaired; and a Gerstmann syndrome may be present.
- Gerstmann and angular gyrus syndrome: Anomia, alexia, agraphia, acalculia, right–left disorientation, finger agnosia, constructional apraxia, right visual field defect, and possible mild, fluent aphasia.
- Pure alexia without agraphia: Normal speech patterns with color-naming impairment; comprehension, repetition, and writing are spared but reading is impaired; right hemianopia is present.
- Aphasic alexia: A term of art that refers to alexia associated with left frontal lesions and global or Broca's aphasia.
- Psycholinguistic alexia syndromes: Letter-by-letter reading and various dyslexias.

D. Agraphias
- Aphasic agraphia: Writing typically mimics spoken language in aphasics.
- Lexical agraphia: Words are misspelled but phonologically plausible ("spaid" for "spade" or "flud" for "flood").
- Phonological aphasia: Patients cannot spell nonwords and cannot spell words they did not know before their injury.
- Deep agraphia: Writing errors of semantically related words ("chair" for "desk," etc.).
- Semantic agraphia: Patients confuse homonyms while writing to dictation. (e.g., "doe" instead of "dough").

E. Acalculia
- Three types: (1) Inability to read and write numbers, (2) inability to keep numbers in columns, and (3) true loss of ability to perform mental arithmetic.

F. Dysprosody: Receptive and Expressive
- The paralinguistic elements of discourse.

more general mental retardation syndrome. Second, the classical aphasias, including acquired aphasias from TBI, exclude motor speech disorders, which disturb only spoken language output rather than the formation of language within the brain. In motor speech disorders, the comprehension of both spoken and written language remains intact. Muteness is especially difficult to diagnose. A patient who is mute is not always aphasic, and other causes of muteness include severe dysarthria, laryngeal disorders, frontal lobe syndromes with akinetic mutism, extrapyramidal disorders seen in Parkinson's disease and psychogenic states such as catatonia or the uncooperative malingering patient. A patient who can understand language and write normally is probably not aphasic. In the mute patient, the diagnosis may require the detection of "neighborhood signs" of left hemisphere injury such as a right hemiparesis with right hemianopia. Third, disorders of language secondary to psychiatric disorders must be excluded. These can mimic the posterior aphasias of Wernicke's area. The fluent speech of a severe Wernicke aphasic may resemble that of psychotic language. Usually the bizarreness or delusional content of language will help the examiner separate psychiatric disorders from Wernicke's aphasia or posterior transcortical aphasia. A key difference between psychosis and aphasia is in the patient's nonlinguistic behavior. The behavior of the psychotic patient is often very abnormal and inappropriate, whereas an aphasic patient usually behaves appropriately but is unable to communicate effectively.

Broca's aphasia is described classically in clinical descriptions of Paul Broca's two original patients. They could comprehend language but could produce only stereotyped utterances such as "tan, tan." The person with typical Broca's aphasia speaks hesitantly. The expressive speech is agrammatical or "telegraphic." A Broca's aphasic might say, "Go fishing Sun Saturday," to express his plans for the weekend leaving out connectors and articles. Naming is typically impaired in Broca's aphasia. Repetition is generally impaired as well. Auditory comprehension often seems normal, but a true Broca's aphasic may reveal deficits in syntactic decoding using complex grammatical structures. For example, the sentence, "The present that Jane gave to Arthur was gaudy," may cause major difficulty, and the patient may not be able to answer questions regarding who received the present and who gave it.[140] Most patients presenting with classic Broca's aphasia will have hemiparesis or hemiplegia of the right arm and leg making it difficult for the person to write with their dominant right hand. Usually there is near total inability to write, and when a Broca's aphasic is asked to attempt writing with the nondominant or left hand, they often will refuse to do so. The inability of a Broca's aphasic to write is not a motor disorder but rather is a part of the language disorder and should not be confused with malingering behavior. Associated neurological deficits that often present with Broca's aphasia include weakness of the right facial muscles, right arm and right leg with sensory loss on the right side of the body. The visual fields are often spared in stroke syndromes, but depending on the nature of the TBI and the tissue destruction associated with it, a right visual defect could present in a TBI-caused Broca's aphasia. Anatomically, the lesions that produce Broca's aphasia classically involve the posterior two-thirds of the inferior frontal convolutions, the pars triangularis, the pars opercularis, and Brodmann's areas 44 and 45 (see Figure 6.2). In classic stroke syndromes causing Broca's aphasia, much of speech may return as vascularity improves following the stroke. This may not be the case in TBI patients with substantial structural injury from trauma. Patients with aphemia often demonstrate right facial weakness but have no major motor deficits and no visual field defects. The lesions may involve the face area of the motor cortex. In strict terms, aphemia is not a true language disorder but is a disorder of motor speech.[145]

Wernicke's aphasia was described by the German physician Karl Wernicke in 1874.[140] Wernicke's aphasia is characterized by a fluent effortless speech output often with normal or even increased number of words per unit time (logorrhea). The speech content is empty and carries very little meaning, as nouns and verbs are often omitted, and paraphasic areas of phonemic (sounds) and semantic (verbal) types occur. Some authors describe Wernicke's aphasia as "jargon aphasia," as the sound resembles that of street jargon. Naming is impaired and may involve bizarre productions unrelated to the target word. Repetition is impaired and may contain paraphasic substitutions. Reading comprehension is usually impaired as is auditory comprehension. Some patients with

Wernicke's aphasia can comprehend printed words better than spoken language, or may present with the reverse.[146] The patient with Wernicke's aphasia can usually write with well-formed letters, but the writing is filled with many misspellings, empty phrases, and nonwords. The associated neurological deficits with Wernicke's aphasia usually are slighter than those seen in Broca's aphasia. Some patients may demonstrate right visual field deficits, but usually there is no significant weakness or sensory loss on the right side. This is often what causes Wernicke's aphasia to be mistaken for a psychosis or an acute confusional state. In contrast to the Broca's aphasics who may appear depressed, Wernicke's aphasics rarely do so. The anatomical lesion in Wernicke's aphasia classically involves the left superior temporal gyrus. Some authors include the inferior parietal lobule (supramarginal and angular gyri, Brodmann's areas 39 and 40) as part of Wernicke's area. Modern brain imaging studies have confirmed the left superior temporal gyrus as a structural deficit in Wernicke's aphasia, but Brodmann's areas 39 and 40 remain controversial as to whether they should be included. Electrical stimulation studies have confirmed that activation of the left superior temporal gyrus by surface electrodes interferes temporarily with language comprehension; patients can report hearing sounds and lack the ability to comprehend them.[147]

Pure word deafness is a selective deafness for auditory language. Pure word deafness is classically seen with bilateral lesions involving the Heschl gyrus. This causes loss of both word comprehension and identification of other meaningful sounds. Global aphasia is, from a practical standpoint, the confluence of Broca's aphasia with Wernicke's aphasia. The patient presents with loss of all the elementary language functions for both expression and reception. Patients may be mute or speak only with a verbal stereotyped phrase.[5] There are always associated severe motor and sensory deficits of right hemianopia, right hemiparesis, and right hemisensory loss. In general, patients with global aphasia neuroanatomically demonstrate extensive damage in the left frontal, temporal, and parietal lobes. There are almost always stroke syndromes associated with infarctions secondary to embolic occlusion of the middle cerebral artery or occlusion of the left internal carotid artery. Massive head trauma can cause global aphasia.[140] Conduction aphasia can be thought of primarily as a disorder of repetition, because this function is impaired out of proportion to other language deficits. Speech in conduction aphasia is usually fluent. Naming is variable, but auditory comprehension must be intact for conduction aphasia to be diagnosed. Reading for meaning is generally intact, but reading aloud may produce errors representing repetition. Many of these patients have right hemiparesis and right-sided sensory loss, and many present with ideomotor apraxia. The lesions found in conduction aphasia usually involve the superior temporal lobe or the inferior parietal lobe. Conduction aphasia is an example of a "disconnection syndrome," originally postulated by Wernicke but later revived by Geschwind.[141] Anomic aphasia is a syndrome in which naming difficulty is a primary abnormality. Patients can present with word production anomia or word selection anomia. In the former, the patient has difficulty eliciting words, and in the latter, the patient cannot produce the word or benefit from cues to produce a word, but they can point to the object if given the name. This deficit may correlate with lesions in the left temporal lobe, but usually does not involve the anatomy of Wernicke's area. The naming of nouns is more affected than verbs with temporal lesions, and if the lesion is in the frontal lobes, the reverse may occur. The lesions of anomic aphasia are extremely variable. Anomia is common in TBI and can be a sign of a localized disorder such as a left subdural hematoma, though it is also seen in acute confusional states, Alzheimer's disease and Pick's disease.[140]

The transcortical aphasias are not in the primary language cortex. These spare the perisylvian language circuit. The key method for detecting transcortical aphasia is that the patient always can repeat well. Transcortical motor aphasia resembles Broca's aphasia with repetition preserved, and transcortical sensory aphasia resembles Wernicke's aphasia with repetition preserved. Subcortical aphasias do occur in TBI where lesions affect the subcortical structures, the internal capsule or deep white matter areas. Thalamic injuries can produce a thalamic aphasia. The language is usually fluent with paraphasic errors, but there is better comprehension and repetition than seen in Wernicke's aphasia. There may be an altered awareness in this disorder, and patients may appear alert for a period of time with coherent speech and then become somnolent and mumble unintelligible paraphasic speech. The posterior thalamic area has extensive projections to Wernicke's area. This disorder usually correlates with an ischemic infarction within the territory of the tuberothalamic artery,[148] but it has been seen in TBI. The anterior subcortical aphasia syndrome presents with lesions of the caudate nucleus, putamen, and the adjacent white matter. The language disorder is usually nonfluent associated with dysarthria. Abnormalities are usually mild, and many patients have an associated right hemiparesis. The neuroanatomy of this syndrome likely involves disruption in the caudate nucleus or anterior limb of fibers projecting to the caudate from the temporal cortex and from the caudate to the globus pallidus, ventral lateral thalamus, and premotor cortex.[149]

Alexia is an acquired disorder of reading. The syndrome of alexia with agraphia was first described by the French physician Dejerine in 1891.[140] Reading and writing are both disrupted without significant dysfunction of other language modalities. Repetition and auditory comprehension are preserved. Occasional cases of alexia with agraphia evolve from an initial deficit of Wernicke's aphasia, but this can exist as a pure disorder. Writing is usually affected totally, such that patients cannot write or spell even single words. Some patients can copy but cannot write sentences spontaneously or to dictation. The lesion in alexia with agraphia involves the left inferior parietal lobule, and in particular the left angular gyrus (Brodmann's area 39). This syndrome may be seen in strokes involving the inferior division of the left middle cerebral artery or after a watershed infarct between the left middle and posterior cerebral arteries from vascular occlusion, hypoxia, or toxic brain poisoning. It has been associated with traumatic injuries and arteriovenous malformation.[140] The classic Gerstmann's syndrome is associated with an angular gyrus disorder (BA 39). In 1930, when Gerstmann described this syndrome, it consisted of agraphia, right–left confusion, disorientation, acalculia, and finger agnosia. Finger agnosia refers to the inability to identify topographically which fingers are being touched while the patient is blindfolded. This disorder indicates a left inferior parietal lesion. The angular gyrus syndrome is a variant of Gerstmann's syndrome and may mimic dementia. This can be confused with Alzheimer's disease, as a patient with a single lesion in the left angular gyrus, documented by PET scan but not by CT scan, has combined deficits of anomia, fluent aphasia, alexia, agraphia, acalculia, right–left disorientation, finger agnosia, and constructional apraxia.[140] As the reader probably knows, posterior metabolic defects are common in Alzheimer's disease patients examined by PET scan in these same anatomic areas described above.

Pure alexia without agraphia was also described by Dejerine in 1892.[140] In patients presenting with this disorder, spontaneous speech is usually normal and naming may be mildly impaired for colors. Auditory comprehension and repetition are typically intact and oral spelling and comprehension is impaired in almost all other syndromes; since they are not impaired in this syndrome, their presence is a useful guide in the diagnosis of pure alexia without agraphia. Most patients presenting with this disorder will have a visual defect, either a hemianopia or a right upper quadrant defect. Rarely, visual fields are intact. Some of these patients lose color vision in the right visual field (hemiachromatopsia).[150] The Damasios point out that these visual defects are important to test, as they may be the only neurological deficits present to aid in the detection of this syndrome.[150] Associated behavioral deficits include color anomia, visual agnosia, and memory loss. The inability of these patients to name colors is not a perceptual problem, as they can match and sort colors normally. They can also name colors in the abstract, such as the color of the inside of a watermelon; so the problem is not anomia. The deficit is an inability to associate and perceive a specific color with its name. This has been termed "color agnosia."[140] Alexia without agraphia is specific for a consistent lesion site: the left posterior cerebral artery distribution and the medial occipital and medial temporal lobes, often including the splenium of the corpus callosum. The left occipital lobe lesion produces a right homonymous hemianopia, whereas the lesion in the corpus callosum prevents visual information from the right occipital lobe from reaching the left hemisphere language centers. This is another example of a "disconnection syndrome." The short-term memory loss seen in some pure alexic patients correlates with medial temporal involvement, especially within the hippocampus. This deficit may contribute to the inability of patients with pure alexia to be able to read a sentence they have just written. The term "aphasic alexia" is a term of art and refers to alexia associated with left frontal lesions and global or Broca's aphasia. Psycholinguistic alexic syndromes are involved in the sequential cognitive steps required for reading. Analysis of these syndromes requires the assistance of a reading specialist in most cases unless the neuropsychiatric examiner is particularly skilled in the associated syndromes noted in Table 6.13. These include letter-by-letter reading, phonological alexia, and patients who can read only phonetically. They read nonsense syllables normally but cannot read irregularly spelled words such as "colonel" or "yacht."

The agraphias are defined as a disruption of previously intact writing skills due to brain damage. In the aphasia syndromes, writing is often the most severely impaired language modality and should always be tested in any person being screened for a disruption of language function. The reader is referred to standard behavioral neurology or neuropsychiatry texts for more careful delineation of this complex area of language function. Lastly, acalculia is the loss of ability to calculate. Studies have confirmed that calculation disorders are most common in the posterior left hemisphere lesions, though they occur with lesions in other varied sites. They are considered parts of language function rather than an isolated mathematical ability. If the reader will note, the arithmetic scale on the Wechsler Adult Intelligence Scale-III is within the group of verbal tests, rather than performance tests.

A word about bilingual patients: with increased globalization, it is more and more likely that an examiner will encounter a traumatically brain-injured patient who is multilingual. A recent German study examined the question whether verbal memory processing in two unrelated languages is mediated by a common neural system or by distinct cortical areas. Subjects skilled in both the Finnish language and the English language, who had acquired the second language after the age of 10, were PET scanned while encoding or retrieving word pairs in their mother tongue (Finnish) or in a foreign language (English). A PET scan using oxygen-15-water was obtained in each person. Encoding was associated with prefrontal and hippocampal activation. During memory retrieval of words, the precuneus showed a consistent activation in both languages and for both highly imaginable and abstract words. However, differential activations were found in Broca's area and in the cerebellum as well as in the angular-supramarginal gyri, depending on the language being used.[151] This offers some explanation for the fact that in a multilingual person who sustains a TBI, if an aphasic syndrome is involved, the aphasia is worse in the most recently acquired language and is least apparent in the mother tongue (a very useful point in a forensic examination). In the auditory recognition of language, there is evidence that there are sex-linked differences in the anatomy of primary and association auditory cortices. Women exhibit left hemisphere asymmetry of the planum temporale, whereas men do not exhibit this asymmetry. This is based on volumetric MRI studies of Heschl's gyrus, planum temporale, and the posterior temporal gyrus.[152]

One difficulty often noted following TBI is that patients lose the ability to verbally self-monitor. A study in the United Kingdom using oxygen-15-water as a tracer of regional cerebral blood flow found that self-generated and externally generated speech are processed in similar regions of the temporal cortex. The monitoring of self-generated speech involves the temporal cortex bilaterally and areas associated with the processing of speech, which has been generated outside the patient.[153] This is consistent with the known likelihood of injury to the temporal cortex during closed head TBI (see Chapter 1).

Whereas language studies have classically followed the models of Broca and Wernicke, more recent information indicates that sites external to the perisylvian area are involved in language processing as well and may be injured during TBI. For instance, a recent Northwestern University study demonstrated that the putamen engages in cortical initiation of language while the cerebellum amplifies and refines the signal to facilitate correct decision making in phonological processing. This was based on fMRI studies obtained during a rhyming judgment task in adults using dynamic causal modeling. These results demonstrated that the cerebellum has reciprocal connections with both the left inferior frontal gyrus and the left lateral temporal cortex, whereas the putamen has unidirectional connections into these two brain regions.[154] An interesting study recently gave insight into the neural anatomical areas responsible for auditory verbal hallucinations. Eighteen medicated schizophrenic patients (8 with auditory verbal hallucinations) and 12 healthy control subjects were scanned with oxygen-15-water PET under two conditions: reading aloud English nouns or passively looking at English nouns without reading them. The healthy control subjects demonstrated higher activation in Wernicke's area during the reading condition. However, this was reversed in those patients with auditory verbal hallucinations. They activated the supplemental motor area in the frontal lobes. The authors suggested that the abnormal laterality of the supplemental motor area actively accounts for the failure of a person to attribute speech generated by one's own brain to one's self. The activation of Wernicke's area in normal subjects accounts for the perceptual nature of hearing one's auditory experience.[155] The reader is referred to Chapter 2 for a discussion of psychosis following TBI. Some psychotic patients following TBI do experience auditory verbal hallucinations.

The last aspect of language disorders to be considered includes issues of prosody. Recall from Chapter 4 that a nonverbal language system operates parallel to the verbal-based system located in the left hemisphere. The nonverbal language system is primarily in the right hemisphere. Prosody is an important feature of language, and it comprises affective content, intonation, loudness, tempo, facial expression, hand gestures, and other nonlinguistic elements of discourse. Emotional prosodic processing forms an integral part of our social interactions, and the term "reading someone" comes from the general societal recognition that we unconsciously can determine the emotional responses of another person. The right hemisphere posterior areas decode the emotions of other people and the affective components of their language in the same way that Wernicke's area decodes and comprehends spoken language. The posterior temporal lobe responses to the emotional aspects of another person's language are relatively right-lateralized with or without semantic information. This has been confirmed by fMRI studies in the United Kingdom.[156] As we interact with others, our language and associated actions occur concurrently. Speech and gestures that people use in everyday communication seem well coordinated. Functional MRI studies from the Netherlands have indicated a coordination that gestural action and language share a high-level integration system using Brodmann's areas 45 and 47, and premotor areas (BA 6).[157] As we have seen earlier in this text, many patients are dysarthric following TBI. The dysarthria at times is a marker of dysprosody. Dysarthric patients in particular have impairments of speaking rate and the emphatic stress placed upon language components.[158]

The clinical syndromes that arise from language disturbances in the right hemisphere are collectively termed "the aprosodias." It is now scientifically accepted that right hemisphere injury may interfere with discourse. That is, the skill with which one can organize a narrative story, make a joke, or write a letter.[159] Imagine the difficulty with communication if a TBI negatively affects the production of words and sentences which provide meaning that goes beyond their basic dictionary descriptions.[142]

MRI structural brain studies have generally shown that patients with impaired spontaneous affective prosody (anterior dysprosody) had lesions involving the posterior–inferior frontal lobe, which included the pars opercularis and triangularis. These regions are anatomically similar to Broca's areas in the left hemisphere. Those patients with more posterior lesions impairing comprehension of affective prosody ("reading other people") had lesions involving the posterior–superior temporal lobe. This region is similar anatomically to Wernicke's area in the left hemisphere. This indicates that there is a dual-highway language system with symbolic language produced and decoded primarily in the left hemisphere while the affective components of language are produced and decoded primarily in the right hemisphere.[144] Table 6.14 summarizes the known neuroanatomy of human language function.

The Neuropsychological Measurement of Language

The assessment of language following TBI can be done relatively expertly using the bedside language examination techniques in Table 6.13. This will allow the neuropsychiatric examiner to

TABLE 6.14

The Neuroanatomy of Language

Function	Purported Location
Brain activation by speech sounds	Heschl's gyrus, planum temporale, dorsal superior temporal gyrus, lateral superior temporal gyrus, and superior temporal sulcus[160,161]
Brain activation by written symbols	Calcarine cortex and medial occipital extrastriate region[162,163]
Letter processing	Posterior fusiform and inferior occipital gyrus, left > right[163,164]
Phoneme processing	Left frontal operculum (anterior insula and Brodmann's area 45) and inferior frontal gyrus (Brodmann's areas 6 and 44)[165]
Prosody	Parallel right-hemisphere system mirroring Broca's and Wernicke's left-hemisphere areas[144]
Semantic (meaning) analysis	Brodmann's area 39 (angular gyrus)[141]
Self-generated word production	Frontal operculum, inferior frontal gyrus, middle frontal gyrus, inferior frontal sulcus, and mid-dorsal frontal sulcus (Brodmann's areas 6, 8, 44–47)[160]

screen for language dysfunction and determine whether a more precise evaluation of language should be undertaken. Due to the complexity and time demands of most language disorder batteries (see Table 6.15), a full language assessment is usually not required nor performed during an ordinary neurocognitive evaluation following TBI. In those selected cases where the patient has an obvious aphasia, or where neuroimaging and physical examination reveal the likelihood of substantial structural injury in the perisylvian area, the full language battery should probably be administered to the patient. Lezak suggests that six elements should be performed during the neuropsychological assessment of language.[8] These include (1) spontaneous speech, (2) repetition of words, phrases, and sentences, (3) speech comprehension, (4) naming of objects and their parts, (5) reading for accuracy and comprehension, and (6) writing by copying, dictation, and composition of a sentence. Goodglass[166] has pointed out the importance of attending to ease and quantity of verbal production (fluency), articulatory ability (pronunciation with tongue and mouth parts), speech rhythms and intonation (prosody), grammar and syntax, and the presence of misspoken words (paraphasias).

The assessment of language in bilingual or multilingual persons presents substantial difficulties to the examiner. Screening with bedside techniques may be the most that can be accomplished in these situations. However, with the large Spanish-speaking population in the United States,

TABLE 6.15

Neuropsychological Tests of Language

Test	Measurement
Aphasia Screening Test	A language screening test of the Halstead–Reitan battery. Lezak says to "junk it altogether."[8]
Boston Diagnostic Aphasia Examination (BDAE-3)	Available in English, Spanish, and French. Requires diagnostic skills in aphasia to use properly. The gold standard for full language assessment.
Boston Naming Test	Effectively elicits an anomia if present.
Controlled Oral Word Association Test	Assesses word fluency: Measures frontal lobe word output ability.
Multilingual Aphasia Examination	Revised by Benton and is a full language battery. Requires less time for administration than the BDAE. Spanish version is available.
Token Test	Assesses ability to perform spoken commands. Detects comprehension.
Western Aphasia Battery	A full language assessment battery. The diagnostic classification poorly describes patients with mixed language disorders.

currently there are available two large batteries that can be administered in Spanish. These include the Boston Diagnostic Aphasia Examination and the Multilingual Aphasia Examination.[167–169]

Boston Diagnostic Aphasia Examination-III

This is the third edition of the classic Boston Diagnostic Aphasia Examination (BDAE-III). It was published in 2000, and it is devised to examine the components of language.[169] This test battery provides for a systematic assessment of communication and communication-related functioning in twelve areas that have been defined by factor analysis. This produces a total of 34 subtests. A complete examination requires from 1 to 4 h, depending on the neuropsychological and language intactness of the patient. Many examiners use portions of this test selectively. The BDAE-III has a new short form that takes only an hour or less. The extended version of the BDAE-III contains instructions for examining praxis problems, which often accompany aphasia. An Aphasia Severity Rating Scale can be derived from the BDAE-III within a five-point range based on examiner ratings and patient responses to a semi-structured interview and free conversation. The range and sensitivity of this battery make it an excellent tool for the description of aphasic disorders and for treatment planning with patients. However, examiners are cautioned that they must be experienced to use it diagnostically. Ordinary psychological or psychiatric training generally does not provide sufficient skills to use this test battery effectively, and it is recommended that examiners have special interest and training in language disorders in order to gain full utility from this instrument. In those seriously injured patients, one has to consider motivational factors and fatigue as confounding variables in the test. Spordone and Saul warn, as well as Lezak, that neuropsychologists need strong backgrounds in the study of language disturbances and aphasias to use the examination well.[8,18]

Boston Naming Test

This test consists of sixty large ink drawings of items ranging in familiarity from common figures such as "tree" or "pencil" at the beginning of the test to more complex figures such as "Sphinx" and "trellis" near the end of the test.[170] It is a subcomponent of the BDAE. The revised edition published in 2000 has a 15-item short version as well as the standard 60-item picture set. The new edition also has a multiple-choice format for recognition testing, which can be used when items are missed. Nine error types are coded. The same picture set is used in the new edition as was used in the first edition. The data on this test indicate that no appreciable score declination occurs in normals until the late 70s when the drop is slight.[8] Standard deviations by age group increased steadily from age 60 on, indicating a greater variability for naming skill within the normal older population. The newer edition has better norms relative to the first edition. Poor scores on this test can be due to a variety of factors including a limited cultural or language background, low intellectual functioning, low level of education, or a psychiatric disturbance.[18]

Controlled Oral Word Association Test

Controlled Oral Word Association (COWA) Test was originally published by Benton and Hamsher as a variation from the Multilingual Aphasia Examination. Spreen and Strauss[172] and Ivnik et al.[171] have provided additional means and standard deviations for different ages and educational groups, and Tombaugh et al.[173] report means and standard deviations for large normal samples ranging from 20 to 89 years with percentiles stratified by age and education. Norms are also available stratified for education and sex by Ruff et al.[174] This test consists of three word-naming trials using words beginning with the letters F-A-S. The Multilingual Aphasia Examination edition provides norms for two sets of letters, C-F-L and P-R-W.

To administer the test, the examiner asks patients to say as many words as they can think of that begin with the given letter of the alphabet excluding proper nouns, numbers, and the same word with a different suffix. Word fluency is measured by the COWA, and similar techniques calling for generation of a word list, have proven to be sensitive indicators of brain dysfunction. Frontal lobe lesions, regardless of laterality, tend to depress fluency scores with left frontal lesions resulting in lower word production than right frontal lesions.[8] Poor performance also can occur in patients who are suffering from anxiety, depression, sleep deprivation, cultural deprivation and poor language skills.[18]

Token Test

The Token Test is extremely simple to administer and to score. It can be completed by almost every nonaphasic person who has completed the 4th grade, and these individuals will perform with few if any errors. It is remarkably sensitive to the disrupted linguistic processes that are central to aphasia, even when much of the patient's communication behaviors remained intact. Scores on the Token Test correlate highly with scores on tests of auditory comprehension. This test measures a person's ability to comprehend and perform commands that are presented orally.[175]

Twenty tokens made from heavy construction paper or thin sheets of plastic or wood make up the test materials. They come in two shapes (circles and squares), two sizes (large and small), and five colors. The tokens are laid out horizontally in four parallel rows of large circles, large squares, small circles, and small squares, with colors in random order. The only requirement this test makes on the patient is the ability to comprehend the token names, and the verbs and prepositions in the instructions. Almost all brain-injured persons can respond to these simple instructions. The examiner instructs the patient with direct commands or complex commands such as "Touch the white square," or "Before touching the yellow circle, pick up the red square." This test is sensitive for examining patients with receptive language skills following TBI, and it has been used to evaluate children and adolescents who have sustained head injuries.[172,176] Performance on this test can be confounded in those patients who have hearing loss, attentional deficits, psychiatric disorders, or pain disorders. Table 6.15 lists tests useful for measuring language following TBI.

Multilingual Aphasia Examination

This consists of a seven-part battery, and currently the Token Test and the Controlled Oral Word Association test are components of the Multilingual Aphasia Examination and its variations. This test comes from the Benton school of neuropsychology. One advantage is that most of the tests in this battery have two or three forms, which can assist in reducing practice effects if repeated administrations are required. For each test, age and education effects are dealt with by means of a correction score, which is added to the raw score and gives an adjusted score. Internal statistics have been corrected on this test so that scores on each of the subtests are psychometrically comparable.[171] This enables each subtest to be used as a stand alone test if one chooses. For instance, verbal fluency or verbal memory could be measured using this test instrument in a patient who is not aphasic. A Spanish version of this test is also available.[208]

MEASURING VISUAL–SPATIAL ABILITY

From a neuropsychiatric or behavioral neurology perspective, visual dysfunction is categorized somewhat differently than neuropsychologists such as Lezak would classify. Table 6.16 categorizes defects of visual processing. The cerebral organization of visual processing involves two distinct components: (1) a serial relay of information from the retina to the lateral geniculate nucleus and then to striate cortex (area V1 of the occipital lobe) and (2) after the striate cortex receives visual data, visual information then fans out in multiple projections to various areas in an interconnected hierarchal network of extrastriate cortical areas. As information proceeds through this hierarchy, the visual areas become increasingly specialized for specific types of visual analysis, and topographic representation becomes coarser with many neurons in high-level areas responding to stimuli from a wide expanse of both ipsilateral and contralateral visual fields.[177]

The Neuroanatomical and Neuroimaging Bases of Visual–Spatial Ability

Tasks of visual processing are extremely complex. They occupy a vast amount of neural tissue, and visual processing tasks are some of the most complicated neuroanatomical functional areas within the brain. Recent evaluations using slow-cortical potentials and low-resolution electromagnetic

TABLE 6.16

Visual Processing Dysfunctions

A. Disorders of Color
- Dyschromatopsia: Color perception is faded or reduced in range of hues.
- Color anomia and agnosia: Patients can discriminate colors but not name or recognize them.

B. Visual Agnosia
- Inability to recognize objects one has seen before.

C. Acquired Alexia

D. Disorders of Facial Perception
- Prosopagnosia: Patients cannot recognize previously known faces or learn new ones.
- Anterograde prosopagnosia: Patients can recognize previously known faces but not new ones.
- Developmental prosopagnosia: Patients cannot judge facial age, gender, or affective expressions.

E. Akinetopsia
- Impaired perception of motion.

F. Bálint Syndrome
- Simultanagnosia, optic ataxia, and ocular motor apraxia.

G. Topographagnosia
- Getting lost in familiar surroundings.

H. Constructional Defects
- Inability to draw or copy familiar simple objects. This skill combines visual perception with motor and spatial abilities.

tomography have confirmed that visual–spatial processing involves a complex distributed network of extrastriate occipital, superior parietal, temporal, medial frontal, and prefrontal areas during task solving.[183] The initial input to the striate cortex occurs at about 50–55 ms after the stimulus is introduced. It does not appear to be modulated by attention. There is a second facilitation of signals observed in extrastriate visual areas at 70–75 ms later. Recent studies suggest that there is reentrant feedback from higher visual areas involved in this initial processing.[184] The recognition of visual-spatial information also includes frontal lobe function. A fMRI study demonstrated that common areas used were the frontal eye fields, the presupplementary motor area complex, the precentral gyri and the horizontal and descending branches of the intraparietal sulcus.[185] Thus, as we explore further visual processing dysfunctions, the reader should be aware that in TBI, it is probably not possible for an ordinary neuropsychiatric examiner to parse out all the various elements involved in visual processing defects. The analysis and testing would be too complex for most patients to endure.

In Chapter 2, we learned that most individuals who suffer a closed TBI display relatively normal visual-perceptual abilities. This statement does not hold for those individuals who have sustained brain contusions, hematomas, or penetration into specific visual processing areas, and they are the most likely persons to demonstrate disorders of visual processing. For a more complex understanding of visual processing defects, two recent texts will be useful for further study.[177,178]

If a person develops achromatopsia, they see the world in shades of gray. Color perception may not be entirely abolished and may be presented with a faded or reduced range of hues to the patient.[179] Testing color perception is difficult, and asking patients to name colors is not sufficient. This will confuse color anomia with achromatopsia. The detection of this disorder probably requires expert ophthalmologic consultation. The anatomical areas that subserve achromatopsia are in the lingual and fusiform gyri. Lesions of the middle third of the lingual gyrus or the white matter behind the posterior tip of the lateral ventricle may be critical in causing this disorder. Functional MRI has confirmed the participation of this region in normal color perception.[180] Unilateral lesions cause a contralateral hemiachromatopsia. Complete achromatopsia requires bilateral lesions. These are most commonly seen in posterior cerebral arterial strokes but conceivably could occur in TBI with significant intraparenchymal contusion into the lingual and fusiform gyri.

For color anomia and color agnosia, patients can discriminate colors but not name or recognize them. PET studies have shown that color words activate the posterior–inferior ventral temporal lobe just anterior to the zone activated by color perception, the parietal–occipital junction, and the left lingual gyrus.[181] Color anomia can occur without other linguistic dysfunction. Color agnosia is rare. These patients are similar to those demonstrating color anomia, but they cannot color line drawings correctly or learn associations between objects and their colors.[182]

Patients with visual agnosia cannot recognize objects they have seen before. They cannot name a previously familiar but unrecognized object, and they will demonstrate no knowledge of its use, the context in which they have seen it previously, or their history of using the object. If the visual agnosia is pure, it is possible the patient could recognize an object through other sensory modalities such as hearing (a clock or watch) or touch (a hammer or screwdriver). One of the common causes of visual agnosia is a watershed injury to the brain by diffuse anoxia such as seen with carbon monoxide poisoning. It may also be associated with alexia and prosopagnosia.[177,186] Alexia has been discussed previously in this chapter and will not be further analyzed with regard to visual processing.

Disorders of face perception are intriguing and extremely interesting to most behavioral neurologists or neuropsychiatrists. The patient presenting to an examiner with prosopagnosia cannot recognize the faces of familiar people or learn new faces. The testing of face recognition usually involves a battery of photographs of public persons well known either in the person's individual country or worldwide. Sometimes these tests have unfamiliar faces as foils. One common test is the Benton Face Recognition Test[187] in which patients are shown anonymous faces and are asked to find the matching face in an array of faces that differ either in lighting or viewpoint. Damasio et al. believe that prosopagnosia almost always involves bilateral lesions.[178] A recent Harvard Medical School study was able to apportion function in individuals with prosopagnosia. This study concluded that a person's imagery for facial shape, but not features, was degraded by lesions of the right hemisphere's fusiform face area, with severely impaired perception of facial configuration. On the other hand, imagery for features of the face was degraded only when there was an associated occipital–temporal damage in the lingual and fusiform gyri. This study suggests that although the anterior temporal cortex may be the site of facial memory stores, these data support hypotheses that perceptual areas of the fusiform face area have parallel contributions to mental imagery.[188] Patients with prosopagnosia can recognize that a face is a face, but they are unable to say whose face it is. This basic-level object recognition dysfunction distinguishes these patients from those with severe generalized visual agnosia. Prosopagnosia is caused by lesions of either the lingual and fusiform gyri or the more anterior temporal cortex. Functional MRI has confirmed face identity-related activity in the right fusiform gyrus. Bilateral lesions have been reported in many cases at autopsy and neuroimaging. Evidence from pathology and neuroimaging indicates that a right-sided occipital lesion can cause prosopagnosia alone and bilaterality is not required.[189–191]

There is a rare group of patients who present with variants of disorders of face perception. One rare disorder is described as anterograde prosopagnosia. This occurs with bilateral damage to the amygdalae and has been reported following epilepsy surgery. There is an associated dysnomia, and patients cannot judge facial expressions or the direction of gaze, which is consistent with the role the amygdala plays in social behavior.[192] A second rare developmental prosopagnosia exists. This is commonly encountered in patients with Asperger's syndrome. These individuals have difficulty with face perception and also demonstrate problems judging facial age, gender, and facial expressions; they perform very slowly on tests of facial matching. Developmental prosopagnosia has also been reported as an autosomal dominant trait. Neuroimaging may not show a lesion.[193] There is a related disorder known as Capgras syndrome. In this disorder, a patient believes that familiar people have been replaced by imposters. It can be seen in Alzheimer's disease and other psychiatric syndromes. There are also cases from neurologic origin. Frontal lesions are common; they are often bilateral and sometimes are combined with right posterior hemispheric lesions. These individuals often do not have classic lesions consistent with prosopagnosia.[177]

Disorders of motion perception are termed akinetopsia. Patients who have a unilateral lesion may be asymptomatic or give subtle complaints to the examiner, such as "feeling disturbed by visually cluttered moving scenes," and have difficulty judging the speed and direction of cars while driving.[194] In most cases with unilateral lesions, the defect is in the extrastriate cortex. Some patients have been reported to have lesions in the lateral occipitotemporal cortex or the inferior parietal lobule. A special disorder of spatial perception is called Bálint's syndrome. This classically has been described in patients who present with simultanagnosia, optic ataxia, and ocular motor apraxia. These patients have a deficit in distributing visual-spatial attention. They cannot pay attention to more than a few objects at a time, and they have difficulty with attentionally demanding visual search tasks and in maintaining attentional surveillance consistently over large regions of visual space. Simultanagnosia is the inability to interpret a complex scene with multiple interrelated elements, despite being able to perceive those elements individually. Optic ataxia is the inability to control hand movements under visual guidance to a target despite normal motor function in the limb and normal proprioception. The patient misreaches while attempting to touch a target. In ocular motor apraxia, the patient has difficulty initiating visual saccades to targets. When the patient is prompted by a verbal command to visually follow a target, he or she is unable to do so. To diagnose Bálint's syndrome, the examiner must carefully exclude more general cognitive dysfunction, hemineglect, and elementary visual defects in acuity and peripheral fields. Ophthalmologists may have difficulty performing perimetry on these patients due to their inability to attend and due to the associated fatigue and difficulty maintaining visual fixation that is present. Simultanagnosia is usually tested by asking the patient to report all items in a complex visual display and describe the events depicted. One excellent test to determine this is the cookie theft picture from the Boston Diagnostic Aphasia Examination.[169] Patients will omit elements and they will fail to grasp the story being told pictorially. At the bedside, patients can be asked to pick up a number of coins scattered on a table. To test for optic ataxia, easily seen items are placed at different locations within arm's reach of the patient who is then asked to touch or grasp them with each hand tested separately. Affected patients will misreach for the visual targets. This misreaching must be differentiated from cerebellar dysmetria, but the latter is usually accompanied by intention tremor and dysdiadocokinesia. Ocular motor apraxia is confirmed by comparing the patient's difficulty in making saccades to command with ease in making reflex saccades to sudden targets in the natural environment such as an unexpected hand clapping or person walking down the hall.[177]

Patients with topographagnosia get lost in familiar surroundings. Lesions in this disorder are usually within the ventral or dorsal association cortices (Brodmann's areas 18 and 19). Lesions in the ventral area present with prosopagnosia and achromatopsia and reflect agnosia for familiar landmarks and buildings, whereas dorsal lesions present with impaired spatial processing and inability to describe, follow or memorize routes and maps. These are usually preferential in the right hemisphere.[195] Recent anatomical work has found that the subiculum plays a role in topographagnoisa.[196] Also, another anatomical study has demonstrated that spatial memory is dependent on the hippocampus no matter how long ago the information was acquired.[196,197]

Lastly, under the rubric Visual Processing Dysfunctions is the inability to construct items by drawing or copying. This defect is seen in persons who cannot draw a clock and place the hands, or cannot draw familiar simple objects such as intersecting pentagons and Greek crosses. It is a more complex disorder than a pure visual processing dysfunction, as this ability combines perception with motor responses, and it has a spatial component. However, it is a visual-perceptual defect. Laterality is often present, and patients with right hemisphere lesions are more likely to demonstrate constructional impairment than are patients with left hemisphere lesions. The site of the lesions along the anterior–posterior axis affects the expression of constructional impairment. The primary differences are in the qualitative aspects of the drawings. For instance, patients with left-sided lesions may get the overall idea of the item to be copied, and the proportions they construct may be correct, but their drawings tend to omit details and generally they turn out a shabby production. Unlike patients with right hemisphere dysfunction, those with lesions on the left may do better when presented with

TABLE 6.17

The Neuroanatomy of Visuoperception

Function	Purported Location
Prosopagnosia	Lingual and fusiform gyri: Subjacent white matter (inferior and mesial visual association cortex)[177]
Topographic disorientation	Parahippocampal place area[198]
Bálint's syndrome	Bilateral occipitoparietal areas[199]
Judgment of orientation and direction of lines	Occipitoparietal areas[200]
Face selection	Fusiform face area (mid-fusiform gyrus)[190,201]
Emotional expression in faces	Amgydalae[202]

a model as opposed to drawing to command, and their performance will often improve with repetition. Patients with right hemisphere lesions often proceed from right-to-left on drawing or assembly tasks rather than in the more common approach of working from left-to-right.[8] Table 6.17 summarizes the known neuroanatomy of visual processing dysfunctions. For a recent review of the complex topic of visual recognition, the reader is referred to Kanwisher et al.[203]

The Neuropsychological Measurement of Visual Processing

Lezak[8] warns that many aspects of visual perception may be impaired by brain disease. Typically, brain impairment involving one visual function will affect a cluster of functions. It is infrequent that disorders of visual perception are confined to a single or a small set of dysfunctions. Neuropsychologically, the measurement of visual functions can be broadly divided along the lines of verbal/symbolic and configural stimuli. When examining using visually presented material, the examiner cannot categorically assume that the right brain is doing most of the processing when the stimuli are pictures or figures, or that the right brain is not engaged in distinguishing the shapes of words or numbers. Visual symbolic stimuli have spatial dimensions and other visual characteristics that lend themselves to processing as configurations. Most of what we see, including pictorial or design material, can be given a label. The psychological test materials used for measuring visual-perceptual functions do not conform to a strict verbal-configurational dichotomy any more than do the visual stimuli of the real world that the patient experiences. Moreover, impairment of very basic visual functions such as acuity and oculomotor skills are likely to result in poor performance on more complex visual-perceptual tasks. Visuoperception is often impaired by brain injury. Typically, if one visual function is affected following brain injury, a cluster of functions will secondarily be affected as well.[204] There is some visual activity that occurs within the left hemisphere as well.[5] See Table 6.17 for a survey of purported visuoperceptual neuroanatomy.

Bender-Gestalt Test

Lezak places the Bender-Gestalt Test within the domain of construction.[5] Others note that this test evaluates the patient's visuoperceputal and visuoconstructional skills.[205,206] It is one of the most frequently used psychological tests in the United States; it has been used for over 60 years, and there are more than 1000 studies concerning its validity and reliability. However, it is only a screening test and it may be misused. Most experts feel that it should never be used as a stand alone test or a test upon which to conclude that organic brain injury is present.[18]

The test consists of nine geometric designs that are presented individually to the person being examined. The patient is then asked to draw an accurate reproduction of the figure on a piece of blank paper.[5] A number of different scoring systems exist based on the accuracy and organization of the reproduced drawing. However, there is a substantial amount of subjectiveness within this test, as its effective use depends upon the skill of the examiner.[207]

Benton Facial Recognition Test

This test is designed to measure a person's ability to compare photographs of faces. The patient is shown a photograph of a person's face, and directly below the photograph are six other photographs containing someone's face. The initial part of the test simply is to identify the person in the first six photographs. The second portion of the test reveals only three quarters of a person's face, and the patient has to determine which face is present. In the third portion of the test, the patient must match the original photograph of faces to photographs that have been taken under low lighting conditions.

This test is quick to administer and requires about 15 min of testing time.[208] Patients who have right parietal lesions perform more poorly than patients with right temporal lesions. Lezak suggests that this demonstrates a substantial visuospatial processing component to the test.[5] Thus, this test tends to be particularly sensitive to patients who have sustained left hemisphere or frontal lobe damage. Psychiatric conditions can lead to poor performance on this test. It is not a stand alone examination, and Spordone and Saul[18] recommend that other neuropsychological measures be taken at the same time as this test is administered.

Benton Judgment of Line Orientation Test

During this test administration, the patient is asked to match a pair of angled lines, which are shown on a card, to 1 of 11 numbered lines below it.[209] Essentially, the patient has to match the angle of the stimulus line to the correct angle of 1 of the 11 numbered control lines. While performing this test, cerebral blood flow in temporo-occipital areas increases bilaterally. However, the greatest increase is on the right side.[210] Most patients with left hemisphere damage alone perform this test within an average range, whereas patients with right hemisphere damage are more likely to provide impaired scores, particularly if they have posterior lesions.

Poor performance on this test can be caused by impaired visual acuity, psychiatric disorder, significant pain, impairment of visual attention, and fatigue.[18] This test may not detect brain damage located in the left hemisphere, and it requires the administration of other neuropsychological tests to improve the overall neuropsychological screening.

Block Design Test

This test consists of assembling 1-in. blocks with red and white colors to reproduce a specific printed design from a stimulus card. The task may require the use of four to nine blocks. It is one of the performance subtests of the Wechsler Adult Intelligence Scales. It is a timed test, and each design becomes more difficult than the prior design.[211] This test is generally recognized as the best measure of visuospatial organization within the Wechsler Scales.[5] It reflects a general ability in most individuals so that cognitively capable persons who are academically or culturally limited will frequently obtain their highest score among the 11 subtests. However, Block Design scores tend to be lower in the presence of any kind of brain dysfunction. It is particularly sensitive to detection when the injury is located in the frontal or parietal lobes. In normal subjects, Block Design performance is associated with an increased glucose metabolism in the posterior parietal regions when measured by PET scan. Generally, the more intense metabolic activation is in the right cerebral hemisphere.[212]

Edith Kaplan argues that the examiner should note whether lateralized errors on this test tend to occur more at the top or the bottom of the constructions, as the upper visual fields have a temporal lobe component, whereas the lower visual fields have parietal components. Thus, a pattern of errors clustering at the top or the bottom corner can give some indication of the anatomical site and extent of the lesion.[5] By taking a qualitative rather than a quantitative approach to Block Design analysis, other information may be detected. For instance, patients with left hemisphere, particularly parietal lesions, tend to show confusion and simplification while handling the design in a concrete fashion. However, their approach to the designs is likely to be orderly; they typically work from left to right, as do intact subjects, and their construction usually preserves the square shape of the design. However, their greatest difficulty may be in placing the last block, which most often will be on their right. On the other hand, patients with right-sided lesions may begin at the right of the design and work to their left. The visuospatial defect reveals itself in disorientation, design distortions, and misperceptions. Left visuospatial inattention may compound this design-copying problem, resulting in two- or three-block solutions to the four-block designs.[5]

Hooper Visual Organization Test

The Hooper Visual Organization Test consists of showing the patient 30 pictures of objects that have been cut up and placed in different positions.[213] The patient must visually examine each picture and then decide what it would represent if it were assembled. The patient must write down the name of the object, such as a fish, ball, or key. Most individuals can complete this test in approximately 15 min.[18]

Cognitively intact persons generally fail no more than six items on this test. More than 11 failures usually indicate organic brain pathology. The test appears sensitive to bilateral posterior brain dysfunction, or in some instances, dysfunction of the right frontal lobe. These patients tend to examine only one object singly rather than visually organize the different objects into a cohesive visual whole. Poor performance on this test also can be caused by low intellectual ability, psychiatric disease, or poor effort.

Object Assembly Test

The Object Assembly Test is another subtest of the WAIS-III.[211] It requires the patient to assemble cardboard figures of familiar objects. There are timed portions of this test, and the patient must form the puzzle parts into a man, a face profile, an elephant, a house, and a butterfly. The patient is not told the name or nature of the object and must identify the object during the assembly process.

The speed component of this test renders it relatively vulnerable to brain damage generally.[5] It tests constructional ability and visuospatial perception and is sensitive to posterior brain lesions, more so on the right side than the left. In terms of internal correlations on the WAIS-III, the Object Assembly and Block Design subtests correlate more highly with one another than do any of the other Wechsler subscale tests.

Patients who have posterior right hemisphere damage typically will perform poorly on this test, and patients with frontal lobe injuries may show poor organization and planning skills in their approach to the test. If the brain injury is significant, the patient may not comprehend the test instructions and possibly could require extra examples, such as described in the WAIS-III test manual.

Visual Form Discrimination Test

This test consists of a series of three geometric figures that the patient must match to one of four sets of designs.[214] It is a multiple-choice test of visual recognition. Of the four sets of designs, one of the designs is an exact replica of the stimulus figure, while the others may vary to a subtle degree. This is a visual recognition test, and it is sensitive to posterior brain injury, particularly in the right parietal lobe. One of its strengths is that it can be administered to patients who are unable to speak English, as the patient only must point to one of four sets of figures on a sheet of cardboard. Visual memory plays little role in this test. A number of factors may interfere with test performance. These include impaired visual acuity, psychiatric disturbances, visual field defects, and poor motivation. Poor performance on this test alone may be sufficient to provide gross evidence of brain injury.[18] Please refer to Table 6.18 to review tests of visual-spatial and constructional ability.

MEASURING SOMATOSENSORY AND MOTOR FUNCTION

The Neuroanatomical and Neuroimaging Bases of Somatosensory and Motor Function

The four major modalities in the somatosensory system are (1) discriminative touch (a sense of texture and shape of objects and their movement across the skin), (2) proprioception (a sense of static position and movement of the limbs and body), (3) nociception (the signaling of tissue damage or chemical irritation, typically perceived as pain or itch), and (4) temperature sense

TABLE 6.18

Tests of Visuospatial and Constructional Skills

Test	Measurement
Bender-Gestalt Test	Visual perceptual and visual constructional skills, R > L parietal lobe
Benton Facial Recognition Test	Subtle perceptual/visual discrimination, R > L parietal lobe
Benton Judgment of Line Orientation Test	Ability to estimate angular relationships between line segments, rCBF increases in bilateral temporal–occipital areas, R > L[211]
Block Design Test (WAIS)	Visuospatial organization skills, glucose metabolism increases in posterior parietal lobe, R > L[213]
Clock Drawing Test	Visual neglect, right parietal dysfunction
Hooper Visual Organization Test	Visual perceptual fragmentation from bilateral posterior brain dysfunction or right frontal dysfunction
Object Assembly Test (WAIS)	Constructional ability, visuospatial perception, posterior brain R > L
Visual Form Discrimination Test	Visual recognition, posterior brain injury, particularly left parietal lobe

Note: rCBF stands for regional cerebral blood flow.

(warmth and cold).[215] Each modality is mediated by a distinct system of peripheral sensory pathways to the brain. There is a somatosensory map of the body created in the central nervous system by the topographic arrangement of afferent inputs from the dorsal root ganglion cells. The contralateral half of the body is represented in a precise but disproportionate manner as a sensory homunculus in the primary sensory cortex. The primary somatosensory cortex (S1) is located in the postcentral gyrus of the parietal lobe (Brodmann's areas 1, 2, and 3) and in the posterior part of the paracentral lobule. Area 3 is subdivided into two parts: 3a in the depths of the central sulcus, and 3b on the posterior wall of the central sulcus. Neurons in areas 3b and 1 predominantly mediate the sense of touch, while neurons in area 3a predominately mediate the sense of position. Neurons in area 2 mediate both touch and position sense. The association cortex for this region lies within Brodmann's areas 5 and 7, and a portion of it is in the anterior segment of Brodmann's area 40. The posterior insula is often included in this association cortex as well. The somatosensory association cortex plays an essential role to guide the finer aspects of touch localization and the active manual exploration of objects. The somatosensory coordination of reaching and grasping and the encoding of complex somatosensory memories are also subserved by this anatomical area.[216] Area 5 is unimodal association cortex, and area 7 is heteromodal association cortex, and they are located in the anterior and posterior portions of the posterior parietal lobe. Areas 5 and 7 project to the S2 area, which is important for shape perception, to the dorsolateral portion of the frontal lobe (important for sensorimotor transformation), to multimodal association areas in the inferior parietal lobe, and to the supramarginal angular gyri (areas 39 and 40), which are important for intermodal integration and multisensory perceptions.

Neurons in nonmesial area 5 have bilateral hand representation and integration information necessary for the cooperative actions of our two hands. They also determine the information of the spatial relationship between the body and the limbs at rest and in motion, which can be used for grasping and reaching in the dark. These neurons integrate tactile inputs from mechanoreceptors in the skin with proprioceptive input from the fingers to encode the shape of objects grasped and explored by both hands. When an object is palpated, these neurons process sensory and proprio-ceptive cues and interact with premotor and motor regions to direct a series of coordinated movements necessary to construct a tactile image of the object within the brain. The projection of area 5 to the premotor cortex is believed to be important for tactile exploration. A lesion in this area may result in defective shape perception or in abnormal sensory-motor transformation seen in tactile apraxia.[217]

Cells in area 7 of the somatosensory association cortex receive tactile and visual input about the current position and configuration of the eyes, head, body, and limbs. These cells aid in the performance of computations necessary for transforming visually perceived locations into body-centered coordinates. They enable us to know where we are in space relative to what we perceive visually. These cells receive information about body part relationships from area 5. Functional MRI studies reveal activation of area 7 during reaching tasks. Lesions in this area may result in abnormal sensorimotor transformations and may play a role in optic ataxia and Bálint's syndrome.[215] In addition to their involvement in building frames of references necessary for sensory-motor trans-formations, areas 5 and 7 are also involved in awareness and knowledge about the body in general. The supramarginal angular gyri (Brodmann's areas 39 and 40) are multimodal association areas that receive inputs from visual, auditory, and tactile modalities. Lesions in these areas can result in the Gertmann syndrome (see above).[215]

In humans, S1 is bound ventral laterally by S2, which is located on the most inferior aspect of the postcentral gyrus and in the depth of the lateral sulcus (parietal operculum). S2 responds to low threshold somatosensory stimuli. This is sometimes called a ventral stream or the "what" pathway. Information from S1 converges and integrates in S2, which contributes to tactile perception ("what"). The naming of palpated objects is mediated through the connection of S2 to the language areas ipsilaterally or through corpus callosum connections contralaterally. Lesions in these areas can result in asteroagnosia, tactile agnosia, or tactile anomia.[215]

The motor association cortex includes the premotor area (within Brodmann's area 6), the frontal eye fields within Brodmann's area 6, the supplemental motor area (SMA) in the medial wall of the cerebral hemisphere (mostly in Brodmann's area 6), the supplementary eye fields, the posterior part of Brodmann's area 44 and perhaps parts of Brodmann's area 8.[216] The primary motor area is termed M1. For a simple action like moving fingers, a distributed network of cortical and subcortical areas is activated. Functional imaging studies show that the sensory motor cortex is invariably involved. However, depending on the nature of the task, activity may be seen in the basal ganglia, thalamus, supplementary motor area, cerebellum, premotor area, or parietal areas.[218] The right motor cortex is activated primarily during left bodily movements, and the left motor cortex is activated with right-sided movements and some during ipsilateral finger movements. There is anatomical evidence for 10%–15% of uncrossed fibers in the lateral corticospinal tract. Functional MRI has shown activation of the motor network when the person is only imaging finger movements.[219] An fMRI study found distinct hand, foot, and facial representations in the putamen.[220] Table 6.19 details known anatomy of somatosensory and motor function. Table 6.20 lists common somatosensory dysfunctions and their definitions.

Astereoagnosia can result from damage to any level of the somatosensory system including the peripheral nerves (this may be seen in large-fiber peripheral neuropathies or spinal cord disorders).

TABLE 6.19

The Neuroanatomy of Somatosensory and Motor Function

Function	Purported Lesion
Coordination of complex movements	Superior parietal lobule projecting to dorsal premotor cortex.[221]
Touch localization and active manual exploration	Brodmann's areas 1, 2, and 3; Brodmann's areas 5, 7, and 40; and posterior insula.[216]
Complex movement and modulation of sensory guidance, initiation, planning, and learning of complex movement	Premotor area (in Brodmann's area 6), frontal eye fields (in area 6), supplemental motor area (in area 6), supplementary motor area, posterior part of Brodmann's area 44, and perhaps part of Brodmann's area 8.[216,222]
Mental rehearsal of movements	Supplemental motor area.[223]

TABLE 6.20
Somatosensory Dysfunctions

A. Astereognosia
- Patients cannot tactually recognize objects because of their inability to perceive texture or shape.

B. Tactile Agnosia
- Apperceptive agnosia: Patients cannot recognize an object they are touching, but they can draw the object (e.g., cannot correctly name a hammer; may call it a tool).
- Associative agnosia: Patients cannot attribute meaning to an object. They correctly perceive by tactile manipulation (e.g., cannot describe the use of a hammer).

C. Tactile Anomia
- Inability to name a tactually recognized object in the absence of aphasic anomia (e.g., can classify an object as a tool but cannot name it as a hammer).

D. Graphesthesia
- Inability to tactually recognize letters or numbers written on the skin.

E. Tactile Apraxia
- A defect of motor sensory transformation motion. Patients cannot guide their fingers to explore objects tactually.

Astereoagnosia is generally more severe when caused by a cortical lesion, and it is the inability to tactually recognize objects based on their texture or shape. If peripheral sensation is preserved, then this disorder is of central origin. It is generally more severe when caused by a cortical lesion than a peripheral lesion. Tactile agnosias are of two types. The first type is the inability to recognize an object tactually. The second type is the inability to attribute meaning or use to an object tactually. Apperceptive tactile agnosia is usually a unilateral disorder, and it will affect the left or right hand from a contralateral lesion. This disorder is generally nondisabling since patients can compensate by describing the object in approximate terms such as a "safety pin" for a paper clip or a "tool" for a hammer. Apperceptive tactile agnosia is usually related to lesions in the S2 somatosensory region. In contrast, patients who cannot attribute meaning to an object (associative tactile agnosia) have lesions in the connections from S2 to the semantic memory area in the inferior temporal lobe. For example, there may be damage in the arcuate fasciculus or inferior longitudinal fasciculus in the subcortical regions of the angular gyrus. Tactile anomia can occur due to disconnection of the tactile recognition system from language areas. Lesions of the corpus callosum can result in a clinical syndrome wherein objects presented to the left hand are well recognized but cannot be named by the linguistically deprived right hemisphere. Graphesthesia is usually associated with lesions of the left interparietal sulcus. Tactile apraxia is usually caused by lesions in the projections from area 5, particularly from the anterior interparietal sulcus to premotor and supplementary areas.[213]

The Neuropsychological Measurement of Somatosensory and Motor Function

Finger Tapping Test

The Finger Tapping Test is a measure of motor speed and is one of the components of the Halstead–Reitan Battery. It was originally developed by Halstead and improved by Retain and Wolfson.[93] This is probably the most widely used test of finger manual dexterity. It consists of tapping the key of a device that records the number of taps. The score for each hand is the average of five trials. Traumatic brain injury, if it produces motor slowing, often will have an adverse affect on finger-tapping rate. Lateralized lesions usually result in slowing of the tapping rate of the contralateral hand. There are norms for this test based on sex, age, and educational background.[224]

This test is sensitive to unilateral lesions, particularly in the posterior frontal lobes. However, it is sensitive to many conditions besides TBI, including AIDS, Huntington's disease, Parkinson's disease, and other neurological, metabolic, or neurodegenerative disorders that produce slow hand speed. It is also susceptible to false positives in severely depressed patients who display psychomotor slowing or in individuals taking medications that produce motor slowing (e.g., neuroleptics or antipsychotics).

Grip Strength Test

The Grip Strength Test is also called the hand dynamometer test. It is used to assess grip strength in each hand.[93] It is a subtest within the Halstead–Reitan Battery. The test is based on the assumption that lateralized brain damage may affect strength of the contralateral hand. It is easily administered in approximately 5 min. However, this is a very effort-dependent test, and there is no method for determining validity. It can be consciously manipulated. Moreover, persons who have orthopedic injuries (e.g., cervical radiculopathy or carpal tunnel syndrome) or arthritis in the hands may perform poorly on this test. It is not a test used alone to detect brain injury or lateralized injury. It is performed with a dynamometer, and the force exerted in kilograms for each hand is averaged for two trials. One generally expects a 10% difference in strength between hands in normal persons, with the dominant hand showing the superior strength.

Grooved Pegboard Test

This test is a subtest within the Wisconsin Neuropsychological Test Battery. It was developed by Kløve in 1963.[225] The test consists of a small board that contains a 5×5 matrix of slotted holes. These function like keyholes, and each peg has a key ridge along one side that requires it to be rotated into position before it may be inserted. It is actually quite a complex task, which makes it very sensitive for measuring general slowing, whether it is due to medication, neurodegenerative disease, parkinsonism, or other disorders. It can aid in identifying lateralized impairment. The method of scoring is based on the time to completion of the test. Generally, both hands are tested, but only one hand may be used if the examiner only wishes to know about motor speed. If measurements of lateralization of brain injury are required, both hands should be tested. Norms are available for both hands.[5,226]

Finger Localization and Fingertip Number Writing Test

This is a subtest of the Halstead–Retian Battery and is part of the Sensory-Perceptual Examination. The finger localization portion of this test is a measure of finger agnosia. It is administered by blindfolding the patient and touching her fingers. There is a standardized format for touching fingers, and then the patient must report the name and number of each finger as it is touched. In the fingertip-writing portion, the examiner writes the numbers 3, 4, 5, or 6 in a standardized order, again with the patient blindfolded, until a total of 20 numbers have been written on the fingertips of each hand. The patient must identify which number the examiner has written. A significant number of errors are consistent with sensory impairment of either the peripheral nerves to the fingers or the contralateral parietal lobe. In the examination of a brain-injured patient, assuming peripheral nerve function is intact, this test will identify contralateral parietal lobe dysfunction.[93,227]

Sensory-Perceptual Examination

This test is a component of the Halstead–Reitan Test Battery.[93] It contains a number of clinical tests to determine tactile stimulation and possible suppression, auditory stimulation and possible suppression, and the visual fields. In the tactile perception test, the patient's hands are placed on a table in front of the examiner with the palms down. The eyes are closed or blindfolded, and the examiner touches either the back of each hand or both hands lightly in a random sequence. After each side has been examined, the examiner then touches either the hand, the face, or both hand and face simultaneously and asks the patient to indicate which side was touched. If the patient gives evidence of a suppression error, this suggests a contralateral brain injury.

A similar procedure is used for assessing perception of auditory stimuli. The examiner stands directly behind the patient who has his eyes closed or blindfolded. A small noise is produced by rubbing the fingers together approximately 6 in. from the patient's left or right ear. This is performed for each side to determine if the patient can perceive the auditory stimulus. Following this, the examiner simultaneously rubs the fingers of both hands together near both of the patient's

TABLE 6.21

Tests of Sensorimotor Function

Test	Measurement
Motor	
Finger Tapping Test	Manual dexterity and finger motor speed
Grip Strength Test	Lateralized difference in hand strength
Grooved Pegboard Test	Fine motor coordination and manual dexterity
Sensory	
Finger Localization and Fingertip	Finger agnosia, fingertip number
Number Writing Tests	Perception (parietal lobes)
Sensory-Perceptual Examination	Perception of tactile sensation, tactile inattention, auditory suppression, and visual fields

ears, interspersed with auditory stimuli on solely the right or left. If the patient consistently fails to identify the sound arriving at one of the ears on the bilateral stimulation trials, then it is likely that a suppression of the sound in that ear has occurred as a result of injury to the contralateral hemisphere. See Table 6.21 for a listing of commonly used somatosensory and motor tests.

The last portion of the test includes visual field examination. The examiner sits approximately 4 ft in front of the patient and stretches her arms while the patient's eyes are focused directly on the examiner's nose. The examiner then instructs her to indicate whether she notices anything moving at the periphery of the visual field while focus is maintained upon the examiner's nose. The upper, middle, and lower visual fields are tested while the examiner makes slight movements with her fingers. This examination is performed separately for each side. Interspersed with these unilateral stimulation trials, the examiner makes simultaneous movements of the fingers on both hands again in the upper, mild, and lower visual fields, to evaluate for suppressions. Mostly, this test proceeds in the same fashion as that which physicians normally use for confrontational visual field testing.

MEASURING EXECUTIVE AND FRONTAL LOBE FUNCTION

The reader should recall that the case of Phineas Gage leads us to our first classical understandings of the relationship of frontal lobe injury to human behavior.[228] The human frontal lobe is divided grossly into primary motor, premotor, and prefrontal regions. These are anatomically, histologically, and functionally distinct areas.[229] The primary motor area is closely linked with the premotor cortex and primary somatosensory cortex as well as the basal ganglia. Not only is it involved in the generation and control of movement, it is the origin of the outgoing pyramidal motor system and gives rise to the pyramidal tracts, which descend through the internal capsule, brainstem, and into the spinal cord. The premotor area is located immediately rostral to the primary motor cortex. It receives projections from other cortical regions, and it is a convergence zone for primary motor cortex activation. This includes motor planning, anticipation of a motor act, programming of motor sequences and motor memory. Broca's area is also located in the lower portion of this cortex in the left hemisphere in the region of the pars triangularis. Both the primary motor and premotor cortexes are organized with the human homunculus overlaid across the cortex. The prefrontal area is quite different from either the primary motor or the premotor regions. It is a cortical association area, but it does not receive any primary sensory input, except for smell, into a small portion of the orbital surface. It does receive extensive projections from all other association cortex, and these include the sensory-perceptual systems, the unimodal and multimodal cortical association areas for visual, auditory, somatosensory, olfactory, and gustatory functions. It also receives extensive projections from the limbic system structures mediating memory and emotion, and from the brainstem regions related to visceral autonomic, hormonal, vegetative, and cognitive functions.[229]

TABLE 6.22

Functional Neuroanatomy of Three Major Frontal Lobe Circuits

Dorsolateral

1. Brodmann's areas 9 and 10 ↑
   ↓ ↑
2. Dorsolateral caudate ↑
   ↓ ↑
3. Dorsomedial globus pallidus, substantia nigra ↑
   ↓ ↑
4. Ventral anterior and dorsomedial thalamic nuclei ↑

Orbitofrontal

1. Brodmann's areas 11 and 10 ↑
   ↓ ↑
2. Ventromedial caudate ↑
   ↓ ↑
3. Dorsomedial globus pallidus, substantia nigra ↑
   ↓ ↑
4. Ventral anterior and dorsomedial thalamic nuclei ↑

Anterior Cingulate

1. Brodmann's area 24 ↑
   ↓ ↑
2. Ventromedial caudate, ventral putamen, nucleus accumbens, olfactory tubercle
   ↓ ↑
3. Rostromedial globus pallidus, ventral globus pallidus ↑
   ↓ ↑
4. Dorsomedial thalamic nuclei ↑

Extensive work over the last 30 years has elucidated the functional neuroanatomy of the frontal lobe circuits within the dorsolateral frontal region, the orbitofrontal region, and the anterior cingulate region. Table 6.22 outlines the circuitry of these three major frontal areas.[230] The dorsolateral region begins in Brodmann's areas 9 and 10 and moves to the caudate, globus pallidus, and the ventral anterior and dorsomedial thalamic nuclei and then circles back to Brodmann's areas 9 and 10. The orbitofrontal area begins in Brodmann's areas 11 and 10 and proceeds to the ventral medial caudate nucleus, onto the globus pallidus and substantial nigra, to the ventral anterior and dorsomedial thalamic nuclei, and then back to Brodmann's areas 11 and 10. The anterior cingulate comprises Brodmann area 24 and projects to the ventral medial caudate, the ventral putamen, the nucleus accumbens, and the olfactory tubercle. From there, it proceeds to the rostromedial globus pallidus and the ventral globus pallidus moving onto the dorsomedial thalamic nuclei. From the thalamus, the circuitry swings back to Brodmann area 24.[230]

The Neuroanatomical Bases of Executive and Frontal Lobe Function

It is beyond the scope of this chapter to cover in any extensive detail the massive amount of neuroimaging literature that has evolved regarding studies of executive function. Table 6.23 categorizes executive function and the various associated tasks relating to each of these functions. Also included in Table 6.23 are the psychological tests that measure certain portions of executive function. A comprehensive neuropsychiatric examination of TBI requires that the examiner makes efforts to carefully measure executive function. Of all the higher order cognitive processes that occur, executive dysfunction is the most likely to lead to morbidity in a patient following TBI. The executive functions listed in Table 6.23 are those where the most extensive literature exists demonstrating by functional neuroimaging a probable anatomical locus.[231] Working memory arises

TABLE 6.23

Executive Functions and Associated Tasks

Category	Tasks
Strategic control of memory	Source memory, (future memory, recent memory)
Stimulus–response interference	Stroop Test
Response inhibition	Go or no-go
Undetermined responding	Verb generation, random number generation
Performance monitoring	WCST, Gambling task
Task management	Task switching, dual-task coordination
Higher cognition	Progressive matrices

in the dorsal premotor areas and supports maintenance and manipulation of data.[232] The superior frontal gyrus in particular is activated during working memory tasks.[233] The executive function for strategic control of memory has been extensively studied. Most neuroimaging literature provides evidence that the prefrontal cortex, particularly the lateral areas, subserve such strategic processes. In particular, the activation of anterior prefrontal cortex regions in Brodmann's area 10 are thought to reflect control operations that act to structure how memory retrieval occurs by way of engaging a sustained retrieval mode.[234] The strategic control of memory is important for source memory of facts, prospective memory for the future, and recent memory such as that involved in episodic memory of autobiographical information. The encoding of divided-attention is also involved in the category of strategic control of memory as well as constantly updating the information contained in working memory.[235]

Stimulus–response interference is the category of executive function that deals with attention control. In other words, it involves keeping attention focused on a task-relevant stimulus in the face of distracting information. This is the so-called multitasking that is *en vogue* in modern human behavior. One of the best ways to test stimulus–response interference is by use of the Stroop Test. The Stroop Test is used in numerous neuroimaging tasks, and at the time of the writing of this chapter, there are well over 100 papers published studying neuroimaging during mental processing by the Stroop Test.[234]

The third category of executive function noted in Table 6.23 is that of response inhibition. This is particularly noted in persons who sustained infraorbital frontal lobe injury. A common observation in these persons is their inability to withhold strong responses that are socially inappropriate. These individuals often exhibit disinhibition syndromes (see Chapter 2) and often cannot stop themselves from making inappropriate statements or social actions. Go or no-go paradigms have become favorite tools for investigating individuals with this behavior.[234] Recent studies suggest that the dorsolateral and inferior prefrontal cortex regions are impaired in individuals who have difficulty with go or no-go task performance.[236]

The fourth item from Table 6.23 is undetermined responding. One good way to test this function is by verb generation tasks. In a verb generation paradigm, the patient is required to verbally generate an appropriate action to a noun that is presented visually (e.g., say "bake" if the word "cake" is presented).[237] A common finding across functional neuroimaging studies is activation in the medial frontal regions such as the anterior cingulate and the pre-SMA, and in the left lateral prefrontal cortex.[235]

The fifth category from Table 6.23, performance monitoring, is the task of dynamically monitoring and adjusting one's own behavior in order to optimally achieve task goals.[235] The classic way to measure this is the Wisconsin Card Sorting Test. Although this task is multicomponent in nature, the greatest demand on executive function probably centers on the requirement for the patient to adjust an internal task set or decision rule based on ambiguous feedback information.

The perseverative error score reliably observed by patients with prefrontal cortex damage, and other patient groups with executive control impairments, appears to involve a failure to appropriately process or utilize such feedback signals to adjust cognitive strategy. Neuroimaging studies using the WCST have confirmed the role of the prefrontal cortex in this performance, particularly the dorsolateral area.[238]

The sixth task in the listing from Table 6.23 is that of task management. Task management collectively provides a regulating force on information processing and the action selection therefrom.[239] Studies indicate that posterior prefrontal cortex regions in the inferior frontal junction, BA-44 and BA-6, seem to play an important role in task-switching environments. However, the activity studied appears to index more general processes associated with cued tasks, and these may not be specific to all task switches.[235]

The last category of function from Table 6.23 is that of higher cognition. This is a generic, all-encompassing activity of executive function. Higher cognition represents the pinnacle of human cognitive skills and achievements, setting man apart from all other thinking animals on the planet. The mental processes in this category include planning, the solving of novel problems, and abstract reasoning. These are typically thought to reflect the essence of higher intellect, and in particular they represent the concept of "emotional intelligence." Elements of this category can be measured by the Tower of London Test or the Raven Progressive Matrices Test. The Tower of London planning task is adapted from the well-known Tower of Hanoi problem in cognitive psychology.[235] Neuroimaging studies using the Tower of London Test are associated with selectively increased activity in the anterior prefrontal regions, particularly BA-10.[240] Similar activation of the prefrontal cortex region has been found when using Raven's Progressive Matrices.[241]

A recent Cornell University study evaluated go or no-go decisions based on "what," "when," and "where" related information using an fMRI study.[242] Subjects were imaged during the performance of a perceptual go or no-go task for which instructions were based on spatial (where), temporal (when), or object (what) stimulus features. Activity within the inferior middle occipital gyri and the middle temporal gyrus, during the "what" and "when" tasks was biased toward the left hemisphere, and toward the right hemisphere during the "where" task. This lateralization was observed regardless of whether the response was executed or merely imagined. The ability to exert control over automatic behavior is of particular importance, as it allows us to interrupt our behavior when the automatic response is no longer adequate or even dangerous. Trinity College at Dublin recently evaluated this concept by way of a visual search task that enabled participants to automatize according to defined criteria within three hours of practice. The participants were then required to reassert control without changing the stimulus set. Activation in all frontal areas and in the inferior parietal lobule decreased significantly with practice. In other words, as the individuals learned more and more of the task, less brain activation was required. Only Brodmann's areas 9, 46, and 8, and parietal areas BA-39 and 40 were specifically reactivated when executive control was required. This underlines the crucial role of the dorsolateral prefrontal cortex in executive control to guide our behavior.[243]

The Neuropsychological Measurement of Executive and Frontal Lobe Function

The measurement of executive and frontal lobe function has been primarily developed by neuropsychologists. Their view of executive and frontal lobe function differs somewhat from neuropsychiatrists, behavioral neurologists, and cognitive neuroscientists. For instance, Lezak has probably a more narrow view of this matter with regard to the measurement of performance than neuroscience physicians. She conceptualizes the executive functions as having four components: (1) volition, (2) planning, (3) purposive action, and (4) affective performance.[8] As can be seen from the preceding view of frontal lobe function by neuroimaging experts, her categories are more restrictive. However, that does not prevent reasonable measurement of executive function by neuropsychological means. When neuropsychologically examining executive function, the paradoxical need to structure a situation in which patients can show whether or how well they can make structure for themselves is a major obstacle. Most cognitive tests employed by neuropsychologists allow the patient little room for discretionary behavior. This is a weakness in the examination and calls into question whether executive function neuropsychological tests are "ecologically valid." In other words, do they measure a set of tasks that are important for daily function, and can impairments detected by these tasks be translated into evidence of real-world dysfunction? A complete evaluation of executive function within the context of a neuropsychiatric TBI examination is beyond the scope of most medical examinations. The following is a list of screening tests that may be of assistance in detecting specific executive dysfunctions.

Category Test

The Category Test is used in the Halstead–Reitan Test Battery.[9] Lezak[5] describes this as a test of abstracting ability. It consists of 208 visually presented items in six sets. Each set is organized on the basis of different principles. From all the tests in the Halstead battery, this test is considered the most sensitive to the presence of brain damage, regardless of its nature or location. A reevaluation of Halstead's original data indicates that while the Category Test's greatest sensitivity is to left frontal lesions, in some cases, 35%–40% of nonfrontal patients also performed abnormally.[244] This test is quite sensitive for detecting brain damage in the frontal lobes with variable specificity. It requires 30 min to 1 h to administer. Severely brain-damaged persons may require longer times. There appears to be considerable variability in the performance of healthy normal controls on this test. This suggests that false-positive errors can occur.[18]

The Raven Progressive Matrices Test

The Raven Progressive Matrices Test was originally developed in England, but it has been used widely in the United States, as well as many other countries throughout the world since it is essentially language-free. This test does not require the patient to perform skilled movements or to verbalize responses but simply to point. Therefore, it can be used to assess persons whose cultural or language background would be disadvantageous if they were administered the Wechsler Intelligence Scales. It also can be administered to individuals with significant motor limitations or those who are hearing impaired.[245]

This test serves to measure inductive reasoning, and it requires the patient to conceptualize spatial design and numerical relationships. There are three forms of the test: standard, colored, and advanced. The standard version consists of 60 items, which are grouped in 5 sets. The patient is to select the correct pattern from either six or eight pictures. Spreen and Strauss[38] find this test particularly useful for persons who are poorly fluent in English or in those who do not understand English. They have also used this test for those who are aphasic or have cerebral palsy. Therefore, while it is not a first-choice test for measuring intellectual functioning, in the severely impaired brain-injured patient, it may be a best second choice.

While this test assesses mainly nonverbal and visuospatial problem-solving skills, the more difficult items contain mathematical concepts that involve analytic reasoning required by the left cerebral hemisphere. Persons with right-sided brain lesions are more likely to show poor performance on the visuospatial tasks, whereas patients with left hemisphere injuries may have greater difficulty with the analytical reasoning portion of the test. This test is not recommended for discriminating right from left brain damage in patients or for assessing individual visuospatial abilities.[5]

Stroop Test

Please see the section "The Neuropsychological Measurement of Attention."

The Tower of London Test

The test version described provides instructions and norms for both children and adults.[246] This test uses two boards. On the first board, the examiner places three colored wooden balls (red, blue, and green) in the goal position, and the other board contains three colored wooden balls that the patient rearranges from a standard "start" position to the examiner's model.[8] Ten problems occur at each level, whether it is the child or adult form. They are administered in order of increasing difficulty. Two minutes are allowed for each trial. Seven different scores (or indexes) can be obtained for both number of moves and successful completions. There is extensive theory and interpretation literature based on studies of this test instrument. There is a recent computerized format that is available, and it appears equivalent to older picture copying formats.[247]

Wisconsin Card Sorting Test

The Wisconsin Card Sorting Test (WCST) was originally developed by Berg[248] and later revised by Heaton et al.[249] There is little question when administering this test that patients with frontal lobe damage will make more perseverative errors.[250] The current version of this test consists of 128 cards containing one to four symbols (triangle, star, cross and/or circle), which are printed in one of four colors (red, green, yellow, or blue). The examiner places four cards into a horizontal array in front of the patient. The patient must match the top card in a pack of 64 cards by placing it directly below one of the four cards lying above. Only minimal instructions are given to the patient, as the premise of this test is to determine if the patient can deduce the underlying sorting principle based on color, form, or number. The patient is given a maximum of 128 cards in which to complete six categories. After the patient has made 10 consecutive correct responses, the underlying category automatically changes and the patient is expected to deduce the change. Error scores are kept and perseverative responses are noted.

This test has been shown to be sensitive to dorsolateral lesions in the frontal lobes, but it is relatively insensitive to orbitofrontal lesions.[251] Similar to the Category Test, patients with diffuse brain damage may perform as poorly on this test as patients with frontal lobe pathology. However, the WCST is widely used in PET studies to measure frontal function. The manual contains norms for normal controls, patients with frontal lobe pathology, patients with brain injuries that do not include the frontal lobes and patients with diffuse brain damage, so the examiner can make some discrimination. Many patients with posttraumatic orbitofrontal syndromes frequently perform well on this test. Poor performance can be caused by visual impairment, color blindness, visual-perceptual difficulties, impaired hearing, psychiatric disease, and poor effort or malingering.[18]

MEASURING INTELLECTUAL FUNCTIONING

In the early years of psychology, intellectual testing was designated as a measure of mental ability. Since those early years, the use of intellectual testing has advanced considerably and has become much broader in its application. No good neuropsychological evaluation would be complete without a measure of intellectual functioning. Most neuropsychologists will administer the Wechsler Intelligence Scales for Adults (WIS-A). The current edition of that test is the Wechsler Adult Intelligence Scale-III (WAIS-III). Originally, psychologists treated "intelligence" as a unitary function. However, as experience was gained using various intellectual assessment instruments, it became obvious that what is termed "intelligence" is made up of numerous components. Intellectual testing broadened in its assessment capacities following the work of David Wechsler. When he developed the original Wechsler scales, he maintained the notion of intelligence as a unitary entity (thus his use of IQ scores), but those scores were based on aggregate or specific abilities that are more or less complex and qualitatively distinct.[8,252] From a neuroscience standpoint, one of the first persons to challenge psychological views of intelligence was Francis Crick, the codiscoverer of DNA structure. Following his seminal work in molecular biology, he turned his attention to the study of the human brain and in particular the study of brain-based intelligence. His *Scientific American* article in 1979 is still a classic.[253] Hawkins has expanded upon the work of Crick in his pursuit of understanding the brain in terms of artificial intelligence models being developed for computer science.[254]

Unlike the prior portions of this chapter that look at specific neuroanatomical substrates as areas of brain activated during particular cognitive tasks, there is no known unitary neuroanatomical site

---

TABLE 6.24

Tests to Assess Intelligence in Adults

- Kaufman Brief Test of Intelligence (KBIT)
- Raven Progressive Matrices Test
- Test of Nonverbal Intelligence (TONI)
- Wechsler Adult Intelligence Scale-III (WAIS-III)

---

for what is termed test intelligence. It is not possible using fMRI, PET or other functional imaging techniques to determine an anatomical location of intelligence. Therefore, no single test instrument is currently capable of comprehensively measuring human intellect. The examiner should be aware that the time required to test individuals with an intellectual assessment instrument varies inversely with the severity level of brain injury. For example, severely brain-injured persons will test rapidly, as they will fail early the subtest requirements of most intellectual test instruments. Also, persons of low intelligence will complete fewer items of testing and require shorter test times. Table 6.24 lists test instruments of value in the neuropsychological assessment of TBI.

Kaufman's Brief Test of Intelligence

Kaufman's Brief Test of Intelligence (KBIT) is an individually administered intelligence test for persons whose ages range from 4 to 90. It is useful for assessing verbal and nonverbal abilities.[255] The Vocabulary subtest is broken into expressive vocabulary and definitions. Nonverbal abilities are assessed by the Matrices subtest, which consists of items involving visual stimuli that require the person being tested to determine the relationship between the stimuli using a multiple-choice format. This test is quick to administer and requires 15–30 min depending on the age, intelligence capacity, and impairment level of the person being tested. Individual subtest scores are converted to standard scores with a mean of 100 and a standard deviation of 15 for both the Vocabulary and Matrices subtests to determine if any differences between the two are statistically significant.

The norms for this test come from a sample of 2022 individuals stratified according to U.S. Census data on or about 1990. These data include four variables: gender, geographic region, socioeconomic status, and race or ethnic group. For certain brain-injured patients, this test of intelligence offers an advantage over others. Unlike the Wechsler Scales, it does not require a motor response from the patient. Thus, it is well suited for determining intelligence in brain-injured persons who are physically handicapped or have significant motoric limitations of the dominant extremity. The main limitation of this test instrument is that it provides less of a differentiation between verbal and nonverbal intellectual functions than the Wechsler Scales. It may also produce a spuriously low estimate of verbal intelligence in some persons.[172,256]

The Raven Progressive Matrices Test

The reader is referred to the section "Neuropsychological Measurement of Executive and Frontal Lobe Function."

Test of Nonverbal Intelligence

The Test of Nonverbal Intelligence (TONI) is a language-free measure of abstract problem-solving skills.[257] It is normed for persons ranging from 5 to 85 years. Similar to the Raven Test, it is an untimed test and requires approximately 15 min to administer. The format for administration is completely free of language. No listening, speaking, reading, or writing is required, and the person needs to make only a minimal motor response to the test items.

This test was specifically designed to measure intellectual functioning in individuals who are not functional in English and in those persons who have been raised in non-American cultures. Therefore, when assessing TBI in immigrant persons, this may be the preferred intellectual test instrument relative to Kaufman's Brief Test of Intelligence or other Wechsler Intelligence Scales. During testing, the person attempts to identify relationships among abstract figures and then solve problems created by the cognitive manipulation of these relationships. The person must complete patterns by selecting correct responses from among four or six alternatives. The test items contain characteristics of shapes, direction, contiguity, position, rotation. shading, size, figure patterns, links, and movement.[257] The difficulty of test items is increased as the person progresses through the testing. The person must identify the rule or rules that are operating among the figures and thereby select appropriate responses. There are two forms for this test (TONI-1 and TONI-2), and they are useful in situations where the person must be retested at a later date. This, of course, avoids test–retest issues.

Obviously a major strength of this test is its ability to evaluate brain-injured persons for whom the Wechsler Intelligence Scales are not appropriate. It can be administered to brain-injured persons who have language dysfunction, hearing impairment, poor English skills or cultural differences. It may be difficult for patients who have significant visual impairment. Thus, a patient who has a visual field cut or a neglect syndrome may not be appropriate for this examination. Moreover, it will not provide a measure of verbal skill, and its ability to measure intellectual functioning is not equivalent to the Wechsler Scales.[18]

Wechsler Adult Intelligence Scale-III

The Wechsler Adult Intelligence Scale-III (WAIS-III)[211] is the most recent revision of the Wechsler Intelligence Scale-Revised. This instrument contains 14 subtests. Eleven of these were retained from the Wechsler Adult Intelligence Scale-Revised. The Symbol Search Scale was adapted from the Wechsler Intelligence Scale for Children-III (WISC-III). Two new subtests were added: Matrix Reasoning and Letter–Number Sequencing.

Three functionally distinct factors have consistently emerged in research on all of the published forms of the Wechsler Scales. The first is a verbal factor, usually called verbal comprehension, and it has its highest statistical weightings on the information, comprehension, similarities, and vocabulary subscales. A second factor, the perceptual organization factor, always statistically loads on the Block Design and Object Assembly subscales, and it statistically contributes to the Digit Symbol subtest and sometimes the Picture Completion or Picture Arrangement subtests. The third factor, a memory or freedom from distractibility factor, weights significantly on the Arithmetic and Digit Span subscales, and to some extent on the Digit Symbol subscale.[5]

There is some general tendency for verbal scale IQ scores to be reduced relative to performance scale IQ scores when the injury is predominately or only in the left hemisphere. However, this decline does not occur regularly enough, nor is it typically large enough, for reliable distinctions or predictions to be made.[258] A lower performance scale IQ score is even less useful as an indicator of right hemisphere damage due to the time-dependent requirements of completing the performance scales. Thus, these scales are sensitive to any cerebral disorder that impairs the brain's efficiency, as they call upon more unfamiliar activities than the subtests within the verbal scale test. Confounding reduction of the performance scale IQ score can occur with patients having extensive right hemisphere damage, left hemisphere lesions, bilateral brain damage, certain neurodegenerative disorders, and the cognitive disorders associated with depression.[258] Moreover, a person's inherent intellectual capacity plays a role in the verbal-performance differences, if any. There is a strong tendency for verbal scale IQ scores to be relatively high in those persons whose full-scale IQ socres are in the superior or higher range. This tendency is reversed in favor of higher performance scale IQ scores in those persons whose full-scale IQ scores are below 100.[259]

The WAIS-III contains new index scores that were not present in the prior forms of the Wechsler Scales. These index scores are developed for verbal comprehension, perceptual organization, working memory, and processing speed. The Verbal Comprehension Index is composed of the vocabulary, similarities, and information subtests. The Perceptual Organization Index is composed of the picture completion, block design and matrix reasoning subtests. The Working Memory Index is composed of the Arithmetic, Digit Span and Letter–Number Sequencing subtests. The Processing Speed Index is based on the Digit Symbol-Coding and Symbol Search subtests.[211]

The WAIS-III has norms for ages 16–89 years. This is a substantial lengthening of the upper age limit from the WAIS-R, which includes norms only to age 74. The updated test contains a powerful and useful function in the assessment of TBI in that it is specifically designed to be used in conjunction with the WMS-III. Moreover, from a cultural standpoint, for each age group in the standardization samples of 2450 adults, the proportions of Caucasians, African-Americans, Hispanics, Asians, and Native Americans is based on those same proportions of individuals within each age group of the United States population using 1995 Census data. The normative samples also were stratified by educational background ranging from fewer than 8 years of education to greater than 16 years of education.[211]

The disadvantage of the WAIS-III, relative to the WAIS-R, is that the administration time of the third edition appears to have been increased by approximately 30 min. This, of course, is a result of increasing the number of subtests from 11 to 14. This test may require up to 2 h to administer, and it may be particularly difficult for patients who have significant TBI, since their performance may deteriorate over time due to mental fatigue while they are taking the test. This test also may not be suitable for individuals with significant motor impairment or for those who have poor English skills. The test is very inflexible in administration requirements also. If a patient is fatigued or anxious during a subtest, a break cannot be taken, or it violates the manner in which the original test norms were obtained. Thus, it may not be particularly suitable for patients who have sustained significant brain damage affecting mental endurance or mood.[18] Moreover, in the standardization sample, 24% of normal individuals who were tested durign the development of the WAIS-III had verbal and performance IQ scores that differed by 15 points or more (greater than 1 SD). Since a difference of greater than 1 SD can be found in approximately one of four normal individuals, these IQ scale differences should not be used to determine whether a patient has brain damage.[18] Also, when comparing this test with the WAIS-R, it should be remembered that full-scale IQ determined on the WAIS-III is 3 points less than full-scale IQ determined by the WAIS-R. Moreover, the verbal and performance IQs of the WAIS-III are 1.2 and 4.8 points less than the comparable WAIS-R verbal and performance IQs, respectively.[211] Standard scores are classified as very superior (<130), superior (120–129), high average (110–119), average (90–109), and low average (80–89). Other changes have been incorporated into the WAIS-III in order to improve this battery for neuropsychological assessment. Slowing is a normal consequence of the aging brain, and a number of the items in the WAIS-III are time-based. Therefore, the number of time-based bonus points was decreased to compensate for changes associated with aging. Matrix Reasoning was added to replace Object Assembly from the WAIS-R. The "floors" for each subtest were lowered to allow greater performance discrimination among patients with mild to moderate impairments. Moreover, as noted in the section of memory measurement, 1200 subjects in the original database for the WAIS-III were also tested using the Wechsler Memory Scale-III. This allows a more direct comparison of performance across these tests since they were normed together.[8]

CHILD NEUROCOGNITIVE ASSESSMENT

MEASURING COGNITIVE DISTORTION

Few tests are available to measure cognitive distortion in the pediatric age group. Historically, child psychiatrists, child psychologists, and neuropsychologists testing children have felt that it is not possible for a child to malinger on a neurocognitive examination. As discussed in the forensic section of this text, the neuropsychiatric examiner seeing children in a forensic setting must be aware that children can malinger by proxy. In other words, subtle cues could have been given to the child by the parent. For instance, the mother could say, "If we don't win this lawsuit we're not going to have a house over our heads." The child may then reduce effective performance during neuropsychological testing in order to be of assistance to the parent. Also, if the child is medicated, motivation and effort must be considered within the context of dulling of senses from medication. Children should probably be tested for effort with at least one effort instrument during neuropsychological testing, but few are available for use. The Victoria Symptom Validity Test (VSVT) has been found useful for determining motivation in children, as it is a test based on probability theory even though it was not originally devised for children.[31] Recently, the Test of Memory Malingering[28] (TOMM), has been administered to children. In Grand Rapids, Michigan, the TOMM was evaluated in a sample of 100 consecutively referred 6- to 16-year-old children with a wide range of clinical diagnoses. In this sample, 97 children met actuarially defined criteria for sufficient effort on the TOMM. Two children were correctly identified as providing suboptimal effort, and one case was possibly a false positive. The children were retested, and performance on the second trial of the TOMM did not vary with gender, ethnicity, parental occupation, performance on an independent memory test, or length of coma. Younger children tended to perform somewhat less efficiently on the TOMM than older children, but more than 90% of children in the age range of 6–8 years met criteria originally developed for adults for sufficient effort on the TOMM. The author concluded that the TOMM is a potentially useful measure of effort in the clinical neuropsychological evaluation of school-age children.[260] Table 6.25 lists age ranges for tests commonly used to assess neuropsychological function in children.

Establishing a Pre-Injury Cognitive Baseline

A pre-injury cognitive baseline can be routinely established in children of school age with the use of reading scores such as was described for establishing a pre-injury cognitive baseline in adults. For the child between ages 3 and 5 years, this may be more difficult to accomplish. High school age children, and even some middle school children, in the United States have completed the ACT, PSAT, or SAT. These scores can be used to establish a pre-injury cognitive baseline, as they are based on United States norms, and those norms are equivalent across states. The Wechsler Individual Achievement Test-II (WIAT-II) has been found useful for children between ages 4 and 8 years.[261]

Wechsler Individual Achievement Test-II

This test is extremely useful in child assessment following TBI. The second edition of this test is also a direct link to the WISC-IV and other editions of the Wechsler Intelligence Scales for Children.[8] Lezak notes that the mathematics reasoning task of this battery assesses more applied mathematics and simple computational ability, and it may be a more ecologically valid method for assessing mathematical skills than the WRAT-III arithmetic subtest. The WIAT-II has been normed on children aged 4 onward to adult. It was nationally standardized on 5586 individuals, and it uses normative information based on age and grade level. The reading subtests are useful for prediction of pre-injury ability. A word of caution regarding Lezak's analysis of the mathematics reasoning section; as noted previously in this book, mathematics is the most likely academic skill to be adversely impacted by brain trauma in a child, and therefore it is not recommended that the mathematics section be used as a pre-injury cognitive baseline. Only reading scores are recommended for that analysis. The WIAT-II is composed of four composite scales: reading, mathematics, written language and oral language. The Reading Composite Scale consists of the subtests word reading, reading comprehension, and pseudo-word decoding. The Mathematics Composite Scale contains the subtests of spelling and written expression. The Oral Language Composite Scale contains the subtests of listening comprehension and oral expression. The scores are presented as standard scores with a mean of 100 and a standard deviation of 15, which comports with the WISC-IV. The WIAT-II measures aspects of the learning process that take place in traditional academic settings. It should provide a reasonably accurate measure of information learned by children and adults before brain injury, assuming that it is

TABLE 6.25

Neuropsychological Test Instruments for Children

Test Category	Age Range (Years)[a]
Achievement tests (premorbid reading ability)	
Wide Range Achievement Test-III	5–74
Wechsler Individual Achievement Test-II	4–85
Attention tests	
Continuous Performance Test-II	5–90
Kiddie Continuous Performance Test	4–5
Memory tests	
Children's Memory Scale	5–16
Wide Range Assessment of Memory and Learning	5–17
Language tests	
Boston Naming Test	4–13
Controlled Oral Word Association Test	6–90
Expressive Vocabulary Test	2½–90
Peabody Picture Vocabulary Test-III	2½–90
Token Test	6–13
Visuoperceptual tests	
Hooper Visual Organization Test	5–13
Rey Complex Figure Test	6–89
WISC-IV Performance Scales (Block Design, Object Assembly, Picture Completion)	6–16
Sensorimotor tests	
Finger Tapping Test	5–7, 12–80
Grip Dynamometer Test	5–7, 12–80
Executive function tests	
Delis–Kaplan Executive Function System	8–89
Stroop Test	7–80
Tower of London Test	8–89
Trails for Children	8–15
Wisconsin Card Sorting Test	6–89
Intelligence function	
Cognitive Assessment System	5–17
Kaufman Brief Intelligence Test	4–90
Wechsler Intelligence Scale for Children-IV	6–16
Wechsler Preschool and Primary Scale of Intelligence-III	2½–7½
Young child's neuropsychological test battery	
NEPSY	3–12

[a] Norms for various ages may be derived from sources other than the published testing manuals.[172,224,226]

administered reasonably close to the time of the injury (for instance, within the first year) so that intercurrent learning factors do not affect the predictive outcomes of the test.

MEASURING ATTENTION IN CHILDREN

Limited research has investigated specific attentional sequelae following pediatric TBI. Little is known to date about the effects of TBI upon sustained, selective, and shifting attention, as well as speed of processing. Catroppa and Anderson's group in Melbourne has made significant progress in this area recently. They examined attentional abilities in the acute phase and at 6, 12, and 24 months post-injury in a group of 71 children who had sustained either a mild, moderate or severe TBI. Their results indicated that children who sustained a severe TBI generally performed the poorest, but they also showed the most recovery over time.[262] Yeates' group at Ohio State University reviewed long-term attentional problems and their cognitive correlates following childhood TBI. Their recent data examined 41 children with severe TBI, 41 children with moderate TBI and 50 children with orthopedic injury as controls. These children ranged from 6 to 12 years of age at the time of their injury. Hierarchal linear and logistic regression analyses indicated that the severe TBI group displayed significantly more attentional problems than the orthopedic injury group at 4 years post-injury. At the end of 4 years, 46% of the severe TBI child group displayed significant attentional problems. This was opposed to 26% of the orthopedic group. The authors concluded that childhood TBI exacerbates premorbid attentional problems if they are present.[263] Anderson and Catroppa continued their studies of attentional deficits in children following TBI out to 30 months, and later to 5 years. In their 30 month study[264] they found severe TBI to be associated with reduced accuracy and slowed mental processing. Children with mild and moderate TBI had better outcomes. When their research was extended to a 5-year follow-up in children injured between the ages of 2 and 7, attentional and processing speed deficits persisted up to 5 years, particularly in those children who were severely brain injured.[265] A study from the Netherlands has followed children up to 7 years following TBI and found that most problems were in the domains of attention, memory, and executive functioning. At follow-up more than half of the children (54%) attended a regular school or had a regular job. However, that means that 46% did not attend a regular school and were not employed in a normal fashion.[266] Max's group at the University of California San Diego has noted that attention deficit hyperactivity disorder occurs in children and adolescents following TBI.[267] The confusing issue for the neuropsychiatric examiner is the outcome of a child who is afflicted with ADHD before TBI. Does TBI worsen this condition? It has been previously unknown whether children with TBI and ADHD have greater neuropsychological impairments than children with TBI alone. A recent study examined attention, executive function and memory in children with TBI-only and TBI + ADHD. Children underwent neuropsychological testing one year after injury. Compared with the TBI-only group, children with TBI + ADHD had worse performance on measures of attention, executive function and memory. The authors concluded that pre-injury ADHD is an added burden to a child who sustains a brain injury.[268]

The Kiddie Continuous Performance Test

The Conners Continuous Performance Test-II works well for youngsters 6 years old and above and, of course, is used in adults, as noted in the adult section earlier. However, it was determined that the 14 min duration of the CPT-II was problematic for youngsters aged 4 and 5 years. At that age, even children with no signs of attention deficits produced false positives. As a result, the Kiddie Continuous Performance Test (K-CPT) was set to run at 7½ min on a computer system.[269] This provided the necessary balance for 4- and 5-year-old youngsters. Moreover, the stimuli used on the K-CPT are a series of pictures that are readily familiar to children of a very young age. Whereas the CPT-II uses letters, these stimuli were inappropriate for very young children.

The K-CPT was specially designed to assist with the assessment of attention disorders in 4- and 5-year-old children. However, even though the K-CPT is appropriate for use with children aged 4 or 5 years, some children with severe cognitive impairment cannot complete this test instrument. If the child cannot understand the simple instructions, he or she is likely to perform poorly on the tasks regardless of whether attention problems are present.

This test is administered on a computer, and it uses a short practice test to familiarize the child with the procedures. Familiar pictures are projected onto the computer screen (e.g., sailboat, horse, scissors, soccer ball, etc.) rather than letters. The child is required to press the space bar or mouse whenever any picture except the soccer ball appears. The K-CPT measures include omission and commission errors, average reaction time for hits, risk taking, perceptual sensitivity, and overall reaction time. Scores can be obtained immediately.

For the child 6 years of age and above, the Continuous Performance Test-II may be administered. The examiner should recall that the Ruff 2 & 7 Test is used for persons aged 16 years and above, and the Brief Test of Attention is used for persons aged 17 and above. The Seashore Rhythm Test of the Halstead–Reitan Battery could be used as an alternative to assess attention in persons aged 15 years and above.

MEASURING MEMORY IN CHILDREN

While attention clearly is impaired in children following TBI, memory deficits also are very common, particularly after severe pediatric TBI. They tend to persist for at least a year and in some children may lead to academic failure as a result of inability to assimilate new information.[270] In a pediatric population, immediate, and short-term memory deficits are common in certain developmental disorders or in attention deficit hyperactivity disorder. Although it is unusual for long-term memory deficits to be seen in developmental disorders, they are significantly common in pediatric brain injury. The reader may wish to review again the memory schema from Figure 2.1. With that in mind, a Spanish group has examined declarative memory dysfunctions in early TBI. MRI imaging and volumetric analysis was performed in 16 adolescents following severe TBI and compared to 16 matched normal controls. Verbal memory was assessed by Rey's Auditory Verbal Learning Test and visual memory by the Rey's Complex Figure Test. The adolescent brain-injured group demonstrated decreased white matter volume and compensatory increased ventricular volume. TBI patients performed significantly worse than controls in both verbal and visual memory.[271] A German team has evaluated the recovery of spatial memory and spatial orientation after TBI during childhood.[272] Eighteen children with TBI were matched against eighteen controls. These children were in a rehabilitation facility, and the testing was done 4 years after injury. Children were assessed with the Kiel Locomotor Maze. They had to remember to find locations in an experimental chamber with completely controlled intra-maze and extra-maze cues until the learning criterion was reached. Four years after injury, spatial learning appeared to be functionally recovered, but cognitive mapping skills were still impaired. The authors concluded that prior studies of children who survived a severe TBI may have overestimated the healing of children with similar injuries.

A question that may confront the neuropsychiatric examiner seeing children following TBI is whether or not memory function is more compromised in children who have premorbid learning problems versus children who do not. A University of Missouri School of Medicine study attempted to address this problem. The researchers examined memory functioning of 25 children who sustained a TBI and who had prior learning impairment and compared them with 48 TBI children who did not have prior learning problems and used a control group of 23 noninjured children. The children with TBI and prior learning impairment displayed significantly worsened memory abilities than both the control participants and the children with TBI absent prior learning problems.[273] A Michigan study evaluated 167 children with TBI selected from an 8-year series of consecutive referrals to a midwestern rehabilitation hospital. They used the California Verbal Learning Test-Children's Version (CVLT-C) and found evidence of proactive interference. This is defined as performance on the second list of words that was at least 1.5 standard deviations below that on the first list. This difference was much more likely in the traumatic brain-injured children. Other performance discrepancies found included retroactive interference, rapid forgetting and retrieval problems. However, there was no significant difference between the TBI sample and the controls. Children with anterior cerebral lesions were about three times less likely to have a large proactive interference effect than children without such lesions. Adults with anterior cerebral lesions usually show increased risk for proactive interference. In children with anterior cerebral lesions, the memory difficulty seems to be related mostly to speed of information processing, and this deficit is primarily responsible for the learning deficits seen on the CVLT-C after pediatric TBI.[274] The examiner of children should be aware that at the present time, there are no standardized memory instruments other than the NEPSY for accurately measuring memory function in children younger than age 5 following TBI.

Children's Memory Scale

The Children's Memory Scale (CMS) is a comprehensive learning and memory assessment instrument designed to evaluate learning and memory functioning in individuals 5 through 16 years.[275] Nine CMS subtests are used to assess functioning in each of three domains: (1) auditory and verbal learning and memory, (2) visual and nonverbal learning and memory, and (3) attention and concentration. Each domain is assessed through two core subtests and one supplemental test. The core subtest battery can be administered in about 30–35 min. The supplemental battery takes an additional 9–15 min to administer. There is approximately 30 min delay between the immediate memory and the delayed memory portion of each subtest. Many portions of the testing are further subdivided by age with three basic age levels: (1) ages 5–8, (2) ages 9–12, and (3) ages 13–16. Eight indices result from the administration of this test; they are presented as standard scores with a mean of 100 and a standard deviation of 15.

The General Memory Index globally measures memory function in much the same way that the full-scale IQ score of the WISC-IV is viewed as a global measure of general intellectual ability. The Attention/Concentration Index assesses the ability to sustain and direct attention and concentration, processing speed and working memory. The Verbal Immediate Index measures immediate and working memory span for auditory verbal material. The Visual Immediate Index measures immediate and working memory span for visual and nonverbal material. The Verbal Delayed Index measures the ability to consolidate, store, and retrieve newly learned auditory verbal material. The Visual Delayed Index assesses the ability to consolidate, store, and retrieve newly learned visual and nonverbal material. The Delayed Recognition Index enables one to determine whether impaired performance on the Verbal Delayed Index is the result of an encoding and storage deficit or a retrieval deficit. The Learning Index is a summation of the child's performance across three learning trials of the Word Pairs (verbal) subtest and the Dot Locations (visual) subtest.

Wide Range Assessment of Memory and Learning

The Wide Range Assessment of Memory and Learning (WRAML) allows the examiner to evaluate a child's ability to actively learn and memorize a variety of information.[276] The WRAML is normed for children aged 5–17 years. The structure of the test is based upon three major divisions. The first division makes a distinction between memory and learning. The second division evaluates competencies in both verbal and visual, modalities. The third division evaluates delayed recall. There are three verbal, three visual, and three learning subtests that yield three indices: (1) Verbal Memory Index, (2) Visual Memory Index, and (3) Learning Index. When combined, the nine subtests yield a General Memory Index. Standard scores and percentiles are derived from the subtests and allow an age-based comparison of performance. The normative data are divided into two main age groups, children aged 5–8 and children aged 9 and older.

MEASURING LANGUAGE IN CHILDREN

Unlike adults, children who sustain injury to language centers do not demonstrate the classic aphasia syndromes of Broca or Wernicke. Children may demonstrate more subtle abnormalities, but their deficits carry a significant adverse social impact. The pragmatic aspects of child language are often involved following TBI, and ordinary discourse among children is also impaired. Ewing-Cobbs' group at the University of Texas-Houston studied these issues for many years. Young children who sustain severe TBI are particularly vulnerable to linguistic deficits of both lexical and discourse levels. Traumatic brain injury in older children and adolescents preferentially disrupts higher-order discourse functions.[277] A cross-sectional and prospective study of children admitted to the hospital with nonaccidental head injury in Scotland demonstrated a very large variance among the numerous linguistic problems. Sixty-eight percent of these children were neurologically abnormal at an average follow-up of 59 months. A wide range of speech and language difficulties were present in 64% of the study group. The authors pointed out that in the nonaccidental head injury group of children, the spectrum and degree of severity of neurological abnormalities is extremely variable with the majority of these children demonstrating moderate or severe impairments. They point out that these children require the support of a multidisciplinary team in the community. Moreover, as in the United States, complex medicolegal issues usually arise as treaters attempt to help these youngsters.[278] Harvey Levin's group at the University of Texas-Dallas analyzed a group of brain-injured children at least 2 years post-injury to determine their macro-level processing abilities of discourse language. Compared to the control group, the TBI group could condense information written in text to a similar extent. However, when these children were asked to summarize information, they had significantly less skill doing so. They demonstrated substantial deficits in the ability to transform information into a more useable form.[279] Catroppa and Anderson in Melbourne evaluated language skills in a group of 68 children who had sustained mild, moderate, or severe TBI. They evaluated these children at least 24 months post-TBI. Predictors of outcome at 24 months included pre-injury communication skills, socioeconomic status at the time of injury, and vocabulary as measured by the Wechsler Intelligence Scale for Children (WISC-III). There was a dose–response relationship where severe TBI was associated with poorest performance, and mild TBI was associated with the least deficits.[280] One question for the examiner that may arise is regarding the impact of pediatric TBI on academic achievement scores during post-TBI education. A study of children ages 5–15 years of age who sustained mild, moderate or severe TBI was undertaken. Achievement scores were collected from baseline out to 5 years following the TBI and were subjected to individual growth curve analysis. Children's scores improved significantly over the follow-up period relative to normative data from the standardization sample of the test. However, children with severe TBI demonstrated persistent deficits on all achievement scores when compared to children with mild-moderate TBI.[281] Language testing of children below the age of 5 or 6 will be discussed within the description of the NEPSY. The following is a discussion of useful language instruments.

Expressive Vocabulary Test

The Expressive Vocabulary Test (EVT) is an individually administered assessment of expressive vocabulary and word retrieval for children and adults aged 2½–90 years.[283] This test has been conormed with the Peabody Picture Vocabulary Test-III (PPVT-III).[282] The EVT measures expressive vocabulary knowledge with two types of items—labeling and synonyms. Word retrieval is evaluated by comparing expressive and receptive vocabulary skills using standard score differences between the EVT and PPVT-III.[283] The conorming of the EVT and PPVT-III provides a very useful anterior and posterior language assessment in very young children and allows direct comparisons of expressive and receptive vocabulary.

The EVT is an untimed test that can be completed in about 15 min. Generally, the younger the child is, the shorter the testing time. Examinees are administered only items that most closely approximate their ability levels. The EVT does not require the child to read, write or give lengthy oral responses. EVT results can be reported as standard scores (with a mean of 100 and a standard deviation of 15) that range from 40 to 160. These standard scores can allow comparisons to be made between EVT scores and scores earned on tests of oral language, academic achievement, and cognitive ability. If needed, EVT scores can be expressed as percentiles, normal curve equivalents, stanines, and test-age equivalents.

Peabody Picture Vocabulary Test

This test is designed for persons aged 2½ through 90+ years. It serves two purposes: (1) as an achievement test of receptive (auditory) vocabulary attainment for standard English and (2) as a screening test of verbal ability. It was standardized nationally on a stratified sample of 2725 persons including 2000 children and adolescents. Raw scores can be converted to standard scores, percentiles, stanines, normal curve equivalents, and age equivalents.[282]

This test instrument is very easy to administer and is highly reliable, even at the youngest ages. It is extremely useful in testing preschool children. Because no reading or writing is required, it can be used in children who have written-language difficulty or impairment of the writing hand. For individuals with language impairments, particularly those with expressive vocabulary problems, it provides a measure of linguistic potential because it is a pure measure of receptive vocabulary. It may be used in children who are withdrawn or those who have significant cognitive impairment because there is no need to speak or interact verbally with the examiner. Even children who are hemiparetic and language impaired can be tested reliably with this instrument.

MEASURING VISUOPERCEPTUAL ABILITY IN CHILDREN

Children who are brain-injured and sustain impairments in the visuoperceptual domains may also demonstrate weaknesses in spatial abilities, social judgment, or other nonverbal functions. Moreover, children may demonstrate weaknesses in the visuoperceptual area within the context of relatively intact elementary verbal skills. Routine vision screening generally confirms that impairments in visual acuity or other primary sensory capacities are not present.[284]

The Block Design, Object Assembly, and Picture Arrangement subtests of the WISC-IV may be used for assessing visuoperceptual and visuospatial skills. The analogs of these tests used for adults have been discussed previously in the adult cognitive measurement section. The essential findings in adults are generally the same as in children. However, these WISC-IV subtests have been specifically normed upon children, and the children's version should be used. The WISC-IV is normed for measuring cognitive function in children aged 6–16 years, 11 months.

Hooper Visual Organization Test

This test consists of showing children 30 pictures of objects that have been cut up and placed in different positions. Norms exist in order to assess children as young as age 5 years.[213] The child is required to visually examine each picture, decide what it would be if it were assembled, and write down the name of the particular object, such as fish, ball or key. Test items are arranged in order of increasing difficulty, and most children can complete the test in approximately 15 min. It is sensitive to posterior brain damage. Poor performance on this test can be due to poor visual acuity, low intellectual functioning, psychiatric disease, and poor effort.[18]

Rey–Osterrieth Complex Figure Test

The Rey-Osterrieth Complex Figure Test consists of instructing the patient to copy a complex geometric figure onto a sheet of white paper. The amount of time taken initially to copy the figure is recorded. Standard procedures usually have the person draw the figure again from memory after a delay of 3 min and again after 30 min or 1 h. Norms are available on this test in order to measure children as young as 6 years. A scoring system was developed by Taylor that was adapted from the original work of Osterrieth.[285]

Traumatically brain-injured patients, including children, have difficulty on recall trials of the complex figure test. Even patients with mild head injuries may show significant deficits on 3 min recall trials within the first 2 years of injury. Moderately to severely injured patients have been shown to have impaired functioning more than 2–5 years after trauma. However, clearly there is a memory component to this test as well as a visuoperceptual component, and visual memory is one element being measured, among others.[5]

This test has some discriminating ability for lesion location. Patients with posterior brain damage, particularly on the right side, are more likely to have problems with spatial organization, whereas patients with frontal lobe pathology are more likely to have difficulty in the planning and organization of their drawing. Patients with right hemisphere damage tend to perform more poorly on the recall section than patients with predominately left hemisphere brain damage.[18] This test is easy to administer and score, but nonneurological etiologies can produce impaired scores.

MEASURING SENSORIMOTOR FUNCTION IN CHILDREN

In the first edition of this text, it was pointed out that little in the way of research studies comparing traumatically brain-injured children with controls is available regarding their sensorimotor function. However, one recent study from Germany did evaluate by gait analysis the outcome of brain-injured children. The age ranged from 4 years, 7 months to 15 years, 10 months. These children were measured not only in terms of gait but also in terms of hand ability. More than half of the children had a Glasgow Coma Scale score below 8, and the remainder had Glasgow Scale scores from 8–10. Compared with healthy control children the same age and sex, significant reductions of gait velocity, stride length, cadence, and balance were noted. Spatiotemporal abilities with hands were also impaired.[286] The same German group had previously developed methods for evaluating sensorimotor functions in children. Those have been refined further by this German research department, but limited studies are available in other parts of the world, and most pediatric rehabilitation centers do not have the kinematic and video assessment techniques used by the German group.[287] Thus, norms on children are noticeably lacking. Grip strength and finger tapping tests used for adults can be used in children aged 6–8 and ages 12 and older, if the norms of Spreen and Strauss are used. For children 3–12 years of age, since other norms are lacking, the NEPSY can be used for sensorimotor assessment in this age range. There are some earlier studies that have noted that approximately 25% of children with severe TBI display deficits on tests of stereognosis, finger localization and graphesthesia. Timed motor skills may also be degraded in youngsters following TBI.[288,289]

MEASURING EXECUTIVE FUNCTION IN CHILDREN

The impact of TBI on executive function in children is an evolving area of research. Executive deficits in children are defined as cognitive processes that include voluntary initiation and inhibition of behavior, selective attention, planning, organization, and ability to switch sets. These deficits usually result from damage to the prefrontal regions or to their connections, as well as due to diffuse injury. The advanced organizing functional ability of the frontal lobes in a child may not be reasonably active until ages 12–15 years, or even into early adulthood. Some human studies provide support for the development of core frontal lobe skills as early as 6–9 months in humans. This parallels findings in monkeys, on an age and species corrected basis, as well. In children, neuro-psychological evidence of executive function deficits following TBI has been identified that clinically correlates with both CT and MRI findings.[270,290]

Experts in child development are also recommending that evaluation of executive function in children include not only neuropsychological testing but a multilevel approach to understanding childhood executive function deficits. This includes traditional test-based measures of executive function, real-world behavioral manifestations of executive dysfunction and the environmental system factors that impact the child.[291] Anderson and Catroppa in Australia recently evaluated how executive skills are recovered following pediatric TBI. They followed children for 2 years. They noted that the younger the child at the time of injury, the more likely the child was to sustain permanent executive dysfunction. Moreover, children with severe brain injury demonstrated substantial deficits at 2 years post-TBI.[292] Slomine and others have noted recently that children who have pre-injury ADHD and then go on to develop executive dysfunction following TBI have a worse outcome than children with TBI who do not have pre-injury ADHD.[268]

As with adults, children who sustain TBI, particularly frontal parts, frequently demonstrate executive dysfunction. However, the studies of children with these disorders are minimal. The Wisconsin Card Sorting Test can be used to assess frontal function, particularly the dorsolateral brain areas, in children as young as 6 years. The Stroop Test has norms available for measuring response inhibition in children as young as 7 years. The Delis–Kaplan Executive Function System (D-KEFS) has norms beginning at age 8 for children.[293] For very young children, the NEPSY measures executive function in youngsters as young as 3 years of age. Levin and others have found that children with traumatic brain injuries display deficits on various tasks meant to assess executive functions. These include the Tower of London (in the Delis–Kaplan test), which measures planning skills, and the Controlled Oral Word Association Test, which measures verbal fluency. The Twenty Questions Test (see D-KEFS section next) measures concept formation and mental flexibility and has been used to assess executive function in children as well.[294] Levin's group also has measured the magnitude of deficits within executive function tasks and found a correlation with the volume of lesions in the frontal lobes, but very poor or no correlation with lesion volume outside frontal lobe areas when using tests specifically designed to measure planning skills, verbal fluency, concept formation and mental flexibility.[295]

Delis–Kaplan Executive Function System

The D-KEFS was standardized on a nationally representative stratified sample of 1750 children, adolescents, and adults, ages 8 to 89 years. Stratification was based on age, sex, race, ethnicity, years of education and geographic region. The 2000 U.S. Census figures were used as target values for composition of the D-KEFS normative sample.[293] The D-KEFS consists of nine subtests, each of which may stand on its own merit independently: (1) Trailmaking Test, (2) Verbal Fluency Test, (3) Design Fluency Test, (4) Color-Word Interference Test, (5) Sorting Test, (6) 20 Questions, (7) Word Context Test, (8) Tower Test, and (9) Proverb Test. Raw scores are converted to scaled scores, with a mean of 10 and an SD of 3.

The key objective of the D-KEFS is to provide psychologists with a larger and more diverse armamentarium of executive function tests for assessing the complex and multifactorial domain of cognition in a more comprehensive manner. The overall philosophy of this testing system uses three approaches: (1) relatively new tests that were developed by the authors, (2) modification of tasks that have been used previously in the past experimental studies but not developed into standardized clinical instruments, and (3) modifications of existing clinical instruments. Historically, the Wisconsin Card Sorting Test has been the gold standard of executive function tests.[249] However, Kaplan[296] has argued that the use of a single-score method such as that used in the Wisconsin Card Sorting Test for quantifying performance on a cognitive instrument will mask the multiple natures of cognitive function that are required for successful performance. She argues that the single-score method is especially problematic with executive function tasks because such tests typically tap a host of fundamental and higher-level cognition skills. This is purportedly avoided in the D-KEFS.

Particularly with children, the D-KEFS instruments measure several key components of executive function. These include (1) initiation of problem-solving behavior, (2) verbal concept-formation skills, (3) nonverbal concept-formation skills, (4) transfer of concepts into action, (5) abstract expression of conceptual relationships, (6) flexibility of thinking, and (7) flexibility of behavioral response.

The Tower of London Test

The Tower of London is a subcomponent of the Delis–Kaplan Executive Function System. It is described in the adult section of this chapter, and it is normed for children as well.

MEASURING INTELLECTUAL FUNCTIONING IN CHILDREN

Intellectual deficits are found in children who sustain traumatic brain injuries whether they are compared with normal controls or with children who have received orthopedic trauma not involving the head. The magnitude of the deficits is generally directly proportional to injury severity. IQ scores that reflect nonverbal skills, relative to verbal skills, are particularly likely to be depressed.[284] While it is not an invariable finding, performance intelligence on standard IQ tests in children seems more vulnerable to change following head injury than the verbal portions. This dissociation probably reflects different demands of the two major IQ scales. Performance IQ subtests are more likely to require fluid problem-solving skills, and they generally involve speeded motor input and timed performance, whereas verbal IQ subtests are more likely to measure previously acquired verbal knowledge and more crystallized skills. They make few demands for response requiring speed or motor control.[284]

IQ scores tend to increase from an injury baseline over time following TBI in children. The largest increases occur among children who are more severely injured. The greatest improvement in IQ scores is immediately after injury, and the scores tend to plateau after approximately 1–2 years. Improvements have been shown to occur for periods up to 5 years. However, even with substantial recovery, IQ scores often continue to be depressed relative to pre-injury intelligence, particularly among children with severe injuries.[297–299] If it is necessary for the examiner to determine if there have been practice effects from prior intellectual assessments administered to the child, the current best reference for determining potential changes is found in the recent work by McCaffrey et al.[44]

Cognitive Assessment System

The Cognitive Assessment System (CAS) has been used to evaluate children and adolescents with TBI. Children with TBI earned significantly lower scores in the domains of planning and attention than matched control groups. The results of studies using this test instrument are consistent with previous medical literature demonstrating poor performance on measures of attention and executive function among children who have experienced TBI.[300] The Cognitive Assessment System is an assessment battery designed to evaluate cognitive processing in children aged 5–17 years. This test is based upon the PASS theory (planning, attention, simultaneous, and successive). These four processing areas of cognitive function complete the four scales that make up the CAS.

The CAS has two forms: a standard battery and a basic battery. Each of the two forms is composed of planning, attention, simultaneous, and successive scales. In the standard battery, these scales are defined by three subtests each. In the basic battery, these scales are composed of two subtests each. Each subtest yields a scaled score with a mean of 10 and a standard deviation of 3, similar to that derived from the subtests of the Wechsler Intelligence Scale for Children-IV (WISC-IV). The subtest scaled scores with each PASS scale are combined to yield a standard score with a mean of 100 and a standard deviation of 15. The standard battery consists of 12 subtests, and the basic battery consists of 8 subtests; both yield a full-scale standard score that is derived from the sum of the subtest scaled scores.[301]

The Planning subtests contain three test components: (1) matching numbers, (2) planned codes, and (3) planned connections. The Simultaneous subtests contain three test components: (1) nonverbal matrices, (2) verbal-spatial relations, and (3) figure memory. The Attention subtests are composed of these components: (1) expressive attention, (2) number detection, and (3) repetitive attention. The Successive subtests contain four components: (1) word series, (2) sentence repetition, (3) speech rate that is normed for ages 5–7 only, and (4) sentence questions that are normed for ages 8 to 17 only.

The materials and instructions for each subtest are divided into age-appropriate item sets. Younger children (ages 5–7) are administered different item sets than are older children (ages 8–17). The test is very explicit in that it requires subtests to be administered as they were during the standardization data collection and in the order prescribed in the manual. Administering the tests out of order may invalidate the results. The logic for this is that the Planning subscales are administered first because they are the least structured, giving the child maximum latitude to solve them in any manner thought best. This is in contrast to the Attention subtests, which are highly structured and have instructions that impose considerable constraints on the child.

The standard scores from the CAS are presented in the same manner as deviation IQs are presented following administration of the WISC-IV. The classification of descriptive categories are also the same as those of the WISC-IV. For instance, an attained standard score of 130 and above is classified as very superior, whereas 120–129 is superior. High average classification is made for standard scores 110–119, average for scores 90–109, low average for scores 80–89, below average for scores 70–79, and well below average for scores 69 and below. The standardization sample percentiles for each classification range fit closely to the theoretical normal distribution.[301]

Wechsler Intelligence Scale for Children-IV

When the first edition of this text was written, the Wechsler Intelligence Scale for Children-III (WISC-III) was the test most recent test of intellect in the Wechsler Scales for Children. The WISC-IV has been in use since 2003. As the current manual points out,[302] much of the debate over intellectual assessment during the last 60 years has focused on the existence of an underlying, global aspect of intelligence that influences an individual's performance across cognitive domains. Recent factor analytic investigations of cognitive ability demonstrate that the evidence for a general factor of intelligence is overwhelming. The trend toward an emphasis on multiple, more narrowly defined cognitive abilities has not caused the rejection of a general factor of intelligence. Currently, intelligence in children and adults is widely viewed as having a hierarchical structure with more specific abilities comprising several broad domains.[302] The WISC-IV has 10 core subtests and five supplemental subtests. The three subtests that comprise the Verbal Comprehension Index are Similarities, Vocabulary, and Comprehension. The three core Perceptual Reasoning subtests are Block Design, Picture Concepts, and Matrix Reasoning. Digit Span and Letter–Number Sequencing are the two core Working Memory subtests, while Coding and Symbol Search are the two core Processing Speed subtests. All 10 core subtests comprising the four indices contribute equally to the full-scale IQ score.[302] In addition to the subtests and composite scores, several additional process scores providing more detailed information about a child's performance are available. The fourth edition improved upon the third edition by introducing new subtests to improve measurement of fluid reasoning, working memory, and processing speed. Moreover, this test instrument has made a statistical linkage to measures of achievement. The WISC-IV is linked directly, by statistical means, to the Wechsler Individual Achievement Test—2nd edition (WIAT-II).[261] The test authors have also endeavored to increase developmental appropriateness of this instrument. Whenever possible, the authors took the more difficult concepts and reworded them to simplify those concepts. Every subtest incorporates teaching samples and practice items. With regard to the timed performance sections, subtests that were not primarily designed to measure processing speed were removed. For instance, Picture Arrangement, Object Assembly, and Mazes from the WISC-III were removed from this edition. The number of Block Design items with time-bonus scores has been significantly reduced, and the time-bonus scores for the Arithmetic subtest were removed altogether. This will be particularly beneficial to those children being tested following TBI where performance speed decrements may actually interfere with their ability to be examined.

The WISC-IV normative data was established using a sample collected from August 2001 to October 2002. This sample was stratified on key demographic variables (i.e., age, sex, race/ethnicity, parent education level and geographic region) according to the March 2000 U.S. Census data. Increased attention to the floors and ceilings of the subtests was improved to ensure adequate coverage of a wide range of cognitive abilities from those of a 6-year-old child with moderate mental retardation to that of a 16-year-old child who is intellectually gifted. Contemporary methodologies for testing item bias were used for WISC-IV item selection, and problematic items that were identified were deleted on the basis of formal expert review of items and empirical data from statistical and bias analyses. The user friendliness of this test has been improved relative to the WISC-III. The full WISC-IV requires the administration of 10 subtests to obtain all five composite scores. To obtain the full-scale IQ and index scores on the WISC-III, 12 subtests are administered.[302]

Following testing, the psychologist performs a profile analysis. Five scores are usually reported. These include the full-scale IQ score and four indexes. The indexes include a measure of verbal concept formation (VCI), a measure of perceptual and fluid reasoning, spatial processing and visual-motor integration (PRI), a measure of working memory ability (WMI) and a measure of processing speed (PSI).

With regard to TBI, the WISC-IV has a unique feature among children's intellectual assessment instruments. The WISC-IV was administered to a total of 43 children, ages 6–16, identified with a history of moderate or severe TBI. Children identified with a previous TBI of mild severity were also included if an abnormality was present on CT or MRI. Children who had sustained a TBI within six months before the time of testing were excluded, as well as those children with estimated or measured intelligence in the range expected for children with mental retardation. The group consisted of those with open-head injury and closed-head injury. The reader is referred to the manual[302] for analysis of mean performance of open-head injury and matched control groups, and mean performance of closed-head injury and matched control groups.

MEASURING COGNITIVE INJURY IN THE VERY YOUNG CHILD

As noted earlier, the research base for neuropsychological assessment of traumatically brain-injured children is very weak relative to the databases available for adult patients. Moreover, the younger the child, the more sparse are the databases of assessment techniques. There has been a recent addition to the techniques available for measuring cognition of very young children. The NEPSY[303] was introduced in 1998.

The NEPSY is a comprehensive instrument that was designed to assess neuropsychological development in preschool and school-age children. The authors chose NEPSY as an acronym formed from the words neuropsychology and psychology. The subtests of this instrument are designed specifically for children between the ages of 3 and 12 years. Compared with other neuropsychological tests for children, the NEPSY is unique in that not only can it measure cognitive function of very young children, but the subtests were also standardized on a single sample of children and administered in conjunction with a number of other validity measures, including the Wechsler Preschool and Primary Scale of Intelligence-Revised, the WISC-III and the WIAT. A broad range of subtests is included in the NEPSY to assess neuropsychological development in five functional domains: (1) attention or executive functions, (2) language functions, (3) sensorimotor functions, (4) visuospatial processing, and (5) memory and learning.

One of the major purposes for developing the NEPSY was to create an instrument that could be used for follow-up of children with congenital or acquired brain damage (including TBI). Recovery of function in children who sustained TBI needs to be evaluated over time in order to identify improving functioning, as well as persistent deficits that may require attention. Particularly in a psychoeducational framework, the NEPSY may be used to adapt interventions to the child's changing needs.

Much of the inspiration for the NEPSY was Luria's approach to assessing cognitive function in adults who had sustained brain damage.[304] Luria's work stimulated a Finnish version of the NEPSY developed in the 1980s.[305] The initial process of adapting the Finnish NEPSY for publication in the United States began in the spring of 1987. The U.S. pilot version was administered to 160 children in New York, New Jersey, Connecticut, and Pennsylvania during the fall of 1987. A tryout phase and new subtests were developed. The U.S. national tryout was undertaken in 1991–1992 and was administered to a sample of 300 children between the ages of 2 and 12. The sample was further stratified by race/ethnicity, gender, parent education, and geographical region. The review of these data established the age range for the present NEPSY at 3–12 years, and the subtests designed for 2-year-olds were eliminated. The standardization and validation phase was conducted by The Psychological Corporation from 1994 to 1996. The standardization version of the NEPSY was composed of 38 subtests and administered to 1500 children between the ages of 3 and 12. This sample was again stratified by age, race/ethnicity, gender, parent education and geographic region. Oversampling was included for minority groups. Validation studies were carried out with clinical populations. Following the standardization and validation of data, the final section of the subtests for each of the five functional domains was made.[303]

The NEPSY provides standard scores for the five domains noted previously. These are composite scores derived from specified subtests in each of the domains. The mean of the core domain scores is 100 with a standard deviation of 15. The subtest scaled scores within each core domain score have a mean of 10 and an SD of 3. The standard scores allow the NEPSY core domain scores and subtest scaled scores to be compared with other types of normalized scores (e.g., WISC-III or CAS scores). Supplemental scores are also available that enable the examiner to evaluate a child's performance in more detail and to identify factors that could account for or contribute to the child's poor performance. Qualitative observations are also recorded, much in the same manner that Luria emphasized during his career. The reader is referred to the NEPSY manual[303] for a more complex understanding of the only multidomain neuropsychological test instrument developed to date for very young children.

REFERENCES

1. Meyer, A., *Outlines of Examinations*, Bloomingdale Hospital Press, New York, 1918.
2. Harry, M. and Schroder, R., *Six Sigma: The Breakthrough Management Strategy Revolutionizing the World's Top Corporations*, Doubleday, New York, 2000.
3. Rush, A.J., Pincus, H.A., First, M.B., et al., *Handbook of Psychiatric Measures*, American Psychiatric Association, Washington, D.C., 2000.
4. Meyer, G.J., Finn, S.E., Eyde, L.D., et al., Psychological testing in psychological assessment: A review of evidence and issues. *Am. Psychol.*, 56, 128, 2001.
5. Lezak, M.D., *Neuropsychological Assessment*, 3rd edition, Oxford University Press, New York, 1995.
6. Anastasi, A., *Psychological Testing*, 6th edition, Macmillan Publishing Company, New York, 1988.
7. Sax, G., *Principles of Educational and Psychological Measurement and Evaluation*, 3rd edition, Wadsworth Publishing Company, Belmont, CA, 1989.
8. Lezak, M.D., Howieson, D.B., and Loring, D.W., *Neuropsychological Assessment*, 4th edition, Oxford University Press, New York, 2004.
9. Reitan, R.M. and Wolfson, D., *The Halstead–Reitan Neuropsychlogical Test Battery: Theory and Clinical Interpretation*, Neuropsychological Press, Tucson, AZ, 1993.
10. Orsini, D.L., van Gorp, W.G., and Boone, K.B., *The Neuropsychology Case Book*, Springer-Verlag, New York, 1988.
11. Reitan, R.M. and Wolfson, D., Theoretical, methodological and validation bases of the Halstead–Reitan neuropsychological test battery, in *Neuropsychological Assessment of Neuropsychiatric Disorders*, 2nd edition, Grant, I. and Adams, K.M., Eds., Oxford University Press, New York, 1996, p. 3.
12. Golden, C.J., Purisch, A.D., and Hammeke, T.A., *Luira-Nebraska Neuropsychological Test Battery: Forms I and II*, Western Psychological Services, Los Angeles, CA, 1985.
13. Korkman, M., NEPSY: A proposed neuropsychological test battery for young developmentally disabled children: Theory and evaluation, academic dissertation, University of Helsinki, Helsinki, Finland, 1988.
14. McKenna, P. and Warrington, E.K., The analytical approach to neuropsychological assessment, in *Neuropsychological Assessment of Neuropsychiatric Disorders*, 2nd edition, Grant, I. and Adams, K.M., Eds., Oxford University Press, New York, 1996, p. 43.
15. Milberg, W.P., Hebben, N., and Kaplan, E., The Boston process approach to neuropsychologial assessment, in *Neuropsychological Assessment of Neuropsychiatric Disorders*, 2nd edition, Grant, I. and Adams, K.M., Eds., Oxford University Press, New York, 1996, p. 58.

16. Tranel, D., The Iowa-Benton school of neuropsychological assessment, in *Neuropsychological Assessment of Neuropsychiatric Disorders*, 2nd edition, Grant, I. and Adams, K.M., Eds., Oxford University Press, New York, 1996, p. 811.
17. Mitrushina, M. and Fuld, P.A., Cognitive screening methods, in *Neuropsychological Assessment of Neuropsychiatric Disorders*, 2nd edition, Grant, I. and Adams, K.M., Eds., Oxford University Press, New York, 1996, p. 118.
18. Spordone, R.J. and Saul, R.E., *Neuropsychology for Health Care Professionals and Attorneys*, 2nd edition, CRC Press, Boca Raton, FL, 2000.
19. Granacher, R.P. and Berry, D.T.R., Feigned medical presentations, in *Clinical Assessment of Malingering and Deception*, 3rd edition, Rogers, R., Ed., Guilford Press, New York, 2007.
20. Vickery, C.D., Berry, D.T.R., Inman, T.H., et al., Detection of inadequate effort on neuropsychological testing: A meta-analytic review of selected procedures. *Arch. Clin. Neuropsychol.*, 16, 45, 2001.
21. Rey, A., L'examen psycholgique dans les cas d'encéphalopathie traumatique. *Arch. Psychol.*, 28, 286, 1941.
22. Rey, A., *L'examen Cinique en Psychologie*, Presses Universitaires de France, Paris, 1964.
23. Cercy, S.P., Schretlen, D.J., and Brandt, J., Simulated amnesia and the pseudomemory phenomena, in *Clinical Assessment of Malingering and Deception*, 2nd edition, Rogers, R., Ed., Guilford Press, New York, 1997, p. 85.
24. Pankratz, L. and Binder, L.M., Malingering on intellectual and neuropsychological measures, in *Clinical Assessment of Malingering and Deception*, 2nd edition, Rogers, R., Ed., Guilford Press, New York, 1997, p. 223.
25. Paul, D.S., Franzen, M.D., Cohen, S.H., et al., An investigation into the reliability and validity of two tests used in the detection of dissimulation. *Int. J. Clin. Neuropsychol.*, 14, 1, 1992.
26. Hiscock, M. and Hiscock, C.K., Refining the forced-choice method for the detection of malingering. *J. Clin. Exp. Neuropsychol.*, 11, 967, 1989.
27. Binder, L.M., *Portland Digit Recognition Test Manual*, 2nd edition, Binder, L.M., Portland, OR, 1993.
28. Tombaugh, T.N., *TOMM: Test of Memory Malingering*, Multi-Health Systems, North Tonawanda, NY, 1996.
29. Brown, L., Sherbenou, R.J., and Johnsen, S.K., *Test of Nonverbal Intelligence*, Pro-Ed, Austin, TX, 1982.
30. Frederick, R.I., *VIP: Validity Indicator Profile, Manual*. National Computer Systems, Minneapolis, MN, 1997.
31. Slick, D., Hopp, G., Strauss, E., et al., *Victoria Symptom Validity Test: Professional Manual*, Psychological Assessment Resources, Odessa, FL, 1997.
32. Green, P., Allen, L.M., and Astner, K., *The Word Memory Test: A User's Guide to the Oral and Computer-Administered Forms*, Cognisyst, Durham, NC, 1996.
33. Green, P., Iverson, G.L., and Allen, L., Detecting malingering in head injury litigation with the word memory test. *Brain Inj.*, 13, 813, 1999.
34. Wilson, R.S., Rosenbaum, G., and Brown, G., The problem of premorbid intelligence in neuropsychological assessment. *J. Clin. Neuropsychol.*, 1, 49, 1979.
35. Barona, A., Reynolds, C.R., and Chastain, R., A demographically based index of premorbid intelligence for the WAIS-R. *J. Consult. Clin. Psychol.*, 52, 885, 1984.
36. Krull, K.R., Scott, J.G., and Sherer, M., Estimation of premorbid intelligence from combined performance and demographic variables. *Clin. Neuropsychologist*, 9, 83, 1995.
37. Nelson, H.E. and Willison, J.R., *National Adult Reading Test (NART): Test Manual*, 2nd edition, NFER-Nelson Publishing Company, Berkshire, UK, 1991.
38. Spreen, O. and Strauss, E., *A Compendium of Neuropsychological Tests: Administration, Norms and Commentary*, Oxford University Press, New York, 1991.
39. Wilkinson, G.S., *Wide Range Achievement Test-3: Administration Manual*, 1993 edition. Wide Range, Wilmington, DE, 1993.
40. Wechsler Test of Adult Reading, Manual, *The Psychological Corporation*, San Antonio, TX, 2001.
41. Sweet, J., *Personal Communication*, San Diego, CA, February 21, 2006.
42. Mittenberg, W.W., Patton, C.C., Canyock, E.M., et al., Base rates of malingering and symptom exaggeration. *J. Clin. Exp. Neuropsychol.*, 24, 1094, 2002.
43. Millis, S.R. and Volinsky, C.T., Assessment of response bias and mild head injury: Beyond malingering tests. *J. Clin. Exp. Neuropsychol.*, 23, 809, 2001.

44. McCaffrey, R.J., Duff, K., and Westervelt, H.J., *Practitioner's Guide to Evaluating Change With Intellectual Assessment Instruments*, Kluwer Academic/Plenum Press, New York, 2000.

45. McCaffrey, R.J., Duff, K., and Westervelt, H.J., *Practitioner's Guide to Evaluating Change With Neuropsychological Assessment Instruments*, Kluwer Academic/Plenum Press, New York, 2000.

46. Cimino, C.R., Principles of neuropsychological interpretation, in *Clinician's Guide to Neuropsychological Assessment*, Vanderploeg, R.D., Ed., Erlbaum, Hillsdale, NJ, 1994.

47. McCaffrey, R.J., Ortega, A., Orsillo, S.M., et al., Practice effects in repeated neuropsychological assessments. *Clin. Neuropsychologist*, 6, 32, 1992.

48. Shatz, M.W., WAIS practice effects in clinical neuropsychology. *J. Clin. Neuropsychol.*, 3, 171, 1981.

49. Mesulam, M.M., Attentional networks, confusional states and neglect syndromes, in *Principles of Behavioral and Cognitive Neurology*, 2nd edition, Mesulam, M.M., Ed., Oxford University Press, New York, 2000, p. 174.

50. Mesulam, M.M., Geula, C., Bothwell, M.A., et al., Human reticular formation: Cholinergic neurons of the pedunculopontine and laterodorsal tegmental nuclei and some cytochemical comparisons to forebrain cholinergic neurons. *J. Comp. Neurol.*, 283, 611, 1989.

51. Vecera, S.P. and Rizzo, M., Attention: Normal and disordered processes, in *Principles and Practice of Behavioral Neurology and Neuropsychology*, Rizzo, M. and Eslinger, P.J., W.B. Saunders, Philadelphia, PA, 2004, p. 223.

52. Posner, M.I., Orienting of attention. *Q. J. Exp. Psychol.*, 32, 3, 1980.

53. Heilman, K.M., Watson, R.T., and Valenstein, E., Neglect and related disorders, in *Clinical Neuropsychology*, 3rd edition, Heilman, K.M. and Valenstein, E., Eds., Oxford University Press, New York, 1993, p. 279.

54. Heilman, K.M., Watson, R.T., and Valenstein, E., Neglect I: Clinical and anatomic issues, in *Patient-Based Approaches to Cognitive Neuroscience*, Farah, M.J. and Feinberg, T.E., Eds., MIT Press, Cambridge, MA, 2000, p. 115.

55. Bartolomeo, P., Sièroff, E., Decaix, C., et al., Modulating the attentional bias and unilateral neglect: The effects of the strategic set. *Exp. Brain Res.*, 137, 432, 2001.

56. Rafal, R. and Grimm, R.J., Progressive supranuclear palsy: Functional analysis of the response to methysergide and anti-Parkinsonian agents. *Neurology*, 31, 1507, 1981.

57. Rafal, R.D. and Posner, M.I., Deficits in human visual spatial attention following thalamic lesions. *Proc. Natl. Acad. Sci. U.S.A.*, 84, 7349, 1987.

58. Vecera, S.P., Toward a biased competition account of object-based segregation and attention. *Brain Mind*, 1, 353, 2000.

59. Egly, R., Driver, J., and Rafal, R.D., Shifting visual attention between objects and locations: Evidence from normal and parietal lesion subjects. *J. Exp. Psychol. Gen.*, 123, 161, 1994.

60. Husain, M., Shapiro, K., Martin, J., et al., Abnormal temporal dynamics of visual attention in spatial neglect patients. *Nature*, 385, 154, 1997.

61. Sturm, W. and Willmes, K., On the functional neuroanatomy of intrinsic and phasic alertness. *Neuroimage*, 14 (1 pt. 2), s76, 2001.

62. Nielson, K.A., Langenecker, S.A., and Garavan, H., Differences in the functional neuroanatomy of inhibitory control across the adult life span. *Psychol. Aging*, 17, 56, 2002.

63. Gerton, V.K., Brown, T.T., Myer-Lindenberg, A., et al., Shared and distinct neurophysiological components of the digits forward and backward tasks as revealed by functional neuroimaging. *Neuropsychologia*, 42, 1781, 2004.

64. Muller, N.G. and Knight, R.T., The functional neuroanatomy of working memory: Contributions of human brain lesions studies. *Neuroscience*, 139, 51, 2006.

65. Giesbrecht, B., Kingstone, A., Handy, T.C., et al., Functional neuroimaging of attention, in *Handbook of Functional Neuroimaging of Cognition*, 2nd edition, Cabeza, R. and Kingstone, A., Eds., MIT Press, Cambridge, MA, 2006, p. 85.

66. Woldorff, M.G., Hazlett, C.J., Fichtenholz, H.N., et al., Functional parcellation of attentional control regions of the brain. *J. Cogn. Neurosci.*, 16, 149, 2004.

67. vanZomeren, A.H. and Brouwer, W.H., Assessment of attention, in *A Handbook of Neuropsychological Assessment*, Crawford, J.R., Parker, D.M., and McKinlay, W.W., Eds., Lawrence Erlbaum Associates, Hove, UK, 1992.

68. Stuss, D.T., Stethem, L.L., Hugenholtz, H., et al., Traumatic brain injury. *Clin. Neuropsychol.*, 3, 145, 1989.

69. Ballard, J.C., Assessing attention: Comparison of response-inhibition and traditional continuous performance tests. *J. Clin. Exp. Neuropsychol.*, 23, 331, 2001.

70. McDowell, S., Whyte, J., and D'Esposito, M., Working memory impairments in traumatic brain injury: Evidence from a dual-task paradigm. *Neuropsychologia*, 35, 1341, 1997.

71. Bakker, K. and Anderson, V., Assessment of attention following preschool traumatic brain injury: A behavioural attention measure. *Pediatr. Rehabil.*, 3, 149, 1999.

72. Keller, M., Hiltbrunner, B., Dill, C., et al., Reversible neuropsychological deficits after mild traumatic brain injury. *J. Neurol. Neurosurg. Psychiatry*, 68, 761, 2000.

73. Schretlen, D., *Brief Test of Attention: Professional Manual*, Psychological Assessment Resources, Odessa, FL, 1997.

74. Keyl, P.M., Rebok, G.W., and Gallo, J.J., Screening elderly drivers in general medical settings: Toward the development of valid and feasible assessment procedure. Andrus Foundation, NRTA/AARP, Los Angeles, CA, 1996.

75. Lezak, M.D., *Neuropsychological Assessment*, 2nd edition, Oxford University Press, New York, 1983.

76. Ruff, R.M. and Allen, C.C., *Ruff 2 & 7 Selective Attention Test: Professional Manual*, Psychological Assessment Resources, Odessa, FL, 1996.

77. Ruff, R.M., Niemann, H., Allen, C.C., et al., The Ruff 2 & 7 selective attention test: A neuropsychological application. *Percept. Mot. Skills*, 75, 1311, 1992.

78. Ruff, R.M., Allen, C.C., Farrow, C.E., et al., Differential impairment in patients with left versus right frontal lobe lesions. *Arch. Clin. Neuropsychol.*, 9, 41, 1994.

79. McCarthy, G., Puce, A., Constable, R.T., et al., Activation of human prefrontal cortex during spatial and nonspatial working memory tasks measured by functional MRI. *Cereb. Cortex*, 6, 600, 1996.

80. Risberg, J. and Ingvar, D.H., Patterns of activation in the gray matter of the dominant hemisphere during memorizing and reasoning: A study of regional cerebral blood flow changes during psychological testing in a group of neurologically normal patients. *Brain*, 96, 737, 1973.

81. Morris, J.S., Friston, K.J., Buchel, C., et al., A neuromodulatory role for the human amygdale in processing emotional facial expressions. *Brain*, 121, 47, 1998.

82. Naito, E., Kinomura, S., Kawashima, R., et al., Correlation of the rCBF in anterior cingulate cortex with reaction time. *Neuroimage*, 7 s948, 1998.

83. Medina, J.L., Rubino, F.L., and Ross, A., Agitated delirium caused by infarction of the hippocampal formation and fusiform and lingual gyri: A case report. *Neurology*, 24, 1181, 1974.

84. Pardo, J.V., Fox, P.T., and Raichle, N.E., Localization of a human system for sustained attention by positron emission tomography. *Nature*, 349, 61, 1991.

85. Spiers, P.A., Schomer, D.L., Blume, H.W., et al., Visual neglect during intracarotid amobarbital testing. *Neurology*, 40, 1600, 1990.

86. Snyder, L.H., Batista, A.P., and Anderson, R.A., Change in motor plan, without a change in the spatial locus of attention, modulates activity in the posterior parietal cortex. *J. Neurophysiol.*, 79, 2814, 1988.

87. Corbetta, M., Shulman, G.L., Miezin, F.M., et al., Superior parietal cortex activation during spatial attention shifts and visual feature conjunction. *Science*, 270, 802, 1995.

88. Coull, J.T. and Nobre, A.C., Where and when to pay attention: The neural systems for directing attention to spatial locations and to the time intervals as related by both PET and fMRI. *J. Neurosci.*, 18, 7426, 1998.

89. Cicerone, K.D., Attention deficits in dual task demands after mild traumatic brain injury. *Brain Inj.*, 10, 79, 1996.

90. Conners, C.K., *Conners Continuous Performance Test II*, Multi-health Systems, Toronto, 2000.

91. Wilkinson, G.S. and Robertson, G.J., *WRAT-4: Wide Range Achievement Test: Professional Manual*, Psychological Assessment Resources, Lutz, FL, 2006.

92. Golden, C.J. and Freshwater, S.N., *Stroop Color and Word Test, Revised: Examiner's Manual*, Stoelting, Wood Dale, IL, 2002.

93. Jarvis, P.E. and Barth, J.T., *Halstead–Reitan Test Battery: An Interpretive Guide*, Psychological Assessment Resources, Odessa, FL, 1985.

94. Segal, M., Changing views of Cajal's neuron: The case of the dendritic spine. *Prog. Brain Res.*, 136, 101, 2002.

95. Takahashi, H., Kato, M., Hayashi, M., et al., Memory and frontal lobe functions: Possible relations with dopamine D2 receptors in the hippocampus. *Neuroimage*, 34, 1643, 2006.

96. Small, G.W., Kepe, V., Ercoli, L.M., et al., PET of brain amyloid and tau in mild cognitive impairment. *N. Engl. J. Med.*, 355, 2652, 2006.

97. Squire, L.R., Stark, C.E., and Clark, R.E., The medial temporal lobe. *Annu. Rev. Neurosci.*, 27, 279, 2004.

98. Gold, J.J. and Squire, L.R., The anatomy of amnesia: Neurohistological analysis of three new cases. *Learn. Mem.*, 13, 699, 2006.

99. Schott, B.H., Richardson-Klavehn, A., Henson, R.N., et al., Neuroanatomical dissociation of encoding processes related to priming and explicit memory. *J. Neurosci.*, 26, 792, 2006.

100. Mackiewicz, K.L., Sarinopoulos, I., Cleven, K.L., et al., The effect of anticipation and the specificity of sex differences for amygdala and hippocampus function in emotional memory. *Proc. Natl. Acad. Sci. U.S.A.*, 103, 14200, 2006.

101. Kelly, S., Lloyd, D., Nurmikko, T., et al., Retrieving autobiographical memories of painful events activates the anterior cingulate cortex and inferior frontal gyrus. *J. Pain*, 8, 307, 2006.

102. Dobbins, I.G. and Davachi, L., Functional neuroimaging of episodic memory, in *Handbook of Functional Neuroimaging of Cognition*, 2nd edition, Cabeza, R. and Kingstone, A., Eds., MIT Press, Cambridge, MA, 2006, p. 229.

103. Simons, D.J. and Rensink, R.A., Change blindness: Past, present, and future. *Trends Cogn. Sci.*, 9, 16, 2005.

104. Poldrack, R.A., Wagner, A.D., Prull, M.W., et al., Functional specialization for semantic and phonological processing in the left inferior prefrontal cortex. *Neuroimage*, 10, 15, 1999.

105. Kelley, W.M., Miezin, F.N., McDermott, K.B., et al., Hemispheric specialization in human dorsal frontal cortex and medial temporal lobe for verbal and nonverbal memory encoding. *Neuron*, 20, 927, 1998.

106. Lepage, M., Ghaffar, O., Nyberg, L., et al., Prefrontal cortex and episodic memory retrieval mode. *Proc. Natl. Acad. Sci U.S.A.*, 97, 506, 2000.

107. Cabeza, R. and Nyberg, L., Imaging cognition: An empirical review of PET studies with normal subjects. *J. Cogn. Neurosci.*, 9, 1, 1997.

108. Dobbins, I.G., Foley, H., Schacter, D., et al., Executive control during retrieval: Multiple prefrontal processes subserve source memory. *Neuron*, 35, 989, 2002.

109. Nolde, S.F., Johnson, M.K., and D'Esposito, M., Left prefrontal activation during episodic remembering: An event-related fMRI study. *NeuroReport*, 9, 3509, 1998.

110. Tulving, E., Episodic and semantic memory, in *Organization of Memory*, Tulving, E. and Donaldson, W., Eds., Academic Press, New York, 1972, p. 386.

111. Thompson-Schill, S.L., Kan, I.P., and Oliver, R.T., Functional neuroimaging of semantic memory, in *Handbook of Functional Neuroimaging of Cognition*, 2nd edition, Cabeza, R. and Kingstone, A., Eds., MIT Press, Cambridge, MA, 2006, p. 149.

112. Tulving, E., Précis of elements of episodic memory. *Behav. Brain Sci.*, 7, 223, 1984.

113. D'Esposito, M., Detre, J.A., Aguirre, G.K., et al., A functional MRI study of mental image generation. *Neuropsychologia*, 35, 725, 1997.

114. Kellenbach, M.L., Brett, M., and Patterson, K., Large, colorful or noisy? Attribute- and modality-specific activations during retrieval of perceptual attribute knowledge. *Cogn. Affect. Behav. Neurosci.*, 1, 207, 2001.

115. Buccino, G., Lui, F., Canessa, N., et al., Neural circuits involved in the recognition of actions performed by non-specifics: An fMRI study. *J. Cogn. Neurosci.*, 16, 114, 2004.

116. Oliver, R.T. and Thompson-Schill, S.L., Dorsal stream activation during retrieval of object size and shape. *Cogn. Affect. Behav. Neurosci.*, 3, 309, 2003.

117. Pietrini, P., Furey, M.L., Ricciardi, E., et al., Beyond sensory images: Object-based representation in the human ventral pathway. *Proc. Natl. Acad. Sci. U.S.A.*, 101, 5658, 2004.

118. Chao, L. and Martin, A., Representation of manipulable man-made objects in the dorsal stream. *Neuroimage*, 12, 478, 2000.

119. Boronat, C.B., Buxbaum, L.J., Coslett, H.B., et al., Distinctions between manipulation and function knowledge of objects: Evidence from functional magnetic resonance imaging. *Cogn. Brain Res.*, 23, 361, 2005.

120. Cerf-Ducastel, B. and Murphy, C., fMRI brain activation and response to odors is reduced to primary olfactory areas of elderly subjects. *Brain Res.*, 986, 39, 2003.

121. Rogers, T.T., Lambon-Ralph, M.A., Garrard, P., et al., Structure and deterioration of semantic memory: A neuropsychological and computational investigation. *Psychol. Rev.*, 111, 2005, 2004.

122. Milner, B., Corkin, S., and Teuber, H.L., Further analysis of the hippocampal amnesia syndrome. *Neuropsychologia*, 6, 215, 1968.

123. Poldrack, R.A. and Willingham, D.T., Functional neuroimaging of skill learning, in *Handbook of Functional Neuroimaging of Cognition*, 2nd edition, Cabeza, R. and Kingstone, A., Eds., MIT Press, Cambridge, MA, 2006, p. 113.
124. Saint-Cyr, J.A. and Taylor, A.E., The mobilization of procedural learning: The "key signature" of the basal ganglia, in *Neuropsychology of Memory*, 2nd edition, Squire, L.R. and Butters, N., Eds., Guilford, New York, 1992, p. 188.
125. Alexander, G.E., DeLong, M.R., and Strick, P.L., Parallel organization of functionally segregated circuits linking basal ganglia and cortex. *Ann. Rev. Neurosci.*, 9, 357, 1986.
126. Toni, I. and Passingham, R.E., Pre-frontal basal ganglia pathways are involved in the learning of arbitrary visuomotor associations: A PET study. *Exp. Brain Res.*, 127, 19, 1999.
127. Boake, C., Edouard claparède and the auditory-verbal learning test, *J. Clin. Exp. Neuropsychol.*, 22, 286, 2000.
128. Ross, S.R., Millis, S.R., and Rosenthal, M., Neuropsychological predication of psychosocial outcome after traumatic brain injury. *Appl. Neuropsychol.*, 4, 165, 1997.
129. Molinari, M., Leggio, M.G., Solida, A., et al., Cerebellum and procedural learning: Evidence from focal cerebellar lesions. *Brain*, 120, 1753, 1997.
130. Thompson, R.F. and Kim, J.J., Memory systems in the brain and localization of memory. *Proc. Natl. Acad. Sci. U.S.A.*, 93, 13428, 1996.
131. Seeck, M., Mainwaring, N., Cosgrove, N.D., et al., Neurophysiologic correlates of implicit face memory in intracranial visual evoked potentials. *Neurology*, 49, 1312, 1997.
132. Fletcher, P.C., Frith, C.D., and Rugg, M.D., The functional neuroanatomy of episodic memory. *Trends Neurosci.*, 20, 213, 1997.
133. Tulving, E., Kapur, S., Craik, F.I.M., et al., Hemispheric encoding/retrieval asymmetry and episodic memory: Positron emission tomography findings. *Proc. Natl. Acad. Sci. U.S.A.*, 91, 2016, 1994.
134. Zelkowicz, B.J., Herbster, A.N., Nebes, R.D., et al., An examination of regional cerebral blood flow during object naming tasks. *J. Int. Neuropsychol. Soc.*, 4, 160, 1998.
135. Martin, A., Functional neuroimaging of semantic memory, in *Handbook of Functional Neuroimaging of Cognition*, Cabeza, R. and Kingstone, A., Eds., MIT Press, Cambridge, MA, 2001, p. 153.
136. Binder, J.R., Frost, J.A., Hammeke, T.A., et al., Human brain language areas identified by functional magnetic resonance imaging. *J. Neurosci.*, 17, 353, 1997.
137. Ruff, R.M. and Allen, C.C., *Ruff-Light Trail Learning Test: Professional Manual*, Psychological Assessment Resources, Odessa, FL, 1999.
138. *Wechsler Memory Scale–Third Edition: Administration and Scoring Manual*, The Psychological Corporation, Orlando, FL, 1997.
139. Damasio, A.R. and Damasio, H., Aphasia and the neural basis of language, in *Principles of Behavioral and Cognitive Neurology*, 2nd edition, Mesulam, M.M., Ed., Oxford University Press, New York, 2000, p. 294.
140. Kirshner, H.S., Aphasia, alexia, agraphia, acalculia, in *Principles and Practice of Behavioral Neurology and Neuropsychology*, Rizzo, M. and Eslinger, P.J., Eds., W.B. Saunders, New York, 2004, p. 389.
141. Geschwind, N., Disconnexion syndromes in animals and man. *Brain*, 88, 237, 1965.
142. Ross, E.D. and Mesulam, M.M., Dominant language functions of the right hemispheres? Prosody and emotional gesturing. *Arch. Neurol.*, 36, 144, 1979.
143. Ross, E.D., Affective prosody and the aprosodias, in *Principles of Behavioral and Cognitive Neurology*, 2nd edition, Mesulam, M.M., Ed., Oxford University Press, New York, 2000, p. 316.
144. Ross, E.D., Orbelo, D.M., Burgard, M., et al., Functional–anatomical correlates of aprosodic deficits in patients with right brain damage. *Neurology*, 50 (Suppl. 4), A363, 1998.
145. Alexander, M.P., Naeser, M.A., and Palumbo, C.L., Broca's area aphasias: Aphasia after lesions including the frontal operculum. *Neurology*, 40, 353, 1990.
146. Kirshner, H.S., Casey, P.F., Henson, J., et al., Behavioural features and lesion localization in Wernicke's aphasia. *Aphasiology*, 3, 169, 1989.
147. Boatman, D., Gordon, B., Hart, J., et al., Transcortical sensory aphasia: Revisited and revised. *Brain*, 123, 1634, 2000.
148. Bogousslavsky, J., Regli, F., and Uske, A., Thalamic infarcts: Clinical syndromes, etiology and prognosis. *Neurology*, 38, 837, 1988.
149. Alexander, M.P., Naeser, M.A., and Palumbo, C.L., Correlations of subcortical CT lesion sites and aphasia profiles. *Brain*, 110, 961, 1987.

150. Damasio, A.R. and Damasio, H., The anatomic basis of pure alexia. *Neurology*, 33, 1573, 1983.
151. Halsband, U., Bilingual and multilingual language processing. *J. Physiol.* (Paris), 99, 355, 2006.
152. Knaus, T.A., Bollich, A.M., Corey, D.M., et al, Sex-linked differences in the anatomy of the perisylvian language cortex: A volumetric MRI study of gray matter volumes. *Neuropsychology*, 18, 738, 2004.
153. McGuire, P.K., Silbersweig, D.A., and Frith, C.D., Functional neuroanatomy of verbal self-monitoring. *Brain*, 119, 907, 1996.
154. Booth, J.R., Wood, L., Lu, D., et al., The role of the basal ganglia and cerebellum in language processing. *Brain Res.*, 1133, 136, 2006.
155. Stephane, M., Hagen, M.C., Lee, J.T., et al., About the mechanism of auditory verbal hallucinations: A positron emission tomography study. *J. Psychiatry Neurosci.*, 31, 396, 2006.
156. Mitchell, R.L., Elliott, R., Barry, M., et al., The neural response to emotional prosody as revealed by functional magnetic resonance imaging. *Neuropsychologia*, 41, 1410, 2003.
157. Willems, R.M., Ozyurek, A., and Hagoort, P., When language meets action: The neural integration of gesture and speech. *Cereb. Cortex*, 17, 2322, 2007.
158. Wang, Y.T., Kent, R.D., Duffy, J.R., et al., Dysarthria associated with traumatic brain injury: Speaking rate and emphatic stress. *J. Commun. Disord.*, 38, 231, 2005.
159. Gardner, H., Brownell, H.H., Wapner, W., et al., Missing the point: The role of the right hemisphere in the processing of complex linguistic materials, in *Cognitive Processing in the Right Hemisphere*, Perecman, E., Ed., Academic Press, New York, 1983, p. 169.
160. Binder, J. and Price, C.J., Functional neuroimaging of language, in *Handbook of Functional Neuroimaging of Cognition*, Cabeza, R. and Kingstone, A., Eds., MIT Press, Cambridge, MA, 2001, p. 187.
161. Binder, J.R., Frost, J.A., Hammeke, T.A., et al., Function of the left planum temporale in auditory and linguistic processing. *Brain*, 119, 1239, 1996.
162. Indefrey, P., Kleinschmidt, A., Merboldt, K.D., et al., Equivalent responses ot lexical and nonlexical visual stimuli in occipital cortex: A functional magnetic resonance imaging study. *Neuroimage*, 5, 78, 1997.
163. Puce, A., Allison, T., Asgari, M., et al., Differential sensitivity of human visual cortex to faces, letter strings, and textures: A functional magnetic resonance imaging study. *J. Neurosci.*, 16, 5205, 1996.
164. Petersen, S.E., Fox, P.T., Snyder, A.Z., et al., Activation of extrastriate and frontal cortical areas by visual words and word-like stimuli. *Science*, 249, 1041, 1990.
165. Price, C.J., Wise, R.J.S., Warburton, E.A., et al., Hearing and saying: The functional neuroanatomy of auditory word processing. *Brain*, 119, 919, 1996.
166. Goodglass, H., The assessment of language after brain damage, in *Handbook of Clinical Neuropsychology, Volume 2*, Filskov, S.B., Boll, T.J., John Wiley & Sons, New York, 1986.
167. Rey, G.J. and Benton, A.L., *Multilingual Aphasia Examination-Spanish*, Psychological Corporation, San Antonio, TX, 1991.
168. Goodglass, H. and Kaplan, E., *Boston Diagnostic Aphasia Examination*, Lea and Febiger, Philadelphia, PA, 1983.
169. Goodglass, H., Kaplan, E., and Barresi, B., *The Boston Diagnostic Aphasia Examination (BDAE-III)*, 3rd edition, Lippincott, Philadelphia, PA, 2000.
170. Goodglass, H. and Kaplan, E., *Boston Naming Test*, Lippincott, Williams & Wilkins, Philadelphia, PA, 2000.
171. Ivnik, R.J., Malec, J.F., Smith, G.E., et al., Neuropsychological test norms above age 55: COWAT, BAE, MAE, Token, WRAT-R reading, AMNART, Stroop, TMT and JLO. *Clin. Neuropsychol.*, 10, 262, 1996.
172. Spreen, O. and Strauss, E., *A Compendium of Neuropsychological Tests*, 2nd edition, Oxford University Press, New York, 1998.
173. Tombaugh, T.N., Kozak, J., and Rees, L., Normative data stratified by age and education for two measures of verbal fluency: FAS and Animal Naming. *Arch. Clin. Neuropsychol.*, 14, 167, 1999.
174. Ruff, R.M., Light, R.H., Parker, S.B., et al., Benton controlled oral word association test: Reliability and updated norms. *Arch. Clin. Neuropsychol.*, 11, 329, 1996.
175. DeRenzi, E. and Vignolo, L.A., The token test: A sensitive test to detect disturbances in aphasics. *Brain*, 85, 665, 1962.
176. Boller, F. and Vignolo, L., Latent sensory aphasia in hemisphere-damaged patients: An experimental study with the token test. *Brain*, 89, 815, 1966.
177. Barton, J.J.S., Visual dysfunction, in *Principles and Practice of Behavioral Neurology and Neuropsychology*, Rizzo, M. and Eslinger, P.J., Eds., W.B. Saunders, New York, 2004, p. 267.

178. Damasio, A.R., Tranel, D., and Rizzo, M., Disorders of complex visual processing, in *Principles of Behavioral and Cognitive Neurology*, 2nd edition, Mesulam, M.M., Ed., Oxford University Press, New York, 2000, p. 332.
179. Heywood, C.A., Cowey, A., and Newcombe, F., Chromatic discrimination in a cortically colourblind observer. *Eur. J. Neurosci.*, 3, 802, 1991.
180. Merigan, W., Freeman, A., and Meyers, S.P., Parallel processing streams in human visual cortex. *Neuroreport*, 8, 3895, 1997.
181. Martin, A., Haxby, J.V., Lalonde, F.M., et al., Discreet cortical regions associated with knowledge of color and knowledge of action. *Science*, 270, 102, 1995.
182. Kinsbourne, M. and Warrington, E.K., Observations of colour agnosia. *J. Neurol. Neurosurg. Psychiatry*, 27, 296, 1964.
183. Lamm, C., Fischmeister, F.P., and Bauer, H., Individual differences in brain activity during visuo-spatial processing assessed by slow-cortical potentials and LORETA. *Brain Res. Cogn., Brain, Res.*, 25, 900, 2005.
184. Martinez, A., Anllo-Vento, L., Sereno, M.I., et al., Involvement of striate and extrastriate visual cortical areas in spatial attention. *Nat. Neurosci.*, 2, 364, 1999.
185. Pollmann, S. and von Cramon, D.Y., Object working memory and visuospatial processing: Functional neuroanatomy analyzed by event-related fMRI. *Exp. Brain Res.*, 133, 12, 2000.
186. Sparr, S., Jay, M., Drislane, F., et al., A historic case of visual agnosia revisited after forty years. *Brain*, 114, 789, 1991.
187. Benton, A. and vanAllen, M., Prosopagnosia and facial discrimination. *J. Neurol. Sci.*, 15, 167, 1972.
188. Barton, J.J. and Cherkasova, M., Face imagery and its relation to perception and covert recognition in prosopagnosia. *Neurology*, 61, 220, 2003.
189. Evans, J., Heggs, A., Antoun, N., et al., Regressive prosopagnosia associated with selective right temporal lobe atrophy. *Brain*, 118, 1, 1995.
190. Kanwisher, N., McDermott, J., and Chun, M., The fusiform face area: A module in human extrastriate cortex specialized for face perception. *J. Neurosci.*, 17, 4302, 1997.
191. Meadows, J., The anatomical basis of prosopagnosia. *J. Neurol. Neurosurg. Psychiatry*, 37, 489, 1974.
192. Young, A., Aggleton, J., Hellawell, D., et al., Face processing impairments after amygdalotomy. *Brain*, 118, 15, 1995.
193. Kracke, I., Developmental prosopagnosia in Asperger's syndrome: Presentation and discussion of an individual case. *Dev. Med. Child Neurol.*, 36, 873, 1994.
194. Vaina, L., Makris, N., Kennedy, D., et al., The selective impairment or the perception of first-order motion by unilateral cortical brain damage. *Vis. Neurosci.*, 15, 333, 1998.
195. Pai, M., Topographic disorientation: Two cases. *J. Foremos. Med. Assoc.*, 96, 660, 1997.
196. O'Mara, S., The subiculum: What it does, what it might do, and what neuroanatomy has yet to tell us. *J. Anat.*, 207, 271, 2005.
197. Moscovitch, M., Rosenbaum, R.S., Gilboa, A., et al., Functional neuroanatomy of remote episodic, semantic and spatial memory: A unified account based on multiple trace theory. *J. Anat.*, 207, 35, 2005.
198. Epstein, R. and Kanwisher, N., A cortical representation of the local visual environment. *Nature*, 392, 598, 1998.
199. Bálint, R., Seelenlähmung des "Schauens", optische Ataxia, räumliche Störung der Aufmerksamkeit, *Monatsschr. Psychiatr. Neurol.*, 25, 51, 1909.
200. Benton, A.L., Varney, N.R., and Hamsher, K., Visuospatial judgment: A clinical test. *Arch. Neurol.*, 35, 364, 1978.
201. Kohler, S., Kapur, S., Moscovitch, M., et al., Dissociation of pathways for objects and spatial vision: A PET study in humans. *Neuroreport*, 6, 1865, 1995.
202. Whalen, P.J., Rauch, S.L., Etcoff, N.L., et al., Masked presentations of emotional facial expressions modulate amygdala activity without explicit knowledge. *J. Neurosci.*, 18, 411, 1998.
203. Kanwisher, N., Downing, P., Epsetin, R., et al., Functional neuroimaging of visual recognition, in *Handbook of Functional Neuroimaging of Cognition*, Cabeza, R. and Kingstone, A., Eds., MIT Press, Cambridge, MA, 2001, p. 109.
204. Zihl, J., Cerebral disturbances of elementary visual functions, in *Neuropsychology of Visual Perception*, Brown, J.W., Ed., IRBN Press, New York, 1989.
205. Bender, L., A visuomotor Gestalt test and its clinical use. *Am. Orthopsychiatr. Assoc. Res. Monogr.*, 3, 1998.

206. Hutt, M.L., *The Hutt Adaptation of the Bender-Gestalt Test: Rapid Screening and Intensive Diagnosis*, 4th edition, Grune and Stratton, Orlando, FL, 1985.
207. Whitworth, R.H., Bender Visuomotor Gestalt Test, in *Test Critiques, Vol. 1*, Keyser, D.J. and Sweetland, R.C., Eds., Test Corporation of America, Kansas City, KS, 1984, p. 90.
208. Benton, A.L., Hamsher, K., Rey, G.J., et al., *Multilingual Aphasia Examination*, 3rd edition, A.J.A. Associates, Iowa City, IA, 1994.
209. Benton, A.L., Hannay, H.J., and Varney, N.R., Visual perception of line direction in patients with unilateral brain disease. *Neurology*, 25, 907, 1975.
210. Hannay, H.J., Falgout, J.C., Leli, D.A., et al., Focal right temporo-occipital blood flow changes associated with judgment of line orientation. *Neuropsychology*, 25, 755, 1987.
211. Wechsler, D., *Wechsler Adult Intelligence Scale*, 3rd edition, Psychological Corporation, San Antonio, TX, 1997.
212. Chase, T.N., Fedio, P., Foster, N.L., et al., Wechsler Adult Intelligence Scale performance: Cortical localization by fluorodeoxyglucose F 18-positron emission tomography. *Arch. Neurol.*, 41, 1244, 1984.
213. Hooper, H.E., *Hooper Visual Organization Test (VOT)*, Western Psychological Services, Los Angeles, 1983.
214. Benton, A.L., Sivam, A.B., Hamsher, K. deS., et al., *Contributions to Neuropsychological Assessment*, 2nd edition, Oxford University Press, New York, 1994, p. 65.
215. Razavi, M., Somatosensory system, in *Principles and Practice of Behavioral Neurology and Neuropsychology*, Rizzo, M. and Eslinger, P.J., Eds., W.B. Saunders, New York, 2004, p. 305.
216. Mesulam, M.M., Behavioral neuroanatomy: Large-scale networks, association cortex, frontal syndromes, the limbic system, and hemispheric specializations, in *Principles of Behavioral and Cognitive Neurology*, 2nd edition, Mesulam, M.M., Ed., Oxford University Press, New York, 2000, p. 1.
217. Binkofski, E., Kunesch, E., Classen, J., et al., Tactile apraxia unimodal apractic disorder of tactile object exploration associated with parietal lobe lesions. *Brain*, 124, 132, 2001.
218. Patterson, J.C. and Kotrla, K.J., Functional neuroimaging in psychiatry, in *The American Psychiatric Publishing Textbook of Neuropsychiatry and Clinical Neurosciences*, 4th edition, Yudofsky, S.C. and Hales, R.E., Eds., American Psychiatry Publishing, Washington, D.C., 2002, p. 285.
219. Maillard, L., Ishii, K., Bushara, K., et al., Mapping of the basal ganglia: fMRI evidence for somatotopic representation of face, hand, and foot. *Neurology*, 55, 377, 2000.
220. Rao, S.M., Binder, J.R., Bandettini, P.A., et al., Functional magnetic resonance imaging of complex human movements. *Neurology*, 43, 2311, 1993.
221. Wise, S.P., Boussaoud, D., Johnson, P.B., et al., Premotor and parietal cortex: Corticocortical connectivity in combinational computations. *Ann. Rev. Neurosci.*, 20, 25, 1997.
222. Brinkman, C. and Porter, R., Supplementary motor area and premotor area of monkey's cerebral cortex: functional organization and activities of single neurons during performance of a learned movement, in *Motor Control Mechanisms in Health and Disease*, Desmedt, J.E., Ed., Raven Press, New York, 1983.
223. Stephan, T.M., Fink, G.R., Passingham, R.E., et al., Functional anatomy of the mental representation of upper extremity movements in healthy subjects. *J. Neurophysiol.*, 73, 373, 1995.
224. Heaton, R.K., Graham, I., and Matthews, C.G., *Comprehensive Norms for an Expanded Halstead–Reitan Battery: Demographic Corrections, Research Findings, and Clinical Applications*, Psychological Assessment Resources, Odessa, FL, 1991.
225. Kløve, H., Clinical neuropsychology, in *The Medical Clinics of North America*, Forester, F.M., Ed., W.B. Saunders, New York, 1963.
226. Mitrushina, M.N., Boone, K.B., and D'Elia, L.F., *Handbook of Normative Data for Neuropsychological Assessment*, Oxford University Press, New York, 1999.
227. Golden, C.J., *Clinical Interpretation of Objective Psychological Tests*, Grune and Stratton, New York, 1979.
228. Harlow, J.M., Recovery from the passage of an iron bar through the head. *Pub. Mass. Med. Soc.*, 2, 327, 1868.
229. Eslinger, P.J. and Chakara, F., Frontal lobe and executive functions, in *Principles and Practice of Behavioral Neurology and Neuropsychology*, Rizzo, M. and Eslinger, P.J., Eds., W.B. Saunders, Philadelphia, PA, 2004, p. 435.
230. Burruss, J.W., Hurley, R.A., Taber, K.H., et al., Special report: Functional neuroanatomy of the frontal lobe circuits. *Radiology*, 214, 227, 2000.
231. Curtis, C.E. and D'Esposito, M., Functional neuroimaging of working memory, in *Handbook of Functional Neuroimaging of Cognition*, 2nd edition, Cabeza, R. and Kingstone, A., Eds., MIT Press, Cambridge, MA, 2006, p. 269.

232. Mohr, H.M., Goebel, R., and Linden, D.E., Content- and task-specific dissociations of frontal activity during maintenance and manipulation in visual working memory. *J. Neurosci.*, 26, 4465, 2006.
233. du Boisgueheneuc, F., Levy, R., Volle, E., et al., Functions of the left superior frontal gyrus in humans: A lesion study. *Brain*, 129 (pt. 12), 3315, 2006.
234. Velanova, K., Jacoby, L.L., Wheeler, M.E., et al., Functional-anatomic correlates of sustained and transient processing components engaged during controlled retrieval. *J. Neurosci.*, 23, 8460, 2003.
235. Braver, T.S. and Ruge, H., Functional neuroimaging of executive functions, in *Handbook of Functional Neuroimaging of Cognition*, 2nd edition, Cabeza, R. and Kingstone, A., Eds., MIT Press, Cambridge, MA, 2006, p. 307.
236. Durston, S., Davidson, M.C., Thomas, K.M., et al., Parametric manipulation of conflict and response competition using rapid mixed-trial event-related fMRI. *Neuroimage*, 20, 2135, 2003.
237. Petersen, S.E., Fox, P.T., Posner, M.I., et al., Positron emission tomographic studies of the processing of single words. *J. Cogn. Neurosci.*, 1, 153, 1989.
238. Berman, K.F., Ostram, J.L., Randolph, C., et al., Physiological activation of a cortical network during performance of the Wisconsin Card Sorting Test: A positron emission tomography study. *Neuropsychologia*, 33, 1027, 1995.
239. Bunge, S.A., How we use rules to select actions: A review of evidence from cognitive neuroscience. *Cog. Affect. Behav. Neurosci.*, 4, 564, 2004.
240. van den Hauvel, O.A., Groenevegen, H.J., Barkhof, F., et al., Frontostriatal system in planning complexity: A parametric functional magnetic resonance version of tower of London task. *Neuroimage*, 18, 367, 2003.
241. Kroger, J.K., Sabb, F.W., Falas, C.L., et al., Recruitment of anterior dorsolateral prefrontal cortex in human reasoning: A parametric study of relational complexity. *Cereb. Cortex*, 12, 477, 2002.
242. Talati, A. and Hirsch, J., Functional specialization within the medial frontal gyrus for perceptual go or no-go decisions based on "what," "when," and "where" related information: An fMRI study. *J. Cogn. Neurosci.*, 17, 981, 2005.
243. Kubler, A., Dixon, V., and Garavan, H., Automaticity and reestablishment of executive control—a fMRI study. *J. Cogn. Neurosci.*, 18, 1331, 2006.
244. Wang, P.L., Concept formation in frontal lobe function, in *Frontal Lobes Revisited*, Perecman, E., Ed., IRBN Press, New York, 1987.
245. Raven, J.C., *Guide to Standard Progressive Matrices*, H.K., Lewis, London, 1960.
246. Culbertson, W.C. and Zillmer, E.A., *Tower of London: Drexel University (TOL$_{DX}$)*, Multi-Health Systems, North Tonawanda, NY, 2001.
247. Mataix-Cols, D. and Bartres-Faz, D., Is the use of the wooden and computerized versions of the Tower of Hanoi puzzle equivalent? *Appl. Neuropsychol.*, 9, 117, 2002.
248. Berg, E.A., A simple objective technique for measuring flexibility in thinking. *J. Gen. Psychol.*, 39, 15, 1948.
249. Heaton, R.K., Chelune, J.J., Talley, J.L., et al., *Wisconsin Card Sorting Test Manual: Revised and Expanded*, Psychological Assessment Resources, Odessa, FL, 1993.
250. Grafman, J., Jonas, B., and Salazar, A., Wisconsin Card Sorting Test performance based on location and size in neuroanatomical lesion in Vietnam veterans with penetrating head injury. *Percept. Mot. Skills*, 71, 1120, 1990.
251. Stuss, D.T. and Benson, D.F., *The Frontal Lobes*, Raven Press, New York, 1986.
252. Wechsler, D., *The Measurement of Adult Intelligence*, Williams & Wilkins, Baltimore, MD, 1939.
253. Crick, F.H.C., Thinking about the brain. *Sci. Am.*, 241, 181, 1979.
254. Hawkins, J., *On Intelligence*, Henry Holt and Co., New York, 2004.
255. Kaufman, A.S. and Kaufman, N.L., *Kaufman Brief Intelligence Test Manual*, American Guidance Service, Circle Pines, MN, 1990.
256. Burton, D.D., Maughe, R.I., and Schuster, J.M., A structural equation analysis of the Kaufman brief intelligence test and the Wechsler intelligence scale-revised. *Psychol. Assess.*, 7, 538, 1995.
257. Brown, L., Sherbenou, R.J., and Johnsen, S.K., *Test of Nonverbal Intelligence*, 2nd edition, Pro-Ed., Austin, TX, 1990.
258. Borstein, R.A., Vrebal I.Q.-performance I.Q. discrepancies on the Wechsler adult intelligence scale-revised in patients with unilateral or bilateral cerebral dysfunction. *J. Consult. Clin. Psychol.*, 51, 779, 1983.
259. Smith, A., Intellectual functions in patients with lateralized frontal tumors. *J. Neurol. Neurosurg. Psychiatry*, 29, 52, 1966.

260. Donders, J., Performance on the test of memory malingering in a mixed pediatric sample. *Child Neuropsychol.*, 11, 221, 2005.
261. *Wechsler Individual Achievement Test*, 2nd edition, Examiner's manual, The Psychological Corporation, San Antonio, TX, 2001.
262. Catroppa, C. and Anderson, V., A prospective study of the recovery of attention from acute to 2 years following pediatric traumatic brain injury. *J. Int. Neuropsychol. Soc.*, 11, 84, 2005.
263. Yeates, K.O., Armstrong, K., Janusz, J., et al., Long-term attention problems in children with traumatic brain injury. *J. Am. Acad. Child Adolesc. Psychiatry*, 44, 574, 2005.
264. Anderson, V., Catroppa, C., Morse, S., et al., Attention and processing skills following traumatic brain injury and early childhood. *Brain Inj.*, 19, 699, 2005.
265. Catroppa, C., Anderson, V., Morse, S.A., et al., Children's attentional skills 5 years post-TBI. *J. Pediatr. Psychol.*, July 13, 32, 354, 2006.
266. van Heughten, C.N., Hendricksen, J., Rasquin, S., et al., Long-term neuropsychological performance in a cohort of children and adolescents after severe paediatric traumatic brain injury. *Brain Inj.*, 20, 895, 2006.
267. Max, J.E., Lansing, A.E., Koele, S.L., et al., Attention deficit hyperactivity disorder in children and adolescents following traumatic brain injury. *Dev. Neuropsychol.*, 25, 159, 2004.
268. Slomine, B.S., Salorio, C.F., Grados, M.A., et al., Differences in attention, executive function and memory in children with and without ADHD after severe traumatic brain injury. *J. Int. Neuropsychol. Soc.*, 11, 645, 2005.
269. Connor's Kiddie Continuous Performance Test (K-CPT): *Technical Guide and Software Manual*, Multi-Health Systems, North Tonawanda, NY, 2001.
270. Arffa, S., Traumatic brain injury, in *Pediatric Neuropsychiatry*, Coffey, C.E. and Brumback, R.A., Eds., Lippincott, Williams & Wilkins, Philadelphia, PA, 2006, p. 507.
271. Serra-Grabulosa, J.M., Junque, C., Verger, K., et al., Cerebral correlates of declarative memory dysfunctions in early traumatic brain injury. *J. Neurol. Neurosurg. Psychiatry*, 76, 129, 2005.
272. Lehnung, M., Leplow, B., Ekroll, V., et al., Recovery of spatial memory and persistence of spatial orientation deficits after traumatic brain injury during childhood. *Brain Inj.*, 17, 855, 2003.
273. Farmer, J.E., Kanne, S.M., Haut, J.S., et al., Memory functioning following traumatic brain injury in children with premorbid learning problems. *Dev. Neuropsychol.*, 22, 455, 2002.
274. Donders, J. and Minnema, M.T., Performance discrepancies on the California verbal learning test—Children's version (CVLT-C) in children with traumatic brain injury. *J. Int. Neuropsychol. Soc.*, 10, 482, 2004.
275. Cohen, M.J., *Children's Memory Scale: Manual*, Psychological Corporation, San Antonio, TX, 1997.
276. Sheslow, D. and Adams, W., *Wide Range Assessment of Memory and Learning: Administration Manual*, Jastak Associates, Wilmington, DE, 1990.
277. Ewing-Cobbs, L. and Barnes, M., Linguistic outcomes following traumatic brain injury in children. *Semin. Pediatr. Neurol.*, 9, 209, 2002.
278. Barlow, K., Thompson, E., Johnson, D., et al., The neurological outcome of non-accidental head injury. *Pedatr. Rehabil.*, 7, 195, 2004.
279. Chapman, S.B., Sparks, G., Levin, H.S., et al., Discourse macro-level processing after severe pediatric traumatic brain injury. *Dev. Neuropsychol.*, 25, 37, 2004.
280. Catroppa, C. and Anderson, V., Recovery and predictors of language skills two years following pediatric traumatic brain injury. *Brain-Lang.*, 88, 68, 2004.
281. Ewing-Cobbs, L., Barnes, M., Fletcher, J.M., et al., Modeling of longitudinal academic achievement scores after pediatric traumatic brain injury. *Dev. Neuropsychol.*, 25, 107, 2004.
282. Dunn, L.M. and Dunn, L.M., *Peabody Picture Vocabulary Test*, 3rd edition, American Guidance Service, Circle Pines, MN, 1997.
283. Williams, K.T., *Expressive Vocabulary Test: Manual*, American Guidance Service, Circle Press, MN, 1997.
284. Yeates, K.O., Closed-head injury, in *Pediatric Neuropsychology: Research, Theory, and Practice*, Yeates, K.O., Ris, M.D., and Taylor, H.G., Eds., Guilford Press, New York, 2000, p. 92.
285. Taylor, L.D., Localization of cerebral lesions by psychological testing. *Clin. Neurosurg.*, 16, 269, 1969.
286. Kuhtz-Buschbeck, J.P., Hoppe, P., et al., Sensorimotor recovery in children after traumatic brain injury: Analyses of gait, gross motor and fine motor skills. *Dev. Med. Child. Neurol.*, 45, 821, 2003.
287. Johnk, K., Kuhtz-Buschbeck, J.P., Stolze, H., et al., Assessment of sensorimotor functions after traumatic brain injury (TBI) in childhood: Methodological aspects. *Restor. Neurol. Neurosci.*, 14, 143, 1999.

288. Levin, H.S. and Eisenberg, H.M., Neuropsychological impairment after closed head injury in children and adolescents. *J. Pedatr. Psychol.*, 4, 389, 1979.
289. Bawden, H.N., Knights, R.M., and Winogron, H.W., Speeded performance following head injury in children. *J. Clin. Neuropsychol.*, 7, 39, 1985.
290. Slomine, B.S., Gerring, J.P., Grados, M.A., et al., Performance on measures of 'executive function' following pediatric traumatic brain injury. *Brain Inj.*, 16, 759, 2002.
291. Gioia, G.A. and Isquith, T.K., Ecological assessment of executive function in traumatic brain injury. *Dev. Neuropsychol.*, 25, 135, 2004.
292. Anderson, V. and Catroppa, C., Recovery of executive skills following paediatric traumatic brain injury (TBI): A two year follow-up. *Brain Inj.*, 19, 459, 2005.
293. Delis, D.C., Kaplan, E., and Kramer, J.H., *Delis–Kaplan Executive Function System, Examiner's and Technical Manuals*, The Psychological Corporation, San Antonio, TX, 2001.
294. Levin, H.S., Ewing-Cobbs, L., and Eisenberg, H.M., Neurobehavioral outcome of pediatric closed head injury, in *Traumatic Head Injury in Children*, Broman, S.H. and Michel, M.D., Eds., Oxford University Press, New York, 1995, p. 70.
295. Levin, H.S., Sonj., J., Scheibel, R.S., et al., Concept formation and problem solving following closed head injury in children. *J. Int. Neuropsychol. Soc.*, 3, 598, 1997.
296. Kaplan, E., A process approach to neuropsychological assessment, in *Clinical Neuropsychology and Brain Function: Research Measurement, and Practice*, Boll, T. and Bryant, B.K., Eds., American Psychological Association, Washington, D.C., 1988, p. 125.
297. Chadwick, O., Rutter, M., Brown, G., et al., A prospective study of children with head injuries: II. Cognitive sequelae, *Psychol. Med.*, 11, 40, 1981.
298. Klonoff, H., Low, M.D., and Clark, C., Head injuries in children: A prospective five-year follow-up. *J. Neurol. Neurosurg. Psychiatry*, 40, 1211, 1977.
299. Costeff, H., Abraham, E., Brenner, T., et al., Late neuropsychologic status after childhood head trauma. *Brain Dev.*, 10, 371, 1988.
300. Gutentag, S.S., Naglieri, J.A., and Yeates, K.O., Peformance of children with traumatic brain injury on the Cognitive Assessment System, *Assessment*, 5, 263, 1998.
301. Naglieri, J.A. and Das, J.P., *Cognitive Assessment System: Administration and Scoring Manual*, Riverside Publishing, Itasca, IL, 1997.
302. Wechsler, D., *WISC-IV: Technical and Interpretive Manual*, Psychological Corporation, San Antonio, TX, 2003.
303. Korkman, M., Kirk, U., and Kemp, S., *NEPSY: A Developmental Neuropsychological Assessment: Manual*, The Psychological Corporation, San Antonio, TX, 1998.
304. Luria, A.R., *Higher Cortical Functions in Man*, Haigh, B., *Trans.*, Basic Books, New York, 1966.
305. Korkman, M., *A Proposed Neuropsychological Test Battery for Young Developmentally Disabled Children: Theory and Evaluation*, Academic dissertation, University of Helsinki, Helsinki, Finland, 1988.

7 Behavioral Assessment following Traumatic Brain Injury

INTRODUCTION

An emerging body of psychiatric evidence over the last 15–20 years confirms an increased relative risk of developing a psychiatric condition following a traumatic brain injury (TBI). These risks include mood and anxiety disorders, psychotic disorders, substance-induced disorders, sexual misbehavior, and aggression. The most common psychiatric diagnoses are those associated with depression, substance abuse, and anxiety disorders. The base rates for lifetime and current risk exceed those found in the epidemiologic catchment area studies. The rates of lifetime depression, panic disorder, and psychotic disorder following TBI are 26%, 8%, and 8%, respectively. The rates of current depression, current panic disorder, and current psychotic disorder following TBI are 10%, 6%, and 8%, respectively.[1]

THE ADULT

AFFECT AND MOOD CHANGES FOLLOWING TBI

Depression is the commonest mood disorder following brain injury, and it has been estimated to occur in 25%–60% of individuals with TBI within 8 years of injury.[2] Jorge and Starkstein at the University of Iowa have looked further at hospitalization of persons following TBI and found that major depression is present in about 40% of those studied. They also found high rates of anxiety disorders, substance abuse, dysregulation of emotional expression, and aggressive outbursts comorbid with major depression.[3] Jorge reports also that behavioral and psychiatric disturbances are the more frequent consequences of brain injury, and these are the major determinants for the quality of life of patients following TBI.[4] Jorge et al. have recently explored the impact of reduced hippocampal volume on mood disorders after TBI. They studied 37 patients with closed head injury and evaluated them at 3, 6, and 12 months after trauma. They made psychiatric diagnoses with a structured clinical interview using *DSM-IV* (*Diagnostic and Statistical Manual of Mental Disorders*, 4th edition) criteria. Quantitative magnetic resonance imaging scans were obtained at 3 months follow-up to measure hippocampal volume. Patients with moderate to severe head injury had significantly lower hippocampal volumes than patients with mild TBI. Patients who developed mood disorders had significantly lower hippocampal volumes than patients without mood disorders. This group postulated that patients following TBI had a "double-hit" mechanism by which neural and glial elements affected by trauma were further compromised by functional changes associated with mood disorders (e.g., the neurotoxic effects of increased levels of cortisol or excitotoxic damage resulting from overactivation of the glutaminergic pathways).[5] These findings suggest that significant major depression following TBI is an added physiological contributor to the neurochemical and microcellular changes that occur following brain injury.

Geriatric patients may also show considerable changes in mood following TBI. Rapoport's group in Toronto found that TBI, particularly of moderate severity, led to poorer cognitive and psychosocial functioning 1 year post-injury among older adults. This group found a rate of major depression of 16% following TBI in geriatric patients. This was associated with higher degrees of psychological distress, psychosocial dysfunction, and postconcussive syndromes. Major depression in the first few months after TBI in older adults had persisting adverse affects on outcome as they attempted to rehabilitate.[6,7] As the examiner completes a neuropsychiatric assessment of an adult after TBI, it should be remembered that major depression in and of itself may contribute to poor cognitive outcome as well as other localized cognitive deficits. This has been evaluated and documented by Chamelian and Feinstein.[8]

Anxiety is a common complaint in injured persons and noninjured persons alike. There does not seem to be any distinguishing features that separate anxiety disorders following trauma from anxiety disorders occurring in nontraumatic civilian life. Many different patterns of anxiety present including generalized anxiety disorder, panic disorder, phobic disorders, obsessive-compulsive disorder, and posttraumatic stress disorder (PTSD). Few studies are available to address the incidence or prevalence of these disorders after TBI.[1] A recent review from the University of Nebraska at Lincoln suggests that mild TBI plays a notable role in the emergence and expression of anxiety. However, this meta-analysis noted that mild TBI research is rife with inconsistencies concerning prevalence rates, the magnitude and implications of the issue, and in the case of PTSD whether these diagnoses can exist at all.[9] As discussed in Chapter 1, the current conflicts in Iraq and Afghanistan are producing numerous trauma survivors for the U.S. military. Traumatic brain injury is an important source of morbidity from these conflicts, and the reader is referred to the overpressure explosion or blast injury data presented earlier in this text. Moreover, a number of these returning veterans have been found to have anxiety disorders. The exact prevalence of those with anxiety is not known at this time. The Defense and Veterans Brain Injury Center at the Walter Reed Army Medical Center in Washington DC maintains an ongoing database of these individuals much as it did after the Vietnam War.[10] The Centers for Disease Control and Prevention in Atlanta, at their national center for injury prevention and control, has reviewed recently data from Georgia and North Carolina in the model brain injury systems database. Almost 200 patients with mild (19%), moderate (21%), and severe (60%) TBI were interviewed by telephone at 6 and 12 months post-injury. The Impact of Events Scale was used to identify intrusion and avoidance symptoms. Symptoms consistent with severe posttrauma stress increased from 11% at 6 months to 16% at 12 months post-injury. Obviously, this is only one out of six persons and not as high a level of incidence as one might have suspected. However, the authors of this study concluded that survivors of TBI are at risk for developing symptoms consistent with posttrauma stress, and amnesia for the injury event is not protective against developing such symptoms.[11] Traumatic memories are putatively the mechanisms by which PTSD occurs even though biological mechanisms underlie the condition. However, it is not possible to develop empirically based studies to test hypotheses of PTSD in TBI, and we are limited to naturalistic models.[12] Since PTSD and TBI almost invariably involve memory disorders in combination with the expression of posttraumatic symptoms, the true elucidation of prevalence and incidence figures for this condition remains enigmatic. A recent Seattle, Washington, study again confirms that the incidence of PTSD following TBI is low relative to other psychiatric conditions. The authors determined the rate and phenomenology of PTSD symptoms in the 6 months after TBI by conducting a prospective cohort study of 124 subjects who completed the PTSD Checklist-Civilian Version. The cumulative incidence of meeting PTSD symptom criteria at 6 months was 11%, and only 5.6% for full criteria. Prevalence peaked at 1 month (10%). Of these subjects, 86% had another psychiatric disorder, and 29% had a prior history of PTSD. Symptoms were associated with not completing high school, prior assault, recalling being terrified or helpless, and a positive toxicology at the time of the injury.[13] A very recent study from Oxford University in the United Kingdom investigated trauma narratives of road traffic accident survivors prospectively at 1 week, 6 weeks, and 3 months posttrauma. Interestingly, at 1 and 6 weeks, narratives of survivors with acute stress disorder or PTSD were less coherent and included more dissociation content. By 3 months, their narratives also contained more repetition, more nonconsecutive chunks of memory, and more sensory words. It appears that as people recover from acute stress disorder or PTSD, their narratives do not necessarily become less disorganized. No measures of incidence or prevalence were performed in these studies.[14] Therefore, complaints of PTSD following TBI are seen but apparently the disorder is not nearly as prevalent as one might predict. Also, particularly when examiners are reviewing patient data for forensic purposes, one must be very cautious in concluding PTSD as present, as the apparent base rate of PTSD following TBI is low relative to what would seem to be logical expectations for its occurrence.

Comorbid substance abuse, or substance abuse issues following TBI, is extremely common. As has been noted, depression, anxiety, and substance abuse issues are the most common psychiatric conditions cited following TBI. A recent meta-analysis from the University of Wales at Bangor reviewed world literature on prevalence rates for alcohol intoxication at the time of injury. This review found most of the studies had been performed in the United States, and the prevalence for alcohol intoxication at the time of TBI varied from 36% to 51%. Prior TBI history of alcohol misuse ranged from 37% to 51%. Outcome findings correlated with alcohol misuse producing higher levels of poor outcomes.[15] For the psychiatric and psychological examiner, issues of substance abuse in mild TBI cause particular concern in forensic evaluations or lawsuits regarding motor vehicle accident injury. The Department of Psychiatry at the University of British Columbia studied neuropsychological test performance on 73 patients with acute, uncomplicated mild TBI and compared them to a sample of 73 patients from an inpatient substance abuse program. To these patients, 10 cognitive measures were administered including the trailmaking test and selected subtests from the Wechsler Memory Scale-Revised. Only on the Digits Backwards and Trailmaking Test A did patients with mild TBI demonstrate poorer performance than substance abusers. This is interesting, as Trailmaking Test B is the more difficult of the trailmaking tests, and there was no statistical difference between mild TBI and substance abusers. The authors concluded from their study that patients with uncomplicated mild TBI could not be reliably differentiated from patients with substance abuse problems on measures of concentration, memory, and processing speed.[16] The Minneapolis Veterans Administration Medical Center reviewed 550 voluntary patients undergoing treatment for substance abuse disorder. These were compared for clinical and demographic variables based on report of TBI. Among the 218 (40%) patients reporting TBI, 61% were men and 39% were women. Childhood conduct problems and loss of a parent were strongly associated with the occurrence of adult TBI. Patients with TBI had more severe substance abuse disorders and higher rates of depressive and anxiety symptoms, somatic concerns, physical trauma, attempted suicide, and antisocial personality disorder. Men had a higher rate of TBI than women, but women with substance abuse disorder had an increased relative risk of TBI compared to women in the general population.[17] Another veterans administration study from the Veterans Affairs Medical Center in Charleston, South Carolina, determined patterns of alcohol use 1 year after TBI in 1606 adults identified by a review of a South Carolina statewide hospital discharge dataset. Criteria from the Centers for Disease Control defining TBI were used to screen candidates who were interviewed by telephone 1 year after their hospital discharge. Heavy alcohol drinking in the month before the interview was reported by 15.4% of participants, while 14.3% reported moderate drinking (almost 30% total). Risk factors for heavy drinking included male gender, younger age, history of substance abuse before TBI, diagnosis of depression since TBI, fair/moderate mental health function, and better physical functioning. An interesting outcome of the study revealed no association between drinking patterns and severity of TBI.[18] Jorge and Robinson's group at the University of Iowa have reviewed alcohol misuse and its relationship to mood disorders. Previous alcohol abuse increases the risk of developing mood disorders after TBI, and emotional disturbances, in turn, increase the risk of alcohol abuse relapse following TBI. Alcohol's neurotoxic effects probably interact with TBI to produce greater disruption of the neural circuits that modulate reward, mood, and executive functions.[19]

In Chapters 3 and 4, assessment of suicidal and self-harm risk was stressed. Findings from the New Haven NIMH Epidemiologic Catchment Area study indicated that the lifetime risk of suicide attempt was greater in those who had suffered head injury versus those who had not suffered head injury.[20] A study from Liverpool Hospital in New South Wales reviewed 172 outpatients with TBI. These patients were screened for suicidal ideation and hopelessness using the Beck Scale for Suicidal Ideation and the Beck Hopelessness Scale. A substantial proportion of participants had clinically significant levels of hopelessness (35%) and suicide ideations (23%), while 18% had made a suicide attempt following their injury. There was a high degree of comorbidity between suicide attempts and psychiatric disturbances.[21] However, the premorbid history of patients with TBI is probably the highest predictor of suicide risk following TBI. The same population from New South Wales was evaluated for suicide attempts. The data pool had collectively 172 patients of which 45 had made a lifetime total of 80 suicide attempts. The odds ratio of respondents with a comorbid post-injury history of psychiatric disturbance and substance abuse was 21 times higher for an attempt following TBI compared with respondents with no such history.[22] A similar study using more sophisticated statistical techniques was obtained at the New York Psychiatric Institute, where 325 depressed patients presenting for treatment were evaluated for psychopathology, traumatic history, and suicidal behavior. A backward stepwise logistic model examined the relationship between attempter status and variables that differed in the TBI and non-TBI patients. Of all these subjects, 44% reported mild TBI. Subjects with TBI were more likely to be male, have a history of substance abuse, have Cluster B personality disorder (*DSM-IV*), and be more aggressive and hostile compared to subjects without TBI. They were also more likely to be suicide attempters, although their suicidal behavior was not different from that of persons without TBI. Attempt status was mostly predicted by two variables: aggression and hostility, but not the presence of TBI itself. For males, a history of TBI increased the likelihood of being a suicide attempter, whereas the risk was elevated for females regardless of whether they had a TBI or not. These data suggest that suicidal behavior and TBI share antecedent risk factors of hostility and aggression.[23] With regard to suicide as a cause of death following TBI, a very large study has been completed utilizing data from the TBI Model Systems national database, the Social Security Death Index, death certificates, and the U.S. population age-race-gender-cause-specific mortality rates for 1994. This study reviewed data of 2140 individuals with TBI who completed inpatient rehabilitation in one of the 15 national institutes on disability and rehabilitation research-funded TBI model systems of care between 1998 and 2001. They were surveyed beyond 1 year post-injury. The primary cause of death did not include suicide at a significant degree. The findings revealed that individuals with TBI were about 37 times more likely to die of seizures, 12 times more likely to die of septicemia, 4 times more likely to die of pneumonia, and about 3 times more likely to die of other respiratory conditions excluding pneumonia, digestive conditions, and all external causes of injury/poisoning than were individuals in the general population of similar age, gender, and race.[24] However, it is incumbent among those professionals treating persons following TBI to keep a high index of suspicion regarding suicide risk in impulsive persons. The reader is referred to Chapter 4 for specific guidelines regarding suicide risk assessment. Leon-Carrion et al. have noted that during the recovery period following TBI the risk of suicide is high. The profile of these patients reveals an emotional person with cognitive difficulties demonstrating problems with reality interpretation. The patients try to understand what is happening around them but are unable to cope. These patients often demonstrate concrete thinking and, although they have difficulty in solving problems, they have few intellectual resources to cope with their surroundings. They are particularly unable to distance themselves from the emotional aspects of situations.[25] The reader may wish to review a suicide prevention strategy recently developed specifically for families and patients following TBI.[26]

MEASURING MOOD CHANGES

There is no substitute for a face-to-face examination of an individual when determining elements of mood disturbance. We have seen in the early parts of this chapter that TBI results in significant rates of depression, anxiety, substance use disorders, and even some suicidal risk. Chapters 3 and 4 stressed the taking of a proper history and face-to-face mental examination. Assessment of mood disorders cannot be deferred to standardized psychological tests. However, in the course of a complete neuropsychiatric assessment following TBI, it is important to confirm mood disorders using standardized psychological tests as noted below. Also, if the examiner is conducting a forensic examination, without question one must use standardized mood assessment instruments to rule out symptom magnification, exaggeration, or outright malingering (see Chapter 9).

Beck Anxiety Inventory

The Beck Anxiety Inventory (BAI) is designed to measure subjective symptoms of anxiety in adolescents and adults. It is a self-administered inventory and contains 21 descriptive symptoms of anxiety which the patient rates on a 4 point scale: 0—not at all; 1—mildly, it did not bother me much; 2—moderately, it was very unpleasant but I could stand it; and 3—severely, I could barely stand it. Scoring is performed by adding the raw scores for each of the 21 symptoms and the maximum score the patient can achieve on this test is 63 points. Minimal anxiety ranges from scores of 0 to 7 points, mild anxiety ranges from scores of 8 to 15 points, moderate anxiety ranges from scores of 16 to 25 points, and greater than 26 points is consistent with severe anxiety.[27]

This inventory provides only an estimate of overall severity of anxiety. Since the test contains only 21 items, its discriminating power is thus weak as far as psychological tests go. Therefore, it is recommended that this test instrument be administered in association with the Beck Depression Inventory-II or the Beck Hopelessness Scale as this will provide a more comprehensive assessment of the patient's subjective emotional difficulties. The examiner is warned that there are no internal validity controls on this test instrument. Therefore, the individual's score on the Beck Anxiety Inventory must be consistent with other personality tests noted below that contain internal validity controls, such as the MMPI-2, the Millon Clinical Multiaxial Inventory, or the Personality Assessment Inventory. Moreover, this test may not be appropriate for patients who have sustained severe TBIs as organic denial (anosognosia) may interfere with awareness of the emotional problems.[28]

Beck Depression Inventory-II

Like the BAI, the Beck Depression Inventory-II (BDI-II) test instrument is based upon the original work of Aaron Beck.[29] The Beck Depression Inventory contains 21 forced-choice statements regarding depressive symptoms. It is useful for measuring the severity of depression in adults and adolescents age 13 years and older. The BDI-II was developed to correspond with diagnostic criteria in the *DSM-IV*.[30] The BDI-II is an outgrowth of the original BDI which became the BDI-1A. For the new, revised version of the BDI-II, four of the original items (weight loss, body image change, somatic preoccupation, and work difficulty) were dropped and have been replaced by four new items (agitation, worthlessness, concentration difficulty, and loss of energy) to index symptoms more typical of severe depression or depression warranting hospitalization. Two other items were changed to allow for increases as well as decreases in appetite and sleep. Many of the statements and their alternatives were reworded. Unlike the BDI-1A, the BDI-II constitutes a substantial revision of the original BDI.[31]

This test is easy to administer and requires about 5–10 min. It is also easily scored but it should be used only by professionals who are well schooled in the assessment of depressed persons. Patients with severe closed head injuries may not test as depressed because they may be unaware of their cognitive deficits in a fashion similar to that noted above for the Beck Anxiety Inventory. For those performing forensic examinations, one of the major limitations of this test is that individuals involved in litigation who are being evaluated by the courts may purposely test as severely, if not profoundly, depressed, because of the test's obvious face validity for depression.[28] The statistical bases for this test instrument are much stronger than for the two previous versions of the Beck Depression Inventory.

Millon Clinical Multiaxial Inventory-III

The Millon Clinical Multiaxial Inventory-III (MCMI-III) is a personality inventory containing 175 questions. Unlike during the administration of the MMPI-2, the questions and the patient's responses are contained within the same booklet. This test is designed to be used with patients who are ages 17 or older. Unlike the MMPI and its versions, it attempts to directly assess preexisting personality traits or disorders and, as a consequence, it may be valuable in forensic assessment of brain injury cases where prior personality function may be an issue.[28]

Version III of the MCMI contains a total of 175 test items which is far less than the 567 items in the MMPI-II. It has been produced to reduce objectionable statements. The reading and vocabulary skill level is approximately eighth grade. The test is constructed as an operational measure of personality syndromes derived from the theory of personality and psychopathology developed by Theodore Millon.[32] The MCMI-III includes changes to comport more closely to the diagnostic criteria contained in the *DSM-IV*.[30] Software is available from the manufacturer to allow a computer-generated interpretive narrative report or the test may be mailed to the manufacturer for grading. However, this may not be advisable in forensic assessments.

The MCMI-III has been shown to be a valid test. However, the cross validation sample techniques were developed by its authors. It has a limited database relative to the extraordinarily long and thorough analysis of the MMPI and subsequent revisions. Like the MMPI test instruments, the MCMI-III was not designed to identify or to diagnose brain injury. Its primary value in the assessment of TBI lies in its ability to describe the various emotional and adjustment problems seen in patients following brain trauma. Moreover, as noted in Chapters 2 and 3, it may be useful in determining if premorbid personality dysfunction has been exacerbated by the effects of TBI. However, the examiner is cautioned not to assume that the Axis II profile produced by this test, which purports to describe premorbid or long-standing personality traits and accurately reflects those traits after a significant duration of time has elapsed between the time of the injury or the accident and when the patient is actually tested. For example, Spordone and Saul[28] point out that Item 43, "My own bad temper has been a big cause of my troubles," was designed to identify long-standing antisocial or borderline personality traits. If after sustaining a TBI this results in poor frustration tolerance, irritability, and aggressive outbursts toward others, the patient recognizes this problem and responds, "Yes," the patient is likely to be diagnosed as having long-standing antisocial or borderline personality traits. As we saw in Chapter 2, this could be "acquired sociopathy" often seen following orbitofrontal brain trauma. Thus, great skill is required in drawing conclusions of Axis II profiles on the MCMI-III and relating those to the presence of premorbid personality dysfunction. Such a determination should not be based solely on the results of the MCMI-III, and this personality delineation will require a thorough investigation of prior academic, legal, medical, military, and occupational records as well as a face-to-face examination before an assessment of this nature is complete.

Minnesota Multiphasic Personality Inventory-2

The Minnesota Multiphasic Personality Inventory-2 (MMPI-2) was used recently to explore the relationship with the length of consciousness and the severity of cognitive impairment to personality changes after head trauma. This study included 320 chronic TBI patients. A multivariate analysis was conducted using the Halstead-Reitan Neuropsychological Battery and a modified Halstead-Reitan Impairment Index as independent variables, and 30 scales from the MMPI-2 as the dependent variables. Loss of consciousness was found to be a stronger predictor of personality change than was the Halstead-Reitan Neuropsychological Battery at milder levels of severity.[37] Depression is a significant outcome of TBI. The MMPI-2 depression scale has been used to evaluate depression in persons with TBI, and Lezak et al.[38] write that all competent neuropsychological batteries include some behavioral measurement, such as the MMPI-2. The MMPI-2 depression scale is the gold standard against which other tests purported to measure depression following TBI are compared.[39]

The original MMPI was published in 1943 after extensive research studies at the University of Minnesota. It was developed by the psychologist and psychiatrist, Hathaway and McKinley.[33] All versions of the MMPI contain three validity scales, the L (lie), the F (frequency), and the K (defensiveness). The MMPI-2 contains the more recently added scales VRIN (inconsistency), TRIN (response bias), and F_p (psychopathology). A patient's profile on these scales can provide valuable insights as to whether the patient is exaggerating, denying psychological problems, defensive, seeking out help for emotional problems, or faking a mental disorder. The use of these validity scales generally requires consultation with a psychologist who is an expert and trained in the MMPI instruments. A more extensive review of specific applications of these scales to faking and symptom magnification is discussed in the forensic portions of this text (Chapter 9).

The MMPI-2 contains 10 clinical scales: 1 (Hs: hypochondriasis), 2 (D: depression), 3 (Hy: hysteria), 4 (Pd: psychopathic deviate), 5 (Mf: masculinity/femininity), 6 (Pa: paranoia), 7 (Pt: psychasthenia), 8 (Sc: schizophrenia), 9 (Ma: mania), and 0 (Si: social introversion). This test may be scored by using special templates over the patient's answer sheet or by entering the patient's raw scores into computer software produced by the University of Minnesota Corporation. The psychologist can examine the relative elevations of each of these scales in relationship to the others and determine the clinical significance of the patient's profile as well as judge the overall test responses for validity. The content scales can provide an adjunct to the traditional empirically derived clinical scales. If the reader wishes a more thorough understanding of MMPI-2 scoring and analysis, it is recommended to consult with some of the standard texts on the matter such as Graham.[34]

The MMPI-2 has been administered to individuals with moderate to severe TBI.[35] Individuals following brain trauma tend to show elevated scores on the schizophrenia (8) and mania (9) scales. However, patients who have sustained mild TBI tend to show elevations on scales 1, 2, and 3 (hypochondriasis, depression, and hysteria). Elevation on scale 1 and a low score on scale 5 tend to predict low likelihood for resumption of employment following a TBI. The MMPI-2 was not designed specifically to diagnose brain damage. Unfortunately, some psychiatrists and psychologists rely on the patient's MMPI-2 profile to diagnose brain damage or "organicity."[28] This should not be done. However, a patient's profile on the MMPI-2 may be used to determine the presence of significant emotional problems which may account, at least in part, for relatively poor performance on neuropsychological testing or be an outcome of TBI itself. Thus, the MMPI-2 appears to have usefulness for measures of outcome following TBI but it lacks specificity for the diagnosis of TBI.

When administering the MMPI-2, it should be remembered that another person is not to be interposed between the test questions and the patient. In other words, the examiner, or a surrogate, should not read the test items to the patient. If the patient's reading ability (a sixth grade reading level is required to understand MMPI-2 items) is insufficient to take the test unaided, special auditory tapes containing an oral repetition of the test items can be obtained from the test manufacturer. This is a perfectly valid way to administer the test to those with poor reading skills. Moreover, there are available Spanish language and French language editions if required. It is probably wise in clinical situations to make a measure of reading recognition such as with the Wide Range Achievement Test-III or other similar test instrument, before administering the MMPI to ensure minimal reading proficiency. For forensic assessment, as discussed more fully later in the text, it may be necessary to further measure reading comprehension as well as recognition of language.

If using a version other than English, the norms may not be appropriate for the patient and psychological consultation may be required to determine if appropriate norms are being used. The patient's responses to languages other than English may reflect cultural factors which were not part of the original database for the MMPI-2 even though it is demographically correct and corresponds to the average demographics of the United States in 1989.[36] Many psychologists numerically score this test on a computer, which actually is probably more reliable than hand scoring using the templates. However, care must be exercised when using the narrative descriptive scoring procedures in addition to numerical scoring and it is recommended that the narrative descriptors never be used alone without extensive face-to-face evaluation of the patient. Moreover, the examiner should not rely solely on the MMPI-2 to determine whether an individual has psychological or psychiatric impairment. The neuropsychiatric examination of TBI should be based on a detailed clinical and background history, behavioral observations, interviews with collateral sources if needed, brain imaging and neurological examination, and a thorough review of medical and psychiatric records.

Personality Assessment Inventory

A very recent study of 95 individuals used the Personality Assessment Inventory (PAI) to determine if it could evaluate psychopathology following TBI when compared to research literature on the MMPI-2. The highest mean clinical scale elevations in 95 individuals who had suffered a TBI included somatic complaints, depression, and borderline features.[40] This test instrument was developed by Morey,[41] and it is a self-administered objective test of personality and psychopathology. Unlike the MMPI, this test is based upon clinical syndromes and it is more consistent with contemporary diagnostic practices.[42] The PAI is useful for patients from ages 18 through adulthood. There is no data to support the interpretation of the test scores for adolescents, unlike the Minnesota Multiphasic Personality Inventory-A. This test has a wider range of utility than the MMPI-2 at the lower end of the intellectual and educational scales as the reading level necessary to take the PAI is at the fourth grade. The test usually can be administered in 45–60 min, unlike the one and one-half hours or more generally required for the MMPI-2. That is because this test contains 344 test items instead of 567 test items for the MMPI-2. There are four validity scales, eleven clinical scales, five treatment scales, and two interpersonal scales. The clinical scales contain a number of subscales.

It is being argued more and more in the psychological literature that the PAI is psychometrically superior to the MMPI-2 and more clinically relevant. The test questions are more straightforward than those on the MMPI-2. However, like the MMPI-2, this test instrument was not designed to establish the presence of brain damage and it should not be used for this purpose. Patients with impaired cognitive abilities as a result of brain trauma should be tested with caution and it may not be appropriate for patients who are confused or have significant psychomotor retardation.[28] As with the caveat noted above for the MMPI-2, determination of the psychological or psychiatric state should not solely rest on the use of this test instrument and a thorough examination should be made concurrently. A computerized interpretive profile and narrative report are commercially available from the test manufacturer. The test can be computer scored.

State–Trait Anxiety Inventory

Construction of the State–Trait Anxiety Inventory (STAI) began in 1964 with the goal of developing a single set of items to provide objective measures of state and trait anxiety. The concepts of state and trait anxiety were first introduced by Cattell.[43] State anxiety and trait anxiety are analogous in certain respects to kinetic and potential energy. The anxiety state, like kinetic energy, refers to a palpable reaction or process taking place at a given time. On the other hand, anxiety traits, like potential energy, refers to individual differences in reactions.[44]

The STAI was designed to be self-administering. It contains 40 items with 20 items on Form Y-1 and 20 items on Form Y-2. The patient circles one of the four responses to each question based on the following categories: almost never, sometimes, often, and almost always. The test may be administered to adults ranging in age from 19 through 69 years. Normative data for Form Y are from working adults, college students, high school students, and military recruits. Form X norms are available within the Form Y manual for male neuropsychiatric patients, general medical and surgical patients, and young prisoners. However, these norms are not based on representative or stratified samples. One useful function of the STAI is for following patients during treatment. Since it only takes 6–7 min to administer this test, it can be used serially to evaluate levels of anxiety throughout the rehabilitation and treatment process.

AGGRESSION

Recall from earlier discussions in this chapter that anger and hostility as premorbid personality characteristics can adversely affect outcomes following TBI. Moreover, aggression can occur as a de novo outcome of TBI as well. Aggression or agitated behavior is a major source of disability to individuals with brain injury and a major source of stress to families of persons who have been injured. These behaviors endanger not only the safety of patients and their families, but also professionals providing care to them. It is usually not possible for a single individual to manage aggressive behaviors in the brain-injured population, and a multimodal, multidisciplinary, collaborative approach is necessary in most cases.[45] It is essential that the neuropsychiatric examiner determines the mental status of the patient before the agitated or aggressive event begins, the nature of the precipitant if any, and the physical and social environment in which the aggression occurs. It is also important to determine if there are any primary or secondary gains related to the subject's agitation and aggression.[45] Aggression following TBI begs the question "how common is common?" In an attempt to answer this, a study out of Sydney, Australia, performed a mixed cross-sectional and longitudinal review of data from a 5 year follow-up study of discharged TBI patients that were analyzed retrospectively. A total of 228 patients with moderate to severe TBI were evaluated at 6, 24, and 60 months postdischarge to assess the prevalence and predictors of aggressive behavior. Measurements included the Overt Aggression Scale and injury-related variables, along with a battery of postdischarge questionnaires including the Beck Depression Inventory. At any given followup period, 25% of the participants were classified as aggressive. Aggression, when it was present, was consistently associated with depression, concurrent traumatic complaints, younger age at injury, and low satisfaction with life. Depression was the factor that was most significantly associated with aggressive behavior at all times post-injury. The second most frequent variable was younger age at the time of injury. The authors concluded that aggression is a common, fluctuating, and long-term problem following TBI.[46] Another recent study from Wales, United Kingdom, evaluated cognitive variables associated with aggression. In a prospective cohort study of 134 brain-injured individuals who exhibited aggression, these persons were compared to 153 individuals who had sustained comparable injuries but were not aggressive. In the aggressive group, specific deficits were identified in verbal memory and visuoperceptual skills, and these persons also displayed impaired executive-attention functions. Low premorbid IQ, low premorbid socioeconomic status, and male gender increased the likelihood of aggression.[47]

Disinhibited aggressive behavior occurs following TBI. The disinhibited behavior is often called "impulsive aggression." Where this has been studied, there is noted to be a higher incidence of premorbid aggressive behavior and the aggressive persons generally are younger. They also had more pre-injury impulsive, irritable, and antisocial features than nonaggressive controls.[48] A review of data from the Vietnam Head Injury Study revealed that patients with frontal ventral medial lesions consistently demonstrated more aggressive and violent tendencies than control patients or patients with lesions in other brain areas. The optimistic news from this study is that most of the aggression was by verbal confrontation rather than physical assault. However, this type of behavior did have a significant adverse impact and disruptive influence upon family activities.[49] When one looks at outcomes of TBI regarding criminal activity, there is noted to be a direct relationship between the level of alcohol use and the level of criminal arrest rates.[50] There was found in this particular study, to be a relatively high incidence of heavy drinking both before and after injury among patients with a history of criminal arrest. One additional finding was that those persons with relatively high levels of aggressive behaviors and arrests had a strong association with a greater likelihood of psychiatric treatment. Should it become necessary, there is a framework of forensic evaluation to determine the relevance of the association of TBI and the ultimate commission of a crime.[51] This is discussed more fully in the forensic sections of this text. However, for clinical evaluations, neuropsychiatric assessment often requires a detailed determination of aggression risk before placing patients into the home or other care facilities.

Measuring Aggression

Aggression Questionnaire

The Aggression Questionnaire (AQ) is an updated version of the Buss–Durkee Hostility Inventory.[53] Buss contributed to the development of the Aggression Questionnaire more than 40 years later.[52] It is a brief measure consisting of only 34 items scored on five scales: physical aggression (PHY), verbal aggression (VER), anger (ANG), hostility (HOS), and indirect aggression (IND). An AQ total score is also provided, along with an inconsistent responding (INC) index score as a validity indicator. The individual taking the test rates the item description on a scale from $1 =$ "not at all like me" to $5 =$ "completely like me." The items on this test instrument can be read and understood easily by any person with at least a third grade reading ability. The norms are based on a standardization sample of 2138 persons ranging in age from 9 to 88 years. The inconsistent responding index, although unlikely to uncover sophisticated fakers, may help to identify unusual levels of inconsistency in item responses that can result when a test taker attempts to "fool the test." It is also useful to detect persons who are careless in completing the form or who lack consistent attention as a result of brain injury.

The AQ total score is based on the person's responses to all 34 AQ items. It is a good summary measure of the general level of anger and aggression the individual has reported. Statistically, the AQ total score is most closely associated with the physical aggression and anger subscale scores. When the AQ total score is high, it is important to examine the individual's subscale scores and other information available to the examiner to understand what kind of experiences the individual has reported and to assess the level of risk for aggression. If the picture is dominated by high levels of anger and hostility, for example, but relatively low levels of physical or verbal aggression, the implications for follow-up assessment and intervention are likely to differ from what is called for when the picture is dominated by high levels of physical or verbal aggression.[52] As for the subscales, it should be noted that those who obtain high PHY scores tend to justify their aggressive acts in their own minds. They perceive themselves as being provoked by others and they are more likely than others to respond aggressively when they feel ashamed or humiliated. Low PHY scores may indicate a relative absence of physically aggressive behavior and a relatively strong ability to control physically aggressive impulses.

Individuals with high scores on the VER scale are commonly aroused to anger by situations they perceive to be unfair. Persons with a preexisting antisocial personality will tend to obtain high scores on the VER scale. Low VER scores are obtained by individuals who do not perceive themselves as argumentative. The ANG subscale describes aspects of anger. Persons who score high on ANG may benefit from relaxation training, as well as cognitive-behavioral and other arousal-reducing strategies or psychotherapy. Thus, this scale may be useful to predict those who might respond to treatment techniques aimed at reducing anger. The HOS subscale is most closely associated with pervasive social maladjustment, as well as severe psychopathology. It is probably wise to review this scale with elements on the MMPI-2. Predictors of violence from the MMPI-2 subtests are more fully explained in the forensic sections of this text. Persons with elevated HOS scores are more likely to demonstrate affective disturbance and social isolation. Extremely low HOS scores are consistent with individuals who feel comfortable in their current social surroundings. The IND scale measures the tendency to express anger and actions that avoid direct confrontation. Youngsters who score high on IND may be identified as oppositional or avoidant, and they often have disrupted peer relationships. Adults with antisocial personality characteristics tend to obtain high IND scores. People with low IND scores are likely to be willing to use direct confrontation to resolve conflicts in their lives.

With respect to psychiatric disturbances, individuals with anxiety disorders often obtain elevated VER and HOS scores in combination. Persons identified as antisocial will often have high VER, HOS, and IND scores relative to other AQ scores. Children who have attention deficit disorder with hyperactivity may obtain high scores on both the PHY and HOS scales.[52]

Buss–Durkee Hostility Inventory

The Buss–Durkee Hostility Inventory was originally published in 1957 and it still has some usefulness in the evaluation of hostile behaviors.[53] This inventory contains 75 items from an original inventory of 105 items. The 75 items were determined following measures of internal consistency that rejected 30 of the original items. The questions are answered in a true–false format. Factor analyses on college men and women revealed two factors: an attitudinal component of hostility (resentment and suspicion) and a motor component (assault, indirect hostility, irritability, and verbal hostility). This inventory is still used today but only in limited forms as the Aggression Questionnaire is supplanting it.

State–Trait Anger Expression Inventory-2

The original State–Trait Anger Expression Inventory (STAXI) was published in 1988.[54] The new version, the STAXI-2, provides concise measures of the experience, expression, and control of anger. The STAXI-2 was developed for two primary reasons: (1) to assess the components of anger for detailed evaluations of normal and abnormal personality, and (2) to provide a means of measuring the contributions of various components of anger to the development of medical conditions, particularly hypertension, coronary heart disease, and cancer.[55]

Anger expression and anger control within the STAXI-2 instrument are conceptualized as having four major components: (1) Anger Expression-Out involves the expression of anger toward other persons or objects in the environment, (2) Anger Expression-In is anger directed inward, (3) Anger Control-Out is based on the control of angry feelings by preventing the expression of anger toward other persons or objects in the environment, and (4) Anger Control-In is related to the control of suppressed angry feelings by calming down or cooling off when angered. Thus, since anger following TBI is so pervasively destructive to relationships and family dynamics, this instrument may prove useful for the assessment of traumatically brain-injured persons who are being considered for family or personal psychotherapy to reduce hostility.

Separate norms are provided for females and males in three age groups: 16–19 years, 20–29 years, and 30 years and older. Appendix A of the manual also provides percentiles based on scores of a psychiatric patient sample. T-scores are provided with a mean of 50 and a standard deviation of 10, similar to the T-scores used for the MMPI-2. Guidelines exist for interpreting high scores on the STAXI-2 scales and subscales. The STAXI-2 consists of six scales, five subscales, and an Anger Expression Index, which provides an overall measure of the expression and control of anger. Persons taking the test rate themselves on a 4 point scale that assesses either the intensity of their angry feelings at a particular time or how frequently anger is experienced, expressed, suppressed, or controlled. Completion of the STAXI-2 generally requires 12–15 min. If an examinee does not understand an item, it is acceptable for the psychologist to provide simple definitions of the words or issues of concern. If 10 or more of the 57 items are missing, the protocol should be considered invalid. The test instrument enables the examiner to determine state and trait anger versus anger expression and the ability to control oneself when angry. Table 7.1 lists adult tests useful for behavioral evaluation following brain injury.

EFFECTS OF BRAIN INJURY UPON SEXUAL BEHAVIOR

There are two major issues of sexual behavior following TBI. The first issue is that of inducing sexual dysfunction in a man or a woman as a result of the TBI itself. The second issue, and a critical one, is whether or not TBI increases the risk of sexual offenses perpetrated primarily by men. With regard to the sexual response cycle itself, there is significant evidence that multiple factors following TBI and also accompanying bodily trauma can affect sexual behavior significantly.[56] There is limited literature in this area and few well-controlled studies to assist the treater in developing

---

TABLE 7.1

Adult Behavioral Tests that Are Useful in Traumatic Brain Injury

Mood/Affect
Beck Anxiety Inventory
Beck Depression Inventory-II
Millon Clinical Multiaxial Inventory-III
Minnesota Multiphasic Personality Inventory-2
Personality Assessment Inventory
State–Trait Anxiety Inventory

Aggression
Aggression Questionnaire
Buss–Durkee Hostility Inventory
State–Trait Anger Expression Inventory

Emotional Intelligence
Behavioral Assessment of Dysexecutive Syndrome
Bar-On Emotional Quotient Inventory

Neurobehavioral Function
Neurobehavioral Functioning Inventory

---

treatment plans for persons with sexual dysfunction following TBI. For the person with any disabling disease, including TBI, questions of sexuality are complex. Usually multiple interrelated impairments coexist after TBI, and specific questions regarding the etiologies of sexual dysfunction remain unanswered. The questions that are begged are: what is the pathophysiologic process in the individual? What are the alterations in sexual desire, drive, arousal or sexual response that are due to organic factors, and which of these can be attributed to secondary factors such as cognitive, emotional, behavioral, and communication impairments? Do mobility deficits that result from the TBI affect sexuality?[56] No well-designed studies have established clear links between the various impairments that frequently occur and the putative sexual dysfunction. Questions that need answers, and questions that will prove difficult for the neuropsychiatric examiner, include the following: Do communication defects affect the interpersonal relationship such that it results in sexual dysfunction? What is the role of depression or other psychological factors upon interpersonal sexuality? What are the deleterious effects of medications used to treat cognitive or behavioral dysfunctions following TBI? What is the impact of the TBI upon the romantic relationship? Are there anatomical correlates of sexual dysfunction? Hibbard et al.[57] have recently extensively examined the sexual response cycle and difficulties encountered in men and women with and without TBI. Men with TBI experienced significantly more difficulties on self-ratings of sexual energy, sexual drive, the ability to initiate sexual activity, the ability to experience orgasm, and the ability to maintain an erection. On the other hand, women following TBI experience significantly more difficulties than women without TBI on self-ratings of sexual energy, sexual drive, initiation of sexual activity, arousal, pain during sexual activity, ability to masturbate, ability to experience orgasm, and the functionality of vaginal lubrication.[57] Sandel et al. examined sexual functioning following TBI more specifically to questions of posttraumatic amnesia and location of brain lesions. This group examined sexual functioning in male and female outpatients who had sustained severe TBIs (average length of PTA was 54 days). Sexual function was consistently lower than in the normal population, but it only affected to a significant degree orgasm and sexual drive and desire. The location of the brain injury was relevant. Patients with frontal lesions and right hemisphere lesions reported higher sexual satisfaction and higher function. No correlations of sexual function were found between dysfunction and cognitive measures.[58]

Of more difficult concern to the examiner is the issue of aberrant sexual behavior following TBI. Simpson and colleagues at Liverpool Hospital in New South Wales, Australia, reviewed 5 years of admissions to the brain injury rehabilitation unit at their hospital. Out of 477 patients, they identified a sample of 29 males who committed 128 incidents of sex offending. Alcohol was a factor in only three of the incidents, and only 2 of the 29 males had a pre-injury history of sexual offending. The most common offenses were touching others, followed by exhibitionism and overt sexual aggression. While the patients were inpatients, staff members were the most common targets, and members of the general public or family while the patients were outpatients. The authors concluded that sex offending is a significant clinical problem among a small minority of men after TBI. Since alcohol and pre-injury histories of sexual offending were so low in this study group, the authors concluded further that sequelae of TBI were a significant etiological factor underlying their offenses.[59] A more recent study by Langevin[60] sampled 476 male sexual offenders seen in a university psychiatric hospital for forensic assessment. Forty-nine percent of these men sustained head injuries that led to unconsciousness, and of this group, 23% sustained significant neurological insults. The brain-injured group was convicted of a diverse and wide range of sexual offenses, and nothing seemed specific. The brain-injured men, compared to a noninjury group, were more likely to offend against adults than against children. They also demonstrated more exhibiting and polymorphous sexual behaviors than the noninjured population. We are reminded that while inappropriate sexual behavior following TBI is less prevalent than other behavioral sequelae, its impact on patients, physicians, and caregivers can be significant.[61] Also, it is important to remember that brain-injured persons are far more likely to be victims of sexual abuse by others than to perpetrate sexual crimes against persons.[62]

PSYCHOSOCIAL FUNCTIONING

As we shall see below, emotional intelligence is often adversely affected by TBI in both adults and children. This translates into observable alterations of psychosocial functioning. It is necessary when taking the neuropsychiatric history to focus significantly upon changes in the social life and social behavior of the patient following TBI. Moreover, the social history provides significant and important data on the patient's current level of functioning. Since many brain-injured persons are very susceptible to psychosocial stressors, it is important to determine these specifically and also to determine their adaptation to social stressors following TBI. Some of the psychopathology observed following TBI is related directly to the adverse impact of social stressors upon the patient. One important marker of these possible adverse outcomes is the integrity of the patient's social integration following injury. It is extremely difficult for many patients following TBI to reintegrate into the family, their social network, the occupational and employment environment, and any other important social structure that were used previously by the patients. With the child, absent the family, the most important area for social functioning is the school. Careful inquiries must be made of the child and family about post-TBI school performance and problems that may be associated with reintegration into the school system. For instance, it may be necessary to develop an individualized educational plan (IEP) following TBI. Moreover, children are learning social skills and social integration as they grow, and TBI may interfere with this progress.

There is evidence that the use of maladaptive coping strategies following TBI is associated with increased depression and a lower productivity status. A scientific measure of this has been made recently by Dawson et al.[63] This group evaluated 73 significant others of TBI survivors. They reported on their friend/family member's pre-injury functioning and their 6 month coping behaviors following TBI using the Coping with Health Injuries and Problems Scale. They were able to detect a statistically significant difference in coping strategies following brain injury compared to pre-injury functioning. Ponsford's group in Australia also evaluated these issues. Their study found a strong association between the style of coping used to manage stress and emotional adjustment, suggesting the possibility that emotional adjustment might be improved by the facilitation of more adaptive coping styles with patients. Following TBI, many patients cope by avoidance, worry, wishful thinking, self-blame, and substance abuse. This, in turn, leads to higher levels of anxiety, depression, and psychosocial dysfunction with lower levels of self-esteem.[64] A recent University of Wales study found by measuring demographic factors and cognitive impairment 10 years after injury that injury severity predicted life satisfaction gender and relationship status predicted community integration and age at injury predicted employment status.[65] Teasdale's group at the University of Glasgow leaves us some hope in assisting patients with substantial psychosocial impairment following TBI. This group notes that it is expected that improvement occurs 1–2 years after head injury, but the pattern thereafter is unclear. Prior studies have not examined representative head injury populations and typically report findings in terms of functioning across social, psychological, neurobehavioral, or cognitive domains rather than by global outcome. The University of Glasgow, Department of Neurosurgery, studied late outcome of participants admitted to hospital after a head injury occurring 5–7 years previously. The studies on 475 survivors at 1 year post-injury revealed a significantly high death rate. Twenty-four percent (115 participants) had died by 7 years later. In those survivors at 5–7 years, disability remained frequent (53%), and the rate was very similar to that found at 1 year post-injury (57%). Sixty-three participants (29%) had improved, but 55 participants (25%) had deteriorated. The persistence of disability and its development after previous recovery each showed stronger associations with indices of depression, anxiety, and low self-esteem than with the initial severity of injury or the level of persisting cognitive impairment. The researchers concluded that admission to hospital after head injury is followed 5–7 years later by disability in a high proportion of survivors. Persistence of disability and development of new disabilities are strongly associated with psychosocial factors that may be open to remediation, even later after injury.[66]

TRAUMATIC BRAIN INJURY AND IMPACT UPON EMOTIONAL INTELLIGENCE

Emotional intelligence is a term of art rather than a cognitive or behavioral domain. Sternberg[67] attempted to identify the operations used in solving standard intelligence tests in hope that this would describe the intelligence of daily living. Gardner made further attempts at this discovery with his theory of multiple intelligences.[68] He noted that damage to the frontal lobes of an adult exerts only relatively minor effects on the individual's ability to solve problems such as those found on a standard intelligence test but it may wreak severe damage on the person's personality. The individual may no longer be recognizable as the same person known by others before the injury. In fact, Gardner believes that this kind of injury can cause a pathology of personhood.

Daniel Goleman[69] brought to public awareness the concept of emotional intelligence. He describes emotional intelligence as abilities representing five main domains:

(1) Knowing one's emotions: This includes self-awareness and recognizing a feeling as it happens.
(2) Managing emotions: This is the ability to handle feelings so they are appropriate and build upon self-awareness. In particular, this describes the capacity to soothe oneself, to shake off rampant anxiety, gloom, or irritability. People who are poor in this ability are constantly battling feelings of distress.
(3) Motivating oneself: This has been described in Chapters 2 and 4 in association with executive function. Self-motivation is part of self-mastery and creativity. The ability to exercise self-control and delay gratification and stifle impulsiveness underlies accomplishment of every sort.
(4) Recognizing emotions in others: Empathy builds on emotional self-awareness and is the fundamental "people skill." This may be a feature of right brain nonverbal function discussed in Chapter 4 but people who are empathic are more attuned to the subtle social signals that indicate what others need or want.

(5) Handling relationships: The art of relationships is, in large part, a skill at managing emotions in others. This is the ability that underlies popularity, leadership, and interpersonal effectiveness.

Antonio Damasio has reviewed the famous story of Phineas Gage.[70] A short review of the alteration of Gage's emotional intelligence after the tamping rod was blown through his brain offers a fascinating 150-year-old review of TBI and the impact it has upon emotional intelligence (see Chapter 2). Dr. Harlow spent much of his life exploring the behavior of Phineas Gage after his injury.[71] Following injury, Gage could touch, hear, and see and was not paralyzed. He did lose vision in the left eye as the tamping rod passed under the zygomatic bone, severing the optic nerve, and exited the posterior frontal skull. He is described as walking firmly, using his hands with dexterity, and he had no noticeable difficulty with speech or language. Before his injury, he was described as having "temperate habits" and "considerable energy of character." Following the accident, he was described as "fitful, irreverent, indulging at times in the grossest profanity which was not previously his custom, manifesting but little deference for his fellows, impatient of restraint or advice when it conflicts with his desires, at times pertinaciously obstinate, yet capricious and vacillating, devising many plans of future operation, which are no longer arranged than they are abandoned." He was so different in his personality following his injury that his railroad employers had to terminate his employment shortly after he returned from sick leave, for they "considered the change in his mind so marked that they could not give him his place again." The change in his employment status was not due to lack of physical ability or skill; it was due to a change in behavior and emotional intelligence.

Emotional intelligence has been studied scientifically to see its relationship to everyday life. There is a large scientific basis that affirms the ecological validity of emotional intelligence.[72] Research with brain-damaged patients shows that people who cannot experience affective reactions because of isolated frontal lobe damage also tend to make disastrous social decisions and their social relationships suffer accordingly, even though intellectual abilities remain unimpaired. Adolphs and Damasio[73] have posited that affective processing is an evolutionary antecedent to more complex forms of information processing. They believe that higher cognition requires the guidance provided by affective processing. Traumatic brain injury often injures affective processing as we have seen previously in this text.

Bar-On has argued that emotional intelligence is critical to human self-actualization.[74] He has conducted extensive research on emotional intelligence and his cross-cultural findings strongly suggest that the best predictors of self-actualization are the following factors and facilitators which he lists in their order of importance: happiness, optimism, self-regard, independence, problem solving, social responsibility, assertiveness, and emotional self-awareness. Many of these behavioral descriptors and facilitators are altered following TBI.

MEASURING ASPECTS OF EMOTIONAL INTELLIGENCE FOLLOWING BRAIN INJURY

Behavioral Assessment of the Dysexecutive Syndrome

This test was developed to predict problems in everyday functioning arising from impaired executive function. The test battery consists of a collection of six novel tests and a questionnaire. These are similar to real-life activities likely to be problematic for persons who have impaired executive ability. The entire test can be administered in approximately 30 min, so it requires little time for completion. Some of the test items have timed components:

1. Rule Shift Cards Test: This examines the patient's ability to respond correctly to a rule and shift from one rule to another.
2. Action Program Test: This requires the patient to obtain a cork from within a tube without using any of the objects in front of the patient. The patients are not allowed to lift the stand,

the tube, or the glass beaker containing water and must perform the activity without touching the lid with their fingers.

3. Key Search Test: This requires the patient to develop a strategy to locate lost keys in an imaginary large square field.

4. Temporal Judgment Test: This section contains four open-ended questions.

5. Zoo Map Test: In this test, the patients are shown how to visit a series of designated locations on a map at a zoo and they must follow certain rules.

6. Modified Six Elements Test: In this section, the patient must perform three tasks, each of which is divided into two parts. The patient must attempt some portion within each subtest within a 10-min period without violating any rules.

7. Dysexecutive Questionnaire: This 20-item questionnaire samples the patient's emotional and personality changes, motivational changes, behavioral changes, and cognitive changes.

Spordone[15] believes this test is a useful tool for the evaluation of impaired executive functions in traumatically brain-injured patients. It is particularly useful in those persons who appear to be cognitively well preserved and function well in highly structured settings. In fact, research has shown that this test is a better predictor of a patient's executive function in real-world situations than is the Wisconsin Card Sorting Test.[75] The test apparently is able to differentiate patients with neurological disorders as a result of closed head injuries from normal, healthy control patients. The test also seems to correlate well with behavioral ratings of executive functions made by the patient's family or significant others. However, in terms of statistical analysis, the test–retest reliability is low. This is because in general, there is a tendency for traumatically brain-injured patients to improve on follow-up testing. This may not be a sensitive test for patients who have sustained only a mild TBI or patients who are depressed, have significant hearing or visual impairments, or are significantly anxious.[28]

Bar-On Emotional Quotient Inventory

The evolution of the Emotional Quotient Inventory (EQ-i) began in 1980 with the independent development of a theoretically eclectic and multifactorial approach to operationally defining and quantitatively describing emotional intelligence.[76] The EQ-i has been used to evaluate the emotional intelligence of people suffering from severe medical problems, such as heart disease, cancer, and AIDS. However, since there is no significant database on the EQ-i in TBI at this time, its primary usefulness is to determine the effect of TBI upon emotional intelligence, particularly in the regulation of emotions, and then apply this information to psychotherapy directed at individuals coping with the outcomes of brain injury. This is primarily true in an effort to apply emotional intelligence to the improvement of health and mental function.[77] It is recommended that the EQ-i be used as part of a larger evaluation process as delineated within this text.

Within the EQ-i there are 15 conceptual components of emotional intelligence that are measured by the subscales. These include:

1. Emotional self-awareness: This is the ability to recognize one's feelings. It also is used to differentiate between the feelings and to know what one is feeling and why and know what caused the feelings. This lack of ability is termed alexithymia (inability to express feelings verbally).[78]

2. Assertiveness: This subscale measures the ability to express feelings, beliefs, and thoughts and defend one's rights in a nondestructive manner. This ability is very difficult for traumatically brain-injured persons to manage due to the poor modulation of affect following some TBIs.

3. Self-regard: This measures the ability to respect and accept oneself as basically good. Following TBI, self-esteem is often impaired, particularly due to problems of interpersonal relatedness.

4. Self-actualization: This pertains to the ability to realize one's potential capacities. As the person rehabilitates, this subscale may be useful in monitoring general improvement during rehabilitation or psychotherapy.

5. Independence: The ability to be self-directed and self-controlled in one's thinking and actions and to be free of emotional dependency is an important aspect of this subscale. Traumatic brain injury often robs people of their independence and this subscale is a useful factor in measuring improved independence through cognitive rehabilitation and psychotherapy.

6. Empathy: To be aware of, to understand, and to appreciate the feelings of others are the core of empathy. Being empathetic means being able to "emotionally read" other people. Since TBI often interferes with right brain cerebral processing and the nonverbal aspects of interpreting other people, this is an important subscale for determining the impact of behavioral disturbance related to right cerebral hemisphere injury.

7. Interpersonal relationships: This involves the ability to establish and maintain mutually satisfying relationships that are characterized by intimacy and by giving and receiving affection. Since relationships are often traumatically influenced following brain injury, this subscale may tap into the variables involved in problematic relationships following TBI.

8. Social responsibility: The ability to demonstrate oneself as a cooperative, contributing, and constructive member of one's social group is manifested as social responsibility. This component of the EQ-i relates to the ability to do things for and with others, accepting others, acting in accordance with one's conscience and upholding social rules. As discussed earlier in this text, "acquired sociopathy" may occur due to infraorbital brain injury and this subscale may assist in the measurement of poor social outcomes following infraorbital injury.

9. Problem solving: Problem solving is multiphasic in nature and is the ability to identify and define problems as well as to generate and implement potentially effective solutions. Owing to the significant aspects of frontal injury in TBI, this aptitude often is impaired.

10. Reality testing: Following brain injury, many persons appear paranoid due to difficulty with reality testing. This subscale measures the ability to assess the correspondence between what is experienced and what objectively exists. It involves "tuning in" to the immediate situation, attempting to keep things in the correct perspective, and experiencing things as they really are, without excessive fantasizing or daydreaming about them. These abilities often are seriously impaired following TBI and this subscale assists in the assessment of those functions.

11. Flexibility: The ability to adjust one's emotions, thoughts, and behavior to changing situations and conditions is consistent with flexibility. As noted in Chapter 6, cognitive flexibility is often impaired following TBI to frontal brain systems. This subscale may assist in the delineation of behaviors affected by lack of flexibility.

12. Stress tolerance: Many persons following TBI will tell their treaters and therapists that they cannot deal with stressful situations. This subscale measures the ability to withstand adverse events and stressful situations without "falling apart" by actively and positively coping with stress. It may assist therapists and rehabilitation counselors in assessing a brain-injured patient's ability to tolerate stressful situations.

13. Impulse control: This is the ability to resist or delay an impulse, drive, or temptation to act. Chapter 2 explained the difficulties of persons with orbitofrontal brain trauma. This subscale may help delineate behaviors associated with inferior frontal brain injury.

14. Happiness: Many brain-injured patients tell their therapists, counselors, and physicians how unhappy they are following brain injury. This unhappiness spills over into the family relationships. This subscale in the EQ-i measures the ability to feel satisfied with one's life, to enjoy oneself and others, and to have fun.

15. Optimism: Optimism is the opposite of pessimism, which is a common symptom of depression and a common feature of suicidal people. It is the ability to look at the brighter side of life and to maintain a positive attitude, even in the face of adversity. This subscale

may be useful to assist in the screening of persons who are having substantial behavioral difficulty with affect regulation.

The EQ-i takes about 30–40 min for most people to complete as it is short and contains only 133 items. A significantly brain-injured person may require a longer time. However, there are no imposed time limits for completing the EQ-i. Patients should complete the inventory in one sitting though. Professionals using the EQ-i can obtain software support from the test manufacturer to assist in scoring and display of the results.

There are validity controls within the EQ-i. The omission rate is tabulated and should be near 0%. If more than 6% of answers are omitted, the results are considered invalid. An inconsistency index will identify those persons who cannot maintain their concentration or comprehension well enough to complete the test. The Positive Impression and Negative Impression scales will identify those persons who are excessively optimistic or attempting to make themselves appear worse than they are validity indicators. If either the Positive or Negative Impression scale score exceeds two standard deviations from the mean, the protocol is invalid. The age range for this test instrument is persons 16 years of age and older. The reading level required is approximately sixth to seventh grade (12–13 years of age). Even though the reading level is this low, the EQ-i should not be administered to youngsters under the age of 16.

THE CHILD

AFFECT AND MOOD CHANGES AFTER TBI

It has been determined repeatedly and reported in the pediatric literature that new psychiatric disorders occur at a higher rate following pediatric TBI.[79] Yeates' group has noted that an inverse relationship exists between the frequency of depression in children following TBI and the level of socioeconomic prosperity in their family.[80] The seminal work by Max et al.[81,82] is instructive in teaching us about the development of psychiatric disorders in children and adolescents following TBI. More recent data support the premise that the development of a mood or anxiety disorder following pediatric head injury is mediated by multiple determinants. However, early psychosocial assessment and interventions aimed at increasing a child's coping ability may attenuate the emotional consequences of pediatric TBI.[83] The most common anxiety disorder of childhood TBI is PTSD. Max et al. have added to our understanding of this disorder as well as from their work in childhood depression.[84] His group at the University of Iowa followed 50 children, aged 6–14 years, who were hospitalized after TBI. They were assessed soon after the TBI regarding their injury severity, pre-injury psychiatric, socioeconomic, family functioning, and family psychiatric history status. Neuroimaging was also analyzed. Assessments were then repeated at 3, 6, 12, and 24 months following TBI. Of 46 children who completed the study, only 2 (4%) developed PTSD. However, many PTSD-like symptoms were experienced by children in the first 3 months following injury. About 68% of these children demonstrated one or more posttraumatic symptoms. When the study was analyzed at 2 years, the rate of PTSD symptomatology (not a full-blown PTSD) was approximately 12%. Max et al. concluded that PTSD and subsyndromal posttraumatic stress disturbances occur even in those children who may demonstrate posttraumatic amnesia. He recommends that these problems be treated, particularly if the symptoms persist beyond 3 months.[84]

A more recent study than that of Max has compared children with mild TBI against children without TBI following motor vehicle accidents. These children were compared to see if differences could be detected in PTSD.[85] Their results were significant, and it was concluded that the presence of mild TBI did not influence the likelihood of experiencing PTSD symptomatology following a traffic accident. There were no statistically significant group differences between those children with TBI and those children without TBI who reported PTSD symptomatology following the injury. The Department of Psychiatry at Johns Hopkins University School of Medicine published recent data that provide some intriguing neuroimaging correlates of anxiety following pediatric TBI. Children who sustain primarily orbitofrontal cortex damage have a decreased likelihood of developing anxiety outcomes. On the other hand, children with temporal lobe damage demonstrate a positive correlation with PTSD. This study comprised 95 children and adolescents who were followed for 1 year post-injury. Pre-injury and 1 year post-injury anxiety status was obtained from the parent. MRI was performed to evaluate brain lesions. Regression models were used to determine relationships between brain lesions and anxiety outcomes.[86]

MEASURING MOOD CHANGES IN CHILDREN

Adolescent Psychopathology Scale

The Adolescent Psychopathology Scale (APS) was developed and standardized for use in the clinical assessment of adolescents aged 12–19 years. The APS consists of 346 items, and it requires approximately 45–60 min to complete. A significantly impaired adolescent may take somewhat longer for completion. The standardization sample of this test instrument does not include individuals under the age of 12 years or over the age of 19 years. Therefore, this test should not be used for children or young adults outside those age ranges.[87] Reading level requirements are at about third grade level. However, the test author advises that years of completed education are not a reliable indicator of reading ability and it is recommended that the youngster be administered an appropriate reading test such as described in Chapter 6.

This is a self-report measure of psychopathology and the test instrument has been devised to comport with the majority of *DSM-IV* Axis I clinical disorders and five of the *DSM-IV* Axis II personality disorders. The APS was designed specifically for adolescents and it is not a downward extension of adult scales from other test instruments. It assesses four broad content domains: (1) clinical disorders, (2) personality disorders, (3) psychosocial problems, and (4) response style indicators. The APS scales further provide the perspective of internalizing/externalizing domains which are based on a factor analysis of the scales. Specific analytical procedures for performing this function are contained within the technical manual and a well-trained psychologist experienced with this test instrument should have no difficulty with interpretation. The clinical disorder scales deal with 20 *DSM-IV* diagnoses: attention-deficit/hyperactivity disorder, conduct disorder, oppositional defiant disorder, adjustment disorder, substance abuse disorder, anorexia nervosa, bulimia nervosa, sleep disorders, somatization disorder, panic disorder, obsessive-compulsive disorder, generalized anxiety disorder, social phobia, separation anxiety disorder, posttraumatic stress disorder, major depression, dysthymic disorder, mania, depersonalization disorder, and schizophrenia. The personality disorder scales evaluate pervasive aspects of inner sense, feelings, affect, and thoughts, as well as behaviors that deviate significantly from normal characteristics of adolescence. The five personality disorder scales include: Avoidant Personality Disorder, Obsessive-Compulsive Personality Disorder, Borderline Personality Disorder, Schizotypal Personality Disorder, and Paranoid Personality Disorder.

The psychosocial problem content scales function primarily as targets for intervention. These scales are categorized along the internalizing–externalizing dimension noted above. The psychosocial problem content scales include: Self-Concept, Psychosocial Substance Use Difficulties, Introversion, Alienation-Boredom, Anger, Aggression, Interpersonal Problems, Emotional Lability, Disorientation, Suicide, and Social Adaptation. A number of these problems are important in the assessment of children following TBI and they would include the Anger, Aggression, Emotional Lability, and Suicide scales.

The response style indicator scales are used for validity checks. They include four scales: (1) Lie Response, (2) Consistency Response, (3) Infrequency Response, and (4) Critical Item Endorsement. The Lie Response scale assesses the adolescent's openness and willingness to give honest answers. The Consistency Response scale measures the youngster's understanding of item content and serves as a potential screener for random responding or inattention. Inattention could occur due to poor reading comprehension or serious brain injury and that should be kept in mind. The Infrequency Response scale contains items that generally are not endorsed by normal adolescents. They represent unusual and bizarre behaviors, affect, and cognition. The Critical Item Endorsement scale consists of 63 of the 346 items on the APS. They are designated as critical items for their ability to differentiate clinical from nonclinical individuals.

Behavior Assessment System for Children-II

The Behavior Assessment System for Children-II (BASC-II) has supplanted the Behavior Assessment System for Children (BASC) since the first edition of this book. The first edition of this test was published in 1985, and the current edition was published in 2004. The BASC-II is a multimethod, multidimensional system used to evaluate the behavior and self-perceptions of children and young adults, aged 2 through 25 years. The BASC-II is multimethod in that it has the following five components that may be used individually or in any combination: (1) a teacher rating scale, (2) a parent rating scale, (3) a self-report scale used by a child or young adult, (4) a structured developmental history form, and (5) a form for recording and classifying directly observed classroom behavior. The examiner can choose any one of these methods for examination, and it is not required that it all be completed to gain useful information. The BASC-II was designed to facilitate the differential diagnosis or educational classification of a variety of emotional and behavioral disorders of children and to aid in the design of treatment plans. When used as a total system, the BASC-II provides information about a child from a variety of sources.[88]

The author has some recommendations about use of the teacher rating scales in the assessment of children following TBI, particularly if the assessment data are to be used for litigation purposes. Teachers are significantly concerned about identifying a child with special needs. If they do, this triggers U.S. government regulations regarding the provision of special services to children. Therefore, there is no accurate way to provide effort controls on the teacher rating system, and it is the author's experience that significant biases may be introduced into the assessment. Therefore, it is probably better to use this instrument with child or parent rating scales and supplement information from the child's academic record, such as standardized test scores and academic grades rather than relying on teacher inferences. This is not to condemn teachers, as none of us would have gotten very far in life without their assistance. However, teachers are not motivated to describe a child's behavior being significantly different following brain injury than it was before brain injury for numerous reasons. Moreover, if teachers know that a child is in litigation or at risk for being involved in litigation, they are often loathe to provide information, as they may be asked to testify.

The standardization and norming of this instrument took place from August 2002 through May 2004. The general norm samples include a total of more than 13,000 cases from ages 2 through 18 years. The overall standardization sample came from over 375 sites in 257 cities and 40 states. Thus, this test is highly representative of the contemporary U.S. child population. Educational professionals were recruited as site coordinators for the data collection. Site coordinators recruited teachers to participate in the project. Norms were represented by sex, race/ethnicity, mother's education level, geographic region, and special education classification level. There are also norms for young adults. The authors included these norms specifically because schools may be required to provide children needing special services a continuation of services into young adulthood. The administration forms come in three formats: hand-scored, computer entry, and optical scanning. There are also forms in Spanish. Audio recordings are available from the test manufacturer for administration of the BASC-II parent rating scales and self-report of personality scales to parents or respondents who may have a reading impairment. Use of audio recordings is preferable to reading items to the individual, and the manufacturer does not recommend doing this. Having the examiner read aloud the items and observe the marking of responses may alter how parents, and especially children, respond to the test items. There are two computer programs available to assist with scoring and reporting. Each program generates profiles, calculates validity indices, identifies strengths and weaknesses, and computes multirater comparisons and progress reports.[88] The test manual for this system demonstrates well that the normative samples and psychometric properties of the BASC-II are substantially superior to the BASC.

Minnesota Multiphasic Personality Inventory-Adolescent

The Minnesota Multiphasic Personality Inventory-Adolescent (MMPI-A) was developed because many studies of the MMPI test instruments have demonstrated the importance of using adolescent norms for young people. The use of adult norms applied to adolescents tends to over report pathology or make adolescents appear more disturbed than they actually are. Thus, the MMPI-A is an outgrowth of the MMPI Adolescent Project Committee of the University of Minnesota which was specifically appointed to develop the MMPI-A.[89]

The MMPI-A contains 478 items. All of the basic clinical scale items, as well as those that are unique to the adolescent form, appear among the first 350 questions. Thus, scores for F2, F, VRIN, TRIN, the Content Scales, and the supplementary scales are not obtainable in the first 350 items, but require complete administration of the test booklet. The clinical sample for the normative base included 420 boys and 293 girls, ages 14–18. It is recommended that the MMPI-A be used with 14- to 18-year-olds. The grade level of the clinical sample ranges from 7 to 12 and all normative subjects were enrolled in school; although, some were attending school in a psychiatric treatment facility. When scored on the basis of the original MMPI norms, this clinical sample produced clinical scale profiles that were very similar to those of the previous clinical sample used by Marks et al.[90] to develop the MMPI code-type data for adolescents.

It is thought to be possible that bright, mature younger 12- or 13-year-old adolescents can comprehend and respond validly to the MMPI-A. However, ethically it must be reported by the examiner that these age levels are outside the normative database. Also, for adolescents age 19, the MMPI-2 should be used rather than the MMPI-A. For 18-year-olds, the maturity level allows the clinician to make some judgment about whether to use the MMPI-A or the MMPI-2 during examination.

An essential requirement is adequate English language reading comprehension. This could prove especially troublesome for a youngster who is learning disabled or has attention deficit disorder before TBI. Alternative test instruments may be required for this group of youngsters. Some brain-injured youngsters may be too easily distracted, hyperactive, or impulsive to complete 478 items in a single testing session. Thus, frequent breaks may be required. The majority of MMPI-A items are at the fifth to seventh grade reading level. The author recommends that all adolescents be screened for reading skill before administration of the test instrument.

The validity indicators contain some differences between those of the MMPI-2. Those that are similar to the MMPI-2 are the Cannot Say, L, F, K, VRIN, and TRIN scales. Two new validity scales, F1 and F2, are unique to the MMPI-A. The Cannot Say measures the total number of items that the adolescent failed to answer true or false. The L scale may be used as a measure of naive defensiveness in adolescents. F, the Infrequency scale, is divided into a 33-item F1 scale and a 33-item F2 scale. The F1 scale is a direct descendant of the traditional F scale from the original MMPI. The F2 scale consists of items that occur in the latter half of the test booklet. Thus, the F1 and F2 scales for the MMPI-A may be used in an interpretive strategy similar to that recommended for the F and Fb scales in the MMPI-2. Because all of the F1 scale items appear in the first 350 items of the MMPI-A booklet, this measure provides a method for evaluating the acceptability of the response pattern for the basic MMPI-A scales. The F2 scale operates like the Fb scale of the MMPI-2 in that it provides an index of the acceptability of the test record in relation to the MMPI-A Content and supplementary scales. F1 will enable the psychologist to determine the likelihood of significant symptom magnification or even malingering of psychological problems.

The K scale is a basic validity indicator in the MMPI-A, but few descriptors are available from the normative samples. The test manufacturer recommends that interpretation of K profiles with elevated T-scores (>65) includes a cautionary statement about the possibility of a defensive test-taking attitude. The test authors recommend that TRIN should be used to clarify elevations on this scale and psychological consultation will be necessary to complete this analysis. The VRIN and TRIN scales are new validity scales developed with the second edition of the MMPI-2. They are quite different from the traditional L, F, and K scales. VRIN and TRIN scores indicate the tendency of a person to respond to items in ways that are inconsistent or contradictory. TRIN is made up exclusively of pairs that are opposite in content. Thus, this scale can be used to determine whether the adolescent is acquiescent or nonacquiescent to true or false responses. VRIN is useful to determine if the adolescent is answering the questions carelessly or is confused. Moreover, it can be useful for determining symptom magnification or malingering. A high F1, with a normal or low VRIN, is consistent with the adolescent understanding the responses and deliberately skewing the responses of the test items either to represent symptom magnification or even malingering. Whereas, a high elevation on VRIN accompanied by a high elevation on F1 may be consistent with a disorganized or confused adolescent who cannot attend to the test items or comprehend the test items. Psychological consultation is required for the neuropsychiatric examiner to fully use the validity scales on the MMPI-A.

The MMPI-A contains 10 clinical scales. These have the same names as the MMPI-2 or the original MMPI scales and they include: 1 (Hs: Hypochondriasis), 2 (D: Depression), 3 (Hy: Hysteria), 4 (Pd: Psychopathic Deviate), 5 (Mf: Masculinity/Femininity), 6 (Pa: Paranoia), 7 (Pt: Psychasthenia), 8 (Sc: Schizophrenia), 9 (Ma: Hypomania), and 0 (Si: Social Introversion). As is true for the interpretation of the MMPI and MMPI-2 with adults, the adolescent MMPI-A interpretation is often done by code type. The only published empirically developed code type for the MMPI-A is by Marks.[91] There is a later publication of code-type frequency data for 1762 adolescent patients who received the original form of the MMPI and were scored using the Marks et al. norms and the MMPI-A norms.[91]

The scoring and interpretation of the MMPI-A have options specific for adolescents which are not present for the adult interpretive schemes. For instance, the potential for school problems can be determined by two of the MMPI-A Content scales (A-SCH and A-LAS). Several other MMPI-A scales also include school problems (See MMPI-A Manual, 1992). Scale 0 (Si) and its subscales are helpful for describing problems of social relationships. These of course occur very frequently in adolescents following TBI. Predictions about family problems can be made from the A-FAM scale. Alienation (A-ALN) and cynicism (A-CYN) are covered by the MMPI-A Content scales. Negative peer-group influences can be inferred from elevations on the PRO scale, given its item content. The IMM scale also provides information relating to interpersonal style and capacity to develop meaningful relationships. Elevations on the A-TRT scale can be interpreted as an indication of the presence of negative attitudes toward mental health treatment that may interfere with building a therapeutic relationship.[89] As with the adult MMPI-2, psychological consultation is recommended when using the MMPI-A.

Multidimensional Anxiety Scale for Children

The Multidimensional Anxiety Scale for Children (MASC) is an easily administered, self-report instrument that assesses the major dimensions of anxiety in young persons. One weakness of this test is that it is based on *DSM-III-R* criteria rather than *DSM-IV* criteria. The author particularly chose to do this, as he believes the *DSM-IV* criteria sets do not generally reflect a developmental perspective, and therefore it is the responsibility of the clinician to translate the *DSM-IV* into terms that are relevant for the age, gender, and cultural background of the youngster.[92] For physicians providing TBI examinations of children, it is worth noting that Dr. March, at the time he wrote this manual, was director of the Child and Adolescent Anxiety Disorders Program at Duke University Medical Center, and of course he is a child psychiatrist. The MASC consists of 39 items distributed across four basic scales: Physical Symptoms, Harm Avoidance, Social Anxiety, and Separation/ Panic. The test produces three indexes: Total Anxiety Scale, Anxiety Disorders Index, and Inconsistency Index. The MASC generates 12 raw scores (not including the Inconsistency Index).

The MASC is used for children in three age groups: ages 8 to 11, ages 12 to 15, and ages 16 to 19. These groups made up the normative sample, which consisted of 2698 children and adolescents (1261 males and 1437 females) who ranged in age from 8 to 19 years. The demographics were 53.3% Caucasian, 39.2% African-American, 0.7% Hispanic, 1.4% Asian, 2.4% Native-American, and 3.0% other ethnic backgrounds. This test is easy to administer and score, and the entire assessment can be completed by a child or adolescent in under 15 min. The clinician can score and profile the results in less than 10 min.

Multiscore Depression Inventory for Children

The Multiscore Depression Inventory for Children (MDI-C) is a 79-item questionnaire in the form of brief sentences presented in a true–false response format. The administration time is about 15–20 min. This test instrument is standardized for ages 8–17 and it allows children to indicate their own feelings and beliefs about themselves. It is an unusual test in that it is the first behaviorally oriented test for children that was written by children in their own words.[93] The MDI-C is reported to be useful both as a screening instrument and to identify high risk children within clinical assessments. It yields scores on 8 scales, as well as a total score measuring the general severity of depression. It may be scored on a computer, by sending the score sheet by fax to the manufacturer, or by mail-in scoring.

The MDI-C scales are: Anxiety, Self-Esteem, Sad Mood, Instrumental Helplessness, Social Introversion, Low Energy, Pessimism, Defiance, and Total. The Anxiety scale measures cognitive and somatic aspects of anxiety. The Self-Esteem scale reflects children's perceptions of themselves. Sad Mood is basically what it says. The Instrumental Helplessness scale measures children's perceptions of their abilities to manipulate social situations in order to receive ordinary benefits. The Social Introversion scale reflects the tendency to withdraw from social situations and social contact. The Low Energy scale measures cognitive intensity and somatic vigor. The Pessimism scale gauges children's outlook to the future. The Defiance scale measures irritability and other behavior problems. The Total scale sums all 79 items, including a Suicide Risk indicator and is an overall measure of depression. The scale items have a third grade reading level. Most children have few problems understanding the content since it was written by children. There are scales to determine faking good and faking bad as response biases. Children are more likely to have a defensive response or a "faking good" response as they may be worried how adults or professionals will react to their problems. Children with high scores on the Infrequency Index are either "faking bad" or suffering extreme forms of depression. This instrument includes scales that address features widely agreed to accompany depression or contribute to it. The scores are displayed as T-scores exactly analogous to the T-score presentation with the MMPI-A. On this test instrument, the most reliable and valid confirmation of depression in a child is the Total score of the MDI-C. This score is a measure of severity of childhood depression. Children with total scores greater than 65T have sad or blue moods often. They may be irritable, helpless, hopeless, and lack energy. Vegetative signs of depression may be present. On the subscale for Suicidal Ideation, children with Total scores above 65T should be carefully evaluated for suicidal behaviors and ideas. Item 45 from this test instrument contains a Suicide Risk Indicator ("I have a suicide plan"). Furthermore, the test manufacturer recommends evaluating the child's answers to Item 5 ("I think about death a lot"), Item 11 ("I hate myself"), Item 26 ("I do not want to live"), Item 36 ("I worry about death"), and Item 56 ("No one would care if I died").

State–Trait Anxiety Inventory for Children

The State–Trait Anxiety Inventory for Children (STAIC) was initially developed as a research tool for the study of anxiety in elementary school children. It consists of separate, self-report scales for measuring two distinct anxiety concepts: State Anxiety (S-Anxiety) and Trait Anxiety (T-Anxiety). This measurement is very similar to the adult test described previously (STAI).

TABLE 7.2

Child Behavioral Tests That Are Useful in Traumatic Brain Injury

Mood/Affect

Adolescent Psychopathology Scale (12–19 years)

Behavioral Assessment System for Children-II
  (2–25 years)

Minnesota Multiphasic Personality Inventory-
  Adolescent (14–18 years)

Multidimensional Anxiety Scale for Children
  (8–19 years)

Multiscore Depression Inventory for Children
  (8–17 years)

State–Trait Anxiety Inventory for Children (9–12 years)

Neurobehavioral Function

Neurobehavioral functioning inventory (16–82 years)

The original STAIC was constructed to measure anxiety in 9–12 year old children but it may also be used with younger children who possess average or above average reading ability and with older children who are below average in their reading ability.[94]

The S-Anxiety scale measures transitory anxiety states. These are subjective, consciously perceived feelings of apprehension, tension, and worry that vary in intensity and fluctuate over time. On the other hand, the T-Anxiety scale measures a relatively stable individual difference in childhood anxiety proneness. High T-Anxiety children are more prone to respond to situations perceived as threatening with elevations in S-Anxiety intensity than low T-Anxiety children. Thus, this test instrument may be useful in the highly traumatized child who is also being screened for possible PTSD.

There are no internal validity scales for this test instrument. There are foreign language adaptations and translations of the test that are available from the manufacturer. There is a wide variety of languages available, including Hindi, Chinese, Czech, German, Greek, Hebrew, Japanese, Russian, Spanish, Turkish, and others. There is also a Spanish language version used in Puerto Rico, Mexico, and the Mexican-American population of Texas. The East Indian versions have been standardized with college students at Punjab University in India. The scores are provided as T-scores with the usual mean of 50 and a standard deviation of 10. Table 7.2 lists behavioral tests useful during evaluation of children.

AGGRESSION

Aggression syndromes in children are substantially different than those seen in adults. Unfortunately, there are no well-developed and well-normed aggression psychological test instruments specifically designed to measure aggression in children. However, personality change is common after childhood TBI, and there are affective instability and rage subtypes within these personality changes.[95] The affective instability and aggressive types frequently occur together.[96] The affective instability and rage subtypes of personality change are generally treated with mood stabilizing medications. What has been described by Max's group and others as personality change, may also be an inability to self-regulate mood. A recent study of 65 children with moderate to severe TBI and 65 children without TBI demonstrated that those children with TBI displayed deficits in self-regulation and social and behavioral functioning, after controlling for their socioeconomic status. The magnitude of the deficits in self-regulation was not related to injury severity. However, the impairment of self-regulation accounted for a significant amount of the variance in the child's social and behavioral functioning.[97] Also, a study out of Wales cautions us that the assessment of the child's personality change after injury may be particularly influenced by how relatives judge that personality change. There are no research studies to guide examiners in determining the accuracy of personality assessment when made by parents or other relatives.[98] Moreover, a family's ability to adapt to their injured child and the burden that the child places upon them may adversely affect their ability to detect accurately personality changes. Aggressive behaviors may be an outcome of altered family dynamics as much as related directly to the brain lesion. It must be remembered that families of children with severe TBI experience long-standing injury-related burdens.[99] When the child demonstrates long-term maladaptive behaviors containing aggressive and antisocial features, these are highly predictive in causing problems with reintegration into classroom settings.[100] It is beyond the scope of this book to describe, but specific interventions to manage classroom children with aggressive tendencies will require a pediatric psychologist to assist. These interventions include contingency management, stimulus control, problem solving, social skills training, relaxation training, anger management, and parent–child training.[101]

PSYCHOSOCIAL FUNCTIONING IN BRAIN-INJURED CHILDREN

Post-injury psychiatric disorders can be predicted by a variety of injury and psychosocial variables. These lend themselves to measurement soon after injury.[95] Children with TBI who are at high risk for impairing psychopathology are readily identifiable before these problems manifest themselves. Therefore, there is hope that the psychosocial burden of TBI upon children can be reduced by identifying these behaviors. There is also a close relationship between the level of family dysfunction and the psychiatric disorders that manifest themselves in children. Children who grow up with physical disabilities or illness face challenges when trying to reintegrate with their peers.[102] Children with TBI are at substantial risk for both acute and chronic social problems.[103,104] A University of Texas at Houston study evaluated social competence in young children with inflicted TBI. They examined social and cognitive competence in 25 infants, aged 3–23 months, who sustained moderate to severe TBI secondary to physical abuse. These youngsters were compared to 22 healthy community children. Early brain injury caused significant disruption in the TBI survivors' behaviors and impaired their ability to regulate initiation and responsiveness in social contexts.[105] Thus, these children are deprived very early of the ability to develop the necessary social reciprocity and social understanding that will guide them through the remainder of their life. Yeates and his colleague have evaluated social problem-solving skills in children with TBI. They evaluated 35 children with severe TBI, 40 children with moderate TBI, and compared them to 46 children with orthopedic injuries. These youngsters were followed longitudinally. They ranged in age from 9 to 18 years and were approximately 4 years post-injury at the time of evaluation. They were administered a semistructured interview used in previous research in social problem solving to assess the developmental level of their responses to hypothetical dilemmas involving social conflict. Children in the severe TBI group were able to solve social dilemmas and generate alternative strategies at the same developmental level as children in the orthopedic group. However, they articulated lower level strategies as the best way to solve the dilemmas and used lower level reasoning to evaluate the effectiveness of their strategies. These children were controlled for race, socioeconomic status, IQ, and age. These findings demonstrated that children with severe TBI show selective, long-term deficits that reduce them to a lower level ability in their social problem-solving skills which may account for their poor social and academic outcomes following brain injury.[106]

During examination of the child with TBI, it must be remembered that traumatically brain-injured children often have comorbid orthopedic or other multisystem injuries. The psychosocial impact of these injuries, as well as the complications from TBI, may be a substantial burden both to the child and to the child's family. Comorbid orthopedic injuries and TBIs may play a significant negative role in the family's ability to adjust to the child's needs. This has been demonstrated to be very high for those children in the age range of 6–12 years. In families who were socially or behaviorally dysfunctional before the child's trauma, TBIs and concurrent orthopedic injuries have a magnified negative impact upon the family system.[107]

DYNAMICS OF TRAUMATIC BRAIN INJURY WITHIN THE FAMILY OR WITH SIGNIFICANT OTHERS

THE ADULT

Lezak wrote a classic article in 1978, which provides observations on what family members experience while living with the "characterologically altered" person who has sustained a brain injury.[108] She noted the personality changes that have primary impact on the family. These included an impaired capacity for social perceptiveness, concrete thinking, impaired capacity for control and self-regulation, emotional alterations such as apathy, irritability, and changes in sexual ability, and an inability to profit from experience. As a result, family members may feel trapped, isolated, or abandoned by outside relatives and may feel even abused, certainly at an emotional level. Recent studies have confirmed Lezak's early assertions about the negative impact of TBI upon family systems and caregivers. Path analysis is being used to determine the structural effect of neurobehavioral problems following TBI upon family members.[109] It has been noted that spouse/caregivers report partners with TBI as having high levels of behavioral and cognitive problems, which then produces high levels of unhealthy family functioning.[109] These findings of substantial caregiver stress seem unrelated to culture, as a recent Brazilian study and Israeli study have confirmed the observations of Lezak and others.[110,111]

There are some predictors and indicators of caregiver distress. A Wayne State University study demonstrated that neurobehavioral disturbance in the afflicted person is the strongest predictor of caregiver distress. This study also demonstrated that social support services showed a direct and linear relationship to improving family functioning.[112] An Australian study[113] sampled 135 people derived from a statewide cohort of persons with TBI recruited to the multicenter Brain Injury Outcome Study. The authors used path analysis to examine the varying contributions of impairment, participation, and support variables to both relatives' distress and disturbances in family functioning. The overall model accounted for substantial proportions of the variance in psychological distress and family functioning. The important finding of this study is that the distress experienced by the relatives was not due to the direct impact of the neurobehavioral impairments. Most of the variance was due to the effect of these impairments mediated by the degree of community participation achieved by the person with TBI. In other words, if the injured person could be reintegrated into the community at a reasonably successful level, this markedly reduced caregiver stress.[113] An earlier Australian study extended research into primary, secondary, and tertiary caregivers following TBI in a family member.[114] This study used a cross-sectional design to gather outcome data from individuals with TBI and their primary, secondary and tertiary caregivers 19 months and 10 days after trauma. Multivariate analyses of variance were used to determine differences in levels of psychological distress and family satisfaction within families. The results indicated that primary caregivers, particularly a wife, are at greatest risk of poor psychosocial outcome. However, male relatives, the majority of whom were secondary or tertiary caregivers, may report their distress in terms of anger and fatigue rather than depression and anxiety, which was seen in the wives.

If the examiner wants to measure caregiver stress, that has been attempted fairly successfully. Models in the brain injury literature have used the Neurobehavioral Functioning Inventory (NFI). This inventory is comprised of six scales with items describing symptoms and daily living problems. The findings of studies using this instrument indicate general agreement between family members and patients regarding everyday problems within the patient. For instance, the Medical College of Virginia used this inventory to study a group of brain-injured persons. Their findings did not support the theory that patients tend to underestimate their difficulties, and the agreement level between patient and families related to injury severity and outcome was good.[115] Some studies have used the Caregiver Appraisal Scale in attempts to directly measure caregiver stress. It demonstrates adequate concurrent validity, and it is a potential instrument to be used by a neuropsychiatric examiner.[116] If the examiner is determining caregiver burden, a clinical examination of the patients and their family is necessary. The examiner should first determine the nature of care needed by collateral interviews with family members. Inquiries should be made concerning the stress and burden experienced in the family home or the caregiving home and how individuals caring for the loved one are coping.[117] As noted from some of the research reports above, the main goal is to develop a trajectory for caregivers that will reintegrate the injured person into their families, and it is hoped also into the community.[118] A recent successful intervention strategy has focused upon mentoring. It is useful to find those who have established caregiving duties and allow those individuals to mentor the person attempting to deal with a loved one with a recent brain injury.[119] It is important to keep in mind the gender differences in caregiver stress as represented by men versus women.[114]

THE CHILD

It seems intuitive that good family functioning would influence the outcome of children who have sustained TBI. Stanton[120] has reviewed a number of medical factors within various research protocols that have attempted to answer this question. While there are methodological problems in some of the studies and analytical differences among studies, there is good evidence that family functioning influences directly the behavioral adjustment and adaptive functioning of a child after TBI.[120] A study from Louisville, Kentucky, examined not only the effects of TBI in a youngster on family dynamics but also examined the impact upon finances. This research group at the Department of Pediatrics at the University of Louisville designed a 30-item survey to determine the effects of the injury on the child, parents, and siblings, and whether parents were retrospectively content with the decisions related to the aggressiveness of care provided by physicians and others. The mean patient age at the time of injury was 8.7 years. The mean time since the child was injured was 3 years, and the mean Glasgow Coma Scale (GCS) score at injury was 3.7. Approximately one-third of the children in the 46 families studied had disabilities related to education, socialization, or self-care skills. These youngsters required multiple healthcare visits each month, and they required prescription medications. The study demonstrated that 30% of families reported deterioration in finances or loss of job in one of the parents. Sixteen percent reported a worsening in the relationship between adults. In 13 of 32 cases, housing required modification or new housing was required to facilitate care for the child. Siblings were adversely affected in approximately 16 of 28 families, and they exhibited behavioral problems such as increased fear and withdraw from the injured child. Only one of the 32 families stated that they would have asked caregivers to provide less aggressive treatment to their child, even if it led to the child's death.[121] A Case Western Reserve University study has demonstrated that severe TBI in a child is a source of considerable caregiver morbidity. The caregivers of children with severe TBI have persistent stress associated with the child's injury, as well as stress associated with the reactions of other family members. There is a relative risk of clinically significant psychological problems in these caregivers, and they have twice the probability of developing psychological problems as parents who care for severely orthopedically injured children.[122]

As the examiner collects data, obviously how to intervene in the family with an injured child is a prominent question. A recent University of Arkansas study in the Department of Pediatrics reviewed the needs of children and their families following TBI with audiotaped semistructured interviews. The conclusions from this study revealed that the family dynamics could be improved by attention to constructive communication and clarification of the system of care by the physician provider, continued family-centered care, and development of peer support programs to meet the needs of caregivers and therefore facilitate improvement in the pediatric recovery. Again, the use of support systems and peer influences appears prominently in the outcomes of this study.[123] This study was continued to develop further research on family intervention of children who had sustained TBI. It found that a program consisting of the following three components was the most effective for intervention: (1) efforts to increase coordination of discharge care at the time the child leaves the hospital, (2) establishment of structured educational protocols for the family, and (3) the implementation of support groups and a peer support program for families.[124]

As the neuropsychiatric examiner assesses the family, care should be taken to determine the current and preaccident mood states of primary caregivers where that is appropriate.[125] There is evidence that the greater the number of adverse events or effects occurring in the patient with TBI as well as the patient's impact upon the family, the more likely the caregiver is to develop depression.[126] There is further evidence to suggest that the rate of depression in caregivers may exceed 50% when measured using the Beck Depression Scales.[127] Other studies have shown that the depression rate may be as high as 60% in caregivers attempting to meet the needs of a traumatically brain-injured loved one.[128]

MEASUREMENT OF PATIENT NEUROBEHAVIORAL FUNCTION WITHIN THE FAMILY SYSTEM

Neurobehavioral Functioning Inventory

The Neurobehavioral Functioning Inventory (NFI) was developed in three phases. It grew out of the 105 item Brain Injury Problem Checklist, developed in the 1980s. This inventory was based on face validity and organized into five categories: somatic, cognitive, behavior, communication, and social problems. Patients or family members rated the frequency of patient problems. The present NFI consists of two forms, one for patients and one for family members or other knowledgeable informants. Both forms consist of 76 items on a 5-point Likert scale that measures the frequency of behaviors exhibited by the patient. The Likert-type response choices include the follwing: never, rarely, sometimes, often, and always.[129]

It is essential to attain responses from both the patient and a relative. Differing perspectives may be useful to the examiner. When more than one informant is available, the examiner may consider soliciting the opinion of the person who knows the patient best. This usually will be the primary caregiver, but examiners may wish to solicit questions from different family members and compare their responses. The age range for administration is 16–82 years. However, this inventory has an interesting component in that it is standardized to accept responses from patients who were ages 4–81 at the time of their injury. The standardization sample also was multiethnic and comprised of varying levels of brain injury severity existing between 0 and 195 days post-injury.

The NFI contains six clinical scales: (1) depression, (2) somatic, (3) memory/attention, (4) communication, (5) aggression, and (6) motor. The data are presented as T-scores with a mean of 50 and a standard deviation of 10. The examiner may find it useful to look at responses to individual test items as they offer a wealth of information regarding overall neurobehavioral functioning.

REFERENCES

1. McAllister, T.W., Neuropsychiatric aspects of TBI, in *Brain Injury Medicine: Principles and Practice*, Zasler, N.D., Katz, D.I., and Zafonte, R.D., Eds., Demos, New York, 2006, p. 835.
2. Jorge, R.E., Robinson, R.G., Moser, D., et al., Major depression following traumatic brain injury. *Arch. Gen. Psychiatry*, 61, 42, 2004.
3. Jorge, R.E. and Starkstein, S.E., Pathophysiologic aspects of major depression following traumatic brain injury. *J. Head Trauma Rehabil.*, 20, 475, 2005.
4. Jorge, R.E., Neuropsychiatric consequences of traumatic brain injury: A review of recent findings. *Curr. Opin. Psychiatry*, 18, 289, 2005.
5. Jorge, R.E., Acion, L., Starkstein, S.E., et al., Hippocampal volume and mood disorders after traumatic brain injury. *Biol. Psychiatry*, Nov. 20 [Epub ahead of print], 2006.
6. Rapoport, M.J., Herrmann, N., Shammi, P., et al., Outcome after traumatic brain injury sustained in older adulthood: A one-year longitudinal study. *Am. J. Geriatr. Psychiatry*, 14, 456, 2006.
7. Rapoport, M.J., Kiss, A., and Feinstein, A., The impacts of major depression on outcome following mild-to-moderate traumatic brain injury in older adults. *J. Affect. Dis.*, 92, 273, 2006.

8. Chamelian, L. and Feinstein, A., The effect of major depression on subjective and objective cognitive deficits in mild-to-moderate traumatic brain injury. *J. Neuropsychiatr. Clin. Neurosci.*, 18, 33, 2006.

9. Moore, E.L., Terryberry-Spohr, L., and Hope, D.A., Mild traumatic brain injury and anxiety sequelae: A review of the literature. *Brain Inj.*, 20, 117, 2006.

10. Warden, D., Military TBI during the Iraq and Afghanistan wars. *J. Head Trauma Rehabil.*, 21, 398, 2006.

11. Greenspan, A.I., Stringer, A.Y., Phillips, V.L., et al., Symptoms of post-traumatic stress: Intrusion and avoidance 6 and 12 months after TBI. *Brain Inj.*, 20, 733, 2006.

12. Gil, S., Caspi, Y., Ben-Ari, I., et al., Memory of the traumatic event as a risk factor for the development of PTSD: Lessons from the study of trauma brain injury. *C.N.S. Spectr.*, 11, 603, 2006.

13. Bombardier, C.H., Fann, J.R., Temkin, N., et al., Posttraumatic stress disorder symptoms during the first six months after traumatic brain injury. *J. Neuropsychiatr. Clin. Neurosci.*, 18, 501, 2006.

14. Jones, C., Harvey, A.G., and Brewin, C.R., The organisation and content of trauma memories in survivors of road accidents. *Beh. Res. Ther.*, 45, 151, 2007.

15. Parry-Jones, V.L., Vaughan, F.L., and MilesCox, W., Traumatic brain injury and substance misuse: A systematic review of prevalence and outcomes research (1994–2004). *Neuropsychol. Rehabil.*, 16, 537, 2006.

16. Iverson, G.L., Lange, R.T., and Franzen, M.D., Effects of mild traumatic brain injury cannot be differentiated from substance abuse. *Brain Inj.*, 19, 11, 2005.

17. Felde, A.B., Westermeyer, J., and Thuas, P., Co-morbid traumatic brain injury in substance use disorder: Childhood predictors and adult correlates. *Brain Inj.*, 20, 41, 2006.

18. Horner, M.D., Furguson, P.L., Celassie, A.W., et al., Patterns of alcohol use one year after traumatic brain injury: A population-based epidemiological study. *J. Int. Neuropsychol. Soc.*, 11, 322, 2005.

19. Jorge, R.E., Starkstein, S.E., Arndt, S., et al., Alcohol misuse and mood disorders following traumatic brain injury. *Arch. Gen. Psychiatry*, 62, 742, 2005.

20. Silver, J.M., Kramer, R., Greenwald, S., et al., The association between head injuries and psychiatric disorders: Findings from the New Haven NIMH Epidemiologic Catchment Area study. *Brain Inj.*, 15, 935, 2001.

21. Simpson, G. and Tate, R., Suicidality after traumatic brain injury: Demographic, injury and clinical correlates. *Psychol. Med.*, 32, 687, 2002.

22. Simpson, G. and Tate, R., Clinical features of suicide attempts after traumatic brain injury. *J. Nerv. Ment. Dis.*, 193, 680, 2005.

23. Oquendo, M.A., Friedman, J.H., Grunebaum, M.F., et al., Suicidal behavior and mild traumatic brain injury in major depression. *J. Ment. Nerv. Dis.*, 192, 430, 2004.

24. Harrison-Felix, C., Whiteneck, G., Devivo, M.J., et al., Causes of death following one year postinjury among individuals with traumatic brain injury. *J. Head Trauma Rehabil.*, 21, 22, 2006.

25. Leon-Carrion, J., DeSerdio-Arias, M.L., Cabezas, F.M., et al., Neurobehavioral and cognitive profile of traumatic brain injury patients with stroke, traumatic brain injury, myocardial infarction, and spinal cord injury. *Psychosomatics*, 42, 382, 2001.

26. Kuipers, P. and Lancaster, A., Developing a suicide prevention strategy based on the perspectives of people with brain injuries. *J. Head Trauma Rehabil.*, 15, 1275, 2000.

27. Beck, A.T. and Steer, R.A., *Beck Depression Inventory*, Psychological Corporation, San Antonio, TX, 1993.

28. Spordone, R.J. and Saul, R.E., *Neuropsychology for Health Care Professionals and Attorneys*, 2nd edition, CRC Press, Boca Raton, FL, 2000.

29. Beck, A.T., *Depression: Causes and Treatment*, University of Pennsylvania Press, Philadelphia, PA, 1967.

30. *Diagnostic and Statistical Manual of Mental Disorders*, 4th edition, American Psychiatric Association, Washington, D.C., 1994.

31. Beck, A.T., Steer, R.A., and Brown, G.K., *Beck Depression Inventory-II Manual*, The Psychological Corporation, San Antonio, TX, 1996.

32. Millon, T., *Toward a New Personology*, John Wiley & Sons, New York, 1990.

33. Hathaway, S.R. and McKinley, J.C., *Booklet for the Minnesota Multiphasic Personality Inventory*, Psychological Corporation, New York, 1943.

34. Graham, J.R., *MMPI-2: Assessing Personality and Psychopathology*, 2nd edition, Oxford University Press, New York, 1993.

35. Goldstein, D. and Primeau, M., Neuropsychological and personality predictors of employment after traumatic brain injury. *J. Int. Neuropsychol. Soc.*, 1, 370 (abstract), 1995.

36. Hathaway, S.R., McKinley, J.C., Butcher, J.N., et al., *Minnesota Multiphasic Personality Inventory: Manual for Administration and Scoring*, University of Minnesota Press, Minneapolis, MN, 1989.
37. Golden, Z. and Golden, C.J., Impact of brain injury severity on personality dysfunction. *Int. J. Neurosci.*, 113, 733, 2003.
38. Lezak, M.D., Howieson, D.B., and Loring, D.W., *Neuropsychological Assessment*, 4th edition, Oxford University Press, New York, 2004.
39. Seel, R.T. and Kreutzer, J.S., Depression assessment after traumatic brain injury: An empirically-based classification method. *Arch. Phys. Med. Rehabil.*, 84, 1621, 2003.
40. Demakis, G.J., Hammond, F., Knotts, A., et al., The personality assessment inventory in individuals with traumatic brain injury. *Arch. Clin. Neuropsychol.*, 22, 123, 2006.
41. Morey, L.C., *Personality Assessment Inventory Manual*, Psychological Assessment Resources, Odessa, FL, 1991.
42. Morey, L.C., *An Interpretive Guide to the Personality Assessment Inventory (PAI)*, Psychological Assessment Resources, Odessa, FL, 1996.
43. Cattell, R.B., *Handbook of Multivariate Experimental Psychology*, Rand McNally, Chicago, IL, 1966.
44. Spielberger, C.D., *State–Trait Anxiety Inventory (Form Y)*, Mindgarden, Redwood City, CA, 1983.
45. Silver, J.M. and Arciniegas, D.B., Pharmacotherapy of neuropsychiatric disturbances, in *Brain Injury Medicine: Principles and Practice*, Zasler, N.D., Katz, D.I., and Zafonte, R.D., Eds., Demos, New York, 2006, p. 963.
46. Baguley, I.J., Cooper, J., and Felmingham, K., Aggressive behavior following traumatic brain injury: How common is common? *J. Head Trauma Rehabil.*, 21, 45, 2006.
47. Wood, R.L. and Liossi, C., Neuropsychological and neurobehavioral correlates of aggression following traumatic brain injury. *J. Neuropsychiatr. Clin. Neurosci.*, 18, 333, 2006.
48. Greve, K.W., Sherwin, E., Stanford, M.S., et al., Personality and neurocognitive correlates of impulsive aggression in long-term survivors of severe traumatic brain injury. *Brain Inj.*, 15, 255, 2001.
49. Grafman, J., Schwab, K., Warden, D., et al., Frontal lobe injuries, violence, and aggression: A report of the Vietnam Head Injury Study. *Neurology*, 46, 1231, 1996.
50. Kreutzer, J.S., Marwitz, J.H., and Witol, A.D., Interrelationships between crime, substance abuse, and aggressive behaviors among persons with traumatic brain injury. *Brain Inj.*, 9, 757, 1995.
51. Diaz, F.G., Traumatic brain injury and criminal behavior. *Med. Law*, 14, 131, 1995.
52. Buss, A.H. and Warren, W.L., *Aggression Questionnaire*, Western Psychological Services, Los Angeles, CA, 2000.
53. Buss, A.H. and Durkee, A., An inventory for assessing different kinds of hostility. *J. Cons. Psychol.*, 21, 343, 1957.
54. Spielberger, C.D., *Manual for the State–Trait Anger Expression Inventory*, Psychological Assessment Resources, Odessa, FL, 1988.
55. Spielberger, C.D., *State–Trait Anger Expression Inventory-2, Professional Manual*, Psychological Assessment Resources, Odessa, FL, 1999.
56. Sandel, M.E., Delmonico, R., and Kotch, M.J., Sexuality, reproduction and neuroendocrine disorders following TBI, in *Brain Injury Medicine: Principles and Practice*, Zasler, N.D., Katz, D.I., and Zafonte, R.D., Eds., Demos, New York, 2006, p. 673.
57. Hibbard, M.R., Gordon, W.A., Flanagan, S., et al., Sexual dysfunction after traumatic brain injury. *NeuroRehabilitation*, 15, 107, 2000.
58. Sandel, M.E., Williams, K.S., Dellapietra, L., et al., Sexual functioning following traumatic brain injury. *Brain Inj.*, 10, 719, 1996.
59. Simpson, G., Blaszczynski, A., and Hodgkinson, A., Sex offending as a psychosocial sequela of traumatic brain injury. *J. Head Trauma Rehabil.*, 14, 567, 1999.
60. Langevin, R., Sexual offenses in traumatic brain injury. *Brain Cogn.*, 60, 206, 2006.
61. Johnson, C., Knight, C., and Alderman, N., Challenges associated with the definition and assessment of inappropriate sexual behavior amongst individuals with an acquired neurological impairment. *Brain Inj.*, 20, 687, 2006.
62. Cole, S., Facing the challenges of sexual abuse in persons with disabilities. *J. Sex. Disabil.*, 7, 71, 1986.
63. Dawson, D.R., Cantanzaro, A.M., Firestone, J., et al., Changes in coping style following traumatic brain injury and their relationship to productivity status. *Brain Cogn.*, 60, 214, 2006.

64. Anson, K. and Ponsford, J., Coping and emotional adjustment following traumatic brain injury. *J. Head Trauma Rehabil.*, 21, 248, 2006.
65. Wood, R.L. and Rutterford, N.A., Demographic and cognitive predictors of long-term psychosocial outcome following traumatic brain injury. *J. Int. Neuropsychol. Soc.*, 12, 350, 2006.
66. Whitnall, L.L., McMillan, T.M., Murray, G.D., et al., Disability in young people and adults after head injury: 5–7 year followup of a prospective cohort study. *J. Neurol. Neurosurg. Psychiatry*, 77, 640, 2006.
67. Sternberg, R., The nature of mental abilities. *Am. Psychol.*, 34, 214, 1979.
68. Gardner, H., *Frames of Mind: The Theory of Multiple Intelligences*, Basic Books, New York, 1983.
69. Goleman, D., *Emotional Intelligence: Why It Can Matter More Than I.Q.*, Bantam Books, New York, 1995.
70. Damasio, A.R., *Descartes' Error: Emotion, Reason and the Human Brain*, G.P. Putnam, New York, 1994.
71. Harlow, J.M., Recovery from the passage of an iron bar through the head. *Publ. Mass. Med. Soc.*, 2, 327, 1848.
72. *Emotional Intelligence in Everyday Life: A Scientific Inquiry*, Ciarrochi, J., Forgas, J.P., and Mayer, J.D., Eds., Psychology Press, Philadelphia, PA, 2001.
73. Adolphs, R. and Damasio, A., The interaction of affect and cognition: A neurobiological perspective, in *The Handbook of Affect and Social Cognition*, Forgas, J.P., Ed., Erlbaum, Mahwah, NJ, 2001.
74. Bar-On, R., Emotional intelligence and self-actualization, in *Emotional Intelligence in Everyday Life: A Scientific Inquiry*, Ciarrochi, J., Forgas, J.P., and Mayer, J.D., Eds., Psychology Press, Philadelphia, PA, 2001, p. 82.
75. Wilson, B.A., Alderman, N., Burgess, P.W., et al., *Behavioral Assessment of the Dysexecutive Syndrome*, Thames Valley Test Company, Bury St. Edmunds, UK, 1996.
76. Bar-On, R., *Bar-On Emotional Quotient Inventory: Technical Manual*, Multi-Health Systems, North Tonawanda, NY, 1997.
77. Sternberg, R.J., Measuring the intelligence of an idea: How intelligent is the idea of emotional intelligence? in *Emotional Intelligence in Everyday Life: A Scientific Inquiry*, Ciarrochi, J., Forgas, J.P., and Mayer, J.D., Eds., Psychology Press, Philadelphia, PA, 2001, p. 187.
78. Taylor, G.J., Low emotional intelligence and mental illness, in *Emotional Intelligence in Everyday Life: A Scientific Inquiry*, Ciarrochi, J., Forgas, J.P., and Mayer, J.D., Eds., Psychology Press, Philadelphia, PA, 2001, p. 67.
79. Bloom, D.R., Levin, H.S., Ewing-Cobbs, L., et al., Lifetime and novel psychiatric disorders after pediatric traumatic brain injury. *J. Am. Acad. Child Adolesc. Psychiatry*, 40, 572, 2001.
80. Kirkwood, M., Janusz, J., Yeates, K.O., et al., Prevalence and correlates of depressive symptoms following traumatic brain injuries in children. *Neuropsychol. Dev. Cogn. Sect. C Child Neuropsychol.*, 6, 195, 2000.
81. Max, J.E., Lindgren, S.D., Robin, D.A., et al., Traumatic brain injury in children and adolescents: Psychiatric disorders in the second three months. *J. Nerv. Ment. Dis.*, 185, 394, 1997.
82. Max, J.E., Robin, D.A., Lindgren, S.D., et al., Traumatic brain injury in children and adolescents: Psychiatric disorders at two years. *J. Am. Acad. Child Adol. Psychiatry*, 36, 1278, 1997.
83. Luis, C.A. and Mittenberg, W., Mood and anxiety disorders following pediatric traumatic brain injury: A prospective study. *J. Clin. Exp. Neuropsychol.*, 24, 270, 2002.
84. Max, J.E., Castillo, C.S., Robin, D.A., et al., Posttraumatic stress symptomatology after childhood traumatic brain injury. *J. Nerv. Ment. Dis.*, 186, 589, 1998.
85. Mather, F.J., Tate, R.L., and Hannan, T.J., Posttraumatic stress disorder in children following road traffic accidents: A comparison of those with and without mild traumatic brain injury. *Brain Inj.*, 17, 1077, 2003.
86. Vasa, R.A., Grados, M., Slomine, B., et al., Neuroimaging correlates of anxiety after pediatric traumatic brain injury. *Biol. Psychiatry*, 55, 208, 2004.
87. Reynolds, W.M., *Adolescent Psychopathology Scale: Administration and Interpretation Manual*, Psychological Assessment Resources, Odessa, FL, 1998.
88. Reynolds, C.R. and Camphaus, R.W., *Behavior Assessment System for Children*, 2nd edition, *Manual*, AGS Publishing, Circle Pines, MN, 2004.
89. Butcher, J.N., Williams, C.L., Graham, J.R., et al., *Minnesota Multiphasic Personality Inventory-Adolescent: Manual for Administration, Scoring and Interpretation*, University of Minnesota Press, Minneapolis, MN, 1992.

90. Marks, P.A., Seeman, W., and Haller, D., *The Actuarial Use of the MMPI with Adolescents and Adults*, Oxford University Press, New York, 1974.

91. Archer, R.P. and Klinefelter, D., Relationships between *MMPI* codetypes and MAC scale elevations in adolescent psychometric samples. *J. Pers. Assess.*, 58, 149, 1992.

92. March, J.S., *Multidimensional Anxiety Scale for Children, Technical Manual*, Multi-Health Systems Inc., North Tonawanda, NY, 1997.

93. Berndt, D.J. and Kaiser, C.F., *Multidepression Inventory for Children: Manual*, Western Psychological Services, Los Angeles, CA, 1996.

94. Spielberger, C.D., *State–Trait Anxiety Inventory for Children (STAIC): Professional Manual*, Mind Garden, Redwood City, CA, 1973.

95. Max, J.E., Children and adolescents, in *Textbook of Traumatic Brain Injury*, Silver, J.M., McAllister, T.W., and Yudofsky, S.C., Eds., American Psychiatric Press, Washington, D.C., 2005, p. 77.

96. Max, J.E., Robertson, B.A.M., and Lansing, A.E., The phenomenology of personality change due to traumatic brain injury in children and adolescents. *J. Neuropsychiatr. Clin. Neurosci.*, 13, 161, 2001.

97. Ganesalingam, K., Sanson, A., Anderson, V., et al., Self-regulation and social and behavioral functioning following childhood traumatic brain injury. *J. Int. Neuropsychol. Soc.*, 12, 609, 2006.

98. Weddell, R.A. and Leggett, J.A., Factors triggering relatives' judgments of personality change after traumatic brain injury. *Brain Inj.*, 20, 1221, 2006.

99. Wade, S.L., Gerry Taylor, H., Yeates, K.O., et al., Long-term parental and family adaptation following pediatric brain injury. *J. Pediatr. Psychol.*, 31, 1072, 2006.

100. Andrews, T., Rose, F.D., and Johnson, D.A., Social and behavioural effects of traumatic brain injury in children. *Brain Inj.*, 12, 133, 1988.

101. Teichner, G., Golden, C.J., and Giannaris, W.J., A multimodal approach to treatment of aggression in a severely brain-injured adolescent. *Rehabil. Nurs.*, 24, 207, 1999.

102. Harper, D.C., Social psychology of difference: Stigma, spread, and stereotypes in childhood. *Rehabil. Psychol.*, 44, 131, 1999.

103. Donders, J. and Ballard, E., Psychological adjustment characteristics of children before and after moderate to severe traumatic brain injury. *J. Head Trauma Rehabil.*, 11, 67, 1996.

104. Ris, M.D. and Noll, R.B., Long-term neurobehavioral outcome in pediatric brain-tumor patients: Review and methodological critique. *J. Clin. Exp. Neuropsychol.*, 16, 21, 1994.

105. Landry, S.H., Swank, P., Stuebing, K., et al., Social competence in young children with inflicted traumatic brain injury. *Dev. Neuropsychol.*, 26, 707, 2004.

106. Janusz, J.A., Kirkwood, M.W., Yeates, K.O., et al., Social problem-solving skills in children with traumatic brain injury: Long-term outcomes and prediction of social competence. *Child Neuropsychol.*, 8, 179, 2002.

107. Stancin, T., Taylor, H.G., Thompson, G.H., et al., Acute psychosocial impact of pediatric orthopedic trauma with and without accompanying brain injuries. *J. Trauma*, 45, 1031, 1998.

108. Lezak, M.D., Living with the characterologically altered brain-injured patient. *J. Clin. Psychiatry*, 39, 592, 1978.

109. Anderson, M.I., Parmenter, T.R., and Mok, M., The relationships between neurobehavioral problems of severe traumatic brain injury (TBI), family functioning and the psychological well-being of the spouse/caregiver: Path model analysis. *Brain Inj.*, 16, 743, 2002.

110. Hora, E.C. and de Sousa, R.M., Effect of the behavioral disorders of victims of traumatic brain injury on the family caregiver. *Rev. Lat. Am. Enfermagem.*, 13, 93, 2005.

111. Katz, S., Kravetz, S., and Grynbaum, F., Wives' coping flexibility, time since husbands' injury and the perceived burden of wives of men with traumatic brain injury. *Brain Inj.*, 19, 59, 2005.

112. Ergh, T.C., Rapport, L.J., Coleman, R.D., et al., Predictors of caregiver and family functioning following traumatic brain injury: Social support moderates caregiver distress. *J. Head Trauma Rehabil.*, 17, 155, 2002.

113. Winstanley, J., Simpson, G., Tate, R., et al., Early indicators and contributors to psychological distress in relatives during rehabilitation following severe traumatic brain injury: Findings from the Brain Injury Outcome Study. *J. Head Trauma Rehabil.*, 21, 53, 2006.

114. Perlesz, A., Kinsella, G., and Crowe, S., Psychological distress and family satisfaction following traumatic brain injury: Injured individuals and their primary, secondary, and tertiary carers. *J. Head Trauma Rehabil.*, 15, 909, 2000.

115. Seel, R.T., Kreutzer, J.S., and Sander, A.M., Concordance of patients' and family members' ratings of neurobehavioral functioning after traumatic brain injury. *Arch. Phys. Med. Rehabil.*, 78, 1254, 1997.

116. Struchen, M.A., Atchison, T.B., Roebuck, T.M., et al., A multidimensional measure of caregiving appraisal: Validation of the Caregiver Appraisal Scale in traumatic brain injury. *J. Head Trauma Rehabil.*, 17, 132, 2002.

117. Degeneffe, C.E., Family caregiving in traumatic brain injury. *Health Soc. Work*, 26, 257, 2001.

118. Brzuzy, S. and Speziali, B.A., Persons with traumatic brain injuries in their families: Living arrangements and well-being postinjury. *Soc. Work Health Care*, 26, 77, 1997.

119. Hibbard, M.R., Cantor, J., Charatz, H., et al., Peer support in the community: Initial findings of a mentoring program for individuals with traumatic brain injury in their families. *J. Head Trauma Rehabil.*, 17, 112, 2002.

120. Stanton, B.R., Does family functioning affect outcome in children with neurological disorders? *Pediatr. Rehabil.*, 3, 193, 1999.

121. Montgomery, V., Oliver, R., Reisner, A., et al., The effect of severe traumatic brain injury on the family. *J. Trauma.*, 52, 1121, 2002.

122. Wade, S.L., Taylor, H.G., Drotar, D., et al., Family burden and adaptation during the initial year after traumatic brain injury in children. *Pediatrics*, 102, 110, 1998.

123. Aitken, M.E., Mele, N., and Barrett, K.W., Recovery of injured children: Parent perspectives on family needs. *Arch. Phys. Med. Rehabil.*, 85, 467, 2004.

124. Aitken, M.E., Korehbandi, P., Parnell, D., et al., Experiences from the development of a comprehensive family support program for pediatric trauma and rehabilitation patients. *Arch. Phys. Med. Rehabil.*, 86, 175, 2005.

125. Gillen, R., Tennen, H., Affleck, G., et al., Distress, depressive symptoms, and depressive disorder among caregivers of patients with brain injury. *J. Head Trauma Rehabil.*, 13, 31, 1998.

126. Harris, J.K., Godfrey, H.P., Partridge, F.M., et al., Caregiver depression following traumatic brain injury (TBI): A consequence of adverse effects on family members? *Brain Inj.*, 15, 223, 2001.

127. Mintz, M.C., van Horn, K.R., and Lavine, M.J., Developmental models of social cognition in assessing the role of family stress in relatives predictions following traumatic brain injury. *Brain Inj.*, 9, 173, 1995.

128. Douglas, J.M. and Spellacy, F.J., Correlates of depression in adults with severe traumatic brain injury and their carers. *Brain Inj.*, 14, 71, 2000.

129. Kreutzer, J.S., Seel, R.T., and Marwitz, J.H., *Neurobehavioral Functioning Inventory*, The Psychological Corporation, San Antonio, TX, 1999.

8 Neurobehavioral Analysis and Treatment Planning following Traumatic Brain Injury

INTRODUCTION

The reader has seen in the first seven chapters of this text a systematic development of the medical dataset through which information is collected in order to proceed with the neurobehavioral analysis. Neurobehavioral analysis is a term of art describing the analytical procedures used by the neuropsychiatric examiner to summarize an examination of a patient in order to provide effective treatment planning and assistance. It is suggested that the components of the neurobehavioral analysis include all items developed in the first seven chapters of this text, unless they have been adequately performed by other qualified persons, and that data are available to the neuropsychiatric examiners at the time they assess the patients following traumatic brain injury (TBI). For instance, the dataset for neurobehavioral analysis should in most cases include (1) a complete neuropsychiatric history, (2) a neuropsychiatric mental status examination, (3) a neurological examination, (4) neuroimaging, (5) a standardized neurocognitive assessment, (6) a standardized behavioral assessment, and (7) a review of the ambulance report, police records, emergency department records, hospital records, rehabilitation records, and outpatient treatment records that were developed at the time of the accident and thereafter. This chapter will focus upon the analysis of these various elements as they comprise the dataset following the examination. The schema described in Chapter 8 is neither exhaustive nor required, and it depends upon the particular medical orientation of the examiners as to how they wish to use these suggestions. For instance, a physiatrist may take an approach different than a neuropsychiatrist, and those approaches in turn will probably be different from that of a neurologist. Obviously, a neuropsychologist will have an approach different from that of most medical professions. That is not to say that one is better than the other, but it is still suggested that the seven elements above be included in the assessment. If they are not developed by the examiner at the time of his or her examination, the data should be sought from other sources to supplant the examiner's analysis.

ANALYSIS OF THE DATA

THE INJURY RECORDS

It is suggested that the neuropsychiatric examiner obtain the police record if the brain injury was caused by a reportable accident. In worker's compensation cases, it is best to obtain the employer's report of injury, which is required virtually in all states. Thus, motor vehicle accidents in the United States causing significant injury to others are almost always evaluated first by a police entity. If the patient was injured in a criminal action, there should be a record of the investigation as well. This record should be examined carefully to determine what biomechanical factors may have played a role in the injury to the patient. Many times this will have little relevance to a treating physician.

However, it is a good idea to perform this in case the treating physician is called as a fact witness in litigation. If the purposes of the brain injury examination are for forensic use, then at all times the police record should be scrutinized. For instance, an individual may be claiming a substantial brain injury, and by examination of the police report one can find that the patient was sitting in his vehicle at a stop light when his bumper was tapped by a vehicle behind, yet he was allowed to drive his vehicle away from the scene to his home. This, of course, would be consistent with no probability of causing a brain injury. If, on the other hand, the police record indicates that the individual's vehicle was struck from behind with force sufficient to fracture the driver's seat, then obviously severe force was supplied to the patient's vehicle.

It is wise to develop a treatment timeline of a patient when brain trauma is suspected. This enables the neuropsychiatric examiner to develop a comprehensive understanding of the injury factors as well as the various steps in the treatment process that the patient has experienced. With that in mind, the next record to scrutinize carefully is that of the emergency medical squad or EMT personnel. Within that document, the examiner will generally find the Glasgow Coma Scale score (GCS). It may not be stated explicitly; depending on how the records are written and printed, instead of GCS, it may merely say "EMV." The reader will recall from Chapter 1 that the three subcomponents of the GCS are eyes, verbal, and motor function. For instance, if the neuropsychiatric examiner sees in the EMT records "GCS = 10," then it should be understood that at the time of the accident, the patient had a substantially abnormal presentation to the emergency medical technicians. Other trauma records generated by EMTs may state $E = 3$, $V = 4$, and $M = 4$. This, of course, would translate to a GCS score of 11. The reader is referred to Chapter 1 for the scoring and classification of the GCS.

Another important variable often displayed in the initial emergency medical squad records is the Revised Trauma Score (RTS). This score is composed of data from the GCS, systolic blood pressure, and respiratory rate. The reader is referred to Table 8.1 for a schema of the clinical neuropsychiatric data collection and review, and Table 8.2 indicating the components and scoring details of the RTS. The RTS is scored from 12 (best possible score) to 0 (worst possible score). As the reader will recall from Chapter 1, the GCS is scored from a low of 3 to a high of 15.

The Ambulance Run Sheet (ARS) should be evaluated further to see if the GCS score was determined on more than one occasion. If the patient is traveling a great distance, or if the patient is transported by air, frequently serial recordings of the GCS are made. This enables the neuropsychiatric

---

TABLE 8.1

Schema of the Clinical Neuropsychiatric Data Collection and Review

Police report	Review for level of force to patient vehicle and whether extraction required. If criminal acts caused injury, what level of force was used?
Employer injury report	Was the injury by fall, explosion, battery, crush, etc.?
Ambulance report	Review for level of consciousness, Glasgow Coma Scale (GCS).
Emergency department	Review for GCS, Trauma Score, and level of mental/cognitive function. What injuries were documented; what is the result of neuroimaging?
Hospital record	Review ICU records, neurosurgical/neurological consultation, and any subsequent neuroimaging. Is there evidence of secondary causes of brain injury?
Rehabilitation record	Review deficits at admission and "Rancho" level at discharge. Review reports of speech/language, occupation therapy, and physical therapy assessments. Was neuropsychological assessment performed?
Outpatient treatment	Review continuing treatments by physiatrists, neurologists, psychiatrists, or psychologists. Is speech/language therapy still in place?
Neuropsychiatric examination	Review history, mental status examination, neurological examination, brain imaging, standardized mental assessment, and laboratory testing

TABLE 8.2
Revised Trauma Score

Glasgow Coma Scale (GCS)	Systolic Blood Pressure (SBP)	Respiratory Rate (RR)	Score
13–15	>89	10–29	4
9–12	76–89	>29	3
6–8	50–75	6–9	2
4–5	1–49	1–5	1
3	0	0	0

Note: RTS score = GCS + SBP + RR; best score = 12, worse score = 0.

examiner to determine if there was an improvement or deterioration of function in the patient during transport. For instance, if the initial GCS score = 13, and by the time the patient arrived at the receiving hospital it had deteriorated to a score of 7, further analysis would be required to determine why that occurred. On the other hand, it is not uncommon for a GCS score of 13 at the scene to have improved to a GCS score of 15 by the time the patient arrives at an emergency department. This, of course, would indicate improvement rather than deterioration. The causes of primary trauma to the brain, with resulting sequelae, have been discussed thoroughly in Chapters 1 and 2. With regard to secondary brain injury (see Chapter 1), the ARS or the emergency medical squad records should be reviewed carefully to see if the patient required intubation, developed respiratory failure, had significant bleeding, was hypotensive, required intravenous fluids, required pressor agents, or underwent other interventions that would indicate the potential for secondary injury. Some neurotrauma centers in sophisticated urban centers are in contact with emergency medical personnel by voice, and a trauma physician may provide orders to the personnel en route. Where this is implemented, it has been shown to reduce mortality in almost every country where it has been instituted.[1,2] For instance, hypotension and hypoxia in the field are proven secondary injury insults that are associated with poor outcomes. Hypotension is considerably more detrimental to the brain than hypoxia, and both of these should be treated and prevented if possible.[3] The records should be scrutinized further to determine if the pupil size was obtained before the administration of sedatives or paralytic drugs. Paralytic drugs would be used for intubation in most instances. It is also important from a factual basis to determine if extraction was required. This should be evident either in the police records or the EMT records. That is not so the neuropsychiatric examiner can be a reconstruction specialist, but again, it supplies useful information to determine whether the trauma was sufficient to have produced the complaints the patient expresses. In other words, it is another form of clinical correlation. The third record to review in this sequence is that of the emergency department. Upon arrival in the emergency room, it is recommended to utilize the Advanced Trauma Life Support (ATLS) protocol following the recommendations of the American College of Surgeons.[4] This protocol stresses a systematic approach to the evaluation of trauma injury. Airway, breathing, and circulation are assessed first. Once fluid resuscitation is addressed, a neurologic assessment is made by using the GCS score, pupillary exam, and lateralizing signs. Again, this should be done preferably before any sedation or paralytic agent being used. A lateral cervical spine and chest x-ray should be performed. A computed tomography (CT) scan of the head should be performed as rapidly as possible in any patient with suspected or confirmed loss of consciousness, skull fracture, or focal neurological examination. If the GCS score is less than 15, it is recommended that a CT scan of the head be obtained. As noted in Chapter 5, CT scanning is the diagnostic procedure of choice for the initial assessment of intracranial injury. It will accurately demonstrate acute blood, and it is able to identify most skull fractures. Current ATLS protocol recommends that patients with mild TBI who are neurologically normal with a negative head CT can be discharged home safely.[4] Other patients, especially those with altered mental status or collections of blood on their CT scans, should be admitted for observation and possible serial CT imaging. Patients with isolated skull fractures and normal neurological exams can possibly be discharged to home; however, this is a controversial disposition, and it should be assessed on a case-by-case basis.[5]

With regard to emergency department records, it is important to determine if there has been a change, either up or down, in the severity level of the GCS score. Obviously, a deteriorating GCS is important, and the records should be scrutinized carefully to determine the cause for this and the subsequent interventions made. Other useful information in the emergency department record includes the presence of comorbid conditions. Many persons who sustain head trauma also sustain significant orthopedic and abdominal trauma (see Chapters 1 and 2). In cases of motor vehicle accident, on-the-job injuries, and injuries occurring under the auspices of the U.S. Department of Transportation, blood alcohol levels and urine drug screens will usually be obtained. The neuro-psychiatric examiner should review the records for the presence of these. Recall the discussions in Chapter 5, and the reader is referred to the CT imaging demonstrating evidence of acute contusion and blood. The CT scan of the head remains the single most important neuroimaging study to obtain in a patient with a significant head injury.[2,6] Most neuroimaging today is being stored on computer disc (CD), and thus it is easy for the neuropsychiatric examiner to order a CD of imaging and review it himself or herself. Recall from Chapter 1 that if a lesion is found on a CT scan following trauma to the head the patient is scored as a moderate head injury even if the GCS score is greater than 12. The neuropsychiatric examiners should obtain their own neuroimaging and then compare these findings to the original trauma neuroimaging.

After the patient leaves the emergency department, if admitted to hospital, there is variance in how the patient receives care. Depending on the level of care available, the patient may be transferred to a general surgical unit, specialized trauma unit, neurosurgical intensive care unit (NICU), or trauma center. The level of hospital care and whether or not neurosurgeons are available at the facility will often dictate the care setting and care received. Level I trauma centers in the United States have the availability of immediate neurosurgical care, whereas lesser specialized centers generally must transfer patients for expert neurosurgical assistance.

The neuropsychiatric examiner should review the hospital record carefully. Operative therapy is indicated in patients where intracerebral collections are exerting a significant mass effect. Traditionally, this has been defined as greater than 5 mm of midline shift.[7] It is further recommended that epidural hemorrhages greater than 30 cc in volume should be evacuated regardless of whether the patient is symptomatic. Those patients with a GCS score less than 9 with associated pupillary dilation and an epidural hematoma should undergo decompression as soon as possible. Intracerebral contusion may be life-threatening. Patients with contusions who demonstrate progressive neurologic deterioration secondary to the contusion, or are found to have refractory intracranial hypertension, should be treated operatively. Comatose patients with frontal or temporal contusions greater than 20 cc in volume with a midline shift of 5 mm or cisternal compression on CT scan and those with a contusion greater than 50 cc in volume should be treated operatively. These numbers are general guidelines.[4] Open depressed skull fractures greater than the thickness of the skull with evidence of dural laceration should be operated acutely to lower the risk of infection. Closed skull fractures can be managed nonoperatively.

A review of the hospital records often indicates that the patient has had placed an intracerebral pressure (ICP) monitoring device for the treatment of elevated intracerebral pressure. Using the Guidelines for the Management of Severe Traumatic Brain Injury, ICP monitoring is appropriate in patients with GCS scores below or equal to 8 with a head CT demonstrating hemorrhages, contusions, edema, or compressed basilar cisterns.[8] Interestingly, there are no significant prospective research data to this date demonstrating that ICP monitoring improves clinical outcomes. However, there is considerable evidence favoring its use in the management of patients with severe TBI based on retrospective series and trauma data bank studies.[4] Controversy remains regarding the efficacy of ICP monitoring versus empiric therapies for head injuries (e.g., mannitol administration).[4] Regardless, the neuropsychiatric examiner will find numerous hospital records of patients indicating that they have received ICP monitoring. Many neurosurgeons follow the recommendations of Narayan et al., which define those patients likely to develop ICP elevations.[9] Be that as it may, ventriculostomy (external ventricular drain) insertion is the ICP monitoring procedure of choice in adults with severe TBI. It permits both monitoring of pressure by transduction of a continuous flow column from the ventricles, and it also permits cerebral spinal fluid drainage, usually into the abdomen. Sometimes fiberoptic monitors are used for determining ICP, but they do not allow CSF drainage. A threshold of 20–25 mmHg can be used to define an elevated ICP.[4]

The neuropsychiatric examiner should review medical records to determine if mannitol was used for lowering ICP. It is the mainstay in this regard presently.[4] It works by dehydrating the brain, especially in areas of cerebral edema, and by altering cerebral viscosity. Unfortunately, it loses some of its efficacy with time, and it has some potentially serious side effects such as renal failure and pulmonary edema. Hyperventilation was advocated in past years to lower ICP. However, current neurosurgical recommendations are modest in suggesting its use. Hyperventilation functions to lower ICP by causing cerebral vasoconstriction. This reduces ICP, but the secondary side effect can be an increase in cerebral ischemia. Current neurosurgical recommendations are for avoidance of the use of prophylactic hyperventilation in the first 24 h after severe TBI. It is reserved for treatment of patients with established ICP elevations between 30–35 mmHg, and more aggressive hyperventilation is reserved for those patients with refractory ICP elevation and in those demonstrating neurologic extremis.[8] In a few cases, the neuropsychiatric examiners may notice that a decompressive craniectomy has been performed. If the person is refractory to attempts to lower ICP, the neurosurgeon may decompress the brain by unilaterally or bilaterally opening large areas of skull with duraplasty. If the reader will review the gunshot neuroimaging figures in Chapter 5, a left craniectomy for decompression can be noted.

The examiner may notice in the neurosurgical ICU other forms of treatment to assist patients following severe TBI. For instance, it has become the mainstay in the management of severe TBI to maintain cerebral perfusion pressure above 60 mmHg in patients with elevated ICP. Intravenous fluids should be isotonic solutions such as normal saline. Dextrose-containing solutions should be avoided, as hyperglycemia has been shown to be associated with worse outcomes in TBI.[10] Similarly, the surgical team usually avoids glucose abnormalities, as these are secondary insults to the brain. Sodium values must be followed carefully, as it is not unusual for the syndrome of inappropriate antidiuretic hormone producing diabetes insipidus to occur. Early posttraumatic seizures may present within the first 7 days after TBI. These are more common in younger people, and their risk of occurrence increases in the presence of hematomas, contusion, prolonged unconsciousness, and focal neurologic signs.[4] Current recommendations are for prophylactic treatment of seizures in the TBI patient undergoing craniotomy, or at risk for seizures, with phenytoin or carbamazepine for one week. The examiner should review records to see if these pharmaceutical products were used. Further exploration of the records should be undertaken to determine if intravenous nutrition was used. Deep venous thrombosis (DVT) is a common complication, and review of the records for methods to reduce DVT should be undertaken. The neuropsychiatric examiner may note that jugular venous oxygen saturation was monitored. This is used in an effort to detect increases in oxygen consumption and as a result, globally increase oxygen extraction by the brain. This is measured by placing a catheter tip (equipped with a fiberoptic monitor) in the dominant jugular bulb, and it is reserved for those patients who have sustained severe TBI. Current recommendations are to maintain jugular venous saturation between 55% and 75%. Desaturations below 50% are associated with significant increases in patient mortality.[4] More recently, various neurosurgical intensive care centers routinely use methods to measure cerebral blood flow. These are still considered experimental techniques in the management of severe TBI, but the neuropsychiatric examiner may find evidence of these in certain cases. These include intermittent measurement techniques such as xenon (including inhalational, intravenous, and xenon, or CT scanning), nitrous oxide saturation techniques, single-photon emission computed tomography (SPECT), and

PET scanning, gradient echo-planar imaging (EPI) using magnetic resonance imaging (MRI) technology, and transcranial doppler (TCD) monitoring.[4]

Once the patient is removed from the intensive care unit (ICU) and transferred to the hospital floor, the records should be reviewed to determine what ancillary therapies were required, as these may be important indicators of the severity and significance of TBI. For instance, was speech–language therapy required? Was there a need for occupational therapy? Was physical therapy required due to immobilization syndrome, hemiparesis, spasticity, or orthopedic injury? Was psychiatric intervention required because of delirium, severe behavioral difficulties, agitation, or aggression? Was neurological assessment or neurophysiologic monitoring required due to peripheral nerve injuries or seizures? What was the patient's level of self-care and ambulation?

If the patient has been severely injured, the rehabilitation specialists will play a pivotal role in the treatment of those sustaining TBI. Moreover, the examiner will notice in the hospital record that the rehabilitation specialist has been consulted to assist with discharge planning for rehabilitation. Rehabilitation has been thought to be optimal if started early rather than later, with resultant improved mobility and decreased length of acute rehabilitation stay.[11] The neuropsychiatric examiner will notice that acute rehabilitation for patients with severe TBI starts in the comatose and early arousal states with goals of preventing orthopedic and visceral complications. Immobilization syndromes are frequent following lengthy coma. Subsequent inpatient rehabilitation is designed to help impairments recover and to teach patients to compensate for their disabilities. There is often a wealth of information within the rehabilitation records. In addition to the special needs already cited, it is important to determine if the patient required audiometry, vision screening, and examination for ability to drive a motor vehicle. Brain injury physiatrists are very skilled at determining cognition levels, and these data usually are entered into the patient record on the Rancho Scale (see Chapter 1). The examiner can detect what skill deficits are present in the TBI patient during rehabilitation and what activities of daily living are the most impaired. Further review of rehabilitation techniques can be found in Chapter 10 of this text where forensic issues and outcome issues are discussed. The neuropsychiatric examiner should review carefully the nursing record during rehabilitation, as this often provides a significant database for the neuropsychiatric examiners to use during evaluation.[12] Also, issues during cognitive rehabilitation are important to detect. Usually cognitive rehabilitation can be divided generally into two levels: functional and generic. At the functional level, the patient is trained to use activities necessary for the orderly execution of practical skills of daily living. These include dressing, preparing meals, getting items off a shelf, going up and down stairs, etc. At the second level, generic cognitive skills focus on specific mental domains such as attention, memory, and executive function.[13,14]

THE NEUROPSYCHIATRIC EXAMINATION DATABASE

History

The reader may wish to review Chapter 3 at this point. The comprehensive neuropsychiatric history in adult or child brain injury assessment is extremely important. It is now time for the examiner to return to the history obtained, review it carefully, and catalog the post-TBI neurocognitive and behavioral symptoms expressed by the patient or their family. The posttrauma symptoms should be reviewed with specific detail paid to the cognitive and behavioral complaints. Potential risk to self or others should not be overlooked. It is also important to review what outpatient treatments have transpired since the person left the emergency department, hospital, or rehabilitation unit. In particular, the neuropsychiatric examiner should review carefully the current ability for activities of daily living. Nothing provides greater information regarding real-world function than how an individual is able to perform the usual and customary activities that we all use in our lives for grooming, self-preservation, feeding, toileting, occupational endeavors, etc. Past medical history should be reviewed carefully, as it is necessary to distinguish posttrauma difficulties from those that occurred before trauma.

Moreover, once a TBI develops, it may become comorbid with other serious pre-injury difficulties such as diabetes, cardiovascular diseases or prior orthopedic injuries. The past neuropsychiatric history may reveal evidence for pre-injury childhood attention deficit disorder, pre-injury antisocial behaviors, pre-injury substance abuse, or pre-injury learning disability. Developing a family history helps determine if there are genetic loadings. For instance, a prior family history of Alzheimer's disease may be an important marker for the determination of apolipoprotein-E (see Chapter 1). As noted in Chapter 7, psychosocial difficulties are prominent following TBI. Also, it was learned in Chapter 7 that pre-injury psychosocial difficulties augment post-TBI psychosocial dysfunction when it occurs. As is true of any medical problem, it must be placed in context within the patient's social fabric. It is important to have a reasonable understanding of family dynamics, demographics, social, and occupational functioning, and other important aspects of the patient's social life in order to understand properly the impact of TBI upon the person and the person's environment. A careful examination of the review of systems is important. At this point, the examiner will determine current symptoms in all organ systems, as this is necessary to understand in order to judge the interplay between the TBI and the patient's overall health functioning.

Turning to the child, historical information is likewise very important. However, in contrast to the adult, the history analysis focuses upon the impact to the neurodeveloping youngster. As stressed earlier in this text, the neuropsychiatric examiners should review pre- and post-injury academic records where available. It may be necessary to obtain and review school records and any individualized educational plans that have been provided to the child since injury. These records will assist in the development of cognitive and behavioral baselines, but their use is even more critical for the longitudinal evaluation and recommendations regarding academic function and educational needs of the child. Further analysis is required of the child's activities of daily living. It is important to determine if these activities are consistent with the developmental level of the child and whether or not they are having a negative impact upon peer relationships and the child's role within his family. It is important at this point to review and analyze the past pediatric history, past pediatric neuropsychiatric history, and the family and social history of the child. In particular, the child with pre-injury learning disorders, pre-injury neurodevelopmental disorders, pre-injury academic difficulties, or learning impairments provides a particular challenge to the neuropsychiatric examiners. Has there been an augmentation of pre-injury difficulties as a result of the TBI? Is there a substantial genetic loading to this child, which may present itself as an additive disorder as the child ages? Is the child on a trajectory of declining academic performance that will reduce the child's effectiveness in the work force or in pursuing further academic attainment?

When examining the database for the child, it is necessary to take a neurodevelopmental approach rather than the more linear approach of the adult. The history since the accident should focus significantly upon academic performance, as this is the "work of the child." As noted in Chapter 6, there are many issues that may arise following TBI in a child that affect not only the education of the child but also the ability to educate the child. As was discussed in Chapters 3, 4, and 6, neurocognitive symptoms following TBI in the child play a very different role than similar disorders play in the rehabilitation or treatment of an older adolescent or adult. Recall the neuropsychiatric developmental history from Chapter 3 as well as the past pediatric history and past pediatric neuropsychiatric history. It is important to review these at the time one performs a data analysis following neuropsychiatric examination of a child. Further guidelines for examining the database of a child are included in Larsen's chapter.[15] Also, analysis of the child's activities of daily living is quite different than a similar analysis in the adult. In the preschool child, the analysis of daily activities will center primarily on play. It is important to review again whether the child had pre-injury learning difficulty or pre-injury psychiatric conditions. In the older child, it is important to determine whether attention deficit disorder was present with or without hyperactivity. The social history of the child plays substantially more importance in treatment planning than for the adult. By definition, the child is a dependent person, and without adequate parental, home, school, and other support systems, rehabilitation of the child following TBI is extraordinarily difficult at best.

Mental Status Examination

In Chapter 2, we explored the numerous neuropsychiatric and psychiatric conditions that may result following TBI in adults and children. In Chapter 4, we focused upon the mental and neurological examination of adults and children following TBI. Therefore, after the examiner has collected these data, a review of the findings is required. As was noted in Chapters 6 and 7, analysis of the neuropsychiatric mental status examination should be divided into cognitive and behavioral spheres. The examiner should review the notes and data acquired during the face-to-face examination and determine on a clinical basis which domains of cognitive and behavioral functions appear abnormal. With regard to the cognitive portions of the mental status examination first, the various domains of cognitive function should be reviewed including attention, speech and language, memory and orientation, visuospatial and constructional ability, executive function, and apparent intellectual capacity. The examiner should have described the patient's appearance, level of consciousness, and orientation. Obviously, a review of one's notes of the mental examination will provide only a rudimentary analysis of potential cognitive difficulties. As stressed throughout this text, it is necessary to measure neuropsychologically in order to quantify the deficits. At this point, the examiner will develop a qualitative determination of probable areas of cognitive concern. Then, as we shall see later, it will be important to clinically correlate these findings with neuropsychological data, neurological examination data, and neuroimaging data. An overall analysis of these various data will enable the examiner to describe the patient's cognitive deficits.[15–21]

Once the examiner has reviewed the cognitive data from the face-to-face mental examination, a second review should incorporate behavioral information. Did the examiner detect changes in affect and mood? Are there alterations in thought processing, content, or perception? Is there evidence that the individual being examined is at risk to oneself or to others? Is there a tone suggestive of aggressive tendencies? Are suicidal ideas or plans present? These issues are important to delineate, as they will also require clinical correlation with whatever behavioral measures were used, as outlined in Chapter 7.[17–19]

With regard to the child, the examiner should review cognitive data from the face-to-face mental examination in the same fashion as is done with an adult. Obviously, allowances have to be made for neurodevelopmental level and age of the child.[15,20] The cognitive domains of the child that were reviewed in Chapter 4 should be scrutinized carefully. These include attention, speech and language ability, memory and orientation level, visuospatial and constructional ability, executive function and apparent intellectual functioning. These data should be recorded and analyzed with specific measurements by neuropsychological assessment, neuroimaging, and physical examination to determine their clinical correlation.

The behavioral assessment of the child should focus upon those issues discussed previously in Chapter 4. These include affect and mood, and general motor behavior during the examination. As has been discussed previously, stability of mood in children usually becomes evident by age 2 or 3 years. Recall the simple questions of Weinberg et al. from Chapter 4.[21] Larsen also provides significant guidelines in this regard.[15]

Neurological Examination

The neurological examination will provide a wealth of data for the neuropsychiatric examiner to use in the neurobehavioral analysis. The absence of focal findings is good news for the patient. While it does not obviate the possibility that a mild TBI has occurred, it certainly will not correlate in most instances with severe brain trauma. On the other hand, if focal neurological deficits are present, the neuropsychiatric examiner must clinically correlate these with neuroimaging, neurocognitive, behavioral, and other data. It is probably wise to systematically review the neurological examination data much as it was reviewed in Chapter 4. It may be useful to the examiner to systematically go from top to bottom and attempt to clinically correlate any focal findings. For instance, if the patient demonstrates cranial nerve alteration, do these correlate with facial fractures, if they occurred? If visual deficits are present, do they fit a confrontational pattern consistent with a homonymous hemianopsia? Does that, in turn, correlate with neuroimaging lesions in the contralateral hemisphere or occipital lobe? While reviewing the motor examination, is there evidence of abnormal involuntary movements that correlate with subcortical or basal ganglia injury? If the patient has been injured in such a manner as to produce an upper motor neuron lesion, the examiner should suspect spasticity and hyperreflexia in the contralateral arm or leg or both. These findings are merely guides; as has been stressed earlier, the neuropsychiatric examiners are not expected to be, nor should they function as a neurologist. However, obvious focal neurological deficits must be clinically correlated with neuropsychiatric findings. A review of muscular coordination as well as gait abnormalities is important. These, of course, are focal neurological findings. Many persons following TBI have alterations of balance. Do these translate to tandem-walk dystaxia? Are there findings on balance assessment that may correlate with traumatic vestibular apparatus injury? It is important at this point to review the prior work of our neuroscience colleagues. For instance, is there evidence within the injury examinations by neurosurgeons, neurologists, or physiatrists of focal neurological findings that may have abated or disappeared by the time the neuropsychiatric examiners complete their examination? It may be helpful at this point to review the adult neurological examination in Chapter 4.

If the examination is that of a child, the examiner should attempt to clinically correlate any focal neurological findings with other data developed within the assessment of the child. Are there neurological deficits in the child that have an impact upon sports activity, education, peer relationships, and future development? If the child has been injured substantially from a neurological standpoint, the assessment should be thorough in reviewing whether appropriate remediation steps have been taken and what special challenges these deficits present to parents, caregivers, and teachers. As stressed for the adult, the neuropsychiatric examiners are expected only to discern whether focal neurological deficits are present and then attempt to correlate these clinically with the remainder of the neuropsychiatric examination. Their treatment and remediation is best left to pediatric specialists in neurology, neurosurgery, physiatry, and neurobehavioral medicine.

Brain Neuroimaging

The overall goal of a neuropsychiatric review of brain imaging is simple. Can one see two general relationships and their clinical correlations? In the first instance, is there a clinical correlation between lesions found by neuroimaging during the current neuropsychiatric evaluation that compare and clinically correlate with lesions noted at the time of the original brain injury, usually noted by CT scan? In the second instance, do any lesions found during neuroimaging within the neuropsychiatric examination correlate clinically with neuropsychological deficits, neurological examination deficits, or cognitive and behavioral deficits? In order to answer these questions, it is necessary for the neuropsychiatric examiners to review, where possible, the original neuroimaging data at the time of the injury. That data should be included in the original injury records of the emergency department, hospital, or rehabilitation facility. With regard to neuroimaging obtained during the neuropsychiatric examination, it is necessary for the examiners to review the findings of neuroimaging with the particular person involved in its interpretation. This usually will consist of a radiologist, nuclear medicine physician, or neurologist specially trained in neuroimaging. This, of course, depends on whether the neuroimaging was structural or functional. Moreover, if electroencephalogram (EEG) analysis is used during the neuropsychiatric examination, it may be necessary to review that with the neurologist who interpreted the data.

Now we return to the differences between neuroimaging at the time of the injury versus neuroimaging at the time of the neuropsychiatric examination. There may have been an interval change between imaging, and if so, the neuropsychiatric examiner should make note. For instance, it would be expected that an epidural or subdural hematoma has resolved in most instances 2 years following injury. As noted in Chapter 5, posttraumatic changes may occur over time. Is there evidence that hemosiderin is present at prior lesion sites within an MRI obtained during the neuropsychiatric examination? Have contusions noted on CT scan at the time of the original injury now progressed to encephalomalacia? If findings on neuroimaging are present at the time of the neuropsychiatric examination, do they correlate clinically with the cognitive and behavioral data? At the time of the neuropsychiatric examination, particularly if it is being used for forensic purposes, the neuroimaging may be critically important for not only treatment planning and prognostic considerations, but it may also be necessary to assist the patient with a disability determination, worker's compensation finding, or application for Social Security Administration benefits.

It may be necessary to review again the findings in Chapter 5. It should be remembered that most acute brain trauma is imaged by CT. On the other hand, most remote examinations of cognitive status following brain trauma rely primarily on MRI. Also, the examiners should remember that the American College of Radiology guidelines finds little use for PET and SPECT imaging in TBI except in special circumstances. The reader may wish to review again those guidelines as expressed in Chapter 5. If the examiners choose to use PET or SPECT imaging during the neuropsychiatric assessment, the findings should clinically correlate with structural imaging. The weakness of most neuropsychiatric examinations using functional neuroimaging lies in the lack of clinical correlation. While this may not be highly significant in clinical examinations for treatment purposes, this lack of correlation is highly important in a forensic assessment. An EEG should be obtained by the neuropsychiatric examiners if there is any question of posttraumatic seizures or if the neuropsychiatric history reveals evidence of uncal fits, olfactory or gustatory paroxysmal episodes, or abrupt episodic alterations of consciousness. Any history of paroxysmal intermittent disturbances in awareness should probably be evaluated by EEG as well.[22]

Neurocognitive Measures

The examiner should have a close working relationship with a psychologist or neuropsychologist who has wide experience in the evaluation of persons who have sustained TBI. Most psychologists do not have this experience, and some neuropsychologists have limited experience and have worked mostly in stroke units or in pediatric neurodevelopmental units. Therefore, the neuropsychiatric examiner should carefully vet the qualifications of the psychologist. Once that has been obtained, it is mandatory that cognitive assessment includes a measurement of cognitive status by metrical means. If the neuropsychiatric examiner does not employ psychologists or does not have immediate access to psychologists, it is necessary to establish a working relationship with a psychologist off-site who can provide neurocognitive examination data to the neuropsychiatric examiner. As was discussed in Chapter 6, it is currently the standard of care to provide a measurement of cognitive effort at the time neurocognitive assessment is made psychologically. Not to do so is outside the standard of care. Moreover, if the neuropsychiatric examination is to be used for forensic purposes, it may not withstand a *Daubert* challenge (see Chapter 9). It is important to clinically correlate the neuropsychological findings with the historical, mental status, neurological, and neuroimaging findings obtained during the neuropsychiatric examination.

It should be remembered by the examiner that neuropsychological or psychological test data to the physician is no different than any other laboratory assessment. The contemporary practice of medicine is that a physician orders a test to confirm a diagnosis. That test is obtained in a laboratory setting, such as neuroimaging, chemical laboratory assessment, electroencephalogram, electrocardiogram, etc. The physician providing laboratory services to the neuropsychiatric physician functions as a laboratory consultant. The same is true for a psychologist assisting a physician in an examination. In the practice of medicine, there is no distinction between using the services of a psychologist and using the services of an electrocardiographer or radiologist.

When the psychological data are returned to the neuropsychiatric examiner, the first item to review is cognitive distortion. The readers may wish to refer back to Chapter 6 at this point and reacquaint themselves with the various cognitive measures of effort. One should scrutinize the psychological data to ensure that the assessment of cognitive effort is probability based using binomial probability theory or forced-choice methods. If the patient did not provide optimal cognitive effort, then consultation will be required between the physician examiner and the psychologist or neuropsychologist to determine the bases for lack of cognitive effort. This will be discussed more fully in Chapter 9 for those persons providing forensic examinations. For the treating neuroscience physician, it may be wise also to refer to Chapter 9 for further clarification on these important issues. Assuming the patient provided optimal cognitive effort, it is necessary secondly to establish a pre-injury cognitive baseline. The psychologist or neuropsychologist should have completed that form of examination for the physician. Recall, tests such as the Wechsler Test of Adult Reading (WTAR) can be used.[23] Another way to establish a pre-injury cognitive baseline is through historical information or examination of work product. If the physician is examining a lawyer, for instance, a review of pre-injury briefs written by the lawyer or a review of a deposition cross-examination made by that lawyer might be helpful to contrast with post-injury cognitive data. For injured students, ACT scores, SAT scores, or military records may be of use to establish a cognitive baseline. It is also important to determine historically whether the person has ever been psychologically tested before the injury, as these would be more definitive measures than any of the potential extrapolated measures. Thus, it is particularly important to review rehabilitation records if they exist. Oftentimes, there is speech-pathology data, occupational therapy data, or neuropsychology data within those records. While examining data, it is important to remember discussions previously made in this book. One expects after TBI that the cognitive disorder plateaus. Maximal cognitive improvement is expected at about 6–12 months. After 12 months, only small incremental improvements are noted. Therefore, if the examiner is seeing a patient 14 months post-TBI, the cognitive disorder at that point should be static and essentially unchanging. If, for instance, the neuropsychiatric examination at 14 months is more impaired than one made at 5 months post-injury, suspicions about the effort of the patient should be explored. Again, these issues are discussed further in Chapter 9. Once the examiner has determined pre-injury cognitive capacity and determined that cognitive effort was optimal, then the specific neuropsychological test data should be reviewed. The various domains of mental function discussed in Chapters 2 and 6 should be reviewed. These include test data measuring attention, memory, language, visuoperceptual abilities, sensorimotor function, executive function, and intellectual functioning. The numerical findings from these measurements are then collated into the neuropsychiatric database of neuroimaging, history, mental, and neurological examination, and laboratory testing to provide the entire database for drawing neuropsychiatric conclusions following examination.

With regard to the analysis of child neurocognitive data, obviously alterations of the analysis must be undertaken to account for neurodevelopmental level, social factors and age of the child. In Chapter 6, it was noted that the Wechsler Individual Achievement Test-II may be used to establish reading ability and pre-injury cognitive capacity in children aged 4 and up.[24] Other data may be useful to establish pre-injury cognitive capacity such as pre-injury school performance, pre-injury academic testing, and if the child has been referred for school psychological assessment, those data should be reviewed. It is particularly important to review the child's pediatric history to determine whether there was evidence of pre-injury neurodevelopmental delay, learning disability, prematurity, or parental abuse or neglect. These adverse factors will impact the analysis of a neuropsychiatric TBI examination. Once the pre-injury cognitive ability has been predicted, then the neurocognitive testing domains are reviewed individually in the same manner as for the adult. These include attention, memory, language, visuoperceptual ability, sensorimotor function, executive function, and intellectual functioning. The findings from the child neurocognitive examination are then collated with the entire neuropsychiatric database in the same fashion as discussed above for the adult.

Behavioral Measures

Chapter 2 instructs on the various behavioral issues that may arise following TBI in the adult or child. Chapter 7 describes more fully the measurement and confirmation by measurement of behavioral domains following TBI. The historical data, face-to-face mental examination data and behavioral measurement data will beg certain questions of the neuropsychiatric examiner. For instance, is there pre-injury evidence of a prior psychiatric or neuropsychiatric condition? Is there evidence of pre-injury brain injury that resulted in changes in behavior? In the adult, is there evidence that the patient was a substance abuser of significant proportions, was learning disabled, or in the child was there evidence of neurodevelopmental delay? Are the current expressed behaviors such as impulsivity, hyperactivity, aggression, or antisocial behaviors, an outcome of a TBI or do they reflect pre-injury personality or behavioral dysfunction?[25] When the examiners have answered these questions to their satisfaction, then it is important to establish first the psychiatric diagnosis following TBI. The guidelines in Chapter 2 may be of assistance at this point. Sometimes, only syndromal descriptors can be made, and a precise psychiatric diagnosis may not be offered. However, most insurance companies and lawyers, if litigation is in process, are uncomfortable with this. Therefore, the physician should make all efforts to establish a psychiatric diagnosis that most closely fits the history and face-to-face examination data obtained during the neuropsychiatric examination. Usually, by reviewing all of the available data, the neuropsychiatric examiner will be able to establish whether a behavioral syndrome such as depression, anxiety, posttraumatic stress disorder (PTSD), or other behavioral disorder as a result of TBI is present.

With the child, this proves to be more difficult. The *DSM-IV-TR* is most inadequate in attempting to describe childhood behaviors following TBI. However, the examiners should do the best of their ability to come up with a diagnosis. The historical database may be more expansive for the child than the adult, and it may be necessary to obtain collateral behavioral information from caregivers, school teachers, parents, and grandparents. One cannot rely on psychological testing alone to determine the behavioral impact of TBI upon the child, and the observations of others in the child's life may be of significant importance to the neuropsychiatric examiner.

Impact of the Brain Injury upon Caregivers

The neuropsychiatric examination focuses mostly upon the patient. Its purpose is to collect data in order to establish a diagnosis and then design a treatment plan. However, since the patient usually functions in a system, most likely a family system, it is necessary not to overlook the caregivers of the injured patient. One cannot provide an optimal outcome during treatment of one's patient if the family system or the social system of the patient is adverse to the quality of outcome. Kay and Cavallo have outlined five impacts upon the family system that often occur as a result of TBI:[26] (1) TBI inevitably causes profound changes in every family system; (2) these changes dramatically influence the functional recovery of the person with brain injury; (3) the impact of the brain injury continues over the life-cycle of the family, long after the initial adjustment to disability is made; (4) the lives of individual family members may be profoundly affected by a brain injury in another family member; and (5) family assessment and intervention are crucial at all stages of rehabilitation and adjustment after brain injury, even when a pathological response is not present in the patient. Thus, the examiner should review carefully the family system for elements of stress within it.

Recall from Chapter 7, Lezak's observation in her classic paper from 1978 regarding what it is like for family members to live with a brain-injured person who has undergone substantial changes in personality.[27] She described these as (1) an impaired capacity for social perceptiveness; (2) a stimulus-bound behavioral style or concrete thinking; (3) an impaired capacity for control, self-monitoring, and self-regulation; (4) significant alteration of emotional expression including apathy, irritability, and changes in sexual behavior; and (5) an inability for the patient to profit from experience and a tendency for him or her to repeat maladaptive patterns.

When the primary caregiver to the TBI patient is a spouse, this can extract enormous emotional and physical costs. Life has changed forever for either spouse. Healthcare providers have been notoriously poor at recognizing needs of the spouse for individual psychotherapy or treatment for depression or anxiety.[28] Table 8.3 summarizes a suggested approach to systematically collecting cognitive and behavioral data about the patient and his or her caregivers in order to develop and formulate a successful treatment plan.

TABLE 8.3

Systematizing Clinical Neuropsychiatric Deficits

	Cognitive	Behavioral
History	Are there symptoms of inattention, speech/language dysfunction, memory impairment, disorientation, visuospatial/constructional dysfunction, sensorimotor or executive dysfunction? Is there a pre-injury learning disorder, psychiatric or neurologic illness, or substance abuse disorder?	Are there symptoms of affective/mood changes, aggression/agitation, thought/perception dysfunction, high risk behaviors/disinhibition, or altered emotional intelligence? Is there a pre-injury learning disorder, psychiatric or neurologic illness, or substance abuse disorder?
Mental status examination	Are there signs of altered consciousness, inattention, speech/language dysfunction, memory impairment, visuospatial/constructional inability, sensorimotor impairment, or executive impairments?	Are there signs of abnormal affective modulation, abnormal thought processing or content, abnormal perceptions, or admissions of suicidal ideations or plans?
Neurological examination	Are there abnormalities in function of cranial nerves, motor/sensory abilities, tendon reflexes, muscle strength/tone, cerebellar ability, or posture/gait?	Are there abnormalities of neurological function?
Brain imaging	Are there abnormal CT or MRI images from the acute care setting? What are the structural and functional imaging findings from the neuropsychiatric evaluation? Do they correlate with cognitive deficits (e.g., frontal lobe injury and deficits of working memory, executive function)?	Are there abnormal CT or MRI images from the acute care setting? Do structural or functional image abnormalities from the neuropsychiatric evaluation correlate with behavioral abnormalities (e.g., infraorbital brain injury and orbital frontal disinhibition syndrome or aggression)?
Cognitive measures	Is there good effort during testing? If so, are there quantitative impairments of attention, speech/language, memory, sensorimotor, visuospatial/constructional skill, executive functions, or intellectual functions?	
Behavioral measures		Is there evidence of symptom magnification or malingering? If not, does psychological testing confirm the presence of depression, mania, anxiety, or psychosis? Is there test confirmation of aggression or self-destructive ideas?
Family/caregiver interviews	Does the family or caregiver report impairments in the patient's ability to understand, follow directions, pay attention, remain oriented, use language, remember, plan, organize or complete activities of daily living? Is the family/caregiver stressed or depressed by the patient's cognitive impairments?	Does the family or caregiver report behavior problems in the patient such as aggression, anger, depression, euphoria, anxiety, delusions, perceptual distortions, disinhibition, apathy, hypersomnolence, suicidal ideas, or plans? Is the family/caregiver stressed or depressed by the patient's behavior?

ESTABLISHING NEUROPSYCHIATRIC DEFICITS

Medical examination has historically developed four areas of inquiry. These include (1) symptoms, (2) signs of mental or physical disorder, (3) measurement of functioning, and (4) the development of a differential diagnosis. Using this model, one should be able to support conclusions that particular neuropsychiatric deficits are present. This must be done before one can establish an effective treatment plan. From a neuropsychiatric perspective, it is useful to look at the four aspects of neuropsychiatric assessment within a biopsychosocial model. Using this model, one can integrate clinical data along three parallel tracks. These are (1) disturbances in brain function due to alteration of tissue integrity; (2) the establishment of emotional and psychological reactions to impairments in cognition and behavior as a result of brain trauma, including the presence of denial or acceptance of these deficits; and (3) disruptions of interpersonal relationships, family interactions and systems, and the lack of capacity of the patient to work.[29] It should be obvious that the classic four aspects of a medical examination have been enlarged and modified for the particular needs of patients following TBI.

While this text stresses the use of neuropsychological and psychological data and measurement to establish evidence of injury and to establish the parameters of injury, it should be remembered that neuropsychologists have substantial limitations upon their ability to establish the gamut of deficits following TBI. As has been stated previously in this text, neuropsychologists are constrained by the limits of their profession, that is, a neuropsychologist takes a history and performs a neuropsychological examination. These examinations by their very nature are effort dependent and introduce both strengths and weaknesses into their abilities to assess fully the outcomes of TBI. On the other hand, the neuropsychiatrist or physician examining a person following TBI has the added benefit of using the medical model to enlarge upon what our neuropsychology colleagues have developed as an assessment model. Our ability as physicians to include physical examination data, neuroimaging data, genetic measurement data, and other laboratory assessments within the medical system is a distinct advantage in developing an overall treatment plan for our patients following TBI. Neuropsychologists, on the other hand, such as Lezak,[30] emphasize that it is primarily deficiencies caused by dysfunctional alterations of cognition, emotionality, and self-direction that produce the social and personal deficiencies in patients following TBI. Regardless of one's professional orientation, the ultimate goal for physicians is to provide a comprehensive assessment and develop a treatment plan to optimize the strengths of the patient and reduce the deficits in cognitive and behavioral capacity of the patient.

NEUROPSYCHIATRIC TREATMENT PLANNING

Table 8.4 lists a suggested approach to reviewing cognitive and behavioral data in order to define a treatment plan for a patient following TBI. This table lists approaches to the cognitive and behavioral domains as well as addressing the needs of families and caregivers; it focuses specifically on distinct issues with the child. As neuropsychiatric or physician examiners, we must remember that we are often part of a medical team. Nothing stated in this text is to be construed as a comprehensive or all-inclusive plan of treatment for our injured patients. For instance, as has been learned from the first seven chapters of this text, patients may present with comorbid physical impairments, visual impairments, ambulatory impairments or suffer the impact of comorbid diseases that were present at the time they were victims of TBI. A truly comprehensive plan is outside the scope of a mere neuropsychiatric evaluation for treatment. It is necessary for the physician to maintain a collegial and working relationship with neurologists, physiatrists, psychologists, social workers, occupational therapists, speech-pathology therapists, nurses, educators, etc. One cannot name all of the potential professionals that may be needed in a person's life following TBI. The more networking that is performed on the behalf of one's patient, the more likely the outcome will be positive for the patient and rewarding to the physician.

The neuropsychiatric examination is by its very nature limited in scope, primarily to the behavioral and cognitive changes in the patient and the impact of TBI and the resulting impairments upon the family system or caregivers. The stress placed upon networking with other professionals notwithstanding, it is also important to educate TBI patients and their families about resources available to them. The neuropsychiatric examiners should acquaint themselves with advocacy groups, support groups, and others who can be of assistance to the patient, caregivers, or family for both support and advice. Most states within the United States have brain injury associations. It is recommended that the physician examiner put the patient or family in contact with these resources during treatment.

TABLE 8.4

Neuropsychiatric Treatment Planning after Traumatic Brain Injury (TBI)

Cognitive	1.	Identify specific cognitive domains (attention, language, memory, visuospatial, sensorimotor, executive, or intellectual) found to be impaired during the neuropsychiatric examination.
	2.	Review school records and work products, if possible.
	3.	Determine appropriate pharmacologic, cognitive, behavioral, and family interventions.
Behavioral	1.	Identify specific disorders of mood, thought, or perception found to be impaired during the neuropsychiatric examination.
	2.	Identify whether patterns of aggression, anger, disinhibition, impaired emotional intelligence, or self-destruction are present.
	3.	Determine appropriate pharmacologic, psychotherapeutic, behavioral, and family interventions.
Family/caregiver	1.	Identify specifically from family interviews the impact of the patient's TBI upon the family or caregiver system.
	2.	Determine if the spouse, parent or caregiver is in need of pharmacologic, social, or psychotherapeutic assistance.
	3.	Provide appropriate intervention to improve the patient's family/caregiver support and to assist the caregiver if stressed or depressed.
The child	1.	Identify specific cognitive, behavioral, and caregiver impairments from the neuropsychiatric examination.
	2.	Review preschool or school performance, if possible.
	3.	Provide appropriate pharmacologic, psychotherapeutic, cognitive, behavioral, educational, social, and parental interventions.

Again, it must be emphasized that there is currently a lack of evidence-based guidelines for practitioners to use in the pharmacological treatment of neurobehavioral problems that commonly occur after TBI. Three panels of leading researchers in the field of brain injury were formed to review the current literature on pharmacological treatment for TBI sequelae in the topical areas of affective-anxiety-psychotic disorders, cognitive disorders, and aggression. A comprehensive Medline literature search was performed by each group to establish the content of pertinent articles. Additional articles were obtained from bibliography searches of the primary articles that were gained from the original search. Group members then independently reviewed these articles and established a consensus rating. Despite reviewing a very large number of studies on drug treatment of neurobehavioral sequelae after TBI, the quality of evidence did not support any treatment standards and few guidelines due to a number of recurrent methodological problems. Guidelines were established for the use of methylphenidate in the treatment of deficits in attention and speed of information processing as well as for the use of beta-blockers in the treatment of aggression following TBI. Optional guidelines were recommended in the treatment of depression, bipolar-like disorders, psychosis, aggression, general cognitive functions and deficits in attention, speed of mental processing, and memory impairment after TBI. The evidence-based guidelines and options established by this working group may help guide practitioners in the pharmacological treatment of patients who experience neurobehavioral sequelae following TBI. This working group called for well-designed randomized control trials to be established in order to produce treatment guidelines for the common problems after TBI and also to establish definitive treatment standards for this patient population.[32]

PHARMACOLOGIC MANAGEMENT OF COGNITIVE DISORDERS FOLLOWING TRAUMATIC BRAIN INJURY

At the time the first edition of this book was prepared, there was almost no Class I evidence (randomized controlled trials) of pharmacologic agents and their applications to the symptoms and signs of patients following TBI. Unfortunately, that statement stands today. There continues to be a limited psychopharmacologic research base for the use of brain-specific medications in the treatment of TBI. As with the use of any pharmacologic agent in treating a patient, a risk–benefit analysis must be made of the pharmacologic agent to be used and the expected beneficial outcome for the patient. This must be weighed against potential side effects or deleterious outcomes from the use of a particular medication.[31]

Cholinergic Enhancers

Virtually all of the available cholinergic enhancers that can be prescribed to patients following TBI are based on acetylcholinesterase inhibition. There are no evidence-based studies available using acetylcholine precursors such as lecithin or choline. Moreover, the use of centrally selective nicotinic or muscarinic receptor agonists have not been studied in brain-injured populations on a controlled basis. The reader is cautioned again that there is a paucity of evidence-based studies in general regarding medications used to treat post-TBI symptoms, and this includes cholinergic enhancers.

The cholinergic enhancing standard is physostigmine. Physostigmine is a potent acetylcholinesterase inhibitor, and it exerts its principle pharmacologic effect by inhibiting synaptic acetylcholinesterase. It also has some effect on nicotinic receptors similar to that of galantamine.[33] However, the therapeutic index for physostigmine is very small, and it is prone to substantial cholinergic toxicity; its use is not recommended in TBI.[34] The commonly used and prescribed cholinergic enhancers today include donepezil, rivastigmine, and galantamine. Early open-label studies of donepezil appeared in 2001 and 2003.[35–37] They putatively reveal that some aspects of memory and behavior in persons with chronic TBI were improved by the use of donepezil.

The Masanic et al. study treated four patients with donepezil, 5 mg daily for 8 weeks and then donepezil, 10 mg daily for an additional 4 weeks.[35] The Morey et al. study[36] treated seven patients with TBI averaging 33 months post-injury. They were given donepezil, 5 mg daily for one month followed by donepezil, 10 mg daily for an additional 5 months. A 6-week washout period followed, and then patients were treated for an additional 6 months with donepezil, 5 mg daily. Kaye et al.[37] performed an 8-week open-label study of 10 persons in an outpatient setting using a forced titration protocol of 5 mg daily for 4 weeks followed by 10 mg daily for 4 weeks. All three open-label studies reported improvement in cognitive function at the duration of the study. More recently, donepezil was evaluated in an acute rehabilitation facility. Thirty-six patients with moderate to severe TBI were evaluated within 90 days of injury. Donepezil was administered beginning at 5 mg daily with titration to 10 mg daily based on perceived clinical response. The evidence from this study[38] suggested that donepezil administration early in the rehabilitation stay may have advantageous treatment effects.

The research data to date on cognitive enhancers in TBI reveals a significant paucity of controlled studies. A recent Japanese study reviewed the measurement of short-interval intracortical inhibition (SICI), intracortical facilitation (ICF), and short-latency afferent inhibition (SAI) to evaluate motor cortex excitability in 16 diffuse axonal injury (DAI) patients with memory impairment and compared the data with those of 16 healthy controls. SAI was reduced in patients compared with controls ($p < .0001$), using an unpaired T-test. DAI patients tended to have a higher resting motor threshold and less pronounced SICI and ICF than controls, but these differences were not significant. A single oral dose (3 mg) of donepezil improved SAI in DAI patients with wide individual variations. The authors concluded that measuring SAI may provide a means of probing the integrity of cholinergic networks in an injured human brain.[39] A recent study from Finland reviewed the use of central acetylcholinesterase inhibitors in the treatment of chronic TBI. An outpatient study was conducted of 111 individuals who had chronic stable TBI and at least one of the following target symptoms: fatigue, poor memory, diminished attention, or diminished initiation. Patients received in random order, donepezil, galantamine, or rivastigmine. The evaluation of the treatment response was based on the subjective view of the patients. There were no controls and no crossover. As first treatment, 27 patients received donepezil, 30 patients received galantamine, and 54 received rivastigmine. All together, 41 patients tried more than one drug in a nonrandomized fashion, but only 3 patients tried all three alternatives. In total, 61% of patients had a marked positive response, and 39% had a modest or no response. The clearest effect was in almost all responders a better vigilance and attention causing better general function. About one-half of the patients volunteered to continue therapy with one of these drugs. The mean dose on maintenance therapy was 7.2 mg daily for donepezil, 5.0 mg twice daily for galantamine, and 2.3 mg twice daily for rivastigmine.[40]

A study from San Antonio, Texas, used donepezil in a randomized, placebo-controlled double-blind crossover trial. The duration was 24 weeks, and the patients were derived from outpatient clinics and two teaching hospitals, where 18 postacute TBI patients with cognitive impairment were enrolled. Patients were randomly assigned to Group A or Group B. Patients in Group A received donepezil for the first 10 weeks and then a placebo for another 10 weeks. The two treatment phases were separated by a washout period of 4 weeks. Patients in Group B received the preparations in the opposite order. The measures were short-term memory and sustained attention. These were assessed by the Auditory Immediate Index and Visual Immediate Index of the Wechsler Memory Scale (WMS)-III and the Paced Auditory Serial Addition Test. At baseline, week 10, and week 24, measures were made. The intragroup comparison of different phases of the trial in both groups show that donepezil significantly increased the testing scores on all three test measures compared with the baseline. There was no significant change in the testing scores between assessment at baseline and the end of the placebo phase in Group B. Intragroup comparison at the 10 week assessment showed significantly improved testing scores in Group A with donepezil over Group B with the placebo. The authors concluded that donepezil increased neuropsychological testing scores in short-term memory and sustained attention in postacute TBI patients.[41]

To date, there is only one significant study of acetylcholinesterase inhibitors in children. The Kennedy Krieger Institute in Baltimore, Maryland, studied three adolescents with TBI on and off medications using 5 mg and 10 mg donepezil. Four variables were examined: total recall, long-term storage, consistency of long-term retrieval, and delayed memory. On medication, three out of three participants demonstrated better memory. Two showed greatest improvement on 10 mg donepezil. All participants demonstrated improvement in total recall and long-term storage. Two participants demonstrated improved consistency of long-term retrieval. No participants displayed improvement in delayed memory. No adverse side effects were reported.[42]

At the time of the writing of this text, the largest study of acetylcholinesterase inhibitors in TBI patients has been conducted by Jon Silvers' group at New York University School of Medicine. The study authors compared the efficacy and safety of rivastigmine (3–6 mg daily) versus a placebo over 12 weeks in patients with TBI and persistent cognitive impairment. The study design was a prospective, randomized, double-blind, placebo-controlled study. One hundred and fifty-seven patients were enrolled at least 12 months after injury. The primary efficacy measures were the Cambridge Neuropsychological Test Automated Battery (CANTAB), Rapid Visual Information Processing (RVIP), and the Hopkins Verbal Learning Test (HVLT). The primary efficacy outcome measured was the proportion of patients who demonstrated 1 SD or greater improvement from baseline at week 12. The percentage of responders at week 12 on the CANTAB, the RVIP or the HVLT was 48.7% for rivastigmine, and 49.3% for placebo ($p = .940$). Furthermore, for the overall study population, there were no significant differences for any of the secondary efficacy variables. In a subgroup of patients with moderate to severe memory impairment ($n = 81$), defined as 25% impairment or greater on the HVLT at baseline, rivastigmine was significantly better than placebo for a number of measures including a proportion of HVLT responders and CANTAB and RVIP mean latencies. Rivastigmine was found to be safe and well tolerated. Rivastigmine shows promising results in the subgroup of TBI patients with moderate to severe memory deficits.[43]

Galantamine has not been tested to any significant degree in TBI. One of the earliest uses of this cholinergic agent was by Luria the esteemed Russian physician and neuropsychologist.[44]

TABLE 8.5

Cholinergic Enhancers and Traumatic Brain Injury (TBI)

- The beneficial effects, if any, depend upon the level of central cholinergic deficit.
- Not all persons with TBI have central cholinergic deficits.[130]
- Donepezil: start 5 mg/day. Titrate to 10 mg/day over 2- to 4-week period.
- Rivastigmine: shorter T 1/2 than donepezil. Start 1.5 mg b.i.d. and increase by 1.5 mg b.i.d. increments to maximum benefit.
- Galantamine: shorter T 1/2 than donepezil. Start 4 mg b.i.d. and increase by 4 mg b.i.d. increments to maximum benefit.

A recent article in the *Journal of Psychopharmacology* added galantamine to risperidone in patients presenting with schizophrenia-like psychosis after TBI.[45] The authors concluded in this open-label study that the addition of galantamine to risperidone improved negative and cognitive symptoms. Table 8.5 lists useful guidelines when administering cholinergic enhancers to patients following TBI.

Dopamine Agonists and Amantadine

This section will review three major medications used as dopamine enhancers following TBI. These include amantadine, levodopa, and bromocriptine. A study at the University of Alabama at Birmingham reviewed the use of amantadine in 35 subjects who had a TBI in a transportation accident and were initially seen with a GCS score of 10 or less within the first 24 h after admission to hospital. They were randomly assigned to a double-blind placebo-controlled crossover design trial. Amantadine, 200 mg or placebo was each administered for 6 weeks (12 weeks total) to patients who were recruited consecutively. Measurements included the Mini-Mental Status Examination (MMSE), Disability Rating Scale (DRS), Glasgow Outcome Scale (GOS), and the FIM Cognitive Score. There was an improvement in all measures in consecutive order at a statistically significant level ($p < .0185, .0022, .0077$, and $.0033$) for the amantadine group but not the placebo group. This study was continued in other groups, and the authors concluded that there was a consistent trend toward a more rapid functional improvement regardless of when a patient with DAI-associated TBI was started on amantadine in the first 3 months after injury.[46]

A positron emission tomography (PET) study from the Department of Psychiatry at the University of Illinois evaluated the effects of amantadine (thought to be both a dopaminergic agent and NMDA antagonist) on TBI patients. The primary hypotheses were that amantadine treatment would result in executive function improvement and increased activity in the prefrontal cortex. An open-label design was used. Twenty-two subjects underwent neuropsychological testing before and after 12 weeks of treatment. Six subjects also underwent PET scanning. Amantadine, 400 mg was administered daily. Significant improvements on tests of executive function were observed with treatment. Analysis of PET data demonstrated a significant increase in left prefrontal cortex glucose metabolism. There was a significant positive correlation between executive domain scores and left prefrontal glucose metabolism measured by PET. This is the first known study to assess amantadine in chronic TBI patients using PET, and the data were consistent with the authors' hypotheses before study.[47]

With regard to pediatric patients, amantadine and the psychostimulants have been the pharmacologic agents studied in the greatest frequency. A University of Michigan study was performed in a retrospective, case-controlled fashion. Fifty-four patients aged 3–18 years were admitted to the study and treated with amantadine. Nine percent of participants had excess side effects which included hallucinations, delusions, increased aggression, nausea, and vomiting. These side effects discontinued when the medicine was discontinued or the dosage decreased. Patients were measured using the Rancho Los Amigos level (see Chapter 1) during their admission and followed over time. The authors reported that subjective improvements were noted in the majority of the patients administered amantadine, and the amantadine group showed a greater improvement in Ranchos

Los Amigos level during admission, suggesting that it may be effective. Of course the weakness in this study is that there was no placebo arm, no crossover, no washout, and lack of controls.[48] A small study from the Western Psychiatric Institute at the University of Pittsburgh did perform a controlled study using amantadine in youngsters. Children were age- and severity-matched following TBI and randomized to amantadine or usual care without amantadine. The authors completed behavioral scales and neuropsychological testing. Effect sizes measured the treatment effect within subjects and between groups. Side effects were tracked over the 12-week study duration. Behavior improved in the amantadine group, but only those 2 years or less post-injury showed a treatment effect on cognitive tests. The authors concluded that this 12-week course of amantadine was safe, and according to reports from parents, behavior improved.[49] A recent comparison trial at the University of Virginia Children's Hospital tested amantadine against pramipexole. Ten children and adolescents aged 8–21 years (mean = 16.7 years) with TBI sustained at least 1 month previously and remaining at a low response state (Rancho Los Amigos scale level = 3) received either pramipexole or amantadine. Medication dosage was increased over 4 weeks and weaned over 2 weeks before being discontinued. At baseline and weekly during the study the children were evaluated with the Coma or Near Coma Scale, Western NeuroSensory Stimulation Profile and the Disability Rating Scale. Scores improved significantly from baseline to the medication phase on the Coma or Near Coma Scale, Western NeuroSensory Stimulation Profile and Disability Rating Scale ($p < .005$). The weekly rate of change was significantly better for all three measures on medication than off medication ($p < .05$). Rancho Los Amigos scale levels improved significantly on medication as well ($p < .005$). No difference in efficacy between amantadine and pramipexole was detected. No unexpected or significant side effects were observed with either drug.[50] Obviously, further randomized controlled studies of dopamine agonists in children is warranted.

Studies of L-dopa following TBI have been almost entirely in those patients in coma or vegetative states. One of the earliest studies of L-dopa in coma was reported in 1974.[51] Fifteen patients were selected for this study. The degree of consciousness impairment and level of coma varied among the patients. In all of them, however, the comatose state persisted unchanged for at least 6 days before beginning L-dopa treatment. A gradual and progressive improvement in the level of consciousness as well as of the EEG patterns followed the administration of L-dopa in patients. On the other hand, the authors questioned the results of the treatment's effects upon sequelae of coma (apallic syndrome, coma vigil, or akinetic mutism). This was not a controlled study.[51] An Israeli study recently reviewed the use of L-dopa in vegetative state TBI patients (VS-TBI). A prospective study of eight patients, aged 25–50 years, with a mean duration of 104 days of vegetative state, was performed by investigating changes within their state of consciousness while they were treated with L-dopa. Initial improvement was observed in all patients within a mean of 13 days after onset of treatment. Seven patients recovered consciousness after a mean time of 31 days of treatment. The remaining patients showed only slight improvement to a minimally conscious state. The authors concluded that clinical awareness to the structured order of responses and to the effective dosage can help clinicians in early assessment of response to dopaminergic treatment in vegetative state patients.[52] Matsuda et al. in Kyoto[53] have found levodopa to be effective in those vegetative states with Parkinson signs or T2-MRI evidence of injury to dopamine pathways.

Lastly, bromocriptine appears to act directly on postsynaptic D2 receptors, and it serves as an agonist in cerebral systems mediated by dopamine. Limited studies are available on this compound in patients following TBI. McDowell et al.[54] have studied the effect of bromocriptine in a double-blind, placebo-controlled crossover design. They found that bromocriptine improved performance on some frontally mediated tasks and also upon executive function and dual-task performance. This study did not show an improvement in working memory. A very recent study evaluated bromocriptine in 11 patients, but this was an open-trial in six men and five women.[55] These individuals had either TBI or subarachnoid hemorrhage, and thus the patients' population is mixed. Assessments were repeated at increasing doses of bromocriptine, during maintenance of bromocriptine, and after withdrawal of medication. Measures of anxiety and depression along with

TABLE 8.6

Dopamine Agonists and Amantadine Usage in Traumatic Brain Injury (TBI)

- Dopamine agonists may enhance functional recovery and improve dysexecutive syndromes.[132]
- Amantadine seems to improve tremors, visual inattention, concentration, and speed of mental operations. However, it may lower seizure threshold.
- Amantadine may be combined with levodopa to decrease impulsivity-perseveration and to improve executive function. It is usually initiated at 50 mg b.i.d. and increased weekly by 100 mg/day. Do not exceed a daily dose of 400 mg.
- Carbidopa/L-dopa treatment usually starts at 10/100 mg b.i.d. and is gradually titrated to 25/250 mg q.i.d.

cognitive tests sensitive to motivation and frontal lobe involvement were administered. The authors reported that bromocriptine treatment was followed by improved scores on all measures other than mood. Improvement was maintained after bromocriptine withdrawal in 8 of the 11 patients. The authors concluded that poor motivation in patients following TBI may result from dysfunction in the mesolimbic or mesocortical dopaminergic circuitry giving rise to associated deficiencies in reward responsiveness and frontal cognitive function. Table 8.6 lists clinical approaches to using dopamine agonists or amantadine following TBI.

Glutamate-Based Treatment

Memantine is the paradigm agent in glutamate-based therapy. Rat studies have shown that memantine causes a neuroprotective response to prevent TBI-induced neuronal damage. A University of Wisconsin study investigated whether memantine was neuroprotective after TBI induced in adult rats with a controlled cortical impact device. TBI in these animals led to significant neuronal death in hippocampal regions CA2 and CA3 by 7 days after the injury. The rats in this study were treated with memantine, 10 and 20 mg/kg, intraperitoneally immediately after the injury. This significantly prevented the neuronal loss in both regions CA2 and CA3. This is thought to be the first study showing the neuroprotective potential of memantine to prevent TBI-induced neuronal damage.[56] A Turkish study evaluated the affect of memantine on lipid peroxidation following closed-head trauma in rats. A total of 132 adult male Sprague–Dawley rats were randomly divided into four groups: sham-operated, closed-head trauma, closed-head trauma plus saline, closed-head trauma plus memantine. The dosage was 10 mg/kg intraperitoneally. A cranial impact was delivered to the skull just in front of the coronal suture over the left hemisphere from a height of 7 cm. Saline or memantine was injected 15 min after trauma. Rats were euthanized 0.5, 1, 2, 6, 24, and 48 h after trauma. Brain tissue samples were taken 5 mm distance from the left frontal pole and also from the corresponding point of the contralateral hemisphere. Memantine treatment significantly reduced lipid peroxidation levels in the treatment group compared with other groups ($p < .01$).[57]

A University of Glasgow group has reviewed the world literature on stroke and TBI trials of more than 9000 patients treated with NMDA antagonists. Several of the synthetic NMDA antagonist development programs have been abandoned due to concerns about drug toxicity, particularly in stroke. Systematic reviews in stroke and TBI have shown that definitive conclusions cannot be drawn for most of these agents owing to early termination of trials. To date, memantine has shown some benefit only in dementia associated with Alzheimer's disease. Other therapeutic areas of promise, including the use of memantine in TBI, remain inadequately explored at present.[58] Table 8.7 describes current thinking regarding the use of glutamate-based agents following TBI.

Hypothalamic Agents

Underarousal, fatigue, and hypersomnolence are often common outcomes following TBI. The reader will recall from Chapter 2 that hypersomnolence can be quite impairing following TBI, and the disorder of central nervous system hypersomnolence has been causally connected to TBI. Modafinil is

TABLE 8.7
Gultamate-Based Agents and Traumatic Brain Injury (TBI)

- Memantine is the only currently used agent in this category.
- Its use is empiric and no studies to date document a human neuroprotective effect in TBI.
- It is dosed as if it were being used for Alzheimer's disease.

the representative agent in this category. The exact mechanism of action of modafinil is poorly understood at this time, but it is thought to exert influences in the hypothalamus, and this may be attributable to activation of hypocretin neurons in the lateral hypothalamus. There is also evidence that it has functions in the preoptic area and posterior thalamus.[59,60] Clinically, the emergence of modafinil as a possible activating medication came following reports that it was helpful in the treatment of fatigue in patients with multiple sclerosis.[61] Elovic first reported the use of provigil for underarousal following TBI.[62] Teitelman reported off-label uses of modafinil, and included in these uses was a recommendation for patients with TBI-induced underarousal.[63] The University of Toronto recently completed a study reviewing the evidence surrounding the pharmacological management of arousal state following acute and chronic head injury for the years 1986–2002. The authors concluded that the quality of the evidence was generally poor for many agents, including modafinil, and sometimes conflicting. The spotty results of research lead to indecisive guidelines for treating patients who are underaroused following TBI.[64] Table 8.8 gives guidelines for the use of modafinil following TBI.

Monoamine Oxidase Inhibitors

The representative agent in this class of treatment is selegiline (L-deprenyl). Initial studies in rats have been shown to rescue axotomized immature facial motoneurons comparable to that of neurotrophic factor. A Canadian study in the 1990s tested this proposal in an *in vitro* model consisting of a mixed astrocyte population of flat and processed-bearing astroglia taken from postnatal day-2 or postnatal day-5 cerebral cortex. Deprenyl was shown to increase ciliary neuro-trophic factor mRNA content. This study was thought to be the first report of an agent that can upregulate CNTF gene expression in astroglial cell culture as well as influence the process length of the glial cell.[65] Povlischock's group at the Department of Anatomy, Medical College of Virginia has also used L-deprenyl in fluid percussion TBI models with rats. Post-injury motor assessment showed no effect of L-deprenyl treatment. Cognitive performance was assessed on days 11–15 post-injury, and brains from the same cases were examined for dopamine beta-hydroxylase immunoreactivity and acetylcholinesterase histochemistry. Significant cognitive improvement relative to the untreated cases was observed in both TBI groups following L-deprenyl treatment. These rats were treated with L-deprenyl beginning 24 h after TBI alone and 15 min after a bilateral entorhinal cortical lesion was induced. After TBI and entorhinal lesion induction L-deprenyl increased acetylcholinesterase in the dentate molecular layer of the hippocampus relative to untreated injured cases. These results suggest that dopaminergic or noradrenergic enhancement facilitates cognitive recovery after brain injury,

TABLE 8.8
Hypothalamic Agents and Traumatic Brain Injury (TBI)

- Modafanil is the only agent in this category at this time.
- Increased emotional instability has been reported in TBI patients.[63]
- When modafanil is used, start at 100 mg in the morning and titrate by 100-mg daily increments to a maximum of 400 mg/day.

TABLE 8.9

Selegeline and Traumatic Brain Injury (TBI)

- Selegeline is a monoamine oxidase inhibitor (MAOI) and it may improve post-TBI apathy.[67]
- Even though tyramine risk is low, MAOI diet and medication cautions should be followed (e.g., avoid aged foods and drugs that are substrates for MAO metabolism).
- Start dosage at 5 mg/day. Titrate 5-mg increases per week. Do not exceed 40 mg/day. Avoid concomitant antidepressants.

---

and that noradrenergic fiber integrity is correlated with enhanced synaptic plasticity in the injured hippocampus.[66] A New Zealand study reviewed the use of selegiline in humans in an open-label trial. Four patients were evaluated using the Apathy Evaluation Scale and overall clinical functional improvement. They were placed on selegiline, and in all cases selegiline was well tolerated. They were compared in the same trial against methamphetamine, which was not well tolerated. The authors concluded, based on this series of four patients only, that selegiline shows potential for the management of apathy following TBI. They concluded further that this provided evidence that impaired dopaminergic processes are prominent in the genesis of apathetic symptoms.[67] No controlled studies of selegiline and TBI have been reported to date. Refer to Table 8.9 for guidelines using selegiline following TBI.

Neutraceuticals

Neutraceuticals are in the class of nutritional supplements not prescribed by attending physicians. Increasingly, patients are buying these without the advice of a physician and adding them to their treatment regimens. The use of St. John's Wort around the world is a case in point. Commonly used substances include cytidine 5′-diphosphocholine (CDP-choline). The physicians may notice that their patients obtain and try choline, phosphatidycholine, *Ginkgo biloba*, pyritonol, piracetam, carnitine, dimethylaminoethanol, pantothenic acid, lucidril, and vinpocetine. These will not be discussed in this text, but the physician should be aware that they may be used by patients following TBI or recommended by family members. The one compound that has been studied in a controlled fashion is CDP-choline (cytidine 5′-diphosphocholine). CDP-choline is an essential intermediate in the biosynthetic pathway of phospholipids, which are then incorporated into cell membranes. When CDP-choline is ingested, it is metabolized into cytidine and choline. CDP-choline putatively activates the synthesis of structural phospholipids in neuronal membranes, increases cerebral metabolism and enhances the activity of neurotransmitters dopamine, norepinephrine, and acetylcholine.[68]

An early study performed a single-blind randomized examination of 216 patients with moderate to severe TBI during the acute post-injury period. The researchers noted improvements in motor, cognitive, and psychiatric function while the patients were receiving CDP-choline. They reported further that the use of CDP-choline reduced the hospital length of stay.[69] A second study conducted a double-blind, placebo-controlled study of 14 patients to evaluate CDP-choline effectiveness while treating postconcussional symptoms in the first month after mild to moderate TBI. One gram of CDP-choline was administered orally, and a placebo control group was matched for age, education, and severity of the initial injury. The authors reported that CDP-choline reduces severity of postconcussional symptoms and improves recognition memory for visual designs. Other neuro-psychological test performance in this study was not significantly enhanced.[70]

There is no FDA approval of CDP-choline as a pharmacologic agent in the United States. This product is available as an over-the-counter nutritional supplement in health food stores within the United States. Its most common formulation is 250-mg capsules. There are no quality control standards to enable a consumer to determine whether variants exist among formulations or among manufacturers. However, there are no published warnings that this product is toxic if used according to the directions by the health food supplement manufacturer.

Psychostimulants

The two representative psychostimulants used in TBI are methylphenidate and dextroamphetamine. Both of these increase the release of the monoamines dopamine and norepinephrine at ordinary doses, and at higher doses they block the reuptake of these substances. There is some evidence that they inhibit monoamine oxidase, which may increase the effectiveness of monoaminergic neuro-transmission. Most of the controlled studies available in the recent world literature include methyl-phenidate. Fewer controlled studies of dextroamphetamine in TBI patients exist. Probably the first controlled study of methylphenidate for treatment of TBI was conducted by Levin's group at the University of Texas Medical School in Houston. This study was double-blind and placebo-controlled with random assignment. Patients were enrolled when their Galveston Orientation and Amnesia Test score was at least 65. Drug/placebo treatment began the day following baseline cognitive assessment and continued for 30 consecutive days. Follow-up evaluations were conducted at 30 days and 90 days after baseline, and after discontinuation of either the drug or placebo. These patients were recruited from a Level I trauma center. Twenty-three patients ranging in age from 16 to 64 years were included, and the severity ranged from moderately severe to complicated mild (GCS score = 8 or below to GCS score = 13–15) with positive CT brain scans. Thirty day follow-up included 12 patients, and 90 day follow-up included 9 patients. Methylphenidate was administered twice daily at a dose of 0.30 mg/kg. Placebo administration was on the same schedule as the methylphenidate and was administered in identical capsules. Measures included the DRS, and a test of attention, memory, and vigilance. The methylphenidate group was significantly better at 30 days on the DRS ($p < .02$), and on tests of attention ($p < .03$) and motor performance ($p < .05$). No significant differences were noted between placebo or methylphenidate groups at 90 days. The authors concluded that subacute administration of methylphenidate after moderately severe head injury appeared to enhance the rate but not the ultimate level of recovery as measured by the DRS and other tests of vigilance.[71] The Moss Rehabilitation Research Institute in Philadelphia conducted a randomized placebo-controlled trial of methylphenidate after TBI. This study was double-blind, placebo-controlled, and a repeated crossover design using five different tasks to measure various facets of attentional function. The results suggested that methylphenidate may be a useful treatment in TBI, but the study results caused the authors to conclude that its use was primarily for symptoms that can be attributed to slow mental processing.[72]

The Moss Rehabilitation Research Institute provided an updated study 7 years later on methyl-phenidate's effect on attention deficits following TBI. These researchers entered a total of 34 adults with moderate to severe TBI that had attentional complaints in the postacute phase of recovery. They were enrolled in a 6-week, double-blind, placebo-controlled repeated crossover study of methylphenidate administered at a dose of 0.3 mg/kg twice daily. A wide range of attentional measures were gathered on a weekly basis including videotaped analysis. Twenty-four subjects completed the study. A total of 54 dependent variables were reduced to 13 composite factors and 13 remaining individual variables. Of the 13 attentional factors, 5 showed suggestive treatment effects. Of these, three showed statistically significant treatment effects. These included speed of informa-tion processing, attentiveness during individual work tasks, and caregiver ratings of attention in the patient. No treatment related improvement was seen in divided attention, sustained attention or susceptibility to distraction. Improvements in processing speed, however, did not seem to come at the expense of accuracy. The authors concluded that methylphenidate dosed at 0.3 mg/kg twice daily, to individuals with attentional complaints after TBI, seemed to have clinically significant positive effects on speed of processing, caregiver ratings of attention, and some aspects of on-task behavior in naturalistic settings such as at work.[73]

A very recent Republic of Korea study from the Chonnam National University Medical School compared methylphenidate, sertraline, and placebo in a 4-week, double-blind, parallel-group trial. Thirty patients with mild to moderate TBI were randomly allocated to one of three treatment groups with matching age, gender, and education controls. The methylphenidate dosage varied from 5 to 20 mg/day. Sertraline was titrated from 25 mg/day to 100 mg/day. Both drugs were compared to placebo. Behavioral assessments using the Beck Depression Inventory (BDI) and Hamilton Depression Rating Scale (HDRS) were used. Postconcussional symptoms were evaluated using the Rivermeade Postconcussion Symptoms Questionnaire. Performance tests included numerous short neuropsychological measures. The authors concluded that daytime sleepiness was reduced by methylphenidate while it was not by sertraline. Methylphenidate had significant and similar effects on depressive symptoms as sertraline. However, methylphenidate seemed to be more beneficial in improving cognitive function and maintaining daytime alertness. Methylphenidate also showed better tolerability among patients than sertraline.[74]

A second Korean study at the Sungkyunwan University School of Medicine in Seoul was undertaken to determine the effect of a single dose of methylphenidate on the cognitive performance of patients with TBI. This study examined particularly working memory and visuospatial attention using a double-blind placebo-controlled method. Eighteen subjects with TBI (16 male and 2 female) were enrolled. The patients were given a single 20-mg methylphenidate dose or a placebo. Cognitive assessments were performed three times: before medication use, 2 h after medication use, and at follow-up (48 h later). Cognitive assessments consisted of working memory tasks and visuospatial attention tasks using computer simulation. Response accuracy and reaction times were measured. There were significant improvements in response accuracy in the methylphenidate when compared with the placebo group for both the working memory and visuospatial attention tasks. A significant decrease in reaction time was also observed in the methylphenidate group only for the working memory tasks. The authors concluded that the administration of a single dose of methylphenidate has an effect in improving cognitive function following TBI, most prominently regarding the reaction time of working memory.[75]

A very recent study from Iran found that methylphenidate reduced ICU and hospital length of stay by 23% in severely injured TBI patients. These findings were statistically significant. Severely and moderately injured TBI patients were randomized to treatment and control groups. The treatment group received methylphenidate, 0.3 mg/kg twice daily by the second day of admission until their time of discharge from hospital. The control group received only a placebo. Forty patients with a GCS score of 5–8 and 40 patients with a GCS score of 9–12 were randomly divided into treatment and control groups on their day of admission.[76] A recent and very interesting study of methylphenidate's effects on the sleep–wake cycle has come to us from Oman. This was a retrospective chart review of 30 patients diagnosed with TBI who were observed in a rehabilitation facility for at least 10 days. Seventeen of these patients had been administered methylphenidate on clinical grounds, and they served as the experimental group. The unmedicated patients ($n = 13$) served as controls. Sleep–wake cycles were arbitrarily designated as nighttime and daytime, respectively. The average number of hours of sleep during a 24-h period was not significantly different for the two cohorts. Similar trends emerged for the nighttime and daytime observations. On the whole, methylphenidate appeared not to have unfavorable effects on sleep–wake cycles, presently defined as nighttime, daytime, and 24 h in the TBI population. Thus, the authors concluded that administration of methylphenidate does not appear to have an adverse effect on sleep–wake quantity in persons who have sustained TBI.[77]

With regard to children, there are two studies, both conducted in the 1990s, that describe the use of methylphenidate in the treatment of children and adolescents who have post-TBI cognitive impairment. The first was by Mahalick et al.[78] who administered in a crossover design study of 14 children (ages 5–14 years) methylphenidate 0.3 mg/kg twice daily. The children were observed on measures of vigilance, mental processing speed, and distractibility. Statistically significant improvements in all three measures were noted. The second study was by Williams et al.[79] who examined 10 patients, ages 5–16 years who were 2 years post-injury. The level of severity of their injury is not specified. They were dosed 5–10 mg twice daily based on their weight. These authors reported improvement in behavioral measures as assessed by teachers using the Connor's Rating Scale (see Chapter 6). Parent ratings in this scale did not correlate with teacher ratings. Obviously, the studies on children with methylphenidate are few and poorly designed to date.

Studies of dextroamphetamine following TBI are sparse. An early study by Lipper and Tuchman,[80] a single-case study using dextroamphetamine, is probably the first reported case in the TBI literature. The authors claimed dextroamphetamine improved confusion, paranoia, and short-term memory deficit in a young adult with chronic organic brain syndrome secondary to trauma.[80] A chart review of 29 TBI patients during rehabilitation suggested that amphetamine treatment enhanced the recovery and functional status of 15 patients. This was at Helen Hayes Hospital in New York State. However, there was no placebo arm, no controls, and poor methodology.[81] The National Institute of Neurological Disorders and Stroke, an arm of the NIH in Bethesda, Maryland, has attempted to document the effects of dextroamphetamine on use-dependent plasticity. Healthy human volunteers underwent a training period of voluntary thumb movements under the effects of placebo or dextroamphetamine in different sessions in randomized double-blind, counterbalanced design trials. Previous work by this agency found that in a drug-naive condition, subjects given such training produced changes in the direction of thumb movements evoked by transcranial magnetic stimulation and in transcranial magnetic stimulation-evoked electromyographic responses. The input measure of this specific study was the magnitude of training-induced changes in transcranial magnetic stimulation-evoked kinematic and electromyographic responses in the dextroamphetamine and in the placebo conditions. Motor training resulted in increased magnitude, faster development and longer lasting duration of use-dependent plasticity under dextroamphetamine use compared to the placebo session. The authors of this study concluded that dextroamphetamine caused a facilitator effect on use-dependent plasticity. They argued that this was a possible mechanism mediating the beneficial effect of dextroamphetamine on functional recovery after cortical lesions.[82]

While the use of psychostimulants, particularly methylphenidate, seems to offer some benefit to TBI patients, the results are muted when one evaluates all available data. The Cochrane Database System at the University of Newcastle upon Tyne has spent considerable effort reviewing the available world literature on monoaminergic agonist use in TBI.[83] In 2003, they concluded there was insufficient evidence to support the routine use of methylphenidate or other amphetamines to promote recovery from TBI. In 2006 they concluded, that at present, "there is insufficient evidence to support the routine use of monoamines to promote recovery after TBI."[84] However, the clinical data suggest they may have usefulness. Table 8.10 provides dosing guidelines for psychostimulant use in TBI patients.

TABLE 8.10

Psychostimulant Use following Traumatic Brain Injury (TBI)

- Psychostimulants improve symptoms of inattention, distractibility, disorganization, hyperactivity, disinhibition, impulsiveness, and emotional lability in properly selected TBI patients.[71,133]
- Methylphenidate is useful for slowed mental processing, and it may enhance the rate of recovery.[73,75]
- Stimulants may be combined with amantadine, levodopa, and antidepressants.[134]
- Methylphenidate dosage starts at 5 mg b.i.d. Dosage titration is 5 mg b.i.d. per week. Doses higher than 40 mg b.i.d. daily are not recommended.
- Dextroamphetamine can be dosed initially at 5 mg b.i.d., titrated slowly to a maximum of 20–30 mg b.i.d.

Pharmacologic Management of Behavioral Symptoms following Traumatic Brain Injury

The commonest psychiatric condition following TBI is depression (see Chapter 2). Depression occurs frequently in patients with neurologic disorders, and by 1990, psychopharmacologic treatments were found to be safe and efficacious in the treatment of depression in patients with neurologic illness, including TBI, even though there was a dearth of controlled studies.[85] Things are not much better in the psychopharmacologic treatment of depression 17 years later. A recent review of the various literature databases in worldwide medicine as well as the Cochrane Library databases between 1990 and 2003 revealed a significant absence of Type I–III evidence for psychopharmacologic use in TBI. There was no strong evidence either way to suggest that drugs are effective in the treatment of behavioral disorders in patients with TBI. The authors of this recent review concluded there was weak evidence, primarily based on case studies, that psychostimulants are effective in the treatment of apathy, inattention, and slowness. High-dose β-blockers appear useful in the treatment of agitation and aggression. Also, anticonvulsants and antidepressants (particularly SSRIs) have some evidence of effectiveness in the treatment of agitation and aggression, particularly in the context of an affective disorder.[86]

Antidepressants

Mood disorders are a frequent complication of TBI, and they exert a deleterious effect on the recovery process and psychosocial outcome of brain injury patients. Preliminary studies have suggested that selective serotonin reuptake inhibitors such as sertraline, mood stabilizers such as sodium valproate, as well as stimulants and ECT, may be useful in treating these disorders.[87] Recent guidelines for the use of antidepressant medication following acquired brain injury has been established by the British Society of Rehabilitation Medicine, the British Geriatric Society, and the Royal College of Physicians.[88] On the American side of the "pond," a recent article offers a practical approach to the evaluation and treatment of depression following TBI.[89] The reader is referred to these guidelines and suggestions for more complete information than can be provided in this text.

Tricyclic antidepressants were, of course, first used for treating depression following TBI. A small study examined desipramine treatment in a randomly assigned placebo-controlled study. Patients were assigned to either desipramine treatment or a placebo lead-in. Patients starting with desipramine stayed on that drug, and patients starting with a placebo lead-in were blindly crossed over to desipramine after one month if there was no significant improvement demonstrated by DSM-III-R criteria. Of all patients that could be evaluated, 6 of 7 demonstrated resolution of depression and depressed mood during desipramine treatment. Three of these received desipramine throughout the study, and three others began desipramine after one month of placebo exposure when they crossed over to desipramine. There was a statically significant improvement over time ($p < .001$).[90] Amitriptyline has been used to treat depression following TBI, but it has also been used to treat agitation.[91–93] Protriptyline was touted as an alternative stimulant medication in patients with brain injury.[94]

The SSRIs have become the mainstay for treating depression and even anxiety following TBI. They are easier to use, more user friendly for both patient and physician, and they do not carry the anticholinergic cognitive load of the tricyclic antidepressants that may further worsen short-term memory function. They are preferred in most instances of treating depression and anxiety in the brain-injured population.[95] Fluoxetine was studied in an open-label pilot investigation at 20–60 mg daily. It was administered to a heterogeneous group of five head-injured patients. The preliminary results showed that fluoxetine improved mood in addition to improving performance on the Trailmaking Test Part A.[96] In addition to depression, pathological crying following TBI seems quite amenable to treatment using SSRIs. Paroxetine was tested against citalopram in the treatment of pathological crying. A series of 26 consecutive patients with acquired brain damage and episodes of involuntary crying were placed into the study. The first 13 patients were treated with paroxetine, and the second 13 patients were treated with citalopram in single daily doses of 10–40 mg. The authors reported rapid-onset (within 1–3 days) and highly significant ($p < .001$) improvements of emotionalism after both paroxetine and citalopram. There were no differences in efficacy between the two products. The only adverse effect after paroxetine was nausea, and citalopram was tolerated without adverse effects.[97] There is also a single case study of citalopram being used to treat a 6-year-old boy who had pathological crying following a stroke. This youngster sustained a traumatic right-sided hemorrhage into the basal ganglia following a head injury. The citalopram is reported to have had a dramatic effect on his pathological crying and sleep disturbance.[98]

Most of the studies of SSRI use following TBI involve sertraline. One study at the University of Alabama in Birmingham used 11 subjects with severe TBI (GCS score $\leq$ 8) with presumed DAI and randomized them to receive sertraline, 100 mg daily, or placebo for 2 weeks. The reader should understand that this study was in a tertiary care inpatient rehabilitation center directly attached to a Level I trauma center. All subjects were within 2 weeks of acute injury, which may have biased the study since most antidepressants are used late in the course of treatment. This pilot study failed to establish whether the early use of sertraline improved alertness, decreased agitation, or improved recall of material. However, it is important to note that there were no complications with the use of sertraline and no apparent detrimental effect on recovery.[99] An 8-week nonrandomized single-blind placebo run-in trial of sertraline was conducted on 15 patients diagnosed with major depression between 3 and 24 months after mild TBI. This study was completed at the University of Washington in Seattle. Thirteen (87%) had a decrease in the Hamilton Rating Scale for Depression greater than or equal to 50%. Ten patients (67%) achieved a score of less than or equal to 7, which qualified for remission by 8 weeks of sertraline. There was statistically significant improvement in psychological distress, anger, and aggression; functioning was improved; and postconcussion symptoms were less with treatment.[100] The most complicated controlled study of sertraline used in brain injury depression comes out of St. Mark's Hospital Trust at Harrow in Middlesex, United Kingdom. This facility used an integrated care pathway (ICP) to describe the characteristics of patients presenting with depression in a brain injury rehabilitation program. It was also used to further assess patients' response to treatment with sertraline. A prospective cohort study included 82 patients admitted to the unit during the 15-month period between September 1999 and December 2000. Response to sertraline was assessed in an open-label, before-and-after study design. All admissions were screened for depression before entering the ICP. Of 82 admissions, 41% were managed using the ICP and 27 of those patients were either started on sertraline at admission or changed to sertraline after admission for depression. All of the depressed patients improved clinically at some level, and no significant side effects were observed. The ICP was practical to use and provided systematic data on assessment of depression and response to treatment in "real life" clinical practice in a brain injury rehabilitation setting.[101] While this appears correct, the weakness of this study is lack of randomization and lack of a placebo control. At this time, there remains still a lack of substantial controlled studies demonstrating the effectiveness of antidepressants in depression following TBI. The reader is referred to Table 8.11 for guidelines to using antidepressants in TBI depression.

TABLE 8.11

Antidepressant Approaches to Traumatic Brain Injury (TBI)

- Following TBI, the risk of depression remains elevated for decades.[135]
- Most depressions begin the first post-injury year.[136]
- The choice of antidepressant depends predominantly upon the desired side-effect profile.[137]
- Maprotiline and bupropion carry enhanced seizure risk.[138,139]
- ECT may be required in extreme cases.[95,140]
- SSRIs can, in some, produce excessive activation, irritability, or mania.[141]
- "Start low and go slow" to reduce side-effect risk.
- Mood disorders may respond, whereas, cognitive symptoms may not.
- Dosing follows standard pharmacologic guidelines for each antidepressant.

Antiepileptic Drugs

As with all drugs used to treat TBI, antiepileptic drugs are no different in that there is an extreme paucity of controlled studies regarding the use of these agents. The common folklore among psychiatrists is that they assist in the treatment of aggression and agitation following TBI. The Good Shepherd Rehabilitation Hospital in Allentown, Pennsylvania, studied 13 patients. These patients were on various anticonvulsant medications and were switched to lamotrigine. This cohort of patients had been transferred to a rehabilitation unit and started lamotrigine on average about 88 days after acute brain injury. This was an open-label, nonplacebo controlled study. It was an experiential study, and the authors concluded that 10 patients were discharged to the community and fewer to skilled nursing facilities than were expected because of their response to lamotrigine.[102] Lamotrigine was also reported in a single patient from the Brain Injury Rehabilitation Prevention Program at Alberta Hospital, Alberta, Canada. This 40-year-old male sustained severe TBI. A significant decrease in problematic behaviors and significant improvement in neurobehavioral function was observed after lamotrigine treatment.[103] No placebo-controlled trials of lamotrigine have been found to date for treating TBI.

Mania following TBI has been reported to respond to carbamazepine treatment. However, sometimes the response is seen only after addition of lithium or antipsychotics. A word of caution: carbamazepine has been known to produce or exacerbate cognitive impairment among patients with TBI. Additionally, there is evidence that persons using carbamazepine following TBI are at increased risk for neurotoxicity induced by combination therapy with carbamazepine and lithium.[95] Recently, an Italian study evaluated carbamazepine with citalopram in 20 post-TBI patients who were diagnosed as being depressed by two independent neuropsychiatric observers. These subjects were divided into two subgroups depending on the time elapsed from trauma. The first group was within 6 months of trauma, and the second group was 24 to 36 months after trauma. Rating at baseline included GCS score on hospital admission, length of coma, length of hospitalization, score on the Brief Psychiatric Rating Scale (BRPS), and score on the Clinical Global Impression (CGI) Scale. The BPRS and CGI were repeated after 12 weeks of oral administration of citalopram, 20 mg daily and oral administration of carbamazepine, 600 mg daily. The authors concluded that citalopram combined with carbamazepine is effective in reducing depression and behavioral disorders following TBI. They concluded further that these disturbances should be addressed as soon as possible during the acute rehabilitation period.[104]

While valproic acid has been used the most in treating aggressive and agitation syndromes following TBI, there is no advantage to be found in well-controlled studies for this product. In 1994, Geracioti[105] reported using valproic acid to treat episodic explosiveness related to brain injury. Wroblewski et al.[106] reported five patients with acquired brain injury. In an open study, they determined that in all cases valproic acid was effective after other pharmacologic interventions were not, and that improvement was seen often within 1–2 weeks. Valproate has also been used for TBI-induced rapid-cycling affective disorder.[107] Probably the largest valproate trial to date was at the Department of Rehabilitation Medicine at the University of Washington in Seattle. Dikmen et al.[108] studied 279 adult patients in whom valproate was given to prevent posttraumatic seizures. This was a randomized, double-masked, parallel group clinical trial. The study question was to compare the seizure prevention and neuropsychological effects of 1 or 6 months of valproate against 1 week of phenytoin. The patients were randomized within 24 h of injury and examined with a battery of neuropsychological measures at 1, 6, and 12 months post-injury. Drug effects were cross-sectionally examined at 1, 6, and 12 months and longitudinally by examining differential change from 1 to 6 months and from 6 to 12 months as a function of protocol-dictated changes in treatment. The results of the study demonstrated no significant adverse or no beneficial neuropsychological effects while using valproate. The authors concluded that valproate has a benign neuropsychological side-effect profile and is a cognitively safe antiepileptic drug to use for controlling established seizures or stabilizing mood. However, based on their study, the authors concluded further that valproate should not be used for prophylaxis of posttraumatic seizure because it does not prevent them. Moreover, in the rehabilitation population, they noted a trend toward more deaths in the valproate group, and it did not improve cognition. However, it is noteworthy that patients underwent this study very early, and unlike the neuropsychiatric use of valproate for aggression or agitation, the study question was the impact upon seizures, and neuropsychological side effects were an incidental study finding.

A case series of 29 patients were used to evaluate divalproex for agitation symptoms. This was an open-label study from Allentown, Pennsylvania, and chart information was abstracted retrospectively for all patients who received valproate for agitated symptoms during a 22-month period during one inpatient brain injury rehabilitation unit. For 26 of the 29 patients, valproate appeared effective within 7 days after a typical 1250 mg/day dose. Ninety-three percent of the patients were discharged to their home or community sites. The authors concluded that valproate was an efficacious alternative to neuroleptics and benzodiazepines for impulsive and disinhibited brain injury patients.[109] Lastly, a retrospective chart review was conducted on 11 patients at the Robert Wood Johnson Medical School in New Jersey. These individuals had been referred for psychiatric treatment. They were treated in an open fashion based on clinical grounds with valproate alone or in combination with other psychotropic medications. The patient base had a variety of psychiatric symptoms and frequently received concomitant medications. The average daily dose of valproate was $1818 \text{ mg} \pm 791 \text{ mg}$ per day. The average serum level of valproate was 85.6 ± 29.6 mcg/ml. Improvement on the Clinical Global Impression Scale was 1.9 ± 0.5 points. The authors concluded that valproate was well tolerated and effective in reducing a broad range of neurobehavioral symptoms in psychiatric patients with a remote history of TBI.[110] Please refer to Table 8.12 for guidelines using antiepileptic drugs following TBI.

Anxiolytic Medications

Anxiety disorders are common after TBI. The classical issues of these disorders were discussed prominently in Chapter 2. The commonest clinical anxiety disorder that the neuropsychiatric examiner will face is PTSD within the context of a TBI. It is not unusual for PTSD to be comorbid with TBI. The treatment of anxiety disorders following TBI may require medications. However, it is probably wise to use SSRIs for the treatment of anxiety rather than benzodiazepines. Benzodiazepines may disinhibit the patient, produce sedation, and are known to impair memory even at therapeutic doses and particularly in impaired patients who have sustained TBI.[95] It is not recommended that benzodiazepines be used as a first-line treatment for anxiety following TBI. If it is necessary to resort to benzodiazepines in selected TBI patients, those agents with short half-lives

---

TABLE 8.12

Use of Antiepileptic Drugs (AEDs) following Traumatic Brain Injury

- These are generally used for (1) posttraumatic seizures, (2) behavioral dyscontrol syndromes, and (3) neuropathic pain.[95]
- For psychiatric use, AEDs may assist to manage mania or disinhibition.[134]
- Valproate will not prevent posttraumatic seizures.[108]
- Secondary effects of brain injury may alter by enzyme induction the pharmacokinetics of valproate and phenytoin in adults and children, respectively.[142,143]
- Appropriate laboratory monitoring should accompany the use of valproate, phenytoin, carbamazepine, and lamotrigine.
- Lamotrigine may modify metabolism of multiple other AEDs.
- Dosage guidelines are individualized for each AED.

TABLE 8.13

Anxiolytic Agents in Traumatic Brain Injury (TBI)

- SSRIs are preferred for posttraumatic stress disorder (PTSD) and anxiety after TBI.[95]
- Benzodiazepines may be needed as an adjunct to treat severe PTSD. Their use as first-line agents is discouraged.[95]
- Buspirone may have usefulness in treating post-TBI anxiety.[112]

and limited active metabolites are preferred (lorazepam or oxazepam). Very short half-life drugs should be avoided, as they may cause rebound anxiety and reinforce overuse.

Gualtieri reported buspirone to be effective for decreasing anxiety, depression, irritability, somatic preoccupation, inattention, and distractibility among 4 of 7 patients who sustained concussion. Buspirone appears to carry less risk of worsening cognitive function in patients with TBI than benzodiazepines. The use of buspirone is not associated with dependency, and it causes no rebound anxiety should it be discontinued prematurely. However, since buspirone is a 5-HT1A receptor partial agonist, it requires a number of weeks to achieve optimal response.[95,111-112] Please see Table 8.13 for guidelines while using anxiolytic agents in patients who have sustained TBI.

There is one large retrospective study out of the College of Pharmacy at the University of Texas at Austin regarding buspirone's efficacy in organic-induced aggression. A retrospective medical records review was conducted on all patients who were admitted to a psychiatric rehabilitation facility over a 36-month period at the University of Texas. The College of Pharmacy researchers identified all patients who received buspirone therapy during their hospital stay. Monthly behavioral records were used to determine the quality and quantity of aggression-related behaviors. The study endpoint was reached in each subject when the buspirone was discontinued or when records were unavailable. Twenty subjects were selected ranging in age from 15 to 35 years. Of these subjects, 9 of 10 subjects for whom data were available for at least 3 months showed an improvement in behavior by study endpoint; six patients showed at least a 50% reduction in behavioral symptoms by study endpoint. The authors concluded that buspirone was well tolerated and might be effective in the treatment of aggression and other maladaptive behaviors in individuals with an organic component to their psychiatric illness, particularly in those who had sustained TBI.[113]

While benzodiazepines are not recommended in patients following TBI, they are occasionally used. There is available a randomized, double-blinded crossover trial performed at a tertiary care rehabilitation inpatient unit in a teaching hospital.[114] A total of 18 brain-injured and stroke patients were administered lorazepam, 0.5–1.0 mg orally at bedtime as needed for seven days, along with zopiclone, 3.75–7.5 mg orally at bedtime as needed for seven days. Total sleep time and characteristics of sleep were measured. Effects on cognition were measured using the Folstein Mini-Mental Status Examination. There was no difference in average sleep duration or in subjective measures of sleep. Cognition as assessed revealed no differences in the zopiclone arm compared with the lorazepam arm. The authors concluded that zopiclone was equally effective as lorazepam in the treatment of insomnia and stroke in brain-injured patients. The weakness of this study is the small number of 18 patients and also the lack of any sophisticated neuropsychological assessment.

Lithium

A study out of the New England Medical Center in 1989 used lithium to treat 10 brain-injured patients with severe, unremitting, aggressive, combative or self-destructive behavior, or severe affective instability.[115] Five patients in an open-label trial reportedly had a dramatic response that resulted in significant improvement in their participation in a rehabilitation program. A two-case study, one 4 years post-injury and the other 17 years post-injury, comes from the Buffalo Psychiatric Center. The patients were treated with lithium over a 2-year period, and the authors claim to have

---

TABLE 8.14

Lithium Use following Traumatic Brain Injury

- Useful for bipolar-like mania or chronic aggression following TBI.[95]
- TBI increases sensitivity to lithium neurotoxicity.[144]
- TBI increases side effects due to lithium and probably lowers seizure threshold.[145]
- Start dosing at 300 mg daily and titrate carefully.

---

demonstrated the efficacy of lithium carbonate in treating aggressive behaviors in brain-injured patients within a state psychiatric hospital. However, lithium was added to other medications, and the study was open and nonblinded.[116] Lastly, a single-case study of a 48-year-old woman in Kyoto, Japan was treated for rapid-cycling bipolar disorder subsequent to TBI. Neuroradiological examination revealed a circumscribed lesion in the left temporal pole. Her mood swings were successfully treated with the coadministration of valproate and lithium.[117] Table 8.14 suggests guidelines while using lithium in patients who may exhibit aggressive or bipolar symptomatology following TBI.

Neuroleptics (Typical and Atypical Antipsychotics)

The medical literature is sparse with reports of using neuroleptics or antipsychotic medications in persons with TBI. In fact, there is evidence that neuroleptics may cause their own cognitive load and further worsen cognition. A study from the College of Pharmacy at the University of Texas evaluated patients before, during, and after discontinuation of antipsychotic agents in inpatients undergoing rehabilitation for TBI. These patients were treated with either thioridazine or haloperidol. The evaluation revealed that selected areas of cognition improved after antipsychotic discontinuation in subjects with TBI. The magnitude of improvement appeared to be greater after discontinuation of thioridazine when compared with haloperidol.[118] Obviously, this is probably due to the significant inherent anticholinergic effect of thioridazine and the lack of anticholinergic potency in haloperidol. A recent study out of the Virginia Commonwealth University in Richmond evaluated haloperidol and olanzapine in rats. Rats received an intraperitoneal injection beginning 24 h after a brain injury was induced, and this administration continued daily for the duration of the study. Their cognitive performance was evaluated in the Morris Watermaze Performance Test on days 11–15 post-injury. Haloperidol exacerbated the cognitive deficits induced by the injury, as injured rats treated with 0.30 mg/kg haloperidol performed worse in the Morris Watermaze than injured rats treated with vehicle. The use of olanzapine did not adversely affect cognition in the same manner as haloperidol.[119] Another rat study from the University of Pittsburgh evaluated differential effects of single versus multiple administration of haloperidol and risperidone on functional outcome after experimental brain trauma. A total of 60 adult male Sprague–Dawley rats received either a cortical impact or sham injury and then were randomly assigned to five TBI groups (0.045 mg/kg, 0.45 mg/kg, or 4.5 mg/kg risperidone; 0.5 mg/kg haloperidol; or 1 ml/kg vehicle). The experiment consisted of three phases. In the first phase, a single treatment was provided intraperitoneally 24 h after surgery, and motor and cognitive function was assessed on postoperative days 1–5 and 14–18, respectively. During the second phase, after completion of the initial behavioral task, the same rats were treated once daily for five days and behavior was reevaluated. During the third phase, treatments were discontinued, and three days later the rats were assessed one final time. The rats were assessed on their time to maintain beam balance, time to traverse an elevated beam, and time to locate a submerged platform in a Morris Watermaze. Neither motor nor cognitive performance was affected after a single treatment by either agent. In contrast, both behavioral deficits reoccurred after daily treatments of risperidone and haloperidol. This was significant at $p < .05$. The cognitive deficits persisted even after a 3-day washout period during the third phase. The authors concluded that these data suggest that although single or multiple low doses of risperidone or haloperidol may be innocuous to subsequent recovery after TBI, chronic high-dose treatments are detrimental.[120]

TABLE 8.15

Use of Neuroleptics following Traumatic Brain Injury

- Brain injury is a risk factor for tardive dyskinesia.[146]
- If psychosis occurs after brain injury, neuroleptics generally must be prescribed.[147]
- Withdrawal of typical neuroleptics, if appropriate, may lead to an improvement in cognition or reduce abulia.[148]
- Routine use of neuroleptics acutely may segue into long-term treatment with little evidence-based data to support the usage.[134]
- Observe carefully for neuroleptic malignant syndrome (muscular rigidity, catatonia, fever, increased white cell count, sweating, etc.).
- Seizure threshold may be lowered.
- Neuroleptics probably delay recovery.[119,120]

Risperidone has been used to treat insatiable appetite following hypothalamic injury of TBI.[121] Risperidone has been noted to have a beneficial effect on sleep disturbance and psychosis following TBI.[122] A study out of Leeds, in the United Kingdom, reported successful treatment of a case of posttraumatic delirium and delusion following TBI using risperidone.[123] Olanzapine has been used to treat intractable hiccups following severe TBI,[124] and quetiapine was reported in a pilot study of 6 weeks open-label to effectively treat aggression due to TBI.[125] Dosages of 25–300 mg daily were used. The literature for using neuroleptics or antipsychotic medications in children following TBI is entirely lacking. The reader is referred to Table 8.15 for guidelines while using neuroleptics following TBI.

Propranolol

As noted above, the Cochrane Database has indicated that propranolol is probably effective for treating aggression following TBI. This has been demonstrated in a double-blind, placebo-controlled study of 100 patients with severe TBI.[126] In this study, the Overt Aggression Scale was used to measure patient behavior. The intensity of the episodes and number of episodes were less after propranolol use. Another double-blind study was completed by Greendyke et al.[127] This was a randomized placebo-controlled crossover study of propranolol in ten patients with aggression. An average dose of 520 mg daily was used. However, this study has limitations, as only 5 of the 10 patients had TBI. Other authors have reviewed the use of propranolol in the management of aggression in multiple states including those of TBI.[128,129] Table 8.16 gives suggested guidelines for using propranolol to treat aggression following TBI.

TABLE 8.16

Propranolol for Aggression following Traumatic Brain Injury (TBI)

- Complete a thorough medical evaluation and avoid contraindications for beta-blocker use.
- Give trial dose of 20 mg/day.
- If no untoward effects, increase dosage 20 mg every 3 days.
- When 60 mg/day dosage is reached, increase dosage 60 mg every 3 days.
- Keep resting pulse rate above 50/min and resting systolic blood pressure above 90 mmHg. Monitor for dizziness, ataxia, or wheezing.
- Target dose is 12 mg/kg body weight. Dosages above 800 mg daily are not required usually.
- Give at least an 8-week trial at appropriate dosage. Depression is a rare side effect.
- Monitor plasma levels of antipsychotic and antiepileptic drugs while using propranolol.

Source: From Silver, J.M. and Arciniegas, D.B. in *Brain Injury Medicine*, Zasler, N.D., Katz, D.I., and Zafonte, R.D., Eds., Demos, New York, 2007, p. 963.

Psychotherapy following Traumatic Brain Injury

If one reviews the psychiatric literature of the last 100 years for approaches to TBI using psychotherapy, little useful information will be found. The psychiatric profession has historically neglected to provide any analysis of the psychotherapeutic needs of patients following TBI. In fact, the great schools of psychoanalytic theory taught for years that psychotherapy is of no benefit to persons without insight; it derives from that, that persons with TBI probably do not have insight and therefore are not candidates for psychotherapy. Of course, nothing could be farther from the truth. Not only do most medical schools provide little if any instructional time to their students about the ramifications of TBI, most psychiatric residency programs treat TBI with the same short shrift. Psychiatric residents are afforded little to no opportunity to provide any form of psychotherapeutic services to the traumatically brain-injured unless there is a viable neuropsychiatry program within the department of psychiatry where residents are being trained. Most quality neuropsychiatric training programs today do recognize the importance of psychotherapy to those persons afflicted with TBI.

The traditional approach to psychotherapy has been that the inner psychological life of the person is the primary source of emotional problems. Obviously, within a neuropsychiatric model, this is not a tenable premise. The neuropsychiatric model posits that brain dysfunction caused by TBI is responsible for altered mental processing and altered emotional experiences. On the other hand, the life experiences of persons with brain injuries are not so different from those of noninjured persons.[149] People who have sustained TBI have similar struggles to others, and these include unresolved internalized conflicts, irrational assumptions about themselves, feelings of anxiety, depression, phobias, and obsessions. They often feel alienated and complain of lack of feeling. They are confronted by environmental circumstances over which they feel they have little control. All of these conditions are amenable to psychotherapy, even if only at a supportive level. Pollack[150] has recommended that psychotherapy with a brain-injured person should begin, assuming the patient is mentally competent enough, with reassurance to the patient that a brain injury is causing the behavioral or emotional disturbances, and it is not due to a neurotic or psychotic process. Of course, this assumes that the person is not psychotic at the time the initial psychotherapy evaluation is undertaken. Pollack recommends further that the patient's complaint should be heard carefully by the therapist and that the injury and its causation of emotional difficulty should be explained in nontechnical language and in a manner that the patient will understand. Positive and proactive language should be used with persons following brain injury. No therapist can predict outcome, and it must be recognized that any positive changes will be slow in coming. Therapists must be extremely flexible if they choose to work with a TBI patient due to the lability of emotions, difficulty with executive function, and poor motivation and apathy, which may interfere with the psychotherapeutic process.

Recently, psychotherapy is noted to be used within several models of neurorehabilitation, and it is becoming a core part of the posttrauma rehabilitative process.[151] Other forms of psychotherapy with the brain-injured population are taking place in natural settings. The more traditional forms of one-on-one psychotherapy are being redesigned.[152] Other studies have noted that it is important to select patients well. For instance, a recent study from Toronto concluded that routine treatment of all mild TBI patients with psychotherapy provides little benefit. It is better to focus on individuals who have pre-injury psychiatric problems that have been worsened as a result of TBI.[153] Studies have focused on what type of approach is best, and a recent evaluation reviewed operant behavioral approaches versus relational approaches. Both of these approaches were within the context of a neurobehavioral program. It was suggested by this study[154] that the relational neurobehavioral approach is more likely to engage or reengage persons who have sustained TBI. Often these individuals are resistant to behavioral change, and the relational approach appears to provide better rapport and increased likelihood of a positive outcome. A University of Victoria approach advises that acquired brain injury commonly results in both cognitive and emotional sequelae. Certainly, that should be clear to the reader by now at this point in this text. Consequently, interventions directed at only cognitive rehabilitation, or at only emotional distress, may be confounded by the interaction of cognitive and emotional issues. It is believed that cognitive rehabilitation must integrate both cognitive and emotional aspects with their interventions in order to be effective in assisting the patient with change.[155]

Psychotherapy with children presents its own particular difficulties, and obviously caregivers or family members should be included. A recent study from Schenectady, New York evaluated children receiving psychotherapy services due to behavioral concerns after TBI. This was a single-subject reversal design used to document the effects of combined behavioral, cognitive, and executive function intervention on dependent variables of frequency and intensity of aggressive behaviors and the amount of therapy work accomplished. The authors concluded that their program had potential for successfully treating behavior disorders in young children with TBI if the program combined behavioral, cognitive, and executive function components.[156] In order to enhance the interaction of families following TBI, a University of Cincinnati Children's Hospital study examined whether an online problem-solving intervention could improve parental adjustment following pediatric TBI. Families of children with moderate-to-severe TBI were recruited from the trauma registry of this large children's hospital and randomly assigned to receive online family problem-solving therapy or internet resources only. There were 20 persons in each group. The group receiving family problem-solving reported significantly less global distress, less depressive symptoms, and fewer anxiety symptoms at follow-up than did the group that received only Internet resources. The online family group also reported significant improvements in their problem-solving skills. The authors concluded that their findings suggest that an online skill-building approach can be effective in facilitating parental adaptation after TBI in their child.[157]

Overall, it is still necessary for the therapist treating an adult or child after TBI to pay attention to transference and countertransference issues. The usual components of trauma must be evaluated and dealt with. This includes denial, conditions that occur as a result of catastrophic injury and the guilt, shame, and feelings of punishment that injured persons often experience. Moreover, it is important to review with the patient the feelings of stigmatization or the feeling that they are being marginalized in society as a result of their disability. For the individual who has a limited social support structure of family, loneliness is a primary consideration and often may be the major focus of therapy.[149] Pollack also recommends that reasonable risk taking should be encouraged. It goes without saying that in a disinhibited orbitofrontal syndrome patient, this may be inappropriate, but many patients following TBI can take social risks in order to learn and grow. It has been noted that without the possibility of failure, a person can never achieve true independence or the right to make choices on one's behalf.[158]

FAMILY INTERVENTIONS AND THERAPY

As noted above, Lezak in 1978[27] described poignantly what it is like to live with a characterologically altered brain-injured patient. There are numerous literature and family system studies available presently that enable us to understand that TBI causes significant role changes and negative impact to spouses, parents, children, siblings, and extended family members.[159] Modern family systems experts working with TBI patients have broadly defined the stages of intervention for families afflicted by TBI at three stages: (1) acute care, (2) rehabilitation care, and (3) community reintegration. In the acute care phase, families organize around the injured person. It is at this point that expectations are often unrealistic, and emotional support may be lacking from the family. Rehabilitation is the more intermediate phase after acute care treatment. During this stage, families reportedly have worked past the initial grief of injury and are relieved that their loved one has survived. The hope for improvement is often very unrealistic at this stage. Families require careful and tender assistance so that they may learn of the realities and needs of the patient. Lastly, community reintegration is the stage at which family pathology is most likely to present. It is at this point when the family members become discouraged and depressed, and mourning for the loss of their injured loved one's function emerges. This is a crucial point for family intervention.

The goal is to help families become an effective and functional system in order to help the injured party. However, many families are unable to do so. Families may be separated, poorly structured, or have multiple social and financial demands upon them that limit their emotional and physical effectiveness at helping the injured patient. Even if therapy and support help families make a transition so the normal family trajectory and lifecycle reestablishes itself, there will be transition points where crises may occur. Episodic loss and mourning may emerge when the injured child attempts reintegration into school or the injured father reattempts employment. Failures at this point will reawaken family difficulties and produce an intense sense of mourning and loss. Moreover, the injured family member often loses contact with friends and community services. As time progresses, the family may become more and more pathological.

A recent study reviewed 57 caregivers of persons with TBI who were at least 4 years post-injury and who resided in Virginia.[160] These caregivers were primarily women ranging in age from 19 to 82 years and were primarily of the Caucasian race. The investigation noted that unmet family needs extend well beyond the acute care setting and extend many years after the original injury. The study further noted that caregiver life quality tended to diminish over time. The authors concluded that long-term life quality issues should not be underestimated following TBI in a family member. A study from Wales examined the impact of head injury and its neurobehavioral sequelae on personal relationships. Twenty-three couples who had divorced or separated from their brain-injured partner in the years following injury were placed into a "separated" group, while twenty-five others still in the marital relationship at the time data were collected comprised the "together" group. This study was interesting in that only mood swings accounted for a significant difference between groups. The findings concluded, at a statistically significant level, that unpredictable patterns of behavior, as perceived by partners of brain-injured individuals, imposed the greatest burden on personal relationships and may contribute to relationship failure.[161] Some brain injury rehabilitation units are recognizing the long-term needs in families and are developing structured interventions to assist. One recent system development is the Brain Injury Family Intervention Program at the Medical College of Virginia in Richmond, Virginia. This rehabilitation group has found that a structured approach, well tested and applied to all families in need, can help mitigate community-encountered problems as the injured person attempts community reintegration.[162]

The child injured by TBI poses particular challenges to therapists attempting to help families cope following TBI. A recent study from Brazil evaluated direct clinician-delivered services versus indirect family-supported rehabilitation of children following TBI. This was a randomized controlled trial in which children aged 5–12 years in the chronic phase of their recovery were randomly assigned to a clinician-delivered caregiver or to a family-supported intervention group. Both groups received intensive services for 1 year. Physical outcome was measured by structured physical therapy scales, and cognitive outcome was measured by WISC-III measures. Patients in the family-supported intervention sample efficiently acquired the skills needed to deliver physical and cognitive interventions to the child. The family's level of education was not a factor in success. Although both groups demonstrated improvements, only the children in the family-supported intervention group demonstrated statistically significant improvements on both outcome measures. The authors concluded that their study supported the effectiveness of children receiving care within the everyday routines of their lives, including intensive support for their families.[163]

In keeping with modern technology, the Cincinnati Children's Hospital has tested a web-based family intervention system in children with TBI. This hospital reported 8 parents and 6 children with moderate-to-severe TBI who were injured more than 15 months before the study. The families were given computers, web cameras, and high-speed Internet access. Weekly video conferences with the therapists were conducted after they completed self-guided web exercises on clinical problem-solving, communication, and antecedent behavior and management strategies. Statistical tests using paired t-tests compared pre- and post-intervention scores. Findings revealed significant improvements in injury-related burden, parental psychiatric symptoms, depression, and parenting stress. There was also a significant reduction in antisocial behaviors in the injured child but not in the child's self-reported depressive symptoms. The authors concluded that computer-based intervention might successfully be used to improve both parent and child outcomes following TBI in children.[164] Studies of this type herald the emergence of more efficient ways to deliver care using web-based systems, and it is probable that the use of these methods will accelerate in the future.

COGNITIVE REHABILITATION

In the first edition of this text, there were no significant evidence-based data to support the effectiveness of cognitive rehabilitation following TBI. This seems intuitively wrong, but the evidence is what it is. Since the last edition of this text, unfortunately little has changed. The use of hospital-based cognitive rehabilitation remains significantly questionable. If cognitive rehabilitation is to be offered, most experts now suggest that it be community based. The *Cochrane Database Systems Reviews* looked at multidisciplinary rehabilitation for acquired brain injury in adults of working age.[165] These studies reviewed the data for acute brain injury in adults aged 16–65 years. A wide range of sources were explored from 1966 through 2004. Randomized controlled trials comparing multidisciplinary rehabilitation with either routinely available local services or lower levels of intervention, or trials comparing intervention in different settings or at different levels of intensity, were evaluated. Quasi-randomized and quasi-experimental designs also were included provided they met predefined methodological criteria. Trials were selected by two authors independently, and their methodological quality was rated, again by two different independent authors. A third reviewer arbitrated when disagreements occurred. A "best evidence" synthesis was performed by attributing levels of evidence based on methodological quality.

Using this methodology, only 10 trials were identified of good methodological quality and four of lower quality. Within the subgroup of predominately mild brain injury, "strong evidence" suggested that most patients make a good recovery with provision of appropriate information and without additional specific intervention. For moderate-to-severe brain injury, there is "strong evidence" of benefit from formal intervention. For patients with moderate-to-severe acute brain injury already in rehabilitation, there is "strong evidence" that more intensive programs are associated with earlier functional gains, and "moderate evidence" that continued outpatient therapy helped to sustain gains made in early postacute rehabilitation. There is "limited evidence" that specialist inpatient rehabilitation and specialist multidisciplinary rehabilitation may provide additional functional gains, but the study served to highlight the particular practical and ethical restraints on randomization of severely injured individuals for whom there are no realistic alternatives to specialist intervention. The authors concluded that patients presenting acutely to hospital with moderate-to-severe brain injury should be routinely followed to assess their need for rehabilitation. Intensive intervention appeared to lead to earlier gains. The balance between intensity and cost-effectiveness has yet to be determined. Patients discharged from inpatient rehabilitation should have access to outpatient or community-based services appropriate to their needs. Those with milder brain injury benefit from follow-up and appropriate information and advice. There are important questions still to be answered, and future research should employ the appropriate methodology.[165]

In America, the J.F.K.-Johnson Rehabilitation Institute in Edison, New Jersey reviewed evidence-based cognitive rehabilitation from 1998 through 2002.[166] One hundred and eighteen articles were initially selected. Thirty-one studies were excluded. Articles were assigned to one of seven categories reflecting the primary area of intervention: attention, visual perception, apraxia, language, and communication, memory, executive function, problem-solving, and awareness, and comprehensive or holistic cognitive rehabilitation. Of 87 studies evaluated, 17 were rated as Class I, 8 as Class II, and 62 as Class III evidence-based studies. The authors of this review concluded that there is substantial evidence to support cognitive-linguistic therapies for people with language deficits after left hemisphere stroke and training for apraxia after left hemisphere stroke. They went on to state that there was substantial evidence to support cognitive rehabilitation for people with TBI, including strategy training for mild memory impairment, strategy training for postacute attention deficits, and interventions for functional communication deficits.[166] Unfortunately, this study is heavily weighted toward stroke patients, and the data supporting interventions in TBI are limited.

European rehabilitation specialists recently reviewed guidelines on cognitive rehabilitation. They reviewed the available evidence about effectiveness of cognitive rehabilitation. They found a limited number of generally low quality randomized clinical trials in this particular area of therapeutic intervention. The task force examined the available Cochrane reviews. They also considered evidence from small-group or single-case studies including an appropriate statistical evaluation of effect sizes. This study included stroke patients as well as TBI patients. They concluded that for TBI patients, there was evidence of efficacy for attentional training in the postacute stage after TBI, evidence for the use of electronic memory aids in memory disorders (databooks and computers), and the treatment of apraxia with compensatory strategies. They noted a lack of adequately designed studies in this area.[167]

With regard to the cognitive rehabilitation of children with acquired brain injury, a review from the United Kingdom examined all published interventions targeting cognitive domains of attention, memory, and executive function that could be identified. Eleven papers, involving 54 children and adolescents receiving intervention, were identified. The authors concluded that there was an absence of randomized control trials and a very limited number of studies using other methodological approaches at this time. They could find no conclusive evidence for the efficacy of cognitive rehabilitation for children with acquired brain injury, but they did discover a clear need to address a range of methodological difficulties in this field of study.[168]

What can safely be said is that there is a dearth of randomized controlled trials demonstrating the effectiveness of cognitive rehabilitation following TBI. It has never been answered if a person is better off with natural healing following TBI or is improved substantially with so-called modern rehabilitation techniques. The question is still open. This question has limited practical usefulness to the neuropsychiatrist treating TBI. Most neuropsychiatrists are not trained in brain rehabilitation, and their focus will be upon attempting to improve the behavioral and cognitive lives of their patients. On the other hand, as we will see in later chapters, the issue of the effectiveness of cognitive rehabilitation has important considerations for brain injury litigation. Most plaintiff lawyers include large demands for extensive and prolonged cognitive rehabilitation of patients who suffer a compensable brain injury. The need and expense for those services remains a substantial open question, and if a neuropsychiatric examiner is evaluating persons within the context of litigation, it is wise to be familiar with the significant limitations in effectiveness of cognitive rehabilitation following TBI. Most studies of rehabilitation on adults or children following TBI will not meet *Daubert* standards with regard to efficacy. For a thorough review of modern cognitive rehabilitation techniques, the reader is referred to Cicerone.[169]

CLINICAL NEUROBEHAVIORAL ANALYSIS OF CASE DATA

CASE 8.1:   MILD TRAUMATIC BRAIN INJURY AS A RESULT OF MOTOR VEHICLE ACCIDENT

Introduction

M.A. was a 31-year-old female from the Central United States at the time of TBI examination. She was sent by a worker's compensation management system to determine an optimization of her treatment plan following a motor vehicle accident. She was examined 28 months following her injury.

History of the Accident

At the time of her injury, M.A. was employed customarily as an emergency medical technician. She was involved in a motor vehicle accident, which produced significant injury to her. She required transport by helicopter to a university hospital. At admission to that hospital, her GCS = 10, with

$E = 3$, $M = 5$, and $V = 2$. Initial CT of the head revealed a small amount of traumatic subarachnoid hemorrhage in the right cerebral hemisphere. CT was repeated one week after admission to hospital and demonstrated evolution of encephalomalacia in the right posterior-cerebellar hemisphere.

She required inpatient treatment at the university hospital for 13 days. Further information was obtained while in hospital, and it was noted she had been ejected from the vehicle and that she had a positive loss of consciousness. During her hospital stay, evaluation revealed bilateral mandibular fractures, facial lacerations, right maxillary sinus fracture, left fifth metacarpal fracture, and left lateral epicondyle fracture. She became depressed during hospitalization and was placed on fluoxetine. She was transferred to a nearby rehabilitation hospital at discharge. At that facility, she demonstrated poor short-term memory and fair long-term memory. Deep tendon reflexes were increased bilaterally in the lower extremities, greater on the left side than the right side. Toes were upgoing bilaterally. She was discharged from inpatient rehabilitation 5 weeks after her original injury. Her discharge diagnoses included mild closed-head injury, prior history of depression, and history of asthma.

History of Present Symptoms

She continued to complain of depression while at the rehabilitation facility. When examined neuropsychiatrically, she was treated by a family physician and an anesthesiologist pain physician. Her depression improved slightly, but she remained unable to work. She denied plans or thoughts of suicide, but she did complain of depression, sadness, and nervousness associated with poor concentration and memory difficulty. She reported word-finding difficulty, feelings of excessive anger, and irritability. Her sleep was not normal, and she reported difficulty maintaining sleep with a sleep continuity disturbance and nighttime awakenings. Her left hand remained dysfunctional, and she could not close her left hand to make a fist. She complained of poor coordination and balance and that she fell easily. She reported she had fallen a number of times since her injury.

Activities of Daily Living

She lived with her husband and two children. Her time of arising was about 6:00 a.m., and she retired at about 10:00 p.m. She was able to fix her own breakfast, and she was able to drive the family truck. She was able to use a checkbook. She could attend church if she chose. She enjoyed walking, and she was recovering her ability to read. She enjoyed reading mysteries. She was able to perform light housecleaning and performed laundry duties for her family. She was able to eat outside the home socially a couple of times monthly. She could use the telephone effectively. She was able to dress and bathe herself independently, and she retained sexual function with her husband.

Past Medical History

She did not know her birth weight, but she denied she was born prematurely and she had no birth injury. Her developmental milestones were normal, and she had no difficulty learning to read in school. She was able to sit still in her seat at school and keep her mind on task.

As an adult, before this injury, M.A. had demonstrated anemia and hypertension. She denied any other motor vehicle injuries. She denied any history of prior fractures. Her surgeries related to this accident included (1) open reduction and internal fixation of mandible, (2) tendon repair, left wrist, (3) elbow repair for right epicondylar fracture, and (4) left hand reconstruction.

Her current medications were as follows:

1. Fluoxetine, 20 mg daily
2. Pregabalin, 75 mg, twice daily
3. Topirimate, 100 mg, twice daily

She gave a pre-injury history of migraine headaches beginning at age 15, and her most recent treatment for those headaches was topirimate. She claimed her migraine headaches had worsened since her injury. Before the subject accident, M.A. had separated from her husband, and she had been treated with fluoxetine for depression. She reported allergies to atropine-containing medications and morphine. She denied using tobacco products, alcoholic beverages, or drugs of abuse. She drank three cups of coffee daily and two caffeinated soft drinks daily. She had two pregnancies and produced two living children by caesarean section; she maintained regular menstrual periods.

Past Psychiatric History

M.A. denied she had ever been hospitalized for psychiatric, drug abuse, alcohol, or mental problems. She denied using antidepressants as a youngster or at any other time in her life until the pre-injury separation from her husband. She denied she had ever received counseling or psychotherapy. She denied she had ever intentionally overdosed herself on drugs or medicines, and she had never made an attempt to take her life. She denied she had ever intentionally cut, burned, or disfigured herself.

Family and Social History

Her father was 68 years of age, and her mother was 55 years of age at the time of the evaluation. Her father had undergone repair of an atrial septal defect, and her mother had mitral valve prolapse syndrome. M.A.'s 7-year-old son had been diagnosed with Wolff-Parkinson-White syndrome. A sister had undergone repair of an atrial septal defect and also had been diagnosed with mitral valve prolapse syndrome. Another sister had a prior history of anorexia nervosa. Both sons were treated for asthma, and one son was treated for comorbid attention deficit disorder. Her brother was alcohol dependent. She denied any family history of suicides, homicides, violence towards others, child abuse, or spouse abuse. No one in her family had been diagnosed with epilepsy, neurological disease, Alzheimer's disease, or strokes.

She was born in a midwestern state, and she was one of three children. She had a sister and a brother. When she was a youngster living at home, her father was employed in the construction industry, and her mother was a homemaker. She denied that her father abused her mother and denied she had ever been sexually or physically abused. There were no guns in the home, and she denied any plans to harm herself or harm others. After graduating high school, she obtained a 2 year degree from a local state university and later completed emergency medical technician training. She had been married for 14 years, and the marriage produced two sons who were of ages 7 and 11 years at the time of this examination. She claimed her marital history had improved following her accident, because she rented a home and moved her family away from his parents; her husband followed her and their relationship improved. She admitted to interference from her in-laws.

Legal and Employment History

She had never been convicted of a felony or misdemeanor. She had never been a party in a lawsuit, restraining order, or emergency protective order. She had never been charged with spouse abuse, child abuse, or terroristic threatening. However, she had previously declared bankruptcy. Her employment history was that of an emergency medical technician for 7 years before the subject injury. Before that, she had worked as an account assistant at a university and also as a university secretary. She had no military history.

Review of Systems

In her general review, she had gained about 15 lb since the accident. Her HEENT review was positive for chronic migraine headaches since adolescence. Her chest, cardiovascular, gastrointestinal, and genitourinary reviews were negative. In her gynecological review, she reported some menstrual irregularity. Her psychiatric and sleep reviews are noted within the body of the report above. In her pain review, she complained of head and jaw pain along with pain radiating into the left arm, left hand, and left shoulder. In her neurological review, she complained of poor balance since the accident and poor coordination.

Mental Status Examination

M.A. completed independently a complex 22-page medical questionnaire. She was right handed, and she demonstrated cursive handwriting without evidence of tremor or micrographia. She was a capable historian, and she was pleasant and cooperative.

All current complaints were subjective. Objectively, she demonstrated reduced and constricted affective range, but she was never tearful. Thought and motor speed were mildly reduced. She made good eye contact with the examiner, and she denied specifically suicidal ideas or plans. There was no evidence of delusions or hallucinations. There was no evidence of loose associations or circumstantial thinking, and no formal thought disorder was present.

Articulatory agility was good, and there was no evidence of dysarthria, dysphonia, dysprosody, or dysphasia. The melodic line was slightly truncated. Phrase length was reasonably normal. There was no evidence of word-finding impairment and no evidence of paraphasias. Cognitive evaluation was deferred to the neuropsychological testing reported below.

Neurological Examination

Her weight was 234 pounds, and her blood pressure was 126/86 mmHg in the left arm sitting position. No bruits were present in the head or neck. The face was symmetrical and revealed no obvious signs of trauma. Hand dominance was to the right hand.

On cranial nerve inspection, there was no evidence of focal deficits. Nerve I was intact to anise and peppermint oils. Tuning fork sound was heard well in the left ear and the right ear, but the Weber sign lateralized to the left. Corneal reflexes were intact, and extraocular movements were full. Bulk and tone were good, but strength was reduced in the left grip. Outstretched arms revealed no pronator drift. Deep tendon reflexes were symmetrical. Light touch and pinprick were intact in the sensory examination. Vibratory and position sensations were intact bilaterally. The Romberg sign revealed no sway. Nystagmus was not present. Finger-to-nose function was intact, and heel-shin function was intact. There was no evidence of dysdiadochokinesia. Gait analysis revealed normal stride with some widening of gait due to obesity of the thighs. Arm swing was normal in excursion, and motor speed was normal. Tandem walking was without dystaxia, even though she complained of poor balance.

Neuroimaging

Magnetic resonance imaging of the brain was obtained without infusion. Images were interpreted by a board-certified radiologist and were then overread by the neuropsychiatrist. The reader is referred to Figures 8.1 and 8.2, where it can be noted that there is an area of abnormal axial FLAIR signal in the right cerebellar hemisphere. This is consistent with an area of encephalomalacia. There is also a small area of abnormal axial FLAIR signal involving the right temporal tip, consistent with encephalomalacia.

Standardized Mental Assessment

The psychologist noted that M.A. was friendly and cooperative, and she had a fair attitude toward the assessment procedure. Her speech was coherent and characterized by an accent typical of her geographic region. She became tearful on a few occasions, such as when discussing her employment or health since the accident. Testing was conducted over a 1.5-day period, and all tests were administered in a standardized manner. She demonstrated optimal effort throughout the evaluation.

During nonverbal test items, M.A. utilized both hands when manipulating objects such as blocks and picture cards. She approached tasks in a trial-and-error manner, and she attempted to

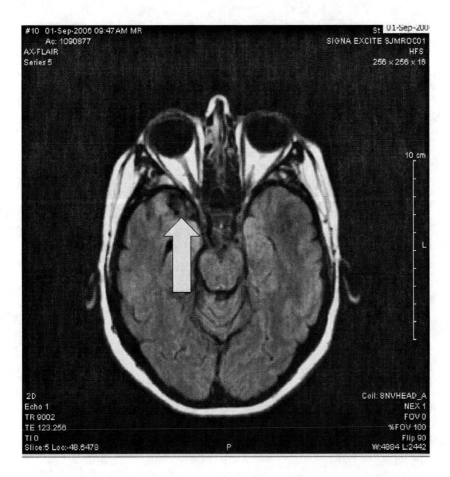

FIGURE 8.1 Axial FLAIR MRI demonstrating encephalomalacia at the right temporal tip.

work in a speedy fashion. On a subtest requiring her to reproduce a three-dimensional block design (Block Design subtest of the Wechsler Adult Intelligence Test, WAIS-III), she displayed much difficulty and had problems recognizing and correcting her errors. On a picture arrangement task (of the WAIS-III) she again displayed difficulty and was noted to state, "This doesn't make any sense."

On assessing measures requiring verbal responses, she often struggled to adequately express herself. She engaged in long pauses. She attempted to elaborate or further explain but often responded with, "I don't know" as test items became more difficult in content. On a test measuring word fluency (Controlled Oral Word Association test), she was able to produce only 13 words over three separate 1-min trials.

Otherwise, she readily comprehended and followed instructions. She occasionally closed her eyes during tests that required extra concentration. She reported some pain and discomfort in the left wrist during testing. Although she was right-hand dominant, she had obvious difficulty on tests of motor skill requiring her to use the left hand. On measures of cognitive distortion, she produced a score within normal limits on the Test of Memory and Malingering (TOMM), and she had scores within the valid range on the Victoria Symptom Validity Test (VSVT).

Results of the Minnesota Multiphasic Personality Inventory (MMPI-2) validity measures were interpreted to indicate a questionably valid profile characterized by a partial acquiescent response set and an overly positive self-presentation. The psychologist advised that particular attention should be paid to scales L, K, and S; these scores may be artificially deflated owing to the acquiescent

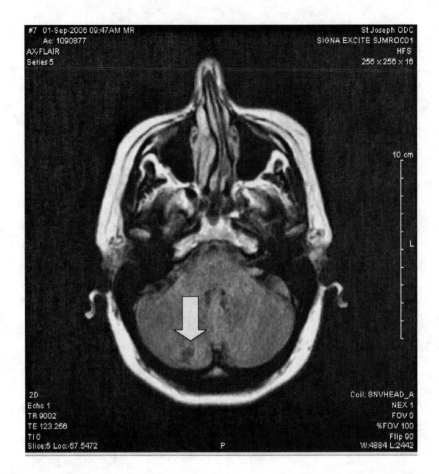

FIGURE 8.2 The southward-facing arrow highlights right cerebellar hemisphere encephalomalacia.

response set. Consequently, the results of the MMPI-2 profile may not accurately represent existing psychopathology. The MMPI-2 Fake Bad Scale (FBS) was within normal limits.

On the Minnesota Multiphasic Personality Inventory-II (MMPI-II), she produced the following validity profile:

	VRIN	TRIN	F	F(B)	Fp	L	K	S
T-score	54	65	61	66	65	66	39	48

Measures Providing Estimate of Pre-injury Function

The Wechsler Test of Adult Reading (WTAR) was administered to M.A. She produced the following demographic predicted (WAIS-III) and Wechsler Memory Scale-III (WMS-III) indices:

WTAR Demographic Predicted WAIS-III and WMS-III Indices:

	Standard Score	Percentile	Classification
WAIS-III VIQ	106	66	Average
WAIS-III PIQ	106	66	Average
WAIS-III FSIQ	107	68	Average
WAIS-III VCI	106	66	Average
WAIS-III POI	105	63	Average
WAIS-III WMI	104	61	Average
WAIS-III PSI	108	70	Average
WMS-III immediate memory index	105	63	Average
WMS-III general memory index	107	68	Average
WMS-III working memory index	103	58	Average

Attention and Concentration

The Ruff 2 & 7 Selective Attention Test was administered to determine visual attention, and the Brief Test of Attention was administered to determine auditory attention. The Digit Span subtest of the Wechsler Intelligence Scale (WIS) was also used to determine working memory for digit span.

Ruff 2 & 7 Selective Attention Test

Measure	Sum of *T*-Scores	*T*-Score	Percentile	Classification
Total speed	73	38	12	Mildly impaired
Total accuracy	110	55	70	Above average

Brief Test of Attention

	Percentile	Interpretation
BTA total score	>74	Above average

WAIS-III Digit Span Subtest

	Standard Score	Percentile	Classification
Longest digit span forward	104	61	Average
Longest digit span backward	91	27	Average
Digit span scaled score	95	37	Average

Language and Language-Related Skills

M.A. was administered the Boston Naming Test and the Controlled Oral Word Association Test to determine naming skill and the ability to produce specific words under timed conditions.

Boston Naming Test

T-score	53
Classification	Average
Percentile	63

Controlled Oral Word Association Test

T-score	18
Percentile	0.1
Classification	Severely Impaired

Memory

M.A. was administered the WMS-III to determine auditory, visual, and working memory abilities.

Wechsler Memory Scale - III

	Scale Score Sum	Index Score	Percentile	Classification
Auditory immediate	19	97	42	Average
Visual immediate	19	97	42	Average
Immediate memory	38	96	39	Average
Auditory delayed	19	97	42	Average
Visual delayed	16	88	21	Low average
Auditory recognition delayed	08	90	25	Average
General memory	43	89	23	Low average
Working memory	13	81	10	Low average

Sensory Perceptual Skills

M.A. was administered the Reitan–Kløve Sensory Perceptual Examination. She was administered tests to determine bilateral simultaneous sensory stimulation, fingertip writing and tactile finger recognition. Her *T*-scores are noted below:

Sensory Perceptual Examination

	T-Score	Classification	Percentile
Total right errors	32	Mildly to moderately impaired	04
Total left errors	40	Below average	16
Sensory perceptual total	34	Mildly to moderately impaired	06

Motor and Visual Motor Skills

M.A. was tested with the Grooved Pegboard Test, Grip Dynamometer, and the Finger Tapping Test. She produced the following scores:

Grooved Pegboard Test

	T-Score	Classification	Percentile
Dominant right hand	28	Moderately impaired	1.0
Nondominant left hand	14	Severely injured	0.04

Grip Dynamometer

	T-Score	Classification	Percentile
Dominant right-hand strength	54	Average	68
Nondominant left-hand strength	23	Moderately to severely impaired	0.8

Finger Tapping Test

	T-Score	Classification	Percentile
Dominant right hand	51	Average	55
Nondominant left hand	45	Average	32

Executive Functions

Her executive ability was tested by using the Wisconsin Card Sorting Test and Trailmaking Tests A and B. She produced the following *T*-scores and injury classifications:

Wisconsin Card Sorting Test

	Standard Score	T-Score	Percentile	Classification
Total errors	<55	<20	<1	Severely impaired
Perseverative responses	<55	<20	<1	Severely impaired

Trailmaking Test A

T-Score	Classification	Percentile
42	Below average	23

Trailmaking Test B

T-Score	Classification	Percentile
22	Moderately to severely impaired	0.7

Test Intelligence

This was measured using the WAIS-III. Her age-adjusted scaled scores, deviation IQs, and index scores are noted below:

Wechsler Adult Intelligence Scale-III

Subtests	Age-Adjusted Scaled Scores					
	Verbal	Performance	VC	PO	WM	PS
Picture completion		04		04		
Vocabulary	10		10			
Digit symbol-coding		07				07
Similarities	10		10			

(*continued*)

Wechsler Adult Intelligence Scale-III (continued)

Subtests	Verbal	Performance	VC	PO	WM	PS
		Age-Adjusted Scaled Scores				
Block design		06		06		
Arithmetic	07				07	
Matrix reasoning		05		05		
Digit span	09				09	
Information	08		08			
Picture arrangement		05				
Comprehension	09					
Symbol search		(04)				04
Letter–number sequencing	(10)				10	
Sum of Scaled Scores	**53**	**27**	**28**	**15**	**26**	**11**

Deviation IQs

	Standard Score	Classification	Percentile	Range
Verbal IQ	92	Average	30	87–97
Performance IQ	72	Borderline	03	67–80
Full scale IQ	81	Low average	10	77–85

WAIS-III Index Scores

	Standard Score	Classification	Percentile	Range
Verbal comprehension	96	Average	39	91–102
Perceptual organization	70	Borderline	02	65–79
Working memory	92	Average	30	86–99
Processing speed	76	Borderline	05	70–88

Psychopathology

For detection of psychopathology, the MMPI-2 was administered. The clinical scores are noted below with their appropriate T-scores represented:

Minnesota Multiphasic Personality Inventory-2

Scale	VRIN	TRIN	F	F(B)	Fp	L	K	S	
T-Score	54	65	61	66	65	66	39	48	

Scale	1	2	3	4	5	6	7	8	9	0
T-score	67	70	54	51	45	63	68	60	41	75

Records Reviewed

The records were fairly extensive in this case, and they included the original police traffic collision report, forms supplied to her worker's compensation carrier, and the records from the university hospital where she was treated. The record database also included the original scoring sheets from the helicopter transport and the records from the rehabilitation hospital wherein she was treated following injury.

She was followed by a medical case manager who produced monthly reports. These were reviewed for the neuropsychiatric examination. The records of her occupational therapist, physical therapist, speech therapist, pain physician, and an independent neurosurgical examiner were reviewed. Because of her mandibular fractures, she required extensive dental reconstruction, and those records were reviewed as well.

Diagnoses

Neuropsychiatrically, she was diagnosed with dementia due to head trauma (294.1x, ICD-9-CM) and cognitive disorder not otherwise specified (294.9, ICD-9-CM). She also demonstrates symptoms consistent with mood disorder (major depression) due to brain injury (293.83, *DSM-IV*).

Neurobehavioral Analysis

The reader is asked to review the data from the original injury. It can be seen that the GCS score was equal to 10. Recall from Chapter 1 that this is potentially consistent with a moderate injury. This case turned out to be a mild injury based on outcome criteria. However, recall from Chapter 1 that if any lesion is found on CT scan, the minimal level of severity is a moderate injury. She did not require significant resuscitation. The initial CT of the head revealed a small amount of traumatic subarachnoid hemorrhage, and a repeat CT on the eighth injury day demonstrated encephalomalacia in the right posterior cerebellar hemisphere. The encephalomalacia detected at neuropsychiatric examination was not yet apparent when she was treated at the university hospital, and no follow-up neuroimaging was obtained during rehabilitation so this was not known until her neuropsychiatric examination.

As has been stressed in this book, TBI is often a comorbid condition. This lady demonstrates significantly that she had multiple head and body orthopedic injuries, which are comorbid with her TBI, and these must be factored into assessing her neuropsychiatric needs and treatment planning. She sustained bilateral mandibular fractures, facial laceration, right maxillary sinus fracture, left fifth metacarpal fracture, and left lateral epicondyle fracture. She required four orthopedic surgeries for these injuries.

When she was evaluated at the rehabilitation hospital, she had a significantly abnormal neurological examination. At the time of the neuropsychiatric examination, most of these focal neurological signs were no longer present. Her complaints at the time of the neuropsychiatric examination were primarily behavioral, memory, concentration, and sleep.

By reviewing her past psychiatric history, it is obvious that she had a pre-injury depressive disorder that required pharmacologic treatment. Recall from prior statements in this text that the likelihood of her developing a post-TBI mood disorder is therefore higher, and that appears to have occurred in this case. However, at the time of the neuropsychiatric examination, her mood state had not been optimized. She continued with her inability to be employed, and she was struggling to maintain her role as a wife and mother.

If the reader will review Figures 8.1 and 8.2, the right temporal encephalomalacia and the right cerebellar encephalomalacia persist. Since it is more than 2 years following her injury, these are permanent tissue deficits, and they are static at the time of the neuropsychiatric examination. With regard to her emotional and cognitive state, there are significant abnormalities within the neuropsychological assessment. As has been discussed in Chapters 6 and 7 what first must be determined is her level of effort. She provided good cognitive effort, and there is no evidence of significant symptom magnification or a malingering pattern (see Chapter 9) on the MMPI-2. Therefore, her complaints probably accurately represent her true cognitive and behavioral state.

The reader should review carefully the data from the WTAR demographic-predicted WAIS-III and WMS-III indices. In the United States, this is often the standard for determining pre-injury cognitive capacity. This test is statistically correlated with the Wechsler IQ scales and the WMS (see Chapter 6). As the reader can see, M.A. is predicted to be average for the WAIS-III indices noted and average for immediate memory, general memory, and working memory. These now become the standards for comparison with her actual scores. Therefore, we expected that her pre-injury cognitive capacity was in the average range, and if she deviates substantially from average, those can be considered to be deficits as a result of this injury, as there is no other competent cause.

After reviewing the data from the Ruff 2 & 7 Selective Attention Test, it can be seen that M.A. is mildly impaired in her ability to rapidly acquire visual targets. While her accuracy is above average, her speed of visual pursuit is below average. On the other hand, based on the results of the BTA, there does not seem to be any impairment of auditory attention. Moreover, her Digit Span subtest scores are in the average range and consistent with predicted cognitive capacity. On the measures of language and language-related skills, the Boston Naming Test score is in the average range. However, she is showing substantial impairment of verbal fluency on the Controlled Oral Word Association Test, and her ability to produce words from the frontal parts of her brain is severely impaired.

Moving to the WMS-III, it is noted that visual delayed memory, general memory, and working memory are in the low average range. These are not expected deviations and are consistent with mild impairment. On sensory perceptual examination, it can be seen that she shows right-sided errors. These are not easily explainable, as the brain deficits are in the right brain, and if the sensory deficits were due to a central lesion, it would be expected that they would refer to the contralateral side. However, on measures of motor skill, she shows a left-sided deficiency on the Grooved Pegboard Test and the Grip Strength Test, consistent with the injury to her left hand and elbow and the necessary surgery required.

The reader may wish to review Chapter 6 regarding executive function. This lady shows severe impairment on the Wisconsin Card Sorting Test and moderate to severe impairment on Trailmaking Test B. These findings are consistent with substantial executive dysfunction as a result of her injury. The findings of executive dysfunction show good clinical correlation with the abnormal T2 signal involving the right inferior frontal lobe and the right temporal tip. Right-sided frontal lesions often significantly affect adversely executive function, and that seems to have occurred in this case.

With regard to test intelligence, M.A. shows substantial deviations in performance IQ and full scale IQ, which do not meet predicted values for her pre-injury cognitive capacity. This apparent drop in intellectual capacity forms the basis for the diagnosis of dementia due to TBI. The term "dementia" is being used in somewhat of a loose fashion in this case to represent an acquired loss of intelligence. If one bores into the subtest data of the WAIS-III, it is noteworthy that she is well below expected ability on Picture Completion, Matrix Reasoning, Picture Arrangement, and Symbol Search. These low scores reflect a substantial impairment to her general cognitive ability. If the reader will also review the index scores of the WAIS-III, it can be seen that she is significantly low on the perceptual index and the processing index.

With regard to her behavioral state, if the reader will review the T-score of the clinical scales 1–0 of the MMPI-2, it can be seen that scales 1, 2, 7, and 0 exceed the statistical cutoff of 65T. Scale 2 measures mood components and areas of mental function normally associated with depression. Scale 1 is often elevated in persons who have physical dysfunction, and scale 7 is within the behavioral domain commonly noted as anxiety. The elevation on scale 0 reflects probable difficulty with self-integration into society.

Treatment Planning

M.A. had shown a limited response to fluoxetine, and she had been taking this agent since before her TBI. She was switched to escitalopram, 20 mg daily. After approximately 8 weeks, she began to show a positive mood response. She was placed into individual psychotherapy helping her focus upon vocational reattainment. Also, family therapy was offered to her husband and children who were having difficulty coping with her lack of employment and her altered mood and cognition.

After approximately 5 months of treatment with the escitalopram and psychotherapy, she was placed into a work-hardening program. She did very well, and she was able to find employment with two ambulance companies, and she is now working more than 40 h weekly as an emergency medical technician.

Case 8.2: Moderate Brain Injury due to Slip-and-Fall

Introduction

This case concerns a man aged 72 at the time of his injury. He was exploring a construction site during off-hours. There were no warning signs or barriers around a storm-draining culvert, and he fell approximately 7 ft from a roadway to the bottom of the culvert. This case is instructive, as W.R. demonstrated a severe language disturbance as a result of his fall, and this case is used to illustrate the evaluation of a language disturbance within the context of TBI.

History of the Accident

W.R. fell from a roadway into an open storm drainage culvert. It is not clear how he was discovered, and he may have lain at the bottom of the culvert for quite some time. When attended by the emergency medical squad, his GCS score totaled 11, with $E=4$, $M=5$, and $V=2$. He was transported to a university Level I trauma center. His functions deteriorated during transport, and when received at the emergency department, his GCS score was 9, with $E=4$, $M=4$, and $V=1$. CT scan of the head was obtained and revealed an area of hemorrhagic contusion in the right temporal lobe with associated pneumocephalus. Blood was seen in the mastoid air cells. The evaluating physician determined that the neuroimaging findings were consistent with a probable occult fracture of the right temporal bone. CT scan was repeated 8 days following injury, and it revealed an evolving contusion of the temporal lobes bilaterally. During the interim, a ventricular catheter was placed into the right brain.

The emergency department records revealed that he was combative, and he had decreased oxygen saturation. He required placement of a chest tube due to a pneumothorax. He had a prolonged neurointensive care unit hospitalization, which was complicated by Pseudomonas pneumonia and methicillin-resistant *Staphylococcus aureus* (MRSA). He required a tracheostomy. His pneumonia eventually resolved, but his mental status improved only slightly. He was not discharged from hospital until $3\frac{1}{2}$ weeks post-injury. At that time, he was transferred to a university-affiliated TBI unit.

At the time of admission to the rehabilitation unit, W.R. was examined by an attending physician and a resident physician. They found that W.R. was nonverbal on mental examination. He would follow less than 25% of commands, and he was agitated. He could not comply with or understand portions of the physical examination. He was hospitalized in the rehabilitation unit for 1 month, and during that time he developed diabetes mellitus requiring sliding-scale insulin and NPH insulin. He had difficulty feeding himself. Cognitive ability was markedly diminished.

History of Present Symptoms

At the time of his neuropsychiatric examination, which was 21 months following his original injury, he was not capable of providing independently his own history. His wife of many years provided collateral information. She reported that W.R. had significant difficulty with short-term memory and language. He would use incorrect words to describe objects. He communicated to his wife poorly and in a halting fashion. She reported that W.R. understood poorly, and he had difficulty with oral comprehension. If information was conveyed to him orally, he was able to receive the information better if he read it, and she often wrote notes for him to do so. His wife reported that reading comprehension was better than auditory comprehension, but he required reading the material repeatedly to retain the information. His wife denied any form of motor impairment, and in fact, he walked in his neighborhood two or three times daily. While verbal ability was markedly diminished, he was able to cut his own grass with a lawnmower. However, he was significantly hypersomnolent following his injury, and he slept much more than he used to. His prior agitation had abated.

Activities of Daily Living

W.R. lives with his wife, and he is not employed. He was retired at the time of his injury. His time of arising is about 6:00 a.m., and his wife fixes his breakfast. He is not able to drive a vehicle; he cannot use a checkbook; he does sign checks, but his wife has to complete them. Most Sundays he is able to attend church. He dislikes sitting, and he has always been an active man. He is able to read the newspaper, but comprehension and retention of information is very poor. He can write only slightly. He spends most of his day watching television. He is able to take out the garbage if his wife asks him to do so. He is able to make minor repairs around the house based on old knowledge that he had before he was injured. He often eats outside the home socially but always accompanied by his wife. He rarely uses the telephone. He can dress and bathe himself independently. He has lost all sexual function with his wife, yet he was sexually active with her before this injury.

Past Medical and Psychiatric History

His birth weight was unknown, but he was not born prematurely and his developmental milestones were normal. Physically and mentally he did well in school. His diabetes was probably stress related at the time of his original injury, and at the time of the neuropsychiatric examination he no longer required diabetic treatment. He developed hypertension while hospitalized with his brain injury, but that dissipated following injury. At the time of the neuropsychiatric examination, he was normo-tensive. He was being treated with no medication of any kind at the time of this examination. His pre-injury health had been very good, and he rarely required the attention of a physician. He had no prior history of injury in motor vehicle accidents, and he had no prior history of brain injury, loss of consciousness or coma. He had a shoulder separation approximately 45 years before the current examination, but he had no complications therefrom. He had never undergone surgery until he required the tracheostomy following his brain injury. He had no known allergies to drugs or medicines. He did not use tobacco products, alcoholic beverages, or illegal drugs. He did not drink coffee, but he did consume iced tea and caffeinated colas.

He had never been hospitalized for psychiatric, drug abuse, alcohol or mental problems. He had never been prescribed any form of psychiatric medicine, antidepressant, or tranquilizer before the subject injury. He had never needed any form of psychiatric or psychological services, and he had never undergone counseling or psychotherapy. He had never made an intentional attempt to overdose on drugs or medicines, and he had never made an attempt to take his life. He had never intentionally cut, burned, or disfigured himself.

Family and Social History

His father died in his 80s, but the cause of death was not known. His mother died in her 80s of an unspecified cancer. There was no family history of mental illness, depression, or substance abuse. A nephew committed suicide the year before this examination, but no details of the nephew's mental health history, if any, were known. There was no family history of homicides, violence toward others, child abuse, spouse abuse, epilepsy, neurological disease, Alzheimer's disease, or strokes.

He was born in a midwestern area. He grew up in a home where his father was employed as a bricklayer, and his mother was employed as a housekeeper at a university facility. Both parents were present in the home when he was young, and he gave no history of physical or sexual abuse as a youngster. He did possess a handgun in his home, but he denied plans to harm himself or harm others, and this was confirmed by his wife. He was a high school graduate, and he did not require any form of special education classes or remedial education. He and his wife had been married 41 years at the time of his injury. They had no children together, but he had a daughter by a prior relationship. His wife had a son by a prior marriage, but that son was deceased.

His legal history was negative, and he had never been convicted of a felony or misdemeanor. He had never been a party in a lawsuit. When he fractured his arm in 1958, there may have been a worker's compensation claim at that time. He had never declared bankruptcy.

He served in the United States Navy in the 1950s and following that worked in construction as a hod carrier for about 10 years. For the remaining 30 years of his work life, he worked for the United States Postal Service. He served honorably in the United States Navy for 4 years, and he functioned as a crew member of a minesweeper.

Review of Systems

His general and HEENT reviews were negative. His chest review at the time of the neuropsychiatric examination was benign for any remnants of the prior pneumothorax. His cardiovascular, gastrointestinal, and genitourinary reviews were negative. His psychiatric, neurological, and sleep reviews are noted within the body of text above.

Mental Status Examination

He was poorly oriented as to the purpose of the neuropsychiatric examination. His speech was characterized with effortful and nonfluent language, and he made a notable number of semantic paraphasias. He had altered pronunciation skills. He could not say the word "minesweeper," and the word for "mine" was substituted by the word "main." This was thought to be a phonemic paraphasia. Phrase length was shortened, and oral output was diminished.

There was no objective evidence of a mood disturbance. He had a good affective range, and he smiled easily. Language comprehension was very poor. He deferred most questions to his wife, and he displayed obvious dependent behavior toward her. He denied specifically suicidal ideas or plans. There was no evidence of thought disturbance and no loose associations or circumstantiality was noted. However, his language output was so sparse that form of thought could not be adequately determined. There was no evidence of delusions or hallucinations. His articulatory agility was very poor, and the melodic line was altered by obvious dysphasia. Dysarthria was present, but there was no evidence of dysphonia or dyspraxia.

Neurological Examination

His weight was 211 pounds, and his blood pressure was 128/72 mmHg in the left arm sitting position. Oxygen saturation was 93% on room air. His face was symmetrical and hand dominance was to the right. On the cranial nerve examination, there was no evidence of visual field cuts. Pupils were equal and reactive to light and accommodation. Funduscopic examination was benign. The mastoid and temporalis muscles were intact. No nasal speech was present. The gag reflex was intact, and the sternocleidomastoid and trapezius muscles were intact. The tongue protruded to the midline and was without atrophy or fasciculation. Anise and peppermint oils were poorly appreciated. Tuning fork sound was heard well in both ears. The Weber sign lateralized to the right. The corneal reflexes were intact.

Bulk and tone was fair. Strength was symmetrical, and outstretched arms revealed no pronator drift. There was no hyperrefelxia, and deep tendon reflexes were symmetrical. Light touch and pinprick was intact, but his comprehension was sufficiently impaired that the sensory examination was not adequately reported. The Romberg position revealed no sway. Nystagmus was not present. Finger–nose and heel–shin functions were intact. Dysdiadochokinesia was not present. Gait analysis revealed a normal stride, but he had dystaxia on turning. Tandem walking revealed dystaxia.

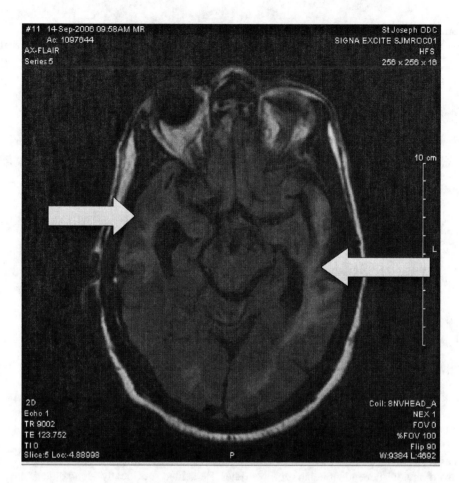

FIGURE 8.3 The eastward facing arrow depicts inferior-anterior temporal encephalomalacia. The westward-facing arrow reveals similar left temporal signal change. Note the bilateral occipital encephalomalacia.

Neuroimaging

MRI of the brain without contrast was obtained concurrently with the neuropsychiatric evaluation. As the reader can see in Figure 8.3, this is a significantly abnormal MRI. There are areas of encephalomalacia bilaterally in the temporal lobes. The loss of tissue is greater on the right than the left. Note the enlargement of the hippocampal cisterns. There was noted to be a localized area of abnormal signal within the right frontal lobe, which is probably posttraumatic in origin but could be related to chronic ischemic changes. Both lateral ventricles were enlarged. These images are not shown. There is evidence of superimposed moderate levels of chronic angiopathic ischemic changes throughout the brain (Figure 8.4).

Laboratory Studies

A blood sample for apolipoprotein-E was obtained. Analysis of chromosome 19 revealed two alleles of apolipoprotein E, genotype ε4.

Standardized Mental Assessment

During assessment, the psychologists noted that W.R. was pleasant and cooperative. He attempted to apply his best effort. Affect was blank and unresponsive for most of the examination. He did make

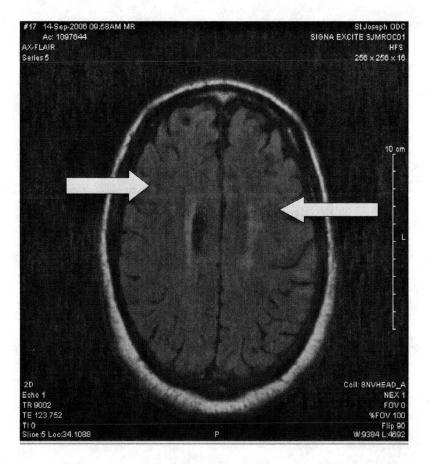

FIGURE 8.4 The small punctuate areas of increased white matter signal (within centrum semiovale) represents concomitant and incidental microangiopathy.

several comments indicating that he was concerned about his test performance. He exhibited moderately severe impairment of receptive and expressive language abilities. It was often necessary to repeat questions and statements multiple times. After multiple repetitions, W.R. would usually grasp the question being asked and then respond in an appropriate manner. However, he had difficulty with specific words, and he transposed the word "dog" with the word "God." He was never able to repeat the word "dog" correctly. A similar pattern was observed with the word "chair," which he continually repeated as "tare." He showed evidence of difficulty with orientation, and he was occasionally unable to comprehend complex test instructions despite multiple repetitions.

He demonstrated a tendency to perseverate in his responses. He occasionally would repeat the same response that he provided from a previous question, despite the fact that his response did not relate to the question currently asked. He demonstrated impaired reading ability and severely impaired spelling ability. He could not write descriptively. He demonstrated severe impairment of higher-order cognitive function, and he had great difficulty responding to questions that involved reasoning or abstraction. He appeared to have comparatively minimal difficulty responding to questions that related to visuospatial praxis or constructional skills.

Measures of Cognitive and Psychological Effort
Because of obvious and severe language impairment, it was elected not to measure cognitive and psychological effort. He was unable to comprehend at an adequate level the English language even when presented to him auditorily or in writing.

Language and Language-Related Skills

W.R. was administered the Boston Diagnostic Aphasia Examination, Short Form. His results are noted below.

Boston Diagnostic Aphasia Examination, Short Form

Scale	Percentile	Classification
Severity rating	50	Impaired
Fluency		
Phrase length	100	Normal
Melodic line	30	Impaired
Grammatical form	20	Impaired
Conversation/expository speech		
Simple social responses	10	Impaired
Auditory comprehension		
Basic word discrimination	40	Impaired
Commands	20	Impaired
Complex ideational material	20	Impaired
Articulation		
Articulatory agility	30	Impaired
Recitation		
Automatized sequences	30	Impaired
Repetition		
Words	20	Impaired
Sentences	30	Impaired
Naming		
Responsive naming	40	Impaired
Special categories	100	Normal
Paraphasia		
Rating from speech profile	30	Impaired
Phonemic	30	Impaired
Verbal	70	Impaired
Neologistic	100	Normal
Multi-word	20	Impaired
Reading		
Matching cases and scripts	100	Normal
Number matching	100	Normal
Picture–word matching	40	Impaired
Oral word reading	40	Impaired
Oral sentence reading	30	Impaired
Oral sentence comprehension	10	Impaired
Sentence/paragraph comprehension	100	Normal
Writing		
Form	100	Normal
Letter choice	30	Impaired
Motor facility	100	Normal
Primer words	20	Impaired
Regular phonics	30	Impaired
Common irregular words	20	Impaired
Written picture naming	20	Impaired
Narrative writing	10	Impaired

Verbal Learning and Memory
He was administered the HVLT-Revised, and those results are presented below.

Hopkins Verbal Learning Test-Revised

	T-Score	Percentile	Classification
Total recall	≤20	<1	Severely impaired
Delayed recall	≤20	<1	Severely impaired
Retention	≤20	<1	Severely impaired
Recognition discrimination index	≤20	<1	Severely impaired

Global Cognitive Function

The Mini-Mental Status Examination (MMSE) by Folstein was administered. The raw score was converted to a *T*-score, a percentile, and placed into a normative classification system. Those results are noted below.

Mini-Mental State Examination

T-Score	Percentile	Classification
19	<1	Mild dementia

The Dementia Rating Scale-II was administered. The subscores and raw score are noted below.

Dementia Rating Scale-II

Scale	Scaled Score	Percentile	Classification
Attention	2	<1	Severely impaired
Initiation/perseveration	2	<1	Severely impaired
Construction	10	41–59	Below average
Conceptualization	2	<1	Severely impaired
Memory	4	2	Moderately impaired
DRS-2 total score	2	<1	Severely impaired

Records Reviewed

Photographs had been made of the construction site, and they were reviewed to understand the biomechanics of his injury and the distance he fell. Emergency medical squad records were available. Records from the examination at the level I trauma center and the university neurointensive care unit were reviewed. Lengthy records from the rehabilitation hospital were available.

Diagnoses

He was diagnosed with a cognitive disorder due to brain trauma, language disorder due to brain trauma, dementia due to brain trauma, and personality change due to brain trauma.

Neurobehavioral Analysis

This case instructs us at three levels: (1) this gentleman is a geriatric patient, (2) W.R. had a primary brain injury with the opportunity for secondary injury because of lung impairment, and (3) he probably had secondary injury from edema and mass effect requiring a ventricular catheter. To complicate conditions further, he developed Pseudomonas pneumonia and MRSA. He required tracheostomy.

He was severely impaired when admitted to a rehabilitation unit 3½ weeks after his original injury. He demonstrated substantial impairment of language, and he could only follow 25% of commands. These findings are consistent with severe brain injury, even though his GCS score remained at 9 or higher. This illustrates how the GCS cannot be used to predict outcome with any specificity. When neuropsychiatrically examined almost 2 years following his injury, he was independent for many functions, but due to substantial dementia, aphasia, and lack of cognitive capacity, he was not capable of providing an independent living environment and was dependent upon his wife.

A review of Figures 8.3 and 8.4 shows that the MRI findings 2 years after injury are consistent with substantial bitemporal brain damage. The right side appears worse than the left, but yet he remains with substantial language impairment. Another noteworthy factor is that this man was old enough that he was demonstrating significant ischemic changes in his brain due to microangiopathy (Figure 8.4). That finding has contributed to the worsened outcome from his injury. He also has two alleles of apolipoprotein-E, ε4, which has aggravated his condition (see Chapter 1).

This case is also instructive to us from the standpoint of difficulty with neuropsychological assessment in a person who presents with dysphasia. As a result of his dysphasia, ordinary reading scores (such as the WTAR) cannot be used to determine pre-injury cognitive capacity. That is a weakness of this particular neuropsychiatric examination. As has been stressed elsewhere in this text, it is usually necessary to determine pre-injury cognitive capacity. There were no methodologies available at the time of neuropsychiatric examination due to his dense dysphasia.

From a review of the results of the Boston Diagnostic Aphasia Examination (BDAE), it can be seen that he has multiple areas of language disturbance. He is nonfluent. He is impaired in auditory comprehension and articulation. Note from prior chapters that when repetition is impaired, the injury is in the perisylvian area. His repetition for words and sentences was substantially impaired, and repetition for words is only at the 20th percentile and for sentences only at the 30th percentile. The paraphasias that can be detected on face-to-face mental status examination are confirmed on the BDAE. His reading varied from normal findings on some portions of reading to significantly impaired on others. In particular, oral sentence comprehension was only at the 10th percentile. His ability to write in a narrative fashion was substantially impaired, and he produced narrative writing only at the 10th percentile. Recall from prior discussions of aphasia that the writing tends to mimic the oral content of dysphasic speech.

As would be expected from bitemporal injuries, the ability to learn verbal information should be impaired. This is confirmed on the HVLT. If the reader reviews those findings, on all areas of this test instrument he is severely impaired, and he scores below the 1st percentile on each subtest. With regard to overall cognitive function, he is below the 1st percentile on the MMSE results, and on the Dementia Rating Scale-II, he is also below the 1st percentile.

At this point, the reader may be confused as to why this is categorized as a moderate brain injury. The moderate rating has to do with outcome. Even though he is significantly demented, his daily life and daily function are not impaired to a severe degree but rather to a moderate degree. Those issues are discussed more fully in Chapters 9 and 10 of this text, as impairment rating and disability determination are better left to forensic matters rather than those of a treating physician. Due to his severe language impairment, no attempt was made to test behavioral function. His reading comprehension is too impaired to provide adequate scores on the MMPI-2 or the Personality Assessment Inventory (PAI). One of these ordinarily would be administered as part of a neuropsychiatric examination.

Treatment Planning

He was administered cognitive enhancers. The addition of donepezil provided evidence over time of improved behavioral functioning. This was confirmed by his wife. However, at the time of the writing of this text, he has never developed fully independent functioning, and he remains a person dependent upon his wife. She also was offered the opportunity for counseling directed at her obvious caregiver stress. She found this helpful to her. Further assistance was provided to her for respite services at least once weekly to allow her the opportunity to see to her own personal needs and give her a timeout from the dependency of her husband. Unlike discussions of risk to marriage earlier in this text, their marriage has remained intact and preserved.

CASE 8.3: SEVERE BRAIN INJURY AS A RESULT OF A TRACTOR-TRAILER TRUCK ACCIDENT

Introduction

K.R. was 43 years old at the time of an 18-wheel truck accident. He was injured in a northern midwestern state, and he was found to have a left open depressed tempoparietal skull fracture with intracerebral hematoma.

History of the Accident

Approximately 19 months before the neuropsychiatric examination, K.R. was involved in a large truck accident. He was found to be severely confused by the EMS squad at the time of his injury. His GCS score was 7 at the time he was initially attended. He was transported to a tertiary care receiving hospital in a northern midwestern state. When admitted to the emergency department, CT scan of his head revealed numerous skull fractures present with the greatest displacement of skull fractures in the left skull, near the periphery of the left frontal lobe. This fracture was inwardly displaced by 7 mm. Inferior to the fractured skull bone, there was a 3.5 cm parenchymal hematoma consistent with a hemorrhagic contusion. A small amount of subarachnoid hemorrhage was present, and intraventricular hemorrhage was present within the left lateral ventricle. There was noted to be mild, diffuse cerebral edema, and there was mild effacement of the left lateral ventricular system. No midline shift was present. He remained within the neurosurgical unit for ten days and was then discharged to a neurospecialty unit at another hospital within his state. He remained at that facility for 7 weeks.

While at the level I trauma center, he developed respiratory failure requiring mechanical ventilation and later a tracheostomy. He required placement of a feeding tube for nutritional needs, and he was noted to have obvious cognitive and language difficulty. He developed a situational depression associated with anxiety, and he also developed an infection of the right first metatarsal area.

History of Present Symptoms

At the time of his neuropsychiatric examination, K.R. was unable to provide the majority of his history. His wife assisted with providing collateral information. His wife reported that when he came out of coma, he was very depressed. He was physically disfigured, and he would say to her, "I'm ugly; you'll leave me." That feeling eventually dissipated, but some elements of it remained at the time of the neuropsychiatric examination. His wife noted further that his sleep was very disturbed and continued to be disturbed. He was hypersomnolent in the daytime, and he could not stay awake while sitting. He had severe snoring that bothered others. He had not been evaluated for obstructive sleep apnea (see Chapter 2, as this is a complication following head injury), and it was recommended to his wife that he be evaluated for that disorder.

He developed a posttraumatic seizure disorder a number of months following his original injury. At the time of his neuropsychiatric examination, he was treated with valproate, 1000 mg daily, and levetiracetam, 500 mg twice daily. His wife reported significant remaining cognitive impairment associated with chronic complaints of double vision. He had significant issues with double vision in the left eye immediately following his injury. Before the neuropsychiatric examination, he had a prism placed in the left lens of his eyeglasses. He reported also numbness, tingling, and weakness in his legs associated with poor balance and poor coordination.

Activities of Daily Living

At the time of the neuropsychiatric examination, he was living with his wife and daughter. He was not able to be employed. He generally arose about 5:45 a.m., and he retired about 8:00 p.m. His wife fixed his breakfast. He was not able to drive a vehicle, and he was not able to use a checkbook. His wife paid the bills and cleaned the home. He did attend church with her weekly. He was not able to engage in any prior hobbies. He would sit in front of the television at least 8 h daily, but it is not clear how much of this he comprehended. He performed no work around the home. He would eat outside the home socially with his family approximately once a week. He was able to use a telephone, but did so rarely and generally never more than once weekly. He could dress and bathe himself independently, but he had lost his sexual function with his wife.

Past Medical and Psychiatric History

He was born a 9 lb, 12 oz baby with no prematurity and no birth injury. He was happy as a child, but he was diagnosed with dyslexia while in school. There was no formal test data available to verify this. His last seizure was approximately 6 months before the neuropsychiatric examination, and he had been seizure-free in that interim. He had never been involved in prior motor vehicle accidents, and he had no prior history of head or brain injury or periods of unconsciousness. He had never been in a coma before. He had no prior history of seizures, and he had no prior history of requiring prescribed medications. He did not use tobacco products, alcoholic beverages, or drugs of abuse. He drank one cup of coffee daily and two caffeinated soft drinks daily.

In his psychiatric history, he had never been hospitalized for psychiatric, drug abuse, alcohol, or mental problems. He had been treated with mirtazepine, 15 mg daily, while in the rehabilitation hospital. He had never intentionally overdosed himself on drugs or medicines. He had never made an attempt to take his life, and he had never intentionally cut, burned, or disfigured himself.

Family and Social History

K.R.'s father was 71 years old, and he was afflicted with parkinsonism and hypertension. His mother was 71 years old and was hypertensive. He was born in a midwestern state, and he grew up in a home with a sister and two brothers. His father retired from the military and then worked as a tobacco company foreman. His mother was a homemaker, and both parents were present in the home when he was young. His father did not abuse his mother. He had no history of violence toward others.

After graduating from high school, he obtained a commercial driver's license. He had been married three times, and his present marriage had been in place for approximately 20 years. He and his wife had one child together.

His legal history was negative. He has never declared bankruptcy. He was receiving Social Security Disability benefits at the time of this examination. He had worked as a truck driver for his company approximately 6 years at the time of his accident. Before that, he had worked as a truck driver for other companies for about 10 years. He served 4 years in the U.S. Army and received an honorable discharge.

Review of Systems

In his general review, he reported chronic fatigue since his brain injury. He lost a considerable amount of weight following his injury, but it had stabilized at 163 lb at the time of this examination. His HEENT review was positive for diplopia in the left eye due to apparent third nerve palsy. His chest, cardiovascular, and gastrointestinal reviews were negative at the time of this examination.

In his genitourinary review, he required tolterodine due to excessive urination since his injury. His psychiatric, neurologic, and sleep reviews are noted above within the text. His sexual review is also noted above.

Mental Status Examination

He was a pleasant, cooperative, docile man who was obviously confused. He could not complete his medical questionnaire, and this information was obtained from his wife. He could not give the examiner the name of his physician or his physician's specialty practice. He could not recite his current medications. He was able to give the year, but when asked the month he perseverated and could not answer. When asked for the day of the week, he said, "thirty." He eventually was able to name the day but with great difficulty. When asked for the governor of his state, he gave the name of the president of the United States.

He demonstrated significant phonemic paraphasia and word-finding difficulty. He showed evidence of a comprehension deficit. He was emotionally withdrawn, and he demonstrated conceptual disorganization. His recent memory was obviously impaired. He demonstrated motor retardation, blunted affect, and tension. He had an obvious speech articulation defect with dysarthria present.

Neurological Examination

Weight was 163 lb and blood pressure was 100/64 mmHg in the left arm sitting position. There were no bruits in the head or neck. There was evidence of prior trauma to the head, and the calvarium was asymmetric. A left skull defect could be palpated. He had a left eyelid droop and left temporal muscle concavity. Hand dominance was to the right.

There were no visual field cuts present, but ocular motility was impaired superiorly and laterally. Funduscopic examination was benign. The branchiomotor group of muscles revealed no deficits. He did demonstrate anosmia to anise and peppermint oils. Tuning fork sound was reduced in the left ear. The Weber sign lateralized to the right. Corneal reflexes were intact.

His bulk and tone were normal, but strength was reduced in his right arm and leg. Outstretched arms revealed a right pronator drift. Deep tendon reflexes were increased in the right arm and right leg. Light touch and pinprick could not be adequately determined due to his comprehension dysphasia. The Romberg position revealed circular sway. He had nystagmus present to right-ward gaze. Figure–nose function was dystaxic on the right, and dysdiadochokinesia was present in the right hand. His gait revealed a right hemiparetic circumduction with widening of the base. Arm swing was leaden. Motor speed was reduced. He demonstrated severe dystaxia on heel–toe walking.

Neuroimaging

As Figures 8.5 and 8.6 show, on the T2 FLAIR axial images, there is extensive abnormal signal noted within the left posteriotemporal and posterioparietal lobes. The signal noted in these regions is consistent with cystic encephalomalacia and probable gliosis. There is noted to be asymmetric enlargement of the posterior horn of the left lateral ventricle present and also enlargement of the temporal horn of the left lateral ventricle. These findings are consistent with *ex vacuo* dilatation.

Standardized Mental Assessment

The psychologist noted that he was casually dressed and appropriately groomed, but he appeared to be older than his stated age. He was cordial and cooperative. He maintained a rather neutral facial expression and rarely showed emotion. It was noted that he had significant expressive dysphasia. He did not initiate conversation but did respond to direct questions. Response latencies were excessively long, and he had to be prompted to respond. Speech was primarily nonfluent and effortful

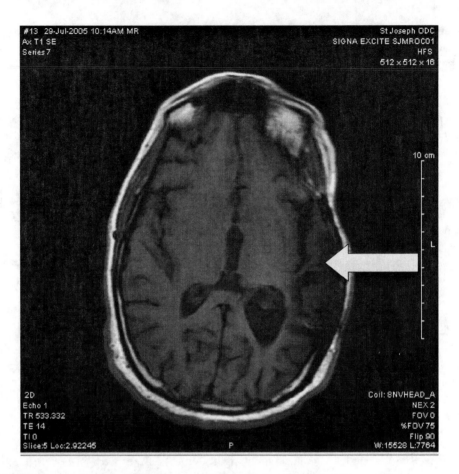

FIGURE 8.5 Prominent cystic encephalomalacia of the left temporal lobe.

characterized by a slow rate of delivery, a tendency to perseverate, long pauses and articulation difficulties. He occasionally made word substitutions such as "rain" for "rent." He had difficulty providing verbal names for visually presented objects. He did improve his performance with phonemic cues. He performed slightly better when written multiple choice options were given. He ambulated slowly and cautiously. Gait was unsteady, and he indicated that his right side was considerably weaker than his left side. He demonstrated much difficulty on verbal and visual recall, and he frequently required prompting to respond. He would state, "I can't remember." After short delays and even with verbal cues, he was not able to recall any information from previously presented short stories. He had difficulty with demographic and orientation information. Due to the severity of his language impairment, it was elected not to administer the MMPI-2.

Measures of Cognitive Distortion
He was administered the Test of Memory and Malingering and the Victoria Symptom Validity Test. On both tests he provided valid and normal effort.

Measures Providing Estimates of Pre-injury Function
Due to language difficulties, he was not administered the Wechsler Test of Adult Reading. He was administered the Wide Range Achievement Test-III. However, as the reader can see below, his scores are not useable due to severe reading recognition impairment.

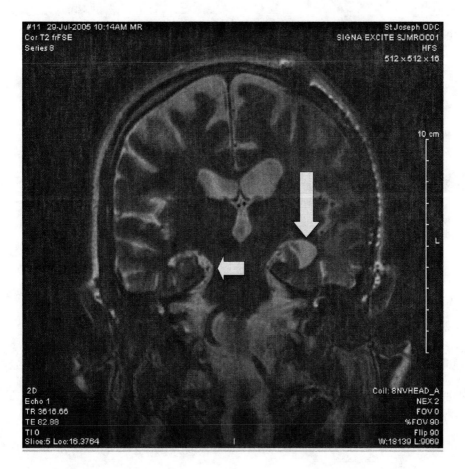

FIGURE 8.6 Bilateral hippocampal atrophy, left > right.

Wide Range Achievement Test-III

	Standard Score	Percentile	Grade Equivalence
Reading	<45	<0.02	1

Attention and Concentration
The Ruff 2 & 7 Selective Attention Test was administered to determine visual attention, and the Brief Test of Attention was administered to determine auditory attention. The Digit Span subtest and the Spatial Span subtest of the Wechsler Memory Scale-III were also used to determine working memory for digit span.

Ruff 2 & 7 Selective Attention Test

Measure	Sum of *T*-Scores	*T*-Score	Percentile	Classification
Total speed	44	23	<1	Moderately to severely impaired
Total accuracy	94	47	39	Average

Brief Test of Attention

	Percentile	Interpretation
BTA total score	<2	Impaired

WMS-III Digit Span Subtest

	Standard Score	Percentile	Classification
Longest digit span forward	50	0.07	Extremely low
Longest digit span backward	71	03	Borderline
Digit span scaled score	60	<1	Extremely low

WMS-III Spatial Span Subtest

	Standard Score	Percentile	Classification
Longest spatial span forward	80	09	Low average
Longest spatial span backward	110	75	High average
Spatial span scaled score	100	50	Average

Language and Language Related Skills

K.R. was administered the Boston Naming Test and the Controlled Oral Word Association Test to determine naming skill and the ability to produce specific words under timed conditions. He was also administered the Boston Diagnostic Aphasia Examination, Short Form.

Boston Naming Test

T-score	17
Classification	Severely impaired
Percentile	<0.02

Controlled Oral Word Association Test

T-score	17
Percentile	0.07
Classification	Severely impaired

Boston Diagnostic Aphasia Examination, Short Form

Scale	Percentile	Classification
Severity rating	40	Low
Fluency		
Phrase Length	25	Low
Melodic Line	10	Low
Grammatical Form	25	Low
Conversation/expository speech		
Simple social responses	50	Low
Auditory comprehension		
Basic word discrimination	40	Low
Commands	100	Normal
Complex ideational material	50	Low

Boston Diagnostic Aphasia Examination, Short Form (continued)

Scale	Percentile	Classification
Articulation		
Articulatory agility	30	Low
Recitation		
Automatized sequences	100	Normal
Repetition		
Words	30	Low
Sentences	30	Low
Naming		
Responsive naming	25	Low
Boston naming test	25	Low
Special categories	30	Low
Paraphasia		
Rating from speech profile	40	Low
Reading		
Matching cases and scripts	100	Normal
Number matching	100	Normal
Picture–word matching	20	Low
Oral word reading	15	Low
Oral sentence reading	20	Low
Oral sentence comprehension	50	Low
Sentence/paragraph comprehension	70	Low
Writing		
Form	45	Low
Letter choice	60	Low
Motor facility	40	Low
Primer words	100	Normal
Regular phonics	30	Low
Common irregular words	40	Low
Written picture naming	30	Low
Narrative writing	15	Low

Memory

K.R. was administered the Wechsler Memory Scale-III to determine auditory, visual, and working memory abilities.

Wechsler Memory Scale-III

	Scale Score Sum	Index Score	Percentile	Classification
Auditory immediate	04	53	<1	Extremely low
Visual immediate	09	65	1	Extremely low
Immediate memory	13	49	<1	Extremely low
Auditory delayed	05	55	<1	Extremely low
Visual delayed	10	68	2	Extremely low
Auditory recognition delayed	01	55	<1	Extremely low
General memory	16	52	<1	Extremely low
Working memory	12	79	8	Borderline

Motor and Visuomotor Skills

K.R. was tested with the Grooved Pegboard Test, Grip Dynanometer, and the Finger Tapping Test. He produced the following scores:

Grooved Pegboard Test

	T-Score	Classification	Percentile
Dominant right hand	10	Severely impaired	<0.02
Nondominant left hand	19	Severely impaired	0.2

Grip Dynamometer

	T-Score	Classification	Percentile
Dominant right-hand strength	12	Severely impaired	<0.02
Nondominant left-hand strength	18	Severely impaired	0.1

Finger Tapping Test

	T-Score	Classification	Percentile
Dominant right hand	27	Moderately impaired	01
Nondominant left hand	22	Moderately to severely impaired	0.7

Executive Functions

His executive ability was tested the WCST and Trailmaking Tests A and B. He produced the following *T*-scores and injury classifications:

Wisconsin Card Sorting Test

	Standard Score	T-Score	Percentile	Classification
Total errors	<55	<20	<1	Severely impaired
Perseverative responses	73	32	04	Mildly to moderately impaired

Trailmaking Test A

T-Score	Classification	Percentile
15	Severely impaired	0.05

Trailmaking Test B

T-Score	Classification	Percentile
18	Severely impaired	0.1

Test Intelligence

Intelligence was measured using the Kaufman Brief Intelligence Test-2.

Kaufman Brief Intelligence Test-2

	Standard Score	Percentile	Classification
Verbal	43	<0.1	Lower extreme
Nonverbal	68	02	Lower extreme
IQ composite	54	0.1	Lower extreme

Records Reviewed

At the time of the neuropsychiatric examination, there were seven treating physician records available and one record of audiology examination. The entire neurosurgical file was available as well as his rehabilitation records.

Diagnoses

He was diagnosed with a cognitive disorder, dementia, expressive, receptive dysphasia, and mood disorder, all due to brain trauma. He also had an incidental posttraumatic seizure disorder, but this was not evaluated at the time of the neuropsychiatric examination.

Neurobehavioral Analysis

If the reader will review the facts of his original injury, obviously he had multiple skull fractures. This case differs significantly from the two prior cases in that he sustained a depressed skull fracture. The reader may wish to review neuropathological findings from Chapter 1 related to brain trauma and depressed skull fractures. He eventually required a left hemicranioplasty. That is not stated explicitly above, but about $2\frac{1}{2}$ months after his original injury, he had an elevation of the depressed fracture. The hemicranioplasty measured 15 cm. He required significant improvement of his medical status before it was felt he could tolerate the revision surgery. Also, recall that he had diffuse cerebral edema at the time of his original injury. Therefore, this case represents both primary and direct injury to brain tissue as well as secondary factors of severe respiratory failure, diffuse cerebral edema and post-injury hemicranioplasty.

If the reader will review the MRI findings, it can be seen that almost all of the injury is in the left hemisphere, and the *ex vacuo* dilatation is a marker for substantial loss of tissue in the left hemisphere. This clinically correlates well with the obvious language findings noted on neuro-psychological assessment and face-to-face mental examination. The findings on neurological examination are obviously consistent with left hemisphere injury. Thus, the dysphasia and right hemiparesis are strikingly correlated with neuroimaging findings.

In reviewing the neuropsychological data, on the TOMM and VSVT he provided adequate effort. This is excellent evidence that even severely injured persons can provide adequate cognitive effort at the time of an examination if they choose to do so. On the other hand, it is not possible to estimate his pre-injury cognitive capacity based on reading scores due to his dysphasia. This case is an excellent example of how posttraumatic dysphasia interferes with the ability to use reading as a measure of pre-injury cognitive capacity.

On the Ruff 2 & 7 Selective Attention Test, he is severely impaired in speed but his accuracy of visual search is in the average range. On the other hand, his ability to attend to an auditory stimulus is very impaired on the Brief Test of Attention. He also shows impairment of working memory on the WMS-III Digit Span subtest.

With regard to his language ability, he is severely impaired in naming and severely impaired in fluency. The fluency test is the COWA Test. Overall, his scores on the BDAE are uniformly low and consistent with the dysphasia detectable by face-to-face examination. His memory is significantly impaired. His memory scores are at the 2nd percentile or below, and even his working memory is only at the 8th percentile. Thus, effectively, this man has lost ordinary memory capacity as well as language function.

His motor impairments correlate with the right hemiparesis. Executive function is very impaired on both the WCST and Trailmaking Tests A and B. His intellectual capacity appears to have reduced considerably. By demographic variables and estimation of function as a truck driver, he probably functioned in the average range of cognitive capacity. His current level of intellectual capacity is in the mentally retarded range.

Treatment Planning

It was recommended that his mirtazapine dosage be increased to 30 mg daily. A prior physician had placed him on topirimate to reduce his appetite. However, he was having difficulty maintaining weight, and it was recommended that topirimate be discontinued. It was thought that the antihistamine effect of mirtazapine would enhance his appetite with increased dosage. That turned out to be the case, and he was able to gain to a more appropriate body mass index. He was also placed on rivastigmine for cognitive enhancement. His mood seemed to improve with the use of this medication, and his wife reported that she thought his memory had become slightly more effective. He was not interested in psychotherapy, but his wife was interested. She was placed with a therapist to provide to her supportive care to assist with the stress she was feeling from his increased dependency upon her and the negative impact of his illness upon their marriage.

CASE 8.4:   CHILD TRAUMATIC BRAIN INJURY

Introduction

D.H. was $3\frac{1}{2}$ years old at the time he was riding as a passenger in an extended cab pickup truck. His vehicle was struck in the rear by a large tractor-trailer truck traveling on an interstate highway. There was a significant second impact by a second truck.

History of Present Symptoms

The ambulance crew arrived on the scene shortly after his injury, and he was found to have a GCS score of 10, with $E = 2$, $M = 5$, and $V = 3$. He was transported to a tertiary care hospital providing neurosurgical services. His GCS score deteriorated on the way to the hospital, and on three separate measures, his GCS score equaled 8.

Unfortunately, this youngster was not restrained in a car seat or booster seat. He had a positive loss of consciousness and was then minimally responsive to bystanders. His head was atraumatic and normocephalic. The left pupil was 2–3 mm in size and reactive, but sluggish. The right pupil was 1–2 mm in size and was minimally reactive. No blood or cerebrospinal fluid was visualized in the ear canals. A CT scan of the head revealed a punctuate focus of hemorrhage within the medial right temporal lobe, which was thought to be representative of a small area of hemorrhagic contusion. There was also noted to be hemorrhage within the upper right quadrigeminal cistern. No epidural or subdural hematoma was visualized. There was evidence of a nondisplaced fracture along the inferior orbital rim and the anterior maxillary sinus. There was a suggestion of a minimal amount of intraventricular hemorrhage within the dependent aspect of the occipital horn on the right. An MRI of the brain was obtained after he was transferred to a children's hospital in a large university city. This MRI was obtained almost 3 weeks following his injury and revealed a punctuate focus of signal loss within the right internal capsule in a subnuclear location. It was almost 2 weeks post-injury until D.H. revealed increased sensory activity and decreased agitation. At that time, he was noted to have some left-sided weakness. He was discharged from the children's hospital more than a month following his injury.

Thereafter, he was placed into pediatric rehabilitation. At this neuropsychiatric examination, his mother noted that he had been severely irritable since his injury, and he would get mad too easily. He had frequent tantrums and was very short-fused compared to his behavior before injury. His mother noted that his concentration was diminished, and he had become exceedingly dependent on his parents and refused to have them out of his sight. He also developed significant tremors of the hand, and he had to eat with weighted utensils as a result. He required assistance getting on and off the commode, or he would fall to the floor. He would fall while bending in an attempt to pull up his pants. He had to wear 1-lb wrist weights in order to write or use scissors at school. His mother reported that he was weak in the left hand.

Activities of Daily Living

At the time of the neuropsychiatric examination, he was 4 years of age. He was attending an early childhood school, and he arose about 7:30 a.m. and would retire about 9:30 p.m. He often attended physical therapy after school. He enjoyed watching cartoons on television, and he enjoyed playing a Nintendo game. He was able to attend ballgames with his parents. He was able to fish if he chose. He could eat outside the home with his family, and he was able to talk to others on the telephone.

Past Medical History

D.H. was born by caesarean section at approximately 28 weeks gestation. His mother had toxemia and early renal failure, and the pregnancy was terminated early. He weighed 3 lb, 12 oz at birth and required a ventilator while in the neonatal intensive care unit for a few weeks. He could sit alone at 9 months, crawl at 13 months, and pull himself up at 15 months. He stood alone at 8 months. He walked alone at 20 months and was potty-trained at $2\frac{1}{2}$ years. Presently, he was demonstrating difficulty learning in school and difficulty keeping his mind on tasks. An individualized educational plan had been put in place for him, and he was receiving school-based assistance with speech therapy, occupational therapy, and physical therapy. His teachers had not complained that he was hyperactive.

He had never been injured in a prior motor vehicle accident. In the subject accident, he had fractured his maxillary sinus, right clavicle, and right first rib. He had required no surgery. However, since the sinus fracture, he had chronic rhinitis, and he was treated with antihistamines. He was using no over-the-counter medicines and no herbs or natural products. He had no known allergies to drugs or medicines.

Past Medical and Past Psychiatric History

He had never been hospitalized for psychiatric, drug abuse, alcohol, or mental problems. He had never been prescribed any form of psychiatric medicine, cognitive enhancer, or stimulant before or after his injury. His family had not been advised to take him for psychiatric care. He had never had counseling or psychological intervention.

Family and Social History

At the time of this examination, D.H.'s father was 31 years of age, and his mother was 31 years of age. Neither parent had any chronic medical illnesses. However, his mother had sustained a serious neck injury in the subject accident. There was no history of suicides, homicides, violence toward others, child abuse, or spouse abuse in his family. There was no history of epilepsy, neurological disease, Alzheimer's disease, or strokes in his relatives.

He was born in a large midwestern city, and he had two older brothers. His father was employed as a coalminer, and his mother was not employed outside the home. Both parents were present in his home, and his father did not abuse his mother. There is no evidence that D.H. had ever been sexually or physically abused. He had no history of violence toward others, and there was no access to guns or weapons in his home. He had no juvenile court record.

Review of Systems

In his general review, he had a chronic tremor of the hands since this injury. His HEENT review was positive for chronic nasal stuffiness and runny nose treated with antihistamines. His chest, cardio-vascular, gastrointestinal, and genitourinary reviews were negative. His psychiatric, neurological, and musculoskeletal reviews are noted within the text above.

Mental Status and Neurological Examination

His mother completed a medical questionnaire on his behalf. He was a shy young man who weighed 54 lb in ordinary clothing, and he had a 54-cm head circumference. He demonstrated a noticeable drift in the left outstretched arm with intorting of the left hand. There was diminished strength in the left arm versus the right. Hyperreflexia could not be detected in the left arm or leg. His gait was widened, and he was dystaxic on turns. He walked in an antalgic fashion as a result of his widened gait.

His demeanor was relatively placid, but he tended to irritability. He became very irritated during examination when the psychologist commented to the physician that he was having difficulty with hand function. He became angry and told the psychologist to "shut-up." This was done in an abrupt impulsive fashion. He also developed separation anxiety when an effort was made to remove him from his parents. It was not possible to examine him at any time out of the eyesight of his parents.

Neuroimaging

MRI of the brain was obtained at the time of this neuropsychiatric examination. He was sedated with 1cc of chloral hydrate and standard brain injury sequences were obtained. The ventricles and sulci were noted to be within normal limits. On the inversion recovery sequences, there was no evidence of a retained injury pattern. However, the reader is referred to Figures 8.7 and 8.8, as those show representative samples of the original CT scans when he came to the trauma hospital. The reader

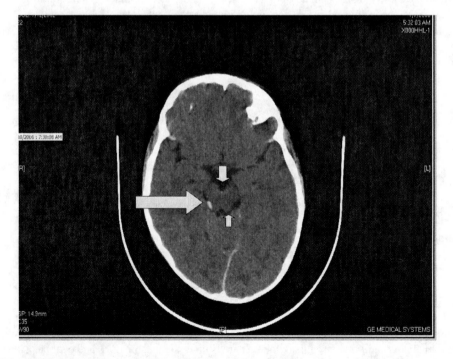

FIGURE 8.7 The eastward-facing arrow marks right subarachnoid hemorrhage within the ambient cistern. The southward-facing arrow marks the interpeduncular fossa and the northward-facing arrow depicts the midbrain tectum.

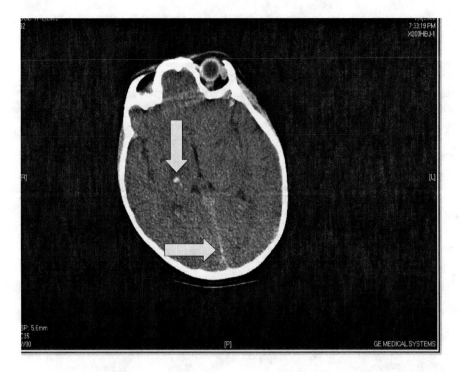

FIGURE 8.8 Note the right lenticular hemorrhage (southward-facing arrow) and the blood along the falx cerebri (eastward-facing arrow).

should be able to note the subarachnoid hemorrhage layering along the falx and also the hemorrhage in the vicinity of the quadrigeminal plate on the right side. There is also evidence of a shear injury in the right lenticular area.

Standardized Mental Assessment

The psychologist noted that D.H. was shy, but he would make good eye contact and followed the examiner to the testing room. His ability to cooperate with the evaluation varied during the examination, as his attention span was noticeably short. If he became disinterested in a test, he required much encouragement to redirect his focus. During the afternoon sessions, he became noticeably fatigued and began yawning. He required frequent breaks during the day. His attention span was usually better following a break but only for a short period of time.

He often engaged in off-task behaviors. He was somewhat stimulus bound, and he would become fascinated by objects in the examination office. He would leave his seat and wander around the room. It was difficult to reengage him in the testing process at this point, and usually a break was required.

He had significant difficulty understanding some of the tasks on the NEPSY. He had difficulty attentively listening to a story, freely recalling a story, and then answering specific questions regarding the story on a specific task measuring memory. Often, he did not respond at all to the examiner's questions concerning the story. During motor examination, he was not able to maintain a statue-like body position with his eyes closed in order to assess motor persistence and inhibition.

He demonstrated minor language difficulties throughout testing. Receptively, he showed little difficulty with comprehension. Expressively, though, his speech was often difficult to understand, and his parents had to translate meaning at times. On nonverbal assessments, he was observed to heavily favor his dominant right hand when manipulating objects, pointing, or copying. He did exhibit a slight hand tremor. Weights were not required during this examination. Moreover, his entire left side appeared weaker than his right side during the psychological examination.

Attention and Concentration

The Connor's Kiddie Continuous Performance Test (K-CPT) is a computerized test designed to assess attention problems in children. Published in 2001, the normative sample of this test consists of 454 children, aged 4–5. The K-CPT allows for comparison of responses to general population norms and ADHD norms. Results are presented in the form of *T*-scores and percentiles. D.H. produced the following profile:

Connor's Kiddie Continuous Performance Test

Measure	*T*-Score	Percentile	Guideline
# Omissions	54	32	Within average range
# Commissions	54	33	Within average range
Hit RT	51	43	Within average range
Hit RT Std error	57	21	Within average range
Variability	62	10	Mildly atypical
Detectability (d')	53	35	Within average range
Response style (B)	45	67	Within average range
Perseverations	54	32	Within average range
Hit RT block change	47	60	Within average range
Hit SE block change	63	8	Mildly atypical
Hit RT ISI change	45	68	Within average range
Hit SE ISI change	53	37	Within average range

Please note that to be consistent with other test results, CPT-II percentile scores have been inverted from the values presented in the CPT-II computer-based score report. Thus, lower percentile scores reflect lower levels of performance in the table above. *T*-scores have not been inverted.

Neuropsychological Functioning

D.H. was administered the NEPSY. His particular scaled scores and core domain scores are noted below.

NEPSY Scaled Scores

Subtest	Attn/Exec	Language	Sensorimotor	Visuospatial	Memory
Body part naming		09			
Design copying				09	
Phonological processing		10			
Visual attention	06				
Comprehension of instructions		09			
Imitating hand position			07		
Visuomotor precision			11		
Narrative memory					07
Block construction				04	
Sentence repetition					05
Statue	06				
Sum scaled scores	12	28	18	13	12

	Core Domain Score	Percentile	Classification
Attn/exec functions	74	04	Below expected level
Language	96	39	At expected level
Sensorimotor functions	94	34	At expected level
Visuospatial processing	77	06	Below expected level
Memory and learning	74	04	Below expected level

Test Intelligence

He was administered the Wechsler Preschool and Primary Scale of Intelligence-III. The age-adjusted scaled scores and composite scores are noted below.

Wechsler Preschool and Primary Scale of Intelligence-III

Subtests	Age-Adjusted Scaled Scores			
	Verbal	Performance	Pr. Spd.	GLC
Block design		04		
Information	08			
Matrix reasoning		03		
Vocabulary	09			
Picture concepts		10		
Symbol search			09	
Word reasoning	05			
Coding			07	
Similarities	(08)			
Receptive vocabulary				08
Picture naming				06

Wechsler Preschool and Primary Scale of Intelligence-III

	Composite Score	Classification	Percentile	Range
Verbal composite	85	Low average	16	80–92
Performance composite	73	Borderline	04	68–81
Processing speed	88	Low average	21	81–98
Full-scale IQ	77	Borderline	06	73–83
General language	83	Low average	13	77–92

Records Reviewed

The records reviewed included the ambulance run sheet and the neurosurgical records from the tertiary care hospital where he was treated and admitted initially. Further review was made of the children's hospital records, photographs of the accident site, the police traffic collision report, and records of his personal physician.

Diagnoses

D.H. demonstrates numerous cognitive difficulties including dementia due to brain trauma, executive dysfunction disorder due to brain trauma, visuospatial processing disorder due to brain disorder,

Wechsler Adult Intelligence Scale-III

Subtests	Age-Adjusted Scaled Scores					
	Verbal	Performance	VC	PO	WM	PS
Picture completion		04		04		
Vocabulary	10		10			
Digit symbol-coding		07				07
Similarities	10		10			
Block design		06		06		
Arithmetic	07				07	
Matrix reasoning		05		05		
Digit span	09				09	
Information	08		08			
Picture arrangement		05				
Comprehension	09					
Symbol search		(04)				04
Letter–number sequencing	(10)				10	
Sum of scaled scores	**53**	**27**	**28**	**15**	**26**	**11**

and amnestic and learning disorder due to brain trauma. Not all of these diagnoses comport to either ICD-9 or DSM-IV criteria for children. As has been reported earlier in this text, neuropsychiatric injuries from TBI often do not fit within the contemporary diagnostic nosologies.

Neurobehavioral Analysis

A review of all the digital neuroimaging made at the original neurosurgical hospital indicated numerous areas of brain injury, which can no longer be detected structurally by MRI. There was evidence of diffuse axonal injury in the mediotemporal region of the internal capsule. There was also evidence of blood in the brainstem cistern and blood along the left falx in the posterior head. It was thought that there was blood in the occipital horn of the right ventricle. Recall from Chapter 1 that this intraventricular hemorrhage is consistent with diffuse axonal injury. An MRI obtained at the children's hospital indicated damage to brain tissue in the right internal capsule. This correlates presently with the left hemiparesis and reduction of strength in the left hand and left arm.

In order to best estimate his preinjury cognitive capacity, the highest score method was used taking the highest scores from the NEPSY core domain scores and the Wechsler Preschool and Primary Scale of Intelligence-III scores. If the reader will refer to those tests, it can be seen that his core domain language and sensory motor function scores were both above a standard score of 96 and at the 39th and 34th percentiles, respectively. On the Wechsler Preschool and Primary Scale of Intelligence-III, he produced an age-adjusted scale score of 10 on picture concepts and 9 on Symbol Search. Thus, his preinjury cognitive capacity was probably in the average range using these methods. Obviously, there is possible error in this estimation, but with a child of $3\frac{1}{2}$ years at the time of injury, it is probably the best estimate that can be made.

Overall, the results of this assessment are consistent with dementia. Normally, children are not diagnosed with dementia, but the common sense use of the term "dementia" is that of an acquired loss of intellectual capacity. Certainly, this youngster qualifies for that. If the reader will note on examination of his test intelligence, his full scale IQ score measures only 77, which places him at the 6th percentile on a national basis. Using the highest score method, this is consistent with a loss of intellectual capacity, as in all probability, his pre-injury intellectual ability was in the average range. On the remainder of neuropsychological testing, he shows evidence of impairment in areas of attention/executive function, visuospatial processing, memory, and learning, and nonverbal reasoning. Results of the Continuous Performance Test suggest some element of inattentiveness as well as limitations with vigilance (attention sustained over time). His neurological examination is abnormal and indicates injury to the right brain motor system affecting left-sided motor abilities. His abnormality of station and gait is more complex and may relate to subtle brainstem injury. Recall that there was evidence of blood around the quadrigeminal plates.

Treatment Planning

As noted above, an individualized educational plan had already been established by his school system, and he was receiving occupational, speech, and physical therapy assistance. At the conclusion of this examination, it was recommended to his parents and to his physician that he be placed in the care of a pediatric neurologist who could organize and foster his care. With no lack of respect meant to his personal physician, the facilities in this youngster's small town did not allow comprehensive services to be offered to him. Obviously, at his young age, he required referral to a more comprehensive center. It was recommended that he be seen in the pediatric neurology department of one of the two major university medical schools near his home. The greatest distance his parents would have to travel was approximately 100 miles, which was within their abilities. It was recommended that he be evaluated on a yearly basis. Unlike the pharmacological treatment noted earlier in this chapter, there is limited data for using these drugs in youngsters. However, as he ages and becomes older, the opportunity to assist him pharmacologically may be improved. Moreover, recall from previous discussion in the text that a youngster with TBI is at very high risk for developing a major mental disorder. It was also recommended that he have subspecialty care from a child psychiatrist associated with the pediatric neurology department where he was to be treated.

REFERENCES

1. Klauber, M.R., Marshall, L.F., Toole, B.M., et al., Cause of decline in head injury mortality rate in San Diego County, CA. *J. Neurosurg.*, 62, 528, 1985.
2. Colohan, A.R.T., Alves, W.M., Gross, C.R., et al., Head injury mortality in two centers with different emergency medical services and intensive care. *J. Neurosurg.*, 71, 202, 1989.
3. Chesnut, R.M., Marshall, L.F., Klauber, M.R., et al., The role of secondary brain injury in determining outcome from severe head injury. *J. Trauma*, 34, 216, 1993.
4. Baron, E.M. and Jallo, J.I., TBI: Pathology, pathophysiology, acute care and surgical management, critical care principles and outcomes, in *Brain Injury Medicine*, Zasler, N.D., Katz, D.I., and Zafonte, R.D., Eds., Demos, New York, 2007, p. 265.
5. Hutchinson, P.J., Kirkpatrick, P.J., Addison, J., et al., The management of minor traumatic brain injury. *J. Accid. Emerg. Med.*, 115, 84, 1998.
6. Johnson, N.H. and Lee, S.H., Computed tomography of acute cerebral trauma. *Radiol. Clin. North Am.*, 30, 325, 1992.
7. Narayan, R.K., Head trauma, in *Advanced Trauma Life Support for Doctors*, Krantz, B.E., Ali, J., Aprahamin, C., et al., Eds., American College of Surgeons, Chicago, IL, 1997, p. 181.
8. Bullock, M.R., Chesnut, R.M., Clifton, G.L., et al., *Management, and Prognosis of Severe Traumatic Brain Injury*. Brain Trauma Foundation, New York, revised 2003.
9. Narayan, R.K., Kishore, P.R., Becker, D.P., et al., Intracranial pressure: To monitor or not to monitor? A review of our experience with severe head injury. *J. Neurosurg.*, 56, 650, 1982.
10. Rovlias, A. and Kotsou, S., The influence of hyperglycemia on neurological outcome in patients with severe head injury. *Neurosurgery*, 46, 335, 2000.
11. Wagner, A.K., Fabio, T., Zafonte, R.D., et al., Physical medicine and rehabilitation consultation: Relationships with acute functional outcome, length of stay and discharge planning after traumatic brain injury. *Am. J. Phys. Med. Rehabil.*, 82, 526, 2003.
12. Krych, D.K. and Ashley, M.J., An overview of traumatic brain injury rehabilitation: The field evaluation, in *Traumatic Brain Injury Rehabilitation*, Ashley, M.J. and Krych, D.K., Eds., CRC Press, Boca Raton, FL, 1995, p. 1.

13. Rattok, J. and Ross, B.P., Cognitive rehabilitation, in *Neuropsychiatry of Traumatic Brain Injury*, Silver, J.M., Yudofsky, S.C., and Hales, R.E., Eds., American Psychiatric Press, Washington, D.C., 1994, p. 703.

14. McAllister, T.W. and Flashman, L.A., Mild brain injury and mood disorders: Causal connections, assessment, and treatment, in *The Evaluation and Treatment of Mild Traumatic Brain Injury*, Varney, N.R. and Roberts, R.J., Eds., Lawrence Erlbaum Associates, Mahwah, NJ, 1999, p. 347.

15. Larsen, P.D., Clinical neuropsychiatric assessment of children and adolescents, in *Pediatric Neuropsychiatry*, Coffey, C.E. and Brumback, R.A., Eds., Lippincott, Williams & Wilkins, Philadelphia, PA, 2006, p. 49.

16. Strub, R.L. and Black, F.W., *The Mental Status Examination in Neurology*, 4th edition, F.A. Davis Company, Philadelphia, PA, 2000.

17. Trzepacz, P.T. and Baker, R.W., *The Psychiatric Mental Status Examination*, Oxford University Press, New York, 1993.

18. Lishman, W.A., *Organic Psychiatry: The Psychological Consequences of Cerebral Disorder*, 2nd edition, Blackwell Scientific Publications, Oxford, UK, 1987.

19. Fish, F., *Fish's Clinical Psychopathology: Signs and Symptoms in Psychiatry,* Hamilton, M., Ed., John Wright and Sons, Bristol, UK, 1974.

20. Kestenbaum, C.J., The clinical interview of the child, in *Textbook of Child and Adolescent Psychiatry*, 2nd edition, Wiener, J.M., Ed., American Psychiatric Press, Washington, D.C., 1997, p. 79.

21. Weinberg, W.A., Harper, C.R., and Brumback, R.A., Examination II: Clinical evaluation of cognitive or behavioral function, in *Textbook of Pediatric Neuropsychiatry*, Coffey, C.E. and Brumback, R.A., Eds., American Psychiatric Press, Washington, D.C., 1998, p. 171.

22. *Principles of Behavioral and Cognitive Neurology*, 2nd edition, Mesulam, M.M., Ed., Oxford University Press, New York, 2000.

23. *Wechsler Test of Adult Reading, Manual*, The Psychological Corporation, San Antonio, TX, 2001.

24. *Wechsler Individual Achievement Test*, 2nd edition, Examiner's Manual, The Psychological Corporation, San Antonio, TX, 2001.

25. McAllister, T.W., Neuropsychiatric aspects of TBI, in *Brain Injury Medicine,* Zasler, N.D., Katz, D.I., and Zafonte, R.D., Eds., Demos, New York, 2007, p. 835.

26. Kay, T. and Cavallo, M.M., The family system: Impact, assessment, and intervention, in *Neuropsychiatry of Traumatic Brain Injury*, Silver, J.M., Yudofsky, S.C., and Hales, R.E., Eds., American Psychiatric Press, Washington, D.C., 1994, p. 533.

27. Lezak, M.D., Living with a characterologically altered brain injured patient, *J. Clin. Psychiatry*, 39, 592, 1978.

28. Siders, C.T., Therapy for spouses of head injured patients, in *The Evaluation and Treatment of Mild Traumatic Brain Injury*, Varney, N.R. and Roberts, R.J., Eds., Lawrence Erlbaum Associates, Mahwah, NJ, 1999, p. 483.

29. Taylor, C.A. and Price, T.R.P., Neuropsychiatric assessment, in *Neuropsychiatry of Traumatic Brain Injury*, Silver, J.M., Yudofsky, S.C., and Hales, R.E., Eds., American Psychiatric Press, Washington, D.C., 1994, p. 81.

30. Lezak, M.D., *Neuropsychological Assessment*, 3rd edition, Oxford University Press, New York, 1995, p. 97.

31. Ericksen, J., Cifu, D.X., and Burnett, D., The role of neuropharmacologic agents in return to work after traumatic brain injury, *Brain Inj. Source*, 5, 32, 2001.

32. Warden, D.L., Gordon, B., McAllister, T.W., et al., Guidelines for the pharmacologic treatment of neurobehavioral sequelae of traumatic brain injury. *J. Neurotrauma*, 23, 1468, 2006.

33. Maelicke, A. and Albuquerque, E.X., Allosteric modulation of nicotinic choline receptors as a treatment strategy for Alzheimer's disease. *Eur. J. Pharmacol.*, 393, 165, 2000.

34. Granacher, R.P. and Baldessarini, R.J., Physostigmine: Its use in acute anticholinergic syndrome with antidepressant and antiparkinsonian drugs, *Arch. Gen. Psychiatry*, 23, 375, 1975.

35. Masanic, C.A., Bayley, M.T., VanReekum, R., et al., Open-label study of donepezil in traumatic brain injury. *Arch. Phys. Med. Rehabil.*, 82, 896, 2001.

36. Morey, C.E., Cilo, M., Berry, J., et al., The effect of Aricept in persons with persistent memory disorder in traumatic brain injury: A pilot study. *Brain Inj.*, 17, 809, 2003.

37. Kaye, N.S., Townsend, J.B., and Ivins, R., An open-label trial of donepezil (aricept) in the treatment of persons with mild traumatic brain injury. *J. Neuropsychiatr. Neurosci.*, 15, 383, 2003.

38. Walker, W., Seel, R., Gibellato, M., et al., The effects of donepezil on traumatic brain injury acute rehabilitation outcomes. *Brain Inj.*, 18, 739, 2004.
39. Fujiki, M., Hikawa, T., Abe, T., et al., Reduced short-latency afferent inhibition in diffuse axonal injury patients with memory impairment. *Neurosci. Lett.*, 405, 226, 2006.
40. Tenovuo, O., Central acetylcholinesterase inhibitors in the treatment of chronic traumatic brain injury—clinical experience in 111 patients. *Prog. Neuropsychopharmacol. Biol. Psychiatry*, 29, 61, 2005.
41. Zhang, L., Plotkin, R.C., Wang, G., et al., Cholinergic augmentation with donepezil enhances recovery and short-term memory and sustained attention after traumatic brain injury. *Arch. Phys. Med. Rehabil.*, 85, 1050, 2004.
42. Trovato, M., Slomine, B., Pidcock, F., et al., The efficacy of donepezil hydrochloride on memory functioning in three adolescents with severe traumatic brain injury. *Brain Inj.*, 20, 339, 2006.
43. Silver, J.M., Koumaras, B., Chen, M., et al., Effects of rivastigmine on cognitive function in patients with traumatic brain injury. *Neurology*, 67, 748, 2006.
44. Luria, A., Naydin, V., Tsvetkova, L., et al., Restoration of higher cortical function following local brain damage, in *Handbook of Clinical Neurology*, Vinkin, R.J. and Bruyn, G.W., Eds., North Holland, Amsterdam, 1968, p. 368.
45. Bennouna, M., Greene, V.B., and Defranoux, L., Adjuvant galantamine to risperidone improves negative and cognitive symptoms in a patient presenting with schizophrenialike psychosis after traumatic brain injury. *J. Clin. Psychopharmacol.*, 25, 505, 2005.
46. Meythaler, J.M., Brunner, R.C., Johnson, A., et al., Amantadine to improve neurorecovery in traumatic brain injury-associated diffuse axonal injury: A pilot double-blind randomized trial. *J. Head Trauma Rehabil.*, 17, 300, 2002.
47. Kraus, M.F., Smith, G.S., Butters, M., et al., Effects of the domamenergic agent and NMDA receptor antagonist amantadine on cognitive function, cerebral glucose metabolism and D2 receptor availability in chronic traumatic brain injury: A study using positron emission tomography (PET). *Brain Inj.*, 19, 471, 2005.
48. Green, L.B., Hornyak, J.E., and Hurvitz, E.A., Amantadine in pediatric patients with traumatic brain injury: A retrospective, case-controlled study. *Am. J. Phys. Med. Rehabil.*, 83, 893, 2004.
49. Beers, S.R., Skold, A., Dixson, C.E., et al., Neurobehavioral effects of amantadine after pediatric traumatic brain injury: A preliminary report. *J. Head Trauma Rehabil.*, 20, 450, 2005.
50. Patrick, P.D., Blackman, J.A., Mabry, J.L., et al., Dopamine agonist therapy in low-response children following traumatic brain injury. *J. Child Neurol.*, 21, 879, 2006.
51. Di Rocco, C., Maira, G., Meglio, M., et al., L-dopa treatment of comatose states due to cerebral lesions. Preliminary findings. *J. Neurosurg. Sci.*, 18, 169, 1974.
52. Krimchanski, B.Z., Keren, O., Sazbon, L., et al., Differential time and related appearance of signs, indicating improvement in the state of consciousness in vegetative state traumatic brain injury (VS-TBI) patients after initiation of dopamine treatment. *Brain Inj.*, 18, 1099, 2004.
53. Matsuda, W., Komatsu, Y., Yanaka, K., et al., Levo-dopa treatment in persistent vegetative or minimally conscious states. *Neuropsychol. Rehabil.*, 15, 414, 2005.
54. McDowell, S., White, J., and D'Esposito, M., Differential effect of a dopamenergic agonist on prefrontal function in traumatic brain injury patients. *Brain*, 121, 1155, 1998.
55. Powell, J.H., al-Adawi, S., Morgan, J., et al., Motivational deficits after brain injury: Effects of bromocriptine in 11 patients. *J. Neurol. Neurosurg. Psychiatry*, 60, 416, 1996.
56. Rao, V.L., Dogan, A., Todd, K.G., et al., Neuroprotection by memantine, a non-competitive NMDA receptor antagonist after traumatic brain injury in rats. *Brain Res.*, 911, 96, 2001.
57. Ozsuer, H., Gorgulu, A., Kiris, T., et al., The effects of memantine on lipid peroxidation following closed-head trauma in rats. *Neurosurg. Rev.*, 28, 143, 2005.
58. Muir, K.W., Glutamate-based therapeutic approaches: Clinical trials with NMDA antagonists. *Curr. Opin. Pharmacol.*, 6, 53, 2006.
59. Chemelli, R.M., Willie, J.T., Sinton, C.M., et al., Narcolepsy, and orexin knock out mice: Molecular genetics of sleep regulation. *Cell*, 98, 437, 1999.
60. Ferraro, L., Tanganelli, S., O'Connor, W.T., et al., The vigilance promoting drug modafinil decreases GABA release in the medial preoptic area and in the posterior hypothalamus of the awake rat: Possible involvement of the serotonergic 5-HT3 receptor. *Neurosci. Lett.*, 220, 5, 1996.

61. Rammonhan, K.W., Rosenberg, J.H., Lynn, D.J., et al., Efficacy, and safety of modafinil (Provigil) for treatment of fatigue in multiple sclerosis: A two-centre phase 2 study. *J. Neurol. Neurosurg. Psychiatry*, 72, 179, 2002.

62. Elovic, E., Use of provigil for underarousal following TBI. *J. Head Trauma Rehabil.*, 15, 1068, 2000.

63. Teitelman, E., Off-label uses of modafinil. *Am. J. Psychiatry*, 158, 1341, 2001.

64. DeMarchi, R., Bansal, V., Hung, A., et al., Review of awakening agents. *Can. J. Neurol. Sci.*, 32, 4, 2005.

65. Seniuk, N.A., Henderson, J.T., Tatton, W.G., et al., Increased CNTF gene expression in process-bearing astrocytes following injury as augmented by R(-)deprenyl. *J. Neurosci. Res.*, 37, 278, 1994.

66. Zhu, J., Hamm, R.J., Reeves, T.M., et al., Postinjury administration of L-deprenyl improves cognitive function and enhances neural plasticity after traumatic brain injury. *Exp. Neurol.*, 166, 136, 2000.

67. Newburn, G. and Newburn, D., Selegiline, and the management of apathy following traumatic brain injury. *Brain Inj.*, 19, 149, 2005.

68. Dixon, C.E., Ma, X., and Marion, D.W., Effects of CDP-choline treatment on neurobehavioral deficits after TBI and on hippocampal and neocortical acetylcholine release. *J. Neurotrauma*, 14, 161, 1997.

69. Calatayud, M., Calatayud, V., Perez, J.B., et al., Effects of CDP-choline on recovery of patients with head injury. *J. Neurol. Sci.*, 103 (suppl.), S15, 1991.

70. Levin, H.S., Treatment of postconcussional symptoms with CDP-choline. *J. Neurol. Sci.*, 103 (suppl.), S39, 1991.

71. Plenger, P.M., Dixon, C.E., Castillo, R.M., et al., Subacute methylphenidate treatment for moderate to moderately severe traumatic brain injury: A preliminary double-blind placebo-controlled study. *Arch. Phys. Med. Rehabil.*, 77, 536, 1996.

72. Whyte, J., Hart, T., Schuster, K., et al., Effects of methylphenidate on attentional function after traumatic brain injury. A randomized, placebo-controlled trial. *Am. J. Phys. Med. Rehabil.*, 76, 440, 1997.

73. Whyte, J., Hart, T., Vaccaro, M., et al., Effects of methylphenidate on attention deficits after traumatic brain injury: A multidimensional, randomized, controlled trial. *Am. J. Phys. Med. Rehabil.*, 83, 401, 2004.

74. Lee, H., Kim, S.W., Kim, J.M., et al., Comparing effects of methylphenidate, sertraline, and placebo on neuropsychiatric sequelae in patients with traumatic brain injury. *Hum. Psychopharmacol.*, 20, 97, 2005.

75. Kim, Y.H., Ko, M.H., Na, S.Y., et al., Effects of single-dose methylphenidate on cognitive performance in patients with traumatic brain injury: A double-blind, placebo-controlled study. *Clin. Rehabil.*, 20, 24, 2006.

76. Moein, H., Khalili, H.A., and Keramatin, K., Effect of methylphenidate on ICU and hospital length of stay in patients with severe and moderate traumatic brain injury. *Clin. Neurol. Neurosurg.*, 108, 539, 2006.

77. Al-Adawi, S., Burke, D.T., and Dorvlo, A.S., The effect of methylphenidate on the sleep–wake cycle of brain-injured patients undergoing rehabilitation. *Sleep Med.*, 7, 287, 2006.

78. Mahalick, D.M., Carmel, P.W., Greenberg, J.P., et al., Psychopharmacologic treatment of acquired attention disorders in children with brain injury. *Pediatr. Neurosurg.*, 29, 121, 1998.

79. Williams, S.E., Ris, M.D., Ayyangar, R., et al., Recovery in pediatric brain injury: Is psychostimulant medication beneficial? *J. Head Trauma Rehabil.*, 13, 73, 1998.

80. Lipper, S. and Tuchman, M.M., Treatment of chronic posttraumatic organic brain syndrome with dextroamphetamine: First reported case. *J. Nerv. Ment. Dis.*, 162, 366, 1976.

81. Hornstein, A., Lennihan, L., Seliger, G., et al., Amphetamine, and recovery from brain injury. *Brain Inj.*, 10, 145, 1996.

82. Butefisch, C.M., Davis, B.C., Sawaki, L., et al., Modulation of use-dependent plasticity by d-amphetamine. *Ann. Neurol.*, 51, 59, 2002.

83. Forsyth, R. and Jayamoni, B., Noradrenergic agonists for acute traumatic brain injury. *Cochrane Database Syst. Rev.*, CD003984, 2003.

84. Forsyth, R.J., Jayamoni, B., and Paine, T.C., Monoaminergic agonists for acute traumatic brain injury. *Cochrane Database Syst. Rev.*, CD003984, 2006.

85. Silver, J.M., Hales, R.E., and Yudofsky, S.C., Psychopharmacology of depression and neurologic disorders. *J. Clin. Psychiatry*, 51 (suppl.), 33, 1990.

86. Deb, S. and Crownshaw, T., The role of pharmacotherapy in the management of behaviour disorders in traumatic brain injury patients. *Brain Inj.*, 18, 1, 2004.

87. Jorge, R. and Robinson, R.G., Mood disorders following traumatic brain injury. *Int. Rev. Psychiatry*, 15, 317, 2003.

88. Turner-Stokes, L. and MacWalter, R., Guideline Development Group of the British Society of Rehabilitation Medicine; British Geriatric Society; Royal College of Physicians, London, Use of Antidepressant medication following acquired brain injury: Concise guidance. *Clin. Med.*, 5, 268, 2005.
89. Alderfer, B.S., Arciniegas, D.B., and Silver, J.M., Treatment of depression following traumatic brain injury. *J. Head Trauma Rehabil.*, 20, 544, 2005.
90. Wroblewski, V.A., Joseph, A.B., and Cornblatt, R.R., Antidepressant pharmacotherapy in the treatment of depression in patients with severe traumatic brain injury: A controlled, prospective study. *J. Clin. Psychiatry*, 57, 582, 1996.
91. Reinhard, D.L., Whyte, J., and Sandel, M.E., Improved arousal and initiation following tricyclic antidepressant use in severe brain injury. *Arch. Phys. Med. Rehabil.*, 77, 80, 1996.
92. Jackson, R.D., Corrigan, J.D., and Arnett, J.A., Amitriptyline for agitation in head injury. *Arch. Phys. Med. Rehabil.*, 66, 180, 1985.
93. Mysiw, W.J., Jackson, R.D., and Corrigan, J.D., Amitriptyline for post-traumatic agitation. *Am. J. Phys. Med. Rehabil.*, 67, 29, 1988.
94. Wroblewsky, B., Glenn, M.B., Cornblatt, R., et al., Protriptyline as an alternative stimulant medication in patients with brain injury: A series of case reports. *Brain Inj.*, 7, 353, 1993.
95. Silver, J.M. and Arciniegas, D.B., Pharmacotherapy of neuropsychiatric disturbances, in *Brain Injury Medicine*, Zasler, N.D., Katz, D.I., and Zafonte, R.D., Eds., Demos, New York, 2007, p. 963.
96. Horsfield, S.A., Rosse, R.B., Thomasino, V., et al., Fluoxetine's effects on cognitive performance in patients with traumatic brain injury. *Int. J. Psychiatry Med.*, 32, 337, 2002.
97. Muller, U., Murai, T., Bauer-Wittmund, T., et al., Paroxetine versus citalopram treatment of pathological crying after brain injury. *Brain Inj.*, 13, 805, 1999.
98. Andersen, G., Stylsvig, M., and Sunde, N., Citalopram treatment of traumatic brain damage in a 6-year-old boy. *J. Neurotrauma*, 16, 341, 1999.
99. Meythaler, J.M., Depalma, L., Devivo, M.J., et al., Sertraline to improve arousal and alertness in severe traumatic brain injury secondary to motor vehicle crashes. *Brain Inj.*, 15, 321, 2001.
100. Fann, J.R., Uomoto, J.M., and Katon, W.J., Sertraline in the treatment of major depression following mild traumatic brain injury. *J. Neuropsychiatr. Clin. Neurosci.*, 12, 226, 2000.
101. Turner-Stokes, L., Hassan, N., Pierce, K., et al., Managing depression in brain injury rehabilitation: The use of an integrated care pathway and preliminary report of response to sertraline. *Clin. Rehabil.*, 16, 261, 2002.
102. Showalter, P.E. and Kimmel, D.N., Stimulating consciousness and cognition following severe brain injury: A new potential clinical use for lamotrigine. *Brain Inj.*, 14, 997, 2000.
103. Pachet, A., Friesen, S., Winkelaar, D., et al., Beneficial behavioural effects of lamotrigine in traumatic brain injury. *Brain Inj.*, 17, 715, 2003.
104. Perino, C., Rago, R., Cicolini, A., et al., Mood, and behavioral disorders following traumatic brain injury: Clinical evaluation and pharmacological management. *Brain Inj.*, 15, 139, 2001.
105. Geracioti, T.D., Valproic acid treatment of episodic explosiveness related to brain injury. *J. Clin. Psychiatry*, 55, 416, 1994.
106. Wroblewski, V.A., Joseph, A.B., Kubfer, J., et al., Effectiveness of valproic acid on destructive and aggressive behaviours in patients with acquired brain injury. *Brain Inj.*, 11, 37, 1997.
107. Monji, A., Yoshida, I., Koga, H., et al., Brain injury-induced rapid-cycling affective disorder successfully treated with valproate. *Psychosomatics*, 40, 448, 1999.
108. Dikmen, S.S., Machamer, J.E., Winn, H.R., et al., Neuropsychological effects of valproate in traumatic brain injury: A randomized trial. *Neurology*, 54, 895, 2000.
109. Chatham, Showalter, P.E., and Kimmel, D.N., Agitated symptom responses to divalproex following acute brain injury. *J. Neuropsychiatr. Clin. Neurosci.*, 12, 395, 2000.
110. Kim, E. and Humaran, T.J., Divalproex in the management of neuropsychiatric complications of a remote acquired brain injury. *J. Neuropsychiatr. Clin. Neurosci.*, 14, 202, 2002.
111. Gualtieri, C.T., Buspirone for the behavior problems of patients with organic brain disorders. *J. Clin. Psychopharmacol.*, 11, 280, 1991.
112. Gualtieri, C.T., Buspirone: Neuropsychiatric effects. *J. Head Trauma Rehabil.*, 6, 90, 1991.
113. Stanislav, S.W., Fabre, T., Crismon, M.L., et al., Buspirone's efficacy in organic-induced aggression. *J. Clin. Psychopharmacol.*, 14, 126, 1994.
114. Li Pi Shan, R.S. and Ashworth, N.L., Comparison of lorazepam and zopiclone for insomnia in patients with stroke and brain injury: A randomized, crossover, double-blinded trial. *Am. J. Phys. Med. Rehabil.*, 83, 421, 2004.

115. Glenn, N.B., Wroblewski, B., Parziale, J., et al., Lithium carbonate for aggressive behavior or affective instability in ten brain-injured patients. *Am. J. Phys. Med. Rehabil.*, 68, 221, 1989.

116. Bellus, S.B., Stewart, D., Vergo, J.G., et al., The use of lithium in the treatment of aggressive behaviours with two brain-injured individuals in a state psychiatric hospital. *Brain Inj.*, 10, 849, 1996.

117. Murai, T. and Fujimoto, S., Rapid-cycling bipolar disorder after left temporal polar damage. *Brain Inj.*, 17, 355, 2003.

118. Stanislav, S.W., Cognitive effects of antipsychotic agents in persons with traumatic brain injury. *Brain Inj.*, 11, 335, 1997.

119. Wilson, M.S., Gibson, C.J., and Hamm, R.J., Haloperidol, but not olanzapine, impairs cognitive performance after traumatic brain injury in rats. *Am J. Phys. Med. Rehabil.*, 82, 871, 2003.

120. Kline, A.E., Massucci, J.L., Zafonte, R.D., et al., Differential effects of single versus multiple administration of haloperidol and risperidone on functional outcome after experimental brain trauma. *Crit. Care Med.*, 35, 919, 2007.

121. Bates, J.B., Effectiveness of risperidone in insatiable appetite following hypothalamic injury. *J. Neuropsychiatr. Clin. Neurosci.*, 9, 626, 1997.

122. Schreiber, S., Klag, E., Gross, Y., et al., Beneficial effects of risperidone on sleep disturbance and psychosis following traumatic brain injury. *Int. Clin. Psychopharmacol.*, 13, 273, 1998.

123. Temple, M.J., Use of atypical antipsychotics in the management of posttraumatic confusional states in traumatic brain injury. *J. R. Army Med. Corps*, 149, 54, 2003.

124. Alderfer, V.S. and Arciniegas, D.B., Treatment of intractable hiccups with olanzapine following recent severe traumatic brain injury. *J. Neuropsychiatr. Clin. Neurosci.*, 18, 551, 2006.

125. Kim, E. and Bijlani, M., A pilot study of quetiapine treatment of aggression due to traumatic brain injury. *J. Neuropsychiatr. Clin. Neurosci.*, 18, 547, 2006.

126. Brooke, M.M., Questad, K.A., Patterson, D.R., et al., Agitation, and restlessness after closed head injury: A prospective study of 100 consecutive admissions. *Arch. Phys. Med. Rehabil.*, 73, 320, 1992.

127. Greendyke, R.M., Kanter, D.R., Schuster, D.B., et al., Propranolol treatment of assaultive patients with organic brain disease: A double-blind crossover, placebo-control study. *J. Nerv. Ment. Dis.*, 174, 290, 1986.

128. Yudofsky, S.C., Silver, J.M., and Schneider, S.E., Pharmacologic treatment of aggression. *Psychiatr. Ann.*, 17, 397, 1987.

129. Haspel, T., Beta-blockers in the treatment of aggression. *Harv. Rev. Psychiatry*, 2, 274, 1995.

130. Murdoch, I., Nicoll, J.A., Graham, D.I., et al., Nucleus basalis of Meynert pathology in the human brain after fatal head injury. *J. Neurotrauma*, 19, 279, 2002.

131. Rogers, S.I. and Friedhoff, L.T., Pharmacokinetic, and pharmacodynamic profile of donepezil HCl following single oral doses. *Br. J. Clin. Pharmacol.*, 46 (suppl. 1), 1, 1998.

132. Karli, D.C., Burke, D.T., Kim, H.J., et al., Effects of dopaminergic combination therapy for frontal lobe dysfunction in traumatic brain injury rehabilitation. *Brain Inj.*, 13, 63, 1999.

133. Evans, R.W., Gualtieri, C.T., and Patterson, D.R., Treatment of chronic closed head injury with psychostimulant drugs: A controlled case study in an appropriate evaluation procedure. *J. Nerv. Ment. Dis.*, 175, 106, 1987.

134. Gualtieri, C.T., *Brain Injury and Mental Retardation: Psychopharmacology and Neuropsychiatry*, Lippincott, Williams & Wilkins, Philadelphia, PA, 2002.

135. Holsinger, T., Steffens, D.C., Phillips, C., et al., Head injury in early adulthood and the lifetime risk of depression. *Arch. Gen. Psychiatry*, 59, 17, 2002.

136. Gualtieri, C.T., The pharmacologic treatment of mild brain injury, in *The Evaluation and Treatment of Mild Traumatic Brain Injury*, Varney, N.R. and Roberts, R.J., Eds., Lawrence Erlbaum Associates, Mahwah, NJ, 1999, p. 411.

137. Silver, J.M. and Yudofsky, S.C., Psychopharmacology, in *Neuropsychiatry of Traumatic Brain Injury*, Silver, J.M., Yudofsky, S.C., and Hales, R.E., Eds., American Psychiatric Press, Washington, D.C., 1994, p. 631.

138. Davidson, J., Seizures, and bupropion: A review. *J. Clin. Psychiatry*, 50, 256, 1989.

139. Pinder, R.M., Brogden, R.N., Speight, T.M., et al., Maprotiline: A review of its pharmacological properties and therapeutic efficacy in mental states, *Drugs*, 13, 321, 1977.

140. Ruedrich, I., Chu, C.C., and Moore, S.I., ECT for major depression in a patient with acute brain trauma. *Am. J. Psychiatry*, 140, 928, 1983.

141. Jones, K.T., Zwil, A.S., McAllister, T., et al., Mania secondary to antidepressant medications in brain-injured patients. *J. Neuropsychiatr. Clin. Neurosci.*, 7, 417, 1995.
142. Anderson, G.D., Awan, A.B., Adams, C.A., et al., Increases in metabolism of valproate and excretion of 6 beta-hydroxycortisol in patients with traumatic brain injury. *Br. J. Clin. Pharmacol.*, 45, 101, 1998.
143. Stowe, C.D., Lee, K.R., Storgion, S.A., et al., Altered phenytoin pharmacokinetics in children with severe, acute traumatic brain injury. *J. Clin. Pharmacol.*, 40, 1452, 2000.
144. Hornstein, A. and Seliger, G., Cognitive side effects of lithium in closed head injury. *J. Neuropsychiatr. Clin. Neurosci.*, 1, 446, 1989.
145. Massey, E.W. and Folger, W.N., Seizures activated by therapeutic levels of lithium carbonate. *South. Med. J.*, 77, 1173, 1984.
146. O'Shanick, G.J., Clinical aspects of psychopharmacologic treatment in head-injured patients. *J. Head Trauma Rehabil.*, 2, 59, 1987.
147. Neppe, V.M., Integration of the evaluation and management of the transient closed head injury patient: Some directions, in *The Evaluation and Treatment of Mild Traumatic Brain Injury*, Varney, N.R. and Roberts, R.J., Eds., Lawrence Erlbaum Associates, Mahwah, NJ, 1999, p. 421.
148. Stanislav, S.W., Cognitive effects of antipsychotic agents in persons with traumatic brain injury. *Brain Inj.*, 11, 335, 1997.
149. Pollack, I.W., Psychotherapy, in *Textbook of Traumatic Brain Injury*, Silver, J.M., McAllister, T.W., and Yudofsky, S.C., Eds., American Psychiatric Press, Washington, D.C., 2002, p. 641.
150. Pollack, I.W., Individual psychotherapy, in *Neuropsychiatry of Traumatic Brain Injury*, Silver, J.M., Yudofsky, S.C., and Hales, R.E., Eds., American Psychiatric Press, Washington, D.C., 1994, p. 671.
151. Coetzer, R., Psychotherapy following traumatic brain injury: Integrating theory and practice. *J. Head Trauma Rehabil.*, 22, 39, 2007.
152. Carnevale, G.J., Anselmi, B., Johnston, M.V., et al., The natural setting behavior management program for persons with acquired brain injury: A randomized clinical trial. *Arch. Phys. Med. Rehabil.*, 87, 1289, 2006.
153. Ghaffar, O., McCullagh, S., Ouchterlony, D., et al., Randomized treatment trial in mild traumatic brain injury. *J. Psychosom. Res.*, 61, 153, 2006.
154. Giles, G.M. and Manchester, D., Two approaches to behavior disorder after traumatic brain injury. *J. Head Trauma Rehabil.*, 21, 168, 2006.
155. Mateer, C.A., Sira, C.S., and O'Connell, M.E., Putting Humpty Dumpty together again: The importance of integrating cognitive and emotional interventions. *J. Head Trauma Rehabil.*, 20, 62, 2005.
156. Feeney, T. and Ylvisaker, M., Context-sensitive cognitive-behavioural supports for young children with TBI: A replication study. *Brain Inj.*, 20, 629, 2006.
157. Wade, S.L., Carey, J., and Wolfe, C.R., An online family intervention to reduce parental distress following pediatric brain injury. *J. Consult. Clin. Psychol.*, 74, 445, 2006.
158. Banga, J.D., Independence, and rehabilitation: A philosophic perspective. *Arch. Phys. Med. Rehabil.*, 69, 381, 1988.
159. Cavallo, M.M. and Kay, T., The family system, in *Textbook of Traumatic Brain Injury*, Silver, J.M., McAllister, T.W., and Yudofsky, S.C., Ed., American Psychiatric Press, Washington, D.C., 2002, p. 533.
160. Kolakowsky-Hayner, S.A., Miner, K.D., and Kreutzer, J.S., Long-term life quality and family needs after traumatic brain injury. *J. Head Trauma Rehabil.*, 16, 374, 2001.
161. Wood, R.L., Liossi, C., and Wood, L., The impact of head injury neurobehavioural sequelae on personal relationships: Preliminary findings. *Brain Inj.*, 19, 845, 2005.
162. Kreutzer, J.S., Kolakowsky-Hayner, S.A., Demm, S.R., et al., A structured approach to family intervention after brain injury. *J. Head Trauma Rehabil.*, 17, 349, 2002.
163. Braga, L.W., DaPaz, A.C., and Ylviskaker, M., Direct clinician-delivered versus indirect family-supported rehabilitation of children with traumatic brain injury: A randomized controlled trial. *Brain Inj.*, 19, 819, 2005.
164. Wade, S.L., Wolfe, C., Brown, T.M., et al., Putting the pieces together: Preliminary efficacy of web-based family intervention for children with traumatic brain injury. *J. Pediatr. Psychol.*, 30, 437, 2005.
165. Turner-Stokes, L., Disler, P.B., Nair, A., et al., Multi-disciplinary rehabilitation for acquired brain injury in adults of working age. *Cochrane Database Syst. Rev.*, 20, CD04170, 2005.

166. Cicerone, K.D., Dahlberg, C., Malec, J.F., et al., Evidence-based cognitive rehabilitation: Updated review of the literature from 1998 through 2002. *Arch. Phys. Med. Rehabil.*, 86, 1681, 2005.
167. Cappa, S.F., Benke, T., Clarke, S., et al., E.F.N.S. guidelines on cognitive rehabilitation: A report of an E.F.N.S. task force. *Eur. J. Neurol.*, 12, 665, 2005.
168. Limond, J. and Leeke, R., Practitoner review: Cognitive rehabilitation for children with acquired brain injury. *J. Child Psychol. Psychiatry*, 46, 339, 2005.
169. Cicerone, K.D., Cognitive rehabilitation, in *Brain Injury Medicine*, Zasler, N.D., Katz, D.I., and Zafonte, R.D., Eds., Demos, New York, 2007, p. 765.

9 Forensic Examinations: Distinctions from Examinations for Treatment and the Detection of Deception

INTRODUCTION

Examination of a traumatically brain-injured person for treatment differs in many distinct ways from the examination designed to provide information to a trier of fact within a court of law (jury, judge, or administrative law judge). The role of the treating physician vis-à-vis a patient is sacrosanct. Hippocrates, one of the early practitioners of medicine and upon whom the modern practitioners of medicine model themselves, stated in his text, *Epidemics*, Book 1, Section XI, "As to diseases, make a habit of two things, to help or at least to do no harm." At a later time, the remarkable physician Galen wrote on this subject and translated this phrase into Latin as *primum non nocere*. His statement translates from Latin as "first do no harm."

Practicing physicians take these admonitions seriously. We are ethically required to act as healthcare advocates for our patients, and we are to strive always to do what is in the best medical interest for our patient. On the other hand, there is a clear distinction between those benevolent and compassionate roles of the physician practitioner and the very different role assumed by a physician who examines a person within the context of a legal action or litigation. For treatment examinations, the neuropsychiatrist or other physician is unconcerned about legal issues such as causation, damages, potential malingering, impairment ratings, or disability (see Chapter 10). The first eight chapters of this text have focused the physician examiner upon the steps necessary to ensure a comprehensive and adequate neuropsychiatric examination for treatment purposes. Those same steps are applied in a forensic examination, and the techniques for examining a traumatic brain injury (TBI) case in a forensic evaluation are exactly the same as for examining a patient with TBI. How the information is used varies considerably, and the relationship of the physician to the examinee (to distinguish this person from a patient) is significantly different.

The Ethical Principles of the American Academy of Psychiatry and the Law, the professional body representing forensic psychiatrists, state that in most cases a treating psychiatrist should not be an expert witness in a forensic matter.[1] Physicians are ethically required to assist in the application of the judicial process and to assist courts in carrying out the matters before them. We have an ethical obligation to testify on behalf of our patients if asked to do so, but when testifying as a treating physician, we are a fact witness. This means that we testify about the facts of a case wherein we have treated a patient, and we should avoid getting into issues of malingering, ratable disability impairment, whether the patient is telling the truth, and other issues of legal importance. To do otherwise puts at risk the doctor–patient relationship. We should never allow that to happen. In the same regard, a physician examining a person within the context of a lawsuit or other form of litigation should never imply to the examinee that a doctor–patient relationship exists. Persons who come to us for examination are not familiar with these concepts. The authoritative nature of the physician, and the respect society holds for physicians, places the examinee in a disadvantageous position. The examinee assumes the physician is there to provide assistance. That is not the case in a forensic examination; the physician is acting as an agent for the person who hired him to perform the examination, and while the physician should treat the examinee with compassion and appropriate respect, there is no question for whom the physician is employed. It is not the patient. As we shall see in Chapter 10, it is wise to advise the examinee of this difference and the full nature of the examination at the outset. It is suggested that this be done in writing as well as verbally (see warning statements in Chapter 10).

If the physician has a treatment relationship with a patient, while it may be necessary for the physician to testify on behalf of the patient as a fact witness, it is probably wise if an impairment rating is required that the physician defers that to a more objective examiner. Many physicians practicing today will advise a lawyer that if an impairment rating is needed, the patient's lawyer should secure the services of another physician. This avoids any potential conflict of interest. This also helps the physician maintain the doctor–patient boundary effectively. Nothing could be worse than for a treating physician to provide testimony to a court and discover within the context of treatment that the patient is lying to the doctor about the nature of the case. This produces a severe crisis of faith in the physician, and that should not be allowed to happen within a doctor–patient relationship. Therefore, it is much easier to defer examinations for disability and impairment to physicians who do not have a doctor–patient relationship.

CRITICAL DIFFERENCES BETWEEN TREATMENT EXAMINATIONS AND FORENSIC ASSESSMENT OF TRAUMATIC BRAIN INJURY

ARE YOU EXAMINING A PATIENT OR AN EXAMINEE?

This has been addressed above. However, there are further issues that the physician should understand before undertaking a forensic examination of a person alleging TBI. If one agrees to provide a TBI examination to a lawyer, a court, an administrative law judge, or other legal body or entity, the physician expert is always functioning as a consultant. The consultant role occurs very early in the relationship between the physician and the person who hires the physician to perform the examination. The expert physician is providing consultation and education to the attorney or other entity, and that person generally is not as knowledgeable about brain injury as the physician. When the examination is undertaken, the physician obviously is aware that the possibility of being called as an expert witness at court is a core portion of the implicit understanding in the contractual relationship.[2] The physician must understand that when an agreement is made to perform a TBI forensic examination, a business relationship is established with the person hiring the physician. The experts are selling their time, skill, medical knowledge, and advice. Testimony is never for sale, and that goes without saying. Only the physician's specific expertise, skill at examination of TBI, possible forensic understanding, knowledge, and time are sold contractually within the context of a forensic examination. This is a clear contradistinction to the doctor–patient relationship. In that instance, the physicians have a contractual relationship between themselves and the patient, and either the patient pays the doctors' fee or the fee is paid by a third party entity contracted to the patient to pay the fee (such as a commercial insurance company, Medicare or Medicaid). It is suggested that forensic physicians see themselves as teachers and consultants. They teach the lawyer about the medical aspects of the TBI case, and if called upon will teach a jury or other trier of fact about the elements of the case.

While it is not only permissible, but also mandatory, that physicians act as healthcare advocates for their patients, they should never be an advocate in a legal matter. The only advocacy allowed by physician experts is advocacy for their opinions. Courts clearly do not want physician experts acting as advocates, and that is disdained before the law. The physician expert is never to be an advocate for the examinee or an advocate for the person who hired the physician (such as the lawyer or judge). The physicians are to apply their best skill at the neuropsychiatric examination of the alleged TBI victim, provide a comprehensive assessment, provide a detailed report of that assessment, and provide clear and understandable opinions about the TBI case if asked to do so.

When treating a patient, in most instances fees are stated explicitly either to the patient or to the insurance carrier and are generally not negotiable but prearranged by the insurance company, Medicare, Medicaid, or other payor source. Those rules differ dramatically in a forensic examination. The physician expert can negotiate fees if requested, and the physician expert can ask for fees up front, before the examination, if wished (this is recommended). This would never occur in a doctor–patient relationship and would be considered practicing medicine on a contingency fee basis, which is unethical. On the other hand, lawyers expect physicians to ask for a retainer to take a case and to bill against that retainer. That is perfectly acceptable and fully ethical. Moreover, it helps the physician maintain objectivity, as there is no question as to whether the physician will be paid for his services. While we should respect our lawyer colleagues in forensic matters, it is an incontrovertible fact that at times lawyers will attempt to take advantage of physicians and fee arrangements or outright refuse to pay the fee if they do not like the outcome of the case. Therefore, retainer fees avoid these potential difficulties.

The Ethical Principles of the American Academy of Psychiatry and the Law[1] advise examining psychiatrists that a forensic neuropsychiatric examination must strive always for honesty and objectivity. We owe courts and triers of facts our undying pledge that we will provide this type of service when we perform an examination of a forensic nature. The fee relationship described above is very helpful to the physician to maintain these ethical principles. Also, the fees should always be paid by the person or organization for whom the physician is acting. The fees should not come from the examinee, as that may provide evidence that a physician–patient relationship has been established. Therefore, if the physician is hired by an attorney, the fee should come from either the attorney or the attorney's law firm and never from the person being examined or a family member of the examinee. If the attorney wishes to get monies from the examinee or an examinee's family member, that is between the attorney and the party he represents. That is ethical for lawyers to arrange, but physicians should not be included in that loop. This will provide assurance that the forensic evaluator is not the agent of the examinee, even if the examinee is ultimately paying the bill to the attorney.[3]

ETHICS AND BOUNDARY ISSUES OF THE FORENSIC NEUROPSYCHIATRIC EXAMINATION

Remembering again that the practice of forensic medicine is a business, one must negotiate with the attorney, or other legal entity, the time necessary to evaluate and prepare a case. If the examining physician has a standard framework for completing a neuropsychiatric examination, it may be worthwhile to give the requesting attorney a base rate for the examination. For instance, if it takes the neuropsychiatric examiner 9–10 h to complete the entire examination suggested in this book, the physician can provide a base rate for that type of examination and use that as a standard fee. It is recommended that other aspects of the examination be billed on an hourly basis. Attorneys often will call and ask for an estimated fee for reviewing records, for instance. The examiners should have a clear idea of how fast they read and how fast they can review medical records. An experienced physician should be able to determine that. It is probably wise to ask the lawyer how many records are to be sent. Lawyers often defer record preparation to paralegals or other clerical personnel in their office, and they may have limited understanding of the size of the record. While some readers may think it is humorous, it is reasonable to ask the lawyer how many inches thick the records are, and if the examiner is aware of how many sheets per hour he can read, then this enables the physician examiner to provide a reasonable estimation of time to the lawyer. It should be remembered, for instance, that the standard package of copier paper is 500 pages. Five hundred pages is a lot of material and is equivalent to the average book. Therefore, the examiner should not underestimate the amount of time necessary to carefully review large amounts of records. It is not unusual for a lawyer to send 3000 pages of medical records and depositions to be read in preparation of the case.

Let us return to the ethics of the relationship between the physician examiner and the examinee. As noted above, persons being examined by physicians do not have a clear understanding of the distinctions between an examination for treatment and an examination for forensic purposes. Therefore, the physician must strive for extreme clarity with the examinee regarding the boundaries of the examination. The physician examiner is ethically obligated to advise the examinee that since the medical examination is not for treatment and is within the context of a legal case, the normal protections of confidentiality do not apply (see Table 10.5). For instance, in almost all jurisdictions, the law recognizes that if a person raises her mental state as an issue in a legal matter, she cannot then claim confidentiality between herself and the physician who examines them. This should be explicitly stated, and it is suggested that the reader review Chapter 10 to read the warnings placed upon the medical questionnaire. These warnings should be stated again orally to the examinee at the time of the examination. Some examinees will be illiterate and incapable of understanding the written material. Other factors may arise during the examination as well. It is not unusual for the examinee to ask the advice of the examining physician about treatment or whether the care they received from other doctors has been appropriate. The physician examiner should politely decline answering such questions, as again these are providing consultation directly to the examinee, and this is not an appropriate boundary to cross. It is also wise, when questions of this nature are asked, to remind the examinee that he has the right to obtain a copy of the evaluation report that will be provided, and this can be secured through efforts of his lawyer.

It is recommended further that in forensic examinations the physician considers audio recording the examination interview. It is not unheard of for the lawyer of an examinee to raise a claim that his client was handled poorly by the physician examiner or in fact, even abused. A documentation of what was said to the examinee at the time of the TBI neuropsychiatric examination can be preserved on tape or CD and provided at a later date should issues of this nature arise. It is necessary at all times for the examining physicians to maintain distance between themselves and the examinees. This distance must be maintained after the examination as well. It is not uncommon for an examinee to leave the physician's office and later call requesting specific information about the examination or that neuroimaging or other laboratory tests be sent to their personal physician. This should never be done, and all information regarding the examination should be first conveyed to the person who hired the physician to perform the examination. If calls are received requesting information, they should be politely declined, and the party calling should be referred to their lawyer. A word of caution, since by nature most physicians are compassionate individuals who strive to provide the best care possible to their patients, it is very difficult for some physicians to switch modes into the forensic examination arena. While it is necessary to maintain compassion at all times during a forensic examination, it cannot be overstressed that the boundaries particular to a forensic examination must be maintained, and that they are distinct and apart from boundaries that occur in a doctor–patient relationship.

While in most instances written consent is not required to perform a forensic examination, it is probably wise to obtain the written consent of the examinee. When the examinee presents to the physician's office in a legal context, that individual in almost all cases is represented by an attorney who will see to the examinee's legal and personal interests. However, it is recommended that the physician follow the guidelines in Chapter 10. A review of the medical questionnaire (see Chapter 3) will demonstrate that certain waivers are asked at the time of the neuropsychiatric examination. For instance, the examinee or his guardian should sign a waiver for the physician to examine the patient. This prevents any later claims of assault or battery. It may seem inappropriate to raise these issues in this text, but they have occurred to nontreating physicians. The examinee should also sign a waiver for psychological testing to be performed if that is a portion of the neuropsychiatric examination. Obviously, it has been recommended earlier in this text that psychological testing be undertaken. The examinees should be asked to sign a statement certifying that they are telling the physicians the truth regarding the history. A fourth waiver should be obtained allowing the physician to send a report to the party requesting the examination. Again, this is not specifically required, but it is probably wise to obtain this consent anyway. If neuroimaging and laboratory assessment are obtained, waivers for those examinations will be obtained at the laboratory facility or radiology facility providing the services.

LEGAL RULES GOVERNING THE ADMISSIBILITY OF SCIENTIFIC EVIDENCE AT COURT

United States Supreme Court Justice Stephen Breyer has advised us cogently that legal disputes before us increasingly involve the principles and tools of science. Proper resolution of those disputes is important not only to the litigants involved, but also to the general public. Those of us who live in our technologically complex society, and whom the law must serve, have a vested interest in how science is applied in the courtroom. Legal decisions should reflect proper scientific and technical understanding so the law can respond to the needs of the public.[4] Expert testimony in courts of law extends back more than 2000 years. Our earliest record of this is from Roman times wherein a judge had discretion to bring experts to the court to inform about unknown "scientific" phenomena. These testimonies were probably no better than that of witch doctors or shamans. In France, about 1606, Henry IV appointed coroners in cities and important towns. This was probably the first establishment of a true coroner system in the world. These coroners were entrusted with the duty of examining all murdered persons, and their findings were reported to the court. Emperor Charles V at Ratisbon, in 1552, required that all murder cases produce expert opinion to the court. At that time, the basic common law test regarding the admissibility of expert testimony was simple. If the person offered to the court as a witness was qualified as an expert in his field, that person was competent to render expert testimony.[5] In modern times in the United States, the courts have become increasingly concerned about the production of "junk science" into the courtroom.[6] In the United States, about 1923, the *Frye* test became the standard of general acceptance for evidence produced in court within a particular scientific field.[7] Modern law in the United States regarding the admissibility of scientific evidence focuses on product liability cases. Bendectin was a commonly used antinausea agent prescribed by physicians for vomiting during pregnancy. The Merrell Dow Pharmaceutical Company was sued alleging a birth defect in a child as a result of the mother consuming Bendectin during pregnancy. The lower court in the original trial case had excluded the plaintiff's medical experts from testimony, and a judgment was entered on behalf of Merrell Dow Pharmaceutical Company. Legal appeals ensued, and the case eventually went to the United States Supreme Court to produce what is currently termed the *Daubert* rule.

The mythology surrounding expert witnesses is that there are large numbers of expert witnesses obtained through advertisements who devote most of their time and make a substantial amount of money by testifying. The empirical research does not, however, support this mythology.[8] The use of advertisements or referral firms is not how most lawyers identify experts. They usually rely primarily on advice from other lawyers, personal contacts, or through searches of prior testimony. Most experts who testify spend the majority of their time within their fields of expertise. Professor Shuman, law professor at Southern Methodist University, believes that at most this stereotype may apply to 5% or fewer of expert witnesses.[8] There is an advantage for witnesses who testify regularly. That advantage is that they are experienced and tested, and their testimony is present in the public record in many cases for review and potential impeachment of prior statements. They are also familiar with courtroom logistics and relevant legal issues and processes. If these witnesses were not effective in front of juries, competent attorneys would not continue to hire them. There are disadvantages to these witnesses, however. That is, the same experience may identify them ideologically or financially with one side, thereby limiting their credibility. In addition, if they spend significant time testifying and do not treat patients, their professional activities may become vulnerable to attack on this aspect of their experience.[8]

There is a natural conflict when scientific testimony is presented within the courtroom. The presentation of scientific evidence in a court of law is similar to a shotgun marriage between the disciplines of medicine and law. Both are forced to some extent to yield the central imperatives of the other's way of doing business. It is often that neither will be shown in its best light. The *Daubert* decision, discussed below, is an attempt to regulate that encounter and an attempt to improve upon the *Frye* test (discussed below). Judges are asked to decide the "evidential reliability" of the intended testimony based not on the conclusions to be offered but on the methods used to reach those conclusions.[9]

FRYE V. UNITED STATES: GENERAL ACCEPTANCE STANDARDS

The issue in *Frye v. United States* was the defendant's offer of an expert witness to testify that the defendant was truthful when he denied he had committed the charged crime. The expert reached a conclusion by using a systolic blood pressure deception test. This was a crude precursor of the current polygraph or lie detector machine. The case was heard in the District of Columbia Circuit Court in 1923. The opinion of the court stated "Just when a scientific principle or discovery crosses the line between the experimental and demonstrable stages is difficult to define. Somewhere in this twilight zone the evidential force of the principle must be recognized, and while the courts will go a long way in admitting expert testimony deduced from a well-recognized scientific principle or discovery, the thing from which the deduction is made must be sufficiently established to have gained general acceptance in the particular field in which it belongs."[7] The court concluded that the systolic blood pressure test had not yet gained such general acceptance. *Frye* received little attention initially. However, after World War II, courts were flooded with newer forms of expert testimony and *Frye* was rediscovered suddenly by lawyers. Initially, *Frye* was applied only in criminal cases and it was used to determine the admissibility of opinions derived from voice prints, neutron activation analyses, gunshot residue tests, bite mark comparisons, use of sodium pentothal for interview, scanning electron microscope analysis, and many other forms of scientific inquiry.[10–15] It was not until 1984 that *Frye* first was applied in a civil case.[16] *Frye* became more and more established as a standard in civil cases and in the 1980s and early 1990s it was thought that the general acceptance test under *Frye* would eliminate the need for hearings on the validity of innovative techniques.[17]

Frye endured from 1923 until 1993, but it was strongly criticized throughout that time period. It was argued that it worked too well and it resulted in not only the exclusion of unreliable evidence but also potentially reliable evidence as well.[17] Courts also faced a daunting problem of identifying which scientific field would "generally accept" a new test. Since new scientific tests and evidence approach old problems, many scientific techniques thus overlap and involve two or more academic disciplines or professional fields. A professional in one field might well develop a new test that lies on the fringes of an existing discipline and spawn an entirely new profession. This has been seen clearly in medicine with the advent of CT scanning which is in the realm of radiology, whereas MRI scanning is not only in the realm of radiology, but since it does not use radiation, it overlaps into the imaging field in general. SPECT scans and PET scans are not x-rays but rather rely upon radioactive tracers, thereby belonging in the nuclear medicine field which is a field distinct and apart from that of diagnostic radiology. Yet, as we have seen in Chapter 5, CT, MRI, SPECT, PET, and the newer techniques of fMRI and MRS have evolved and continue to evolve. These rapid changes in scientific techniques applied to brain injury pose challenges to the admission of scientific evidence at trial.

DAUBERT V. MERRELL DOW PHARMACEUTICALS, INC.

As we saw above, the *Frye* case became known as the "general acceptance" test for the admissibility of scientific evidence at trial. In some federal circuits, the *Frye* test had already been supplanted in the United States before *Daubert*. The Federal Rules of Evidence had superseded *Frye* regarding rules of scientific admissibility. In *Daubert*,[18] the plaintiffs were two infants who sued Merrell Dow Pharmaceuticals alleging they had suffered phocomelia (a reduction in the size of their limbs) birth defects as a proximate cause to their mother's ingestion of Bendectin, a pharmaceutical product manufactured by the defendant, Merrell Dow. At the trial, Merrell Dow's lawyers moved for summary judgment based on the testimony of Stephen Lamm, MD. He had served as a birth defect epidemiologist for the National Center for Health Statistics, and he was well published in the scientific areas of teratology risk from exposure to chemicals and biological substances.[18] The plaintiffs did not dispute Lamm's testimony that the relevant medical literature contained no studies concluding that Bendectin caused human birth defects. They responded to Lamm's testimony by presenting eight experts of their own who concluded that Bendectin could cause birth defects. However, the plaintiffs' experts based their conclusions on studies upon animal cells, studies upon live animals, and by analyses of chemical structures. They also recalculated prior data that had been presented in the medical literature that had previously found no causal connection between Bendectin and birth defects. Even in light of this evidence, the trial court granted to the defendant a motion for summary judgment. The trial court concluded that Bendectin did not cause birth defects and that the plaintiffs' expert opinions were not admissible. Moreover, the trial court concluded that it was not sufficiently established that the plaintiffs' expert testimony had a general acceptance in the field to which it belonged. The recalculations of prior statistical data offered by the plaintiffs' experts were judged to be inadmissible since they had never been published in a peer-reviewed medical journal.

This case eventually found its way to the United States Supreme Court. The majority opinion in *Daubert* set forth major themes. They established that the trial court is the "gatekeeper" who must screen proffered expertise, and the objective of the screening is to ensure that what is admitted "is not only relevant but also reliable." The majority opinion in *Daubert* stated further that the trial court has not only the power but also the obligation to act as gatekeeper.[19] The United States Supreme Court went on further to consider the relevancy and reliability of scientific evidence offered at trial. With regard to relevancy, the Court explained that expert testimony cannot assist the trier in resolving a factual dispute unless the expert's theory is tied sufficiently to the facts of the case. To determine whether proffered scientific testimony or evidence satisfies the standard of evidentiary reliability, a judge must ascertain whether it is grounded in the methods and procedures of science. The *Daubert* decision went on to explain by a list of four factors whether a theory or technique has been derived by the scientific method. Also mentioned by the Court in *Daubert* as indicators of good science are peer review or publication of the claimed scientific theories, the existence of known or potential error rates and standards for controlling the operation of a scientific technique.

How does this decision apply to a physician performing a neuropsychiatric examination of TBI to prepare for testimony at trial? Table 9.1 lists elements derived from the *Daubert* decision that should be followed by a physician preparing to give expert scientific testimony at trial. Obviously, the physician must be qualified by training and experience to provide an examination of TBI. The expert should possess sufficient knowledge and expertise in the areas of TBI and should have treated and examined a reasonable number of persons who have sustained TBI. It is incumbent upon the examining physician to be able to demonstrate personal experience in the examination and treatment of persons with TBI, and that physician would be expected to have demonstrated expertise in the laboratory techniques, neuroimaging, and neuropsychological applications to a neuropsychiatric examination of a traumatically brain-injured person. If the physician experts will offer testimony regarding TBI, the experts should have a sufficient familiarity with the medical scientific literature to be able to demonstrate for the court that their opinions can be tested against published opinions,

TABLE 9.1
The *Daubert* Rule

* The witness must be qualified by training, study, or experience to express an expert opinion.
* The witness must have personal experience dealing with the specific technical and scientific application that is the subject of the court's inquiry (TBI).
* Can the expert's basis for opinion be tested or has it been tested?
* Have the expert's techniques, theories, or scientific concepts been published in peer-reviewed journals?
* What are the known potential rates of error or standards controlling the expert's examination techniques in a TBI case?

or they have in fact been tested by their own prior publications in peer-reviewed journals. Any theories, opinions, or scientific evidence to be presented at trial by the expert should have a reasonable scientific underpinning in peer-reviewed medical journals. If, for instance, the expert witness plans to testify about subdural hematoma and the subsequent production of TBI, the known potential errors for the diagnosis of subdural hematoma and the known potential errors for extrapolating brain injury from the diagnosis of subdural hematoma should be known by the expert. This information is widely available in the medical literature, much of it is available in this textbook, and a reasonably qualified TBI physician can easily meet the requirements of *Daubert*.

GENERAL ELECTRIC COMPANY V. JOINER

As we shall see, initiation of the *Daubert* rule led to what has come to be called the Supreme Court's trilogy on admissibility of expert testimony. The second case in the trilogy is *General Electric Company v. Joiner*.[20] In *Joiner,* a 37-year-old plaintiff, who was a longtime cigarettesmoker with a family history of lung cancer, claimed that exposure to polychlorinated biphenyls (PCBs) and their derivatives had promoted the development of his small-cell lung cancer. The trial court in this case applied *Daubert* criteria and excluded the opinions of the plaintiff's experts. It granted the defendant's motion for summary judgment.[21] Joiner appealed, and the United States Court of Appeals reversed the decision stating that because the federal rules of evidence governing expert testimony displayed a preference for admissibility, the court applied a particularly stringent standard of review to the trial judge's exclusion of expert testimony.[22] When this case was appealed to the United States Supreme Court, all the justices joined Chief Justice Rehnquist in holding that abuse of discretion is the correct standard for an appellate court to apply and reviewing a district court's evidentiary ruling, regardless of whether the ruling allowed or excluded expert testimony.[20] Justice Breyer, in writing his opinion in the *Joiner* case, urged judges to avail themselves of techniques such as the use of court-appointed experts that would assist them in making determinations about the admissibility of complex scientific or technical evidence. The Justices did something quite different from what they had done in the *Daubert* case. They examined the court record and found that the plaintiff's expert had been properly excluded. They then reversed the appellate decision without sending the case back to be retried. The Court concluded that it was within the district court's discretion to find that the statements of the plaintiff's experts with regard to causation were nothing more than speculation. The Court noted that the plaintiff had never explained how and why the experts could have extrapolated their opinions from animal studies far removed from the circumstances of the plaintiff's exposure. This apparently had been done in an effort to explain how PCBs caused Joiner's lung cancer with no human evidence presented at trial to show causation. What the plaintiff and Joiner had done at trial was argued that four epidemiological studies, if they were pooled together, showed a link between PCBs and cancer in Joiner. Obviously, that is not a testable scientific conclusion; one cannot take epidemiological studies, transfer those, and apply them to a single person. The *Joiner* case is interesting because the *New England Journal of Medicine* filed an amicus curiae (friend of the court) brief, noting that judges should be encouraged strongly to make greater use of their inherent authority to appoint experts. They recommended that experts be sent to court by established scientific organizations such as the National Academy of Sciences and the American Association for the Advancement of Science. However, after *Daubert* and *Joiner*, the legal community raised concerns that the threshold for junk science to be introduced at trial was still too low.

KUMHO TIRE COMPANY V. CARMICHAEL

In *Kumho*,[23] the plaintiffs brought suit after a tire blew out on a minivan causing an accident in which one passenger died and others were seriously injured. The tire was manufactured in 1988 and had been installed on the minivan sometime before it was purchased as a used car by the plaintiffs in 1993. The plaintiff claimed that the tire was defective when the vehicle was bought. To support their allegation, the plaintiffs relied primarily on deposition testimony by Dennis Carlson, Jr., an expert in tire-failure analysis. He concluded, on the basis of a visual inspection of the tire, that the blowout was caused by a defect in the tire's manufacturer or design. The defendant moved to exclude Carlson's testimony. The district court agreed with the defendant that the *Daubert* rule's gate-keeping obligation applied not only to scientific knowledge but also to "technical analyses." The trial court examined Carlson's visual-inspection methodology in light of the four factors that had been mentioned in *Daubert*: the theory's testability; whether it was the subject of peer review or publication; its known or potential rate of error; and its general acceptance as a theory within the relevant scientific community. After concluding that Carlson satisfied none of the *Daubert* factors, his testimony was excluded, and the defendant's motion for summary judgment was granted. The plaintiffs asked for reconsideration, arguing that the trial court's application of the *Daubert* factors was too inflexible. The Court granted the plaintiff's request and agreed that it had erred in treating the four factors as mandatory rather than for illustrative purposes. However, the trial court reaffirmed its earlier order and excluded Carlson's expert testimony and granted summary judgment again.

The case went to the United States Court of Appeals, and this court stressed the difference between expert testimony that relies on the application of scientific theories or principles, and testimony that is based on the expert's "skill or experience-based observations." The Court went on to state that Carlson's testimony was nonscientific. He based his opinions on no scientific theory of physics or chemistry. Instead, Carlson's opinion relied on his personal experience in analyzing failed tires. After years of looking at the mangled carcasses of blown-out tires, Carlson claimed that he could identify telltale markings revealing whether a tire failed because of abuse or a defect. The Appeals Court concluded that Carlson's testimony fell outside the scope of *Daubert* and that the district court had erred as a matter of law by applying *Daubert* to this particular case, since it was based on experience rather than science. However, the 11th Circuit Court of Appeals did not conclude that Carlson's testimony was admissible. Instead, it directed the district court to determine if Carlson's testimony was sufficiently reliable and relevant enough to assist a jury. Thus, the Appeals Court upheld the circuit court decision that the trial court had a gatekeeping obligation. Its quarrel with the district court was over the court's assumption that *Daubert*'s four factors had to be considered.

When the case went to the United States Supreme Court, the Court found that the trial court's gatekeeping obligation extended to all expert testimony, and it unanimously rejected the 11th Circuit Court of Appeals' dichotomy between the expert who "relies on the application of scientific principles" and the expert who "relies on skills or experience-based observation." The Supreme Court noted that Federal Rule of Evidence 702 "makes no relevant distinction between scientific knowledge and technical or other specialized knowledge, and applies its reliability standard to all matters within its scope."[19,23] Thus, the bottom line of these three cases in terms of its application to an expert witness in a TBI case is that in most instances, the expert witnesses' scientific evidence, if challenged at court, will be reviewed in terms of the four factors of the original *Daubert* rule.

In light of *Daubert*, *Joiner*, and *Kumho*, Gutheil and Simon[3] have offered suggestions wherein an expert examiner may address questions of scientific validity regarding the expert's own opinions. They note that expert opinion is strengthened by drawing upon recognized clinical entities (such as the diagnostic and clinical categories noted in Chapter 2 that are associated with TBI). They further point out that literature review and the use of citations that are "on point" are extremely useful techniques for meeting the requirements of both a general acceptance standard and a scientific reliability standard. A forensic expert functioning in a TBI case should be able to provide empirical, scientific, or consensus bases for opinions. Data useful for fulfilling these functions might be taken, for example, from clinical studies of TBI, task force reports from the neurosurgical, neurological, neuropsychiatric, and psychiatric literature, official practice guidelines from medical disciplines relevant to the evaluation and treatment of TBI, and other relevant sources. The question to be asked by the neuropsychiatric examiner is "Do my medical discipline and examination techniques have anything to say about this case at all?" If the answer to the question is yes, the examiner must then consider whether their particular expertise can assist the fact finder to understand some relevance to the legal issues regarding the brain injury at hand. In complex cases, Gutheil and Simon suggest peer consultation. However, they caution that it is unclear whether such consultation might be legally discoverable.

DETECTION OF DECEPTION DURING NEUROPSYCHIATRIC EXAMINATION OF TRAUMATIC BRAIN INJURY

The forensic examiner is obligated to consider the possibility of malingering in a forensic assessment done for any purpose.[3] This, of course, includes examination for cognitive and behavioral effects of TBI. Failure to consider malingering constitutes substandard practice for a forensic neuropsychiatric examination.[24,25] Malingering and factitious disorders are legitimate psychiatric diagnoses and are found in the current *Diagnostic and Statistical Manual of Mental Disorders*.[26] The detection of malingering is becoming increasingly scientific and reliable, and malingering should never be an exclusion diagnosis arrived at merely because certain symptoms are or are not present.[3] Even with children, distortion and effort factors must be considered when psychic trauma is an issue in civil litigation.[26]

MALINGERING

Malingering as defined by the *DSM-IV*[26] is a condition not attributable to a mental or physical disorder. It is defined as the intentional production of falsely or grossly exaggerated physical or psychological symptoms motivated by external incentives, such as financial compensation. In contrast, factitious disorders involve the intentional production of symptoms in order to assume a patient role or a sick role. Both disorders require a deceitful state of mind.[26,29] Resnick[28] describes a number of subcategories of malingering. He defines pure malingering as the feigning of disease when it does not exist at all in the particular person. Partial malingering is the conscious exaggeration of existing symptoms or the fraudulent allegation that prior genuine symptoms are still present. This is the most likely presentation of malingering in worker's compensation and disability claims. He reports a third category, false imputation. He defines this as the ascribing of actual symptoms to a cause consciously recognized by the person to have no relationship to the symptoms. For instance, a cognitive or behavioral symptom due to severe stress within the family or a grief reaction may be falsely attributed to a TBI. Resnick describes causations for malingering a mental disorder, and he reports that they generally present for one of five purposes: (1) criminals may seek to avoid punishment by pretending to be incompetent to stand trial or insane at the time of the crime, (2) malingerers may seek to avoid induction into military service, avoid combat, or be relieved from undesirable military assignments, (3) malingerers may seek financial gain from social security disability, veterans administration benefits, workers compensation, or legal damages, (4) prisoners may malinger to obtain drugs or to be transferred to a psychiatric hospital, and (5) malingerers may seek admission to a psychiatric hospital to avoid arrest, to obtain free room and board, or to seek medication.[28]

When a person presents to a physician who is conducting an examination for TBI, there are three basic ways to malinger this evaluation: (1) to present false cognitive or neuropsychological signs or symptoms, (2) to present false psychiatric signs and symptoms, and (3) to present false somatic or physical signs and symptoms.[98] Hall and Poirier[30] have summarized the response styles that malingerers may present to a medical examiner to produce false cognitive, neuropsychological, or psychiatric symptoms. (1) Present realistic symptoms: The faker may employ a common sense or popularly understood schema of what brain-damaged persons are thought to be like. They will present symptoms with that naïve view. It is hoped that the expert evaluator will have a more objective and detailed view of realistic neurological and neuropsychological symptoms to see through the charade. (2) Distribute errors: Fakers tend to make a deliberate number of mistakes throughout their evaluation rather than miss only difficult items. They attempt to seek a balance between missing too many items and appearing too impaired by missing too many items on the tests. From a practical standpoint, fakers are unable to maintain a realistic percentage of errors and they can be detected in this fashion. (3) Protests that tasks are too difficult or they feign confusion and frustration: The faker may appear confused, angry, or display other emotions that are superimposed upon reasonably adequate cooperation and task compliance. (4) Perform in a crudely estimated fraction of their actual ability: Speed may be deliberately decreased. Since many neuro-psychological assessments have a time component, this is an excellent way to fake the examination. The evaluator should search for failures on easy test items in the neuropsychological assessment. The physician forensic examiner will need to rely upon the neuropsychologist or psychologist for assistance in this regard. (5) Errant affective style: Many traumatic brain injuries will produce changes in the expressed affect (see Chapter 2). Fakers may employ changes in affect as part of their malingering strategy. This can be a difficult response style to detect but the psychological validity measures described below will assist the examiner in determining whether or not this has occurred. The Minnesota Multiphasic Personality Inventory-2 (MMPI-2) in particular will provide the examiner with valuable information regarding behavioral, emotional, and psychiatric issues. The scales determining response bias on the MMPI-2 are particularly useful if affective coloring is being used as a deception technique during the cognitive portion of the testing.[31]

When a neuropsychiatric examiner must testify about malingering, recall that the four factors of *Daubert* may be used to challenge the expert's testimony. There are known base rates for malinger-ing. Recall Mittenberg et al.[32] from prior discussions in this text (Chapter 6). His group surveyed members of the American Board of Clinical Neuropsychology, and estimates of base rates of probable malingering and symptom exaggeration were derived from 33,531 annual cases. Diagnos-tic impressions of probable malingering were reported in 39% of mild head injury cases, 35% of fibromyalgia or chronic fatigue cases, 31% of chronic pain cases, 27% of neurotoxic cases, and 22% of electrical injury claims. At the time of the writing of this text, there are no diagnostic criteria for malingered behavioral or physical symptoms, with the exception of the Waddell signs (discussed below). Slick et al.[33] have provided diagnostic criteria for malingered neurocognitive dysfunction (which would apply to TBI), and these are increasingly being applied to the evaluation of medical conditions wherein cognitive disorders may be presented. The Slick categories[33] separate neuro-cognitive malingering into three groups: (1) definite malingering neurocognitive dysfunction, (2) probable malingering neurocognitive dysfunction, and (3) possible malingering neurocognitive dysfunction. These criteria can be applied to the neurocognitive examination of an alleged TBI. Definite malingering neurocognitive dysfunction (MND) is indicated by the presence of clear and compelling evidence of volitional exaggeration or fabrication of cognitive dysfunction in the absence of alternative explanations on one or more forced-choice measures of cognitive function at a below-chance performance level ($p < .05$). This would include any of the forced-choice measures described in Chapter 6, such as the Test of Memory Malingering (TOMM), the Victoria

Symptom Validity Test, etc. Probable MND is indicated by the presence of evidence strongly suggesting volitional exaggeration or fabrication of cognitive dysfunction in the absence of plausible alternative explanations (performance on one or more well-validated psychometric tests designated to measure feigning of cognitive deficits is consistent with fabrication). Possible MND is indicated by the presence of evidence suggesting volitional exaggeration or fabrication of cognitive dysfunction in the absence of plausible alternative explanations. To these categories for MND, Slick et al.[33] supply four criteria. Criterion A is the presence of a substantial external incentive for exaggeration or fabrication of symptoms (e.g., personal injury settlement, disability pension, evasion of criminal prosecution, or release from military service). Criterion B is evidence from neuropsychological testing of exaggeration or fabrication of cognitive dysfunction during neuropsychological test output. Criterion C is evidence from self-reports. These include self-reported history, which is discrepant with the documented history; self-reported symptoms discrepant with known patterns of brain functioning; self-reported symptoms discrepant with behavioral observations; self-reported symptoms discrepant with information derived from collateral informants and where there is evidence of exaggerated or fabricated psychological dysfunction. Criterion D is a rule-out criterion wherein behaviors meeting necessary criteria from groups B or C are not fully accounted for by psychiatric, neurological, or developmental factors. Thus, of the three potential forms of malingering presentations during a neuropsychiatric evaluation, the detection of neurocognitive malingering has the greatest evidence-based development at this time. Detection strategies for psychological and physical malingering are less well developed, but they are discussed below, and the capabilities of their detection are improving.

The neuropsychiatric examiner must be particularly suspicious of PTSD claims in association with a brain injury claim where the evidence for injury is slight or nonexistent. It is extremely easy to be coached on the details of posttraumatic stress disorder and most skilled plaintiff attorneys have a copy of the *DSM*. On the other hand, as noted in Chapter 2, PTSD is a frequent outcome and often associated with a TBI. However, defense attorneys often assume an attitude of disbelief when PTSD is raised as an issue and they imply that the individual is not suffering from any genuine psychiatric symptoms. The examiner also should consider the issue of partial malingering, i.e., a person with an actual TBI who is exaggerating the psychological component of the injury in order to enlarge the claim by including false elements of PTSD.

With regard to children, the examiner must consider, within the evaluation context, either malingering by proxy or Munchausen syndrome by proxy.[27] Young children are extremely coachable and suggestible.[34] With the Munchausen by proxy disorder, suggestibility also plays a role. Munchausen syndrome is a recognized mental disorder and is a factitious disorder. The parent or guardian, through the child, intentionally produces or feigns physical or psychological signs or symptoms. The motivation is to assume the sick role. However, in some instances, assuming the sick role becomes the genesis for a litigation which then moves the Munchausen disorder from a factitious illness to a malingered disorder. Thus, if the child is being seen repeatedly in emergency rooms or doctors' offices with a claim of brain injury and there is no evidence for financial gain or litigation, the child and its parent or guardian would properly be placed in the category of factitious disorder. If on the other hand, there is obvious economic gain, litigation, or pursuit of insurance monies, then the disorder may be transformed to malingering by proxy.[35] Table 9.2 categorizes types of false mental symptoms.

DETECTION OF COGNITIVE MALINGERING

For a forensic evaluation, the neuropsychiatric examiner must assume that the person being examined has been coached by his attorney. This may seem a contentious statement to make. However, there is significant evidence now that coaching occurs by Internet, and that Internet sites have been established to help plaintiffs learn the signs and symptoms of TBI. Moreover, this has been empirically tested. Wetter and Corrigan conducted a survey of 70 attorneys and 150 law

TABLE 9.2
Syndromes of False Mental Symptoms Common to Forensic Neuropsychiatric Assessment

Conversion disorder	Symptoms or deficits that mimic a motor or sensory neurologic disorder, or other medical conditions. The disorder is not voluntary and is unconsciously produced.[26]
Symptom magnification	Conscious exaggeration of existing symptoms or the fraudulent allegation that a prior genuine psychological or cognitive disorder is still present.[28]
False imputation	Ascribing actual symptoms to a cause consciously recognized to have no relationship to the symptoms (e.g., marital stress falsely attributed to a traumatic event in the workplace).[28]
Factitious disorder	Intentional production of physical or psychological signs or symptoms. The motivation is to assume the sick role.[26]
Malingering	Intentional production of false or grossly exaggerated physical or psychological symptoms. Motivation is to fake for an external incentive.[26]
Ganser syndrome	A form of mental malingering often seen in criminals awaiting trial. It is characterized by approximate answers (e.g., How many legs on a three-legged stool? Answer, 4; What color is snow? Answer, green.). This has been termed "Vorbeireden."[36]

students with respect to whether they brief their clients before they were administered psychological tests. Attorneys and law students considered it their responsibility to consult with their clients on testing beforehand to prepare them for the evaluation.[37] Moreover, it is increasingly common for lawyers to query, with the court's permission, the neuropsychiatric examiner and demand beforehand a list of tests that will be administered to their client. These tests are ordered to be submitted before the client presents to the examiner for assessment. These procedures by attorneys beg the question: Can individuals successfully fake the results of their psychological tests if they are informed in advance about the validity scales? Rogers et al.[38] found that criminal legal clients can be instructed in strategies that will allow them to present a fake clinical pattern on the MMPI-2 and avoid detection by the MMPI-2 validity indicators such as the F scale. The MMPI-2 F scale was ineffective for detecting coached simulators from genuine patients with schizophrenia. However, others have not replicated the findings of Rogers et al. Storm and Graham[39] found that the Fp scale was effective in detecting both uncoached and coached malingerers. Pope et al. believe that the coaching of symptoms does not appear to influence the detection of malingering.[40] As noted earlier in this text, neuropsychological tests are sensitive to both effort and timing. Merely by slowing down, one can reduce test performance.

It is probably wise for the reader of this book to consult Chapter 6 at this point. The detection of cognitive malingering is well outlined in that section, and the examiner should utilize or have utilized instruments such as the Test of Memory Malingering, the Portland Digit Recognition Test, the Victoria Symptom Validity Test, or the Letter Memory Test. Other tests may be equally as effective and could be utilized as well. The physician performing a TBI forensic examination should understand that a person with actual TBI is expected to perform well with regard to cognitive effort. There is nothing intrinsic about a TBI that destroys the ability of an individual to provide effective cognitive effort. It is recommended that at a minimum three tests of cognitive effort be administered in a forensic brain injury evaluation.[41] If the examinee fails one test and passes the second, a third test can be administered to be used as a "tie-breaker." To satisfy *Daubert* and other standards, the neuropsychiatric examiner should ensure that forced-choice and symptom validity techniques follow appropriate current psychological standards.

The forensic examiner must be particularly wary when examining persons claiming mild traumatic brain injury (MTBI). Since most cases of MTBI do not present with physical impairment, focal neurological signs, or neuroimaging findings, there are little if any objective medical standards that can be applied to a case of this type. Almost all litigation cases of MTBI rely on neuropsychological test data only. Therefore, it is critically important that the forensic examiner review carefully the original case record (see Chapter 11), the original medical evidence, and the emergency department or hospital for whether or not a TBI was present, and any other collateral information that may have a bearing on the function of the individual following the alleged injury. The use of neuropsychological test data alone to support the evidence of MTBI may have merit, but it is also fraught with scientific uncertainty. Moreover, financial incentives and litigation issues themselves may play a role in the induction and maintenance of symptomatology in persons claiming TBI. This is much more likely to occur if the head trauma is mild rather than moderate or severe. Data previously published have revealed a higher level of abnormal presentations and disability in patients with financial incentives, despite less severe head injuries. One study examined demographic, injury-related, and symptom variables at time of first examination, at 3 months post-injury, and at 12 months post-injury. The authors compared 50 treated adults with TBI who were not seeking or receiving financial compensation against 18 litigants who were seeking financial reward. The compensation seekers reported symptom incidence and severity at approximately 1 SD higher at each of the testing intervals. The level of variance between the groups did not significantly differ over the 12-month period. No demographic variables distinguished the groups. No injury-related variables other than more immediate post-injury prescription use were predictive of the greater symptom complaints for the patients seeking or receiving compensation. Medication effects did not explain away the compensation effect when medication use was covaried in the analysis.[42] That is not to say that persons in litigation cannot have a true brain injury. Of course, they can. However, even people in litigation who have valid TBI should demonstrate true cognitive and psychological deficits if adequate controls are in place within the examination. A comprehensive neuropsychiatric assessment should strive to uncover issues such as impression management, symptom magnification, or malingering.[43-48] Please refer to Table 9.3, which outlines principles of cognitive malingering detection.

Detecting False Memory Complaints

The reader at this point may wish to review Ribot's law and its discussion elsewhere in this text (Chapter 2). This is a very basic and important principle of human memory, and when Ribot's law is violated during a neuropsychiatric examination, it is mandatory that the examiner pursue further efforts to detect memory malingering. As noted in Chapter 6, the Test of Memory Malingering has been widely used as a screening tool for deceptive expressions of memory during examination. This instrument has been repeatedly tested recently and found to be valid and reliable. Haber and Fichtenberg recently evaluated the TOMM in a TBI and head trauma sample. These authors selected 50 cases from two different participant pools: medically documented TBI patients and compensation-seeking mild head trauma cases. Their results replicated and expanded those found originally by Tombaugh.[49] Greve's group at the University of New Orleans evaluated the Test of Memory Malingering in persons reporting exposure to environmental and industrial toxins. Thirty-three patients who met Slick et al.'s criteria for malingered neurocognitive dysfunction[33] were compared to 17 toxic exposure patients negative for evidence of malingering, 14 TBI patients, and 22 memory disorder

---

TABLE 9.3

Principles of Cognitive Malingering Detection

- At least three probability-based cognitive effort tests should be used during cognitive assessment.
- Multiple sources of information and data should be gathered in malingering analysis.
- These sources include historical indicators (prior history of deception), marked discrepancy between claimed and measurable cognitive deficits, interference with the examination, memory disorder or amnestic claims which deviate from Ribot's law, and failure of performance during cognitive effort measures.

patients. The findings from this examination indicated that the TOMM can be used with confidence as an indicator of negative response bias in cases of cognitive deficits attributed to exposure to alleged neurotoxic substances.[50] Greve's group evaluated more extensively the TOMM in detecting cognitive malingering in TBI. Forty-one of 161 TBI patients at the University of New Orleans met Slick et al. criteria[33] for malingered neurocognitive dysfunction (MND). Of the 161 TBI patients, 22 no-incentive memory disorder patients were also included in the study group. The original cutoffs for the Trial 2 and the Retention Trial of the TOMM demonstrated excellent specificity (<5% false positive error rate) and impressive sensitivity (>45%). However, these authors found the cutoffs were very conservative in the context of mild TBI. Over 90% of the non-MND mild TBI sample scored 48 or higher on the Retention Trial and none scored less than 46. On the other hand, 60% of the MND patients claiming mild TBI were detected at malingering level cutoffs.[51]

A study from Texas Tech University evaluated the TOMM against the Word Memory Test. This study attempted to estimate the positive predictive value and negative predictive value of the TOMM. When the Word Memory Test was used as the gold standard and compared against the TOMM, the TOMM achieved a very high predictive value (0.98) and an acceptable negative predictive value (0.78).[52]

When neuropsychiatric examiners are evaluating persons with TBI and depression, lawyers often question the validity of using a cognitive malingering screening device such as the TOMM. A recent West Virginia University study evaluated the effects of severe depression on TOMM performance among those seeking disability. Twenty participants with high levels of depression, as measured by the Beck Depression Inventory, 2nd Edition (BDI-II), with a current psychiatric diagnosis of major depression were evaluated. The study hypothesis was that the depressed patients would perform significantly worse on the TOMM than a control group of nondepressed persons. The study results revealed that the depressed and control groups did not have significant mean group differences on TOMM performance. Of the 20 depressed participants, only two persons on Trial 2 and one person on the Retention Trial scored below the cutoff of 45. None of the control participants performed within this range. The results indicated that the TOMM can be used with even severely depressed participants with only slight caution.[53] While the TOMM is widely used across the United States for the detection of malingered memory complaints, the Letter Memory Test is also widely used. A recent University of Kentucky study evaluated and cross-validated the Victoria Symptom Validity Test, the Test of Memory Malingering, the Digit Span subtest of the WAIS-III, and the Letter Memory Test. Compensation-seeking neuropsychological evaluees were classified into "honest" ($n = 37$) or "probable cognitive feigning" ($n = 53$) groups based on the results from using the methods of testing noted. The groups were generally comparable on demographic, background, and injury severity characteristics. Honest TBI participants were significantly more likely to have a documented loss of consciousness, whereas the probable cognitive feigning participants were significantly more likely to be currently on disability. Those who were cognitively feigning showed significantly lower scores on many neuropsychological tests, particularly on tests of memory as well as producing higher scores on most MMPI-2 clinical scales than the honest group. Results from the Letter Memory Test were significantly lower for the probable cognitive feigning group, and using the recommended cutting score, specificity was 0.984, whereas sensitivity was 0.640. This suggested adequate performance on cross-validation of the Letter Memory Test.[54]

The reader should have noted by now that there are numerous tests designed specifically to detect cognitive malingering, and in particular, the detection of memory malingering. Some of these tests have been outlined extensively in Chapter 6. However, it may not be understood by many physicians that tests measuring memory specifically rather than tests used to detect malingering can also be used to detect memory malingering. The California Verbal Learning Test-2nd Edition (CVLT-II) has been used repeatedly for the detection of memory malingering. As noted in Chapter 6, it is also an excellent test for measuring verbal memory. However, numerous authors have proved convincingly that this test is quite a skillful measure of memory malingering. For instance, Greve's group at the University of

New Orleans recently used a well-defined TBI population, a mixed neurological population (other than TBI), and psychiatric patients to examine the specificity and sensitivity to malingered neurocognitive dysfunction (by the methods of Slick et al.[33]) using four individual California Verbal Learning Test variables and eight composite CVLT-II malingering indicators. The participants were 275 TBI patients and 352 general clinical patients seen for neuropsychological evaluation. The TBI patients were assigned to one of the five groups using the Slick et al. criteria. These groups included no incentive, incentive only, suspect, and malingering (both probable and definite). Within the TBI population, persons with the strongest evidence for malingering had the most extreme scores. Good sensitivity (approximately 50%) in the context of excellent specificity (>95%) was found in the TBI samples.[55] Slick et al. have noted that the CVLT-II may add useful data over and above those obtained from using symptom validity testing alone. However, he cautions that using the CVLT-II scores alone may be associated with a higher than acceptable false positive error rate.[56]

Other recent studies have confirmed the use of the CVLT-II as a screening tool for memory malingering.[57,58]

Detecting False Executive Function Complaints

This is a more difficult analysis to perform than testing memory effort. However, it is rare to find pure executive function complaints in the absence of memory complaints. Moreover, remember discussions from Chapter 6 that working memory is a component of executive function. Therefore, methods to detect false complaints of working memory are useful in the screening of individuals who may falsely complain of executive dysfunction.

The Wisconsin Card Sorting Test (WCST) does have validity indicators within it. These are not self-evident. However, it has been researched with regard to invalid performances, a subset of which in a forensic context could be associated with malingering. Prior research studies[59,60] have noted, by multivariate approaches, variables that may assist in the detection of malingering using the WCST. Recently, King et al. at Northwestern University reviewed the WCST in a multivariate approach in an attempt to find patients with probable insufficient effort. However, while these techniques are useful from a statistical standpoint, they do not have ease of transfer to the ordinary forensic examination.[61]

A much simpler approach to the screening for executive effort is the Digit Span from the Wechsler Adult Intelligence Scale–III. Recent studies have noted that the Digit Span scaled score is the best discriminating index of all methods for using the digit span subtest. A cutoff score of less than or equal to 7 accurately classifies 75% of persons providing incomplete or poor effort.[62] Greve's group has also evaluated Digit Span scores and found valuable data supporting their use in detection and diagnosis of malingering.[63]

As noted above under the memory section of this chapter, in addition to standardized tests of cognitive effort, tests intrinsic to the measurement of executive function can themselves be used in the detection of malingering. For instance, the number of categories completed and failure to maintain set will usually distinguish malingers from controls who are administered the Wisconsin Card Sorting Test.[64] High false positive error rates are usually observed in most samples when comparing normal college students asked to fake with neurological patients used as controls.[65] Thus, the Wisconsin Card Sorting Test can be used as an alternative estimator of malingering in addition to the cognitive effort tests such as the Test of Memory Malingering, Victoria Symptom Validity Test, and other cognitive effort measures noted in Chapter 6. When administering the Trailmaking Tests, performance errors and inflated time scores may be useful in the assessment of malingering.[66]

DETECTION OF PSYCHOLOGICAL MALINGERING

Virtually any psychological state can be malingered. With regard to TBI, the most likely syndromes or diseases to be malingered are depression and posttraumatic stress disorder. In the modern litigation climate, the neuropsychiatric examiner must be extremely vigilant regarding psychological malingering. Many individuals who present to physicians with a claim of TBI have been briefed by their lawyer about the reasons and rationales for the tests that they will take. Moreover, as noted above, many times the examiner will have to provide a list of tests to be administered to the plaintiff lawyer before the lawyer will allow his client to appear for examination. Lees-Haley[67] wrote, "Attorneys influence psychological data by a variety of means. They advise their clients how to respond to psychological tests, make suggestions of what to tell examining psychologists and what to emphasize, and lead patients not to disclose certain information important to psychologists." We have seen above that Wetter and Corrigan[37] conducted a survey and found that almost 50% of the attorneys and over 33% of the law students believed that clients referred for testing always or usually should be informed of validity scales on tests. At the time of the writing of this text, it is still not known what percentage of attorneys actually brief their clients in these particular areas of testing and how much information about the MMPI-2, for instance, they actually provide. A recent review of the Internet found that on one site, a psychologist posted test stimuli of many popular neuro-psychological instruments, and another site contained an accurate facsimile of the Rorschach inkblot cards with detailed information on how the results are interpreted and instructions on how to respond appropriately. A set of Rorschach plates, which are generally restricted from unauthorized purchase, were also for sale on a popular Internet auction site. In another instance, a website provided explicit instructions on how to avoid dissimulation on certain psychological tests. For example, this site provided detailed information about the MMPI-2 and the Rorschach. This information included pictures of the inkblots as well as the detection strategies used on both instruments to identify pathology and malingering. Sites provided information about the purpose of the independent medical evaluation and provided advice to potential examinees on how to present themselves in a manner to obtain disability benefits.[68–70]

Actually, a number of recent studies suggest that attorneys will have a difficult time in coaching their clients. Research on the topic of fakability of the MMPI-2 to date suggests that briefings of clients with respect to the validity scales can affect the results of testing in unknown ways. Coaching symptoms do not appear to influence the detection of malingering.[71] Two recent studies reviewed the capacity of the MMPI-2 and the Personality Assessment Inventory (PAI) validity scales and indexes to detect coached and uncoached faking.[72,73] These researchers found that coaching had no effect on the ability of the research participants to fake more successfully than those participants who received no coaching. For the MMPI-2, the F scale, or the F(p) scale, proves to be the best at distinguishing psychiatric patients from research participants instructed to malinger. It is extremely difficult for a neuropsychiatric examiner to inquire about the potential of prior coaching. It is not ethical, or within the bounds of attorney–client privilege, for the examiner to intrude into communications between a lawyer and client that may be privileged.

The MMPI-2 in Detection of Psychological Malingering

In most instances, the neuropsychiatric examiner will not possess a license in psychology and, therefore, consultation with a psychologist or neuropsychologist is required. However, the same caveats apply in psychological assessment as in neuropsychological assessment. It is incumbent upon the neuropsychiatric examiner to determine if the consulting psychologist or neuropsychologist is appropriately skilled in the interpretation of the MMPI-2. In general, individuals who possess one course in graduate school regarding the MMPI-2, and subsequent limited experience in the utilization of this test instrument, are poor choices for consultation in neuropsychiatric assessment. As with medical procedures, the heart surgeon performing 200–300 procedures annually is generally more competent than one performing 25 procedures annually. The same is true of the psychologist. Therefore, the neuropsychiatric examiner may want to determine the base rate of MMPI inter-pretations performed by the psychologist in any given year. This will help the neuropsychiatric examiner determine, at least in part, the experience base of the psychologist. Moreover, in a forensic setting, the use of computerized interpretive templates for the MMPI-2 is not recom-mended. The most credible use of the MMPI-2 in court rests upon careful individual interpretation by the psychology examiner who also examined the injury claimant at the request of the neuro-psychiatric examiner. A case in point lies in substantial elevations on Scale 8 of the MMPI-2 which is often an outcome of significant TBI. A computerized interpretation of the MMPI-2 generally will default to a diagnosis of "schizophrenia" or some schizophrenia-like process. In fact, the MMPI-2 is responding to the disordered thinking being reported by the examinee as a result of impaired attentional and frontal systems following TBI. Clinical psychologists who are inexperienced in TBI may overlook this point but if the examining physician testifies in court about the MMPI-2 and the finding of schizophrenia, this in all likelihood discredits the examiner and causes significant complications to the production of accurate medical testimony regarding the behavioral effects of TBI.

"Cannot Say" Score

The use of this scale determines how many questions the examinee failed to answer during MMPI administration. It is generally accepted that if more than 30 test questions are not answered, this will attenuate the profile. Most psychology experts believe the MMPI profile should not be interpreted if 30 or more items are omitted. Therefore, it is incumbent upon the psychology examiner to insure that post-test-taking interviews are performed to answer questions the examinee may have regarding omitted items so that they can be completed at the time of the examination. Moreover, it is extremely important that the neuropsychiatric examiner insures that the examinee completed the MMPI-2 uninterrupted by interference from others. If the examinee reads poorly, the University of Minnesota Press provides auditory tapes that may be used for the administration of the MMPI-2. In almost no instance should an MMPI-2 be read to the examinee by a second party. This will usually invalidate the protocol for forensic purposes. If English is a second or third language, the MMPI-2 may require deletion from the test protocol unless appropriate other language forms are used. The examinee may be loathe to answer certain questions in the face of a second party. The reading requirements and other testing standards for the MMPI are discussed further in Chapter 7.

If asked, the neuropsychiatric examiner should be aware that possible reasons for omitting items during administration of the MMPI include poor cooperation, defensiveness, indecisiveness, fatigue, depression, carelessness, poor reading comprehension, and the perception of examinees that the items are not relevant to them. It is recommended that no items be omitted as even 5 or 6 omitted items, on a particular scale, can affect the reliability and validity of that scale.[40] On the other hand, if most of the omitted items occur toward the end of the booklet (after item 370 on the MMPI-2 or after item 350 on the MMPI-A), some validity and all clinical scales can be interpreted. The newer validity scales such as VRIN cannot be used in this instance. Also, the forensic examiner cannot use data from the Supplementary or Content scales which are included in items found toward the end of the test question booklet.

The Lie Scale

If the examinee elevates the Lie (L) scale (>65T), the examinee is probably involved in impression management of the testing situation. However, the L scale cannot measure lying per se. It is not a truth detector. Elevations on the L scale suggest the examinee has responded to other items in the MMPI-2 in such a manner as to deny personal weakness and present the most favorable image to the examiner. Elevation on the L scale may not be as important in the neuropsychiatric examination of TBI as it would be in a custody evaluation or a criminal evaluation. However, if the score exceeds 72T, this suggests clear distortion of item responding on the L scale in order to manipulate what the examiner thinks of the examinee. If the examinee is attempting to create a particular pattern of disability (e.g., brain injury), elevations of the L scale associated with other elevated MMPI-2 scores are consistent with that interpretation. Review of the TRIN scale (inconsistent true or false responding) can aid in determining whether the elevated L score is due to a frequent false response. Baer et al.[74] reviewed measures of underreporting psychopathology on the original MMPI. They did not find any substantial differences in the function of the L score on the MMPI-2 relative to the MMPI.

In addition to the above-mentioned reasons for elevation of the L scale, this scale may also be elevated in persons who are unrealistically proclaiming virtue. Other causes of elevation are hypermorality, a naïve self-view, an effort to deceive others about motives or adjustment, personality adjustment problems, and a lack of willingness to admit even minor flaws in one's personality or character (poor self-disclosure).

The K Scale
Elevations on the K scale indicate the tendency to present a favorable self-report.[40] This scale can be influenced by one's socioeconomic class or educational level.[75] Elevations on the K scale greater than 65T suggest possible defensive responding. For instance, the individual is presenting a more favorable image than is practical. This is commonly seen in family custody evaluations or criminal proceedings and rarely in TBI evaluations but it may occur. Persons who are poorly educated below high school level tend to produce lower K scores than more educated persons. Causes for elevated K scores include defensiveness, a great need on the part of the examinee to present as very well adjusted, or overresponding falsely. False responding can be ruled out by examining the TRIN scale.

The Infrequency (F) Scale
This is clearly the most important validity scale on the MMPI. While it cannot be interpreted in isolation, it has the greatest scientific database of all of the MMPI validity scales available to psychologists. It has been modified substantially in the MMPI-2 and MMPI-A relative to the original MMPI. Four original items were dropped from the scale because of their objectionable content. The new F scale was empirically normed using linear T-scores as opposed to the rationally derived setting of scale values with the original F scale development. An additional infrequency scale has been added, the back-page F scale or F(b). This was developed to rule out a measure of infrequency for the items that appear in the back of the booklet (after item 370) because the original F scale contains only items that occur in the front half of the item booklet.[40] The F scale for the MMPI-A was further revised to address more fully the tendency of adolescents to endorse items differently than adults.[76]

Concern over elevations on the F scale generally is not present until the scale exceeds 80T. A score between 60T and 79T usually reflects that the examinee is approaching the items in a problem-oriented fashion. If the F scale exceeds 80T, this indicates an exaggerated response set and probably represents an attempt to claim excessive problems. This would be consistent with symptom magnification. The examiner can review the VRIN T-score and if it is below 79, this rules out the probability of inconsistent responding. If the F scale T-score ranges from 90T to 109T, the profile may be invalid. If the F score exceeds 110T, this is an uninterpretable profile and consistent with extreme item endorsement. Where the F scale is elevated, possible causes include confusion, illiteracy, responding to the items in a random fashion, severe mental illness, symptom exaggeration, faking psychological problems, and malingering.[77]

A new F scale was added to the current edition of the MMPI-A and was specifically developed for persons between the ages of 14 and 18. The F1 scale functions similar to the F scale on the adult version of the MMPI-2. The F2 scale corresponds to the F(b) on the adult form of the MMPI-2. In other words, F2 allows one to assess responding toward the end of the booklet versus toward the front of the booklet with the adolescent test in the same fashion as is accomplished with the adult MMPI-2. With the F and F(b) scales of the MMPI-2, Berry et al. have found that these scales will significantly differentiate patients seeking compensation for head injuries from closed head injury patients not seeking compensation, in terms of greater scale elevation in the former.[78]

The VRIN Scale
This new scale was added to the MMPI-2 and the MMPI-A during their development. VRIN does not exist in the original edition of the MMPI. It is a very useful scale for determining careless, inconsistent, or random responding. Its most important interpretation is made in combination with the F scale. The VRIN scale is an empirically derived measure. Throughout the MMPI-2 and

MMPI-A, there are pairs of items for which some responses are semantically inconsistent. As noted above, very high elevations on the F scale are the most sensitive indicators of psychological malingering. The VRIN scale enables the psychologist to determine if extreme elevations on the F scale are in fact malingering or due to other complications within the examinee's approach to the MMPI-2 or MMPI-A. If the individual has a high score on the F scale and a low to moderate score on the VRIN scale, reasons other than randomly responding or inconsistent responding must be considered to explain the high F score. A high F score in these cases, with a relatively reduced VRIN score, may represent actual or faked psychopathology. If the F scale score is extremely elevated and the VRIN scale score also is extremely elevated, these findings are consistent with confusion, random responding, or inconsistency in the examinee's approach to the testing. If the VRIN T-score exceeds 80T on the MMPI-2, or exceeds 75T on the MMPI-A, this indicates inconsistent random responding that invalidates the MMPI profiles. If the VRIN scores range from 70T to 79T on the MMPI-2 and 70T to 74T on the MMPI-A, this suggests a possibly invalid profile due to inconsistent responding.[77]

The TRIN Scale
This scale, True Response Inconsistency scale, was designed to measure the tendency for some individuals to respond in an inconsistent manner by endorsing many items in the same direction (either true or false).[40] Scoring for the TRIN scale is very complicated. Most MMPI experts feel that TRIN should be computer scored rather than hand scored to reduce scoring errors. The TRIN score is particularly useful when one interprets scores on scales L and K because all but one of the items on these two scales is keyed "false." Thus, if a person engages in an inconsistent false response set, this may produce elevated scores on scales L and K that have nothing to do with being defensive or with an attempt to fake good. Conversely, an individual who answers the MMPI-2 items inconsistently "true" may produce very low scores on L and K that have nothing to do with being excessively open, self-critical, or overwhelmed by stress. Thus, whenever extreme scores appear on scales L and K, the psychologist should make a careful examination of the score on TRIN. Pope et al. believe this is essential if L and K scores are in the extreme ranges.[40] As with VRIN, TRIN scores greater than 80T on the MMPI-2 or greater than 75T on the MMPI-A indicate inconsistent responding and probably invalidate the test protocol. In like fashion, respective scores 70T–79T on the MMPI-2 or 70T–74T on the MMPI-A suggest possible inconsistent responding,

Pope et al.[40] have described four major ways that the validity scales of MMPI-2 may raise the issue of malingering. These faking responses are (1) rare responding, (2) defensive responding, (3) inconsistent responding, and (4) atypical MMPI-2 patterns. The F scale is the most sensitive scale in the MMPI for detecting rare responding. Defensive responding is a common indicator of complaints without actual organic problems.[79] Defensive individuals often respond to the test items on the MMPI-2 by claiming a high degree of virtue and denying or minimizing faults. This response set will produce high L and K scores so that their claims of physical problems will seem more credible. It is an attempt to manipulate what the examiner thinks of the person or to create a particular pattern of disability within the context of the neuropsychiatric examination. Rogers has noted[80] that inconsistent responding on the MMPI test items can reflect a general pattern of malingering. Some individuals will attempt to endorse extreme symptoms in an unselected fashion and endorse randomly, or respond in an "all true" or "all false" response set. The VRIN and TRIN scales on the MMPI-2 will help detect these types of malingering. The fourth possible indicator of malingering, atypical MMPI-2 patterns, requires consultation with a psychologist very experienced and educated in the use of the MMPI-2. This is the most difficult pattern to analyze. To detect malingering, the psychologist must match behavior or symptoms from the examinee's responses to that of expected clinical patterns established by research on the particular sample involved or by the base rates for the relevant population.[81] There are modal or expected MMPI-2 performances that can be identified for a variety of clinical situations or phenomena and those are published in the major texts on interpretation of the MMPI-2 (see references in Chapter 7).

The F(p) Scale

The F and F(b) scales are effective at detecting extreme item endorsement on the MMPI-2. However, in the more moderate ranges, they are not useful for differentiating symptom exaggeration or malingering from a person who is actually quite seriously mentally ill. The examiner must understand that mentally ill or psychologically disturbed persons can elevate scores on F and F(b) even though they are not exaggerating or malingering. After the original publication of the MMPI-2 in 1989, Arbisi and Ben-Porath[82,83] developed the scale now called F(p) to help with that differentiation. If the T-score on F(p) ranges from 60T to 79T, this generally reflects a problem-oriented approach to the items and the person may have true psychopathology. Scores ranging from 80T to 89T indicate an extremely exaggerated response set in which the examinee is attempting to claim extreme or unusual psychiatric symptoms. If the T-score elevates to 90T–109T, the profile may be invalid as a result of the examinee claiming an extreme number of rare psychiatric symptoms. In those instances where F(p) is greater than 110T, this indicates likely malingering of psychiatric symptoms and it results in an uninterpretable profile because of the extreme item endorsements. Elevated F(p) scores (greater than 90T) usually represent symptom exaggeration, faking psychological problems, or malingering psychiatric illnesses.[77]

The F-K Index

This dissimulation index was first proposed by Gough in 1947.[84] However, Gough set the cutoff at 9. In other words, he advised taking the raw score on F and subtracting the raw score from K. If that score exceeded +8 (+9 or greater), the examinee was considered to have faked the MMPI-2. Later research suggested that this index was too low and it has been recommended that profiles with an F-K score of +12 or above be considered invalid.[85] The F-K index has been supported by various studies in forensic assessment that have demonstrated it will accurately detect malingering.[86–88] However, it is not as effective as the T-scores of the F scale taken alone.[89]

There are numerous other scales which have been reported to be of assistance in the detection of malingering or dissimulation during psychological, psychiatric, and neuropsychiatric examinations. Those include the Fake Bad Scale (FBS), the Superlative Self-Presentation Scale (S), and others that are outside the scope of this text. The reader is referred to Pope et al. for more extensive data on the use of the MMPI-2 or the MMPI-A in court.[40] The reader can also refer to Nelson[90] for use of the MMPI-2 in forensic neuropsychological evaluation. Table 9.4 lists methods whereby the MMPI-2 may assist in the detection of deception.

The Millon Clinical Multiaxial Inventory-2 in Detection of Psychological Malingering

The Millon Clinical Multiaxial Inventory-2 (MCMI-2) is not particularly useful in the forensic neuropsychiatric assessment of TBI. That statement is not meant to discredit this inventory. It is very useful for personality assessment and for the assessment of persons in psychotherapy.

TABLE 9.4

Using the Minnesota Multiphasic Personality Inventory-2 (MMPI-2) and Minnesota Multiphasic Personality Inventory (MMPI-A) to Detect Malingering

- Consult with a psychologist expert in MMPI administration and interpretation.
- Is there evidence of rare responding? Review the MMPI profile to detect high F T-scores and high F-K raw scores. If they are elevated significantly, confirm that VRIN is also not elevated (confusion or random responding if VRIN elevated).
- Is there evidence of defensive responding? Are L and K scores significantly elevated to make claims of impairment more credible? Determine from TRIN scores whether a false response set is present.
- Is inconsistent responding present? Review VRIN and TRIN scores for all true or all false response sets.
- Are atypical MMPI-2 or MMPI-A patterns present?

However, the database for this test instrument in brain injury is slight and not nearly as strong as the MMPI-2, the Personality Assessment Inventory, or the Structured Interview of Reported Symptoms.

There are four validity scales on the MCMI-2 specifically designed to assess exaggeration or minimizing of problems. Those four validity indicators on the MCMI-2 are (1) the Validity Index, (2) Scale X (disclosure), (3) Scale Y (desirability), and (4) Scale Z (debasement). Bagby et al. have independently examined all four MCMI-2 validity scales in distinguishing honest, fake bad, and fake good response sets by discriminate function analyses. Their results revealed that the MCMI was capable of not only classifying fake-bad profiles accurately, but also identifying fake-good and honest profiles with much accuracy. Apparently, the MCMI-2 demonstrates a slight tendency to identify faking-bad profiles more accurately than honest or faking-good profiles.[91,92]

The neuropsychiatric examiner should realize that the MCMI-2 is theory based rather than empirically based. In other words, it is based on theories of psychological functioning by Theodore Millon and is not based on empirically derived samples from mentally ill persons. This provides some potential weakness when using this instrument in forensic settings and as a result, may be inconsistent with *Daubert* standards.

The Personality Assessment Inventory in Detection of Psychological Malingering

Morey[93] describes random responding and malingering as negative distortion. As noted in Chapter 7, the PAI, when contrasted with the MMPI-2, is much more clinically based. However, unlike the MMPI-2, there is no adolescent form for this test instrument and it is not normed on persons younger than 18 years. This test appears to be psychometrically superior to the MMPI-2.[94]

The PAI contains four major validity scales: (1) Infrequency, (2) Inconsistency, (3) Negative Impression, and (4) Positive Impression. The Infrequency scale determines if the examinee is responding carelessly or randomly. The Inconsistency scale determines if the examinee is answering questions consistently throughout the task. The Negative Impression (NIM) scale determines whether the examinee is psychologically exaggerating or malingering. The Positive Impression scale determines whether the examinee is trying to make a very favorable impression or is reluctant to admit to minor flaws.

Infrequency Scale
This scale is used for the identification of examinees who complete the PAI in an atypical way due to carelessness, confusion, reading impairment, or other sources of random responding. The scale consists of items that were designed to be answered similarly by all examinees, regardless of their clinical status. Half of the items are expected to be answered "totally false;" whereas, the other half should be answered "very true." Infrequency (INF) scale items are placed evenly throughout the PAI to identify potentially problematic responding. Infrequency scale items have been written specifically to provide item content that would be infrequent, yet would not sound bizarre, for instance, "I have never seen a building."

The INF scale is primarily a measure of carelessness in responding. However, examinees also could answer the PAI items in a very idiosyncratic way. If the psychologist makes a quick review of the INF items, it is easy to distinguish between these two potential sources of elevation. High scores on INF ($\geq$75T) are consistent with the examinee attending inappropriately to item content while responding to the items on the PAI. The completely random response will result in an average INF score of 86T. The neuropsychiatric examiner should be aware that several potential reasons for scores in this range may occur such as reading impairment, random responding, confusion, errors in scoring the scale, or failure to follow the test instructions. Test results with INF scores in this range are assumed to be invalid and no clinical interpretation of the PAI is recommended.[93]

Inconsistency Scale
This is an empirically derived scale that reflects the consistency with which the examinee completed items with similar content. One commonly observed problem that can cause elevations on Inconsistency

(ICN) scale is a failure to attend to item statements that contain the word "not." There are few items with negative statements on the PAI, but these items are overrepresented on the ICN scale in order to specifically examine how such items are interpreted. If the examinee is paying attention poorly, an elevated scale should alert the interpreter that the examinee may not have been reading the items carefully when completing the inventory. High scores on ICN ($\geq$73T) suggest that the examinee did not attend consistently or appropriately to item content in responding to the PAI items. If the examinee answers the questions in a completely random fashion, this generally results in an average ICN score of approximately 73T. The potential causes for scores in this range include carelessness, reading difficulties, confusion, errors in scoring, or failure to follow the test instructions. Regardless of the etiology, test results should be assumed to be invalid and no clinical interpretation of the PAI is recommended when ICN scores are in the range of 73T or higher.[93]

Negative Impression Scale

Morey indicates that the starting point in the detection of malingering while using the PAI is this scale.[93] The self-report of a high score on Negative Impression (NIM) scale is probably more pathological than an objective observer would report. However, patients with actual mental illness will score higher on this scale than individuals without mental illness due to negative perceptions that covary with the presence of some mental illnesses.

The NIM scale includes two types of items: some are presented as an exaggerated distorted impression of self while others represent extremely bizarre and unlikely symptoms. Either of these tendencies may cause distortion of a self-report in a negative direction. Scores on the NIM scale lower than 73T indicate there is little distortion in a negative direction on the clinical scales. Moreover, the examinee probably did not attempt to present a more negative impression than the clinical picture would warrant. Moderate elevations (73T–84T) are consistent with an element of exaggeration of complaints and problems. Elevations on NIM in the range of 84T to 92T may be consistent with a "cry for help" or an extremely negative evaluation of self. This scale range also is consistent with a deliberate distortion of the clinical picture (symptom magnification or false attribution). High scores on NIM ($\geq$92T) are consistent with examinees' attempts to portray themselves in an especially negative manner. This score is consistent with careless responding, extremely negative self-presentation or malingering. A completely random completion of the PAI would result in an average NIM score of 96T.

Positive Impression Scale

The content of Positive Impression (PIM) scale items includes the presentation of a very favorable impression or the denial of relatively minor faults. Morey advises that it should be recognized that the tendency for favorable self-presentation is fairly common in the normal population. Positive Impression scale scores represent the level examinees attempting to manage their clinical impression to the examiner in a positive direction. Thus, this scale roughly corresponds to the L and K scales of the MMPI and MMPI-2 in terms of measuring defensiveness or positive impression management strategies. Low scores on PIM below 44T are consistent with honest responding. Scores between 44T and 57T suggest the examinee did not attempt to present an unrealistically favorable impression. Moderate elevations ranging from 57T to 66T suggest that the examinee responded in a manner to portray lack of common shortcomings. A PIM score of 66T is two standard deviations above the mean for clinical patients. Thus, scores $\geq$66T are consistent with the examinee's attempts to present as exceptionally free of common shortcomings to which most individuals will admit. The validity of the entire PAI clinical scales is seriously questioned when PIM scores exceed 66T.[93]

The PAI Malingering Index

This is a specific indicator of malingering with higher specificity than NIM. It is comprised of eight configural features of the PAI profile. The reader should refer to the *PAI Manual* or the *PAI Interpretive Guide* authored by Morey for further details and appropriate applications of this

---

TABLE 9.5

Using the Personality Assessment Inventory (PAI) to Detect Malingering

- Consult with a psychologist expert in PAI administration and interpretation.
- Review the Infrequency scale (INF). Is there evidence of careless or random responding?
- Review the Inconsistency scale (ICN). Is there evidence of inconsistent responding?
- Review the Negative Impression scale (NIM). Is there evidence the examinee is presenting a very negative image?
- If the NIM scale exceeds or equals 92T, does the Malingering Index (MAL) indicate malingering?

---

index.[93] However, simply put, the PAI Malingering (MAL) Index scores of 3 or above should raise questions of malingering, whereas scores of 5 or more are highly unusual in clinical samples, and they tend to occur only when mental disorder is being faked severely. Table 9.5 gives guidelines for using the PAI validity scales in the detection of distortion and malingering.

The Structured Interview of Reported Symptoms

Richard Rogers developed the Structured Interview of Reported Symptoms (SIRS). It was first developed in 1985, and it has gone through several important revisions. The SIRS is a 172-item structured interview that is composed of (1) Detailed Inquiries that address specific symptomatology and its severity; (2) Repeated Inquiries that parallel the Detailed Inquiries and tests for response consistency; and (3) General Inquiries that probe specific symptoms, general psychological problems, and symptom patterns. These items are then organized into eight primary scales for the evaluation of feigning.[95] At the time of the writing of this book, the Structured Interview of Reported Symptoms is under revision, and Dr. Rogers is incorporating a civil population to the standardization base. Moreover, his edited book, *The Assessment of Malingering and Deception*[95] is currently in revision, and the third edition is to be published shortly. Two important summaries provide comprehensive and detailed analysis of the SIRS and its use in the detection of psychological malingering.[96,97]

The SIRS must be administered by a psychologist or another professional who has sophisticated training in the use of structured interviewing techniques. Rogers notes that it is imperative that interviewers be familiar with the structure of the SIRS and well practiced in its administration. Mechanics of the SIRS administration differ greatly from many other assessment techniques used in psychology. The SIRS classifies the responses of examinees at two levels of classification certainty. Of the eight primary scales, those classified as "probable feigning" accurately differentiate 75% of the criterion groups, and those classified as "definite feigning" accurately classify 90% or more of individual subjects. There are two ways to use the SIRS data: the threshold model or the clinical decision model. These recommendations are from Rogers and are based on statistical analysis of proper decisions regarding malingering. Rogers points out that the determination of malingering is a multimethod assessment that incorporates and integrates data from unstructured interviews, psychological tests, and collateral sources. He warns that despite the unmatched accuracy of the SIRS for the classification of feigning psychopathology, such an important determination should not rely solely on single measures. Therefore, if one uses the clinical decision model, this requires confirmatory data in addition to using the SIRS.[95]

By following the standard in the *SIRS* manual,[96] some individuals cannot be classified as either feigners or honest responders. In such cases, the examiner will be left with an "indeterminate" classification. The neuropsychiatric examiner, and other physicians using this instrument, must remember that the primary emphasis of the SIRS is on the determination and classification of faking. It is not a psychological test used to detect mental pathology. It should not be used as a stand-alone instrument to measure one's mental state. Its most important addition to the assessment of feigning (faking) is its ability to provide an overview of potential malingering. For instance, the examiner may wish to have a cutoff score on the MMPI-2 (for instance, F scale >90) and then use a default decision to administer the SIRS in those cases where F exceeds 90. Many experts in the fields of psychology and psychiatry consider the SIRS presently to be the gold standard assessment instrument for the detection of psychological malingering when used within a comprehensive psychological or psychiatric evaluation. It is best used when the issue of malingering has been raised by the clinical presentation of the examinee, by distortion of validity indices on other standardized psychological test instruments, by inconsistent historical information, or by inconsistencies detected during the mental status examination.

DETECTION OF SOMATIC (PHYSICAL) MALINGERING

As noted above, there are three basic ways to malinger a medical examination.[98] It is also worth noting above the response styles that malingerers present to medical examiners.[30] Persons malingering physical presentations often present a diagnostic challenge because the presentations may mimic a neurological disorder (such as in feigned TBI). It is necessary to separate conversion disorders from physical malingering. Neurologists view conversion disorders as a temporary disorder of mental, voluntary, motor, or sensory functions that mimic neurological disease, but are caused by unconscious determinants, not by organic lesions in the neuroanatomic sites that should produce the dysfunction being presented.[99] Psychiatry has classically described conversion disorders (hysteria) as arising from unconscious mental mechanisms that relieve overwhelming anxiety by converting it to physical symptoms. These symptoms provide primary and secondary gain.[100] The primary gain consists of the relief of anxiety, whereas the secondary gain consists of a manipulative control over the expressed emotional responses, the attention that may be received from others, and the sympathetic actions of other people. Relief of responsibility is a frequent secondary gain. The MMPI-2 is extremely helpful in differentiating conversion disorder from faking. If the validity indicators are in good order, the examiner would expect a "conversion V" pattern on scales 1, 3, and 2. It is worthwhile reviewing again Mittenberg's base rates of probable malingering and symptom exaggeration in various medical–legal cases noted above.[32] Table 9.6 lists possible psychogenic presentations of physical malingering. The reader will note that the vast majority of these present as a disorder of neurological functioning. Any physical disorder that can be conceived could also be malingered. Some presentations of malingering defy proof. For instance, patients who present with pain or headache cannot be proved. However, a suspicion of malingering can be refuted if a genuine source of pain can be established. Many of the disorders presenting in Table 9.6 can be detected by physical examination. It is beyond the scope of this chapter to present all possible ways to detect the disorders noted in Table 9.6. For highly puzzling cases, it may be necessary for the neuropsychiatric examiner to consult with a clinical neurologist. If necessary, more detailed analyses and detection of these presentations are available.[98,99]

The Fake Bad Scale

Larrabee[101] has argued that somatic complaints, such as pain, parasthesia, and malaise, are common and are not captured well by the ordinary validity scales of the MMPI-2. He demonstrated that the Lees-Haley Fake Bad Scale (FBS) was the one MMPI-2 scale most sensitive to somatic malingering. Boone and Lu[102] have presented evidence that somatic malingering during forensic examinations is not adequately identified by traditional MMPI-2 validity scales. However, their work has demonstrated that the FBS could detect somatic malingering in the absence of adequate MMPI-2 validity scale detection. A recent large meta-analysis by Sweet's group at Northwestern University reviewed a pooled sample size of 3664 subjects. These studies were weighted for effect size differences among the FBS and other commonly used MMPI-2 validity scales. The largest grand

TABLE 9.6
Possible Presentations of Physical Malingering

A. Oculomotor signs
 • Blinking, squinting (blepharospasm), volitional eye crossing, volitional eyelid drooping
B. Dysfunctions of voice, swallowing, and breathing
  • Mutism
  • Spasmodic hoarseness (dysphonia)
  • Choking (dysphagia)
  • Hyperventilation with apnea
C. Vomiting
D. Disturbances of station (standing) and gait
  • Inability to stand (astasia)
  • Inability to walk (abasia)
  • Incomplete paralysis on one side (hemiparesis)
  • Complete paralysis on one side (hemiplegia)
  • Dragging one leg (monoplegia)
  • Apparent paralysis of arms and legs (paraplegia)
E. Tremors
F. Disorders of vision
  • Blindness (monocular or binocular)
  • Visual field defects
  • Double vision (diplopia)
  • Pain in eyes with light exposure (photophobia)
G. Disorders of sensation
  • Deafness
  • Non-anatomic sensory loss
  • Inability to smell (anosmia)
  • Inability to taste (ageusia)
H. Seizures (pseudoepilepsy)
 I. Fevers
 J. Pain
  • Headaches
  • Backaches

effect sizes were observed for FBS (0.96).[103] With regard to TBI in particular, a recent study found evidence that the FBS has high sensitivity and specificity in identifying incomplete effort in mild head injury.[104] Greiffenstein's group has noted that the reason the F scales' (F, FB, and F(p)) show insensitivity to real-world exaggeration may be due to using student simulators for most of the validation studies, and the content is reflective of psychotic simulation. His group argues that the superiority of the FBS in applied forensic settings could derive from its development in actual litigant subjects and content that is reflective of nonpsychotic exaggerations.[105] As an aside to TBI, a behavioral medicine clinic in Denver, Colorado, has noted that the FBS is useful for detecting feigning in litigants claiming an idiopathic environmental tolerance (exposure to multiple toxins).[106]

It should be noted that Butcher's group, who has published a tremendous amount of work on using the MMPI-2 for malingering detection, is vocal in its criticism that the FBS is not a good instrument for detecting somatic malingering. They have made repeated public claims that it should not be used for this.[107] A review of recent psychological literature, 2003–2007, finds that most psychologists disagree with Butcher's assertions regarding the FBS, and most psychologists working in the field of malingering detection believe it is a valuable addition for detecting physical malingering.

REFERENCES

1. American Academy of Psychiatry and the Law, *Ethical Guidelines for the Practice of Forensic Psychiatry*, Adopted May, 1987, Last revised 1995.
2. Weinstock, R. and Garrick, T., The forensic psychiatrist as consultant, in *Principles and Practice of Forensic Psychiatry*, Rosner, R., Ed., Chapman & Hall, New York, 1994, p. 47.
3. Gutheil, T.G. and Simon, R.I., *Mastering Forensic Psychiatric Practice: Advanced Strategies for the Expert Witness*, American Psychiatric Press, Washington, D.C., 2002.
4. Breyer, S., Introduction, in *Reference Manual on Scientific Evidence*, 2nd edition, Federal Judicial Center, Washington, D.C., 2000, p. 1.
5. Wecht, C., Admissibility of scientific evidence under the post-*Daubert* rules, *Forensic Sciences*, Matthew Bender, New York, 1998, pp. 19–23.
6. Huber, P., *Galileo's Revenge: Junk Science in the Courtroom*, Basic Books, New York, 1991.
7. *Frye v. United States*, 293 F. 1013 (D.C. Cir. 1923).
8. Shuman, D.W., *Psychiatric and Psychological Evidence*, 3rd edition, Thomson-West, New York, 2005.
9. Goodstein, D., How science works, in *Reference Manual on Scientific Evidence*, 2nd edition, Federal Judicial Center, Washington, D.C., 2000, p. 67.
10. *United States v. Addison*, 498 F. 2d 741 (D.C. Cir. 1974).
11. *United States v. Stifel*, 433 F. 2d 431 (6th Cir. 1970).
12. *State v. Smith*, 50 2d 183 (Ohio App. 1976).
13. *People v. Slone*, 76 3d 611 (Cal. App. 1978).
14. *Lindsey v. United States*, 237 F 2d 893 (9th Cir. 1956).
15. *People v. Palmer*, 80 3d 239 (Cal. App. 1978).
16. *Barrel of Fun, Inc. v. State Farm Fire and Casualty Company*, 739 F. 2d 1028 (5th Cir. 1984).
17. Giannelli, L., The admissibility of novel scientific evidence: *Frye v. United States*, a half-century later. *Colum. L. Rev.*, 80, 1197, 1980.
18. *Daubert v. Merrell Dow*, 509, 579 (U.S. 1993).
19. Berger, M.A., The Supreme Court's trilogy on the admissibility of expert testimony, Federal Judicial Center, Washington, D.C., 2000, p. 9.
20. *General Electric Company v. Joiner*, 118, 512 (S. Ct., 1997).
21. *Joiner v. General Electric Company*, 864 F. Supp. 1310 (N.D. GA. 1994).
22. *Joiner v. General Electric Company*, 78 F. 3d 524, 529 (11th Cir. 1996).
23. *Kumho Tire v. Carmichael*, 19, 1167 (S. Ct., 1999).
24. Gutheil, T.G., *The Psychiatrist as Expert Witness*, American Psychiatric Press, Washington, D.C., 1998.
25. Gutheil, T.G. and Sutherland, P.K., Forensic assessment, witness credibility and a search for truth through expert testimony in the courtroom. *J. Psychiatr. Law*, 27, 289, 1999.
26. *Diagnostic and Statistical Manual of Mental Disorders*, 4th edition, *Text Revision*, American Psychiatric Association, Washington, D.C., 2000.
27. Schetky, D.H. and Guyer, M.J., Psychic trauma and civil litigation, in *Principles and Practice of Child and Adolescent Forensic Psychiatry*, Schetky, D.H. and Benedict, E.P., Eds., American Psychiatric Press, Washington, D.C., 2002, p. 355.
28. Resnick, P.J., Malingering, in *Principles and Practice of Forensic Psychiatry*, Rosner, R., Ed., Chapman & Hall, New York, 1994, p. 417.
29. Resnick, P.J., The detection of malingered mental illness. *Behav. Sci. Law*, 2, 21, 1984.
30. Hall, H.V. and Poirier, J.G., *Detecting Malingering and Deception: Forensic Distortion Analysis*, 2nd edition, CRC Press, Boca Raton, FL, 2001.
31. Lamb, D.G., Berry, D.T.R., Wetter, M.W., et al., Effects of two types of information on malingering of closed head injury on the *MMPI-2*: An analog investigation. *Psychol. Assess.*, 6, 8, 1994.
32. Mittenberg, W., Patton, C., Cranyock, E.M., et al., Base rates of malingering and symptom exaggeration. *J. Clin. Exp. Neuropsychol.*, 24, 1094, 2002.
33. Slick, D.J., Sherman, E.M.S. and Iverson, G.L., Diagnostic criteria for malingered neurocognitive dysfunction: Proposed standards for clinical practice and research. *Clin. Neuropsychol.*, 13, 345, 1999.
34. Ceci, S.J. and Bruck, M., *Jeopardy in the Courtroom: A Scientific Analysis of Children's Testimony*, American Psychological Association, Washington, D.C., 1995.

35. Artingstall, K., *Practical Aspects of Munchausen by Proxy and Munchausen Syndrome Investigation*, CRC Press, Boca Raton, FL, 1999.
36. Fish, F., *Fish's Clinical Psychopathology: Signs and Symptoms in Psychiatry*, Hamilton, M., Ed., John Wright and Sons, Bristol, UK, 1974, p. 52.
37. Wetter, M.W. and Corrigan, S.K., Providing information to clients about psychological tests: A survey of attorneys' and law students' attitudes. *Prof. Psychol.*, 26, 465, 1995.
38. Rogers, R., Bagsby, R.N., and Chakraborty, D., Feigning schizophrenic disorders on the *MMPI-2*: Detection of coached simulators. *J. Pers. Assess.*, 60, 215, 1993.
39. Storm, J. and Graham, J.R., The effects of validity scale coaching on the ability to malinger psychopathology, *Paper presented at the 33rd Annual Symposium on Recent Developments in the Use of the MMPI-2*, Clearwater, FL, 1998.
40. Pope, H.S., Butcher, J.N., and Seelen, J., *The MMPI, MMPI-2 and MMPI-A in Court: A Practical Guide for Expert Witnesses and Attorneys*, 2nd edition, American Psychological Association, Washington, D.C., 2000.
41. Andrikopoulos, J., Malingering disorientation to time, personal information, and place in mild head injured litigants. *Clin. Neuropsychol.*, 15, 393, 2001.
42. Bordini, E.J., Chaknis, M.M., Ekman-Turner, R.M., et al., Advances and issues in the diagnostic differential of malingering versus brain injury. *NeuroRehabilitation*, 17, 93, 2002.
43. Meyers, J.E., Galinsky, A.M., and Volbrecht, M., Malingering, and mild brain injury: How low is too low? *App. Neuropsychol.*, 6, 208, 1999.
44. Iverson, G.L. and Binder, L.M., Detecting exaggeration and malingering in neuropsychological assessment. *J. Head Trauma Rehabil.*, 15, 829, 2000.
45. Klimczak, N.J., Donovick, P.J., and Burright, R., The malingering of multiple sclerosis and mild traumatic brain injury. *Brain Inj.*, 11, 343, 1997.
46. Green, P. and Iverson, G.L., Validation of the computer assessment of response bias in litigating patients with head injuries. *Clin. Neuropsychol.*, 15, 492, 2001.
47. Green, P., Iverson, G.L., and Allen, L., Detecting malingering in head injury litigation with the Word Memory Test. *Brain Inj.*, 13, 813, 1999.
48. Bianchini, K.J., Mathias, C.W., Greeve, K.W., et al., Classification accuracy of the Portland Digit Recognition Test in traumatic brain injury. *Clin. Neuropsychol.*, 15, 461, 2001.
49. Haber, A.H. and Fichtenberg, N.L., Replication of the Test of Memory Malingering (TOMM) in a traumatic brain injury and head trauma sample. *Clin. Neuropsychol.*, 20, 524, 2006.
50. Greve, K.W., Bianchini, K.J., Black, F.W., et al., Classification accuracy of the Test of Memory Malingering in persons reporting exposure to environmental and industrial toxins: Results of a known-groups analysis. *Arch. Clin. Neuropsychol.*, 21, 439, 2006.
51. Greve, K.W., Bianchini, K.J., and Doane, B.M., Classification accuracy of the Test of Memory Malingering in traumatic brain injury: Results of a known-groups analysis. *J. Clin. Exp. Neuropsychol.*, 28, 1176, 2006.
52. O'Bryant, S.E. and Lucas, J.A., Estimating the predictive value of the Test of Memory Malingering: An illustrative example for clinicians. *Clin. Neuropsychol.*, 20, 533, 2006.
53. Yanez, Y.T., Fremouw, W., Tennant, J., et al., Effects of severe depression on TOMM performance among disability-seeking outpatients. *Arch. Clin. Neuropsychol.*, 21, 161, 2006.
54. Vagnini, V.L., Sollman, M.J., Berry, D.T., et al., Known-groups cross-validation of the Letter Memory Test in a compensation-seeking mixed neurological sample. *Clin. Neuropsychol.*, 20, 289, 2006.
55. Curtis, K.L., Greve, K.W., Bianchini, K.J., et al., California Verbal Learning Test indicators of malingered neurocognitive dysfunction: Sensitivity and specificity in traumatic brain injury. *Assessment*, 13, 46, 2006.
56. Slick, D.J., Iverson, G.L., and Green, P., California Verbal Learning Test indicators of suboptimal performance in a sample of head-injury litigants. *J. Clin. Exp. Neuropsychol.*, 22, 569, 2000.
57. Moore, B.A. and Donders, J., Predictors of invalid neuropsychological test performance after traumatic brain injury. *Brain Inj.*, 18, 975, 2004.
58. Root, J.C., Robbins, R.N., Chang, L., et al., Detection of inadequate effort on the California Verbal Learning Test-2nd edition: Forced-choice recognition and critical item analysis. *J. Int. Neuorpsychol. Soc.*, 12, 688, 2006.
59. Bernard, L.C., McGrath, M.J., and Houston, W., The differential effects of simulating malingering, closed head injury, and other CNS pathology on the Wisconsin Card Sorting Test: Support for the "pattern of performance" hypothesis. *Arch. Clin. Neuropsychol.*, 11, 231, 1996.

60. Suhr, J.A. and Boyer, D., Use of the Wisconsin Card Sorting Test in the detection of malingering in student simulator and patient samples. *J. Clin. Exp. Neuropsychol.*, 21, 701, 1999.

61. King, J.H., Sweet, J.J., Sherer, M., et al., Validity indicators within the Wisconsin Card Sorting Test: Application of new and previously researched multivariate procedures and multiple traumatic brain injury samples. *Clin. Neuropsychol.*, 16, 506, 2002.

62. Axelrod, B.B., Fichtenberg, N.L., Millis, S.R., et al., Detecting incomplete effort with the digit span from the Wechsler Adult Intelligence Scale-3rd edition. *Clin. Neuropsychol.*, 20, 513, 2006.

63. Heinly, M.T., Greve, K.W., Bianchini, K.J., et al., WAIS digit span-based indicators of malingered neurocognitive dysfunction: Classification, accuracy, and traumatic brain injury. *Assessment*, 12, 429, 2005.

64. Gorman, W.F., *Legal Neurology and Malingering: Cases and Techniques*, Warren H. Green, St. Louis, MO, 1993.

65. Rapport, L.J., Farchione, T.J., Coleman, R.D., et al., Effects of coaching on malingered motor function profiles. *J. Clin. Exp. Neuropsychol.*, 20, 89, 1998.

66. Greiffenstein, M.F., Baker, W.J., and Gola, T., Motor dysfunction profiles in traumatic brain injury and postconcussion syndrome. *J. Int. Neuropsychol. Soc.*, 2, 477, 1996.

67. Lees-Haley, P.R., Attorneys influence expert evidence in forensic psychological and neuropsychological examinations. *Assessment*, 4, 321, 1997.

68. Ruiz, M.A., Drake, E.B., Glass, A., et al., Trying to beat the system: Misuse of the Internet to assist in avoiding the detection of psychological symptom dissimulation. *Prof. Psychol. Res. Pract.*, 33, 294, 2002.

69. Victor, T.L. and Abeles, N., Coaching clients to take psychological and neuropsychological tests: A clash of ethical obligations. *Prof. Psychol. Res. Pract.*, 35, 373, 2004.

70. Pope, K.S., Butcher, J.N., and Seelen, J., *The MMPI, MMPI-2 and MMPI-A in Court*, 3rd edition: *A Practical Guide for Expert Witnesses and Attorneys*, American Psychological Association, Washington, D.C., 2006.

71. Moyer, D.M., Burkhardt, B., and Gordon, R.M., Faking PTSD from a motor vehicle accident on the MMPI-2. *Am. J. For. Psychol.*, 20, 81, 2002.

72. Bagby, R.M., Nicholson, R.A., Bacchiochi, J.R., et al., The predictive capacity of the MMPI-2 and PAI validity scales and indexes to detect coached and uncoached feigning. *J. Per. Assess.*, 78, 69, 2002.

73. Morey, L.C., *Essentials of PAI Assessment*, John Wiley & Sons, New York, 2003.

74. Baer, R., Wetter, M., and Berry, D.T.R., Effects of information about validity scales on underreporting of symptoms on the MMPI-2: An analog investigation. *Assessment*, 2, 189, 1995.

75. Baer, R.A., Wetter, M.W., Nichols, D., et al., Sensitivity of MMPI-2 validity scales to underreporting of symptoms. *Psychol. Assess.*, 7, 419, 1995.

76. Butcher, J.N., Williams, C.L., Graham, J.R., et al., *MMPI-A Manual for Administration, Scoring, and Interpretation*, University of Minnesota Press, Minneapolis, MN, 1992.

77. Butcher, J.N. and Williams, C.L., *Essentials of MMPI-2 and MMPI-A Interpretation*, University of Minnesota Press, Minneapolis, MN, 1992.

78. Berry, D.T.R., Wetter, M.W., Baer, R.A., et al., Overreporting of closed-head injury symptoms on the MMPI-2. *Psychol. Assess.*, 7, 517, 1995.

79. Butcher, J.N. and Miller, K.B., Personality assessment in personal injury litigation, in *Handbook of Forensic Psychology*, 2nd edition, Hess, A. and Weiner, I., Eds., John Wiley & Sons, New York, 1998, p. 104.

80. Rogers, R., Towards an empirical model of malingering and deception. *Behav. Sci. Law*, 2, 93, 1984.

81. Butcher, J.N., Frequency of MMPI-2 scores in forensic evaluations. *MMPI-2 News Profiles*, 8, 2, 1997.

82. Arbisi, P. and Ben-Porath, Y.S., Characteristics of the MMPI-2 F(p) scale as a function of diagnosis in an in-patient sample of veterans. *Psychol. Assess.*, 9, 102, 1997.

83. Arbisi, P. and Ben-Porath, Y.S., An MMPI-2 infrequency scale for use with psychopathological populations: The Infrequency-Psychopathology Scale, F(p), *Psychol. Assess.*, 7, 424, 1995.

84. Gough, H.G., Simulated patterns on the MMPI. *J. Abnor. Soc. Psychol.*, 42, 215, 1947.

85. Lachar, D., The prediction of early USAF freshman cadet adaptation with the MMPI. *J. Counsel. Psychol.*, 21, 404, 1974.

86. Bagby, R.M., Nicholson, R.A., Rogers, R., et al., Effectiveness of the MMPI-2 validity indicators in the detection of defensive responding in clinical and nonclinical samples. *Psychol. Assess.*, 9, 406, 1997.

87. Berry, D.T., Wetter, M.W., Baer, R.A., et al., Detection of random responding on the MMPI-2: Utility of F, back F, and VRIN scales. *Psychol. Assess.: J. Consul. Clin. Psychol.*, 3, 418, 1991.

88. Hawk, G. and Cornell, D., MMPI profiles of malingerers diagnosed in pretrial forensic evaluations. *J. Clin. Psychol.*, 45, 673, 1989.

89. Schretlen, D. and Arkowitz, H., A psychological test battery to detect prison inmates who fake insanity or mental retardation. *Behav. Sci. Law*, 8, 75, 1990.

90. Nelson, L.D., Use of the MMPI and the MMPI-2 in forensic neuropsychological evaluations, in *Forensic Applications of the MMPI-2*, Ben-Porath, Y.S., Graham, J.R., Hall, G.C.N., et al., Eds., Sage Publications, Thousand Oaks, CA, 1995, p. 202.

91. Bagby, R.M., Gillis, J.R., and Dickens, S., Detection of dissimulation with the new generation of objective personality measures. *Behav. Sci. Law*, 8, 93, 1990.

92. McCann, J.T. and Dyer, F.J., *Forensic Assessment with the Millon Inventories*, Guilford Press, New York, 1996, p. 69.

93. Morey, L.C., *An Interpretive Guide to the Personality Assessment Inventory (PAI)*, Psychological Assessment Resources, Odessa, FL, 1996, p. 105.

94. Spordone, R.J. and Saul, R.E., *Neuropsychology for Health Care Professionals and Attorneys*, 2nd edition, CRC Press, Boca Raton, FL, 2000, p. 274.

95. Rogers, R., Structured interviews and dissimulation, in *Clinical Assessment of Malingering and Deception*, 2nd edition, Rogers, R., Ed., Guilford Press, New York, 1997, p. 301.

96. Rogers, R., Bagby, R.M., and Dickens, S.E., *Structured Interview of Reported Symptoms (SIRS) and Professional Manual*, Psychological Assessment Resources, Odessa, FL, 1992.

97. Rogers, R., *Diagnostic and Structured Interviewing: A Handbook for Psychologists*, Psychological Assessment Resources, Odessa, FL, 1995.

98. Granacher, R.P. and Berry, D.T.R., Feigned medical presentations, in *Clinical Assessment of Malingering and Deception*, 3rd edition, Rogers, R., Ed., Guilford Press, New York, 2007.

99. DeMyer, W.E., *Technique of the Neurologic Examination*, 5th edition, McGraw-Hill, New York, 2004.

100. Weintraub, M.I., Malingering and conversion reactions. *Neurol. Clin.*, 13, 229, 1995.

101. Larrabee, G.J., Somatic malingering on the MMPI and MMPI-2 in personal injury litigants. *Clin. Neuropsychol.*, 12, 179, 1998.

102. Boone, K.B. and Lu, P.H., Impact of somatoform symptomatology on credibility of cognitive performance. *Clin. Neuropsychol.*, 13, 414, 1999.

103. Nelson, N.W., Sweet, J.J., and Demakis, G.J., Meta-analysis of the MMPI-2 Fake Bad Scale: Utility and forensic practice. *Clin. Neuropsychol.*, 20, 39, 2006.

104. Ross, S.R., Millis, S.R., Krukowski, R.A., et al., Detecting incomplete effort on the MMPI-2: An examination of the *Fake Bad Scale* and mild head injury. *J. Clin. Exp. Neuropsychol.*, 26, 115, 2004.

105. Greiffenstein, M.F., Baker, W.J., Axelrod, B., et al., The Fake Bad Scale on the MMPI-2 F-family in detection of implausible psychological trauma claims. *Clin. Neuropsychol.*, 18, 573, 2004.

106. Staudenmayer, H. and Phillips, S., MMPI-2 validity, clinical and content scales, and the Fake Bad Scale for personal injury litigants claiming idiopathic environmental intolerance. *J. Psychosom. Res.*, 62, 61, 2007.

107. Butcher, J.N., Arbisi, P.A., Atlis, M.M., et al., The construct validity of the Lees-Haley Fake Bad Scale. Does this scale measure somatic malingering and feigned emotional distress? *Arch. Clin. Neuropsychol.*, 18, 473, 2003.

10 Causation, Damages, Outcome, and Impairment Determination following Traumatic Brain Injury

INTRODUCTION

The most likely legal scenarios in which the physician examiner will see traumatic brain injury (TBI) will be in personal injury litigation, workers' compensation claims, criminal proceedings where responsibility or competency is an issue, general competency, and testamentary capacity. There are other scenarios possible, of course. Before the law, personal injury litigation is treated as a tort. A tort is a private or civil wrong. A personal tort is one involving an injury to the person or to the reputation of the person. It is distinguished from an injury or damage to real or personal property, which is called a property tort. When TBI cases are brought to a civil court as a personal injury, they are claimed by a plaintiff. The defendant will be the tortfeasor, the person or entity causing the injury. By taking a claim of TBI to court, the injured party asks the court to provide a remedy in the form of an action for damages. Damages are compensation (usually money) that may be recovered in the courts by a person who has suffered a loss, detriment, or injury to his person as a result of TBI. Depending on the jurisdiction, the plaintiff is entitled to compensation not just for mental distress and pain, but for suffering, anxiety, depression, and fear. From a TBI standpoint, the person is compensated for the loss of brain function as a result of TBI. Other causes of action which may demand damages in a TBI case would include depression, posttraumatic stress disorder, or more classical psychiatric disorders produced by TBI. Thus, any of the diagnoses discussed in Chapter 2 conceivably could become a claim for damages in a tort action raised by alleged TBI.[1]

Traumatic brain injury is a frequent occurrence in the workplace. The workers' compensation system is a state-created statutory scheme designed to compensate a worker who experiences an injury that has a substantial causal nexus to an accident that occurred while the worker was employed.[2] Workers' compensation is a no-fault system. As a result, it does not involve a jury or findings of blame, and the decisions are made by an administrative law judge (the fact finder). This places generally severe limits on damages for mental or emotional injuries. Traumatic brain injury is easier for workers' compensation judges to adjudicate than pure psychiatric claims because of the physical aspects of the injury, less reliance on emotional claim only, and often the availability of neuroimaging documentation of injury. Physical injury or trauma causing mental or emotional injuries compensable in a workers' compensation claim are in virtually all states.[2] However, some jurisdictions have strict limits that the injury be traceable to a definite time and place and that a definite cause be ascertainable.[3] This is a more stringent legal requirement than personal injury litigation in a civil court.

A criminal defense attorney, judge, or the prosecutor may raise the issue of a criminal defendant's competency to stand trial as a result of a TBI at any point during criminal proceedings.

In practice, it is usually the defense attorney that raises this issue. Obviously, competency can become an issue at a criminal trial of a defendant who has sustained a substantial TBI. It makes no difference whether the traumatic brain injury occurred before the criminal act or after the criminal act; the issue of competency as a result of TBI may still be raised. Moreover, once the trial begins, the court may question the defendant's competency to stand trial if the defendant behaves irrationally or exhibits an unusual demeanor at trial assumed to be a result of TBI.[4] With regard to an issue of criminal responsibility, obviously the TBI would have had to occur before the criminal act or it could not be judged to play a role in the criminal act. The procedure for forensic evaluation of a TBI would be the same as described in the first eight chapters of this book. However, after the level of TBI is determined, it is then necessary for the forensic examiner to determine the exact legal and sanity standards used in the jurisdiction where the case is to be tried. The physician can obtain these standards from the court, prosecutor, or defense attorney who referred the defendant for assessment. Then, the physician must get sufficient information from other sources regarding observations of the defendant made at the time of the offense. This would include information from witnesses, victim statements if alive, and police reports of the defendant's behavior. A personal interview of the defendant regarding issues of responsibility should be made at the time of the TBI evaluation.[5]

With regard to competency other than for trial, this will be discussed more fully later in this chapter. The competence of an individual may be general or specific. The question of the person's general competence may be raised when an allegation is made that the individual no longer has the mental capacity to make decisions about the entire range of his affairs. Specific competence may apply to a very focused matter, such as competence to consent to treatment, competence to make a contract, or competence to draft a living will.[6]

Testamentary capacity is the mental capacity necessary to make a will. A will can be written out in hand (a holographic will) or produced at great length by a lawyer. Regardless of how a will is made, the testator must be of sound mind at the time of the execution of the will. Various expressions of the specific elements of the sound mind requirement exist, but all follow in good measure from the English case of *Banks v. Goodfellow*. The court in *Banks* stated that testamentary capacity requires that at the time of the making of the will, the testator must know that he is making a will, know the nature and extent of his property subject to distribution of the will, know how the will would distribute that property, and know those blood relatives and others who would normally be expected to benefit from this distribution.[7] In almost all instances before the physician, the issue of the will and the person's testamentary capacity will come after the person has died. Thus, the physician will be required to reconstruct the mental capacity of the individual making the will on or about the date the will was made. This will require an expert forensic analysis of available records before and after the fact of making the will, eyewitness testimony, and possibly collateral interviewing of individuals who were witnesses to the will or assisted the testator to make the will (such as his lawyer). The issue of TBI should be clear on the records, and there should be clear evidence after gathering the facts that as a result of TBI, the testator could not meet the criteria of *Banks v. Goodfellow*.[8]

The remainder of this chapter will explore the medical–legal issues of causation and damages. Further information will be imparted to the reader in the analysis of outcomes from TBI and how to make a reasoned determination of residual impairment following TBI. For evaluation of impairment, this text will follow the *American Medical Association's Guides to the Evaluation of Permanent Impairment* definition.[9]

CAUSATION

When examining a subject in a personal injury case, causation will be an issue. Physicians think of causation within an entirely different framework than do lawyers. Clinical causation in medical practice is often thought of as multifactorial. Many factors may play a role including environmental, genetic, biological, psychological, or molecular. All these may contribute to the eventual formation of a disease process or an outcome. In contrast, within a legal setting, the claimant must prove that the incident or trauma that caused the TBI either *de novo* produced a "change in the organism," or precipitated, aggravated, or hastened a condition (such as preexisting depression).[10,11] Legal causation includes two findings. First, it must be determined that the defendant's acts or omissions are the cause, in fact, of the injuries causing the TBI (the but-for test). The but-for test requires a finding that, had the defendant's actions not occurred, the injury would not have happened to the individual. This is somewhat of a paradox, as this test implies causation forward into eternity; however, it is accepted as a basic finding in courts of law. The second component of causation developed as a result of this potential philosophical issue. It is called proximate cause and represents a policy determination that the defendant, even one who has behaved negligently, should not automatically be liable for all consequences of his act. Proximate cause is a very complicated legal concept that has defied clear delineation to this time. In its simplest form, proximate cause can be equated with foreseeability: if the consequences of a defendant's actions are unforeseeable, no causation will be found.[11] The reader may wish to refer to Danner and Sagall[10] for further elucidation.

While issues of causation in TBI cases are usually very straightforward, depending on the jurisdiction and depending on whether the case is at federal court in the United States, there are two other issues that could arise. One is general causation versus specific causation. General causation is usually applied to toxic torts (criminal wrongs due to chemicals or noxious substances). One cannot argue that an act specifically caused a TBI unless it is accepted that the accident in question would be expected generally to cause a TBI in reasonable persons. Epidemiologists use causation to mean that an increase in the incidence of disease among the exposed subjects would not have occurred had they not been exposed to the agent (the trauma). Thus, exposure to trauma is a necessary condition to produce a TBI.[12] The physician examiner will be asked to determine specific causation in most TBI cases. In other words, the plaintiff must establish not only that the defendant's injury is capable of causing a TBI but also that it did cause the plaintiff's TBI. This causation analysis will depend on an assessment of the individual's exposure to trauma, including the force of trauma and the temporal relationship between the trauma to the head and body and the production of TBI. This information, particularly in issues of mild traumatic brain injury (MTBI), may be compared with other scientific data on the relationship between a similar accident scenario and the likelihood of producing a TBI. The certainty of the expert physician's opinion will depend on the strength of research data demonstrating a relationship between the level of trauma and the TBI and the force in question in the absence of other confounding factors.[12]

Physicians do not need to concern themselves with complex legal points upon which causation turns. However, an examining physician hired to evaluate a person who may have sustained a TBI, by and large will be used by the hiring attorney as a causation expert for the plaintiff, or in the case of the defendant, to either refute causation or attempt to show that no injury occurred. Personal injury lawyers tend to follow a sequence to prove causation by using an expert who offers an opinion that the trauma caused by the defendant was a substantial or material contributing factor in producing the plaintiff's current symptoms.[13] An expert (such as a physician who examined the victim for TBI) will be presented by either the plaintiff's or defendant's lawyer at trial to support or refute a claim for mental, emotional, or cognitive injuries, depending on the nature of the relationship between the accident and the injuries. If the relationship of the patient's cognitive and psychological state, subsequent to the brain injury, is not a matter of common knowledge likely to be possessed by the average judge or juror, expert testimony is required to avoid a directed verdict for the defense on the item of damages.[14,15] Traumatic brain injuries, and their resulting psychological and cognitive sequelae, are not likely to be understood by a typical judge or jury as necessarily following from physical trauma. Generally, the central issue in a TBI trial is the degree of relationship between the physical trauma and the organic brain injury. These cases typically turn on the requirement of reasonable medical certainty or reasonable medical probability. If an expert physician expresses uncertainty about the causal relationship between the physical injury and the organic brain injury, exclusion of the testimony and a directed verdict for the defense on the issue may result.[16]

DAMAGES

The neuropsychiatric examination will form the basis, in most instances, of damages assessment following TBI. The physician providing a neuropsychiatric examination will determine the level of cognitive and behavioral injury. This in turn will be translated by further analysis into a determination of economic loss. The defendant's harmful act that produced the TBI has reduced the plaintiff's earnings, earning capacity, or stream of economic value. The stream of economic value may take the form of compensation received by a worker, the profit earned by a business, or one-time receipts such as the proceeds from the sale of property. These are measured net of any associated costs.[17]

Another issue of damages is the amount it will cost to treat the outcome of TBI: the medical costs over the injured party's lifetime, the actual costs of treatment received at the time of the TBI, and the future rehabilitation needs or appliances required. For instance, if the individual is rendered hemiplegic following TBI, it may be necessary to factor in purchases for walkers or canes. If the person is so injured that an electric lift is required, this would be an additional medical appliance cost. The reader should be able to see that each individual case would have to be analyzed on its own merits to determine what costs will be required. Thus, the first step in a legal damages study is the translation of the legal theory of the harmful event into an analysis of the economic impact of that event upon the victim. This analysis considers the difference between the plaintiff's economic position if the harmful event had not occurred, and the plaintiff's actual economic position after the event has occurred. The damages study restates the plaintiff's position "but-for" the harmful event. Damages are the difference between the but-for value and the actual value usually projected over one's lifetime.

Once the neuropsychiatrist has established the level of damage to the brain and also established the medical treatment required over one's lifetime, the plaintiff lawyer will turn the data from the neuropsychiatric examination over to a PhD economist or an expert with business or accounting background. These individuals may have an MBA degree, CPA credentials, or both. The lawyer will make this determination and hire these individuals, and the neuropsychiatrist, if hired by the plaintiff's lawyer, will generally be asked to provide consultation to the individual performing the economic analysis.

For physicians neuropsychiatrically evaluating TBI, the major issue in the extent of damages will be outcome and prognosis. Later in this text we will review known outcomes from TBI. With regard to outcomes, the major question to the neuropsychiatric physician will be, "What are the medical outcomes of the TBI that the plaintiff either does or does not possess?" The physician examiner will testify on the causation of cognitive and behavioral damages. The remainder of the damage presentation to a trier of fact (usually a jury) will be made by individuals developing a life care plan and individuals who provide an economic analysis.

When performing a neuropsychiatric examination of a TBI victim to assess damages for a lawyer, it is necessary for the physician to explore carefully for preexisting emotional conditions that may have been aggravated or play a role in the current symptomatology. If preexisting conditions are determined, this presents a substantial challenge to the neuropsychiatric examiner. The law generally dictates that victims of injuries are taken "as they are found." Thus, even though the examinee may have had a prior injury or prior mental disorder before the TBI, this is not a defense. If the tortfeasor has harmed the person with a preexisting condition, that added harm is compensable under the law. Any added aggravation or exacerbation is compensable under the law. On the other hand, it is common for a defense lawyer to argue that the preexisting condition is the cause for any cognitive or behavioral difficulties in the victim. It will be up to the neuropsychiatric examiner to parse out and apportion the contribution of before-injury disease or damage and the results of the TBI at hand.

Another common presentation by the plaintiff lawyer, for a plaintiff who had a preexisting condition prior to TBI, is to argue that the alleged brain injury was "the straw that broke the camel's back" or the lawyer will argue a "cracked-egg theory."[13] Thus, it is incumbent upon the neuropsychiatric examiner to attempt to delineate what the plaintiff was like cognitively and behaviorally before the alleged brain injury. These issues have been explored somewhat in Chapters 6 and 7. In particular, it will be necessary to establish a pre-injury cognitive prediction (pre-injury baseline), and establish pre-injury cognitive capacity based on pre-injury records, SAT scores, academic information, work product, etc. The neuropsychiatric examiner may also need to assist the attorney with answers to two questions: Was the preexisting condition latent? Was the preexisting condition stable or degenerative? A brain trauma can trigger or activate a dormant condition (such as white matter disease from advanced hypertension or a prior resolved subdural hematoma).[18] Whether or not the preexisting condition was stable or degenerative can become a major legal issue, since stability before the TBI must be established or the defense can argue that the present symptoms are merely the result of a preexisting progressive condition.[19]

Determination of damages at trial, and an award for those damages, can come about only if liability can be established. Lawyers often use a term of art that "liability provokes damages" or "damages provoke liability." To win at trial, the alleged TBI victim must demonstrate an organic physical loss due to the TBI and show that any preexisting susceptibility was either aggravated or worsened by the TBI and prove that the current level of brain functioning has changed relative to the individual's premorbid central nervous system status. In most jurisdictions in the United States, at trial the neuropsychiatric examiner will be expected to produce a medical diagnosis that is producing the damage. It is also expected, as discussed previously in this text that the neuropsychiatric examiner, during the course of a competent neuropsychiatric evaluation for forensic purposes, will have determined if there are secondary gain mechanisms at work perpetuating the symptoms. Furthermore, the physician will be expected to have determined whether malingering or symptom magnification is an issue and if there is a direct and continuous medical relationship between the examinee's claim of TBI and a demonstrable neuropsychiatric cause. From a prognosis standpoint, the medical outcome of the TBI will be one of the most important pieces of information that the neuropsychiatric examiner can present to a jury.

OUTCOMES FOLLOWING TRAUMATIC BRAIN INJURY

There is no universally agreed definition of mild traumatic brain injury. The most commonly used definitions are similar. The American Congress of Rehabilitation Medicine has defined MTBI with loss of consciousness (LOC) lasting less than 30 min, an initial Glasgow Coma Scale score (GCS) of 13–15, and posttraumatic amnesia lasting less than 24 h.[20] Some researchers have differentiated MTBI between complicated and uncomplicated.[21] A complicated MTBI is diagnosed if the person has a GCS score of 13–15 but demonstrates at least one brain abnormality (edema, hematoma, or contusion) on the initial CT scan. Skull fractures are also considered characteristics of complicated MTBI. Williams et al.[21] have noted that patients with complicated MTBIs are more likely to have persistent cognitive and psychological symptoms, and their 6 months recovery pattern is more similar to persons with moderate head injury than those with uncomplicated MTBI. The uncomplicated MTBI is characterized by having no intracranial abnormality or skull fracture, with all other severity criteria in the mild range. It has been assumed (although not well studied) that the person who is dazed may have lost consciousness for a few seconds and is much more likely to experience a rapid and complete recovery than a person who is unconscious for 20 min and has a posttraumatic amnesia for 12 h.[22]

There are currently three major working definitions for MTBI used within North America. These include the definition of the American Congress of Rehabilitation Medicine (ACRM),[20] the National Center for Injury Prevention and Control conceptual definition of MTBI,[23] and the CDC Working Group Limited Criteria for identifying MTBI.[23] The World Health Organization has recently provided a comprehensive review of methodological problems in MTBI research and recommendations for improving such research.[24]

The definition provided by the American Congress of Rehabilitation Medicine in 1993[20] attempted to provide a scientific basis to determine whether an MTBI has occurred, by establishing injury severity criteria. This definition is widely cited in clinical practice and research. However, it has significant limitations. It includes a broad range of injury severity. Unfortunately, this definition ranges from a trivial injury involving seconds of confusion to a complicated MTBI involving 20–30 min of unconsciousness, several hours of posttraumatic amnesia, and a focal contusion. By GCS standards, this latter definition would be termed a moderate brain injury and no longer would be in the mild category. The definition by the ACRM of MTBI is any loss of consciousness; any loss of memory for events immediately before or after the accident; any alteration in mental state at the time of the accident; and focal neurological deficits that may or may not be transient; but where the severity of the injury does not exceed 30 min loss of consciousness, initial GCS score of 13–15, and posttraumatic amnesia not greater than 24 h.

The Centers for Disease Control provided a report to the United States Congress in 2003.[23] This working group also proposed limited criteria for identifying MTBI relevant impairment, functional limitations, disability, and persistent symptoms in population-based surveys. These criteria are

- Problems with memory
- Problems with concentration
- Problems with emotional control
- Headaches
- Fatigue
- Irritability
- Dizziness
- Blurred vision
- Seizures

They also proposed current limitations in functional status reported to be a consequence of the MTBI

- Limitations in personal care, ambulation, travel, etc.
- Impairment of major activities such as work, school, homemaking, etc.
- Impairment of leisure and recreation abilities
- Impairment of social integration
- Impairment of financial independence

The CDC working group cautioned Congress that most of these symptoms and limitations noted directly above are associated with many other conditions and comorbid illnesses, not just MTBI. The working group expressed concern regarding the limitations associated with the lack of specificity of the symptoms and functional limitations, but thought that these problems could be partially mitigated by the careful selection of appropriate comparison groups, cautious interpretation of findings, and by evaluating pre- and post-injury symptom reporting.[22]

The most recent definition available for MTBI comes from a comprehensive review of the literature on MTBI published in a series of articles in the *Journal of Rehabilitation Medicine*.[25–28] The World Health Organization Collaborating Centre Task Force on Mild Traumatic Brain Injury provided a definition of MTBI in concert with these articles:

MTBI is an acute brain injury resulting from mechanical injury to the head from external physical forces. Operational criteria for clinical identification include: (1) one or more of the following: confusion or disorientation, loss of consciousness for 30 min or less, posttraumatic amnesia for less than 24 h, or other transient neurological abnormalities such as focal signs, seizure, and intracranial lesion not requiring surgery, and (2) Glasgow Coma Scale score of 13–15 after 30 min postinjury or later upon presentation for healthcare. These manifestations of MTBI must not be due to drugs, alcohol, medications, caused by other injuries, or treatment for other injuries (e.g., systemic injuries, facial injuries or intubation), caused by other problems (e.g., psychological trauma, language barrier, or coexisting medical conditions) or caused by penetrating craniocerebral injury.[24, p. 115]

The neuropsychological outcome of MTBI remains confusing in the medical literature. However, it is well established that a concussion can occur without loss of consciousness. The vast majority of injuries in sports and many injuries in medical trauma settings are not associated with LOC.[22] The presence or duration of LOC is not always used as a criterion for MTBI in research studies, and this leads to further confusion.[24] The question in litigation of TBI is whether brief loss of consciousness is associated with worse outcome. Gennarelli et al. conducted an extraordinary series of primate studies illustrating that both the presence of diffuse axonal injury and functional outcome are associated linearly with duration of unconsciousness.[29] It is well established that an extended period of unconsciousness or coma in humans is associated with poor long-term outcome. There are repeated demonstrations in the medical literature of worse outcome associated with more severe brain injuries, as defined by duration of coma.[22] As a general rule, patients with comas lasting 1–2 weeks have worse outcome than patients with comas lasting less than 24 h.[30] However, this logic should not be assumed to hold true for MTBI.[22] Researchers studying trauma patients have reported that there is no association between brief loss of consciousness and short-term neuropsychological outcome or vocational outcome.[22] For instance, athletes who sustain concussions, as a rule, recover quickly and fully.[31] Therefore, it is a mistake to assume that brief loss of consciousness is a reliable predictor of outcome in MTBI.[22]

A recent Swedish study reviewed the impact of early intervention on late sequelae from MTBI. This was a large 1 year follow-up of 1719 consecutive patients with MTBI. Of this cohort, 395 individuals ages 16–60 met the MTBI definition. Persons with significant pre-injury brain disorders and substance abuse histories were deleted from the study. There was a control group of 131 patients, and the intervention group of MTBI was 264 patients. The initial problems identified were difficulties in daily activities and postconcussion symptoms. Individualized tailored treatment was given, primarily through occupational therapy. The primary measured endpoint was the change in the rate of postconcussion symptoms and in life satisfaction at 1 year follow-up. No statistical differences were found between the intervention group and the control group. Patients who experienced few postconcussion symptoms 2 to 8 weeks after the injury and declined rehabilitation recovered and returned to their pre-injury status. Patients who suffered several postconcussion symptoms and accepted rehabilitation did not recover after 1 year. In this particular MTBI sample, early active rehabilitioan did not change the outcome to a statistically significant degree.[32]

A study from Switzerland compared patients with MTBI who had CT scan lesions versus those who did not. Their definition of MTBI was a GCS score of 14 or 15. Two hundred and five patients with MTBI underwent a CT scan and then were examined with neurocognitive testing. The patients were followed for 1 year and assessed by phone interviews. The neurocognitive tests showed significant deficits only in 51% of patients, and there was no difference for patients between GCS scores of 14 and 15. There was no difference between patients with an intracranial lesion and those without. However, after 1 year, patients who had sustained an intracranial lesion had significantly more complaints than patients who did not. The most frequent complaints were headache and memory deficits. No correlation was found between GCS scores or intracranial lesions in the neurocognitive tests upon admission. After 1 year, patients with intracranial lesions demonstrated significantly more complaints than patients without these. No cost savings resulted by doing an immediate CT scan on all patients.[33]

An Australian study has demonstrated that there is a relationship between psychological and cognitive factors and the use of opioids in the development of the postconcussion syndrome.

The association between postconcussion syndrome and neuropsychological and psychological outcome was investigated in 122 general trauma patients, many of whom had orthopedic injuries following the MTBI. Apart from verbal fluency, the participants in this study with postconcussion syndrome did not differ in their performance on neuropsychological measures compared to those without a postconcussion syndrome (PCS). Individuals with a PCS reported significantly more psychological symptoms. Large effect sizes showed that persons had more psychological complaints than neuropsychological complaints. Analysis revealed a relationship between opioid analgesia and depression, anxiety and stress, and also a relationship between opioids and reduced learning.[34]

Iverson[35] has provided us a significant review of the MTBI literature. He notes that the MTBI literature is enormous, complex, methodologically flawed, and controversial. Overall, his review indicates that during the first week after injury, the brain undergoes a dynamic restorative process. Athletes typically return to pre-injury functioning within 2 to 14 days. Trauma patients usually take longer to return to their pre-injury functioning. In these patients, recovery can be incomplete and complicated by preexisting psychiatric or substance abuse problems, poor general health, concurrent orthopedic injuries, or comorbid problems of pain, depression, substance abuse, life stress, unemployment, and protracted litigation (these are important issues for exploration in any MTBI presenting in a litigation context).[35]

A recent Norwegian study examined a group of patients 25 years after sustaining mild brain injury as children and adolescents. Forty-five subjects were assessed with a standardized neuropsychological test battery 25 years after sustaining mild to moderate head injury as children. Unfortunately, including moderate head injury patients in this group confounds the results, and it is difficult to determine the contribution of MTBI. However, overall the group scores were in the normal range. There was a significant linear relationship between the head injury severity and current neuropsychological function. In other words, those patients with minimal MTBI had the least, if any, neuropsychological findings. The most important predictors of poor outcome were length of posttraumatic amnesia at injury, whether the EEG was pathological, and the length of loss of consciousness at the time of injury.[36] A Quebec study examined the relationship among demographic, social, neurological, and clinical factors, and whether or not persons returned to work following MTBI. Eighty-five MTBI patients between ages 16 and 65 years were examined. These individuals came from the emergency department of the Trois-Rivieres Regional Hospital Centre in Quebec. The demographic and social variables were collected, and patients were tested with the Paced Auditory Serial Addition Task, Stroop Color and Word Task, and California Verbal Learning Test. Patients were followed 12–36 months after trauma. Only the total number of symptoms reported at follow-up was related to vocational status. The majority of individuals with MTBI had returned to work within 1 year. Individuals who had not returned to work reported the greatest number of symptoms.[37]

With regard to litigation, MTBI is the most controversial aspect of brain injury cases which come to the court. Plaintiff lawyers often bring MTBI cases with no evidence of loss of consciousness, little to no evidence of head injury, no evidence of posttraumatic amnesia, fully normal functioning after injury (such as the plaintiff driving his automobile from the scene), and lack of intracranial pathology on head CT. Many studies have reviewed the effects of litigation on the continuation of MTBI symptoms. A study at the University of Toronto examined a consecutive sample of 100 patients with MTBI coming to the Sunnybrook Hospital Clinic. Cognitive screening was obtained and measures of psychological distress were obtained. The Rivermead Head Injury Follow-Up Questionnaire was administered. Litigants were significantly more anxious, depressed, had greater social dysfunction, and had poorer outcome on the Glasgow Coma Outcome Scale and the Rivermead scale. There were no cognitive differences between the two groups. The authors concluded that the data demonstrated an association between litigation and an increased psychological distress at the outset of the litigation process. The TBI-related differences between litigants and nonlitigants suggest that the pursuit of compensation may influence the subjective expression of symptoms following MTBI.[38] A second study, also from Canada, comes from a rehabilitation hospital in Alberta. Ninety-seven patients with MTBI were examined at 3 and 12 months, and measures were made to determine the days taken to return to pre-injury vocational activity. Those in litigation at intake generally continued to be in litigation at 3 and 12 months post-injury. Those seeking or receiving compensation from sick pay or workers' compensation were generally not seeking or receiving compensation 3 months later, as was the case for most of those not seeking any financial compensation at intake. There was a strong relationship between financial compensation-seeking and slow return to work in this MTBI group. The authors recommended that examination for the presence or absence of financial compensation-seeking after MTBI be routinely evaluated when return to work is an issue.[39]

There is a specific reason for examining litigation factors among our Canadian friends. It is often argued that the U.S. litigation system increases the likelihood that persons will prolong symptoms following MTBI. Based on the Canadian experience, this may be a universal phenomenon of human beings and therefore should be a consideration given in any case of litigation where MTBI symptoms seem to persist far longer than they should. Another study from Alberta is a meta-analysis of 428 studies related to prognosis after MTBI. One hundred and twenty of these were accepted for a critical review. For adults, cognitive deficits and symptoms are common in the acute stage, but the majority of studies report recovery from most within 3 to 12 months. Where symptoms persisted, compensation or litigation was a factor, but there is little consistent evidence for predictors other than compensation or litigation for prolonging symptoms.[40] A Vancouver study noted that patients with uncomplicated MTBIs could not be reliably differentiated from patients with substance abuse problems on neuropsychological measures of concentration, memory, and processing speed.[41] Thus, it is important in a litigation of MTBI that substance abuse factors be investigated considerably.

A University of Utah study examined 67 adults with disappointing recoveries after mild TBI. Most of these occurred in a compensation or litigation context, and these individuals were studied with regard to pre-injury, neurotrauma, physical, emotional, and cognitive variables on outcome. Except for prior psychological traumatization, none of the above factors were related to outcome. The authors concluded that in cases of poor recovery after mild TBI where compensation or litigation may be a factor, most of the variance in recovery seems to be explained by depression, pain, and symptom invalidity rather than by the injury variables themselves.[42] These findings were replicated in a meta-analysis from the Veterans Administration Hospital in Tampa, Florida. This analysis was based on 39 studies involving 1463 cases of MTBI and 1191 control cases. Litigation was associated with stable or worsening cognitive function over time. Those in litigation had greater symptomatology, longer outcomes, and less medical response to treatment than control cases.[43]

Overall, it is not fair to assume that anyone in litigation, following an MTBI, is magnifying his symptoms or prolonging his symptoms merely for compensation. On the other hand, there is overwhelming evidence in the medical literature that this, in fact, is a factor in those individuals who prolong their symptomatology, and litigation issues must be honestly explored; without question, symptom validity must be examined in any person with MTBI presenting for neuropsychiatric examination within the course of a litigation. What can be concluded at this point in medical history is that despite decades of research, slow or incomplete recovery from MTBI is poorly understood. For a substantial majority of people, MTBIs are self-limiting and generally follow a predictable course of improvement. Permanent cognitive, psychological, or psychosocial problems due to the biological effects of this injury are relatively uncommon in trauma patients and rare in athletes.[22,43,44] On the other hand, there are some people who do not appear to recover completely following this injury, and these individuals have been referred to as the "miserable minority."[45]

OUTCOMES FOR ADULTS FOLLOWING MODERATE–SEVERE TRAUMATIC BRAIN INJURY

Outcome from moderate to severe TBI in adults is quite variable. The reader may wish to review the Glasgow Outcome Scale in Chapter 1 for definitions of outcomes. While there is a relationship between the initial GCS score, it is not a linear relationship. These scores are associated with outcome, and lower GCS scores are associated with worse outcomes, but one cannot draw a more specific conclusion solely from the GCS score alone.[46] Recall that a moderate GCS score at the time of the initial injury is 9–12, and a severe GCS score is 8 and below. On the other hand, length of coma correlates in a more linear and direct fashion with outcome than does the GCS. In general, the longer the duration of coma, the worse the outcome. One study has reported that no subject made a good recovery whose length of coma exceeded 14 days.[47] Another predictor is posttraumatic amnesia (PTA). The duration of PTA has long been considered one of the most powerful prognostic factors available to those who provide rehabilitation to patients following TBI.[48] The longest reported duration of posttraumatic amnesia before one could exclude a good recovery was 3 months.[47] There is evidence in a number of studies that a person is unlikely to have an outcome of severe disability if the duration of posttraumatic amnesia is less than 2 months. Conversely, it is unlikely a person will have a good recovery when the duration of posttraumatic amnesia extends beyond 3 months.[46] Age is also a factor for predicting outcome. In a large review of multiple studies, all but two found that the older the patient, the worse the outcome. Age is a powerful prognostic factor. The prognosis worsens significantly after the age of 65.[46] With regard to penetrating injuries of the head, the lower the GCS score, the worse the outcome. Bilateral injury or transventricular injury is associated with worse outcome.[49]

With regard to moderate TBI, outcomes are much clearer than for severe TBI.[50,51] More than 90% of individuals who sustain a moderate TBI will achieve either a moderate disability or a good recovery. The odds are heavily in favor of at least independent living, but possibly not a return to previous levels of function. There are certain risk factors associated with poorer outcomes in moderate brain injury. These include older age and abnormalities on the CT scan. When these are present, patients are more likely to have a moderate disability, or even a severe disability, rather than a good recovery. Although the prognosis after moderate TBI is heartening, it is here that the limits of the higher categories of the Glasgow Outcome Scale leave much to be desired. Note that good recovery on the Glasgow Outcome Scale is still consistent with disability. Studies have shown that even individuals with a good recovery often have neurobehavioral problems that contribute significantly to morbidity.[50,51]

Recall from Chapter 1 that the neurobiology of apolipoprotein E was discussed. For persons sustaining a TBI, the effect of APOE ε4 is at least semidominant in its genetic effect. The relative risk of a poor outcome of subjects with at least one copy of APOE ε4 varies from 3.57-fold in the Glasgow study[52] to 13.93 in the Israeli study.[53] However, there were insufficient numbers of APOE ε4/4 subjects in these studies to allow calculation of the relative risk for homozygotes of ε4. Imperatives of APOE ε4 may also influence cognitive dysfunction that is related to TBI but delayed by years or even decades after the injury.[54] As has been noted previously in this text, several case-controlled studies indicate that head injury is a risk factor for the development of Alzheimer's disease in later life.[55–58] Remarkably, there is significant animal-based data that demonstrate that the presence of APOE ε3 protects against neuronal death.[59]

More recent studies have tested some of these factors noted above. A recent Quebec study from the McGill University Health Center has found by logistic regression that a shorter posttraumatic amnesia decreased the probability of moderate to severe disability. This study was in 339 patients (mild = 239, moderate = 48, and severe = 52). These all came from a Level I trauma center at the McGill University Health Center in the Montreal General Hospital. The outcome measures were the extended Glasgow Outcome Scale and the discharge destination. Discharge directly to home was less probable for patients with positive cerebral imaging.[60] A different slant on prediction of outcome was found by the Japan Neurotrauma Databank. A 4-year study of 1002 cases of traumatic brain injuries in Japan was conducted from 1998 to 2001 at 10 emergency medical centers. Patients with severe head injury and a GCS score of 8 or less were admitted. Children under 5 years of age were excluded. Three hundred and ninety-two items from multifocal viewpoints were evaluated. This study concluded that age at injury and mechanism of injury were the most important factors in the outcome.[61] McGill University recently gathered data from 2327 patients with TBI admitted to the level I trauma hospital at the McGill University. The study recorded data from 1997 to 2003 and divided patients into three age groups: 18–39, 40–59, and 60–99 years. Relative to younger adults with similar TBI severity, elderly patients showed worse outcome. No significant difference was observed between the young and middle-age groups except for cognitive ratings. A higher percentage of elderly patients went to inpatient rehabilitation, the long-term care facilities, or died compared to their young and middle-age counterparts. A higher number of young and middle-age patients were discharged directly to home.[62]

UCLA recently completed a study of 87 patients with moderate to severe TBI. These patients were studied longitudinally for neuropsychological, emotional, and behavioral issues. They were evaluated 12 months post-injury. Neurocognitive compromise played the most prominent role in affecting negatively adaptive function.[63] A subcomponent of this study reviewed verbal memory and information processing speed. The findings suggested that despite the pervasive memory complaints from patients following TBI, it is the impact of neurotrauma on frontal systems that appears to be primarily responsible for patients' difficulties in social and occupational functioning (dysexecutive syndromes).[64]

The neuropsychiatric physician providing examinations of forensic cases, will note that many persons with severe brain injury have had craniotomies or craniectomies. One intriguing question is, "What is the outcome following decompressive craniectomy from malignant swelling?" The University of Maryland School of Medicine evaluated 50 of 967 consecutive patients with closed TBI who experienced diffuse brain swelling and underwent decompressive craniectomy, without removal of clots or contusion, to control intracranial pressure or to reverse dangerous brain shifts. Diffuse injury was demonstrated in 44 of 50 patients. In 40 patients, the procedure was performed after intracranial pressure monitoring had become unresponsive to conventional medical management as outlined in the American Association of Neurological Surgeons Guidelines. Survivors were followed for at least 3 months post-treatment to determine their Glasgow Outcome Scale score. Decompressive craniectomy lowered ICP to less than 20 mmHg in 85% of patients. In the 40 patients who had undergone ICP monitoring before decompression, ICP decreased from a mean of 22.9 to 14.4 mmHg ($p < .001$). Fourteen of 50 patients died, and 16 remained in a vegetative state or were severely disabled. Twenty patients had a good outcome (Glasgow Outcome Scale score of 4–5). The authors concluded that decompressive craniectomy was associated with a better than expected functional outcome in patients with medically uncontrollable ICP or brain herniation compared with outcomes in other control cohorts reported in the neurosurgical literature.[65] Unfortunately, we have no long-term data on these persons to see what their cognitive and behavioral outcome has become.

There are some recent articles which help one to predict the probability of outcome in persons following significant brain injury. A recent German report from a databank of 299 patients with TBI included those who showed an MRI lesion pattern compatible with pure diffuse axonal injury (DAI). All of these patients underwent MRI on the newer 3 T system. Pure DAI was defined by the findings of traumatic microbleeds on T2-weighted gradient-echo images in the absence of otherwise traumatic or nontraumatic MRI abnormalities. Neuropsychological performance in the categories of attention and psychomotor speed, executive functions, learning, and memory, and intellectual capacity at 4–55 months after TBI was measured. All of the patients showed impairments of one or more cognitive subfunctions, and no cognitive domain was fundamentally spared. Memory and executive dysfunctions were the most frequent neuropsychological findings, with memory dysfunction reaching a moderate to severe degree in half the patients. In comparison, deficits of attention, executive functions, and short-term memory were mostly mild. There was no correlation between the amount of traumatic microbleeds detected on MRI and global cognitive performance. The authors concluded that an MRI lesion pattern compatible with isolated DAI is associated with a persistent cognitive impairment. On the other hand, the number of traumatic microbleeds detected by MRI was not a sufficient parameter to assess functional outcome.[66] Baylor University has found by MRI that posttraumatic amnesia predicts long-term cerebral atrophy. Sixty adult patients with mild to severe TBI were included in this study. A logistic regression model with a cutoff determined by normative MRI data confirmed that longer posttraumatic amnesia duration predicts increased ventricle-to-brain ratio. A probability model demonstrated a 6% increase in the odds of developing later atrophy on neuroimaging with each additional day of posttraumatic amnesia. Since PTA has previously proven to be a good indicator of later cognitive recovery and functional outcome, this study is interesting in that PTA also predicts long-term parenchymal change.[67]

Physicians working in litigation areas should be aware that the initial CT findings are probably poor predictors of eventual outcome. That is why it is critically important for the physician performing a forensic brain injury examination to obtain MRI imaging at a minimum, if it has not been performed following the initial head CT. For instance, Bigler's group at Brigham-Young University compared date-of-injury CT findings with acute injury severity markers, disability at acute hospital admission, and discharge from inpatient rehabilitation, injury severity markers, and degree of postacute cerebral atrophy on MRI. This group did a retrospective chart review of 240 consecutive TBI admissions with moderate to severe brain injury. All CT abnormalities on day-of-injury were qualitatively rated. Disability was assessed using the Disability Rating Scale. In a representative subset of these patients, cerebral atrophy was determined by the ventricle-to-brain ratio and quantified from MRI scans 25 or more days post-injury. CT classifications resulted in non-significant differences in Disability Rating Scale at the time of discharge from the rehabilitation unit, except in those patients who had sustained a brainstem injury. At 25 or more days post-injury, the presence of any CT abnormality was associated with larger ventricle-to-brain ratios. Increased ventricle-to-brain ratios as an index of cerebral atrophy were associated with worse rehabilitation discharge using the Disability Rating Scale. The authors concluded that CT findings related poorly to rehabilitation outcome. The presence of date-of-injury CT abnormalities was associated with the development of cerebral atrophy, which was associated with poor rehabilitation discharge scores on the Disability Rating Scale, but could not predict the level of outcomes.[68]

There are a couple of neuroanatomical findings which assist with prediction of outcome following significant brain injury. A UCLA study prospectively enrolled trauma patients from 18 centers in North America in the National Emergency X-Radiography Utilization Study (NEXUS) if they received an emergency head computed tomography (CT) scan as determined by the managing physician. Prevalence of intraventricular hemorrhage (IVH) among all trauma patients who received a head CT was 118 in 8374 patients or a rate of 1.41%. Among IVH patients, 70% had a poor outcome and 76% had a combined outcome. A poor outcome was associated with an abnormal GCS score and involvement of the third or fourth ventricle, whereas age appeared to be unrelated. Patients with IVH and no major associated injury on CT tended to do well, and only one of these patients with isolated IVH had a poor outcome. The authors concluded that traumatic IVH is rare and is associated with poor outcomes that seem to be the consequence of associated brain injuries. Isolated IVH patients who were clinically well appeared to have a good functional outcome.[69] Jorge's group recently reviewed hippocampal volumes in TBI. Thirty-seven patients who had sustained closed head injury were evaluated at baseline and 3, 6, and 12 months after trauma. Psychiatric diagnosis was made with a structured clinical interview using *DSM-IV* criteria. Quantitative magnetic resonance imaging scans were obtained at 3 months follow-up. Patients with moderate to severe head injury had significantly lower hippocampal volumes than patients with mild TBI. Patients who developed mood disorders had significantly lower hippocampal volumes than patients without mood disturbance. Furthermore, there was a significant interaction between mood disorders diagnosis and severity of TBI, by which patients with moderate to severe TBI who developed mood disorders had significantly smaller hippocampal volumes than patients with equivalent severe TBI who did not develop a mood disturbance. Reduced hippocampal volumes were associated with poor vocational outcome at 1 year follow-up.[70]

With regard to forensic evaluations of TBI, one of the central issues in outcome measurement and prognostication is to be clear about the outcome of interest. It is very important to ask the lawyer who hires the physician what the questions of outcome are specifically. As has been noted above, there are many outcome measures available. These include survival, physical impairment, ability to perform activities of daily living, cognitive, and behavioral status, return-to-work status, independent living ability, and quality of life.[46] The outcome one chooses depends on the questions necessary for presentation to a trier of fact. We will see later in this chapter how the *Guides to the Evaluation of Permanent Impairment* attempts to guide the physician in determination of impairment level and outcome. In a litigation climate, it is important to make an attempt to answer questions specifically. For instance, is the person unable to live independently because of executive dysfunction, impulsive behavior, or a left hemiparesis? Is the person unable to live independently because of factors that have nothing to do with the brain injury? These would include other disabling physical conditions, lack of financial resources, lack of a home or family support, etc. The broad categories of return-to-work, ability to live independently, or the Glasgow Outcome Scale are simply not designed to identify sequelae such as quality of life, the ability to maintain social relationships, and disturbances of behavior, or cognition.[46] Thus, the physician will have to make very specific measurements to answer very specific questions in order to provide sound opinions to a trier of fact regarding outcome in the adult following a TBI.

OUTCOMES IN CHILDREN FOLLOWING TRAUMATIC BRAIN INJURY

When children sustain a TBI, about 95% survive. However, that includes all forms of TBI, and the number drops to 65% in those children who sustain a severe TBI.[71,72] The highest mortality is in children less than 2 years of age. Then there is a gradual decline in mortality until about age 12. After this, a second peak in mortality is seen at about age 15.[73] As has been noted earlier in this book, children under age 5 do worse than older children. The disorders that seem to contribute mostly to impairment in children are alterations of communication and cognitive function following TBI. A study of 42 children and young adults found that 37% of those injured were independent while 49% were dependent on others in some area of living. Memory problems contributed the most to dependency.[74] One often overlooked outcome of TBI in young children is precocious puberty. A study of 33 children found 7 developed precocious puberty.[75] Another problem with children who receive TBI and orthopedic injury is heterotopic ossification. This has been reported in children and adolescents. The exact incidence is not known, but one study found a 22% positive triple-phase bone scan incidence in pediatric patients who had sustained TBI.[76] The physician performing a neuropsychiatric examination on a child who may have this disorder may notice decreased range of motion in the joints associated with pain and swelling.

Multiple studies have shown that children who sustain TBI require educational support and special education.[77–81] This has been noted earlier in this text, and the reader may refer to Chapters 2, 4, and 6 for a review of these topics. It is noteworthy that children often have difficulty with language. Generally, the more severely affected children have greater deficits in language skills. The negative interrelationship of language, executive function, and self-managing behavior may be so detrimental to the child that social impairments result and are compounded by communication disorders.[82] These social problems may have a significant effect on the youngster's ability to interact in an acceptable manner with peers at school, family members, and in ordinary social situations. If the child is injured young, once puberty is entered, the teenager may have an extraordinarily difficult time. These effects may in turn complicate the family to the point that the parents or guardians develop caregiver stress. This has been discussed previously in this text.

Some children will be so severely injured that they will require decompressive craniectomy. This is performed in an effort to prevent transtentorial herniation of the brain. The Children's Medical Center at the University of Utah reviewed its data on craniectomy following TBI in children between 1996 and 2005. Fifty-one children were identified with an average follow-up length of 18.6 months. Nonaccidental trauma accounted for almost 25% of the cases. The mean presurgery GCS score was 4.6. The mean postoperative GCS score was 9.7. Sixteen of the children died. Posttraumatic hydrocephalus and epilepsy were common complications in the survivors. In children who underwent decompressive surgery for raised intracranial pressure only, and not due to other complications such as depressed skull fracture, the mortality rate was exceedingly high.[83] The Baylor College of Medicine reviewed MRI morphometric findings after moderate to severe TBI in children. This is one of the first studies to complete this type of analysis. MRI volumetry was used to evaluate brain volume differences in the whole brain, and prefrontal, temporal, and posterior regions of children following moderate to severe TBI as compared to an uninjured control group of children of similar age and demographic background. The TBI group had significantly reduced whole brain and prefrontal and temporal regional tissue volumes, as well as increased cerebrospinal fluid space. There also were group difference on gray matter and white matter in the superiomedial and ventromedial prefrontal regions, the lateral frontal region, and the temporal region. Additional analyses comparing volumetric data from typically developing children in subgroups of TBI patients with and without regional focal lesions suggested that gray matter loss in the frontal areas was primarily attributable to focal injury, while white matter loss in the frontal and temporal lobes was related to both diffuse and focal injury. Finally, the volumetric measures of preserved frontotemporal tissue were related to improved functional recovery as measured by the Glasgow Outcome Scale (adapted for children) with greater tissue preservation predicting a better outcome.[84]

A diffusion tensor imaging study (see Chapter 5) was recently completed at the Baylor College of Medicine. The corpus callosum was evaluated in 16 children who were at least 1 year (mean = 3.1 years) postsevere TBI and individually matched against uninjured children as controls. Examiner reliability was tested and was found to be satisfactory. Fractional anisotropy was significantly lower in the patients who had sustained TBI within the genu, body, and splenium of the corpus callosum. Higher fractional anisotropy was related to increased cognitive processing speed and faster interference resolution on an inhibition task. In the TBI patients, the higher the fractional anisotropy, the better functional outcome the children had as measured by the Glasgow Outcome Scale (adapted for children). The authors concluded that diffusion tensor imaging may be useful in identifying biomarkers related to diffuse axonal injury for use in predicting outcome following TBI in children.[85]

It is not clear whether the GCS can be used as a determinant of outcome for children with traumatic brain injuries. A Chinese study from Taiwan attempted to answer this question. The researchers entered 309 children, ages 2–10 years, into the study. Each child underwent GCS measures with brain computed tomography and Glasgow Outcome Scale assessments. The critical point of the GCS was set at 5. This point most strongly correlated with the outcome of pediatric TBI. Subarachnoid hemorrhage with brain swelling and edema, subdural, intracerebral hemorrhage, and basal ganglia lesions was associated with severe injury and poor outcome ($p < .05$). Cortical or gray matter lesions did not affect injury severity and outcome. With regard to secondary injuries, only chest trauma had a tendency to be associated with poorer outcome.[86]

As we learned in Chapter 2, attention deficits are not uncommon after TBI in children, and secondary attention deficit disorder can result. Max's group at the University of California at San Diego reviewed outcome data from 118 children ages 5 through 14 at the time of hospitalization following TBI (severe TBI = 37, mild to moderate TBI = 57). They compared those selected against an orthopedic injury group of 24 children. The children were assessed by standardized psychiatric, adaptive functioning, cognitive functioning, family functioning, and family psychiatric history assessments. Severity of injury and neuroimaging lesion analyses was conducted on TBI participants only. Thirteen of 94 TBI participants and 4 of 24 orthopedic participants had pre-injury ADHD. Secondary ADHD occurred in 13 of 34 eligible participants in the study who had sustained a severe TBI but resolved in 4 of 13 of these participants. Secondary ADHD also occurred in one of the eight eligible moderate TBI participants, only in the presence of pre-injury ADHD traits. Secondary ADHD was significantly associated with the severity of the TBI recorded by categorical and dimensional measures, intellectual, and adaptive functioning deficits, and personality changes. However, it was not associated with the lesion area on neuroimaging or with the location of the lesions. These results suggested that secondary ADHD is a clinically important syndrome after TBI in children and adolescents, and it is unrelated to lesion areas or locations.[87]

A very large study of the characteristics of children who sustain inflicted TBI was undertaken to compare these children against those who sustain noninflicted TBI. A University of Utah study reviewed all children who were hospitalized between January, 2000 and December, 2001 in any of the state's nine pediatric ICUs and who survived a severe TBI that occurred on or before their second birthday. The children were followed over a 1 year period, and the assessment occurred 1 year after injury. Family characteristics were determined through maternal caregiver interviews approximately 1 year after injury. Seventy-two interviews of maternal caregivers were completed among the 112 survivors. Children with inflicted injuries ($n = 41$) had worse outcomes than did children with noninflicted injuries ($n = 31$), as measured with the Pediatric Outcome Performance Category and Stein-Jessup Functional Status II tools. However, approximately 50% of children with inflicted injuries had only mild deficits or better. Children with inflicted injuries used ancillary medical resources at a higher rate. Families caring for the children did not differ substantially between groups. The larger proportion consisted of single working minority mothers in both groups. The authors concluded that children with inflicted TBIs had worse outcomes than did children with other TBIs 1 year after injury. However, outcomes for these children were better than those reported previously. Many families caring for children after severe TBI are socially disadvantaged.[88] The Children's Hospital in Cincinnati[89] recently reviewed long-term parental and family adaptation following pediatric brain injury. Children with severe TBI, moderate TBI, and orthopedic injuries were followed at six time-points from baseline to 6 years post-injury. Parents completed multiple measures of injury-related burden assessments. Mixed-model analysis was used to determine long-term changes. Attrition during the study was higher among families in the severe TBI group. The severe TBI group reported higher injury-related burden over time after injury than the other groups. Families of children with severe TBI and low resources reported deteriorating functioning over the follow-up interval. The authors concluded that families of children who sustain severe TBI experience long-standing injury-related burdens.[89]

Sumich et al.[82] remind us that "children are not small adults." This is particularly true for youngsters who sustain TBI. The unique emotional, social, and developmental needs of children demand a holistic and comprehensive approach by a broad-based team. It is hoped that when a physician conducts a neuropsychiatric examination of a child TBI victim in litigation, that numerous elements of the team will be available so that the neuropsychiatric evaluation will be as comprehensive as possible. It is also important to interview the family at the time of examination where possible. It is also important to remember, as was discussed elsewhere in this text, that children who sustain TBI have higher than expected rates of psychiatric illness as adults.

EVALUATING LEGAL COMPETENCE FOLLOWING TRAUMATIC BRAIN INJURY

ADULT COMPETENCE

The physician may be asked to perform a neuropsychiatric assessment of competence for numerous reasons. It is important that when asked to do so, the physician clarifies exactly the referring party's question. For instance, "Is the examination to determine whether the TBI victim needs a guardian or conservator? Is the examination a question of testamentary capacity in a person now deceased who sustained a TBI before making a will?" Other issues of competency can arise after TBI such as whether or not the individual has the ability to enter a contract. Competence as a concept is an extremely broad term and too broad for general use. The examiner should analytically distinguish between general competence and specific competence. General competence as a term of

TABLE 10.1

Neuropsychiatric Assessment of General Competency

Ability to understand relevant information	Are persons generally aware of their current circumstances? For example, where they live, the sources of income, the general nature of their assets, any significant persons who assist them, and any threats to themselves and financial security (e.g., depletion of their estates).
Ability to understand the issues at hand	Can persons demonstrate a capacity to understand the relevant facts? For instance, do they know that a monthly payment reduction is required to extend the payout period of their IRAs?
Ability to appreciate likely consequences	Do they understand that if their homes are sold to provide an income for life they will no longer be allowed to live there? Do they understand that lack of payment to the water company will result in turning off the water supply?
Ability to manipulate information and communicate a choice	Can persons demonstrate orientation, memory, judgment, logic of thought, and regulation of affect? Can persons demonstrate by explicit examples that they can manipulate data about their assets and express their wishes for their use? Can the person understand, appreciate, reason, and express a choice?
Apply appropriate cognitive, psychological, and imaging measures to confirm clinical findings	Perform appropriate mental status examination, neurological examination, standardized cognitive and psychological testing, brain neuroimaging, and laboratory studies.

art in society usually refers to the ability to handle one's affairs in an adequate manner. On the other hand, specific competence is defined by the mental capacity necessary to engage in a particular act, such as a contract, function as a witness in court, or be tried as a criminal. Table 10.1 provides to the reader a broad outline of issues of general competency and the necessary cognitive abilities that an individual should possess. Within that table are questions as to each of the abilities mentioned, which should be explored by the neuropsychiatric examiner.

If an individual lacks general competency, it may be necessary for the court to appoint a guardian or a conservator. In a general sense, guardianship is used to protect the incompetent person and to assist with management of affairs, whereas a conservatorship is used to conserve the assets of the person for her use in life. The standard for the appointment of a guardian or conservator in most jurisdictions is based on an inability of the TBI victim to make or communicate responsible decisions based on a condition such as lack of mental capacity. This requires a diagnosis of a mental disorder or deficiency as a result of TBI, and this portion of the medical examination is rather straightforward. The second role of an examiner is to explain the effect of that disorder on the capacity of the individual to make or communicate responsible decisions.[90]

As we saw earlier in this chapter, the basis for testamentary capacity is that the testator must be of sound mind at the time of making the will. If an individual writes a will after sustaining a TBI, it is possible the testamentary capacity of the person could be questioned. Recall the English case of *Banks v. Goodfellow* as described in this chapter. The testator must know that he is making a will, know the nature and extent of his property subject to distribution by the will, know how the will would distribute that property, and know those blood relatives and others who would normally be expected to benefit from the distribution. Since in most instances the TBI victim will be dead at the time the will is contested, the forensic examination will be based on an analysis of records made about the person while living and also based upon collateral information that the examiner can obtain from persons who knew the deceased on or about the time the will was made.

It is very important for the neuropsychiatric examiner to remember that a diagnosis of a mental defect as a result of a TBI does not automatically yield a finding of testamentary incapacity. Such a finding must be based on specific lack of capacity to engage in the acts and have the understanding as outlined in *Banks v. Goodfellow*. On the other hand, the neuropsychiatric examiner must remember that even though an individual has not been diagnosed with a mental disorder, or does not appear to be mentally incapacitated by virtue of TBI, those facts do not guarantee that testamentary capacity exists.[90]

Binding legal agreements require the consent of the parties to the agreement. Contractual incapacity based on a mental disorder is a narrow cognitive test. If, at the time of the transaction, as a result of a mental disorder (from TBI), a party to the contract does not understand the nature or consequence of the transactions, contractual capacity does not exist.[91] In some jurisdictions, a prong to the limits of understanding has been added for those who may have bipolar illness. This prong is what courts refer to as "a lucid interval" at the time of the transaction. If that occurs, contractual capacity exists.[92] This is because a person could be psychotic from mania at a time before making a will, but then be perfectly lucid after treatment at the time the will was actually made. In TBI cases, this would apply only to those persons who might have secondary mania (see Chapter 2).

With regard to specific competence, there are many issues besides making a contract that could occur. For physicians, the commonest occurrences are specific competence to consent to a medical treatment, specific competence to consent to an extraordinary medical or surgical procedure, and specific competence to leave the hospital against medical advice. These require a judicial proceeding in some instances, and if an individual became incompetent by virtue of TBI, it might be necessary to provide a forensic neuropsychiatric assessment and testify to a court.[93]

As the neuropsychiatric examiner approaches a brain-injured person regarding competency, there are four general standards that should apply to the examiner's mental assessment for general competence.[94] Table 10.1 outlines a mental examination schema for determining general competency in decision making. Moreover, when performing any type of competency examination within a medical–legal framework, the physician must first be aware of the applicable competency standards in the particular jurisdiction. Legal consultation may be required to determine these standards. The examination then should focus on the four basic capacities of competence: the ability to understand relevant information, the ability to appreciate the nature of the situation and its likely consequences, the ability to manipulate information rationally, and the ability to communicate a choice.[95] A comprehensive mental status examination will be critical to answering the questions in Table 10.1. Moreover, ancillary measures may be required to support findings obtained during the mental status examination. For instance, is there evidence of executive dysfunction on psychological testing? Is there evidence of a significant reduction in intellectual capacity as a result of brain injury? Has the brain injury produced evidence of dementia on measures such as the Mini-Mental State Examination? Ancillary testing is used merely for confirmation of the mental status examination and to add information that may be of use to a court in the determination of competency. In most instances, competency is determined by a judge rather than a jury and, therefore, the examiner's database can be established at a detailed and complex level appropriate for judicial use. Where a person's capacity to consent to medical treatment is called into question, there is a semistructured interview format available for clinical use. The MacArthur Competence Assessment Tool-Treatment (MacCAT-T) is available to assist in either a forensic examination or a clinical examination of this important capacity.[96] However, it is important to recognize that the MacCAT-T does not provide scores that translate directly into determinations of legal competence or incompetence. The examiner's judgment and other forms of examination will be required for a complete assessment of competence to enter into medical treatment.

Lastly, it is important to remember that the United States Constitution prohibits the trial of an incompetent person.[97] The Constitution further prohibits the execution of an incompetent criminal defendant.[98] An incompetent person may not give consent to healthcare or health procedures as just discussed,[99] and a person must have basic competence to execute a will.[7] As the references indicate,

Dusky, Ford, and Canterbury come from the United States Supreme Court or the Federal Court of Appeals. *Banks v. Goodfellow* comes to us by way of our compatriots in England.

CHILD COMPETENCE

Children by definition are dependent persons and have parents or guardians. However, there are occasions wherein a brain-injured child could come under the scrutiny of the juvenile court system. Moreover, older teenagers who commit serious crimes against others are often waived to adult courts and are tried as adults. Children also may at times be witnesses in a civil or criminal court action and the brain-injured child's competency to testify may be rightfully raised as an issue.[100] The credibility of child witnesses often is an issue before the court and if the child witness has sustained a TBI, almost assuredly, the child's credibility will be questioned. Other child issues in a traumatically brain-injured youngster that may come to the attention of an examiner are assessing risk of harm to others. This could be an issue as a direct outcome of TBI, or as is more often the case, a child with oppositional defiant disorder or attention deficit disorder sustains a TBI and then demonstrates some marked exacerbation of behavior. The methods and procedures for evaluating juveniles have their own specific ethical rules and in many instances these are distinct from the ethics involved in adult assessment.[101] However, the basic evaluation of child competence is structurally no different from that of the adult. Thus, the forensic examination of child competence, as described for the adult, should determine the youngster's capacities for understanding, appreciating, reasoning, and expressing a choice.

DETERMINING IMPAIRMENT FOLLOWING TRAUMATIC BRAIN INJURY

At the time of the writing of this text, the American Medical Association is preparing the sixth edition of the *Guides to the Evaluation of Permanent Impairment*. It will probably be published on or about the same time as this text. Unfortunately, that information is not available to include in this book. The information noted below comes from the fifth edition of the *Guides to the Evaluation of Permanent Impairment*.[9]

As described in the Introduction, the physician directly determines impairment. Thus, the physician can determine impairment in one's patient by the methods discussed in Chapters 1 through 8 or the forensic physician can determine impairment at the request of another party for purposes of litigation. With one's patient, the level of impairment determined by the physician may be used by others to assist in disability determination. Determining whether an injury or illness results in a permanent impairment requires a medical assessment performed by a physician.[9] Once an impairment is established, this may lead to functional limitations or the inability to perform activities of daily living. When evaluating a brain-injured individual, an examining physician has two options: consider the individual's healthy pre-injury or preillness state, or the condition of the unaffected side, as normal for the individual, if this is known. The physician also can compare that individual to a normal value defined by population averages of healthy people. Both methods are generally used for impairment determination. With regard to TBI, one cerebral hemisphere may be compared to the other; the cognitive assessment may be compared to normative standards for persons of like age and gender, or the individual's cognitive and psychological state may be compared to an estimate of pre-injury functioning (such as described in Chapter 6). While experts may argue that there are other methods for determining impairment, there is no other impairment rating system used by physicians in the United States that has such wide acceptance and sound scientific database as the *AMA Guides*. However, in assessment of impairment for litigation purposes, the *Daubert* rule must be kept in mind by the examiner. The *Guides*, probably without exception, will meet the standards of that rule. As discussed earlier in this text, during history taking, the physician should inquire as to activities of daily living. These are also called "instrumental activities of daily living" (IADL).[102,103] These activities have been described as (1) self-care and personal hygiene, (2) communication skills, (3) physical activity ability, (4) sensory function ability, (5) nonspecialized hand activities, (6) traveling ability, (7) sexual functioning, and (8) sleep functioning. With regard to a neuropsychiatric assessment, almost all scales for measurement of either instrumental activities of daily living or activities of daily living are based primarily on a physical medicine model. For a significantly brain-injured person, these models work quite well. For the person who has only a mental or behavioral impairment following a brain injury, in the absence of physical impairments, these various rating scales measure poorly. Some of the common activities of living scales in use include the OECD Long-Term Disability Questionnaire, the Health Assessment Questionnaire, the Functional Independence Measure, and the Barthel Index.[104–107]

The *Guides* provides information to assist the examining physician with determination of causation, apportionment, and aggravation. These are important issues in the adjudication of workers' compensation and personal injury claims. Causation used in this medical sense is different from legal causation described above in this chapter. For purposes of using the *Guides*, causation means an identifiable factor (e.g., accident or exposure to hazards of a disease) that results in a medically identified condition.[9] The examining physician needs to be aware that the legal standard for causation in civil litigation and workers' compensation adjudication varies from jurisdiction to jurisdiction. It is the examining physician's responsibility to determine those standards when they are being applied within the context of a forensic medical evaluation.[108]

Apportionment analysis may be required in workers' compensation cases depending on the jurisdiction. This analysis derives from the fact that multiple factors may cause or significantly contribute to the injury or disease resulting in the impairment being assessed by the physician. For instance, the examinee may have a preexisting injury or impairment which plays a role in the genesis of the accident or injury under evaluation by the examiner. The examining physician may be asked by the attorney, workers' compensation carrier, or other third party to apportion or distribute a permanent impairment rating between the effects of the current injury and a prior injury or impairment rating. The *Guides* recommend following a protocol for the analysis of apportionment. The physician needs to verify that all the following information is true for an individual:[9] (1) There is documentation of a prior factor. (2) The current permanent impairment is greater as a result of the prior factor (i.e., prior impairment, prior injury, or illness). (3) There is evidence indicating the prior factor caused or contributed to the impairment, based on a reasonable medical probability (>50% likelihood).

For the forensic neuropsychiatric examiner, this is not an unusual circumstance. Many persons sustaining a brain injury have had a prior head or brain injury. Thus, the physician performing a neuropsychiatric examination following brain injury, in some instances, may need to determine by apportionment analysis the contribution of the first brain injury to the second brain injury. The combined effect of the first and second brain injuries may result in an impairment rating that exceeds the mere additive effects of both. In other words, the outcome may be exponential rather than arithmetically additive. In workers' compensation cases, it often derives from a prior industrial injury that the employer shall be liable only for the additional disability from the injury or occupational disease due to the subsequent injury and not the prior injury.[9,109]

For purposes of using the *Guides*, aggravation refers to a factor, or factors, that alters the course of progression of the medical impairment.[9] With regard to a TBI, this could be an individual who had a substantial attention deficit disorder or learning disorder as a youngster. If this disorder remained manifest into adulthood and that individual then sustained a TBI, the TBI could be an aggravating factor to the pre-injury psychiatric condition. When evaluating a person for impairment, permanency should not be considered until the clinical findings indicate that the medical condition has become static, well stabilized, and reached maximum medical improvement. With regard to TBI, improvement generally becomes static by 12–18 months post-injury. There are, of course, exceptions to this rule but in most instances, and at least within reasonable medical probability, by 18 months the improvement in TBI will have plateaued. Thus, a maximum medical improvement refers to a time specific from which further recovery or deterioration is not anticipated, even though there may be some slight expected changes or improvement. To determine a whole person, or whole body, impairment, the examining physician should first estimate the impairment for the person's most significant injury and evaluate other impairments secondary to or in relation to the primary impairment. If there are two or more significant medical conditions, each impairment rating is calculated separately unless they are related. For instance, following a TBI, a person may have executive dysfunction and dysphasia. However, these would be interrelated conditions as an outcome of the primary brain injury rather than separate mental or cognitive constructs. Where there are separate unrelated conditions, the *Guides* provide a combined values chart for combining impairments.

Following the examination of a brain-injured person, the physician examiner should complete a neurobehavioral analysis taking into account the cognitive and behavioral impairments in the person. Depending on the outcome of the neuropsychiatric evaluation, the physician examiner then may utilize, in most instances, two specific chapters of the *Guides*, fifth edition. These are Chapter 13 (The Central and Peripheral Nervous System) and Chapter 14 (Mental and Behavioral Disorders).[9] With regard to Chapter 13 of the *Guides*, the most relevant section for the neuropsychiatric examiner is 13.3d (Mental Status, Cognition, and Highest Integrative Function). Table 13.5 of the *Guides* enables the neuropsychiatric examiner to determine an impairment level and a Clinical Dementia Rating score. These determinations include memory, orientation, and executive function as well as activities of daily living and self-care. Table 13.6 of the *Guides* provides criteria for Rating Impairment Related to Mental Status wherein the neuropsychiatric examiner can place the examinee into one of the four classes (Table 10.2). The Clinical Dementia Rating system was developed by Morris and provides the physician examiner with a schema for categorizing dementia syndromes as a result of TBI, or other medical causes.[110] Chapter 11 of this text provides the physician with case examples for using these scales to determine impairment following TBI. Tables 10.2 and 10.3 provide criteria for rating impairment related to mental status out of Chapter 13 of the *Guides*. Table 10.4 comes from Chapter 14 of the *Guides* and refers specifically to classes of impairment due to classical psychiatric disorders.

Where an emotional or behavioral impairment is the direct outcome of brain trauma, Section 13.3f (Emotional or Behavioral Impairments) of the *Guides* may be useful to the examining physician. Table 13.8 of the *Guides* describes criteria for rating impairment due to emotional or behavioral disorders into one of the four classes. A Class I impairment describes a person with mild limitation of activities of daily living, whereas, Class II describes a person with moderate limitation of some activities of daily living and some limitation of daily social and interpersonal functioning. Class III impairment is a fairly significant limitation in that the person demonstrates severe

---

TABLE 10.2

Criteria for Rating Impairment Related to Mental Status

Class I 1%–14% Impairment of the Whole Person	Class II 15%–29% Impairment of the Whole Person	Class III 30%–49% Impairment of the Whole Person	Class IV 50%–70% Impairment of the Whole Person
Paroxysmal disorder with preimpairment exists, but is able to perform activities of daily living	Impairment requires direction of some activities of daily living	Impairment requires assistance and supervision for most activities of daily living	Unable to care for self and be safe in any situation without supervision

Source: *Guides to the Evaluation of Permanent Impairment*, 5th edition, AMA Press, Chicago, IL, 2000, p. 320. With permission.

TABLE 10.3
Criteria for Rating Impairment due to Emotional or Behavioral Disorders

Class I 0%–14% Impairment of the Whole Person	Class II 15%–29% Impairment of the Whole Person	Class III 30%–69% Impairment of the Whole Person	Class IV 70%–90% Impairment of the Whole Person
Mild limitation of activities of daily living and daily social and interpersonal functioning	Moderate limitation of some activities of daily living and some daily social and interpersonal functioning	Severe limitation in performing most activities of daily living, impeding useful action in most daily social and interpersonal functioning	Severe limitation of all daily activities, requiring total dependence on another person

Source: *Guides to the Evaluation of Permanent Impairment*, 5th edition, AMA Press, Chicago, IL, 2000, p. 325. With permission.

limitation in performing most activities of daily living that impedes useful action in most daily social and interpersonal functions. A Class IV behavioral impairment due to brain injury would cause severe limitation of all daily activities requiring total dependence upon another person.[9] Thus, an individual with a severe infraorbital behavioral syndrome (see Chapter 2) as a result of a TBI can be aptly described for impairment rating purposes in Chapter 13, Section 13.3f of the *Guides*. On the other hand, if the individual has a mood disorder or posttraumatic stress disorder as a result of a head injury with no evidence of organic mental impairment, Chapter 14 of the *Guides* may prove more useful to the examining physician.

For a purely psychiatric outcome following a TBI, the method of evaluating psychiatric impairment in Chapter 14 is somewhat different than the method used in Chapter 13 of the *Guides*. In Chapter 14, the *Guides* specifically avoid the use of percentage ranges of impairment, whereas they are used in Chapter 13. The *Guides* point out in Chapter 14, "Percentages are not provided to estimate mental impairments in this edition of the *Guides*. Unlike cases with some organ systems, there are no precise measurements of impairment in mental disorders. The use of percentages implies a certainty that does not exist. Percentages are likely to be used inflexibly by adjudicators, who then are less likely to take into account the many factors that influence mental and behavioral

TABLE 10.4
Classes of Impairment due to Mental and Behavioral Disorders

Area or Aspect of Functioning	Class I No Impairment	Class II Mild Impairment	Class III Moderate Impairment	Class IV Marked Impairment	Class V Extreme Impairment
Activities of daily living Social functioning Concentration Adaptation	No impairment noted	Impairment levels are compatible with most useful functioning	Impairment levels are compatible with some, but not all, useful functioning	Impairment levels significantly impede useful functioning	Impairment levels preclude useful functioning

Source: *Guides to the Evaluation of Permanent Impairment*, 5th edition, AMA Press, Chicago, IL, 2000, p. 363. With permission.

impairments. After considering this difficult matter, the Committee on Disability and Rehabilitation of the American Psychiatric Association advised *Guides* contributors against the use of percentages in the chapter on mental and behavioral disorders of the Fourth Edition, and that remains the opinion of the authors of the present chapter."[9] The *Guides* further point out that there is little relationship between psychiatric signs and symptoms identified during a mental status examination and the ability to perform competitive work. There are four categories that may assess areas of function that are related to work ability and these include (1) ability to perform activities of daily living, (2) social functioning, (3) concentration, persistence, and pace, and (4) deterioration or decompensation in work or work-like settings. Thus, Table 14.1 of the *Guides* defines classes of impairment due to mental and behavioral disorders. Unlike Chapter 13, this classification system uses five classes ranging from Class I for no impairment noted to Class V, impairment levels preclude useful functioning. A Class II impairment is at the mild level and impairment levels are compatible with most useful functioning. A Class III mental or behavioral impairment is a moderate level and impairments are compatible with some, but not all useful functioning. A person is assigned to a Class IV, marked impairment level, when impairments significantly impede useful functioning. Table 10.4 lists classes of impairment due to mental and behavioral disorders which may provide useful assistance in the determination of behavioral incapacity following a TBI. The reader is advised that if impairment ratings are part of the customary practice of the physician, frequent consultation with the *Guides* will assist to standardize the examination process. Chapter 11 of this text describes in further detail specific use of the *Guides* for determining impairment levels following TBI.

DISABILITY DETERMINATION FOLLOWING TRAUMATIC BRAIN INJURY

According to a 1997 Institute of Medicine Report, "Disability is a relational outcome, reflecting the individual's capacity to perform a specific task or activity, contingent on the environmental conditions in which they are to be performed."[111] The alternative definition of disability used by the *Guides* is noted above. Since this section deals primarily with forensic issues, disability is described here, yet it is determined judicially or by an administrative law judge. However, it must be stressed that treating physicians, including psychiatrists, may be asked to evaluate their patients for disability within the context of a workers' compensation claim or a social security claim. The physician will determine a level of impairment which can then be used by the adjudicating body to determine whether or not the patient has a disability. When the physician is conducting an independent medical evaluation, and not functioning on behalf of the patient, the evaluation is performed within the context of a forensic or nonpatient centered format.

Social security disability is determined under the Social Security Disability Insurance Benefits Program.[112] The disability standard of this program requires that the claimant demonstrates an "inability to engage in any substantial gainful activity by reason of any medically determinable physical or mental impairment which can be expected to result in death or which has lasted or can be expected to last for a continuous period of not less than 12 months."[9] Within *42 U.S.C.*, is contained the Administration's Listing of Impairments. The mental impairments are found in Listing 12.00 (Mental Disorders). Listing 12.02 contains Organic Mental Disorders. This listing is where persons suffering TBI would be categorized and classified. The listing for organic mental disorders requires satisfaction of requirements A and B:

A. Demonstration of a loss of specific cognitive abilities or affective changes and the medically documented persistence of at least one of the following:
   1. Disorientation to time and place
   2. Memory impairment, either short-term (inability to learn new information), intermediate, or long-term (inability to remember information that was known sometime in the past)

3. Perceptual or thinking disturbances (e.g., hallucinations, delusions)
4. Change in personality
5. Disturbance in mood
6. Emotional lability (e.g., explosive temper outbursts, sudden crying, etc.) and impairment in impulse control
7. Loss of measured intellectual ability of at least 15 IQ points from premorbid levels or overall impairment index clearly within the severely impaired range on neuropsychological testing, e.g., the Luria-Nebraska, Halstead-Reitan, etc.

and

B. Resulting in at least two of the following:
1. Marked restriction of activities of daily living
2. Marked difficulties in maintaining social functioning
3. Deficiencies of concentration, persistence or pace resulting in frequent failure to complete tasks in a timely manner (in work settings or elsewhere)
4. Repeated episodes of deterioration or decompensation in work or work-like settings which cause the individual to withdraw from that situation or to experience exacerbation of signs and symptoms (which may include deterioration of adaptive behaviors)

Should the examinee or patient have a pure psychiatric syndrome due to TBI, other categories of impairments may apply. Listing 12.03 covers schizophrenic, paranoid, and other psychotic disorders. Listing 12.04 covers affective disorders including depressive, manic, or bipolar syndromes. Listing 12.05 covers mental retardation and autism. Listing 12.06 includes anxiety-related disorders. This would include posttraumatic stress disorder if it were present. Listing 12.07 includes somatoform disorders. Listing 12.08 includes personality disorders and would include a personality change due to a TBI. Listing 12.09 contains the criteria for substance addiction disorders.

Druss et al. recently reviewed the 1994–1995 National Health Interview Survey of Disability, the largest disability survey ever conducted in the United States. Their review noted that 1.1% of adults reported a functional disability from a mental condition versus 4.8% of adults who reported a disability from a general medical condition. They estimated that 3 million Americans (one-third of all disabled people) reported that a mental condition contributes to their disability.[113] However, review of this data does not allow one to determine what percentage of those with mental disability are disabled by virtue of TBI. The *Federal Register* routinely publishes criteria for evaluating mental disorders in TBI as they are revised.[114] Rules for determining medical equivalents in childhood disability claims when a child has marked limitations in cognition and speech are also routinely reported in the *Federal Register* as a social security ruling.[115]

When the physician is performing an examination for social security disability as a result of a TBI, it is recommended that the criteria of Listing 12.02 be followed. Both criteria A and B in that listing enable the examining physician to determine by mental status examination, cognitive testing, and an examination of activities of daily living the current functioning of either a patient or an examinee. The report written on behalf of the patient or for the person who hired the physician to perform the IME, should be clear and direct and to the point in describing which of the specific criteria are met by the examination and the bases for the determination.

FORSENSIC MEDICAL HISTORY

The reader should refer to Chapter 3. The adult and child medical history formats are listed. Those have been designed by the author to provide dual purpose assistance. In the first instance, these forms are very suitable for a treating psychiatrist or psychologist to use when taking the medical history within the context of a TBI examination to be used for treatment. On the other hand, they are

TABLE 10.5
Warnings to Be Applied When Taking a Forensic Medical History

Warning: Because you are being examined for purposes of your mental fitness or a legal action (workers' compensation, social security, civil rights, civil or criminal, etc.), please be aware that the information you supply in this questionnaire, or tell the doctor, may not be confidential.

This is a medical–legal or an independent medical examination. Forensic Doctor, MD, will not have a doctor–patient relationship with you. This examination is not for treatment or counseling. Forensic Doctor, MD, may video- or audiotape-record the interview. If the doctor does so, your lawyer can request a copy of the tape.

equally effective in taking the medical history during a forensic examination. There are no technical differences between a history for a forensic examination versus a treatment examination with the exception of focusing on issues of motivation, deception, and other factors that may play a role in a forensic examination. The reader is referred to Table 10.5. This table contains warnings, which should be applied to the medical history questionnaire when used for forensic purposes. The warnings are entirely distinct from those used for treatment for reasons discussed elsewhere in this text.

REFERENCES

1. Firestone, M., Personal injury in the legal process, in *The American Psychiatric Publishing Textbook of Forensic Psychiatry*, Simon, R.I. and Gold, L.H., Eds., American Psychiatric Press, Washington, D.C., 2004, p. 263.
2. Shuman, D.W., *Psychiatric and Psychological Evidence,* 3rd edition, Thomson, New York, 2005.
3. *Cunningham v. Shelton Sec. Service, Inc.*, 46 S.W.3d 131 (Tennessee, 2001).
4. *Drope v. Missouri*, 420 US 163 (1974).
5. Resnick, P.J. and Noffsinger, S., Competency to stand trial in the insanity defense, in *The American Psychiatric Publishing Textbook of Forensic Psychiatry*, Simon, R.I. and Gold, L.H., Eds., American Psychiatric Press, Washington, D.C., 2004, p. 329.
6. Gutheil, T.G. and Appelbaum, P.S., *Clinical Handbook of Psychiatry and the Law,* 3rd edition, Lippincott, Williams & Wilkins, Philadelphia, PA, 2000.
7. *Banks v. Goodfellow*, 5 QB 549 (1870).
8. Slovenko, R., Civil competency, in *The American Psychiatric Publishing Textbook of Forensic Psychiatry*, Simon, R.I. and Gold, L.H., Eds., American Psychiatric Press, Washington, D.C., 2004, p. 205.
9. *Guides to the Evaluation of Permanent Impairment,* 5th edition, Cocchiarella, L. and Andersson, G.B.J., Eds., AMA Press, Chicago, IL, 2000.
10. Danner, D. and Sagall, E.L., Medicolegal causation: A source of professional misunderstanding. *Am. J. Law Med.*, 3, 303, 1977.
11. Gerbasi, J.B., Forensic assessment in personal litigation, in *The American Psychiatric Publishing Textbook of Forensic Psychiatry*, Simon, R.I. and Gold, L.H., Eds., American Psychiatric Press, Washington, D.C., 2004, p. 231.
12. Green, N.D., Freedman, D.M., and Gordis, L., Reference guide on epidemiology, in *Reference Manual on Scientific Evidence,* 2nd edition, Federal Judicial Center, Washington, D.C., 2000.
13. Barton, W.A., *Recovering for Psychological Injuries,* 2nd edition, ATLA Press, Washington, D.C., 1990.
14. *Stafford v. Neurological Medicine, Inc.*, 811 F2d 470 (8th Cir. 1987).
15. *Fox-Kirk v. Hannon*, 542 S.E. 2d 346 (North Carolina. App. 2001).
16. Shuman, D.W., *Psychiatric and Psychological Evidence*, 2nd edition, West Group, New York, 2001.
17. Hall, R.E. and Lazear, V.A., Reference guide on estimation of economic losses in damages awards, in *Reference Manual on Scientific Evidence,* 2nd edition, Federal Judicial Center, Washington, D.C., 2000, p. 277.
18. *Immekus v. Quigg*, 406 S.W. 2d 298 (Mo. 1966).
19. *State v. Scott*, 189 S.W. 1191 (Missouri. App. 1916).

20. American Congress of Rehabilitation Medicine: Definition of mild traumatic brain injury. *J. Head Trauma Rehabil.*, 8, 86, 1993.
21. Williams, D.H., Levin, H.S., and Eisenberg, H.M., Mild head injury classification. *Neurosurgery*, 27, 422, 1990.
22. Iverson, G.L., Lange, R.T., Gaetz, M., et al., Mild TBI, in *Brain Injury Medicine: Principles and Practice*, Zasler, M.D., Katz, D.I., and Zafonte, R.D., Eds., Demos, New York, 2007, p. 333.
23. National Center for Injury Prevention and Control, *Report to Congress on Mild Traumatic Brain Injury in the United States: Steps to Prevent a Serious Public Health Problem.* Centers for Disease Control and Prevention, Atlanta, GA, 2003.
24. Carroll, L.J., Cassidy, J.D., Holm, L., et al., Methodological issues and research recommendations for mild traumatic brain injury: The WHO Collaborative Centre Task Force on Mild Traumatic Brain Injury. *J. Rehabil. Med.*, (43 Suppl.), 113, 2004.
25. Peloso, P.M., Carroll, L.J., Cassidy, J.D., et al., Critical evaluation of the existing guidelines in mild traumatic brain injury. *J. Rehabil. Med.* (43 Suppl.), 106, 2004.
26. Borg, J., Holm, L., Peloso, P.M., et al., Non-surgical intervention and cost for mild traumatic brain injury: Results of the WHO Collaborative Centre Task Force on Mild Traumatic Brain Injury. *J. Rehabil. Med.* (43 Suppl.), 76, 2004.
27. Borg, J., Holm, L., Cassidy, J.D., et al., Diagnostic procedures in mild traumatic brain injury: Results of the WHO Collaborative Centre Task Force on Mild Traumatic Brain Injury. *J. Rehabil. Med.* (43 Suppl.), 61, 2004.
28. Cassidy, J.D., Carroll, L.J., Peloso, P.M., et al., Incidence, risk factors, and prevention of mild traumatic brain injury: Results of the WHO Collaborative Centre Task Force on Mild Traumatic Brain Injury. *J. Rehabil. Med.* (43 Suppl.), 28, 2004.
29. Gennarelli, T.A., Thibault, L.E., Adams, J.H., et al., Diffuse axonal injury in traumatic coma in the primate. *Ann. Neurol.*, 12, 564, 1982.
30. Dikmen, S.S., Machamer, J.E., Winn, R., et al., Neuropsychological outcome one-year post head injury. *Neuropsychology*, 9, 80, 1995.
31. Collins, M.W., Iverson, G., Gaetz, M., et al., Sport-related concussion, in *Brain Injury Medicine: Principles and Practice*, Zasler, M.D., Katz, D.I., and Zafonte, R.D., Eds., Demos, New York, 2007, p. 407.
32. Elgmark, A.E., Emanuelson, I., Bjorklund, R., et al., Mild traumatic brain injuries: The impact of early intervention on late sequelae. A randomized control trial. *Acta Neurochir. (Wien)*, 149, 151, 2007.
33. Sadowski-Cron, C., Schneider, J., Senn, P., et al., Patients with mild traumatic brain injury: Immediate and long-term outcome compared to intra-cranial injuries on CT scan. *Brain Inj.*, 20, 1131, 2006.
34. Meares, S., Shores, E.A., Batchelor, J., et al., The relationship of psychological and cognitive factors and opioids in the development of postconcussion syndrome in general trauma patients with mild traumatic brain injury. *J. Int. Neuropsychol. Soc.*, 12, 792, 2006.
35. Iverson, G.L., Outcome from mild traumatic brain injury. *Curr. Opin. Psychiatry*, 18, 301, 2005.
36. Hessen, E., Nestvold, K., and Sundet, K., Neuropsychological function in a group of patients 25 years after sustaining minor head injuries as children and adolescents. *Scand. J. Psychol.*, 47, 245, 2006.
37. Nolin, P. and Heroux, L., Relations among sociodemographic, neurologic, clinical, and neuropsychological variables in vocational status following mild traumatic brain injury: A follow-up study. *J. Head Trauma Rehabil.*, 21, 514, 2006.
38. Feinstein, A., Ouchterlony, D., Somerville, J., et al., The effects of litigation on symptom expression: A prospective study following mild traumatic brain injury. *Med. Sci. Law*, 41, 116, 2001.
39. Reynolds, S., Paniak, C., Toller-Lobe, G., et al., A longitudinal study of compensation-seeking and return to work in a treated mild traumatic brain injury sample. *J. Head Trauma Rehabil.*, 18, 139, 2003.
40. Carroll, L.J., Cassidy, J.D., Peloso, P.M., et al., Prognosis for mild traumatic brain injury: Results of the WHO collaborative centre task force on mild traumatic brain injury. *J. Rehabil. Med.* (43 Suppl.), 84, 2004.
41. Iverson, G.L., Lange, R.T., and Franzen, N.D., Effects of mild traumatic brain injury cannot be differentiated from substance abuse. *Brain Inj.*, 19, 11, 2005.
42. Mooney, G., Speed, J., and Sheppard, S., Factors related to recovery after mild traumatic brain injury. *Brain Inj.*, 19, 975, 2005.

43. Belanger, H.G., Curtiss, G., Demery, J.A., et al., Factors moderating neuropsychological outcomes following mild traumatic brain injury: A meta-analysis. *J. Int. Neuropsychol. Soc.*, 11, 215, 2005.

44. Belanger, H.G. and Vanderploeg, R.D., The neuropsychological impact of sports-related concussions: A meta-analysis. *J. Int. Neuropsychol. Soc.*, 11, 345, 2005.

45. Ruff, R.M., Camenzuli, L., and Mueller, J., Miserable minority: Emotional risk factors that influence the outcome of a mild traumatic brain injury. *Brain Inj.*, 10, 551, 1996.

46. Kothari, S., Prognosis after severe TBI: A practical, evidence-based approach, in *Brain Injury Medicine: Principles and Practice*, Zasler, M.D., Katz, D.I., and Zafonte, R.D., Eds., Demos, New York, 2007, p. 169.

47. Katz, D.I. and Alexander, M.P., Traumatic brain injury: Predicting course of recovery and outcome for patients admitted to rehabilitation. *Arch. Neurol.*, 51, 661, 1994.

48. Greenwood, R., Value of recording duration of posttraumatic amnesia. *Lancet*, 349, 1041, 1997.

49. Levy, M.I., Masri, L.S., Lavine, S., et al., Outcome prediction after penetrating craniocerebral injury in a civilian population: Aggressive surgical management in patients with admission *Glasgow Coma Scale* scores of 3, 4, or 5. *Neurosurgery*, 35, 77, 1994.

50. van der Naalt, J., Prediction of outcome in mild to moderate head injury: A review. *J. Clin. Exp. Neuropsychol.*, 23, 837, 2001.

51. Stein, S.C., Outcome from moderate head injury, in *Neurotrauma*, Narayan, R.K., Wilberger, J.E., and Povlishock, J.T., Eds., McGraw-Hill, New York, 1996, p. 755.

52. Teasdale, G.M., Nicoll, J.A.R., Murray, G., et al., Association of apolipoprotein E polymorphism with outcome after head injury. *Lancet*, 350, 1069, 1997.

53. Friedman, G., Froom, P., Sazbon, L., et al., Apolipoprotein E ε4 genotype predicts a poor outcome in survivors of traumatic brain injury. *Neurology*, 52, 244, 1999.

54. Starkstein, S.E. and Jorge, R., Dementia after traumatic brain injury. *Int. Psychogeriatr.*, 17 (Suppl.), S93, 2005.

55. Mortimer, J.A., French, L.R., Hutton, J.T., et al., Head injury as a risk for Alzheimer's disease. *Neurology*, 35, 264, 1985.

56. Mortimer, J.A., van Duijn, C.M., Chandra, V., et al., Head trauma as a risk factor for Alzheimer's disease: A collaborative reanalysis of case-control studies. EURODEM Risk Factors Research Group. *Int. J. Epidemiol.*, 20 (Suppl. 2), S28, 1991.

57. Graves, A.B., White, E., Koepsell, T.D., et al., The association between head trauma and Alzheimer's disease. *Am. J. Epidemiol.*, 131, 491, 1990.

58. Mayeux, R., Ottman, R., Tang, M.X., et al., Genetic susceptibility in head injury as risk factors for Alzheimer's disease among community-dwelling elderly persons and their first degree relatives. *Ann. Neurol.*, 33, 494, 1993.

59. Diaz-Arrastia, R. and Baxter, V.K., Genetic factors and outcome after traumatic brain injury: What the human genome project can teach us about brain trauma. *J. Head Trauma Rehabil.*, 21, 361, 2006.

60. deGuise, E., LeBlanc, J., Feyz, N., et al., Prediction of outcome at discharge from acute care following traumatic brain injury. *J. Head Trauma Rehabil.*, 21, 527, 2006.

61. Nakamura, N., Yamaura, A., Shigemori, M., et al., Final report of the Japan Neurotrauma Databank project, 1998–2001: 1002 cases of traumatic brain injury. *Neurol. Med. Chir. (Tokyo)*, 46, 567, 2006.

62. LaBlanc, J., deGuise, E., Gosselin, N., et al., Comparison of functional outcome following acute care in young, middle-aged and elderly patients with traumatic brain injury. *Brain Inj.*, 20, 779, 2006.

63. Rassovsky, Y., Satz, P., Alfano, M.S., et al., Functional outcome in TBI I: Neuropsychological, emotional and behavioral mediators. *J. Clin. Exp. Neuropsychol.*, 28, 567, 2006.

64. Rassovsky, Y., Satz, P., Alfano, M.S., et al., Functional outcome in TBI II: Verbal memory and information processing speed mediators. *J. Clin. Exp. Neuropsychol.*, 28, 581, 2006.

65. Aarabi, B., Hesdorffer, D.C., Ahn, E.S., et al., Outcome following decompressive craniectomy from malignant swelling due to severe head injury. *J. Neurosurg.*, 104, 469, 2006.

66. Scheid, R., Walther, K., Guthke, T., et al., Cognitive sequelae of diffuse axonal injury. *Arch. Neurol.*, 63, 418, 2006.

67. Wilde, E.A., Bigler, E.D., Pedroza, C., et al., Post-traumatic amnesia predicts long-term cerebral atrophy in traumatic brain injury. *Brain Inj.*, 20, 695, 2006.

68. Bigler, E.D., Ryser, D.K., Gandhi, P., et al., Date-of-injury computed tomography, rehabilitation status, and development of cerebral atrophy in persons with traumatic brain injury. *Am. J. Phys. Med. Rehabil.*, 85, 793, 2006.

69. Atzema, C., Mower, W.R., Hoffman, J.R., et al., Prevalence and prognosis of traumatic intraventricular hemorrhage in patients with blunt head trauma. *J. Trauma*, 60, 1010, 2006.

70. Jorge, R.E., Acion, L., Starkstein, S.E., et al., Hippocampal volume in mood disorders after traumatic brain injury. *Biol. Psychiatry*, 62, 332, 2006.

71. Kraus, J.F., Rock, A., and Hemyari, P., Brain injuries among infants, children, adolescents, and young adults. *Am. J. Dis. Child*, 144, 684, 1990.

72. Berger, M.S., Pitts, L.H., Lovely, M., et al., Outcome from severe head injury in children and adolescents. *J. Neurosurg.*, 62, 194, 1985.

73. Luerssen, T.G., Klauber, N.R., and Marshall, L.F., Outcome from head injury related to patient's age: A longitudinal prospective study of adult and pediatric head injury. *J. Neurosurg.*, 68, 409, 1988.

74. Eiben, C.F., Anderson, T.P., Lockman, L., et al., Functional outcome of closed head injury in children and young adults. *Arch. Phys. Med. Rehabil.*, 65, 168, 1984.

75. Sockalosky, J.J., Kriel, R.L., Krach, L.E., et al., Precocious puberty after traumatic brain injury. *J. Pediatr.*, 110, 373, 1987.

76. Hurvitz, E.A., Mandac, B.R., Davidoff, G., et al., Risk factors for heterotopic ossification in children and adolescents with severe traumatic brain injury. *Arch. Phys. Med. Rehabil.*, 73, 459, 1992.

77. Greenspan, A.I. and Mackenzie, E.J., Functional outcome after pediatric head injury. *Pediatrics*, 94, 425, 1994.

78. Berger, E., Worgotter, G., and Oppolzer, A., Neurological rehabilitation in children and adolescents. *Pediatr. Rehabil.*, 4, 229, 1997.

79. Boyer, M.G. and Edwards, P., Outcome one to three years after severe traumatic brain injury in children and adolescents. *Injury*, 22, 315, 1991.

80. Tomlin, P., Clarke, M., Robinson, G., et al., Rehabilitation and severe head injury in children: Outcome and provision of care. *Dev. Med. Child Neurol.*, 44, 828, 2002.

81. Hawley, C.A., Ward, A.B., Magnay, A.R., et al., Children's brain injury: A postal follow-up of 525 children from one health region in the UK, *Brain Inj.*, 16, 969, 2002.

82. Sumich, A., Nelson, M.R., and McDeavitt, J.T., TBI: A pediatric perspective, in *Brain Injury Medicine: Principles and Practice*, Zasler, M.D., Katz, D.I., and Zafonte, R.D., Eds., Demos, New York, 2007, p. 305.

83. Kan, P., Amini, A., Hansen, K., et al., Outcomes after decompressive craniectomy for severe traumatic brain injury in children. *J. Neurosurg.*, 105 (5 Suppl.), 337, 2006.

84. Wilde, E.A., Hunter, J.V., Newsome, M.R., et al., Frontal and temporal morphometric findings on MRI in children after moderate to severe traumatic brain injury. *J. Neurotrauma*, 22, 333, 2005.

85. Wilde, E.A., Chu, Z., Bigler, E.D., et al., Diffusion tensor imaging in the corpus callosum in children after moderate to severe traumatic brain injury. *J. Neurotrauma*, 23, 1412, 2006.

86. Chung, C.Y., Chen, C.L., Cheng, P.T., et al., Critical score of Glasgow Coma Scale for pediatric traumatic brain injury. *Pediatr. Neurol.*, 34, 379, 2006.

87. Max, J.E., Lansing, A.E., Koele, S.L., et al., Attention deficit hyperactivity disorder in children and adolescents following traumatic brain injury. *Dev. Neuropsychol.*, 25, 159, 2004.

88. Keenan, H.T., Runyan, D.K., and Nocera, M., Child outcomes and family characteristics one year after severe inflicted or non-inflicted traumatic brain injury. *Pediatrics*, 117, 317, 2006.

89. Wade, S.L., Gerry-Taylor, H., Yeates, K.L., et al., Long-term parental and family adaptation following pediatric brain injury. *J. Pediatr. Psychol.*, 31, 1072, 2006.

90. Shuman, D.W., *Psychiatric and Psychological Evidence,* 3rd edition, Thompson-West, New York, 2005.

91. *People v. Cain*, 238 Mich. App. 95, 605 NW2d 28, 46 (1999).

92. *Landmark Medical Center v. Gauthier*, 635 A2d 1145 (Rhode Island, 1994).

93. Appelbaum, P.S. and Gutheil, T.G., *Clinical Handbook of Psychiatry and the Law*, 4th edition, Wolters Kluver/Lippincott Williams & Wilkins, Philadelphia, PA, 2007.

94. Appelbaum, P.S. and Roth, L.H., Clinical issues in the assessment of competency. *Am. J. Psychiatry*, 138, 1462, 1981.

95. Shuman, D.W., Competence in mental impairment, in *Retrospective Assessment of Mental States in Litigation: Predicting the Past*, Simon, R.I. and Shuman, D.W., Eds., American Psychiatric Press, Washington, D.C., 2002, p. 425.

96. Grisso, T. and Appelbaum, P.S., *Assessing Competence to Consent to Treatment: A Guide for Physicians and Other Health Professionals*, Oxford University Press, New York, 1998.

97. *Dusky v. United States*, 362, 402 (US 1960).
98. *Ford v. Wainwright*, 477, 399 (US 1986).
99. *Canterbury v. Spence*, 464 F2d 772 (DC Cir. 1972).
100. Quinn, K.M., The child witness, in *Clinical Handbook of Child Psychiatry and the Law*, Shetky, D.H. and Benedek, E.P., Eds., Williams & Wilkins, Baltimore, MD., 1992, p. 249.
101. Grisso, T., *Forensic Evaluation of Juveniles*, Professional Resource Press, Sarasota, FL, 1998.
102. *Guides to the Evaluation of Permanent Impairment,* 2nd edition, American Medical Association, Chicago, IL, 1984.
103. McDowell, I. and Newell, C., *Measuring Health: A Guide to Rating Scales and Questionnaires,* 2nd edition, Oxford University Press, New York, 1996.
104. McWhinnie, J.R., Disability assessment and population surveys: Results of the OECD common development effort. *Rev. Epidemiol. Sante Publique,* 29, 413, 1981.
105. Fries, J.F., Spitz, P.W., and Young, D.Y., The dimensions of health outcomes: The Health Assessment Questionnaire, disability and pain scales. *J. Rheumatol.,* 9, 789, 1982.
106. Hamilton, B.B., Granger, C.V., Sherwin, F.S., et al., A uniform national data system for medical rehabilitation, in *Rehabilitation Outcomes: Analysis and Measurement*, Fuhrer, M.J., Ed., Paul, H. Brooks, Baltimore, MD, 1987, p. 137.
107. Mahoney, F.I., Wood, O.H., and Barthel, D.W., Rehabilitation of chronically ill patients: The influence of complications and the final goal. *South. Med. J.,* 51, 605, 1958.
108. *Utah's 1997 Impairment Guides*, The Industrial Commission of Utah, Salt Lake City, 1997.
109. *Idaho Code*, Section 406 (1).
110. Morris, J.C., The Clinical Dementia Rating (CDR): Current version and scoring rules. *Neurology*, 43, 2412, 1993.
111. Brandt, E.N. and Pope, A.M., *Enabling America: Assessing the Role of Rehabilitation Science and Engineering*, National Academy Press, Washington, D.C., 1997.
112. *42 U.S.C.*, § 423.
113. Druss, B.G., Marcus, S.C., Rosenheck, R.A., et al., Understanding disability in mental and general medical conditions. *Am. J. Psychiatry*, 157, 1485, 2000.
114. Revised Medical Criteria for Evaluating Mental Disorders in Traumatic Brain Injury. Social Security Administration. Final Rules. *Fed. Regist.*, 65, 50746, 2000.
115. Social Security Ruling, SSR 98-1p; Tile XVI: Determining medical equivalents in childhood disability claims when a child has marked limitations in cognition and speech—SSA. Notice of Social Security Ruling. *Fed. Regist.*, 63, 15248, 1998.

11 Forensic Neurobehavioral Analysis of Traumatic Brain Injury Data

INTRODUCTION

In Chapter 8, the reader was introduced to the neurobehavioral analysis of clinical data regarding one's patient. This chapter takes a different view and focuses upon forensic issues in persons with traumatic brain injury (TBI) who are in litigation, applying for disability, have criminal charges against them, or where competency may be an issue. In Chapter 8, Chapters 1 through 7 were distilled into the essential elements necessary for examination of a patient following TBI, preparing an accurate diagnosis, and developing a treatment plan for the patient or his family. Recall in Chapter 9 critical differences between the neuropsychiatric examination for treatment were delineated from the neuropsychiatric examination for forensic purposes. Forensic neurobehavioral analysis within a legal context is primarily focused to determining causation, the nature of damages, and assisting the legal profession in a disposition of a case. Recall that the medical documents used to gather history in Chapter 3 are exactly the same medical documents that are used for gathering medical history in a forensic TBI evaluation. The goal of a forensic neurobehavioral analysis following TBI is to develop a forensic database upon which an examining expert may rely to provide sound opinions at trial or settlement, if requested.

This chapter presents three cases for analysis. The first case is a severely injured young college woman who had massive trauma to the center of the face, which secondarily produced brain trauma. The second case is a real-world situation that often arises. A young man developed a TBI following an assault and battery. During his neuropsychiatric examination for forensic purposes, he provided very poor cognitive and psychological effort, and yet there was overwhelming medical evidence that he had a permanent brain injury. The third case is instructive from the standpoint of malingering detection. It provides an interesting demonstration of how little clinical correlation is often present in a case of true faking.

ANALYSIS OF THE FORENSIC DATA FOLLOWING TRAUMATIC BRAIN INJURY

THE POLICE RECORD OR INJURY REPORT

Table 11.1 outlines a suggested schema for collecting data following TBI where forensic issues are raised. This data collection is extremely important and oftentimes of far greater importance in a forensic case than in a treatment case. The police report forms a basis for the initial gathering of factual information in issues of personal injury or criminal acts. For workers' compensation cases, it will be the employer's first report of injury. In competency issues or testamentary capacity, there generally is no police record or injury record, and the establishment of a medical history and life trajectory is the most important data to gather.

TABLE 11.1

Schema for Forensic Neuropsychiatric Data Collection and Review

Police report	This document is important to lawyers as it aids in establishing liability. For the forensic examiner, it aids in establishing causation of brain injury. Review for contributing factors: drugs, alcohol, violence, rape, etc.
Photographs	If the examinee was injured in a motor vehicle accident, what is the extent of obvious force applied to the victim's vehicle? Were photographs of the examinee's body obtained? What is the visual evidence of the trauma?
Ambulance report	Review for the Glasgow Coma Scale (GCS), Revised Trauma Score (RTS) and documentation of apparent injury. Did the GCS or RTS improve or worsen during transport? Was intubation required?
Emergency department	What were the GCS and RTS? Does neuroimaging aid in establishing causation? Do focal neurological signs or mental status changes aid in establishing causation? Was hospitalization required? If discharged from the E.D., were head injury instructions given? Was a follow-up with a neurologist or neurosurgeon ordered?
Hospital record	Was ICU required? Is there evidence of respiratory failure? Were secondary injuries present (e.g., hypovolemia, blood loss, cardiac or lung contusion, organ trauma or failure, etc.)?
Rehabilitation record	What was the "Rancho" score at discharge? Was there evidence of cognitive/behavioral impairment? Was speech/language therapy required? Could the examinee complete ADLs by discharge? Was neuropsychological assessment provided? Was assisted ventilation required? Were neuronal salvage medications administered?
Outpatient record	Is there evidence of posttraumatic seizures, headaches or hypersomnolence? Is focal neurologic dysfunction present? Was neuropsychological assessment obtained? Was the examinee independent in ADLs? Was speech/language therapy continued? Was psychiatric treatment required? Was there evidence of family or caregiver stress?
School record	An important marker of damages in the child is alteration or reduction in school performance. Was an individual educational plan required after brain injury? Was an educational diagnostic evaluation required?
Pre-injury records	These are important for determining damages due to intellectual changes, reduction in employability, change in work product, reduction of school performance or requirement for added medical treatments. These also are important in order to establish pre-injury conditions which may have been aggravated (e.g., learning disorder, ADHD, PTSD, etc.) or which contribute to a poorer outcome (e.g., Alzheimer's disease, prior brain injury, prior psychiatric illness, substance abuse, diabetes, etc.).

Where TBI is associated with vehicular accident, in every state in the United States a police report is required. Unless the injured party has left the scene of the accident before police were called, there is almost always a police record. The police record provides little medical information, but it is important to review, as it is a matter of record for issues of liability. For instance, which vehicle struck which vehicle? It is also important to review the police record in motor vehicle trauma to determine the amount of force involved in the accident. This is necessary for determination of clinical correlation in case the alleged outcome does not match the original evidence of injury. For instance, a recent case occurred when an attorney was driving her automobile in a parking lot. Her vehicle was bumped by an 86-year-old man driving his 84-year-old wife. The police were not called, and the elderly gentleman drove his vehicle home, then the lawyer drove her vehicle to the jail to interview a client. She traversed more than 10 miles through city streets making numerous turns and negotiating various stoplights. She then argued in a lawsuit that she had posttraumatic amnesia and a TBI. Thus, evidence of this type is extremely useful in determining clinical correlation and possible deception.

The police traffic accident report generally will give a location on the document that indicates the type of injury the examinee sustained. It generally lists whether or not the person required transport to a hospital, whether the examinee was wearing a restraint device, and whether airbags deployed. The police record will also describe how the accident scene was disposed, who transported the examinee from the accident site, and whether the vehicle remained in service or required a tow truck. This information can be very important to the neuropsychiatric examiner attempting to determine causation. In cases of significant injury, the police record will generally document the level of damage to the examinee's vehicle, whether mechanical extrication was required, and how the examinee was transported to the hospital. Many times the police officer will follow the examinee to the hospital and interview the person after medical treatment.

In workplace injuries, employers are required to document injury. This document will describe the nature of the accident, the location wherein it occurred at the workplace, whether witnesses observed the accident, and a general description of the nature of the injuries. The document usually describes the disposition and whether or not the person required emergency treatment or hospitalization. The document can be very useful, again for clinical correlation, where there is limited evidence of injury, for instance, if the person remained at the worksite and did not seek medical attention or the individual returned to her work shift. On the other hand, if a worker has been seriously injured, the record generally will adequately document that. When youngsters are injured at school, the school is required to write an injury report. This will provide very useful information to the neuropsychiatric examiner, and as in an employer's document, it will list the nature of the injury and how the child's condition was disposed.

INVESTIGATION FILE

Where an individual is injured in a criminal action, there is usually an investigation file on the nature of the injury. If the victim was seriously injured, the neuropsychiatric examiner can get the prosecutor's file in some jurisdictions but not others. Many states in the United States now have victims' advocates and victims' services. Those records should be available with the examinee's permission for review by the physician. This can provide substantial firsthand evidence and witness statements regarding the nature of the injury and how it transpired. If, on the other hand, the physician examiner is hired by a prosecutor in a case where an individual is claiming TBI interferes with criminal responsibility or competency to be tried, the physician will have access to the investigation file and will see all reports of police investigations and summaries, forensic laboratory data, and evidence of examination and treatment that the perpetrator may have received at the time of head injury.

PHOTOGRAPHS

Most police today take photographs of a motor vehicle accident scene, and those should be available to the physician examiner. Many times photographs are made of an individual who sustained significant facial trauma, and these are part of the medical record. Thus, the physician examining a person 18 months after a TBI may have firsthand photographic evidence of the nature of the injury. The reader may be interested in the case of E.L. noted below and the graphic features of the three-dimensional CT reconstruction of her facial fractures after trauma. Many times photographs are made of workplace events at the time of injury. Photographs may be available in criminal cases. The availability of photographs may be unknown to the physician examiner, and it is worthwhile asking the party who hired the physician to assist in determining whether photographs are available.

AMBULANCE REPORT

In cases of accidental injury, this is one of the most important records for the physician to review. This is generally the first recording of the Glasgow Coma Scale (GCS), which will be important in establishing the level of consciousness and function at the time of the alleged TBI. This record is also useful in determining whether there is a possibility of secondary injury (see Chapter 1). Did the injured party require intubation? Were paralytic drugs required? Did the person's GCS deteriorate during transport? Was the person confused, combative, or disoriented, or show other signs of cerebral injury? What is the nature of the Revised Trauma Score? Was there evidence of significant hypotension, blood loss, respiratory failure, abdominal injury, severe orthopedic injuries, or other signs in the physical assessment that might be consistent with secondary injury?

As has been discussed previously in this text regarding the GCS, the examiner should not be surprised if this scale does not correlate clinically with outcome. Also, it is important to remember that an individual can have GCS score of 15 and yet still sustain a mild traumatic brain injury (MTBI). On the other hand, a person can score a GCS score of 3, be in coma or unconscious, and not have sustained a TBI at all (e.g., blood loss syncope). Good analysis is required to be clear about the value of the GCS from the ambulance report.

The usefulness of emergency medical services cannot be overstated regarding the benefit to victims of TBI. The American College of Surgeons first developed criteria for the establishment of Level 1 trauma centers in the United States and further developed a trauma system based on regional needs.[1] The Joint Section of Trauma of the American Association of Neurological Surgeons and the Congress of Neurological Surgeons supported these original criteria and they have further endorsed the establishment of regional neurotrauma centers throughout the United States.[2] Research studies have shown a marked reduction in the incidence of preventable deaths as a result of trauma since the establishment of these centers.[3,4] Unfortunately, not all citizens live near a Level 1 trauma center. Even if the destination hospital is not a designated trauma center, outcome is enhanced with the use of the acute central nervous system injury clinical pathway, in which an emergency physician, neuroradiologist, neurosurgeon, and intensivist are promptly available as the victim reaches the emergency department.[5,6] Generally ambulance transport is used within a 50-mi radius of injury, assuming the roadway traffic is not a limiting factor in transport time. Helicopter transport is often used for distances between 51 and approximately 150–200 mi, while a fixed-wing aircraft may be used for longer distances in very large states, when available, after the ambulance transports the person to an airport.[7] As the physician reviews the ambulance and EMS records, he should carefully evaluate the various forms of therapy provided in the field. Multiple studies have shown that having physicians in the field is no advantage whatsoever unless the person is in cardiac arrest, and that prompt delivery of a TBI patient to a neurointensive facility gives the best chance for good recovery to the patient.[7]

EMERGENCY DEPARTMENT RECORDS

After the patient arrives in the emergency department, the GCS will be repeated. The neuropsychiatric examiner should review this record carefully. It is important to detect whether there has been a diminishment in the level of consciousness during transport by the emergency medical services. Also, this may be the last GCS available. From a forensic standpoint, the GCS, while not predictive of outcome, does give the examiner in a forensic situation a reasonable window to know the victim's mental state and neurological state at the time emergency services were provided. Recall from the discussion of mild head injury in Chapter 10, most patients with mild head injury will have GCS scores of 13–15. Also, it is not unusual for a person who has sustained a mild head trauma to have GCS score of 14 at the accident scene and have all subsequent GCS scores equal 15.

As discussed in Chapter 5, the initial neuroimaging examination will almost always be CT of the head. The CT scan should be reviewed. In a forensic situation, it is probably wise for the examiner to obtain a CD of the original CT (most radiology departments in the United States today do not use film, and images are now in digital format). The CT of the head will reveal pathology if present, in most instances (review Chapter 5 if necessary). If the CT does not demonstrate pathology, and the GCS score is equal to 15, the examiner has evidence that at worse the individual sustained an MTBI or concussion. This is important to document by examining emergency department records, as if litigation ensues, it is not unusual for the examiner to find over time embellishment of the alleged level of injury. As the examinee goes from examination to examination, the symptoms become progressively worse, which is not consistent with the known clinical course of MTBI. If the head trauma is mild, the victim is generally discharged to home from the emergency department. Review the latter part of the emergency department record carefully. It is important to note whether or not the person was sent home with a head injury sheet, and it is also important to note whether follow-up examinations were made with a neurosurgeon or neurologist. If these are absent, this indicates a low likelihood that any significant brain injury occurred. Obviously, a person with known or suspected brain trauma of significant proportions will be admitted to hospital.

THE HOSPITAL RECORD

If the individual is admitted to hospital, this record should be scrutinized carefully. The first items to determine are whether or not the person has secondary injury factors which may have contributed to or exacerbated the TBI. For instance, was intubation required? Was it necessary for the individual to be placed in a neurointensive care unit? Was there evidence of substantial orthopedic injuries producing complications to the patient (see Chapters 1 and 2)? What is the evidence of other consultants? Was speech pathology consulted? Were neurological services required? Did the individual develop markers of substantial brain trauma such as hypothalamic and pituitary failure, diabetes insipidus syndrome, or was a prolonged coma evident? Was there evidence of focal neurological signs? Was there evidence of pulmonary or cardiac contusion, injury to abdominal organs, or other injuries contributing to the morbidity of the patient?

The nursing records and neurointensive care flow sheet records will be very important to the neuropsychiatric examiner in an effort to determine length of posttraumatic amnesia. Conversations between the patient and hospital personnel may be revealing of the cognitive state, level of ability to communicate, and other signs of cognitive importance. Oftentimes if the individual is in a life-threatening situation, explicit statements about cognitive status may not be documented, and the neuropsychiatric examiner will need creativity to glean from the record the probable cognitive state of the individual and the time line of the neurobehavioral status of the patient. Neurointensivists and neurosurgeons are concerned with the welfare of their patient, the improvement in health of the patient, and avoidance of death; they therefore may pay little attention to cognitive status.

REHABILITATION RECORDS

If the patient sustained a serious injury and is poorly ambulatory or unable to meet activities of daily living, she will be referred to a rehabilitation facility after inpatient hospitalization. The intake examination generally will be performed by a physiatrist skilled in TBI, and the physiatrist will focus upon the individual's cognitive status, neurological status, and dependency needs. It is at this point in the review of records that the neuropsychiatric examiner likely will begin finding medical evidence of cognitive status. Usually a significantly brain-injured person is not able to provide sufficient information to hospital healthcare personnel to determine cognitive status, and only at the point of rehabilitation is the person verbal and communicative enough to obtain an accurate assessment of cognitive status. At the rehabilitation facility, records often will appear from occupational therapists, speech pathologists, physiatrists, and psychologists. These records can be most useful within the context of a forensic neuropsychiatric examination, particularly in determining a clinical correlation between the person's mental state in the rehabilitation facility and mental state at the time of the neuropsychiatric examination. Refer again to Chapter 1, which outlines the Rancho Los Amigos Scale.[8] This 8-point scale will enable the neuropsychiatric examiner to understand the patient's ability to meet daily living needs at the time of discharge.

The rehabilitation records also will enable the neuropsychiatric examiner to determine whether elements of aggression and agitation are present. These may be predictive of future cognitive and behavioral complications. Also, if psychotropic agents are used such as cognitive enhancers, stimulants, or dopamine agonists, the rehabilitation hospital is probably the location where these will be introduced to the patient first. At this facility, the neuropsychiatric examiner should be able to find evidence of musculoskeletal and medical needs such as complications due to spasticity, dysphagia, inability to eat, bowel and bladder difficulties, respiratory impairment, orthopedic impairment, neuroendocrine disorders, dysautonomia, and other potential complications as a result of TBI.[9]

NEUROPSYCHOLOGY RECORDS

Within the rehabilitation facility is probably the first time the patient will be sufficiently cognitively aware that neuropsychological assessment can be made. This often will be brief, as a significantly injured person cannot sustain a 1- or 2-day neuropsychological assessment at this point. Be aware also that litigation may already be in place during the time the person is in the rehabilitation facility. That is not to say the patient will necessarily be aware of this, but lawyers and family members may already be involved to assist the patient at this point. Therefore, if neuropsychological assessment is made, a careful scrutiny of the record is required, as in most instances cognitive effort measures are not made at rehabilitation. The neuropsychologist in a rehabilitation center is not concerned about potential litigation. Even though good psychological practice recommends that cognitive effort be measured at the time cognitive tests are administered, this is not always done at rehabilitation facilities, and the neuropsychiatric examiner should carefully evaluate the record to see whether or not this was completed. Also, the neuropsychology examination during rehabilitation can have important ramifications during a litigation process. If the neuropsychiatric examiner discovers that neuropsychological test results worsen 1 year after injury when compared to a neuropsychological assessment made 6 weeks after injury in a rehabilitation facility, suspicion should be high that poor effort or litigation factors are involved.

It is important to be aware that a neuropsychological assessment made within the first 6 months of recovery following TBI, may not be predictive of eventual outcome. It also is not a precise baseline, as the brain is in a state of recovery (see Chapter1), and the recovery trajectory is producing a positive slope on the recovery time line. This must be taken into account when data from the neuropsychological assessment in a rehabilitation center is compared to neuropsychological data obtained 1 or 2 years post-injury. Also, a neuropsychological assessment made at the time of rehabilitation is usually limited, and the examiner should determine if all cognitive domains were assessed at the time of examination. The psychology records should be scrutinized carefully to determine if scores were prorated and if certain measures were not made but then statistically predicted observations were entered into the record. This, of course, is not the same as a direct measurement, and for forensic purposes, prorated measures should not be used. If the patient is severely injured, most neuropsychologists will perform a limited examination during rehabilitation.[10]

OUTPATIENT TREATMENT

Within the context of a forensic examination, this is another area where the neuropsychiatric examiner must be most careful. In a patient who may spuriously produce evidence of a TBI, the development of that information will likely occur well after hospitalization. This is most likely to occur with MTBI and not moderate or severe TBI. In the MTBI case, the neuropsychiatric examiner should be particularly wary if multiple and extensive evaluations are made by examiners hired by the plaintiff's lawyer. Obviously, any citizen who brings a claim to court has a right to have his or her own examination. However, many of these examiners have strong relationships with a national network of TBI advocates. Many so-called brain advocacy groups were initiated by plaintiff lawyers not by physicians or healthcare providers. For instance, if the initial injury records indicate minimal chance of significant TBI but yet the plaintiff brings forth a multimillion dollar claim for damages, immediate suspicion should be aroused. If reviewing the emergency department records indicates that the individual had a slight laceration to the head, no obvious loss of consciousness, no focal neurological findings, and no requirement for any significant treatment or admission to hospital, these findings are inconsistent with moderate or severe TBI.

For the truly injured patient, it is important not to overlook treatments that occur following rehabilitation. These include prolonged physical therapy, continuing speech and language therapy, cognitive rehabilitation, and efforts to address orthopedic and other comorbid injuries. With regard to a neuropsychiatric examination, the forensic examiner should focus particularly upon psychiatric or psychological data within outpatient records. It is important to establish within the psychiatric-psychological database if there is evidence that the individual had a pre-injury psychiatric illness that may currently play a role in the claim of cognitive and behavioral disturbance following alleged TBI. For instance, if the individual showed evidence of previous repeated treatments for depression, antisocial personality disorder, or prior posttraumatic stress disorder (PTSD), significant inquiry will be required in order to apportion pre-injury factors from post-injury factors.

Outpatient needs will be particularly important as the forensic examiner develops a damages assessment. The needs of the patient following a moderate or severe TBI may be significant, and the outpatient records will provide markers for the forensic examiner in order to develop a damages database. Review of neurological records is most important. Is there evidence of posttraumatic seizures, focal neurological injuries, or residual effects from neurosurgical procedures? Is there consistency in histories given to outpatient providers after alleged TBI? If the forensic examiner finds significant variance in histories given to various treating doctors versus examiners hired by the plaintiff attorney, it will be necessary to determine carefully at the time of the neuropsychiatric examination what is the basis for these inconsistencies. It is not unusual to find an embellishment in the historical record of outpatient treatment following the filing of a lawsuit.

In the truly injured patient, the outpatient record will be most important for the forensic examiner to develop neuropsychiatric data that can be used by a life care planner if the TBI patient is going to require long-term needs. Obviously, if at the time of the neuropsychiatric examination, the forensic examiner observes an individual with a left hemiparesis requiring leg braces, ambulation devices, and assistance with activities of daily living, it will be important to provide to the life care planner information about this person that can be used to properly compensate the individual for damages. The damages will be long-term and lifelong in most instances.

The outpatient record will be of significant assistance to the forensic examiner to determine whether there is evidence of upper airway dysfunction, swallowing dysfunction, need for orthotic devices, need for devices to assist with transfers, or other substantial environmental needs that the patient may have. Can the individual function independently? Can the individual prepare his own meals or see to his health and safety needs? Can the individual operate an automobile? Is there evidence since the injury that the individual has required assessment for driving skills? In a child, are there substantial academic needs present? Are tutors needed?

ANALYSIS OF THE FORENSIC NEUROPSYCHIATRIC DATABASE

After the examinee has left the forensic examiner's office, it is wise to reflect carefully on each element of the neuropsychiatric examination. One should start at the beginning, and as is true with most medical practice, one should start with the history. The history obtained will contain two major elements useful in the data analysis. The first element is the history reported directly to the forensic examiner by the examinee. The second major history is the one developed by the forensic physician during collection of all data from all sources, independent of information obtained during the face-to-face interview of the examinee. These data will include medical records of the accident and its aftermath, pre-injury medical records, information from collateral sources, academic, military, and employment records, prior legal records, current legal records (if this is a criminal examination in particular), and depositions that have been taken in the case since the injury.

As has been stressed repeatedly in this text, the forensic examiner should ask some important questions: Does the neuropsychiatric examination data clinically correlate with the allegation of TBI? Do the expressed symptoms of the examinee clinically correlate with an expected outcome of TBI? Was the effort during cognitive and psychological testing of good validity? Does the mental status examination demonstrate elements consistent with TBI? Does analysis of the treatment records corroborate a TBI? Is there evidence from the examinee, or the examinee lawyer's theories, that the legal claims do not clinically correlate with the medical evidence? Does the neurological examination clinically correlate with the examinee's claims? Does brain imaging clinically correlate with medical evidence in the original treatment records and the claims of the examinee? Does the neuropsychological test data obtained by the forensic examiner clinically correlate with the claims of the examinee, neuroimaging, and the treatment medical record? The forensic examiner should be able to see where this analysis is going. All potential questions cannot be listed in this text, and it requires creativity on the physician's part to develop rhetorical questions after the neuropsychiatric examination on a case by case basis depending on the nature of the particular alleged injury.

While neuroimaging is not a *sine qua non* of TBI assessment, it is the only objective finding that cannot be manipulated by the examinee (except in functional neuroimaging). Thus, structural neuroimaging, such as CT and magnetic resonance imaging (MRI), and functional neuroimaging, such as magnetic resonance spectroscopy (MRS), cannot be manipulated by the patient, as they are not subject to issues of blood flow or metabolism. Plaintiff attorneys always ask a simple question if the facts are not on their side or there is limited evidence that their client truly sustained a TBI. That question is: "Doctor, isn't it possible that a person can have a TBI and show no evidence of injury on CT or MRI?" The obvious answer is, yes. This places the forensic examiner back into the major gray area that occurs in MTBI litigation (see Chapter 10). Thus, it will be at the jury's discretion, if the case is tried, whether the plaintiff lawyer's theories and demands for compensation are consistent with a TBI in most MTBI cases. The remainder of this chapter will focus the forensic examiner on other sources of important information and assist with the elucidation of causation and damages analysis during a forensic neuropsychiatric examination. Representative cases are used to assist the forensic examiner in determining issues of significant forensic importance.

COLLATERAL HISTORY SOURCES

Collateral sources may or may not be needed during a forensic neuropsychiatric examination. The examination type that most likely requires collateral sources is the criminal forensic neuropsychiatric examination. That would be the examination where an individual sustained a TBI at some time prior to a criminal act and then claims in court that he is either not competent to be tried or lacks the responsibility for the crime by virtue of the TBI. This is a complex evaluation that requires first a complete neuropsychiatric examination to see if brain injury can be verified. A second analysis is required to determine mental competency to be tried, responsibility for the crime, or both, depending on the needs of the defendant's lawyer or the court. Collateral information might come from interviews of family members, potentially eyewitnesses, or other persons who may come forward to assist with the examination. The second most likely TBI forensic neuropsychiatric examination that would need collateral information is with the child. Parents or guardians at a minimum should be interviewed within the context of a child forensic neuropsychiatric examination. The child who is claiming brain injury in a civil court may speak directly with the neuropsychiatric examiner, but since the child is not of legal age, it would also be necessary to speak with one or more parents, grandparents, or other legal guardians.

When collateral information is taken during a forensic neuropsychiatric examination, it must be weighted by the forensic examiner as to its usefulness, veracity, and overall assistance to the examination. Many times collateral informants have a vested interest in the outcome of the case, and therefore they may skew the information they provide to the forensic examiner. An injured male worker who is asserting a TBI from a fall at work may ask the forensic examiner to speak with his wife. He may or may not have sustained a TBI, and she may have a vested interest in assisting him either in gaining compensation or disability. The same can be said for parents of a small child. The child will be ill-equipped and unable to provide the necessary information to the examiner, and the entire examination could be skewed by the parents. That is not to say that either of these scenarios will occur, but certainly the forensic examiner must provide a thorough and comprehensive examination keeping in mind at all times that it is difficult for plaintiffs bringing a lawsuit, or defendants attempting to avoid responsibility of a crime, not to be biased to their own best interests.

PRE-INJURY MEDICAL RECORDS

These records will have great importance in a forensic examination, relative to a treatment examination. In a civil action, the plaintiff claiming a TBI may have had a psychiatric condition or a prior TBI, which has a direct bearing on causation and damages. Therefore, the forensic examiner should review any pre-injury medical records that are available. In a workers' compensation claim, in some states, the employer is not responsible for preexisting conditions, and if a worker sustains a TBI on the job, a preexisting condition may reduce the compensation due to them for a work injury. The same can be said in a civil suit for TBI in a motor vehicle accident. If the individual was struck as a pedestrian at age 15 and sustained a right frontal brain contusion, that may play a direct role in causation and damages of a motor vehicle accident occurring to them at age 37 producing an alleged TBI.

Other items to consider are pre-injury neuroimaging. Particularly in older persons who may have sustained a TBI, it is important to gain insight from pre-injury neuroimaging that might show evidence of cortical atrophy, alcoholic neurodegeneration, white matter gliosis or microangiopathy, hippocampal atrophy from severe bipolar illness, etc. The forensic examiner should see the importance of reviewing these pre-injury records.

ACADEMIC AND EMPLOYMENT RECORDS

The reader may wish to review Chapter 6 wherein it was discussed how to determine pre-injury cognitive capacity. In other words, the cognitive baseline of the individual prior to injury must be determined. This is critically important in a civil lawsuit where an alleged victim is claiming TBI. As has been noted in previous portions of this text, academic information may provide ACT or SAT score. Military records may contain cognitive scores. The employment record may allow one to determine work product. For instance, if the plaintiff in a TBI lawsuit is an attorney, it would be worthwhile for the forensic examiner to review pre-injury briefs or other legal information written by the attorney in an effort to determine pre-injury cognitive capacity. This is particularly important when the forensic examiner is evaluating a person of high intelligence, high education, or high level of professional skill. The pre-injury work product may be as useful, or more useful, in helping the forensic examiner develop a pre-injury cognitive baseline than anything else available.

Many defense lawyers place great emphasis on a person's grades in an effort to determine pre-injury cognitive capacity. While these are useful, they are not as useful as metrics. They will not supplant ACT scores, SAT scores, military entrance examination scores, GRE scores, and other nationally standardized metrics. School grades contain a significant motivational component. Most physicians recall that some of their colleagues in medical school were brilliant but yet produced mediocre grades. On the other hand, some of their less intellectually endowed medical school colleagues made superior grades by overwork. Therefore, grades must be weighted as they are not a direct metric of cognitive capacity, and they are subject to bias.

Employment records can provide other significant and useful information in a forensic examination. Sometimes a plaintiff may omit a preexisting medical condition that is not otherwise detectable. However, most corporations hiring individuals require an employment medical history so that the worker can obtain medical insurance. It is very useful at times to find that employment medical document, as it oftentimes contains accurate information about the person's pre-injury medical history that may not be available from other sources. School records often contain important demographic variables or information about learning struggles that a youngster experienced while in elementary or high school. These may be useful factors in establishing a pre-injury cognitive baseline. Moreover, school records will contain psychological and cognitive assessment of youngsters if they were referred for school-based assistance with tutors, special education, or if they sustained a childhood injury that affected their learning capacity.

LEGAL RECORDS

Legal records may or may not have relevance in a forensic neuropsychiatric TBI examination. They, of course, will have great relevance if the examination is within the context of a criminal evaluation. With regard to a civil suit for brain injury, they could provide useful information with regard to personality and pre-injury behavior. For instance, if an individual has a long history of legal conflicts due to alcohol-induced misbehavior, this record would be highly relevant to the forensic examination. Also, legal records may enable the forensic examiner to determine how aggressive the individual was prior to injury and whether there are markers for physical violence. Recall elsewhere in this text that aggression and physical violence before brain injury is highly predictive of the same behaviors after brain injury. Thus, an apportionment might need to be made. Legal records may enable a forensic examiner to determine whether this individual is a litigious person. Do they have a prior history of separate lawsuits in different years for "slip-and-falls" in department stores? If the examinee is in a civil lawsuit for TBI occurring by motor vehicle accident or other civil action, the examiner should not forget to inquire about prior workers' compensation records. These may be very useful in helping to determine the presence of pre-injury TBI or head injury, and those records might not be available with an ordinary request for medical records. Sometimes workers' compensation records are separate and apart from ordinary medical records.

MILITARY RECORDS

Military records have two basic uses in a forensic neuropsychiatric examination. They are useful first for determining preexisting personality problems. The individual may have been expelled from the military, discharged as unfit for military duty, court marshaled due to aggressive or substance-abusing behavior, or for other reasons that are relevant to the individual's pre-injury personality state. Military records can be quite revealing in this regard. The examiner should understand that it may take months to acquire these records in the United States, and it is not an efficient process. The second major use of the military records is to obtain the scores from the military entrance examination. These scores are based on national norms, and they carry the same predictive weight of cognitive capacity as SAT or ACT scores. They are quite useful for the determination of pre-injury cognitive capacity.

DEPOSITIONS

Depositions are sworn testimony taken in the context of a legal action, and they carry the same weight as if testimony were made directly to a jury or a judge. They are very useful to the forensic examiner in determining facts that may be missed by interview or record review alone. Moreover, the context of a deposition is entirely different than the context of a forensic medical examination. History taken by the forensic examiner is not evidence to be directly entered at court, since it is not sworn to be true. On the other hand, a deposition is fact evidence that can be introduced directly to a court of a law, and it is assumed to be true since the deponent swore that it was true. It is a much more powerful information from a fact standpoint than a medical history. In a TBI examination, the most useful information to be gained from a deposition is that it is an indirect mental status examination. If a person alleges injury from a rear-end collision while sitting in her vehicle at a stoplight and then provides a 4 h grueling cross-examination testimony, it is difficult to conclude that she sustained any significant brain injury, particularly any that affects verbal ability or set switching ability. The forensic examiner can gain significant information by careful review of a plaintiff's deposition looking particularly at the major elements of language, executive function, and memory as discussed in Chapter 4. How well did the deponent handle mentally the questions posed by the cross-examining attorney? Could the examinee (deponent) follow the logic of the questions as presented by the attorney? Is there evidence that the answers were circumstantial or tangential? Was the deponent able to spend long periods of time answering questions to the lawyers, or is there evidence that the deponent tired easily and required a break every 15 or 20 min? One of the greatest strengths of the deposition is that it enables the forensic examiner to determine if there are inconsistencies in what the examinee expressed during sworn testimony versus what the examinee expressed during medical history taking.

In terms of causation analysis, depositions of witnesses and bystanders to an accident are extremely helpful. Again, these may provide evidence that the examinee provided inconsistent history. They may provide evidence that the alleged injury was so slight that no reasonable person would be expected to have sustained a brain injury. On the other hand, they may confirm that the examinee was extremely confused and combative after the injury, and they may further confirm that cognitive capacity and physical ability were seriously compromised immediately after the injury.

CAUSATION ANALYSIS

The reader should review the information in Chapter 9. Causation analysis is a civil issue and not a criminal issue. Causation refers to the legal term proximate cause. In a civil legal case, liability must be established first. The forensic examiner usually has no role to play in the determination of liability. For instance, in a motor vehicle accident, an accident reconstruction engineer, highway engineer, or other such person may establish whether or not a particular actor was negligent in striking the plaintiff's motor vehicle. Police information is also used to assist in the determination of liability. If liability is proved at court, then the neuropsychiatric physician may be asked to testify regarding issues of causation with regard to TBI. If the physician has been hired by the plaintiff's lawyer, this individual would be interested in establishing a proximate cause of the brain injury, if one exists. If hired by the defense lawyer, this physician will attempt to demonstrate medically that there is no proximate cause to the allegation of TBI. The original concept of proximate cause is traced to Lord Chancellor Bacon and is found in the Law of Torts.[11] Law school dean, William Prosser noted that the term proximate cause is confusing and suggests that it is best to use terms such as legal cause and perhaps even responsible cause. The physician does not need to concern himself or herself with these issues, but it is worthwhile knowing the legal mechanics of their use.

From a medical standpoint, causation is usually fairly simple to determine in a brain injury case. Even in an allegation of MTBI where causation is fairly simple to determine, the problem arises with the determination of damages, outcomes, and needs for long-term care. With regard to a straight-forward TBI, the causation will be established again by reviewing the original medical record. The physician should start at the scene of the injury with the EMS report. If information in the EMS report is consistent that an injury occurred as described, then that is the initial point for determination of causation. The physician will probably want to review police records, eyewitness statements, and other information in order to verify the physical aspects of the injury that caused the EMS to be called to the scene. The importance of reviewing these initial records cannot be overemphasized. If a patient is then taken straightaway to an emergency department and there is an obvious right frontal brain hematoma, then there is incontrovertible medical evidence that the facts at the accident scene will support. With regard to MTBI, the issues are less clear. However, the original injury records will be most helpful in delineation of causation of an alleged MTBI. As a case in point, if an individual is in a motor vehicle accident and claims a year later a MTBI, the records may show a low likelihood that one existed. For instance, if the physician reviews the police record and finds that the plaintiff spoke directly to the police officer at the scene, was ambulatory and walking around his car inspecting for damage, and provided a lengthy witness statement to the police officer, it can be reasonably demonstrated factually that no significant brain injury occurred.

TABLE 11.2

Records Useful for Determining Causation or Damages

The Record	Primary Forensic Uses
Police report	Causation
Injury report	Causation, deception, detection
Emergency medical services	Causation
Hospitalization	Causation, damages
Rehabilitation/outpatient	Causation, damages
Neuropsychological	Causation, damages, deception detection
Neuropsychiatric	Causation, damages, deception detection
Collateral sources	Causation, damages
Pre-injury documents	Causation, deception detection
Academic/employment	Causation, damages
Legal records	Causation, deception detection
Military records	Causation, deception detection
Depositions	Causation, deception detection

Recall from the discussion above regarding mental status information within a deposition. This likewise is mental status information within the context of the police record. The same can be said for the EMS record. If this same individual provided a complete health history to the EMS squad, was not confused, did not require restraint, and was transported to an emergency department as an exercise in caution, then the physician should find no significant evidence that a TBI occurred. If the emergency department record confirms that there were no focal neurological findings, the plaintiff gave his own history to the physician, neuroimaging was without evidence of lesions, and he was discharged from the emergency department to home with a prescription for acetaminophen, then the facts support that there is not a probable TBI. (Recall that in the law, physicians testify using the standard of reasonable medical probability). Be prepared for the plaintiff's lawyer to ask, "Doctor, isn't it possible this individual sustained a TBI?" The answer to this is, of course, yes. However, the possibility has no value before the law, only probability is acceptable.

Table 11.2 provides useful information for the value of various records following TBI. Some records are useful for causation analysis, whereas other records are useful for damages analysis or the detection of deception and inconsistent history. Table 11.3 provides simple steps for the

TABLE 11.3

Analysis of Brain Injury Medical Causation

Early records: police, emergency services, injury reports, and emergency department evaluation	Does the police report document an injury to the head or body? Do the EMS records document alterations of behavior or cognition and evidence of trauma or injury? Is an injury report consistent with trauma? Does the emergency department document mental, neurological, or brain imaging abnormalities? Are the medical deficits continuously and temporally related to the trauma?
Intermediate records: hospital, outpatient, rehabilitation, and neuropsychological	Was hospitalization required as a direct result of trauma? Is outpatient or rehabilitation treatment a direct result of the trauma? Is neuropsychological assessment completed as a direct result of the trauma?
Is there an intervening cause?	Did another trauma or disease occur between the original trauma and the date of the neuropsychiatric examination?
Is there a pre-injury cause or contributing factor?	Is there a pre-injury psychiatric or neurological disease which better accounts for the present psychiatric or cognitive complaints? Has a pre-injury condition been exacerbated by the trauma?

physician examiner to use while making a medical causation analysis of data from a neuro-psychiatric examination. There are some pitfalls of which the physician should be aware when making a causation analysis. There are a number of head injuries occurring each year that come to the attention of an emergency department wherein a TBI is not diagnosed either due to lack of skill on the part of the physician, or the individual had other significant injuries that precluded detection of the TBI at the time of examination. Other important factors to consider are that many individuals may be left with a residual cognitive symptomatology from a blow to the head when the GCS score at the scene was measured to be 15. Recall from Chapter 1 that a GCS score of 15 does not equate to "normal." It is the highest score obtainable on the GCS, but it is not an absolute measure of whether injury occurred. However, the early records (police, EMS, and emergency department) are the most important for determining causation of TBI unless it can be conclusively demonstrated that a TBI was overlooked initially.

DAMAGES ANALYSIS

Damages analysis will be discussed in much more detail within the context of the three cases provided within the remainder of this chapter. The reader may wish to review Chapter 10 with regard to damages. Outcome analysis is the primary contributor to the medical assessment of damages following TBI, and these are discussed at length in Chapter 10. It is the damages analysis to which the neuropsychiatric examiner will provide the greatest contribution to a court in TBI litigation.

If asked to testify, it is expected that the forensic examiner will provide significant medical information regarding damages. This should be most useful to the trier of fact (judge or jury) as to the effects and outcomes of the residual brain injury and the impact upon the plaintiff and family members. Recall from prior information in chapters beforehand that the primary determinant of damages is twofold: (1) the impact of measured deficits upon daily functioning and (2) the costs associated with providing medical services directly related to the TBI. This information should be provided within the examining physician's report, and if oral testimony is required, it should be provided in a clear and succinct manner. The issue before the court is one of ecological validity: "How do the TBI deficits affect the plaintiff's ability to function socially, personally, and occupationally?" Table 11.4 provides a short schema for analysis of brain injury damages.

For example, an examinee who has sustained a substantial frontal brain injury, and who demonstrates significant executive dysfunction, may appear perfectly normal sitting in a courtroom in front

---

TABLE 11.4
Analysis of Brain Injury Damages

What is the medical evidence of damage?	What symptoms does the examinee express? What is abnormal in the mental status examination? Are there focal neurological findings? Are there neuropsychological deficits consistent with brain injury? Do the medical records document neuropsychiatric injury? Is there brain imaging evidence of injury? Is malingering or symptom magnification absent?
Can the damage be quantified?	Can the deficits be measured and compared to a normative database? Can an accurate pre-injury cognitive and behavioral baseline be established in the examinee?
How do deficits affect daily cognitive, behavioral, social, and occupational function?	Can the examinee attend, remember, use language, demonstrate executive function, and remain oriented? Can the examinee maintain normal mood, display appropriate behavior, communicate normally, and think rationally? Can the examinee relate to others, function in a social setting, and maintain relationships? Can the examinee maintain work pace, complete tasks, and maintain behavior in a work setting?

of a jury. Even while he testifies, the average layman may note little wrong with the individual. Thus, it is incumbent upon the examining physician to communicate effectively to the trier of fact the components of an executive disorder and how that translates to impairment of daily functioning. The disturbances of goal setting, planning, future memory, response inhibition, modulation of behavior, self monitoring, and other features of dysexecutive syndromes should be explained in a narrative fashion such that a layman can understand how these deficits preclude normal functioning. This requires much greater skill on the part of the examining physician than presenting a patient to a jury with an obvious left hemiparesis and structural deformities of the head as a result of skull fractures.

CASE 11.1:   SEVERE CENTRAL FACIAL FRACTURES RESULTING IN TRAUMATIC BRAIN INJURY

This case demonstrates how impact to the central face can also result in TBI. As the reader can see in Figure 11.1, this young woman sustained very severe trauma to the center of her face sufficient to tear away the anterior maxilla and crush the central portion of the facial bones. She sustained substantial TBI as well.

HISTORY FROM THE MEDICAL RECORDS

E.L. was 18 years old at the time of this accident. She was attending a moderate-sized midwest state university. She was returning to her home for the weekend to visit her parents and wash her laundry. She was driving a small automobile, and her motor vehicle slid under the rear of the defendant's truck bed causing the bumper of his vehicle to crush the windshield area of her automobile. She sustained immediate and massive injury to the anterior central face. A review of the ambulance record notes that the passenger compartment of her automobile was described to be severely

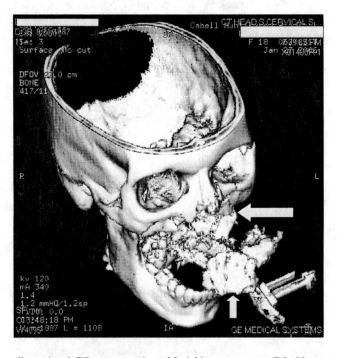

FIGURE 11.1 Three-dimensional CT reconstruction of facial bone trauma to E.L. Note anterior teeth pointing northward as anterior maxilla was fractured and displaced (northward-facing arrow). The westward-facing arrow marks the massive loss of central facial structures.

damaged. Her airbag did not deploy. She was unresponsive when attended by the ambulance staff, and her GCS score was 3. She was transported to a small city community hospital near her area where she was stabilized, fully immobilized, and sent by helicopter to the nearest major trauma center in another state. She was pharmacologically paralyzed and sedated for the flight.

She was hospitalized more than 20 days. Her initial examination revealed bilateral dislocation of the mandible, fracture of the mandibular angle, and fracture of the left zygomatic arch, and left margin of the left orbit. She had the anterior maxilla torn free of its bony connection. She required tracheostomy and percutaneous endoscopic gastrostomy tube placement. Referring again to Figure 11.1, the three-dimensional CT construction reveals severe loss of bony structures to the central face. CT scan of the head revealed that a small volume of the left central convexity was covered by a subarachnoid hemorrhage. No parenchymal hematoma was noted at this examination. However, on about the seventh hospital day, a follow-up CT revealed an interval development of a hematoma within the right temporal lobe. There was substantial edema noted throughout the brain, but no evidence of herniation. The subarachnoid hemorrhage continued to be prominent.

After hospitalization, she returned to her hometown for medical care. She was followed by a neurologist who obtained an MRI of her brain approximately 9 weeks post-injury. There were now present focal areas of encephalomalacia involving the right temporal lobe and to a lesser extent the right occipital lobe and upper convexity of both cerebral hemispheres. The ventricular systems and cisterns were unremarkable. She required placement of prosthetic metal in her skull in an effort to reconstruct her face. This precluded obtaining further MRIs at the time of this neuropsychiatric examination, which was completed approximately 9 months post-injury.

History from the Examinee

At the time of the neuropsychiatric examination, E.L. noted her last memory prior to impact was carrying clothes to her car while leaving college. She did not remember the impact and did not remember driving away from her university. Since her accident was a number of miles beyond her university, there remained a substantial level of retrograde amnesia of approximately 1 h. She reported anterograde amnesia of probably more than 10 days. Her first memories came to her while in a hospital bed observing a nurse changing her diaper. She spent approximately 12 days in the ICU, and her first clear memories were after leaving the ICU and being placed into a hospital room.

She denied flashbacks and denied nightmares, as she had no memory of the accident or her severe difficulties while in the hospital. However, she demonstrated substantial emotional distress over her cosmetic disfigurement. She provided to the examiner a picture of herself as a senior in high school, and the disfigurement as a result of this injury was striking. She was concerned over the loss of a romantic relationship that she had enjoyed for 2½ years. The outcome of her injury was so extreme that he did not remain with her. Her cosmetic disfigurement was so extreme that when she presented her driver's license for identification purposes, her present appearance did not match the picture, and she had been challenged numerous times for apparently providing improper identification.

She reported significant receptive dysprosody. She could not interpret other persons' emotions. Moreover, she demonstrated alexithymia, and she could not put proper emotional words to her feelings. She described herself as impatient and irritable. She reported herself to be weaker on the left side than the right side of her body. She developed a significant tremor in her handwriting after this accident. If she wrote for any significant time, she developed writer's cramp, and she could not write quickly since the accident. Her left hand developed chronically hyperextended fingers, and she reported her left grip to be weak. If she attempted to manipulate or bend her left hand, it caused significant pain. She reported chronic trembling in both legs, greater on the left than the right side. She also reported substantial pain in her head, right and left arm, left hand, and low back. Her sleep became very disordered after the injury, and she required a hypnotic in order to obtain sleep. She also complained of "crazy dreams." Following the accident she was slightly hypersomnic, and she would sleep more than 9 h nightly.

ACTIVITIES OF DAILY LIVING

At the time of the neuropsychiatric examination she was living with her parents, and she had been unable to return to college. She arose about 9:00 a.m. and retired about midnight. She was not yet driving an automobile at the time of this examination. She was able to attend church weekly, and she was able to use her computer, watch television, and read. Shortly after her injury, she could not watch television at all, as she could not concentrate. She continued to report some concentrating difficulty while reading. She was able to assist her mother with very light housekeeping, and she could perform laundry duties and other tasks. She could use the telephone, and she could dress and bathe herself independently.

PAST MEDICAL HISTORY

She weighed 8 lb 2 oz at birth, and she was not born prematurely. She sustained no birth injury, and her developmental milestones were normal. She was able to sit in class as a youngster, and she had no difficulty learning to read. Since her trauma, she had some difficulty with breathing due to a chest injury and pneumothorax with fractured ribs she sustained in the accident. Her medications at the time of the examination consisted of citalopram, 20 mg daily; methylphenidate; 40 mg daily, propranolol, 40 mg daily; and baclofen, 30 mg daily.

She demonstrated memory difficulty and could not recite the dosages of the medications herself. She did not use drugs of abuse, and she had no history of doing so. She used only moderate levels of caffeine. She had never been pregnant, and she had no alteration of menstrual regularity following the accident.

PAST PSYCHIATRIC HISTORY

She had never required a hospitalization for psychiatric, drug abuse, alcohol, or mental problems. She was seeing a physiatrist in her hometown. Because of significant impairment with attention span, he had placed her on methylphenidate. About 7 months prior to this examination, her family physician placed her on citalopram, as she was crying significantly and reported depression. She had recently begun counseling with a clinical social worker. She had no history of ever overdosing herself on drugs or medicines, and she had never made an attempt to take her life. She had never intentionally cut, burned, or disfigured herself.

FAMILY AND SOCIAL HISTORY

Her father was 38 years old, and her mother was 40 years old. Both parents became significantly depressed following her injuries, and both parents were treated with serotonin-specific antidepressants. There was no family history of suicides, homicides, violence toward others, child abuse, or spouse abuse. There was no history of epilepsy, neurological disease, Alzheimer's disease, or strokes in her family.

Socially, she was born in her hometown, and she had one sister. She was the youngest in the birth order. Her father was employed in the coal mining industry, and her mother was employed as an administrative assistant in a medical center. Both parents were present in her home, and her father did not abuse her mother. She denied any history of sexual or physical abuse. She had no history of violence toward others.

She was a high school graduate, and she maintained a 4.0 grade point average while in high school. She had attended her university for one semester prior to this injury, and she had made perfect grades that first semester. She was majoring in nursing and wanted to be a certified nurse anesthetist. However, she had changed her opinion following her accident, and she did not believe she would be able to tolerate the nursing profession because of her experiences. She was thinking of pursuing a major in physical therapy, speech pathology, or rehabilitation counseling. She had never been married.

Her legal history was negative. She had never been in a previous lawsuit. She had never been involved in a restraining order or emergency protective order. She had never been charged with abuse, terroristic threatening, or other criminal charges. She had never filed a workers' compensation claim, and she had never declared bankruptcy.

She had worked part-time to earn money for college, and she had been employed in restaurant work and in a retail store. She had never tried to enter military service or a service academy.

REVIEW OF SYSTEMS

She had lost a considerable amount of weight since her injury. Her standard weight was approximately 130 lb at the time of her injury. At the time of this examination, she weighed 115 lb. Her lowest weight after injury was 108 lb. She reported very significant fatigue. Her HEENT review revealed headaches three times weekly. She also had visual disturbance from optic nerve damage in the left eye. Her chest review was positive for chronic congestion following her chest injury. Her cardiovascular review was negative. Her gastrointestinal review was positive for loss of appetite. Her genitourinary and gynecological reviews were negative. Her psychiatric, neurological, pain, and sleep reviews are noted above.

MENTAL STATUS EXAMINATION

She was a pleasant, cooperative young woman who presented with obvious facial deformities. She had significant retrognathia due to loss of maxillary tissue, and she had a retroplacement of the nose due to maxillary tissue loss. Prominent facial scars were present, and there was evidence of reconstructive plastic surgery. Her left extremity revealed excessive pronation and hyperextension of the fingers. Her handwriting revealed a substantial tremor, but she was able to complete independently a complex 22-page medical questionnaire such as demonstrated in Chapter 3. No micrographia was present.

Her affective range was significantly diminished. There was a paucity of language output, and the melodic line was constricted. She subjectively reported a lack of prosodic comprehension of others. She denied specifically suicidal ideas or plans. Her mood was subjectively depressed, and her affective range was subjectively flattened and depressive. There was no evidence of delusions or hallucinations.

Dysarthria was present and articulatory agility was very poor due to the physical injuries to her upper maxilla. She had no teeth in the upper mouth, which affected tongue placement for pronunciation. No specific paraphasias were present. There was evidence of word-finding difficulty for emotional expression and emotional terms.

NEUROLOGICAL EXAMINATION

Her weight was 118 lb. Her blood pressure was 116/78 mmHg in the left arm. There were no bruits in the neck or head. Her face was asymmetrical. The central face was concave. A tracheostomy tube was in place. The anterior maxillary ridge was absent. A feeding tube was in place through the abdominal wall into the stomach. On cranial nerve examination, there was a left homonymous visual field cut. Ocular motility was full, and the pupils were equal to light and accommodation. The mastoid and temporalis muscles were intact. The forehead rose equally, the eyelids would close, and the lips pursed. The gag reflex was present. "E" was well phonated, and there was no other evidence of cranial nerve dysfunction with the exception of Nerve I. She could not detect anise and peppermint oils.

On examination of the motor and sensory system, bulk and tone were reasonably normal. However, motor strength was weaker on the left than the right side. Outstretched arms revealed a mild left arm pronation with hyperextended fingers. Deep tendon reflexes were hyperreflexive bilaterally in the biceps, brachioradialis, triceps, patellar tendons, and ankle jerks. Light touch and pinprick were reduced over the facial trauma areas. The vibratory and position senses were intact. The Romberg position revealed no sway. Nystagmus was not present, and finger–nose function was normal. Dysdiadochokinesia was not present. The Babinski sign was negative. Her gait was reasonably normal, but heel rising was dystaxic, and she was dystaxic when she attempted to rise on her toes. Balance testing produced dystaxia. Arm swing was reduced on the left side, and motor speed was generally reduced.

NEUROIMAGING

CT of the head was obtained without contrast at the time of this examination. The reader is referred to Figure 5.3. There is focal encephalomalacia in the right anterior temporal lobe, and focal encephalomalacia was also seen in the right posterior temporal lobe, left frontal lobe, right superior frontal lobe, and the right anterior–superior frontal lobe. Mild encephalomalacia was present in the right parietal occipital lobe. It is not possible to provide all visualizations of her encephalomalacia in this book.

A PET scan was obtained by injection of F-18 FDG. Multiple focal areas of decreased metabolism were seen within the brain. These are partially represented in Figure 5.12. This image demonstrates bilateral loss of frontal metabolism and loss of metabolism in the inferior right temporal lobe on this particular coronal view. Other areas of hypometabolism were present, which correlated visually with the findings on CT.

LABORATORY STUDIES

Chromosome 19 was assayed for apolipoprotein-E genotyping. E.L. had two alleles of apolipoprotein-E ε3.

STANDARDIZED MENTAL ASSESSMENT

Behavioral Observations during Testing

E.L. was casually dressed, appropriately groomed, and appeared older than her stated age of 18. She was pleasant, cooperative, and displayed a good attitude toward the evaluation. Speech was coherent but dysarthric. No evidence of significant language deficits was detected. She was initially shy but became more verbal as her comfort level increased.

She exhibited a left hemiparesis and demonstrated bilateral shaking of the lower extremities. She did not complain of physical discomfort. She maintained a neutral facial expression and occasionally attempted to smile. She was fatigued and sluggish during the first day of testing. Mood was dysthymic but rapport was good.

Her entire testing and examination was conducted over a 1.75-day period. On nonverbal assessment measures, she preferred her dominant right hand when manipulating objects and picture cards. She worked slowly, precisely, and carefully. Her initial approach to performance tasks was usually organized, but as the tests became more complex, she used a more trial and error strategy. Both mental and motor speed were reduced, and she demonstrated an awkward grip of the pencil. She demonstrated difficulty on the more complex items of the block design reproduction task. She could not always successfully recognize and correct errors during that task.

On the assessments requiring verbal responses, she was usually reflective and displayed intact verbal expression and receptive skills. However, she exhibited significant difficulty on a task requiring her to provide a verbal name for visually presented objects. When given assistance in the form of stimulus cue, she was able to provide an accurate response only to 25% of the items. When given a phonemic cue, she was able to provide a correct response to approximately 57% of the items. On tests measuring motor skills, she demonstrated much difficulty. During a pegboard task, her motor movements were very slow and laborious. She demonstrated spasticity bilaterally in the upper extremities, and she exhibited significantly impaired dexterity in hand strength, greater on the left than the right. Fine motor speed was significantly reduced. Although she had use of all digits on her dominant right hand, she was able only to use her thumb and forefinger on her left hand. The remaining digits of this hand were hyperextended and essentially nonfunctional for manipulation of objects.

She exhibited intact ability to attend to testing stimuli. She occasionally requested that test items be repeated, and she was observed occasionally to close her eyes during tasks requiring extra concentration. She completed a self-report inventory in an independent and timely manner. Testing progressed at a consistent pace, and she remained friendly and compliant throughout the procedures.

Measures of Cognitive and Psychological Effort

E.L. was administered the Test of Memory Malingering (TOMM) and the Victoria Symptom Validity Test (VSVT). She produced scores within normal limits on the TOMM, and overall the measures on the VSVT were within the valid range. On the MMPI-2, she produced the following validity indicators:

	VRIN	TRIN	F	F(B)	Fp	L	K	S
T-score	46	65	55	42	49	47	54	47

Measures Providing Estimates of Pre-Injury Function

On the Wide Range Achievement Test-III, Reading Subtest, E.L. produced the following results:

Wide Range Achievement Test-III

	Standard Score	Percentile	Grade Equivalence
Reading	<45	<0.02	1

On the Wechsler Test of Adult Reading (WTAR), E.L. produced the following predicted classifications:

WTAR Standard Score = 104

WTAR Demographic Predicted WAIS-III and WMS-III Indices

Standard	Score	Percentile	Classification
WAIS-III VIQ	101	53	Average
WAIS-III PIQ	100	50	Average
WAIS-III FSIQ	99	47	Average
WAIS-III VCI	100	50	Average
WAIS-III POI	100	50	Average
WAIS-III WMI	102	55	Average
WAIS-III PSI	103	58	Average
WMS-III immediate memory index	103	58	Average
WMS-III general memory index	103	58	Average
WMS-III working memory index	101	53	Average

On the Vocabulary Subtest of the Wechsler Adult Intelligence Scale-III (WAIS-III), E.L. produced the following scores:

WAIS-III Subtest

Subtest	Scaled Score	Standard Score	Percentile	Classification
Vocabulary	13	115	84	High average

Attention and Concentration

Visual attention was measured using the Ruff 2 & 7 Selective Attention Test. E.L. produced the following scores and classifications:

Ruff 2 & 7 Selective Attention Test

Measure	Sum of *T*-Scores	*T*-Score	Percentile	Classification
Total speed	49	25	1	Moderately impaired
Total accuracy	66	33	5	Mildly to moderately impaired

Auditory attention was measured using the Brief Test of Attention. E.L. produced the following percentile interpretation:

Brief Test of Attention

	Percentile	Interpretation
BTA total score	10–24	Low average

On another measure of auditory attention, E.L. was administered the Digit Span Subtest of the WAIS-III. She produced the following scores:

WAIS-III Digit Span Subtest

	Standard Score	Percentile	Classification
Longest digit span forward	115	84	High Average
Longest digit span backward	110	75	High Average
Digit span scaled score	115	84	High Average

Language and Language-Related Skills

On the Boston Naming Test, E.L. produced the following scores:

Boston Naming Test

T-score	24
Classification	Moderately to severely impaired
Percentile	0.9

In order to measure verbal fluency, E.L. was administered the Controlled Oral Word Association Test. She produced the following scores:

Controlled Oral Word Association Test

T-score	42
Percentile	23
Classification	Below average

Memory

Memory was measured using the Wechsler Memory Scale-III. E.L. produced the following scores:

Wechsler Memory Scale-III

	Scale Score Sum	Index Score	Percentile	Classification
Auditory immediate	27	120	91	Superior
Visual immediate	15	84	14	Low average
Immediate memory	42	103	58	Average
Auditory delayed	28	124	95	Superior
Visual delayed	17	91	27	Average
Auditory recognition delayed	12	110	75	High average
General memory	57	109	73	Average
Working memory	24	111	77	High average

Motor and Visuomotor Skills

On a measure of manipulative dexterity, E.L. was administered the Grooved Pegboard Test. Her scores are noted below:

Grooved Pegboard Test

	T-Score	Classification	Percentile
Dominant right hand	15	Severely impaired	<0.02
Nondominant left hand	17	Severely impaired	<0.02

Grip strength was tested on the grip dynamometer, and she produced the following scores:

Grip Dynamometer

	T-Score	Classification	Percentile
Dominant right-hand strength	30	Mildly to moderately impaired	3
Nondominant left-hand strength	25	Moderately impaired	1

Finger tapping speed was assessed using the Finger Tapping Test from the Halstead–Reitan Battery. E.L. produced the following scores:

Finger Tapping Test

	T-Score	Classification	Percentile
Dominant right hand	25	Moderately impaired	55
Nondominant left hand	33	Mildly to moderately impaired	32

Executive Function

Executive function was measured using the Wisconsin Card Sorting Test (WCST). E.L. produced the following scores:

Wisconsin Card Sorting Test

	Standard Score	T-Score	Percentile	Classification
Total errors	116	61	86	Above average
Perseverative responses	125	67	95	Above average

A second test of executive function was administered using Trailmaking Tests A and B. She produced the following scores:

Trailmaking Test A

T-Score	Classification	Percentile
28	Moderately impaired	1

Trailmaking Test B

T-Score	Classification	Percentile
27	Moderately impaired	1

Test Intelligence

Test intelligence was measured using the Wechsler Adult Intelligence Scale-III. E.L. produced the following scaled scores and deviation standard scores:

Subtests	Age-Adjusted Scaled Scores					
	Verbal	Performance	VC	PO	WM	PS
Picture completion		05		05		
Vocabulary	13		13			
Digit symbol-coding		03				03
Similarities	12		12			
Block design		07		07		
Arithmetic	10				10	
Matrix reasoning		13		13		
Digit span	13				13	
Information	12		12			
Picture arrangement		07				
Comprehension	11					
Symbol search		08				08
Letter–number sequencing	12				12	
Sum of Scaled Scores	71	35	37	25	35	11

Deviation IQs

	Standard Score	Classification	Percentile	Range
Verbal IQ	111	High average	77	106–116
Performance IQ	80	Low average	09	74–88
Full scale IQ	97	Average	42	93–101

WAIS-III Index Scores

	Standard Score	Classification	Percentile	Range
Verbal comprehension	112	High average	79	106–117
Perceptual organization	89	Low average	23	83–97
Working memory	109	Average	73	102–115
Processing speed	76	Borderline	05	70–88

Psychopathology

As a measure of psychopathology, she was administered the MMPI-2. Her scores are noted below:

Minnesota Multiphasic Personality Inventory-2

Scale	VRIN	TRIN	F	F(B)	Fp	L	K	S		
T-score	46	65	55	42	49	47	54	47		

Scale	1	2	3	4	5	6	7	8	9	0
T-score	84	72	80	53	50	56	66	59	41	60

RECORDS REVIEWED

There was a wealth of medical evidence available for this examination. It included photographs of her face taken at the time of the accident and before her plastic surgery began. The Uniform Police Traffic Collision Report was available, and the ambulance run report was reviewed. The triage initially at the community hospital was available, records from the helicopter were available, and records from the trauma center were reviewed. There were 15 physician and dentist records available for review as well as her transcripts from the university and her high school. Multiple neuroimaging data were available prior to the neuropsychiatric examination.

DIAGNOSES

E.L. was diagnosed with dementia due to brain trauma, cognitive disorder due to brain trauma, mood disorder due to brain trauma, and personality change due to brain trauma.

FORENSIC NEUROBEHAVIORAL ANALYSIS

The reader may find it useful to review Table 11.1. The police report confirmed the nature of her accident, and the ambulance run revealed a GCS score of 3. Thus, she was comatose at the scene. She remained comatose during transport by helicopter to the trauma center in another state. She required more than a 20-day hospitalization, and she was found to have severe and substantial central facial trauma. CT scans were made on repeated occasions, which revealed subarachnoid hemorrhage. Focal areas of encephalomalacia began to appear approximately a week after her injury. She had a posttraumatic amnesia of at least 10 days in length. Further review of the emergency department records, ICU records, neurosurgical ICU records, and her hospital records demonstrated that she had a severe brain injury using GCS criteria.

Reviewing her treatment medical records revealed that she had demonstrated personality and behavioral changes following this accident. She reported substantial impairment of language prosody, which was probably related to right cerebral hemisphere injury, and she demonstrated alexithymia (see elsewhere in this book). All physicians who treated her noted left hemiparesis and left hemianopia with significant tremor throughout her body. Her left hand was chronically dysfunctional with a weak left grip. She reported significant attentional problems.

If the reader will review neuroimaging obtained at the time of her neuropsychiatric examination in Figure 5.3, it can be seen that there are multiple areas of encephalomalacia on the CT scan. These correlate to large areas of hypometabolism on the PET scan (Figure 5.12). These in turn correlate to the level of trauma sustained in Figure 11.1, as evidenced by the CT three-dimensional reconstruction of her facial fractures. Thus, all available medical evidence indicated that she sustained a very severe central trauma to the head producing diffuse brain contusion and resulting in encephalomalacia.

There are interesting findings in this examination. The reader should note that on the Wisconsin Card Sorting Test, she shows a superior score, consistent with her pre-injury cognitive capacity, and there is no evidence of executive dysfunction on that instrument. However, when one reviews her ability to demonstrate visual-optical scanning ability, immediate number identification ability, basic motor skills, and mental flexibility to switch sets under timed constraints, she failed miserably (Trailmaking Tests A and B). This is an important lesson for examiners, as a single executive test may be insufficient to detect executive dysfunction. The Wisconsin Card Sorting Test, remembering from Chapter 6, is somewhat of a focal test, and it is most likely to demonstrate impairment with dorsolateral frontal lesions, which she does not demonstrate. Also, it should be noted that most memory functions remain well preserved with the exception of visual immediate and visual delayed memory. These memory scores are not at the pre-injury predicted level, and thus represent impairments as a result of her brain injury. On the other hand, her auditory memory is excellent and probably at levels which were present before injury. Moreover, her working memory, and executive function, is in the high average range.

Her visual system has been substantially impaired. There is a physiological marker of homonymous hemianopsia present on a measure of visual attention, of which she is moderately impaired, whereas she is less impaired on auditory attention. Language and language-related skills are impaired for naming and fluency when compared to pre-injury cognitive levels.

Recall that the best estimate of pre-injury cognitive capacity comes from the Wechsler Test of Adult Reading, the Wide Range Achievement Test-III Reading Recognition score, and the Vocabulary subtest of the WAIS-III presented above. The evidence is that she functioned in the average to high average range for cognitive capacity prior to her injury.

If the reader will review test intelligence, there is evidence that she has lost intellectual ability. Recall from Chapter 6 that IQ scores are poor indicators of brain trauma, and the best indicators are the scaled scores. Her performance scaled scores have been substantially impacted by her brain injury; if the reader will review those, relative to pre-injury cognitive capacity, she is impaired on the Picture Completion subtest, the Digit Symbol-Coding subtest, the Block Design subtest and the Picture Arrangement subtest, as she produced age-adjusted scaled scores of 5, 3, 7, and 7, respectively. There is a 31-point difference between her verbal IQ of 111 and her performance IQ of 80. This difference is probably related to brain trauma, and it forms the basis for the diagnosis of dementia. Also, her index scores from the WAIS-III reveal that mental processing has been impaired, and perceptual organization has been impaired.

On the MMPI-2, her validity indicators are in reasonably good order. The only scale elevations are 1, 2, and 3, with a very slight elevation on scale 7 (T-score $= 66$). Scales 1, 2, and 3 form a "V" pattern, which is not uncommonly found following TBI. What is unusual on this MMPI-2 is that in many brain-injured persons, Scale 8 is elevated, and hers is not.

CAUSATION ANALYSIS

Please review Table 11.3. From a neuropsychiatric standpoint, the proximate cause of her brain injury was the motor vehicle accident she sustained while driving home from college. From Table 11.3, the police, emergency services records, emergency department evaluation, and helicopter trauma team evaluation all point to this motor vehicle accident as the proximate cause. She had visually confirmed massive trauma to the central face and head, which was confirmed by imaging in the emergency department, and she had documented evidence of coma, with a GCS score of 3. This provides unequivocal medical evidence for the neuropsychiatric examiner that the proximate cause of her brain injury was the subject motor vehicle accident.

DAMAGES ANALYSIS

The reader should refer to Table 11.4. The evidence of damage lies in her symptoms and complaints, which have been confirmed during the neuropsychiatric examination by careful history, mental status examination, neurological examination, neuroimaging, and neuropsychological assessment. Her mental status examination was abnormal. Her neurological examination revealed focal neurological findings. There are numerous neuropsychological deficits compared to her pre-injury estimated cognitive capacity from the neuropsychological data. Her medical records document neurological, neuropsychiatric, and neuropsychological deficits consistent with brain trauma. There is no evidence of malingering or symptom magnification. Her cognitive and psychological effort was excellent.

A quantification of her impairment comes from an analysis within the *Guides to the Evaluation of Permanent Impairment*.[12] The impairment rating comes from the determination at the neuropsychiatric examination that she had a Class II impairment. That is found in Chapter 13 of the *Guides*. Specifically, it is found in Table 13.6 of the *Guides*. The definition of Class II impairment is that the impairment requires direction of some activities of daily living. E.L. continued to require significant direction from her parents. In particular, she had concreteness of abstract thinking, and she lacked the capacity to be self-directed in many of her decisions regarding her own health and need for medical treatment. It was determined that she was at the upper end of Class II, which as the reader can see by referring to the *Guides*, ranges from 15% to 29% impairment. Therefore, it is judged that she had a 20% whole-body neuropsychiatric impairment due to the TBI. Her neurologic impairment is additive to the 20% rating. The remainder of the damages analysis focuses on her specific mental weaknesses. At trial, it would be necessary for the neuropsychiatric examiner to point out the various domains of neuropsychological weakness. Without referring to specific neuropsychological tests, E.L. demonstrated impairment in verbal object naming, visual search and sequencing, shifting of perceptual set, dominant fine motor speed and nondominant hand strength. Mental processing speed was within the borderline range. Visual attention, dominant hand strength, and dominant fine motor speed were mildly to moderately impaired. In addition, there was neuropsychological evidence to suggest that working memory, expressive language, verbal reasoning and abstract nonverbal reasoning, and problem-solving abilities were areas of relative strength, whereas visual motor coordination and graphomotor speed represented areas of individual weakness. Recall that formal memory assessment indicated that immediate and delayed recall ability was better for verbal material than for visual material. With regard to the MMPI-2, this confirmed evidence of the unhappiness and depression that she associated with cosmetic disfigurement as well as depression probably emanating directly from damage to mood centers in her brain. Further damages analysis would require that the neuropsychiatric examiner provide information to a life care planner, as this young woman will require continuing facial reconstruction for many years as well as remedial services for her many neurocognitive deficits. Should she choose to return to college, she probably will require significant tutorial help and possibly a mentor.

CASE 11.2:   MULTIPLE BRAIN TRAUMAS AS A RESULT OF ASSAULT AND BATTERY

M.S. was 23 years old at the time of his injury. He was assaulted and struck about the head numerous times with a baseball bat. This case is very instructive to us, as it demonstrates an incontrovertible brain injury, but yet the examinee produced invalid cognitive effort and invalid psychological effort. This is a real-world dilemma that occurs in forensic evaluations frequently. That is to say, a person sustains a bonafide brain injury but yet, for not always explainable reasons, interferes with the validity indicators at the time of the neuropsychiatric examination.

HISTORY FROM THE MEDICAL RECORDS

M.S. was 23 years old at the time of his injury and was living in a midwestern city. He was an employed person and was assaulted and battered at work by assailants unknown to him. After injury, he was transported to a level 1 trauma center at a university hospital. His admission GCS score was 7. CT of the head without contrast demonstrated a small right parietal contusion with multiple punctuate right temporal hemorrhagic contusions and a right temporoparietal subarachnoid hemorrhage. There was evidence at this examination of a skull-based fracture extending from the right lateral occipital bone through the mastoid antrum and petrous temporal bone. After stabilization, he required placement of a left frontal-ventricular drain. A follow-up CT was made on the third hospital day, which demonstrated extensive hemorrhagic contusions involving the right frontal, right temporal, and right parietal lobes with a small amount of scattered subarachnoid hemorrhage over the right convexity. On the sixth hospital day, a third CT of the head was obtained. There was evidence of both low and high attenuation within the right temporal lobe. M.S. was discharged from the university hospital on the 14th hospital day.

Following hospitalization, M.S. was admitted to a university rehabilitation center. He underwent neuropsychological evaluation between the second and third week post-injury. At that time he demonstrated an unsteady and very slow gait. He required 24 h supervision with monitoring. WAIS-III IQ scores revealed a VIQ of 69, a PIQ of 75, and a FSIQ of 69. His mental processing speed score was equal to 79. On the WMS-III, memory scores ranged from a low of 72 for visual-delayed memory to a high of 110 for auditory recognition delayed memory (see Chapter 6). On working memory, he produced a standard score of 91. His memory scores in general were higher than his cognitive-capacity scores on the IQ test. He underwent an MRI of the brain, which revealed an evolving and resolving right inferolateral-temporal parenchymal hemorrhagic contusion with findings of gliosis. Minimal residual blood products were present, and there was evidence of volume loss of the brain in that region.

After discharge from the rehabilitation unit, he underwent a functional capacity evaluation approximately 8 months post-injury. He still demonstrated limitations with walking tolerance, and he had a significant increase of headaches as he exerted. He was relatively intolerant of physical activity. He was also found to have a conductive hearing loss on the right. Approximately a year and a half after injury, he underwent a right tympanoplasty with partial ossicular chain reconstruction with prosthesis. His ear, nose, and throat records indicate that he had a significant prior difficulty with his ears, and he had an ossicular discontinuity that had been repaired several years previous to this assault and battery. The last neuropsychological evaluation before this neuropsychiatric examination was obtained approximately 1½ years after injury. He demonstrated significantly variable motivation throughout that testing. He had very high levels of anger and resentment toward his caretakers. He had a minimal engagement in the psychotherapy that was offered to him. His prognostic indicators were poor. The neuropsychologist noted that the possibility of secondary gain issues could not be entirely ruled out.

History from the Examinee

As noted below, M.S. was not fully cooperative with the neuropsychiatric examination, probably because of disinhibition. Information was taken from his "girlfriend." He provided no historical information, and he appeared to be significantly unaware of his deficits or he was choosing not to provide information.

Activities of Daily Living

He was not employed at the time of the neuropsychiatric examination. His times of arising and going to bed were extremely variable. However, he was able to drive a vehicle, and he did live with a girlfriend. She described his hobbies as fishing and playing video games. He was able to watch television. He was able to eat outside the home if he chose. He was able to receive friends or family visitors in the home, and he was able to use a telephone. He could dress and bathe himself independently. His girlfriend confirmed that he was sexually dysfunctional.

Past Medical History

He was unable to describe his birth weight, but he volunteered that he was not born prematurely. He developed normally but had substantial difficulty with his ears, and he underwent multiple reconstructive procedures to his ears. These were based apparently upon an ossicular discontinuity disorder. He denied that he was sad as a child. He was able to sit still in school and keep his mind on tasks. He learned to read effectively.

Since his brain injury, he developed hypertension. He denied any prior injuries or motor vehicle accidents. He denied any prior head injuries, and he had never broken any bones prior to the skull fracture. He had never undergone prior surgical procedures. His medication at the time of the neuropsychiatric examination was a transdermal clonidine patch. He was unable to tell the examiner the dosage. He denied using over the counter medicines, herbs, or natural products. He claimed not to remember if he were allergic to drugs or medicines. He denied using any form of tobacco or alcohol. He denied any current use of drugs of abuse. He denied drinking caffeinated beverages.

PAST PSYCHIATRIC HISTORY

M.S. denied any prior treatment for a psychiatric condition. Since his injury, various physicians had prescribed sertraline, paroxetine, and valproate. He developed an allergy to valproate. At the time of this examination, he was using no form of psychiatric medicine and no form of cognitive enhancer, stimulant, dopamine agonist, or other brain therapy medication. He had received counseling and cognitive rehabilitation after his injury, but he was unable to tell the examiner who provided it or where it was provided. He denied he had ever intentionally overdosed himself on drugs or medicines. He denied he had ever made an attempt to take his life. He denied he had ever intentionally cut, burned, or disfigured himself.

FAMILY AND SOCIAL HISTORY

He was not able to give his father's or mother's age. His father had hypertension while living, and he died of lymphoma. His mother was living at the time of the neuropsychiatric examination, but he could not describe her health status. He denied that there were any suicides, homicides, violence toward others, child abuse, or spouse abuse among his relatives. He denied that anyone in his family had epilepsy, neurological disease, Alzheimer's disease, or stroke.

He came from a family of three boys. He denied that his home life was abusive or threatening. He denied that he had ever been sexually or physically abused. He denied any history of violence toward others and denied that any guns were currently in his home. He dropped out of school after the 10th grade. He probably failed the 9th grade, and he may have had other grade failures, but he claimed not to know of these. He had never been married, but he had one child by a woman other than his current girlfriend.

He had never been convicted of a felony or misdemeanor, and he had never been involved in a prior lawsuit. He had never been a party in a restraining order or emergency protective order. He had never been charged with spouse abuse, child abuse, or terroristic threatening. He had never declared bankruptcy. His current source of income was from his girlfriend's paycheck. He was unable to provide the examiner with a chronology of his work history. He had never attempted to enter military service.

REVIEW OF SYSTEMS

In his HEENT review, he complained of headaches, blurred vision, and tinnitus. He also complained of a brown drainage from the left ear canal. His chest, cardiovascular, gastrointestinal, and genitourinary reviews were negative. His psychiatric review is noted above, even though it is sketchy. In his neurological review, he complained of weakness and dizziness if he became over-heated. His pain review was negative. His sleep review was not clear. His sexual review was positive for dysfunction, as noted above.

MENTAL STATUS EXAMINATION

He could not complete a complex 22-page medical questionnaire (see Chapter 3), and he received assistance from his girlfriend. He was very disinhibited and inappropriate when met in the waiting room. He was socially inappropriate during conversation. His attention wandered. He did not display worry or fear, but he described posttraumatic symptomatology and nightmares about the attack with the baseball bat. His memory and attention could not be adequately examined face-to-face. He demonstrated no depressive affect. He denied mood changes. If anything, he demonstrated a pseudoeuphoric affect in association with behavioral disinhibition. He demonstrated substantial evidence of a dysexecutive syndrome. There was no evidence of motor retardation or blunted affect. There was not presence of dysarthria or articulation defect. He was easily excitable, but mood was not labile. He showed no evidence of dysphonia, dyspraxia, or dysphasia.

NEUROLOGICAL EXAMINATION

His weight was 187 lb, and he was approximately 6 ft in height. His blood pressure was 152/94 mmHg in the left arm sitting position. No bruits in the head or neck were detected. His face and head revealed evidence of prior contusions and lacerations. However, facial structures were generally symmetrical.

In examination of the cranial nerves, there were deficits present. Nerve I was intact to anise and peppermint oils. Tuning fork sound was reduced to the left ear. The Weber sign lateralized to the left. In the somatic motor system, bulk and tone were normal. There was no lateralization of weakness and no drift of outstretched arms. Deep tendon reflexes were generally symmetrical. In the sensory examination, light touch and pinprick exhibited normal dermatomal pattern. Vibratory and position sense were intact, and the Romberg sign revealed no sway. Nystagmus was not present. Finger–nose function was normal, and heel–shin function was normal. Dysdiadochokinesia was not present. His gait revealed a normal stride, and heels were placed on the midline while walking. There was no dystaxia on turning. Squatting and rising were normal. He was able to raise his heels and raise his toes. The Babinski sign was not present.

NEUROIMAGING

MRI of the brain was obtained, and this examination occurred 3½ years after his injury. There was an area of abnormal signal involving the lateral aspect of the right temporal lobe, which extended superiorly to the right parietal lobe. The reader should review Figures 11.2 and 11.3. There was also an area of abnormal signal in the lateral aspect of the right cerebellar hemisphere, which is not shown in these figures. The areas represented encephalomalacia secondary to trauma. On the MRI views, the left mastoid air cells were opacified, probably related to prior ear surgery. Figure 11.3 represents loss of hippocampal volume in the right hemisphere in association with the substantial encephalomalacia noted in the right temporal lobe.

STANDARDIZED MENTAL ASSESSMENT

Behavioral Observations during Testing

He was somewhat late for his initial appointment. He was generally pleasant and cooperative but exhibited a neutral facial expression. He did not appear to be overly anxious. He occasionally initiated conversation, and he told the psychologist that he felt dizzy and requested water. He occasionally requested breaks from the neuropsychological assessment. No impairment of expressive or receptive language ability was detected. He readily comprehended test instructions. He recognized that he had been administered previously some of the same neuropsychological instruments. He could not provide to the psychologist the approximate dates of the last assessment. When records were checked, there was no significant chance of practice effect, as he had not been tested in almost 2 years prior to this examination.

He generally exhibited reasonably rapid rates of response to test questions. However, he was slow in his rate of his response to forced-choice test questions and tended to pause for a period of time before indicating his responses. On the VSVT, he stopped the assessment and asked to use the restroom. He was asked to identify his response to the test item before he left, and he responded appropriately when he returned. A storm approached in the afternoon; he became very distracted, intermittently rising from his chair in the middle of testing to see if it had begun to rain. He generally

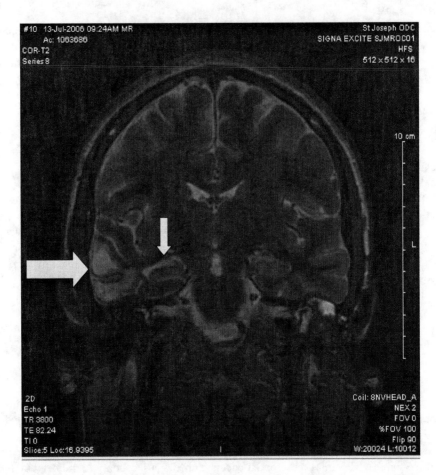

FIGURE 11.2 The southward-facing arrow marks increased T2 signal from an enlarged right hippocampal cistern. The eastward-facing arrow denotes lateral inferior right temporal lobe encephalomalacia (increased T2 signal).

provided good attention to the assessment questions. On the second day of evaluation, he complained that he felt ill and that he had vomited during the night.

Measures of Cognitive Distortion

On the TOMM, VSVT, and LMT, he provided abnormal responses or performance at chance levels. On the MMPI-2 validity indices, he produced the following scores:

	VRIN	TRIN	F	F(B)	Fp	L	K	S
T-score	69	65	92	108	48	56	30	36

Measures Providing Estimate of Pre-Injury Function

He was administered the Wide Range Achievement Test-III and the Vocabulary subtest of the WAIS-III. His reading scores and standard scores are noted below:

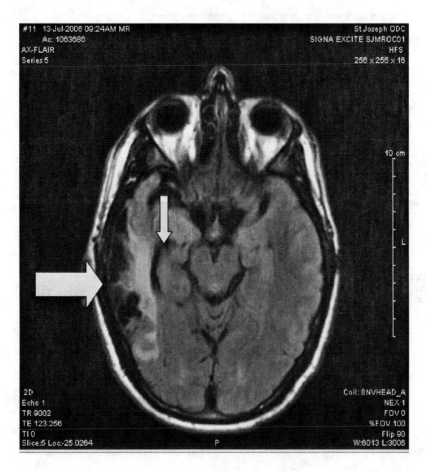

FIGURE 11.3 Cystic encephalomalacia on axial FLAIR MRI (eastward-facing arrow) and enlarged right hippocampal cistern (southward-facing arrow).

Wide Range Achievement Test-III

	Standard Score	Percentile	Grade Equivalence
Reading	73	4	4

WAIS-III Subtest

Subtest	Scaled Score	Standard Score	Percentile	Classification
Vocabulary	5	75	5	Borderline

Attention and Concentration

He was administered the Digit Span subtest of the WAIS-III. He produced the following scores:

WAIS-III Digit Span Subtest

	Standard Score	Percentile	Classification
Longest digit span forward	79	08	Borderline
Longest digit span backward	89	23	Low average
Digit span scaled score	90	25	Average

Executive Functions

He was administered the Wisconsin Card Sorting Test. His scores are noted below:

Wisconsin Card Sorting Test

	Standard Score	T-Score	Percentile	Classification
Total errors	119	63	90	Above average
Perseverative responses	>145	>80	>99	Above average

Test Intelligence

He was administered the Wechsler Adult Intelligence Scale-III. His age-adjusted scaled scores, IQ scores, and index scores are noted below:

Wechsler Adult Intelligence Scale-III

Subtests	Age-Adjusted Scaled Scores					
	Verbal	Performance	VC	PO	WM	PS
Picture completion		09		09		
Vocabulary	05		05			
Digit symbol-coding		07				07
Similarities	08		08			
Block design		10		10		
Arithmetic	10				10	
Matrix reasoning		11		11		
Digit span	08				08	
Information	06		06			
Picture arrangement		10				
Comprehension	07					
Symbol search		10				10
Letter–number sequencing	08				08	
Sum of scaled scores	**44**	**47**	**19**	**30**	**26**	**17**

Deviation IQs

	Standard Score	Classification	Percentile	Range
Verbal IQ	84	Low average	14	80–89
Performance IQ	95	Average	37	89–102
Full scale IQ	88	Low average	21	84–92

WAIS-III Index Scores

	Standard Score	Classification	Percentile	Range
Verbal comprehension	80	Low average	09	75–86
Perceptual organization	99	Average	47	92–106
Working memory	92	Average	30	86–99
Processing speed	91	Average	27	83–101

Psychopathology

He was administered the Minnesota Multiphasic Personality Inventory-2. His scores are noted below:

Minnesota Multiphasic Personality Inventory-2

Scale	VRIN	TRIN	F	F(B)	Fp	L	K	S		
T-score	69	65	92	108	48	56	30	36		
Scale	1	2	3	4	5	6	7	8	9	0
T-score	77	87	76	54	48	75	94	86	56	76

RECORDS REVIEWED

His complete records from the university hospital were available. The university rehabilitation service records were available as well. Further records were available from a neurosurgeon; ophthalmologist; ear, nose, and throat surgeon; internal medicine physician; neuropsychologist; and his family physician. Surgery records were reviewed. Speech pathology records were available. A job description from his employer was reviewed, and his deposition was reviewed.

DIAGNOSES

The diagnoses in this case were cognitive disorder due to brain trauma, mood disorder due to brain trauma, personality change due to brain trauma, and elements of PTSD due to assault and battery. He was also noted to have provided poor cognitive effort. Under Axis IV, he was judged not to be employable. Under Axis V, his GAF was rated at 40–45.

FORENSIC NEUROBEHAVIORAL ANALYSIS

On the basis of GCS criteria, when he was received at the university hospital, he had evidence of a severe brain injury (GCS = 7). His initial CT scans demonstrated substantial and multiple areas of brain injury, which were primarily within the right cerebral hemisphere. He had a skull-based fracture extending from the right lateral occipital bone into the petrous bone. He required a left frontal-ventricular brain shunt for pressure monitoring and because of edema. The MRI obtained at the time of this neuropsychiatric examination indicated permanent changes in the temporal and parietal lobes. There was also a small lesion in the right cerebellum and evidence of right hippocampal atrophy. His behavior was quite abnormal. Yet there was no significant evidence on MRI of frontal lobe injury, and the reader is referred to the superior scores he obtained on the Wisconsin Card Sorting Test.

Were it not for the availability of extensive and substantial medical records, as well as the previous neuroimaging available, it would have been very difficult to assess M.S. within the context of his workers' compensation claim. As the reader can see, his performance on the three measures of cognitive distortion was in the abnormal range on all three measures. If the reader will refer to the MMPI-2 scores, it is noted that VRIN is elevated with a score of 69, and TRIN is elevated with a score of 65. Obviously, F and Fb are elevated as well. However, recall from Chapter 7 that the elevation on VRIN indicates that he was confused and having difficulty conceptualizing his responses to the test questions on this instrument. The elevated TRIN score indicated that he was acquiescing to item content. His validity indicators did not allow an interpretation of the MMPI-2. It is also noteworthy that this was not a complete neuropsychological examination. The reader probably noticed that a memory assessment was not made and that certain other neuropsychological tests were omitted when compared to case 11.1. This was because of his behavior and the difficulty in keeping him engaged throughout the day.

While his Wisconsin Card Sorting Test is within normal limits, there was still substantial evidence of a dysexecutive syndrome and a behavior disorder associated with this. He demonstrated pseudoeuphoric behavior but without evidence of an infraorbital frontal injury. This case demonstrates the complexity of behavioral syndromes following TBI and that they do not always follow textbook descriptors. Overall, he was judged to be moderately to severely impaired.

CAUSATION ANALYSIS

This was a workers' compensation case. Therefore, to qualify for benefits, he had to be on the job. His employer did not contest that he was in fact employed and functioning in a work capacity at the time he was beaten with a baseball bat. He worked for an oil company, and he was managing gasoline pumps. He was apparently beaten in an effort to rob the company. There is clear evidence in the employer's records and the university hospital records that his brain injury stemmed directly from a workplace assault and battery. Therefore, medical causation was established.

DAMAGES ANALYSIS

Damages analysis is a more difficult situation than the causation analysis. He had less than optimal testing performance. Chapter 13 of the *Guides to the Evaluation of Permanent Impairment* was consulted in this case. The reader is referred to Table 13.6 in the *Guides*. He was judged by the examiner to be a Class III impairment and at a 35% impairment of the whole person. The definition for Class III impairment is noted in Table 10.2. While it might be argued that he did not require assistance or supervision, the examiner discussed the situation with his girlfriend, and she was of the opinion that if he did not have someone to assist him in his life, he would be at a substantial disadvantage socially and that he lacked the necessary judgment and insight to see to his personal needs.

Based on the Wide Range Achievement Test-III score and the WAIS-III Vocabulary subtest score, he probably functioned at a marginal level cognitively prior to his injury. Based on those two tests, the evidence is that he functioned at the borderline level of cognitive capacity. On the other hand, recall from Chapter 6 that the highest score obtained can be used in equivocal cases to make a judgment about pre-injury cognitive capacity. If the reader will refer to the age-adjusted scaled scores from his WAIS-III, it can be seen that he has three scaled scores at 10 and one scaled score at 11. These are at average levels. One could make an equally effective argument that he was probably learning disabled for reading and that his true cognitive capacity prior to his injury was in the low average if not in the average range. In looking at his index scores from the WAIS-III, three of four scores are in the average range. Therefore, probably he was functioning in the average range from a cognitive standpoint prior to his injury. It was also learned from his girlfriend that he probably had a learning disorder for reading while in school. This evidence buttresses the opinion that he probably had average cognitive capacity prior to his injury.

Table 13.8 from the *Guides* was used for rating impairment due to emotional and behavioral disorders. He was found to be Class II for behavioral impairment. Table 10.3 gives the definition of this class. He was judged to have a 20% whole-body impairment due to the behavioral disorder.

In order to determine his full level of impairment, it is necessary for the reader to consult with the combined values chart of the *Guides*. This is found in the rear of the text. The impairment rating is derived from the formula $A + B(1-A) =$ combined value of A and B, where A and B are the decimal equivalents of the impairment ratings. For example, to combine a 35% cognitive impairment with a 20% behavioral impairment, the examiner reads down the side of the combined values chart until one comes to the larger value, in this case 35%. Then the examiner reads across the 35% row until he comes to the column indicated by 20%. In this case, 35% combined with 20% is 48%. Thus, his overall level of neuropsychiatric impairment was judged to be 48% to the whole body.

These data were provided to the administrative law judge in his workers' compensation claim. The examiner had been asked to evaluate him on behalf of his employer. For obvious reasons, the examiner's deposition was not taken.

CASE 11.3: FAKING A BRAIN INJURY IN ORDER TO OBTAIN WORKERS' COMPENSATION BENEFITS

The examinee was 52 years old at the time of the neuropsychiatric assessment. He was being examined at the request of his employer to determine if he retained neuropsychiatric impairment as a result of an alleged workplace injury.

History from the Medical Records

At the time of the neuropsychiatric examination, J.B. was 52 years old and was alleging two work injuries. He was alleging an injury to the right foot and ankle 17 months prior to the neuropsychiatric examination, and an injury to the head affecting his cognitive state also 17 months prior to the neuropsychiatric examination.

Seventeen months prior to this examination J.B. was employed by a hardware distribution company. His records were received by the neuropsychiatric examiner before he appeared for examination. After reviewing the records, it appeared that it was questionable whether he had in fact sustained a TBI. Therefore, considerable detail was requested from J.B. about the nature of his accident. The purpose in doing this was to determine his memory for the accident itself. Recall from prior writings in this text that a TBI is almost always worse immediately following the injury and causes the greatest cognitive impairment, and then the individual progressively improves over time to a plateau.

J.B. advised the examiner that he was five stories up on a building working off a ladder and that he was 15–20 ft high on the ladder at the time of his injury. He was painting the outside of a building with a power sprayer, and the base of the ladder was standing on the roof of another building nearby. From that roof, he had leaned the ladder against the wall that he was painting. He had placed concrete blocks above him to hold plastic in place so that the paint did not get outside the range of what he was painting. Apparently, one of the concrete blocks fell between 5 and 10 ft and struck him on the forehead. After being struck, he was not knocked from the ladder, nor was he knocked unconscious. He was not addled. He held onto the ladder after he was struck. Apparently he had looked up before being struck and his helmet had fallen off, which enabled him to be cut by the falling block. The medical evidence revealed it was a glancing blow.

He climbed down the ladder unassisted. There were no witnesses to this accident. While standing on the roof supporting the ladder, he then walked to a door and entered a breakroom to clean himself of blood on his head. He tried to clean his head with water, but there was no mirror in the breakroom. He put a wet cloth on his head and walked two flights of stairs to a bathroom. He then cleansed himself, left the bathroom, and walked 25–30 ft to a customer service desk nearby. He talked to the owner of the business and to a customer service receptionist. Both told J.B. that he needed immediate medical attention and that they would drive him to a nearby urgent care center.

Another person at the business drove him to the urgent care center and waited with him until he was seen by a physician. He received a small number of stitches to the forehead and upper scalp. He was then taken to his pickup truck whereupon he drove himself home independently. He had to leave a large midwestern city, enter an interstate highway, exit to a second county, and drive himself to his home. He drove a total of 20 mi one way after leaving the medical treatment facility. At the medical treatment facility, he was diagnosed with a closed head injury with forehead and scalp lacerations. He was not diagnosed with a TBI. No neuroimaging was obtained at that examination.

HISTORY FROM THE EXAMINEE

At the time of the neuropsychiatric examination, J.B. was claiming multiple injuries. He was claiming he was depressed, sad, and nervous, and that he had thoughts of suicide without a suicidal plan. He claimed poor concentration, impaired memory, and word-finding impairment. He claimed at times that he was unable to know the month or the year. He reported constant ringing in his ears, dizziness, and stumbling. He reported pain that did not follow any distribution associated with his alleged injury, and he claimed pain in the neck radiating into both arms and hands, both shoulders, the mid and low back, both hips, both thighs, both knees, the right ankle, and the right foot. He claimed his sleep was disordered and that he could not maintain sleep.

Collateral history was obtained from his girlfriend at the time of the neuropsychiatric examination. She reported that he quit breathing at night and that she had to awaken him due to apnea. She reported further that he could not stay awake while sitting and that he had sleep paralysis after awakening at times.

ACTIVITIES OF DAILY LIVING

This examination occurred 17 months after his injury, and he had not worked since that time. He lived with his girlfriend, but she had recently asked him to move out of the home. He was providing no support to her. He denied any hobbies. He claimed he could barely read, but he was able to watch television. He denied engaging in any activities, renting movies, attending ball games, or eating outside the home. He did admit that he was able to dress and bathe himself independently.

PAST MEDICAL HISTORY

He was unable to give his birth weight, but he denied premature birth or birth injury. He described his childhood as happy, which was inconsistent with information reported below. He admitted he had difficulty keeping his mind on tasks as a child. Teachers complained that he was hyperactive. As an adult, he denied he had ever been injured in a motor vehicle accident or had any other form of brain or head injury. He had told numerous physicians after the accident that he had been knocked unconscious, and many of the medical records obtained indicated a positive loss of consciousness based on his history. He denied he had ever been in a coma, and he had never broken any bones. His only surgery was a childhood tonsillectomy. At the time of the neuropsychiatric examination, he was treated with oxycodone, 20 mg daily, and ibuprofen, 1800–2400 mg daily. He was taking no other medications. He reported an allergy to codeine. He denied using tobacco products, alcoholic beverages, or illegal drugs. He denied using caffeine.

PAST PSYCHIATRIC HISTORY

He denied he had ever been hospitalized for psychiatric, drug abuse, alcohol, or mental difficulties. He denied he had ever been prescribed any form of psychiatric medicine. He had a prior neuropsychological assessment, and he claimed to the neuropsychiatric examiner that the psychologist had told him that he should be treated psychiatrically. He denied he had ever received counseling or psychotherapy previously. He denied he had ever intentionally overdosed himself on drugs or medicines. He stated he had never made an attempt to take his life, and he had never intentionally cut, burned or disfigured himself.

FAMILY AND SOCIAL HISTORY

His father was living at age 82 and was described as a chronic alcoholic. He claimed that his father was violent and had killed three men who had tried to rob him. He also described his father as abusive to his mother and his children. He admitted that his father had severely beaten him numerous times as a child. His mother had died of liver cancer 4 years prior to this examination, and a brother had recently been diagnosed with throat cancer.

J.B. was born in a southern state, and he had one sister and three brothers. His father was a drill sergeant in the army and a salesman. His mother was a homemaker. He described his home life as a child as abusive and threatening, and that it made him depressed. This, of course, was inconsistent with his claim of having a happy childhood. He denied that he had ever been sexually or physically abused. He denied any history of violence toward others. He owned a shotgun but denied plans to harm himself or harm others.

He graduated from high school and reported his grades were average to above average. He had never been married. He denied fathering any children. The romantic relationship at the time of the neuropsychiatric examination had been in place 5½ years, but his girlfriend was asking him to leave. At the time of the examination, he had recently moved to share an apartment with another man.

He was not able to produce a driver's license at the time of his examination. He admitted to at least 25 speeding tickets in his life, and he had not had a driver's license since the last speeding violation. It was probably more than 2 years since he had a valid license, but obviously on the day of the injury he drove himself home with an invalid license. He denied that he had ever been convicted of a felony or misdemeanor. He denied he had ever been a party in a lawsuit, restraining order, or emergency protective order. He denied he had ever been charged with any form of abuse or terroristic threatening. He denied he had ever filed a prior workers' compensation claim or declared bankruptcy.

Prior to the employment wherein he was injured, he had worked as a loader of milk, and he had worked in a slaughterhouse. He had also worked at a large grocery chain and as a maintenance person. At the time of this examination, he was supporting himself with savings and by selling personal items. He denied he had ever attempted to enter military service.

REVIEW OF SYSTEMS

In his general review, he reported a gain in weight since his injury. In his HEENT review, he claimed visual changes, blurred vision, and tinnitus. In his chest review, he reported that he "choked a lot," consistent with obstructive sleep apnea. In his cardiovascular review, he complained of shortness of breath and that he had to clear his throat quite often (also consistent with obstructive sleep apnea). In his gastrointestinal review, he complained of difficulty swallowing and heartburn. His genitourinary review was positive for difficulty initiating urination and then difficulty retaining urine. His psychiatric, neurological, sleep, and pain reviews are reported above.

MENTAL STATUS EXAMINATION

He was able to complete independently a complex 22-page medical questionnaire (see Chapter 3). His writing was printed and was large, without tremor. He required no assistance in providing social security number, phone number, address, or zip code. He dressed bizarrely in all black and used a black cane. He kept a cap on his head throughout the day, and he wore dark sunglasses and did not remove them at any time. He walked with a plastic bag tied to his cane, and within the plastic bag was a 64 oz container of soft drink.

He reported depression. However, he spoke excessively and with great force. He had a good range of affect and a strong voice. His voice pattern and facial expressions were not consistent with depression. He denied suicidal ideas or plans. There was no evidence of loose associations or circumstantial thinking present. There was no evidence of delusions or hallucinations. Articulatory agility was good and without dysarthria. There was no evidence of dysphonia, dyspraxia, or dysphasia. No word-finding difficulties were present. The melodic line was well preserved, and no paraphasias were present.

NEUROIMAGING

Neuroimaging was not completed at this neuropsychiatric examination. The examiner had available a prior CT scan of the brain and a prior MRI of the brain. The CT scan of the brain was obtained 9 days after his original injury, and the MRI of the brain was obtained 2½ months after the original injury.

The CT examination demonstrated no signs of intracranial mass. The ventricles and cortical sulci were normal in appearance. No focal ischemic changes were present in any area of the brain. There was nothing to suggest an intracranial hemorrhage, and no extraaxial collection of fluid or blood was noted. The skull was intact without evidence of fracture.

The MRI revealed the skull, orbits, and sinuses to be unremarkable. Intracranially, there was no evidence of mass lesions or shift of the midline structures. The ventricular system and basilar cisterns were normal. There were no abnormal areas of increased or decreased signal intensity in the brain parenchyma. No extraaxial fluid collections were seen, and the posterior fossa structures were intact and normal. The brainstem and cerebellum was intact.

STANDARDIZED MENTAL ASSESSMENT

Behavioral Observations during Testing

The behavioral observations of the psychologist indicated that J.B. was pleasant and cooperative. He demonstrated a serious facial expression but occasionally would smile. He was not overly anxious. He walked extremely slowly and unsteadily using his cane. He carried a large pillow with him, which he placed on his chair throughout the day. Occasionally he would stand up at intervals claiming back pain. He claimed an inability to read, and reading glasses were provided to him. However, he wore the reading glasses over his sunglasses. He stated that the reading glasses helped his vision considerably. He complained that lights were bothersome, and that the bright light used to take his photograph would induce a headache. Therefore, his identification picture was taken without a flash.

He was very talkative with the psychologist, and he spent excessive time discussing the purpose of this evaluation. He reported that this was his fourth neuropsychological assessment. There was no impairment of expressive or receptive language noted. He demonstrated an above average vocabulary while talking with the psychologist. However, on certain test portions, he would respond incorrectly to very easy vocabulary questions. Despite evidence of a large and extensive vocabulary, J.B. often responded to questions in a vague manner or would not address the content of the question. He seemed to comprehend all test instructions.

During the administration of the VSVT and the LMT, J.B. was observed to fall asleep. He needed to be awakened and reoriented to the test. During the LMT, it was necessary to prompt him to wake up on several occasions. He referred to these sleep episodes as "blacking out." He was encouraged to drink coffee to help his state of alertness. He did so. He stated that it made him sleepier.

Measures of Cognitive and Psychological Effort

On the TOMM, VSVT, and the LMT, J.B. produced abnormal scores. On the VSVT, Difficult Items scale, he performed at chance levels.

His MMPI-2 validity indices are noted below:

	VRIN	TRIN	F	F(B)	Fp	L	K	S
T-score	88	72	92	79	63	61	47	48

Structured Interview of Reported Symptoms

The SIRS (see Chapter 9) was administered. It is standard practice in individuals who exceed a *T*-score of 90 on the F scale of the MMPI-2 to be administered the Structured Interview of Reported Symptoms. This was done in J.B.'s case, and he produced the following classifications:

Structured Interview of Reported Symptoms

Primary Scale	Classification
Rare symptoms (RS)	Honest
Symptom combinations (SC)	Honest
Improbable or absurd symptoms (IA)	Honest
Blatant symptoms (BL)	Probable
Subtle symptoms (SU)	Probable
Selectivity of symptoms (SEL)	Indeterminate
Severity of symptoms (SEV)	Probable
Reported vs. observed symptoms (RO)	Honest

Measures Providing Estimate of Pre-Injury Function

J.B. was administered the Wide Range Achievement Test-III and the Vocabulary subtest of the WAIS-III. His scores are noted below:

Wide Range Achievement Test-III

	Standard Score	Percentile	Grade Equivalence
Reading	88	21	High school

WAIS-III Subtest

Subtest	Scaled Score	Standard Score	Percentile	Classification
Vocabulary	7	85	16	Low average

Attention and Concentration

The Digit Span subtest of the WAIS-III was administered. His scores are noted below:

WAIS-III Digit Span Subtest

	Standard Score	Percentile	Classification
Longest digit span forward	94	34	Average
Longest digit span backward	92	30	Average
Digit span scaled score	95	37	Average

Because the effort measures are given early within the neuropsychological evaluation, if an individual is documented to be providing invalid or suboptimal effort, a complete neuropsychological evaluation is not administered. The person being examined is generally unaware that the examination is being substantially truncated so as not to give away to them the fact that their obvious poor performance has been detected.

Test Intelligence

The Wechsler Adult Intelligence Scale-III was administered, and the age-adjusted scaled scores, IQ scores, and index score are noted below:

Wechsler Adult Intelligence Scale-III

Subtests	Verbal	Performance	VC	PO	WM	PS
Picture completion		06		06		
Vocabulary	07		07			
Digit symbol-coding		05				05
Similarities	10		10			
Block design		09		09		
Arithmetic	08				08	
Matrix reasoning		11		11		
Digit span	09				09	
Information	07		07			
Picture arrangement	06					
Comprehension	07					
Symbol search		(05)				05
Letter–number sequencing	(06)				06	
Sum of scaled scores	**48**	**37**	**24**	**26**	**23**	**10**

Age-Adjusted Scaled Scores

Deviation IQs

	Standard Score	Classification	Percentile	Range
Verbal IQ	88	Low average	21	83–93
Performance IQ	83	Low average	13	77–91
Full scale IQ	85	Low average	16	81–89

WAIS-III Index Scores

	Standard Score	Classification	Percentile	Range
Verbal comprehension	89	Low average	23	84–95
Perceptual organization	91	Average	27	84–99
Working memory	86	Low average	18	80–94
Processing speed	73	Borderline	04	67–85

Psychopathology

J.B. was administered the MMPI-2, and those scores are noted below:

Minnesota Multiphasic Personality Inventory-2

Scale	VRIN	TRIN	F	F(B)	Fp	L	K	S		
T-score	88	72	92	79	63	61	47	48		
Scale	**1**	**2**	**3**	**4**	**5**	**6**	**7**	**8**	**9**	**0**
T-score	92	80	94	79	38	75	74	93	72	60

RECORDS REVIEWED

There were a number of post-injury treating physicians' records present, and none indicated brain injury. A neuropsychologist had examined J.B. about 14 to 15 months after his original injury. The neuropsychologist claimed evidence of a cognitive impairment and a depressive disorder. A reexamination of the neuropsychology data at the time of the neuropsychiatric examination revealed that not a single item within the neuropsychological assessment was within the impaired range. No effort measures had been applied.

FORENSIC NEUROBEHAVIORAL ANALYSIS

Recall the term clinical correlation from previous discussions in this text. This man's complaints do not clinically correlate with the original injury record. For instance, the reader may wish to review again how this man was struck in the head but yet brought himself down 15 ft of ladder, walked down two flights of stairs, had multiple conversations with people, rode to a medical treatment facility, and thereafter drove himself 20 mi to his own home. It was not even considered to obtain a CT of his head until more than a week after his injury. All neuroimaging was within normal limits.

His constellation of symptoms and complaints do not clinically correlate with the facts of his injury and his behavior immediately following the injury. Moreover, J.B. failed 3/3 cognitive effort tests. Therefore, his entire examination was suspect. His MMPI-2 F scale was substantially elevated (F = 92). Therefore, he was administered the Structured Interview of Reported Symptoms. On this test, his combination of elevated scores was characteristic of a person who was feigning a mental disorder, and this pattern is rarely seen in persons responding truthfully.

DIAGNOSES

He was diagnosed with malingering a mental disorder following a workplace injury. On Axis III there was no evidence of brain trauma. On Axis IV, he had evidence of current stressors, as his girlfriend had asked him to move out. On face-to-face examination, while his behavior was bizarre, there was no evidence of a cognitive disturbance.

Causation Analysis

It could not be concluded that he had a neuropsychiatric condition as a result of a TBI. There was no evidence of TBI, and as noted above, the lack of clinical correlation therefore did not support a medical causation. It was determined neuropsychiatrically that while he had received a blow to the head that required stitches to the scalp, this had not produced a TBI. It is scientifically accurate to say that most blows to the head, even those that lacerate the scalp, do not result in a TBI.

Damages Analysis

In a case of malingering, there is no impairment that can be assessed. The reader may wish to review prior discussions of the complex psychological and medical issues of malingering. Also, the reader may wish to review in Chapter 9 the high level of malingering reported by Mittenburg's study.[13]

REFERENCES

1. Committee on Trauma: Hospital and pre-hospital resources for the care of the injured patient, *Bull. Am. Coll. Surg.*, 71, 4, 1986.
2. Pitts, L.H., Ojemann, R.G., and Quest, D.O., Neurotrauma care and the neurosurgeon: A statement from the joint section of trauma of the AANS and CNS, *J. Neurosurg.*, 67, 783, 1987.
3. West, J.G., Cales, R.H., and Grazzaniga, A.B., Impact of regionalization: The Orange County experience, *Arch. Surg.*, 118, 740, 1983.
4. Shackford, S.R., Hollingworth-Fridlund, P., Cooper, G.F., et al., The effect of regionalization upon the quality of trauma care as assessed by concurrent audit before and after institution of a trauma system, *J. Trauma*, 26, 812, 1986.
5. Kish, D.L., Pre-hospital management of spinal trauma: An evolution, *Crit. Care Nurs. Q.*, 22, 36, 1999.
6. *Pre-hospital Trauma Life Support Committee of the National Association of Emergency Medical Technicians in Cooperation with the Committee on Trauma of the American College of Surgeons. PHTLS: Basic and Advance Pre-hospital Trauma Life Support,* 4th edition, Mosby, St. Louis, 1999.
7. Gabrielli, A., Idris, A.H., and Layon, A.J., Pre-hospital care of the patient with neurologic injury, in *Textbook of Neurointensive Care*, Layon, A.J., Gabrielli, A., and Friedman, W.A., Eds., W.B. Saunders, Philadelphia, PA, 2004, p. 439.
8. Gouvier, W.D., Blanton, P.D., Laporte, K.K., et al., Reliability and validity of the disability rating scale and the levels of the cognitive functioning scale in monitoring recovery from severe head injury, *Arch. Phys. Med. Rehabil.*, 68, 94, 1987.
9. Bonke, C.F., Zasler, N.D., and Boake, C., Rehabilitation of the head-injured patient, in *Neurotrauma*, Narayan, R.K., Wilberger, J.E., and Povlishock, J.T., Eds., McGraw-Hill, New York, 1996, p. 841.
10. Hannay, H.J. and Sherer, M., Assessment of outcome from head injury, in *Neurotrauma*, Narayan, R.K., Wilberger, J.E., and Povlishock, J.T., Eds., McGraw-Hill, New York, 1996, p. 723.
11. Prosser, W. and Keeton, W., *The Law of Torts,* 5th edition, West Publishing Company, New York, 1984.
12. Cocchiarella, L. and Andersson, G.B.J., Eds., *Guides to the Evaluation of Permanent Impairment,* 5th edition, AMA Press, Chicago, IL, 2001.
13. Mittenburg, W., Patton, C., Cranyock, E.M., et al., Base rates of malingering and symptom exaggeration, *J. Clin. Exp. Neuropsychol.*, 24, p. 1094, 2002.

Index

A

DISCOVERY LIBRARY
LEVEL 5 SWCC
DERRIFORD HOSPITAL
DERRIFORD ROAD
PLYMOUTH
PL6 8DH